Marsh Family

South Africa

THE ROUGH GUIDE

D1048843

There are more than one hundred and fifty Rough Guide titles
covering destinations from Amsterdam to Zimbabwe

Forthcoming titles include

Cuba • Dominican Republic • Las Vegas • Sardinia • Switzerland

Rough Guide Reference Series

Classical Music • Drum 'n' Bass • European Football • House
The Internet • Jazz • Music USA • Opera • Reggae
Rock Music • World Music

Rough Guide Phrasebooks

Czech • European • Dutch • French • German • Greek • Hindi & Urdu
Hungarian • Indonesian • Italian • Japanese • Mandarin Chinese
Mexican Spanish • Polish • Portuguese • Russian • Spanish • Swahili
Thai • Turkish • Vietnamese

Rough Guides on the Internet
www.roughguides.com

ROUGH GUIDE CREDITS

Text editor: Geoff Howard
Series editor: Mark Ellingham
Editorial: Martin Dunford, Jonathan Buckley, Jo Mead, Kate Berens, Amanda Tomlin, Ann-Marie Shaw, Paul Gray, Helena Smith, Judith Bamber, Kieran Falconer, Orla Duane, Olivia Eccleshall, Ruth Blackmore, Sophie Martin, Claire Saunders, Gavin Thomas, Alexander Mark Rogers, Polly Thomas, Joe Staines, Lisa Nellis, Andrew Tomičić (UK); Andrew Rosenberg, Mary Beth Maioli (US)
Production: Susanne Hillen, Andy Hilliard, Link Hall, Helen Ostick, Julia Bovis, Michelle Draycott, Anna Wray, Katie Pringle, Robert Evers

Cartography: Melissa Baker, Maxine Burke, Nichola Goodliffe, Ed Wright
Picture research: Louise Boulton, Catherine Marshall
Online editors: Alan Spicer, Kate Hands (UK); Kelly Cross (US)
Finance: John Fisher, Katy Miesiaczek, Gary Singh, Ed Downey, Catherine Robertson
Marketing & Publicity: Richard Trillo, Simon Carloss, Niki Smith, David Wearn, Jemima Broadbridge (UK); Jean-Marie Kelly, Myra Campolo (US)
Administration: Tania Hummel, Charlotte Marriott, Demelza Dallow

....

PUBLISHING INFORMATION

This second edition published September 1999 by Rough Guides Ltd, 62–70 Shorts Gardens, London, WC2H 9AB.
Distributed by the Penguin Group:
Penguin Books Ltd, 27 Wrights Lane, London W8 5TZ
Penguin Books USA Inc., 375 Hudson Street, New York 10014, USA
Penguin Books Australia Ltd, 487 Maroondah Highway, PO Box 257, Ringwood, Victoria 3134, Australia
Penguin Books Canada Ltd, 10 Alcorn Avenue, Toronto, Ontario, Canada M4V 1E4
Penguin Books (NZ) Ltd, 182–190 Wairau Road, Auckland 10, New Zealand
Typeset in Linotron Univers and Century Old Style to an original design by Andrew Oliver.
Printed in England by Clays Ltd, St Ives PLC
Illustrations in Part One and Part Three by Edward Briant.

Illustrations on p.1 & p.683 by Henry Iles
© Tony Pinchuck, Barbara McCrea, Donald Reid and Greg Mthembu-Salter 1999
No part of this book may be reproduced in any form without permission from the publisher except for the quotation of brief passages in reviews.
784pp – Includes index
A catalogue record for this book is available from the British Library
ISBN 1-85828-460-0

....

South Africa

THE ROUGH GUIDE

written and researched by

Tony Pinchuck, Barbara McCrea, Donald Reid and Greg Mthembu-Salter

with additional contributions by

Roger Field

THE ROUGH GUIDES

THE ROUGH GUIDES

TRAVEL GUIDES • PHRASEBOOKS • MUSIC AND REFERENCE GUIDES

 We set out to do something different when the first Rough Guide was published in 1982. Mark Ellingham, just out of university, was travelling in Greece. He brought along the popular guides of the day, but found they were all lacking in some way. They were either strong on ruins and museums but went on for pages without mentioning a beach or taverna. Or they were so conscious of the need to save money that they lost sight of Greece's cultural and historical significance. Also, none of the books told him anything about Greece's contemporary life – its politics, its culture, its people, and how they lived.

So with no job in prospect, Mark decided to write his own guidebook, one which aimed to provide practical information that was second to none, detailing the best beaches and the hottest clubs and restaurants, while also giving hard-hitting accounts of every sight, both famous and obscure, and providing up-to-the-minute information on contemporary culture. It was a guide that encouraged independent travellers to find the best of Greece, and was a great success, getting shortlisted for the Thomas Cook travel guide award, and encouraging Mark, along with three friends, to expand the series.

The Rough Guide list grew rapidly and the letters flooded in, indicating a much broader readership than had been anticipated, but one which uniformly appreciated the Rough Guide mix of practical detail and humour, irreverence and enthusiasm. Things haven't changed. The same four friends who began the series are still the caretakers of the Rough Guide mission today: to provide the most reliable, up-to-date and entertaining information to independent-minded travellers of all ages, on all budgets.

We now publish more than 150 titles and have offices in London and New York. The travel guides are written and researched by a dedicated team of more than 100 authors, based in Britain, Europe, the USA and Australia. We have also created a unique series of phrasebooks to accompany the travel series, along with an acclaimed series of music guides, and a best-selling pocket guide to the Internet and World Wide Web. We also publish comprehensive travel information on our Web site:

www.roughguides.com

HELP US UPDATE

We've gone to a lot of effort to ensure that the second edition of *The Rough Guide to South Africa* is accurate and up-to-date. However, things change — places get "discovered", opening hours are notoriously fickle, restaurants and rooms raise prices or lower standards. If you feel we've got it wrong or left something out, we'd like to know, and if you can remember the address, the price, the time, the phone number, so much the better.

We'll credit all contributions, and send a copy of the next edition (or any other Rough Guide if you prefer) for the best letters. Please mark letters: "Rough Guide South Africa Update" and send to:
Rough Guides, 62–70 Shorts Gardens, London WC2H 9AB, or Rough Guides, 375 Hudson St, 9th floor, New York NY 10014.
Or send email to: mail@roughguides.co.uk
Online updates about this book can be found on Rough Guides' Web site at www.roughguides.com

ACKNOWLEDGEMENTS

The editor would like to thank Cameron Wilson and Nick Thomson for extra Basics research; Elaine Pollard for proofreading; Maxine Burke and Kingston Presentation Graphics for cartography; and Susanne Hillen, Julia Bovis and Anna Wray for all the time and effort they put into production.

Barbara and Tony would like to thank: our families in South Africa, especially our mothers Pat McCrea and Lily Pinchuck for unstinting generosity while we based ourselves with them; Peta Lee for her invaluable contribution to KwaZulu-Natal; Patch Pinnock for Cape Town updates; Bronwyn Kaplan for the same in the Eastern Cape; Nita Ross for advice on the Wild Coast; Lew Elias for restaurant tips in the Eastern Cape; Roger Field; Steve Jaffee; the very many unmentioned people within the tourist industry; as well as friends, who gave us time and local insights, which have made a huge contribution to this book. We'd like to make a special mention of David Bristow for infallible orientating and steering, as well as our editor, Geoff Howard, for his sure hand, careful editing and limitless attention to detail, which kept us constantly on our toes.

Donald would like to thank: his parents for their love and support over many diverse projects over many years, but especially this last one, when it wasn't easy; also to Mo for being there and here and for her enthusiasm. In Cape Town I'd like to thank a fantastic bunch of friends and acquaintances, particularly Janey for not setting the alarm clock and Trace, Daniel and Isabella for keeping me insane. Around South Africa thanks to all those who have assisted along the way, including Johaan van Shalwyk, Murdoch Ross, Dirk Potgeiter and Hendrick van Zyl in the Northern Cape; Darron and Anita Raw, Roland Thorne, Rod and Lungile de Vletta, Richard Patricks in Swaziland; Peter and Bushy, Marnie Heim-Stafford, Johannes Van Breda and Knowledge Makhware in Gauteng; Di and Mick Jones, Ivan and Ndabesi Yaholnitsky in Lesotho; Renette Volckmar in Northwest; Arrie Horn, Chris Olivier, Damian Ruth and Shelly and Morris in Northern Province; and Dougie and Pam in Bloem. A big thanks also to Ruth and Joe Shone and Derek Schuurman for keeping an eye out for me in big bad Johannesburg. Finally thanks to Tony and Barbara for their loyalty and inspiration and to the folk at Rough Guides, particularly Geoff Howard for his patience and for holding it all together.

Greg would like to thank: my mother Elizabeth, wife Lindiwe and son Lungelo, and Rob Allingham for the music.

Finally, this edition would have been much poorer without all the readers who sent in their comments, advice, criticisms and recommendations.

THE AUTHORS

Tony Pinchuck launched his travels hitching around South Africa when he was fifteen. At university he studied African politics, and also drew political cartoon strips, several of which were banned by the apartheid government, after which he left for the UK. He has since lived in London and Sydney, earning a living as a designer, cartoonist, editor and writer, and has published articles on southern Africa, as well as nine books, including the *Rough Guide to Zimbabwe and Botswana*, and *Mandela for Beginners*. Since the installation of democracy in South Africa, he has returned to the country on several occasions to teach journalism, coordinate a workshop for African newspaper editors, and to work as a consultant on establishing a travel-writing course at Rhodes University. His latest project has been an experiment in travelling with a child, using his young son, Gabriel, as a guinea pig.

Barbara McCrea was born in Zimbabwe and went to university in South Africa, going on to teach African literature at the University Durban-Westville for two years, before coming to London in 1983. Driven by homesickness, she first wrote the *Rough Guide to Zimbabwe and Botswana* with Tony Pinchuck, before tackling even lengthier travels for the *South Africa* guide. Besides writing and travelling between South Africa, London and Sydney, she works as a movement education teacher, and looks after toddler Gabriel.

Donald Reid was born and brought up in Glasgow, studied law at Edinburgh University and left the country soon afterwards to avoid the threat of an office. Having worked on an island in the Caribbean and as a trawler fisherman in Australia, he floated into Cape Town one misty December morning in 1993 and took a notion to hang around, working on books, magazines and newspapers in South Africa for the next three years. He now lives in Edinburgh once again, working as a freelance writer and editor. He is the co-author of *The Rough Guide to Scotland*.

Greg Mthembu-Salter first went to South Africa in 1989 in search of gospel music, and has kept going back ever since for all manner of reasons. Now he's there to live, work less, and surf whenever time permits. So far, he's married, with a Capetonian son, and a still unsatisfied desire to run the city's first Congolese music nightclub.

CONTENTS

Introduction xi

● CHAPTER 3: THE NORTHERN CAPE 239–277

● CHAPTER 4: THE EASTERN CAPE 278–362

● CHAPTER 5: KWAZULU-NATAL 363–457

• CHAPTER 10: NORTHERN PROVINCE 590–618

• CHAPTER 11: LESOTHO 619–657

• CHAPTER 12: SWAZILAND 658–681

PART THREE   CONTEXTS   683

LIST OF MAPS

MAP SYMBOLS

N8	National road	◉	Hotel	�	Public gardens
R27	Regional road	▲	Campsite	⊞	Hospital
M5	Metropolitan road	⌂	Rest camp	ⓘ	Information centre
	Minor road	⊼	Picnic site	⊠	Post office
	Untarred road	⍟	Vineyard	☻	Swimming pool
	Pedestrianized road	⚔	Battlefield	⌘	Golf course
....	Road under construction	❢	Museum	★	Public transport stop
	Railway	⌒	Cave	◆	Other point of interest
- - - - -	Path	▣	Hide	■	Building
▬ ▬ ▬	International border	⚐	Viewpoint	⊞	Church
▬ ▬ ▬	Province border	⍭	Waterfall	⁺⁺⁺	Cemetery
- - - -	Chapter division boundary	⍦	Marshland		National park/nature reserve
⭭	Border post	▲	Mountain peak		Park
✕	Airport	⌃⌃	Mountain range		Beach

INTRODUCTION

South Africa is a large and massively diverse country. The size of France and Spain combined, it varies from the picturesque Garden Route towns of the Western Cape to the raw stretch of subtropical coast in northern KwaZulu-Natal. It's also one of the great cultural meeting points of the African continent, a fact obscured by years of enforced racial segregation, but now manifest in its big cities.

Above all this is an incredibly beautiful country. But it's also something of an enigma, and a visit presents some uniquely South African challenges; it has the best travel facilities on the African continent but also the most difficult surface to scratch. After so long as an international pariah, the "rainbow nation" is still struggling to find its identity.

Many visitors are pleasantly surprised by South Africa's **excellent infrastructure**, which draws favourable comparison with countries such as Australia or the United States. Good air links and bus networks, excellent roads and a growing number of first-class B&Bs make South Africa perfect touring country. For those on a budget, rapidly mushrooming **backpackers' hostels** and a couple of backpacker buses provide an efficient means of exploring. The picture isn't all rosy, however. Apartheid may be dead, but its heritage still shapes South Africa in a very physical way. The country was organized for the benefit of whites, so it's easy to get a very white-orientated experience of Africa. Nowhere is this more in evidence than in the layout of towns and cities, where African areas (often desperately poor) are usually tucked out of sight. As a visitor, you'll have to make an effort to meet members of the country's African majority on equal terms, and you'll need to take a special tour to visit the black townships – or even to know they exist.

South Africa's **population** doesn't simply reduce to black and white. The country's majority group are the **Africans** (76 percent of the population); **whites** make up 13 percent, followed by **coloureds** (8.5 percent) – descendants of white settlers, slaves and Africans, who speak English and Afrikaans and make up the majority in the Western Cape. **Indians** (2.5 percent), most of whom live in KwaZulu-Natal, came to South Africa around the turn of the century as indentured labourers.

Although a growing number of theme parks pander to a tourist appetite for ethnic **culture**, South Africa draws as much from global influences as it does from homegrown sources; you won't be able to tell a power-dressed Xhosa from a jeans-wearing Zulu in downtown Johannesburg. **Music** is one area where South Africans really hold their own, and there's nowhere better than Jo'burg to go clubbing. Up in the Drakensberg, the countless images painted thousands of years ago onto rock faces by **San** people (the now-extinct first South Africans) give a glimpse into the country's rich artistic heritage.

Crime isn't the indiscriminate phenomenon that press reports suggest, but it is an issue. Really, it's a question of perspective – taking care but not becoming paranoid. Patterns of crime aren't uniform and, statistically at least, the odds of becoming a victim are highest in downtown Johannesburg, where violent crime is a daily reality. Other cities aren't exempt, but present a reduced risk – similar to, say, some parts of the United States; many country areas are safe by any standards.

Where to go

While you could circuit the whole of South Africa in a matter of weeks, a more satisfying approach is to focus your attention on one section of the country. Every one of thenine provinces (plus Lesotho and Swaziland) holds at least a couple of compelling reasons to visit, although, depending on the time of year and your interests, you'd be wise to concentrate on either the **west** or the **east**.

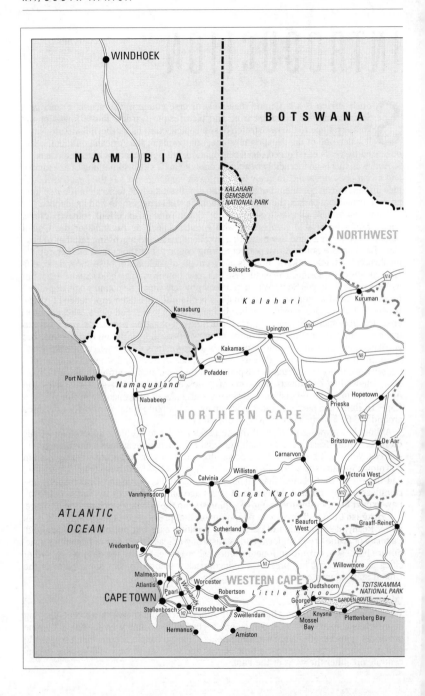

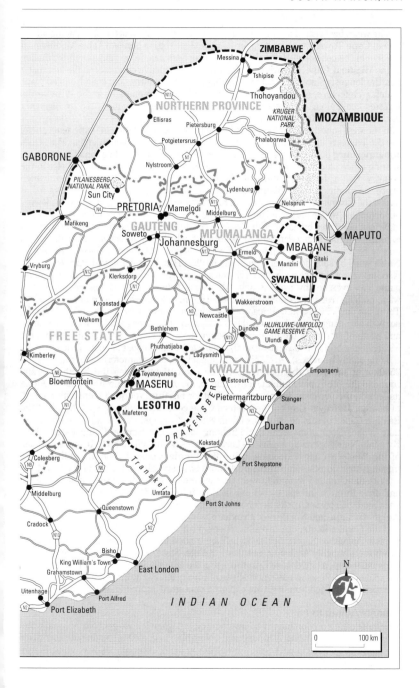

The **west**, best visited in the warmer months (Nov–April), has the outstanding attraction of **Cape Town**, worth visiting for its matchless setting beneath Table Mountain, at the foot of the continent. Half a day's drive from here can deliver any other destination in the **Western Cape**, a province which owes its distinctive character to the fact that it has the longest-established colonial heritage in the country. You'll find gabled Cape Dutch architecture, historic towns and vineyard-draped mountains in the **Winelands**; forested coast along the **Garden Route**; and a dry interior punctuated by Afrikaner *dorps* in the **Little Karoo**.

If the west sounds a bit too pretty and you're after a more "African" experience, head for the **eastern** flank of the country, best visited in the cooler months (May–Oct). **Johannesburg** is likely to be your point of entry to this area, and its frenetic street life, soaring office blocks and lively mix of people make it quite unlike anywhere else in the country. Half a day away by car lie the Northern Province and Mpumalanga, which share the mighty **Kruger National Park**. Of South Africa's roughly two dozen major parks, the Kruger flashes like a beacon to first-time visitors homing in on game-viewing opportunities, and is unrivalled on the continent for its cross-section of mammal species.

Kruger combines brilliantly with KwaZulu-Natal to the south, and an excellent short cut is to drive through tiny, landlocked **Swaziland**, which has attractions all of its own; a unique Swazi culture and a number of well-managed game parks. Once in **KwaZulu-Natal**, you'll be spoilt for superb game and birdlife; **Hluhluwe-Umfolozi Park** is the best place in the world to see endangered rhinos and there are several other outstanding **small game reserves** nearby, such as Itala, Mkuzi and Ndumo. If it's hiking and nature you want, nothing rivals the soaring **Drakensberg** range. Meanwhile **Durban** is, after Cape Town, the only city in South Africa worth visiting in its own right; a busy, cultural melting pot with a bustling Indian district and lively beachfront. The long stretch of beaches north and south of Durban is the most developed in the country; but head north towards the Mozambique border and you'll be on the wildest stretch of **coast** in South Africa.

Long sandy **beaches**, developed only in pockets, are characteristic of much of the 2500km of shoreline that curves from the cool Atlantic along the Northern Cape round to the subtropical Indian Ocean that foams onto KwaZulu-Natal's shores. Along its length, the pumping waves are excellent for **surfing**, yet don't teem with a crush of boards; **Jeffrey's Bay** on the Eastern Cape coast is a favourite spot. Much of the Eastern Cape coast is equally appealing, whether you just want to stroll, sunbathe or take in backdrops of mountains and hulking sand dunes. **Scuba-diving**, especially in KwaZulu-Natal, opens up a world of coral reefs rich with colourful **fish**, and southeast of the Western Cape winelands, along the **Whale Coast**, is one of South Africa's unsung attractions – some of the best shore-based **whale-watching** in the world.

With time in hand you might want to leave the big cities, the coast and game parks, and drive through the sparse but exhilarating **interior**, with its open horizons, switchback mountain passes, rocks, scrubby vegetation and isolated *dorps*. The offerings of the **Northern Cape** and **Northwest Province**, while less obvious than Kruger, Cape Town and the Garden Route, can reveal surprises. Visit the western section of the Northern Cape in August or September, and you'll be treated to a riot of colourful **wildflowers**. From the staunchly Afrikaner heartland of **Free State**, you're well poised to visit the very undeveloped kingdom of **Lesotho**, set in the mountains between the Free State and KwaZulu-Natal. Lesotho has few vestiges of royalty left today, but it does offer plenty of spectacular highland scenery, best explored on a sturdy, sure-footed Lesotho pony.

Climate: when to go

South Africa is a predominantly sunny country, but when it does get cold you really feel it, because indoor heating is limited and everything is geared to the fine weather that's the norm. You'll need to pack with the weather in mind, especially if you're going in winter. Southern hemisphere seasons are the reverse of the north, with **midwinter** occurring in June and July and **midsummer** over December and January, when the country shuts down for its annual holiday.

South Africa has distinct climatic zones. **Cape Town** and the **Garden Route** coastal belt have a so-called Mediterranean climate, influenced by winds blowing in from the South Atlantic. Summers tend to be warm, mild and a little unpredictable, but temperatures generally keep below 26°C (79°F). Rain can fall at any time of year and winter days can be cold and wet. Nagging winds are a feature of the Cape Town climate and sweep down for days at a time, especially in summer. Many Capetonians regard March to May as the perfect season; this is when the winds drop, it's beautifully mild and the tourists have all gone home.

KwaZulu-Natal puts on a highly convincing impression of a "tropical province", with warm winters, coral reefs and tepid seas. In fact it's well south of the tropics and is really subtropical – a technicality that won't concern you when you're enjoying its fabulous winter sunshine. Summers on average are only a degree or two above Cape Town's, but can be uncomfortably humid. The region is best visited in midwinter, when Durban's average daytime temperature is around 22°C (72°F) compared with Cape Town's 17°C (63°F) and Johannesburg's 16°C (61°F). The province's Drakensberg range has a climate similar to the Highveld, only some degrees cooler, with snow on the mountains in winter and misty days in the summer.

Johannesburg and **Pretoria** lie on a plateau and have a near-perfect climate. Despite being several hundred kilometres closer to the equator than Durban, these cities experience similar summer temperatures, but none of the humidity. Hot summer days are relieved by pyrotechnic afternoon thunderstorms with lightning flashing across slatey skies, and intense downpours of rain. Winters are dry, with chilly night temperatures. Winter days start off brisk, but by midday temperatures are rarely below the mid-teens (15°C).

East of Johannesburg, the **Lowveld**, the low-lying wedge along the Mozambique border that includes the **Kruger National Park**, is subject to similar summer and winter rainfall patterns to the Highveld, but experiences far greater extremes of temperature because of its considerably lower altitude. The average night-time low for winter is 6°C (43°F) while the daytime high is 25°C (77°F). Throughout most of the summer, you can expect daytime temperatures nudging 30°C (86°F), with peaks that soar into the high thirties. Despite this, you should take along a warm jacket for winter nights and early mornings; both can get a lot chillier than you might expect.

AVERAGE MAXIMUM TEMPERATURES (°C)											
	Jan	Feb	Mar	Apr	May	June	July	Aug	Sept	Oct	Nov	Dec
Cape Town	27	27	26	23	20	19	17	18	19	22	24	26
Durban	27	28	27	26	24	23	22	22	23	24	25	26
Johannesburg	26	26	24	22	19	16	16	20	23	25	25	26
Kimberley	33	31	28	25	21	19	19	22	25	28	30	32
Port Elizabeth	25	26	25	23	22	20	20	20	20	21	22	24
Skukuza (Kruger National Park)	31	31	30	29	27	25	25	26	29	29	30	30
Maseru (Lesotho)	20	17	14	11	9	7	7	9	11	14	17	20
Mbabane (Swaziland)	25	25	24	23	21	19	19	21	23	24	24	25

PART ONE

THE

BASICS

GETTING THERE FROM BRITAIN AND IRELAND

Most people travel to South Africa by air and it has never been cheaper or easier to get there, with an increase in the number of scheduled flights and plunging prices following the end of apartheid in the Nineties. From London there are direct flights to Johannesburg, Cape Town and Durban; the cheapest usually go via mainland Europe or Africa and involve changes of plane.

Fares depend on which **season** you're flying. To give a rough idea, the rock-bottom **basic season** is in April and May (the South African autumn); a rung up, the **low season** runs from June to November (winter and early spring); the more expensive **shoulder season** covers mid-January to the end of March; while by far the most expensive is **high season**, which falls over the first half of January and most of December (midsummer). Expect some variation on these dates from one airline to the next.

Also worth considering is an **"open-jaw" ticket**, which allows you to fly into one South African destination and out from another (say Johannesburg and Cape Town) or even to fly out from another African country. On some airlines these fares are no more expensive than a straightforward return ticket, and they have the great advantage of avoiding tedious backtracking if you're touring.

Overland options (see p.7) include journeys via East Africa, either driving or travelling by rail

---

AIRLINES IN THE UK

Air France, 10 Warwick St, 1st Floor, London W1R 5RA (☎0181/742 6600, *www.airfrance.fr*).

Air Namibia, 3 Premier House, Betts Way, Crawley, West Sussex, RH10 2GB (☎01293/596654).

Air Zimbabwe, Colette House, 52–55 Piccadilly, London W1V SAA (☎0171/491 0009).

Alitalia, 4 Portman Square, London W1H 9PS (☎0171/602 7111, *www.alitalia.it*).

Balkan Bulgarian Airlines, 322 Regent St, London W1R 5AB (☎0171/637 7637).

Britannia Airways, London Luton Airport, Luton, Beds LU2 9ND (☎01582/424155, bookings through Bluebird ☎0990/320000, *www.britanniaairways.com*).

British Airways, 156 Regent St, London W1R 5TA, and branches throughout the UK (all enquiries ☎0345/222111, *www.british-airways.com*).

Egyptair, 29–31 Piccadilly, London W1V OPT (☎0171/734 2395).

Emirates Airlines, 95 Cromwell Rd, London SW7 4DL (☎0171/808 0808, *www.emirates.com*).

Ethiopian Airlines, 4th Floor, 166 Piccadilly, London W1V 9DE (☎0171/491 9119).

Iberia Airlines of Spain, Venture House, 3rd floor, 27–29 Glasshouse St, London W1R 6SU (☎0171/830 0011, *www.iberia.com*).

KLM Royal Dutch Airlines, ticket office at Terminal 4, Heathrow (reservations ☎0990/750900, *www.klm.nl*).

Kenya Airways, Cirrus House, CFC Building, Bedfont Rd, London Heathrow Airport, Staines, Middlesex TW19 7NL (☎01784/888222, *www.kenyaairways.co.uk*).

Lufthansa German Airlines, 7–8 Conduit St, London W1R 9TG (☎0345/737747, *www.lufthansa.co.uk*).

Olympic Airways, 11 Conduit St, London W1R OLP (☎0171/409 3400).

Sabena, 10 Putney Hill, London SW15 6AA (☎0345/581291, *www.sabena.com*).

South African Airways, St Georges House, 61 Conduit St, London W1R ONE (☎0171/312 5000, *www.saa.co.za*).

Swissair, Swiss Centre, 10 Wardour St, London W1V 4BJ (☎0171/434 7300, *www.swissair.com*).

Virgin Atlantic Airways, Virgin Megastore, 14 Oxford St, London W1 (☎01293/747747, *www.flyvirgin.com/atlantic/*).

TOUR OPERATORS IN THE UK

Abercrombie and Kent, Sloane Square House, Holbein Place, London SW1W 8NS (☎0171/730 9600, *www.abercrombiekent.com*). Large upmarket operator with comprehensive and professional programmes in southern Africa.

Acacia Expeditions 23A Craven Terrace, Lancaster Gate, London W2 3QH (☎0171/706 4700, *www.acacia-africa.com*). Camping-based trips along classic South African routes, with some trips linking to Swaziland, Mozambique and Namibia.

Africa Travel Centre, 21 Leigh St, London WC1H 9QX (☎0171/387 1211, *www.africatravel.co.uk*). Experienced and knowledgeable Africa specialists with a variety of tailor-made itineraries. Agents for many South Africa-based overland operators, including Drifters.

Art of Travel, 21 The Bakehouse, Bakery Place, 119 Altenberg Gardens, London SW11 (☎0171/738 2038, *www.artoftravel.co.uk*). Highly flexible specialist agent offering fully inclusive holidays to South Africa, including Swaziland, to suit a range of budgets, using tried and tested local operators.

Discover the World, 29 Nork Way, Banstead, Surrey SM7 1PB (☎01737/218800, *www.artic-discover.co.uk*). Well-established safari holiday specialist. Tempting packages include a twenty-day train journey from Johannesburg to Cape Town, with safari excursions en route.

Grenadier Safaris, 11–12 West Stockwell St, Colchester CO1 1HN (☎01206/549585). Small but expert agent with genuine knowledge of South Africa and an affection for the region based on several years' residence. Highly personalized, upmarket trips with great attention to detail.

Hayes & Jarvis, Hayes House, 152 King St, London W6 0QU (☎0181/748 5050). Long-established operator, whose wide-ranging options stretch from budget self-catering and no-frills safaris to luxury tours. Exotic weddings organized.

Kuoni Worldwide, Kuoni House, Dorking, Surrey RH5 4AZ (Africa ☎01306/743000); 33 Maddox St London W1R (☎0171/499 8636); 2a Barton St, Manchester M2 (☎0161/832 0667). Flexible packages from this reputable long-haul operator, with good deals for families.

Okavango Tours and Safaris, Gadd House, Arcadia Ave, London N3 2TJ (☎0181/343 3283, *www.okavango.com*). Old hands with on-the-ground knowledge of the subcontinent, offering fully flexible and individual tours across South Africa.

Rainbow Tours, 64 Essex Rd, London N1 8LR (☎0171/226 1004, *rainbow@gn.apc.org*). South African specialists with trips emphasizing eco-friendly and community-based tourism.

Safari Consultants, Orchard House, Upper Road, Little Cornard, Sudbury, Suffolk CO10 0NZ (☎01787/228494, *bill.safcon@pop3.hiway.co.uk*). Individually tailored holidays across southern Africa, with particular expertise in activity-based holidays, including walking safaris.

South African Airways Holidays, 12 Coningsby Rd, Peterborough PE3 8XP (☎0870/ 607 1364). Fly-drive and tailor-made tours using SAA and other main carriers.

Sunvil Discovery, Sunvil House, Upper Square, Old Isleworth, Middlesex TW7 7BJ (☎0181/232 9797, *www.itsnet.co.uk/si/sunvil.htm*). Tailored holidays throughout southern Africa.

Thomas Cook Holidays, 12 Coningsby Rd, Peterborough PE3 8XP (☎01733/418650), plus branches throughout Britain. Fly-drive packages with South African or British Airways from Heathrow to Johannesburg, Cape Town or Durban.

Virgin Holidays, The Galleria, Ground Floor, Station Rd, Crawley, West Sussex RH10 1WW (☎01293/617181, *www.virginholidays.co.uk*). Fly-drive packages in conjunction with Virgin Atlantic Airlines.

Worldwide Journeys and Expeditions, 8 Comeragh Rd, London W14 9HP (☎0171/381 8638). Outstanding tailor-made travel programmes by a company that will steer you to the smaller, better-value options. One popular itinerary is their fifteen-day "Highlights of South Africa", which includes game viewing in Kruger, touring the Drakensberg, and then down to the Garden Route and Cape Town.

or on economy buses and converted trucks. Organized trips that show you the sights run on a number of routes, some starting in Europe.

DIRECT FLIGHTS FROM BRITAIN

South African Airways (SAA), British Airways (BA) and Virgin Atlantic fly daily from Heathrow direct to **Johannesburg**, a journey taking eleven-and-a-half hours – the fastest available. Both SAA and BA operate direct flights to **Cape Town** (12hr 30min) six times a week and to **Durban** (14hr), via Johannesburg, three times a week. Basic/high season scheduled fares – APEX – go for £690/£1025 to Johannesburg; and £733/£1065 to Cape Town.

You can usually pick up fares for a lot less by booking through travel **agents** (see box below), who will often be able to sell you the same scheduled seat cheaper or do you a deal on a direct **charter flight**, although you'll have to start planning this several weeks in advance during peak season. For the latest cheap deals, look through the travel sections of the weekend newspapers – the *Sunday Times* and *Observer* especially – and if you live in London, *Time Out* magazine and the *Evening Standard* newspaper; you may be able to pick up a return flight to Johannesburg for around £400–500 direct and to Cape Town for around £500 direct in basic season. Keep an eye out also for "seat sales"

TRAVEL AGENTS IN THE UK

Bridge the World, 47 Chalk Farm Rd, London NW1 8AN (☎0171/209 9494, *www.b-t-w.co.uk*). Specializes in round-the-world tickets, with good deals aimed at the backpacker market.

Council Travel, 28a Poland St, London W1V 3DB (☎0171/437 7767, *www.ciee.org*). Flights, with student discounts.

Flightbookers, 177–178 Tottenham Court Rd, London W1P 0LX (☎0171/757 2444); Gatwick Airport, South Terminal inside the British Rail Station (☎01293/568300); on the Web at *www.flightbookers.net*. Low fares on an extensive offering of scheduled flights.

The London Flight Centre, 131 Earls Court Rd, London SW5 9RH (☎0171/244 6411); 47 Notting Hill Gate, London W11 3JS (☎0171/727 4290); Shop 33, The Broadway Centre, Hammersmith, London W6 9YE (☎0181/748 6777). Long-established agent dealing in discount flights.

North South Travel, Moulsham Mill Centre, Parkway, Chelmsford, Essex CM2 7PX (☎01245/492882). Friendly, competitive agency offering discounted fares worldwide. Profits are used to support projects in the developing world, especially the promotion of sustainable tourism.

STA Travel, 86 Old Brompton Rd, London SW7 3LH; 117 Euston Rd, London NW1 2SX; 38 Store St, London WC1E 7BZ; 11 Goodge St, London W1P 1FE; 85 Shaftesbury Av, London W1; 40 Bernard St, London WC1N (all London enquiries ☎0171/361 6262); 38 North St, Brighton (☎01273/728282); 25 Queens Rd, Bristol BS8 1QE (☎0117/929 4399); 38 Sidney St, Cambridge CB2 3HX (☎01223/366966); 27 Forrest Rd, Edinburgh EH1 (☎0131/226 7747); 184 Byres Rd, Glasgow G1 1JH (☎0141/338 6000); 88 Vicar Lane, Leeds LS1 7JH (☎0113/244 9212); 75 Deansgate, Manchester M3 2BW (☎0161/834 0668); 36 George St, Oxford OX1 2OJ (☎01865/792800); 9 St Mary's Place, Newcastle-upon-Tyne NE1 7PG (☎0191/233 2111); on the Web at *www.statravel.co.uk*; plus branches on university campuses throughout Britain. Worldwide specialists in low-cost flights and tours for students and under-26s, though other customers are welcome.

Trailfinders, 42–50 Earls Court Rd, London W8 6FT (☎0171/938 3366); 194 Kensington High St, London W8 7RG (☎0171/938 3939); 58 Deansgate, Manchester M3 2FF (☎0161/839 6969); 254–284 Sauchiehall St, Glasgow G2 3EH (☎0141/353 2224); 22–24 The Priory Queensway, Birmingham B4 6BS (☎0121/236 1234); 48 Corn St, Bristol BS1 1HQ (☎0117/929 9000); on the Web at; *www.trailfinders.com*. One of the best-informed and most efficient agents for independent travellers. They produce a very useful quarterly magazine worth scrutinizing for round-the-world routes (for a free copy call ☎0171/938 3366).

Travel Bag, 52 Regent St, London W1R 6DX; 373–375 The Strand, opposite the Savoy Hotel, London WC2R 0JF; 12 High St, Alton, Hants GU34 1BN (southern Africa enquiries, ☎0171/287 5535). Discount flights worldwide.

The Travel Bug, 125 Gloucester Rd, London SW7 4SF (☎0171/835 2000); 597 Cheetham Hill Rd, Manchester M8 5EJ (☎0161/721 4000). Their Web address is *www.travel-bug.co.uk*. Large range of discounted tickets. Official South African Airways agent.

Travel Cuts, 295 Regent St, London W1 (☎0171/255 2082, *www.travelcuts.co.uk*). Specialists in student/youth travel and round-the-world tickets.

Travel Horizon, 107 Great Portland St, London W1N 5FA (☎0171/580 5000). Agents for Air Namibia and SAA.

Usit Campus, 52 Grosvenor Gdns, London SW1W 0AG (☎0171/730 8111); 541 Bristol Rd, Selly Oak, Birmingham B29 6AU (☎0121/414 1848); 61 Ditchling Rd, Brighton BN1 4SD (☎01273/570226); 37–39 Queen's Rd, Clifton, Bristol BS8 1QE (☎0117/929 2494); 5 Emmanuel St, Cambridge CB1 1NE (☎01223/324283); 53 Forest Rd, Edinburgh EH1 2QP (☎0131/225 6111, telesales 668 3303); 166 Deansgate, Manchester M3 3FE (☎0161/833 2046, telesales 273 1721); 105–106 St Aldates, Oxford OX1 1DD (☎01865/242067); on the Web at; *www.usitcampsco.uk*. Student/youth travel specialists, with branches also in YHA shops and on university campuses all over Britain.

OVERLAND OPERATORS IN THE UK

Dragoman, 97 Camp Green, Debenham, Stowmarket, Suffolk IP14 6LA (☎01728/861133, *www.dragoman.co.uk*). Extended journeys in purpose-built expedition vehicles through Africa. Shorter camping and hotel-based safaris also offered.

Encounter Overland, 267 Old Brompton Rd, London SW5 9JA (☎0171/370 6845, *www.encounter-overland.com*). Wide range of routes in southern Africa including six-month treks from London to Cape Town via Nairobi.

Exodus, 9 Weir Rd, London SW12 0LT (reservations ☎0181/675 5550, brochures ☎0181/673 0859, *www.exodustravels.co.uk*). Experienced adventure-tour operators running nine-week trips from Kenya to Cape Town and short tours in South Africa, including backed-up mountain biking in the Western Cape.

Explore Worldwide, 1 Frederick St, Aldershot, Hampshire GU11 1LQ (reservations ☎01252/760 000, brochures ☎01252/760 100, *www.explore.co.uk*). Journeys inside southern Africa, with a popular trip starting in Cape Town and heading along the Garden Route and through Swaziland to Johannesburg. They also offer routes that take in Namibia, Botswana and Zimbabwe.

Guerba Expeditions, Wessex House, Station Rd, Westbury, Wiltshire BA13 3JN (☎01373/826611, *www.guerba.co.uk*). Range of trans-African overland routes including Nairobi to Cape Town and shorter pick-and-mix trips in southern Africa.

Kumuka Expeditions, 40 Earls Court Rd, London W8 6EJ (☎0171/937 8855, *www.kumuka.co.uk*). Seven-week journeys from Nairobi to Cape Town, and three-week trips from Victoria Falls to Cape Town, plus short tours around South Africa using local operators.

Oasis Overland, 33 Travellers Way, Hounslow, London TW4 7QB (☎0181/759 5597, *oasisoverland@travellersway.demon.co.uk*). One of the smaller overland companies, with low prices, such as a three-week "Deserts and Game Parks" tour through Botswana and Namibia to Cape Town for £500 all-in.

Truck Africa, 37 Ranelagh Gardens Mansions, Ranelagh Gardens, Fulham, London SW6 3UQ (☎0171/731 6142, *www.truckafrica.com*). Young and fun, with trips that include one-against-the-grain from Cape Town to Harare, plus an itinerary running through northern South Africa and Swaziland to Mozambique.

from the airlines throughout the year, which sometimes bring fares in basic season down to around £400, as well as "seat auctions" run by some airlines on their Web sites.

FLIGHTS VIA EUROPE

The growing popularity of South Africa means there's a choice of easy flights from London **via Europe**. Convenient transfers and discounted prices make these definitely worth considering, although you pay the price of longer journey times and lingering in transit lounges. London to Johannesburg tickets on a number of European carriers, including Air France via Paris, Lufthansa via Frankfurt, KLM via Amsterdam, Olympic Airways via Athens and Sabena via Brussels, sometimes come up for under £350 in low season. Some of these airlines continue on to Cape Town after stopping in Johannesburg.

FLIGHTS VIA AFRICA

Cheap flights from London are also often available **via other African countries**. One of the best carriers is Air Namibia, which flies from London to Windhoek several times a week and frequently offers competitive fares on to Johannesburg or Cape Town (special prices can be as low as £350 return from London to Johannesburg). Air Namibia has good African regional connections and is also useful if you're exploring the subcontinent beyond South Africa. Air Zimbabwe flies from Gatwick to Harare with onward flights to Cape Town (once a week), Durban (once a week) and Johannesburg (twice a week). A number of other airlines, such as Kenya Airways, via Nairobi, Egyptair via Cairo, and Emirates via Dubai, offer connections to Johannesburg.

ROUND-THE-WORLD TICKETS

Round-the-world tickets provide an extremely economical way of travelling if you want to include South Africa in an extended tour taking in several continents. Routings almost always include Australia; but that aside, there's a wide choice of destinations. A popular combination is London–Johannesburg–Perth (own arrangements to Sydney)–Sydney–Los Angeles–London, which costs under £650 in May and June, or around £950 in September and October. For the same price you can fly to Harare (or another African destination)

AIRLINES, AGENTS AND TOUR OPERATORS IN IRELAND

AIRLINES

Aer Lingus, Northern Ireland reservations (☎0645/737 747); Dublin reservations (☎01/705 3333). Branches at: 41 Upper O'Connell St, Dublin; 13 St Stephen's Green, Dublin 2; 12 Upper St George's St, Dun Laoghaire; 2 Academy St, Cork (☎021/327 155); and 136 O'Connell St, Limerick (☎061/474 239).

British Midland, Northern Ireland reservations (☎0345/554 554); Dublin reservations (☎01/283 8833).

KLM UK, Reservations in Northern Ireland (☎0990/074074); in the Republic (☎0345/445588).

Lufthansa, Dublin airport (☎01/814 4755).

Olympic Airways, Franklin House, 140/142 Pembroke Rd, Ballsbridge, Dublin 4 (☎01/608 0090).

Sabena Airlines, Dublin airport (☎01/844 5454).

Virgin Atlantic, Club Travel Offices, 30 Lower Abbey St, Dublin 1 (☎01/873 3388).

AGENTS AND TOUR OPERATORS

Liffey Travel, 12 Upper O'Connell St, Dublin 1 (☎01/878 8322). Package tour specialists.

Thomas Cook, 11 Donegall Place, Belfast (☎01232/550232 or 554455); 118 Grafton St, Dublin 2 (☎01/677 1721). Package holiday and flight agent with occasional discount offers.

Trailfinders, 4–5 Dawson St, Dublin 2 (☎01/677 7888, www.trailfinders.com). Competitive fares out of all Irish airports, as well as deals on hotels, insurance, tours and car rental worldwide.

USIT, Fountain Centre, College St, Belfast BT1 6ET (☎01232/324073); 10 Market Parade, Patrick St, Cork (☎021/270900); 33 Ferryquay St, Derry (☎01504/371888); Aston Quay, Dublin 2 (☎01/602 1777 or 677 8117); Victoria Place, Eyre Square, Galway (☎091/565177); Central Buildings, O'Connell St, Limerick (☎061/415064); 36 Georges St, Waterford (☎051/872601); on the Web at www.campustravel.co.uk. Student and youth specialists.

---

and make your way overland to Johannesburg, from where you can fly out to Perth.

PACKAGES AND ORGANIZED TOURS

There are few traditional sea-and-sun **packages** to South Africa. After all, there's not much point flying for at least eleven hours just to cool out on a beach for a couple of weeks when you can do it far cheaper much closer to home. Package tours therefore tend to include some form of travelling around the country. The least imaginative of these are highly organized sightseeing **bus tours**, with punishing whistle-stop itineraries that promise more interaction with the other passengers than with local people. These through-the-window holidays can be booked at most of the large high-street travel agents, such as Thomas Cook or Going Places.

A more satisfactory alternative are **tailor-made packages** that prearrange all or part of your holiday, but leave you to travel on your own. Quite a number of well-informed tour operators and travel agents have an excellent knowledge of South Africa and specialize in such packages. If time is tighter than money, it's definitely worth drawing on their years of knowledge and expertise.

Fly-drive packages are also worth considering if you want to simply have your transport taken care of, but want the freedom to arrange the rest of your visit. Packages are available in conjunction

with BA, SAA and Virgin – the three airlines that fly direct from Heathrow to South Africa. Prices for a one-week basic package for two people travelling together range from £700 to £1000 per person (depending on season). Car rental can be extended for around £200 a week.

ORGANIZED OVERLAND TRIPS

Several overland operators run **trans-Africa routes** starting in Britain, Europe or Nairobi and working their way down to Cape Town. Some companies have stopped traversing the full length of the continent, due to the impassibility of Sudan and the Congo, but others simply fly clients over the awkward sections. A 28-week trip from **London to Cape Town** via West Africa and Nairobi costs in the region of £4500–5000 (land arrangements only); other routes go via Istanbul, Egypt and Nairobi. For a more modest eleven-week trip from **Nairobi to Cape Town** via Harare, expect to pay in the region of £2000, or around £800 for a three-week trip from **Harare to Cape Town** via Victoria Falls and Namibia. An increasing number of operators are also offering overland trips within southern Africa, taking in **South Africa and its neighbours**. Other trips just take in the well-worn **South African routes** from Cape Town, down the Garden Route through to the Kruger National Park and on to Johannesburg.

FLIGHTS FROM IRELAND

There are no direct flights **from Ireland** to South Africa and prices tend to be higher than nonstop routings from Britain. With the frequency of connections from Belfast and, to an even greater extent, from Dublin to London and several cities on mainland Europe, you shouldn't have a problem arranging a convenient **connection** if you book well in advance.

From Belfast to Johannesburg, KLM fly via Amsterdam and Olympic Airways via Athens, but these can involve a longish delay between flights (anywhere between two and eight hours).

From Dublin, the choice of flights to Johannesburg is a lot wider and the interval between connections much shorter. Among the airlines flying this route are: Aer Lingus, connecting the main European carriers in Amsterdam, Frankfurt and Zurich; British Midland, connecting with SAA at Heathrow; and Sabena, changing planes at Brussels. Apart from these, your travel agent should be able to arrange a routing to suit you.

When it comes to **packages**, you're best off contacting one of the British-based companies listed on p.4, or booking through one of the agents in the box p.7.

GETTING THERE FROM THE US AND CANADA

It's possible to fly direct from New York to Johannesburg or from Miami to Capetown in about fourteen-and-a-half hours. South African Airways (SAA), in partnership with American Airlines, operate daily nonstop flights from both airports, except for the Tuesday flight from New York, which makes a short stop for refuelling – as do all flights from South Africa to the USA.

Most other flights stop off in Europe and involve a change of plane. Daily flights are operated by **British Airways** and **Virgin Atlantic Airways** via London; **Sabena** via Brussels; **Air France** via Paris; **KLM/Northwest** via Amsterdam; and **Swissair** via Zurich. Check the waiting time between connecting flights to avoid

a long layover. The domestic carriers (see box opposite), in partnership with SAA or one of the European carriers, will provide connections from all the major US cities.

From Canada you don't have much of a choice. Daily services from Toronto or Vancouver to Johannesburg are operated by **British Airways** via London, and **KLM/Northwest** via Amsterdam.

The **high season** for travel from North America to South Africa, when fares are generally most expensive, is from mid-June to mid-September and early December to mid-January. The rest of the year is low season (most airlines have no shoulder season).

SHOPPING FOR TICKETS

Barring special offers, the cheapest of the airlines' published fares is usually an **APEX** ticket, although this carries certain restrictions. You have to book – and pay – at least 21 days before departure and spend a minimum of seven days abroad (maximum stay three months). Some airlines issue **Special APEX** tickets to **under-24s**, often extending the maximum stay to a year. Many also offer youth or student fares to **under-26s**; a passport or driving licence are sufficient proof of age, though these tickets are subject to availability and can have eccentric booking conditions. It's worth remembering that most cheap return fares involve spending at least one

AGENTS AND OPERATORS IN THE US AND CANADA

DISCOUNT AGENTS AND COURIER BROKERS

Air Brokers International, 150 Post St, Suite 620, San Francisco, CA 94108 (☎1-800/883-3273 or 415/397-1383, www.airbrokers.com). Consolidator.

Air Courier Association, 15000 W6th Ave, Suite 203, Golden, CO 80206 (☎1-800/282-1202 or 303/215-0900, www.aircourier.org). Courier flight broker.

Council Travel, 205 E 42nd St, New York, NY 10017 (☎1-800/226-8624 or 888/COUNCIL or 212/822-2700, www.ciee.com); plus branches in cities across the US. Specialists in student travel.

Educational Travel Center, 438 N Frances St, Madison, WI 53703 (☎1-800/747-5551 or 608/256-5551, www.edtrav.com). Student/youth and consolidator fares.

High Adventure Travel, 442 Post St, 4th Floor, San Francisco, CA 94102 (☎1-800/350-0612 or 415/912-5600, www.highadv.com). Round-the-world tickets. Their Web site lets you build and price your own RTW itinerary.

Now Voyager, 74 Varick St, Suite 307, New York, NY10013 (☎212/431-1616, www.nowvoyagertravel.com). Courier flight broker and consolidator.

STA Travel, 10 Downing St, New York, NY 10014 (☎1-800/777-0112 or 212/627-3111; www.sta-travel.com), plus branches in cities across the US. Worldwide discount travel firm specializing in student/youth fares; also student IDs, travel insurance, car rental etc.

Travel Cuts, 187 College St, Toronto, ON M5T 1P7 (☎1-800/667-2887 or 416/979-2406, www.travelcuts.com); plus branches in cities across Canada. Discount travel organization.

Traveler's Advantage, 3033 S Parker Rd, Suite 900, Aurora, CO 80014 (☎1-800/548-1116, www.travelersadvantage.com). Discount travel club.

TOUR OPERATORS

Although phone numbers are given here, you're better off making tour reservations through your **local travel agent**. An agent will make all the phone calls, sort out the snafus and arrange flights, insurance and the like – all at no extra cost to you.

Abercrombie and Kent (☎1-800/323-7308, www.abercrombiekent.com). Leading upscale operator with over thirty years of experience organizing African safaris. Package options include a twelve-day "Highlights of South Africa" from US$3795, and a twelve-day "Family Safari" from US$3215 for adults and US$1460 for kids (both packages are land only).

Adventure Center (☎1-800/227-8747, www.adventure-center.com). Wide variety of affordable packages, ranging from a three-day "Kruger Park Experience" from US$520, to a twelve-day "South African Panorama" from US$1675 (both land only).

Adventures Abroad (☎1-800/665-3998, www.adventures-abroad.com). Canada-based company offering small group and activity tours to South Africa and the neighbouring regions.

AfricaTours (☎1-800/235-3692, www.africasafaris.com). Moderate to high-end customized tours.

Backroads (☎1-800/462-2848, www.backroads.com). Eleven-day hiking/inn trip for US$4498 (land only).

Big Five Tours and Expeditions (☎1-888/244-3483, www.bigfive.com). Range of photographic safaris, including an eleven-day "Long Walk to Freedom" from US$2995 (including flights).

Bushtracks (1-800/995-8689 or 650/326-8689, www.bushtracks.com). Upmarket, customized tours for travellers interested in wildlife photography, at around US$400–$450 per day.

International Gay and Lesbian Travel Association (☎1-800/448-8550, www.iglta.org). Trade group with lists of gay-owned or gay-friendly travel agents, accommodations and other travel businesses.

Safaricentre (☎1-800/223-6046, www.safaricentre.com). Wide choice of packages from budget to upmarket, from a five-day camping tour of the Bushveld at US$425 per person, to an eighteen-day package with game viewing, hiking, a visit to Swaziland and a day in the Winelands, for US$1375 (land only).

Saga Holidays (☎1-800/343-0273). Specialists in group travel for seniors. Saga, and their more education-oriented subsidiary Road Scholar, offer a choice of packages including "South Africa: A Nation Reborn" (fifteen nights from US$3599, including flights).

Wilderness Travel (☎1-800/368-2794, www.wildernesstravel.com). Small group tours, including a fifteen-day luxury hiking tour for US$4895 (land only).

Worldwide Adventures/Quest Nature Tours (☎1-800/387-1483, www.worldwidequest.com). Packages include a nineteen-day mixed-accommodation hiking/game viewing/cultural tour for US$1495, and a more upscale fourteen-day hotel/lodge-accommodated, game viewing and bird-watching tour for US$3495 (both land only).

Saturday night away and that many will only give a percentage refund if you need to cancel or alter your journey, so check the restrictions carefully before buying.

You can normally cut costs further by going through a **specialist flight agent**. This can be either a **consolidator**, who buys up blocks of tickets from the airlines and sells them at a discount; or a **discount agent**, who in addition to dealing with discounted flights may also offer special student and youth fares and other travel-related services, such as insurance, car rental and tours. If you travel a lot, **discount travel clubs** are another option – the annual membership fee may be worth it for benefits such as cut-price air tickets and car rental.

Don't automatically assume that tickets purchased through a travel specialist will be cheapest – once you get a quote, check with the airlines for special offers and you may turn up an even better deal. Be advised also that the pool of travel companies is swimming with sharks – *never* deal with a company that demands cash up front or refuses to accept payment by credit card.

A further possibility is to see if you can arrange a **courier flight**, often from New York to Johannesburg or Cape Town. The hit-or-miss nature of these makes them most suitable for the single traveller who travels light and has a very flexible schedule. In return for shepherding a parcel through customs and possibly giving up your baggage allowance, you can expect to get a deeply discounted ticket. You'll probably also be restricted in the duration of your stay. Also worth considering is an **"open-jaw" ticket**, which allows you to arrive in one city, travel overland, then depart from another. Flying from New York into Johannesburg and out of Cape Town in low/high seasons costs around US$1299/1699.

If South Africa is only one stop on a longer journey, you might want to consider buying a **round-the-world (RTW) ticket**. Some travel agents can sell you an "off-the-shelf" RTW ticket that will have you touching down in a handful of cities; a typical itinerary would be Boston–London –Johannesburg–Buenos Aires–Lima–New York (US$1950). Others will tailor one to your needs but it's apt to be more expensive.

ROUND-TRIP FARES

Prices quoted below are for round-trips and exclude taxes (roughly US$50–65/CDN$30). They also assume midweek travel; for **weekend travel** check if the airline hikes its fares on its South Africa routes. SAA, for example, charge the same rates seven days a week, whereas British Airways fares are around US$25 more expensive (each direction) at weekends.

Typical lowest standard APEX **fares** to Johannesburg for low/high seasons are: Chicago (US$1649/2049); Los Angeles (US$1729/2129); New York (US$1299/1699); Toronto (CDN$2650/2915); Vancouver (CDN$3070/3335). From New York or Miami to Durban, fares are roughly US$1370/1770; to Cape Town they're about US$1299/1699.

Low-/high-season **discount/student rates** can be found for New York to Johannesburg for about US$945/1350, and to Cape Town or Durban for roughly US$995/1400.

GETTING THERE FROM AUSTRALIA & NEW ZEALAND

Southern Africa is an undeniably expensive destination for travellers from Australia and New Zealand. Fares are steep, and a ticket to Europe with a stopover in South Africa, or even a round-the-world (RTW) ticket, generally represents better value than a straightforward return.

There are flights from the eastern states and Western Australia to Johannesburg and Cape Town, but New Zealanders fly via Sydney. South African Airways (SAA), Qantas, Air New Zealand and British Airways all fly to South Africa; some of the Asian (Air Lanka, Malaysia Airlines, Singapore Airlines and Thai Airways) and Middle Eastern (Gulf Air) airlines tend to be less expensive, but their routings often entail more stopovers en route.

FARES

Whatever kind of ticket you're after, your first call should be to a **specialist travel agent** (see box overleaf), who can fill you in on all the latest **fares** and any special offers. If you're a student or under 26, you may be able to undercut some of the prices given here; STA is a good place to start. All the fares quoted are for travel during low or shoulder seasons; flying at peak times (primarily mid-May to 31 Aug & Dec to mid-Jan) can add substantially to these prices.

Johannesburg is the main South African gateway airport for flights from Australia and New Zealand, though there are also services to Cape Town, which tend to cost another A$100–200. When the airlines have surplus capacity, special fares can be as low as A$1689. Otherwise, the best return fares you're likely to find are around A$1899 from the eastern states, A$1629 from Western Australia. From New Zealand, fares start at NZ$2220.

"**Open-jaw**" tickets enable you to fly into Johannesburg and out of Cape Town (or vice versa), which can save valuable time spent backtracking; a special SAA fare costs A$1930 from the east coast (around A$200 less from Perth). If you plan to visit South Africa **en route to Europe**, you can expect to pay in the region of A$2299/NZ$2649.

ROUND-THE-WORLD TICKETS

Round-the-world tickets that take in South Africa are worth considering, especially if you

---

TOUR OPERATORS IN AUSTRALIA AND NEW ZEALAND

Abercrombie and Kent, 90 Bridport St, Albert Park, Melbourne (☎03/9699 9766); 14/17 Victoria St, Auckland (☎09/358 4200). Luxury tours of southern Africa.

African Wildlife Safaris, 1/259 Coventry St, Melbourne (☎03/9696 2899). Upmarket camping and lodge-based safaris to southern Africa.

Bench International, 36 Clarence St, Sydney (☎02/9290 2877 or 1800/221 451). African tours, focusing on wildlife and safaris.

Contiki Holidays for 18–35s, 35 Spring St, Bondi Junction, Sydney (☎02/9511 2200). Frenetic tours for the young and adventurous.

Encounter, Suite 15, 600 Lonsdale St, Melbourne

(☎03/9670 1123 or 1800/654 152). Overland tours – from seven days to 34 weeks.

Explore Worldwide, book through Adventure World, 73 Walker St, North Sydney (☎02/9956 7766 or 1800/221 931), plus branches in Melbourne, Brisbane, Adelaide and Perth; 101 Great South Rd, Remuera, Auckland (☎09/524 5118). Small-group tours and treks.

Peregrine Adventures, 258 Lonsdale St, Melbourne (☎03/9663 8611), plus offices in Brisbane, Sydney, Adelaide and Perth. Adventure tours and all-inclusive game safaris throughout Africa.

have the time to make the most of a few stopovers. Ultimately, your choice of route will depend on where else you want to visit besides South Africa, but possible itineraries include: starting from either **Melbourne**, **Sydney or Brisbane**, flying to Johannesburg, then travelling overland to Cape Town, before flying to London, and taking in Amsterdam, New York and San Francisco on the way back home (from A$2249); or, starting from **Perth,** flying to Denpasar, Casablanca, Istanbul, Nairobi, then down to Cape Town and Johannesburg on the return leg to Perth (from A$2199).

From New Zealand, you could fly from Auckland to Sydney, Bangkok and London, returning via Johannesburg and Perth to Auckland. Fares for this route start at NZ$2799.

PACKAGES AND ORGANIZED TOURS

Package holidays from Australia and New Zealand to South Africa tend to be either expensive

or of the extended **overland** variety, although airlines are beginning to put together bargain fly-drive options as demand increases. At the luxury end of the market, tailor-made **safaris** will set you back around A$6499/NZ$7200 for a two-week trip. Bench International's "Safari and Cape Town Special" is a slightly more affordable option, their fourteen-day coach tour taking in Kruger National Park, Zululand, Swaziland, Durban, plus other stops between Jo'burg and Cape Town (from A$2030, excluding flights). **Fly-drive** deals can often be found for little more than the cost of a flight alone: Qantas Holidays, for example, offer return flights to Johannesburg, seven days' car rental and your first night's accommodation for A$2000–2499 (depending on season).

Adventure tours are worth considering if you want to cover a lot of ground or get to places that could be difficult to reach independently. Contiki offer fully inclusive fourteen-day bus tours, with prices starting from A$4450, including return flights. Companies such as Encounter Overland, Explore Worldwide and Peregrine Adventures run extended camping trips taking in the Kruger National Park, Swaziland, the Drakensberg mountains and the Garden Route to Cape Town (20–28 days, A$1990–2250, air fares extra).

RED TAPE AND VISAS

EU nationals, as well as those of the USA, Canada, Australia and New Zealand, need only a valid passport to stay for up to three months in South Africa. All visitors need a valid return ticket; if you try to enter South Africa without one, you may be required to deposit the equivalent of your fare home with customs (the money will be refunded to you after you have left the country). Visitors may also need to prove that they have sufficient funds to cover their stay.

Citizens of some African and former Eastern Bloc countries do require a visa to enter South Africa, and this must be purchased before arrival, as visas are not issued at the border. If you come under this category and plan on travelling to Lesotho and Swaziland during your trip, you'll need a **multi-entry visa** to get back into South Africa. If you don't have one, it it will be issued free of charge on return, although this can be time-consuming.

For longer stays in South Africa, **visa extensions** (around R50) may be granted by the Aliens Control Section at one of the main

SOUTH AFRICAN DIPLOMATIC MISSIONS ABROAD

Australia Rhodes Place, Yarralumla, Canberra, ACT 2600 (☎02/6273 2424).

Botswana Plot 5131, Kopanyo House, Nelson Mandela Drive, Gaborone (☎304 800).

Canada High Commission, 15 Sussex Drive, Ottawa, ON K1M 1M8 (☎613/744 0330); Consulate General, Suite 2615, 1 Place Ville Marie, Montreal, Quebec H3B 4S3 (☎514/878 7231).

Ireland, 2nd floor, Alexandra House, Earlssort Terrace, Dublin 2 (☎01/661 5553).

Malawi Mpico Bldg, City Centre, Capital City, Lilongwe (☎78 3722)

Mozambique Avenue Eduardo Mondlane 41, Maputo (☎01/491614).

Namibia RSA House, corner of Jan Jonker and Nelson Mandela avenues, Windhoek (☎064/229 765).

New Zealand no representative.

UK South Africa House, Trafalgar Square, London WC2N 5DP (☎0171/930 4488).

USA Embassy, 3051 Massachusetts Ave NW, Washington, DC (☎202/232 4400); Consulates: 333 E38th St, 9th Floor, New York, NY 10016 (☎212/213 4880); 200 South Michigan Ave, 6th Floor, Chicago, IL 60604 (☎312/939 7929).

Zimbabwe Temple Bar House, corner of Baker Ave and Angwa, Harare (☎04/753147).

KINGDOM OF LESOTHO DIPLOMATIC MISSIONS ABROAD

South Africa 391 Anderson St, Menlo Park, Pretoria (☎012/46 7648).

UK 7 Chesham Place, Belgravia, London SW1 8HN (☎0171/235 5686).

USA 2511 Massachusetts Ave NW, Washington DC 20008 (☎202/797-5533).

KINGDOM OF SWAZILAND DIPLOMATIC MISSIONS ABROAD

Canada 130 Albert St, Ottawa, Ontario ON K1P 5G4 (☎613/567-1480).

South Africa Infotech Bldg, 1090 Arcadia St, Hatfield, Pretoria 0083 (☎012/342 5784).

UK 20 Buckingham Gate, London SW1E 6LB (☎0171/630 6611).

USA 3400 International Drive, Washington DC 20008 (☎202/362-6683).

offices of the Department of Home Affairs, where you will be quizzed about your intentions and your funds. In Cape Town, the Department of Home Affairs office is at 56 Barrack St (☎021/462 4970); in Johannesburg, you'll find it at 77 Harrison St (☎011/836 3228); they also have offices in quite a few towns – check in the telephone directory, and make sure that they are able to grant extensions.

Very few citizens need a **visa** to enter **Swaziland** – and those that do will be issued with one free of charge at the border. Visa requirements for **Lesotho** have a habit of changing from time to time, but the recent trend has been that citizens of Commonwealth countries,

most EU nations, the USA and Canada, do not need visas. For extended stays beyond the standard fourteen days granted at the border, contact the Department of Immigration and Passport Services, Kingsway, Maseru (☎31 7339).

CUSTOMS

At present the **duty free** allowance in South Africa is as follows: two litres of wine and one litre of spirits, 400 cigarettes and 50 cigars and 250g of tobacco per person.

South Africa, Lesotho and Swaziland are members of the Southern African Common Customs Union, which means that there is no internal **customs control** between those countries.

HEALTH

You can put aside most of the health fears that may be justified in some parts of Africa; run-down hospitals and bizarre tropical diseases aren't typical of South Africa. As in the rest of Africa, however, HIV is rampant, but there's little chance of catching it other than through intravenous drug taking or unprotected sex.

There are generally high standards of hygiene and safe **drinking water** in all tourist areas. The only hazard you're likely to encounter, and the one the majority of visitors are most blasé about, is the **sun**, which can cause short- and long-term illness. In some parts of the country there is a risk of catching **malaria**, and you will need to take precautions. See p.17 for details.

INOCULATIONS

Although no specific **inoculations** are compulsory if you arrive from the West, it's wise to ensure that your **polio** and **tetanus** jabs are up to date. A **yellow fever** vaccination certificate is necessary if you've come from a country where the disease is endemic, such as Kenya or Tanzania or tropical South America.

In addition to these, the Hospital for Tropical Diseases in London recommends a course of shots against **typhoid** and a Havrix injection against **hepatitis A**, which is caught from contaminated food or water. This is a worst-case scenario, as you probably won't be travelling in areas where these illnesses pose a serious threat. The

cholera vaccination is unpleasant, pretty ineffective and not recommended unless you are going to be working for a period in very deprived areas. In any case, despite their terrible reputation, typhoid fever and cholera are both eminently curable and few, if any, visitors to South Africa ever catch them. Hepatitis B vaccine is essential only for people involved in health work. The disease is spread by the transfer of blood products, usually dirty needles, so most travellers need not worry about it. If you decide to have an armful of jabs, start organizing them six weeks before departure.

If you're going to another African country first and need the yellow fever jab, remember that a yellow fever certificate only becomes valid ten days after you've had the shot.

STAYING HEALTHY

The surest way of staying healthy is to keep your resistance up by eating a **balanced regular diet** and by avoiding **stress** – sometimes more easily said than done. The following tips should help you to stay well on your travels and assist you over the illness if you do succumb.

WATER – AND STOMACH UPSETS

Stomach upsets from food are rare. Salad and ice – the danger items in many other Third World countries – are only found in hotels and restaurants. Both are perfectly safe. As anywhere, though, don't keep food for too long, be sure to

MEDICAL RESOURCES FOR TRAVELLERS

For a comprehensive and sobering account of the health problems which travellers encounter worldwide, consult the regularly updated *Traveller's Health*, edited by Dr Richard Dawood (OUP; Viking Penguin).

AUSTRALIA AND NEW ZEALAND

Travellers' Medical and Vaccination Centre, 7/428 George St, Sydney (☎02/9221 7133); 2/393 Little Bourke St, Melbourne (☎03/9602 5788); 6/29 Gilbert Place, Adelaide (☎08/8212 7522); 6/247 Adelaide St, Brisbane (☎07/3221 9066); 5 Mill St, Perth (☎08/9321 1977); *www.tmvc.com.au*. Up-to-date information on health-risk areas, recommended inoculations and preventative measures for travellers and so on.

Auckland Hospital, Park Rd, Grafton, Auckland (☎09/379 7440). Similar services as above.

BRITAIN AND IRELAND

British Airways Travel Clinic, 156 Regent St, London W1 7RA (Mon–Fri 9.30am–5.15pm, Sat 10am–4pm; ☎0171/439 9584); plus the clinic within Flightbookers, 177 Tottenham Court Rd, London W1P 0LX (Mon–Fri 9.30am–6.30pm, Sat 10am–2pm; ☎0171/757 2504); both are walk-in services, but appointments are available. There are appointment-only branches at 101 Cheapside, London EC2 (Mon–Fri 9am–4.30pm; ☎0171/606 2977); and at the BA terminal in London's Victoria Station (Mon–Fri 8.15–11.30am & 12.30–3.30pm; ☎0171/233 6661). BA also operate around forty regional clinics throughout the country (for the one nearest to you ☎01276/685040, or consult *www.britishairways.com*), plus at Gatwick and Heathrow airports. There are also BA Travel Clinics in South Africa, in Johannesburg, Cape Town and Knysna (in South Africa ☎011/807 3132, *www.travelclinic.co.za/*).

Healthline (☎0839/337733; 49p per minute; code for South Africa ☎73) and **Health-Fax** (☎0991/991992; £1.50 per minute; code for South Africa ☎235). Up-to-the-minute recorded advice provided by the Hospital for Tropical Diseases on how to stay healthy abroad. Computer-operated system dishes out detailed health information about South Africa and all its neighbouring countries. Health-Fax sends the same information to a fax number you specify, which actually works out cheaper.

Hospital for Tropical Diseases, St Pancras Hospital, 4 St Pancras Way, London NW1 0PE (☎0171/388 9600). Travel clinic offering consultations, jabs and any other medical gear you might need such as mosquito nets or anti-malaria pills. Consultations cost £15, a fee that is waived if you have jabs as well. Most jabs cost around £10.

MASTA (Medical Advisory Services for Travellers Abroad), School of Hygiene and Tropical Diseases, Keppel St, London WC1E 7HT (☎0171/631 4408). Commercial service providing detailed "health briefs" for all countries, and a Travellers' Healthline (☎0891/224100; 49p per minute) providing written information tailored to your journey by return of post.

Trailfinders Immunization Centre, 194 Kensington High St, London W8 7RG (Mon–Wed & Fri 9am–5pm, Thurs 9am–6pm, Sat 9.30am–4pm; ☎0171/938 3999). Walk-in advice and inoculation service operated by the respected and knowledgeable travel agency.

USA AND CANADA

Canadian Society for International Health, 1 Nicholas St, Suite 1105, Ottawa ON K1N 7B7 (☎613/241-5785). Distributes a free pamphlet *Health Information for Canadian Travellers*, containing an extensive list of travel health centres in Canada.

Center for Disease Control, 1600 Clifton Rd, NE, Atlanta, GA 30333 (☎404/639-3311, International Travelers Hotline ☎1-888/232-3228, *www.cdc.gov/travel/travel.html*). Publishes outbreak warnings, suggested inoculations, precautions and other background information for travellers.

International Association for Medical Assistance to Travellers (**IAMAT**), 417 Center St, Lewiston, NY 14092 (☎716/754-4883), and 40 Regal Rd, Guelph, ON N1K 1B5 (☎519/836-0102). Non-profit organization supported by donations, and providing a list of English-speaking doctors in South Africa, climate charts and leaflets on various diseases and inoculations.

Travel Medicine, 351 Pleasant St, Suite 312, Northampton, MA 01060 (☎1-800/872-8633). Sells first-aid kits, mosquito netting, water filters and other health-related travel products.

Travelers Medical Center, 31 Washington Square, New York, NY 10011 (☎212/982-1600). Consultation service on immunizations and treatment of diseases for people travelling to developing countries.

---

wash fruit and vegetables as thoroughly as possible, and don't overindulge on fruit – no matter how tempting – when you first arrive.

If you do get a **stomach bug**, the best cure is lots of water and rest. Papayas, the flesh as well as the pips, are a good tonic to offset the runs.

Most medicines and medical gear can be bought in pharmacies all over South Africa, so there's no need to lumber yourself with too heavy a **medical kit**. Only in deeply rural areas where few visitors ever go are you likely to be caught short. If you need specialized drugs bring your own supply, but any first-aid items can be easily replaced. A very **basic kit** should include:

Antibiotics Potentially useful if you're heading off the beaten track. A broad-spectrum variety is best.

Antiseptic cream *Bacitracin* is a reliable brand. *Nelson's* natural calendular ointment is invaluable for stings, rashes, cuts, sores or cracked skin.

Bandages One wide and one narrow.

Eyedrops Wonderfully soothing if you're travelling on dusty roads.

Fine tweezers Useful for removing thorns or glass.

Insect repellent Essential in malarial areas (see opposite).

Lip salve/chapstick Invaluable for dry lips.

Paracetamol Safer than aspirin for pain and fever relief.

Sticking plasters

Otherwise, most chemists should have name-brand anti-diarrhoea remedies. These – Lomotil, Codeine phosphate, etc – shouldn't be overused.

Avoid jumping for **antibiotics** at the first sign of illness: keep them as a last resort – they don't work on viruses and annihilate your "gut flora" (most of which you want to keep), making you more susceptible next time round. Most upsets will resolve themselves by adopting a sensible fat-free diet for a couple of days, but if they do persist unabated (or are accompanied by other unusual symptoms) then see a doctor as soon as possible.

THE SUN

The **sun** is likely to be the worst hazard you'll encounter in southern Africa, particularly if you have a fair skin. The danger of overexposure to the sun is something white South Africans haven't yet caught onto; locals still regard their tans as more important than their health.

The sun in the southern hemisphere is far more intense and transmits far more ultraviolet than it does in the north (even in the sunshine states of the USA). It's wise to limit your exposure to this major cause of **skin cancer**. If on returning home you notice any changes to any mole on your body you should see your doctor, as melanomas can be removed if caught early, but malignant melanomas can prove fatal if ignored.

Short-term effects of **overexposure** to the sun include burning, nausea and headaches. This usually comes from overeager tanning and has the nasty side effect of leaving you looking like a lobster. The fairer your skin the slower you should take tanning. Start with short periods of exposure and **high protection suncreen** (at least SPF 15),

and gradually increase your time in the sun and decrease the factor of your screen. Many people with fair skins, especially those who freckle easily, should take extra care, starting with a very high factor screen (SPF 25–30) and continue using at least SPF 15 for the rest of their stay. There's no shame in smearing sensitive areas of your face with total block cream, which contains zinc and has been made fashionable by cricketers and skiers.

Overexposure to the sun can cause sunburn to the surface of the eye, inflammation of the cornea and can result in serious short- and long-term damage. Good **sunglasses** can reduce ultraviolet light exposure to the eye by 50 percent. Look for a pair that absorbs at least 95 percent of UVR (which is invisible to the human eye) as well as UVB. A **broad-brimmed hat** is also recommended.

These last meaures are especially true for children, who should ideally be kept well-covered at the seaside. Don't be lulled into complacency on cloudy days, as this is when UV levels can be especially high. UV-protective clothing is available locally, but it's best to buy before you arrive; some excellent ranges are made in Australia. If you don't come with this gear, make sure children wear T-shirts (preferably a close-weave fabric) at the beach, and use SPF 30 sun screen liberally and often.

AIDS AND SEXUALLY TRANSMITTED DISEASES

Your biggest chance of catching **HIV** in South Africa is through unprotected sex. HIV/AIDS and other venereal diseases are widespread in southern Africa in both men and women. The chance of catching the virus through sexual contact is very real. Follow the usual precautions regarding safer sex: abstain – or at the very least use a condom. There's no special risk from medical treatment in the country, but if you're travelling overland and you want to play it safe take your own needle and transfusion kit.

BILHARZIA

One ailment that you need to take seriously throughout sub-Saharan Africa is **bilharzia**, carried in most of South Africa's fresh waterways except in the mountains. Bilharzia (schistosomiasis) is spread by a tiny, waterborne parasite. These worm-like flukes leave their water-snail hosts and burrow into human skin to multiply in the bloodstream. They work their way to the walls of the intestine or bladder where they begin to lay eggs.

Avoid swimming in dams and rivers where possible. If you're canoeing or can't avoid the water, have a test when you return home. White water is no guarantee of safety; although the snails favour sheltered areas, the flukes can be swept downstream. The chances are you'll have avoided bilharzia even if you swam in the Orange River, but it's best to be sure.

Symptoms may be no more than a feeling of lassitude and ill health. Once infection is established, abdominal pain and blood in the urine and stools are common. Fortunately it's easily and effectively treated these days with praziquantel, although the drug can make you feel ill for a few days. No vaccine is available and none foreseen.

MALARIA

Most of South Africa is free of **malaria**, a potentially lethal disease that is widespread in tropical and sub-tropical Africa, where it's a major killer. In South Africa there is a risk in **northern and northeastern Mpumalanga**, notably the **Kruger National Park**, as well as **northern KwaZulu-Natal**, in the border regions of **Northwest and Northern provinces**, and in low-lying areas of **Swaziland**. Protection against malaria is essential if you're planning on travelling to these areas. The **highest risk** is during the hot, rainy months from **November to April**. The risk is reduced during the cooler, dry months from May to October, and some people decide not to take prophylaxis during this period.

Malaria is caused by a parasite carried in the saliva of the female anopheles mosquito. It has a variable incubation period of a few days to several weeks, so you can become ill long after being bitten. If you go down with it, you may at first mistake it for flu: the **symptoms** can start off relatively mildly with a variable combination that includes fever, aching limbs and shivering, which come in waves, usually beginning in the early evening. Deterioration can be rapid as the parasites in the bloodstream proliferate: get **medical help** without delay if you go down with flu-like symptoms within a week of entering or three months of leaving a malarial area. Malaria is not infectious but it can be dangerous and even fatal if not treated quickly.

PREVENTION

No antimalarial drug is totally effective – your only sure-fire protection is to **avoid getting bitten**. Malaria-carrying mosquitoes are active between dusk and dawn, so avoid being out at this time, or at least cover yourself well.

Sleep under a **mosquito net** when possible, making sure to tuck it under the mattress, and burn **mosquito coils** (which you can buy everywhere) for a peaceful, if noxious, night. Whenever the mosquitoes are particularly bad – and that's not often – cover your exposed parts with something strong. **Insect repellents** containing diethyltoluamide work well. Other locally produced repellents such as Peaceful Sleep are widely available.

Electric mosquito-destroyers which you fit with a pad every night are less pungent than mosquito coils, but you need electricity. Mosquito "buzzers" are useless.

Doctors can advise on which kind of **antimalarial tablets** to take – generally the latest anti-resistant creation – and you can buy most without a prescription at a pharmacy before you leave. It's important to keep a routine and cover the period before and after your trip with doses. The combination of chloroquine and proguanil is the prophylactic recommended for **South Africa** by the World Health Organization. For the low-lying areas of **Swaziland**, the WHO recommends mefloquine (Larium). However, the UK Public Health Laboratory Service recommends caution to doctors prescribing this drug, which, in a tiny number of users, has serious psychiatric or psychological side effects, including depression, panic attacks, agression and psychosis. They suggest that treatment should be commenced two to three weeks before travel to enable any adverse reaction to be identified and an alternative prescribed.

TEETH AND EYES

Dental care in South Africa is well up to British and North American standards and is generally no more expensive. You'll find **dentists** in all the cities and most smaller towns. Dentists are listed after doctors at the beginning of each town in the telephone directory. You can buy cleaning kit for most types of **contact lenses** in the larger centres.

SNAKES, INSECTS AND OTHER UNDESIRABLES

South Africa features all sorts of potential bites, stings and rashes – which rarely, if ever, materialize.

Snakes are present, but hardly ever seen as they move out of the way quickly. Puff and Berg adders are the most dangerous because they lie in paths and don't move, but they're not commonly encountered by travellers. The best advice if you get bitten is to remember what the snake looked like and get yourself to a clinic or hospital. Most bites are not fatal and the worst thing is to panic: desperate measures with razor blades and tourniquets risk doing more harm than good.

Tick-bite fever is occasionally contracted from walking in the bush, particularly in long wet grass. The offending ticks can be minute and you may not spot them. Symptoms appear a week later – swollen glands and severe aching of the bones, backache and fever. Since it is a self-limiting disease, it will run its course in three or four days. Ticks you may find on yourself are not dangerous; just repulsive at first. Make sure you pull out the head as well as the body (it's not painful). A good way of removing small ones is to smear Vaseline or grease over them, making them release their hold.

Scorpions and spiders abound, but are hardly ever seen unless you turn over logs and stones. If you're collecting wood for a campfire, knock or shake it before picking it up. Contrary to popular myth, scorpion stings and spider bites are painful but almost never fatal. Most are harmless and should be left alone. A simple precaution when camping is to shake out your shoes and clothes in the morning before you get dressed.

Rabies is present throughout southern Africa. Be wary of strange animals and go immediately to a clinic if bitten. Rabies can be treated effectively with a course of injections.

HOSPITALS AND DOCTORS

Public **hospitals** in South Africa are fairly well-equipped and attempt to maintain standards, but they are facing huge pressures under which they are unfortunately buckling. Expect long waits and frequently indifferent treatment. Private hospitals or clinics, which conform more closely to British or North American standards, are usually a better option for travellers. You're likely to get more personal treatment and the costs are nowhere as prohibitive as in the US; besides which, if you're adequately insured these shouldn't pose a problem. Private hospitals are given in the town listings throughout the Guide.

TRAVEL INSURANCE

It's very important to take out a good travel insurance policy for a trip to South Africa. The policy can be quite comprehensive, anticipating anything from lost or stolen baggage and missed connections to charter companies going bankrupt; however, certain policies (notably in North America) only cover medical costs.

If you plan to participate in adventure activities, watersports or do some hiking, you'll probably have to pay an extra premium; check carefully that any insurance policy you are considering will cover you in case of an accident. Note also that very few insurers will arrange on-the-spot payments in the event of a major expense or loss; you will usually be reimbursed only after going home. In all cases of loss or theft of goods, you will have to contact the local police to have a report made out so that your insurer can process the claim.

BRITAIN

Most British and Irish travel agents and tour operators will offer you insurance when you book your flight or holiday, and some may insist you take it. These policies are usually reasonable value, though as ever you should **check the small print**. If you feel the cover is inadequate, or you want to compare prices, insurance brokers and banks should be able to help. Most companies offer at least two tiers, the more basic essentially covering medical expenses and limited loss of property,

while the upper tier will include things like loss of money, delayed flights or baggage and will promise to pay out more on lost property and medical expenses. The cheapest basic cover for South Africa starts at around £30 for seventeen days, £50 for a month, and £85 for three months – but it's always worth shopping around. If you have a good "all risks" **home insurance policy** it may well cover your possessions against loss or theft even when overseas, and many **private medical schemes** also cover you when abroad – make sure you know the procedure and the helpline number.

US AND CANADA

Before buying an insurance policy, check that you're not already covered. **Canadian provincial health plans** typically provide some overseas medical coverage, although they are unlikely to pick up the full tab in the event of a mishap. Holders of official **student/teacher/youth cards** are entitled to accident coverage and hospital in-patient benefits – the annual membership is far less than the cost of comparable insurance. **Students** may also find that their student health coverage extends during the vacations and for one term beyond the date of last enrolment. Bank and credit cards (particularly American Express) often provide certain levels of medical or other insurance, and travel insurance may also be included if you use a major credit or charge card to pay for your trip. **Homeowners'** or **renters'** insurance often covers theft or loss of documents, money and valuables while overseas.

After exhausting the possibilities above, you might want to contact a **specialist travel insurance** company; your travel agent can usually recommend one, or see the box overleaf.

Travel insurance **policies** vary. Some are comprehensive, while others cover only certain risks (accidents, illnesses, delayed or lost luggage, cancelled flights, etc.). In particular, ask whether the policy pays **medical costs** up front or reimburses you later, and whether it provides for medical evacuation to your home country. For policies that include lost or stolen luggage, check exactly what is and isn't covered, and

TRAVEL INSURANCE

AUSTRALIA AND NEW ZEALAND
Cover More, 9/32 Walker St, North Sydney (☎02/9202 8000 or 1800/251 881).
Ready Plan, 141 Walker St, Dandenong, Melbourne (☎1300/555 017); 10/63 Albert St, Auckland (☎09/379 3208).

BRITAIN
Columbus Travel Insurance, 17 Devonshire Square, London EC2M 4SQ (☎0171/375 0011, *www.columbusdirect.co.uk*).
Endsleigh Insurance, 97–107 Southampton Row, London WC1B 4AG (☎0171/436 4451, *www.endsleigh.co.uk*).
Frizzell Insurance, Frizzell House, County Gates, Bournemouth, Dorset BH1 2NF (☎01202/292 333).

Worldwide Travel Insurance Services Limited, The Business Centre, 1–7 Commercial Rd, Tonbridge, Kent TN12 6YT (☎01892/833 338, *www.wwtis.co.uk*).

USA AND CANADA
Access America, PO Box 90310, Richmond, VA 23230 (☎1-800/284-8300).
Carefree Travel Insurance,100 Garden City Plaza, PO Box 9366, Garden City, NY 11530 (☎1-800/323-3149).
Desjardins Travel Insurance Canada ☎1-800/463-7830.
Travel Guard, 1145 Clark St, Stevens Point, WI 54481 (☎1-800/826-1300, *www.noelgroup.com*).
Travel Insurance Services, 2930 Camino Diablo, Suite 200, Walnut Creek, CA 94596 (☎1-

make sure the per-article limit will cover your most valuable possession. Most policies cover only items lost, stolen or damaged while in the custody of an identifiable, responsible third party – hotel porters, airlines, luggage consignment and so on.

The best **premiums** are usually to be had through student/youth travel agencies – rates for STA policies, for example (see p.9), are US$35 for up to seven days; US$55 for 8–15 days; US$115 for one month; and US$180 for two months.

AUSTRALIA AND NEW ZEALAND

Travel insurance is available from most **travel agents** (see p.12) or direct from **insurance companies** (see box above) for periods ranging from a few days to a year or even longer. Most policies are similar in premium and coverage. Two weeks' cover for a trip to southern Africa should cost roughly A$130/NZ$145, while you can expect to pay around A$190/NZ$210 for a stay of one month, A$270/NZ$310 for two months and A$300/NZ$340 for three months.

COSTS, MONEY AND BANKS

Visitors coming from Europe, North America or Australasia will find South Africa cheap by comparison. Since the twenty percent fall in the rand in 1998, foreign visitors have found that their money goes a lot further here than at home. However, South Africa is more expensive than other African countries.

What you spend depends on the kind of trip you want to have. If If you're prepared to stay in backpackers' lodges, travel on public or backpacker transport and eat cheaply, you can get by on under **US$30/£20** a day – less if you're camping. If you plan on staying in B&Bs and guesthouses, and on eating out regularly, you should allow for anything between **US$30** and **US$60 (£20–40)** a day. In luxury hotels and game lodges, expect to pay upwards of **US$100/£60** per day. Extras such as car rental, scuba diving, horse-riding and safaris will obviously add to these figures substantially.

You'll almost always find a decent **place to stay** for under US$25/£15 a night, especially if there are two of you. Backpackers' lodges currently cost under US$7/£5 per person and most B&Bs charge less than US$25/£15 per head for a couple. A hotel costing US$50/£30 or over per head should have something special to justify the price, although, in Cape Town particularly, this cannot be guaranteed. Prices tend to be highest over the Christmas and Easter holidays, especially at the coast.

Food and **drink** are both good value, especially if you by from pavement-side stalls and markets. Most **restaurants** cost US$5–10 (£3–7) for a reasonable three-course meal. Cape Town and the Winelands are more expensive: an average meal will cost you around US$20/£13, and you can expect to fork out up to US$30/£19 per person at an upmarket restaurant. At restaurants used by working-class blacks, you can fill up on hearty stews for less than US$1/60p, although such places can feel rather intimidating to travellers new to the country. Almost all imported goods, books and international phone calls are very expensive.

Despite the size of the country, **transport** is inexpensive, especially compared to Europe, Australia and the US. Even using luxury and tourist **bus** services will not set you back much, considering the distances that are usually involved. If you're travelling around on Intercape or Translux buses, it makes sense to buy one of their variety of passes (see "Getting around" on p.26), which will save you money. Internal **flights** can be pricey; pre-planning as far in advance as possible will help keep costs down. **Driving** may not be the cheapest way of getting around, given the cost of car rental, but in many parts of the country it's the only realistic option. For this reason, you might consider buying a used car for around US$4500/£2800. **Rental cars** usually cost US$30–45 (£18–30) a day. **Fuel**, though rising in price, is still very inexpensive; roughly US35c/25p a litre.

What you'll pay **on safari** will depend very much on whether you stay in government-run national parks, where accommodation in a rondavel can cost as little as US$6/£4 per night, or fully catered for on an upmarket private reserve, where prices can rocket up to as much as US$500/£320 a night.

Most **museums** and **art galleries** charge an entry fee, usually quite low. Because prices – and the rand – tend to fluctuate, we haven't included exact entry fees for museums and galleries, but have indicated whether or not you will need to pay something to get in. Few other than the most sophisticated attractions charge more than R10.

MONEY AND THE EXCHANGE RATE

South Africa's currency is the **rand** (R), often called the "buck". Notes come in R10, 20, 50, 100 and 200 denominations and there are coins of 1,

2, 5, 10, 20 and 50 cents, as well as R1, 2 and 5. At the time of writing, the **exchange rate** was around R10 to the pound sterling, R6 to the US dollar and R4 to the Australian dollar.

All but the tiniest settlement has a **bank** where you can **change money** swiftly and easily. **Banking hours** are Monday to Friday 9am to 3.30pm, and Saturday 9am to 11am, with banks in smaller towns usually closing down for lunch. In major cities, some banks operate bureaux de change that stay open until 7pm.

Outside banking hours, some hotels will change money, although you can expect to pay a fairly hefty commission. You can also change money at branches of American Express and Rennies Travel.

TRAVELLER'S CHEQUES, CASH AND CREDIT CARDS

Travellers' cheques are the safest way to carry your funds into South Africa, as they can be replaced if lost or stolen. American Express, Visa and Thomas Cook are all widely recognized.

However, they'll be useless if you're heading into remote areas, where you'll need to carry **cash**, preferably in a very safe place, such as a leather pouch under your waistband.

Credit cards can come in very handy for hotel bookings and for paying for more mainstream and upmarket tourist facilities, and they are essential for car rental. Visa and Mastercard are the cards most widely accepted in major cities, while American Express is not. Like travellers' cheques though, credit cards won't be accepted in small *dorps* and rural areas such as the Wild Coast and Northern Cape, where again, you'll need cash for most transactions.

Visa, Mastercard and most international ATM cards (check with your bank before departing) can be used to withdraw money at **automatic teller machines** (ATMs), open 24 hours a day in the cities. When the ATM asks what type of account you have, press "cheque". Curiously, this works better with the ATMs at smaller banks like Nedbank, Volksas and United Bank than at the larger ones such as First National Bank and Standard Bank.

MAPS, INFORMATION AND WEB SITES

South Africa is experiencing a boom in tourism, and you should have no difficulty finding maps, books and brochures before you leave. The South African Tourism Board (SATOUR) is reasonably well organized: if there's an office near you, it's worth paying a visit to pick up their free map and browse through their information on hotels and organized tours. Alternatively, you can surf through South Africa's growing Internet presence for up-to-date travel details, and maps you can print out.

MAPS

Many place names in South Africa were changed after the 1994 elections – and changes continue to be made – so if you buy a **map** before you leave make sure that it's up to date. Bartholomew produce an excellent map of **South Africa**, including Lesotho and Swaziland (1:2,000,000), as part of their World Travel Map series. Also worth investing in are MapStudio's "Miniplan" maps of major cities such as Cape Town, Durban and Pretoria: these are a convenient size and have useful details, such as hotels, cinemas, post offices and hospitals. MapStudio also produce good regional maps, featuring scenic routes and street maps of major towns, and a fine Natal Drakensberg map which shows hiking trails, picnic spots, campsites and places of interest.

South Africa's motoring organization, the Automobile Association (AA) offer a wide selection of maps, free to members, which you can pick up from their offices. Their *New South African Book of the Road* is an invaluable combination of good **road maps**, a large range of city and town maps alongside information about South African flora, fauna and architecture, and troubleshooting for your car.

INFORMATION IN SOUTH AFRICA

Nearly every town in South Africa, even down to the sleepiest *dorp*, has some sort of **tourist information office** – sometimes connected to the museum or post office – where you can pick up local maps, lists of B&Bs and travel advice. In larger cities such as Cape Town and Durban, you'll find several branches offering everything from hotel bookings to organized safari trips.

We've given precise **opening hours** of tourist information offices in most cases; they generally adhere to a standard schedule of 8.30am to noon and 2pm to 5pm, Monday to Friday, with many offices also open from 9am to noon on Saturdays.

In this fast-changing country, often the best way of finding out what's happening is by word of mouth, and for this **backpackers' hostels** are invaluable. If you're planning on seeing South Africa on a budget, rest assured that the useful notice boards, constant traveller traffic and largely helpful and friendly staff you'll encounter in the hostels will greatly smooth your travels.

SOUTH AFRICA ON THE INTERNET

The tourism industry is one of the most vibrant adopters of online technogy and its range is vast, from individuals posting their B&Bs to byzantine sites with vast numbers of links. Most of the sites listed here provide good information on practicalities and background, while others, such as the Ananzi and *Mail & Guardian* sites, are excellent lead-ins to other South African topics.

SOUTH AFRICAN TOURIST OFFICES

Head office 442 Rigel Avenue South, Erasmusrand 0181, Private Bag X164, Pretoria 0001 (☎012/347 0600, fax 45 4889).
Australia 6/285 Clarence St, Sydney, NSW 2000 (☎02/9261 3424, fax 9261 3414).
UK 5–6 Alt Grove, Wimbledon SW19 4DZ (☎0181/944 8080, fax 944 6705).
USA 500 Fifth Ave, Suite 2040, New York, NY 10110 (☎1-800/822-5368 or 212/730-2929, fax 764-1980, *www.satour.org*).

SPECIALIST BOOK AND MAP SUPPLIERS

AUSTRALIA AND NEW ZEALAND
Adelaide The Map Shop, 16a Peel St (☎08/8231 2033).
Auckland Specialty Maps, 58 Albert St (☎09/307 2217).
Brisbane Worldwide Maps and Guides, 187 George St (☎07/3221 4330).
Melbourne Mapland, 372 Little Bourke St (☎03/9670 4383).
Perth Perth Map Centre, 884 Hay St (☎08/9322 5733).
Sydney Travel Bookshop, Shop 3, 175 Liverpool St (☎02/9261 8200).

BRITAIN
Bristol Stanfords, 29 Corn Street, BS1 1HT (☎0117/929 9966).
Cambridge Heffers Map Shop, 3rd Floor, 19 Sidney St, CB2 3HL (☎01223/568467, www.heffers.co.uk).
Glasgow John Smith and Sons, 57–61 St Vincent St, G2 5TB (☎0141/221 7472, www.johnsmith.co.uk).
Inverness James Thin Melven's Bookshop, 29 Union St, IV1 1QA (☎01463/233500, www.jthin.co.uk).
Leicester The Map Shop, 30a Belvoir St, LE1 6QH (☎0116/2471400).
London Daunt Books, 83 Marylebone High St, W1M 3DE (☎0171/224 2295), and 193 Haverstock Hill, NW3 4QL (☎0171/794 4006); National Map Centre, 22–24 Caxton St, SW1H 0QU (☎0171/222 2466, www.mapsworld.com); Stanfords, 12–14 Long Acre, WC2E 9LP (☎0171/836 1321, sales@stanfords.co.uk); The Travel Bookshop, 13–15 Blenheim Crescent, W11 2EE (☎0171/229 5260, www.thetravelbookshop.co.uk).
Manchester Waterstone's, 91 Deansgate, M3 2BW (☎0161/832 1992, www.waterstones.co.uk).
Newcastle upon Tyne Newcastle Map Centre, 55 Grey St, NE1 6EF (☎0191/261 5622).
Oxford Blackwell's Map and Travel Shop, 53 Broad St, OX1 3BQ (☎01865/792792, bookshop.blackwell.co.uk).

CANADA
Montréal Ulysses Travel Bookshop, 4176 St-Denis, Montreal H2W 2M5 (☎514/843-9447, www.ulysses.ca).

Toronto Open Air Books and Maps, 25 Toronto St, Toronto, ON M5C 2R1 (☎416/363-0719).
Vancouver International Travel Maps & Books, 552 Seymour St, Vancouver, V6B 3J5 (☎604/687-3320).

IRELAND
Easons Bookshop, 40 O'Connell St, Dublin 1 (☎01/873 3811).
Fred Hanna's Bookshop, 27–29 Nassau St, Dublin 2 (☎01/677 1255).
Waterstone's, Queens Bldg, 8 Royal Ave, Belfast BT1 1DA (☎01232/247 355); 7 Dawson St, Dublin 2 (☎01/679 1415); 69 Patrick St, Cork (☎021/276 522).

USA
California Book Passage, 51 Tamal Vista Blvd, Corte Madera, CA 94925 (☎1-800/999-7909 or 415/927-0960); The Complete Traveler Bookstore, 3207 Fillmore St, San Francisco, CA 94123 (☎415/923-1511, www.completetraveler.com); Map Link Inc, 30 S La Patera Lane, Unit 5, Santa Barbara, CA 93117 (☎805/692-6777, www.maplink.com); Phileas Fogg's Books & Maps, #87 Stanford Shopping Center, Palo Alto, CA 94304 (☎1-800/533-FOGG, www.foggs.com); Sierra Club Bookstore, 6014 College Ave, Oakland, CA 94618 (☎510/658-7470, www.sierraclubbookstore.com); Rand McNally, 595 Market St, San Francisco, CA 94105 (☎415/777-3131).
Chicago Rand McNally, 444 N Michigan Ave (☎312/321-1751, www.randmcnallystore.com).
New York The Complete Traveller Bookstore, 199 Madison Ave (☎212/685-9007); Rand McNally, 150 E 52nd St (☎212/758-7488).
Seattle Elliott Bay Book Company, 101 S Main St (☎1-800/962-5311 or 206/624-6600, www.elliottbaybook.com/ebbco/).
Washington DC The Map Store Inc, 1636 ISt NW, Washington, DC 20006 (☎1-800/544-2659 or 202/628-2608); Travel Books & Language Center, 4437 Wisconsin Ave ☎1-800/220-2665.

Note: Rand McNally now have more than 20 stores across the US; call ☎1-800/234-0679 for the address of your nearest store, or for **direct mail** maps.

Ananzi South Africa www.ananzi.co.za
South Africa's own search engine and the fastest way to research the myriad of local Web sites, with menus covering city guides, destinations, accommodation, safaris, tour operators, transport and more.

ANC Homepage www.anc.org.za
Dry but informative official Web site of the ANC, with daily news briefings, government documents, and links to other African Web sites.
British Airways Travel Clinic www.travelclinic.co.za

Authoritative health advice and tips from the South African branch of BATC. It draws a distinction between the health risks in South Africa and the rest of the continent – a less paranoid spin on the bugs, bites and bacteria than you'll get in Britain or the US.

Business Day *www.bday.co.za*
A solid, reliable source of daily local news (not just about business), from the sister paper of Britain's *Financial Times.*

Daily Mail & Guardian *www.mg.co.za*
The weekly *Mail & Guardian*'s homepage includes daily news and a homepage dedicated to surveying South Africa's online travel resources, as well as Jump *Start (*www.mg.co.za/mg/za1/jump.html*), its excellent launch pad for exploring other links.

Ecoafrica.com *www.ecoafrica.com*
Excellent site for nature and adventure travel, with information and booking forms for most of the major KwaZulu-Natal parks, plus the national parks in South Africa.

The Mandela Page
www.anc.org.za/people/mandela
Fine Web site packed with information on Mandela, with selected speeches and writings, articles, plus excerpts from his autobiography and the chance to write to him.

The Mbeki Page
www.anc.org.za/ancdocs/history/mbeki/index.html
Less scintillating than Mandela's page, the one devoted to his successor is nevertheless a good starting point for biographical information and a collection of his speeches and writings.

South African National Parks
www.parks-sa.co.za
Comprehensive information on parks operated by SANP, with prices and online booking. A Webcam trained on a waterhole in the Kruger National Park offers a bit of extra fun. The major shortcoming is the number of pages you have to navigate through.

Satour *www.satour.co.za*
Attractive site from the official tourism agency, though surprisingly thin on content.

South African Airways
www.saa.co.za
Current flight info, with offers and seat auctions.

Spoornet *www.spoornet.co.za*
Route details, with a useful map and timetables of all services run by the national rail utility.

The Universal Currency Converter
www.xe.net/currency
Up-to-date rates from any currency you can think of.

GETTING AROUND

Despite the large distances, travelling around most of South Africa is fairly straightforward, with a well-organized network of public transport, a good range of car rental companies, the best road system in Africa, and the continent's most comprehensive network of internal flights. The only weak point is public transport in urban areas, which is almost universally poor and often dangerous. Urban South Africans who can afford to do so tend to use private transport, and if you are planning to spend much time in any one town you'd be well advised to do the same. It's virtually impossible to get to the national parks and places off the beaten track by public transport; even if you do manage, you'll most likely need a car once you're there.

BUSES

South Africa's three established **intercity bus companies** are Greyhound, Intercape and Translux, which between them reach most towns in the country. Travel on these buses (commonly

---

ENGLISH/AFRIKAANS STREET NAMES

Many towns have **bilingual street names** with English and Afrikaans alternatives sometimes appearing along the same road. This applies particularly in Afrikaans areas away from the large cities, where direct translations are sometimes used. Some common variations you may encounter are listed in "Language" (see p.749).

---

called coaches) is safe, comfortable and good value. Fares vary according to distances covered. Generally, you can expect to pay a peak fare of roughly R360 (US$60/£36) from Johannesburg to Cape Town (1434km), and a similar amount from Cape Town to Durban (1639km). Peak fares correspond approximately to school holidays, and you can expect about thirty percent off at other times.

If you're planning on making several long journeys, it's worth investing in a **pass**. By joining Greyhound's Frequent Traveller Club (fill in the form at one of their offices), each journey you make earns you points that can eventually buy you a free bus journey. Greyhound also offer a pass that gives seven days' unlimited travel over a thirty-day period for around R950 (US$160/£95); fifteen days over thirty days for R1825 (US$350/£180); or thirty days over sixty days for R2890 (US$480/£290). If you make fifteen bus journeys with Translux, present your tickets at one of their offices and you'll get your next journey free. Their Lux Travel Pass offers seven days' unlimited travel over a thirty-day period for R1200 (US$200/£120); ten days over one month for R1600; fifteen days over one month for R2800 (US$470/£280); or thirty days over a two month period for R3400 (US$570/£340). Intercape do not offer any passes.

The **Baz Bus** operates an extremely useful hop-on/hop-off system aimed at backpackers and budget travellers. The Baz route runs up and down the coast in both directions between Cape Town and Durban. From Durban, it follows a loop through Zululand and Swaziland to Johannesburg and Pretoria, from where it heads down via the northern Drakensberg and Pietermaritzburg to Durban. It picks up and drops off at backpacker accommodation, except in instances where the place is too remote – in which case the owner of the relevant backpackers' lodge generally comes to pick you up. The only drawback, apart from occasionally erratic timing, is that the people you'll meet on them will almost exclusively be other backpackers, rather than locals.

As well as the major bus companies, there is a national network of more **inexpensive buses**, some of which are operated by Translux's sister company Transcity (sometimes called Transtate), and others operated by a host of small private companies. It's difficult to get much information about them from travel agents and tourist

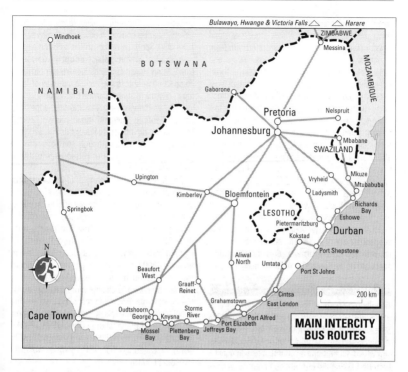

Bulawayo, Hwange & Victoria Falls △ △ Harare

MAIN INTERCITY BUS ROUTES

information offices, though Translux offer some information about the Transcity service. To find out more – and to enquire about other private company services – enquire at the main bus station the day before you travel. Apart from saving money, travelling on these buses also enables you to meet black South African travellers, who are distinctly thin on the ground on the luxury coaches.

All bus journeys can be **booked** at no extra charge through Computicket (Cape Town ☎021/918 8950, Durban ☎031/304 5560, Jo'burg ☎011/445 8300), the national booking service that also offers cinema and concert seats.

MINIBUS TAXIS

Minibus taxis travel absolutely everywhere in South Africa, covering relatively short hops from

---

INTERCITY BUS COMPANYS

Baz Bus National (☎021/439 2323, fax 439 2343). Bookings can also be made through hostels or the Baz offices at the central tourist information centres in Cape Town or Durban. Their Web site (*www.bazbus.com*) has route and pricing information.
Greyhound Cape Town (☎021/418 4310); Bloemfontein (☎051/430 2361); Durban (☎03/309 7830); Johannesburg (☎011/830 1301); Port Elizabeth (☎041/56 4879). Their Web site (*www.intercape.co.za*) has contact information, routes and prices.

Intercape Cape Town (☎021/386 4400); Port Elizabeth (☎041/56 0055); Pretoria (☎012/654 4114. Their Web site (*www.intercape.co.za*) has contact numbers.
Translux Cape Town (☎021/405 3333); Durban (☎031/361 8333); East London (☎0431/44 1999); Johannesburg (☎011/774 3333); Port Elizabeth (☎041/507 1333); Pretoria (☎012/315 2333). A useful Web site (*www.translux.co.za*) covers pricing, passes and routes.

town to town, commuter trips from township to town and back, and routes within larger towns and cities. However, the problems associated with them – unroadworthy vehicles, dangerous drivers and violent feuds between the different taxi associations who compete for custom – mean that, at least in busy urban areas, you should avoid using them. This is particularly true in cities, where minibus taxi ranks tend to be a magnet for petty criminals. The other problem with minibus taxis is that there is rarely much room to put luggage. However, despite all these drawbacks, don't rule out using this form of transport altogether. Without a car, minibus taxis will often be your only option for getting around in remote areas, where you're unlikely to encounter trouble. You should, however, be prepared for some long waits. **Fares** are very low. Try to have the exact change, and pass your fare to the row of passengers in front of you; eventually all the fares end up with the conductor, who dishes any change. There are no passes available for minibus taxis.

TRAINS

Travelling by **train** is just about the slowest way of getting around South Africa: the journey from Johannesburg to Cape Town, for example, takes 27 hours – compared to 19 hours by bus. Unless you've got a lot of time on your hands, you may be better off taking the bus, although rail travel does give you a free night's accommodation.

First- and second-class travel is in compartments equipped with washbasins and with seats that convert into bunks at night. The principal distinction between the two is that second-class cabins accommodate up to six people, while first-class takes a maximum of four, has a shower in each carriage and tends to be quieter. Coupés, which take two people in first or three people in second (although you pay for three if you want it to yourself), are ideal if you're travelling as a couple. Third-class travel isn't recommended. Seating in first and second classes is comfortable and so are the bunks, which offer the real possibility of getting a good night's sleep. If you don't have a sleeping bag, you can rent fresh cotton sheets and blankets for the night, which are brought around by a bedding attendant who'll make up your bed in the evening. It's best to buy your bedding voucher when you book your train ticket.

Spoornet (*www.spoornet.co.za*) run most of the intercity rail services. **Ticket prices** for first-class seats are comparable to the cost of a bus journey over the same distance, with second-class

compartments costing considerably less. Train tickets must be booked in advance at railway stations or at Spoornet offices in the large cities.

A word of warning about **security** on trains. Don't leave your valuables unattended in your compartment, unless you have some way of locking it, and make sure you close the window before you go, as thieves work the stations, especially around Gauteng. This may mean you won't want to eat in the dining car, so it's worth bringing your own food and drink, although someone usually comes round selling tea or coffee once or twice during the journey.

South Africa offers a handful of **luxury trains** worth considering if you want to travel in plush surroundings, often through wonderful scenery, and don't mind paying through the nose for the privilege. The celebrated **Blue Train** runs from Pretoria to Cape Town, and from Pretoria to Victoria Falls. The full Pretoria–Cape Town fare is around R4500 for the 29-hour journey. Passengers must be dressed in "smart casual" clothes during the day, and have to change into formal wear for the evening meal. You can reserve a seat on this popular train by booking through Blue Train's offices in Johannesburg (☎011/773 7631); Pretoria (☎012/315 3038); Cape Town (☎021/405 2672) or Durban (☎031/361 7550); or toll-free (☎0800/11 7715).

Another luxury rail option is offered by **Rovos Rail** (Pretoria ☎012/323 6052; Cape Town ☎021/21 4020; *len@rovos.co.za*), which runs trips from Cape Town to: Pretoria for around R5500 US$920/£550); Knysna for R3300 (US$550/£330); or if you have time on your hands, as far as Dar es Salaam in Tanzania for US$7200. Rovos also go from Pretoria to Komatipoort, for the Kruger National Park, with road transfers from there to Skukuza rest camp, for R2600 (US$435/£260); to Victoria Falls; and to Swakopmund in Namibia.

INTERNAL FLIGHTS

Flying between destinations in South Africa is an attractive option if time is short and, though not particularly cheap, it compares favourably with the money you'll spend covering long distances in a rented car, stopping over at places en route. By far the biggest airline offering domestic flights in South Africa is South African Airways (SAA) with its two associates SA Airlink and SA Express (all of which form a seamless whole, with reservations going through SAA). Other significant airlines are British

AIRLINES IN SOUTH AFRICA

British Airways/Comair Durban (toll-free ☎0800/131 4155); East and Western Cape (toll-free ☎0800/961 1196); Johannesburg (☎011/921 0222). **Sabena/Nationwide Air** Johannesburg (☎011/390 1660).

South African Airways Johannesburg (☎011/978 1111). **Sun Air** Cape Town (☎021/ 936 9111); Durban (☎031/469 3444); Johannesburg (☎011/397 2244).

Airways/Comair, Sabena/Nationwide and Sun Air, which usually work out cheaper than SAA.

Discounts are available on all airlines, the general rule being that the earlier you book the greater the saving. Subject to availability, you can expect 50 percent off if you book a month in advance and 30 percent off for booking two weeks ahead. Booking through travel agents is the best idea, as they'll know of the cheapest available fares; there's little benefit shopping around different agents as the only variation in price is going to be between airlines.

SAA and its associates have the most extensive flight network, serving the major hubs of Johannesburg, Cape Town and Durban, as well as Bloemfontein, East London, George, Kimberley, Margate, Mmabatho, Nelspruit, Phalaborwa, Pietermaritzburg, Pietersburg, Plettenberg Bay, Skukuza (Kruger National Park), Sun City, Ulundi, Umtata and Upington. As a rough guide, expect to pay just under R1000 (US$160/£100) for a one-way tourist-class fare from Johannesburg to Cape Town, or from Cape Town to Durban.

On the smaller airlines fares are sometimes as much as 25 percent cheaper than SAA. **British Airways/Comair** serve Cape Town, Durban, Johannesburg and Port Elizabeth within South Africa; and beyond its borders Harare, Victoria Falls and Windhoek. **Sabena/Nationwide** fly from Johannesburg to Cape Town, Durban and George; and smallest of all, **Sun Air** connect Johannesburg, Cape Town and Durban to each other.

If you expect to fly a fair amount, there are a number of **passes** that can save money. All the carriers operate **frequent-flyer programmes**, for which you must first fill out forms available at travel agents. None of the airlines offer discounts for students or pensioners.

Travellers expecting to make more than four flights in and around South Africa will save considerably with the **African Explorer Pass**, available on SAA and SA Express internal and regional flights. To qualify for the pass, you need an international flight to South Africa on any airline, and must quote your ticket number to your travel

agent or SAA. The pass, valid for 45 days from the date of issue, gives up to sixty percent savings when you book between four and eight flights, plus you save on VAT.

DRIVING

Given the excellent bus services, you won't need to **drive** to get between the major centres in South Africa, but it's the only way to get to national parks or remote areas where public transport is sporadic. South Africa has a generally well-maintained network of highways and a high proportion of its secondary and tertiary roads are tarred and drivable at speed. The only real challenge you'll face is **other drivers**.

If your visit is a long one – six weeks or more – it's worth considering **buying a vehicle**, which you can then sell at the end of your trip. On shorter trips, **renting a vehicle**, though not cheap, will enable you to explore areas in depth and at your own pace.

The usual **fuel** in coastal areas is **97** and **93 octane** on the highveld, with most filling stations now offering **unleaded** too.

Filling stations are frequent on the major routes of the country, and usually open 24 hours a day, so it's hard to run out of fuel. If you wander off these, though, stations are less frequent, so do fill up regularly if you're on a long journey. Stations are rarely self-service. Instead, poorly paid attendants will fill up your car, check oil, water and tyre pressure if you ask them to, and often clean your windscreen even if you don't. A tip is always appreciated, though not obligatory. The transition from lowveld to highveld affects the timing of a small proportion of engines, so it's a good idea to have a quick retuning if you notice a loss of power.

REGULATIONS AND DRIVING TIPS

Foreign **licences** are valid in South Africa for up to six months provided that they are printed in English. If you don't have such a licence, you'll need to get an International Driving Permit before arriving in South Africa (available from national motoring organizations). When driving, make sure you have your driving licence and your passport on you at all times.

INTERNATIONAL CAR RENTAL AGENCIES

UK

Avis ☎0990/900 500
Budget ☎0800/181 181
Europcar ☎0345/222 525

Hertz ☎0990/996 699
Holiday Autos ☎0990/300400

AUSTRALIA

Avis ☎1800/225 533
Budget ☎132 727

Hertz ☎133 039

NEW ZEALAND

Avis ☎09/526 2847
Budget ☎09/375 2222

Hertz ☎09/309 0989

NORTH AMERICA

Avis ☎1-800/331-1084
Budget ☎1-800/527-0700

Hertz ☎1-800/654-3001;
in Canada ☎1-800/263-0600
Kemwel Holiday Autos ☎1-800/422-7737

You drive on the **left-hand side**; **speed limits** range from 60kph in built-up areas to 100kph on rural roads and 120kph on highways and major arteries. Note that traffic lights are called **robots** in South Africa.

You won't find many roundabouts in the country; instead, there are **four-way stops**, where the rule is that the person who got there first leaves first, and you are not expected to give way to the right.

South Africa has among the world's worst road accident statistics – the result of reckless driving, **drunken drivers** or defective, overloaded vehicles. Keep your distance from cars in front, as domino-style pile-ups are particularly common. Watch out also for overtaking traffic coming towards you; overtakers often assume that you will head for the hard shoulder to avoid an accident – it is legal to do this, but it's also dangerous, so be careful. If you do pull into the hard shoulder to let a car overtake, the other driver will probably thank you by flashing the hazard lights. If oncoming cars flash their headlights at you, it probably means that there is a speed trap up ahead.

Other potential **hazards** include animals on the road in rural areas. This can be especially dangerous at night, so drive slowly at that time. Finally, the large **distances** between major towns means that falling asleep at the wheel, especially when travelling through long stretches of flat landscape in the Karoo or the Free State, is a real danger. Plan your car journeys carefully to include plenty of breaks and stopovers. Driving in Johannesburg, you risk the danger of being **carjacked**; see p.53 for safety hints.

CAR RENTAL

Renting a car can be quite expensive, but it's recommended if you want to travel widely and don't fancy being governed by public transport timetables. Prebooking your car with a travel agent before flying out is the cheapest way of doing it, and will provide more favourable terms and conditions (such as unlimited mileage and lower insurance excesses).

The major car rental companies present in South Africa are Avis (☎0800/021 111), Budget (☎0800/01 6622), Europcar (☎0800/01 1344), Hertz (☎0800/02 1515), Imperial (☎0800/13 1000) and Tempest (☎0800/03 1666) – see box above for international phone numbers. As a rough guideline, for a one-week rental you can expect to **pay** upwards of R1200 (US$200/£120) including collision damage and theft waivers, as well as about 1400 free kilometres. Most companies stipulate that drivers must be a **minimum age** of 21.

The advantage of renting through major companies is that you do not have to return the car to where you hired it from, but can deposit it in some other major centre instead; though rental companies will usually levy a charge for this. If you're planning on driving into **Lesotho** and **Swaziland**, check that the company allows it – some don't. Insurance often doesn't cover you if you drive off the tar, so check for this too. Local firms are almost always cheaper, but usually have restrictions on how far away from base you can go.

Camper vans can be a good idea for getting to remote places where accommodation is scarce. Expect to pay around R800 (US$135/£80) per day for a vehicle that sleeps three. Some companies offer standby rates that knock fifteen to twenty percent off the price if you book at short notice (one week or less ahead). Vans come fully equipped with crockery, cutlery and linen and usually a toilet. The downside of camper vans is that they struggle up hills and guzzle a lot of fuel (15 litres per 100km in the smaller vans, and 20 litres per 100km in the larger ones), which could partly offset any savings on accommodation.

One of the biggest **camper-van rental companies** is Britz Africa (toll-free ☎0800/11 7460, *britzafr@iafrica.com*), which has branches in Cape Town (☎021/981 8947, fax 981 8946), Durban (☎031/72 9326, fax 72 9329) and Johannesburg (☎011/396 1860, fax 396 1937), and will pick you up from the airport and return you for about R70. Rainbow Camper Hire is another company with offices in Cape Town (☎021/948 0743, fax 949 7515) and Johannesburg (☎011/396 1445, fax 396 1757). One of the cheapest companies is Knysna Camper Hire (☎044/382 2444, fax 382 5887, *knysnacampers@pixie.co.za*) in Knysna, who charge R600 per day, with up to twenty-five percent discount for long-term rentals .

BUYING A CAR

Suprisingly, **buying a used vehicle** in South Africa is more expensive than in most Western countries, and you will have to spend at least R20,000 (US$3350/£2000) to be sure of getting something reliable. However, you should be able to get most of your money back when you sell it, providing you haven't paid over the odds for the vehicle in the first place, although it can take a few weeks to get the price you deserve.

Buying from a **dealer** will generally up the price by ten to twenty percent, but should enable you to get a warranty for the vehicle. Bear in mind that this is only worth having if you are able to return the car to the dealer who issued it, which is likely to be tricky if you're travelling around the country.

Alternatively, you can buy a car through the **small ads** in the newspapers or in the growing number of free ads papers. If you do this, it helps to know something about the kind of vehicle you are buying, as no guarantee will be offered for its roadworthiness. If you don't trust your own mechanical abilities, enlist the services of the AA, who check out cars for about R400 (US$65/£40). Go for a car that still has a few months of its road tax left to save forking out for another year's worth of tax when you register the car.

Beware of **rust**: cars from coastal regions, particularly those from Cape Town, are most likely to be on the rusty side. The least rusty vehicles are usually from the Northern Cape or somewhere equally dry.

When you buy, make sure you get the **registration document** from the previous owner, as you'll need it when you come to register the vehicle in your name. Make sure you have a contact number for the previous owner too, just in case the car turns out to have been stolen. After buying the car, you need to ensure that it's **roadworthy**. This involves taking it to the nearest testing station and paying for it to be put through a series of pretty basic tests. One possible problem that can arise is that the engine serial numbers do not all match up. If this happens, you'll have to take the vehicle to a police testing station where they run a series of computer checks to see if the car has been stolen.

Once you've got the roadworthy certificate, head for the nearest vehicle registration centre with your certificate, registration document, driving licence, passport and about R100 (US$16/£10): all this is enough to procure you your own registration document for the vehicle.

Selling a vehicle is a lot more simple than buying one. All you need is the registration document to give to the new owner, a completed form for the transfer of ownership (which you can pick up from any vehicle registration centre), and a photocopy of the new owner's ID book or passport. Once you have handed over the keys and the new owner has driven away, you need to present the completed form and photocopy to a vehicle registration centre.

Most South Africans drive without any form of **insurance** but you would be foolish to do the same. Aim to buy a third-party insurance policy, preferably comprehensive, as soon as you take charge of a new vehicle. **Joining the AA** is a good idea, and you can join for a year for about R300 (US$50/£30). Their maps, travel advice and emergency services can be invaluable when driving around.

CYCLING

It's easy to see why **cycling** is popular in South Africa: you can get to stunning destinations on good roads unclogged by traffic, and many towns have decent cycle shops for spares and equipment. You'll need to be fit though, as South Africa is a hilly place and many roads climb punishing gradients. The weather can make life difficult too: if it isn't raining, there is a good chance of it being very hot, so carry plenty of liquids. An increasing number of backpackers' hostels rent out mountain bikes for reasonable rates, making it easy to do plenty of cycling without having to transport your bike into the country. Cycling on the main roads is not recommended.

HITCHING

Generally speaking, **hitching** in most areas of South Africa is not a good idea, particularly in large towns and cities. Even in rural areas it's risky and, while you might encounter wonderful hospitality and interesting companions, it's advisable not to hitch if you have any doubts at all.

If you must hitchhike, it's essential to take a number of precautions to maximize your safety. Avoid hitching alone, and being dropped off in isolated areas between *dorps*. Ask drivers where they are going before you say where you want to go, and keep your bags with you: having them locked in the boot makes a hasty escape more difficult. Check the notice boards in backpackers' lodges for people offering or looking to share lifts – that way, you can meet the driver in advance.

ACCOMMODATION

While you shouldn't expect the kind of bargains found in other Third World countries, accommodation in South Africa does offer good value for money. On average B&B prices are quite a bit cheaper than they are in Britain, and you'll invariably find that you get a lot more for your money. Except for the cheapest of rooms, you'll almost always get a private bath or shower, and you'll often have the use of a garden or swimming pool. The continuing growth in backpacker accommodation means that you should be able to find a hostel in most areas, and many will offer excellent facilities. Finally, at the camping and self-catering end of the scale, you'll be spoilt for choice: this is the preferred form of holiday accommodation of

South Africans themselves and the country is amply supplied with caravan parks, camping resorts and self-catering apartments and cottages.

Advance booking is vital if you're planning on staying in a national park or in popular areas such as Cape Town or the Garden Route, or if you're visiting during high season. South Africa's **peak season** is during the midsummer Christmas school holiday period (roughly Dec 4–Jan 21), which coincides with many foreign tourists piling in to catch their winter tan. The Easter school holiday (March 20–April 15) is a shorter and less intense period, when South African families migrate to the coast and inland resorts. At both Christmas and Easter, **prices** for budget and mid-priced accommodation (but not camping or backpacking) can as much as double, and most places get booked up months ahead.

There's a lull in the midwinter **low season** (June–Aug), during which time you should have no problem finding plenty of good-value places to stay, at least outside Cape Town and the Garden Route.

HOTELS

Most of South Africa's cheaper **hotels** are throwbacks to the Fifties and Sixties and are being left behind by the growing profusion of guesthouses and B&Bs – many have degenerated into watering holes that earn most of their keep from their bar. Hotels are really only worth considering at the middle to the top end of the scale, and then only if

ACCOMMODATION PRICE CODES

All the accommodation listed in the Guide has been categorized into one of nine price bands, as set out below. The rates quoted represent what you can expect to pay for much of the summer **per person**, and unless otherwise stated, are based on two sharing. Rooms are generally en suite. Expect prices in some areas to be significantly higher in peak season (Dec–Jan & Easter), and look out for discounts during the winter.

① **Up to R50**. Camping and dorms at backpackers' lodges, with shared washing and cooking facilities.

② **R50–100**. At the bottom end of this range are doubles at backpackers' lodges, and downmarket B&Bs, both with shared bathrooms. At the top end you'll get slightly run-down hotels, good self-catering accommodation on farms, at resorts and in towns, and good budget B&Bs offering rooms with bath in less touristy areas. The most basic national parks accommodation in rondavels with shared washing and cooking facilities also fall into the upper end of this range.

③ **R100–150**. Basic mid-range hotels, good B&Bs and guesthouses, which should have a degree of style and will usually have a garden and swimming pool. Some en-suite self-catering national parks chalets are within the top half of this range.

④ **R150–200**. Stylish B&Bs and guesthouses in popular areas, and exceptional places off the beaten track. This category also includes good mid-range hotels and the best en-suite national parks accommodation.

⑤ **R200–250**. The starting range for comfort and style, whether in a guesthouse, upmarket hotel or country lodge. Expect spacious rooms, gardens with swimming pools, the occasional Jacuzzi, first-class service and above-average food.

⑥ **R250–300**. As above, but the location ought to be outstanding, perhaps with sea or mountain views.

⑦ **R300–400**. Very few establishments in the Guide fall into this band, though it does include the odd exceptional guesthouse and luxury hotel.

⑧ **R400–500**. Excellent places to stay, and there's really no need to pay more than this for top-notch hotels. You'll also find exceptional country hotels and lodges with full-board rates.

⑨ **Over R500**. The sky's the limit here. Virtually every private lodge in the Kruger National Park and other game reserves fall into this band. We only recommend urban accommodation in this range if it's truly out of the ordinary.

you want plenty of facilities and luxurious accommodation and are prepared to pay through the nose for it. At some of the most expensive places you'll be paying for the social cachet of the name and may find equal facilities nearby far cheaper.

At the **bottom end** you can expect unremarkable en-suite rooms from around US$16/£10 per person. In smaller places off the tourist routes, you'll often have a choice of one or two hotels of this type, and these are rarely good value. There are exceptions of course: hotels with real charm in *dorps* where you'd least expect them, and we've included many of those in this guide.

At **mid-range** hotels you'll usually pay between US$20–40/£12–25, and you can expect decent, frequently excellent, standards, often in old and characterful buildings that have been refurbished. Many hotels in this middle category are comparable to guesthouses for the same price, but they offer an acceptable alternative if you prefer hotel anonymity and facilities such as room service, private telephone and TV. Many mid-priced hotels – especially those on main routes in the interior – get fully booked up during the week

by travelling salesmen; but over the weekends, when they're often empty, you can often negotiate reasonable discounts. Along the coastal holiday strips such as the Garden Route and southern KwaZulu-Natal and all the major seaside towns in between, medium-priced hotels are ubiquitous and frequently offer rooms right on the beachfront.

South Africa's main hotel chains include Holiday Inn, Protea, Southern Sun and Karos, all of which offer reliable but rather soulless accommodation. At this **upmarket** end of the scale, prices can be pretty high but for US$80–90/£50–60, you should have no problem at all enjoying the height of luxury. If conspicuous consumption is as important to you as comfort, then you could find yourself shelling out over US$160/£100 per person to stay somewhere like Cape Town's *Mount Nelson*.

If you're going to dig that deep in your pocket, you may be better off at one of the many pleasant country hotels with beautiful gardens tucked away in scenic parts of the country, such as the Garden Route and the KwaZulu-Natal Midlands. It's worth being warned about South Africa's idiosyncrasy over "smart casual" wear, which is demanded by many posher hotels after 6pm. The directive applies mainly to men, and in practice means you'll need a pair of slacks, a decent shirt with a collar and closed shoes.

CARAVAN PARKS, RESORTS AND CAMPING

Caravanning was once the favourite way of enjoying a cheap family holiday in South Africa, and this accounts for the very large number of caravan parks dotted across the length and breadth of the country. However, their popularity has declined and with it the standard of many of the country's **municipal caravan parks and campsites**. Today, municipal campsites are generally pretty scruffy places, though you may find the odd pleasant one in rural areas, or near small *dorps*. Staying in a municipal campsite adjoining a city or large town will often be more grief than it's worth; not only will facilities generally be run-down, but theft is a big risk. In most municipal sites you can expect to pay roughly US$8/£5 per site.

All in all, you're best off heading for the better-organized **privately owned resorts**, where for roughly the same price you'll get greater comfort and a lot more facilities. Although private resorts sometimes give off a holiday-camp vibe, they usually have good washing and cooking facilities, self-catering chalets, shops selling basic goods, *braai* stands and swimming pools.

Virtually all **national parks** in the country – and many provincial reserves – have campsites

and in some of the really remote places, such as parts of KwaZulu-Natal, camping may be your only option. A site is unlikely to cost more than US$12/£8. At national parks you can rely on well-maintained washing facilities and there are often communal kitchen areas or at the very least a *braai* stand and running water as well as decent communal shower, toilet and washing facilities (known locally as "ablutions").

Camping rough is not recommended anywhere in the country, and with so many proper campsites, even in very remote areas, it's very unlikely you'll have to pitch a tent anywhere else.

BACKPACKERS' LODGES AND YOUTH HOSTELS

Backpackers' lodges comprise the fastest-growing category of accommodation in South Africa and their quality is improving all the time. Most offer basic hostel accommodation in a dormitory for under US$8/£5 per person, and many have some doubles, which cost a little more. They usually have communal kitchens, an on-site restaurant or café, TV, Internet facilities and bike rental.

The lodges are invariably good meeting points, with large notice boards filled with advertisements for hostels and backpacker facilities, and a constant stream of travellers passing through. Many lodges operate reasonably priced excursions into the surrounding areas, and will pick you up from railway stations or bus stops (especially Baz bus stops) if you phone in advance. The only drawback with staying in this

YOUTH HOSTEL ASSOCIATIONS

South Africa, Hostelling International South Africa, 3rd Floor, St George's House, 73 St George's Mall, Cape Town 8001 (☎021/424 2511, fax 424 4119, *info@hisa.org.za*).

England and Wales, Youth Hostel Association (YHA), Trevelyan House, 8 St Stephen's Hill, St Albans, Herts AL1 2DY (☎01727/855 215, *www.yha.org.uk*); YHA International Booking Network ☎01629/581 418; shop and membership desk, 14 Southampton St, London WC2 7HY (☎0171/379 0597).

Northern Ireland, Youth Hostel Association of Northern Ireland, 22 Donegal Rd, Belfast BT12 5JN (☎01232/324 733).

Ireland, An Oige, 61 Mountjoy St, Dublin 7 (☎01/830 4555, *www.irelandyha.org*).

Scotland, Scottish Youth Hostel Association, 7 Glebe Crescent, Stirling FK8 2JA (☎01786/451 181, *www.syha.org.uk*)

Canada, Canada Hostelling Association, Room 400, 205 Catherine St, Ottawa, ON K2P (☎1-800/663-5777).

USA, Hostelling International-American Youth Hostels (HI-AYH), 733 15th St NW, Suite 840, PO Box 37613, Washington DC 20005 (☎202/783-6161, *www.hostels.com*).

Australia, Australia Youth Hostels Association, 422 Kent St, Sydney (☎02/9261 1111, *www.yha.org.au*); 205 King St, Melbourne (☎03/9670 9611); 236 William St, Perth (☎08/9227 5122).

New Zealand, Youth Hostels Association of New Zealand, 173 Gloucester St, Christchurch (☎03/379 9970, *www.yha.org.nz*).

YHA BOOKINGS

The following hostels and lodges in the Guide can be **booked in advance** through your local Youth Hostel Association office:

WESTERN CAPE
Cape Town *Abe Bailey Youth Hostel, The Albergo, Ashanti Lodge, City Slickers, Cloudbreak Backpackers' Lodge, The Green Elephant, Overseas Visitors Club Hostel* and *Riverview Guest Lodge.*
Hermanus *Zoete Inval.*
Knysna *Highfield Backpackers Guest House.*
Mossel Bay *Mossel Bay Backpackers* and *Santos Express.*
Plettenberg Bay *Albergo for Backpackers.*
Stellenbosch *Backpackers Inn* and *Stumble Inn.*

EASTERN CAPE
Cintsa *Buccaneer's Retreat.*
Jeffreys Bay *Jeffrey's Bay Backpackers.*
Port Alfred *Sherwood Shack.*
Port Elizabeth *Jikeleza Lodge* and *Port Elizabeth Backpackers.*

KWAZULU-NATAL
Durban *Durban Beach Youth Hostel* and *Tekweni Backpackers.*

MPUMALANGA
Sabie *Jock of the Bushveld Hostel.*
Hazyview *Kruger Park Backpackers.*
Nelspruit *Nelspruit Backpackers.*
Phalaborwa *Elephant Walk.*

GAUTENG
Johannesburg *Backpacker's Ritz* and *The Explorer's Club.*
Pretoria *Mazuri Backpackers* and *Pretoria Backpackers.*

NORTHERN CAPE
Kimberley *Gum Tree Lodge.*

SWAZILAND
Mlilwane Wildlife Sanctuary *Sondzela Backpackers' Lodge.*

kind of accommodation is that you tend to meet the same people over and over again as you travel around.

An **upmarket** variant on backpackers' lodges is still something of a fledgling development, aimed at thirtysomethings who want reasonably priced, casual accommodation, but are looking for something a little more stylish and sedate. At these places you'll get a very decent double for under US$13/£8, and can still expect congenial communal areas. They are still rare, so don't count on finding one in every town.

South Africa's **youth hostel** scene is on the small side, with around fifty backpackers' lodges affiliated to Hostelling International South Africa (HISA), part of the international Youth Hostel Association network. Located in all the major tourist centres, some of these can be prebooked and prepaid for via the International Booking Network (see box).

HISA has also put together a "Go-as-you-please" package for YHA members, comprising prepaid dormitory vouchers (valid for up to a year) and discounted passes for Translux intercity buses.

SELF-CATERING

Away from the resorts, **self-catering accommodation** in cottages, apartments and small complexes provides the cheapest option outside of staying in a backpackers' lodge. A self-catering holiday almost always clocks up at less than US$16/£10 per person per night for two people sharing. Apartments often sleep up to six, and because rates are mostly quoted for entire units this can be extremely economical if you're travelling as a family or in a group. Even though you don't usually get breakfast (although this is sometimes offered for a small extra charge), you can save a lot of money by cooking for yourself, and you'll get a sense of freedom and privacy missing from the nicest guesthouse or B&B.

Apart from chalets at the ropiest of municipal caravan parks, standards of self-catering accommodation are usually quite high. Cottages or apartments generally come fully equipped with crockery and cutlery – and even microwaves and TVs in the more modern places. Linen and towels are often, but not always, provided – check before you book in.

One of the best things about self-catering is the wide choice of location you'll get. There are self-catering options on farms, near beaches, in forests and in wilderness areas, as well as in practically every town and city. We've listed many places throughout this guide – however, they are so widespread that it's always worth enquiring locally at tourist information bureaus if our recommendations are full.

B&BS, GUESTHOUSES AND FARMSTAYS

More and more South Africans are opening their homes to visitors, and in some places you'll be spoilt for choice. The most basic **B&B** consists of just one or two rooms inside a house, where you share washing facilities with the owners and pay around about US$16/£10 per person. Far more common are the efficiently run B&Bs with en-suite rooms, often in garden cottages or annexes to the main house, and frequently with tea-making facilities and the use of a garden; for these you can expect to pay around about US$16–40/£10–25. In several places, Cape Town being the most notable, B&Bs are not allowed to display signs outside, but they usually have sign-posts in their front gardens, and often there will also be clear official signs pointing from the main street. It's worth asking to see your room first and get a feel for the place; South Africans are highly hospitable and at some B&Bs you run a real risk of being overwhelmed by attentive hosts and having little privacy.

For decades the homes of black South Africans were deliberately kept hidden from tourist trails, a state that has changed dramatically with the proliferation of township tours. Since the late Nineties, township dwellers have begun offering accommodation, opening up new possibilities for experiencing South Africa. **Township B&Bs** are still few in number, but this is a sector that's bound to grow, and we've tried to cover as many as possible that exist at the time of writing. Expect to pay around US$13/£8 for this type of accommodation.

The defining line between a B&B and a **guesthouse** can seem a little hazy. According to official definition, guesthouses are professionally run establishments without a public bar that rent out between four and fourteen rooms – they are dedicated lodgings rather than offshoots of someone's home. For practical purposes guesthouses fall somewhere between B&Bs and better hotels in facilities, atmosphere and cost. Prices start at around US$30/£20 per person and many offer half board.

Along many roads in the countryside you will see signs for "*Bed en Ontbyd*" (Afrikaans for "bed and breakfast") – this signals **farmstay** accommodation. As with urban B&Bs you will either be in rooms in the main homestead or in a cottage in its garden. On a farmstay you can usually expect a hearty Afrikaner breakfast and prices a little below urban B&Bs. Some offer hiking, horse-riding, and other activities and excursions – there are some real gems dotted about, which we've listed in this guide. Tourist information bureaus will almost always have lists of farms in the area that rent out rooms or cottages.

NATIONAL PARKS ACCOMMODATION

Almost every **national park** in the country has a choice of several types of accommodation. Classic pre-Seventies accommodation is often arranged in circles facing inward without a view – a pity as national parks are invariably in beautiful settings. However, there will always be one or two that do have vistas and it's worth your while trying to secure a bed in one of these. Fortunately, recent fashion has been towards architect-designed rest camps with imaginative accommodation of a good standard, that makes the most of the site while emphasizing privacy (something the KwaZulu-Natal parks excel at).

Accommodation options include **campsites**, which cost about about US$12/£8 per site; one-room **rondavels** with shared washing and cooking facilities for US$8–13/£5–8 per person; **safari tents** at some of the Kruger and some KwaZulu-Natal rest camps in the region of US$10–13/£6-8; and self-contained **chalets** with private bath or shower and cooking facilities, which come out at about US$23–30/£14–18 per person. For groups of four there are self-contained **family cottages** with private bath and kitchen, where the price of the whole unit is around US$100/£60; and if there are five or six of you, you can aim for one of the **guest cottages** that go for US$100–150/£60–90 – this can work out fairly reasonably for a group.

In all national parks accommodation (apart from camping) you get bedding, towels, a fridge and basic cooking utensils. The ultimate wildlife accommodation is in the **private game reserves**, most of which are around the Kruger National Park. Here you'll pay big bucks, but will get a far more intimate experience of the wild. At this level accommodation is almost always luxurious and can be in large en-suite walk-in tents, small thatched rondavels, or plush rooms with air conditioning in the larger and most expensive lodges. Prices start with a handful of places that charge US$125/£75 per person per night; but more commonly you can expect to pay upwards of US$160/£100, rising to several times that amount at the most fashionable spots. It's worth remembering that, high as these prices are, all your meals and game drives are included and you're essentially paying for an exclusive experience of the bush rather than for just a bed (see p.40 for more details).

PARKS RESERVES AND WILDERNESS AREAS

No other African country has as rich a variety of parks, reserves and wilderness areas as South Africa. Literally hundreds of game reserves and state forests pepper the terrain, creating a bewildering but enticing choice. While there are dozens of unsung treasures among these, the big destinations amount to just over a dozen parks protecting the country's major game reserves and wilderness areas. With few exceptions these fall under KwaZulu-Natal Conservation Services, who control most of the public reserves in KwaZulu-Natal, and the South African National Parks, who cover the rest of the country.

It's important to realize that only some national parks are also game reserves; the chart overleaf details what to expect from the major parks. **Wildlife** is what most people come for, and here again South Africa excels. But don't let the Big Five (buffalo, elephant, leopard, lion and rhino) blinker you into missing out on the marvellous **wilderness areas** that take in dramatic landscapes and less-publicized animal life. There are parks protecting marine and coastal areas, wetlands, endangered species, forests,

MAJOR PARKS AND WILDERNESS AREAS

MAJOR PARKS AND WILDERNESS AREAS

KEY	PARK	PRINCIPAL FOCUS	DESCRIPTION AND HIGHLIGHTS	DETAILS
WESTERN CAPE				
1	Karoo NP	Desert reserve	Arid mountainous landscape with ancient fossils, herbivores and wild flowers in spring.	p.177
2	Tsitsikamma NP	Marine and coastal	Cliff, tidal pools, deep gorges and evergreen forests. Snorkelling, scuba and forest trails.	p.222
3	Wilderness NP	Marine and coastal	Lakes, rivers, lagoons, forest, fynbos, beaches and the sea.	p.205
4	West Coast NP	Marine and coastal	Wetland wilderness with birding and watersports.	p.230
EASTERN CAPE				
5	Addo Elephant NP	Endangered species	Home to more than 200 elephants, Cape buffaloes and various antelopes.	p.291
6	Mountain Zebra NP	Endangered species	Dramatic hilly landscape in flat country with rare mountain zebras and other herbivores.	p.315
NORTHERN CAPE				
7	Kalahari-Gemsbok NP	Desert/game reserve	Remote desert with rust-red dunes, desert lions, shy leopards and thousands of antelopes.	p.260
8	Augrabies Falls NP	Desert reserve	Orange River plummets down a deep ravine. Rhinos, antelopes and prolific birdlife.	p.258
FREE STATE				
9	Golden Gate NP	Mountain enclave	Resort at the foot of rich sandstone formations in the heart of the Maluti Mountains. Trails.	p.471
NORTHWEST				
10	Pilanesberg NP	Game reserve	Mountain-encircled grassland trampled by the Big Five, accessible from Johannesburg.	p.538
NORTHERN PROVINCE/MPUMALANGA				
11	Kruger NP	Game reserve	The largest, best-stocked and most popular game reserve in the subcontinent.	p.573
KWAZULU-NATAL				
12	Greater St Lucia	Coastal wetland	Vast patchwork of wetlands, wilderness, coast and game reserves.	p.428
13	Hluhluwe-Umfolozi GR	Game reserve	KwaZulu-Natal's hillier, smaller answer to Kruger is among the top African spots for rhinos.	p.425
14	Itala GR	Game reserve	Lesser-known small gem of a game reserve in mountainous country.	p.442
15	Mkuzi GR	Game/bird reserve	Top birding venue, excellent for rhinos and other herbivores. Walks in wild fig forest.	p.434
16	Natal Drakensberg Pk	Mountain reserve	A series of parks covering the highest, most stirring and most dramatic peaks in SA.	p.420

deserts and mountains, usually with the added attraction of animals, birds, insects, reptiles or marine mammals.

If you had to choose just one of the country's top three parks, **Kruger**, stretching up the east flank of Mpumalanga and Northern Province, would lead the pack for its sheer size (it's larger than Wales), its range of animals, its varied Lowveld habitats and unbeatable game-viewing opportunities. After Kruger, the **Tsitsikamma**, in the Western Cape, attracts large numbers of visitors for its ancient forests, cliff-faced oceans, the surging Storms River Mouth as well as its Otter Trail, South Africa's most popular **hike**. For epic mountain landscapes, nowhere in the country can touch the **Natal Drakensberg Park**, which takes in a series of reserves on the KwaZulu-Natal border with Lesotho and offers gentle hikes along watercourses as well as ambitious mountaineering for serious climbers.

The unchallenged status of Kruger National Park as the place for packing in elephants, lions and casts of thousands of animals, tends to put the **KwaZulu-Natal parks** in the shade; quite undeservedly, as they have several points going for them. As well as offering the best places (in the world) for seeing **rhino**, these parks feel less developed than Kruger, often provide superior (but no more expensive) accommodation, and are just as accessible for self-driving. Both Kruger and KwaZulu-Natal parks offer guided **wildlife trails** and **night drives**, a popular way to catch sight of the elusive denizens that creep around after dark.

SAFARIS

If it's **wildlife** you've come to see, you'll find South Africa hard to beat. The country has the best-managed **national parks** in Africa, with well-organized rest camps, developed over four decades to provide cheap holidays for white South African families, and offering reasonably priced accommodation, campsites and good self-catering facilities.

Game viewing isn't a cheap business, and mostly you get what you pay for. The **least expensive** way of experiencing a game park is by renting a car and **self-driving** around a national park, taking advantage of the self-catering and camping facilities. Nearby backpackers' lodges, and occasionally hotels and B&Bs, will often offer **safari excursions**. The disadvantages of these are that you miss out on the experience of waking up in the wild and you spend considerably more time on the road. But during South African school holidays, when Kruger, for example, is booked to capacity, you may have no other option. Another budget alternative for the Kruger, worth considering if you're alone and have no transport, is to stay outside the park and take game drives with a safari company into the park or a **budget tour** from Johannesburg or one of the gateway towns.

In addition to the state-run parks there are expensive **private reserves**, frequently abutting onto them and sharing the same wildlife population. For your money you'll see the same animals, but under more exclusive conditions, staying at luxurious game lodges staffed by well-informed rangers who lead game-viewing outings in open-topped Land-Rovers. If you're new to the African bush and its wildlife, consider shelling out and spending at least two nights at one of the safari lodges on the private reserves abutting Kruger and then set out on your own. If money's no object, don't bother with self-driving at all.

A word of warning: be wary of any cheap deals on "safari farms" in the vicinity of Kruger. These are generally fine if you want to see animals in what are essentially huge zoos and make an acceptable overnight stop en route to Kruger, but are no substitute for a real wilderness experience – sooner or later you hit fences and gates on your game drive. Some of the better places in this category are given in the relevant chapters.

Spotting game takes skill and experience. It's easier than you'd think to mistake a rhino for a large boulder, or to miss the king of the beasts in the tall, lion-coloured grass – African game is after all designed with camouflage in mind. Don't expect the volume of animals you get in wildlife documentaries, which edit months of filming into half an hour: what you see is always a matter of luck, patience and skill. The section of the Guide on Kruger National Park (see p.573) gives advice on how to go about spotting game and how to enjoy and understand what you do see – whether it's a brightly coloured lizard in a rest camp, head-butting giraffes at a waterhole or dust-kicking rhinos. For other **books** that can enhance your visit to a game reserve, see p.737.

Although the Kruger is the focus for most of South Africa's safari activity, particularly for venturing into the wilderness with skilled guides, the KwaZulu-Natal game reserves – foremost among them **Hluhluwe-Umfolozi**, **Mkuzi** and **Itala** – offer rewarding opportunities for self-drive touring. The same applies to the **Pilanesberg Game Reserve** in Northwest Province, while the remote **Kalahari-Gemsbok National Park** on the border of Botswana promises truly exciting wilderness driving. A number of extremely upmarket operations offer the whole game-lodge experience on private reserves, where your vehicle stays in the car park and you walk or are driven around by a guide. Among the most prestigious of these are **Phinda** in KwaZulu-Natal and **Tswalu** in the Northern Cape.

SELF-DRIVE SAFARIS

Self-driving involves the thrill of spotting game yourself, rather than relying on a game ranger, and gives you the freedom to stick around for as long as you like. For people with **children** it's the principal way to get into a game reserve, as most of the upmarket lodges don't admit under-twelves. You also have the advantage of going at your own pace, and may choose to cover a route that takes in both

the Mpumalanga reserves and those in KwaZulu-Natal, just a few hours away – an appealing combination of one large and some more intimate reserves, which will cover very different terrain.

As far as **accommodation** at the state reserves is concerned, you'll usually have a broad choice of camping; basic chalets with shared washing facilities; safari tents; or comfortable en-suite units (see p.36 for prices). En-suite accommodation is in serviced, thatched rondavels with linen provided. The cheaper units usually don't have their own kitchen, although everywhere you go will have a fridge, tea-making facilities and somewhere to *braai*. In several of the KwaZulu-Natal parks rest camps you aren't allowed to use the kitchen, but give your food to the camp chef and attendants who prepare your meal for you, serve you and wash up, at no extra cost. **Advance booking** is essential to secure a place to stay in a national park – this is especially true during holiday season.

Most game reserve rest camps have a **shop** selling supplies for picnics or *braais*, as well as a **restaurant**.

If you plan to self-drive, consider investing in good animal and bird field **guides**; once in the park, you'll find them indispensible for identification and learning about what you see. The same applies to a decent pair of **binoculars** – one pair per person is recommended if you want to keep your relationships on a friendly footing. Finally, whether you're cooking or not, it's worth taking a thermos for tea and a cool bag to keep water cold.

The one real disadvantage of self-driving is that you can end up jostling with other cars to get a view, especially when it comes to lion-watching. Also, you may not know what signs to look out for in order to spot game; and unless you travel in a minibus or 4WD vehicle you're unlikely to be high enough off the ground to be able to see across the *veld*.

PRIVATE RESERVES AND LODGES

If you choose well, the ultimate South African game experience has to be in a **private reserve** or **lodge**. The advantage of private reserves is that you spend time in a small group and relax while your game-viewing activities are organized, and because you rarely see other visitors you get a stronger sense of the wild than you ever could at one of the big Kruger rest camps. Most of all, you get the benefit of knowledgeable rangers, who can explain the terrain and small-scale wildlife as they drive you around looking for game.

Nowhere are the private reserves more developed than along the west flank of the **Kruger**, where you'll find the top-dollar prestigious lodges as well as some places offering more bang for fewer bucks.

Smaller private reserves accommodate between ten and sixteen guests, which gives you very close contact with your hosts and the opportunity to ask about flora and fauna around meal tables and at teatimes. Larger camps often cater to two or three times as many people, and resemble hotels in the bush, though you'll always have a game ranger and see the same quantity of game. Many safari lodges have their own waterholes, overlooked by the bar, from which you can watch animals drinking.

Accommodation is in luxurious safari tents with private bathrooms, or in a variety of chalets – some thatch and brick, some stylish luxury suites. A couple of places have "bush-showers" (a hoisted bucket of hot water with a shower nozzle attached) behind reed screens but open to the sky – one of the great thrills of the bush is taking a shower under the southern sky. Some chalets or tents have gaslights or lanterns in the absence of electricity. **Food** is usually good and plentiful, and vegetarians can be catered for.

A **typical day** at a private camp or lodge starts at dawn for tea or coffee followed by guided game viewing on foot, or driving. After a mid-morning brunch/breakfast, there's the chance to spend time on a viewing platform or in a hide, quietly watching the passing scene. Late-afternoon game viewing is a repeat of early morning but culminates with sundowners as the light fades, and often turns into a night drive with spotlights out looking for nocturnal creatures.

Prices, which include accommodation, meals and all game activities, vary widely, though expensive doesn't necessarily mean better. You might find that the cheaper camps in the same areas are more to your taste, simply because of the plainer and wilder atmosphere that is more in keeping with the bush. The ultra-expensive camps offer more luxury and social cachet, but not necessarily better game viewing.

FOOD AND DRINK

South Africa doesn't really have a coherent indigenous cuisine, although attempts have been made to elevate Cape Cuisine to this status. Traditional African food tends to focus around stiff grain porridge (similar to Italian *polenta*) accompanied by meat or vegetable-based sauces. Among white South Africans, Afrikaners have evolved a style of cooking known as *boerekos*

("farmer's food") that tends to be cholesterol-rich and can be heavy-going if you're not used to it. People of British extraction favour the traditional English style of meat and overcooked vegetables.

With its thousands of kilometres of coast, South Africa is blessed with a vast array of seafoods, from oysters to numerous species of fish – and this is where you should focus your culinary attention. In all the major cities you'll find reasonably priced restaurants covering an ever-increasing range of international styles and eclectic local adaptations.

SOUTH AFRICAN FOOD

Although South Africa's indigenous offerings are few, you can still expect to eat well in this country. The variety of food available is huge and context is always important – you may not want to eat *boerewors* at a restaurant; but at a *braai* under the stars, accompanied by a few beers, it's almost obligatory.

CAPE CUISINE

Styles of cooking brought by Asian slaves have evolved into **Cape Cuisine** (sometimes known as

THE BRAAI AND BOEREKOS

Braai (which rhymes with "dry" and is an abbreviation of *braaivleis*), is an Afrikaans word literally translated as "meat grill" and is probably the only place you'll catch an unreconstructed white South African man cooking. A *braai* is basically a barbecue, but white South Africans have perfected the form, and at any national park, nature reserve or resort you'll never be far from a permanent *braai* stand.

Barbecuing is an intensely social activity and is usually done among family and friends accompanied by gallons of beer. You can *braai* anything, but a traditional barbecue meal consists of huge slabs of steak, lamb cutlets and **boerewors** ("farmer's sausage"), a deliciously spicy South African speciality. Potatoes and onions wrapped in aluminium foil and placed in the embers are a usual accompaniment. The real skill comes in knowing when the coals are hot enough to cook the meat and in concocting the marinades and sauces. A variant on the *braai* is **potjiekos** ("pot food"), in which the food is cooked, preferably outdoor over an open fire, in a three-legged cast-iron cauldron.

In a similar vein, but cooked indoors is **boerekos**, a diet eaten mainly by Afrikaners. Much of it is similar to English food, but taken to cholesterol-rich extremes, with even the vegetables prepared with sugar and butter. Should you spend the night on an Afrikaans farm, you could well find yourself waking up to a breakfast of several eggs, steak, piles of bacon and *boerewors*. *Boerekos* comes into its own in its variety of over-the-top desserts, including *koeksisters* (plaited doughnuts saturated with syrup) and *melktert* ("milk tart"), a solid rich custard in a flan case.

Cape Malay food — a misnomer given that few slaves came from Malaysia). Characterized by sweet aromatic curries, Cape Cuisine is worth sampling at least once, especially in Cape Town, where it developed and is associated with the Muslim community. Although it can be delicious, there isn't that much variety and few restaurants specialize in it. Despite this, most of the dishes considered as Cape Cuisine have actually crept into the South African diet, many becoming part of the Afrikaner culinary vocabulary. For details of particular dishes see p.121.

OTHER ETHNIC AND REGIONAL INFLUENCES

Although there's nothing as distinct as regional cuisines in South Africa, you will find changes of emphasis and local specialities in different parts of the country. **KwaZulu-Natal**, for instance, particularly around Durban and Pietermaritzburg, is especially good for Indian food. The South African contribution to this great multifaceted tradition is the humble **bunny chow**, a cheap takeaway consisting of a hollowed out half-loaf of white bread originally filled with curried beans, but nowadays with anything from curried chicken to sardines (see p.384).

Because of its proximity to Mozambique, **Portuguese food** made early inroads into South Africa, predominantly through the use of hot and spicy peri-peri seasoning, which goes extremely well with *braais*. The best-known example of this is delicious **peri-peri chicken**, which you will find all over. **Italian food** has also been around

for a while, brought over with POWs from the North Africa campaign who were incarcerated here and stayed on after World War II. You'll find some excellent Italian restaurants in the cities, from small pizzerias to smarter restaurants going the whole hog.

Eastern European **Jewish food** came with turn-of-the-century refugees and you'll find bagels, chopped liver and chopped herring at delis and some supermarkets.

VEGETARIAN FOOD

While not quite a **vegetarian** paradise, South Africa is nevertheless vegetarian-savvy and you'll find at least one concession to meatless food on most menus. Even steakhouses will have something palatable on offer and generally offer the best salad bars around; especially at the Spur chain, where you can fill up on greens for not much more than US$2/£1. If you're self-catering in the larger cities, head for the delicious dips and breads at delis and Woolworth's and Pick'n'Pay supermarkets. South Africa's choice of vegetables and fruit is wide and inexpensive compared to Europe.

PLACES AND PRICES

Restaurants in South Africa offer outstanding value compared with Britain or North America. In every city you'll find places where you can eat a good main course for well under US$8/£5 and for US$16/£10 you can splurge on the best. Restaurants with imaginative menus are found in all the larger centres. **Franschhoek**, a small town in the Winelands, has established itself as a culinary centre for the country, where you'll find some fine eateries in extremely close proximity. As a rule restaurants are licensed, but Muslim establishments serving Cape Cuisine don't allow alcohol at all.

An attractive phenomenon in the big cities, especially Cape Town, has been the rise of the continental-style **cafés** – easy-going, informal places where you can eat just as well as you would in a regular restaurant, but also drink coffee all night without the feeling that you're expected to order food. A reasonable meal in a café is unlikely to set you back more than US$7/£4. Café service tends to be slick and friendly, and opening hours long. Make sure you don't confuse this new type of café with the traditional South African café found in even the tiniest country town. The equivalent of a corner store elsewhere, they commonly sell a few magazines, soft drinks, sweets, crisps and an odd collection of tins and dry goods. Their only concession to ready-to-eat food is normally a meat pie heated in a microwave oven or a leg of chicken that spent a little too long incubating in the warmer.

If popularity is the yardstick, then South Africa's real national cuisine is to be found in its **franchise restaurants**, which you'll find in every town of any size. The usual international names like KFC and Wimpy are omnipresent, but these are no match for South Africa's own home-grown American-style steakhouses, such as **Spurs**, **Steers** and **Saddles**, projecting a wholesome Wild West image that has successfully been roping in South African families for decades. South Africa's great contribution to the world of fast food is the **Nando's Chickenland** chain, which grills excellent Portuguese-style chicken, served under a variety of spicy sauces. Expect to pay around US$3/£2 for a filling burger and chips or chicken meal at any of these places and somwhere around US$5/£3 for a good-sized steak.

DRINKING

Although South Africa yearns to be a major wine-producing country, **beer** is indisputably the national drink. Beer is as much an emblem of South African manhood as the *braai* is for whites – and unlike the *braai* it cuts through all race and class divisions. Pubs and bars are not the centres of social activity they are in the US or the UK, although in the African townships **shebeens** or informal bars do occupy this position. Whites tend to do their drinking at home. In city centres, **bars** have traditionally been rough, men-only places, women being corralled into stiff lounges or ladies' bars attached to hotels. The **Irish/British-style pub** is beginning to make an appearance under the invasion of a series of franchised names, but has no deep roots in South African culture. Beer, wines and spirits can be bought at supermarkets and bottle stores (the equivalent of the British off-licence), which generally keep normal shopping hours, although some stay open until 6.30pm. Don't expect be able to buy liquor at night or on Sundays.

BEER

South Africans tend to be fiercely loyal to their brand of **beer**, though they all taste pretty much the same, given that virtually all beer in the country is produced by the huge South African Breweries monopoly. **Lager** is the predominant style, and to a British palate is likely to taste a bit thin and bland, though it can be wonderfully refreshing drunk ice-cold on a sweltering day. One or two microbreweries have sprung up, best known of which is Mitchell's in Knysna, which produces some distinctive ales. These can be found at some bottle stores and bars between Cape Town and Port Elizabeth. **Imported beers** are starting to make an appearance, but they're rather expensive by comparison with the local product.

WINES

South Africa's **wine industry** is rising out of years in the doldrums, casting aside a 350-year-old tradition of trying to make French wine, and is starting to take a pride in the **Cape wine** label. Exports are rising and, though South African wines haven't reached the general standards of Australian wine (yet), make no mistake: this country produces some excellent wines that can give the Aussies a good run for their money – and it's dead cheap.

Prices for quaffable bottles start below US$3/£2 and you won't find many over US$15/£10. At twice this price you can expect the best, although anything over about US$6/£4 is considered outrageously expensive by locals. This means that anyone with an adventurous streak can indulge in a bacchanalia of sampling without breaking the bank. Wine is available throughout the country, although prices rise as you move out of the Western Cape – and not always to levels that appear accountable just to transport costs.

The best way to sample wines is by visiting **wineries**, some of which charge a small tasting fee to discourage freeloading. The oldest and most rewarding wine-producing regions are the **Constantia estates** in Cape Town (see p.104) and the region known as the **Winelands** around the towns of Stellenbosch (see p.140), Paarl (see p.148) and Franschhoek (see p.155), which all have institutionalized wine routes. Other wine-producing areas include the Klein Karoo (see p.159), Robertson (see p.163), the Swartland (see p.227), the Orange River (see p.255) and Walker Bay (see p.186).

SOFT DRINKS AND FRUIT JUICE

There are no surprises when it comes to **soft drinks**, with all the usual names available. What does stand out is South African **fruit juice**. The range is broad and includes what must be one of the most extensive selections of unsweetened juices in the world under the Liquifruit and Ceres labels.

POST, PHONES AND EMAIL SERVICES

Most towns of any size have a post office, generally open Monday to Friday 8.30am to 4.30pm and Saturday 8am to 11.30am (closing earlier in some places). The deceptively familiar feel of South African post offices can lull you into expecting an efficient British- or US-style service. In fact, post within the country is slow, erratic and unreliable, and money and valuables are frequently stolen en route. For important items, it makes sense to use one of the private courier services such as Federal Express, which are more expensive, but far more reliable.

Expect domestic delivery times from one city to another of about a week – longer if a rural town is involved at either end. **International airmail** deliveries are often quicker, especially if you're sending or receiving at Johannesburg, Cape Town or Durban – the cities with direct flights to London. By surface mail you can expect your letter or package to take anything up to six weeks to get from South Africa to London. **Stamps** are available at post offices and newsagents, such as the CNA chain, and postage is relatively inexpensive compared to Britain or North America. You'll find **poste restante** facilities at the main post office in most larger centres, and in many backpackers' hostels.

PHONES

South Africa's **telephone system**, operated by the state monopoly, Telkom, works well and public phone booths are easily found in every city and town, with increasing numbers being installed in rural areas – a tangible result of the new government's policy of taking services to the people. There are two types of Telkom phone: coin- or card-operated. International calls can be made

CHANGES TO PHONE NUMBERS

Phone numbers in various areas of the country are being changed as South Africa progessively upgrades and expands its network. Some of the numbers given in this book may go out of date during its lifetime. If you have a problem getting through, contact the directory enquiry service on ☎1023.

DIRECTORY ENQUIRIES AND INTERNATIONAL CODES

Telkom operates an extremely useful **directory enquiry service** (☎1023). However, English is not the first language of many of the operators and, with standards of literacy quite a lot lower than in Europe or North America, be prepared to be patient and to help the operator with spelling. Also remember that the English accent people are accustomed to here may be very different to your own – so talk slowly and clearly.

INTERNATIONAL CALLS

To call southern Africa **from overseas**, dial the international access code (☎00 from the UK; ☎011 from the US and Canada; ☎0011 from Australia) followed by the country code. Remember to leave out any zeros in front of domestic area codes. The international codes are:

South Africa ☎27   Lesotho ☎266   Swaziland ☎268

To dial **out of South Africa**, the international access code is ☎09. To dial **out of Lesotho and Swaziland**, the code is ☎00. Remember to omit any zeros in front of the city, town or area code of the place you're phoning. Outgoing international codes from South Africa include:

Australia ☎09 6   Ireland ☎09 353   New Zealand ☎09 64   UK ☎09 44   USA and Canada ☎09 1

from virtually any of them, and for this it helps to have a card, as you'll be lucky to stay on the line for more than a minute or two for R15. **Cards** are available at Telkom offices, post offices and newsagents, and come in R15, 20, 50 and 100 denominations.

The cheapest time to make **international calls** is Monday to Friday 8pm to 8am and during the weekends. **Reverse-charge calls** are made through the International Operator Service (☎0900).

If you need to use the phone while staying at a **hotel**, be sure to ask what their rate is – the surcharge is often extortionate. In cities you'll find **private phone bureaus**, where you can make your call on a normal phone and pay afterwards, but, while it's more comfortable to sit down, these cost considerably more than a Telkom phone booth. Some of these bureaus will also send and receive **faxes** for you, which though expensive, may turn out cheaper than making a phone call. Many newsagents also offer fax services, which they advertise in their windows.

Mobile phones (known locally as cellular or cell phones) operate on the GSM digital system and are well-established in South Africa, with two competing networks covering all the main areas and the national roads connecting them. If you want to use your GSM phone in South Africa you

will need to arrange a **roaming agreement** with your provider at home – but be warned this is likely to be expensive. An alternative is to buy **prepaid cards** offered by both networks, which carry a code to key into your handset when you want to start using them. Mobile phone **rental** can be arranged at the airports in the main cities as well as through other providers in town. If you are phoning someone who is on a mobile phone, remember that calls are usually more expensive than the Telkom network, for you as well as the recipient.

EMAIL

The unreliability of mail and the expense of phones have provided the motivation for early adoption of **email** and the Internet: both are remarkably well-established for this relatively poor country. Many hotels, safari lodges and tourism service providers have email addresses, and this is the cheapest way to make contact over distance. If you're planning on using a computer for email in South Africa, find out whether your service provider has any agreements with local companies. Alternatively, set up a **free email address** – something you'll be able to do from one of the many **cybercafés** that now exist. Every city has at least one, and increasing numbers of **backpackers' hostels** have Internet and email facilities.

THE MEDIA

South Africa's press is rather parochial, with one or two notable exceptions. Unlike Britain, the country lacks a strong tradition of national papers and instead has many regional papers of varying quality. Meanwhile, television is still in the process of transforming itself from an apartheid mouthpiece into a democratic voice – no mean task. Radio is where South Africa is finding it easiest to meet the multicultural needs of a diverse and scattered audience, and deregulation of the airwaves has brought to life scores of new stations.

NEWSPAPERS

Of the roughly twenty **daily newspapers**, most of which are published in English or Afrikaans, the only one that qualifies as a national is the weekly *Mail & Guardian*, which is available throughout the country, and benefits enormously from its close association with the London *Guardian* (from which it draws most of its international coverage). The *Mail & Guardian* is unquestionably the country's intellectual heavyweight, although its dense reporting can be a bit stodgy. The *Sowetan*, targeted at a mainly black Jo'burg audience, is also widely available across the country and provides a less exclusively white perspective on South African issues.

Of the English dailies, the *Star* in Johannesburg is one of the best, while *Business Day*, with it's solid coverage of local and international news as well as commerce, is South Africa's equivalent of the *Financial Times* or the *Wall Street Journal*. **Local papers** are useful for listings; in Cape Town you'll find the *Cape Times*, and the *Cape Argus*, sister paper to the *Star*, which identifies itself with issues local to the mother city. Durban brings out the *Daily News* and the *Natal Mercury* in the morning and evening, while Port Elizabeth offers the *Eastern Province Herald* – a gossipy broadsheet which beats with the heart of a tabloid. Finally, East London has the *Daily Dispatch*, an Eastern Cape paper packed with local news, which earned some fame in the Seventies for its sympathetic coverage of black consciousness leader, Steve Biko.

The easiest places for **buying newspapers** are corner stores and newsagents, especially the CNA chain. These places also sell **international press**, such as *Time* and *Newsweek*, and the weekly editions of the London *Daily Mail*, the *Telegraph* and the *Express*.

TELEVISION

Every day twelve million South African adults tune into the SABC's three public **TV** channels, which churn out a mixed bag of domestic dramas, game shows, soaps and documentaries, filled out with lashings of familiar imports. **SABC 1, 2** and **3** share the unenviable task of trying to deliver an integrated service, while having to split their time between the eleven official languages. This massive mission would tax the resources of even a rich, industrialized country, but for a Third World one like South Africa it's a crippling project. In practice English turns out to be most widely used, with SABC 3 broadcasting almost exclusively in the language, while SABC 2 and SABC 1 spread themselves thinly across all the remaining ten languages with some English creeping in even here. A selection of sports, movies, news and specialist channels are available to subscribers to the **M-Net** satellite service, which you'll find piped into many hotels. South Africa's first and only free-to-air independent commercial channel **e.tv** won its franchise in 1998 on the promise of providing a showcase for local productions, a pledge it has signally failed to meet – its output, in its first year at least, has consisted substantially of uninspired and uninspiring imports.

RADIO

Given South Africa's low literacy rate and widespread poverty, it's little surprise that **radio** is its most popular medium, since receivers are cheap and broadcasts can penetrate into even the remotest rural area. The SABC operates a national radio station for each of the eleven official language groups. The English-language service, **SAfm** is of a generally high standard; its best offerings are the highly polished evening and morning news programmes. The SABC also runs **5FM Stereo**, a national pop station broadcasting Top 40 tracks, while their **Radio Metro** is targeted at black urban

BBC WORLD SERVICES AND VOA

The **BBC World Service** gives wider coverage than local South African stations, and broadcasts some excellent programmes in its **Africa Service**. There can be considerable variation in reception, so it's worth surfing the airwaves to find the sharpest frequency. As a rule of thumb, the short wave ones (below 7000kHz) tend to provide better reception from late afternoon and throughout the evening, while the higher ones are usually better during the early morning till about midday. **Frequencies** tend to change seasonally, so it's best to find out current wavelengths from the World Service's Web site (*www.bbc.co.uk/worldservice/schedules/safrica.htm*), or by simply experimenting. Having said that, the medium wave transmissions on 1197kHz (daily local time 1pm–7.15am) have remained consistently in service and also tend to offer the best reception.

The **Voice of America**'s English-language service to Africa broadcasts throughout the day on 909kHz (medium wave) as well as on a number of short-wave frequencies. A complete list of current schedules is available on their Web site (*www.voa.gov/allsked.html*).

listeners. These aside, there are scores of regional, commercial and community stations, broadcasting a range of material, which makes surfing the airwaves an enjoyably serendipitous experience, wherever you are in the country. See p.508 for new stations operating in the Gauteng area.

OPENING HOURS AND HOLIDAYS

The working day starts and finishes early in South Africa: shops and businesses generally open on weekdays at 8.30am and close at 4.30pm or 5pm. In small towns, many places close for an hour over lunch. Shops and businesses close around noon on Saturdays for the day, and most shops are closed on Sundays. However, in every neighbourhood, you'll find what South Africans call "cafés" – not places where you get coffee, but corner stores where you can buy milk, bread and essentials after hours.

It's always best get out early and do business in the morning. **Banking hours** are generally Monday to Friday 8.30am to 3.30pm, Saturday 8am to 11am, but you'll find **bureaux de change** in the major cities open until at least 5pm (see "Listings" for each city for late openings) and open at the international airports to meet flights. Post offices are generally open 8.30am to 4.30pm on weekdays, and Saturdays 8am to 11.30am. Government departments are open 8am to 4pm weekdays.

HOLIDAYS

School holidays in South Africa can disrupt your plans, especially if you want to camp, or stay in

the national parks and the cheaper end of accommodation (self-catering, cheaper B&Bs, etc), all of which are likely to be booked solid during that period. If you do travel to South Africa over the school holidays, book your accommodation well in advance – especially for the national parks.

The longest and busiest holiday period is **Christmas (summer)**, which for schools stretches from around December 4 to January 21. Flights and train berths can be hard to get from December 16 to January 2, when many businesses and offices close for their annual

SOUTH AFRICAN PUBLIC HOLIDAYS

January 1 New Year's Day
March 21 Human Rights Day
Good Friday
Easter Sunday
Easter Monday
April 27 Freedom Day
May 1 Workers' Day
June 16 Youth Day
August 9 National Women's Day
September 24 Heritage Day
December 16 Day of Reconciliation
Christmas Day
December 26 Day of Goodwill

break. You should book your flights – long-haul and domestic – as early as six months in advance for the Christmas period. The provinces stagger their school holidays, but as a general rule, the remaining school holidays cover the following periods: **Easter**, March 20–April 15; **winter**, June 20–July 21; and **spring**, Sept 19 –Oct 7.

PHOTOGRAPHY

South Africa is outstandingly photogenic and you won't need to be a professional to get striking photographs. What kind of camera you take depends on how much weight you're prepared to carry around, how much of a tourist you want to look, and whether or not you plan to photograph animals.

Small, compact cameras are handy as you can keep them unobtrusively in your pocket and whip them out for a quick shot. But they're hopeless for wildlife – a nearby lion will end up a furry speck in savannah. Compacts are also potentially dangerous – tales abound of tourists with little cameras sneaking up too close for comfort to big game and ending up hurt.

If you take your photography seriously, you'll probably want a single-lens reflex camera (SLR) and two or three lenses – a heavy and cumbersome option. For decent wildlife photography you definitely need a **telephoto lens**. A 300mm lens is a good all-rounder: any bigger and you'll need a tripod. The smallest you could get away with for animals is 200mm, while 400mm is the best for birds. All long lenses need fast film, or you'll find you're restricted to the largest apertures, and hence the narrowest depth of focus. If you simply want good snaps from your SLR, think about one well-chosen zoom lens.

PROTECTION

The biggest problem can be **dust**, which tends to penetrate straight into a normal camera case or cloth bag. When travelling in dry, dusty regions, cameras need to be inside sealed plastic bags, or in some dustproof container, and taken out only for the business of taking pictures. You'll need to carry a blower-brush to blow dust off lenses.

Another problem is South Africa's **heat**. Never leave your camera or films lying in the sun. The film in a camera left exposed on a car seat, for instance, will be completely ruined. Keep rolls of film cool in the middle of your clothes or sleeping bag.

LIGHT READING

You really have to rely on a judicious combination of the camera's **light readings** and your own common sense. The contrast between light and shade can be huge, so expose for the subject and not the general scene. This can mean setting your camera to manual, approaching the subject to get a reading and then using that. With a zoom you can zoom in for a reading and then return. Some of the new multi-mode cameras will do much of this for you.

If you're photographing black people, especially in strong light, use more exposure than usual, otherwise they'll be underexposed; the light and your eyes (which are more sophisticated than any camera) can deceive you.

Early morning and late afternoon are the best times for photography. At midday, with the sun overhead, the light is flat and everything is lost in glare.

FILM

Film is readily available in South Africa. Don't let anyone tell you it's unnecessary to have fast film because the sun is so bright in Africa. Even if you opt for a compact with a fast lens (ie one that's very light-sensitive) you'll need at least some 400 ASA film if you want to take pictures at dawn and dusk and in heavy cloud or forest. With long lenses on an SLR, fast film is essential.

SUBJECTS AND PEOPLE

Photographing animals is a question of patience and resisting taking endless pictures of nothing happening. If you can't get close enough, don't waste your film. While taking photos, try keeping both eyes open and, in a vehicle, always turn off your engine.

You should always ask before taking photographs of **people** or, for example, of a dwelling decorated with colourful paintings. Some kind of interaction and exchange is customarily implied: people often ask for a copy of the photograph and you'll end up with several names and addresses and a list of promises.

SPECTATOR SPORTS

South Africa is a sports-fanatical nation, where devotion has been heightened by the re-entrance of the national teams into international competitions since the lifting of the sports boycott during the first half of the Nineties. The big spectator sports are soccer, rugby and cricket, with horse racing also a firm favourite and, since the 1996 Olympics, athletics too.

Soccer is the country's most popular game, with a primarily black and coloured following, and it is only now starting to attract the kind of serious money that could one day see South Africa as one of the world's top soccer nations. The professional season runs from August to May, with teams competing in the **Premier Soccer League** (PSL) and the relatively new knockout **Rothman's Cup** competition, with big prize money. Unlike rugby teams, soccer teams do not own their own grounds and are forced to rent them for specific fixtures. In most places, there is only one choice of ground so it does not make much difference to the fans, but in Gauteng, the heartland of South African soccer, all the big clubs have to use the same grounds, which has prevented the development of the kind of terrace fan culture you find elsewhere. Nonetheless, soccer crowds are generally witty and good-spirited, perhaps because alcohol is banned, though violence is now on the increase at Gauteng games. A remarkable feature of South African soccer games is the absence of police, as the clubs themselves provide the security. The two big club names in South African soccer are undoubtedly the **Kaiser Chiefs** and the **Orlando Pirates**. They are both Sowetan clubs, but have a nationwide following, and their derbies are the highlight of the PSL's fixture list. Games are played on weekday evenings (usually at 7.30pm or 8.30pm) and at 3pm on Saturdays, and cost about R15. The national squad, nicknamed **Bafana Bafana** (literally "boys boys" but connoting "our lads") took African soccer by storm in 1996 when it won the African Cup of Nations. They followed this up by coming second to Egypt in the 1998 clash of the African giants, but this success has failed to translate into the larger international arena; the local euphoria resulting from their admission to the 1998 World Cup was swiftly deflated after they failed to progress beyond the first round. Bafana play typically South African soccer – imaginative and strong on spectacular athletic feats that have the crowd cheering, but a tendency to run out of energy in the second half and thus risk throwing the game away. Even games they should win have that element of unpredictability that makes for great spectator sport.

Rugby is hugely popular with whites, especially Afrikaners, though the South African **Springboks**' victory in the 1995 World Cup greatly broadened the game's appeal. The competition attracted fanatical attention nationwide, particularly when President Nelson Mandela donned a Springbok jersey (long associated exclusively with whites) to present the cup to the winning side. Since then the goodwill has dissipated to be replaced by an acrimonious struggle to transform the traditionally white sports (cricket and rugby) into something more representative of all race groups, with the government threatening to introduce legislation enforcing racial quotas in national squads.

Despite this, the fact remains that South Africa is extraordinarily good at rugby, and you are likely to witness high-quality, if brutal play when you watch either inter-regional or international games. The main domestic competition has traditionally been the **Vodacom Currie Cup**, with games played from March to October, almost always on Saturdays at around 3.30pm. Admission is around R50. The second half of the Nineties has seen this overshadowed by the **Super 12**, in which four teams apiece from South Africa, New Zealand and Australia compete.

Matches are staged annually from late February to the end of May in all three countries, and in South Africa you'll catch a fair bit of action in the major centres of Johannesburg, Cape Town and Durban, though smaller places such as Port Elizabeth, East London, Bloemfontein and George sometimes get a look in. More conventional **internationals** are played throughout the year and are invariably popular, so you will need to get tickets well in advance.

Cricket is dominated by the one-day game, at which the country excels, although three-day contests are played at inter-provincial level. The provincial season runs from October to April, and the main one-day competition is the **Standard Bank Cup**. Games are played throughout the week, and admission is around R25 for standing and R35 for a seat. You stand a good chance of being around for an international test or one-day series if you are in the country for a month or more. South African cricket teams have historically been almost solidly white, but a few coloureds and Africans are now playing. Attempts to promote the game in black townships have been on the go for a few years now, though it will be some time before they bear fruit.

South Africa is very strong at **long distance running**, a tradition that reached its apotheosis at the 1996 Atlanta Olympics when Josiah Thugwane won the marathon, the first black South African ever to bag Olympic gold. The biggest single sports event in South Africa, the **Comrades Marathon**, attracts nearly 15,000 participants, among them some of the world's leading international ultra-marathon runners. The 90km course crosses the hilly country between Durban and Pietermaritzburg with a drop of almost 800m between the town and the coast. Run annually on May 31, the race alternates direction each year and is notable for having been non-racial since 1975, although it took till 1989 for a South African, Samuel Tshabalala, to win it. Since then black athletes have begun to dominate the front rankings.

On the subject of racing you'll find huge interest among rich and poor South Africans in **horse racing**, with totes and tracks in all the main cities. Its popularity is partly due to the fact that this was the only form of public gambling that South Africa's Afrikaner Calvinist rulers allowed – on the pretext that it involved skill not chance. The highlight of the racing calendar is the **Rothman's Durban July Handicap** held at Durban's Greyville racecourse. A flamboyant event, it attracts huge crowds, massive purses, socialites in outrageous headgear and vast amounts of media attention.

ACTIVITIES AND OUTDOOR PURSUITS

South Africa's diverse landscape of mountains, forests, rugged coast and sandy beaches, as well as miles of veld and game-trampled national parks, make this supreme outdoor terrain, a fact that hasn't been missed by the South Africans themselves, who have been playing in the outdoors for decades. The result is a well-developed infrastructure for activities, an impressive national network of hiking trails and plenty of commercial operators selling adventure sports.

HIKING TRAILS

Over the past twenty years **hiking** has taken off in a big way in South Africa, and this country has the most comprehensive system of footpaths in Africa (inspired by the US Appalachian Hiking Trail).

Wherever you are – even in the middle of Johannesburg – you won't be far from some sort of trail. The best ones are in wilderness areas, where you'll find waymarked paths that vary from half-hour strolls to major hiking expeditions of two to seven days that take you right into the heart of some of the most beautiful parts of the country. Overnight hiking trails are normally well laid out, with painted footprints or other markers to indicate the route and campsites or huts along the way (but you need to carry all your own equipment). Numbers are limited on most, and many trails are so popular that they become booked up many months in advance, so it's worth arranging these beforehand – although you can often find a place by just turning up and hoping for a cancellation. If you want to do a fair amount of walking but don't want to launch out on a long expedition, consider basing yourself in one of the wilderness areas such as the **Drakensberg**, where you can stay in chalets and set off on a series of day walks, returning each night.

Unique to Africa are **guided wilderness trails**, where you walk in game country (such as the Kruger National Park), accompanied by an armed guide. These walks should be regarded as a way to get a feel for the wild rather than actually see any wildlife, as you'll encounter far fewer animals on foot than from a vehicle. Specialist trails include mountain biking, canoeing, horseback trails and camel trails. A handful of trails have also been set up specifically for **people with disabilities**, mostly for the visually impaired or people confined to wheelchairs.

WATERSPORTS

Don't expect balmy Mediterranean seas in South Africa: of its 2500km of coastline, only the stretch along the Indian Ocean seaboard of KwaZulu-Natal can be considered tropical, and along the entire coast an energetic surf pounds the shore. In **Cape Town**, sea bathing is only comfortable between November and March. Generally, the further east you go from here the warmer the water becomes and the longer the bathing season. Sea temperatures that rarely drop below 18°C make the **KwaZulu-Natal** coast warm enough for a dip at any time of year. A word of warning: dangerous undertows and riptides are present along the coast and you should try to bathe where lifeguards are present. Failing that (and guards aren't that common away from main resorts out of season) you should follow local advice, never swim alone and always treat the ocean with respect.

The pumping surf is of course precisely what makes South Africa among the world's finest spots for **surfing**. The country's perfect wave at

TRAIL BOOKS

Numerous books exist covering hikes in specific regions of South Africa, but these two general guides are extremely useful.
Jaynee Levy *The Complete Guide to Walks & Trails in Southern Africa* (Struik). Levy was important in helping establish the system of trails, and this is the most comprehensive guide to the region as a whole, with all the basic information and contact addresses you'll need to trail anywhere in the subcontinent.
Willie and Sandra Olivier *Hiking Trails of Southern Africa* (Southern). Covers less ground than Levy, dealing with only the 44 most important trails, but writes them up with greater depth and gives excellent natural history commentary on each trail.

Jeffrey's Bay was immortalized on celluloid in the Sixties cult movie *Endless Summer*, but any surfer will tell you that there are equal, if not better, breaks all the way along the coast from the Namibian to the Mozambique border. Surfers can be a cliquey bunch, but the South African community has a reputation for being among the friendliest in the world and, provided you pay your dues, you should find yourself easily accepted. Some of the world's top shapers work here and you can pick up an excellent board at a fraction of European or US prices. If you can face the humiliation of being regarded by the pro-surfers as a "tea bag" or "doormat", boogie-boarding and body-surfing make easy alternatives to the real thing, require less skill or dedication and are great fun. **Windsurfing** (or sailboarding) is another popular sport you'll find at many resorts, where you can rent gear.

Scuba diving is a recreation that's growing in popularity and South Africa is one of the cheapest places in the world to get an internationally recognized open-water certificate, with courses at all the coastal cities as well as a number of other resorts. The most rewarding diving is along the St Lucia Marine Reserve in northern KwaZulu-Natal coast, where 100,000 dives go under every year for its coral reefs and fluorescent fish. You won't find corals and bright colours along the Cape coast, but the huge number of sunken vessels makes wreck-diving popular and you can encounter the swaying rhythms of giant kelp forests.

KwaZulu-Natal is also good for **snorkelling** and there are some underwater trails elsewhere in the country, most notable of which is in the Tsitsikamma National Park.

Fishing is another well-developed South African activity and the coasts yield 250 species caught through rock, bay or surf angling. The confluence of the warm Indian and cooler Atlantic east of the Cape Peninsula, brings one of the highest concentrations of game fish in the world, including longfin, tunny and marlin. Inland you'll find plenty of rivers and dams stocked with freshwater fish, while trout fishing is extremely well-established in Mpumalanga, the northern sections of the Eastern Cape and the KwaZulu-Natal Midlands.

If you want to find out how it feels to be bait, there are a couple of places along the southern Cape and Garden Route where you can go on **shark-cage dives** and come face to face with deadly great whites.

On inland waterways, South African holidaymakers are keen **speedboaters**, an activity that goes hand in hand with **waterskiing**. **Kayaking** and **canoeing** are also very popular and you can often rent craft at resorts or national parks that lie along rivers. For the more adventurous, there's **white-water rafting**, with some decent trips along the Tugela River in KwaZulu-Natal and on the Orange River.

OTHER ACTIVITIES

There are ample opportunities for aerial activities in South Africa. In the Winelands you can go **ballooning**; and **paragliding** offers a thrilling way to see Cape Town, by diving off Lion's Head and riding the thermals. More down-to-earth options include **mountaineering** and **rock climbing**, both of which have a huge following in South Africa. If you decide to go **skiing** at one or two resorts in the Eastern and Western Cape, you'll be able to go home with a quirky experience of Africa. And finally, if you can't choose between being airborne or earthbound, you can always bounce between the two by **bungee jumping** off the Gouritz River Bridge near Mossel Bay – the world's highest commercial jump.

Horse-riding is a sport you'll find at virtually every resort, whether inland or along the coast, for two hours or two days. You can ride in the Drakensberg from the Natal parks, or go pony trekking for several days in Lesotho. Take your own hat, as not everyone provides them. **Bird-watching** is another activity you can do almost anywhere, either casually on your own, or as part of a guided trip with one of the several experts operating in South Africa. Among the very best bird-watching spots are Mkuzi and Ndumo game reserves in KwaZulu-Natal. **Golf** lovers will have a fabulous time in South Africa as courses are prolific and are frequently in stunningly beautiful locations.

TROUBLE AND THE POLICE

Despite horror stories of sky-high crime rates, most people visit South Africa without incident. This is not to minimize the problem – crime is probably the most serious difficulty facing the country and it is unacceptably high by any standards. However, once you realize that crime follows demographic patterns, the scale becomes less terrifying. The greatest proportion of violent crime takes place in the poorer areas – predominantly townships – and in Johannesburg, where the dangers are the worst in the country. Be careful, but don't be paranoid.

While levels of crime in major centres outside Gauteng, such as Port Elizabeth, Cape Town or Durban, are probably higher than (say) the metropolitan United States, many other areas such as the Garden Route are safer than most places in

the world. Outside city centres and major tourist venues, **police presence** is almost non-existent, and the police have a rather poor image. It's best to rely on your own resources. This is exactly what many middle-class people now do, by subscribing to the services of armed, **private security firms** to protect their property. Protecting property and "security" are major national obsessions, and it's difficult to imagine what many South Africans would discuss at their dinner parties if the problem disappeared. The other obvious manifestation of this obsession is the huge number of alarms, bars, high walls and electronically controlled gates you'll find, not just in the suburbs, but even in less deprived areas of some townships.

Guns, both licensed and illicit, are an everyday part of life, routinely and openly carried by police

---

SAFETY TIPS

In general
• Try not to look like a tourist.
• Dress down.
• Don't carry a camera or video openly visible in cities.
• Avoid wearing jewellery or expensive watches.
• Leave your expensive designer shades at home – they are sometimes pulled off people's faces.
• Remain calm and co-operative if you are robbed.

On foot
• Grasp bags firmly under your arm.
• Don't carry excessive sums of money on you (but have a small amount to satisfy a mugger).
• Don't put your wallet in your back trouser pocket.
• Always know where your valuables are.
• Don't leave valuables exposed (on a seat or the ground) while having a meal or drink.
• Develop an awareness of what people in the street around you are doing.
• Don't let anyone get too close to you – especially people in groups.
• In big cities, travel around in pairs or groups.

On the beach
• Take only the bare essentials to the beach.
• Don't leave valuables, especially cameras, unattended.
• Some people pin car keys to their swimming gear, or you can put them in a waterproof wallet

or splash box and take them into the water with you.

On the road
• Lock all your car doors, especially in cities.
• Keep your rear windows sufficiently rolled up to keep out opportunistic hands.
• Never leave anything worth stealing in view when your car is unattended.

At cash machines
Automatic teller machines (ATMs) are favourite hunting grounds for sophisticated conmen who use cunning rather than force to steal money. Never underestimate their ability and don't get drawn into any interaction at an ATM, no matter how well-spoken, friendly or distressed the other person appears. You can avoid trouble by following the pointers below.
• Never help anyone who claims to be having problem with a cash machine – tell them to contact the bank.
• Never accept help from strangers if you have a problem at a cash machine.
• Don't allow people to crowd you while withdrawing money.
• If in doubt, go to another machine.
• Never allow anyone to see you punch in your personal identification number (PIN).
• If your card gets swallowed, report it without delay.

– and often citizens. In many high streets you'll spot firearm shops rubbing shoulders with places selling clothes or books; and you'll come across notices asking you to deposit your weapon before entering the premises.

If you fall victim to a **mugging**, you should take very seriously the usual advice not to resist and do as you're told. The chances of this happening can be greatly minimized by using common sense and following a few simple rules. If you're staying in Johannesburg, it pays to be extra alert. For specific guidelines, see our box on previous page

POLICE

For many black South Africans, the **South African Police** (SAP) still carry strong associations of collaboration with apartheid and a lot of public relations work has yet to be done to turn the police into a genuine people's law enforcement agency. Poorly paid, shot at (and frequently hit), underfunded, badly equipped, barely respected and demoralized, the police keep a low profile. If you ever get stopped, at a roadblock for example (one of the likeliest encounters), always be courteous. And remember that under South African law you are required to carry your **driver's licence** at all times. If you are robbed, don't expect too much crime-cracking enthusiasm (and don't expect to get your property back), but you will need to report the incident to the police, who should give you a case reference for insurance purposes.

DRUGS, DRINKING AND DRIVING

Dagga (cannabis in dried leaf form) is South Africa's most widely produced and widely used drug. The quality is generally good, but this doesn't alter the fact that it is illegal. Grown in hot regions like KwaZulu-Natal (the source of Durban Poison), Swaziland (Swazi Gold) and as a cash crop in parts of the former Transkei, it is fairly easily available, but you should take particular care when scoring as people have run into trouble dealing with unfamilar local conditions. Otherwise, if you're reasonably discreet you should encounter no problems. Rave culture is big in South Africa, and together with **ecstasy** is principally a white, middle-class thing.

Strangely, for a country that sometimes seems to be on one massive binge, South Africa has laws that prohibit **drinking** in public – not that anyone pays any attention to them. The **drink-drive laws** are also routinely and brazenly flouted, making the country's roads the one real danger you should be concerned about. Levels of alcohol consumption go some way to explaining why during the Christmas holidays over a thousand people die in an annual orgy of carnage on the roads. People routinely stock up their cars with booze for long journeys and even at filling stations you'll find places selling liquor.

WOMEN AND SEXUAL HARASSMENT

South Africa's extremely high incidence of **rape** doesn't as a rule affect tourists. In fact you're very unlikely to need to fend off the unwanted attentions of men. However, women should avoid travelling on their own, nor should they hitchhike or walk alone in deserted areas. This applies equally to cities, the countryside or anywhere after dark. Minibus taxis should be ruled out as a means of transport after dark, especially if you're not exactly sure of local geography. **Sexual harassment** is rare, but you should nevertheless walk assertively in crowded areas such as minibus taxi termini in big cities. At heart the majority of the country's males, regardless of race, hold on to fairly sexist attitudes. Sometimes your eagerness to be friendly may be taken as a sexual overture – always be sensitive to potential crossed wires and unintended signals.

TRAVELLERS WITH DISABILITIES

Facilities for disabled travellers in South Africa are not as sophisticated as you'd get in the First World, but overall they are sufficient to ensure you have a satisfactory visit.

By accident, rather than design, you'll find pretty good accessibility to many buildings, as South Africans tend to build low (single-storey bungalows are the norm), with the result that you'll have to deal with fewer stairs than you may be accustomed to. Because the car is king, you'll frequently find that you can drive to, and park right outside, your destination.

A growing number of popular tourist attractions are being designed to facilitate **disabled access**. For example, the Kirstenbosch Botanical Gardens in Cape Town have Braille and wheelchair trails, while trails aimed specifically at disabled travellers are on offer at Kamberg Nature Reserve in the Drakensberg and in the Karoo National Park. The longest trail so far is a six-kilometre walk with a tapping rail and guide ropes in the Palmiet Nature Reserve in Durban. Cape Town's Waterfront, one of the top national attractions, has specially designed parking bays as well as ramps and broad walkways around the development itself. Sun City in Northwest Province, as well as a growing number of national parks, is also disability-friendly.

PLANNING A HOLIDAY

There are **organized tours** and holidays specifically for people with disabilities – the contacts in the box below and overleaf will be able to put you in touch with specialists for trips to South Africa. If you want to be more independent, it's important to become an authority on where you must be self-reliant and where you can expect help, especially regarding transport and accommodation. It is also vital to be honest – to know your limitations and make sure others know them. If you do not use a wheelchair all the time but your walking capabilities are limited, remember that you are likely to need to cover greater distances while travelling (often over rougher terrain and in hotter temperatures) than you are used to. If you do use a wheelchair, have it serviced before you go and take a repair kit with you.

Read your **travel insurance** small print carefully to make sure that people with a pre-existing medical condition are not excluded. *Tripscope* (see box overleaf) can provide a current list of appropriate insurers. Use your travel

USEFUL CONTACTS IN SOUTH AFRICA

Carpe Diem Tours, PO Box 248, Lutzville 8165 (☎ & fax 02725/71125). One- to four-day tours in the Western and Northern Cape provinces by specially equipped bus.

Eco-Access, PO Box 1377, Roosevelt Park 2129 (☎011/477 3676, fax 477 3675, *eco-access@cis.co.za*). Agency working for improved facilities for disabled people to take part in eco-tourism in South Africa. Contact Rob and Julie Filmer or Catherine Anderson.

Independent Living Centre, PO Box 248, Auckland Park 2006, Johannesburg (☎011/482 5474, fax 482 5565). An organization that is compiling details of accessible holiday accommodation in South Africa, and can provide information on equipment and issue disabled parking permits for the Johannesburg area.

KwaZulu-Natal Conservation Services PO Box 13069, Cascades, Pietermaritzburg 3202 (☎0331/845 1000, fax 846 1001). Information about facilities in game reserves and parks in KwaZulu-Natal.

National Council for the Physically Disabled in South Africa, PO Box 426, Melville 2109 (☎011/726 8040, fax 726 5705, *ncppdsa@cis.co.za*). Advice on where to rent wheelchairs and other equipment in the major cities.

South African National Parks, PO Box 787, Pretoria 0001 (☎012/343 1991, fax 343 0905); PO Box 7400, Roggebaai 8012, Cape Town (☎021/422 2810, fax 424 6211, *reservations@parks-sa.co.za*). Up-to-date information about facilities at rest camps in the national parks

Titch Travel Ltd, PO Box 671, Rondebosch 7700, Cape Town (☎021/689 4151, fax 689 3760; *titcheve@iafrica.com*). Travel agent for physically disabled and visually impaired people.

Wilderness Wheels Africa, 117 St Georges Rd, Observatory 2198, Johannesburg (☎ 011/648 5737, fax 648 6769). Adventure safaris for paraplegics and other disabled travellers and their families.

BEFORE YOU LEAVE: USEFUL ORGANIZATIONS

AUSTRALIA AND NEW ZEALAND
ACROD (Australian Council for Rehabilitation of the Disabled), PO Box 60, Curtin, ACT 2605 (☎02/6282 4333). General travel information.
Disabled Persons Assembly, 173–175 Victoria St, Wellington (☎04/811 9100). Advice and travel information.

CANADA
Jewish Rehabilitation Hospital, 3205 Place Alton Goldbloom, Chomedy Laval, PQ H7V 1R2 (☎514/688 9550, ext 226). Guidebooks and travel information.
Kéroul, 4545 Ave. Pierre de Coubertin, CP 1000, Station M, Montréal, PQ H1V 3R2 (☎514/252-3104). Organization promoting and facilitating travel for mobility-impaired people, primarily in Quebec.
Twin Peaks Press, Box 129, Vancouver, WA 98666 (☎206/694-2462 or 1-800/637-2256). Publisher of the *Directory of Travel Agencies for the Disabled* (CDN$19.95), listing more than 370 agencies worldwide; *Travel for the Disabled* (CDN$19.95); the *Directory of Accessible Van Rentals* (CDN$12.95); and *Wheelchair Vagabond* (CDN$18.95), loaded with personal tips. Postage and packing CDN$5 for first title, CDN$3 each extra one.

UK
Access Travel, 16 Haweswater Ave, Astley, Lancashire M29 7BL (☎01942/888 844). Tour operator that can arrange flights, transfer and accommodation. This is a small business: staff personally check out places before recommendation and can provide first-hand impressions on conditions in South Africa, guarantee accommodation standards and recommend suitable places to stay on

game farms as well as other places of interest. ATOL bonded and established for five years.
Holiday Care Service, 2nd Floor, Imperial Building, Victoria Rd, Horley, Surrey RH6 7PZ (☎01293/774535). Provides free lists of accessible accommodation abroad – European, American and long-haul destinations, including South Africa – plus a list of accessible attractions in the UK. Information on financial help for holidays available.
RADAR (Royal Association for Disability and Rehabilitation), 12 City Forum, 250 City Rd, London EC1V 8AF (☎0171/250 3222; Minicom ☎0171/250 4119). Produce an annual holiday guide for long-haul destinations including South Africa, but information tends to be rather basic (£7.50 inc. p&p).
Tripscope, The Courtyard, Evelyn Rd, London W4 5JL (☎0181/994 9294). Registered charity providing a national telephone information service offering useful advice for first-time disabled air travellers, and they can provide an up-to-date list of insurers offering appropriate policies for your needs.

USA
Mobility International USA, PO Box 10767, Eugene, OR 97440 (voice & TDD ☎541/343-1284). Information and referral services, access guides, tours and exchange programs. Annual membership US$35 (includes quarterly newsletter).
SATH (Society for the Advancement of Travel for the Handicapped), 347 5th Ave, New York, NY 10016 (☎212/447-7284). Non-profit-making travel industry referral service that passes queries on to its members.
Travel Information Service (☎215/456-9600). Telephone-only information and referral service for disabled travellers.

agent to make your journey as straightforward as possible; airline or bus companies can cope better if they are expecting you, with a wheelchair provided at airports and staff primed to help. A **medical certificate** of your fitness to travel, provided by your doctor, is also extremely useful, and some airlines or insurance companies may insist on it. Make sure you have extra supplies of drugs – carried with you if you fly – and a prescription including the generic name in case of emergency. Carry spares of any clothing or equipment that might be hard to find; if there's an association representing people with your disability, contact them early in the planning process.

TRANSPORT

All the major **airlines** flying to South Africa can provide assistance for disabled passengers, but you should give them notice of your needs when booking. As far as domestic air travel is concerned, South African Airways provides passenger aid units at all principal airports.

Car rental of automatics with hand controls can be arranged for no extra charge through Avis or Budget (see p.30) at all the major centres, but a month's prior notice is recommended. Many garages along the main routes, especially along the N1 between Johannesburg and Cape Town, have wheelchair-accessible **toilets**. A Special

Parking Disc, which allows **parking** concessions to people with severe mobility impairment, can be obtained for the Johannesburg area through the Independent Living Centre (see box on previous page) and for elsewhere in the country through the local traffic department. You should bring any appropriate disc or badge from your home country, which can be used to get a temporary disc.

ACCOMMODATION

South Africa has a growing number of **hotels** with facilities for disabled people. The South African Tourism Board publishes an accommodation guide, available from all their offices (see p.23), which includes up-to-date information about disability-friendly establishments. In the national parks, specially adapted huts are available in the Kruger and Karoo national parks. For further details of facilities in other parks, contact the National Parks Board and Natal Parks Board (see p.39 for addresses).

ACTIVITIES AND TOURS

Activities and tours are opening up for disabled travellers to South Africa, ranging from the relatively sedate to the more energetic. Organized tours offer the possibility for wheelchair-bound visitors to take part in safaris, sport and a vast range of adventure activities, including whitewater rafting, horse-riding and parasailing. Tours can either be taken as self-drive trips or group packages.

GAY AND LESBIAN TRAVELLERS

South Africa has the world's first and only gay- and lesbian-friendly constitution, and Africa's most developed and diverse gay and lesbian scene. Not only is homosexuality legal between consenting adults of 18 or over, but the constitution outlaws any discrimination on the grounds of sexual orientation. This means that, for once, you have the law on your side.

Outside the big cities, however, South Africa is a pretty conservative place where open displays of public affection by gays and lesbians are unlikely to go down well; many whites will find it un-Christian, while blacks will think it un-African. Satour (the official tourism organization), on the other hand, has recently woken up to the potential of the pink pound (and dollar) and is wooing gay travellers with *The Pink Map*, which lists gay-friendly and gay-owned places in Cape Town, with a view to turning the mother city into an African Sydney.

Outright (☎011/476 1580 or 678 5981) is a bimonthly glossy lifestyle **magazine** aimed at gay and lesbian readers (though with an emphasis on men), with a separate travel and accommodation section, as well as features, up-to-date information on the national club scene and advertisements for gay-owned or gay-friendly restaurants and shops. Available at South Africa's international airports, as well as the CNA newsagent chain, it serves as a good starting point for making contacts or finding out where to go. Also worth keeping an eye out for is the monthly newspaper *Exit*, which has club listings, but is of interest more for its political focus.

A useful contact is the **National Coalition For Gay and Lesbian Equality** (☎021/423 5026, fax 423 5046, *josie@ncgle.org.za*), a powerful lobbying organization that also works to advance the interests of black gays and lesbians. Staff here can let you know about new contact groups in other parts of the country.

CAPE TOWN

Cape Town is South Africa's – and indeed, the African continent's – gay capital. The country's only gay **travel agent**, *Gay esCape*, 105 High Level Road, Greenpoint (☎021/439 3829, fax 439 3861, *gayesc@cis.co.za*), is a quick and sure way of finding out the latest on the scene throughout South Africa. They stock the popular, free biannual *Cape Town Gay Guide*, which lists gay-owned accommodation establishments, bars, restaurants, clubs and massage parlours, along with a handy city map. There's also *The Pink Map* (see above). The Cape Town **Gay Help and Information line** (☎021/222 500, daily 1–5pm) is another excellent source of information with a resource directory on tap covering organizations as well as entertainment.

The city hosts an annual **Queer Party**, a hugely popular event usually held in mid-December at the *River Club* (☎021/448 6117) in Observatory. People dress as outrageously as possible according to a theme (past ones have included "on safari", and "underwater"). While in town, be sure to tune into Bush Radio's (89.5FM) gay programme, called **In the Pink**, every Thursday 8–10pm. Like much else in the city, Cape Town's gay scene is white-dominated, though there are a few gay-friendly clubs starting to emerge in the surrounding townships.

JOHANNESBURG AND PRETORIA

The gay scene is a lot more multiracial in **Johannesburg**, especially in the clubs. Useful contacts here include Glow (Gay and Lesbian Organization of the Witwatersrand; ☎011/ 648 5873), which has information about where to go and what to do, as well as the low-down on political issues. The National Coalition for Gay and Lesbian Equality has a Johannesburg office (36 Grafton Road, Yeoville (☎011/487 3811, fax 487 1670, *mazibuko@ncgle.org.za*). If you're near Johannesburg in September, make sure you check out the **Pride Parade** through the streets of the city.

The **Pretoria** gay and lesbian scene has grown enormously over the past few years and now outdoes Johannesburg. Glop (Gay and Lesbian Organization of Pretoria; information Mon–Fri 10am–3pm, ☎011/344 6501; counselling Mon–Thurs 7–10pm, ☎011/344 6500) has put together a very handy map showing places to go, and is an excellent contact once you're in Gauteng.

TRAVELLING WITH CHILDREN

Holidaying with children is straightforward in South Africa, whether you want to explore a city, kick back on the beach, or find peace in the mountains. You'll find people friendly, attentive and accepting of babies and young children. The following is aimed principally at families with under-fives.

Flying to South Africa with toddlers is the only considerable challenge, especially as the long-haul flight is bound to disrupt sleeping and eating routines. Although children up to 24 months only pay ten percent of the adult fare, the illusion that this is a bargain rapidly evaporates when you realize that they get no seat or baggage allowance. Given this, you'd be well advised to secure bulkhead seats and reserve a **basinet** or sky cot, which can be attached to the bulkhead. Basinets are usually allocated to babies under six months, though some airlines use weight (under 10kg) as the criterion. When you reconfirm your flights, check that your seat and basinet are still available. A child who has a seat will usually be charged fifty percent of the adult fare and is entitled to a full baggage allowance. For getting to and from the aircraft, and for use during your stay, take a light-weight collapsible **buggy** – not counted as part of your luggage allowance. A child-carrier backpack is another useful accessory.

Given the size of the country, you're likely to be **driving** long distances, something you should think about carefully to avoid grizzly children. Aim to go slowly and plan a route that allows frequent stops – or perhaps take trains or flights between centres. The Garden Route, for example, is an ideal drive, with easy stops for picnics, particularly on the section between Mossel Bay and Storms River. The route between Johannesburg and Cape Town, conversely, is tedious.

Game viewing can also be boring for young children, since it too involves a lot of driving – and disappointment, should the promised beasts fail to put in an appearance. Plus, of course, toddlers won't particularly enjoy watching animals from afar and through a window. If they are old enough to enjoy the experience, make sure they have their own binoculars. To get in closer, some animal parks, such as Tsukudu near Kruger, have semi-tame animals that should do the trick, while snake and reptile parks are an old South African favourite that you'll encounter all over the place.

Family accommodation is plentiful and hotels often have rooms with extra beds or interconnecting rooms. Kids usually stay for half price.

Self-catering options are worth considering, as most such establishments have a good deal of space to play in, and there'll often be a pool. A number of resorts are specifically aimed at families with **older children**, with activities on offer. Pick of the bunch is the Aventura chain, which has places in beautiful settings, including Keurboomstrand near Plettenberg Bay, and two close to the Blyde River Canyon in Mpumalanga. Note that many safari camps don't allow children under twelve, so you'll have to self-cater or camp at the national parks and those in Kwa-Zulu Natal.

Eating out with a baby or toddler is easy, particularly if you go to an outdoor venue where they can get on unhindered with their exploration of the world. Some restaurants have high chairs and do small portions. If in doubt there's always the ubiquitous family-oriented chains such as Spur or Wimpy. Breast feeding is practised by the majority of mothers wherever they are, though you won't see many white women doing it in public. Be discreet, especially in more conservative white areas – which is most of the country outside middle-class Cape Town, Johannesburg or Durban. There are very few **baby rooms** in public places for changing or feeding.

You can buy disposable **nappies** wherever you go (imported brands are best), as well as wipes, bottles, formula and dummies. High-street chemists and the Clicks chain are the best places to buy baby goods. If you run out of **clothes**, Woolworths has good-quality stuff, but for trendy gear there are a number of creative children's clothes outlets, especially in Cape Town and Knysna.

Health and hygiene standards are high and there are plenty of good doctors and hospitals should you need them. **Malaria** affects only a small part of the country (see p.17), but think carefully about visiting such areas as the preventatives aren't recommended for under-twos. For toddlers, chloroquine is available as a syrup, while proguanil is only available in tablet form – not the easiest thing to get down little throats. Avoid most of the major game reserves, particularly the Kruger National Park and those in KwaZulu-Natal, Northwest and Northern provinces and Swaziland, and opt instead for malaria-free reserves in the Western and Eastern Cape, such as Addo Elephant National Park. Malarial zones carry a considerably reduced risk in winter, when it's unusual to find mosquitoes, so if you're set on going, this is the best time. Take mosquito nets, cover children from head to toe between dusk and dawn, and use a good repellent.

Tuberculosis (TB) is widespread in South Africa, mostly (but by no means exclusively) affecting the poor, so make sure your child has had a BCG jab.

For protection against **the sun**, see p.16.

DIRECTORY

AIRPORT TAX An arrival tax of between R20 and R70 (depending on whether your flight is domestic, regional or international) is included in all air fares.

BARGAINING Haggling at markets and with street traders isn't a part of South African shopping culture. Most marketeers are trying to earn an honest living and are generally not trying to rip you off, so bargaining just isn't expected.

BEGGING The coexistence of poverty and wealth in close proximity, and the absence of a social security safety net, make begging a widespread and inevitable phenomenon in South Africa. What you do when confronted by someone asking for money (or even food) is a sticky matter of conscience, but giving to every beggar you encounter is simply not a workable possibility. Your choices are to not give at all, to give selectively, or to make a donation to one of the recognized charities that is trying to alleviate the worst consequences of deprivation – the way many middle-class South Africans salve their consciences. An extension of begging is people offering services you may not have asked for. Common examples are self-appointed car attendants who hang around parking places, direct you into your parking bay and offer to look after your vehicle while you're away – essentially an offer you can't refuse. Agree to pay when you return (around R3–5 should do the trick) provided they've done their job. Offers to clean your car are also very common (R10 is standard).

CONTRACEPTION Despite a serious HIV/AIDS problem, South Africa is remarkably coy about contraception and you shouldn't expect to find condoms anywhere other than in pharmacies. As far as the pill goes, this can also be bought through a pharmacy, but only with a doctor's prescription. The safest option is to bring your own supply.

ELECTRICITY Electricity runs on 220/230V, 50Hz AC and sockets take unique round-pinned plugs. Most hotel rooms have sockets that will take 110V electric razors, but for other appliances US visitors will need a transformer.

EMERGENCIES Police ☎10111, Ambulance ☎10177.

LAUNDRIES Most towns have self-operated launderettes where for a reasonable sum you can also often have a serviced wash which can include ironing.

TAX Value-added tax (VAT) of fourteen percent is levied on most goods and services, though it's usually already included in any quoted price. Foreign visitors can claim back VAT on any goods over R250. To do this you must present the tax invoice and your passport at the airport just before you fly out.

TIME There is only one time zone, two hours ahead of GMT, throughout the region. If you're flying from anywhere in Europe you shouldn't experience any jet lag, as you'll be travelling virtually due south, which won't mess with your body clock.

TIPPING Ten to fifteen percent of the tab is the normal tip at restaurants and for taxis – but don't feel obliged if the service has been shoddy. Keep in mind that many of the people who'll be serving you will be black South Africans, who rely on tips to supplement a meagre wage on which they support huge extended families. When in doubt, err on the side of generosity, as gratuities are seldom unwelcome. Porters at hotels normally get about R3 per bag. There are no self-service garages in South Africa; someone will always be on hand to fill your vehicle and clean your windscreen, for which you should tip around R3–5. It is also usual at hotels to leave some money for the person who services your room. Many establishments, especially private game lodges, take (voluntary) communal tips when you check out – by far the fairest system, which ensures that all the low-profile staff behind the scenes get their share.

WEIGHTS AND MEASURES South Africa is fully metricated, and kilometres, grammes, kilogrammes, litres and degrees Celsius are the norm. Shoe sizes follow the British system.

METRIC CONVERSION TABLE

1 centimetre (cm) = 0.394in
1 inch (in) = 2.54cm
1 foot (ft) = 30.48cm

1 metre (m) = 100cm
1 metre = 39.37in
1 yard (yd) = 0.91m

1 kilometre (km) = 1000m
1 kilometre = 0.621 miles
1 mile = 1610m

1 hectare = 10,000 square metres

1 hectare = 2.471 acres

1 acre = 0.4 hectares

1 UK gallon (gal) = 4.55 litres

1 litre = 0.26 US gal

1 US gallon (gal) = 5.46 litres

1 gramme (g) = 0.035oz
1 ounce (oz) = 28.57 g

1 kilogramme (kg) = 1000g
1 kilogramme = 2.2lb

1 pound (lb) = 454g

PART TWO

THE

GUIDE

CHAPTER ONE

CAPE TOWN AND THE PENINSULA

CAPE TOWN is southern Africa's most beautiful, most romantic and most visited city. Indeed, few urban centres anywhere can match its setting along the mountainous **Cape Peninsula** spine, which slides like the mighty tail of the continent into the Atlantic Ocean. By far the most striking – and famous – of its sights is **Table Mountain**, frequently mantled by clouds, and rearing up from the middle of the city to provide a constantly changing vista to the suburbs below.

More than a scenic backdrop, Table Mountain is the solid core of Cape Town, dividing the city into distinct zones with public gardens, wilderness, forests, hiking routes, vineyards and desirable residential areas trailing down its lower slopes. Standing on the tabletop, you can look north for a giddy view of the **city centre**, its docks filled with matchbox ships. Looking west, beyond the mountainous Twelve Apostles, the drop is sheer and your eye will sweep across Africa's priciest real estate, clinging to the slopes along the chilly but spectacularly beautiful Atlantic seaboard. Turning south, the mountainsides are forested and several historic vineyards and the marvellous Botanical Gardens creep up the lower slopes. Beyond the oak-lined suburbs of Newlands and Constantia, lies the warmer but more distant **False Bay seaboard**, which curves around before fading off to **Cape Point**. Finally, relegated to the grim industrial east, are the coloured **townships** and black **ghettos**, spluttering in winter under the smoky pall of coal fires – your stark introduction to Cape Town when driving in.

To appreciate Cape Town you need to spend time **outdoors**, as Capetonians do, hiking, picnicking or sunbathing, or often choosing mountain bikes in preference to cars and turning **adventure activities** into an obsession. Sailboarders from around the world head for Table Bay for some of the world's best windsurfing, and the brave (or unhinged) jump off Lion's Head and paraglide down close to the Clifton beachfront. But the city offers sedate pleasures as well, along its hundreds of walks and 150km of beaches.

Cape Town's rich urban texture is immediately apparent in the diverse **architecture**: an indigenous Cape Dutch style, rooted in the Netherlands, finds its apotheosis in the Constantia wine estates, which were themselves brought to new heights by French refugees in the seventeenth century; Muslim slaves, freed in the nineteenth century, added their minarets to the skyline; and the English, who invaded and freed these slaves, introduced their Georgian and Victorian buildings. In the tightly packed terraces of twentieth-century Bo-Kaap and the tenements of District Six, coloured descendants of slaves evolved a unique brand of jazz, which is still played in the Cape Flats and some city-centre clubs.

Sadly, when most travellers expound the unarguable delights of the city, they are referring only to genteel Cape Town – the formerly whites-only areas. The harsh reality for most Capetonians is one of crowded **shantytowns**, sky-high murder rates, taxi wars, racketeering and gangland terror. In the second half of the Nineties this violence

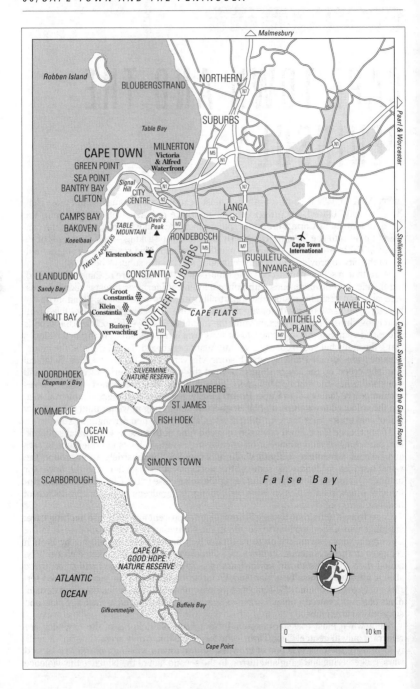

PAGAD

In 1996, a Cape Flats-based organization calling itself **Pagad** (People Against Gangsterism and Drugs) exploded onto the front pages of the national press when it took the law into its own hands, lynching a leading drugs baron and declaring war on the gangs. As one of the more grisly events in the tableau of violence that has been part of daily life in the Cape Flats (almost since its creation as an apartheid dumping ground for coloureds in the Sixties), it has made existence even more unbearable for many residents caught in the crossfire. It's by no means clear as to who is involved and to what end, and to complicate things Pagad has splintered into a number of factions. Some of these talk the language of Muslim fundamentalism, while at the same time there are gangsters who claim to have gone straight and have formed a representative organization to publicize their new-found righteousness. In 1999 there were even suggestions that Pagad had been infiltrated by gangsters as part of a complex war to control turf. What is not in doubt, though, is the fact that the cycle of attack and counter-attack has accelerated with drive-by shootings, assassinations and hundreds of incidents involving pipe bombs, some targeting police stations. Apart from a spectacularly horrific and widely publicized bombing of the *Planet Hollywood* restaurant on the V&A Waterfront in 1998, these events have been restricted to the Cape Flats and haven't touched tourists.

has been characterized by a complex and bloody war between coloured gangs and Pagad (see box above), an organization that appears to have begun with the aim of stamping out crime. Fortunately this conflict has remained largely restricted to the Cape Flats and isn't something you need to be unduly concerned about. Having said that, petty crime is nonetheless a problem in central Cape Town, but it's a risk you can minimize by taking a few simple precautions (see Basics, p.53).

Some history

San hunter-gatherers, South Africa's first human inhabitants, moved freely through the Cape Peninsula for tens of millennia before being edged into the interior some 2000 years ago by the arrival of sheep-herding **Khoikhoi** migrants from the north. Over the next 1600 years the Khoikhoi held sway over the Cape pastures. **Portuguese** mariners, in search of a stopoff point en route to East Africa and the East Indies, first rounded the Cape in the 1480s, and named it Cabo de Boa Esperanza (Cape of Good Hope), but their attempts at trading with the Khoikhoi were short-lived, and no Europeans seriously attempted to create a permanent stopping-off point until the **Dutch East India Company** (VOC) cruised into Table Bay in 1652 and set up shop.

The VOC, the world's largest corporation at the time, planned little more at the Cape than a halfway stop to provide fresh produce to their ships travelling between Europe and the East in search of spices, slaves and profit. Their small landing party, led by **Jan van Riebeeck**, built a mud fort where the Grand Parade now stands and established **vegetable gardens**, which they hoped to work with Khoikhoi labour.

The Khoikhoi were understandably reluctant to exchange their perfectly satisfactory lives for the restrictions of formal employment, so van Riebeeck began to import **slaves** in 1658. The growth of the Dutch settlement alarmed the Khoikhoi, who declared war in 1659 to drive the Europeans out, but were defeated and had to cede the Peninsula to the colonists.

During the early eighteenth century, Western Cape Khoikhoi society disintegrated, **German** and **French** religious refugees swelled the European population, and slavery became the economic backbone of the colony, which was now a minor colonial village of canals and low, whitewashed, flat-roofed houses. By 1750, Cape Town had become a town of over 1000 buildings, with 2500 inhabitants.

In 1795, **Britain**, deeply concerned by Napoleonic expansionism, grabbed Cape Town to secure the strategic sea route to the East. This was not welcomed by the settlement's

Calvinist Dutch burghers, but was better news for the substantially Muslim slave population, as Britain ordered the **abolition of slavery** and allowed **freedom of religion**. It wasn't long before South Africa's first mosque, built by freed slaves, shot up in Dorp Street in the Bo-Kaap.

By the turn of the nineteenth century, Cape Town had become one of the most cosmopolitan places anywhere and a sea port of major significance, growing under the influence of the British Empire. The Commercial Exchange went up in 1819, followed by department stores, banks and insurance company buildings. In the 1860s the docks were begun, Victoria Road from the city to Sea Point was built, and the suburban railway line to Wynberg was laid. Since slavery had been abolished, Victorian Cape Town had to be built with **convict labour** and that of prisoners of war transported from the colonial frontier in Eastern Cape. Racial segregation wasn't far behind, and an outbreak of bubonic plague in 1901 gave the town council an excuse to establish **Ndabeni**, Cape Town's first black location, near Maitland.

In 1910, Cape Town was drawn into the political centre of the newly federated South Africa (see p.690) when it became the **legislative capital** of the Union. Africans and coloureds, excluded from the cosy deal between Boers and Brits, had to find expression in the workplace, flexing their collective muscle on the docks in 1919, where they formed the mighty **Industrial and Commercial Union**, which boasted 200,000 members in its heyday.

Increasing industrialization brought an influx of black workers, who were housed in the locations of **Guguletu** and **Nyanga**, built in 1945. Three years later, the National Party came to power, promising a fearful white electorate that it would reverse the flow of Africans to the cities. In Cape Town it introduced a policy favouring coloureds for jobs, admitting only African men with work and forbidding the construction of family accommodation for Africans.

Langa township became a stronghold of the **Pan Africanist Congress** (PAC), which organized a peaceful anti-pass demonstration in Cape Town on April 8, 1960. Police fired on the crowd, killing three and wounding many more, and the government declared a state of emergency, and banned anti-apartheid opposition groups, including the PAC and ANC.

In 1966 the notorious **Group Areas Act** was used to uproot whole coloured communities from District Six and to move them to the desolate **Cape Flats**, where rampant gangsterism took vicious root and today remains one of Cape Town's most pressing problems. Compounding the injury, the National Party stripped away coloured representation on the town council in 1972.

Eleven years later, at a huge meeting on the Cape Flats, the extra-parliamentary opposition defied government repression and re-formed as the **United Democratic Front**, heralding a period of intensified struggle to topple apartheid. In 1986 one of the major pillars crumbled when the government was forced to scrap influx control; and blacks began pouring into Cape Town seeking work and erecting shantytowns, making Cape Town one of the fastest-growing cities in the world. On February 11, 1990, the city's history took a neat twist, when, just hours after being released from prison, **Nelson Mandela** made his first public speech from the balcony of City Hall to a jubilant crowd spilling across the Grand Parade, the very site of the first Dutch fort. Four years later he entered the formerly whites-only Parliament, 500m away, as South Africa's first democratically elected president.

Despite five years of non-racial democracy, on the eve of the 1999 elections, Cape Town remained a divided city, with whites continuing to enjoy a leafy existence in the suburbs along the two coasts and the slopes of Table Mountain, while the **V&A Waterfront** complex continued to develop apace. On the desolate **Cape Flats**, some progress had been made in bringing electricity to the shanty towns, but the shacks were still there – and spreading. Despite white fears about crime, it was still blacks and coloureds who were overwhelmingly and disproprtionately the victims of protracted violence, much of it gang related (see box on p.67).

Some attempts were made to foster cultural interaction and to forge a more integrated city. In 1999, the *Cape Times* launched a highly popular "One City, Many Cultures" campaign, which featured regular articles highlighting the richness of Cape Town's different ethnic and religious groups. To the same end the city's local government began being restructured. The city's 69 racially segregated bodies were rationalized into six councils that deliberately linked the wealthy and disadvantaged and brought black, white and coloured areas under common administrations for the first time ever. Part of the process included plans to turn Cape Town into what was described as a "unicity" by the end of 2000, though its exact shape and size were the subject of heated dispute.

> The **telephone code** for Cape Town is ☎021.

Arrival and information

One of the world's great moments of **arrival** is cruising into Table Bay on a luxury liner. For most, however, the approach is much less picturesque – indeed, it can be something of a shock. Whether you come in by air or road, there's small chance of avoiding the grey, industrial sprawl and the miles of squatter camps that line the N2 into town.

The airport

Cape Town International Airport (flight information ☎934 0407) is on the Cape Flats, 22km and half an hour's drive (longer during rush hour: 7–9am & 4–5.30pm) from the city centre.

Intercape (at the airport ☎934 0802, from the city centre ☎419 8888), at the domestic terminal, operate two types of **shuttle** (6am–6.30pm) to and from the airport: from the domestic terminal (in the same complex as the international terminal) there's a **scheduled service** to the main train station, running on the half hour (and on the hour for the return journey) and costing R30. From their office in the international terminal office they operate a door-to-door **transfer service**, which goes to anywhere on the Peninsula and as far east as Stellenbosch on request. The price (R80–120 per person) depends on the distance and number of people in a group.

A cheaper door-to-door option is the 24-hour **Backpackers Airport Shuttle**, based at Extreme Sports, 220 Long Street, city centre (bookings 8am–10pm, mobile ☎083/528 2690), a minibus that takes passengers from the airport to anywhere in the city centre, City Bowl or Sea Point. The service operates in response to demand, which means you'll either need to prebook or wait up to 45 minutes for them to get to the airport. Between 7am and 7pm it costs R40 per person, falling to R25 each for four or more passengers; at other times you'll pay R30–60. Metered **taxis** rank in reasonable numbers outside both terminals and cost about R100. Inside the terminals, you'll find the desks of the major **car rental** firms. There are no trains from the airport.

A **bureau de change** is open to coincide with international arrivals, but exchange rates are more advantageous at banks in the city. The **Cape Town Tourism** desk (daily 7am–5pm) can provide information on accommodation.

Intercity buses and trains

Greyhound, Intercape and Translux **intercity buses**, and mainline **trains** from other provinces, all terminate in the centre of town around the interlinked central complex that includes the **railway station** and **Golden Acre** shopping mall, at the junction of Strand and Adderley streets. Note that Intercape and Translux arrive on the northeast side of the station, off Adderley Street, while Greyhound arrive on the northwest side in Adderley itself. The Golden Acre shopping complex can be a confusing muddle, but this is where all rail and bus transport – both intercity and from elsewhere in the city – and most minibus taxis converge, and if you use public transport at all, you're bound to find yourself here at some stage. Everything you need for your next move is within two or three blocks of here, inlcuding information; the **left-luggage** facilities at the station (Mon 8am–7pm, Tues–Thurs 8am–4pm, Fri 6am–6pm, Sat & Sun 8am–3pm; ☎449 2611) might come in handy while you sort yourself out.

Information

The best place for **information** is the Cape Town Tourism office, corner of Burg and Castle streets (Mon–Fri 8am–5pm, Sat 8.30am–1pm, Sun 9am–1pm; ☎426 4260, fax 426 4266, *captour@iafrica.com*), a five-minute walk and couple of blocks northwest of the station. It operates a comprehensive accommodation booking service and can provide very cheap city maps.

There are also a couple of alternative sources of information that are especially good for backpackers and within easy walking distance of the station. Closer of the two is **Purple Turtle**, First Floor, Purple Turtle Building, corner of Long and Shortmarket streets, a wacky hangout that consists of a backpackers' travel agency (where you'll get good independent advice on lodges and tours), a friendly cybercafé and a collection of hip shops selling records, clothes and what-have-you. **One World Travellers' Space**, 309 Long St (Mon–Fri 9am–5pm; ☎ & fax 423 0777), at the south end of Long, makes bookings for tours and is also a place where you'll get sympathetic advice on all backpacker-ish matters. Services include baggage storage (same hours as office), a travellers' notice board, and mail-holding facilities. You can also chill out in their armchairs, have a coffee, and listen to (and buy) CDs from their extensive selection of African music.

If you're planning to explore beyond the confines of the city centre, you'll need to invest in a detailed **street atlas**, found at most bookshops, including the ubiquitous CNA chain. MapStudio's *A to Z Streetmap* is the cheapest and adequate for the centre and most of the suburbs, although it doesn't cover Simon's Town. There are countless **guide books** on walks around Cape Town, hikes up Table Mountain, dive sites, fishing locations, surfing breaks and windsurfing spots. For the best-stocked shelves and nicest atmosphere, head for the three Exclusive Books stores, one in Claremont and the other at the Victoria and Alfred Waterfront; you'll also find some useful books on all aspects of South Africa at the second-hand bookshops down Longmarket Street. See p.131 for addresses and details.

City transport

Although Cape Town's city centre is compact enough to get around on foot, much of what you'll want to see is spread along the considerable length of the Peninsula, so to make the most of your visit you'll need to use **taxis**, **rent transport**, take a **tour**, or make do with the pretty skeletal public transport system. Inner-city areas west of the centre are better served by **buses** than other central suburbs, but transport north along the Atlantic coast is negligible. There is, however, a **train** service that cuts through the southern suburbs and continues all the way down to Simon's Town. It's fairly reliable and well-used, though the rolling stock is looking a little battered (which it is, by vandals who dismantle the train interiors to sell the elements such as window frames for scrap). A concerted programme is underway to upgrade and vandal-proof carriages.

Note that although travellers do use public transport **after dark** without incident, there's always a risk attached. If in any doubt, make every effort to take metered taxis at night, and if you're forced to use public transport take sensible precautions, such as travelling in a group (especially women) and avoiding third-class carriages on trains.

Buses

Within the central area, **buses** can be a convenient way of getting around, especially those serving the Waterfront, Sea Point and Camps Bay, and there's also a regular though infrequent service to Hout Bay and World of Birds. Don't, however, attempt to

---

USEFUL BUS SERVICES

CITY TO:

Sea Point (direct): Golden Acre–Mouille Point–Main Road Sea Point. *Mon–Sat at least 13 daily.*

Table Mountain (for cableway) (circular): Golden Acre–Adderley St–Wale St–Buitengragt St–New Church St–Kloofnek Rd–Kloofnek Terminus. *Mon–Fri 1–2 hourly; Sat hourly.*

Hout Bay: Golden Acre–Lower Plein St–Darling Rd–Adderley St–Green Point, Main Rd–Sea Point–Camps Bay, Victoria Road–Hout Bay Beach–Hout Bay Harbour. *Mon–Fri 4 hourly to Sea Point, 14 daily to Hout Bay; Sat 3 hourly to Sea Point, 6 daily to Hout Bay; Sun 3 daily to Hout Bay.*

Kirstenbosch: Adderley St–Hout Bay–World of Birds–Kirstenbosch. *Daily at 7.30am (returns at 3.30pm).*

Waterfront: Cape Town Station–Riebeeck St–Buitengragt St–V&A Waterfront. *Daily every 10min; Sun every 15min.*

V&A WATERFRONT TO:

City: V&A Waterfront–Buitengragt St–Riebeeck St–Cape Town Station. *Daily every 10min; Sun every 15min*

Sea Point: V&A Waterfront–Mouille Point–Green Point–Three Anchor Bay–Beach Road Sea Point. *Daily every 20min.*

MOWBRAY TO:

Kirstenbosch: Mowbray bus terminus-Kirstenbosch. *Mon–Fri 6 daily.*

CITY BUS TERMINALS

Adderley Street, outside OK Bazaars supermarket: buses to Sea Point, Hout Bay and southern suburbs.
Cape Town Station, Adderley Street: buses to Waterfront.
Golden Acre Bus Terminus, outside

Golden Acre Shopping Centre in Adderley Street: buses to Table Mountain, Camps Bay and Table Bay.
Grand Parade, in Strand Street behind the railway station: the main bus station, where all other services depart from.

catch a bus to the southern suburbs – take the train, unless you have a penchant for slow journeys in old rigs.

All the principal terminals are around Adderley Street and Golden Acre (see box on previous page). **Tickets** are sold on buses by the driver, and if you're planning on using them frequently, consider buying a **Ten-Ride Clip Card**, which will save you around 25 percent; a card covering the route from the city to Sea Point, for example, costs around R20, and around R30 to Camps Bay. The card is valid for fourteen days. For **timetables**, enquire at the Golden Arrow **information booth** (toll-free ☎0801/21 2111) at the Grand Parade **central bus terminal**, or at Cape Town Tourism, on the corner of Burg and Castle streets. It's always advisable to reconfirm the timetabled times and points of departure at the booth, as these periodically change inexplicably. Having said that, you can't rely on someone always being in attendance, in which case you'll have to chance your luck or ask people waiting at the stops.

Taxis, minibus taxis and rikkis

The term "**taxi**" is no less ambiguous in Cape Town than elsewhere in South Africa: it's used to refer to conventional metered cars, jam-packed minibuses and their more upmarket cousins, rikkis.

Metered taxis

Metered taxis, regulated by the Cape Town Municipality, don't cruise up and down looking for fares; you'll need to go to the taxi ranks around town, including the Waterfront, the train station and Greenmarket Square. Alternatively, you can phone to be picked up (see "Listings", p.133). Taxis must have the driver's name and identification clearly on display and the meter clearly visible. Fares work out at around R10 a kilometre. This is expensive compared to other forms of transport, but worth it at night, when metered taxis are the safest way of getting around.

Minibus taxis

Minibus taxis are cheap, frequent and bomb up and down the main routes at tearaway speeds. As well as the crazed driving, be prepared for the pickpockets who work the taxi ranks. Minibus taxis can be hailed from the street or boarded at the central taxi rank, adjacent to the railway station. Once you've boarded, pay the *guardjie* (assistant), who sits near the driver, and tell him when you want to get off. Fares should be under R4 for most trips. A word of warning: minibus taxi companies throughout South Africa are riven by factions, which from time to time become engaged in violent campaigns of vendetta. Ask at your accommodation for the current situation.

Rikkis

Rikkis are more visitor-friendly versions of minibus taxis, carrying not more than eight passengers, and aimed principally at tourists. In Cape Town (7am–7pm; ☎423 4888 or 423 4892) they are restricted to the City Bowl, the Waterfront and the Atlantic seaboard as far as Camps Bay – they don't go into the suburbs. Fares are kept down by picking up and dropping off passengers along the way (between R6 and R15). Rikkis also operate mini-tours to destinations that include Cape Point and Stellenbosch, for which they charge R60–80 an hour for a whole vehicle.

Trains

Cape Town's Metro Rail **train** service (enquiries ☎449 2991, timetable information toll-free ☎0800/656 463) is a relatively reliable, if slightly tatty, urban line that runs from the city's central station, through the **southern suburbs** and all the way down to Simon's Town. Highly recommended as an outing in its own right, and undoubtedly one of the great urban train journeys of the world, it reaches the False Bay coast at Muizenberg and continues south, sometimes so spectacularly close to the ocean that you can feel the spray and peer into rock pools.

Trains run overground, and there are no signposts on the streets, so you'll have to look at a map or ask around to find the stations. Useful stations to locate include Observatory and Newlands, where you might well be staying, while from Mowbray there are buses to Kirstenbosch. Tickets must be bought at the station before boarding. You're best off in the reasonably priced first-class carriages; curiously, there's no second class, and third class is not recommended for security reasons. A first-class single from Cape Town to Muizenberg works out at a little under R7. Returns cost double.

Suburban trains tend to run approximately to the published **timetable**, which can be bought from newsagents or stations. There are departures every ten minutes at peak times (Mon–Fri 5.30–8am & 3.30–6pm) along the line for the southern suburbs to Retreat, and every twenty minutes to Fish Hoek; at other times there are one to two trains per hour, the last one at 10.30pm. One to two trains an hour, the last one leaving at 9.40pm, go all the way down the line to Simon's Town, where rikkis (☎786 2136) meet every service between 6.40am and 6.20pm (Mon–Sat). Three other lines run east from Cape Town to Strand (through Bellville) and to the outlying towns of Stellenbosch and Wellington, but as they run through the Flats some sections are not as safe as the journey to Simon's Town. The only times you're likely to need these trains is to get to Stellenbosch or Paarl and apart from undertaking these journeys, they aren't recommended. In general, trains, like buses, aren't recommended after dark – take a taxi instead.

Driving

Cape Town is car-friendly, with good roads and several fast **freeways** that can whisk you across town in next to no time, even if these latter routes appear to have been conceived by a manic fairground designer. Take care approaching: the access roads frequently feed directly into the fast lane (and Capetonians have no compunction in exceeding the 100kph freeway and 120kph highway speed limits). Signs on freeways make no concession to outsiders. There's often little warning of branches off to the suburbs, only the final destination of the freeway being given. Your best bet is to plan your journey, and make sure you know exactly where you're going. On the plus side, the obvious landmarks of Table Mountain and two seaboards make orientation a cinch, particularly south of the centre, and some wonderful journeys postively demand your attention, the most notable being Chapman's Peak Drive, a narrow winding cliff-edge route that affords wonderful views of the Atlantic breaking hundreds of metres below.

The usual precautions for defensive **driving** in South Africa are in order, especially since Cape Town has a few peculiarities all of its own. The unwritten rule of the road on the Peninsula is that minibus taxis have the right of way. Don't mess with them: their vehicles are bigger than yours, they carry handguns and will often run red lights (as will many Capetonians). Don't assume green means safe: pretend you're a pedestrian (look left, look right and left again), then cross if it's safe.

Car and bike rental

There are dozens of **car rental** companies in Cape Town. To find out who's currently operating and to get the best deal, either pick up one of the brochures at the Captour office (see "Arrival and information" on p.69) or look in the Yellow Pages telephone directory. Cheapest are Discount Drive Car Hire (☎439 2078), who rent out older vehicles for as little as half the price of the others. For one-way rental (to drive down the Garden Route and fly out of Port Elizabeth, for example), you'll have to rely on one of the bigger companies, which are pricier but have nationwide offices, such as Avis (☎423 0823), Hertz (☎386 1560) and Imperial (☎421 5190).

For **motorbike rental**, Le Cap Motorcycle Hire, 3 Carisbrook St (☎423 0823), can provide all the necessary gear and rent out bikes (from R150 a day, plus 60c/km), as well as automatic scooters (R120 a day). **Mountain bikes** are available from Rent 'n' Ride, Park Rd, Mouille Point (☎434 1122; R50 per day). Fly Bike, on the corner of Somerset and Chiappini roads, on the northern outskirts of the city centre, near the Waterfront (☎421 1328), rent out automatic **scooters** (R150 per day), including a helmet.

Tours

Guided tours enable you to orientate yourself quickly and get to the highlights in a hurry – a good option if time is limited. Mother City Tours (☎448 3817, fax 448 3844) offer half- and full-day tours of the City, Cape Point, Table Mountain and the Winelands; Hylton Ross Tours (☎511 1784, fax 511 2401) cover all the popular sites in and around town; and Intercape (☎419 8888) offer customized tours of Cape Point, the Peninsula and Winelands for any size group. All three companies will collect you from your residence and take you home again; prices range from R120 to R240 per person. (For tours of the Cape Flats townships and Bo-Kaap, see pp.120 and 96 respectively). For specialist **natural history tours**, which look at, among other things, fynbos (see box on p.117) and the Cape floral kingdom, Dr Penny Mostert's Cape Specialist Ecotourism (☎ & fax 689 2978) is highly recommended.

Accommodation

Finding a **place to stay** in Cape Town isn't always easy, especially with the city's growing popularity, and there are few signs that this will change. December to January (the main annual school holidays) is peak season, when many South Africans head for the coast and you should expect to pay up to twice as much as at other times. The foreign tourist season, too, is progressively stretching and now extends throughout summer from October to March. The only way to guarantee the kind of place you want is to **book ahead**.

There are a few **accommodation agencies** that may be able to help if you're stuck: Cape Town Tourism runs a Hotel and Accommodation Booking Centre from its office on the corner of Burg and Castle streets (Mon–Fri 8am–5pm, Sat 8.30am–1pm, Sun 9am–1pm; ☎418 5214, fax 418 5227, *captour@iafrica.com*); Bed 'n' Breakfast, 17 Talana Rd, Claremont (☎683 3505, fax 683 5159); and A–Z Holiday Accommodation, 11 Elgin Rd, Milnerton (☎551 2785). Home Accommodation (☎757 7130, fax 712 3340) produce a comprehensive guide of accommodation – choose your place and book directly with the hosts.

ACCOMMODATION PRICE CODES

All the accommodation listed in the Guide has been categorized into one of nine price bands, as set out below. The rates quoted represent what you can expect to pay for much of the summer **per person**, and unless otherwise stated, are based on two sharing. Rooms are generally en suite. Expect prices in some areas to be significantly higher in peak season (Dec–Jan & Easter), and look out for discounts during the winter. For further details, see p.33.

① up to R50	⑥ R250–300
② R50–100	⑦ R300–400
③ R100–150	⑧ R400–500
④ R150–200	⑨ over R500
⑤ R200–250	

City Bowl and the Waterfront

The greatest concentration of accommodation is around the **City Bowl** and the adjacent seaside strip as far as Sea Point. The City Bowl, creeping up towards Table Mountain, along Kloof Nek Road, includes the **city centre**, the down-at-heel and lively suburb of **Gardens**, and the desirable inner-city suburbs of **Tamboerskloof** and **Oranjezicht**, which are close to the centre and ten minutes' drive over the mountain to the stunning Camps Bay coast. A cluster of backpackers' lodges are concentrated on **Long Street** in the city centre, and at the lower end of its continuation up **Kloof Street**. Further up, the sweaty ranks of apartment blocks dissolve into leafier suburbs, and you'll find the pricier and more comfortable B&Bs, guesthouses and hotels.

Backpackers' lodges

The Albergo, 5 Beckham St, Gardens (☎422 1849, fax 423 0515). Pleasant converted house along a side street, just off the main drag. Dorms ①; triples and doubles ②.

Ashanti Lodge, 11 Hof St, Gardens (☎423 8721, fax 423 8790, *ashanti@iafrica.com*). Well-located lodge, just behind the *Mount Nelson Hotel*, with a nice garden, swimming pool and courtyard. Dorms ①; doubles ②.

The Backpack, 74 New Church St, Tamboerskloof (☎23 4530, fax 23 0065). Dorms in a stylishly decorated house, with a courtyard, swimming pool and bar. Internet access available. ①.

Bob's Backpack, 187 Long St (☎424 3584, fax 424 8223). All-in-one bistro/bar/hostel offering mini dorms with their own kitchens and bathrooms. Friendly but slightly grubby. ①.

Cat & Moose, 305 Long St (☎ & fax 423 7638, *cat&moose@hotmail.com*). Most characterful of the Long St lodges, run by interesting and informed Capetonians. Dorms ①, doubles ②.

City Slickers, 25 Rose St (☎422 2357, fax 422 2355). Purpose-built, professionally run backpackers' lodge, with small lockable double rooms mostly with bunks, 5min from Adderley St. Roof garden with views of Table Mountain. ①.

Cloudbreak Backpackers' Lodge, 219 Upper Buitenkant St, Gardens (☎461 6892, fax 461 1458, *cloudbrk@gem.co.za*). Friendly and fun place with a garden on a busy road close to a large shopping centre. Full travel and booking centre. Dorms ①; doubles ②.

Lion's Den, 255 Long St (☎423 9003, fax 423 9166, *lionsden@iafrica.com*). Dorms and doubles on offer at this friendly, respectable establishment, in a Victorian building converted into a lodge. Dorms ①; doubles ②.

Long Street Backpackers, 209 Long St (☎423 0615, fax 423 1842, *longstbp@mweb.co.za*). The oldest Long St backpackers' lodge, in a former apartment block converted into dorms and doubles. Safe, clean and basic. ①.

Oak Lodge, 21 Breda St, Gardens (☎465 6182, fax 465 6305, *oaklodge@lantic.co.za*). More an event than a lodge, this 1860s' Victorian house has dramatic dungeons, dragon murals, and a lively atmosphere. Spacious, well serviced, and with an immaculate kitchen. Dorms ①; doubles ②.

Overseas Visitors' Club Hostel, 230 Upper Long St (☎724 6800, fax 423 4870, *hross@ovc.co.za*). Airy high ceilings and dorms with balconies. ①.

Zebra Crossing, 82 New Church St (☎ & fax 422 1265). Standard backpackers' lodge, with a lively café and a full kitchen in two converted houses on a main road. Dorms ①; doubles ②.

Guesthouses and B&Bs

African Sun, 3 Florida Rd, Vredehoek (☎ & fax 461 1601, *afpress@iafrica.com*). Small, secluded, self-catering apartment close to the city centre, furnished with pared-back ethnic decor and run by friendly, well-informed owners. Good value. ③.

Ambleside Guesthouse, 11 Forest Rd, Oranjezicht (☎465 2503, fax 465 3814). Inexpensive, slightly stuffy rooms, some with bath, in a nice part of town. ②.

Belmont House, 10 Belmont Ave, Oranjezicht (☎461 5417, fax 461 6642, *belmont@dockside.co.za*). Tastefully restored 1920s' house with clear, fresh rooms, each with its own shower or bath and use of kitchen. Discount to *Rough Guide* readers. ③.

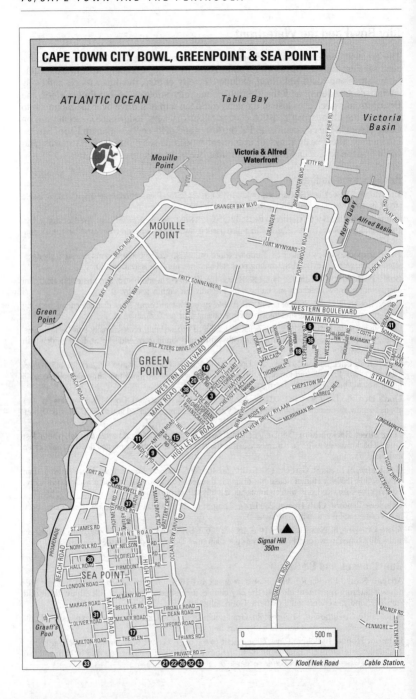

CAPE TOWN CITY BOWL, GREENPOINT & SEA POINT

ATLANTIC OCEAN

Table Bay

Victoria Basin

Mouille Point

Victoria & Alfred Waterfront

GRANGER BAY BLVD

MOUILLE POINT

BEACH ROAD

BAY ROAD

STEPHAN WAY

VLEI ROAD

FRITZ SONNENBERG

Green Point

BILL PETERS DRIVE/RYLAAN

GREEN POINT

WESTERN BOULEVARD

BEACH ROAD

MAIN ROAD

WESTERN BOULEVARD

MAIN ROAD

CHEPSTOW RD

OCEAN VIEW DRIVE / RYLAAN

MERRIMAN RD

HIGH LEVEL ROAD

ANTRIM ROAD

ST BEDE'S

FORT RD

CAMBERWELL RD

KLOEMEYER RD

FRERE RD

WHITLEY RD

RHINE ROAD

ST JAMES RD

MT. NELSON

NORFOLK RD

OLDFIELD

HALL ROAD

FIRMOUNT

LONDON ROAD

SEA POINT

MARAIS ROAD

ALBANY RD

BELLEVUE RD

MAIN ROAD

OLIVER ROAD

MILNER ROAD

FIRDALE ROAD

DEAN ROAD

CLIFFORD ROAD

FRIARS RD

THE GLEN

MILTON ROAD

PROMENADE

BEACH ROAD

Graaff's Pool

PRIVATE RD

Signal Hill 350m

SIGNAL HILL RD

LONGMARKET

YUSUF DRIVE

VOETBOOG

STRAND

SOMERSET

MILNER RD

KENMORE

DEVENPORT

Kloof Nek Road

Cable Station,

0   500 m

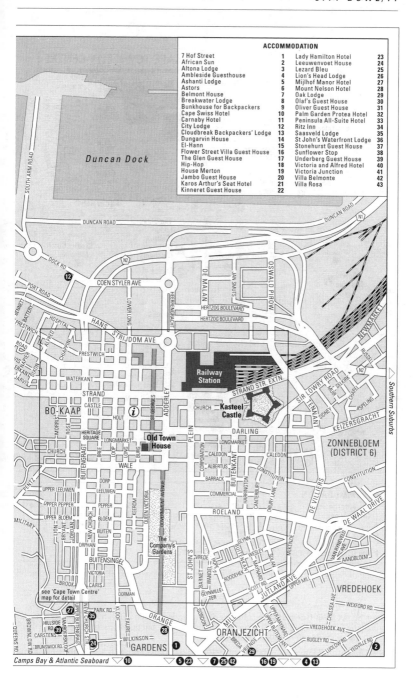

ACCOMMODATION

7 Hof Street	1
African Sun	2
Altona Lodge	3
Ambleside Guesthouse	4
Ashanti Lodge	5
Astors	6
Belmont House	7
Breakwater Lodge	8
Bunkhouse for Backpackers	9
Cape Swiss Hotel	10
Carnaby Hotel	11
City Lodge	12
Cloudbreak Backpackers' Lodge	13
Dungarvin House	14
El-Hann	15
Flower Street Villa Guest House	16
The Glen Guest House	17
Hip-Hop	18
House Merton	19
Jambo Guest House	20
Karos Arthur's Seat Hotel	21
Kinneret Guest House	22
Lady Hamilton Hotel	23
Leeuwenvoet House	24
Lezard Bleu	25
Lion's Head Lodge	26
Mijlhof Manor Hotel	27
Mount Nelson Hotel	28
Oak Lodge	29
Olaf's Guest House	30
Oliver Guest House	31
Palm Garden Protea Hotel	32
Peninsula All-Suite Hotel	33
Ritz Inn	34
Saasveld Lodge	35
St John's Waterfront Lodge	36
Stonehurst Guest House	37
Sunflower Stop	38
Underberg Guest House	39
Victoria and Alfred Hotel	40
Victoria Junction	41
Villa Belmonte	42
Villa Rosa	43

CAPE TOWN CITY CENTRE

ACCOMMODATION

1 The Albergo	**7** City Slickers	**13** St Paul's B&B Guest House
2 The Backpack	**8** Holiday Inn Garden Court	**14** Travellers Inn
3 Bob's Backpack	**9** Holiday Inn Waterfront	**15** Tudor House Hotel
4 Cat & Moose	**10** Lion's Den	**16** Tulbagh Protea Hotel
5 Cape Gardens Hotel	**11** Long Street Backpackers	**17** Zebra Crossing
6 The Cape Heritage Hotel	**12** Overseas Visitors' Club Hostel	

Flower Street Villa Guest House, 3 Flower St, Oranjezicht (☎465 7517). Spacious rooms in a former nursing home. There's a small extra charge for breakfast, but guests have use of kitchen there. Doubles and triples (with or without bathroom) ②.

House Merton, 12 Forest Rd, Oranjezicht (☎465 6417). Rooms with bath in a comfortable private house. ③.

Leeuwenvoet House, 93 New Church St, Tamboerskloof (☎424 1133, fax 424 0495, *leeuwen@iafrica.com*). Tranquil guesthouse along a main drag, with lots of oregon pine and wicker. All rooms have bath. ⑤.

Lezard Bleu, 30 Upper Orange St, Oranjezicht (☎461 4601, fax 461 4657, *welcome@lezardbleu.co.za*). En-suite rooms in a spacious, relaxed place in a pleasant part of town with a changing exhibition of contemporary art. Good views, pool and generous breakfast. ③.

Room in the Garden, 2 Invermark Crescent, Oranjezicht (☎24 2536). Thoughtful service at a B&B (or self-catering accommodation) halfway up Table Mountain with great views of the city. ③.

Saasveld Lodge, 73 Kloof St, Tamboerskloof (☎424 6169, fax 424 5397). Clean but rather impersonal lodge on a noisy thoroughfare, with TV and phone in rooms. No breakfast. ③.

St Paul's B&B Guest House, 182 Bree St (☎23 4420, fax 23 1580). Charming, well-managed guest house with spacious rooms, in a beautifully restored building attached to the historic St Paul's Church. Shared bathroom facilities. ③.

7 Hof Street, 7 Hof St, Gardens (☎424 4984). Room in a private house in a nice part of town. ③.

Travellers Inn, 208 Long St (☎424 9272, fax 424 9278). Somewhere between a backpackers' lodge and a guesthouse in character, you won't be swinging many cats in their small rooms. Shared showers and toilets. ②.

Underberg Guest House, 6 Tamboerskloof Rd, Tamboerskloof (☎426 2262, fax 424 4059, *underberg@netactive.co.za*). Centrally located, fairly large Victorian guesthouse. ⑤.

Hotels

Breakwater Lodge, Portswood Rd, Waterfront (☎406 1911, fax 406 1070, *brkwater@fortesking-hotels. co.za*). Sparklingly clean hotel in the city's old prison building. Excellent value, 5min from the Waterfront. Rate excludes breakfast. ④.

Cape Gardens Hotel, 88 Queen Victoria St, Gardens (☎423 1260, fax 423 2088, *lodge@dockside.co.za*). Functional hotel, bang in the centre, opposite the Botanical Gardens. ④.

The Cape Heritage Hotel, 90 Bree St (☎424 4646, fax 424 4949, *chrelais@satis.co.za*). Elegant and tastefully restored hotel in Heritage Square, just below the Bo-Kaap, with spacious rooms each uniquely furnished to a theme, among them African, Japanese and Dutch. ⑨.

Cape Swiss Hotel, corner of Kloof and Camp streets, Tamboerskloof (☎423 8190, fax 426 1795). Three-star comfort in this high-rise hotel on the corner of two main roads, in a trendy part of town. ④.

City Lodge, corner of Alfred and Dock roads, Waterfront (☎419 9450, fax 419 0460). Rather austere but perfectly adequate hotel in the Waterfront development. ⑤.

Holiday Inn Garden Court, 10 Greenmarket Square (☎423 2040, fax 423 3664). Just what you'd expect from the assembly-line chain, remarkable only for its central setting on the famous Greenmarket Square. Rate excludes breakfast. ⑤.

Holiday Inn Waterfront, Buitengragt Extension (☎409 4000, fax 409 4444, *sandras@southernsun.com*). One of Cape Town's newest hotels offers sweeping views across Cape Town and Table Mountain. Rate excludes breakfast. ⑦.

Lady Hamilton Hotel, Union St, Gardens (☎424 1460, fax 423 7788). Reasonably priced, smart hotel with swimming pool, restaurant and karaoke bar. ④.

Mijlhof Manor Hotel, 2A Milner Rd, Tamboerskloof (☎426 1476, fax 422 2046, *mijlof@grm.co.za*). Fairly decent hotel in a nice area near town. Rate excludes breakfast. ⑤.

Mount Nelson Hotel, 76 Orange St, Gardens (☎423 1000, fax 424 7472 *nelress@iafrica.com*). Cape Town's *grande dame*: a fine and famous establishment that takes itself very seriously and overcharges accordingly. Rate excludes breakfast. ⑨.

Tudor House Hotel, 153 Longmarket St, Greenmarket Square (☎421 5140, fax 423 1198). Terrifically situated rooms with baths and balconies, overlooking attractive Greenmarket Square. ③.

Tulbagh Protea Hotel, 9 Ryk Tulbagh Square, Hans Strydom Ave (☎421 5140, fax 421 4648). Centrally situated member of a respectable South African chain, but in a somewhat desolate location on the Foreshore. ⑥.

Victoria and Alfred Hotel, Pierhead, Waterfront (☎419 6677, fax 419 8955, *resvanda@ambassador. co.za*). Squeaky-clean atmosphere, bang in the middle of the Waterfront development. ⑨.

Villa Belmonte, 33 Belmont Ave, Oranjezicht (☎462 1576, fax 462 1579, *villabel@iafrica.com*). South Africa's smallest four-star hotel feels like a country lodge in the middle of the city. Wonderful views of the sea and Table Mountain. Rooms are themed and prices vary according to size. Book six months ahead for balcony rooms. ⑧–⑨.

Southern suburbs

The southern suburbs – the formerly whites-only areas closest to the mountain – are convenient for the Simon's Town train line, providing easy access to both the city centre and the False Bay seaboard. Closest to town, **Observatory**, with its narrow streets, tightly packed Victorian cottages and large student population, has a bohemian ambience, and some congenial bars and restaurants, while the more southerly areas of **Rosebank, Claremont, Newlands** and **Rondebosch** become greener and more suburban the further from town you go. Poshest of all are the semi-rural areas close to the mountain and along the road to Hout Bay. Of these, **Constantia** is the oldest and most salubrious suburb in Cape Town, boasting functioning wine estates and country-style hotels. Although there is a limited bus service along Hout Bay Main Road, generally you'll need your own transport.

Budget self-catering and backpackers' lodges

Allandale Holiday Cottages, 72 Swaanswyk Rd, Tokai (☎75 3320, fax 72 9744, *allandale@iafrica.com*). Sixteen one-, two- and three-bedroom self-catering brick cottages on the slopes of the Constantiaberg, right next to Tokai Forest, with a pool and tennis courts. ③.

The Green Elephant, 57 Milton Rd, Observatory (☎ & fax 448 6359, *greenele@iafrica.com*). Basic dorms and doubles in a large, vibey house just off Main Rd, with a Jacuzzi, braai and Internet facilities. The owner leads outdoor expeditions around Cape Town. Camping and dorms ①; doubles ②.

Ivydene, off Glebe Rd, Rondebosch (☎685 1747, *ivydene@mweb.co.za*). Delightful old Cape Dutch farmhouse near the university, with an artisitic and friendly atmosphere, divided into self-catering apartments. Garden and swimming pool. ③.

The Lodge, 36 Milton Rd, Observatory (☎ & fax 448 6536). Clean, quiet and homely house with a pool; good value for a couple sharing. Linen included. Dorms ①, doubles ②.

Guesthouses and B&Bs

Camelia Cottage, 17 Talana Rd, Claremont (☎683 3505, fax 683 5159). All rooms with bath in a quiet suburban street, a 20min walk from the station and Cavendish Square shops. ③.

Carmichael House, 11 Wolmunster Rd, Rosebank (☎689 8350, fax 689 8097, *carmichael@webmaster.co.za*). Turn-of-the-century house with nice big rooms and a pool, near the Baxter Theatre. ④.

Constantia Lodge, Duntaw Close, off Rhodes Drive, Constantia (☎794 2410, fax 794 2418, *constantialodge@intekom.co.za*). Luxurious and beautifully situated guesthouse, close to Cecilia Forest. ④–⑤.

Constantia Uitsig Country Hotel, Spaanschemat River Rd, Constantia (☎794 6500, fax 794 7605, *res@ilink.co.za*). Charming cottages on a wine estate. ⑨.

The Coach House, 20 Mortimer Rd, Wynberg (☎761 6493, *scgiles@iafrica.com*). Cottage in converted barn near shops and Wynberg station. ②.

Elephant Eye Lodge, 9 Sunwood Drive, Tokai (☎ & fax 752 432, *orsmond@iafrica.com*). Friendly B&B in converted Cape farmhouse, minutes' walk from Tokai Forest and with its own large grounds. ④.

Gloucester House Bed & Breakfast, 54 Weltevreden Ave, Rondebosch (☎ & fax 689 3894). Self-catering rooms conveniently close to Rondebosch station, with a swimming pool and *braai* area. Slightly less expensive rooms available without baths. Price excludes breakfast. ②.

Houtkapperspoort, Hout Bay Rd (☎794 5216, fax 794 2907, *houtkap@iafrica.com*). A great rural feel at these 26 one- and two-bedroom stone and brick self-catering cottages close to Constantia Nek, with paths leading onto the mountain. Highly recommended. ③–④.

Kenilworth Guest House, 38 Greenfield Rd, Kenilworth (☎761 6181, fax 761 6185). Victorian house, nicely furnished, with tranquil garden and rooms without bath. Very convenient for the station. ③.

Koornhoop Manor House, corner of Wrensch and Nuttal roads, Observatory (☎ & fax 448 0595). Immaculate rooms in this Victorian house with a quiet garden, close to the station. ③.

Little Ruo, 11 Willow Rd, Constantia (☎794 2052, fax 794 1981, *ruo@netactive.co.za*). Very pleasant and reasonably priced B&B and self-catering units set in huge grounds in landscaped garden with willows, a stream and a saltwater pool. Self-catering units ⑤, B&B ④.

Riverview Guest Lodge, 5 Anson Rd, Observatory (☎47 9056, fax 47 5192). Large and extremely reasonably priced guesthouse, handy for transport. ②.

Rodenburg Guest House, 8 Myrtle Rd, Rondebosch (☎689 4852, fax 689 2065, *rodenbrg@iafrica.com*). Gracious Victorian home very close to the station. All rooms with bath. ④.

The Stables, Chantecler Lane, Constantia (☎ & fax 794 3653). Converted farmhouse, with comfortable, English-style rooms with patios and verandahs. Fabulous breakfasts are served. ④.

Walloon Farm, Fairview Rd, off Walloon Close, Constantia (☎794 4406, fax 794 1470, *bevgage@netactive .co.za*). Guesthouse in an area more suburban than some Constantia places, but still very pleasant. ④.

Hotels

Baxter Suites, 20 Lyle Rd, opposite Baxter Theatre, Rondebosch (☎689 7070, fax 689 7295, *baxter@ambassodor.co.za*). Serviced flats near station and shops, with a lively pub and a pool. ④.

The Courtyard, Liesbeek Ave, Mowbray (☎448 3929, fax 448 5494, *cy#capetown@citylodge.co.za*) . The height of luxury in an exceptionally beautiful eighteenth-century Cape Dutch homestead under thatch, with terracotta floors and large lawns in a semi-rural setting. Breakfast is extra. ⑤.

Greenways Hotel, Torquay Ave, Claremont (☎761 1792, fax 761 0878, *greenways@intekom.co.za*). Small, private hotel in a historic Cape Dutch house. All rooms with bath. Prices depend on size of room and view. ⑥–⑧.

Vineyard Hotel, Colinton Rd, Newlands (☎683 3044, fax 683 3365, *hotel@vineyard.co.za*). For total colonial elegance, this historic Cape Dutch house offers unequalled views and is one of Cape Town's best, at half the price of the *Mount Nelson Hotel*. The mountain-facing rooms are dearer. ⑦–⑧.

Atlantic seaboard

Down the Atlantic seaboard the urban ribbon extends through the inner-city seaside suburbs of **Green Point** and **Sea Point**, historically Cape Town's hotel and high-rise land, now a dense conglomeration of every type of accommodation. At night, Green Point is a magnet for the city's hookers, and petty crime is a problem, but its proximity to the rapidly expanding Waterfront gives a sense that this area is on the way to becoming revamped and revitalized. Sea Point mixes tacky and gentrified and has many of Cape Town's best restaurants, as well as a leading gay cruising zone along the seaside promenade. Rikkis operate as far as Sea Point, and buses to the centre are regular and take under ten minutes. Moving south along Victoria Drive, the luxury mountainside suburb of **Camps Bay** has soaring views over the Atlantic, while the nearby **Llandudno** has similar vistas but fewer places to stay. Further down the coast, **Hout Bay** is the main urban concentration along the lower half of the peninsula, with its own harbour, a pleasant waterfront development, and the only public transport beyond Camps Bay, with direct buses from the centre along the coast, or across the mountain via the southern suburbs. South of Hout Bay is the semi-rural settlement of **Noordhoek**, which has the best walking beach along the coast and is close to the Cape of Good Hope Nature Reserve. The quiet but windy village of **Scarborough**, nestled around Smit's Bay, is the last settlement on the Atlantic coastline before Cape Point, and offers a couple of places to stay.

Green Point and Sea Point

Crammed with a wide range of hostels and hotels, **Green Point** and **Sea Point** are good places to head for if your budget is tight. Sea Point also boasts lively restaurants and trendy coffee shops along its bustling Main Road.

BACKPACKERS' LODGES

Astors, 37 Main Rd, Green Point (☎439 9045, fax 439 9046, *astor@iafrica.com*). Bright murals in a slightly musty hostel with cramped dorms on a busy road, mitigated by a pleasant garden. Dorms ①; doubles with linen ②.

Bunkhouse for Backpackers, 23 Antrim Rd, Sea Point (☎ & fax 434 5695). One of the best-run lodges in the area: sociable and busy, with a swimming pool, pool table, and lockers in each room. ①.

Hip-Hop, 11 Vesperdene Rd, Green Point (☎439 2104, fax 439 8688). Pleasantly decorated and lively lodge, though it can be noisy and not always as clean as you might wish. Camping and dorms ①; doubles with linen ②.

St John's Waterfront Lodge, 4–6 Braemar Rd, Green Point (☎439 1404, fax 439 1424). Expertly run by friendly and helpful staff, with two pools and a great garden. Highly recommended, despite being in a bit of a red-light area. Dorms, triples and doubles ②.

Sunflower Stop, 179 Main Rd, Green Point (☎434 6535, fax 434 6501). Tightly packed but clean dorms in a bright, lively converted house with pool, *braai* area and spacious kitchen. Offers airport shuttle and full laundry facilities. ②.

GUESTHOUSES AND B&BS

Altona Lodge, 19 Croxteth Rd, Green Point (☎ & fax 434 2572). Quiet and friendly guest house close to the city centre, offering first-class service and very reasonable rates. ③.

Dungarvin House, 163 Main Rd, Green Point (☎ & fax 434 0677, *kom@ilink.nis.za*). An Edwardian villa on a busy road, with gracious, well-appointed rooms. ⑤.

El-Hann, 5 Scholtz Rd, Three Anchor Bay (☎434 0968, fax 439 4128, *elhann@dockside.co.za*). Repro furniture and rooms with bath in a quiet cul-de-sac. ④.

The Glen Guest House, 3 The Glen, Sea Point (☎439 0086, fax 439 3552, *theglen@mweb.co.za*). Seriously upmarket establishment with large airy rooms, all with bath. ⑥.

Jambo Guest House, 1 Grove Rd, Green Point (☎439 4219, fax 434 0672). Atmospheric, small establishment, where the service is excellent and there's a delightfully relaxing enclosed garden with a pond. Recommended. ④.

Kinneret Guest House, 11 Arthur's Rd, Sea Point (☎439 9237, fax 434 8998). Comfortable doubles amid outrageously camp interior decor. Love it or hate it, it's perfect for the promenade and beachfront. ④.

Leeuwenzee Guest House, 199 High Level Rd, Sea Point (☎439 9516, fax 439 9550, *leeuwenzee@icon.co.za*). Small, clean rooms somewhat devoid of character, with a swimming pool. ⑤.

Olaf's Guest House, 24 Wisbeach Rd, Sea Point (☎439 8943, fax 439 5057, *olafs@icon.co.za*). Clean, comfortable Victorian house, nicely decorated, and run by a friendly owner.

Oliver Guest House, 8 Oliver Rd, Sea Point (☎439 9237, fax 434 8998). Sister to the *Kinneret Guest House*, but more plainly furnished and better value. ④.

Stonehurst Guest House, 3 Frere Rd (☎434 9670, fax 439 8131). Airy Victorian residence with original fittings and Cape furniture. No meals provided, but there's a kitchen and guest lounge. Not all rooms have bath. ②–③.

Villa Rosa, 277 High Level Rd, Sea Point (☎ & fax 434 2768). Friendly guesthouse decorated with simplicity and style. Some rooms have sea views, but the main drawback is the busy road. ④.

HOTELS

Carnaby Hotel, corner of Main and St Bede's roads, Three Anchor Bay (☎439 7410, fax 439 1222). Clean, good-value hotel with small rooms. Shared facilities ②, en suite ③.

Karos Arthur's Seat Hotel, Arthur's Rd, Sea Point (☎434 1187). Excellent, and convenient for the beach, but pricey. ⑦.

Lion's Head Lodge, 319 Main Rd, Sea Point (☎434 4163, fax 439 3818, *lionhead@cif.co.za*). No-nonsense, functional rooms that serve the purpose, but have no flair. The lodge also offers fully equipped apartments sleeping two. Rooms and apartment ③.

Palm Garden Protea Hotel, 75 Regent Rd, Sea Point (☎439 1171, fax 434 1662). In central Sea Point, with grand views of Lion's Head. ⑥.

Peninsula All-Suite Hotel, 313 Beach Rd, Sea Point (☎439 8888, fax 439 8886). Very good, upmarket apartments; a fine bet if you can afford it. ⑥.

Ritz Inn, corner of Main and Camberwell roads, Sea Point (☎439 6010, fax 434 0809). Enormous block, best known for its revolving restaurant on the 22nd floor with views of the sea and mountain. With over 200 rooms, you'll never feel alone. Price excludes breakfast. ④.

Victoria Junction, corner of Somerset and Ebenezer roads, Green Point (☎418 1234, fax 418 5678, *vicjunct@icon.co.za*). Standard and loft-apartment style rooms with good views and a trendy atmosphere. No breakfast. Standard rooms ④, others ⑨.

Winchester Mansions Hotel, 221 Beach Rd, Sea Point (☎434 2351, fax 434 0215, *winmanares@mweb.co.za*). Elegant and charming hotel right on the seafront. The pricier sea-facing rooms have the nicest views in Sea Point. ⑦–⑨.

Camps Bay

Bay Hotel, Victoria Rd (☎438 4444, fax 438 4455, *res@thebay.co.za*). Luxurious, glitzy hotel that occasionally hosts the mildly famous, on the fashionable beachfront strip. Mountain-facing rooms ⑥, sea-facing rooms ⑨.

Diamond House, 61 Hely Hutchinson Ave (☎438 1344, fax 438 1557, *bookings@diamondhouse.co.za*). Comfortable rooms with bath, in a house set against the hillside, away from the beach. ⑦.

House Michelitsch, 41 Hely Hutchinson Ave (☎438 9148). Self-contained apartment with its own balcony, halfway up Table Mountain. ⑥.

Lalamandi, corner of 11 Victoria Rd and Houghton Rd, Bakoven (☎ & fax 438 8922). Bright and colourful small flats and doubles, done out with ethnic decor at a friendly, well-run establishment near the sea. Flats ⑥, doubles ⑤.

Leeukop, 25 Sedgemoor Rd (☎438 1361, fax 438 1675). Best B&B accommodation in Camps Bay, in two stylishly arty flats (one larger than the other) near the beach. ③–⑤.

Stan's Halt, The Glen (☎ & fax 438 9037). Cape Town's most tranquil backpackers' hostel has six-bed dorms in a former nineteenth-century hunting lodge in the heart of woodlands, a 15min walk to Clifton beach. The only snag is the 30min walk from the nearest public transport. Take the Kloofnek bus from Adderley St (outside OK Bazaar) and get off at Kloofnek; then walk down to the right towards Clifton, following the hostel signs. ①.

Views, 53 Strathmore Rd (☎ & fax 438 1622). En-suite rooms on the hillside, with magnificent views. ④.

Llandudno

11 Sunset Avenue, Llandudno (☎ & fax 790 2103). Self-contained, open-plan studio and an apartment for four close to the beach, with indigenous garden, a pool, and magnificent sea and mountain views. Apartment ②, studio ③.

Llandudno Apartments, 1 Fisherman's Bend (☎ & fax 790 2656). Self-contained apartment with balcony overlooking the sea. Five–minute walk to the beach. Breakfast included. ④.

Hout Bay

Bayview Manor, 8 Flora Close (☎790 2061, fax 790 5096, *bayviewm@iafrica.com*). Comfortable rooms with baths, set in isolation high on a hill reached by driving through a working-class fishing village with spectacular views of Hout Bay. ④.

Beach House, Royal Ave (☎ & fax 790 4228). Comfortable doubles in a modern guesthouse, close to the beach and near Mariner's Wharf. ③.

Chapman's Peak Hotel, Main Rd (☎790 1036, fax 790 1089). Restaurant with a few rooms with bath, some facing the sea. Not luxurious, but pleasant enough, and one of the best places in town for sunsets. ⑤–⑥.

Dune Lodge, 8 Edward St (☎790 5847). Comfortable and modern, if slightly sterile rooms (with bath) across the road from Mariner's Wharf. ③.

Marlinspike Lodge, 15 Marlin Crescent, Hout Bay (☎790 7757, fax 790 7756, *reservations@marlinspike. com*). You won't meet Captain Haddock here, but you'll find great hospitality and spectacular views from its sea-facing, en-suite rooms. ⑤–⑧.

Noordhoek

Chapman's Peak Caravan Farm, Dassenheuvel Lane (☎789 1225). Three kilometres from the beach, so best with a car. Campsite and on-site caravans (bring your own linen). ②.

Imhoff Caravan Park, 1 Wireless Rd, Kommetjie (☎783 1634). One hundred metres from the beach, this is the nicest campsite in the area. Two-bedroom self-catering chalets (sleeping four) also available. Camping ①, chalets ②.

Monkey Valley Beach, Mountain Rd, Noordhoek (☎789 1391, fax 789 1143, *monkey@iafrica.com*). It's a 10min walk to the beach from these two-roomed, double-storey, thatched cottages (sleeps four people) and double rooms on the slopes of Chapman's Peak. ⑦.

Scarborough and Kommetjie

Bay Cottage, Benning Drive (☎ & fax 783 3601). Choice of delightful spacious B&B or self-catering rooms very close to the beach. ③.

Beach Break, 365 Rooibok St (☎ & fax 780 1517). Well-equipped, self-catering apartment with three rooms, a short walk from the sea, and off to the right of Main Rd. ③.

False Bay seaboard

Down the eastern side of the peninsula, the still-bracing waters of the **False Bay coast** are warmer than the Atlantic, and the public transport is better than anywhere else. This is a good place to stay if you want to be by the sea and away from the centre. The suburban railway runs through the southern suburbs to hit the coast at **Muizenberg**, the oldest and most developed of Cape Town's seaside suburbs. To its south are a series of settlements, including **St James**, **Kalk Bay**, **Fish Hoek** and **Simon's Town**, which, as the third-oldest urban settlement in South Africa, has its own well-established identity.

Muizenberg and St James

Abe Bailey Youth Hostel, corner of Maynard and Westbury roads, Muizenberg (☎ & fax 788 2301, *abeb@new.co.za*). A respectable hostel just a 5min walk from the beach. Dorms ①, doubles ②.

Alexander Mews Guest House, 10 Alexander Rd, Muizenberg (☎788 3541). Somewhat sombre and impersonal guesthouse in one of Muizenberg's less attractive streets. ③.

Greens Hotel, 90 Beach Rd, Muizenberg (☎788 1131, fax 788 7415). Basic hotel with clean en-suite rooms, worth considering for its beachfront position and bottom-of-the range rates. Breakfast extra. ③.

Shrimpton Manor, 19 Alexander Rd, Muizenberg (☎788 5225, fax 788 1128). Lavishly furnished small hotel, a few blocks back from the seafront. Rooms have baths or, less expensively, showers. ③–④.

Sonstraal Guest House, 6 Axminster Rd, Muizenberg (☎ & fax 788 1611). A comfortable establishment 5min from the beach, with kitsch decor and the most extravagantly generous breakfast in Cape Town. ④.

Spray, 105 Main Rd, St James (☎ & fax 788 8018). One of the best-situated and most reasonably priced B&Bs along the False Bay seaboard. The two bedrooms (with bath) are about 30m from the shore, with superb views across the bay. Book well in advance. ③.

Sunbird Lodge, 66 Clovelly Rd, Clovelly (☎782 2778, *crida@mweb.co.za*). Tiny self-catering place that sleeps four, close to beach. ③.

Zandvlei Caravan Park, 1km north of Muizenberg Beach, signposted off the Row (☎788 5215 or 788 5220). Campsites and self-catering bungalows. ①.

Kalk Bay

Castle Hill, 37 Gatesville Rd, Kalk Bay (☎788 2554, fax 788 3843). Stylishly restored Edwardian guesthouse with large, high-ceilinged rooms, and fretwork balconies with unparalleled views of the sun rising across the bay. Magnificent. ④.

Chartfield Guest House, corner of Gatesville and Norman roads, Kalk Bay (☎788 3793, fax 788 8674, *info@chartfield.co.za*). Comfortable and unpretentious accommodation halfway up the hill, offering rooms with baths. Ask for one of the semicircular rooms on the corner with 180-degree views, or the loft. ③.

Harbourside Backpackers, 136 Main Rd, Kalk Bay (☎788 2943, fax 788 6452). Popular hangout with beds on platforms offering views of the harbour. A party atmosphere prevails, but there are quieter doubles on the lower of its upstairs floors. Very cheap restaurant open to public. Dorms ①, doubles.②.

The Innisfail, 6 Dalebrook Rd, Kalk Bay (☎788 8928, fax 788 8929, *innis@iafrica.com*). Modest hotel with simple rooms, off Kalk Bay Main Rd and a few minutes' walk (across the railway line) to the sea. ③.

Fish Hoek

The Avenue Hotel, 7 First Ave, Fish Hoek (☎782 6026, fax 782 5693). Comfortable hotel within walking distance of beach, but without its own sea view. ④.

Beaufort B&B, 34 Main Rd, Fish Hoek (☎782 4037, fax 782 4227). Reasonably priced and clean, with a boarding-house feel. Right on the main road, but plenty of rooms make it a good bet if you're stuck. ②.

Nautilus Lodge, 39 Simon's Town Rd (☎ & fax 782 4168) Magnificent sea views from every suite in this self-catering establishment for four. ③.

Sunny Cove Manor, 72 Simon's Town Rd, Fish Hoek (☎782 2274, fax 782 6043). Outstanding sea views (except for the back room) in this cheerful B&B, 3min from Sunny Cove station. ④.

Tides, 37 Simon's Town Rd, Fish Hoek (☎782 6933, mobile 082/781 4492). Luxury two-storey townhouse on the shore with two double bedrooms each opening out onto a balcony with excellent views of False Bay. Kitchen equipped with dishwasher, microwave and you name it. ④.

Tudor House by the Sea, 43 Simon's Town Rd, Fish Hoek (☎782 6238). Runner-up to the best B&B in South Africa in 1995. Luxury self-catering apartments on the water's edge have slightly stuffy decor, but incredible views. Book as far ahead as possible. Four people ③–⑤.

The Wave Backpackers, 288 Main Rd, Clovelly (☎782 3659). Dorms and doubles and a very reasonable B&B rate, just across the road from the beach. Kitchen for self-catering, free airport pickups and a 5min walk along the beach to Fish Hoek station. ①.

Simon's Town

Ark Studio, 4 Grant Ave, Boulders (☎786 2526, fax 786 3512). Thoroughly comfortable and fully equipped apartments sleeping two, with sweeping views across False Bay. ④.

Blue Lantern Holiday Cabins, Main Rd, Froggy Pond, Simon's Town (☎ & fax 786 2113). Small, fully equipped timber cabins of varying sizes, outside the centre of town. The flimsy walls could be a problem if your neighbours are partying. ②–③.

Boulders Beach Backpackers, 4 Boulders Place, Boulders Beach (☎786 1758, fax 786 1825). A sixteen-bed dorm and a double room, sharing the kitchen and lounge. Breakfast is available at *Penguin Point Restaurant* next door. ①.

Boulders Beach Guest House, Boulders Place, off Bellevue Rd, Simon's Town (☎786 1758). B&B, also with self-catering units, on the parking lot rather than the beach, but 2min walk to the water, and with a sea view. ⑤.

British Hotel Apartments, 90 St George's St, Simon's Town (☎790 4930). Three-bedroom, self-catering apartments in a grand 1898 Victorian hotel. This is an experience rather than just somewhere to stay. Huge units with high ceilings and enormous balconies overlooking the street and the docks and more modest doubles (with bath). ④.

Harbour Lights, 135 Runciman Drive (☎ & fax 786 1119). Clashingly over-decorated and over-full B&B, which is nevertheless comfortable, friendly and blessed with superb views, particularly at night. ③.

Kijabe Lodge, 32 Disa Rd, Murdock Valley (☎786 2433). High on the hillside, a little away from the seafront, with amazing views. Reasonably priced, with exceptionally hospitable owners who welcome mountain bikers and will arrange tours. ③.

Lord Nelson Inn, 58 St George's St (☎786 1386, fax 786 1009). Comfortable little inn overlooking the harbour in the village centre. The best rooms have sea views. ③–④.

Oatlands Holiday Village, Froggy Pond (☎786 1410, fax 786 1162). Slightly cramped, fully equipped self-catering chalets of varying size. ③.

Quayside Lodge, St George's St, off Jubilee Square, Simon's Town (☎786 3838, fax 786 2241, *info@quayside.co.za*). Luxury hotel accomodation awash with nautical references, affording views of the mountain-edged False Bay, the yacht basin and Naval Dock Yard. ⑨.

Sans Tache, 10 Neptune Close (☎ & fax 786 3934). Highly recommended B&B in a hospitable private home, overlooking the harbour with views of False Bay. All rooms en suite. ③.

Seaforth Beach Bungalows, corner of Main and Seaforth roads (☎786 1463). Despite the name, they're not on the beach and there's no sea view, but the strand is a short walk away. Tiny, old-fashioned timber units and flats sleeping six. ①–②.

Whale House, corner of Main Rd and Ixia Crescent, Murdock Valley, Simon's Town (☎ & fax 786 2187). Self-catering family apartment with modern decor, good views and its own terrace, as well as a studio and a B&B unit, all with breakfast. Apartment R300, studio and B&B ③.

Table Bay and the northern suburbs

Around the N2 and north of the city are the **northern suburbs**, the most boring suburban expanse on the entire Cape Peninsula. With the notable exception of **Bloubergstrand**, which has some shred of its origins as a fishing village, and a couple of adjacent places along the edge of Table Bay, which are noted for the ultimate view of Table Mountain, there is every reason to pump hard on the accelerator if you're driving through. Public transport is limited to a handful of buses from the city centre transporting workers to and from the Koeberg nuclear reactor, north of Blouberg, at the beginning and end of the working day.

Blouberg Windsurf & Leisure, 28 Pikkewyn Rd, Bloubergstrand (☎56 1663, *blouwind@mweb.co.za*). Budget self-catering accommodation avaialaeb for a minimum of two weeks, overlooking the sea, and a self-catering unit at 49 Pentz Drive, Tableview, overlooking a lake. Excludes breakfast. ②.

Blue Peter Hotel, Popham Rd, Bloubergstrand (☎56 1956, fax 56 1364). Popular, well-appointed and expensive hotel, right on the beach. ⑤.

Cape View, 50 Sir David Baird Drive, Bloubergstrand (☎ & fax 56 2127). Pick of the area, this well-run and friendly guesthouse offers comfortable rooms and is nicely located, minutes from good restaurants and the beach. ④.

Cotswold Guest House, 6 Cotswold Drive, Milnerton (☎551 3637). Away from the beach, but with luxurious accommodation and pleasant staff. The rooms with views of Table Mountain and the Bay are more expensive. ⑥–⑦.

Dolphin Beach Hotel, Marine Drive, Table Bay (☎557 8140, fax 557 8147). Modern hotel where you pay primarily for the view. Nice long walks on Milnerton Beach. ⑧.

Batavia Street, 8 Batavia St, Bloubergstrand (☎ & fax 56 1169). Self-catering apartments for up to four people, one street away from the sea without the views, but reasonably priced. ①.

Beach Villa Guest House, 43 Harold Ashwell Boulevard, Melkbosstrand (☎553 1296, fax 553 1787). Right on the beach, with a secluded garden leading to the sea. Pool, bar and organized tours. ⑤.

Ou Skip Caravan Park, Otto Du Plessis Drive, Melkbosstrand (☎553 2058). Fully equipped two-bedroom chalets for four, some distance from Cape Town, plus camping. A good deal for families or small groups. Camping ①, chalets ②.

Rockhaven Lodge, 3 Sir David Baird Drive, Bloubergstrand (☎56 2414, fax 56 1501). Pleasant guesthouse close to the beach and restaurants. The pricier rooms have views. ⑤–⑥.

Sunset Lodge, 41 Gull Rd, Bloubergstrand (☎56 1818, fax 56 2592, *clutten@iafrica.com*). Modern house on a hill, with views. ④.

The City

Between two mountainous flanks, reaching away from the docks, through the intense city centre and up the mountain is the **City Bowl** (made up of the Upper and Lower city centres and the Waterfront) where lively areas, like Long Street, the Bo-Kaap and Gardens rub shoulders with the serious new wealth of Tamboerskloof and Oranjezicht. Straggling south from the centre along the eastern slope of the mountain, the predominantly white **southern suburbs** become progressively more affluent as you move from arty Observatory through the comfortably middle-class districts of Rondebosch and Newlands, culminating with the Constantia wine estates. Along the coastal belt, the **Atlantic seaboard** is drier and sunnier, with the wealthiest areas like Clifton and Camps Bay clinging to the mountainside above the sea, white sands and rocky beaches. The **False Bay** coast is wetter, softer and greener, and the sea here usually several degrees warmer than the western peninsula, making Muizenberg, Fish Hoek and Boulder's Beach in Simon's Town the most popular bathing beaches in Cape Town. Curling northeast around Table Bay, the **northern suburbs**, taking in Parow, Milnerton and Bloubergstrand are exceptionally dull suburbs, traditionally with an Afrikaans flavour. South of these, and extending seemingly endlessly along the N2 into the interior, the coloured **Cape Flats townships** jostle with the desolate, litter-strewn **African ghettos** of Nyanga, Langa and Guguletu, which relentlessly overflow into kilometre after kilometre of iron, wood and cardboard shantytowns.

The Upper City Centre

The **Upper City Centre**, the entire area from Strand Street to the southern foot of the mountain, is a collage of Georgian, Cape Dutch, Victorian and twentieth-century architecture, as well as the place where Europe, Asia and Africa meet in markets, alleyways and mosques. Among the substantial drawcards here are **Parliament**, the **Botanical Gardens** and many of Cape Town's major **museums**.

Strand Street marks the edge of Cape Town's original beachfront (though you'd never guess it today), and all urban development to its north stands on reclaimed land. To its south, heading towards Table Mountain, are the remains of the city's 350-year-old historic core, which has survived the ravages of modernization and apartheid-inspired urban clearance to emerge with enough charm to make it South Africa's most pleasing city centre.

Adderley Street, slicing through the Upper City from the railway station in the north to the Gardens in the south, is the obvious orientation axis. To its east, and close to each other just off Strand Street, are the **Castle of Good Hope**, the site of **District Six**, the **Grand Parade** and the **City Hall**. The district to the west of Adderley Street is the closest South Africa gets to a European quarter – a tight network of streets with cafés, buskers, bookstores, street stalls and antique shops congregating around the pedestrianized **St George's Mall** and **Greenmarket Square**. The **Bo-Kaap**, or Muslim district, three blocks further west across Buitengragt (which means the Outer Canal, but is actually a street), exudes a piquant contrast to this, with its minarets, spice shops and cafés selling curried snacks.

South of Adderley Street, where it takes a sharp right into Wale Street, is the symbolic heart of Cape Town (and arguably South Africa), with **Parliament**, museums, archives and De Tuynhuys, the Western Cape office of the President, arranged around the **Botanical Gardens**.

Adderley Street

Once *the* place to shop in Cape Town, **Adderley Street**, lined with centuries of handsome buildings, is still worth a stroll today, for what grand architecture remains. Its attractive streetscape has been wantonly blemished by a series of large Sixties' shopping centres, but just minutes away from crowded malls, among the streets and alleys around Greenmarket Square, you can still find some human scale and historic texture.

Adderley Street was formerly the Heerengracht (Gentlemen's Canal) – a waterway that ran from the Botanical Gardens down to the sea. Low-walled channels, ditches, bridges and sluices ran through Cape Town and earned it the name Little Amsterdam. During the nineteenth century, the canals were buried underground, and in 1850 Heerengracht was renamed Adderley Street (see box opposite). There's little evidence of the canals today, except in name – one section of the street is still called Heerengracht and a parallel street to its west is called Buitengragt (sometimes spelled Buitengracht, after the Dutch style).

The destruction of old Cape Town continued well into the twentieth century, with the razing of many of the older buildings. One of the ugliest newcomers is the **Golden Acre** shopping complex, built in the Seventies, and today Cape Town's unavoidable transport hub. Dominating the north (harbour) end of Adderley Street, Golden Acre employs an unfriendly network of subways and walkways to draw together all the major arrival points into town. The Metrorail urban transit and mainline stations, the central bus terminals, the taxi ranks and tiered parking garages all congregate around this enormous, darkened shopping mall.

Inside sit the **Golden Acre Ruins**, the remains of southern Africa's oldest colonial structure – a reservoir built in 1663 by the Dutch. All that's left is a small bit of wall behind glass, and you might easily walk past and think that the builders who worked on the complex forgot to finish the plastering. Although the mall itself and its environs are anything but picturesque, you will get an authentic taste of ordinary Capetonians doing their shopping, something you just won't catch at the sanitized Victoria and Alfred Waterfront. On Saturday mornings, if you exit through onto Adderley Street, you'll often encounter the spirited sounds of busking brass bands or choirs. Among the sidewalks and pedestrianized sections outside, which run down to the station, you'll find a closely packed **flea market**, where you can browse through curios, crafts and electronic goods (but watch your wallet).

A little further south lies a **flower market**, run by members of the Bo-Kaap Muslim community. As you wander up, two grandiose banks stand on opposite sides of Adderley Street. The fussier of the two is the **Standard Bank**: fronted by Corinthian columns and covered with a tall dome – a temple to the partnership of empire and finance. The **First National Bank**, completed in 1913, was the last South African building designed by Sir Herbert Baker (see the box on p.498). Inside the banking hall, a solid timber circular writing desk, with the original inkwells still in place, resembles an altar.

At the top corner of Adderley Street, just as it veers sharply west into Wale Street, you'll find the **Slave Lodge** (Mon–Sat 9.30am–4.30pm; small entry fee), formerly known as the South African Cultural History Museum. Originally the slammer where the Dutch East India Company kept its human chattels, it also became the colony's main brothel, and was then turned over to another form of entertainment in 1810, when the Supreme Court moved in (and left in 1914), and its proceedings were opened to the public.

THE NAMING OF ADDERLEY STREET

Although the Dutch used Robben Island (see p.99) as a political prison, the South African mainland only narrowly escaped becoming a second Australia, where British felons and enemies of the state could be dumped. By the 1840s, "respectable Australians" were lobbying for a ban on the transportation of criminals to the Antipodes, and the British authorities responded by trying to divert convicts to the Cape. In 1848, the *Neptune*, with a cargo of 282 prisoners, set sail for Cape Town, where the news of their departure was met with outrage. Five thousand citizens gathered on the Grand Parade to hear prominent liberals denounce the British government, and when the ship docked in September, 1849, governor Sir Harry Smith forbade any criminal from landing. In London, politician Charles Adderley successfully addressed Parliament in support of the Cape colonists. In February, 1850, the *Neptune* set off for Tasmania, and grateful Capetonians renamed the city's main thoroughfare **Adderley Street**.

Displays here spread themselves a little thinly over a wide range of topics. The **upper floor** brings together weapons, silver and toys, while the **lower floor** has tasters from a selection of cultures, including Japanese, Tibetan and Dutch. One interesting display downstairs deals with the orginal inhabitants of the Cape, the Khoisan, focusing on their knowledge of plants and herbs, many of which are still in use today. But the most compelling of the downstairs rooms cover topics you aren't likely to see elsewhere, including a social history of Cape Town, displays of coins, paintings, clothes and furniture; a small exhibit illustrates the lives of the slaves who were housed in apalling conditions at the slave lodge. There is a poignant listing, by first name only, of the slaves "resident" in 1693, as well as a scale model of the original lodge itself. The "Cape Kaleidoscope" exhibition is worth taking in for its interesting crash course in the political and economic history of South Africa's first European settlement. Behind the Slave Lodge, on the traffic island in Spin Street, a simple and insconspicuous plinth marks the site of the **Old Slave Tree**, under which slaves were bought and sold.

Castle of Good Hope

From the outside, South Africa's oldest building looks somewhat miserable, and its position on Darling Street, behind the railway station and city bus terminal, does nothing to dispel this. Nevertheless the **Castle of Good Hope** (daily 9am–4pm; R7.5) is well worth the modest entrance fee to experience the meticulous ten-year restoration that has returned the decor to the British Regency style introduced in 1798.

The Castle, as it's commonly known, was built in accordance with seventeenth-century European principles of fortification, comprising strong bastions from which the outside walls could be protected by cross fire. Completed in 1679, it replaced van Riebeeck's earlier mud and timber fort, which stood on the site of the Grand Parade. For 150 years it was the symbolic heart of the Cape adminstration, and the centre of social and economic life. In the late nineteenth century, when the colony had expanded far beyond its walls, there were at least three attempts to demolish it, as it was regarded as a white elephant that was costly to maintain. Inside, there's a powerful atmosphere of calm and a strong sense of order in the Castle's pentagonal plan, though ironically there was nothing ordered about its construction, which lasted over thirteen years, with work constantly coming to a standstill either because of labour shortages or insufficient materials. The original, seaward entrance had to be moved to its present position facing landward, because the spring tide sometimes came crashing in – a remarkable thought given how far aground it is now. This newer entrance is a fine example of seventeenth-century Dutch classicism, and the bell, cast in 1679 by Claude Fremy in Amsterdam, still hangs from its original wooden beams in the tower over the entrance.

There are three interesting collections inside: the **Military Museum** has displays on the conflicts that dogged the early settlement; the **Secunde's House** has furnishings, paintings and *objets d'art* that filled the living space of the deputy governor; and the **William Fehr Collection**, one of the country's most important exhibits of decorative arts, includes paintings of the settlement, eighteenth- and nineteenth-century Dutch and Indonesian furniture, and seventeenth- and eighteenth-century Chinese and Japanese porcelain. **Free tours** (daily 11am, noon & 2pm) are useful for orientation and cover the main features, including the prison cells and dungeons with their centuries-old graffiti painstakingly carved into the surfaces by residents, who clearly had plenty of time to kill. There is a very pleasant tea shop in the Castle courtyard. The Castle is also home to the Defence Force's Western Province Command and you may catch a glimpse of armed soldiers marching in and stepping through the elegant courtyard as Table Mountain peers over the west wall.

The Grand Parade and the City Hall

The **Grand Parade**, on the west of the Castle, is where the residents of District Six used to come to trade. On Wednesdays and Saturdays it still transforms itself into a **market**, where you can buy a whole array of bargains ranging from used clothes to spicy food. The Grand Parade appeared on TV screens throughout the world on February 11, 1990, when 100,000 people gathered to hear **Nelson Mandela** make his first speech, from the balcony of City Hall, after being released from prison. The **City Hall** is a slightly fussy Edwardian building dressed in Bath stone, which, despite its drab surroundings, looks impressive against Table Mountain.

District Six

South of the Castle, in the shadow of Devil's Peak, is a vacant lot shown on maps as the suburb of Zonnebloem. Before being torn out by apartheid two decades ago, it was **District Six**, an impoverished but lively community of 55,000, predominantly coloured people. Once known as the soul of Cape Town, this inner-city slum harboured a rich cultural life in its narrow alleys and crowded tenements. Along the cobbled streets hawkers rubbed shoulders with prostitutes, gangsters, drunks and gamblers, while craftsmen plied their trade in small workshops. This was a rich place of the South African imagination, inspiring novels, poems, jazz and the blockbuster *District Six: The Musical*, by David Kramer, which played to packed houses in South Africa and spawned a series of hits.

In 1966, apartheid ideologues declared District Six a **White Group Area** and the bulldozers moved in, taking fifteen years to drive its presence from the skyline, leaving only the mosques and churches. But, in the wake of the demolition gangs, international and domestic outcry was so great that the area was never redeveloped apart from a few luxury town houses on its fringes and the hefty Cape Technikon, a college that now occupies nearly a quarter of the former suburb. After years of negotiation, original residents will be allowed to move back under a scheme to develop low-cost housing in the district.

On the northern boundary, at 25a Buitenkant St, is the **District Six Museum** (Mon–Sat 10am–4.30pm; donation). Formerly the Central Methodist Mission Church, it offered solidarity and ministry to the victims of forced removals, right up to the Eighties, and was a venue for anti-apartheid gatherings. Today the church houses a collection of documentary photographs, a huge map of the area before the bulldozing, laid out on the floor, and an almost complete collection of original street signs, retrieved at the time of demolition. It is a deeply moving place, hinting at the sense of collective loss experienced by an entire community. This living installation, intended as much for residents as tourists, invites visitors to jot down comments, memories or reflections (as powerfully evocative as the exhibit itself) on any part of the display. There are few places in Cape Town that speak more eloquently of the effect of apartheid on the day-to-day lives of men and women.

Long Street

Seedy but trendy **Long Street** lies at the heart of a lively central area, and is possibly one of Cape Town's most fascinating thoroughfares. At the edge of the Bo-Kaap, its mosques attract Muslims from across the way, while the nightclubs and bars pull tourists, young locals and the old-timers who never stopped coming.

When it was first settled by Muslims, some three hundred years ago, Long Street marked Cape Town's boundary. By the Sixties, it had become a sleazy alley of drinking holes and whorehouses. Miraculously it's all still here, but with a whiff of gentrification. Georgian-style mosques still coexist with Victorian bottle stores, brothels live above old-fashioned locksmiths, pawnbrokers alongside brokers of porn. There are gun shops next to delicatessens, and wonderful antique dealers rubbing shoulders with coffee shops. Also here are several excellent second-hand bookshops and more **backpackers' lodges** per metre than on any other street in Cape Town.

Towards the harbour end of the street, the **South African Missionary Meeting-House Museum** (Mon–Fri 9am–4pm; free), at no. 40, is a wonderfully calm space with a notable neoclassical pulpit, where slaves were instructed in Christianity during the early nineteenth century. Built in 1802, it was the first missionary church in the country, and an interesting permanent exhibit covers the work of the early missionaries and mission stations throughout the Western Cape. Heading up the hill, away from the church, the **Long Street Baths** (Mon–Fri 7am–8pm, Sat 7am–7pm, Sun 8am–6pm) occupy the top of the road, where it hits Buitensingel (Outer Crescent). A Cape Town institution, established in 1906, the steam rooms are great for relaxing on a winter's day and are open on separate days to women (Mon, Thurs & Sat) and men (Tues, Wed, Fri & Sun morning). A four-hour session (R55) gets you a private cubicle and towel, access to the dry or wet steam rooms, the plunge pool and a short massage. Swimming (R6) is communal.

Cross Buitensingel from the baths and you'll find yourself in **Kloof Street**, the trendier and calmer continuation of Long Street. Lined with some interesting shops and galleries, it carries a cosmopolitan range of restaurants, which offer inside or alfresco seating (see p.121). Kloof Road also provides a quick, direct route up to Kloofnek for the cable car (see p.107) and the saddle that separates Table Mountain from Camps Bay.

Greenmarket Square and around

Turning east from Long Street into Shortmarket Street, you'll skim the edge of **Greenmarket Square**, which is worth at least a little exploration to soak up the distinctly European atmosphere, with cobbled streets, coffee shops and grand buildings. As its name implies, the square started as a vegetable market, though it spent many ignominious years as a car park. Human life has returned and it's now a flea market, selling crafts, jewellery and hippie clobber. This is also one of the few places in Cape Town to buy from Congolese (Zairean) traders, selling masks and malachite carvings. On the western side are the solid limewashed walls and small shuttered windows of the **Old Town House** (Feb–Dec daily 10am–5pm; free; ☎424 6367), entered from Longmarket Street. Built in the mid-1700s, this beautiful example of Cape Dutch architecture, with its fine interior, has seen duty as a guard-house, a police station and Cape Town's city hall, and these days houses the Michaelis collection of minor but interesting Dutch and Flemish landscape paintings. Small visiting exhibitions are also displayed, and good evening classical concerts are a regular event; pick up the town house's quarterly newsletter, which lists forthcoming events. Tickets are available at the door immediately prior to the shows.

Heading east of the square you come to **St George's Mall**, a pedestrianized road that runs southwest from Thibault Square, near the railway station, to Wale Street. Coffee shops, snack bars and lots of street traders and buskers make this a pleasanter route between the station and the Company's Gardens than the parallel Adderley Street, while dancers, drummers, choirs and painters add a certain buzz to the place. **Church Street** (which crosses the mall towards it's southern end) and its surrounding area abound with antique dealers, and on the pedestrianized section at its northeastern end you'll find an informal antique market. Prices are competitive and you may pick up unusual pieces of jewellery, bric-a-brac, Africana and even old sheet music. At the southern end of the mall, at Queen Victoria and Wale streets, **St George's Cathedral** is interesting more for its history than for its Herbert Baker Victorian Gothic design; on September 7, 1986, **Desmond Tutu** hammered on its doors symbolically demanding to be enthroned as South Africa's first black archbishop. Three years later, he heralded the last days of apartheid by leading 30,000 people from the Cathedral to the City Hall, where he coined his now famous slogan for the new order: "We are the rainbow people!" he told the crowd, "We are the new people of South Africa!"

Back in Greenmarket Square, if you head northeast down Shortmarket Street and cross Long Street, you'll come to **Cape Heritage Square**, three blocks up, the largest restoration project ever undertaken in Cape Town. Situated on the fringe of the Bo-Kaap, it's home to the Cape Heritage Hotel as well as a conglomeration of restaurants, wine merchants, art galleries, jewellers and fashion shops, many of which are housed in a complex dating back to 1771. Set around a courtyard, in which the oldest known (and still fruit-bearing) vine in South Africa continues to flourish, the square is worth visiting for a glimpse of the superb resoration work and the particularly noteworthy stone walls.

Government Avenue and the Company's Gardens

A stroll down **Government Avenue**, the southwest extension of Adderley Street, makes for one of the most serene walks in central Cape Town (all roads and paths in the Gardens are pedestrianized). This oak-lined boulevard runs past the rear of Parliament through the Gardens, and its benches are frequently occupied by snoring *bergies* (tramps).

Looming on your right as you enter the north end of the avenue, the **South African Library** (Mon–Fri 9am–6pm, Sat 9am–1pm; free) houses one of the country's best collections of antique historical and natural history books, covering southern Africa. Built with revenue from a tax on wine, it opened in 1822 as one of the first free libraries in the world.

Stretching from here to the South African Museum, the **Company's Gardens** were the initial *raison d'être* for the Dutch settlement at the Cape. Established in 1652 to supply fresh greens to Dutch East India Company trading ships travelling between the Netherlands and the East, the Gardens were initially worked by imported slave labour. This proved too expensive, as the slaves had to be shipped in, fed and housed, so the Company phased out its own farming and granted land to free burghers, from whom it bought fresh produce (see p.687). At the end of the seventeenth century, the gardens were turned over to botanical horticulture for Cape Town's growing colonial elite. Ponds, lawns, landscaping and a crisscross web of oak-shaded walkways were introduced. Today, they are full of local plants, the result of long-standing European interest in Cape botany; botanists have been sailing out since the seventeenth century to classify and name specimens.

The gardens are a pleasant place to meander: Cecil Rhodes certainly thought so – it was during a stroll here that he plotted the invasion of Matabeleland and Mashonaland (both of which which became Rhodesia and subsequently Zimbabwe). Rhodes also introduced an army of small, furry colonizers to the gardens: the North American grey squirrels. There's a statue of Rhodes here, as well as an outdoor café.

Continuing along Government Avenue from the South African Library, past the rear of Parliament, you can peer through an iron gate to see the grand buildings and tended flowerbeds of **De Tuynhuys**, the office (but not residence) of the president. One party of tourists, during Mandela's presidency, stood amazed as the great man, who is renowned for his common touch, strolled across the lawns for a friendly chat.

A little further along, the tree-lined walkway opens out into a formal gravel area with ponds and statues, around which are sited the National Gallery, the Jewish Museum and the Great Synagogue to the east, and the South African Museum and Planetarium to the west.

The South African National Gallery

Not far from the southern end of Government Avenue, where it's joined by the tiny Gallery Lane, the **South African National Gallery** (Tues–Sun 10am–5pm; free; ☎465 1628) represents an essential port of call for anyone interested in the local art scene, and includes a small but excellent permanent collection of contemporary South African art. You'll also find a fine display of traditional works from the southeast of the continent, based around a small collection donated by the German government. The exhibits, which include beadwork, carvings and craft objects, were chosen for their aesthetic qualities and rarity, and represent the gallery's policy of focusing on neglected parts of South Africa's heritage. A room of minor works by various British artists includes Pre-Raphaelites, George Romney, Thomas Gainsborough and Joshua Reynolds. The gallery has a good café serving light lunches, snacks, coffees and cakes, as well as an excellent gallery shop.

The Jewish Museum, the Great Synagogue and Bertram House

Housed in South Africa's first synagogue, which dates from 1863, is the **Jewish Museum**, 84 Hatfield St (Tues & Thurs 1.30–5pm, Sun 10.30am–12.30pm; free), just south of the National Gallery, built in the Egyptian revival style that was fleetingly fashionable at the Cape in 1860s. Displays of photographs and other material cover the history of Jews in South Africa, together with some fine religious artefacts. Today there are around twenty thousand Jews in Cape Town, the majority descended from Europern refugees who fled discrimination and pogroms during the late nineteenth and early twentieth centuries. Since 1795, when the occupying British introduced freedom of worship to the Cape, Jews already living in South Africa have faced no legal impediments. However there were one or two instances of semi-official anti-semitism during the twentieth century, the most notable being in the policy of the Nationalist Party while in opposition during the Forties. Before the World War II, elements in the party came under the influence of Nazi ideology, which was being poured into South Africa by the German foreign and propaganda offices, and began to attribute all the ills facing Afrikanderdom to "British-Jewish capitalism". In 1941 the party adopted a policy of ending Jewish immigration and even repatriation of "undesirable immigrants" (read "Jews") as well as stronger controls over naturalization and the introduction of a "vocational permit" system to protect "the original white population against unfair competition." Ironically, in 1947, on the eve of taking power, the party of apartheid turned its back on anti-semitism and one of its first acts after winning the 1948 election was to recognize the newly created state of Israel, with which it maintained close links till it relinquished power in 1994.

Ask the attendant at the museum to be shown through to the magnificent **Great Synagogue** next door, which was erected in 1903 with twin towers, and displays strong influences from the elaborate baroque churches of Eastern Europe.

Continuing to the southernmost end of Government Avenue, you'll come upon **Bertram House** (Tues–Sat 9.30am–4.30pm; small entrance fee), on the corner of Orange St, whose beautiful face-brick facade looks out at passers by across a fragrant herb garden. Built in the 1840s, the museum is the only surviving Georgian house in Cape Town and displays typical furniture and objects of a well-to-do colonial British family in the early half of the nineteenth century.

The South African Museum and Planetarium

The nation's premier museum of natural history and human sciences, the **South African Museum**, west of Government Avenue and across the square from the National Gallery, at 25 Queen Victoria St (daily 10am–5pm; small entry fee), displays a collection that should command anyone's attention. The **ethnographic galleries** downstairs are stunning and include casts of San hunter-gatherers, now virtually extinct in South Africa, and superb dioramas depicting nineteenth-century San life. There are very good displays on the traditional arts and crafts of several African groups, some exceptional examples of rock art (entire chunks of caves sitting in the display cases), and casts of stone birds found at Great Zimbabwe, across South Africa's border. Upstairs, the **natural history galleries** display mounted mammals, dioramas of prehistoric Karoo reptiles, and Table Mountain flora and fauna. The highlight is the four-storey "whale well", in which a collection of beautiful whale skeletons hang like massive mobiles, accompanied by the eerie strains of their song.

The attached **Planetarium** (shows Mon–Fri 1pm, Sat & Sun noon, 1pm & 2.30pm; Tues 8pm; small entrance fee) is recommended for the chance to see the southern sky. There's also a changing programme of often interesting shows covering topics such as San sky myths. Leaflets at the museum provide a list of forthcoming attractions and you can buy a monthly chart of the current night sky, which is very handy, especially if you're staying in an area without streetlights and can actually see the stars.

Houses of Parliament

South Africa's **Houses of Parliament**, east of Government Avenue, on Parliament Street, are not one building but a complex of interlinking ones, with labyrinthine corridors connecting hundreds of offices, debating chambers and miscellaneous other rooms. Many of these are relics of the 1980s' reformist phase of apartheid when, in the interests of racial segregation, there were three distinct legislative complexes sited here to cater to different "races".

The original wing, completed in 1885, is an imposing Victorian neoclassical building which first served as the legislative assembly of the Cape Colony. After the Boer republics and British colonies amalgamated in 1910, it became the Parliament of the Union of South Africa. This is the old Parliament, where over seven decades of repressive legislation, including apartheid laws, were passed. It's also where **Hendrik Verwoerd**, the arch-theorist of apartheid, met his bloody end, not at the hand of a political activist, but stabbed to death by a parliamentary messenger, who inexplicably went off the rails, committing the act because, as he told police, "a tapeworm ordered me to do it." Due to his mental state the assassin escaped the gallows to outlive apartheid – albeit in an institution. Verwoerd's portrait, depicting him as a man of vision and *gravitas*, used to hang over the main entrance to the dining room. In 1996 it was removed "for cleaning", along with paintings of generations of white parliamentarians.

The new chamber was built in 1983 as part of the **tricameral parliament**, P.W. Botha's attempt to avert majority rule by trying to co-opt Indians and coloureds – but in their own separate debating chambers. The "tricameral" chamber, where the three non-African "races" on occasions met together, is now the **National Assembly**, where you can watch sessions of Parliament. One-hour **tours** take in the old and new debating chambers, the library and museum, and should be booked in advance through the Tours Section (tours Mon–Fri 9am; free; ☎403 2537 or 403 2201), which is also the place to contact for day tickets to watch the **debating sessions** – most interesting of which is question time (Wed 3pm onwards), when you can hear ministers being quizzed by MPs if Parliament is sitting. To join a tour, go to the Plein Street entrance to Parliament, opposite the Receiver of Revenue (it's the more southerly of the two entrances in this street); go through a security check, where you should ask for directions to the Poorthuis entrance. From there you'll see arrows indicating the starting point for tours.

The ANC sits to the right of the speaker, so if you want to see them you should enter the gallery at the rear via the right entrance. The minority parties sit opposite. You're most unlikely to see the President, who is not a member of parliament and rarely attends sittings. When he does, for the opening of Parliament or for visits by foreign leaders, seats are invariably already snapped up.

The Bo-Kaap

Minutes from Parliament, on the slopes of Signal Hill, is the **Bo-Kaap**, one of Cape Town's oldest and most fascinating residential areas. Its streets are a facade of brightly coloured nineteenth-century Dutch and Georgian terraces, which conceal a network of alleyways that are the arteries of its **Muslim community**. The Bo-Kaap harbours its own strong identity, made all the more unique by the destruction of District Six, with which it had much in common. A particular dialect of Afrikaans is spoken here, although it is steadily being eroded by English, which has a higher social status and lacks the associations with apartheid.

Bo-Kaap residents are descended from dissidents and slaves imported here by the Dutch in the sixteenth and seventeenth centuries. They became known collectively as "Cape Malays", a term you'll still hear, even though it's a complete misnomer: fewer than one percent of slaves actually came from Malaysia. Most originated from Africa, India, Madagascar and Sri Lanka.

The easiest way to get to the Bo-Kaap is by foot along Wale Street, which trails up from the south end of Adderley Street and across Buitengragt, to become the main drag of the Bo-Kaap. There's a deceptively quaint feel to the area; apart from Wale Street, this is not really a place to explore alone. A good place to head for is the **Bo-Kaap Museum**, 71 Wale St (Mon–Sat 9.30am–4.30pm; small entry fee), near the Buitengragt end. It consists mainly of the family house and possessions of Abu Bakr Effendi, a nineteenth-century religious leader brought out from Turkey by the British as a mediator between feuding Muslim factions. He became an important member of the community, founded an Arabic school and wrote a book in the local vernacular — now regarded as possibly the first book to be published in what can be recognized as Afrikaans. The museum also has exhibits exploring the local brand of Islam, which has its own unique traditions and nearly two dozen *kramats* (shrines) dotted about the peninsula. One block south of the museum, at Dorp Street, is the **Auwal**, South Africa's first official mosque, founded in 1795 by Tuan Guru, nickname of a Muslim activist. Ten more mosques, whose minarets give spice to the quarter's skyline, now serve its 10,000 residents.

Modern, low-cost developments, looking down from the heights of Signal Hill onto the photogenic Bo-Kaap townscape, have helped alleviate the community's housing shortage, but have added nothing to the architectural charm of the protected historic core bounded by Dorp and Strand streets, and Buitengragt and Pentz streets. A small Muslim shantytown, tucked away next to the old quarry below the cemetery, brings the immediacy of South Africa's housing crisis right to the edge of the city centre.

The only way to get under the skin of the Bo-Kaap is on one of the several **tours** that take in the museum and walk you around the district. The best (and cheapest) of these is the two-and-a-half hour walk, costing R33, run by Bo-Kaap Guided Tours (bookings on ☎22 1554) and operated by residents of the area, whose knowledge goes beyond the standard tour-guide script.

Strand Street

At the corner of Strand and Buitengragt streets, which marks the eastern boundary of the Bo-Kaap, the **Evangelical Lutheran Church Complex**, built in 1785, is worth popping into to see some fine examples of eighteenth-century wood-carving. The magnificent pulpit, supported on two life-size Herculean figures, is one of Anton Anreith's masterpieces. A major figure who breathed life into Cape architecure in the late nineteenth and early twentieth centuries, Anreith was born in Germany, where he came under the influence of the Baroque style of sculpture. Other important works at the Cape include the Kat Balcony at the castle and the pediment on the wine cellar at Groot Constantia. South of the church, sandwiched between two office blocks, is **Koopmans De Wet House**, 35 Strand St (Tues–Sat 9.30am–4.30pm; small entrance fee; ☎424 2473), an eighteenth-century neoclassical town-house, once the home of Marie Koopmans De Wet (1834–1906), a prominent figure on the Cape social and political circuit. Now a museum, it houses an outstanding collection of antique furniture and rare porcelain and produces an excellent guide to accompany the exhibits.

The Lower City Centre

The **Lower City Centre** has for centuries been a marginal area between Cape Town and the sea. The area stretches north of Strand Street to the shore, taking in the still-functional **Duncan Dock** and Cape Town's biggest shopping and entertainment complex at the **Victoria and Alfred Waterfront**. In the mid-nineteenth century, the city's middle classes viewed the quarter and its low-life activities with a mixture of alarm and excitement – a tension that remains today.

Lower Long Street divides the area just inland from the docklands into two. To the east is the Foreshore, an ugly post-World War II wasteland of grey corporate architecture, among which is the **Nico Theatre**, Cape Town's prestige arts complex. To the west, in sharp contrast, is the city's densely packed clubbing and pubbing locality.

Clubland: west of Lower Long Street

As long as the docks have existed, there's been life after dark west of Lower Long Street, particularly along **Waterkant Street**, and at the northern ends of **Bree** and **Loop streets**, where they intersect Waterkant. Frequented by sailors and dockers, Cape Town's red-light district used to be a hard-drinking, drugged-up, apartheid-free zone where some of the city's best jazz was played and raids by the police were a regular part of the scene. These days, with its high density of **nightclubs** and **pubs**, the area has become the best place in Cape Town to club-crawl and one of the few places where you're guaranteed action seven nights a week. See p.125 for club details.

The Foreshore

The Foreshore, an area of reclaimed land north of Strand Street, stretching to the docks, and east of Lower Long Street, is a ham-handed post-World War II development, which was intended to turn Cape Town's harbour into a heavily symbolic gateway to Africa, but instead turned out as a series of large concrete boxes surrounded by acres of windswept tarmac parking lots.

Heerengracht, a truncated two-lane carriageway running from Adderley Street to the harbour, and punctuated at either end by massive roundabouts, each solemnly guarded by statues of Jan van Riebeeck and Bartholomeu Dias, was meant to be the ceremonial axis through this grand scheme, joining the city to the sea, but it never quite makes it to the water, coming to a disappointing standstill at the dock perimeter fence, before bearing east under the dismal shadow of the N1 and N2 flyovers.

The only building worth visiting here, when there's something on, is the **Nico Theatre Complex,** Cape Town's major performance venue, in DF Malan Street just east of Heerengracht. Incorporating the large Main Theatre, it also houses the small Arena Theatre and an opera house. The complex is currently making attempts to throw off the burden of a long association with the apartheid establishment (the name derives from Nico Malan, one-time Nationalist Party administrator). In 1999 – to the dismay of traditional opera, ballet and theatre goers – the complex shed its highbrow image relaunched itself as a community arts centre, and it was announced that the name "Nico" would be dropped.

Duncan Dock

North of the Foreshore, **Duncan Dock,** Cape Town's working harbour is a forbidding industrial landscape of large ships and towering cranes cut off from the city by an enormous perimeter fence. It's a fabulous place to take moody photographs of gigantic hulks against Table Mountain, and has an excellent Taiwanese restaurant, the *Jewel Tavern* (see p.122), but is not the kind of area you'd want to linger alone in.

Work started on the dock in 1938, swallowing the city beachfronts at Woodstock and Paarden Island to cater for the growing supertanker traffic that was outstripping the capacity of the Victoria and Alfred Docks (see below).

The V&A Waterfront

The Victoria and Alfred (V&A) Waterfront (known simply as the Waterfront), adjoining the west of Duncan Dock, is Cape Town's original Victorian harbour that, after two decades of stagnation, began redevelopment at the start of the Nineties as the city's central shopping area, its most fashionable eating and drinking venue, the site of an excellent aquarium and the embarkation point for trips to Robben Island – making it the city's most popular attraction. A cocktail of period buildings, neo-Victorian shopping malls, piers with waterside walkways, and a functioning harbour, as well as the magnificent backdrop of Table Mountain, complement the wide range of restaurants, outdoor cafés, pubs, clubs, cinemas, museums and outdoor entertainment.

The Waterfront has drawn fire, though, for presenting a sanitized, Anglo-Saxon version of its history, with little acknowledgement of the thousands of slaves, press-ganged sailors, impoverished fishermen and prostitutes who made the place work and created its real historical atmosphere. Controversy here is nothing new – arguments raged throughout the first half of the nineteenth century over the need for a proper dock. The Cape was often known as the Cape of Storms because of its vicious weather, which left dozens of wrecks littering Table Bay. Many makeshifts were attempted, including the

---

GETTING TO AND FROM THE WATERFRONT

The Waterfront is one of the easiest points to reach in Cape Town by **public transport.** Waterfront Shuttle Buses (☎082/893 0489) leave from outside the Tourism Gateway in Adderley Street every ten minutes (daily 6.30am–10pm) and from Beach Road in Sea Point every twenty minutes, and terminate at Breakwater Boulevard on the Waterfront. If you want to leave by **cab,** head for the taxi rank on Breakwater Boulevard. Arriving by **car,** you'll find yourself well catered for, with several car parks and garages.

TOURS TO ROBBEN ISLAND

The only **tours** allowed onto Robben Island are ones run by the Department of Arts and Culture (daily every hour 9am–noon & 2–4pm; R100; central booking ☎419 1300, *robbenis@netqactiv.co.za*). **Tickets** on these heavily subscribed tours are sold at the Clock Tower Terminal, which is also the embarkation point, and can be booked ahead and paid for by credit card.

The catamaran takes about half an hour to reach this potent symbol of apartheid, where ex-prisoners and ex-warders work as guides, sharing their experiences. The visit takes in Section B of the prison, where you'll see **Mandela's cell** as well as the horrifically crowded **dormitory cells**, which accommodated sixty to seventy prisoners in cramped and sometimes freezing conditions. A bus ride around the island takes in the **leper graveyard**, the **leper church** designed by Sir Herbert Baker, and the **lime quarry**, where Mandela and the other prisoners worked hacking away at the stark, white mineral, ruining their eyes from the relentless glare. Perhaps one of the saddest and most poignant sites is **Robert Sobukwe's house**. Leader of the Pan Africanist Congress (see p.694), Sobukwe was kept here in solitary confinement and not allowed to speak to anyone, even his warder. He was considered such a dangerous political figure that after his sentence expired the apartheid government drummed up the General Amendment Act, specifically to prolong his detention indefinitely.

construction of a lighthouse in 1823, and the start on a jetty at the bottom of Bree Street in 1832. The clamour for a harbour grew with the expansion of sea traffic arriving at the Cape in the 1850s, and reached its peak in 1860, when the Lloyds marine insurance company refused the risk of covering ships dropping anchor in Table Bay.

The British colonial government eventually agreed that a harbour was needed and, on a suitably stormy September day in 1860, at a huge ceremony, the teenage Prince Alfred tipped the first batch of stones into Table Bay to begin the **Breakwater**, the westernmost arm of the harbour, which was subsequently completed with convict labour. In 1869 the dock, consisting of two main basins, was completed and the sea was allowed in.

The **Victoria Basin**, and the smaller **Alfred Basin** to its west, now joined by the even more westerly **New Basin**, create the Waterfront's geography of piers and quays, with most of the activity concentrated around the north side. The **Waterfront Visitors' Centre**, set back from the northwest of the Victoria Basin on Dock Road (☎418 2369, fax 25 2165, *info@waterfront.co.za*), can provide maps, bookings for tours and taxis, and an excellent booklet that guides you round 32 social history display boards dotted about the harbour. If you're simply sauntering, you'll get by without a map, as the Waterfront is replete with visitor-friendly signposts, and the constant presence of Table Mountain makes orientation simple.

Northeast of the visitors' centre, the action centres around **Market Square** and the **Agfa Amphitheatre**, where you can often catch free rock or jazz performances and sometimes hear the Cape Town Symphony Orchestra (details from the Visitors' Centre). Head west from Market Square (away from the water) and you'll find yourself on Dock Road; walk north along here for about 100m and you'll come to the **Imax Cinema** (information ☎419 7365; booking through Computicket, ☎918 8970; tickets at the door), Cape Town's representative of the worldwide family of outsized screens, at the BMW Pavilion on the corner of Portswood Road. It shows visual spectacles such as *Mission to Mir* and wonderful nature documentaries that in the past have covered African elephants, the ocean, the Grand Canyon and the Amazon.

Tours to Robben Island and other trips

A couple of minutes east of the Agfa Amphitheatre brings you to the dockside, and to Quays 4 and 5. **Boat trips** and **cruises** for trips other than to Robben Island, such

ROBBEN ISLAND

Nelson Mandela may have been the most famous Robben Island prisoner, but he certainly wasn't the first. Established in the seventeeth century as a place of banishment for those who offended the political order – first of the **Dutch**, later the **British** and most recently the **Afrikaner Nationalists**. The island's first prisoner was the Strandloper leader **Autshumato**, who learnt English in the early seventeenth century and became an emissary of the British. After the Dutch settlement was established, he was jailed on the island in 1658 by Jan van Riebeeck. The rest of the seventeenth century saw a succession of East Indies political prisoners and Muslim holy men exiled here for opposing Dutch colonial rule (the latter going on to establish Islam at the Cape once they were freed).

During the nineteenth century, the **British** used Robben Island as a dumping ground for deserters, criminals and political prisoners, in much the same way as they used Australia. Captured **Xhosa leaders** who defied the Empire during the Frontier Wars of the early to mid-nineteenth century were transported by sea from the Eastern to the Western Cape to be imprisoned, and many ended up on Robben Island. In 1846, the island's brief was extended to include a whole range of the **socially marginalized**, and criminals and political detainees were joined by vagrants, prostitutes, lunatics and the chronically ill. All were victim to a regime of brutality and maltreatment, even in hospital. In the 1890s, a leper colony existed alongside the social outcasts. Lunatics were removed in 1921 and the lepers in 1930. During World War II the **Defence Force** took over the island to set up defensive guns against a feared Axis invasion, which never came.

Robben Island's greatest era of notoriety began in 1961, when it was taken over by the **Prisons Department**. Prisoners arriving at the island prison were greeted by a slogan on the gate that read: "Welcome to Robben Island: We Serve with Pride." By 1963, when Nelson Mandela arrived, it had become a maximum security prison, and all the warders – and none of the prisoners – were white; prisoners were only allowed to send and receive one letter every six months; and common-law and political prisoners were housed together, until 1971 when they were separated in an attempt to further isolate the politicals. Harsh conditions, including routine beatings and forced hard labour, were exacerbated by geography; there's nothing but sea between the island and the South Pole, so icy winds routinely blow in from across the Atlantic – and inmates were made to wear shorts and flimsy jerseys. Like every other prisoner, Mandela slept on a thin mat on the floor (until 1973, when he was given a bed because he was ill) and was kept in a solitary confinement cell measuring two metres square for sixteen hours a day.

Amazingly, the prisoners found ways of **protesting**, through hunger strikes, publicizing conditions when possible (by visits from International Commitee of the Red Cross, for example) and, remarkably, by taking legal action against the prison authority to stop arbitrary punishments. They won improved conditions over the years and the island also became a university behind bars, where people of different political views and generations met; it was not unknown for prisoners to give academic help to their warders. The last political prisoners were released from Robben Island in 1991 and the remaining common-law prisoners were transferred to the mainland in 1996. On January 1, 1997, control of Robben Island was transferred from the Department of Correctional Services to the Department of the Arts, Culture, Science and Technology, which has now established it as a museum. In 1999, the site was expected to become a UN World Heritage Site.

as cruises around the bay, are available here from outdoor vendors, as well as the office in the Old Port Captain's Building on the adjacent Pierhead, or from more vendors on North Quay, near the Victoria and Alfred Hotel. The dowdy brick building at the end of Quay 5 was once the Department of Correctional Services' embarkation point for prisoners exiled to Robben Island; for tours of Robben Island see box opposite.

From the Pierhead jetty you can catch the **penny ferry** rowing boat, or the motorized **water taxi service**, both of which will take you all over the Waterfront. Look out for Cape Fur seals lying atop the buffer tyres, which hang from the harbour wall.

Two Oceans Aquarium

Bear west from the Pierhead along the adjacent North Quay, past the swanky Victoria and Alfred Hotel and towards the northwest corner of New Basin, and you'll reach what is without question the highlight of the Waterfront – **Two Oceans Aquarium** (daily 9.30am–6pm; R30). Dedicated to exhibiting the unique ecosystem of Africa's southern coast, this museum is great fun and alone justifies a visit to the Waterfront. Downstairs in the auditorium, scheduled videos cover South Africa's marine life and related topics (such as underwater photography); on the same floor, you'll find tanks containing a jaw-dropping array of bizarre sea creatures. You can even have a feel of them – if you are inclined – in the shallow "touch pool". Upstairs, the ambitious River Ecosystem, Kelp Forest and Open Ocean exhibits display complex interactions in a living and changing environment. The first of these has penguins flapping about rocks, and diving and swimming underwater, while sea birds fly about the rafters.

The southern suburbs

The bulk of Cape Town's residential sprawl extends east into South Africa's interior away from Table Mountain and the city centre. It's here that the **southern suburbs**, the formerly whites-only residential areas, cut a swath from town, down the east side of Table Mountain, ending just before Muizenberg on the False Bay coast. All the main suburban attractions are concentrated in this area and, not surprisingly, the best shopping areas and cinemas.

From anywhere in the southern suburbs you can see Table Mountain rising above Cape Town. The area offers some quick escapes from the city heat into forests, gardens and vineyards, all hugging the eastern slopes of the mountain, and its extension, the Constantiaberg. The suburbs themselves are pleasant enough places to stay, eat and shop, but sights are thin on the ground.

Woodstock, Salt River and Observatory

First and oldest of the suburbs as you take an easterly exit from town is **Woodstock**, unleafy and windblown, but redeemed by some nice Victorian buildings, originally occupied by working-class coloureds, and now yuppifying.

To its east, **Salt River** is a harsh, industrial, mainly coloured area, built initially for workers and artisans, while **Observatory**, abutting its southern end, is generally regarded as Cape Town's bohemian hub, a reputation fuelled by its proximity to the University of Cape Town in Rondebosch and its large student population. Many of the houses here are student digs, but the narrow Victorian streets are also home to young professionals, hippies and arty types. The refreshingly unrestored, peeling arcades on Observatory's Lower Main Road, and the streets off it, have some nice cafés and lively bars, as well as a wholefood shop, an African fabrics shop, one of Cape Town's few African restaurants, the *Africa Café* (see p.123), and a couple of antiques emporiums. The huge Groote Schuur Hospital, which overlooks the freeway that sweeps through Observatory, was the site of the world's first heart transplant in 1967.

Mowbray and Rosebank

Heading along Station Road, away from the mountain and south of Observatory, is **Mowbray**, originally called Drie Koppen (Three Heads), after the heads of three slaves impaled there in 1724, but its name was sanitized in the 1840s. In the nineteenth century, this was the home of philologist Willem Bleek, who lived with a group of Khoisan convicts given up by the colonial authorities so that he could study their languages and world-view. Bleek's pioneering work still forms the basis of much of what we know about traditional Khoisan life.

Rosebank, to Mowbray's south, has a substantial student community, some staying in the so-called Tampax Towers, the unmistakable circular residential blocks on Main Road. Just beyond them is the brown-bricked **Baxter Theatre**, one of Cape Town's premier arts complexes (see "Theatre, performance and cinema" on p.128).

Irma Stern Museum

Irma Stern is acknowledged as one of South Africa's pioneering artists of the twentieth century, more for the fact that she brought modern European ideas to the colonies than for any huge contribution she made to world art. The **UCT Irma Stern Museum**, Cecil Rd, Rosebank (Tues–Sat 10am–5pm; small entry fee), was the artist's home for 38 years until her death in 1966. The museum is definitely worth visiting to see Stern's collection of Iberian, African, Oriental and ancient artefacts. The whole house, in fact, reflects the artist's fascination with exoticism, starting with her own Gauguinesque paintings of "native types", the fantastic carved doors she brought back from Zanzibar, and the very untypical garden that brings a touch of the tropics to Cape Town with its exuberant bamboo thickets and palm trees.

Born in a backwater town in South Africa in 1894 to German Jewish parents, Stern studied at Germany's Weimar Academy, against whose conservatism she reacted. She adopted **expressionist distortion** in her paintings, some of which were included in the Neue Sezession Exhibition in Berlin in 1918. Although her work was appreciated in Europe when she returned to South Africa after World War II, critics claimed that her style was simply a cover for technical incompetence. Stern went on several expeditions into Africa in the Forties and Fifities, where she found the source for her intensely sensuous work that shocked contemporary South Africa, but has led historians to regard her as the towering figure of her generation.

Rondebosch and the Rhodes Memorial

South of Rosebank, neighbouring **Rondebosch** is home to the **University of Cape Town** (UCT), handsomely festooned with nineteenth-century creepers and sitting grandly on the mountainside, overlooking Main Road and the M3 highway. Next to the campus north towards the city is the **Rhodes Memorial**, built to resemble a Greek temple, and grandiosely conspicuous against the slopes of Devil's Peak. The monument celebrates Cecil Rhodes' energy with a sculpture of a horse rearing up wildly, and the empire-builder's bust is planted at the top of a towering set of stairs. His large estate, **Groote Schuur**, bordering on Main Road, became the official prime ministerial residence of the Cape, though Nelson Mandela prefered to stay at Genadendal, nearby (his private home is in Houghton, Johannesburg). Even more eye-catching are the herds of wildebeest and zebra, nonchalantly grazing on the slopes around the Memorial, as cars fly past on the M3, and the **Tea Garden**, with terrific views of Cape Town. From here you can walk to the King's Blockhouse, formerly a signalling station to Muizenberg, and onto the contour path which follows the eastern side of the mountain, way above the southern suburbs to Constantia Nek (see "Table Mountain walks", p.107). Below the Memorial, alongside the M3, is the incongruous **Mostert's Mill**, a real mill built two centuries ago, when there were wheat fields here instead of highways.

South of Rondebosch

Continuing **south from Rondebosch** along the Van der Stel Freeway or along the more congested Main Road, you pass some of Cape Town's most prestigious suburbs.

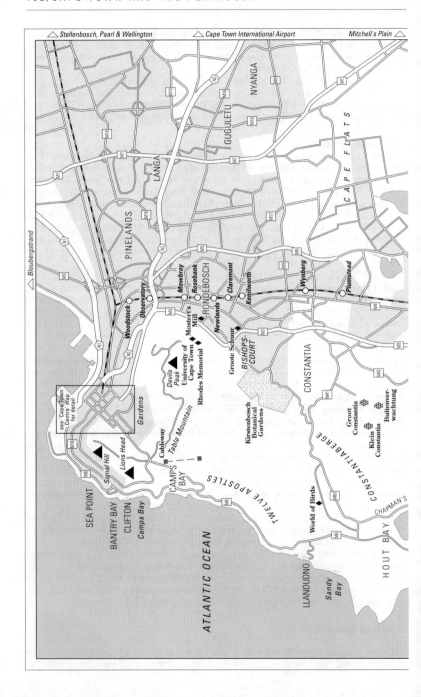

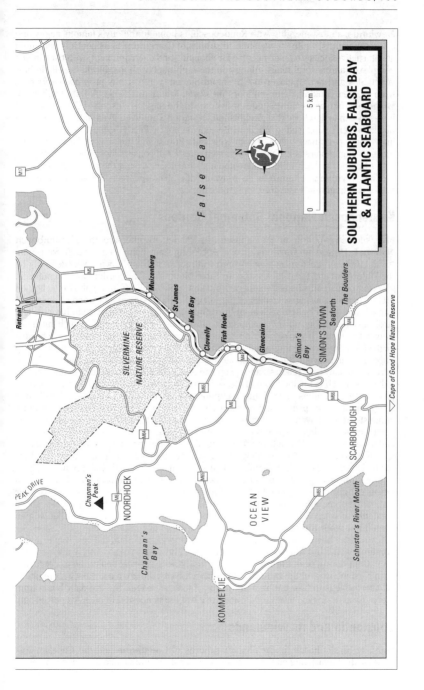

SOUTHERN SUBURBS, FALSE BAY
& ATLANTIC SEABOARD

Newlands, almost merging with Rondebosch, is home to the city's famous rugby and cricket stadiums, while the well-heeled suburb of **Claremont** to its south is becoming an alternative focus to the city centre for shopping and entertainment, with two cinema complexes and several malls. Alongside the high quality shops, hawkers sell clothes, vegetables and herbs; closer to Claremont Station, you can buy tasty *boerewors* rolls from women cooking them outdoors on *skottel braais* (braziers). A little further on, **Bishopscourt**, as its name suggests, is home to the Anglican bishop of Cape Town and it was in a mansion here that Archbishop Desmond Tutu lived even in the years when blacks weren't supposed to live in whites-only suburbs. Partly because of its prime siting – some plots have views of both Newlands Forest and the sea – this is one of the most prestigious areas in Cape Town and a number of consuls live here on huge properties behind the high walls that are about all you'll see passing the area. Further down the line, **Wynberg** is known for its Maynardville Shakespearean open-air theatre (see p.128) and quaint little row of shops and eateries.

Kirstenbosch National Botanical Gardens

Five kilometres south of Rondebosch, in Rhodes Avenue, are the **Kirstenbosch National Botanical Gardens** (daily: April–Aug 8am–6pm; Sept–March 8am–7pm; ☎762 1166), the third most-popular tourist attraction in Cape Town (exceeded only by the Waterfront and the cable-car trip up Table Mountain). The gardens are magnificent, glorying in lush shrubs and exuberant blooms, which trail off into fynbos (see box on p.117), covering a huge expanse of the rugged eastern slopes and wooded ravines of Table Mountain. The setting is quite breathtaking – this is a great place to have tea and stroll around gazing up the mountain, or to wander onto the paths, which meander steeply to the top. If you're here in summer, one of the undoubted delights is to bring a picnic for a Sunday evening **open-air concert**, where you can lie back on the lawn, sip Cape wine and savour the mountain air and sunset light. There's a middling tea house here, open daily for breakfast, and lunch and teas, plus a restaurant and a coffee bar.

Kirstenbosch is the oldest and largest botanical garden in South Africa, and was created by Cecil Rhodes in 1895 (his camphor and fig trees are still here). Today, over 22,000 indigenous plants, and a research unit and library, attract researchers and botanists from all over. There's a nursery selling local plants, while characteristic Cape plants, found nowhere else in the world, are cultivated on the slopes. Little signboards and paved paths guide you through the highlights of the gardens, with trees and plants identified to enhance the rambling. The most interesting route is the one created for blind visitors, with labels in Braille and an abundance of aromatic and textured plants.

The cultivated gardens blend seamlessly into the mountainside, as there are no fences cutting off the way to the top of Table Mountain. From here, you can make your way up the mountain: two popular paths, starting from the Contour Path above Kirstenbosch, are Nursery Ravine and Skeleton Gorge (see p.108). Note that women should **not walk alone** in the isolated upper reaches of Kirstenbosch.

If you don't have a car and don't want to take an organized tour, the best way to **get to Kirstenbosch** is by rikki (☎423 4888 or 423 4892). These will take and fetch you at any time apart from during peak traffic times. Otherwise, it requires real dedication to get to and from Kirstenbosch on the two daily buses from the city, though a marginally more practical alternative is to take the train to Mowbray and then one of the five daily buses from there. If you're driving, take the M5, and leave it at the signposted Rhodes Avenue turnoff.

Constantia and its winelands

South of Kirstenbosch lie the elegant suburbs of **Constantia** and the Cape's oldest **winelands**. Luxuriating on the lower slopes of Table Mountain and the Constantiaberg, with tantalizing views of False Bay, the winelands are an easy drive from town, not more than ten minutes off the Van der Stel Freeway (the M3), which runs between the centre and Muizenberg.

The winelands started cultivated life in 1685 as the farm of **Simon van der Stel**, the governor charged with opening up the fledgling Dutch colony to the interior. Thrusting himself wholeheartedly into the task, he selected for his own use an enormous tract of the choicest land set against the Constantiaberg, the section of the peninsula just south of Table Mountain. He named the estate after his daughter Constancia, and this is now (with a minor change of spelling) the name of Cape Town's oldest and most prestigious residential area. Exuding the easy ambience of landed wealth, Constantia is a green and pleasant place, shaded by oak forests and punctuated with farm stalls, riding schools, designer Cape Dutch-style shopping centres and, of course, the vineyards.

Constantia grapes have been making wine since van der Stel's first ouput in 1705. After his death in 1712, the estate was divided up and sold off as the modern **Groot Constantia**, **Klein Constantia** and **Buitenverwachting**. In 1990, the nearby Steenberg Estate was bought up by a large Johannesburg mining conglomerate and is worth keeping an eye on for its future output. All **four estates** are open to the public and offer tastings; definitely worth devoting a few hours to if you aren't heading further afield to the Winelands proper.

There is no public **transport** to Constantia, but Groot Constantia features on most organized tours of Cape Town or the peninsula. To get to the estates **by car**, take the signposted Groot Constantia exit from the M3 onto Ladies Mile Extension, and keep following the signs to Groot Constantia. Buitenverwachting and Klein Constantia are on Klein Constantia Road, just off Ladies Mile Extension, and are clearly signposted.

Groot Constantia

The largest estate and the one most geared to tourists is **Groot Constantia**, Cape Town's fourth most-visited attraction. Its big pull is that it retains the rump of van der Stel's original estate, as well as the original buildings. Otherwise, there's a pretty average **museum** full of period furniture (daily 10am–5pm; small entry fee), a gift shop, art gallery and two **restaurants**. **Cellar tours** start every hour on the hour (10am–4pm; R6) and there's **wine tasting** between 10am and 4.30pm (R6).

Despite the commercialism, Groot Constantia is impressive, though its portrayal of life in a seventeenth-century colonial chateau makes scant reference to the slave labour that underpinned its operations. The **manor house**, a quintessential Cape Dutch building, was van der Stel's original home, modified at the end of the eighteenth century by the French architect Thibault. Walking straight through it, down the ceremonial axis, you'll come to the cellar, fronted with a carved pediment, depicting a riotous bacchanalia, which represents fertility.

Klein Constantia and Buitenverwachting

Smaller in scale than Groot Constantia, Klein Constantia and Buitenverwachting both offer free wine tasting in less regimented conditions than at the bigger estate, and although the buildings are far humbler the settings are equally beautiful. **Klein Constantia**, Klein Constantia Rd (free wine tasting & sales Mon–Fri 9am–5pm, Sat 9am–1pm; ☎794 5188) has a friendly atmosphere and produces some fine wines. Something of a curiosity is its **Vin de Constance**, the re-creation of an eighteenth-century Constantia wine that was a favourite of Napoleon, Frederick the Great and Bismarck. It's a delicious dessert wine, packaged in a replica of the original bottle, and makes an original souvenir. As well as wine, there's wildlife here: look out for the guinea fowls that roam the estate munching on the beetles that attack young vine leaves; in summer, migrant steppe buzzards prey on unsuspecting starlings, which eat the grapes.

Buitenverwachting, also on Klein Constantia Road (free wine tasting & sales Mon–Fri 9am–5pm, Sat 9am–1pm; ☎794 5190) provides its workers with some of the best living conditions of any South African farm. Unusual labour practices include the provision of two social workers, weekly visits by a doctor to the farm clinic, and worker involvement in the selection of new staff. Buitenverwachting's expensive **restaurant**, *Constantia Uitsig Restaurant* (Tues–Fri noon–3pm & 7pm–midnight), is regularly voted one of South Africa's ten best. For a day out on the farm (they have cattle and horses, too), Buitenverwachting provides **picnic lunches** (Mon–Sat noon–2.30pm), which must be prebooked (☎794 1012 or 794 2122).

Table Mountain

The icon that for hundreds of years and from hundreds of kilometres announced Cape Town to seafarers, **Table Mountain**, a 1087m flat-topped massif with dramatic cliffs and eroded gorges, dominates the northern end of the peninsula. Its north face overlooks the city centre with the distinct formations of **Lion's Head** and **Signal Hill** to the west and **Devil's Peak** to the east. The west face is made up of a series of gabled formations known as the **Twelve Apostles**. The southwest towers over Hout Bay and the east over the southern suburbs.

The mountain is a compelling feature in the middle of the city. It's a wilderness where you'll find wildlife and a substantial 1400 species of **flora**. Indigenous mammals include baboons, dassies (hyraxes) and porcupines, while the animals that resemble

---

TABLE MOUNTAIN SAFETY

MAKE SURE YOU . . .
- Don't climb alone.
- Inform someone you're going up the mountain.
- Tell them your route, when you're leaving and when you expect to be back.
- Leave early enough to give yourself time to complete your route during daylight.
- Don't try to descend via an unknown route. If you get lost in poor weather, seek shelter, keep warm and wait for help.
- Never leave even the tiniest scrap of litter on the mountain.
- Never make fires. No cooking (even on portable stoves) is allowed.

WEAR . . .
- Good footwear. Boots or running shoes are recommended.
- A broad-rimmed hat.

TAKE . . .
- A backpack.
- A water bottle. Allow two litres per person.
- Enough food: sandwiches, glucose sweets, nuts, raisins, juice.
- A warm jersey.
- A windbreaker.
- A raincoat.
- Sunglasses.
- High-factor sunscreen.
- Money for the cable car.
- Plasters for blisters.
- A map (available from Cape Union Mart at the Waterfront, or Cavendish Square Shopping Cente in Claremont).

mountain goats are Himalayan tahrs, descended from specimens introduced by Cecil Rhodes onto his estate, and which escaped to flourish on the mountain.

Reckoned the most-climbed massif in the world, Table Mountain has suffered under the constant pounding of **hikers** and wanton vandalism, though the damage isn't always obvious – certainly not from the dizzying vista at the top. The harm done isn't all one way, either; every year the mountain strikes back, taking its toll of lives. One of the commonest causes of difficulties is people losing the track (often due to sudden mist falling) and ending up trapped. If you plan on tackling one of the hundreds of walks and climbs on its slopes, go properly prepared (see box opposite); you might also like to consider the services of a guide (see "Participation sports" on p.129).

The cable car

The least challenging, but certainly not least interesting, way up the mountain, is via the **cable car**, which offers dizzying views across Table Bay and the Atlantic. The journey is a Cape Town must: don't go home without doing it.

To cope with half a million visitors jostling to ride the cable car to the top of the mountain (at the front of the western table), a state-of-the-art Swiss system was installed in 1997. The floor of the fishbowl-shaped car is designed to complete a 360-degree rotation on its way to the top, giving passengers a full panorama. Departures leave every 10–20 minutes from the lower cableway station (daily: May–Oct 8.30am–6pm; Nov 7.30am–9pm; Dec–April 7.30am–10pm; ☎424 5148 or 424 8181) on Tafelberg Road; note that you'll probably be queuing for anywhere between twenty minutes and an hour, especially in high season (Dec & Jan). **To get there** by public transport you have to take the Kloofnek bus from the Adderley Street terminus to Kloofnek and walk the rest of the way – a fair slog. There's a very irregular shuttle from Kloofnek to the lower cable station, so it's best to take one of the minibus taxis that ply the route from Adderley Street to the lower cable station (around R10 each way); alternatively take a rikki taxi.

Climbs and walks

Climbing the mountain will give you a greater sense of achievement than being ferried up by the cable car, but proceed with extreme caution: it may look sunny and clear when you leave, but at the top you could find a very different story. The weather is subject to rapid changes, both in general and in small localized areas. The main hazards are sun, mist and violent winds. Unless you're going with a knowledgeable guide, attempt only the simplest routes (the ones outlined here).

Signal Hill and Lion's Head

From the roundabout at the top of Kloofnek a road leads all the way along **Signal Hill** to a car park and lookout with good views over Table Bay, the docks and the city. A cannon was formerly used for sending signals to ships at anchor in the bay, and the Noon Gun, still fired from its slopes daily, sends a thunderous rumble through the Bo-Kaap below. Halfway along the road is a sacred Islamic *kramat* (shrine), one of several dotted around the Peninsula which "protect" the city. You can also walk up **Lion's Head**, an unstrenuous and popular hike that seems to bring out half of Cape Town every full moon.

Platteklip Gorge and Maclear's Beacon

The first recorded ascent to the summit of Table Mountain was by the Portuguese captain Antonio de Saldanha, in 1503. He wisely chose **Platteklip Gorge**, the gap visible from the front table (the north side) which, as it turned out, is the most accessible way up. A short and easy extension will get you to Maclear's Beacon which, at 1086m, is the highest point on the mountain. The Platteklip route has the added advantage of depositing you up at the Upper Cable Station, so you can hop on a car to get back down.

The route starts out at the **Lower Cable Station**. From here, walk east along Tafelberg Road until you see a high embankment built from stone and maintained with wire netting. Just beyond and to the left of a small dam is a sign pointing to Platteklip Gorge. A steep fifteen-minute climb brings you onto the **upper contour path**. About 25m east along this, take the path indicated by a sign reading "Contour Path/Platteklip Gorge". The path zigzags from here onwards and is very clear. The gorge is the biggest cleavage on whole mountain, leading directly and safely to the top, but it's a very steep slog which will take **two to three hours** in total if you're reasonably fit. Once on top, turn right and ascend the last short section onto the **front table**, for a breathtaking view of the city. A sign points the way to the **Upper Cable Station** – a fifteen-minute walk along a concrete path thronging with visitors.

Maclear's Beacon is about 35 minutes from the top of the Platteklip Gorge on a path leading eastward; a waymarked path of white squares on little yellow footsteps guides you all the way. The path crosses the front table with Maclear's Beacon visible at all times. From the top you'll get views of False Bay and the Hottentots Holland Mountains to the east.

The Pipe Track

One of the most rewarding and easiest walks along the mountainside takes the **Pipe Track**, a service road which follows water pipes from the mountain reservoirs to Kloofnek. The track runs on the level for roughly 7km, on the west flank of Table Mountain, beneath the Twelve Apostles, following the mountain's contours and offering fantastic views of the Atlantic. The Pipe Track isn't a circular route, so you can turn back at any point. The whole walk can take up to three hours each way.

The route begins at some stone steps at Kloofnek opposite the bus terminus for the cable car, just to the west of Tafelberg Road turn-off (if you're driving, park on Tafelberg Road). Steps lead up alongside forestry staff houses before the road levels off under some pines. The path intersects several climbs up the mountain, useful indicators as to how far you've come. The first, after about 45 minutes, is indicated by a sign to Blinkwater Ravine (closed to the public due to rockfalls). A further ten to fifteen minutes brings you to the Kasteelspoort ascent (signposted under gum trees) followed by Woody Ravine and the last, roughly 25 minutes after Kasteelspoort, at Slangolie Ravine, where the path ends. The rock bed on Slangolie is steep, unstable and to be avoided. Turn back when you see the first of the Woodhead Tunnel danger signs.

Skeleton Gorge and Nursery Ravine

You can combine a visit to the gardens at Kirstenbosch with an ascent up Table Mountain via one route and a descent down another, ending at the Kirstenbosch National Botanical Gardens' **restaurant** for tea. Starting at the restaurant, follow the **Skeleton Gorge** signs, which lead you onto the **Contour Path**. At the Contour Path, a plaque indicates that this is **Smuts' Track**, the route favoured by Jan Smuts, the Boer leader, statesman, philosopher, friend to the British, and South African prime minister. The plaque marks the start of a broad-stepped climb up Skeleton Gorge, involving wooden steps, stone steps, wooden ladders and loose boulders. Be prepared for steep ravines and difficult rock climbs and under no circumstances stray off the path. It requires reasonable fitness, but can take as little as an hour. Skeleton can be an unpleasant way down, especially in the wet season when it gets slippery.

Nursery Ravine is recommended for the descent. At the top of Skeleton Gorge, walk a few metres to your right to a sign indicating **Kasteelspoort**. It's just 35 minutes from the top of Skeleton along this path to the head of Nursery Ravine. The descent returns you to the 310-metre Contour Path, which leads back to Kirstenbosch. This entire walk lasts about five hours.

The Atlantic seaboard

Table Mountain's steep drop into the ocean along much of the western peninsula forces the suburbs along the **Atlantic seaboard** into a ribbon of developments clinging dramatically to the slopes. The sea washing the west side of the peninsula can be very chilly; far colder than on the False Bay seaboard. Although not ideal for bathing, the Atlantic makes up for this with mind-blowing views from some of the most incredible coastal roads in the world, particularly beyond **Sea Point**. The coast itself consists of a series of bays and white-sanded beaches edged with smoothly sculpted bleached rocks; inland, the Twelve Apostles, a series of rocky buttresses, gaze down onto the surf. The beaches are ideal for sunbathing, or sunset picnics – it's from this side of the Peninsula that you can watch the sun sink into the ocean, creating fiery reflections on the sea and mountains behind as it slips away.

Green Point and Sea Point

Inland from the Waterfront and stretching for about a kilometre to the west, **Green Point** is one of the suburbs closest to the city centre, with a growing supply of budget accommodation, but little else to recommend it. Green Point's Main Road is notorious as a major hangout for prostitutes and their pimps, who are conveniently close here to their gangland turf in the Bo-Kaap.

Continuing southwest along Main Road, Green Point merges with the more fashionable **Sea Point**, one of the long-established haunts of Cape Town's gourmands. Middle-class couples, pram-pushing mothers, street kids and drunks living together create a blend of respectability and seediness that dissipates as you move into the wealthier suburbs down the Atlantic seaboard.

Sea Point is Cape Town's most densely populated former white suburb, with high-rise hotels and apartments interspersed with Victorian bungalows, and is one of the best places to find accommodation. The closest seaside to the city centre is a block down from Main Road, although it's too rocky for swimming. Halfway along the kilometre-long beach promenade, running alongside Beach Road, you'll catch views of **Graaff's Pool**, an institutionalized male nudist spot, while at the westernmost end is the only place in the vicinity to swim, at the spanking-new Olympic-sized **saltwater pool**, alongside the crashing surf (see "Participation sports on p.129 for details).

Clifton to Sandy Bay

Suburbia proper begins south of Sea Point at Bantry Bay. Fashionable **Clifton**, on the next cove, is sheltered by Lion's Head. The sea here is good for surfing and safe for swimming, but bone-chillingly cold. Sitting on the most expensive real estate in Africa, Clifton is studded with fabulous seaside apartments and four wonderful sandy **beaches**, reached via steep stairways. First Beach (they're all numbered) is colonized by pneumatic male ball-players, surfers and their female counterparts, so avoid it unless your tan is up to scratch. Second and Third beaches are split between the teenies and thirtysomethings; if in doubt, head for Fourth, which has become the family beach because it has the fewest steps. Hout Bay **buses** go to Clifton from the city centre twelve times a day (a 30min journey).

A little to the south, **Camps Bay** suburb climbs the slopes of Table Mountain and is scooped into a small amphitheatre, bounded by the Lion's Head and the Twelve Apostles sections of the Table Mountain range. This, and the airborne views across the

Atlantic, make Camps Bay one of the most desirable places to live in Cape Town. The main drag, Victoria Road, skirts the coast and is packed with trendy restaurants, while the wide sandy beach is accessible by bus and is consequently enjoyed by families of all shapes and colours. Lined by a row of palms and some grassy verges with welcome shade for picnics, Camps Bay beach positively throngs around the Christmas and Easter breaks. However, it's exposed to the southeaster, and there's the usual Atlantic chill and an occasional dangerous backwash.

There's little development between Camps Bay and **Llandudno**, a wonderful cove, 20km from Cape Town along Victoria Road (not served by public transport). A steep and narrow road winds down past smart homes to the shore, where the sandy beach is punctuated at either end by magnificent granite boulders and rock formations. This is a good sunbathing spot and a choice one for bring-your-own sundowners. The small car park frequently spills over into the suburban streets at peak periods.

Isolated **Sandy Bay**, Cape Town's main nudist beach, can only be reached via a twenty-minute walk from Llandudno. In the apartheid days, the South African police went to ingenious lengths to trap nudists, but nowadays the beach is relaxed, so feel free to come as undressed as feels comfortable. Among the dunes and fynbos (see box on p.117) there are no houses – in fact, no facilities whatsoever – so bring whatever supplies you may need. To get there, take the path from the south end of the Llandudno car park, through fynbos vegetation and across some rocks, to the beach. It's a fairly easy walk, but if you're barefoot watch out for broken glass.

Hout Bay

Although no longer the quaint fishing village it once was, **Hout Bay** still has a functioning fishing harbour and is the centre of the local crayfish industry. Leopards no longer stalk its *kranse* and *koppies*, but their former presence is recalled by a bronze statue looking down from Chapman's Peak Drive. Despite ugly modern development and a growing shantytown, the natural setting is quite awesome. Next to the harbour and car park, the little **Mariner's Wharf** waterfront development shelters the Seafood Emporium selling fresh fish and there's a decent restaurant upstairs. This is a good place to pick up fresh *snoek*, a Western Cape speciality, both at the restaurant and from the Emporium.

The sea off the long slender **beach** is no good for swimming – too cold, too close to the harbour and too prone to fish scales floating in its surf – but the beach is perfect for walking. Away from the harbour, the village is just managing to hang onto its historic ambience, with the **Hout Bay Museum**, 4 St Andrews Rd (Tues–Sat 10am–12.30pm & 2–4.30pm; ☎790 3270), offering good exhibits on Strandloper culture and the local fishing industry. Nearby **World of Birds**, Valley Rd (daily 9am–5pm; R22), is one of the world's largest bird parks, with large walk-through aviaries. It's a great chance to see unusual species like African blue cranes and Australian cassowaries, and there's also a wildlife sanctuary here, as well as a children's "touch" farmyard. Alternatively, go down to the estuary near the harbour to see local birds in their natural environment for free; kingfishers and blacksmith plovers are among commonly sighted residents.

Hout Bay is at a convenient junction for the rest of the peninsula and has the highest concentration of places to stay south of Sea Point, including the upmarket, country-style *Hout Bay Manor*. From Cape Town it's 20km along either the coast or inland via Constantia. At a push you can get there on public transport on one of the couple of **buses** (see p.71) that leave from Adderley Street every day along the latter route and you can also catch minibus taxis. Crossing the peninsula spine from Simon's Town it's 26km (on the Glencairn Expressway).

Chapman's Peak Drive to Scarborough

Continuing south along the coast, **Chapman's Peak Drive** is a thrilling journey along one of the most beautiful drives in the world. For 10km the road carves into the mountainside on the one side, dropping precipitously hundreds of metres to the ocean on the other. Unceasingly spectacular views take in the breadth of Hout Bay to the 331-metre high sentinel on a curved outcrop. Viewpoints are provided along the route, but take care in high winds as it can be dangerous, with occasional rockfalls, although this doesn't seem to bother the scores of cyclists who sweat their way round, making considerate driving a necessity.

Noordhoek, a low-key settlement at the end of the descent from Chapman's Peak Drive, consists of smallholdings in a gentle valley with a long white untamed beach stretching 3km across Chapman's Bay to Kommetjie. The sands are fantastic for walking and horse-riding, but can resemble a sandblaster when the southeaster blows. Swimming is hazardous, though surfers relish the rough waters around the rocks to the north. For refreshment, the only place around here is the excellent *Red Herring* restaurant (see p.123) set back from the sea, about ten minutes on foot from the car park as you head away from the sea, with fine views from its outdoor deck.

Although only a few kilometres south of Noordhoek along the beach, getting to **Kommetjie** by road involves a 15km haul inland up the peninsula spine south along Noordhoek Road, taking a west turn into Kommetjie Road, to descend again. The beach's small basin (*kommetjie*), which is always a few degrees above the surrounding sea temperature, is perfect for swimming. Just to its north, **Long Beach** is a favourite surfing spot, used by devotees even during the chilly winter months.

Almost 10km by road from Kommetjie, the developing village of **Scarborough** is the most far-flung suburb along the peninsula. A long wide beach edges temptingly to its south just beyond Schusters River Lagoon – resist its potentially treacherous sea and stick to the lagoon. A crayfish processing plant, based here, and the local *Camel Rock* **restaurant**, make this a good place to stop and eat.

The False Bay seaboard

In summer, the waters of **False Bay** are several degrees warmer than those on the Atlantic seaboard, which is why Cape Town's oldest and most popular seaside development is along this flank of the peninsula. A series of village-like suburbs, backing onto the mountains, each served by a Metro Rail Station, is dotted all the way south from **Muizenberg**, through **St James**, **Kalk Bay**, **Fish Hoek** and down to **Simon's Town**. Each has its own character with restaurants, shops and places to stay, while Simon's Town, one of South Africa's oldest settlements, is worth taking in as a day-trip and makes a useful base for visiting the **Cape of Good Hope Nature Reserve** and **Cape Point**.

Muizenberg

Once South Africa's most fashionable beachfront, today **Muizenberg**, on the train line and one of the beaches closest to the populous Cape Flats, has become rather tacky, although plans are in the pipeline to upgrade and restore it. Brightly coloured bathing boxes are reminders of a more elegant heyday, when it was visited by the likes of Agatha Christie, who enjoyed riding its waves while holidaying here in the Twenties: "Whenever we could steal time off," she wrote, "we got out our surf boards and went surfing."

Despite the slight air of tawdriness, Muizenberg's gently shelving, sandy **beach** is the most popular along the peninsula for swimming – with good reason. It's safe for

CAPETOWN'S TOP WHALE SPOTS

Cape Town's best **whale-watching spots** are on the warmer **False Bay** side of the peninsula, and you'll need binoculars to get a decent sighting. Along this side, look out for whale signboards, indicating good places to spend time looking for them. The commonest whales along this section of coast are southern rights, but it's worth noting that there are more spectacular spotting opportunities further east, especially around Hermanus (see p.186).

Boyes Drive, running along the mountainside behind Muizenberg and Kalk Bay, provides an outstanding vantage point. To get there **by car**, head out on the M3 from the city centre to Muizenberg, taking a sharp right into Boyes Drive, at Lakeside, from where the road begins to climb, descending finally to join Main Road between Kalk Bay and Fish Hoek. Alternatively, sticking close to the shore along Main Road, the stretch between **Fish Hoek** and **Simon's Town** is recommended, with a particularly nice spot above the rocks at the south end of Fish Hoek Beach, as you walk south towards Glencairn. **Boulders Beach** at the southern end of Simon's Town has a whale signboard, and smooth rocky outcrops above the sea to sit on and gaze out over the sea. Even better vantage points are further down the coast between Simon's Town and **Smitswinkel Bay**, where the road goes higher along the mountainside.

Without a car, it's easy enough to go **by train** to Fish Hoek or Simon's Town and whale-spot from the Jager's Walk beach path that runs along the coast from Fish Hoek to Sunny Cove, just below the railway line.

If you're on a **coach trip**, or **driving** around the peninsula, you could also try your luck looking out to sea at **Chapman's Peak** towards Hout Bay, and between **Llandudno** and **Sea Point**, where the road curves along the ocean. Outside Cape Town, the best place of all is ninety minutes away, at **Hermanus** and the other towns dotted around Walker Bay.

Information on exactly where whales have been sighted in the past 24 hours is available from the **Whale Watch Hotline** (toll-free ☎0800/22 8222).

bathing, the water tends to be flat and warm, and there's good surfing in its breakers. This is also the most developed of the peninsula's beaches, with a pavilion complex around the car park featuring tea shops, a waterslide and minigolf. Along the beachfront and Main Road you'll also find shops, cafés and restaurants catering to the seaside trade. Muizenberg is one of the most heavily policed beaches, particularly at peak times, and there is a secure left-luggage office near the changing rooms.

Getting there is best done by train: from the centre it's a 45-minute journey – the train's first seaside stop as it trundles through the southern suburbs on its way to Simon's Town. By car, take the M3 through the posh suburbs, or the slightly quicker M5 via the less salubrious Cape Flats to Muizenberg. During peak season, finding a place to leave your vehicle can be near impossible.

The Historical Mile

Striking out south from Muizenberg, Main Road and the railway line hug the shore all the way to Simon's Town. A short stretch, starting at Muizenberg station, is known as the **Historical Mile**, dotted with a run of notable buildings and easily explored on foot. **Muizenberg station**, an Edwardian-style edifice completed in 1913, is now a national monument, while further towards Simon's Town is the **Posthuys**, a rugged white-washed and thatched building dating from 1673 and a fine example of the Cape vernacular style. **Rhodes' Cottage Museum** (Tues–Sun 10am–1pm & 2–5pm; free; ☎788 1816), was bought in 1899 by the millionaire politician who dreamt of a railway from the Cape to Cairo through British territory. He died here in 1902 before his grander dwelling next door (closed to the public) could be completed. Rhodes' Cottage contains memorabilia that paint a distinctly rosy portrait of the man, with photographs, a model of the Big Hole in Kimberley (where Rhodes made his fortune at the diamond diggings), and a curious diorama of World's View in Zimbabwe's Matopos Hills, where he lies buried.

Most idiosyncratic of the buildings along the historic mile, and closest to St James, is the **Natale Labia Museum** (Tues–Sun 10am–5pm; ☎788 4106), completed in 1930 as the residence of the Italian Consul, now part of the National Gallery and housing a small collection of artworks and furniture. Built in eighteenth-century Venetian style, it sits incongruously amid the Main Road townscape. Inside, heavy lace obscures the magnificent view, but there's an excellent **restaurant**, which serves up breakfasts, light meals and teas in the ersatz-Baroque interior or on the Italianate patio.

St James

St James, 2km south of Muizenberg, and just one stop away by train, is more upmarket than its northern neighbour, and its pleasing, villagey feel makes it a nice place to hop off the train. The compact beach draws considerable character from its much-photographed Victorian-style bathing boxes, whose bright, primary colours catch your eye as you pass by road or rail. The rocky beaches here don't make for great sea swimming, although it's always sheltered from the wind and there's a tidal pool that is safe for toddlers and great for bathing at high tide, when enormous breakers crash over the sea wall. A paved one-kilometre **coastal path**, connected at intervals to the Historical Mile, ribbons along the ocean from Muizenberg to Fish Hoek and apart from making a thoroughly pleasant way to stretch your legs and take in the stupendous views across the bay, leads conveniently to the Labia Museum (see above) for refreshment.

Kalk Bay

Moving south from Muizenberg, **Kalk Bay**, one of the most southerly and smallest of Cape Town's suburbs, is a lively **working harbour** with wooden fishing vessels, mountain views, and a shopping precinct packed with trendy coffee shops, antique dealers and curiosity shops.

Apart from the larger Hout Bay, Kalk Bay is the only harbour settlement still worked by coloured fishermen. The settlement is arranged around the small docks, where you can watch the boats come in and buy fresh fish, which are flung onto the quayside and noisily auctioned off in a spirited display. Kalk Bay somehow managed to slip through the net of the Group Areas Act, making it one of the few places on the peninsula with an intact coloured community. You can buy fish direct from the boats on the dockside, but what's available depends on the weather. The harbour is busiest on Saturdays and Sundays when Capetonians descend on the harbour to pick up something for a weekend *braai*. You can have the fish gutted and descaled on the spot for a couple of rand.

Perched on the harbour wall in the station building, pounded by waves, is the popular *Brass Bell* **restaurant**, one of Kalk Bay's biggest attractions and one of the few restaurants along the peninsula where you can actually sit next to the sea (see p.124).

Rising up behind the Kalk Bay settlement is **Silvermine Nature Reserve**, which runs across the Peninsula's spine, almost stretching to the west side at Chapman's Peak. Part of the Table Mountain chain, it offers walks and drives with fabulous views of False Bay, the mountains, indigenous forest and montane fynbos (see box on p.117), and is most easily reached via the Ou Kaapseweg (Old Cape Road, the M64) through Tokai. Alongside Silvermine runs **Boyes Drive**, a high-level alternative to the main road between Fish Hoek and Muizenberg offering spectacular views across False Bay to the Hottentots Holland Mountains on the east side of False Bay.

Fish Hoek

In contrast to Kalk Bay, the suburb of **Fish Hoek**, to the south, is one of the dreariest along the entire False Bay coast. Right up till the mid-Nineties, a now-repealed law banned the sale of alcohol here, boosting the town's image as the dull retirement home of the Peninsula. However, it does boast one of the Peninsula's finest family **beaches**. The best and safest swimming is at its southern end, where the surf is moderately warm, tame and much enjoyed by boogie boarders. Facilities include changing rooms, toilets, fresh water, and a surprisingly good **restaurant** right on the beach, the *Fish Hoek Galley Seafood Restaurant* (see p.124). The Cape Town to Simon's Town train stops at Kalk Bay station, just opposite the beach.

From behind the restaurant, **Jager's Walk**, a picturesque concrete pathway (see p.113), skirts the rocky shoreline above the sea for 1km to Sunny Cove, where it continues for 6km as an unpaved track to Simon's Town. The walkway provides a good vantage point for seeing whales if they're in the vicinity.

If you're driving, Fish Hoek is well-placed for access to the Atlantic Seaboard or for heading into the Constantia winelands. Just south of the suburb you can strike west on the Glencairn Expressway (M6), or alternatively take the equally scenic Kommetjie Road (M65) about 4km further south (more convenient than the M6 if you're coming from Simon's Town). The two intersect halfway across the peninsula at Sun Valley, where Kommetjie Road continues west, veering slightly south to the coastal suburban village of Noordhoek. At Sun Valley, the M6 strikes north and splits about a kilometre after the intersection, with the northwesterly branch hitting the coast at Chapman's Point to continue along the precipitously beautiful Chapman's Peak Drive, which eventually reaches the City Bowl along the Atlantic shore. The northeasterly branch heads along the winding treelined Ou Kaapseweg (M64, becoming the M42), passing through the Silvermine Nature Reserve and the winelands.

Simon's Town

South Africa's principal naval base, **Simon's Town** isn't the hard-drinking, raucous place you might expect or hope for. Just 40km from Cape Town, the country's third-oldest European settlement is exceptionally pretty, with a near-perfectly preserved streetscape. It's slightly marred on the ocean side by the domineering **naval dockyard**, but this, and glimpses of naval squaddies square-bashing behind the high walls or strolling to the station in their crisp white uniforms, are what give the place its distinct character.

Roughly halfway down the coast to Cape Point, Simon's Town makes the perfect base for a mellow break along the peninsula, offering easy day-trips by train to Cape Town. Just a few kilometres to the south is the rock-strewn **Boulders Beach**, with its colony of nonchalant African penguins – reason in themselves to venture here.

Some history

Founded in 1687 as the winter anchorage of the Dutch East India Company, Simon's Town was modestly named by **Governor Simon van der Stel** after himself. Its most celebrated visitor was Lord Nelson, who convalesced here as a midshipman while returning home from the East in 1776. Nineteen years later, the British sailed into Simon's Town and occupied it as a bridgehead for their invasion of Cape Town and the **first British occupation of the Cape**. After just seven years they left, only to return in 1806. Simon's Town remained a British base until 1957, when it was handed over to South Africa.

There are fleeting hints, such as the odd mosque, that the town's exclusively white appearance isn't the whole story. In fact, the first **Muslims** arrived from the East Indies in the early eighteenth century, imported as slaves to build the Dutch naval base. After the British banning of the slave trade in 1807, ships were compelled to disgorge their human cargo at Simon's Town, where one district became known as Black Town. In 1967, when Simon's Town was declared a White Group Area, there were 1200 well-established coloured familes descended from these slaves. By 1973 the majority had been **forcibly removed**, because of the Group Areas Act (see "History", p.693), to the desolate township of Ocean View (ironically, one of the few places along the peninsula not to enjoy a sea vista). Their departure made a significant impact, and dwellings were destroyed or allowed to rot, depriving the town of significant historic buildings. In 1973, town clerk Charles Chevalier complained that "the loss of the non-white population has had a depressing effect on the commercial life of the town".

Arrival and information

Trains run from Cape Town roughly every hour during the day. The trip takes an hour, the last twenty minutes from Muizenberg skirting the coast spectacularly close to the shoreline – it's worth going to Simon's Town just for the train ride. Trains are met at Simon's Town by rikkis (☎786 2136), which you can also book for excursions to Cape Point and Boulders. A great outing is to take one of the restaurant trains pulling *Biggsy's Restaurant Carriage & Wine Bar*, which serves lunches, salads and highly recommended breakfasts. *Biggsy's* operate five return trips a day (Tues–Sat) from Platform 1 at Cape Town station, but space is limited so book ahead (☎449 3870). **By car**, the quickest way to get here from Cape Town is via the M3 or M5 freeways to Muizenberg and then follow the coastal road to Simon's Town. There are no buses to Simon's Town.

The Town

A short way south of the station along King George's Street (the main drag through town), a signposted road to the left points to the museums. The **Simon's Town Museum**, Court Rd (Mon–Fri 9am–4pm, Sat 10am–4pm, Sun 11am–4pm; small entry fee; ☎786 3046), is in the Old Residency built in 1772 for the Governor of the Dutch East India Company. It also served as the slave quarters (the dungeons are in the basement) and town brothel. The motley collection includes maritime material and an inordinate amount on Able Seaman Just Nuisance, a much-celebrated seafaring Great Dane adopted as a mascot by the Royal Navy in World War II, and reputed to have enjoyed the odd pint with the sailors he accompanied into Cape Town. At the **South African Naval Museum** (daily 10am–4pm; free; ☎797 4653) next door, lively displays include the inside of a submarine, the bridge of a ship simulating rocking, and loads of official portraits of South African Navy big guns with double-barrelled names, from 1922 to the present.

For the best bread, pastries, pies and everything else you'll need for a **picnic** at Cape Point, pop into *Brad's Food Shop & Bistro* across the street in King George's Road, which also acts as an excellent self-appointed **accommodation** agency for Simon's Town.

A little further down the main road you'll reach **Jubilee Square**, a small collection of craft and coffee shops, and from here steps lead to the **Marina**, a modest development of shops and restaurants, opened in 1998. One of the best reasons to venture onto the quayside is to take a high-speed **catamaran trip** on the *Cape of Good Hope*, which embarks on exhilarating ninety-minute excursions around Cape Point (daily 10am & 2.30pm; R120) and shorter seal-spotting outings to Seal Island (daily noon & 1.15pm; R80). Booking is advisable; contact Tigre Cruises (☎786 1045 or 786 1055).

Just beyond Jubilee Square, St George Way leads off the main road north to the **Noorul Islam Cultural Museum** (Mon–Fri 10am–4pm, Sat 10am–1pm, Sun

10am–6pm; free; ☎786 2302), in Amlay House. The museum relates the rich history of the Muslim community of Simon's Town, who were forcibly kicked out of town during the apartheid removals of the Sixties and Seventies. Photographs document family life from the nineteenth century, and there are interesting displays on Muslim life, some lovely everyday artefacts, a table set for festive occasions, a bridal room, and a *hadj* (pilgrimage) room displaying exquisite pilgrims' garments. The well-informed and welcoming curator tells some interesting and poignant tales of the old Muslim residents.

The beaches

Nearest to the station, **Long Beach** offers no shade and is therefore little used. However, on windless days it can be pleasant for long walks, with views of the Hottentots Holland Mountains, and its tidal pool is safe for bathing. Access is by a number of gaps in a brick wall alongside the main road and about midway along the beach (opposite Hopkirk Way), by a flight of steps. There are changing rooms (free) and toilets nearby, and fresh water.

One of the best beaches for swimming is at **Seaforth**, where clear, deep waters lap around rocks. It's calm, protected and safe, but not pretty (bounded on one side by the looming grey mass of the naval base), but there's plenty of lawn shaded by palm trees.

Two kilometres from the station towards Cape Point takes you out of town and to **Boulders**, the most popular local beach, with a number of places to stay and only one small shop, The Curious Penguin. The area takes its name from the huge, rounded rocks that create a collection of little coves with sandy beaches and clear, natural sea pools. But the main reason people come here is for the **African penguins** (formerly known as jackass penguins), in the **Boulders Coastal Park** (open 24hrs; R10 entry fee 8am–5pm), a fenced reserve on Boulders Beach. Passing sailors used to prey on the quirky birds and their eggs, but the penguins are extremely laid-back, paying little attention to visitors. More recently they have fallen victim to vandals, and some locals who consider them pests, but are now under the protective wing of a semi-official guard. African penguins usually live on islands off the west side of the South African coast; the Boulders birds form one of only two mainland colonies in the world. This is also the only place where the endangered species are actually increasing in numbers, so it's a rare opportunity to get a close look at them.

Almost 5km to the south is the popular **Miller's Point** resort, which has a number of small sandy beaches and a tidal pool protected from the southeaster. There's a **campsite** at the caravan park, with great sea views. Along Main Road, the notable *Black Marlin* seafood **restaurant** attracts busloads of tourists, while the boulders around the point attract rock agama and black zonure lizards and dassies.

The last place before you get to the Cape of Good Hope Nature Reserve is **Smitswinkelbaai**, a little cove with a small beach, which is safe for swimming but feels the full blast of the southeaster. It's not accessible by car, as local property owners fiercely guard their privacy. To get there, you must park next to the road and walk down a seemingly endless succession of stairs.

Cape of Good Hope Nature Reserve

Most people come to **Cape of Good Hope Nature Reserve** (daily: summer 7am–6pm; winter 7am–5pm; R5; ☎780 9100) to see the southernmost tip of Africa and the place where the Indian and Atlantic oceans meet at **Cape Point**. In fact, it's the site of neither, but is nevertheless an awesomely dramatic spot, which should on no account be missed. The reserve sits atop massive sea cliffs with huge views, strong seas, and an even wilder wind, which whips off caps and sunglasses as visitors gaze southwards from the old

FYNBOS

Early Dutch settlers were alarmed by the paucity of good timber on the Cape Peninsula's hillsides, which were covered by nondescript, scrubby bush they described as *fijn bosch* (literally "fine bush") and which is now known by its Afrikaans name **fynbos** (pronounced "fayn-bos"). They set about planting exotics, like the oaks that now shade central Cape Town, and over the ensuing centuries their descendants established pine forests on the sides of Table Mountain in an effort to create a landscape that fulfilled their European idea of the picturesque. It's only relatively recently that Capetonians have come to proudly claim fynbos as part of the peninsula's cultural heritage, and Table Mountain pines have been felled to be recycled as books and articles about fynbos. Fynbos is remarkable for its astonishing variety of plants, making up eighty percent of the vegetation of the **Cape Floral Kingdom**, the smallest and richest of the floral kingdoms; its 8500 species make it one of the world's biodiversity hot spots. Only the South American rainforests come anywhere near matching its incredible concentration of diversity.

The Cape Peninsula alone, measuring less than 500 square kilometres, has 2256 plant species (nearly twice as many as Britain, which is 5000 times bigger). While the other five floral kingdoms cover vast areas such as Australia or the northern hemisphere, the entire Cape kingdom stretches across a relatively narrow coastal crescent from Niewoudville in the west, through Cape Town and across to Grahamstown in the east.

The four basic types of fynbos are: **proteas** (South Africa's national flower you'll see sold in bouquets at the airport if nowhere else); **ericas**, amounting to 600 species of heather (against 26 in the rest of the world); **restios** or reeds; and **geophytes**, including ground orchids and the startling flaming red disas, which can be seen in flower on Table Mountain in late summer.

lighthouse buttress. The continent's real tip is at **Cape Agulhas**, some 300km southeast of here, but Cape Point is a lot easier to get to than Agulhas and a lot more exciting.

There is no public transport to the reserve, although you can rent a Simon's Town **rikki** (☎786 2136) there and back. To get there **by car**, take the M3 to Muizenberg, continuing on the M4 via Simon's Town to the reserve gates, where you'll be given a good **map** that marks the main driving and walking routes, as well as the tidal pools and other facilities.

From the car park, the famous viewpoint is a short, steep walk, crawling with tourists, up to the original lighthouse. A **funicular** runs the less energetic to the top, where

CAPE WILDLIFE

Along with indigenous plants and flowers, you may well spot some of the **animals** that harbour in the Cape of Good Hope Nature Reserve fynbos habitat. **Baboons** lope along the rocky shoreline and can be a menace. Keep your car windows up and watch out, as they're adept at slyly swiping picnics and it's not unknown for them to invade vehicles. There are also **bontebok**, **eland** and **red hartebeest**, as well as **Cape rhebok** and **grysbok** grazing on the heathery slopes. If you're very lucky you may even see some of the extremely rare **Cape mountain zebras**.

Ostriches stride through the low fynbos, and occasionally **African penguins** come ashore. A distinctive bird on the rocky shores is the **black oystercatcher** with a bright red beak, jabbing limpets off the rocks. You'll also see **Cape cormorants** in large flocks on the beach or rocks, often drying their outstretched wings. Running up and down the water's edge are **white-fronted plovers** and **sanderlings** which probe for food left by the receding waves. Finally, as on any other beach walk in the Cape, you'll see piles of shiny brown **ecklonia kelp** on the beach or floating in dark beds in the wave-swells.

there's a curio shop. There's also a functional **restaurant** at the car park, which has outdoor seating (but it's usually too windy to be pleasant) and huge picture windows taking in the drop to the sea below. Most people come to the Point as part of a round-trip, returning via Kommetjie and the especially scenic Chapman's Peak Drive. Numerous **tours** spend a day stopping off at the peninsula highlights; Day Trippers (☎531 3274) run fun tours for R155 (including a picnic lunch), some of which give you the option of cycling part of the way. For general tours that take in the reserve see "Tours", p.74.

Cape Point and around

Cape Point is the treacherous promontory of rocks, winds and swells that navigators since the Portuguese in the fifteenth century had to contend with when they "rounded the Cape" on their way to the East. Plenty of wrecks lie submerged off its coast, and at **Olifantsbos** on the west side you can walk to two wrecks: one a US ship sunk in 1942, and the other a South African coaster which ran aground in 1965. The **Old Lighthouse**, built in 1860, was too often dangerously shrouded in cloud, failing to keep ships off the rocks, so another was built lower down in 1914, not always successful in averting disasters but still the most powerful light beaming onto the sea from South Africa.

The sea and mountain scenery in the reserve are reason enough to travel the 66km from central Cape Town. Most visitors make a beeline for Cape Point, seeing the rest of the reserve through a vehicle window, but walking is the best way to appreciate indigenous **Cape flora**. At first glance the landscape appears rocky and bleak, with short, wind-cropped plants, but the vegetation is surprisingly rich – there are as many plant varieties in this small reserve as in the whole of Britain. Amazingly, many bright blooms in Britain and the US, such as geraniums, freesias, gladioli, daisies, lilies and irises, are hybrids grown from indigenous Cape plants.

Swimming and walking

There are several waymarked **walks** in the Cape of Good Hope Nature Reserve. If you're planning a big hike it's best to set out early, as shade is rare and the wind can be foul, especially during summer, often increasing in intensity as the day goes on. One of the most straightforward **hiking routes** is the signposted forty-minute trek from the car park at **Cape Point** to the more westerly **Cape of Good Hope**. For exploring the shoreline, a clear path runs down the Atlantic side from Hoek van Bobbejaan. A convenient place to join it is at **Gifkommetjie**, which is signposted off Cape Point Road. From the car park, several sandy tracks drop quite steeply down the slope across rocks, and through bushes and milkwood trees to the shore, along which you can walk in either direction. Alternatively, take a copy of the Government Printer's 1:50,000 map 3318 C.D. *Cape Town* for some more intrepid exploration. Take water on any walk in the reserve, as there are no reliable fresh sources.

You'll find the **beaches** along signposted sideroads branching out from Cape Point Road, the main route through the reserve, going from the entrance gate to the car park at Cape Point. The sea is too dangerous for swimming, but there are safe tidal pools at the adjacent **Buffels Bay** and **Bordjiesrif**, midway along the east shore. Both have *braai* stands, but more southerly Buffels Bay is the nicer, with big lawned areas and some sheltered spots to have a picnic.

Table Bay and the northern suburbs

The **northern suburbs**, middle-class and Afrikaner-dominated, curl around the edge of Table Bay, north from Duncan Dock, and east along the N2 freeway. Few tourists see more of this area than the strip along the coast from Milnerton to Blouberg, and with good reason: the main attraction here is the much-snapped view of Table Mountain across the bay, otherwise the northern suburbs are an unappetizing sprawl of starter homes and new developments (this is one of the few areas of Cape Town where there's room for expansion).

Nevertheless, the long sandy beaches are ideal for a sunset walk, when you can watch the glowing orb slip into the sea close to **Robben Island** (see p.98). The sea is cold, and often windy, but windsurfers and kite-fliers do well here. **Big Bay** (Grootbaai), close to the principal resort of **Bloubergstrand** (usually shortened to Blouberg), draws windsurfing enthusiasts from all over the world for annual competitions.

By car, take the N1 from the city centre and the Milnerton/Paarden Island exit to get onto Marina Drive which follows the coast to Milnerton, Tableview, Blouberg, Melkbosstrand, Koeberg nuclear power station and right on up the west coast to the Namibia border.

Milnerton to Melkbosstrand

The beachfront strip at **Milnerton**, closest to central Cape Town, is a banal, neon-lit fast-food haven, offering little reason to stop off, unless you're one of the surfing devotees who brave the water for the break off the lighthouse, undeterred by the debris floating across from the docks.

To the west is **Table View**, noted for its easy access to the beach, beachside parking and its classic view of Table Mountain. Nearby **Bloubergstrand**, 25km from the city, is the only place to draw you out to Table Bay. Once a fishing village, this is a good place to walk and take in the views, and you can sample one of Blouberg's outdoor restaurants for meals or tea.

By the time you get to **Melkbosstrand** and find yourself driving through dry, low scrub, you will feel well and truly out of Cape Town. Melkbos, 30km from Cape Town, has a caravan park and one or two places to stay, but few people choose to, perhaps because the settlement is so close to Koeberg, the country's only **nuclear power station**, which generates electricity for the Western Cape. It's said that the sea around Melkbos is a few degrees warmer than elsewhere around here, heated by the water used to cool the reactor. The radioactive waste itself is currently deposited 600km to the north at Vaalputs, but the national power company, Eskom, is negotiating to store spent fuel on site.

The Cape Flats and the African townships

East of the northern and southern suburbs, among the industrial smokestacks and the windswept Cape Flats, reaching well beyond the airport, is Cape Town's largest residential block, taking in the **coloured districts**, **African townships** and shantytown **squatter camps**, which are only visited on packaged township tours.

The **Cape Flats** are exactly that: barren, windswept and flat. You can't miss them along the N2 as you drive into Cape Town from the airport. Exclusively inhabited by Africans and coloureds, in their own separate areas, they can be both shocking and heartening. If you manage to get inside and talk to people, you'll see unimaginable squalor and hear countless stories of personal courage and stoicism. The safest way inside is via a **tour** (see box overleaf); venturing in on your own isn't a good idea as the apartheid ghettos are crime-ridden, and thanks to them Cape Town has earned an unenviable reputation as the "murder capital of the world".

Some history

The African townships were set up as dormitories to provide labour for white Cape Town, not as places to build a life, which is why they had no facilities and no real hub.

CAPE FLATS TOURS

In the darkest days of apartheid, during the late Eighties, the African townships were no-go areas for outsiders – particularly whites or police. Although today that's over, and many people welcome visitors, your best chance of getting in and coming out safely is to join one of the **township tours**, which will give you a chance to meet local people. The popular One City Tours (☎387 5351) take visitors on a three-hour journey around the African areas of Langa, Khayelitsha, Guguletu and Crossroads; tours leave from Tourism Gateway in Adderley Street and are led by residents of the townships. Western Cape Action Tours (☎461 1371), led by former Umkhonto weSizwe (ANC armed wing) guerillas, focus on the fight against apartheid and take visitors through the townships to sites of political resistance, as well as trips to a traditional healer, housing projects and township markets. AfriCultural Tours (☎423 3321) offer a comprehensive look at Cape Town's "other side"; they also offer a "Slave Route" tour, a tour of San rock art and visits to traditional music makers, dancers and artists, as well as to creative training centres. For a chance to experience the upbeat side of Cape Flats nightlife join their "Vibey Jazz" tour.

The **men-only hostels**, another apartheid relic, are at the root of many of the area's social problems. During the Fifties, the government set out a blueprint to turn the tide of Africans flooding into Cape Town. No African was permitted to settle permanently in the Cape west of a line near the Fish River, the old frontier over 1000km from Cape Town; women were entirely banned from seeking work in Cape Town and men prohibited from bringing their wives to join them. By 1970 there were ten men for every woman in Langa.

In the end, apartheid failed to prevent the influx of work-seekers desperate to come to Cape Town. Where people couldn't find legal accommodation they set up the **squatter camps** of makeshift iron, cardboard and plastic sheeting. During the Seventies and Eighties, the government attempted to eradicate these by demolishing them and destroying anything left inside. But no sooner had the police left than the camps reappeared, and they are now a permanent feature of the Cape Flats. One of the best known of all South Africa's squatter camps is **Crossroads**, whose inhabitants suffered campaigns of harassment that included killings and continuous attempts to bulldoze it out of existence. Through sheer determination – and no little desperation – its residents hung on and eventually won the right to stay. Today, the government is making attempts to improve conditions in the shantytowns by bringing in running water and sanitation. The lack of facilities is starting to change, with families moving in and ad hoc traders beginning to fill the gaps.

Langa and Mitchell's Plain

Langa is the oldest and most central township, lying just east of the white suburb of Pinelands and north of the N2. In this relentlessly grey and random place, without the tiniest patch of green relief, you'll find women selling sheep and goats' heads, alongside state-of-the-art public phone bureaus run by enterprising township businessmen from inside recycled cargo containers. Nuclear families live in smart suburban houses while, not far away, there are former men-only hostels where as many as three families share one room.

South of the African ghettos is **Mitchell's Plain**, a coloured area stretching down to the False Bay coast, which you'll skirt if you take the M5 to Muizenberg. More salubrious than any of the African townships, Mitchell's Plain reflects how under apartheid lighter skins meant better conditions, even if you weren't quite white. But for coloureds the forced removals were no less tragic, many being summarily forced to vacate family homes because their suburb had been declared a White Group Area. Many families were relocated here when District Six was razed, and their communities never fully recovered – one of the symptoms of dislocation are the violent gangs, which have become an everyday part of Mitchell's Plain youth culture.

Eating and drinking

Cape Town scores with its large number of relaxed and convivial restaurants serving imaginative and healthy food of a high quality that doesn't cost an arm and a leg. The range of styles is broad – and widening all the time.

Cape Cuisine, the only truly local food, is a spicy hybrid of the cooking styles brought to South Africa and adapted to local conditions by slaves principally from Asia and Madagascar. While it's definitely a must-try, its lack of variety means the novelty will soon wear thin. Mild and semi-sweet curries with a strong Indonesian influence predominate, and include: *bredie* (stew), of which *waterblommetjiebredie* (made using water hyacinths), is a speciality; *bobotie*, a spicy minced dish served under a savoury custard; and *sosaties*, a local version of kebab using mincemeat. Of the desserts, dates stuffed with almonds make a light and delicious end to a meal, while *malva* pudding is a wickedly rich combination of milk, sugar, cream and apricot jam. There are only one or two restaurants dedicated to this style of cooking, but dishes influenced by Cape Cuisine are relatively common elsewhere. As far as **seafood** goes, Cape Town offers cold-water fish such as kingklip and snoek, not found along the coast to the east. Apart from *smoorsnoek*, a delicious spicy speciality you'll find in restaurants serving Cape Cuisine, on the whole snoek isn't widely available as a main course at restaurants. You will, however, find smoked snoek and snoek pâté as starters, and every fish-and-chip shop in town offers fried snoek as an option in season.

Given Cape Cuisine's strong links with the local (teetotal) Muslim community, you'll rarely be able to enjoy Cape wines at restaurants serving Cape food, particularly in the Bo-Kaap. However, just about everywhere else in Cape Town, **wine** drinking (see p.43 and p.138) is a matter of fierce local loyalty and most meals are accompanied by it. Apart from the Constantia estates, whose restaurants serve their own wines, you'll find much the same choice here as you would in any of the bigger centres, but in no other city in the country does it feel more right to be sampling Cape wines than here under the gaze of Table Mountain. For **self-catering**, see p.132.

Restaurants

The greatest concentration of **restaurants** is in the central district around the **City Bowl**, with **Sea Point** and, more recently, the **Waterfront** having established reputations as places where you'll find quite a few eateries. An even younger newcomer, and one making a concerted attempt to become the eating heart of the city, is **Kloof Street**, with new places springing up along its length by the day. For **Cape Cuisine**, the best places are *Biesmiellah* in the Bo-Kaap, or *Kaapse Tafel* in the city centre. As far as **prices** go, expect to pay under R30 for a main course at an inexpensive restaurant, up to R50 at a medium-priced one, and upwards of that at an expensive one.

City Bowl and the Waterfront

Al Dente, 88 Kloof St (☎423 7617). A sprawling and beautifully decorated restaurant that serves mid-priced fresh and fragrant Mediterranean food. Mon & Wed–Sun 11am–10.30pm.

Aldo's Restaurant, Shop 153, Ground Floor, Victoria Basin, Waterfront (☎421 7876). Good but expensive traditional Italian food. Daily until 10.45pm.

Amigos Mediterranean Restaurant, 158 Kloof St, Gardens (☎423 6805). A tasty mixture of Greek *meze* combined with Italian and Spanish food. Medium-priced and lively, with some tables outside. Daily until midnight.

Anatoli, 24 Napier St, De Waterkant (☎419 2501). Mid-priced Turkish restaurant in a turn-of-the-century warehouse that buzzes with atmosphere. Excellent *meze* include exceptionally delicious dolmades, and there are superb deserts such as pressed dates topped with a puff of cream. Tues–Sun until 11pm.

Bayfront Blu, Two Oceans Aquarium complex, Waterfront (☎419 9068). Traditional African dishes and seafood, overlooking the marina with a stunning panoramic view of Table Mountain and live music Fri and Sat. Open daily for lunch and dinner.

Biesmiellah, corner of Upper Wale and Pentz streets (☎423 0850). One of the oldest and best-known restaurants for medium-priced, traditional Cape Cuisine. No alcohol permitted. Daily noon–3pm & 6–11pm.

The Blue Plate Restaurant and Bar, 35 Kloof St (☎424 1515). Spacious restaurant offering global cuisine and open seven nights a week till late. Friendly and well-informed waiters. Closed lunchtime except Fri.

Buccaneer Steakhouse, 64 Orange St, Gardens (☎424 4966). Good steaks and sauces in an atmosphere bordering on dowdy, making for a supremely relaxed and low-cost evening. Closed Sat & Sun lunchtime.

Café Paradiso, 110 Kloof St (☎423 8653). Good, medium-priced Greek and Mediterranean dishes, including a weigh-your-plate *meze* bar and outside terrace with views up to the mountain and down over the city and docks. Open daily for lunch and dinner.

Col'Cacchio, Seeff House, 42 Hans Strydom Ave, Foreshore. Offbeat, cheap pizza restaurant that also serves pasta and often spills onto the pavement outside. Has over forty different and quite original pizza toppings, such as smoked salmon, sour cream and caviar. Closed Sat & Sun lunchtime.

Floris Smit Huijs, 55 Church St (☎423 3414). The beautiful decor in this eighteenth-century town house is as big an attraction as the mid-priced, eclectic international cuisine. Daily until 10.30pm.

Jewel Tavern, off Vanguard Rd, Duncan Docks (☎448 1977). Unpretentious Taiwanese sailors' eating house, which has been "discovered" by Cape Town's *bon viveurs*. Superb, mid-priced Chinese food, including stunning hot and sour soup and spring rolls made while you watch. Daily mid-morning until 10pm.

Kaapse Tafel, Montreux Building, 90 Queen Victoria St (☎423 1651). Twenty years in the business of traditional Cape Cuisine hasn't diminished this restaurant's excellent reputation. Good for *bobotie* and medium-priced Cape seafood. Closed Sun.

Long Street Café, 259 Long St. Trendy bar/deli/resto with tasteful open-plan décor and lovely, fresh continental-style food.

Mama Africa, 178 Long St (☎424 8634). Mid-priced food from around the continent in a relaxed atmosphere. The highlight is a 12-metre bar in the form of a green mamba. Mon–Sun until late with live music.

Max-Max Global Cuisine, 22 Kloof St (☎424 1424). A touch of Art Deco, with a nice fire on cold nights, and an imaginative eclectic global menu of spicy dishes that includes North Indian balti curries, Mongolian lamb, and Penang chicken cooked in coconut milk. Closed Sat & Sun lunchtime.

Melissa's The Food Shop, 94 Kloof St (☎424 5540). Food emporium, where you can buy medium-priced, freshly made Mediterranean fare, and a small eatery that serves light meals and fine desserts. Daily 8.30am–8pm.

Mexican Kitchen Café, 13 Bloem St (☎423 1541). Cheap, casual restaurant serving up good-value burritos, enchiladas, *calamari fajitas* and *nachos*. They also do deli-style takeaways. Daily until midnight.

Musselcracker Restaurant, Shop 222, First Floor, Victoria Basin, Waterfront (☎425 2157). Eat your way through the fine (and pricey) seafood buffet at one of the few Waterfront restaurants of note. Daily for lunch and dinner.

Ocean Basket Southern Africa, 75 Kloof St (☎ 422 0322). Long queues and unspeakably delicious aromas wafting out of the door speak eloquently of this medium-priced establishment's outstanding fish dishes. Mon–Sat for lunch and every evening for dinner.

Vasco da Gama Tavern, 3 Alfred St (☎425 2157). Known locally as the "Portuguese embassy", this unpretentious restaurant with a blaring TV is a genuine working man's pub. Grilled tongue with bread, accompanied by wine mixed with Coke, are standard. It's also a great seafood restaurant at half the price and better than many of the upmarket joints. Daily 10am–9pm.

Yindees, 22 Camp St, Tamboerskloof (☎422 1012). Undeniably the best Thai in Cape Town. Great, mid-priced food and brilliant spicy prawn soup served by dour waiters. Mon–Sat until late.

Southern suburbs

Africa Café, 213 Lower Main Rd, Observatory (☎47 9553). Sample inexpensive food from around the dark continent in a suitably *fauve* atmosphere. Mon–Sat until midnight.

Constantia Uitsig Restaurant, Spaanschemat River Rd, Constantia (☎794 4480). Very successful, rather pricey restaurant on a wine estate. Views across the Constantia Valley and good Provençale food have made this one of South Africa's top ten restaurants. Daily until late.

Enrica Rocca, 19 Wolfe St, Wynberg. A real Italian – no red-checked tablecloths and straw chianti bottles with candles – with a vast antipasto spread followed by a limited range of interesting mid-priced pasta dishes. Open lunchtimes Tues–Fri, plus evenings Tues–Sat.

Pancho's Mexican Kitchen, 127 Lower Main Rd, Observatory (☎47 4854). Highly popular and inexpensive cantina-style restaurant serving Mexican dishes. Overzealous frying has led to it being described as "Cape Town's other oil depot". Daily until late.

Parks, 114 Constantia Rd, Wynberg (☎797 8202). The most elegant and expensive eating in the southern suburbs outside the wine estates, in a restored Victorian town house with original menu and personal, almost pedantic service and attention to detail. Closed Sat lunchtime & all day Sun.

Atlantic seaboard

Aris Souvlaki, 83a Regent Rd, Sea Point (☎439 6683). Reliable, inexpensive terrace restaurant for Greek *shwarma* and *souvlaki*. You can also get takeaways. Daily until 11pm.

Blues Restaurant, 9 The Promenade, Victoria Rd, Camps Bay (☎438 2040). Spectacular views make this over-rated Californian-style restaurant one of the most popular in town. Brace yourself for poor service and ringing mobile phones, though the pastas and seafood are actually pretty good. Daily until midnight.

Caponero, 142 Main Rd, Sea Point (☎434 9056). Superb, thick-based pizzas with indulgently rich fillings and seafood toppings to remember. Daily until late.

Chicken Bar, 110 Main Rd, Sea Point (☎439 2751). Touch nothing here apart from the chicken, which is very good and reasonably priced. Daily 9am–9pm.

Little Bombay, 245 Main Rd, Three Anchor Bay (☎439 9041). Excellent food at Cape Town's only vegetarian Indian restaurant. Their *thalis* give you a cheap and tasty set meal. Unlicensed, so bring your own booze. Daily until late.

Mario's Restaurant, 89 Main Rd, Green Point (☎439 6644). Excellent mid-priced Italian casseroles and pastas with attitude. Closed Sat lunch & all day Mon.

Nando's Chickenland, 128 Main Rd, Sea Point (☎439 7999). South Africa's answer to KFC. Surprisingly good grilled Portuguese-style *peri-peri* poultry. Daily until 10pm.

Ons Huisie Restaurant, Stadler Rd, Bloubergstrand (☎56 1553). Come to enjoy the romantic 1816 fisherman's cottage (now a national monument), rather than their expensive fish. Closed Tues.

Pizzeria Napoletana, 178 Main Rd, Sea Point. A family business since 1956, the best Italian joint in Cape Town offers solid, good-value and tasty cuisine. Try the Veal Parmigiano or their crayfish – the most generous you'll find on the Peninsula. Closed Mon.

Red Herring, Beach Rd/Pine St, Noordhoek (☎789 1783). Beautiful sea and mountain views at this relaxed, mid-priced, out-of-town restaurant. A good place for line-caught fish. Daily until late.

The Round House, The Glen, Camps Bay (☎438 2320). Nouvelle cuisine at one of the snottiest, but not too expensive, restaurants in town, housed aptly in Lord Charles Somerset's hunting lodge. Daily until late.

San Marco, 92 Main Rd, Sea Point (☎439 2758). Stunning, mid-priced Italian seafood. The grilled *calamari* tossed in chilli and garlic is wonderful, and their antipasto trolley is especially good for vegetarians. They also serve wonderful *gelato*. Closed Tues.

Theo's Steaks, Beach Rd, Mouille Point (☎439 3494). Upmarket ambience right on the beachfront, offering superb mid-priced beef and seafood. Daily until 10pm.

Wooden Bridge, Golf Club, Woodbridge Island, Milnerton (☎52 2423). You'll enjoy a classic postcard view of Table Mountain across the bay at this mid-priced restaurant. Seafood is the speciality, but you'll find all sorts of continental cuisine here. Tues–Sat until 11.30pm.

Zorba, 229d Main Rd, Sea Point. Tasty, good-value Greek dishes, as well as generous tender steaks and delightful salads under a hopelessly kitsch (but delicious) thousand islands dressing. Mon–Sat until 11pm.

False Bay seaboard

Brass Bell, Kalk Bay station, Kalk Bay (☎788 5456). Arguably the best location in town to eat, with views of both Table and the Hottentots Holland mountains, the mid-priced seafood meals don't quite match the magnificent setting. There's also a pub with live music some nights. Daily until late.

Café Matisse, 76 Main Rd, Kalk Bay. Popular, relaxed café serving pizzas and light meals. The work of local artists is exhibited on the walls.

Fish Hoek Galley Seafood Restaurant, Beach Rd, Fish Hoek (☎782 3354). Informal restaurant right on the beach, with an attached bistro and outdoor seating. Their excellent-value seafood platter attracts busloads of Japanese tourists. Daily until 10pm.

Gaylords Indian Cuisine, 65 Main Rd, Muizenberg (☎788 5470). The tacky interior belies an imaginative menu that adapts great Indian cooking and local ingredients to create something unique and inexpensive. Mon & Tues–Wed until 10pm.

Harbour House Restaurant, Kalk Bay Harbour (☎788 4133). Mid-range seafood, and Mediterranean fare, situated spectacularly on the breakwater of Kalk Bay Harbour. Open daily for lunch and dinner.

La Mer Restaurant and Ladies Bar, top floor, Muizenberg Station, Main Rd, Muizenberg (☎788 3251). Good, mid-priced seafood and even better views. Mon–Sat till late, Sun 11.30am–3.30pm.

The Owl and the Pussycat, Shop 2, Shoprite Centre Main Rd, Muizenberg (☎788 6189). Lively medium-priced bar, restaurant and pizzeria. Daily 9.30am till late.

Coffee and snacks

Recently Cape Town's centre has begun to enjoy a renaissance, and **continental-style cafés** are springing up in their numbers, offering easy-going places where you can eat a meal, or just linger over a drink or coffee. Service at these tends to be slick and friendly, and they stay open until around 11pm.

Surprisingly for a warm and sunny city, Cape Town has few **outdoor snack bars** and even fewer seaside ones, which is a pity given the 150km of peninsula coastline. Fortunately the idea is beginning to catch on, and more and more places around town, especially the more relaxed cafés, are managing to create room for a few outdoor tables and chairs during the summer months. You'll always find somewhere with harbour views at the **Waterfront**. For **garden settings**, try the *Company Gardens* in town, the *Jonkerhuis* on the Groot Constantia Wine Estate or Kirstenbosch Botanical Gardens. For **Table Mountain vistas**, try *Aladdin* in Sea Point or *Rhodes Memorial* on its slopes, with panoramas across the city. For **seaside settings** there's the choice of *Mariner's Wharf Bistro* or *Suikerbossie* in Hout Bay, the *Red Herring* at Noordhoek, the *Brass Bell* at Kalk Bay station (see above) or *Wimpy* at Sea Point.

City Bowl and the Waterfront

Aladdin Coffee Shop, Nedbank Centre, 15 Kloof Rd, Sea Point. Patio coffee shop with views of Table Mountain, serving up breakfast and light lunches. Mon–Sat 8am–5pm.

Café Bardeli, Long St Studios, off Kloof St (☎423 4444). Excruciatingly stylish, the epitome of café society where the food is suitably chic but also very good. A film-set favourite, with Cape Town's highest quotient of supermodels per square metre. Open daily for lunch and dinner.

Company Gardens, near the north end. Slow service and standard sandwiches and teas in pleasant surroundings. A good bet if you're already in the centre of town. Daytime only.

Hartlief Gourmet, Gardens Centre, Mill St, Gardens. Essentially a takeaway, this meat-centred deli has an exceptional selection of foods. German specialities include sauerkraut fried with strips of bacon. Mon–Fri until 6pm, Sat until 1pm.

Mr Pickwick's, 158 Long St. Hearty and cheap "tin-plate" meals, including a range of hot and cold "foot-long" sandwiches. Few have been known to finish them, never mind depart hungry. Open so late that no one really knows when, if ever, it closes.

Yellow Pepper, 138 Long St. Good lunch spot near town centre, featuring big plate-glass windows to gawk at bustling Long St, and pasta bakes that will set you fair for a hard afternoon's sightseeing or shopping. Mon–Sat 8.30am–5pm, plus dinner Fri & Sat.

Southern suburbs

Café Carte Blanche, 42a Trill Rd, Observatory. Former curio shop decorated with Eastern artefacts, where you can sip wine under a Persian carpet or quaff beer on a Mongolian bedspread. Small, unique and exotic.

Gardener's Cottage, Montebello Estate, Newlands. Set in a complex of old farm buildings under ancient pine trees, and serving hearty breakfasts and lunches as well as tea and coffee. Worthwhile if you want to browse through the neighbouring arts and crafts workshops. Closed Mon & Sun.

Jonkerhuis, Groot Constantia Wine Estate, Constantia. Enjoy an outdoor lunch or tea surrounded by vineyards and mountains. Daily for breakfast, lunch and dinner.

Kirstenbosch Gardens Tea House, Rhodes Drive, Newlands. Good outdoor English breakfasts and Cape Town's most boring tea (a choice of apple pie or scones) in the lovely gardens at the foot of Table Mountain. Daytime only.

Rhodes Memorial Tea Garden, Rhodes Estate, Rondebosch. Set on the side of Devil's Peak, this is one of Cape Town's best tea gardens, offering views across the city to the sea. Good for snack lunches and teas. Closed Sun morning & Mon.

Atlantic seaboard, Sea Point and Green Point

Chariots Italian Coffee Bar, 107 Main Rd, Green Point. Stylish decor and great, inexpensive food make this a fashionable haunt for Cape Town's yuppies. Come for *focaccia* with simple fillings and good coffee. Daily until 11.30pm.

Giovanni's Deliworld, Main Rd, Green Point. No outdoor seating, but this trendy Italian deli/coffee shop is good for a coffee, snack or takeaway. Daily 8.30am–9pm.

Rieses Delicatessen, 367 Main Rd, Sea Point. Fine sandwiches served up at a local institution, with outdoor seating. Try their salt beef on rye. Daily until mid-evening.

Wimpy, Sea Point Carousel, Beach Rd. Run-down, ramshackle and seedy fast-food outlet with wonderful views.

Fish on the Rocks, beyond Mariner's Wharf, Hout Bay (drive through the dock and factory). Delicious fresh fish and chips, served under red umbrellas or eaten on the rocks overlooking the bay. A fabulous place, during their season, to watch whales. Daily 9am–7pm.

Mariners Wharf Bistro, The Harbour, Hout Bay. Relaxed, well-run place with terrace seating overlooking the harbour. Good for seafood to eat in or take away. Daily 10am–6pm.

Red Herring, corner of Beach Rd and Pine St, Noordhoek. Snacks and drinks on the upstairs deck, which offers marvellous sea and mountain views. Closed Mon.

Suikerbossie, Victoria Drive, Hout Bay. A Cape Town outdoor institution with great views of Hout Bay, making it popular with tourists. This is a fine spot for afternoon tea. Closed evenings and all day Mon.

Nightlife and entertainment

If you've come to Cape Town looking for any especially African or cosmopolitan **entertainment** you're bound to be disappointed. Suburbanites thrive on the usual mid-Atlantic fare of mainstream movies, classical concerts and the odd play, while **clubbing** and **pubbing** tends to cut sharply down ethnic lines with distinct white and coloured venues. The African townships weren't intended by their apartheid planners to be places of pleasure, and never developed much of a club culture.

The fact that segregation still marks out Cape Town's nightlife from Johannesburg's or Durban's may come as a surprise in the legislative capital of the Rainbow Nation, with supposedly the most liberal tradition in the country. However, this owes as much to geography as social attitudes, with Table Mountain, once again, defining the boundary. The City

Bowl is also the **nightlife** centre of Cape Town, with pubs and clubs clustering in the heart of the city and along Kloof Street towards the suburbs.

To find out what's on, check out the daily *Tonight* supplement in the *Cape Argus*, and the Friday *Top of the Times* supplement in the *Cape Times*. Both give fairly comprehensive coverage. Alternatively, look at the *Cape Weekend* supplement to the *Weekend Argus*, which hits the streets on Saturdays and offers similar coverage, with the bonus of quaintly provincial-sounding listings of local activities ranging from big events at the Planetarium to local cake sales.

Pubs, clubs and Cape jazz

The distinction between **clubs** and **pubs** is fuzzy in Cape Town – drinking and dancing often take place at the same venue. Activity is centred around the lower end of **Long and Loop streets**, where you can spend an entire evening strolling around and sampling the nightlife. To a lesser extent the **Waterfront** also holds out the promise of an evening's meandering, with a number of pubs, clubs and coffee bars, but in the more artificial, and safer, mall atmosphere (though some have the distinct plus of overlooking the harbour). The only real indigenous flavour in town, **Cape jazz**, can be found in the coloured clubs on the Cape Flats, where you can also catch **jazzing**, hugely popular ballroom dancing to Fifties' bossa nova and tango. The most famous exponent of the Cape jazz style is the internationally acclaimed **Abdullah Ibrahim** (aka Dollar Brand), but there are scores of other talented performers to look out for.

White clubs in the city centre and inner-city suburbs frequently change names and policy (rather than venue). Cape Town youth is quite capable of getting down and partying, although the sounds and styles tend to be derivative of whatever was going on "overseas" some time ago. The best sources of **information** are the peninsula-wide Good Hope FM (94–97MHz), which specializes in American-style soul and hip-hop and announces forthcoming gigs; and Cape Talk (567kHz), which runs news, features and phone ins. There's also Bush Radio (88.9MHz), a community station that can only be picked up in the city centre and Cape Flats and broadcasts mainly to a coloured audience.

City Bowl and the Waterfront

Angels, The Bronx and Detour, corner of Somerset Rd and Napier St, Green Point. A complex of gay clubs with a courtyard at the back. Daily noon–late.

Club Georgia, 30 Georgia St, off Buitensingel (☎422 0261). Lively over-25s club that celebrates music from across the African continent, including *kwassa kwassa*, *kwaito*, *ndombolo*, *rai*, *kizamba* and *makossa*. Tues–Sat 9.30pm till very late.

Crowbar Pub, 43 Waterkant St. Lively and well-established bar that recreates a London pub.

The Drum Café, 32 Glynn St (☎461 1305). Have a drink and hire a drum for a thumping African cultural experience at this fully licensed venue. Women's Drum Circle on Mon. Light meals available. Cover charge.

The Fireman's Arms, 25 Mechau St. Pub serving first-class steaks at a third of the price of the restaurants.

Green Dolphin Dinner-Jazz Restaurant, Victoria and Alfred Arcade, Waterfront (☎421 7471). Smooth and sophisticated venue with live music every night. Phone to find out about forthcoming attractions.

Kennedy's Cigar Bar, 251 Long St (☎424 1212). Cape Town's best selection of Havana cigars accompanied by good food and live music. Well-ventilated for non-smokers. Mon–Sat noon–2am.

Kimberley Hotel, 48 Roeland St. Frequented by white working-class men, this old pub is full of photographs and memorabilia of Edwardian Cape Town. The delightful upstairs verandah is a good place to survey the passing urban scene.

The Lounge, 194 Long St. Trendy late-night drinking hole in a gorgeous Victorian building. Popular with a twenty-something film-industry set with money to burn.

Manhattan Cafe, 74 Waterkant St. Gay-friendly bar-restaurant serving up cheap eats, where you can sit on the verandah and check out the passing scene or join the throng standing outside with their drinks.

On Broadway, 21 Somerset Rd, Green Point (☎418 8338). Cabaret restaurant-bar with Mediterranean-style food and live performances every night of the week. Drag shows on Sun and Tues.

Perseverance Tavern, 83 Buitenkant St. The oldest pub in town, and mainly a drinking hole for city workers before they trek home to the suburbs. There's a roaring fire in winter and an outdoor patio for warmer weather. Mon–Sat noon–midnight.

The Shebeen on Bree, 25 Bree St. Wire sculptures, and drinks served in tin mugs in a stylized parody of a township drinking dive.

The Stag's Head Hotel, 71 Hope St. Seedy, cockroach-ridden establishment with huge windows looking onto the street. Raucous, rough and sometimes scary. It's bliss for pool players, with tables upstairs and down.

Sweeney's Fun Pub, 94 Strand St. Dark and vibey bar with dancing and pool. The place to come if you're into *kwaito* and hip-hop.

Southern suburbs

Don Pedro's, 113 Roodebloem Rd, Woodstock. Late-night arty hangout that feels like a corner café, with a motley collection of non-matching tables and chairs. Linger all evening over a beer or a coffee without feeling hassled.

Heidelberg Tavern, 94 Station Rd, Observatory. Based on a German bierkeller, this student hangout near the university has long wooden tables and an outdoor beer garden.

Peddars on the Bend, Spaanschemat River Rd, Constantia (☎794 7747). Posh bar at one of the posher restaurants in the poshest suburb with a delightful outdoor area shaded by oaks.

The Planet, 87 Station Rd, Observatory. A local institution and great venue for hanging out until late.

Atlantic seaboard

Ambassador Hotel, 34 Victoria Rd, Bantry Bay. Snotty bar attached to a smart hotel, with stunning cliff and sea views.

Chapman's Peak Hotel, Main Rd, Hout Bay. Beautiful for sunsets over the bay, accompanied by greasy and delicious *calamari*.

Dizzy Jazz Café, 41 Camps Bay Drive, Camps Bay. Crowded and lively nightspot with a big verandah, draught beer and sea views. Live jazz on Fridays and Saturdays.

La Med Bar and Restaurant, Glen Country Club, Victoria Rd, Clifton (☎438 5600). Overlooking the rocks at Clifton, this is a favourite place for hang-gliders from Lion's Head to drop in after landing in the field adjacent to the pub.

False Bay seaboard

Muizenberg Station, Main Rd, Muizenberg. Favoured haunt of local fishermen and great views upstairs at *La Mer* restaurant.

Cape Flats

Baker Street Jazz Club, Halt Rd/28th Ave. Large, live jazz club and one of the best places for jazz dancing. Wed, Fri & Sat.

Blue Note, Club Galaxy, Cine 400, College Rd, Rylands. One of Cape Town's oldest jazz venues, much favoured by serious musicians.

Club Lenin, 2 Old Klipfontein Rd, Athlone (☎696 4144). Resident DJ, good live jazz and R&B. Check the local *Athlone News* for ads featuring what's on. Fri night and Sat afternoon till late.

Club Vibe, corner Castor and Rigel roads, Landsdowne (☎762 8962). Fast Eddi is the resident jock, the sounds are jazz, R&B and beats, and the food includes sausage rolls and pies. Decide how old you feel and pick your slot: Fri night 18–21 year olds; Sat afternoon 16–21; and Sat night strictly for fogeys over 21.

Classical music

Although you won't be coming to Cape Town specifically for its **classical music**, there are a handful of venues with decent programmes. However, the only real reason to go to a concert here is to enjoy the combination of music and wonderful outdoor settings during the summer at the Kirstenbosch National Botanical Gardens and the Josephine Mill. Scan the *Cape Times* or the *Cape Argus* to find out what's on at the venues below.

The Baxter Theatre, Main Rd, Rondebosch (☎685 7880). Occasional opera performances and lunchtime concerts in an impressive auditorium.

Josephine Mill, Boundary Rd, Newlands (☎686 4939). The Nedbank Summer Concert Season delivers a varied menu of outdoor music along the Liesbeek River, including classical and choral performances on Sundays from November to March.

Kirstenbosch Botanical Gardens, Rhodes Drive, Newlands (☎762 1166). A stunning venue, whatever the music, at the foot of Table Mountain. The Appletiser Summer Sunset Concerts provide an eclectic programme to accompany your picnic.

Natale Labia Museum, 192 Main Rd, Muizenberg (☎788 4106). Chamber music on the fourth Sunday of every month, in this imitation Baroque former residence of the Italian consul.

Theatre, performance and cinema

Live performance is suffering in the new South Africa as resources are being directed towards essentials like restructuring education, and away from what is seen as elitist activity, such as **theatre**. While there are some fine playwrights in the country, exciting performances are few and far between. Your best bet of catching something good is by checking out what's on at the province's showpiece theatre, the Nico, or the more innovative Baxter. It's worth keeping an eye on the press, as there are occasional surprises.

Theatres

Baxter Theatre Complex, Main Rd, Rondebosch (☎685 7880). Administered by the University of Cape Town, the Baxter houses three theatres. It has attempted to accommodate the changing face of South Africa by putting on visiting shows from Jo'burg, as well as classical and contemporary material.

Little Theatre, University of Cape Town, Orange St (☎480 7129). Showcase for innovative work from the University drama school.

Maynardville Open-Air Theatre, corner of Church and Wolfe streets, Wynberg (☎421 5470). Exclusively Shakespearean works performed in the park and under the stars during January and February.

Nico Theatre Complex, DF Malan St, Foreshore (☎421 5470). Opera house and two theatres, home to CAPAB, the Western Cape's theatre company. High-quality productions of classical and contemporary theatre, with belated attempts to explore indigenous forms.

Theatre on the Bay, Link St, Camps Bay (☎438 3301). Farces, reviews and lightweight comedies are the standard fare.

Cinema

South Africa's indigenous film industry is fledgling at best, and the local taste for **cinema** runs mostly to mainstream Hollywood. All the major cinemas advertise daily in the *Cape Times* and the *Cape Argus*. The two main movie companies, Ster-Kinekor and

Nu Metro, have a number of multi-screen complexes in the city centre and the suburbs. Most convenient for visitors are the Nu-Metro Victoria and Alfred Waterfront (☎419 9700) in the centre; and the Ster-Kinekor Cavendish Commercial (☎683 6328 or 683 6329) and Ster-Kinekor Cinema Nouveau (☎683 4063 or 683 4064), both in the Cavendish Square shopping complex along Main Road, Claremont, in the southern suburbs.

Cape Town has two art cinemas: the Labia, 68 Orange St (☎424 5927), which has a relaxed atmosphere and is conveniently central just across from the Company's Gardens; and the Baxter, Main Rd, Rondebosch (☎689 1069). Neither advertises widely, so pop in for one of their programmes, or give them a call. Worth noting also is the Imax Cinema at the Waterfront (see p.98).

Outdoor activities

Capetonians take their **leisure** seriously and the city provides every opportunity for pitting yourself against all four elements, whether riding the winds on a sailboard, hangglider or even a kite; tackling the oceans with surfboard or scuba gear; coming down the mountain on a rope or bike; or simply letting everyone else get on with it while you soak in the sun, sink a few beers and watch the cricket.

Spectator sports

Cricket This is keenly followed by many Capetonians, with international and local events taking place at Newlands Cricket Ground, 61 Campground Rd, Newlands (☎64 4146). If there's anything going on in town, it will almost certainly get high-profile coverage in the press.

Rugby Exceeding even cricket as an obsession, rugby manages to bring South Africa's white community to a virtual standstill of TV-watching. Newlands Stadium, on Campground Road in Newlands, is one of the country's major venues for international and provincial contests.

Running The Two Oceans Marathon, another of the Cape's big events, is in fact a 56km marathon and a half, and takes place every April.

Participation sports

Abseiling You can slide off Table Mountain or Chapman's Peak with Abseil Africa (☎424 1580) for around R200 for a half-day trip.

Bird-watching The peninsula's varied habitats attract nearly 400 different species of bird. Fertile ground for the activity is on Lion's Head, in Kirstenbosch Gardens and the Cape of Good Hope Nature Reserve, as well as at Kommetjie and Hout Bay; you can find out about guided outings through the Cape Bird Club (☎686 8795). For a more institutionalized experience, there's World of Birds, Valley Rd, Hout Bay (☎790 2730; see p.110 for more).

Golf The Milnerton course, Bridge Rd, Milnerton (☎52 1047), is tucked in between a lagoon and the Table Bay and boasts classic views of Table Mountain. Other popular local courses are at Rondebosch Golf Club, Klipfontein Rd, Rondebosch (☎689 4176), and Royal Cape Golf Club, 174 Ottery Rd, Wynberg (☎761 6551).

Gyms Health and Racquet clubs are upmarket but well-appointed gyms dotted around the peninsula. Contact their head office (☎710 8500) to find out where the nearest one is to you.

Horse-riding Horse Trail Safaris, Indicator Lodge, Skaapskraal Rd, Ottery (☎73 4396), offer riding along Strandfontein and Muizenberg beaches; and Sleepy Hollow Horse Riding, Sleepy Hollow Lane, Noordhoek (☎789 2341) cover the spectacular Noordhoek Beach. Both cost around R50 for ninety minutes.

Kite-flying The Kite Shop (☎421 6231) can bring you face to face with another friend of the Cape southeaster – power-kite flying. You can harness yourself up to big, powerful kites for some exhilarating adventures on buggies and skis, from R350.

Mountain-biking Downhill Adventures (mobile ☎082 459 2422), whose meeting point is on the corner of Bree and Wale streets in the city centre, take organized mountain biking trips down Table

Mountain, around Cape Point and through the Winelands from R180 for a full day. Also try Rent'n'Ride, 1 Park Rd, Mouille Point (☎434 1122), for bike rental, from R60 a day.

Paragliding Fun 2 Fly (☎557 9735) offer one-day, one-and-a-half day and full-licence courses, from R350 to R2500.

Road cycling The 105km Cape Argus Pick'n'Pay Cycle Tour, the largest individually timed bike race in the world with over 25,000 participants, takes place in early March. Entries close in early January: contact Pedal Power Association (☎689 8420), who also organize fun rides from Sep to May. Otherwise, cycling is popular all over the peninsula, and is a great way to take in the scenery.

Rock climbing You can learn how to rock-climb up Table Mountain's famous facade with the Cape Town School of Mountaineering (☎619 604), who charge R750 for a four-day course.

Inline skating (rollerblading) Especially popular along the long, smooth promenade that runs from Mouille Point to Sea Point, inline skating is a growing activity. You can rent blades from Rent 'n' Ride, 1 Park Rd, Mouille Point (☎434 1122), for about R30 for two hours.

Sailing Cape Town's largest seafaring event is the biennial Cape to Rio Yacht Race, held in January in even years. If this is too long to wait, you might consider one of the more modest cruises, most of which leave from the Waterfront. From here you can pick up countless Robben Island cruises (but only the official one docks at the island, see p.98), sunset outings into Table Bay, and the romantic two-hour trip to Clifton and back that includes a bottle of bubbly.

Scuba diving Cape waters are cold but can be clear and are good for wrecks. For information and arranging courses, equipment, rental and dives, contact: Atlantic Underwater Club, Bay Rd, Mouille Point (☎439 0701 or ☎439 9322); Ocean Divers International, Protea Ritz, Main Rd, Sea Point (☎439 1803); Orca Industries, corner of Herschel and Bowood roads, Claremont (☎61 9673); and Time Out Adventures, Avalon Building, 8 Mill St, Gardens (☎461 2709).

Surfing Top spots include Big Bay at Bloubergstrand, where competitions are held every summer, Llandudno, Muizenberg, Kalk Bay, and Long Beach at Kommetjie and Noordhoek. For further information, contact the Western Province Surfing Association (☎64 2972).

Surf skiing/canoeing/kayaking Contact Coastal Kayak Trails (☎551 8739).

Swimming There are surf livesaver patrols on duty at Milnerton, Camps Bay, Llandudno, Muizenberg and Fish Hoek beaches. Snorkelling trips to swim with seals at Seal Island are arranged by Hout Bay Two Ocean Divers (☎438 9317), from R180, including all gear. For pools, try Long St Swimming Pool, Long St (☎400 3302), Cape Town's only heated indoor pool; Newlands Swimming Pool, corner of Main and San Souci roads, Newlands (☎64 4197), is an Olympic-sized chlorinated pool. Sea Point Swimming Pool, Beach Rd, Sea Point (☎434 3341), is an enormous and wonderful sea-water pool.

Walking and rock climbing The best places for gentle strolls are Newlands Forest, up from Rhodes Memorial, and any beaches. For longer walks, head for anywhere on Table Mountain (see p.107), Tokai Forest, Silvermine Nature Reserve or Cape Point Nature Reserve. For guided rock-climbing (R600 for two maximum) or mountain walks (from R250 each for two, to R125 each for five or more), contact Richard Behne (☎448 2697). Jill Lockley (☎75 6136) is a registered guide who can take you along any of the major Table Mountain ascents and provide informed commentary on natural history; she also does less strenous outings in the Silvermine reserve on the lower slopes of the mountain. You can also try the South African Mountain Guides Association (☎447 8036).

Windsurfing In summer most Capetonians moan about the howling southeaster; if you've got a smile on your face, though, you're probably into windsurfing. Langebaan, 75min north of Cape Town, is one of the best spots; otherwise the place to go is Bloubergstrand. The Blouberg Windsurf Centre (☎56 1663, *blouwind@mweb.co.za*) rents equipment, cars with racks and has long-term accommodation at Bloubergstrand, as well as being able to offer general advice to its clients, such as which airlines offer free carriage of windsurfing equipment. For further help, contact Cape Windsurf Centre, Langebaan (☎022/772 1114).

Shopping

Cape Town's **Waterfront** is the country's most popular **shopping** venue, but beautiful as it is, it lacks the grittier feel of the city centre. You can buy all the functional goods you'll need at the Waterfront and all the most upmarket shops are here too, but you should expect to pay above the odds for everything. For crafts, second-hand books, antiques and food you'll be better off looking to the city centre and the suburban shopping areas.

Arts, crafts, souvenirs and curios

Cape Town is not known for its indigenous **arts and crafts** in the way, say, that Durban is, and much of the stuff you'll buy here is from elsewhere in Africa. Goods from Zimbabwe and Zambia are particularly well represented. There are several places in the city centre and the Waterfront, but you'll often pick up the same arts and crafts for a lot less money at the sidewalk **markets** scattered around town.

African Image, branches at corner of Church and Burg streets, city centre, and Shop 6228 at Victoria Wharf on the Waterfront. Your best port of call for authentic African arts and crafts, from fabrics, antique sculpture to beadwork, but goods are a little overrated and overpriced.

Le Bon Ton...& Art, 209 Bree St, city centre. Art supermarket with exciting new works by as-yet-unknown artists. Light snacks served.

Cape Town Station, Forecourt, Adderley St, city centre. Thronging ranks of market traders selling radios, leather goods and African crafts. Mon–Fri 8am–5pm, Sat 8am–2pm.

Constantia Craft Market, Alphen Common, corner of Spaanschemat River and Ladies Mile roads, Constantia. Sizeable outdoor flea market where you can pick up good local crafts and items from around the continent, ride a camel or a pony and have a cup of tea. First and last Saturday and first Sunday of the month.

Greenmarket Square, Burg St, city centre. Open-air market that's the best place in town for colourful handmade Cape Town beachwear, from T-shirts to shorts and sandals, as well as a venue for antiques and knick-knacks. Mon–Fri 8am–5pm, Sat 8am–2pm.

Holistic Lifestyle Fair, Observatory Community Hall, off Station and Lower Main roads. Busy mix of the new-age, esoteric and wholesome, held on the first Sunday of each month.

Hout Bay Market, just down from the *Hout Bay Manor*. Tightly packed venue where crafters of all shapes and varieties sell their wares every Sunday.

Milnerton Flea Market, alongside the Milnerton Bridge and Lagoon. Cape Town's great car-boot sale held every weekend, where you stand a fair chance of picking up something worthwhile for a song. Farm eggs rub shells with brass pipes and ephemera.

Out of Africa, Shop 125, Victoria Wharf, Waterfront (☎418 5505). Expensive baskets, beads and African arts and antiques, in the pleasant spending fields of the Waterfront.

Rose Korber, 48 Sedgemoor Rd, Camps Bay (☎438 9152). This should be the first stop for the serious collector, with an exceptional selection of top contemporary art and craft from around the continent.

The Pan African Market, 76 Long St. Multicultural hothouse of township and contemporary art, artefacts, curios and craft that's also a great venue for information and media exchange. There's music, a café specializing in African cuisine, a bookshop, a Cameroonian hairbraider and West African tailors.

The Red Shed Craft Workshop, Victoria Wharf, Waterfront. Craft market where craftworkers make and sell ceramics, textiles, candles and jewellery. Mon–Sat 9am–9pm, Sun 10am–9pm.

Victoria Road Market, about 1km south of Bakoven along the coast road. Carvings, beads, fabrics and baskets sold from the most spectacularly sited market anywhere – on a clifftop viewpoint overlooking the Atlantic.

Waterfront Craft Market, Waterfront. High-quality handcrafted items. Daily 9.30am–6pm.

Books

Long Street is the best place for second-hand and remaindered books, with several highly browsable places, plus you'll find useful books on all aspects of the country on Longmarket Street. For new books there are also some pleasant places in the suburbs or at the Waterfront to mooch away half an hour.

Book Warehouse, Main Rd, Rondebosch (☎64 2230). Small shop expertly staffed, with a fine collection. Mon–Fri 9am–5pm, Sat 9am–1pm.

Clarke's Antiquarian, 211 Long St, city centre (☎423 5739). The best in Cape Town for South African books, with a huge selection on tightly packed shelves, and brilliantly well-informed staff. Mon–Fri 8.45am–5pm, Sat 8.45am–1pm.

Exclusive Books. The friendliest bookshop chain for just browsing away an hour, well-stocked with books and magazines. Branches at: Lower Mall, Cavendish Square, Claremont (Mon–Fri 9am–9pm, Sat 9am–11pm, Sun 10am–9pm; ☎64 3030); Victoria Wharf, Victoria and Alfred Waterfront (Mon–Thur 9am–10.30pm, Fri 9am–11pm, Sat 9am–11pm, Sun 10am–9pm; ☎419 0905); Constantia Village Shopping Centre, Spaanschemat River Rd, Constantia (Mon–Sat 9am–9pm, Sun 10am–5pm; ☎794 7800).

Self-catering: food and wine

It should come as no surprise that **self-catering** is the cheapest way to eat in Cape Town, and it can also be good fun. Apart from *braais*, which take place anywhere at any excuse, there are countless places on beaches, in the forests or up the mountain where you can enjoy a terrific picnic, or you may just want to buy stuff to cook back at your accommodation.

Thanks to the city's cosmopolitan population there are some excellent (if pricey) **delicatessens**, several of which are strung along Main Road, Green Point and Sea Point. Among the many are Giovanni's in Green Point, for delicious Italian foods, while the New York Bagel Deli in Sea Point has the best bagels in town and a great selection of Eastern European Jewish fillings.

The easiest places to shop for food are at the large **supermarket chains**, and none is better than Woolworth's, the South African version of the British Marks & Spencer stores. It's excellent for quality fast-cook meals, fresh produce and cold foods, such as olives, houmous and various Mediterranean dips. There are several branches around town, but the most convenient ones are in Adderley Street and at the Claremont shops. In a similar vein, Pick 'n'Pay, which has branches at the Waterfront, Main Road, Camps Bay and Claremont shops, does excellent-value ready-grilled chickens for under R30. The larger branches of the better supermarkets also have fishmonger counters where you can buy **fresh fish**, but by far the most atmospheric way to acquire seafood is at either Kalk Bay or Hout Bay harbours (see pp.110 & 113).

You'll also find delicious food and some unusual **fruit and vegetables** at the more sophisticated farm stalls, such as the Old Cape Farm Stall at the turnoff to Groot Constantia, on Constantia Nek Road. Check out also the fruit and veg sellers on sidewalks and street corners, whose produce is usually cheap and good.

For **wine**, the supermarkets tend to have decent selections at competitive prices, but for more interesting labels and well-informed staff, there are some first-rate specialist wine merchants in town. One of the best known is Vaughan Johnson's, Dock Rd, at the Waterfront, which has a huge range of labels from all over the country, arranged in alphabetical order. There's another good selection at Picardy Liquors, Shop 6, Seeff House, Hans Strydom Avenue, in the city centre.

Listings

Airlines Air France (☎418 8180); Air Namibia (☎421 6685); Air New Zealand (☎419 9382); Air Portugal (☎421 7224); Air Zimbabwe (Compass Tours ☎419 4370); Alitalia (☎418 3386); British Airways (☎683 4203, or toll-free ☎0800/01 1747); KLM Royal Dutch Airlines (☎421 1870 or 934 3495); Lufthansa (☎425 1490 or 934 8534); Nationwide (☎936 2050); Olympic Airways (☎423 0260); Qantas (☎683 4203); SA Airlink (toll-free ☎0800/11 4799); Sabena (☎421 7957); South African Airways (domestic and international ☎936 1111); Sun Air (☎934 0918); Swissair (☎421 4938).

American Express, Thibault House, Thibault Square, city centre (☎21 5586). Full Amex facilities, including help with lost cards.

Banks Main branches are easy to find in the shopping areas of the city centre, the middle-class suburbs and at the Waterfront. Hours are Mon–Fri 8.30am–3.30pm, Sat 8–11am. Wherever you find banks, you'll also find automatic teller machines (ATMs).

Bureaux de change For foreign exchange transactions outside normal banking hours, try one of the following: American Express, Shop 11a, Alfred Mall, Waterfront (Mon–Fri 9am–7pm, Sat & Sun 9am–5pm; ☎419 3917); Rennies Foreign Exchange, Shop 249, main shopping complex, Waterfront (Mon–Sat 9am–7pm, Sun 10am–7pm; ☎418 3744). Rennies Travel, Riebeeck St (Mon–Thurs 8.30am–5pm, Fri 9–11.30am, Sat 9am–noon; ☎425 2370); Trustbank, Cape Town International Airport (open to accommodate international flights; ☎934 0223).

Car parks These are dotted all over the place in this car-friendly city. There are pay-and-display car parks at street level all around the centre, where hustlers will offer to look after your car and clean it for a tip, especially on the Grand Parade and Loop and Church streets. If you want to park in peace, head for one of the multi-storey parking garages; there's one attached to the Golden Acre complex, and another at the north end of Lower Burg St.

Mobile phone rental is available by the day, week or month from Cellucity, Shop 6193, Victoria and Alfred Waterfront (☎418 1306).

Embassies and consulates Australia, 14th Floor, BP Centre, Thibault Square (☎419 5425); Canada, 60 St George's Mall (☎423 5240); UK, Southern Life Centre, 8 Riebeeck St (☎25 3670); USA, 4th Floor, Broadway Centre, Heernegracht (☎21 4280).

Emergencies Ambulance ☎10177; Fire ☎535 1100 or 461 4141; Police (Flying Squad) ☎10111; Police (Tourist Assistance Unit) ☎418 2853; Rape Crisis ☎47 9762.

Gay contacts Gay Escape, 10th Floor, Guarantee House, 37 Burg St (☎23 9001), is a travel agency catering for both men and women, which organizes accommodation, activities and tours as well as providing information on clubs, pubs and parties. There's also the Gay, Lesbian and Bisexual Helpline (☎21 5420).

Hospitals and doctors Doctors are listed in the telephone directory under "Medical". The largest state hospital is Groote Schuur, Hospital Drive, Observatory (☎404 9111), just off the M3. Somerset Hospital, Beach Rd, Mouille Point (☎402 6911), nearer the centre, has outpatient and emergency departments and is convenient for the City Bowl and Atlantic seaboard, although it is generally overcrowded, understaffed and seemingly under-equipped. If you have medical insurance you might prefer to be treated at the private, well-staffed and well-equipped City Park Hospital, Loop St (☎480 6111).

Intercity buses Greyhound, 1 Adderley St (☎418 4312); Intercape, Old Marine Drive (☎386 4400); and Translux, next to Greyhound on Adderley St (☎449 3333).

Pharmacies Hypermed Pharmacy, corner of York and Main roads, Green Point (daily 8.30am–9pm; ☎434 1414); Sunset Pharmacy, Sea Point Medical Centre, Kloof Rd, Sea Point (daily 8.30am–9pm; ☎434 3333); Tamboerskloof Pharmacy, 16 Kloof Nek Rd, Tamboerskloof (daily 9.30am–6pm; ☎424 4450).

Police Head office: Caledon Square, Buitenkant St (☎467 8000); Tourist Assistance Unit, Tulbagh Square (☎418 2853).

Post office The main branch, on Parliament St (Mon, Tues, Thurs & Fri 8am–4.30pm, Wed 8.30am–4.30pm, Sat 8am–noon; ☎464 1700), has a poste restante and enquiry desk.

Taxis There are a number of reliable companies, including Marine Taxi Hire (☎434 0434), Rikkis (☎423 4888 or 423 4892), Sea Point Taxis (☎434 4444), and Unicab (☎448 1720).

Telephones There are phone booths all over Cape Town taking phone cards and coins. For cash calls there are phones at the Main Post Office, Parliament St (Mon–Sat 8am–9.45pm, Sun and public holidays 9.30am–8.30pm).

travel details

Cape Town's undisputed status as the tourism hub of South Africa has meant the development of an excellent network of connections to the rest of the country. **Flying** from Cape Town airport (flight information ☎934 0407) is the quickest though most expensive way of getting around, and useful if you need to cover large distances. As far as overland travel goes, the intercity **express buses**, run by Greyhound (☎418 4312), Intercape (☎386 4400) and Translux (☎449 3333), offer a frequent, comprehensive and inexpensive service connecting Cape Town to major centres in the coastal provinces of **Northern**, **Western** and **Eastern Cape**, and **KwaZulu-Natal**. All have good connections to **Pretoria** and **Johannesburg**, which are on the same route. Besides the intercity express buses detailed above, there are Baz **backpacker buses**, the cheapest way to get around; services run constantly to and fro from Cape Town. The Baz Bus (☎439 2323) leaves Cape Town daily and runs along the coast as far as Port Elizabeth (a 14hr journey), with connections from there to Durban (also a 14hr journey) five times a week. There is little to recommend the long train trips to Johannesburg and Durban, which cross some of South Africa's dreariest terrain, though Spoornet (☎449 3871) run a beautiful weekly **train** journey along the Garden Route between Cape Town and Port Elizabeth.

Trains

Two useful trains are the **Metro Rail** suburban services connecting Cape Town with Stellenbosch and Paarl (both 1hr). Outside peak morning and evening hours, trains are irregular but run at approximately two-hour intervals; check that

they're running on time. **Mainline trains** are slow, but can provide a relaxing way of traversing long routes:

Cape Town to: Bloemfontein (every Mon; 23hr); Durban (every Mon; 36hr 25min); Johannesburg (1 daily; 24hr 55min); Kimberley (1 daily; 16hr 30min); Pietermaritzburg (every Mon; 34hr); Port Elizabeth (every Fri; 24hr); Pretoria (1 daily; 26hr 20min).

Intercity buses

Cape Town to: Bloemfontein (5–6 daily; 13hr); Cradock (1 daily; 10hr); Durban (3 daily; 20hr); East London (3 daily; 15hr 40min); George (4 daily; 6hr); Graaff Reinet (1–2 daily; 9hr); Grahamstown (1 daily; 12hr 25min); Johannesburg (4 daily; 17hr); Kimberley (1 daily except Wed; 11hr 45min); Knysna (4 daily; 6hr 50min); Montagu (3 weekly; 4hr); Mossel Bay (4 daily; 5hr 15min); Oudtshoorn (3 weekly; 6hr 15min); Pietermaritzburg (2 daily; 18hr 40min); Plettenberg Bay (4 daily; 7hr 30min); Port Elizabeth (4 daily; 10hr); Pretoria (4 daily; 18hr); Sedgefield (4 weekly; 6hr 45min); Stellenbosch (1–2 daily; 1hr); Storms River (4 daily; 10hr 10min); Umtata (1 daily; 18hr); Upington (4 weekly; 10hr 30min); Wilderness (4 daily; 6hr 30min); Windhoek (4 weekly; 16hr 30min).

Flights

Cape Town to: Bloemfontein (2–3 daily; 2hr 20min); Durban (10 daily; 2hr); East London (4 daily; 2hr); George (3–4 daily; 1hr); Johannesburg (16 daily; 2hr); Kimberley (1 daily; 3hr); Port Elizabeth (4 daily; 1hr 30min); Upington (6 weekly; 1hr 45min); Walvis Bay (2 weekly; 2hr); Windhoek (5 weekly; 2hr).

CHAPTER TWO

THE WESTERN CAPE

Most mountainous and arguably most beautiful of all South Africa's provinces, the **Western Cape** is also the most popular area of the country among tourists. Curiously, it's also the least African province. Visitors spend weeks here without exhausting its attractions, but frequently find themselves leaving slightly disappointed, never having quite got wind of an African beat. Of South Africa's nine provinces, only the Western Cape and the Northern Cape don't have an African majority; one person in five here is African, and the largest community, making up 55 percent of the population, are coloureds – people of mixed race descended from white settlers, indigenous Khoisan people and slaves from the East.

Although the Western Cape appears to conform more closely to the First World than any other part of the country, the impression is strictly superficial. Beneath the prosperous feel of the Winelands and the Garden Route lies a reality of Third World poverty in **squatter camps** on the outskirts of well-to-do towns and on some farms where nineteenth-century labour practices prevail, despite the end of apartheid.

Nevertheless, you can't fail to be moved by the sensuous physical beauty of the province's mountains, valleys and beaches. The **Winelands**, less than an hour from Cape Town, give full reign to the sybaritic pleasures of eating, drinking and visual feasting. Dutch colonial heritage reaches its peak in this region of gabled homesteads sitting among vineyards against a backdrop of slaty crags.

To the northeast lies the **Breede River Valley**, a region usually bypassed along the N1 en route to Johannesburg, but featuring among its faceless fruit-farming towns some hideaways, such as Greyton and McGregor, favoured by Capetonians as weekend retreats. Further east, the country opens into the timeless landscapes of the **Little Karoo**, the curtain-raiser to the semi-desert that drifts across one-third of South Africa's surface, and is nowhere more rewarding nor more easily accessed than here. Less visited than it deserves, the Little Karoo is skirted by the N1 to its north and the N2 to its south, and offers a succession of dramatic – sometimes hair-raising – **passes** switch-backing across one mountain range after another.

Southeast of the Winelands, the **Overberg** – roughly the area between Arniston and Mossel Bay along the coast, and as far inland as Swellendam – is another region that remains hidden behind the mountains during a hasty journey east. The **Whale Coast**, an angry stretch of Indian Ocean to the south that has claimed hundreds of ships, is known for being the best area in the country for shore-based **whale-watching**, and there are a couple of pleasant coastal towns off the main routes along here.

The best-known name in the Western Cape is the **Garden Route**, a drive along the N2 that technically begins at **Mossel Bay**, where the freeway hits the coast, and continues east for 185km to **Storms River**. In reality it is taken as part of a journey between Cape Town and Port Elizabeth, simply because these are the easiest places to catch flights and to pick up and drop off rental cars. The Garden Route proper can be driven in half a day, but to cover it so quickly would mean missing its essence, which can be found off the road in its coastal towns, lagoons, mountains and ancient forests, the highlight being the **Tsitsikamma National Park**, where the dark Storms River opens spectacularly into the Indian Ocean. Partly because it lies along a single stretch of freeway, **public transport** along the Garden Route is better than anywhere in the

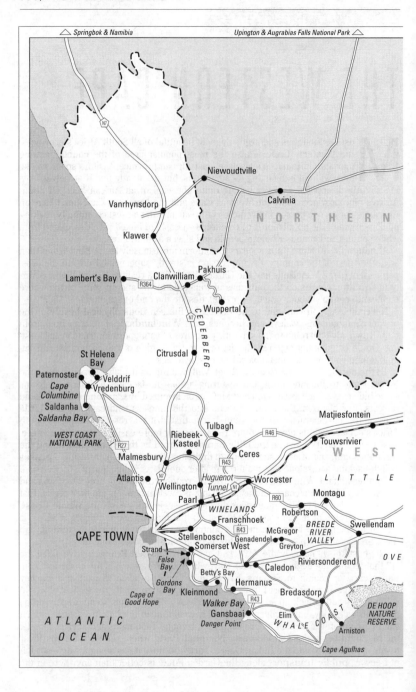

△ Springbok & Namibia
Upington & Augrabies Falls National Park △

Niewoudtville

Calvinia

N O R T H E R N

Vanrhynsdorp

Klawer

Pakhuis

Lambert's Bay   Clanwilliam

Wuppertal

C E D E R B E R G

Citrusdal

St Helena
Bay

Paternoster
Cape
Columbine   Velddrif
Vredenburg

Saldanha
Saldanha Bay

Matjiesfontein

WEST COAST
NATIONAL PARK

Tulbagh

R46

Touwsrivier

Riebeek-
Kasteel

Ceres

W E S T

Malmesbury

R43

L I T T L E

Atlantis

Huguenot
Tunnel

Worcester

Montagu

Wellington

R60

Paarl

WINELANDS

Robertson

Franschhoek

McGregor

Swellendam

CAPE TOWN

Stellenbosch

R43

BREEDE
RIVER
VALLEY

Strand

Somerset West

Genadendel
Greyton

O V E

False
Bay

Gordons
Bay

Betty's Bay

Caledon

Riviersonderend

Cape of
Good Hope

Kleinmond

Hermanus

Bredasdorp

DE HOOP
NATURE
RESERVE

Walker Bay   R43

Gansbaai
Danger Point

Elim

W H A L E   C O A S T

Arniston

ATLANTIC

OCEAN

Cape Agulhas

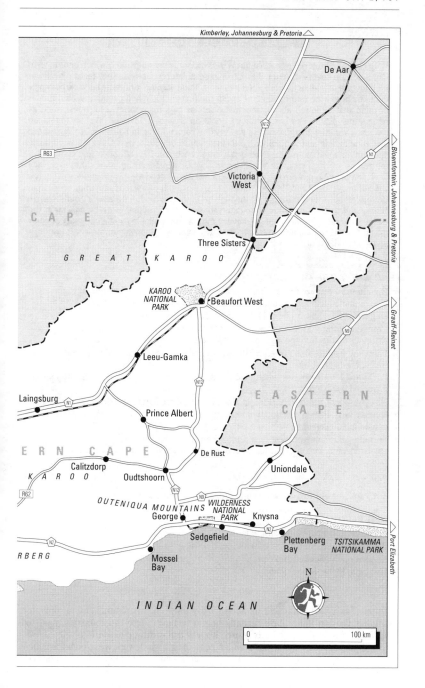

TACKLING THE WINELANDS

With over one hundred estates in the **Winelands**, the big question is which ones to visit. Our selection covers wineries that are of general interest because they feature beautiful architecture or scenery, or are entertaining in some way, not primarily because they produce the best wine (although some are in the first rank). When planning your trip bear in mind that although all the wineries offer tastings many offer a lot more, such as restaurants, picnics and horse-riding. Choose an area to explore and don't try to take on too many wineries in a day unless you want to return home in a dizzy haze. Remember that wine tasting and wine buying are supposed to be fun, so don't take it too seriously and don't take on too much. Even if you aren't a wine buff, you'll often find staff at tasting rooms are happy to talk you through a wine, which can be interesting, especially once you begin to pick up the characteristics of different wines. Most estates will charge a fee of between R2 and R8 for a wine-tasting session. If you plan on anything more than the briefest of tours, think about buying the authoritative John Platter's *South African Wine Guide*, which provides up-to-date ratings of the produce of every winery in the country. *Wine* magazine, published every month and available from all newsagents, has useful features on wineries, places to eat, wine reviews, information on latest bottlings and a diary of events.

ROUGH GUIDE FAVOURITE ESTATES

Boschendal Estate, Franschhoek (see p.158). Best-organized mass-tourist venue offering conducted tours, beautiful buildings, shops and a choice of restaurants.
Delaire, Stellenbosch (see p.148). Best mountain view across the Helshoogte Pass.
Cabrière Estate, Franschhoek (see p.157). Most eccentric uncorking using sabrage – slicing clean through the neck of a bubbly bottle with a sabre.
Fairview Estate, Paarl (see p.154). Great family venue with a famous goat tower, peacocks, cheese and wine.
La Motte Estate, Franschhoek (see p.158). Best tasting room, decorated with marble, glass and oak barrels.
Rhebokskloof Estate, Paarl (see p.154). Trendiest restaurant, overlooking a swan lake.
Rustenberg Estate, Stellenbosch (see p.147). Most bucolic setting, with a historic gabled milking shed.
Vergelegen, Somerset West (see p.148). The estate that has it all: fabulous buildings, a small museum, beautiful gardens, good wines to taste and a choice of restaurants.

ROUGH GUIDE FAVOURITE LABELS

An A to Z of old favourites, rising stars and plain good value

OLD FAVOURITES
Backsberg, Paarl. Whites and reds.
Blaauwklippen, Stellenbosch. Whites and reds.
Kanonkop, Stellenbosch. Reds.
Lievland, Stellenbosch. Reds.

country. Taking advantage of its accessibility and obvious natural charm, operators along the Garden Route have recently begun turning it into the country's most concentrated strip for packaged **adventure sports** and **outdoor activities**.

North of Cape Town, the less popular, remote and windswept **west coast** is usually explored during the wildflower months of August and September, when visitors con-

Meerlust, Stellenbosch. Whites and reds.
Overgaauw, Paarl. Reds.
Rust en Vrede, Stellenbosch. Reds.
Simonsig, Stellenbosch. Whites and reds.
Villiera, Paarl. Whites and reds.

HOT TIPS
Brampton, Rustenberg Estate, Stellenbosch. Whites and reds.
Fairview, Paarl. Whites and reds.
Glen Carlou, Paarl. Whites and reds.
Hartenberg, Stellenbosch. Reds.
Klawervlei, Stellenbosch. Reds.
Klein Constantia, Constantia. Whites and reds.
Morgenhof, Stellenbosch. Whites and reds.
Plaisir de Merle, Simonsberg. Whites and reds.
Saxenburg, Stellenbosch. Reds.
Veenwouden, Paarl. Reds.

RISING STARS
Buitenverwachting, Constantia. Whites and reds.
Grangehurst, Stellenbosch. Reds.
Jordan, Stellenbosch. Whites.
Mulderbosch, Stellenbosch. White and Faithful Hound (red blend).
Stellenzicht, Stellenbosch. Whites and reds.
Thelema, Stellenbosch. Whites and reds.
Vergelegen, Somerset West. Whites and reds.

VALUE FOR MONEY
Backsberg, Paarl. Cabernet Sauvignon, Merlot, Shiraz, Pinotage.
Bergendal, Stellenbosch. Bergenblanc and Bergenrood.
Chateau Libertas, Stellenbosch. Red blend.
De Leuwen Jagt, Paarl. Cabernet Sauvignon-Merlot blend.
Fairview, Paarl. Range of whites and reds.
Fleur du Cap, Bergkleder winery, Stellenbosch. Merlot, Shiraz and noble late-harvest dessert wine.
Hartenberg, Stellenbosch. Cabernet-Shiraz blend.
Lievland, Stellenbosch. Lievlander red blend.
Nederburg, Paarl. Kap Sekt champagne-style bubbly.
Pongrácz, Bergkleder winery, Stellenbosch. Cap classique, champagne-style bubbly.
Villiera, Paarl. Huge range of whites, reds and Tradition (Carte Rouge), a champagne-style bubbly.
Vlottenburg, Stellenbosch. Cabernet Sauvignon, Merlot, Pinotage.

verge on its centrepiece, the **West Coast National Park**. Its other major pull is the **Cederberg** mountain range, 200km north of Cape Town on the N7, a rocky wilderness with hikes and hidden rock-art sites.

Apart from the annual explosion of wild flowers in the north, the Western Cape really scores on wilderness and flora, and is South Africa's **fynbos province**. The plants you'll glimpse from afar all along the coast and up every mountainside look like a non-descript grey-green blur of vegetation, but on closer examination reveal a rich kingdom of delicate flowering species that rival the Amazon Forest for biodiversity.

Several national parks and nature reserves make excellent places to explore fynbos, as do all the hikes mentioned in this chapter, but you shouldn't expect to see much African wildlife here. Most reserves have a few zebra or antelope, but the big game disappeared donkey's years ago – reflecting the fact that South Africa's longest-colonized province was also the first to taste the devastatingly destructive power of firearms. By the same means, indigenous **Khoikhoi and San people** were virtually extinguished in the nineteenth century and **Africans** kept at arm's length, some 1000km away on the "Eastern Frontier", which accounts for their relatively small numbers in the Western Cape.

THE WINELANDS

South Africa has over a dozen recognized wine routes extending to the Karoo and way into the Northern Cape, but the area known as **the Winelands** is restricted to the oldest wineries outside the Peninsula, which are within a sixty-kilometre radius of Cape Town. The district takes in the earliest European settlements at Stellenbosch, Paarl, Franschhoek and Somerset West, each with its own wine route. On the hillsides and in the valleys around these towns you'll find a flawless blending of traditional Cape Dutch **architecture** with landscape.

The Winelands are best covered in your own car, as half the pleasure is the drive through the countryside. Without private transport, your most sensible option is to head for **Stellenbosch**, which is served by regular trains from Cape Town. The most satisfying of the Wineland towns, it enjoys an easy elegance, beautiful streetscapes, a couple of decent museums and plenty of visitor facilities. If you're in a car, one of the region's scenic highlights is the drive along the R310 through the **Helshoogte Pass** between Stellenbosch and Paarl, which can also be reached on the Metro Rail link from Cape Town. The workaday farming town of the region, Paarl is credited as the place where Afrikaans first sprang to recognition, and has an Afrikaans language monument and a museum to honour the fact. Smallest of the Wineland towns, **Franschhoek** has the most magnificent setting at the head of a narrow valley, and has established itself as the culinary capital of the Cape. By contrast, the sprawling town of **Somerset West** has only one drawcard, but it's an outstanding one – **Vergelegen**, by far the most stunning of all the Wineland estates, which can be tacked onto a tour of the Stellenbosch wine route.

Summer is the best time to visit, when days are longer, as are opening hours, the vines are in leaf and there's activity at the wineries. In winter the wine has been made, there are fewer cellar tours and there's not much going on. Several estates offer lunches, while some allow picnics in their grounds – a great idea if you're travelling with children or simply want to drink in the mountainous views in a bucolic haze.

Stellenbosch

Dappled avenues of three-century-old oaks are the defining feature of **STELLENBOSCH**, 46km east of Cape Town – a fact reflected in its Afrikaans nickname Die Eikestad (the oak city). Street frontages of the same vintage, sidewalk cafés, water furrows and a European town layout centred on the Braak, a large village green, add up to a well-rooted urban texture that invites casual exploration. The city is the undisputed heart of the Winelands, having more urban attractions than either Paarl or Franschhoek, while at the same time being at the hub of the largest and oldest of the Cape **wine routes**.

The city is also home to Stellenbosch University, Afrikanerdom's most prestigious educational institution, which does something to enliven the atmosphere. But even the heady promise of plentiful alcohol and thousands of students haven't changed the fact that at heart this is a conservative place, which was once the intellectual engine room of apartheid, and fostered the likes of Dr H.F. Verwoerd, the prime minister who dreamed up Grand Apartheid. Today, the white establishment still has roots firmly in the National Party, the Dutch Reformed Church and the Broederbond (an Afrikaner secret society strongly linked to the National Party).

Some history

One of the first actions of **Simon van der Stel** after arriving at the Cape in November 1679 to take over as Dutch East India commander was to explore the area along the Eerste River (first river), where he came upon an enchanting little valley. Less than a month later it appeared on maps as Stellenbosch (Stel's bush), the first of several places dotted around the Cape, including Simonsberg overlooking the town, which the governor was to name after himself or members of his family.

Charged by the Dutch East India Company directors in the Netherlands with opening up the Cape interior, van der Stel soon settled the first **free burghers** in Stellenbosch. Within eight years, 60 freehold grants had been made and the area was regarded as full. Within 25 years Stellenbosch was established as a prosperous, semi-feudal society dominated by landowners, and in 1702 the Danish traveller, Abraham Bogaert, admired how it had "grown with fine dwellings, and how great a treasure of wine and grain is grown here". Eight years on, some of those fine thatch-roofed houses were destroyed by fire, but were soon rebuilt, and by the end of the century there were over 1000 houses and some substantial burgher estates in and around Stellenbosch, many of which are still standing.

Arrival, information and getting around

Coming to Stellenbosch **by car** gives you the freedom to explore the surrounding wineries at your leisure. The drive from Cape Town takes under an hour along either the N1 or N2. Metro Rail **trains** (information ☎021/449 2991) commute between Cape Town and Stellenbosch roughly every two hours during the day, and take about an hour. Infrequent (and expensive) intercity buses from Cape Town and Port Elizabeth pass through Stellenbosch, calling at the train station; again it's around an hour's journey.

The busy **tourist information** bureau, about 1km from the station at 36 Market St(Mon–Fri 8am–5.30pm, Sat 9am–5pm, Sun 9.30am–4.30pm; ☎021/883 3584, fax 883 8017, *eikestad@iafrica.com*), can provide basic information on local attractions, and can supply you with the *Discover Stellenbosch on Foot* leaflet, which describes a walking tour covering a daunting 62 sites.

The centre of Stellenbosch is small enough to explore on foot, but if you need to get further afield, contact Rikkis (☎021/887 2203), who provide transport in **tuk-tuks** that roam around collecting and dropping off passengers. They also offer excursions to wineries for around R25 per person per farm. For **car rental**, try Premier Rent-a-Car (☎021/883 9103) at 100 Bird St.

For **Winelands tours**, you don't have to be staying at *Stumble Inn* (see "Accommodation" on p.143)) to join their reasonably priced daytime packages (10.45am–5pm); they also do evening outings (6–9.30pm) to Kyamandi African

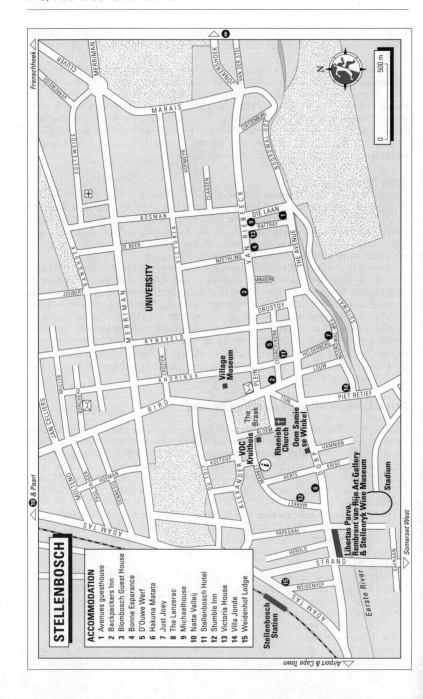

STELLENBOSCH

ACCOMMODATION
1 Avenues guesthouse
2 Backpackers Inn
3 Blombosch Guest House
4 Bonne Esperance
5 D'Ouwe Werf
6 Hakuna Matata
7 Just Joey
8 The Lanzerac
9 Michaelhouse
10 Natte Vallei
11 Stellenbosch Hotel
12 Stumble Inn
13 Victoria House
14 Villa Jonde
15 Weidenhof Lodge

township, including eating and drinking. Roland's Tours & Taxis (mobile ☎082/576 1539) are a slightly pricier alternative for getting around the region's vineyards, but make sense if you want a more customized outing.

Accommodation

Stellenbosch has no shortage of **places to stay** and covers the field from backpackers' lodges to total luxury. Apart from the handful of out-of-town farmstays and the luxurious *Lanzerac*, all the accommodation is within easy walking distance of the town centre.

Backpackers' lodges

Backpackers Inn, De Wet Centre, corner of Bird and Church streets (☎021/887 2020, *bacpac1@global.co.za*). Stellenboschs' most central backpackers' lodge exudes a squeaky-clean atmosphere that attracts travellers of all ages and makes it highly suitable for families. Dorms and doubles ①.

Hakuna Matata, 100 Dorp St (☎021/887 0841, fax 856 2128). Two-storey historic building with a licensed bar, patio *braai* area, and the distinction of having a resident fly-fishing guide who takes trips to local lakes and streams. Dorms ①, en-suite doubles ②.

Stumble Inn, 12 Market St (☎ & fax 021/887 4049, *stumble@iafrica.com*). The town's best and oldest established hostel in two turn-of-the century houses, with friendly, switched-on staff and a chilled atmosphere, just down the road from the tourist information bureau. Also noted for its good-value tours (see "Arrival, information and getting around" on p.141). Doubles ②, dorms and camping ①.

Guesthouses and hotels

Avenues Guest House, 32 The Avenue (☎021/887 1843, fax 887 2733, mobile ☎083/310 2371). Friendly B&B done out in airy yellowwood and pine, with a twist of Laura Ashley, across the road from the Eerste River. An easy walk to the centre and university campus, where guests can use the swimming pool and three-storey gym. ⑦.

Blombosch Guest House, 61 Plein St (☎ & fax 021/883 3674). Central guesthouse with eight budget B&B double rooms, some with balconies. ②.

Bonne Esperance, 17 Van Riebeeck St (☎021/887 0225, fax 887 8328). Colonial elegance in a terrific two-storey Victorian villa. Some larger rooms, good service, a verandah overlooking a lovely front garden, and a courtyard and swimming pool at the rear all help to justify the price. ④–⑤.

D'Ouwe Werf, 30 Church St (☎021/887 1608 or 887 4608, fax 887 4626, *ouwewerf@iafrica.com*). South Africa's oldest country inn, in the middle of town, dates back to the end of the nineteenth century. There are TVs and phones in every room, a swimming pool, and you can eat in their lovely courtyard (see p.145). ⑦.

Just Joey, corner of 13 Noordwal-Wes and Helderberg streets (☎021/887 1799, fax 887 2899, *justjoey@mweb.co.za*). Peachy pink guesthouse, with comfortable rooms glowing with rose-tinted frills and drapes. ④.

ACCOMMODATION PRICE CODES

All the accommodation listed in the Guide has been categorized into one of nine price bands, as set out below. The rates quoted represent what you can expect to pay for much of the summer **per person**, and unless otherwise stated, are based on two sharing. Rooms are generally en suite. Expect prices in some areas to be significantly higher in peak season (Dec–Jan & Easter), and look out for discounts during the winter. For further details, see p.33.

① up to R50	④ R150–200	⑦ R300–400
② R50–100	⑤ R200–250	⑧ R400–500
③ R100–150	⑥ R250–300	⑨ over R500

The Lanzerac, Jonkershoek Rd, 1km east of town (☎021/887 1132, fax 887 2310, *info@lanzerac.co.za*). The last word in Winelands luxury, this hotel wallows in a visual orgy of white-washed buildings surrounded by vineyards and mountains. ⑨.

Michaelhouse, 29 Van Riebeeck St (☎ & fax 021/886 6343). Modern cast-iron decor, with just a hint of the ethnic, offering a relief from the town's ubiquitous soft colours and floral prints. The garden terrace with trellised vines makes the perfect venue for a summery breakfast. ④.

Natte Valleij, on the R44 Klapmuts road, 12km north of town (☎021/875 5171, fax 875 5475). Choice of an en-suite B&B room off a courtyard, a large cottage that sleeps six, or a smaller and less expensive family cottage (R220) attached to an old whitewashed homestead with large gardens in the heart of the Winelands. Breakfast is served on the verandah and there's a swimming pool. ③.

Stellenbosch Hotel, corner of Dorp and Andringa streets (☎021/887 3644, fax 887 3673). Smart town-centre hotel in a restored nineteenth-century house, now declared a National Monument. Brass beds, capacious sofas, starched linen and atmosphere. Room only. ⑤.

Victoria House, 21 Van Riebeeck St (☎ & fax 021/883 2099, mobile ☎082/576 3807, *victoria@adept.co.za*). Comfortably furnished house near the centre, with all the facilities you're likely to need, plus shared lounge, kitchen and bathrooms. Ideal for groups of four. ②.

Villa Jonde, 27 Noorwal-Wes (☎ & fax 021/883 3568). Rambling Edwardian house eccentrically fur-nished and generally unpretentious. Surrounded by a huge jungle of a garden in which you can lose yourself, it offers reasonable value for its price. ③.

Weidenhof Lodge, 24 Weidenhof St (☎021/886 4679, fax 887 2397; *thys_haupt@yahoo.com*). Good-value, compact self-catering apartments with showers, fully equipped kitchens, TVs and linen accommodating two to four people. ②.

The Town

Stellenbosch's attractions lie principally in its setting and streetscape; it's a lovely place to simply wander around. The tourist information bureau in the Rhenish Complex, Market St, is a good place to start your explorations. Heading east up this road you'll soon reach a whitewashed block that was the **VOC Kruithuis** (Jan–May & Aug–Dec Mon–Fri 9.30am–1.30pm & 2–5pm) – the Dutch East India Company's powder maga-zine – which houses a small and unprepossessing collection of four British uniforms, assorted rifles, some intriguing, but unexplained, little laptop-sized cannons and some powder kegs. From here, a right turn south down the side of the **Braak**, the large green that occupies the centre of town, will take you past the **Rhenish Church** in Bloem Street, built in 1823 as a school for slaves and coloured people.

The Village Museum

Head north up Ryneveld Street, and you'll encounter Stellenbosch's highlight, the extremely enjoyable **Village Museum**, 18 Ryneveld St (Mon–Sat 9.30am–5pm, Sun 2–5pm; ☎021/887 2902), which cuts a cross-section through the town's architectural and social heritage by means of a complex of four fortuitously adjacent historical dwellings from different periods. They're beautifully conserved and furnished in peri-od style, and you'll bump into the odd worker dressed in contemporary costume. Earliest of the houses is the homely **Shreuderhuis**, a vernacular cottage built in 1709, with a small courtyard garden filled with aromatic herbs, pomegranate bushes and vine-draped pergolas – bearing more resemblance to the early Cape settlement's European aesthetics than to modern South Africa. Across the garden, Blettermanhuis, built in 1789 for the last Dutch East India Company-appointed magistate of Stellenbosch, is an archetypal eighteenth-century Cape Dutch house, built on an H-plan with six gables. **Grosvenor House**, opposite, was altered to its current form in 1803, and reflects the growing influence of English taste after the 1795 British occupation of the Cape. The neoclassical facade, with fluted pilasters supporting a pedimented entrance, borrows from high fashion then current at the heart of the growing Empire. The more modest **O.M. Bergh House**, across the road, is a typical Victorian dwelling that was once similar to Blettermanhuis, but was "modernized" in the mid-nineteenth century on a rectangular plan with a simplified facade without gables.

Dorp Street and around

From the Village Museum, head back south into **Dorp Street**, Stellenbosch's best-preserved historic axis, well worth a slow stroll just to soak in the ambience of buildings, gables, oaks and roadside water furrows. Heading west along it, you'll spot the **Stellenbosch Wine Tasting Centre** on your left (see overleaf) and next door the much-celebrated **Oom Samie se Winkel**, which amounts to little more than a jam-packed Victorian-style general dealer selling touristy knick-knacks, antiques, comestibles and wines, but is worth popping into if only to sample some fish biltong. On your right, look out for **Krige's Cottages**, an unusual terrace of historic town houses at nos. 37–51, between Aan-die-Wagen-Weg and Krige streets. The houses were built as Cape Dutch cottages in the first half of the nineteenth century, and later Victorian features were added, resulting in an interesting hybrid, with gables housing Victorian attic windows and decorative Victorian verandahs with filigree ironwork fronting the elegant simplicity of Cape Dutch facades.

A left turn into Strand Street brings you to **Libertas Parva**, a fine example of an H-plan Cape Dutch manor, and home to the **Rembrandt van Rijn Art Museum** (Mon–Fri 9am–12.45pm & 2–5pm, Sat 10am–1pm & 2–5pm). Don't let the name fool you into expecting Old Dutch Masters – the museum is funded by the Rembrandt tobacco multinational. The gallery has a small but stimulating collection of South African art, including a wonderful 360-degree panorama of Cape Town rendered in pen, ink and watercolour by Josephus Jones in 1808; *The Conservationists Ball*, an acerbic tryptich by William Kentridge, a leading light among the current generation of South African artists; and a number of Irma Stern paintings and drawings to pad it all out. Adjacent in the same courtyard, the Libertas Parva Cellar houses the **Stellenryck Wine Museum** (Mon–Fri 9am–12.45pm & 2–5pm, Sat 10am–1pm & 2–5pm), which has some moderately interesting ancient amphorae, winepresses, wineglasses and old bottles, but shouldn't keep you nosing around for too long, unless you're a real buff.

Eating and drinking

You'll be spoilt for choices of good places to eat in Stellenbosch, both in the centre and on some of the surrounding estates. In the evenings, the student presence ensures a relaxed and sometimes raucous drinking culture.

De Akker, 90 Dorp St. Good spot for pub lunches and late nights (it hots up after 11pm), in a buzzing joint enjoyed by unshod students with torn jeans and dogs.

De Cameron, 50 Plein St (☎021/883 3331). One of the best restaurants in town, offering southern Italian food, including pasta, pizzas and gnocchi, as well as first-rate seafood.

Lanzerac, *Lanzerac Hotel*, Jonkershoek Rd (☎021/887 1132). Formal restaurant among the vineyards on the outskirts of town, with an internationally inspired à la carte menu that changes once a month.

Mama Roma, Stelmark Centre, Merriman Ave (☎021/886 6064). Good-value restaurant, where you'll get Italian standards such as pizza and pasta as well as seafood, roast lamb, ostrich and their speciality – meat medallions. Closed Sat lunchtime and Sun evening.

D'Ouwe Werf, 30 Church St (☎021/887 1608). In a beautiful courtyard with vines, this restaurant offers traditional Cape Cuisine, including Karoo lamb, *bobotie* and oxtail brewed in red wine sauce. Their Black Forest cake is an excellent accompaniment to tea.

Ralph's, 13 Andringa St (☎021/883 3532). Stellenbosch's top restaurant is run by a master chef and features a terrific international menu that includes ostrich steak. Food is served amid Eighties-style red, white and black decor, and wicker chairs.

Rustic Café, Bird St. Cheap to moderately priced pizzas, nachos, salads and Thai curries.

San Francisco Coffee Roastery, Drostdy Craft Market, Alexander St. A dead cert for a fine cup of coffee, with a choice of blends, flavoured coffees, muffins and light snacks.

Stellenbosch Wine Tasting Centre, 90 Dorp St (☎021/883 3814). Hundreds of Cape wines to taste, buy and quaff.

The Terrace, Shop 12, Drostdy Centre (☎021/887 1942). Centrally located bar-cum-restaurant overlooking the Braak, where you can get pub lunches, burgers and light meals. Frequented by a young crowd and a favoured haunt of backpackers, it's open from mid-morning to the early hours of the next day.

Vinkel en Koljander, *Lanzerac Hotel*, Jonkershoek Rd. Outdoor teas and traditional country dishes (soups, casseroles and light meals) served against a wonderfully scenic backdrop of mountains and vineyards.

Volkskombuis, Aan-de-Wagenweg, off Dorp St (☎021/887 2121). On the banks of the Eerste River, this lunch and dinner venue serves up Cape Cuisine and *boerekos* at acceptable prices. Closed Sun evening.

The Stellenbosch wine estates

Stellenbosch was the first locality in the country to wake up to the marketing potential of a **wine route**, which it launched in 1971. The tactic has been hugely successful and now draws tens of thousands of visitors from all over the world to the wineries, making this the most toured area in the Winelands. Although the region only accounts for fifteen percent of the country that's under vine, its wine route is the most extensive in

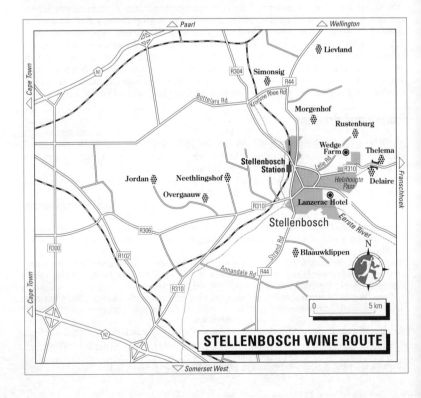

STELLENBOSCH WINE ROUTE

South Africa and offers some of the Cape's best reds and overall the greatest diversity of wines. The wineries are all along a series of roads that radiate out from Stellenbosch. The selection below covers three of these roads, with the wineries arranged from Stellenbosch outwards, making each series easy to cover in a single journey. All the wineries have wine-route signposts along the main road.

Along the R44

Klapmuts Road (the **R44**) north out of Stellenbosch, towards the N1, will lead you, after around 4km, to **Morgenhof** (June–Aug Mon–Fri 9am–4.30pm, Sat 10am–3pm; Sept–May same hours plus Sun 10am–3pm; small tasting charge; ☎021/889 5510). A French-owned chateau-style complex overlooked by the vine-covered Simonsberg, Morgenhof has a light and airy tasting room with a bar. Delicious light lunches are served outside, topped off, when available, by ripe berries and ice cream on the summery lawns. Among the wines worth sampling here are the Merlot, Cabernet Sauvignon and Sauvignon Blanc. Drive north along the Klapmuts Road for about another 4km and you'll reach the turn-off on your left to **Simonsig** (Mon–Fri 8.30am–4.45pm, Sat 8.30am–4.30pm; cellar tours Mon–Fri 10am & 3pm, Sat 10am; small tasting charge; ☎021/882 2044). The winery, just over 2km down Kromme Rhee Road, has an outdoor tasting area under vine-covered pergolas, from where you get majestic views back to Stellenbosch of hazy stone-blue mountains and vineyards. Although there's no restaurant, you can eat your own picnic at tables in a courtyard area cooled by a fountain. Of their first-class wines, their cutting-edge Pinotage is worth a try, as is their Kaapse Vonkel sparkling wine.

Back on the main road, **Lievland** (tasting & sales Mon–Fri 9am–5pm, Sat 9am–1pm; ☎021/875 5226), 4.5km north of the Simonsig turn-off, is the last of the Stellenbosch wineries on this section of the R44 – after this they fall under Paarl (see p.154). In a farm environment, Lievland is an informal place where, if you're keen, you can ask to speak to the winemaker, who is an expert on Shiraz. This, unsurprisingly, is one of the wines you should try in their Cape Dutch tasting room, which dates back to 1823.

Drive straight back through Stellenbosch, and 4km from town along the Strand Road (R44 south) you'll come to **Blaauwklippen** (Mon–Fri 9am–5pm, Sat 9am–1pm; tasting charge; ☎021/880 0133), at the foot of the Stellenboschberg. Although big enough to take tour buses, Blaauwklippen isn't overly commercialized. Apart from the usual Cape Dutch buildings, there are inexpensive carriage rides through the vineyards, a horse-carriage museum, and a little shop selling soft drinks and knick-knacks. A coachman's lunch is served (Mon–Sat) on the verandah. The most celebrated wine from the Blaauwklippen cellar is their Zinfandel, rated South Africa's best of its type, with successive vintages winning international acknowledgement. If you continue south along the R44, you'll eventually reach Somerset West, centre of the Helderberg wine route, the highlight of which is **Vergelegen** (see p.148).

Along the R310

One of the closest estates to central Stellenbosch is **Rustenberg** (tasting & sales 8.30am–4.30pm, Sat 9am–12.30pm; ☎021/887 3153), which isn't a member of the official Stellenbosch wine route but is one of the most alluring wine farms. To get there, join the R310 from the R44 to Paarl, just north of town. After just under 2km along the R310 to Franschhoek, turn into Ida's Valley for a further 2km, which, after a drive through orchards, sheep pastures and tree-lined avenues, brings you to the estate. An unassuming working farm, Rustenberg hangs onto a romantic pastoral atmosphere, with a complex of seventeenth-century buildings, including two National Monuments, and a gabled Cape Dutch milking shed. The first vines were planted here in 1692, but the viniculture looks to the future, with an Australian winemaker bringing in New World know-how to revamp the old labels. Despite the slave bell in the farmyard, their labour practices are among the best in the Cape, with model worker housing and participatory management. No meals are laid on, so you should bring your own picnic to savour under the oaks, and buy one of their wines, of which the Rustenberg Gold, a Bordeaux blend of Cabernet Sauvignon, Merlot and Cabernet Franc, has been coming out tops for years. Also look out for highly drinkable reds and whites under the Brampton brand – their second label.

For the Winelands' best views – though not the best wines – head for **Delaire** (tasting and sales Mon–Sat 10am–5pm; tasting charge; ☎021/885 1756), on the **Helshoogte Pass**, 6km east of Stellenbosch along the R310 to Franschhoek. The drive up from the pass through the slopes of the vineyard-covered hillside brings you to the tasting room and restaurant with views through oaks across the Groot Drakenstein and Simonsig mountains and down into craggy valleys. One of the great mysteries of Delaire is its unexciting wines, given that neighbouring **Thelema** consistently produces some of the Cape's most brilliant reds and whites. Thelema is sadly not worth visiting, as there's little chance you'll find any examples of their best output to taste. In fact, when Britain's Queen Elizabeth II visited South Africa in 1995, the winemaker was forced to raid his private cellar to provide bottles of their world-class Sauvignon Blanc for a state banquet.

Along the R306

Moddergat Road (the R310) heads southwest out of Stellenbosch along the train tracks, branching off 5.5km later onto Polkadraai Road (the **R306**). Half a kilometre later you'll come to the driveway that leads up to **Neethlingshof** (tasting & sales Mon–Fri 9am–5pm, Sat & Sun 10am–4pm; small tasting charge; ☎021/883 8988), which has a beautifully restored Cape Dutch manor dating back to 1814, and two good restaurants (*Palm Terrace* serves light meals). The first vines were planted here in 1692 and Neethlingshof produces some good wines, but hits the high notes with its Noble Late Harvest sweet dessert wines, which are stunners. A further 500m along the R306 takes you to another turn-off to the north, along which after a short distance you'll reach **Overgaauw** (tasting & sales Mon–Fri 9am–12.30pm & 2–5pm, Sat 10am–12.30pm; ☎021/881 3815), notable for having the only Victorian tasting room in the Winelands with an atmosphere that's elegant and understated. A pioneering estate that turns out reds and ports of excellent quality, Overgaauw was the first in the country to produce Merlots and is the only one to make Sylvaner, a well-priced, easy-drinking dry white. None of this has gone to its head and it's a thoroughly convivial place to sample the grape.

Further north along the same road, **Jordan Vineyards** (Mon–Fri 10am–4.30pm, Sat 9am–2.30pm; ☎021/881 3441) is part of the new wave of Cape wineries, with a hi-tech cellar, modern tasting room and friendly service. The drive there is half the fun, taking you into a *kloof* bounded by vineyards that get a whiff of the seas from both False Bay and Table Bay, which has obviously done something for their outstanding Chardonnay and Sauvignon Blanc.

Somerset West and Vergelegen

The only compelling reason to trawl out to the unpromising town of **SOMERSET WEST**, 50km east of Cape Town along the N2, is for **Vergelegen**, Lourensford Rd (daily 9.30am–4pm; entry fee includes wine tasting and cellar tours; ☎021/847 1334), a winery that is fair set on the ascendant and an absolute architectural treasure. Officially part of the Helderberg wine route, Vergelegen can easily be included as an extension to a visit to Stellenbosch, just 14km to the north.

Vergelegen represents a notorious episode of corruption and the arbitrary abuse of power at the Cape in the early years of Dutch East India Company rule. Built by Willem Adriaan van der Stel, who became governor in 1699 after the retirement of his father Simon, it is difficult to overestimate the impact of the estate as a grand Renaissance complex in the middle of the wild backwater that was the Cape at the turn of the eighteenth century. Willem Adriaan got hold of the land illegally and used Dutch East India Company slaves to build Vergelegen as well as Company resources to farm vast tracts of land in the surrounding areas. At the same time he abused his power as governor to corner most of the significant markets at the Cape. When this was brought to the notice of the Dutch East India Company in the Netherlands, Willem Adriaan was sacked and Vergelegen was ordered to be destroyed to discourage future miscreant governors. It's believed that the destruction was never fully carried out and the current building is thought to stand on the foundations of the original.

Vergelegen was the only wine estate visited by the British queen during her 1995 state visit to South Africa – a good choice, as there's enough here to occupy an easy couple of hours. The **interpretive centre**, just across the courtyard from the shop at the building entrance, provides a useful history and background to the estate which you can absorb in about ten minutes. Next door, the **wine-tasting centre** (closed Sun) offers a professionally run sampling with a brief talk through each label. The **homestead**, which was restored in 1917 to its current state by Lady Florence Phillips, wife of a Johannesburg mining magnate, can also be visited. Its pale facade with a classical triangular gable and pilaster-decorated doorways is reached along an axis through an octagonal garden that dances with butterflies in summer. Massive grounds planted with chestnuts and camphor trees and ponds around every corner make this one of the most serene places in the Cape and one where you might want to linger.

Practicalities

Vergelegen is best reached **by car**. Although there are regular Metro Rail trains between Cape Town and Somerset West, the estate is too far from town to make this a serious option, unless you're prepared to hitch. To reach Vergelegen from Cape Town, take the N2 east past the International Airport, and leave the freeway at exit 43, signposted to Somerset West. This will bring you onto the R44, which you should follow into town. Once in Main Street, you'll see the turn-off to Lourensford Road (if you hit the town centre you've missed the turn-off), which you should follow for just over 3km to Vergelegen, which will be on your right.

Given its proximity to far nicer Stellenbosch, there's no reason to stay overnight in Somerset West. For **eating and drinking**, Vergelegen offers two excellent choices: at the chintzy *Lady Phillips Tea Garden* (☎021/847 1346) you can take tea or eat country-cuisine lunches (booking essential) of pies, quiches and pastas with an international flavour, while the less formal *Rose Terrace* offers outdoor light lunches of sandwiches on home-baked bread, cheese platters and wine by the glass.

Paarl

Although **PAARL** is attractively ensconced in a fertile valley brimming with historical monuments, at heart it's a parochial *dorp*, lacking either the sophistication of Stellenbosch or the new-found trendiness of Franschhoek. It can claim some virtue, however, from being a prosperous farming centre that earns its keep from the agricultural light industries – grain silos, canneries and flour mills – on the north side of town, and the cornucopia of grapes, guavas, olives, oranges and maize grown on the surrounding farms. Despite its small-town feel, Paarl has the largest municipality in the Winelands, with its most elite areas on the vined slopes of **Paarl Mountain**, the granite, domed formation that looks down over the town. In stark contrast with the cliquey conservatism of the predominantly white centre, the coloured townships on its periphery bear racy American names such as Chicago and New Orleans.

Some history

In 1657, just five years after the establishment of the Dutch East India Company refreshment station on the Cape Peninsula, a party under **Abraham Gabbema** pitched up in the Berg River Valley to look for trading opportunities with the Khoikhoi, and search for the legendary gold of Monomotapa. They obviously had treasure on the brain, because on awaking after a rainy night to the sight of the silvery dome of granite that dominates the valley, they dubbed it Peerlbergh (pearl mountain), which in its modified form, **Paarl**, became the name of the town.

Thirty years later, commander of the Cape, Simon van der Stel, granted strips of the Khoikhoi lands on the slopes of Paarl Mountain to French Huguenot and Dutch settlers. By the time Paarl was officially granted town status in 1840, it was still an outpost at the edge of the Drakenstein Mountains, a position from which it gained much benefit as a flourishing wagon-making and last-stop provisioning centre. This status was enhanced when the first **train line** in the Cape connected it to the Peninsula in 1863. Following in the spirit of the first Dutch adventurers of 1657, thousands of treasure-seekers brought custom to Paarl as the gateway to the interior during the diamond rush of the 1870s and the gold fever of the 1880s.

In the twentieth century the town holds deep historical significance for the two competing political forces that forged modern South Africa. **Afrikanerdom** regards Paarl as the hallowed ground on which their language movement was born in 1875 (see p.152), while for the **ANC** (and the international community), Paarl will be remembered as the place from which Nelson Mandela made the final steps of his long walk to freedom, when he walked out of **Victor Verster Prison** in 1990.

Arrival and information

Metro Rail and Spoornet **trains** from Cape Town pull in at Huguenot Station in Lady Grey Street at the north end of town, near to the central shops. Greyhound and Intercape intercity **buses** stop at Paarl Station, at the south end of town, close to the Laborie winery.

Paarl's **tourist information** bureau, 216 Main St (☎021/872 3829, fax 872 9376), has a selection of good **maps** and can help with finding accommodation. You can arrange **car rental** through Wine Route Rent-a-Car, 23 Nantes St (☎021/872 8513, fax 872 8523).

Accommodation

Most places to stay in town are either along or just off Main Street, many in historic buildings. Apart from one backpackers' lodge, the cheapest options are the two **resorts** with chalets just outside town. At the other end of the scale, *Roggeland Country House*, which isn't far from central Paarl, is one of South Africa's most outstanding places to stay.

Berg River Resort, 5km south of town on the R45 (☎021/863 1650, fax 863 2583). Rambling, run-down family holiday resort on the banks of the Berg River, with a swimming pool and restaurant. There's an old mini-golf, and canoeing on the river. Bring your own towels. Camping ①, chalets ②.

Berghof, Monte Christo Ave (☎021/871 1099, fax 872 6126). The 22 rooms in this large, modern guesthouse at the top of a hill, are done out in marble, glass and impersonal motel furniture, but the swimming pool commands one of the best sites in Paarl, with soaring views across town to the Drakenstein Mountains. ③.

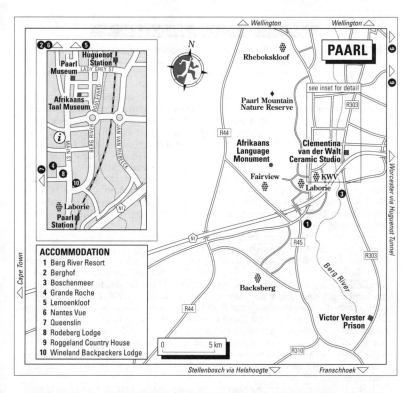

ACCOMMODATION
1 Berg River Resort
2 Berghof
3 Boschenmeer
4 Grande Roche
5 Lemoenkloof
6 Nantes Vue
7 Queenslin
8 Rodeberg Lodge
9 Roggeland Country House
10 Wineland Backpackers Lodge

Boschenmeer, 1km south of the N1 along the R303 (☎021/863 1250, fax 863 3082). Two-bed timber chalets overlooking a dam in a resort that's far more modern than Berg River. The chalets are fully equipped, with microwave and TV. Discounts Mon–Thurs and throughout winter. ③.

De Waenhuis, 8 Patriot St, on the corner of Second St (☎021/872 6643, fax 872 7921). Very central, tiny but fully equipped self-catering cottage a couple of blocks down from the tourist information bureau with TV, swimming pool and private entrance. ②.

Grande Roche, Plantasie St (☎021/863 2727, fax 863 2220, *gr/hotel@adept.co.za*). Stuffy, seriously upmarket hotel in the centre of town, surrounded by vineyards up against Paarl Mountain, with service that is meticulous to a fault and a very good but expensive restaurant (see p.155). ⑨.

Lemoenkloof, 396a Main St (☎021/872 3782 or 872 7520, fax 872 3782, *lemkloof@adept.co.za*). Comfortable and well-run guesthouse in a National Monument that has 1820s' Cape Dutch and Victorian features, a TV and fridge in each room, and a swimming pool. ⑤.

Nantes Vue, 56 Mill St (☎021/872 7311, fax 872 7311). En-suite doubles decorated with artistic flair in a National Monument turned friendly Cape Dutch guesthouse where breakfast is served on the verandah overlooking a small garden. Good value. ③.

Queenslin, 2 Queen St (☎ & fax 021/863 1160, mobile ☎082/577 0635). Two rooms with bath and their own entrances in a family home, set in a quiet part of town bounded on one side by vineyards and towered over by Paarl Rock. Limited self-catering is possible with fridge, kettle and cutlery provided, but no cooker. Breakfast can be provided as an extra. ②.

Rodeberg Lodge, 74 Main St (☎021/863 3202, fax 863 3203, *rodeberg@iafrica.com*). Plain period furnishing gives this huge, centrally located Victorian townhouse a cool, spacious atmosphere. Ask for a room at the back if traffic noise bothers you. ④.

Roggeland Country House, Roggeland Rd, Dal Jospehat Valley (☎021/868 2501, fax 868 2113, *rog@iafrica.com.za*). The accolades keep rolling in for this family-run inn, which somehow manages to

THE HISTORY OF AFRIKAANS

Afrikaans is South Africa's third mother tongue, spoken by fifteen percent of the population and outstripped only by Zulu and Xhosa. English, by contrast, is the mother tongue of only nine percent of South Africans, and ranks fifth in the league of the eleven official languages.

Signs of the emergence of a new southern African dialect appeared as early as 1685, when H.A. van Rheede, a Dutch East India Company official from the Netherlands, complained about a "distorted and incomprehensible" version of Dutch being spoken in the Drakenstein Valley around modern-day Paarl. By absorbing English, French, German, Malay and indigenous words and expressions, the language continued to diverge from mainstream Dutch, and by the nineteenth century was widely used in the Cape by both white and coloured speakers, but was regarded by the elite as an inferior creole, unsuitable for literary or official communication. Even the first attempts by dominee **Stephanus du Toit** and the Genootskap van Regte Afrikaners (League of True Afrikaners) to have Afrikaans recognized as a separate language from Dutch, and their launching in 1875, of *Die Patriot*, the first white Afrikaans **newspaper**, made little impact outside Paarl.

Ironically, it was the British defeat of the Afrikaner republics in the second Anglo-Boer War at the turn of the twentieth century that provided the catalyst for a mass white Afrikaans movement. The scorched-earth policy of the British had driven many Boers from the lands and produced a demoralized and semi-literate Boer underclass. The official British policy of the anglicization of South Africa helped to unite the white Afrikaner proletariat and elite against the common English enemy. In 1905, **Gustav Preller**, a young journalist from a working-class Boer background set about reinventing Afrikaans as a "white man's language". He aimed to eradicate the stigma of its "coloured" ties by substituting Dutch words for those with non-European origins. Preller began publishing the first of a series of populist magazines written in Afrikaans and glorifying Boer history and culture. Through this **Second Language Movement**, whites took spiritual control over Afrikaans and the pressure grew for its recognition as an official language, which came in 1925.

When the National Party took power in 1948, its apartheid policy went hand in hand with promoting the interests of its Afrikaans-speaking supporters and a concerted programme of the **upliftment of poor whites** began. Afrikaners were installed throughout the civil service and filled most posts in the public utilities. Despite the fact that there were more coloured than white Afrikaans speakers, the language quickly became associated with the **apartheid** establishment. This had electrifying consequences in the Seventies, when the government attempted to enforce Afrikaans as the sole medium of instruction in African schools, leading directly to the **Soweto uprising** in 1976, which marked the beginning of the end for Afrikaner hegemony in South Africa. The repressive period throughout the Seventies and Eighties and the forced removals under the Group Areas Act led many coloured Afrikaans speakers to adopt English in preference to their mother tongue, which they felt was tainted by apartheid.

There are few signs that Afrikaans will die out. Under the new constitution, existing **language rights** can't be diminished, which effectively means that Afrikaans will continue to be almost as widely used as before. It is now as much with coloured as white people that the future of the *taal* (language) rests.

combine good service, outstanding food (see p.155) and informality. The homestead is an eighteenth-century masterpiece of Cape Dutch architecture, with bedrooms in outbuildings. Half board ⑧–⑨.

Winelands Backpacker Lodge, 91 Main St (☎021/863 1378, fax 863 2231, *portfoli@iafrica.com*). Small and reasonably priced, purpose-built hostel close to the station with a single eight-bed dorm and *braai* facilities. Bedding can be rented for a small charge. ①.

The Town and around

Unlike Stellenbosch, which is made for wandering, all you're likely to get from strolling around Paarl is a tired pair of legs for relatively little return. The most rewarding sightseeing in the centre can be had by driving down the two oak-lined kilometres of **Main Street**, which has the best-preserved historical frontage in town.

It's here you'll find the **Paarl Museum**, 303 Main St (Mon–Fri 10am–5pm, Sat 10am–noon; small entrance fee), in a handsome, thatched Cape Dutch building with one of the earliest surving gables (1787), in the "new style", characterized by triangular caps. The contents don't quite match up to the exterior, but include some reasonably enlightening panels on the architecture of the town, and several eccentric glass display cases of Victorian bric-a-brac. A token "Road to Reconciliation" exhibit takes on board the new South Africa, with displays of press cuttings covering Paarl during the apartheid years. Among these you'll find passing mention of the fact that Nelson Mandela spent some time here as a "guest" of the town – his last years in jail, in fact.

Heading east down Main Street away from the museum, take a left turn into Van der Lingen Street and then a right into Pastorie Street will bring you to the **Afrikaans Taal Museum** (Mon–Fri 9am–1pm & 2–5pm; free), which chronicles a white Nationalist version of the development of the Afrikaans language (see box opposite). Located in the house of Gideon Malherbe (1833–1921), one of the founders of the League of True Afrikaners, the museum's displays are in Afrikaans, and a leaflet available from the reception desk gives an English summary of exhibits. Some brief material gives an alternative history of Afrikaans, placing new emphasis on the role of slaves and coloured South Africans in its evolution.

On the east side of town, on Jan van Riebeeck Street, is **Clementina van der Walt Ceramic Studio** (Mon–Fri 9am–5pm, Sat 9.30am–3.30pm; ☎021/872 3420), one of the best craft shops in the Winelands, selling tableware from the studio of Clementina van der Walt, who has created a mock-ethnic style with mass appeal. The shop also stocks hand-selected items of cutlery, wonderful fabrics from South Africa and the rest of the continent, and wooden bowls – all well-priced, superior quality stuff, miles away from airport art.

The only other sight of any interest in Paarl itself is the grandiose **Taal Monument** (daily 9am–5pm; free), the controversial memorial to the Afrikaans language, which stands just outside the centre on the top of Paarl Mountain. To get there, drive south along Main Street past the head office of the KWV, and follow the signs to your right up the slope of the mountain. The monument is as important a place of pilgrimage for Afrikaners as the Voortrekker Monument in Pretoria, although when it was erected in 1973 critics joked that monuments were usually erected to the dead. Close up, it's not as intrusive as you might fear, although the best thing is the truly magnificent panorama across to the Peninsula and False Bay in one direction and the Winelands ranges in the other.

Victor Verster Prison

Roughly 9km south of the N1 as it cuts through Paarl, along the R303, the southern extension of Jan van Riebeeck Street, stands **Victor Verster Prison**, Nelson Mandela's last place of incarceration. It was through the gates at Victor Verster (not Pollsmoor in Cape Town or Robben Island as many people believe) that Mandela walked to his freedom on February 11, 1990, and was here that the first images of him in 27 years were bounced around the world – under the Prisons Act not even old pictures of him could be published for his 27 years of incarceration. The jail looks rather like an upmarket boys' school fronted by rugby fields beneath hazy mountains, and there's something bizarre about seeing a prison sign nonchalantly slipped in among all the vineyard and wine route pointers. Since you can't go inside, the usual tourist thing is to have yourself snapped standing in front the of the gates, though raising a clenched fist and shouting "Amandla!" is strictly optional.

The wineries

Retracing your route to town, and turning left into Langenhoven Street and left again into Main Street, will bring you to the entrance of **Laborie**, Taillefert St (Mon–Fri 9am–4.30pm, Sat 9am–1pm; ☎021/807 3095; tasting charge), one of the most impressive Paarl wineries, made all the more remarkable for being right in town. The beautiful manor is fronted by a rose garden, acres of close-cropped lawns, historic buildings and oak trees – all towered over by the Taal Monument. There's a truly wonderful tasting room balcony, jettying out over the vineyards trailing up Paarl Mountain. Try the Chardonnay, Sauvignon Blanc and the Pineau de Laborie, the world's first pot stilled eau de vie made entirely from Pinotage grapes – delicious and well-priced. They also produce a nice Cap Classique, a champagne-style sparkling wine.

Back towards the centre along the main drag, Jan Philips Drive, a dirt track, takes a detour along the hillside past **Paarl Mountain Nature Reserve**, emerging 11km later at the north end of town to rejoin Main Street. If you take a left turn from Jan Philips, after nearly 2km you'll reach **Rhebokskloof** (Mon–Fri 9am–5pm, Sat & Sun 9am–4pm; tasting free; ☎021/863 8386, fax 863 8906, *rhebok@iaccess.co.za*), a highly photogenic wine estate, overlooking a shallow *kloof* that borders on the mountain nature reserve. The estate has a growing reputation for its restaurant (see "Eating and drinking" below), which overlooks an artificial lake with swans. Although wine tasting is free, for a small charge you can book (24hr in advance) for a formal tasting that includes a talk on wine, a video and a cellar tour. The Cabernet Sauvignon, Pinotage and Merlot are well worth sampling.

Back on the southern fringes of town, **Fairview** (Mon–Fri 8.30am–5pm, Sat 8.30am–1pm; tasting free; ☎021/863 2450, fax 863 2591, *fairback@iafrica.com*) promises the most fun of all the Paarl estates, with much more than just wine tasting on offer. To get there, take the R101 (the southwest extension of Main Road) out of town, turning right at the sign and continuing for about 2.5km down a minor road, to the estate entrance. Your arrival is marked by a spiral goat tower, the emblem of the estate, whose inhabitants are publicly milked every afternoon. A deli sells sausages and cold meats for picnics on the lawn, and you can also sample and buy the goat's, sheep's and cow's cheeses made on the estate. As far as wine tasting goes, Fairview is an innovative, family-run place offering interesting tastings, but it can get a bit hectic when the tour buses roll in, so try to phone ahead to find out when they're expected. The first-rate wines here include Shiraz-Merlot, Merlot and Chardonnay – all fabulous and all good value.

From here the **Backsberg Estate** (Mon–Fri 8.30am–5pm, Sat 8.30am–1pm; tasting charge; ☎021/875 5141, fax 875 5144, *backwine@iafrica.com*), south of the R101 along the very minor WR1, can be reached easily by backtracking from Fairview, turning right into the R101, and continuing a short way before turning left. After passing the Simonsvlei winery, go a short way till you strike a T-junction at the WR1, where you turn left and almost immediately get to the winery entrance. Outdoor seating with views of the rose garden and vineyard makes this busy estate a nice place to while away some time. Their wines are of a high standard and, when you can lay hands on them, the Cabernet Sauvignon, Merlot, Shiraz and Pinotage represent good value. For something unusual, sample the Malbec and, if you're into spirits, their international-award-winning brandy.

Eating and drinking

Paarl isn't a gourmet centre, but it does boast one of South Africa's most expensive **restaurants** (at the *Grande Roche*), as well as a couple of outstanding places in the surrounding countryside, where you can enjoy good food accompanied by great views of the vineyards and mountains.

Bizzi Lizzi, Shop 25, Van der Lingen Square. Pleasant coffee shop serving light meals and breakfasts.

Bosman's Restaurant, *Grande Roche Hotel*, Plantasie St (☎021/863 2727). One of the best and most expensive restaurants in the country (winning accolades year after year) offering superb European cuisine with outstanding service that can be a bit stifling.

I Campanelli, 62 Breda St (☎021/872 4397). Low-key Italian restaurant, popular with locals.

The Coffee Place, 191 Main St. Light, seasonal food served indoors or in the garden.

The Country Elephant, Simondium Rd (☎021/874 1355). Provençal-style cuisine served amid bright decor or on a terrace for alfresco summer meals with views of Klein Drakenstein. Choose from a local wine list, tasty starters, and meat, fish or poultry main courses.

Gabi's Coffee Shop, 57 Lady Grey St (☎021/872 5265). Bistro/bar handy for light meals.

Laborie Restaurant & Wine House, Taillefert St (☎021/808 7429). Seasonal à la carte and traditional Cape set-menu lunches every day and dinners. Closed Mon & Sun.

Rhebokskloof Restaurant, Rhebokskloof Minor Rd (☎021/863 8606). Intimate Victorian eatery and a larger Cape Dutch restaurant offering set and à la carte menus with interesting combinations.

Roggeland Country House, Roggeland Rd, Dal Jospehat Valley (☎021/868 2501). Not primarily run as a restaurant, you can sometimes book in here for the imaginative set menu inspired by the regional produce of Paarl, using vegetables and herbs grown in its own gardens. Beautifully prepared dishes are accompanied by a selected wine, each of which you are talked through. Booking is essential.

Saucy Maria's, 127 Main Rd (☎021/863 2285). Mediterranean-inspired restaurant dishing up ravioli, lamb knuckle, and veggie salads. Located in a farmhouse (a National Monument), there's a deli-style café at the front, an informal dining room with fireplace at the back and outdoor seating. Open daily from mid-morning to late.

Wagon Wheels Steakhouse, 57 Lady Grey St (☎021/872 5265). Out-of-the-ordinary steakhouse with surprisingly tasty sauces, and seafood alternatives.

Franschhoek

It's only relatively recently that **FRANSCHHOEK**, 33km from Stellenbosch and 29km from Paarl, has emerged from being the dowdy *dorp* of the Winelands to become the culinary capital of the Western Cape. Its late Victorian architecture, lightly seasoned with bland modern bungalows, can't match the elegance of Stellenbosch, but the terrific setting, hemmed in on three sides by mountains, the vineyards down every other backstreet, and some vigorous myth-making, have created a place fashion-conscious urbanites from Cape Town will drive out to just for Sunday lunch. And, while Capetonians dine here, Jo'burg designers, investors and bankers are buying up the place, as are German industrialists, an Italian count who flies to his estate by helicopter, and President Bongo of Gabon.

Some history

Between 1688 and 1700 about two hundred **French Huguenots**, desperate to escape religious persecution in France, accepted a Dutch East India offer of passage to the Cape and the grant of lands. They made contact with the area's earliest settlers, groups of **Khoi herders**. Conflict between the French newcomers and the Khoi followed familiar lines, with the white settlers gradually dispossessing the herdsmen, and forcing them either further into the hinterland or into servitude on their farms. The establishment of white hegemony was swift and by 1713 the area was known as *de france hoek*, but because of explicit Company policy, French-speaking died out within a generation. However, many of the estates are still known by their original French names. The town itself occupies parts of the original farms of La Cotte and Cabrière and is relatively young, having been established around a church built in 1833.

Arrival, information and accommodation

There's no public transport to Franschhoek or in the town itself; the only way to get here is in your own **car**. The **tourist information** bureau (summer daily 8.30am–6pm; winter Mon–Fri 8.30am–5pm, Sat & Sun 10am–1pm; ☎ & fax 021/876 3603) is in Main Road, just north of the junction with Kruger Street, and can provide information about places to stay in the area and a few hiking maps.

Accommodation

Auberge Bligny, 28 Van Wijk St (☎021/876 3767, fax 876 3483, *bligny@mweb.co.za*). Centrally located Victorian house furnished in country style, with florals and checks and with a nice guest lounge. ④.

Le Ballon Rouge Guest House, 12 Reservoir Rd (☎021/876 2651, fax 876 3743, *info @ballon-rouge.co.za*). Small B&B offering rooms that lead onto a side street-facing verandah, in a Victorian town house with brass bedsteads and floral fabrics. ④.

Chamonix Guest Cottages, Uitkyk St (☎021/876 2498, fax 876 3237, *chamfarm@icon.co.za*). Fully equipped, self-catering cottages surrounded by vineyards on a wine farm. ③.

Chanteclair, signposted just west of the Huguenot Monument along Lambrecht Rd (☎ & fax 021/876 3685, *chantelclair@ct.lia.net*). The best thing about this guesthouse, which stands on a massive property, is that you feel you're in the country, yet are only minutes from town. Unfussy rooms in English country style, and breakfast outside on the verandah looking out onto a lovely garden and orchard. ⑤.

Dassenberg Country House, off Main Rd (☎ & fax 021/876 2107). One family-sized and one single room in a self-catering cottage, in a peaceful and beautiful setting. ③.

Erica Guest House, 4 Erika St (☎021/876 2425, fax 876 2825). Modern, centrally located suburban house with spotless accommodation. One of the cheapest B&Bs in town, offering low-priced rooms with no views, and more expensive ones with small patios leading onto a lawn. All rooms ③.

Le Quartier Français, corner of Berg and Wilhelmina streets (☎021/876 2151, fax 876 3105, *lqf@icon.co.za*). The most luxurious place to stay in Franschhoek, with two suites (one with its own pool) and fifteen huge rooms decorated with sunny fabrics, thick duvets and fireplaces for winter, all arranged around herb and flower gardens and the swimming pool. Child-friendly, and pricey, but worth it for a special occasion. There's a fine restaurant, too (see p.159). ⑦.

Paradise Cottages, Roberstsvlei Rd (☎ & fax 021/876 2160). Among the most inexpensive rooms in the valley in old, basic accommodation on a farm. ②.

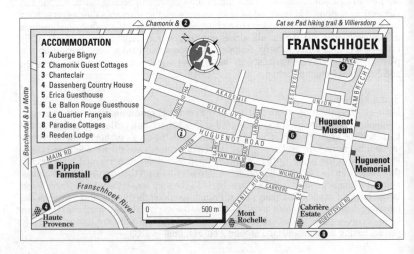

ACCOMMODATION
1 Auberge Bligny
2 Chamonix Guest Cottages
3 Chanteclair
4 Dassenberg Country House
5 Erica Guesthouse
6 Le Ballon Rouge Guesthouse
7 Le Quartier Français
8 Paradise Cottages
9 Reeden Lodge

FRANSCHHOEK

Reeden Lodge, off Cabrière St (☎ & fax 021/876 3174). Three lovely self-catering cottages on a farm, set along a river near Cabrière Estate and within walking distance of town. Very reasonably priced, with a minimum charge based on three people staying. Winter discounts available. ③.

The Town and its wineries

Away from the wining and dining, Franschhoek's attractions are limited to hiking, horse-riding or cycling in the valley, or visiting the institutionalized Huguenot Monument and adjacent museum, which together occupy a prime position at the head of Huguenot Road, where it forms a T-junction with Lambrecht Street. The **Huguenot Monument** consists of three skinny, interlocking arches symbolizing the Holy Trinity, while the **Huguenot Museum** (Mon–Fri 9am–5pm, Sat 9am–1pm & 2–5pm, Sun 2–5pm; small entrance fee) gives comprehensive coverage of Huguenot history, culture and of their contribution to modern South Africa.

The best **hike** in the vicinity is the Cat se Pad (Cat's path), which starts on your left just under a kilometre from the museum as you head out of town up the Franschhoek Pass. The walk leads into fynbos with proteas, and gives instant access to the mountains that surround the valley, with good views. The first two-kilometre section gets you to the top of the pass and you can keep going for another 10km in the direction of Villiersdorp (though you don't actually reach it). To return, simply retrace your steps.

The wineries

Franschhoek's **wineries** are small enough and sufficiently close together to make it a breeze to visit two or three on foot, by mountain bike or even on horseback. Heading north through town from the Huguenot Monument, you'll find virtually all the wineries along branches that are signposted off Huguenot Road and its extension, Main Road.

Close to the Monument, **Cabrière Estate**, on Berg Road (Mon–Fri 8.30am–5pm, Sat 11am–1pm; cellar tours Mon–Fri 11am & 3pm, Sat 11am; ☎021/876 2630), is reached through groves of fruit trees that lead up to the homestead and tasting room. The winery is notable for its Pinot Noirs and colourful wine-maker Achim von Arnim, whose presence on Saturdays guarantees an eventful visit; try to catch him when he slices off the upper neck of a bubbly bottle with a sabre, sending flying the neatly detached cork wrapped in the severed top ring of glass. Next door, **Mont Rochelle**, on Daniel Hugo Road (Mon–Sat 10am–4pm, plus Jan–April & Sept–Dec Sun 11am–1pm; cellar tours Mon–Sat 11am, 12.30pm & 3pm; ☎021/876 3000), has one of the most stunning settings in Franschhoek and an unusual cellar in a converted nineteenth-century fruit-packing shed, edged by eaves decorated with fretwork, stained-glass windows and chandeliers. Look out for the promising new wines under their premium Mont Rochelle label – the first South African wines to be bottled by an all-woman team.

Back on Huguenot Road, keep heading north and turn right into Uitkyk Street to get to **Chamonix** (daily 9.30am–4pm; ☎021/876 2498), which holds its tastings in the cosy Blacksmith's Cottage (where you can also get a light meal). The estate's most consistent wines are their Cabernet Sauvignon and Chardonnay, but they also produce Chamonix schnapps from pear, peach, plum, apple and nectarine, and for teetotallers, Eau de Chamonix. There's a good restaurant here too (see "Eating and drinking", p.159).

Retrace your route back to Hugeunot Road, and a left turn just after the Pippin Farm Stall, where the road merges with Main Street, will bring you to **Haute Provence** (daily 9am–4pm; ☎021/876 3195), across the train tracks. This is one of the most casual and friendly estates, where you can sit in comfy armchairs in a tasting room with a traditional *rietdak* (cane and mud ceiling), surrounded by paintings by well-known South African artists. The estate is best known for Angels' Tears, a fruity blend of Chenin Blanc and Muscat d'Alexandrie grapes, whose name derives from the legend of a French village where angels came at night to taste the new vintage and wept for joy at its brilliance. Although the wine is highly drinkable, come for the genial ambience rather than to hear heavenly sighs. In contrast, **La Motte Estate** (Mon–Fri 9am–4.30pm, Sat 9am–noon; ☎021/876 3119), further along Main Road (here called the R45), presents a supremely cool front, with a superb designer tasting room that looks onto the cellar through a sheer wall of glass. This was the estate that put to rest once and for all the long-held notion that Franschhoek was a poor region for producing red wines. Among the wines, you'll find a good Shiraz and Cabernet Sauvignon and a stunning blend known as Millennium, which sells out quickly.

If you have time for only one estate around here, **Boschendal** (summer Mon–Sat 8.30am–4.30pm; winter Mon–Fri 8.30am–4.30pm, Sat 8.30am–12.30pm; ☎021/874 1031) is the obvious choice. Equidistant between Franschhoek and Stellenbosch at the junction of the R45 and R310, it is geared to absorbing busloads of tourists, who lap up its impressive Cape Dutch buildings, tree-lined avenues, choice of restaurants and cafés (see "Eating and drinking" below), and of course its wines. Now owned by the massive Anglo-American corporation, which has moved from mining to dominate the South African economy, Boschendal is one of the world's longest-established New World wine estates, dating back to 1685, when its lands were granted to Huguenot settler Jean Le Long. The Cape Dutch manor was built in 1812 by Paul de Villiers and his wife, whose initials appear on the front gable. Wine tasting takes place at the Taphuis, where you can sit indoors or sip under shady trees. Of its Reserve range, look out for the Merlot, and Shiraz; and from its extensive regular range, try the Sauvignon Blanc, Chardonnay and the Boschendal brut bubbly.

One- or two-hour **horseback tours** of Franschhoek's wineries for around R50 an hour can be arranged through Mont Rochelle Equestrian Centre (☎021/876 2635, fax 876 2362, mobile ☎083/300 4368); they also do a three-cellar ride (about two-and-a-half hours) for roughly R120, which takes in Clos Cabrière and Haute Provence, at each of which you taste one wine, and ends at Mont Rochelle, where you get to try their whole range; or there's a longer ride (10am–3pm) for R250, which takes in Haute Provence, Rickety Bridge and Moreson, where you have lunch (included in the cost).

Eating and drinking

Eating and drinking is what Franschhoek is all about, so there's little point in making the effort to get here without sampling at least one or two of its excellent **restaurants**, some of which number among the Cape's best. Restaurants in town are concentrated along Huguenot Road, but there are a number of excellent alternatives in the more rustic environment of the surrounding wine estates. **Booking** is essential. Franschhoek's cuisine tends to be French-inspired, but not exclusively so, and salmon trout is a local speciality. For coffee or a sandwich, head for one of the many **cafés** in town, or book a **picnic** hamper at one of the wineries and eat alfresco within sipping distance of the vineyards.

Restaurants

Le Ballon Rouge, 12 Reservoir St (☎021/876 2071). The splash-out menu covers an eclectic range of Mediterranean flavours from Greek starters to their marvellous focaccia filled with smoked chicken breast, five-leaf salad and a sweet curry dressing.

Boschendal, junction of the R45 and R310 to Stellenbosch (☎021/874 1252). Legendary for its pricey but exhaustive daily buffet lunch which will set you up for rest of day. Eat as much as you can from the spread of soup, oysters, kalimari, roasts, casseroles salads, Cape specialities, cheeseboard and desserts.

Bread & Wine, Môreson Farm, Happy Valley Rd, off the R45 (☎021/876 3692). Mediterranean farmhouse lunches accompanied by the estate's own wines in a friendly venue beside a fountain in a courtyard surrounded by orchards and vineyards.

Chez Michel, Huguenot Rd, just north of *Le Quartier Français* and opposite the post office (☎021/876 2671). Franschhoek's oldest eating place is a congenial bistro patronized by locals, in a Victorian house. The emphasis is continental and the mid-range menu incorporates steak, seafood and excellent homemade gateaux.

Haute Cabriére, Franschhoek Pass (☎021/876 3688). A bunker-like venue with an interesting mix-and-match menu planned around Cabrière wines, available by the glass or bottle. There are no starters or main courses but you can order half-portions from a choice that takes in salmon trout, lamb, ratatouille, wonderful desserts and homemade chocolates. There's a helipad on the roof should you wish to fly in.

La Maison de Chamonix, Uitkyk St (☎021/876 2393). French-based menu that includes oysters and smoked salmon trout inside or outdoors on the Chamonix estate surrounded by views of the valley.

La Petite Ferme, Franschhoek Pass (☎021/876 3016). Justifiably one of the most popular Franschhoek lunch venues in a Victorian-style building with superb views across the valley. Country-fare meals include light salads, but their party piece is the deboned smoked salmon trout.

Polfyntjies Country Restaurant, Main Rd (☎021/876 3217). Gourmet versions of South African favourites such as *boerewors*, *bredie* and *bobotie*, as well as local salmon trout in several versions, cold soups and salads. All is served up in an 1860s' farmhouse, with the wine list offering among the best drinking value in Franschhoek. Closed Tues.

Le Quartier Francais, 16 Huguenot Rd (☎021/876 2151). Excellent choice for a no-holds-barred formal meal with a local flavour and an imaginative edge at the place that made Franschhoek synonymous with food. Choose from vegetarian noodles, snoek and lemongrass *sosaties* or grilled salmon trout cutlets with saffron potatoes, followed by delicious desserts.

Light meals, delis and picnics

Boschendal, junction of R45 and R310 to Stellenbosch (☎021/874 1252). *Le Café* does light, sit-down lunches, while *Le Pique Nique* offers deluxe picnic hampers daily under the shady pines. Booking for both is essential.

Dominic's Restaurant & Tea Garden, 66 Huguenot St. Inexpensive, casual place with an alfresco eating area.

Frandeli, Co-op Building, Huguenot Rd. Licensed deli that serves delicious, filled focaccias and bagels accompanied by beer or wine to eat in or take away.

Gideon's Pancake House, 50 Huguenot Rd. Tasty savoury or sweet pancakes with a touch of Cape Muslim flavours.

Mont Rochelle, off Main Rd (☎021/876 3000). Picnic baskets are on offer every day at one of Franschhoek's most scenic wineries.

Pippin Farm Stall, Main Rd. Includes Franschhoek trout among its delicious foods, which you can use to make up your own budget picnic.

Ralf's Country Restaurant & Village Pub, 3 Main Rd. Relaxed and inexpensive joint with an outdoor eating area.

BREEDE RIVER VALLEY AND THE LITTLE KAROO

One of the most rewarding journeys in the Western Cape is an inland counterpart to the Garden Route – the **mountain route** from Cape Town to Port Elizabeth. Nowhere near as well known as the coastal journey, this trip will take you through some of the most dramatic passes and *poorts* (valley routes) in the country and crosses a fading frontier of *dorps* and drylands.

Beyond the Paarl and Stellenbosch winelands, a vast hinterland fans out away from Cape Town. Just outside Paarl, the Huguenot Tunnel punches through the Dutoitsberg mountain range to emerge in the fruit-growing and wine-making country of the **Breede River Valley**, where mountains give way to a jigsaw of valleys, each quite distinct in

PASSES AND POORTS OF THE LITTLE KAROO

The **Little Karoo** is hemmed in to the north by the Langeberg range and to the south the Outeniqua (the range that separates it from the Garden Route). In between lies a gauntlet of mountains and valleys that for centuries made this area virtually impassable for wheeled transport. In the nineteenth century, the British began to tackle the problem and dozens of **passes** were built through the Cape's mountains, 34 of which were engineered by the brilliant road-builder Andrew Geddes Bain and his son Thomas. In 1878, Anthony Trollope commented that the **Outeniqua Pass**, just north of George on the way to Oudtshoorn, equalled "some of the mountain roads through the Pyrenees", a description which just as easily applies today to any number of other Little Karoo passes. In fact, whatever the Little Karoo lacks in museums and art galleries is amply compensated for by the towering drama of these Victorian masterpieces.

In **Afrikaans** there are two words for pass: *pas*, meaning "a route over the mountains" and *poort*, meaning "a valley route", often following a river. Most passes are narrow, winding and steep, and frequently untarred, so they need to be driven slowly. In any case, you won't want to rush past such fantastic views, so it's worth bringing along food and drink to enjoy at the numerous picnic spots along the way. Below, we've listed a selection of some of the best of the passes and *poorts*:

Meiringspoort, just north of De Rust. Tarred road through a gorge in the Swartberg, which keeps crossing a light-brown river, while huge slabs of folded and zigzagging rock rise up on either side. There's a picnic spot at each fording place and a waterfall at Ford 17 (they're all numbered). You can walk from here for 12km into the mountains (see p.174).

Swartberg Pass, between Oudtshoorn and Prince Alfred. Over-the-Swartberg counterpart of Meiringspoort, with 1:7 gradients on narrow untarred roads characterized by precipitous hairpins. Not recommended in poor weather or if you suffer from vertigo (see p.174).

Cogman's Kloof Pass, between Ashton and Montagu. A five-kilometre route that is at its most dramatic as it blasts through a rock face into the Montagu valley (see p.166).

Gamkaskloof Pass, aka Die Hel (The Hell), accessed from the summit of the Swartberg Pass. Arguably the most awesome of all the passes leading into a dramatic and lonely valley. You have to return the same way, as there is no circular route (see p.174).

Prince Alfred's Pass, between the N2 just east of Knysna and Avontuur on the R62.

Du Toit's Kloof Pass, between Paarl and Worcester. The more exciting alternative to the Huguenot Toll Tunnel, with 1:9 gradients (see "Worcester and Ceres", opposite).

character. It's here, not in the more developed Winelands proper, that so many calendar shots are taken of isolated whitewashed homesteads dwarfed by vine-covered hills.

Although the Breede River Valley is part of a through route to the Eastern Cape via Oudtshoorn, its towns also make convenient excursions from Cape Town. **Worcester**, the large functional hub of the region, is only 110km from Cape Town, while to its north, **Tulbagh**, a more promising destination, with a perfectly restored provincial Cape Dutch street, is an easy 130km from the city. South from Worcester, the R60 shadows the groove cut by the Breede River and provides access to the rather dull little town of **Robertson**, centre of yet another wine route. Some 19km south lies **McGregor**, a small, laid-back town with a rural feel, and an excellent choice for a weekend stay. Nearby and a similar distance from the Cape Peninsula, the pleasant historic spa town of **Montagu** is towered over by precipitous red-streaked cliffs that attract serious mountaineers from all over the country.

Continuing east from Montagu, the R62 meanders into the Garden Route's backyard, the **Little Karoo** (or Klein Karoo), a vast and brittle khaki-coloured hinterland (the name is a Khoi word meaning "hard and dry"). The Little Karoo provides the easiest access to the semi-desert that seeps across one-third of South Africa's surface. Open treeless plains, sporadically vegetated with low, wiry scrub, and dotted with flat-topped hills, dissolve eventually into the Great Karoo, which extends into the southern Free State and well into the Eastern and Northern Cape provinces. The Great Karoo is the harsh frontier which a succession of South Africans occupied by turns: San hunters, Khoi herders, Griqua (coloured) farmers and Afrikaner trekkers. Today Afrikaans is the dominant language, used by white and coloured speakers, the latter having absorbed what remained of the Khoi.

The unsung surprise along the way is **Calitzdorp**, a rustic little *dorp*, five to six hours' solid driving from Cape Town, down whose backstreets a few unassuming wine farms produce some of South Africa's best port. Around here you'll find neglected valleys where some of the old Karoo clings on tenuously in an almost feudal relationship between farmsteads and faded scatterings of coloured workers' cottages. By contrast, the well-trumpeted attractions of **Oudtshoorn**, half an hour further on, are the ostrich farms and the massive **Cango Caves**, one of the country's biggest tourist draws. Less than 70km from the coast, with good transport connections, Oudtshoorn marks the convergence of the mountain and coastal roads and is usually treated as a leisurely day-trip away from the Garden Route.

Slicing up through the northernmost third of the Klein Karoo, on its way to Johannesburg, the N1 slips past **Matjiesfontein**, a wonderfully preserved Victorian railway town, and the mountainous **Karoo National Park**, both just off the main road and definitely worth breaking a trip for.

Worcester and Ceres

The fastest way to navigate the mountains from Paarl into the Breede River Valley is via the **Huguenot Toll Tunnel**, which burrows straight through to the other side, but misses the wonderful scenery of driving over the **Du Toit's Kloof Pass**. Much slower but far more interesting, the pass works its way through a series of wonderful mountain ranges with views onto distant farms and villages in the valleys.

WORCESTER, which is 31km from Paarl through the tunnel, is a relatively large town for this part of the world, and features some attractive historic frontage down Church Street, but not enough to demand much of your time. An agricultural centre with a number of factories, it's at the centre of a wine-making region, consisting mostly of co-operatives producing bulk plonk that makes up about one-fifth of national output. There really isn't much reason to dally here, apart from visiting the **Kleinplasie Living Open Air Museum** (Mon–Sat 9am–4.30pm, Sun 10.30am–4.30pm; small entry fee), which depicts the life on the Karoo frontier between 1690 and 1900. Made up of about two dozen reconstructed buildings, with staff in old-style workshops engaged in crafts and home industries, the museum is fairly absorbing. Keep a lookout in particular for the corbelled shepherd's hut, which represents a vernacular style unique to the Karoo, using domed stone roofs rather than beam and lintel construction – a response to the dearth of timber in the treeless expanse. There's a **restaurant** and **café** on site, and next door a wine shop sells a good selection of labels from the Worcester wineries. The museum is just outside the centre of town – to get there, head east along High Street and turn right onto the road to Robertson.

Taking the R43 north from Worcester for 49km brings you to **CERES**, another farming centre which, like several in the vicinity, is highly missable. Its most notable claim to fame is the factory that produces most of South Africa's delicious juices (same fruit, different labels: Ceres, Liquifruit, Just Juice and all the other fruity labels come from one plant on the outskirts of town).

Tulbagh

Altogether the most rewarding destination in the northern section of the Breede River Valley is **TULBAGH**, easily visited in a day from Cape Town, which lies 130km south. You could drive into town, down Van der Stel Street and out the other end, and assume from this unexceptional main street that Tulbagh was just another humdrum *dorp*. But one block west, on **Church Street**, is the most perfectly restored eighteenth- and nineteenth-century streetscape. Although only a fraction of what you see here is the original frontage (the town having been flattened in 1969 by an earthquake), this is no Disneyland, because even if the facades aren't original they're unquestionably authentic and undoubtedly beautiful.

Arrival, information and accommodation

There's no public transport to Tulbagh; the only way you'll make it here is by **car**, taking either the **R43** from Worcester or the **R301** from Paarl. One of the highlights of the drive is crossing the beautiful **Bain's Kloof Pass**, which connects these two routes.

The town's **tourist information** bureau, 4 Church St (May–Aug Mon–Fri 9am–5pm, Sat 10am–4pm, Sun 11am–4pm; Sept–April closed Sun; ☎ & fax 0236/230 1348), can give advice on activities and accommodation in the area. Tulbagh Valley Trails (see box below) offer **mountain-bike rental** – an excellent way to get to wineries or other local attractions.

The cheapest **place to stay** is *Kliprivier Park Holiday Resort* (☎0236/230 0506), one of the nicest municipal caravan parks in the country, with campsites (①) and very basic chalets (②), some of which are on the edge of a dam and have excellent views of the mountains. Good-value B&B accommodation is available at *The Little Courtyards*, 30 Church St (☎ & fax 0236/230 1448, *cook@intekom.co.za*; ③–④), where Tulbagh Valley Trails offer a choice of three en-suite doubles of varying size at the back of a friendly historic house, which has a courtyard under vines. Nearby, *De Oude Herberg*, 6 Church St (☎ & fax 0236/230 0260; ③), is a well-positioned inn offering comfortable rooms with French doors opening onto the communal verandah. Roughly 1.5km north of town along the main road, *Hunter's Retreat* (☎0236/230 0582, fax 230 0057; ④) has plain and airy B&B rooms and spacious two-storey thatched cottages with lounges on a working farm that's home to cattle, ostriches and sheep. Six kilometres south of town, heading towards Wolseley, a signposted turn-off leads you 2km down a dirt track to the family-oriented *Wild Olive Farm* (☎ & fax 0236/230 1160; ②). Offering a choice of six fully equipped self-catering cottages with mountain views, guests are given milk and eggs

---

TULBAGH WILDERNESS TOURS

Instead of just admiring the mountains from afar, you might want to get right into them, and this is possible on a **guided tour** with Tulbagh Valley Trails, 30 Church St (☎ & fax 0236/230 1448, *cook@intekom.co.za*). Dave Cook, a former Natal Parks Board conservationist, leads the way, and focuses on interpreting an environment rich in fynbos, as well as looking at animals and birds. A typical half-day tour takes you into remote parts of the mountains, where you walk for a couple of hours to look for klipspringer and black eagles and explore the vegetation, which, though it appears scruffy and dry, is one of the most diverse floral kingdoms in the world. In summer, swimming is possible at a magnificent waterfall pool. Trips are priced per group and are particularly good value when there are three or more people (from R315).

and can buy meat for *braais*. You can swim in their mountain-stream dam or set out on a free mountain bike to explore the large property. The most luxurious of Tulbagh's accommodation is at *Waterval Country Lodge and Bushcamp* (☎0236/230 0807) off the R46 to Wolseley, on the southern outskirts of Tulbagh. The restored homestead, set in a huge stand of pine plantation, has five en-suite B&B rooms (⑤), each with its own verandah. There's also the choice of staying in luxury en-suite tents or log cabins (④), either of which are cheaper if self-catering.

The Town

The best way to enjoy Tulbagh is to stroll up **Church Street** and take in the houses, gardens and the development in the style of gables that are an essential element of Cape Dutch architecture. After the 1969 earthquake, **restoration** of the buildings took place using salvaged materials from the ruins, following photographic and hand-drawn records. At least six different styles can be distinguished just along this short road. At no. 23, **Paddagang** (frog passage) was originally a *taphuis* (wine house), so it's fitting that it's now a restaurant with a wine house attached (see below), which is recommended for its wonderful labels all featuring comical frogs rather than for the liquor itself. Although the gabled Old Church, built in 1743, is of some interest, you won't be missing much if you don't spend long over the collection of bric-a-brac inside that constitutes the **Oude Kerk Volksmuseum**, 2 Church St (Mon–Fri 8am–1pm & 2–5pm, Sat 10am–1pm & 2–4pm, Sun 11am–1pm & 2–4pm; small entry fee). The museum has three annexes (Mon–Fri 9am–1pm & 2–5pm; all included in entry fee) at nos. 4, 14 and 22, which won't keep you busy for too long either. No. 4 has photographs of old houses in Tulbagh before the earthquake and traces the histories of the families who lived in them.

Outside town, **De Oude Drostdy Museum** (Mon–Sat 10am–1pm & 2–5pm; Sun 2.30–5pm), 4km to the north on the extension of Van der Stel Street, is an impressive Cape Dutch spectacle designed by the French architect Louis-Michel Thibault. Apart from some very nice pieces of furniture and a pleasantly relaxed atmosphere, the museum's main draw is the startling view of the mountains and farmlands that confronts you as you step out through the front doors.

Eating and drinking

Apart from its historic streetscape, Tulbagh's biggest attraction is the *Paddagang Restaurant and Wine House*, 23 Church Street (☎0236/230 0242). Established in 1821 as one of the first taverns in the Cape, it serves moderately priced traditional regional cooking and locally produced wines and has lovely gardens, where you can sit outside under vines. The restaurant is open for breakfast, lunch and tea daily. Traditional curries and country cuisine are on offer at *De Oude Herberg*, Church St, which opens daily for breakfast, lunch, tea and dinner and has terrace seating. *Pieter Potter* (☎0236/230 1626), despite an unpromising location in busy Van der Stel Street, does reasonably priced steak, ribs and excellent fish lunches and dinners from Tuesday to Saturday until late, and lunch only on Sunday. *Le Midi*, at the *Witzenberg Country Inn* in Piet Retief Street, cooks up Cape Mediterranean cuisine.

Robertson and McGregor

ROBERTSON, 77km off the N2, is the largest town in the interesting stretch of the Breede River Valley that connects Worcester to Oudtshoorn. Its size, however, does nothing to mitigate the fact that Robertson is, unfortunately, a big yawn that dies completely over weekends. The only conceivable reason for popping into this fruit-picking town, is to visit the **Robertson Winery** (Mon–Thurs 8am–5pm, Fri 8am–4.30pm, Sat 9am–1pm) just off the R60, which breaks the general co-operative mould by producing some good-value and fairly quaffable Chardonnays and Colombards that are cheaper here than in the shops. In fact the Robertson Valley has its own **wine route**, which extends to McGregor and Bonnievale in the south (see box).

If you're not stocking up on liquor, press straight on to **MCGREGOR**, fifteen minutes to the south, at the end of a minor road signposted off the R60. Although it's been described as South Africa's best-preserved Victorian Karoo village, you certainly shouldn't expect anything like a quaint English hamlet – a description that might just about apply to Greyton on the well-watered side of the mountains (see p.181). Still, dry as it is, McGregor is an attractive enough place, with whitewashed cottages glaring in the summer daylight amid the low rusty steel-wool scrub, and a quiet, relaxed atmos-

---

ROBERTSON VALLEY WINERIES: PICK OF THE BUNCH

The Robertson Valley is responsible for some ten percent of South Africa's vineyards. Its soils have an ideal acidity level for growing grapes, but because it's hot and dry, intense irrigation is necessary. Its best wines tend to be Chenin Blancs and Colombards and it can conjure up some good Muscadels. We've picked out the best of its roughly two dozen wineries.

ALONG THE R317 FROM ROBERTSON TO BONNIEVALE

Bon Courage, about 8km southeast of Robertson, on the right-hand side of the road (Mon–Fri 9am–5pm, Sat 9am–12.30pm; tasting free; ☎02351/4178). Tasting room in a beautiful old homestead along the Breede River. Notable for its sweet whites, and especially its Muscadel.

Van Loveren, roughly 8km south of Bon Courage, on the right-hand side of the road (Mon–Fri 9–1pm & 2–4.30pm, Sat 9.30am–1pm; tasting free; ☎0234/615 1505). Wine tasting in a lovely garden at a friendly estate that produces a quaffable Chardonnay and Pinot Gris.

De Wetshof, 500m south of Van Loveren on the left of the road (Mon–Fri 8.30am–4.30pm, Sat 9.30am–1pm; tasting free; ☎0234/615 1857). Top-notch estate producing several excellent wines including Chardonnay, several variants on Rhine Riesling and their great Finesse.

ALONG THE R60 FROM ROBERTSON TO WORCESTER

Graham Beck, about 7km north of Robertson (May–Sept Mon–Fri 9am–5pm; tasting free; ☎02351/61214). High-flying estate determined to make an international splash – and succeeding big-time with orders from the British supermarket giants, including Tesco and Marks and Spencer. Daringly modern tasting room where you can savour their outstanding Chardonnay and a first-class, pioneering, champagne-style Chardonnay bubbly.

Nuy, turn-off 53km north of Robertson (Mon–Fri 8.30am–4.30pm, Sat 8.30am–12.30pm; tasting free; ☎0231/70272). Not strictly on the Robertson Valley wine route, but one of South Africa's most successful wine-making co-operatives and one that can easily be taken in as part of it. As well as visiting the winery, you can buy, but not taste their wines from the Pitkos Wyne stall, about 32km from Roberston and just beyond the Nuy turn-off. Their lovely Colombard is excellent value and the romantically named Chants de Nuit is a pleasant curiosity, with a hint of pineapple. However, the latter will hit the dust after the 1999 vintage (which should still be available in 2000), because its ingredients include Ferdinand de Lesseps grapes, which have been declared inadmissable by wine-making authorities.

phere that has attracted a small population of spiritual seekers and alternative types. In the shadow of the Dutch Reformed church down the high street, you'll find the **Temenos Retreat Centre** (see "McGregor Practicalities", below) and a Waldorf school. The time to pull out your camera is in the late afternoon, when the sinking sun suffuses the landscape with deeply saturated colours.

McGregor gained some modest prosperity in the nineteenth century by becoming a centre of the whipstock industry, supplying wagoners and transport riders with long bamboo sticks for goading oxen. There aren't too many ox-drawn wagons today and, apart from farming, tourism (which is still quite limited) is beginning to develop. Residents are being urged to build in harmony with existing style and thus maintain the town's character.

Apart from its spare beauty – and it's worth taking a late-afternoon stroll down one of the dirt roads out of town – the main reason people come here is to walk the **Boesmanskloof Traverse** (see p.180), which crosses to Greyton on the other side of the mountain.

McGregor practicalities

Voortrekker Street is McGregor's main thoroughfare, where you'll find a small, clearly signposted **tourist information** bureau (Mon–Fri 10am–5pm, Sat 9am–12.30pm; ☎023/625 1856). The dirt roads around town are perfect for cycling, and you can arrange **bike rental** through *Villagers Art and Coffee Shop*, also in the main road (see below).

All the central **accommodation** is in Voortrekker Street, or clearly indicated off it. Cheapest of the lot is the non-sectarian *Temenos Retreat Centre* (☎023/625 1871, fax 625 1885; ②), on the corner of Voortrekker and Bree streets, which has single rooms where simple vegetarian meals are provided to people seeking the isolation of retreat; they also offer comfortable self-catering cottages, open to anyone, whether on retreat or not. *McGregor House* (☎023/625 1925, fax 625 1620; ③) has some en-suite rooms and others with shared baths; there's also a tea and wine garden. For more flair, head for the friendly *McGregor B&B* (☎023/625 1656, fax 625 1617; ③), which has three attractive en-suite rooms and serves a substantial continental breakfast. For tranquil self-catering, *McGregor Country Cottages* (☎023/625 1816, fax 625 1840; ③) offers a complex of eight workers' dwellings with traditional reed ceilings, surrounded by gardens, orchards and vegetable patches with a pool. The smartest place in town is the *Old Mill Lodge* (☎023/625 1841, fax 625 1941, *1445580@beltel.co.za*; ④), a set of cottages at the southern end of Voortrekker Street, surrounded by vineyards and gardens with a swimming pool.

Outside town you'll find self-catering accommodation at Dove Cottage, on Rhebokskraal Farm (☎023/625 1951, fax 625 1739, or enquire at *Villagers Art and Coffee Shop* on Voortrekker Street; ②), 2km south of town. A restored cottage on a beautiful fruit and grape farm, it's secluded and cosy, with views of mountains and the Karoo, and offers good walking opportunities. Ask for precise directions when you book, as you can't just turn up at the farm. Some 8km from the centre, *Whipstock Farm* (☎ & fax 023/625 1733; full board ④), on the southerly continuation of Voortrekker Street, has restored cottages on an old citrus, almond and grape farm in the mountains. *Whipstock* is 5km from the McGregor side of the Boesmanskloof Traverse (see p.180), and the owners will pick you up from the trail for free. Swimming, bikes and canoes are available free to guests and there's reasonably priced horse-riding too. Another option for walkers is to try the basic semi-equipped huts rented out by Mr Oosthuizen (☎023/625 1735; ②) at the McGregor side of the Traverse; bring your own sleeping bag, towels and supplies.

When it comes to **food**, *Cafe Eremo* (Wed–Sat 10am–5pm), in Voortrekker St, is a delightful place for its excellent coffee, cakes and ciabattas and its stock of magazines. *Villagers*, in the same street, has the advantage of being open daily and is good for daytime snacks and teas with a verandah to watch the passing scene. North of here, the good-value *Lion House Tea Lounge & Dining Room* serves hearty bangers and mash, as well as curries. Light lunches are on offer at the *Old Mill Lodge* (see previous page), where you can also splash out on a four-course set evening meal – though if you want to indulge in the latter, you'll need to have made an advance reservation by lunchtime. On Friday and Saturday nights till 10pm the hottest **drinking** place in town – literally, as it's invariably packed to its capacity of fifteen people – is the extremely popular Irish-themed *Overdraught Pub,* down the main drag. Hosted by the owner of the *McGregor B&B*, it serves draught Guinness and Caffrey's imported from the Emerald Isle, as well as a range of bitters shipped in from England. The absence of a TV or pool table forces you to catch up on local village gossip.

Montagu

Without a doubt **MONTAGU** is the ultimate Breede River Valley destination, and approaching from the south through Cogman's Kloof Gorge numbers among the most dramatic arrivals in the country. A short five-kilometre winding road blasts through a rock face into a tight valley dramatically opening out to Montagu, which is small enough to capture in one glance. Soaring mountains rise up in vast arches of twisted strata that display reds and ochres, and from September to October the gentler tints of peach and apricot blossoms flood the valley. Not only is Montagu very pleasing, with sufficient Victorian architecure to create an historic character, but there's enough to do here to more than justify an overnight stay.

MONTAGU ACTIVITIES

To most people Montagu is best known for its **hot springs**, but serious **rock climbers** come for its cliff faces, which are regarded as among the country's most challenging. You can also explore the mountains on a couple of trails or more effortlessly still on a tractor ride onto one of the peaks that offer stunning panoramas. Montagu is also conveniently positioned for excursions along both the Robertson and Klein Karoo **wine routes** (see p.165).

Three **hikes** begin from the *Old Mill* at the north end of Tanner Street, from where you can also take a gentle meander at the foot of cliffs in a small park; **maps** for the hikes are available from Montagu's tourist information bureau. Shortest is the Lover's Walk, just over a two-kilometre stroll through Bath Kloof (or Badkloof) that follows the Keisie River to the hot springs and is open between 7am and 6pm. More substantial is the twelve-kilometre Cogman's Kloof Hiking Trail, which can be completed in three to six hours; only the first 2km are steep, after which it's an easy walk at a medium altitude, with nice views of Montagu, the ravines and mountains. Most ambitious is the Bloupunt Hiking Trail, at around 15.5km, which gets you up to an altitude of over 1000m and can be completed in six to nine hours. The walk passes through terrain with ravines, mountain streams, craggy cliffs and rock formations and from the summit of Bloupunt you can see as far as McGregor and Robertson. Throughout the year, you will see dassies and klipspringers as well as a large variety of wild flowers because of the presence of perennial streams. The fynbos vegetation includes proteas, ericas, aloes, lilies, watsonias and wild orchids. Carry a waterbottle to fill up at a waterpoint about halfway up the mountain.

If you don't feel like walking up the Langeberg Mountains, you can still get to the top on a highly recommended three-hour **tractor ride** (Wed 10am, Sat 9.30am & 2pm; book at the Montagu tourist information bureau), from Protea Farm, which is 29km along the Koo/Touws River road (R318). Remember to take warm clothes as it can be brisk up there.

The town was named in 1851 after **John Montagu**, the visionary British Secretary of the Cape, who realized that the colony would never develop without decent communications and was responsible for commissioning the first mountain passes that connected remote areas to Cape Town. The grateful farmers of Agter Cogman's Kloof (Behind Cogman's Kloof) leapt at the chance of a snappier name for their village and called it after him.

Arrival, information and accommodation

Intercity **bus** services to Montagu are sparse and inconvenient. The Translux sevice (☎021/405 3333) stops here three times a week on its journey between Cape Town and Port Elizabeth, arriving at the *Avalon Hotel* in Bath Street, either in the late evening or before sunrise. The cheaper and more convenient Munniks (☎021/637 1850) service from Cape Town (a 2hr journey) stops at the *Spur* steakhouse on Wednesday, Friday, Saturday and Sunday, returning the following day. Montagu's **tourist information** bureau, 24 Bath St (Mon–Fri 8.45am–4.45pm, Sat 9am–noon; ☎023/614 2471), is useful for picking up information about local attractions.

Accommodation

Even if you're visiting for the springs, it is far nicer to find somewhere to **stay** in town rather than at the spa, which amounts to little more than a large crowded resort, especially at weekends and school holidays. If you do get stuck, the tourist information bureau can help.

Avalon Springs Hotel (☎023/614 1150, fax 614 1906). One of two options at Montagu Springs, this tacky pink hotel offers B&B rooms and cheaper self-catering flats. Mountain facing ⑤, spa facing ⑦.

Cynthia's, 3 Krom St (☎023/614 2760, fax 614 1326). Six self-catering cottages dotted around the west side of town, all in old houses, with gardens and *braai* areas, and near the starting point for hiking trails. ②.

John Montagu Victorian Guest House, 30 Joubert St (☎ & fax 023/614 1331). En-suite rooms at this guesthouse two streets up from Bath St, with enough period furniture and knick-knacks to create an historic ambience without being oppressive. ④.

Kingna Lodge, 11 Bath St (☎023/614 1066, fax 614 2405). Nelson Mandela's choice when he hit town in 1995, this large period house delivers a Victorian atmosphere with a vengeance. The emphasis is on excellent personal service and excellent food, and there's a verandah for tea and a swimming pool and Jacuzzi at the back. Winter discounts. B&B ⑤, half board ⑦.

Mimosa Lodge, Church St (☎023/614 2351, fax 614 2418, *mimosa@vdu.org.za*). Handsome Edwardian double-storey house just off Bath St, with an emphasis on food using local ingredients. Rooms are en suite, with either shower or bath – the best are upstairs, with a balcony. B&B ④, half board ⑥.

Montagu Caravan Park, at the west end of Bath St, across the Keisie River (☎023/614 2675). Friendly municipal park, with delightful personal touches such as fresh flowers everywhere, offering campsites and basic timber cabins which sleep four. Units have cookers and fridges, but ablution facilities are shared. You can rent bedding, but you'll need to bring your own towels. ①.

Montagu Rose Guest House, 19 Kohler St (☎023/614 2681, fax 614 2780). Well-run guesthouse in a modern home, with very personalized service and a hallway plastered with thank-you notes and cards. All rooms have baths and mountain views. ③.

Montagu Springs (☎023/614 1050, fax 614 2235). The resort has 120 fully-equipped self-catering chalets, some more luxurious than others, that sleep four and (a hot tip) are substantially cheaper from Sunday to Thursday and outside school holidays. ③–④.

Squirrel's Corner, corner of Bloem and Jouberts streets (☎ & fax 023/614 1081). One of the most affordable B&Bs in town, with four comfortable, spotless en-suite rooms in a friendly family house, two blocks from the main road. They also rent out a two-bedroom, self-catering cottage around the corner in Krom St. B&B ③, cottage ②.

The Town and around

Highly photogenic, Montagu is a place in which you can happily foot it around, taking in the interesting buildings or simply enjoying the setting, with its mountains, valleys and farms. There are also a couple of museums, neither of which is outstanding. The best thing about the **Montagu Museum**, 41 Long St (Mon–Fri 9am–1pm & 2–5pm, Sat & Sun 10.30am–12.30pm; small entry fee), housed in a pleasant old church, is its herbal project, which traces back traditional Khoisan knowledge about the medicinal properties of local plants. Work is being done in conjunction with the Pharmacology Department at the University of Cape Town and you can buy *Herbal Remedies: Montagu Museum*, which details some of the findings. The herbs themselves are also on sale, and some of them are grown in the gardens of the **Joubert House Museum** (Mon–Fri 9.30am–1pm & 2–5pm, Sat 10am–noon; small entry fee), one block west at 25 Long St. Built in 1853, this was one of the first houses standing in a vast plot which was originally a town farm, and has peach-pip floors fixed with beeswax, characteristic of the area.

Montagu's main draw is the **Montagu Springs Resort** (daily 8am–11pm; entry fee), about 3km northwest ot town on the R318 (or reached on foot, by following the Keisie River which flows along the north edge of town). Several open-air pools of different temperatures and a couple of Jacuzzis are spectacularly situated at the foot of cliffs – an effect unfortunately not enhanced by the neon lights of a tawdry hotel complex and some fast-food joints. Avoid coming here at weekends if you can – when it becomes a mass of splashing bodies – but first thing in the morning or last thing at night, when the outside air is cooler, the steaming waters provide a wonderfully relaxing alcohol-free nightcap. The springs are popular with coloured and Indian families, who were previously barred under apartheid; this has driven some rednecks to establish a racially exclusive spring on a farm outside town, where only whites are allowed.

Eating and drinking

When it comes to **eating**, Montagu has a number of good places dotted around the town centre. *Something Special Coffee Shop*, Bath St (☎023/614 2436), is a great daytime venue in a listed Cape Dutch building, serving sandwiches, milkshakes and coffee. Two doors along at no. 28, *Jessica's Little Food Emporium* (☎023/614 1805), named after the proprietor's boxer dog, is a small friendly eatery serving reasonably priced bistro-type dishes and a top selection of Robertson wines. *Romano's Continental Restaurant*, on Church Street (closed Sun), is open at lunchtime and evenings for reasonably priced pasta and pizza dishes, while *Preston's Restaurant & Thomas Bain Pub*, in Bath Street (☎023/614 1633), is a small, intimate nightspot that remains open till late every night and is recommended for its sole and oxtail. The ultimate eating experience is the superb set-menu five-course meal, served with silver cutlery and candles, at *Kingna Lodge*, 11 Bath St (☎023/614 1066), where you'll need to book by lunchtime and vegetarians can be catered for. For self-catering and **snacks**, *Montagu Dry Fruit Farmstall*, Bath St (Mon–Fri 7am–6pm, Sat 8am–2pm, Sun 7am–1pm), sells dried fruit, *biltong*, *boerewors*, bread, milk and cheese.

Oudtshoorn and around

The slogan promoting **OUDTSHOORN** as the "ostrich capital of the world" makes one think of a sad bunch of PR consultants with their heads in the sand. The town's surrounds are indeed crammed with ostrich farms, several of which you can visit, and the local souvenir shops keep busy dreaming up 1001 tacky ways to recycle ostrich parts as comestibles and souvenirs. But Oudtshoorn has two other big draws: it's the best base for visiting the nearby **Cango Caves** (see p.171), and the town is known for its sunshine and pleasant climate. Only 63km of tar separate Oudtshoorn from Wilderness on the coast, yet the weather couldn't be more different, and this is especially good news in winter, when a cold downpour along the Garden Route can give the lie to the idea of "sunny South Africa".

Some 50km west of Oudtshoorn, **Calitzdorp** is a delightfully unassuming Victorian village that can be taken as a circular excursion incorporating the scenic **Groenfontein Valley**. Alternatively its wineries and one or two tea shops hold out the chance of a breather if you're travelling on the R62 mountain route through the Little Karoo. A town with similar origins to Calitzdorp, but 35km in the opposite direction, is **De Rust**, which has benefited greatly from lying on the national road connecting the N1 to the Garden Route, but is little more than a pleasant pit stop on a journey north.

Some history

Oudtshoorn started out as a small village named in honour of Geesje Ernestina Johanna van Oudtshoorn, wife of the first civil commissioner for George. By the 1860s, **ostriches**, which live in the wild in Africa, were being raised under the ideal conditions of the Oudtshoorn Valley, where the warm climate and loamy soils enabled lucerne, the favourite diet of the flightless birds, to be grown. The quirky Victorian fashion for large feathers had turned the ostriches into a source of serious wealth, and by the 1880s hundreds of thousands of kilogrammes of feathers were being exported, and birds were changing hands for up to £1000 a pair – an unimaginable sum in those days. On the back of this boom, sharp businessmen made their fortunes, ignorant farmers got ripped off, and labourers drew the shortest straw of all. The latter were mostly coloured descendants of the Outeniqua and Attaqua Khoikhoi and trekboers, who received derisory wages supplemented by rations of food, wine, spirits and tobacco – a practice that still continues on some farms. In the early twentieth century, the most successful farmers and traders built themselves the "feather palaces", ostentatious sandstone Edwardian piles that have become the defining feature of Oudtshoorn.

Arrival and information

Few people other than business travellers arrive in Oudtshoorn by air and there are no shuttles into town from the **airport** (☎044/279 2088), 2km west of the centre, off Park Street. However, there is a payphone at the airport, which is handy if you've arranged for staff at a hotel or lodge to pick you up. Of the **intercity buses**, Intercape pulls in at Stanmar Motors, 187 Langenhoven Rd, and Translux at Queens Riverside Mall, off Voortrekker Street; the Baz **backpacker bus** will drop you off anywhere in town. If you're travelling on the Outeniqua Choo-Tjoe from George (see p.202), your best bet, if you don't have wheels, is to catch one of the **minibus taxis** that commute between Oudtshoorn and George and rank outside the Diskom shop, behind the Spar supermarket.

Oudtshoorn's **tourist information** bureau (Mon–Fri 8am–6pm, Sat 8.30am–1pm; ☎044/279 2532), at the *Queens Hotel*, Baron van Reede St, is good for information about the caves, ostrich farms and local accommodation. *Backpackers Oasis* (see overleaf) is another excellent source of information about what to do in the vicinity. Joyrides, based at the *Oasis*, rent out **bikes**, whether you're staying with them or not and also arrange spectacular **adventurous cycling trips** down the Swartberg Pass, chaperoned with motor vehicle backup.

Accommodation

Oudtshoorn has a number of large hotels catering mainly to tour buses, plenty of good quality B&Bs and guesthouses, a centrally located campsite with chalets, and two of the country's best-run backpackers' lodges. While accommodation is plentiful, it's also in great demand, so you should **book in advance**. The tourist information bureau offers a free accommodation booking service for all budgets.

Adley House, 209 Jan van Riebeeck Rd (☎ & fax 044/272 4533, *adley@pixie.co.za*). A 1905 sandstone home built during the ostrich boom with eight en-suite rooms (all with TV) a swimming pool and garden to relax in. ⑤.

Backpackers Oasis, 3 Church St, Oudtshoorn (☎044/279 1163, *oasisbackpackers@yahoo.com*). Well organized and helpful backpackers' lodge that can provide you with all sorts of information about the area, as well as running cycling trips with bikes, and reasonably priced trips to Cango Caves (see opposite). Every evening there's an ostrich *braai* and a relaxed jamming session on African instruments around the fire. Camping & dorms ①, doubles ②.

Backpackers Paradise, 148 Baron van Reede St (☎044/272 0725, fax 272 0877, *jubilee@pixie.co.za*). Friendly hostel along the main drag, which makes an effort to go the extra few centimetres with three-quarter beds, and an ostrich egg on the house for breakfast in season. Dorms ①, en-suite doubles ②.

Bedstop, 69 van der Riet St (☎044/272 4746, fax 272 2528). Modest rooms with gardens where you can sit outside, and a *braai*. It's slightly cheaper if you don't have breakfast. ②.

Bisibee, 171 Church St (☎044/272 4784, fax 279 2373, *bisibee@hotmail.com*). Good B&B a few blocks from the centre, with five good-value rooms in a colonial-style home with verandahs, a large garden, swimming pool and a *braai* area. ④.

De Oude Meul, signposted off the R328 to Cango Caves, 18km north of Oudtshoorn (☎ & fax 044/272 7190). A row of pleasant rooms facing onto a small lake and hills in Schoemanspoort, on a nursery ostrich farm. B&B and self-catering available, plus very good dinners. ④.

Kannaland Lodge, 126 St John St (☎044/279 2685, fax 279 2686). Reliable if predictable modern hotel-style rooms conveniently located in the centre. You can buy meat packs and *braai* in the garden, and also use the kitchen. ③.

Kleinplaas Holiday Resort, 171 Baron van Reede St (☎044/272 5811, fax 279 2019). Shady camping and fully equipped brick chalets that sleep four, conveniently close to town, with a swimming pool and laundrette. Camping ①, chalets ②.

Old Parsonage, 141 High St (☎ & fax 044/279 1751). Bedrooms with en-suite or shared bathrooms in a fabulous, centrally located, sandstone, double-storey Dutch Reformed Church parsonage that's still in use and has a very pleasant garden. ②

Oue Werf, signposted off the R328 to Cango Caves, 15km north of Oudtshoorn (☎ & fax 044/272 8712). Farmhouse B&B in an old Schoemanshoek Valley farmstead, with good walks, bird-watching and a swimming pool. A good option if you're visiting the caves and want to stay in the country. ④.

Queen's Hotel, Baron van Reede St (☎044/272 2101, fax 272 2104). Nicest of the smart hotels in Oudtshoorn, with all the facilities and right in the centre, next to the museum. *Queens* offers style and cool relief in the summer, with marble floors, a fountain, swimming pool and the expensive *Langenhoven Restaurant*, with an upstairs terrace and ostrich on the menu. ⑤.

Rosenhof Country Lodge, 264 Baron van Reede St (☎044/272 2232, fax 272 3021). The most elegant place to stay in Oudtshoorn, on the edge of town, with twelve white cottages arranged around a restored Victorian house, set in a beautiful rose garden filled with herbs, manicured lawns, a fountain and swimming pool. The lodge has a good though expensive restaurant serving *cordon bleu* food, using local ingredients. ⑥.

The Town and the ostrich farms

Oudtshoorn's town centre is a pretty straightforward place to negotiate, and has little more than a couple of museums worth checking out if you've time to kill. The town's main interest lies in its Victorian and Edwardian sandstone buildings, some of which are unusually grand and elegant for a Karoo *dorp*.

The **C.P. Nel Museum** (Mon–Sat 9am–5pm; entry fee), on the corner of Baron van Reede Street and Voortrekker Road, is a good place to start your explorations. A handsome sandstone building, it was built in 1906 as a boys' school, but now houses an eccentric and fairly intriguing collection of items relating to ostriches. Nearby, **Le Roux Town**

House, on the corner of Loop and High streets (Mon–Fri 9am–1pm & 2–5pm), is a perfectly preserved family town house, and the only way to get a glimpse inside one of the much-vaunted feather palaces. The beautifully preserved furnishings were all imported from Europe between 1900 and 1920, and there is plenty to stroll around and admire here.

Many people come to Oudtshoorn to see, or even ride, **ostriches**. You don't actually have to visit one of the ostrich farms to view Africa's biggest bird, as you're bound to see flocks of them as you drive past farms in the vicinity or past truckloads of them on their way to the butcher (feathers being no longer fashionable, these days ostriches are raised for their low-cholesterol flesh). A number of show farms offer **tours** (45–90min) costing around R20 a person, which include a commentary, the chance to sit on an ostrich and the spectacle of jockeys racing the birds. Best of the bunch is *Cango Ostrich and Butterfly Farm* (☎044/272 4623, fax 272 8241), on the main road between Oudtshoorn and the Cango Caves, which takes only one group (or individuals) of visitors at a time so you don't end up jostling with other twitchers.

Eating and drinking

Oudtshoorn has a choice of several places to eat, mostly strung out along Baron van Reede Street and all catering to the tourist trade – and if you can't last without checking your email for a day, there's even a cybercafé.

Bernard se Taphuis, Baron van Reede St (☎044/22 3208). Opposite the tourist information bureau, this is a large, central restaurant with a pleasant outdoor terrace upstairs. A good place to sample ostrich, game dishes, steaks and Afrikaner specialities at a medium price.

Chatter's Restaurant, 22 Queen's Riverside Mall (☎044/272 0383). Pleasant venue with an indoor fireplace and outdoor verandah for large portions of reasonably priced ostrich, fish and vegetarian meals.

Cyber Ostrich, 12 Plume St (☎044/272 3334, *intercafe@mweb.co.za*). Oudtshoorn's first cybercafé is the obvious place if you want to bury your head in the Web and enjoy a dose of Java.

Fijne Keuken Restaurant, Baron van Reede St. In a house converted into a cosy restaurant with tables in several rooms as well as on the verandah, this is the nicest spot in town for just a drink, or a reasonably priced meal with enormous salads, pasta and the obligatory ostrich dish.

Godfather Restaurant, 61 Voortrekker Rd (☎044/272 5404). Popular eatery with a huge menu, but noted for its medium priced pizzas and springbok steaks.

Headlines, Baron van Reede St, on the corner of St John's St (☎044/272 3434). Good-value coffee shop and restaurant , serving up good sandwiches, ostrich kebabs and steakhouse-style food and fish. A good place to come for a quick lunch.

Santa Fe Spur, Baron van Reede St, between Olivier and St John's streets. Popular chain serving good-value steaks, burgers, salads and cheaper takeaways.

Cango Caves

The **Cango Caves** number among South Africa's most popular ten attractions, drawing a quarter of a million visitors each year to gasp at their fantastic, cavernous spaces, dripping rocks and rising columns of calcite. In the two centuries since they became known to the public, the caves have been seriously battered by human intervention, but they still represent a stunning landscape growing inside the Swartberg foothills. Don't go expecting a serene and contemplative experience, though: the only way of getting inside the caves is on a guided tour accompanied by a hammed-up commentary.

Cango is a Khoi word meaning "a wet place" – spot on, given that the caves' awesome formations are the work of water constantly percolating through rock and dissolving limestone on the way. The solution drips from the roof of the cave and down the walls, depositing calcium carbonate which gradually builds up. Although the caves are many millions of years old, the calcite formations that you see today are geological youngsters, dating back a mere 100,000 years.

Some history

San hunter-gatherers sheltered in the entrance caves for millennia before white settlers arrived, but it's unlikely that they ever made it to the lightless underground chambers. **Jacobus van Zyl**, a Karoo farmer, was probably the first person to penetrate beneath the surface, when he slid down on a rope into the darkness in July 1780, armed with a lamp.

Over the next couple of centuries the caves were visited and pillaged by growing numbers of callers, some of whom were photographed cheerfully carting off wagonloads of limestone columns. In the Sixties and Seventies the caves were made accessible to mass consumption when a restaurant and curio complex were built, the rock-strewn floor was evened out with concrete, ladders and walkways were installed and the caverns were turned into a kitsch extravaganza with coloured lights, piped music and an indecipherable commentary that drew hundreds of thousands of visitors each year. Even apartheid put its hefty boot in: under the premiership of Dr Hendrik Verwoerd, the arch-ideologue of racial segregation, a separate "non-whites" entrance was hacked through one wall, resulting in a disastrous through-draft that began dehydrating the caves.

Fortunately the worst excesses have now ended. Concerts are no longer allowed inside the chambers and the coloured lights have been removed. But the debate over how best to use these geological formations continues. According to David Bristow, editor of the South African travel magazine *Getaway*, "the battle lines have been drawn between those who believe the caves are a lot of attractive rocks that should be at the disposal of the local council for all manner of entertainment and mass tourism, and those who believe they are a fragile ecosystem and should be protected as possibly one of our finest ecotourism destinations".

Practicalities

Apart from the trips organized by *Backpackers Oasis* (see p.170) in Oudtshoorn, there is no transport to the Cango Caves. To **drive** here from Oudtshoorn, head north along Baron van Reede Street, and continue on the R328 for 32km to the caves. The visitors' complex includes a decent **restaurant** with nice views of the mountains and valley, and a souvenir shop, a curio shop, a small-scale diorama of the caves, and a video presentation. Below the complex you'll find shady picnic sites at the edge of a river that cuts its way into the mountains and along which there are hiking trails. The nearest **accommodation** is set beautifully on the river, at Cango Mountain Resort (☎044/272 4506; ②), signposted off the R328 27km from north of Oudtshoorn, 3km off the main road en route to the caves. This is the best self-catering accommodation in the area around Cango, with especially nice timber chalets. A small shop on site sells basics.

Three **tours** leave every hour on the hour (daily 9am–4pm). The half-hour Scenic Tour (R11) takes in the two largest and most spectacular caves, but is too short to give you a decent idea of the whole system. Most people join the one-hour Standard Tour (R22.5), which gets you through the first six chambers. If you're an adrenaline junkie, the ninety-minute Adventure Tour (R28.5) is a must; this takes you into the deepest sections open to the public, where the openings become smaller and smaller. Squeezing through tight openings with names like Lumbago Walk, Devil's Chimney and The Letterbox is not recommended for the overweight, faint-hearted or the claustrophobic, and you should wear oldish clothes and shoes with grip to negotiate the slippery floors.

Calitzdorp and the Groenfontein Valley

Just 50km west of Oudtshoorn, the tiny Karoo village of **CALITZDORP** hangs in a torpor of midday stillness. After the bustle of the "ostrich capital", it comes as a welcome surprise, with its attractive, unpretentious Victorian streets and a handful of wineries.

There's nothing much to do here, apart from have tea, taste some wine and wander through the streets.

The low-key **tourist information** bureau (☎044/213 3312), near the New Byzantine-style Dutch Reformed church, has some first-class brochures about the village and its surrounds, as well as information about the wineries and accommodation. Some of South Africa's best ports are produced at the three modest wineries signposted down sideroads, a few hundred metres from the centre. The most highly recommended is Die Krans (Mon–Fri 8am–5pm, Sat 9am–1pm; ☎044/213 3314, fax 213 3562; tasting free), where you can sample their wines and ports (their vintage reserve port is reckoned to be among the country's top three), and stretch your legs on a thirty-minute vineyard walk in lovely countryside. Boplaas Estate (Mon–Fri 8am–5pm, Sat 9am–3pm; free tasting; ☎044/213 3326, fax 213 3750) also produces some fine ports and is worth a quick look to see their massive reed-ceiling tasting room that feels like a cantina that fell off the set of a spaghetti western. If you've time, head for the Calitzdorp Wine Cellar (Mon–Fri 8am–1pm & 2–5pm, Sat 8am–noon; tasting free; ☎044/213 3301, fax 213 3110), where the main attraction is the stunning view from the tasting room into the Gamka River Valley.

Places to stay include *Lizhof*, 18 Queen St (☎044/213 3183), a nineteenth-century two-storey building with a wrap-around balcony that has backpaers' doubles and B&B (both ②), plus camping (①). There are airy B&B rooms with verandahs at *Die Dorpshuis* (☎044/213 3453; ②), which is centrally located at 4 Van Riebeeck St, opposite the church; the very friendly *Port-Wine Guest House* (☎044/213 3131, *portwine@mweb.co.za*; ④), in a renovated early nineteenth-century homestead on the corner of Queen and Station streets and overlooking the Boplaas Estate; and the comfortable, country-style *Welgevonden Guest House* (☎ & fax 044/213 3642; ③), St Helena Rd, 300m from the main road, on a small Chardonnay farm; St Helena Rd is about 300m west of Queen St, across the river and accessible down Voortrekker St. *Die Dorpshuis* is also a good place to **eat**, serving reasonably priced sandwiches, teas, light meals and heavier traditional Karoo food, such as stews.

Heading east out of town, you can return to Oudtshoorn on the tarred R62, but it would be a pity to miss out on the more circuitous minor route that diverts just outside Calitzdorp and drops into the highly scenic **Groenfontein Valley**. The narrow dirt road twists through the Swartberg foothills, past numerous whitewashed Karoo cottages and farms, and eventually joins the R328 which goes to Oudtshoorn.

De Rust

Hemmed in by Cape fold mountains, **DE RUST**, 35km northeast of Oudtshoorn, is a drive-through town on the N12 that cuts between the Garden Route and the N1 that races to Johannesburg. This accounts for the fact that most of the buildings along the town's small main road all seem to be selling something: teas, crafts, and *biltong* or ostrich products galore. You'll need to reach for your phrase book (or consult our language glossary on p.750) in this very Afrikaans village, which has a safe, calm atmosphere with gardens that make a bright contrast with the surrounding stony, dry hills. De Rust is a nice enough place to stop to stretch your legs and have a drink, but there's little reason to spend the night here.

Greyhound and Translux intercity **buses** from Gauteng stop off on their way to Knysna at the *De Rust Hotel*, while Intercape pull in at the Shell Garage – both central locations. You can **camp** at *De Oude Stal*, Burger St (①), a caravan park that has grassy stands and peacocks and figs in the yard. For beds in town, the clean and cheap *Afsaal Gastehuis* (☎044/241 2134; ②) has two dark, old-fashioned **rooms** facing onto the main road. *Oulap Country House*, some 15km east of town off the R341 to Uniondale (☎044/241 2250, fax 241 2298, *oulap@mweb.co.za*; full board ⑤), is an outstanding place

GO TO HELL

Prince Albert is one of the best places to launch off on a trip into **Die Hel** (also known as Hell, The Hell or Gamkaskloof). Die Hel is not on the way to anywhere and, although it doesn't look very far on the map, by car you'll need to allow for two and a half hours in either direction to make this spectacular but tortuous expedition into the valley. Although the journey is on a dirt road, you won't need a 4WD vehicle, but you should definitely not attempt the drive in the killing heat of December or January. On foot, this makes a thrilling trip of two or three days. Reasonably priced **guided hikes** are operated by the owners of the *Prince Albert of Saxe-Coburg Lodge* in Prince Albert (see "Practicalities" below), but note that they will only take minimum parties of four people. **Accommodation** can be arranged through the Lodge in primitive self-catering huts (②). There's no electricity in the valley and you'll have to heat water using a wood-fired boiler. There are no shops or any other facilities in the valley, so you'll need to stock up on food and supplies before heading off.

to stay, a Karoo farm in the Swartberg Mountains run by Jans Rautenbach, film producer and storyteller, and his wife. Rooms are furnished with antiques and South African paintings. A good base for the Oudtshoorn area, you can also explore the grounds and use the swimming pool. An excellent dinner is included in the rate.

For outdoor **eating**, there are two tea shops in the main road, both with gardens: *Herries*, marked by a purple elephant outside, has pleasant seating under shady trees; and *Country Kitchen*, an acceptable tea stop. For fresh bread, rusks, cakes and indoor **teas**, *Die Groen Bliktrommel*, on the same road, is recommended.

Prince Albert and around

Isolation and poverty have left intact the traditional rural architecture of **PRINCE ALBERT**, an attractive little town 70km north of Oudtshoorn, across the loops and razorbacks of the Swartberg Pass. Although firmly in the thirstlands of the South African interior, occupying the cusp between the Little and Great Karoo, Prince Albert is all the more striking for being quenched by a perennial spring, whose water trickles down furrows along its streets – a gift that propagates fruit trees and gardens.

Supremely old-fashioned displays make window-shopping as much fun as the interior of any country museum, but the essence of Prince Albert is in the fleeting impressions that give the flavour of a Karoo *dorp* like nowhere else: the silver steeple of the Dutch Reformed church puncturing a deep-blue sky, residents sauntering along or progressing slowly down the main street on squeaky bikes. Visitors mostly come to Prince Albert for the drive through its two southerly gateways – the **Swartberg Pass** and **Meiringspoort** – generally driving in one way, spending the night in town, and driving out the other. The town is also an excellent base for some thrilling walks and drives in the mountains – the ultimate being a journey into **Die Hel** (see box above).

Practicalities

The only way to get to Prince Albert is by **car**, but once here the place is easily and most rewardingly handled on foot. A number of moderately priced B&Bs, self-catering places and a good and relatively inexpensive hotel make finding accommodation here a breeze. *Onze Rus*, 47 Church St (☎023/541 1380, fax 541 1666; ②), has cool, thatched **B&B rooms** attached to a restored Cape Dutch house; and *Kuierhuis*, 51 Church St (☎023/541 1675; ②), offers simple rooms with twin beds, in a Cape

Dutch house with a beautiful cottage garden. If you're hiking in the area, head for the *Prince Albert of Saxe-Coburg Lodge*, 60 Church St (☎ & fax 023/541 1267; ②), where the owners hike regularly in the Swartberg Mountains and organize trips to Die Hel (see box opposite). The B&B rooms are in their house, with the best ones opening onto the back garden and duck pond, but they also rent out an entire house at 15 Church St (exclusive to a single party but there's no minimum number; ③) – a National Monument with glowing yellowwood floors, ceilings and timberwork; there are three bedrooms, two bathrooms a spacious lounge-dining room and a beautiful garden. The smartest **hotel** in town is the *Swartberg*, 77 Church St (☎023/541 1332, fax 541 1383; ④), a Victorian two-storey National Monument, set behind behind a lavender hedge. Traditional Karoo dinners are served in an atmospheric dining room, and there's a swimming pool.

When it comes to **eating**, the *Swartberg* is open to non-residents, with an elegant main restaurant, which offers the choice of an à la carte or set menu. Alternatively, there's the hotel's less formal *Boere Bistro*, with traditional Karoo fare and *boerekos* on offer. The *Karoo Kombuis* (Karoo kitchen), a recommended evenings-only spot in Droedrift Street, unsurprisingly also serves traditional fare from this part of the country. For no-nonsense food, which includes fish and chips and other deep-fried delights, served with a singular lack of flair, *CJ's*, a few doors down from the hotel, represents good value. If you want to pick up **snacks**, there's nowhere better than *Sampie se Plaasstal*, at the south end of the main road, where you'll find excellent dried fruit and rusks, as well as local olives which are among the best in South Africa.

The N1 from Worcester to Beaufort West

The **N1** is the main highway between Cape Town and Johannesburg, and with the majority of flights still arriving in Johannesburg it's common for visitors to arrive there and drive down to the coast. This account, however, assumes you'll be starting your journey in Cape Town and heading north. While this route isn't particularly inspiring, and won't take you through the diversity of the country, it does lead you into the Karoo, the huge semi-desert that fills the centre-west of South Africa. The various towns along the way have a couple of interesting historic buildings and some of the flavour of the isolated Karoo in their street scenes – definitely enough to fill an hour if you're looking for a break from the long journey. The most compelling places are undoubtedly the Victorian village of **Matjiesfontein** and **the Karoo National Park** just outside Beaufort West, both of which can be regarded as destinations in their own right.

CAPE TOWN TO JOHANNESBURG ON THE N1

For practical driving purposes, the journey along the **N1** between **Cape Town and Johannesburg**, via Bloemfontein, is just over 1400km – about fifteen to twenty hours' driving time. The halfway point is marked by the small village of **Hanover**, with nearby **Colesburg** offering a wide range of reasonably pleasant places to stay. An alternative route branches off west just north of Three Sisters onto the **N12**, via **Kimberley**, and adds an insignificant 20km on the journey. There is very little by way of halfway stops on the N12, although Kimberley (see p.242) certainly has enough interest to merit a stop on this route. If you're taking the journey slowly, Beaufort West is approximately one-third of the way from Cape Town, with Bloemfontein and Kimberley both about two-thirds of the way. All three main intercity **bus** companies, Greyhound, Intercape and Translux, ply the N1 route (18hr), with the latter two also going along the N12.

Worcester to Beaufort West

Some 30km east of **Worcester**, on the outer edge of the Western Cape mountains, is the **De Doorns Valley**, full of vineyards, small white cottages, farm stalls and strangely contorted mountains, closed in from both ends and often forgotten among the classic valleys of the Cape winelands. Staff at the local **tourist information** bureau (☎02322/2835) in De Doorns Wynkelder (a winery), signposted just off the road about halfway down the valley, are enthusiastic and will help you out if you're keen to explore this tranquil and pleasantly rustic area. **Touwsrivier**, 46km on, is a small, flat town with a service station and not much else, though in the town's hotel you'll find two pillars used by astronomers in 1880 to measure the distance of the sun from the earth.

Matjiesfontein

Pressing on, one of the quirkier manifestations of Victorian colonialism lies 54km east of Touwsrivier at the historic village of **MATJIESFONTEIN** (pronounced "Mikey's-fontayn"). Little more than two dusty streets beside a train track, the village resembles a film set rather than a Karoo *dorp*: every building, including the grand railway station, is a classic period piece, with tin roofs, pastel walls, well-tended gardens and Victorian frills. At the eastern end of the main street is the centrepiece, the *Lord Milner*, a hotel decked out with turrets and balconies and fountains by the entrance. If you're passing by, make sure you stop at least for a look around, and at less than three hours' drive from Cape Town the village is worth considering as a two-day trip of its own.

The origins of this curious place lie in the enterprise of a young Scottish entrepreneur, Jimmy Logan, who came to Cape Town to work on the railways and obtained the concession to sell refreshments to passengers all the way along the line from Cape Town to Bulawayo. He built Matjiesfontein as a health resort – making much play on the clean Karoo air – and it became a gathering point for the wealthy and influential around the turn of the century.

Today the village is doing brisk trade as a treasured relic. You can still come here in the classical manner on the mainline **train** from Cape Town to Jo'burg/Pretoria (although it's a leisurely rather than direct journey), and **stay** at the *Lord Milner* (☎023/551 3011, fax 551 3020; ③), either in one of the grand, antique-filled rooms in the hotel itself, or in one of the annexes in the surrounding houses. Inside the hotel there are huge portraits on the wall, polished brass fittings and, perhaps taking the theme a touch too far, rather surly service from waitresses dressed in black and white, with doilies on their heads. For **eating and drinking**, the hotel has a dimly lit dining room and a wonderfully aged and creaking bar. Along the main street, you'll find a tea room, souvenir shop and post office, all in attractive Victorian houses.

Laingsburg and Leeu-Gamka

There's little incentive to stop at **LAINGSBURG**, a town only 27km further along the N1 that marks the start of the long, lonely spaces of the Karoo. A service station lies on the road as it pulls around the Buffels River, and there are a couple of nondescript hotels and a cosy **caravan park** just up behind the service station, with tiny rondavels (①). As you drive through town, look out for the sign on the central reservation showing the water level during the catastrophic flood here in 1981 – it's level with (if not higher than) the roof of your car. Just outside Laingsburg, beside the road, is an Anglo-Boer War **blockhouse**, still largely intact on the outside and one of the best examples of these you'll see. These were built by the British at frequent intervals along the railway line to protect their main supply route; in all they built some eight thousand blockhouses (at £16 each), prompting Boer General Christiaan de Wet to pass comment on the British "blockhead" system.

One of the longest empty stretches is along the next 124km until you reach **LEEU-GAMKA**, with a filling station and a tiny Anglo-Boer War cemetery that just about has room for the grave of Private Schultz, the tallest man in the British army. Both barrels of the name Leeu-Gamka mean "lion", the first of which is Afrikaans, the second Khoi. But the acquaintanceship of the hamlet with its namesake ended some time ago through the barrel of a gun.

Beaufort West

For over 100km on either side of **BEAUFORT WEST**, the scenery from the N1 is far away and hazy, so the appearance of the Nieuwveld Mountains, which rise up behind town, give the place a certain distinction. Beyond that, however, Beaufort West is not a pretty place, with the N1 traffic trundling through its centre (watch out for speed traps and remember to stop at traffic lights), and it devotes most of its attention to servicing road-weary travellers.

As befits a town which is the oldest municipality in South Africa, most of the old buildings you'll see have a very municipal stolidity to them. Principal among these is the town's **museum**, 87 Donkin St (Mon–Fri 9am–12.45pm & 1.45–4.45pm; entry fee), in the old town hall, which houses an exhibition honouring the glamorous life and achievements of Beaufort West's Professor Christiaan Barnard, who performed the world's first human heart transplant operation at Groote Schuur Hospital in Cape Town in 1967.

Practicalities

The intercity **buses** all pull into the *Oasis Hotel* in Donkin Street. The town's helpful **tourist information** bureau, 63 Donkin St (☎023/415 1160), is one block along from the museum. Beaufort West has no shortage of **accommodation**, though much of it is for mass consumption and fairly characterless. There's a municipal camping and caravan park under some trees on the right as you come into the main part of town on Donkin Street, but as with other camping options along the N1 it's a bit scruffy and unappealing. If you want to **camp**, you're better off going to the Karoo National Park, just a few kilometres out of town (see below). Ideal for backpackers, *Donkin House*, 14 Donkin St (☎023/414 4287; ①), is more of a simple **guesthouse** than a hostel, but has a swimming pool and some communal space to hang out in. Another budget option is the *Formule 1*, 144 Donkin St (☎023/415 2421; ②), part of a fast-bed chain that delivers slick, ultra-modern **rooms** that resemble a ship's cabin. The *Wagon Wheel Country Lodge* (☎023/414 2145), off the N1 on the northern fringe of town, offers clean en-suite motel rooms (③), a few with their own shower, basin and toilet. *Clyde House*, 25 Donkin St (☎023/414 4083; ③), has quite lavish accommodation in a pink, double-storey house built in 1839, and dishes up a good breakfast in the coffee shop downstairs included. For more elegance, make straight for the *Matoppo Inn* (☎023/415 1055, fax 415 1080; ④), on the corner of Bird and Meintjies streets, which has upmarket rooms in the town's old *drostdy*, or magistrate's house.

When it comes to **eating**, you could do worse than the breakfasts and lunches in the coffee shop next to the craft gallery at Clyde House on Donkin Street. For dinner, *Ye Olde Thatch* restaurant, 155 Donkin St, is a bit gloomy inside but the menu is decent enough. Across the road is *Mac Young's*, an upmarket, Scottish-themed restaurant nestled behind a Caltex service station. Popular with Afrikaners, anyone with a Scottish ancestor within five generations will find the cringe factor rather high. Opposite the *Formule 1* hotel is the formulaic but reliable *Saddles Steak House*.

Karoo National Park

Unassuming and undervalued, the **Karoo National Park** (daily 5am–10pm; entry fee) has been emerging in recent years as a reserve with much more to offer than first meets the eye. Although it doesn't immediately feel very Karoo-like (there are too many mountains), the themes of the semi-desert are undoubtedly here, and after a night gazing at the dazzling sky, or a hot day learning about the unexpectedly intricate flora of the region, you'll start to appreciate this park's special value. Many of the slightly graceless facilities are recognizable from national parks elsewhere in South Africa, but here you do get the sense that the management are working hard to help people enjoy the place.

Much of what you take from here is in the landscape and the serene atmosphere: despite the recent introduction of some **black rhino**, big game is limited, although there are some impressive raptors, including the **black eagle**. The designated drives you can take around a limited section of the 600-square-kilometre park aren't terribly exciting; however, a recent innovation is a wider-ranging 4WD trail, with the opportunity to overnight out in the *veld* in a remote mountain hut, for around R200 per person. For bookings, contact South African National Parks (see below).

Near the main rest camp (see "Practicalities" below) there is an environmental **education centre**, along with three **trails**: an eleven-kilometre day-walk; a short but informative tree trail; and a very imaginative fossil trail (designed to accommodate wheelchairs and incorporating Braille boards), which tells the fascinating 250-million-year-old geological history of the area and shows fossils of the unusual animals that lived here in the times when the Karoo was a vast inland sea. Information about these is available at camp reception.

Practicalities

The entrance gate to Karoo National Park is right on the N1, 2km south of Beaufort West. The **reception and rest camp** are a couple of kilometres into the park, hidden among the appealing flat-topped mountains in a way that makes you feel as though you are a million miles from the town and the highway. At reception are a shop selling basic foodstuffs, a **restaurant** (Mon–Sat 8am–8.30pm, Sun 8am–7pm), and there's a pool nearby. Accommodation is in fully equipped **bungalows** that sleep three people (④), strung out on either side of the main complex; the rate is for a minimum of two people and includes breakfast in the restaurant. The **campsite** (①) is hidden away over a rise. If you're intending to overnight in Beaufort West during a long trip, it's well worth considering coming out to the park instead of staying in town. For more **information** about the park, phone ☎023/415 2828. For accommodation **bookings** contact South African National Parks (Pretoria: ☎012/343 1991, fax 343 0905; Cape Town: ☎021/422 2810, fax 424 6211; *reservations@parks-sa.co.za*).

THE OVERBERG INTERIOR AND THE WHALE COAST

East of the Winelands lies a vaguely defined region known as the **Overberg** (Afrikaans for "over the mountain"). In the seventeenth century, when even Stellenbosch, Franschhoek and Paarl were remote outposts, to the Dutch settlers everywhere beyond them was a fuzzy hinterland that drifted off into the arid sands of the Karoo. These days it extends to an imprecise point between Arniston and Mossel Bay on the coast and somewhere east of Swellendam in the interior.

Of the two main routes through the Overberg, the **N2** strikes out across the less interesting interior, a four- to five-hour stretch most people endure rather than enjoy to get to the Garden Route – but you can make it less of a chore with a couple of well-chosen stops along the way. North of the N2 is **Greyton**, a pleasant village used by Capetonians as a relaxing weekend retreat, and the starting point of the **Boesmanskloof Traverse** – a terrific one-day trail across the mountains into the

Karoo. The Moravian mission station of **Genadendal**, five minutes down the road from Greyton, has a strange Afro-Germanic ambience that offers a couple of hours' pleasant strolling. Along the N2 itself the only places that justify a restorative stop are **Caledon**, for its Victorian thermal springs, and **Swellendam**, for its well-preserved streetscape as well as one of South Africa's best country museums.

The real draw of the area is the **Whale Coast**, close enough for an easy outing from Cape Town, yet surprisingly undeveloped. The exception is popular **Hermanus**, which owes its fame to its status as the whale-watching capital of South Africa. The whole of this southern Cape coast, in fact, is prime territory for land-based whale-watching. Also along this section of coast is **Cape Agulhas**, the southernmost place on the continent, which sadly fails to deliver the drama its location promises. Nearby (and far more worthwhile) is **Arniston**, one of the best-preserved fishing villages in the country, and a little to its east the **De Hoop Nature Reserve**, an exciting wilderness of bleached dunes, craggy coast and more whales.

Caledon

The first impression of **CALEDON** is of the huge, cathedral-like grain silos that dwarf its church spires. A declining farming town some 111km east of Cape Town, Caledon built its former prosperity on the wheat, barley and malt trade, but today it's slowly decaying. The town's burghers are gambling on reversing their fortunes through a massive casino and family entertainment complex, currently being built around the town's one natural asset – its **thermal springs**. The public can still wallow in the steaming mineral water at Caledon's terrific historic **Victorian bathhouse** (daily except Thurs 9am–9pm; R10), undergoing restoration as part of the project, in the grounds of the *Overberger Hotel*.

You can make this fascinating rest-stop with only a minor detour from the N2: to get to the spa follow the Overberger sign, which if you're coming from Cape Town is a little way beyond the town-centre indicator. Use of the springs predates by centuries the Victorians, who built the wrought-iron structure in the nineteenth century. When the Dutch arrived here in the eighteenth century, Khoi people were already wallowing in steaming holes dug in the ground – a practice imitated by the settlers. Apart from the spa, Caledon has a couple of other decent attractions. The **museum** (Mon–Fri 8am–1pm & 2–5pm, Sat 9am–1pm; small entry fee), above the tourist information bureau at 16 Constitution St, consists of a collection of mainly domestic items displayed in the old Freemasons Meeting Hall and at a house faithfully restored to "Victorian Caledon style" (1837–1901), diagonally opposite. The most enjoyable way to see the collections is on a guided tour led by curator Tizzie Mangiagalli, whose brilliant, well-informed commentary makes fascinating connections between seemingly trivial household items and the broader tapestry of history – you can also arrange agricultural tours through him.

Caledon's outdoor attraction is the **Wildflower Garden and Nature Reserve**, where you can wander through fynbos, aloes and succulents on a lovely long amble along a rocky, wooded *kloof* into the mountains, or head out on the ten-kilometre Meiring Trail, which goes deep into the nature reserve.

Practicalities

All intercity **buses** stop off at the *Alexandra Hotel* on Market Square in the centre of town. Caledon's **tourist information** bureau, 16 Constitution St (Mon–Fri 8am–1pm & 2–4.30pm, Sat 9am–1pm; ☎028/212 1511), has literature about the area as well as details of places to stay. **Accommodation** is limited but reasonably priced. The cheapest beds in town are in a self-catering cottage, with a verandah, at the *Painted Lady*, 3 Donkin St (☎028/214 1290, evenings 212 2093; ②). Out of town, clearly signposted off the R406 on the way to Greyton, you'll find *Oom Barrie se Huisie* (☎028/214 1080 or 214 8903; ③), a cottage that sleeps six. Extremely rural, the building is set in rolling wheatlands, and has a double room and space for four in the attic. The house has no electricity or phone, although there is hot and cold running water and a fully equipped kitchen, and linen is available on request. The rate more than doubles at the weekend, but it still represents good value, especially for four or more people.

Eating comes down to snacks during the day at the casual *Venster* **restaurant** in the Wildflower Garden. For **self-catering**, you can buy home-baked products, including fresh bread, every Friday at the Museum Shop on Donkin Street, around the corner from the museum.

THE BOESMANSKLOOF TRAVERSE

One of the best reasons to come to Greyton is to walk the fourteen-kilometre **Boesmanskloof Traverse**, which takes you from the gentle, oaked streets of **Greyton** across the Riviersonderend mountain range to the glaring Karoo scrubland around the town of **McGregor**. The stark contrast over so short a distance is staggering, made all the more so by the fact that no direct roads connect the two towns; to drive from one to the other involves a circuitous two hours on the road.

The classic way to cover the Traverse is to walk from Greyton to **Die Galg** (14km from McGregor), where people commonly spend the night, returning the same way to Greyton the following day. The route rises and falls a fair bit so you'll have to contend with some uphill walking, but the whole way can be easily completed in a day if you're reasonably fit. If you don't want to go all the way you can still have a rewarding outing, venturing part of the way and returning to Greyton for the evening. A decent day's walk takes you to **Oak Falls**, 9km from Greyton, the highlight of the route. Composed of a series of cascades, its most impressive feature is a large dark pool, where you can rest and swim in the tannin-coloured water.

The walk takes you through over fifty species of wonderful montane fynbos, and if you come at the right time of year you can find yourself walking through magnificent groves of flowering proteas. Mammals include small antelope, caracals, baboons and dassies, but you're not likely to see many of them, so go for the scenery, with the rugged Riviersonderend Mountains, *kloofs*, streams, waterfalls and pools.

TRAIL PRACTICALITIES

You're free to walk the first 5km of the trail and back, but if you want to complete the whole thing from Greyton to Die Galg you will need a **permit**, which limits numbers to fifty people per day. Over weekends the trail gets extremely full and permits must be arranged in advance through the Manager, Vrolijkheid Nature Reserve, Private Bag X614, 6705 Robertson (☎02353/621 or 671). During the week you can buy a permit on the day of your hike from the Greyton Municipal Offices, Ds Botha St (Mon–Fri 8am–1pm & 2–3.30pm; ☎028/254 9620). You'll get a **map** when you buy the permit, although you don't strictly need one as the Traverse is very clearly marked out. A booklet is available to accompany the interpretation trail, covering the McGregor half of the route. This is keyed to numbered points along the way and helps you to get more out of the walk by drawing your attention to what's around you. The walk isn't particularly strenuous but you should wear good shoes. It's also worth noting that this is a winter rainfall area, and can be wet at that time of year. Summers are hot and dry.

Accommodation on the McGregor side presents two possibilities: staying at the overnight hiking dorms (☎02353/735; ③), equipped with a fridge, cooker and beds (but no bedding) at Die Galg – the other end of trail; or *Whipstock Farm* (see p.165), 4km beyond Die Galg, from where the farm owners will collect you free of charge.

Greyton and the Boesmanskloof Traverse

The best things about **GREYTON**, a small holiday and retirement village 46km north of Caledon, based around a core of Georgian and Victorian buildings, are the unploughed Riviersonderend (Endless River) Mountains, which set it off from the cultivated landscape typical of most of the Western Cape. There's no industry here and the only modern development is the fair quantity of repro Georgian houses along its streets. The calm, bucolic atmosphere created by the shady oaks hides a real tension in the town, between the folk who want to retain the sleepy ambience and keep out economic activity, and those who see a need to create jobs for the 500-strong coloured community who don't have the privilege of living here in golden retirement or on holiday.

Apart from estate agents selling the rural dream to city dwellers who come to set up businesses, so little money changes hands here that there isn't even a bank. The town's big attraction is the superb **Boesmanskloof Traverse** hike (see box opposite), which crosses the mountains to McGregor. Apart from that – and some shorter walks – there's very little to do but stroll down the streets and potter about in the handful of antique and tea shops.

Arrival and information

As there's no public transport to Greyton, the only way to get here is by **car**, the best route being just west of Caledon on the R406, which is tarred all the way. Don't attempt to tackle the untarred route from Riviersonderend, which will hammer your suspension. The **tourist information** bureau (Mon–Sat 10am–noon & 2.30–4.30pm, Sat 10am–noon; ☎ & fax 028/254 9414) is in the public library along the main road as you come into town, and has details of places to stay.

Accommodation

Many of Greyton's holiday homes are rented out by a central **agency** (contact Gerald Shrock on ☎028/254 9046) when not in use by owners. Winters can be cold in this mountainous country; it's worth getting a place with a fireplace if you're here at that time of the year. A brief caution: Greyton municipality renumbered many properties in 1997, but not all. Don't despair if the street numbering appears to obey its own random rules: it's just that some houses may not have corrected their signs yet.

The large **municipal campsite** (☎028/254 9620; ①), 2.5km out of town and signposted off Main Road, is in a lovely setting on the banks of the Riviersonderend, with amenities limited to an ablution block with hot and cold water. Cheapest of the **B&Bs** is *Bullocks*, Main Rd (☎028/254 9948; ②), which has one en-suite room and two others that share a bathroom, and provides a light self-service breakfast. After that, there's *High Hopes B&B*, 89 Main Rd (☎ & fax 028/254 9898; ④), a beautiful country-style home with a magnificent garden and a huge ornamental pond, with afternoon tea and biscuits as well as delicious non-bacon and eggs breakfasts included in the price.

Of the **self-catering** options, you won't find cheaper than *Oak Tree Hikers Loft*, 51 Oak St (☎028/254 9820; ②), a modest holiday house with a very friendly owner, just off the main road with basic rooms supplied with beds and mattresses aimed at hikers doing the Boesmanskloof Traverse. *Webbers*, 1 Main St (☎028/254 9998; ②), is a two-bedroom apartment that sleeps four, attached to a house, with the use of a courtyard; discounts are available for stays of over one night. *Little Mandalay*, Caledon St (☎028/254 9818; ②), just off Main Road, is a 100-year-old fully equipped garden cottage that sleeps two and has a lovely pergola outside.

Cheapest of the **guesthouses** is the *Guinea Fowl*, Ds Botha St (☎028/254 9550; ③), where you'll get a full English breakfast, while the *Post House*, Main Rd (☎028/254 9995, fax 254 9920; ⑤), has en-suite bedrooms, each named after a Beatrix Potter character, furnished with Edwardian and country furniture. The very comfortable *Greyton*

Lodge, 46 Main Rd (☎028/254 9876, fax 254 9672), is the smartest place in town, and should be your first choice if money is no object, with plush standard rooms (⑤) and a "royal suite" with its own lounge and a four-poster bed (⑦).

Eating and drinking

For **meals**, the *Greyton Country Restaurant*, Main Rd (☎028/254 9820), run by a charming French proprietor, serves decent English food during the day throughout the week, and dinners on Tuesday, Friday and Saturday. The licensed *Blue Mountain* (☎028/254 9325; daily noon–3pm & 6–10pm except Mon lunch), 21 Ds Botha Street, opposite the *Guinea Fowl Inn*, serves pizzas, pastas, fish and burgers. In a similar vein *Kwagga's* (☎028/254 9066; Mon & Thurs–Sun till 8.30pm) at 35 Main Rd, is a family-oriented eatery that specializes in steaks and fish. Candle-lit four-course meals are on offer at the *Post House* and *Greyton Lodge*.

When it comes to **drinking**, non-residents can tipple at the *Post House* up to 7pm, after which there's two and a half hours of enforced abstinence till the *Blue Mountain* opens its bar to non-diners at 9.30pm, closing at 2am.

Genadendal

GENADENDAL, whose name means "valley of grace", was established in 1737 and is South Africa's oldest mission station, founded by Moravians (some of the ochre and earthy-pink architecture hints at Central-European influences). The village is essentially an excursion from Greyton, 6km to its west, as there's nowhere to stay in Genadendal itself.

Genadendal's focus is around **Church Square**, which is dominated by a very Germanic church building dating back to 1891. The old bell outside dates back to the eighteenth century, when it became the centre of a flaming row between the local farmers and the mission station. The scrap broke out when missionary Georg Schmidt annoyed the local white farmers by forming a small Christian congregation with impoverished Khoi – who were on the threshold of extinction – and giving refuge to maltreated labourers from local farms. What really got the farmers' goat was the fact that while they, white Christians, were illiterate, Schmidt was teaching blacks, whom they considered uncivilized, to read and write. The Dutch Reformed Church, under the control of the Dutch East India Company, waded in when Schmidt began baptizing converts, and prohibited the mission from ringing the bell which called the faithful to prayer.

At one stage during the eighteenth century, Genadendal was the largest settlement in southern Africa after Cape Town. Although it never became more than a village, Genadendal experienced a golden age in the nineteenth century, with a flourishing economy based on home industries. In 1838 it established the first teacher training college in the country, which the government closed in 1926, on the grounds that coloured people didn't need tertiary education and should be employed as workers on local farms – a policy that effectively ground the community into poverty. In 1995, in recognition of the mission's role, Nelson Mandela renamed his official residence in Cape Town "Genadendal".

Today the population of this principally coloured town numbers around four thousand people adhering to a variety of Christian sects – no longer just Moravianism. The **Mission Museum** (Mon–Thurs 9am–1pm & 2–5pm, Fri 9am–3.30pm, Sat 9am–noon; small entry fee), adjacent to Church Square, is moderately interesting and provides some clues as to why Moravians came here. You should allow up to two hours to explore the museum and wander through the town, down to the rural graveyard, spiked with tombstones dating back to the early nineteenth century. Genadendal offers few visitor facilities, but there is a tea room, just off Church Square, where you can get refreshments.

The Genadendal Trail

While you're here, you can venture a short way from the village into the surrounding countryside along the **Genadendal Trail**. The full twenty-five-kilometre, two-day circular trail requires a high level of fitness, particularly for the first 2km of the second day. But much of the rest is fairly easy-going and passes through montane fynbos inhabited by a variety of small antelope, caracals and the odd leopard. Only 24 people are allowed on the two-day trail at one time, so reservations are essential. **Bookings and permits** (R18) are arranged by post through Vrolijkheid Nature Reserve, Private Bag X614, Robertson 6705 (☎02353/621 or 671); phone before sending off your application (with a cheque or postal order made out to Vrolijkheid Nature Conservation) to check availability.

Overnight **accommodation** can be arranged in a self-catering hikers' cottage on *De Hoek*, a flower farm, halfway along the trail (☎02351/2176; ①). The farm is home to antelope and a wide variety of birds, and you can swim in the farm dam. Book in advance through the owners, Mr and Mrs Okes.

Swellendam

SWELLENDAM, 97km east of Caledon, is an unquestionably attractive historic town at the foot of the Langeberg and has one of the best country museums in South Africa, which makes it a congenial halfway stop along the N2 between Cape Town and the Garden Route. South Africa's third-oldest white settlement, Swellendam was established in 1745 by Baron Gustav van Imhoff, a visiting Dutch East India Company bigwig, who was deeply concerned about the "moral degeneration" of burghers who were trekking further and further from Cape Town and out of Company control. Of no less concern to the Baron was the loss of revenue from these "vagabonds", who were neglecting to pay the Company for the right to hold land and were fiddling their annual tax returns. Following a brief hiccup in 1795, when burghers declared a "free republic" (quickly extinguished when Britain occupied the Cape), the town grew into a prosperous rural centre known for its wagon-making, and for being the last "civilized" port of call for trekboers heading out into the interior.

The income generated from this helped build Swellendam's gracious homes, many of which went up in smoke in the fire of 1865, which razed much of the town centre. In 1950, transport planners ripped out many of the oaks that had survived the blaze to widen the main road. Nevertheless, Swellendam survived with just enough charm to lure you off the national road.

Arrival and information

The Greyhound, Intercape and Translux intercity **buses** travelling between Cape Town and Port Elizabeth all pull in at the *Swellengrebel Hotel*, 91 Voortrek St, in the centre of town, while the Baz backpacker bus will drop you off at any of the central accommodation. Swellendam has a very switched-on **tourist information** bureau, 36 Voortrek St (Mon–Fri 9am–1pm & 2–5pm, Sat 9am–12.30pm; ☎ & fax 028/514 2770), which provides frank and helpful advice about local attractions and will book accommodation. You can easily cover the town centre on foot, which is fortunate as there's no other way of getting around if you don't have your own transport.

Accommodation

Swellendam's budget accommodation starts with the *Swellendam Caravan Park*, Glen Barry Rd (☎028/514 2705, fax 514 2694), which has functional **campsites** (①), and basic en-suite thatched **cottages** (②) that are very cheap if you bring your own bedding and there are four of you sharing. In the same price bracket, but a lot more sociable, *Swellendam Backpackers*, 5 Lichtenstein St (☎028/514 2648), is a friendly place and, of the two **hostels**, is the more geared up for backpackers, with camping, dorms and doubles (all ①); staff can also arrange river rafting and canoeing trips. The other hostel, *Waenhuis Backpackers*, 5 Buitekant St (☎028/514 2281), has only one dorm (①), but also offers reasonably priced B&B rooms (②) in an elegant house.

The nicest **B&Bs** in town are in historic Cape Dutch or Georgian houses. Pick of the bunch is the well-run *Pond Cottage*, 21 Buitekant St (☎028/514 2036; ③), offering a cottage in a lovely garden with a double bed and fully equipped kitchen, and two rooms inside the Pond Cottage itself. Other options include *Moolmanshof*, 217 Voortrek St (☎028/514 3258; ③), with comfortable country-style rooms inside a Cape Dutch homestead, and *Cypress Cottage*, 3 Voortrek St (☎028/514 3296; ②), which has reasonable rooms in a small cottage that's not as grand as you might hope, looking at the main house (one of the oldest in town); the same owners have rooms (②) in the nicer *Tuishuis* next door. The *Old Mill*, 241–243 Voortrek St (☎028/514 2790; ③), has two picturesque cottages and a small restaurant serving light meals during the day. If you're feeling sociable, *Roosje Van De Kaap*, Drostdy St (☎028/514 3001; ③), owned by a chatty couple, makes a convivial choice in a beautiful house, but some of the rooms are tiny. Just outside the centre are Swellendam's best and most expensive lodgings at *Klippe Rivier Homestead* (☎028/514 3341, fax 514 3337; ⑦), off the western end of Voortrek Street and across the Klippe River, with opulent bedrooms in a magnificent 1820 mansion.

The Town

The only building in the centre to survive the town's ravages is the Cape Dutch-style **Oefeningshuis**, 36 Voortrek St, which now houses the tourist information bureau. Built in 1838, it was first used as a place for religious activity, and then as a school for freed slaves, and has surreal-looking stopped clocks carved into either gable end, below which there's a real clock above the entrance. Diagonally opposite and slightly east at no. 11, the **Dutch Reformed Church**, dating from 1910, incorporates Gothic windows, a Baroque spire, Renaissance portico elements and Cape Dutch gables into a wedding cake of a building that, against the odds, agreeably holds its own.

On the east side of town, a short way from the centre, is the excellent **Drostdy Museum**, 18 Swellegrebel St (Mon–Fri 9am–4.45pm, Sat & Sun 10am–3.45pm; small entry fee). One of the finest country museums in South Africa, it is actually a collection of historic buildings arranged around large grounds and a lovely nineteenth-century Cape garden. The centrepiece is the **Drostdy** itself, which was built in 1747 as the seat of the *landdrost*, a magistrate-cum-commissioner sent out by the Dutch East India Company to control the outer reaches of its territory. The building conforms to the beautiful limewashed, thatched and shuttered Cape Dutch style of the eighteenth century, but the furnishings are of nineteenth-century vintage. From the rear garden of the Drostdy you can stroll along a path and across Drostdy St to **Mayville**, a middle-class Victorian homestead from the mid-nineteenth century with an old rose garden. Also part of the complex are the **Old Gaol**, the **jailer's cottage**, and an interesting display of eighteenth- and nineteenth-century farm implements and rural tools. Look out, too, for the old dung circular threshing floor in a low-walled enclosure, into which horses were driven to tramp the wheat.

Strand to Cape Hangklip

The main reason you'd take the coastal route that skirts the eastern shore of False Bay is to get to Hermanus, but scenically the drive has much to recommend it, especially once you get past the commuter settlements close to Cape Town. Leaving the N2 from Cape Town at Somerset West, the first coastal settlement you hit is **STRAND**, a massive industrial centre on the edge of Cape Town. Although it has a good beach, this isn't sufficient reason to stop off and the R44 quickly gets you to the ongoing commuter development of **Gordon's Bay**, your last chance for a decent sea swim for some distance. After here the mountains bear down on the sea and the road works its way around the folding mountainside with the sea crashing against the rocks. Rock-strewn and without a tree in sight, the barren landscape has a raw dramatic quality that takes you just inland of **Cape Hangklip**, the tip of False Bay, which earned its name from the fact that Hangklip frequently fooled Portuguese mariners into thinking they were rounding the Cape of Good Hope. A dirt road takes you down to **HANGKLIP** itself, where a succession of dwellers have made their homes since humans left stone axes here over 20,000 years ago. In the nineteenth century, outlaws hung out in Hangklip's remote caves, but were flushed out in 1852, leaving the area to the baboons that now hole up here.

Betty's Bay and around

Cape Hangklip roughly marks the point at which the commuters become holidaymakers. Just around the corner to the west, **BETTY'S BAY** was developed as a seaside retreat for Capetonians wanting to get away from the city. Prosaically named after Betty Youlden, daughter of the director of the first company to try to develop the area, this rather boring collection of holiday cottages hosts a colony of **African (jackass) penguins**. The best time to see the birds is in the morning or evening between April and June. African penguins mate for life and return to the same nest every year, but here are suffering from interference with their turf by perlemoen (a type of large shellfish) poachers. Residents urge you to tell local shopkeepers if you see poaching taking place.

Betty's Bay is not geared up to visitors, though you can **eat** at the Harold Porter Botanical Garden (see below).

Harold Porter National Botanical Garden

Creeping up the the mountains just above Betty's Bay, **Harold Porter National Botanical Garden** (daily 8am–6pm; small entry fee) is a wild sanctuary of coastal and montane fynbos that makes a good stop along the R44, if only to picnic or have tea at its outdoor **café**. Once here, you'll probably get lured at least some of the way up the *kloof* that runs through the reserve, by both its beauty and the views of the sea you get as you move higher. The relatively compact botanical garden extends over two square kilometres from the mountains, through marshland down to coastal dunes. As you get higher up, you are treated to sea views in one direction and rugged mountains in the other.

Although wildlife in the form of small **antelope, baboons** and **leopards** are present, they are rarely sighted and you should look out instead for the birds and blooms. In January you can see brilliant red disas in all their glory, while the nerine lilies flower in March. Keep an eye open for colourful, nectar-loving sunbirds and scores of other bird **species** that occur here. Four **trails** of between one and three hours meander through the gardens, but you can just as easily take yourself off on an impromptu stroll, up and across the red-stained waters (caused by phenols and tannins leaching from the fynbos) running through Disa Kloof.

Kleinmond

Because of its isolation, **KLEINMOND**, roughly 12km northeast of Betty's Bay, was an outlaws' stronghold for some two hundred years. In the twentieth century, however, relatively easy access has turned the town into a holiday spot for Capetonians and for farmers from the surrounding areas. An impressive confluence of sea, dune, tidal estuary and mountain waterfalls combines with a ten-kilometre crescent **beach** that curves across the Bot River Mouth to Mudge Point, a promontory that completes the vista as you look east. Swimming is safest close to the *Beach House Hotel*, but take care not to venture beyond where you see other bathers.

The cheapest accommodation is at the couple of caravan parks, signposted from the main road, where you can **camp**. Better of the two is the *Palmiet* (☎028/271 4050; ①), which is quieter and closer to the safely swimmable river. The main caravan park, the *Kleinmond* (☎028/271 4010; ①), is unappealingly close to the main road, which slices the village in half. For **self-catering**, *Our Kaia*, 12 5th Ave (☎021/686 8454 or 271 4555; apartment ②, house ③), has an apartment and a house, both with verandahs overlooking the beach. *Sandown Lodge B&B*, 7 Strand St (☎ & fax 028/271 4586; ③), is a family home on the beachfront offering four rooms with private showers but no sea views, and two lounges that have fabulous views of Sandown Bay.

The most luxurious place is *Beach House*, Beach Rd (☎028/271 3130, fax 271 4022; ⑥–⑦), a small **hotel** whose spacious rooms, with king-size beds, white wicker furniture and tastefully understated floral fabrics, look out over Sandown Bay, the lagoon and mountains and enjoy the sound of the endlessly pounding surf; if you are going to fork out to stay here, you may as well stay in one of the luxury sea-facing rooms. *Beach House* is also the best place for eating, with an expensive formal **restaurant**, which serves pleasant English-style food. For something cheaper, there are a couple of **take-away** places along the main road through town.

Hermanus, Walker Bay and around

On the edge of rocky cliffs and backed by mountains, **HERMANUS**, 112km east of Cape Town, sits at the northernmost end of Walker Bay, an inlet whose protective curve attracts calving whales as it slides south to the promontory of Danger Point. The town trumpets itself as the **whale capital** of South Africa and, to prove it, has an official whale crier (apparently the world's only one) who struts around armed with a mobile phone and a dried kelp horn through which he yells the latest sightings. There is still the barest trace of a once-quiet cliff-edge fishing village around the historic harbour and in some understated seaside cottages, but for the most part Hermanus has gorged itself on its whale-generated income that has produced modern shopping malls, supermarkets and craft shops.

Ignoring the hype, **Walker Bay** does provide some of the finest shore-based whale-watching in the world and, even if there are better spots nearby, Hermanus is the best geared-up place in the country to exploit it. From about July, southern right whales (see p.190) start appearing in the warmer sheltered bays of the Western Cape. Whales aside, Hermanus has good swimming and walking **beaches**, three excellent **wineries** you can visit and makes a good base for exploring the rest of the Overberg.

Southeast down Walker Bay, the unprepossessing town of **De Kelders** outshines its smarter neighbour as a whale-watching spot, but at nothing much else; and just inland of it, the wonderful and very upmarket **Grootbos Nature Reserve** is one of the best places in the country to learn about fynbos. Heading further down the bay, you hit the fishing town of **Gansbaai** (Afrikaans for Goose Bay), which these days is far better known for its sharks than its waterfowl. Curving back to Hermanus, Danger Point is the promontory that indicates Walker Bay's southern extent, and marks the spot where HMS *Birkenhead* literally went down in history (see p.192).

An easy excursion from Hermanus takes you through attractive and relatively untrammelled farming country to **Bredasdorp**, a junction town on the R316 that gives you the choice of branching out to Africa's disappointing southern tip at **Cape Agulhas**; the well-preserved Moravian mission town of **Elim**; or the fishing village of **Arniston**, which is the least-developed and nicest town along the Whale Coast.

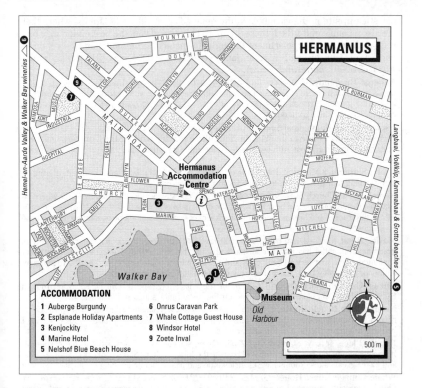

ACCOMMODATION
1 Auberge Burgundy
2 Esplanade Holiday Apartments
3 Kenjockity
4 Marine Hotel
5 Nelshof Blue Beach House
6 Onrus Caravan Park
7 Whale Cottage Guest House
8 Windsor Hotel
9 Zoete Inval

Arrival and information

Scant public transport passes through Hermanus, the exception being a couple of daily **minibuses**: Harvey's Travel (☎028/312 3737), who run from anywhere in Hermanus to Adderley Street and the airport in Cape Town; and Traveller's Joy (☎028/312 3702), who operate a door-to-door service to Cape Town. The Baz **backpacker bus** drops people off at Bot River, 28km to the north on the N2, from where you can arrange to be collected by a licensed **taxi** (see p.191) for about R25 – the bus carries a mobile phone, and can call one while you're en route. Most people come to Hermanus by **car**, which takes about ninety minutes from Cape Town along the N2, or two hours via Gordon's Bay. Travelling along the N2 and striking south onto the R43 at Bot River is the more direct of the two main routes, but the winding road that hugs the coast from Strand, leaving the N2 just before Sir Lowrie's Pass, is the more scenic.

There's a helpful **tourist information** bureau (Mon–Fri 9am–5pm, Sat 9am–3pm, Sun 9am–1pm; ☎028/312 2629, fax 313 0305, *infoburo@hermanus.co.za*) in Main Road, with maps and useful brochures about the area as well. The bureau also operates a free accommodation-finding service.

Accommodation

You'll find very few places to rent along the shore in Hermanus, as they're all in private hands, but there are some **hotels** and **self-catering apartments**. The nearest and nicest **campsite** in the vicinity is in the quiet adjacent village of **Onrus**, where there are also a couple of B&Bs. If there are more than two of you, the best option may be to rent a whole house or apartment through Hermanus Accommodation Centre, on the corner of Church and Myrtle lanes (☎028/313 0004, fax 313 0005, mobile ☎083/651 0001, *hacc@ilink.nis.za*).

Auberge Burgundy, 16 Harbour Rd (☎028/313 1201, fax 313 1204). Imitation-Provençal country house in the town centre projecting a stylish Mediterranean feel, with imported French fabrics and a lavender garden. Breakfast is served across the road at the *Burgundy*, Hermanus's top restauraunt, under the same ownership. ⑨.

Esplanade Holiday Apartments, Marine Drive (☎028/312 3610, fax 313 1125, *clarkbro @hermanus.co.za*). Close to the Windsor Hotel, these recently renovated, self-catering apartments offer good facilities. Those with sea views – unbeatable for whale-watching – are more expensive. ④–⑤.

Green Shutters, 3 Moffat St, Hermanus (☎ & fax 028/312 3117). Fully equipped self-catering cottage sleeping four in a garden set well back from the sea. ④.

Kenjockity, 15 Church St (☎ & fax 028/312 1772). Centrally located and friendly B&B, where you can't see the sea but you can hear the whales at night in season. The best rooms have their own private sitting rooms and are en suite, while backpackers can sometimes be accommodated in smaller, cheaper rooms. ②–③.

Marine Hotel, Marine Drive (☎028/313 1000, fax 313 0160). Recently given a major makeover, this grand seafront hotel has a rather formal ambience, but is certainly Hermanus's best. If you're shelling out, you may as well book early and pay extra for a sea-facing room. There's a Jacuzzi and an indoor swimming pool, and a short way down the cliff is a tidal pool. ⑨.

Onrus Caravan Park (☎028/3161210). In the adjacent village of Onrus, so away from the Hermanus hype, but close enough by taxi for the restaurants, shops and facilities. ①.

Nelshof Blue Beach House, 37 Tenth St (☎028/314 0201). Situated right on Voëlklip Beach in a renovated Victorian house, this is the only B&B in Hermanus where you have a choice of lying in bed or lounging in the Jacuzzi to watch whales. ⑥.

Pendle Place, 44 Luyt St (☎028/312 2556). Quiet, self-contained B&B flatlet in the garden of a house belonging to Brenda Johnson – who wrote the Johannesburg *Star*'s cookery column for years and bakes great cakes. Rooms have electric kettle and fridge, but no cooking facilities. ②.

Whale Cottage Guest House, 20 Main Rd (☎028/313 0929, fax 313 0912, *relmark@iafrica.com*). Simple, pleasantly furnished guesthouse offering five rooms (some larger) decorated with marine themes. The only drawback is it's away from the sea. ③–④.

Windsor Hotel, Marine Drive (☎028/312 3727, fax 312 2181, *windsor@hermanus.co.za*). The town's second hotel has the best location in town – right on the edge of the cliffs – but otherwise isn't a patch on the Marine. Booking is essential, and it's worth paying a little extra for a sea-facing room. ③–④.

Zoete Inval, 23 Main Rd (☎ & fax 028/312 1242, *zoetein@hermanus.co.za*). Excellent-value B&B doubling up as Hermanus's only establishment catering to backpackers. Run by an enthusiastic couple, it has huge amounts of carefully prepared information for guests. The owners can arrange a taxi to pick you up from the Baz bus. Dorms ①, B&B with or without own bath ②.

The Town and around

Main Road, the continuation of the R43, meanders through Hermanus, briefly becoming Seventh Street before again resuming its persona as the national road. **Market Square**, just above the old harbour and to the south of Main Street, is the closest thing to a centre, and here you'll find the heaviest concentration of restaurants, craft shops and flea markets – the principal forms of entertainment in town when the whales are taking time out.

Just below Market Square is the **Old Harbour Museum** (Mon–Sat 9am–1pm & 2–4pm; small entry fee), whose only real attraction is its live transmission of whale calls from a hydrophone anchored in the bay to its audio room (replaced by recordings out of season). Among the other uncompelling displays, you'll find lots of fishing tackle and some sharks' jaws. Outside the museum, a few colourful boats, used by local fishermen from the mid-eighteenth to mid-nineteenth centuries, create a photogenic vignette in the tiny harbour.

An almost continuous five-kilometre cliff path through coastal fynbos hugs the rocky coastline from the old harbour to Grotto Beach in the eastern suburbs. For one short stretch the path heads away from the coast and follows Main Street before returning to the shore. East of the Old Harbour, just below the *Marine Hotel*, a beautiful **tidal pool** offers the only sea swimming around the town centre's craggy coast. For **beaches**, you have to head out east across the Mossel River to the suburbs, where you'll find a decent choice, starting with secluded **Langbaai**, closest to town, a cove beneath cliffs at the bottom of Sixth Avenue. **Voëlklip**, at the bottom of Eighth Avenue, has grassed terraces and is great for picnics if you prefer your sandwiches unseasoned with sand. Adjacent is **Kammabaai**, with the best surfing break around Hermanus, and 1km further east, **Grotto Beach** marks the start of a twelve-kilometre curve of dazzlingly white sand that stretches all the way to De Kelders.

Hemel-en-Aarde Valley: the Walker Bay wineries

On the eastern edge of Hermanus, **Rotary Way** is a fantastic ten-kilometre drive that follows the mountain spine through beautiful montane fynbos offering sweeping views of the town, the Hemel-en-Aarde Valley (Heaven and Earth Valley) and Walker Bay from Kleinmond to Danger Point. To get there from town, turn right just after the sports ground, and take a track straddled by a pair of white gateposts labelled "Rotary Way". The road is tarred for part of the way before becoming dirt, eventually petering out altogether, which means you have to return the same way.

Some of South Africa's top wines come from the adjacent **Hemel-en-Aarde Valley**, about fifteen minutes by car west of Hermanus. Vineyards in the area date back to the early nineteenth century, when the Klein Hemel-en-Aarde Vineyard was part of a Moravian mission station, but winemaking has been established here for little over a decade. Three small **wineries** are dotted along a few gravel kilometres of the R320 to Caledon, which branches off the main road to Cape Town 2km west of Hermanus, and are worth popping into, for their intimate tasting rooms and first-class wines, and to sample the stark scrubby mountains just inland.

Newest of the three wineries, Whale Haven Winery (tastings & sales Mon–Fri 9.30am–5pm, Sat 10.30am–1pm; no tasting charge; ☎028/312 1585), a couple of hundred metres after the Caledon turn-off, released its first vintage in 1995 and its reputation has been growing since. Wines to look out for are the Merlot, which is very highly rated, and the Baleine Noire, a fruity Merlot and Shiraz blend that resembles Beaujolais and is best drunk young.

The longest established of the Walker Bay wineries, Hamilton Russell (tasting & sales Mon–Fri 9am–5pm, Sat 9am–1pm; no tasting charge; ☎028/312 3595) is noted for its exceptionally good Chardonnays and produces South Africa's two priciest wines (a Chardonnay and a Pinot Noir). If you're set on sampling a particular wine, be sure to phone ahead as some vintages sell out fast. Hamilton Russell also bottle a range of wines under the very collectable Southern Right label, which can't be bought at the estate but are available at the town liquor stores, where they quickly sell out as souvenirs. Adjacent to Hamilton Russell, towards Caledon, Bouchard Finlayson (Mon–Fri 9am–5pm, Sat 10.30am–12.30pm; ☎028/312 3515) is another establishment with a formidable reputation, and consistently scores highly with its Pinot Noir, Chardonnays and Sauvignon Blanc.

Eating and drinking

Seafood is the obvious thing to eat in Hermanus, and you'll find plenty of good restaurants serving it. The town's farm stall and deli-style foodshops are very handy if you're

WHALE-WATCHING

The Southern Cape, including Cape Town, provides some of the easiest and best places in the world for **whale-watching**. You don't need to rent a boat or take a pricey tour to get out to sea; if you come at the right time of year, whales are often visible from the shore, although a good pair of binoculars will come in useful for when they are far out.

All nine of the great whale species of the southern hemisphere pass by South Africa's shores, but the most commonly seen off Cape Town are **southern right whales** (their name derives from being the "right" one to kill because of their high oil and bone yields and the fact that, conveniently, they float when dead). Southern right whales are black and easily recognized from their pale, brownish **callosities** (rock gardens). These unappealing patches of raised, roughened skin on their snouts and heads have a distinct pattern on each animal, which helps scientists keep track of some of them. What gives away the presence of a whale is the blow or spout, a tall smoky plume which disperses after a few seconds and is actually the whale breathing out before it surfaces. If luck is on your side, you may see whales breaching – the movement when they thrust high out of the water and fall back with a great splash.

Female whales come inshore for calving in sheltered bays, and stay to nurse their young for up to three months. The period from **August to October** is the best time to see them, although they start appearing in June and some stay around until December. When the calves are big enough, the whales head off south again, to colder, stormy waters, where they feed on enormous quantities of plankton, making up for the nursing months when the females don't eat at all. Though you're most likely to see females and young, you may see **males** early in the season boisterously flopping about the females, though they neither help rear the calves or form lasting bonds with females.

THE OVERBERG'S HOTTEST WHALE SPOTS

In **Hermanus** itself the best vantage points are from the concreted cliff paths, which ring the rocky shore from New Harbour to Grotto Beach. There are interpretation boards at three of the popular vantage points (Gearing's Point, Die Gang and Bientang's Cave). At their worst, you'll find the paths two or three deep with people.

Although Hermanus is best known and most geared up for whale-watching, it's also the most congested venue during the whale season and there are equally good – if not better – spots elsewhere along the Walker Bay coast. Aficionados claim that **De Kelders** (see opposite), some 39km east of Hermanus, is even better, while **De Hoop Nature Reserve** (see p.194), east of Arniston, is reckoned by some to be the ultimate place along the entire southern African coast for whale-watching, with far greater numbers of southern rights breaching here than anywhere else.

DIAL M FOR MARINE MAMMALS

During the season, the Whale Information Hotline (☎083/212 1074) can tell you where the latest sightings have been.

self-catering. One of the best places to stock up on goodies is Hemel-en-Aarde Food, 2 Broad St, which sells cheeses, delicious breads, cakes and organic produce.

Bientang's Cave, off Marine Drive (☎028/312 3454). Next to the old harbour, this is the priciest restaurant in town, and is known for its seafood and fabulous location in a cave on the rocks just above the sea – where you can sit outside. Open daily for lunch during season as well as Fri and Sat nights.

The Burgundy, Marine Drive (☎028/312 2800). Above the old harbour, and arguably Hermanus's top restaurant, serving fairly expensive French-style food in one of the town's oldest buildings. There's indoor as well as shady outdoor seating. Closed Mon.

Fisherman's Cottage, Lemms Corner (☎028/312 3642). Excellent pub off Market Square, with verandah seating in an old cottage. Serves reasonably priced fish and chips. Closed Sun.

Galjoen Restaurant, Shop 3, Village Square, off Old Market Square (☎028/312 2282). Upmarket seafood eatery with a French accent, where the emphasis is on excellent presentation. Pricey but freshly line-caught fish is routinely available and you'll get shellfish and crayfish in season. Closed Tues.

Green's Bistro, 310 Tenth St, Voëlklip Beach (☎028/77 1048). Reasonably priced seafood and home cooking on the east side of town at another good restaurant. Closed all day Mon & Sun evening.

Harbour Rock, Site 24a New Harbour (☎028/312 2920). Great place for sundowners, where you should come for the stunning views from the harbour wall rather than the mid-priced food. Closed Mon.

Hermanus Fish Shoppe, Market Square. Cheap take-away fish and chips, seafood salads and fresh seafood to cook yourself.

Marimba Cafe, 124c Main Rd (☎028/312 2148). Cosy and lively evening joint with a constantly changing mid-price menu from across Africa. Past dishes have included Ethiopean roast lamb seasoned with cardamom and ginger, and *yassa* – Senegalese-style chicken. Booking essential. Closed Tues.

Milkwood Restaurant, Atlantic Drive, Onrus (☎028/316 1516). Nice outdoor family venue, especially recommended for medium-priced steaks and seafood. It's a 5min drive west of Hermanus, on the estuary and shaded by milkwood trees.

Mogg's Country Cookhouse, Hemel-en-Aarde Valley, 12km from Hermanus along the R320 to Caledon (☎028/312 4321). A most unlikely location for one of Hermanus's most successful restaurants – on a working farm in the back country. An intimate, mid-priced place that's always full and unfailingly excellent, it dishes up whatever country-cooking surprises take the chef's fancy, but there's always a choice of three starters, main courses and desserts – all topped off with superb views across the valley. Booking essential. Open Wed–Sun lunch and Fri & Sat evening.

Nautilus, Grotto Beach. Casual old eatery right on the beach, with moderately priced seafood and steaks.

Ouzeri and Trattoria, 60 St Peter's Lane (☎028/313 0532). Fairly standard joint with slow service. The menu switches between Greek and Italian food and includes good-value pizzas and pasta.

Listings

Emergencies Ambulance ☎10177; Fire ☎361 0000; Police (Flying Squad) ☎10111

Hospitals Hermanus Private Hospital, Hospital St, off Main Rd (☎028/312 1166), has a 24hr casualty service.

Pharmacy Hermanus, 145 Main Rd (☎028/312 4039). Opening hours are Mon–Fri 8am–6.30pm, Sat 8am–1pm, Sun 10am–noon & 6.30–7.30pm.

Taxis Bernardus' licensed taxi service (☎028/316 1093) picks up from the Baz bus at Bot River, runs shuttles to and from Cape Town, and can get you around town.

Grootbos and De Kelders

East of Hermanus the R43 takes a detour inland around the Klein River Lagoon, past the riverside hamlet of Stanford, before reaching the private **Grootbos Nature Reserve** (☎02834/40381, fax 40552; minimum stay two nights; ⑨), a highlight of the area, and 33km from Hermanus. Rolling across undulating, fynbos-covered country, this luxury reserve has superb middle-distance views of the coast, and is promoted as a "fynbos lodge", where experts guide you through the Western Cape's unique and richly varied plant kingdom. Outings are available in 4WD vehicles, on foot or on horseback. Accommodation is in self-contained stone cottages with ethnic-chic furnishings, polished granite kitchen surfaces, imported fittings, temperature-controlled showers, multiple sundecks and views of the mountain from one side and the sea from the other. The rate includes a three-course dinner served in the main lodge, breakfast in your own cottage and a choice of activities, including guided horse-rides, walks or drives through the fynbos and conducted beach hikes.

The nearest coast is a couple of kilometres to the east at **DE KELDERS**, a haphazard and treeless hamlet that stares from bleak cliffs across Walker Bay to Hermanus.

Note that **phone numbers** for Grootbos, De Kelders and Gansbaai are due to change throughout 1999 and 2000. If you have any difficulties, call ☎1023.

Despite surpassing fashionable Hermanus as a whale-watching venue and having a marvellous, long, sandy beach, De Kelders has somehow escaped the hype, and this small aggregation of holiday homes remains a backwater devoid of facilities with only a couple of places renting out rooms. *De Kelders* (☎02834/40421, fax 40165; ③) is a typically unsophisticated country **hotel** which has seen little modernization since the Sixties, but has a great verandah for tea, with unbeatable views overlooking the bay, and does cheap pub lunches. The *Mooi Uitsig Guest House*, 124 Cliff Rd (☎02834/41380, fax 41381), has sea-facing **B&B** rooms (④), and cheaper ones (②) at the back, as well as a whale-watching deck with sublime views.

Continuing west past the guesthouse to the end of Cliff Road, you'll reach a car park from which you can clamber down to the **Klipgat strandloper caves**, which were excavated in the early Nineties, unearthing evidence of modern human habitation from 80,000 years ago. It became unoccupied for a few thousand years after which it was again used, by Khoisan people, 20,000 years ago. Shells, middens, tools and bones were uncovered, and some of these are now displayed in the South African Museum in Cape Town (see p.94).

Gansbaai and Danger Point

From the Klipgat caves, the waymarked **Duiwelsgats Hiking Trail** goes east for 7km as far as Gansbaai and is a good way to explore this beautiful coastline. **GANS-BAAI** itself is a workaday place, economically dependent on its fishing industry and the seafood canning factory at the harbour. This all serves to give the place a more gutsy feel than the surrounding holidaylands, but there's little reason to spend time here unless you want to engage in **great white shark safaris**, Gansbaai's other major industry, an appropriately competitive and cutthroat business with a number of operators engaged in a blind feeding frenzy to attract punters. Boats set out from Gansbaai to Dyer Island (see box opposite), east of Danger Point, where great white sharks come to feed on the resident colony of seals. Sharks are baited, but while you do stand a chance of seeing one, sightings are certainly not guaranteed, especially over December and January when the abundance of seal pups keeps the sharks well fed and less inclined to show up for tourists. Even if a shark does come along it may not hang around long enough for all the people on the boat to get into the cage for a viewing (only two can fit in at a time). For more information, contact the Gansbaai **tourist information bureau**.

There's little reason to stay in Gansbaai other than for the budget **accommodation** offered by *Great White Backpackers* (contact Southcoast Seafaris ☎02834/41380, mobile ☎082/553 0999, fax 02834/41381; ①), a pair of Fifties' houses converted into plainly furnished lodges with small dorms and doubles.

Danger Point, the southernmost point of Walker Bay, is where British naval history was allegedly made. True to its name, the Point lured the ill-fated HMS *Birkenhead* onto its hidden rocks on February 26, 1852. As was the custom, the captain of the troopship gave the order: "Every man for himself." Displaying true British pluck, the soldiers are said to have lined up in their ranks on deck where they stood stock-still, knowing that if one man broke ranks it would lead to a rush that might overwhelm the lifeboats carrying women and children to safety. The precedent of "women and children first", which became known as the **Birkenhead Drill**, was thus established, even though 445 lives were lost in the disaster.

DYER ISLAND AND SHARK ALLEY

How a black American came to be living on an island off South Africa in the early nineteenth century is something of a mystery. But according to records **Samson Dyer** arrived here in 1806 and made a living collecting guano on the island that subsequently took his name. Dyer Island is home to substantial **African (jackass) penguin** and **seal breeding colonies**, both of which are prized morsels among great white sharks. So shark-infested is the channel between the island and the mainland at some times of year that it is known as **Shark Alley**, and these waters are used extensively by operators of great white viewing trips. In 1996, a group of West African castaways washed up here having been put out to sea by the unscrupulous skipper of a Taiwanese merchant vessel whom they had paid to take them to the Far East, where they hoped to find work. One of them drowned in the process, but the rest (amazingly) survived five days at sea, including a stint down Shark Alley clinging to pieces of timber and barrels.

Cape Agulhas and Elim

Along the east flank of the Danger Point promontory, the rocky and shallow coastline with heavy swells and strong currents makes this one of South Africa's most treacherous stretches of coast – one that has taken over 250 wrecks and around 2500 lives. Its rocky terrain also accounts for the lack of a coastal road from Gansbaai and Danger Point to **Cape Agulhas** – the southernmost tip of Africa. Apart from this one fact, there's nothing to recommend the place, which is approached through an ugly sprawl of houses. Flat, barren and windswept, it will leave you wishing that you took the left fork to Arniston. To get to Agulhas from Hermanus you have to go inland and take the R316 to Bredasdorp, where the road splits and you take the west branch for 43km to Agulhas or the east one for 24km to Arniston.

A far better reason to venture along the network of dirt roads that crisscrosses the **Whale Coast interior** is to visit **ELIM**, a Moravian mission station 40km northwest of Agulhas, founded in 1824. The whole village is a National Monument of streets lined with thatched, whitewashed houses and fig trees. There's nothing twee about this extraordinarily undeveloped and untouristy place which doesn't have a bottle store or even a tea shop. Facilities amount to a couple of tiny stores where coloured kids play video games. With no museum to visit and no places to stay, this is a place to simply drive or stroll around.

Arniston

After the cool deep blues of the Atlantic to the west, the tepid azure of the Indian Ocean at **ARNISTON** is truly startling; and it's made all the more dazzling by its white dunes interspersed with rocky ledges. This is one of the best places to stay in the Overberg and is refreshingly under-developed compared to Hermanus and places closer to Cape Town. The village is known to locals by its Afrikaans name, Waenhuiskrans (Wagonhouse Cliff), after a huge cave 1.5km south of town, which trekboers reckoned was spacious enough for a wagon and span of oxen (the largest thing they could think of). The English name derives from a British Ship, the *Arniston*, which hit the rocks here in 1815.

Conversely, the shallow seas that are treacherous for vessels give Arniston the safest swimming waters along the Whale Coast. Apart from sea bathing, **Kassiesbaai**, a community of starkly beautiful limewashed cottages, now collectively declared a National Monument, is the principal attraction of this unspoilt hamlet. Its beautifully simple dwellings are invariably the ones that show up in coffee-table books whenever picturesque fishing villages are called for. But as the home to the coloured fishing families that have for generations made their living here, it sits a little uneasily as a living community, as it's a bit of a theme park for visitors, who stalk the streets with their cameras. You can't stay in the cottages; all the holiday accommodation is in the adjacent new section of town, which has managed miraculously to blend in with the spirit of the old village.

The only regular entertainment here is wandering down to the harbour at high tide to watch the fishing boats being shoved down the slipway by a tractor that ends up half submerged. Otherwise, swimming and a few beach walks offer breaks from the supreme languor. You can swim next to the slipway or at **Roman Beach**, the main swimming beach, which is just along the coast as you head south from the harbour. During the whale season, you should also keep your eyes open for the **southern rights** that return here every year to calve.

Heading north through Kassiesbaai, at low tide, you can walk 5km along an unspoilt beach unmarred by buildings until you reach an unassuming fence – resist the temptation to climb over this, as it marks the boundary of the local testing range for military materiel and missiles. Heading south of the harbour for 1.5km along spectacular cliffs and the road, you'll reach the vast **cave** after which the town is named; this is a walk worth doing simply for the fynbos-covered dunes you'll cross on the way. From the car park right by the cave it's a short signposted walk down to the dunes and the cave, which can only be reached at low tide. The rocks can be slippery and have sharp sections, so be sure to wear shoes with tough soles and a good grip. **Dune tours** in a 4WD vehicle are operated by John Midgely of *Southwinds B&B* and can be booked either through them or the *Arniston Hotel* (see below).

Practicalities

As there's no public transport to Arniston, your only option is to **drive** here. Accommodation is limited to one hotel, some self-catering cottages and a handful of B&Bs, which get snapped up quickly during school holidays and over weekends. At the *Waenhuis Caravan Park* (☎028/445 9620), along the main road into Arniston, you can either pitch your own **tent** (①) or stay in small, four-bed en-suite **bungalows** (②), which have no sea views, but are only a couple of minutes' walk to the beach. Cooking equipment is available at a small charge, but you'll need to bring your own bedding and towels. Alternatively, limewashed self-catering mock-Arniston **cottages** can be rented at *Arniston Seaside Cottages* (☎028/445 9772, fax 445 9125; ③), well signposted from the national road, along the street behind the hotel. They're fully equipped and are charged per person out of season – in season (Jan, Easter school holidays & Dec) you pay for the total number of beds in the unit. Just behind the hotel, *Southwinds*, Huxham St (☎ & fax 028/445 9303, *sthwinds@ilink.nis.za*; ③), has three double **B&B** suites looking onto a courtyard garden. The smartest place to stay is the *Arniston* (☎028/445 9000, fax 445 9633, *hotel@arniston.co.za*; ⑤–⑦), a luxurious and well-run **hotel** in a central position along the seafront. Guests are offered extras, such as massage, and this is the only place in the village offering sea views from some rooms.

The village has three **restaurants**, all of which serve fresh fish caught locally. *Waenhuis*, Du Preez St (a continuation of the national road), is the least expensive, and is decorated to resemble a fishermen's tavern. The other two restaurants are at the hotel and have sea views. The informal and reasonably priced *Slipway* serves steaks, burgers and the like, while the hotel's main restaurant is far more formal and quite pricey. You can buy fresh fish from the fishermen at the slipway near the hotel.

De Hoop Nature Reserve

It's surprising that a reserve with as much going for it as **De Hoop** (daily 7am–6pm; small entry fee) has the humble status of a nature reserve, when it's quite probably the wilderness highlight of the Western Cape. Although the reserve makes a relatively easy day outing from Hermanus, you'll find it far more rewarding to come here for a night or more.

Breathtaking coastline is edged by bleached sand dunes that stand 90m high in places, and rocky formations that at one point open to the sea in a massive craggy arch. The flora and fauna are impressive too, encompassing 86 species of mammal, 260 different birds, 1500 varieties of plants, and it's reckoned to be the ultimate place in South Africa (surpassing even Hermanus and De Kelders) to see **southern right whales**. If you're here for a couple of days in season, chances are you'll be in luck, with reports on occasions of a dozen in evidence at one time. July to September is the best time, but you stand a very good chance of a sighting right through June to November. Inland, rare **Cape mountain zebra, bontebok** and other **antelope** congregate on a plain near the reserve accommodation. Apart from swimming and strolling along the length of white sandy beach, there are hiking and mountain-biking trails, but you'll need to bring your own bike as there's nowhere here to rent one.

Practicalities

De Hoop is along a signposted dirt road that spurs off the R319 as it heads out of Bredasdorp, 50km to its west. Accommodation is limited to a **campsite** (①) and equipped or unequipped **self-catering cottages** (②–③) set on an estuary well back from the sea. The unequipped cottages come with a cooker, fridge and electricity, but you'll need to bring your own bedding, and kitchen utensils, whereas the others are fully equipped. Booking should be made through the Manager, De Hoop Nature Reserve, Private Bag X16, 7280 Bredasdorp (☎028/542 1126, fax 542 1679). Overnight visitors must report to the reserve office, about 4km into the reserve, by 4pm. Be sure to stock up on supplies before you come – the nearest shop is 15km away, in the hamlet of Ouplaas.

THE GARDEN ROUTE

The **Garden Route**, a slender stretch of coastal plain between Mossel Bay and Storms River Mouth, bears a legendary status as South Africa's paradise – reflected in local names such as **Garden of Eden** and **Wilderness**. A soft, green forested swath of nearly 200km, cut by rivers from the mountains to the north, which tumble down to its southern rocky shores and sandy beaches, it was heaven to the **Khoi** herders, who lived off its natural bounty and called it Outeniqua ("the man laden with honey").

This Eden was quickly destroyed in the eighteenth century with the arrival of Dutch **woodcutters**, who had exhausted the forests around Cape Town and set about doing the same in Outeniqua, and killing or dispersing the Khoi and San in the process. Birds and animals suffered too from the encroachment of Europeans. The Swedish naturalist Johan Victorin, who came in the 1850s, shot and feasted on the species he had come to study, some of which, including the endangered narina trogon, he noted were "beautiful and good to eat".

Despite the dense appearance of the area, what you see today are only the remnants of one of Africa's great **forests**; much of the indigenous hardwoods have been replaced by exotic pine plantations and the only milk and honey you'll find now is in the many shops that service the Garden Route coastal resorts. **Conservation** may have halted the wholesale destruction of the indigenous woodlands, but a huge growth in tourism and the influx of urbanites seeking a quiet life in the relatively crime-free Garden Route towns threatens to rob the area of its remaining tranquillity.

Most visitors take the Garden Route as a **journey** between Cape Town and Port Elizabeth, dallying for a little more than day or two to do a bit of shopping or sightseeing.

The rapid passage cut by the excellent N2 makes it all too easy to have a fast scenic drive – and end up disappointed because you don't see that much from the road. To make the journey worthwhile, you'll need to slow down, take some detours off the highway and explore a little to find secluded coves, walks in the forests or **mountain passes** in the Karoo.

The Garden Route coast is dominated by three inlets – Mossel Bay, the Knysna Lagoon and Plettenberg Bay – each with its own town. Oldest of these and closest to Cape Town is **Mossel Bay**, an industrial centre of some charm, which marks the official start of the Garden Route. **Knysna**, though younger, exudes a well-rooted urban character and is the nicest of the coastal towns, with one major drawback – unlike **Plettenberg Bay**, its tinselled eastern neighbour, it has no beach of its own. A major draw, though, is the **Knysna Forest**, the awesome remants of the once vast ancient woodlands that still cover some of the hilly country around Knysna.

Between the coastal towns are some ugly modern holiday developments, but also some wonderful empty beaches and tiny coves, such as **Victoria Bay**, **Buffels Bay** and **Nature's Valley**. Best of all is the **Tsitsikamma National Park**, which has it all – indigenous forest, dramatic coastline, the pumping **Storms River Mouth** and South Africa's most popular hike, the **Otter Trail**.

Mossel Bay

MOSSEL BAY, 397km east of Cape Town, gets an undeservedly bad press from most South Africans, mainly because of the industrial facade it presents to the N2. Don't

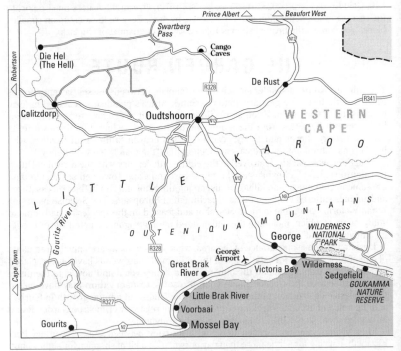

panic – the historic centre is a thoroughly pleasant contrast, set on a hill overlooking the small working harbour and bay, with one of the best **swimming** beaches along the southern Cape coast and an interesting museum. The town takes on a strong Afrikaans flavour over Christmas, when Karoo farmers and their families descend in droves to occupy its caravan parks and chalets. While Mossel Bay's modest attractions are unlikely to hold you for more than a night, it has some decent accommodation and a first-class restaurant, which make it a good place to stop to gather your breath before launching out into the thick of the Garden Route.

Some history

Mossel Bay bears poignant **historical significance** as the place where indigenous Khoi cattle herders encountered the existence of Europeans in a bloody spat that symbolically set the tone for five hundred years of race relations on the subcontinent. A group of Portuguese mariners under captain **Bartholomeu Dias** set sail from Portugal in August 1487 and months later rounded the Cape of Good Hope in search of a sea route to the riches of India. In February 1488, they became the first Europeans to make landfall along the South African coast, when they pulled in for water to the safety of an inlet they called Aguado de São Bras (Watering Place of St Blaize), now Mossel Bay.

The **Khoikhoi** were organized into distinct groups, each under its own chief and each with territorial rights over pastures and water sources. The Portuguese, who were flouting local customs, saw it as "bad manners" when the Khoikhoi tried to drive them off the spring. In a mutual babble of incomprehension the Khoi began stoning the Portuguese, who retaliated with crossbow fire that left one of the herders dead.

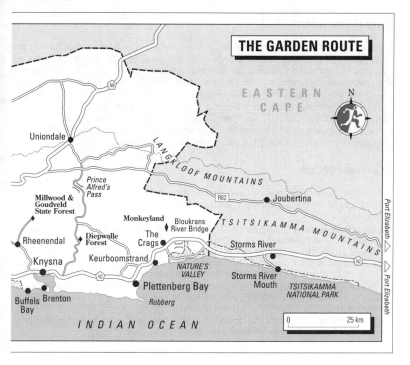

GARDEN ROUTE TRANSPORT

The **Garden Route**, is probably the best-served stretch of South Africa for **transport**. The excellent N2 makes **driving** along here an absolute breeze, and if you take it straight you'd have to try pretty hard to get lost.

Most user-friendly among the public transport options is the Baz **backpacker bus** (daily Cape Town–Port Elizabeth; ☎021/439 2323, fax 439 2343, *info@bazbus.com*), which picks up passengers daily from accommodation (7.15am–8.30am), recommended if you're exploring the Garden Route and want the freedom to get on and off at will. It provides a door-to-door service within the central districts of all the towns along the way, and has the advantage over the large intercity lines that it will happily carry outdoor gear, such as surfboards or mountain bikes. Although the buses take standby passengers if there's space available, you should book ahead if you want to secure your seat.

Intercape, Greyhound and Translux **intercity buses** from Cape Town and Port Elizabeth are better for more direct journeys, stopping only at Mossel Bay, George, Wilderness, Sedgefield, Knysna and Storms River (the village, but not the Mouth, which is some distance away), but often don't go into town, letting passengers off at filling stations on the highway instead.

More of a day out than serious transport, the Outeniqua Choo-Tjoe is a **goods train** with passenger carriages attached, running the 30km between George and Knysna twice daily (Mon–Sat) in both directions. And finally, if time is tight, you may want to go by **air** to George at the west end of the Garden Route, with scheduled services from Cape Town, Johannesburg, Durban and Port Elizabeth. The only other centre served by regular flights is Plettenberg Bay, which is connected to Johannesburg.

Arrival and information

The N2 bypasses Mossel Bay and, of all the buses, only the Baz **backpacker bus** comes right into town, dropping you off anywhere on request. The large **intercity buses** all stop at Shell Voorbaai Service Station, 7km from the centre, at the junction of the national highway and the road into town. The town itself is small enough to negotiate on foot, but should you need transport, Rendezvous Cape run a **taxi** service (☎044/691 3781).

The busy **tourist information bureau** (Mon–Fri 8am–6pm, Sat & Sun 9am–5pm; ☎044/691 2202, fax 690 3077, *info@mb.lia.net*), bang in the centre on the corner of Church and Market streets, has shelves of brochures about Mossel Bay and the rest of the Garden Route, and a small but very adequate **map** of the town.

Accommodation

Mossel Bay has a broad range of **accommodation**, including a number of reasonable B&Bs that can be booked through the tourist information bureau should our recommendations be full.

Allemans Dorpshuis, 94 Montagu St (☎044/690 3621). Comfortable B&B in a nineteenth-century house with Victorian furnishings, on a hill three blocks south of the tourist bureau. ③.

Da Gama Guest House, corner of High and Andrew Joss streets (☎ & fax 044/691 1636). Comfortable rooms in a 134-year-old two-storey colonial house with a generous verandah and balcony that afford views across the bay to the Outeniqua Mountains. ③.

De Bakke, George Rd (☎044/691 2915). Rock-bottom-priced camping at the municipal site just back from the beach, with sea views. Good self-catering chalets sleeping four are also available. Camping ①, chalets ②.

Huijs te Marquette, 1 Marsh St (☎ & fax 044/691 3182). Pleasant, if rather fussily furnished B&B close to the Point, with no views but a lovely courtyard ideal for sundowners. ④.

Mossel Bay Backpackers, 1 Marsh St (☎ & fax 044/691 3182). Cheapest rooms in town, in a small suburban house attached to *Huijs te Marquette*, conveniently located between the centre and the Point. Dorms ①, doubles with or without bath ②.

Mossel Bay Guest House, 61 Bruns Rd (☎044/691 2000, fax 690 4900). Comfortable rooms in a suburban home. ③.

Old Post Office Tree Manor, Bartholomeu Dias Museum Complex, Market St (☎044/691 3738, fax 691 3104). Opposite the tourist bureau and close to Santos Beach and the museums, in an old Cape Dutch manor house, this stylish guesthouse is by far the best place in town, with breakfast served at the *Gannet*, Mossel Bay's nicest restaurant. ⑤–⑥.

Point Caravan Park, Bland St (☎044/690 3501). Along the rocky Point, this is not as nice as the bay's main beach for swimming, but it's close to the start of the St Blaize hiking trail. ①.

Santos Beach Protea Hotel, Santos Rd (☎044/690 7103, fax 691 1945, *santos@mb.lia.net*). Priciest option in town, in a great location overlooking the beach (though some rooms don't face the sea), but with a rate that doesn't include breakfast. ④–⑤.

Santos Express, Santos Beach (☎044/691 1995). A stationary train with the best location in town – on the beach, just metres from the surf. Accommodation is in three-person train compartments and comes with coffee in the morning, but no breakfast. ②.

GARDEN ROUTE ADVENTURES: THE HIGHLIGHTS

The Garden Route is fast losing its reputation as the place to go for sun-soaking idleness or to commune with nature. Adrenaline and adventure are elbowing out these passive pursuits and now thrill-junkies go expressly to throw themselves off bridges, to gape into the jaws of great white sharks and to freewheel down scary mountain passes. The choice is broad – and widely spread across the entire length of the Garden Route. To help you plan, here are some highlights.

Bungee jumping. Leap into the abyss of the world's highest commercial jump at Bloukrans Bridge near The Crags (see p.222). Try bungee swinging, a jump with a twist at Gouritz River Bridge near Mossel Bay (see p.201).

Cycling. Tear down the hair-raising Swartberg Pass, starting out from Oudtshoorn (see p.169), or pedal your way in a slightly calmer fashion round the Homtini Trail in the Knysna Forest (see p.215).

Hiking. Set out on South Africa's oldest and most celebrated hiking route along the long-distance Otter Trail, which leaves from Storms River Mouth (see p.224). Alternatively there's the terrific circular one-day hike along the edge of the Robberg Peninsula (see p.220), with a chance of seeing whales, dolphins and seals. Or take it easy and stroll along the waymarked trails in the Goudveld State or Diepwalle forests near Knysna (see p.215 and p.216).

Horse-riding. Sit cowboy-style in a deep saddle and camp out in the forest, or try a short excursion, at Southern Comfort Western Horse Ranch, between Knysna and Plettenberg Bay (see p.211). Or head out on an English saddle through African countryside near Plettenberg Bay, for fynbos and forest trails (see p.219).

Scenic excursions. Catch the Outeniqua Choo-Tjoe steam train across Knysna Lagoon through beautiful back-country to George (see p.208). If you've got your own transport, try taking the old road just east of The Crags and wind your way down the fantastically scenic route to Nature's Valley (see p.223)

Watersports. Paddle upriver through woodland from Keurboomstrand (see p.221) in a canoe; earn an international scuba diving certificate – or if you already have one, go on a one-off dive – at Mossel Bay (see p.200); or rent a surfboard and take instruction in the art of riding the waves at *Weldon's Kaya*, Plettenberg Bay (see p.219).

Wildlife. Take to the water on a well-informed eco-tour that could encounter a variety of whales and dolphins at Plettenberg Bay (see p.217); or jump into a shark cage for a first-hand encounter with Jaws at Mossel Bay (see p.200). Back on dry land there's family fun in the forest, looking for apes from around the world at Monkeyland (see p.221).

The Town

It's fitting that Mossel Bay's main urban attraction is its **Bartholomeu Dias Museum Complex**, housed in a collection of historic buildings well integrated into the small town centre. The buildings are all within a couple of minutes' walk of each other and the tourist bureau, and are pleasantly diverting. The highlight is the **Maritime Museum** (Mon–Fri 9am–4.45pm, Sat & Sun 10am–4pm), a spiral gallery with displays on the history of Portuguese, Dutch and British seafaring, arranged around a full-size replica of Dias' original caravel (small boarding fee payable at reception). The ship was built in Portugal and sailed from Lisbon to Mossel Bay in 1987 to celebrate the 500th anniversary of Dias' historic journey. You can't fail to be awed by the idea of the original mariners setting out on the high seas into terra incognita on such a small vessel. More astonishingly, the crew were accommodated above deck with only a sailcloth for protection against the elements.

The one Mossel Bay attraction that most South Africans have heard of is the **Post Office Tree**, which grows just outside the Maritime Museum. Sixteenth-century mariners used to leave messages for passing ships in an old boot under a milkwood tree somewhere around here, and the plaque claims that "this may well" be the same tree. You can post mail here in a large, boot-shaped letterbox and have it stamped with a special postmark.

Of the remaining exhibitions, the **Shell Museum and Aquarium** (Mon–Fri 9am–4.45pm, Sat 10am–1pm, Sun 2–5pm; donation), next to the Post Office Tree, is the only one worth taking time to visit. This is your chance to see some of the beautiful shells found off the South African coast, as well as specimens from around the world. Displays of living shellfish, including cowries with their inhabitants still at home, are quite fascinating.

A short walk north down the hill from the Maritime Museum gets you to **Santos Beach**, the main town strand, and the only north-facing beach in South Africa – which gives it exceptionally long sunny afternoons. Adjacent to the small town harbour, the beach provides some of the finest swimming along the Garden Route, with uncharacteristically gentle surf, small waves and a perfect depth for practising your crawl.

East of the harbour, the coast bulges south towards the **Point**, which has a couple of franchised restaurants and a popular bar/restaurant (see "Eating and drinking" opposite) with a deck at the ocean's edge, from which you may see dolphins cruising past, as well as a surreal five-hundred-metre rocky channel known as the **Aquarium**, which is extensively used as a natural tidal pool.

Activities

Given that the seals of **Seal Island**, about 10km northwest of Santos Beach, are a highly popular delicacy among great white sharks, you'd be forgiven for wondering why scuba diving remains so popular off Mossel Bay. In 1990, the unfortunate Monique Price became the first fully kitted scuba diver to fall victim to a great white attack just off the island, and divers are warned to avoid its immediate environs. There are, however, several rewarding **diving and snorkelling** spots around Mossel Bay, and full facilities, including certification courses and one-off dives, are available from Mossel Bay Divers (π & fax 044/691 1441), at the *Santos Protea Hotel*, Santos Rd. These aren't tropical seas, so don't expect clear warm waters, but you do stand a good chance of seeing octopus, squid and sea stars.

If you want to see **sharks** face to face, there are a couple of outfits offering cage dives – the sharks you see most commonly here are the fearsome great whites popularized by *Jaws*. The optimum months for sightings are March to November and the worst January and February, but at no time are encounters guaranteed. One of the best operations in the country is Infante Shark Cage Diving, corner of Upper Cross and Kloof streets (☎ & fax 044/691 3796, mobile ☎082/455 2438); you can either observe from a boat (R300) or go underwater in a cage (R450). If you're not a high roller you can hedge your bets and opt to go for a cage for R600, with the assurance that if the sharks don't show you get half your money back.

Cruises around Seal Island to see the African (jackass) penguin and seal colonies can be taken on the *Romonza* (☎ & fax 044/690 3101) or the *Orpa* (mobile ☎082/702 0655) – medium-sized yachts that launch from the yacht marina in the harbour. On the mainland you check out the coast on the **St Blaize Hiking Trail**, an easy-going fifteen-kilometre walk (roughly 4hr each way) along the southern shore of Mossel Bay. The route starts from Bat's Cave, just below the lighthouse at the Point, and heads west as far as Dana Bay, taking in magnificent coastal views of cliffs, rocks, bays and coves. A **map** is available from the tourist information bureau (see "Arrival and information", p.198).

If jumping off bridges is your bag, the old Gouritz River Bridge, about 40km west of Mossel Bay along the N2, offers a considerably cheaper alternative to the Bloukrans Bridge (see p.222) near Nature's Valley. The major drawback of Gouritz is the fact that you won't be able to boast that you did the highest commercial **bungee jump** in the world, hence its bargain-basement price tag of R150. Gouritz offers the option of a bungee swing, in which the bungee is attached to the back of the same bridge causing you to swing down and under. For further information contact Gouritz Bungy at the bridge (☎044/697 7161), or in Cape Town at the Adventure Village, 229 Long St (☎021/424 1580).

Eating and drinking

As far as eating is concerned, you'll find all the usual **franchised joints**, including *Saddles*, which is at the Point and dishes up predictable steaks and burgers. For **light meals** in town, *Annie's Kitchen*, on Church Street, serves sandwiches and a cheap hot lunch, while *Café Baruch*, Liberty Centre, Bland St, is good for toasted sandwiches and salads and does decent coffee. For **takeaways**, *Snoekies*, Powrie St, is has the best fried fish and chips. Mossel Bay's lively **drinking** spot is *Tidals Waterfront Tavern & Pub*, which buzzes until the early hours on Fridays and Saturdays in a stunning seaside location overlooking cliffs and the open sea.

For more substantial **meals**, the *Gannet* (☎044/691 1885), on Market Street, serves moderately priced seafood dishes with considerable flair, enjoyed all the better in the stylish garden with glimpses across the dusk-washed harbour. Less formal, and superbly located – right on the beach – is the *Pavilion* (☎044/690 4567), a great place for sit-down fish and chips served in a historic, airy conservatory.

George

There's little reason to visit **GEORGE**, 66km northeast of Mossel Bay, unless you're starting or finishing a trip on the Outeniqua Choo-Tjoe. This large inland working town, surrounded by mountains, is a five-kilometre detour northwest off the N2, and 9km from the nearest stretch of ocean at Victoria Bay. Sadly, all that's left of the forests and quaint character that moved Anthony Trollope, during a visit in 1877, to describe it as the "prettiest village on the face of the earth", are some historic buildings, of which the **St Mark's Cathedral**, consecrated in 1850, is the most notable. Other than that, George's claim to recent fame (or notoriety) is the fact that it was the parliamentary seat of former State President **P.W. Botha** (see box on p.203), the last of South Africa's apartheid hardliners and the immediate predecessor of F.W. De Klerk, who negotiated the demise of minority rule. The George Museum once housed the P.W. Botha collection, an exercise in blind adulation for one of the most ruthless proponents of apartheid. Botha removed all his stuff in a fit after having a run-in with the new African-dominated town council.

Practicalities

Arriving in George by **air**, you'll land at the small George Airport, 10km west of town on the N2. There's no public transport from here into town; most tourists flying in pick up a car from one of the rental companies here and push off down the Garden Route. By **train**, scheduled Spoornet and Outeniqua Choo-Tjoe services arrive at George Station (☎044/801 8202), at the southeast end of Market and Hibernia streets. Intercape, Translux and Greyhound **intercity buses** pull in at St Mark's Square in a dubious part of town – if you're arriving here at night, prearrange a pick-up by your accommodation. The Baz **backpacker bus** drops off at the *George Backpackers' Hostel*. **Minibus taxis**, useful mainly for shuttles to and from Oudtshoorn, arrive in Cradock Street.

George's very helpful **tourist information bureau**, 124 York St (Mon–Fri 8am–4.30pm, Sat 9am–noon; ☎ & fax 044/801 9295), can provide town **maps** and help with accommodation bookings.

Accommodation

Places to stay are plentiful. *George Tourist Resort*, York St (☎044/874 5205, fax 044/874 4255), offers **camping** (①) and **chalets** (②) in well-kept pleasant gardens, with a swimming pool, a shop and laundry facilities. You can also camp at the *George Backpackers' Hostel*, 29 York St (☎044/874 7807), 1km south of the town centre, which has **dorms** (①) and doubles (②) in an annexe in the garden. Pick of the budget **B&Bs** is at no. 10 Caledon St (☎044/873 4983, fax 874 6503; ③), a spotless guesthouse in a quiet street around the corner from the museum, featuring balconies with mountain views and a garden to relax in. If you're set on staying in a **hotel**, head for the *King George Protea Hotel*, King George Drive (☎044/874 7659, fax 874 7664; ⑤), slightly out of the centre to the west in a quiet setting, offering comfortable rooms, each with their own verandah.

Eating and drinking

For **meals on a budget**, the *Pancake Tearoom* in George Arcade serves cheap lunches, including *boerewors* roll, meat and veg, or filled pancakes – their speciality. Traditional Afrikaner *boerekos* is served at the good-value *De Oude Werf*, 53 York St, which is open till 8pm during the week and for Sunday lunch. The station restaurant does cheap pub lunches – handy if you're on the midday Outeniqua Choo-Tjoe. The *Copper Pot and Wine Barrel*, 12 Montague St (☎044/870 7378), close to the airport, brings together under one roof one of George's best **restaurants**, which specializes in seafood, and a cheaper bistro-cum-wine-bar. Another recommended seafood eatery is the *King Fisher*, 1 Courtenay St (☎044/873 3127), on the corner of the N12 opposite the Outeniqua High School sports fields, where the specialities include spicy hot Portuguese-style mussels and fresh local fish.

Victoria Bay and Wilderness

Some 9km south of George and 3km off the N2 is **VICTORIA BAY**, a small sandy beach wedged into a cove between cliffs. One of the genuine gems of the Garden Route, during the December holidays it's brimful of day-trippers, and despite its benign aspect of a grassy sunbathing area, safe swimming and a tidal pool, it rates as one of the top **surfing** spots in South Africa. Best of all, because of the cliffs there's only a single row of houses along the beachfront, with some of the most dreamily positioned guest-houses along the coast.

There's no public **transport** to Victoria Bay, although a lot of people **hitch** the few kilometres from the N2. Arriving by **car**, you'll encounter a metal barrier as you drop down the hill to the bay, and you'll have to try and park in a car park that's frequently full (especially in summer). If you're staying at one of the B&Bs, leave your car at the

---

PRESIDENT BOTHA: THE KING CANUTE OF APARTHEID

Pieter Willem Botha is credited with setting up an autocratic "Imperial Presidency" in South Africa, but in retrospect he was actually the King Canute of apartheid, closing his eyes to the incoming tide of democracy and believing that by wagging his finger (his favoured gesture of intimidation) he could turn it back.

A National Party hack from the age of 20, Botha worked his way up through the ranks, getting elected an MP in 1948 when the first apartheid government took power. He became leader of the **National Party** in the **Cape Province** and was promoted through various cabinet posts until he became **Minister of Defence**, a position he used to launch a palace coup in 1978 against his colleague, Prime Minister John Vorster. Botha immediately set about modernizing apartheid, modifying his own role from that of a British-style prime minister, answerable to parliament, to one of an executive president taking vital decisions in the secrecy of a President's Council heavily weighted with army top brass.

Informed by the army that the battle to preserve the apartheid status quo was unwinnable purely by force, Botha embarked on his **Total Strategy**, which involved reforms to peripheral aspects of apartheid and the fostering of a black middle class as a buffer against the ANC, while pumping vast sums of money into building an enormous military machine that crossed South Africa's borders to bully or crush neighbouring countries into submission. South African refugees in Botswana and Zimbabwe were bombed, Angola was invaded, and arms were run to anti-government rebels in Mozambique, reducing it to ruins – a policy that has returned to haunt South Africa with those same weapons now returning across the border and finding their way into the hands of criminals. Inside South Africa, security forces enjoyed a free hand to murder, maim and torture **opponents of apartheid** on a scale that only fully emerged between 1996 and 1998, under the investigations of the Truth and Reconciliation Commission.

Botha's intransigence led to his greatest blunder in 1985, when he responded to international calls for change by hinting that he would announce significant reforms at his party congress that would irreversibly jettison apartheid. In the event, the so-called **Rubicon speech** was a disaster, as Botha proved to have insufficient steel to resist pressure from white right-wing extremists. The speech ruled out meaningful concessions to black South Africans, the immediate result of which was a flight of capital from the country and intensified sanctions. Perhaps worst of all for the apartheid regime, the **Chase Manhattan Bank** refused to roll over its massive loan to South Africa, leaving the country an uncreditworthy pariah.

Botha blustered and wagged his finger at the opposition through the late Eighties, while his bloated military sucked the state coffers dry as it prosecuted its dirty wars. Even National Party stalwarts realized that his policies were leading to ruin, and in 1989, when he suffered a stroke, the party was quick to replace him with **F.W. de Klerk**, who immediately proceeded to announce the reforms the world had expected four years earlier from Botha's Rubicon speech.

Botha lives out his retirement near George, where, it is reported, he still harbours deep resentments against his National Party colleagues, whom he believes betrayed him. He has declined to apologize for any of the brutal actions taken under his presidency to bolster apartheid and, despite being subpoenaed, he refused to testify before the **Truth and Reconcilitaion Commission**, which led in 1998 to him being prosecuted and fined for contempt. In 1999, his appeal against this judgement was successful.

barrier and collect the key from your lodgings to gain access to the private beach road. The only place to buy **food** from is a small beachside kiosk that sells light refreshments and unexciting snacks. However the resort's B&Bs offer a local "dial-a-meal" service at no extra cost, which delivers from several fast-food joints in George.

Accommodation is in somewhat better supply – the cheapest option being *Victoria Bay Caravan Park*, on the left as you approach the beach (☎044/874 4040 or 889 0081; ①), which has magnificently located **camping** on the clifftop overlooking the beach. Budget **self-catering** units are available at *Sea Breeze Holiday Resort* (☎044/889 0098, fax 889 0104; ②), along the main road into the settlement, were you can rent a variety of large, modern double-storey holiday cabanas, sleeping from four to six people. The cabanas have no sea views, but it's an easy stroll to the beach. Just metres from the sea, *The Waves*, Victoria Bay Rd (☎ & fax 044/889 0166; ④, winter discounts), offers two front **rooms** in a high-ceilinged Victorian house in an unbeatable location overlooking the water. Just 6m from the high-water mark, *Sea Shells*, Victoria Bay Rd (☎044/889 0051; ④) has en-suites with a large shared balcony overlooking the sea. A little further along the same road, *Land's End Guest House* (☎044/889 0123, fax 889 0141; ④) has two wonderful self-catering studio **apartments** sleeping two with views out to sea from the bed, and also offers similarly priced **B&B** accommodation.

Wilderness and around

East of Victoria Bay, across the Kaaimans River, the beach at **WILDERNESS** is so close to the N2 that you can pull over for a quick dip and barely interrupt your journey. Unfortunately this is also the worst thing about the place, as it is sliced up by the national road, leaving the village and lakes stranded inland. Tradition has it that Wilderness village earned its name after a young man called van den Berg bought the property in 1830 for £183 as a blind lot at a Cape Town auction. When he got engaged, his fiancée insisted that their first year of marriage should be spent out of town in the wilderness, so he romantically (or perhaps opportunistically) named his property Wilderness and built a hut on it.

If the hut's still there, you'll struggle to find it among the sprawl of retirement homes, holiday houses and 2500 beds for rent in the area. Take your life in your hands and cross the N2 to get to the beach, which is renowned for its long stretch of sand, backed by tall dunes, rudely blighted by holiday houses that compete to outdo each other. Once in the water, stay close to the shoreline: this part of the coast is notorious for its unpredictable currents.

The tiny **village centre**, on the north side of the N2, has a filling station, a few shops and a **tourist information** bureau in Leila's Lane (Mon–Fri 8.30am–12.30pm & 2–5pm, Sat 9am–12.30pm; ☎044/877 0045). One of the cheapest places to stay is *Fairy Knowe Backpackers* (☎ & fax 044/877 1285), an eccentric **hostel** with dorms (①) and doubles (②), set in woodlands near the Touws River, but nowhere near the sea. The Baz bus will drop off here, and the Outeniqua Choo-Tjoe can also make aunscheduled stop at the siding outside (make your request before it departs). Also well away from the ocean, *Island Lake Holiday Resort* (☎ & fax 044/877 1194), Lakes Rd, 2km from the Hoekwil/Island Lake turn-off on the N2, has **camping** and **self-catering** bungalows (①) that sleep four, on one of the quietest and prettiest spots on the lakes. There's good swimming at *Trails End Holiday Resort* (☎044/343 1914, fax 343 2006) on Swartvlei Lake, with pricey camping (②) but budget, fully equipped timber chalets (③). For greater comfort, head for the *Fairy Knowe Hotel* (☎044/877 1100, fax 877 0364; ③–④), on Dumbleton Road (follow the signposts from the N2), an old-fashioned establishment away from the beach, with the best **rooms** facing onto the Touws River and cheaper garden-facing rooms. The best views in Wilderness are from the *Mes-Amis Homestead*, Buxton Close (☎ 044/877 1928, fax 877 1830, *synette@mweb.co.za*; ④) signposted off the

N2 on the coastal side of the road, directly opposite the national park turn-off. The good doubles here each have a terrace and sliding doors that look out to sea.

When it comes to places to **eat**, locals desert Wilderness for Knysna or George, although *Tom's Tavern* (☎044/877 0353) in the village centre, recommended as a decent place for a **drink**, has a range of steaks, pizzas, pasta and seafood of variable quality.

Wilderness National Park

Stretching east from Wilderness village is the **Wilderness National Park** (reception daily Feb–Nov 8am–1pm & 2–5pm; Dec & Jan 7am–8pm; ☎044/877 1197, fax 877 0111; accommodation booking through South African National Parks Pretoria ☎012/343 1991, fax 343 0905; Cape Town ☎021/422 2810, fax 424 6211; entry fee), the least aptly named national park in South Africa, as it never feels very far from the rumbling N2. Although the park takes in beach frontage, it's the **forests** you should come for; the 16km of inland waterways and the variety of habitats that include coastal and montane fynbos, evergreen forests and wetlands which attract 250 species of **birds** and many more holidaymakers. There are several waymarked **trails** lasting from one to four hours, all well worth doing to get a feeling of the indigenous vegetation and escape the N2 and holiday homes – the reception issues trail **maps**. You can also rent **canoes** from reception and take to the water.

There are two **rest camps**, both on the west side of the park and clearly signposted off the N2. *Ebb and Flow – North*, right on the river, is cheap, old-fashioned and away from the hustle. It offers camping (①), fully equipped two-person bungalows with their own showers (②), and slightly cheaper huts with communal washing and toilet facilities (②); there's also a twenty percent seasonal discount here (late Jan to early March & late April to early Dec). *Ebb and Flow – South*, signposted close by, offers camping (①) and modern accommodation in spacious log cabins on stilts and brick bungalows which, although dearer than *North* camp, represent good value. You pay for a minimum of two people in the four-person bungalows (②), both with and without showers; in the larger, fully self-contained family cottages (②), you pay for a minimum of four. There is a **shop** selling milk, bread and basic groceries at reception.

Sedgefield and the Goukamma Reserve

The drive between Wilderness and Sedgefield gives glimpses on your left of dark-coloured lakes which eventually surge out to sea, 21km later, through a lagoon at **SEDGEFIELD**, a lacklustre holiday village with a safe swimming **beach** that makes a refreshing pit stop. Sedgefield's unpromising appearance of shops, restaurants and B&Bs lining the highway belies a gloriously undeveloped beachfront, cut through by a wide lagoon, a few kilometres off the road. The beach is especially beautiful because all the houses are set back and hidden behind the sand dunes.

Sedgefield could be used as a good base from which to explore **Goukamma Nature and Marine Reserve** and the western extent of **Groenvlei**, a freshwater lake that falls within it. An unassuming sanctuary of around 220 square kilometres, Goukamma ranges west as far as the small seaside resort of Buffels Bay to absorb 14km of beach frontage, some of the highest vegetated dunes in the country and walking country covered with coastal fynbos and dense thickets of milkwood, yellowwood and candlewood trees.

The area has long been popular with anglers for the six **fish** species that inhabit Groenvlei. Away from the water you stand a small chance of spotting one of the area's **mammals**, including bushbuck, grysbok, mongoose, vervet monkeys, caracals and otters. Because of the diversity of coastal and wetland habitats, this is also good avifauna territory, with over 220 different kinds of **birds** recorded, including fish eagles, Knysna louries, kingfishers, and very rare African black oystercatchers. Off the shore, southern right **whales** often make an appearance during their August to December breeding season and bottlenose and common **dolphins** can show up at any time of year.

Apart from angling and bird-watching, the Goukamma offers a number of self-guided activities, including safe **swimming** in Groenvlei. There are several day-long hiking **trails** that enable you to explore different habitats – if you plan on hiking you should pick up the Cape Nature Conservation **map** from the *Lake Pleasant Hotel*. A beach walk, which takes around four hours one way, traverses the full 14km of crumbling cliffs and sands between the Platbank car park on the western side and the Rowwehoek one at the other. A slightly longer trek across the dunes also takes you from one end of the reserve to the other, but via an inland route. A shorter circular walk starts at the reserve office and goes through a milkwood forest.

Two roads off the N2 provide **access** to the reserve. At the westernmost side, a dirt road that runs down to Platbank beach takes you past the tiny settlement of Lake Pleasant on the south bank of Groenvlei, which consists of little more than a hotel and holiday resort. On the eastern side, access is via the Buffels Bay road, along which the Goukamma office is reached about halfway. There are no public roads within the reserve.

Practicalities

Despite the forest of holiday homes in **Sedgefield**, there is little **accommodation** away from the N2 for visitors. The one exception is *Landfall Resort* (☎ & fax 044/343 1804), a low-key and old-fashioned place which allows **camping** (①) and rents out on-site **caravans** (②) with attached kitchens, toilets and showers. The resort also rents out more spacious two-bedroom fully equipped **cottages** (②) that sleep six.

Accommodation in **Goukamma Nature Reserve** should be booked well in advance through the Manager, Goukamma Nature and Marine Reserve, PO Box 331, Knysna 6570 (☎044/383 0042). The choice is limited to a basic **bushcamp** (②) on the southern shore of the lake, reached by a road past the hotel turn-off; and on the Buffels Bay side to a thatched **rondavel** (②) overlooking the Goukamma River. At **Lake Pleasant**, on the western edge of the reserve, you have the choice of the *Lake Pleasant Hotel* (☎044/343 1313, fax 343 2040, *lake.pleasant@pixie.co.za*; ⑥), which has country-style public spaces, a lovely garden and simple **rooms** that look onto thick reed-beds around the lake, disturbed by the constant rumble of the N2; the hotel's *Swan Pub* does reasonably priced pub lunches. Within walking distance from here, and good for budget anglers and families, there's the *Lake Pleasant Chalets & Lodges* (☎ & fax 044/343 1985, *lake@mweb.co.za*), which has shady **campsites** (①), three-person self-catering **chalets** (②) and slightly smaller (and cheaper) **lodges**. There's an à la carte **restaurant**, a pub, a store selling basics, and an exceptionally well-stocked anglers' shop. The resort also rents out **mountain bikes**, rowing **boats** and **canoes**.

Another possibility is to stay at **Buffels Bay**, 10km down a turn-off that is 13km east of Sedgefield along the N2, a haphazard little development at the east of the reserve. Cheapest is the *Buffels Bay Caravan Park* at the Point (☎044/383 0045; ①), while the spacious, fully equipped *Buffalo Bay Apartments*, 160 Walker Drive (☎044/383 0218; ②), overlooking the bay, offer some of the best accommodation.

Knysna

South Africa's Nineties tourist boom has rudely shaken **KNYSNA** (pronounced "Nizena") from its gentle backwoods drowse, which for decades made this the hippy and craftwork capital and quiet retirement village of the country. The town, 102km east of Mossel Bay, now stands as the undisputed hub of the Garden Route despite having no beaches of its own, a shortcoming it makes up for through its hilly setting around the lagoon, a broad body of water that fills and drains each day with the tides. The lagoon's narrow mouth is guarded by **the Heads**, a pair of steep rocky promontories, the western side being a private nature reserve and the eastern one an exclusive residential area soaring above the Indian Ocean along dramatic cliffs.

Knysna's distinctive atmosphere derives from its small historic core of Georgian and Victorian buildings, which gives it a character absent from most of the Garden Route holiday towns. Coffee shops, craft galleries, street traders and a modest nightlife add to the attractions, and you may find yourself tempted to stay longer than just one night. That the town has outgrown itself is evident from the cars and tour buses which, especially in December and January, clog Main Street, the constricted artery that merges with the N2 as it toddles into town.

Some history

At the beginning of the nineteenth century, the only white settlements outside Cape Town were a handful of villages that would have considered themselves lucky to have even one horse. Knysna, an undeveloped backwater hidden in the forest, was no exception. The name comes from a Khoi word meaning "hard to reach", and this remained its defining character well into the twentieth century. One important figure was not deterred by the distance – **George Rex**, a colourful colonial administrator, who had placed himself beyond the pale of decent colonial society by taking on a coloured mistress. Shunned by his peers in Britain, he headed for Knysna at the turn of the nineteenth century in the hope of making a killing shipping out hardwood from the Knysna Lagoon.

By the time of Rex's death in 1839, Knysna had become a major **timber centre**, attracting white woodcutters who felled trees with primitive tools for miserly payments, and looked set eventually to destroy the forest. In 1872, **Prince Alfred**, on his visit to the Cape, made his small royal contribution to this wanton destruction when he made a special detour here to come elephant hunting. The forest only narrowly escaped devastation by far-sighted and effective conservation policies introduced in the 1880s.

By the turn of the twentieth century, Knysna was still remote and its forests were inhabited by isolated and inbred communities made up of the impoverished descendants of the woodcutters. As late as 1914, if you travelled from Knysna to George you would have to open and close 58 gates along the 75-kilometre track. Fifteen years on, the passes in the region proved too much for **George Bernard Shaw**, who did some impromptu off-road driving and crashed into a bush, forcing Mrs Shaw to spend a couple of weeks in bed at Knysna's *Royal Hotel* with a broken leg.

Arrival and information

Greyhound, Translux and Intercape **intercity buses** drop passengers off at Bern's Service Station in Main Street, right in the centre of town; the Baz **backpacker bus** will drop passengers off at any of the town's accommodation. The **Outeniqua Choo-Tjoe**, South Africa's last scheduled mixed goods and passenger steam train, runs from George to Knysna twice daily from Monday to Saturday (departing 9.30am & 1pm, a 2hr 45min joiurney; R40 single, R50 return; ☎044/382 1361). For local transport, Rikkis **taxis** (☎044/382 6540) serve Knysna and the surrounding areas as far as Buffalo Bay to the west and Plettenberg Bay to the east; U-Ride (☎ & fax 044/382 7785, mobile ☎083/377 9155) do budget **car and scooter rental** for local use, plus mountain bikes and canoes.

Knysna's **tourist information** bureau, 40 Main St (Mon–Fri 8.30am–5pm, Sat 9am–1pm; ☎044/382 5510, fax 382 1646, *knysna.tourism@pixie.co.za*), Gray St, can provide maps and information about the town and area. The privately operated information kiosk on Pledge Square (Mon–Fri 8.30am–5pm, Sat 8.30am–1pm, Sun 9am–1pm; ☎044/382 5878), just off Main Road, is also useful and can take bookings for a whole range of activities, including ferry cruises on the lagoon and tickets for the Outeniqua Choo-Tjoe.

Knysna Booking Services (☎044/382 6960, fax 382 1609, *knysna_booking @mweb.co.za*), next door to the tourist information bureau, makes reservations for the burgeoning range of **adventure activities** offered around Knysna, from abseiling down the Heads to bungee jumping from the Gouritz River Bridge. The service is free if you phone and there's a small charge for walk-in clients.

Accommodation

Knysna caters well for backpackers, but is short on budget B&Bs. The best places to stay are away from the main road, with views of the Heads or the lagoon; out of town there are some excellent and very reasonably priced self-catering cottages right in the forest, where you can get well away from the town buzz. Knysna Booking Services (see above) run a busy accommodation office, whose staff are extremely knowledgeable about all the options in and around town and can arrange **bookings**.

Town centre

Albatross Guest House, corner of Albatross Rd and Paradise Circle (☎ & fax 044/382 4498). En-suite cottage-style rooms leading onto a garden with a swimming pool, one block up from the lagoon and main road in a quiet wooded area. For scuba divers an added plus is the resident dive master. ③.

The Backpack, 17 Tide St (☎044/382 4362 or 382 7766, fax 382 4362, *backpack@knysna.lia.net*). Clean and sociable backpackers' lodge that attracts travellers keen on mellowing out in the garden and partying, with TV, bar and mountain-bike rental. Dorms ①, doubles ②.

Caboose, corner of Gray and Trotter streets (☎044/382 5850, fax 382 5224, *caboose.kny@pixie.co.za*). Dead-cheap sleepers in spotless but cramped train-style compartments – part of a huge modern timber complex with pleasant open spaces, including a shared lounge, indoor dining areas, a swimming pool and sun deck. Have no illusions though – even though you have your own shower, you'll be using it directly over the toilet. ②.

Gallery Guest House, 10 Hill St (☎044/382 2510, fax 382 5212). Gracious double-storey colonial house within easy walking distance of town, with arty decor and balcony views across the the lagoon to the Heads. ③.

Highfields Backpackers' Guest House, 2 Graham St (☎044/382 6266, fax 382 5799). Best of the backpackers' lodges, with stylish decor, a friendly atmosphere, swimming pool and sun deck. There's no bar, which makes this a good bet if you're after some peace and quiet. Reasonably priced excursions can be arranged to the Heads, the Mitchell's Brewery and Brenton. Dorms ①, doubles ②.

Knysna Backpackers' Hostel, 42 Queen St (☎ & fax 044/382 2554). Claims to be the only backpackers' lodge with a bit of a lagoon view, and this is indeed its principal recommendation. Dorms ①, doubles ②.

Knysna Protea Hotel, 51 Main St (☎044/382 2127, fax 382 3568). Smart hotel offering luxury rooms with air conditioning. Standby discounts are sometimes available. ⑤.

John Benn House, 2 Lake View Ave (☎044/382 2903, fax 382 5753). Budget self-catering double rooms, in an atmospheric Victorian house close to the centre. ②.

Lakeside Guest House, 88 Main St (☎ & fax 044/382 6217, mobile ☎082/416 5635, *lakeside. guesthouse@pixie.co.za*). Bargain pine-panelled en-suite rooms in a mock-Austrian house, close to the centre but with the disadvantage of being on the busy main drag. ②.

Overlander's Lodge, 11 Nelson St (☎ & fax 044/382 5920, *info@gardenroute.co.za*). Popular backpackers' lodge that achieves a delicate balance between being organized and relaxed. Camping is available, and there are clean 18-bed dorms and double rooms inside the house, while outside there's a bar and a fire pit. Can arrange a whole array of outings from hikes to mountain biking and adventure activities. Camping & dorms ①, doubles ②.

Peregrin Backpackers, 16 High St (☎ & fax 044/382 3747, *peregrin@knysna.lia.net*). The biggest hostel in town can accommodate 90 people and offers added-value incentives to potential guests, in

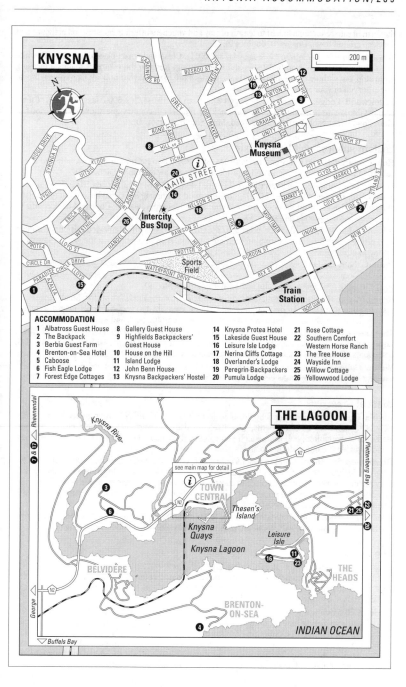

KNYSNA

0   200 m

Knysna Museum

Intercity Bus Stop

Sports Field

Train Station

ACCOMMODATION

1	Albatross Guest House	8	Gallery Guest House	14	Knysna Protea Hotel
2	The Backpack	9	Highfields Backpackers'	15	Lakeside Guest House
3	Berbia Guest Farm		Guest House	16	Leisure Isle Lodge
4	Brenton-on-Sea Hotel	10	House on the Hill	17	Nerina Cliffs Cottage
5	Caboose	11	Island Lodge	18	Overlander's Lodge
6	Fish Eagle Lodge	12	John Benn House	19	Peregrin Backpackers
7	Forest Edge Cottages	13	Knysna Backpackers' Hostel	20	Pumula Lodge

21	Rose Cottage
22	Southern Comfort Western Horse Ranch
23	The Tree House
24	Wayside Inn
25	Willow Cottage
26	Yellowwood Lodge

THE LAGOON

Rheenendal

Knysna River

see main map for detail

TOWN CENTRAL

Thesen's Island

Plettenberg Bay

Knysna Quays

Leisure Isle

Knysna Lagoon

BELVIDERE

George

BRENTON-ON-SEA

THE HEADS

Buffels Bay

INDIAN OCEAN

the form of rate reductions linked to length of stay and vouchers offering discounts on activities and services around town. Dorms ①, doubles ②.

Wayside Inn, Pledge Square (☎ & fax 044/382 6011). Clean and smart place done out with white linen on black wrought-iron bedsteads and sisal matting. Right in the centre, it makes a pleasing night stop, but without communal areas is not somewhere to spend your holiday. Continental breakfast is served in your room on a wicker tray. ④.

Yellowwood Lodge, corner of Handel and Short streets (☎044/382 5906, fax 382 4230). Clean, comfortable rooms in a light and airy, non-smoking, nineteenth-century guesthouse with period furniture, one street back from the main road. May–Sept discounts. ④.

Eastern suburbs and Leisure Isle

House on the Hill, 60 Milkwood Drive (☎044/382 1326). Two B&B rooms in a friendly and cheap suburban house with good views and repro furniture, well away from the action. ②.

Leisure Isle Lodge, 87 Bayswater Drive, Leisure Isle (☎044/384 0462, fax 384 1027). Knysna's top guesthouse, right on the edge of the lagoon at a good swimming spot, exudes a quiet and restful atmosphere. Heated outdoor pool, spacious rooms, under-carpet heating. Choice of back rooms or more expensive lagoon-facing units. ④.

Island Lodge, 12 Parkes Lane (☎ & fax 044/384 0422). The most affordable doubles on the upmarket Leisure Isle in a house that epitomizes high suburbia. A swimming pool in the garden saves you having to stir yourself for the 5min stroll down to the lagoon. ③.

Pumula Lodge, 7 Lindsay St (☎ & fax 044/384 1193, mobile ☎083/228 8594, *pumula@pixie.co.za*). En-suite rooms, each with its own deck overlooking a tranquil garden with a stream – great value if you're looking for somewhere calm and away from the centre. ②.

Rose Cottage, 34 Wilson St (☎044/384 0255, fax 382 7075, *margibas@ilink.nis.za*). Small but immaculate en-suite room ideal for overnighting; and a large, pleasant and good-value self-catering cottage suitable for two adults and a child, with a patio, use of swimming pool, and a garden. Both ③.

The Tree House, 37 Cearn Drive, Leisure Isle (☎ & fax 044/384 0777, mobile ☎082/432 5180). Lovely self-catering cottage on the lagoon near an excellent swimming spot, with two bedrooms, two bathrooms, TV, video and a large sun deck screened by a huge tree. ④.

Willow Cottage, 34a Wilson St (☎ & fax 044/384 0752). Highly recommended double-storey self-catering cottage overlooking a beautiful garden, with clear views of the lagoon from the balcony. ②.

West of town

Berbia Guest Farm, Welbedacht Rd, 6km from Knysna off the N2 towards George (☎ & fax 044/382 5429). Four en-suite rooms, attractively furnished in warm colours, on a farm. All rooms lead onto a swimming pool, from which you can see the lagoon and Heads in the distance. *Braai* stands provide the only catering facilities. ③.

Brenton-on-Sea Hotel, Brenton beachfront (☎ & fax 044/381 0081). The only seaside hotel in the area, overlooking the long curve of Brenton beach, which swings round to Buffalo Bay. Pretty ordinary motel-style rooms make it a place to stay for the location rather than style. May–Nov discounts. Self-catering chalets sleeping six are only worth considering if there are four or more of you. B&B rooms are also available. All accommodation ⑤.

Fish Eagle Lodge, off Welbedacht Rd (☎ & fax 044/382 5431, fax 382 7435). Swiss-style self-catering chalets that come with breakfast, phones, TV and views of the lagoon. April–Aug discounts. ③.

The forest

Forest Edge Cottages, Rheenendal (☎044/388 4704, fax 388 4778). Ideal if you want to be close to the forest itself, these traditional tin-roofed two-bedroomed cottages have verandahs built in the local vernacular style; self-contained, fully equipped and serviced, they sleep four. Forest walks and cycling trails start from the cottage and you can rent mountain bikes. ③.

Nerina Cliffs Cottage, Rheenendal (☎044/388 4624, fax 388 4611). Remote, wonderful place for several adventurous nights' stay on a scenic citrus farm 20min from Knysna. The timber chalet perched on the edge of cliffs overlooks the real Knysna Forest, some distance from the main buildings in a section of the farm wild enough to have the occasional leopard breezing through. A deck jettying out over a chasm is big enough to sleep out on in summer. There's no electricity and the fridge, heater, lights, hot water and cooker all run off gas. You can canoe and swim on the farm lake. ②.

Southern Comfort Western Horse Ranch, 3km along the Fisanthoek road, 17km east of Knysna en route to Plettenberg Bay (☎044/532 7885). Budget accommodation in double rooms with bunk beds, on a farm adjacent to the eastern section of the Knysna Forest. Meals are provided or you can self-cater. A shuttle bus collects guests from either Knysna or Mossel Bay. Western-style riding is also available, from one-hour outings (R60) to overnight trails in the forest sleeping in teepees (R230). Doubles ①.

The Town and around

Knysna wraps around the lagoon, with its oldest part – the town centre – on the north-ern side, while along the eastern shore the exclusive suburbs include **Leisure Isle**, which is connected to the shore by a narrow causeway, and the **Heads**, a network of winding roads curling their way up to the heights overlooking the craggy coast and a wild Indian Ocean.

Main Street is the hub of the city centre, and its principal attraction is the collection of craft and woodwork shops that line up along the road. The **Knysna Museum** (Mon–Fri 9.30am–4.30pm, Sat 9.30am–1pm; small entry fee, includes Angling Museum), on the corner of Queen and Main streets, contains a complex of minor exhibits that can comfortably occupy an undemanding half-hour; attractions here include South Africa's first **Angling Museum**, an extensive collection of antique nets and rods, which traces the changing technology of the activity. Look out for the pre-served coelacanth, one of several specimens in the country of a fish that was long thought to have been extinct, until one turned up in a fishing net in 1939 (see p.305).

A short way from the centre in the industrial area, **Mitchell's Brewery**, Arend Rd, off George Rex Drive via Vigilance and Sandpiper roads, offers thirty-minute tours (Mon–Fri 10.30am), where for next to nothing you get to sample their four kinds of beer, including Foresters Draught, a Pilsner-type lager, and Bosun's Bitter, an ale mod-elled on Yorkshire bitter. The brewery is too far to reach on foot; you're best off taking a Rikki if you don't have your own transport, or staying in town and sampling the beers at one of the pubs.

The main reason to make for **Leisure Isle** is for the excellent swimming it offers in the lagoon and the views out to sea through the gap between the Heads. The best bathing spots are along the southern shore of the island, particularly the western sec-tion along Bayswater Drive; but check a tide table, as the swimming is only good around high tide (and then only in summer).

Continuing south along George Rex Drive gets you to the web of roads that wind up through the small suburban areas of the Heads and Coney Glen to the top of the **east-ern Head**, from which you get fantastic views out to sea.

The beaches

Don't come to Knysna for a beach holiday: the closest sands are 20km away, around the western edge of the lagoon at **Brenton-on-Sea**. On the shores of the beautifully sandy Buffels Bay, this is a tiny settlement with an unexceptional hotel situated on a quite exceptional beach. A few kilometres inland is the quaint and very upmarket settlement of **Belvidere**, through which visitors are prohibited from driving (but you can walk around). Although **Buffels Bay**, the next beach to the west, is along the same continu-ous stretch of sand as Brenton-on-Sea, there's no direct route there; you have to return to the N2 and proceed from there. In the opposite direction from Knysna things are lit-tle better, with the closest patch of sand lying to the east at **Noetzie**, a town known more for its eccentric holiday homes built to look like castles than for its seaside.

Eating, drinking and nightlife

Knysna has a livelier atmosphere than you might expect from a Garden Route town, buzzing at **night** to the strains of pretty good music at *Tin Roof Blues*. As far as food

---

CRUISES

One of the obligatory excursions around Knysna is a **cruise** across the lagoon to the Heads. Knysna Ferries (☎044/382 5520) run six ninety-minute trips a day atound the lagoon from the Tapas Jetty on Thesen's Island. Another option is the larger double-decker MV *John Benn*, which has a bar on board and is the only way to reach the private Featherbed Nature Reserve on the western side of the Heads. The entire MV *John Benn* trip takes four hours and includes a 4WD shuttle to the top of the western Head with the option of walking the 2km back downhill to enjoy spectacular views and see the local flora and fauna, including Knysna louries.

Booking is essential for all ferry trips and can be done through Knysna Booking Services or the information kiosk on Pledge Square (see p.208).

---

goes, oysters are an obvious choice, with the Knysna Oyster Company here being one of the world's largest oyster farms, but you'll also find good **restaurants** catering to other palates and one or two excellent **coffee shops** if you need a caffeine shot on your way through town.

The Anchorage, Garden Route Shopping Centre, Main St (☎044/382 2230). City-centre seafood and steak restaurant, where you can be guaranteed fresh fish every day.

Coffee Connection, Main Rd. The best coffee in town, with a wide choice of blends – including flavoured beans – as well as snacks.

Crab Creek, Belvidere Rd (☎044/386 0011). Worth coming to for the great views on the banks of the lagoon rather than for its average seafood menu.

Cranzgot's, Knysna Heads (☎044/382 3629). Popular young meeting place in an outstanding setting, right on the rocks beneath the Heads. The rather indifferent menu features a selection of coffees, snacks and pizzas.

La Loerie, 57 Main St (☎3044/82 1616). Knysna's top restaurant is a consistently excellent and intimate place, where you can eat fresh lagoon oysters and some of the best fish along the Garden Route.

O Pescador, on the Brenton/Belvidere turn-off from the N2 (☎044/386 0036). Out-of-town restaurant known for its Portuguese cuisine, of which the house speciality is Mozambique prawns. No closing day.

Oyster Tasting Tavern, Thesen's Jetty, Thesen's Island (☎044/382 6941). Tasting tavern at the Knysna Oyster Company, where you can feast on mussels or cultivated oysters served with bread and a choice of sauces. Pickled hake, snoek and angel pâté are on offer, as well as take-away oysters by the dozen, which are best eaten sitting at the edge of the lagoon. Mon–Thurs 8am–5pm, Fri 8am–4pm, Sat & Sun 9am–3pm.

Pink Umbrella, 14 Kingsway, Leisure Island (☎044/384 0135). Highly popular alfresco place done out in sugar-pink decor and renowned for sumptuous chocolate desserts. Serves exclusively seafood and vegetarian dishes, except on Saturday nights when they spit-roast a lamb. Booking is essential.

Sailor Sam, Millwood Place, Main St. Excellent take-away fish and chips as well as sole, squid and prawns. Daily 11am–9pm.

Tin Roof Blues, corner of St George's and Main roads. Good live music performed by local and visiting bands from across the country.

Woodbury's Delicatessen, Woodmill Shopping Lane, off Long and Main streets. Fantastic place to stock up for a gourmet picnic, with the most delicious take-away sandwiches in town (generous fillings in crusty Portuguese rolls). You can eat your tuck at the tables outside in the paved mall.

Listings

Emergencies Ambulance ☎10177; Fire ☎82 5066; Police ☎10111.

Hospitals and doctors The first port of call for medical treatment should be the International Medical Centre, corner of Main and Gray streets (Mon, Tues, Thurs & Fri: 8am–4.30pm, Wed 8am–1pm, Sat 9am–noon; 24hr emergency call out ☎044/382 6366, mobile ☎083/610 0546), which is geared to travellers, and operates an affordable drop-in service for emergencies. The centre incorporates a British Airways Travel Clinic, which offers travel health advice, vaccinations and current malaria prophylaxis. Knysna private hospital, Hunters Drive (☎044/382 7165, fax 382 7280) is well-run with a casualty department open to visitors.

Laundry The Knysna Wash Tub, 20 Gray St. Mon–Fri 7.30am–5.30pm, Sat 7.30am–1pm.

Pharmacy Marine Pharmacy, corner of Main and Grey streets (☎044/382 5614; Mon–Fri 8am–9pm, Sat 8am–1pm & 5–9pm, Sun 9.30am–1pm and 5–9pm.

Knysna Forest

The best reason to come to Knysna is for its **forests**, although these are only the shreds of a once magnificent woodland that was home to **Khoi** clans and harboured a thrilling variety of wildlife, including elephant herds. A marvellous wonderland of strange species and a seemingly boundless timber resource, they attracted European explorers and naturalists, and in their wake woodcutters, businessmen like George Rex and gold-diggers, all bent on making their fortunes here.

French explorer Francois Le Vaillant was one of the first **Europeans** to sample the delights of these forests. He travelled through in the eighteenth century with Khoi trackers, who shot and cooked an elephant; the explorer found the animal's feet so "delicious" that he wagered that "never can our modern epicures have such a dainty at their tables". Two hundred years later, all that's left of the Khoi people are some names of local places. The legendary Knysna elephants have hardly fared better and are teetering on certain extinction.

Eleventh-hour **conservation** has ensured that some of the handsome hardwoods have survived to maturity in reserves of woodland that can still take your breath away. A number of walks have been laid out in several of the forests and this is unquestionably one of the best ways to experience the forests. The devastating success of the nineteenth-century timber industry means that all these reserves are some distance from Knysna itself and require transport to get to.

Goudveld State Forest

The beautiful **Goudveld State Forest** (daily 6am–6pm; small entrance fee), just over 30km northwest of Knysna, is a mixture of plantation and indigenous woodland that

---

THE KNYSNA ELEPHANTS

Traffic signs warning motorists about elephants along the N2 between Knysna and Plettenberg Bay are rather optimistic: it seems that by 1995 there was only one indigenous pachyderm left, a number that may well still hold true. But such is the mystique attached to the **Knysna elephants** that locals tend to be a little cagey about just how few they number. By 1860, the thousands that had formerly wandered the once vast forests were down to five hundred, and by 1920 (twelve years after they were protected by law), there were only twenty animals left. Loss of habitat and consequent malnutrition seem to have been the principal cause rather than full-scale hunting.

An attempt was made in 1995 to create a breeding herd by introducing three young cows from the Kruger National Park, who it was hoped would breed with the Forest's lone bull. The "bull" turned out to also be a cow and fled in terror when confonted with the three teenagers. In the chase that followed, one young elephant died from pneumonia, brought on by stress. By 1997 the two surviving aliens had moved east and were causing destruction to farmland near Plettenberg Bay. South African National Parks, working with local wildlife organizations, decided to relocate them to Shamwari Game Reserve (see p.292), some 300km to the east near Port Elizabeth, where they are doing well.

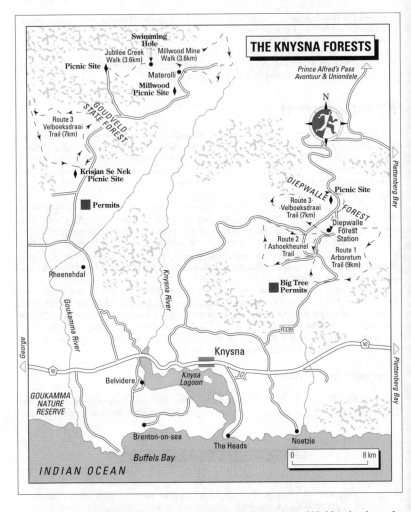

THE KNYSNA FORESTS

Swimming Hole
Jubilee Creek Walk (3.6km)
Millwood Mine Walk (3.6km)
Picnic Site
Materolli
Millwood Picnic Site

Prince Alfred's Pass Avontuur & Uniondale

GOUDVELD STATE FOREST

Route 3 Velboeksdraai Trail (7km)

Krisjan Se Nek Picnic Site

Permits

N

DIEPWALLE FOREST

Picnic Site

Route 3 Velboeksdraai Trail (7km)

Diepwalle Forest Station

Route 2 Ashoekheunel Trail

Route 1 Arboretum Trail (9km)

Rheenehdal

Big Tree Permits

Knysna River

R339

Knysna

N2

Plettenberg Bay

George

Goukamma River

Belvidere

Knysa Lagoon

GOUKAMMA NATURE RESERVE

N2

Brenton-on-sea

The Heads

Noetzie

Buffels Bay

0   8 km

INDIAN OCEAN

takes its name from the gold boom (*goudveld* is Afrikaans for goldfields) that brought hundreds of prospectors to the mining town of **Millwood** in the 1880s. The six hundred small-time diggers who were here by 1886, scouring out the hillsides and panning Jubilee Creek for alluvial gold, were rapidly followed by larger syndicates, and a flourishing little town quickly sprang up, with six hotels, three newspapers and a music hall. The singing and dancing was shortlived and bust followed boom in 1890 after most of the mining companies went to the wall. The ever-hopeful diggers took off for the newly discovered Johannesburg goldfields, and Millwood was left a deserted **ghost town**. Over the years its buildings were demolished or relocated, leaving an old store known as Materolli as the only original building standing. Today, the old town is completely overgrown, apart from signs indicating where the old streets stood. In **Jubilee Creek**, which provides a lovely shady walk along a burbling stream, the holes scraped or blasted out of the hillside are still clearly visible. Some of the old mine works have been restored, as have the original **reduction works** around the co-co pan track, used to carry the ore from the mine to the works, which is still there after a century. The Outeniqua trail passes nearby.

The forest itself is still lovely, featuring tall, indigenous trees, a delightful valley with a stream, and plenty of swimming holes and picnic sites. To **get there** from Knysna, follow the N2 west toward George, turning right onto the Rheenendal road just after the Knysna River, and continue for about 25km, following the Goudveld signposts.

Hiking in the Goudveld

A number of clearly **waymarked hikes** traverse the Goudveld, the most rewarding (and easy going) being along **Jubilee Creek**, which traces the progress of a burbling brook for 3.5km through giant woodland to a gorgeous, deep rock-pool – ideal for cooling off in after your effort. If you are going to encounter **Knysna louries**, there is no better place than here. Keep an eye focused on the branches above for the crimson flash of their flight feathers as they forage for berries, and listen out for their harsh call above the gentler chorus provided by the wide variety of other birdlife here. You can pick up a **map** directing you to the creek from the entrance gate to the reserve (even if there's no one in attendance); note that the waymarked trail is linear, so you have to return via the same route. There's a pleasant **picnic site** along the banks of the stream at the start of the walk.

A more strenuous option is the circular **Woodcutter Walk**, though you can choose either the three- or the nine-kilometre version. Starting at **Krisjan se Nek**, another picnic site not far past the Goudveld entrance gate, it meanders downhill through dense forest, passing through stands of tree ferns and returns uphill again to the starting point. The picnic site is also the starting point for the nineteen-kilometre **Homtini Cycle Route**, which takes you through forest and fynbos and presents wonderful mountain views. Be warned though; you really have to work hard at this, with one particular section climbing over 300m in just 3km. Mountain bikes can be rented from U-Ride in Knysna town (see p.207).

One of the nicest ways to explore is on one of the excellent **guided walk**s organized by Judith Hopley (information ☎044/389 0102, 7–9am & 6–9pm). Balancing information with anecdote, Hopley gives a handle on the forest in terms of identifying the trees and understanding the ecology of the whole system, and passes on Goudveldlore learned from foresters and forest guards. She also does a tour of a furniture factory that works with Knysna hardwoods. To join one of the walks, turn up at the Rheenendal Post Office on Wednesdays or Thursdays at 10am; to get there from Knysna, take the N2 west toward George and turn right onto the Rheenendal road just after the Knysna River. If you are going to strike out by yourself, Hopley's *On Foot in the Garden Route,* available from Kynsna's tourist information bureau (see p.207) and various Garden Route outlets, is a useful guide to fifty relatively easy hikes in the area.

Diepwalle Forest

The only elephants you can expect to see in the **Diepwalle Forest** (daily 6am–6pm; small entry fee), just over 20km northeast of Knysna, are on the painted markers indicating the three main hikes through these woodlands, which are the the last haunt of Knysna's almost extinct elephant population. However, if you're quiet and alert, you do stand a chance of seeing vervet monkeys, bushbuck and blue duiker.

Diepwalle (Deep walls) is one of the highlights of the Knysna area and is renowned for its impressive density of huge trees, especially yellowwoods. Once the budget timber of South Africa, **yellowwood** was considered an inferior local substitute in place of imported pine, and found its way into the structure, floorboards, window frames and doors of thousands of often quite modest nineteenth-century houses in the Western and Eastern Cape. Now its deep golden grain is so sought-after that it commands premium prices at the annual auctions.

The **three main hiking routes** cover between 7km and 9km of terrain, and pass through flat to gently undulating country covered by indigenous forest and montane fynbos. If you're moderately fit, the hikes should take two to two-and-a-half hours. All trails begin at the Forest Station, where you can get a map of them. **To get there** from Knysna, follow the N2 east towards Plettenberg Bay, after 7km turning left onto the R339, which you should take for about 16km in the direction of Avontuur and Uniondale. The Forest Station is 10.5km after the tar gives way to gravel.

The nine-kilometre **Arboretum Trail**, marked by black elephants, starts a short way back along the road you drove in on, and passes down to a stream edged with tree ferns. Across the stream you'll come to the much-photographed **Big Tree**, a 600-year-old Goliath. The easy-going nine-kilometre **Ashoekheuwel Trail**, marked by white elephants, crosses the Gouna River, where there's a large pool allegedly used by real pachyderms. Most difficult of the three hikes is the rewarding seven-kilometre **Velboeksdraai Trail**, marked by red elephants, which passes along the foothills of the Outeniquas. Take care here to stick to the elephant markers, as they overlap with a series of painted footprints marking the Outeniqua Trail, which you shouldn't take. Just before the Veldboeksdraai picnic site, there's another mighty yellowwood regarded by some as the most beautiful in the forest.

Plettenberg Bay and around

Over the Christmas holidays 40,000 residents from Johannesburg's wealthy northern suburbs decamp to **PLETTENBERG BAY** (usually called Plett), 33km east of Knysna, and the flashiest of the Garden Route's seaside towns. This is sufficient reason to give it a miss at Christmas, when prices double, accommodation becomes impossible to find and everything gets very crowded. Yet, during low season, sipping champagne and sucking oysters while watching the sunset from a bar can be wonderful – the banal urban development on the surrounding hills somehow doesn't seem so bad because the bay views really are stupendous. The deep-blue **Tsitsikamma Mountains** drop sharply to the inlet and its large estuary, providing the constant vista to the town and its suburbs. The bay generously curves over several kilometres of white sands, which are separated from the mountains by forest. The proximity of the wooded slopes breathing onto the sea makes this a green and temperate location that receives rainfall throughout the year.

Southern right whales make an appearance every winter and are a seriously underrated attraction. Less particular are the **dolphins** who can be seen hunting or riding the surf, often in substantial numbers, throughout the year. **Swimming** is safe, and though the waters are never tropically warm they reach a comfortable temperature between November and April. River and rock **fishing** yield rewards all year long, and one of the Garden Route's best short **hikes** covers a circuit round the Robberg Peninsula – a great tongue of headland that licks around to contain the western edge of the bay.

Arrival and information

SA Airlink (☎044/533 9041) **flights** from Johannesburg arrive daily at Plettenberg Bay airport. There is no transport from the airport into town, so make arrangements to be picked up by your accommodation. **Intercity buses** stop at the Shell Ultra City service station, just off the N2 in Marine Way, 2km from the town centre; again, prearrange transport. The

---

WHALE-WATCHING AT PLETTENBERG BAY

Elevated ocean panoramas give Plettenberg Bay outstanding vantages for watching **southern right whales** during their breeding season between June and October. Phone the Whale Hotline (☎044/533 3743) for information about their current whereabouts. An especially good watching point is the area between the wreck of the *Athene* at the southern end of Lookout Beach and the Keurbooms River. The Robberg Peninsula is also excellent, looming protectively over this whale nursery and giving a grandstand view of the bay. Other good town watching points are from Beachy Head Road at Robberg Beach; Signal Hill in San Gonzales Street past the post office and police station; the *Beacon Isle Hotel*; and the deck of the *Lookout* restaurant on Lookout Beach. Outside Plett, the Kranshoek viewpoint and hiking trail offers wonderful whale-watching points along the route. To get there, head for Knysna, taking the Harkerville turn-off, and continue for 7km. It's also possible to view the occasional pair (mother and calf) at Nature's Valley, 20km from Plett on the R102, and from Storms River Mouth. For more information about whales, see Hermanus on p.190.

For **guided whale-watching** and eco-trips into the bay, contact Dave Rissik at *Ocean Adventures* (mobile ☎083/701 3583, *oceanadv@global.co.za*), who runs highly recommended three-hour outings (around R200 per person) that frequently run into bottlenose, Indo-Pacific and humpback **dolphins**, as well as Bryde's and humpback whales. The advantage over shore-based watching is that you stand a chance of encounters throughout the year, including species that you'd be unlikely to spot from land. Even if no marine mammals show, you'll still have an interesting trip as Dave is knowledgeable about the geology, archeology, and natural history of the area.

Baz **backpacker bus** drops passengers off at accommodation in town. Plett's **tourist information bureau**, Victoria Cottage, Kloof St (Mon–Fri 8.30am–5pm, Sat 8am–1pm; ☎044/533 4065), has maps of the town and can help with finding accommodation.

Accommodation

Because of the hilly terrain, much of the **accommodation** in Plettenberg Bay has views of the sea and mountains, though you're likely to have to put up with views of holiday developments as well. Surprisingly perhaps, for such an unapologetically upmarket resort, Plett has a number of backpackers' lodges, camping and some cheaper accommodation, with additional self-catering available at **Keurbooms**, just across the river. Rates are sky-high at Christmas and Easter, and several places have two rates throughout the year, depending on the quality of the room. July and August are the cheapest months.

Guesthouses and hotels

Hunter's Country House, off the N2, 10km west of Plett on the way to Knysna (☎044/532 7818, fax 7878, *hunters@pixie.co.za*). Set in a woodland area, this is the best upmarket Garden Route stay, with an emphasis on country comfort rather than seaside glitz, at half the price of the much-vaunted Plettenberg. Accommodation is in thatched cottages set in well-established gardens, each with an open fireplace and private patio. ⑨.

Little Sanctuary, 14 Formosa St (☎044/533 1344, fax 31603; mobile ☎083/741 6259). As close to the beach as you can get, offering bedrooms with showers and private verandahs overlooking the sea. ④.

Pat's Place, 4 Meeding St (☎044/533 3180). One of the cheapest B&Bs in Plett, in an old timber and iron house that's only a 3min walk to Hobie Beach. Rooms don't have bath, but they're pleasantly decorated. In the front rooms you can lie in bed and look out to the sea. ③.

The Plettenberg, 40 Church St, Lookout Rocks (☎044/533 2030, fax 533 2074). Plett's most luxurious hotel offers some unbeatable views straight onto the ocean. But be warned – despite the sky-high room rates you could still end up overlooking the car park. ⑨.

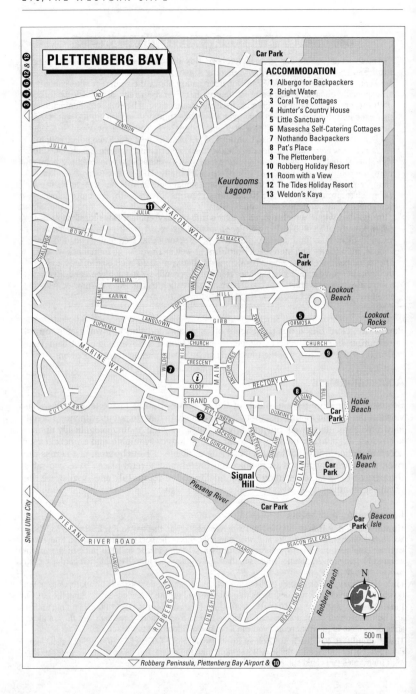

PLETTENBERG BAY

ACCOMMODATION
1 Albergo for Backpackers
2 Bright Water
3 Coral Tree Cottages
4 Hunter's Country House
5 Little Sanctuary
6 Masescha Self-Catering Cottages
7 Nothando Backpackers
8 Pat's Place
9 The Plettenberg
10 Robberg Holiday Resort
11 Room with a View
12 The Tides Holiday Resort
13 Weldon's Kaya

Keurbooms Lagoon

Car Park

Car Park

Lookout Beach

Lookout Rocks

Car Park

Hobie Beach

Main Beach

Signal Hill

Piesang River

Car Park

Car Park

Beacon Isle

Shell Ultra City

Robberg Beach

0   500 m

N

▽ *Robberg Peninsula, Plettenberg Bay Airport &* ⑩

Room with a View, 5 Julia Ave (☎044/533 1836, fax 533 4208, mobile ☎083/261 7587, *almac@pixie.co.za*). Luxury home, back from the beach, but with good views, offering seriously upmarket B&B rooms with TV, video and a champagne breakfast served on your own private deck. ⑥.

Backpackers' lodges and self-catering

Albergo for Backpackers, 8 Church St (☎044/533 4434). Unexceptional backpackers' lodge in the centre of the town, with dorms and a couple of doubles. Canoes, bikes, surf and boogie boards are available to rent, and staff offer rides out to Robberg Nature Reserve. Dorms, double with shared bath ①, en-suite doubles ②.

Bright Water, 15 Jackson St (☎ & fax 044/533 0467). Three en-suite doubles in a centrally located, homely suburban house where you can rent the whole place or just a room, and have use of the kitchen. The owner lives across the road. ④.

Coral Tree Cottages (☎044/532 7822, fax 532 7869). Off the N2, 11km west of Plettenberg Bay. High-quality, well-furnished and spacious self-catering thatched cottages, although unfortunately the roar of the N2 is never absent. ③.

Masescha Self-Catering Cottages, 1km north off the N2, signposted 12km west from Plettenberg Bay (☎044/532 7647, fax 532 7645). Three reasonably priced, self-catering whitewashed cottages, plainly furnished on a farm. The outdoor sitting areas are surrounded by pleasant gardens and a forest, and there's a pool. Good for families or couples, it also has an indigenous plant nursery and natural history bookshop. Breakfast is available as an extra. ③.

Nothando Backpackers, 3 Wilder St (☎044/533 0541, fax 533 0220). Budget accommodation in a bungalow in the centre of town, close to the main shops. Dorms ①, doubles without bath or en suite ②.

Robberg Holiday Resort, Robberg Rd (☎ & fax 044/533 2571). Close to Robberg Nature Reserve and Robberg Beach, this budget option is suitable only if you have your own transport. Camping and self-catering bungalows without bathrooms ①, en-suite bungalows ②.

The Tides Holiday Resort, 2km west of Plett off the N2 (☎ & fax 044/533 2478). Reasonably priced en-suite doubles and slightly more expensive self-catering units, with breakfast offered as an extra charge. ③.

Weldon's Kaya, along the N2, 1km west of Shell Ultra City filling station (☎044/533 2437, fax 533 4364, *info@weldonkaya.co.za*). Probably the most imaginative backpacker accommodation along the Garden Route on a huge property, though with the disadvantage of being some distance from the beach. Rooms are in "African magical" style, constructed using rock, brick and recycled materials. The restaurant has an excellent reputation and there's also a pub, a swimming pool, volleyball and snooker. The owners rent out bikes and can arrange activities such as surfing lessons, bungee jumping, whale-watching and canoeing. Dorms ①, doubles without bath ②, en-suite doubles ③.

The Town and its beaches

Plett's town **centre**, at the top of the hill, consists of a conglomeration of supermarkets, swimwear shops, estate agents and restaurants aimed largely at the holiday trade. It's the **beaches** people come for – and there's a fair choice. Southeast of the town centre on a rocky promontory is **Beacon Isle**, dominated by a Sixties hotel, an eyesore blighting a fabulous location. Beacon Isle Beach, or **Main Beach**, right at the central shore of the bay, is where the fishing boats and seacats anchor a little out to sea. The small waves here make for calm swimming and this is an ideal family spot. To the east is **Lookout Rocks**, which draws surfers to the break off a needle of rocks known as the Point and the predictable surf of **Lookout Beach**, to its east, which is also one of the nicest stretches of sand for bathers, body-surfers or sun lizards. Lookout Beach has the added attraction of a marvellously located restaurant (see "Eating, drinking and nightlife" overleaf), from which you can often catch sight of the **dolphins** that cruise into the bay. From here you can walk several kilometres down the beach towards Keurbooms and the **Keurbooms Lagoon**.

Besides the obvious draw of walking around the protective arm of the Robberg Peninsula (see box overleaf), you can go **horse-riding** through the surrounding forest, fynbos and grassland with Equitrailing (☎044/533 0599, mobile ☎082/955 0373), which runs trails from an hour-and-a-half to half a day, starting from around R70.

Eating, drinking and nightlife

The *Cave*, Plett's young rave spot, is one of the liveliest clubs on the Garden Route, and for some travellers it's the principal draw of the town. You'll also find some pleasant beachside pubs with terrific views, and a handful of decent restaurants serving locally caught fresh fish.

Blue Bay Cafe, Lookout Centre, Main St (☎044/533 1390). A good place for lunches, in a courtyard tucked away under trees and overlooking both the main drag and the sea. Their mid-priced steaks, chicken and fish are all well-prepared.

The Blue Chilli, Noel Centre, Main St (☎044/533 5104). Intimate and reasonably priced bistro with a select but superb Mexican menu. Beware of their "hot" dishes, which positively sizzle. Wash your meal down with a glass of tequila, with or without worm.

The Boardwalk, Yellowwood Centre, corner of Main and Crescent streets (☎044/533 1420). Cosy, eclectic restaurant serving up moderately priced, tasty seafood, steaks and baked potatoes.

Brothers, corner of Main and Marine streets (☎044/533 5056). Medium-priced English cooking with an edge, at a stunning location with views of the ocean and passing trade. Open for breakfast, lunch and dinners, but it's their teas that really shine – try their espresso with muffins, cake of the day or pancake dripping under a blueberry sauce.

The Cave, in the *Arches* hotel, Marine Drive, off the N2 (☎044/533 2118). A young crowd lives it up here, especially at weekends and in the December holidays. Phone to check dates and opening hours.

Cornuti al Mare, Shop 1, Seaview Properties, Perestrella St (☎044/533 1277). Good place to fill up on cheap pasta dishes and pizzas.

Fish Eagle Creek, on the Keurbooms Lagoon, just off the N2 between Plettenberg Bay and Keurbooms (☎044/535 9445). Reasonably priced meals served at this pleasant pub with outdoor seating on the edge of the calm lagoon. Their fresh fish and chips are especially recommended.

Hog's Quaff and Trough, *Formosa Bay Hotel*, along the N2 just west of town (☎044/533 0799). Superb pub grub – in fact the best bar snacks in a 10km radius – at a sports bar with pool tables and loads of TV sets. Steak, egg and chips; sandwiches; and their delicious homemade chicken pies all represent great value.

Islander Eating Place, on the N2 between Plett and Knysna (☎044/532 7776). Popular, high-quality restaurant for seafood – eat as much as you like for a set price. Booking essential.

WALKING IN THE ROBBERG NATURE AND MARINE RESERVE

One of the Garden Route's nicest walks is the four-hour, nine-kilometre circular route around the spectacular rocky peninsula of **Robberg**, where you can completely escape Plett's ugly development and experience the coast in its wildest state, with its enormous horizons and lovely vegetation. Much of the walk takes you along high cliffs, from where you can often look down on seals surfacing near the rocks, dolphins arching through the water and, in winter, whales further out in the bay. If you don't have time for the **full circular walk**, there is a **shorter two-hour hike** and a **thirty-minute ramble**. A map indicating these is available at the reserve gate when you pay to get in (daily: Feb–Nov 7am–5pm; Dec–Jan 7am–8pm; small entry fee).

You'll need sturdy walking shoes as the terrain is rocky and steep in parts, and the walk involves some serious rock-hopping on the west side. Don't forget to bring a hat and a bottle of water, as there's no drinking water for much of the walk and no tea rooms. There's no public transport to the reserve; if you're staying at a backpacker lodge ask about their **transfers**, which are generally reasonably priced. To get there **by car**, take Strand Street towards Beacon Isle, turn right into Piesangs Valley Road, and 200m further on, turn left into Robberg Road. Follow the airport signs, continuing for 3.5km and then turning left toward *Robberg Holiday Resort*; you'll find the gate to the reserve 500m beyond the resort.

The Lookout, Lookout Beach (☎044/533 1379). Marvellous bay views at this casual restaurant-cum-pub right on the beach, where you can eat reasonably priced fresh fish, or more expensive crayfish, and, if you're lucky, watch whales and dolphins rollicking in the surf.

Moby Dick, Main Beach. Pleasant place for a drink, particularly out of season – in summer it draws a lively boogie-board crowd. A wooden deck upstairs gives great views of Central Beach.

Old Nick Tea Garden, on the N2 between Plett and Keurbooms (☎044/533 1395). Good place for outdoor tea, and more especially recommended as the best craft shop in the area, especially for woven goods.

Rusty Nail, Main St (☎044/533 3456). Rough-and-ready fishermen's bar with windows looking out on the bay. Popular with locals rather than holidaymakers.

Keurboomstrand

Some 14km east of Plettenberg Bay, across the Keurbooms River, is the uncluttered resort of **KEURBOOMSTRAND** (Keurbooms for short), which shares the same bay and has equally wonderful beaches, but is less safe for swimming. A calm and attractive place, Keurbooms has few facilities, and if you're intending to stay here you should stock up in Plettenberg Bay beforehand. The safest place for swimming is at **Arch Rock**, in front of the caravan park, though **Picnic Rock Beach** is also pretty good.

If you can tear yourself away from the beach, **canoeing** up the Keurbooms River gives an alternative perspective on the area, but you'll need a permit from Nature Conservation (☎044/533 2125), who rent out fairly basic canoes for day- or overnight trips. The forest comes right down to the river edge, and as the gorge narrows and you go higher the journey gets better, because you leave behind the pleasure boats and water-skiers who are restricted to an area near the caravan park. Don't be put off by the river's Coca-Cola colour (which comes from harmless oxides in the water): it's quite fresh, and wonderful to swim in during the summer. If you're renting a boat, you can stop and **picnic** at any of the little beaches upriver. While you're here, keep an eye out for the pink-flowering Keurboom trees that give their name to the river and resort.

Places to stay include one of the country's best family-oriented campsites, *Keurbooms Aventura* (☎044/535 9309), 6km east of Plett and signposted off the N2. Here you can choose between campsites (①) on the shady banks of the river or self-catering chalets (entire chalet ⑥). Canoes and motorboats are available to rent, and there's a swimming pool. Just a short walk to the sea, *Dune Park*, off Keurbooms Strand Road on the right (☎044/535 9606), offers camping (①) and self-catering timber chalets (entire chalet ⑤), behind the sand dunes, but has no sea view. Finally, *Arch Rock Chalets and Caravan Park* (☎044/535 9409) features a shady campsite and rather old self-catering chalets (entire chalet ④) right on the seashore, but gets packed with families in the summer. The only place in Keurbooms for **eating and drinking** is the reasonably priced *Singing Kettle*, which has an unbeatable location right on the beach and makes a great whale- and dolphin-spotting venue.

The Crags, Monkeyland and Bloukrans River bungee jumping

Little more than a satellite of Plettenberg Bay, **The Crags**, 16km to its east, comprises a collection of smallholdings along the N2, a bottle store and a few other shops on the forest edge. At The Crags (look out for the BP filling station), take the Kurland Village/Forest Hall turn-off for 2km to reach the signposted **Monkeyland** (daily 8am–6pm; entrance free, tours R50; ☎04457/48906), a new primate sanctuary where apes from several continents enjoy a swinging existence in the forest canopy. The animals are free to move around the reserve, looking for food and interacting with each other and their environment in as natural a way as is possible. Visitors are taken on guided walking "safaris" in which they come across water holes, experience a living indigenous forest and have chance encounters with different primates, including lemurs from Madagascar and squirrel monkeys from South America (South Africa has only two native species – vervets and samangos). The day lodge has a restaurant with a forest deck, where you can get refreshments and more substantial meals. It's a child-friendly place with baby sitting and changing facilities.

If you want to try your hand at swinging through the air, then pull in at the **Tsitsikamma Forest Village**, 20km east of The Crags and the Monkeyland turn-off along the N2, where the registration office for the world's highest commercial **bungee jump** is based. The jump takes place off the 216-metre **Bloukrans River Bridge**, 2km beyond the Village down a signposted road that also brings you to a viewpoint. There's no need to book ahead for the jump, which will cost you R500 (including video) for the seven-second descent. For further information contact Bloukrans Bungy (aka Kiwi Extreme) at the bridge (daily 9am–5pm; ☎042/281 1458) or in Cape Town, Adventure Village, 229 Long St (☎021/424 1580).

The Forest Village isn't a village at all but a collection of touristy shops, a less than inspiring restaurant and some offices arranged around an enormous traffic circle-cum-car park. The **tourist information bureau** (daily 9am–5pm) has brochures about the Garden Route. Should you wish to spend the night here, and you could do a lot worse, there's a well-maintained **caravan park** halfway down the road to the bridge with camping (①) and, at the end of the road, a new, well-equipped log-cabin **backpacker lodge**, with two eight-bed dorms (①) and four doubles (②), a couple of hundred metres from the jump site. Both lodge and caravan park are in the midst of verdant indigenous forest and can be booked through the Tsitsikamma Forest Village Trust (☎042/281 1450, fax 281 1457, *juline@intekom.co.za*); their office is a couple of shops away from the tourist information bureau. The Baz **bus** pulls into the Village and will usually take passengers as far as the backpacker lodge and jump site, but if they can't, due to time pressure, the Trust will always be willing to do so.

Other accommodation in the area includes a couple of notable places at either end of the spectrum. Sixteen kilometres east of Plett (or 3km east of The Crags) along the N2, take the Redford turn-off for *Woodgate Farm* (☎04457/48690; ①), signposted 3km down a dirt road; if you don't have your own transport, the owners will pick you up from Tsitsikamma Forest Village. A relaxed **backpackers' lodge** with dorms and doubles (both ①), the farm is set in indigenous forest and has mountain views. Activities on offer include horse-riding, and the owners take hikes to Nature's Valley (see p.223), and take guests to the Bloukrans River Bridge bungee jump and Storms River for blackwater tubing (see p.226). Rather swisher is *Hog Hollow Country Lodge*, Askop Rd, east off the N2 for 4km (☎ & fax 04457/48879, *hoghollow@global.co.za*; ⑦–⑧), recommended for a congenial splurge and its top reputation for food. Each of the ethnic-styled chalets, done out in earthy colours and spiced up with African artefacts, has a bath or shower and its own wooden deck with vistas across the forest and Tsitsikamma Mountains. If you feel up to it you could hike for a couple of hours through forest to Keurbooms Beach – or drive it in fifteen minutes.

Tsitsikamma National Park

The **Tsitsikamma National Park** (open daily; R12 per vehicle, R5 per person; ☎042/541 1651), roughly midway between Plettenberg Bay and Port Elizabeth, is the highlight of any Garden Route trip, and you'd be crazy to pass up its highlight, the **Storm's River Mouth**, which is the most dramatic estuary on this exhilarating stretch of coast. This is where South Africa's ultimate hike, the five-day **Otter Trail**, begins.

Starting from just beyond Keurboomstrand in the west, the national park extends for 68km into the Eastern Cape along a narrow belt of coast, with dramatic foamy surges of rocky coast, deep river gorges and ancient hardwood forest teetering on the edge of tangled, green cliffs. Established in 1964, Tsitsikamma was South Africa's first marine reserve, stretching 5.5km out to sea, with an **underwater trail** open to snorkellers and licensed scuba divers.

Tsitsikamma has two sections: **De Vasselot** in the west and **Storms River Mouth** in the east. Both sections can only be reached down a winding tarred road from the N2 (there's no way of getting from one to the other through the park itself). De Vasselot incorporates **Nature's Valley**, the only resort in the park, and the most low-key settlement on the Garden Route, with a fabulous sandy beach which stretches for 3km.

De Vasselot and Nature's Valley

The **De Vasselot** section, at the western end of Tsitsikamma, extends inland into a rugged and hilly interior incised with narrow valleys and traversed by a series of footpaths. In fact De Vasselot is not a name that trips readily off South African tongues – most people know the section for **Nature's Valley**, the only village inside the national park. **Walking** is the main activity here, and the area is covered with waymarked routes of varying lengths, including the highly popular Otter Trail (see box overleaf). Nature's Valley is a pleasingly old-fashioned settlement on the Groot River Lagoon with 20km of beach. Bypassed by the N2, the intercity buses, tour parties and most motorists, who can't be bothered to contend with the tortuous mountain passes to get down here, this is the right destination if you're after a quiet time along the Garden Route.

There are plenty of good **walks** at Nature's Valley, many starting from the De Vasselot campsite, 1km north of the village, where you can pick up maps and information about birds and trees. One of the loveliest places to head for is **Salt River Mouth**, 3km to the west of Nature's Valley, where you can swim and picnic – though you'll need to ford the tannin-dark river at low tide. This walk starts and ends at the café at Nature's Valley. Also recommended is the circular six-kilometre **Kalanderkloof Trail**, which starts at the De Vasselot campsite, winds up to a lookout point, and descends via a narrow river gorge graced with a profusion of huge Outeniqua yellowwood trees and Cape wild bananas.

Practicalities

Public transport to Nature's Valley is limited to the Baz **backpacker bus**, which deposits passengers at the De Vasselot rest camp or the village centre – little more than a restaurant and small shop that acts as an informal **information bureau** and can help with accommodation.

Most **places to stay** in Nature's Valley are holiday cottages, which means you can forget about finding anywhere during the Christmas holidays, when their owners occupy them. The situation reverses for the rest of the year though, when Ken Corbitt (☎044/531 6725) rents out **self-catering cottages** in and around Nature's Valley. Apart from these, one of the few places in the village geared to travellers is the congenial *Hikers Haven* (☎044/531 6805, *ian.bond@pixie.co.za*), well located just 200m from the sea and the lagoon. Choose between a fourteen-bed backpacker dorm (①), three doubles sharing a bathroom (②), two en-suite rooms (②) – one of which is a family unit – and possibly the least expensive honeymoon suite in the country (③), under thatch and with its own balcony and a sunken bath surrounded by mirrors. Breakfast is an extra R20, whichever accommodation you choose. The backpackers' section has a self-catering kitchen, snooker table, TV lounge and a payphone. Bikes, a canoe, rowing boat, surfboard and windsurfer are available for guests and you can set out from the *Haven* on two- to six-hour hikes along the beaches or through the forests.

MAJOR GARDEN ROUTE HIKES

If you're keen on walking and the outdoors, and want to schedule in at least one long walk somewhere in the country during your holiday, the Garden Route provides some fine possibilities. Indeed, walking is the only way to really experience the Garden Route's forests and coast and escape the clutter of holiday homes and roaring N2.

The **hikes** listed below are two to five days long and are waymarked. You'll need to carry all your food, a sleeping bag for use in the communal hiking huts (mattresses are provided), lightweight cooking utensils and stove, and waterproofs. You should also wear proper, worn-in hiking boots. For day-hikes and walks lasting only a couple of hours, a good bet is Judith Hopley's *On Foot in the Garden Route*, available from Knysna's tourist information bureau (see p.207) and several other outlets on the Garden Route.

OUTENIQUA HIKING TRAIL
Wilderness
Start: Beervlei (old Forest Station – eight overnight huts)
End: Harkerville Forestry Station
Distance: 108km
Duration: seven days (shorter versions possible)
Permit: Department of Forestry, Knysna (☎044/382 3037 or Forestry Office ☎382 5466)
Features: Indigenous forest, including giant yellowwood trees, pine plantations and gold-mining remains at Millwood.

HARKERVILLE COAST HIKING TRAIL
Start and end: Harkerville Forestry Station, 12km west of Plettenberg Bay, signposted off the N2
Distance: 26.5km
Duration: two days
Permit: Department of Forestry, Kynsna (☎0445/23037 or Forestry Office ☎382 5466)
Features: Magnificent rocky coastline, indigenous forest and fynbos. Lots of rock scrambling and some exposed, narrow ledges above the sea. Don't attempt this hike if you're scared of heights or are unfit. Monkeys, baboons and fish eagles are common, and you

On the outskirts of the village, 1km to its north, the **De Vasselot rest camp** has campsites (①) tucked into indigenous forest, and basic two-person forest huts (②) without kitchens and with communal ablution facilities. For bookings contact South African National Parks (Pretoria ☎012/343 1991, fax 343 0905; Cape Town ☎021/422 2810, fax 424 6211; *reservations@parks-sa.co.za*).

If you're **self-catering**, stock up on supplies before you get to Nature's Valley. The only place to buy a meal is at the *Valley Inn* **restaurant**, on the corner of Forest and St Michael streets, which serves seafood, steaks, burgers and toasted sandwiches and provides the only nightlife apart from gazing at the stars.

Storms River Mouth

In contrast to the languid lagoon and long soft sands of Nature's Valley, **Storms River Mouth**, 55km from Plettenberg Bay, presents the elemental face of the Garden Route, where the dark Storms River surges through a gorge to wrestle with the surf. **Storms River Mouth Restcamp**, sited on tended lawns, is poised between a craggy shoreline of black rocks pounded by foamy white surf, and steeply raking forested cliffs, and is without a doubt the ultimate location along the southern Cape coast. Don't confuse this may also spot dolphins or whales. Closer to the roads, this trail isn't as remote in feeling as the Otter Trail, but is a good second-best.

OTTER TRAIL

Tsitsikamma National Park
Start: Storms River Mouth
End: Nature's Valley
Distance: 42km
Duration: five days
Permit: South African National Parks (Pretoria ☎012/343 1991, fax 24 6211; Cape Town ☎ 021/22 2810, fax 343 0905). Bookings are taken up to twelve months in advance. The maximum number of people on the trail is twelve. Cost: R200 per person.
Features: South Africa's first established hiking trail is a coastal walk crossing rivers, tidal pools and indigenous forest. You may see dolphins, whales and seals, and the spoor of the Cape clawless otter – although virtually impossible to spot, they're certainly around. Short daily stretches between log-hut nightstops gives plenty of time to walk slowly, and enjoy the vegetation and birds. Some parts of the hike are steep, so you need to be fit. The Bloukrans River has to be crossed by wading or swimming: go at low tide and waterproof your backpack.

TSITSIKAMMA TRAIL

Tsitsikamma
Start: Nature's Valley Caravan Park
End: Storm's River Bridge
Distance: 64km
Duration: five days, shorter versions possible
Permit: SAFCOL (☎042/391 0393)
Features: Not to be confused with Otter Trail, this is an inland walk through indigenous forest, long stretches of open fynbos and the Tsitsikamma mountain range. Five overnight huts accommodate thirty people. It's not a difficult hike, and you won't cover more than 17km in a day. However, after heavy rains the rivers can be hard to cross.

with **Storms River Village** just off the N2, which is nowhere near the sea, and has little to recommend it, apart from a variety of places to stay if you can't get in at the Mouth.

Walking is the main activity at the Mouth, and at the visitors' office at the rest camp you can get **maps** of short, waymarked trails that leave from here. The trails take in the coast, and there are steep walks up the forested cliffs where you can see 800-year-old yellowwood trees with views onto a wide stretch of ocean. Most rewarding is the **three-kilometre hike** west from the rest camp along the start of the Otter Trail to a fantastic **waterfall** pool at the base of fifty-metre-high falls where you can swim right on the edge of the shore. Less demanding is the kilometre-long **boardwalk stroll** from the restaurant to the suspension bridge to see the river mouth. On your way to the bridge, don't miss the dank *strandloper* (beachcomber) **cave** – hunter-gatherers frequented this area between 5000 and 2000 years ago, living off seafood in wave-cut caves near the river mouth. A modest display shows an excavated midden, with clear layers of little bones and shells.

If you're desperate to walk the **Otter Trail** (see box above), which begins at Storms River, and have been told that it is full, don't despair. As a single person or a couple, you stand a chance of getting in on the back of a last-minute cancellation, so it may be worth hanging out at the Mouth for a night or two. Since the trail is booked long in advance, there is often a chance that someone won't turn up.

Swimming at the Mouth is restricted to a safe and pristine little sandy bay below the restaurant which can be icy in summer if there are easterly winds and cold upwellings of deep water from the continental shelf, only 25 nautical miles off the coast.

Practicalities

Storms River Mouth lies 18km south of Storms River Bridge, where most people stop to gaze into the deep river gorge and fill up at the most beautifully located filling and service station in the country. Even if your time is limited and you can't spend the night at Storms River Mouth, it's still worth nipping down for a meal, a restorative walk or a swim in the summer. You'll need your own wheels though, as there's no public transport to the Mouth.

A wide variety of **accommodation** is available at **Storms River Mouth Restcamp** (☎042/541 1607), all with sea views, including superb campsites (①) just metres from where the surf breaks on the rocks; incredibly good-value two-person cabins (②), which provide bedding, share ablutions and have no catering facilities; comfortable one-bedroom self-catering log cottages, including breakfast (③); oceanette mini-apartments close to the sea, also including breakfast (③); and family oceanettes and cottages for a minimum of four people (③). All are heavily subscribed in season, but are discounted by ten percent from May to the end of August. For **bookings** contact South African National Parks (Pretoria ☎012/343 1991, fax 343 0905; Cape Town ☎021/422 2810, fax 424 6211; *reservations@parks-sa.co.za*).

The only **eating** place is the rest-camp restaurant, which serves breakfasts and à la carte meals, which, alas, are less memorable than the startling views.

Storms River Village

STORMS RIVER VILLAGE lies about a kilometre south of the national road, has a number of places to stay, a general dealer selling basics and some activities, but is little more than a functional stop. There's a fair range of **accommodation**, starting at the cheapest with *Storms River Village Backpackers*, Main Rd, run by Storms River Adventures (☎042/541 1836, fax 541 1609), which has its office next to the post office. The backpackers' **lodge** has packed dorms (①) with twelve bunks in each, a small double room (①), and the use of a kitchen. The recently refurbished *Stormsriver Rainbow Lodge* (☎ & fax 042/541 1530), along the road into the village – turn right at the T-junction – offers affordable **B&B** doubles with shared ablutions (②) and en-suite chalets (③). *Armagh Guest House* (☎042/541 1512, fax 541 1510, *armagh@mweb.co.za*; ④), along the turn-off into the village from the main road, offers slightly more expensive B&B. For something smarter, try the *Tzitzikama Forest Inn* (☎042/541 1711, fax 541 1669, *the-inn@global.co.za*; ⑤), a popular port of call for tour buses. A couple of kilometres east of town along the N2 is the *Tsitsikamma Lodge* (☎042/750 3802, fax 750 3702, *tsitsilodge@pixie.co.za*), which has its eye firmly on the German market, featuring Jacuzzis in every room and a nudist hiking trail.

A **coffee shop** next to the backpackers' lodge sells snacks. Storms River Adventures offers some **activities**, best of which is "blackwater tubing" down the the Storms River canyon for a half-day-trip. This is a far milder version of white-water rafting and goes through the Tsitsikamma National Park to the sea at the Mouth – though you'll need to bring a wet suit, as the water is cold and the river canyon shady.

THE WEST COAST

The **west coast** of South Africa – remote, windswept and flushed by the cold Atlantic ocean demands a special appreciation. For many years the black sheep of Western Cape tourism (a fact borne out by the prominence of industries such as fishing, and the iron-ore terminal at Saldanha Bay) it has been set upon by developers who seem all too ready to spoil the bleached, salty emptiness which many people had just started to value. This is a region roughly cut by nature, with sandy soil and dunes harbouring a distinctive **coastal fynbos** vegetation, a coastline almost devoid of natural inlets or safe harbours, fierce southeasterly winds in summer, dank fogs in the winter, and the ever-miraculous **wild flowers** which appear out of the *veld* in spring.

The southern West Coast region has many links to Namaqualand to the north – not least in the flowers – although this 200km or so of coastline is by far the most densely populated part of the coast and the **Swartland** region immediately inland is unusually fertile. North of Swartland lies the impressive **Cederberg mountain range**, an area of distinctive beauty, and a striking feature on the N7 highway, the main West Coast artery between Cape Town and Namibia. North from **Clanwilliam**, the attractive town at the northern end of the Cederberg, the N7 connects with Vanrhynsdorp, strictly within the Western Cape but for practical purposes linked to the flower routes of Namaqualand in the Northern Cape (see p.226).

Outside the flower months of August and September, the West Coast has a wide range of attractions, particularly during summer when the lure of the sea and the cooler coast is strong. The area is well known for its **seafood**, always fresh, plentiful and much cheaper than in Cape Town, and also for a wide range of activities, most popularly hiking and horse-riding along the coast or in the mountains, various types of watersports, whale-spotting and some excellent bird-watching.

Swartland

Early of a morning it's not uncommon to find a tangy fog smothering the coastal plain inland from Melkbosstrand on the northern edge of Table Bay, but if the visibility is good the N7 highway north from Cape Town leads quickly into the pleasing and fertile **Swartland** landscape. *Swartland* means "black land", but while the rolling countryside takes on some attractive hues at different times of year it is never really black. The accepted theory is that before the area was cultivated the predominant vegetation was a grey-coloured bush called *renosterbos* (rhinoceros bush) which seen from the surrounding ranges of hills gave the area a complexion sufficiently dark to justify the name.

Bounded to the west by the less fertile coastal strandveld and to the east by the tall mountain range running from the Boland mountains by Wellington to the Cederberg, Swartland is known best as a wheat-growing area, although it also supports dairy farms, horse studs, tobacco crops and vineyards famous for earthy red wines.

The N7 skirts a series of towns on its way north, including the largest in the region, **Malmesbury**. If you're travelling south towards Cape Town, look out for some unusual

---

WEST COAST FLOWERS

During August and September you will find displays of **wild flowers** across the West Coast region, with significant displays starting as far south as the inland town of Darling, just 80km north of Cape Town off the main R27 coastal route. Other excellent displays are to be found in the West Coast National Park and the hazy coastal landscapes around Cape Columbine and Lambert's Bay, while inland Clanwilliam is the centre of some good routes. An incredible 4000 flower species are found in the region, most of them members of the daisy and mesembryanthemum groups. For up-to-date advice and guidance, contact Flowerline in Cape Town (☎021/418 3705) or the helpful local information centres in Darling, Saldanha and Clanwilliam. For further tips on flower-viewing, see p.267.

views of Table Mountain, and for tortoises, which you should take care to avoid as they cross the road.

Darling and around

The small country town of **DARLING** lies caught between Swartland and the West Coast, and as a result is famous both for its rolling countryside and dairy products and its displays of wild flowers in spring. Easily reached from Cape Town by the coastal R27 route, Darling boasts some handsome old buildings and has developed recently as a **artists' colony**; one of South Africa's best-loved comedians, Pieter Dirk-Uys, has established his most famous character, **Evita Bezuidenhout** (South Africa's answer to Dame Edna Everidge), as the hostess of a weekend cabaret show at the tiny **old railway station** in the centre of town (for details of shows, bookings and dinner reservations, phone ☎022/492 3145). Local painters are displayed at the well-cared-for **Darling Museum** (daily 9am–1pm & 2–4pm; small entry fee) on the corner of Pastorie and Hill streets, and an "Art Walk" to the homes and studios of local artists, photographers and jewellers is organized on the first weekend of every month (details from the museum).

Just under 20km to the south of Darling at **Mamre**, near the "lost" – or at least oddly adrift – coloured commuter town of Atlantis, an old Moravian **mission station** stands on the northern edge of town. Still active, it includes a series of old thatched mission cottages, a huge church and a working water mill, and remains one of the finest examples in the Western Cape of these pragmatic but bold early nineteenth-century outposts. If you're interested in specialized **tours** of the Mamre mission, contact Mercia Bruce in Cape Town (☎021/576 1296).

Practicalities

Darling's **tourist information bureau** is inside the museum (daily 9am–1pm & 2–4pm; ☎022/492 3361) and can offer useful advice on local attractions. Although Darling is well within the scope of a day-trip from Cape Town, it's also a good spot for a short **stay**. The *Old Buffers*, 9 Station Rd (☎022/492 3008; ③), is a pleasant B&B in an old town house, and more rooms are available at the comfortable *Den Houte*, 25 Long St (☎ & fax 022/492 3000; ③). As well as the old railway station (see above), good **places to eat** include *Zum Schatzi*, a German restaurant on Long Street (☎022/492 3095; closed Mon) or, for snacks and lunches, *Café Mosaic* on Main Road.

Riebeek West

To the northeast of Malmesbury lies an impressive island of hills, **Kasteelberg** (castle mountain), on the far side of which lie two small settlements, **Riebeek Kasteel** and **RIEBEEK WEST**. Roughly 3km north of Riebeek West on the road towards Moorreesburg is a turning to a P.P.C. Cement works. Within the site, rather incongruously set among rumbling conveyor belts and grey dirt heaps, is the whitewashed cottage where **Jan Smuts**, the South African statesman and soldier, was born in 1870. There isn't a great deal to see other than a simple old house with wooden floors and some contemporary artefacts inside, but, if you can suspend for a while the fact that it has been all but gobbled up by an industrial site, there are some pleasant lawns and flowerbeds and a handful of outbuildings to wander around – one of which displays an interesting series of storyboards about the eventful life and times of the man (see box opposite).

Accommodation in Riebeek West is available in a Victorian house, *Carollanns* (☎022/461 2245; ④), visible from the main road, while good **meals** and rooms can also be found in the renovated *Royal Hotel*, 33 Main St (☎022/448 1378; ②), in neighbouring Riebeek Kasteel.

JAN SMUTS

The life of **Jan Christiaan Smuts**, one of South Africa's greatest figures, perhaps embodies more than any other this country's strained relationship with itself in the first half of the twentieth century. Born to an Afrikaner farming family, Smuts spoke English with the distinctive linguistic burr of Swartland and distinguished himself as a scholar at Stellenbosch and then Cambridge universities. During the Anglo-Boer War he waged a wide-ranging and ultimately undefeated guerrilla campaign as the leader of a Boer commando. However, he came to believe in a unified South Africa under a British flag, and was appointed commander-in-chief of imperial forces in East Africa during World War I, attending meetings of the British War Cabinet in the final phases of the war. Smuts was **prime minister** of South Africa between 1919 and 1924 and again between 1939 and 1948, when he led South Africa into World War II on the British side but, rather like his fellow leader and statesman Winston Churchill, he failed to hold together support at home and lost the postwar general election in 1948 to the hardline Afrikaner D.F. Malan, who, coincidentally, grew up on the farm Allesvoloren, a few kilometres from Smuts' birthplace.

Smuts spent much of his career in domestic politics trying to hold together disparate political and social moralities among English and moderate Afrikaans-speaking whites, and is remembered by South Africans as a wily, tainted politician rather than as a great humanitarian. Yet he was, like very few South Africans before or since, a man of global vision and influence who as a 76-year-old played an important role in drafting the United Nations charter in 1946. He also published a philosophical treatise and was known for his love of nature and the outdoors, in particular Table Mountain in Cape Town – one of the popular routes up the mountain carries his name.

Groot Winterhoek

Situated within the often hazy, fortress-like line of mountains on the eastern fringe of Swartland is the three-hundred-square-kilometre **Groot Winterhoek Wilderness Area**, an excellent place for lonely hiking and camping, with sparkling swimming pools, typical Cape mountain fauna such as klipspringer, rhebok and elusive felines, distinctive fynbos vegetation and – as the name suggests – rather formidable winter conditions. It is also an area well worth exploring if you're a mountain biker or paraglider.

As this is a wilderness area, you are free to walk and camp where you wish, although there are a number of suggested trails varying in length from a few hours to a few days, and you must carry a **permit**. For details and **bookings**, contact the Cape Nature Conservation Office in Porterville (Mon–Fri 7.30am–4pm; ☎022/931 2900).

Langebaan Lagoon

To the west of rural Swartland and immediately north of Cape Town's fast-developing northern coastal suburbs of Bloubergstrand and Table View, the west coast of South Africa starts off fairly much as it continues for many hundreds of kilometres north – isolated fishing settlements and sand-dune vegetation of bleak but alluring windswept beauty. Other than river mouths, the only sea inlet and protected deep-water harbour on the entire South African Atlantic seaboard is at **Saldanha Bay**, some 100km north of Cape Town, which is connected to Langebaan Lagoon, the attractive centrepiece to the small but precious **West Coast National Park**.

While the holiday town of **Langebaan**, just to the north of the park on the eastern shore of the lagoon, has managed to keep its focus relatively frivolous and beach-oriented, industrial development has muscled into the northern part of the bay. The structures include a causeway stretching for 1.5km, an iron-ore railway terminal and a fast-rising steel and concrete works, and come as an ugly intrusion after the delicate simplicity of the national park. They also mean that the town of **Saldanha**, which once positioned itself as a sturdy fishing port with historic naval and military ties, is now grim, sullied and eminently avoidable.

West Coast National Park

The **West Coast National Park** (daily 7am–7pm; R8–16; ☎022/772 2144) is one of the best places to savour the simple, unspoilt charm of the West Coast. The park protects over 40 percent of South Africa's remaining pristine strandveld and 35 percent of the country's salt marshes, and incorporates both the majority of Langebaan Lagoon and a Y-shaped area of land immediately around and below it.

Much of the appeal of the park is in what you see and taste soon after driving into it: uplifting views over the still lagoon to an olive-coloured, rocky hillside; the sharp, saline air; the calling gulls and Atlantic mists burning up in the harsh sunlight. This isn't a game park – a few larger antelope are located in the Postberg section of the park, an area open only during the spring flower season – but there are huge numbers of **birds**, including some 70,000 migrating waders. A number of well-organized interpretive walking trails lead through the dunes to the long, smooth, wave-punished Atlantic coastline, offering plenty of opportunity to learn about the hardy fynbos vegetation which so defines the look and feel of the West Coast region.

On the southern tip of the lagoon is a large old farmhouse and steading called **Geelbeck**, where there is an information centre, tea room and accommodation (see "Practicalities" below). There are also a number of bird hides nearby, and all the main **trails** (up to a total of 30km) set out from here. If you continue from Geelbeck up the peninsula on the western side of the lagoon you will come to **Churchhaven**, a tiny village where there are some simple private cottages and where you can swim in the still, relatively warm water of the lagoon. A little further on is the demarcated **Postberg area**, open only during flower season (see box on p.227) but worth visiting at that time to see **zebra**, **gemsbok** and **wildebeest** wandering around among fields of wild flowers. The tip of the peninsula overlooking the mouth of Saldanha Bay is owned by the South African National Defence Force and remains inaccessible. The reserve also includes a number of islands around the mouth of the bay that are home to gannets, penguins, seals and, on one, a colony of albino rabbits.

Practicalities

There are two **entrance gates** to the park: one on the R27, roughly 10km north of the turning to Yzerfontein, and the other south of the town of Langebaan. The park isn't huge; if you're driving you'll cover the extent of the roads in a couple of hours. You can see a good chunk if you enter at one gate and come out at the other – but it's worth taking the roads slowly to enjoy the views, and a visit to the **information centre** (Mon–Fri 7.30am–3.45pm, Sat & Sun 9.30am–3.45pm; R16; ☎022/772 2798 or 772 2799, fax 772 2720) at Geelbeck will allow you to appreciate a bit more of what you're seeing. Overnight **accommodation** is available here, principally for those walking the two-day trail, but there's nothing to stop you simply booking into the simple three- to seven-bed self-catering cottages (①), set attractively near the edge of the lagoon. The **tea room** (daily 10am–3.45pm) on the back patio of the main farmhouse serves snacks and light meals, and there are some nice **picnic** spots around the park. To **book** accommodation call the information centre.

The best time to visit the park is in spring, when the sun is shining and the flowers are out, although this is, inevitably, also the busiest period. Like much of the West Coast, the national park is chilly and wet in winter, and hot and wind-blasted in summer.

Langebaan

Once the home to the largest whaling station in the southern hemisphere, and for a while Cape Town's long-haul passenger flight terminus (when seaplanes from Europe touched down on the lagoon during World War II), **LANGEBAAN** is in some respects the gateway to the West Coast National Park. However, the town appears to have given itself almost entirely to sun, fun, watersports and a motley collection of what only real estate agents (of whom there is no shortage) could dare to call desirable seafront holiday homes. In summer and at weekends the holiday crowds are large, and neon swimsuits, ice creams and speedboats dominate. If you're into **windsurfing** and have been wondering how to harness the big southeaster winds of summer, Langebaan could be just your thing (see "Practicalities" below); right off the beach the water is flat, the sailing winds – as the ragged flags above the centre testify – anywhere from fresh to fearsome, and unless you catch a fast-running tide out towards the Atlantic it's all reasonably safe. Outside summer, the town falls deathly quiet.

Practicalities

Tourist information is available in the library (Mon–Fri 9.30am–4.30pm, Sat 9am–noon; ☎022/772 1515) at the corner of Oostewal (the road in from the R27) and Bree streets, although the presence of a giant papier-mâché seagull outside is a good indication of what Langebaan thinks the tourists want. **Accommodation** is plentiful – it's what the town exists on. The municipal **caravan park** is a couple of blocks from the beach on Suffrens Street, and though it claims not to allow tents without permission you probably won't need to ask when you arrive. Halfway between Langebaan and Saldanha is *Olifantskop* (☎022/772 2326; ③), a **guesthouse** with a restaurant, bar, pool and equestrian centre. On the bay beside this is a burgeoning Greek-village-style **holiday development** called *Club Mykonos* (☎022/772 2101;④–⑥), offering one-, two- and three-bedroom units, the place to go if you feel you're missing a Costa del Cape flavour in your holiday. Langebaan's most upmarket option is *The Farmhouse* (☎022/772 2062; ④), a **luxury guesthouse** with a good restaurant, set on a hill among some new houses at the southern end of town.

As with accommodation, there's a wide selection of **places to eat** in town. *Die Strandloper* (☎022/772 2240 or mobile ☎083/227 7195; bookings essential), just beyond the Cape Windsurf Centre on the road to Saldanha, is a good example of the West Coast's famous open-air seafood restaurants (see box, p.235). On the main beach itself in town, *Pearly's* is a crowded eating, drinking and ogling spot in a prime location, while *La Taverna* (closed Mon), on the corner of Bree and Oostewal streets, serves better food and some mighty, diet-destroying cakes.

If you want to try your hand at any of the watersports on offer here, the Cape Windsurf Centre (daily: summer 9am–7pm; winter 10am–6pm; ☎022/772 1114), on the beach on the northern edge of town, rents out all levels of equipment, including the latest, top-line gear, and offers **windsurfing** lessons. The centre also rents out **mountain bikes** and paddle skis. If you want to rent other **watersports equipment**, such as Hobie Cat sailing dinghies, canoes, jet bikes or boats for **fishing**, try Lagoon Sports (☎022/772 2380) on the beach in the main part of town, beside *Pearly's* restaurant.

Saldanha

SALDANHA is known chiefly for its links to the military (a military academy is sited here) and for the controversial iron-ore loading terminal built here in the Seventies. The iron ore arrives from Sishen in the Northern Cape, 861km away along a purpose-built railway line. The scheme has never been the success it was hoped for, and the latest attempt to paper over the cracks is the erection beside the terminal of a steel plant. This comes with the added bonus of a concrete works, being built to use up the waste material from the steel plant, which will require a ten-kilometre-long conveyor belt to be constructed between it and the coast north of Saldanha. You get the sense that it's in for a penny, in for a pound, leaving the country's environmentalists – the precious ecosystems and bird habitats of the West Coast National Park are only a few kilometres away – with their heads buried in their hands.

The town, seated on the northwestern hook of the bay, thinks of itself as a holiday place, but as an observer it's hard to be convinced. If you do spend time here, though, it's worth taking advantage of the availability of good **fresh seafood** which arrives daily from the fishing fleet. Interspersed with numerous fish-and-chip shops and fast-food chains along the cliff-edge seafront, you'll find some decent **places to eat**, including the unassuming *Hoedjiesbaai Hotel*, or the rather swanky *Meresteijn* (☎022/714 3345) at the top of the hill. Just under 4km north of town, but quickly returning back into the West Coast feel, is *Oranjevlei* (☎022/714 2261), which offers seafood pub lunches (Mon–Sat), **B&B** (④) and plenty of character in one of the oldest farms in the area. For **information**, the West Coast Publicity Association is run from an old cottage called Oorlogsvlei on Van Riebeeck Street (Mon–Fri 9am–1pm & 2–5pm; ☎022/714 2088). Staff here are helpful and frank, and will assist you with information about accommodation or flowers in the wider region.

Around Cape Columbine

The coastline north of Vredenburg is classical West Coast territory: isolated fishing settlements with small, whitewashed cottages and a salty haze hanging over the lazy, glinting ocean. However, despite the quaint image, most of the settlements possess alarmingly expanding holiday developments, offering (naturally) whitewashed cottages in classical West Coast style. Although you can still find the odd lonely coastline and some genuine character in the old villages and their coloured inhabitants, the area feels as though it has reached that sad moment of tilting over from "best-kept secret" to oversubscribed building site.

North of Saldanha is a large inland farming centre, **VREDENBURG**, an unremarkable town in a featureless setting. Nearby are two different **accommodation** options. The first, just past the main crossroads of the R45 from Vredenburg and the R27 from Cape Town, is *Windstone Backpackers* (☎022/766 1645; ①), a house with four- and six-bedded **rooms**, which makes a friendly base for exploring the region, and from which the owners organize horse trails along the coast or up in the Cederberg on request; the second is *Jacobsbaai* (☎ & fax 022/715 3105; ④), an upmarket and comfortable **guesthouse** right on the coast off the R238 between Saldanha Bay and Vredenburg.

The best of the area is to be found around the village of **PATERNOSTER** (whose name comes from the prayer mumbled by Portuguese sailors crawling ashore from a shipwreck in the adjacent bay), and the nature reserves around **Cape Columbine**, **Tieties Bay** and south of **Cape St Martin**. There are some excellent coastal **hiking trails** through these reserves, including two long day-trails (details from West Coast Publicity Association, see above). There is also an attractive, isolated campsite at Tieties Bay (①).

For some choice West Coast delicacies and hospitality, head for the farm stall and **coffee shop**, *Die Winkel op Paternoster* (The shop in Paternoster), by the "Stop" sign on the main road.

St Helena Bay

St Helena Bay was the point where **Vasco da Gama** set foot in what is now South Africa during his epic voyage around the Cape and through to India in 1497. He wasn't the first European to round the Cape of Good Hope, nor the first to land, but his voyage did open up the route to the East, which was to give the Cape its strategic importance for four centuries. Three granite lumps on the shore between the fishing villages of St Helena Bay and Stompneus Bay serve as a memorial to his landing, and a no-expenses-spared **Da Gama Museum** (daily 8.30am–4.30pm; free) has also been established within the largest of the new housing developments in the area at **Shelley Point**. The museum is more a rainy-day affair than a must-see, but does include some well-devised story-boards, a collection of model ships and some early navigation devices.

Throbbing away in the background, as you stand at the granite memorial contemplating three months in a leaky boat, is a **lobster factory**, where you can usually buy fresh or frozen specimens if you enquire at reception. It's illegal to buy the lobsters if they're offered to you on the street, although in season you can obtain a permit to catch them for personal consumption (contact the Department of Sea Fisheries, ☎022/714 1710). Strangely enough, fishermen once thought the lobster that got entangled in their net a pest, and during the nineteenth century sold wagonloads of them to farmers to be ground up and used as fertilizer.

Velddrif

At the northern end of the R27 from Cape Town and 15km east of St Helena Bay is **VELDDRIF**, a fishing town situated at the point where the Great Berg River meets the sea. Each year the Berg River **canoe marathon**, which begins up near Ceres, ends here at a marina development called Port Owen. In the quieter backwaters near the Velddrif bridge, you can still see individual fishermen in small boats landing catches of mullet or horse mackerel which are then dried and salted to make *bokkoms*, called by some a delicacy, but essentially a staple form of cheap protein for fishermen and farm workers on the West Coast. To see the rickety wooden jetties where the boats tie up and the frames and sheds by the shore where *bokkoms* are strung up to dry, turn right at the roundabout just over the bridge coming into town on the R27, and after a kilometre or so take the first right-hand turn down to the riverside.

In town, straight on at the roundabout onto Church Street and then right up a dirt driveway is the **West Coast Gallery** (Mon–Sat 9am–5pm; free), one of the best of its type in the area. Run by a local artist and essentially a shop, it displays a wide selection of art and crafts, including some interesting driftwood collages. You can also have a cup of coffee here, and explore the reed maze or have a game of pétanque in the grounds. Look out for the selection of sea-salt products, including flavoured salts, seaweeds and bath salts, produced on a small pan by the coast nearby.

Further up the Berg River there is a wealth of **birdlife** in the marshes and various wetlands, where you can stay in a **houseboat** (☎ & fax ☎021/462 1902), and there are some pleasant **self-catering cottages** and walking trails on the historic farm of *Langrietvlei* (☎ & fax 022/783 0856; ①), halfway between Velddrif and Hopefield.

Lambert's Bay

The only settlement of any note between Velddrif and Port Nolloth, almost at the Namibian border, is **LAMBERT'S BAY**, 75km north of Velddrif (by indirect dirt road) and 70km due west of Clanwilliam (by tarred road). This is an important **fishing port**, although by the sights and sounds of the harbour you soon become aware that even the fishermen have to stand aside for the impressive colony of **gannets** on Bird Island in the centre of the bay. You can walk out to the island on the causeway which encloses the fishing-boat harbour for a closer look at the tightly packed, petulant, ear-piercing mass of gannets, along with a few disapproving-looking penguins and cormorants.

Lambert's Bay itself is rather short on charm; the fish-processing plant sits on the edge of the harbour, right in the town centre, giving you the feeling you're in a seat behind a pillar at the theatre. Nevertheless, its isolation means that there is some deserted coastline and nature nearby. During the breeding season (July–Jan), the bay plays host to a resident pod of around seven **humpback whales**. This is also the southernmost range of **Heaviside's dolphins** – small, friendly mammals with wedge-shaped beaks (rather than the longer ones more commonly associated with dolphins), with a white, striped patterning reminiscent of killer whales. You can view the cavorting mammals on trips from the fishing port (see below for details).

Practicalities
Tourist information at Lambert's Bay is available from the Sandveld Museum in Kerk Street (Mon–Fri 9am–1pm & 2–5pm, Sat 9am–1pm; ☎027/432 2335). There are a couple of **caravan parks** at either end of town, and no shortage of self-catering apartments, but nothing much by way of charm or character. If you need a proper bed for the night, head for Voortrekker Street in the centre of town, where the neat *Marine Protea* (☎027/432 1126; ④) offers comfortable **hotel** rooms with breakfast on offer as an extra, and *Raston Guesthouse* (☎027/432 2431; ④) has good-quality **B&B** accommodation.

Eating is one of Lambert's Bay's specialities. *Bosduifklip* (☎027/432 2735), an open-air restaurant set inland among some big rock formations 6km out of town along the R364, is a reasonable option, while the original West Coast open-air restaurant, *Muisboskerm* (☎027/432 1017), scores on location – right on the edge of the ocean, 5km south of the town. For a more conventional seafood restaurant, try *Die Kreef Huis* (☎027/432 2235; closed Sun) at the entrance to the harbour on Strand Street. Right on the harbour, *Isabel's Coffee Shop* does the whole gamut from light meals to prawns, but is renowned for its "West Coast breakfast" – a real blowout of a start to the day.

Lamberts Bay Boat Charters (☎027/432 1715) take **whale- and dolphin-watching** trips, with guarantees of an interesting time (even without whale and dolphin sightings, although they say the incidence of encounters is extremely high). Other activities, such as **horse trails**, **bird-watching** and **canoeing** are organized by K'Taaibos Adventure (☎ & fax 0263/684) at **Verlorenvlei**, a wetland inland from Eland's Bay to the south of Lambert's Bay; they also offer rustic B&B **accommodation** in a stone cottage or luxury tents (③).

Cederberg

A bold and jagged outcrop of the Western Cape fold escarpment, the Cederberg mountain range is one of the most magical wilderness areas in the Western Cape. Rising with a striking presence on the eastern side of the Olifants River Valley, around 200km north of Cape Town, these high sandstone mountains and long, dry valleys manage to combine accessibility with remote harshness, offering something for hikers, campers, naturalists, rock climbers and even astronomers. In a number of places the pink-hued sandstone (which can glow with heartbreaking beauty in the light of a low sun) has been weathered into grotesque, gargoyle-like shapes and a number of memorable natural features – including the huge **Wolfberg Arch** and a thirty-metre-high free-standing pillar which is shaped like (and known as) the **Maltese Cross**. Throughout the area there are numerous **San rock-art** sites, an active array of Cape mountain fauna, from baboon and small antelope to leopard, caracal and aardwolf, and some notable montane fynbos flora, including the gnarled and tenacious Clanwilliam cedar and the rare snow protea.

The Cederberg is easily reached from Cape Town by way of the N7: the towns of **Citrusdal** and **Clanwilliam** lie just off the highway near, respectively, the southern and northern tips of the mountain range. Both make attractive bases from which to explore the area, particularly during spring flower season, although you can find simple accommodation right in the mountains themselves. From Clanwilliam, set beside a

---

OPEN-AIR RESTAURANTS

A highlight of a number of West Coast towns is the casual but sumptuous alfresco seafood feast served in **open-air restaurants**, with little more than a canvas shelter held up with driftwood and lengths of fishing twine or a simple wind-cheating brush fence as props. Organized in the style of a beach *braai*, the idea is to serve up endless courses of West Coast delicacies right by the ocean it has just come from. The atmosphere is informal – you eat with your fingers and stand or perch on a rock – and you're likely to hear the waves crashing on the strand a few metres away and feel the sea air rolling in after sundown. A typical menu includes several different kinds of fish cooked in different ways, *bokkoms*, mussels, lobster, paella, *waterblommetjiebredie* (waterlily stew) and homemade breads with jams. Such a meal, without drinks, will cost around R80. For open-air restaurants listed in the text, it's essential that you **book** in advance.

---

man-made dam, there are worthwhile routes out to Lambert's Bay on the coast (see p.233) and over a spectacular mountain pass to the remote and unique mission at **Wuppertal**.

Wuppertal Mission and San rock-art sites

Leaving Clanwilliam to the northeast, the untarred R364 winds up through the northern Cederberg over the **Pakhuis Pass**, a drive worth taking for its lonely roadside scenery and inspiring views. A turn-off from the road after it drops into the Doring River Valley takes you to Wuppertal mission station, but if you keep straight on for another 100km or so it leads though some remote and beautiful landscapes, renowned for their spectacular wild flowers in spring, to Soetwater, on the R27 between Nieuwoudtville and Calvinia (see p.270).

Set deep in the tunefully named Tra-tra valley, the Moravian **mission station at Wuppertal** is one of the oldest in the Western Cape and remains one of the more poetic and untouched settlements in South Africa. A tiny collection of thatched cottages with a few cultivated fields around its fringes, the mission is famous for making *velskoene* (literally "hide shoes"), suede footwear commonly known as *vellies* and part of Afrikaner national dress. You can see the shoes being made and, of course, buy some here.

A couple of places on the R364 north of Clanwilliam, about two kilometres before the Wuppertal turn-off, offer excellent access to ancient **rock-art**, painted by descendants of South Africa's oldest inhabitants, San hunter-gatherers, sometimes known as Bushmen. Good-value, **budget accommodation** is available at *Traveller's Rest* (☎ & fax 027/482 1824, *travrest@kingsley.co.za*; ②), 36km north of Clanwilliam on a farm, where there are various self-catering cottages and the *Khoisan Restaurant* serving local home cooking. The main attraction, apart from its setting in the Cederberg, is that right beside the farm is the four-kilometre **Sevilla Bushman Painting Trail**, which takes in nine separate rock-art sites and offers an easily accessed and varied introduction to rock-art; a leaflet and book, available at *Traveller's Rest*, cover the route. About a kilometre beyond *Traveller's Rest* is *Bushman's Kloof* (☎027/482 2627; bookings ☎021/797 0990, fax 761 5551, *santrack@ilink.nis.za*; ⑨), a **luxury lodge** set in a wilderness area, where the focus is on rock-art with over 125 recorded sites on the property. Rangers here are trained in both wildlife guiding and rock-art interpretation. The rate is reasonable considering that it includes all meals, game drives and guided rock-art trails.

Citrusdal

Heading north from Piketberg on the N7, a long, flat plain reaches out to the line of Olifantsrivierberg Mountains, which the highway crosses by way of the impressive

Piekenierskloof Pass, forged in 1857 by the indomitable road engineer Thomas Bain. Coming down the northern side of the pass, the town of **CITRUSDAL** appears in the rolling countryside of the Olifants River Valley with the dramatic mountainscape of the Cederberg behind. Strange as it may seem now, early Dutch explorers saw huge herds of elephants here as they travelled north towards Namaqualand, so falling upon a suitable name for the river.

There are no roads from Citrusdal into the heart of the Cederberg Wilderness Area – you have to carry on up the N7 to the Algeria turn-off – although there are various routes leading into the foothills justifiably popular with mountain bikers. You can get a **map** outlining these at Sandvelhuise, the town's upbeat **information centre** (Oct–July Mon–Fri 9am–4.30pm, Sat 9am–noon; Aug–Sept daily 9am–4.30pm; ☎022/921 3210) in a small complex off Muller Street, just up from the wide main street, Voortrekker. Staff here can provide useful information about self-catering cottages and guesthouses in the area. The centre also has a **tea room**. If you decide to stay (and Citrusdal is a good place to pause for a break and make some plans), there's a pleasant **campsite** with a pool in town (☎022/921 3145; ①–②), on the left-hand side as you come in over the bridge from the N7, and the garishly coloured *Cederberg Lodge* (☎022/921 2221; ③) has **rooms** on Voortrekker Street. Light **meals** are on offer at *Uitspan*, 66 Voortrekker St, painted a distinctive yellow and purple.

Surrounding Citrusdal is some attractive countryside and farmland, including, as the town's name suggests, plenty of citrus groves. One of the principal attractions of this area is *The Baths* (☎022/921 3609; ①–③), to the south, a laid-back mineral **spa resort** with campsites, chalets and self-catering rooms in a large old stone building set around a series of hot pools. To get to it, turn right off the road leading into Citrusdal from the N7 and drive 16km down a good tarred road past the airfield – incidentally, one of the best places in the Western Cape for parachuting. Given that other hot-spring resorts in the Western Cape tend to be either rather snooty and expensive or tacky and over-crowded, this place hits a nice balance: it will be crowded, certainly, during holidays, but it has retained its simplicity and elegance and is a good spot to relax, particularly if you've been hauling over mountain and rock for a few days.

The Cederberg Wilderness Area

The **Cederberg Wilderness Area**, 710 square kilometres in extent, is reached by a dirt road 28km north of Citrusdal which leads east off the N7 to the forest station at **Algeria**. The **permit** system for the area allows a certain number of people to be in each of three separate parts of the wilderness area, but you do have to arrange permits in advance through the Cape Nature Conservation Office (☎027/482 2812) in Algeria; you can hike or camp where you like within the areas you hold a permit for. There are many designated **trails**, including routes to the main rock features and the two main peaks, **Sneeuberg** and **Tafelberg**. **Camping** is available at a pretty riverside site at Algeria (①), and unsophisticated but fully equipped **self-catering chalets** (②) and unequipped cheaper ones (①), at the bottom of Uitkyk Pass, where you must bring your own bedding and cooking utensils; contact the Cape Nature Conservation Office in Algeria for bookings and information. There are also places to stay on **farms** inside the reserve. *Sanddrif* (☎ & fax 027/482 2825; ②) has fully equipped chalets for four people (though you'll need to bring your own bedding); at *Kromrivier* (☎027/482 2807; ①–②) there are fully equipped chalets that sleep four, with bedding available for a small charge; and *Krakadouw* (☎027/482 2507; ②) has three secluded **cottages**. At Dwarsrivier, by Sanddrif, there is an amateur observatory, which on summer weekend evenings occasionally features an outdoor slide show and some high-powered telescopes for a closer look at the dazzling heavens.

ROOIBOS TEA

Few things in South Africa create such devotion, derision, hype and, among visitors, suspicious bemusement, as **rooibos** (literally, "red bush") **tea**. Still sown and harvested by hand on many farms, rooibos is a type of fynbos plant grown only in the mountainous regions around Clanwilliam and Nieuwoudtville. The tan-coloured tea that is brewed from its leaves has been a traditional South African drink ever since it was developed by Asian slaves two centuries ago, but it is only in the last twenty years that it has broken free from its health-food-shop earnestness and established mainstream credibility as a light, refreshing and healthy (caffeine-free) drink. In homes and tea rooms throughout South Africa you'll find rooibos firmly entrenched alongside regular tea and coffee. Drink it with milk and sugar, or just with a slice of lemon and a teaspoon of honey.

Weather conditions are often extreme in the Cederberg, with frost and snow during winter, and blistering heat in summer. There are a number of rivers, however, which you can safely head to for a **swim**. If something even wetter excites you, the best **white-water rafting trips** in the Western Cape take place on the Doring River in the northern Cederberg from mid-July to mid-September. Weekend trips with River Rafters (☎021/712 5094, *rafters@mweb.co.za*) include one night sleeping under an overhang, and cost around R500 per person.

Clanwilliam

Also on the N7 but at the northern end of the Cederberg, **CLANWILLIAM** is an attractive, assured town that carries off with some aplomb its various roles as a base for the Cederberg Wilderness Area, majestic and ragged behind it; as a centre for spring flowers; as a holiday resort focused on the neighbouring dam; and as a service centre for the lower part of the fertile irrigation schemes of the Olifants River Valley to the north. Established in the last years of the eighteenth century, this is one of the older settlements north of Cape Town, and features a number of historic buildings around town, including an **information centre** and **museum** (Mon–Fri 8.30am–5pm, Sat 8.30am–12.30pm; ☎027/482 2024; small entry fee for museum), situated in the old jail at the far end of Main Street. There are some genuinely interesting attractions in town, including **Kunshuis**, a good commercial art gallery on Main Street; a traditional leather **shoemaking factory** on Ou Kaapseweg; and the country's main **rooibos tea-processing factory** (tours Mon–Fri 10am–noon & 2–4pm) next door (see box above). Just to the south of town is **Ramskop**, a wild-flower reserve set on a hillside inside the entrance to the dam resort.

To add to its charms, Clanwilliam is well-supplied with **accommodation**. You can **camp** on the edge of the dam in the *Clanwilliam Dam Resort* (☎027/482 2133; ①–②), which also has a collection of plain **chalets**. The resort is the only public access point to the **dam** – one of the country's top water-skiing venues – which in summer and at weekends can seem to be monopolized by speedboat louts. There isn't any local rental if you want to join in the **watersports**, unless you're a resident at the *Olifants Dam Motel* (☎027/482 2185; ②) on the N7 side of the dam, which has boats available. Other places to stay include a famous South African institution, *Strassberger's Clanwilliam Hotel* (☎027/482 1101; ③–④), on the town's main street. Dignified and well run, the hotel has an open-air pool, renowned restaurant (*Reinhold's*), a tea room and separate chalets. Finally, *St du Barrys* (☎027/482 1537; ④), on the way out of town on the Pakhuis road, is a country **guesthouse** with an upmarket feel, antique-filled rooms and thatched roofs.

For **evening meals**, *Reinhold's* undoubtedly has the best reputation in town as a place to eat, but if you fancy something a bit more casual head for *Olifantshuis Pizzeria* *and Olde Worlde Pub* (closed Sun), on the corner as you turn into Main Road off Augsburg Drive. For daytime meals and **snacks**, there's *Strassberger's Clanwilliam Hotel*, or you can try *Nancy's Tea Room* (daily 9am–4pm) opposite.

travel details

Most public transport in the Western Cape originates in Cape Town and the main services are outlined in our "Travel details" at the end of Chapter One.

Trains

The most useful trains in the Western Cape are the two Metro Rail services connecting Cape Town with Stellenbosch and Paarl (all a 1hr journey). Outside peak morning and evening hours, trains are irregular, but run at approximately two-hour intervals. Phone the station to confirm times.

Intercity buses

In addition to the major points of departure listed below, the intercity buses stop at a number of intermediate points. Principal routes are Cape Town–Port Elizabeth along the N2 coastal route, with an inland alternative along the Little Karoo mountain route; Cape Town–Johannesburg/Pretoria along the N1; and Knysna–Johannesburg/Pretoria via Mossel Bay and the N12.

George to: Cape Town (6–7 daily; 6hr); Durban (1 daily; 18hr); Johannesburg (1–2 daily; 15hr); Knysna (6–7 daily; 1hr); Mossel Bay (6–7 daily; 45min); Oudtshoorn (3–4 daily; 1hr 30min); Plettenberg Bay (6–7 daily; 1hr 30min); Port Elizabeth (6–7 daily; 4hr 30min); Pretoria (1–2 daily; 16hr).

Knysna to: Cape Town (6–7 daily; 7hr); Durban (1 daily; 17hr); George (6–7 daily; 1hr); Johannesburg (1–2 daily; 16hr); Mossel Bay (6–7 daily; 1hr 15min); Oudtshoorn (1–2 daily; 2hr); Plettenberg Bay (6–7 daily; 1hr 30min); Port Elizabeth (6–7 daily; 4hr 30min); Pretoria (1–2 daily; 17hr).

Mossel Bay to: Cape Town (6–7 daily; 5hr 30min); Durban (1 daily; 18hr 30min); George (6–7 daily; 45min); Johannesburg (1–2 daily; 14hr); Knysna (6–7 daily; 1hr 15min); Oudtshoorn (1–2 daily; 1hr 15min); Plettenberg Bay (6–7 daily; 2hr 15min); Port Elizabeth (6–7 daily; 4hr 30min); Pretoria (1–2 daily; 15hr).

Oudtshoorn to: George (3–4 daily; 1hr 30min); Johannesburg (1–2 daily; 13hr 30min); Knysna (1–2 daily; 2hr); Mossel Bay (1–2 daily; 45min); Pretoria (1–2daily; 14hr 30min).

Paarl to: Beaufort West (4–5 daily; 5hr); Durban (2 daily; 18hr); East London (daily; 11hr 30min); Johannesburg (4–5 daily; 14hr); Pretoria (4–5 daily; 15hr).

Plettenberg Bay to: Cape Town (6–7 daily; 7hr 30min); Durban (1 daily; 16hr); George (6–7 daily; 1hr 30min); Knysna (6–7 daily; 1hr 30min); Mossel Bay (6–7 daily; 2hr 15min); Port Elizabeth (6–7 daily; 2hr 30min).

Backpacker buses

The Baz bus (☎021/439 2323) travels once daily (in both directions) along the N2 between Cape Town and Port Elizabeth. You can be let off anywhere along the national road, and the bus pulls into all the major destinations along the way (with the notable exception of Storms River Mouth).

Cape Town to: Bot River (daily; 1hr 30min); George (daily; 7hr); Hermanus (daily*); Jeffrey's Bay (daily; 12hr 15min); Knysna (daily; 8hr 30min); Mossel Bay (daily; 6hr); Nature's Valley (daily; 10hr); Oudtshoorn (daily*); Plettenberg Bay (daily; 9hr 30min); Port Elizabeth (daily; 13hr 30min); Storms River (10hr 30min); Swellendam (daily; 3hr); Wilderness (daily 7hr 30 min).

*Note: shuttle buses connect with the Baz at Bot River for Hermanus; and at George for Oudtshoorn.

Flights

George to: Cape Town (2–4 daily; 1hr); Durban (daily; 2hr 15min); Johannesburg (2 daily; 1hr 30min); Port Elizabeth (3 weekly; 1hr).

Plettenberg Bay to: Johannesburg (1 daily; 2hr 15min).

CHAPTER THREE

THE NORTHERN CAPE

The vast **Northern Cape**, largest and most disseminated of South Africa's provinces, is not an easy region to tackle as a visitor. From the lonely **Atlantic West Coast** to the provincial capital, **Kimberley**, hard against its eastern border with the Free State, it covers over one-third of the nation's landmass – an area dominated by heat, brown aridity, empty spaces and huge travelling distances. However, while these characteristics themselves possess a surreal attraction, it is for the miracles of the desert you will come – improbable swaths of flowers, diamonds dug from the dirt and wild animals roaming among the dunes.

The most significant of these surprises is the **Orange River**, a large watercourse which flows, often with parched land stretching for hundreds of kilometres on either side, from the Highlands of Lesotho to the Atlantic, where it marks South Africa's northern border with Namibia. The river separates the two sparsely populated semi-desert ecosystems that fill the interior of the Northern Cape – the **Kalahari** and **Great Karoo**. It was by the Orange that **diamonds** were first discovered in the 1860s, although it was in the alluvial deposits of the Vaal River and nearby dry diggings around Kimberley that the story of diamonds would be played out in its most compelling detail.

A no less hard-won economic contribution of the Orange is in the large **irrigation schemes** which have created a stretch of incongruous green along the course of the river, principally around the isolated northern centre of **Upington**. A small but important town, Upington acts as a major gateway to the magnificent **Kalahari-Gemsbok National Park**, part of the Kgalagadi Transfrontier Park and undoubtedly one of the finest game-viewing parks in South Africa, and the smaller **Augrabies Falls National Park**, where the Orange plunges with muscular drama into a large granite gorge.

On the western side of the province, the presence of the Atlantic Ocean means that the land, while still harsh and dry, is subject to different influences. It is in this region, **Namaqualand**, that the brief rains of winter produce one of nature's truly glorious transformations, when in August and September the land is carpeted by a magnificent display of multicoloured **wild flowers**.

Despite these impressive natural attractions, the most commonly encountered part of the Northern Cape is its southeastern corner, where both of the two main routes between Johannesburg and Cape Town, the **N1** and the **N12**, pass before meeting just northeast of Beaufort West in the Great Karoo. The N12, no longer in time or distance than the N1, presents a good opportunity to spend a day or so in Kimberley. Neither route, however, offers particularly inspiring scenery or sights, and anyone hoping to see a cross-section of South Africa by driving between Johannesburg and Cape Town will find themselves hot, tired and rather disappointed. A less obvious, but more attractive option is to take the **N14** from Johannesburg through Upington, passing the atmospheric old mission station at **Kuruman**, and on to **Springbok** and the main west coast route (the N7) to Cape Town. This route is only 400km longer than the N1 or N12 and, while it doesn't offer respite from long, empty landscapes, the sights on the way are more unusual. This route also puts both the Kalahari-Gemsbok National Park and little-visited **Richtersveld National Park** within striking distance and, in August and September, allows you to experience the full

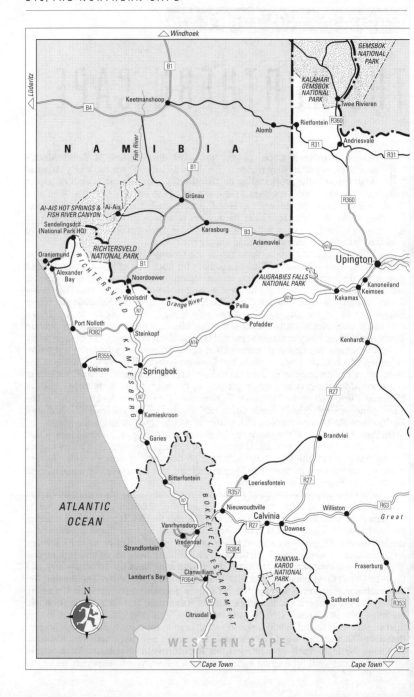

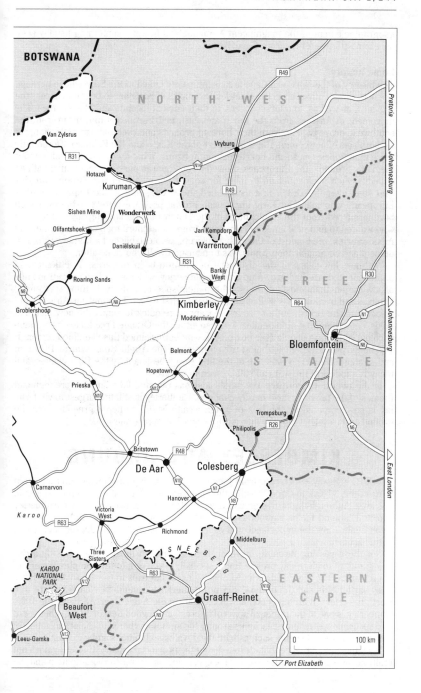

geographic extent of the magnificent Namaqualand flowers, something usually seen only in restrictive forays from Cape Town.

Some history

The history of the Northern Cape area is intimately linked to the **San**, whose heritage is most prominently seen in the countless examples of **rock art** to be found across the province, as well as, to a lesser extent, in their ancient legends and place names. The movement of Africans from the north and east, and Europeans moving in from the southwest, drove the San from their hunting grounds and eventually to extinction, yet for both sets of newcomers the semi-desert of the Karoo and the Kalahari offered little more than hopelessness and heartbreaking horizons. What it did offer – wealth under the dusty ground – the Europeans showed no restraint in pursuing, beginning with an expedition into Namaqualand to mine for copper led by **Governor Simon van der Stel** soon after the Dutch first established their settlement in the Cape. The other Europeans who made an early impression on the province were **trekboers**, Dutch burghers freed from the employment of the Dutch East India Company in the Cape who wanted to find new lands to farm away from the authoritarian company rule, and **missionaries**, the boldest of the early explorers, who established a framework of settlement and communication which was to be used by all who came after.

Within a few years of the discovery of **diamonds** in the area, a settlement of unprecedented size had grown up around Kimberley, which soon had more trappings of civilization than most of the southern hemisphere, with such things as public libraries and tramways, as well as South Africa's first urban "location" for Africans and coloureds. The British authorities in the Cape were quick to annex the new diamond fields, something that didn't endear them to either the Orange Free State or the mainly coloured **Griqua** people (see box p.464), who both claimed this ill-defined region. It was no surprise, therefore, that at the outbreak of the **Anglo-Boer War** in 1899 rich and strategic Kimberley was one of the first towns besieged by the Boer armies, and many reminders of the war can still be seen in the area.

In the **twentieth century** the harsh land has relented little and the predominant themes of the province have hardly changed. Kimberley is still the largest town, farming is still tempered by the lack of water, wealth is still gathered greedily from the ground and travellers into the interior are regarded as rare and bold.

KIMBERLEY AND AROUND

The **N12** highway, which runs from Johannesburg through **Kimberley** and then down to meet the N1 link to Cape Town, is the main reason most visitors find themselves in this area. Although the term suggests a wonderland of romance and riches, Kimberley and its Diamond Fields surrounds are mostly dry and uninspiring, and the city will never again know the importance and glamour it had for two heady decades at the end of the last century.

For those passing through, however, there is enough in the area to justify a day doing a bit of modern-day prospecting, especially if you're into the complex history of South Africa. The biggest draw is Kimberley itself, but trips to the area's **Anglo-Boer War battlefields** and the **alluvial diamond diggings** around the Vaal River are well worth the effort. With the centenary of the start of the Anglo-Boer War falling in 1999, Kimberley is one of the principal areas of interest, and a good deal of effort is being put into sprucing up the tourist facilities around the sites, together with the organization of a number of special events such as battlefield walks, exhibitions and ceremonies.

It's important to realize that, despite being the provincial capital, Kimberley does not really act as a gateway to the Northern Cape, being far nearer to Bloemfontein and the

A SHORT HISTORY OF THE DIAMOND FIELDS

Before 1866, the area now known as the **Diamond Fields** was unpromising farmland, marked by occasional *koppies* inhabited by pioneer farmers and an independent people of mixed race origins called the Griquas. The outlook changed, however, after a fifteen-year-old boy noticed a shiny white pebble on the banks of the Orange River near Hopetown, about 120km southwest of Kimberley. Just as word of that discovery was spreading, another Hopetown resident, Schalk van Niekerk, acquired from a Griqua shepherd a massive 83.5-carat diamond. It is common practice for significant diamonds to be given a name, and these two became known, respectively, as Eureka and The Star of South Africa. The Star was described at the time by the British Colonial Secretary as the "rock on which the future success of South Africa will be built". He was not far off the mark. Certainly in the short term the discoveries provoked wild optimism, as thousands of prospectors made the gruelling trek across the Karoo to begin sifting through the alluvial deposits along the banks of the Orange and Vaal rivers. By 1873 there were an estimated fifty thousand people living in the area.

Although there were plenty of diamonds to be found in the rivers, prospectors also began scratching around in the dry land between them, encouraged by tales of diamonds being found in farmhouse bricks made from local earth. Two of the most promising "dry diggings" were on a farm owned by two brothers, **Johannes** and **Diederick de Beer**. In 1871 the brothers sold the farm, which they had bought a few years previously for £50, to prospectors for the sum of £6300. The two sites were subsequently to become the **Kimberley Mine**, or Big Hole, and the **De Beers Mine**, situated on either side of the city centre of Kimberley. The Big Hole was the focus of the most frenetic mining activity of the early years, and the shantytown that grew up around it, New Rush, was the origin of the present city. In those days it was a heady, rugged place to live, with little authority or structure, but with prizes rich enough to attract bold men with big ideas. Of these, two very different, if equally ambitious, men rose to prominence in the new settlement. **Barney Barnato**, a flamboyant Cockney, established his power base at the Kimberley Mine, while **Cecil John Rhodes**, a parson's son who had come out to join his brother in South Africa to improve his health, gradually took over control of the De Beers Mine. The power struggle between the two men was intense, and culminated in the formation in 1888 of the De Beers Consolidated Mines Limited, an agreement which involved the transfer of over £5 million, an astronomic sum in those days, from Rhodes to Barnato.

This consolidation laid the foundation for De Beers' monopoly of the diamond industry in South Africa, something which has remained intact ever since. The rise of the gold fields on the Witwatersrand soon swamped Kimberley's importance, and although three of the five large mines in the area still produce diamonds, and the alluvial claims along the Vaal are still worked, the firm hand of De Beers has stifled the enterprise which initially gave the area its character.

Free State. The obvious route to the Kalahari and Namaqualand from Johannesburg is along the N14 through Upington, and from Cape Town up the N7 to Springbok.

Kimberley

Despite being a provincial capital and the centre of production of one of the most valuable materials known to man, **KIMBERLEY** is neither a large nor glamorous city. Status and sophistication have been draining from it ever since the days of the diamond rush, when it was the fastest-growing city in the southern hemisphere and **Cecil Rhodes** held in his grip not only the fabulously wealthy diamond industry, but the heart and mind of the British Empire. Even the all-controlling **De Beers Group** (sometimes called the "grandfather" of Kimberley for the number of people it directly and

CECIL JOHN RHODES

When **Cecil John Rhodes** first arrived in the Kimberley Diamond Fields he was 18 years old, a sickly youth sent out to join his brother for the sake of his health. Soon making money buying up claims, he returned to Britain to attend Oxford University, where his illnesses returned and he was given six months to live. He came back out to South Africa, where he was able to improve both his health and his business standing, allowing him to return to Oxford and graduate in 1881, by which time he had already founded the **De Beers Mining Company** and been elected an **MP** in the Cape Parliament. Within a decade Rhodes controlled ninety percent of the world's diamond production and was champing at the bit to expand his mining interests north into Africa, with the British Empire in tow. With much cajoling, bullying, brinkmanship and no little obfuscation in his dealing with imperial governments and African chiefs alike, he brought the territories north of the Limpopo under the control of his South African Company. That land – now Zimbabwe and Zambia – became known as Rhodesia in 1895, the same year as a Rhodes-backed invasion of the Transvaal Republic, the Jameson Raid, failed humiliatingly. Rhodes was forced to resign as prime minister of the Cape Colony, a post he had assumed in 1890 at the age of 37, while the Boers and the British slid towards war. He spent the first part of the war in besieged Kimberley, trying to organize the defences and bickering very publicly with the British commander. A year after the end of the war, aged only 49 and unmarried, he died at Muizenberg near Cape Town and was buried at an outlook called World's End, in the Matopos Hills near Bulawayo in Zimbabwe.

indirectly employs), as part of the mighty Anglo-American corporation, is now itself largely controlled from Johannesburg and the city lives in the chilly shadow of the day when the diamonds finally dry up.

Spend a few hours seeking out some of the many interesting historical buildings which remain, and take the opportunity of an **underground tour** of a working diamond mine, not forgetting to peer into the depths of the **Big Hole**, the remarkable, hand-dug chasm that takes up almost as much land area as the central business district (CBD) of the city itself, and you'll taste some of the opulence and energy which made the city famous.

Arrival, information and orientation

Kimberley's **airport**, serving domestic flights only, lies 7km south of the city centre (information ☎053/851 1241). Arriving by **train**, you'll find yourself within easy walking distance of the town centre, though be warned that the daily service from Cape Town pulls in here at 2am, while trains from Johannesburg arrive at 6pm and 9pm. Other than Greyhound, who pull up at the tourist information office, the main **intercity buses** terminate at the Shell Ultra City service station on the Transvaal Road (N12), an inconvenient 6km north of the city centre. From here your best option is to hitch a lift or call Rikkies Taxis (see opposite), who offer a pick-up service for around R15. If you're arriving by **car** for a fleeting visit, you'll find plenty of parking space outside the tourist information office.

Kimberley's helpful **tourist information office** is in the City Civic Complex on Bulfontein Road (Mon–Fri 8am–5pm, Sat 8.30–11.30am; ☎053/832 7298), and is well worth making use of. The fact that the best-known sight, the Big Hole, is under the ground doesn't make **orientation** immediately easy. However, the tell-tale mounds of dead earth lying immediately to the west of the CBD are a good indication of its location. Another useful landmark is the stern-looking **Harry Oppenheimer House**, often just referred to as HOH, one of the town's few skyscrapers, near the tourist information office.

City transport

Kimberley is poorly served by public transport; beyond the city centre, which is walkable, getting around without a car isn't easy. Note that all the city's **car rental** firms are located at the airport: Avis (☎053/851 1082), Budget (☎053/851 1182) and Imperial (☎053/851 1131). There are a couple of **taxi** companies in town, Rikkies (mobile ☎082/461 8818) and AA Taxis (☎053/861 4015). **Bicycles** can be rented from Alphabeta's in the Sanlam Arcade, 19a Jones St (☎053/831 1059). Unusually for South Africa, Kimberley has a restored **tram** service, but its only function is to transport visitors to the Big Hole. Trams depart regularly from Market Square in the centre.

Accommodation

Kimberley's **accommodation** is targeted at through-traffic and business travellers, but there are a handful of pleasant guesthouses in historic buildings, and because the city isn't regarded as a main centre prices are generally reasonable. While most hotels are within walking distance of the centre, some of the guesthouses, and both the campsites, are over 2km away, and the backpackers' lodge is too far to consider walking if you have luggage to carry. If you get stuck, the tourist information office (see opposite) can provide an accommodation list and will help you find somewhere to stay.

Hotels and guesthouses

Carrington House, 32 Carrington Rd (☎053/833 2219 or mobile ☎083/261 6473). Easy-going and well-priced B&B on the most prestigious street in Kimberley. ②.

Diamond Protea Lodge, 124 Du Toitspan Rd (☎053/831 1281, fax 831 1284). Rather overshadowed by the six-storey *Holiday Inn* next door, the *Diamond* is a bit more intimate, but still aimed primarily at business travellers. ③.

Edgerton House, 5 Egerton Rd (☎053/831 1150, fax 831 1785, *edgerton@kimberley.co.za*). Elegant guesthouse in a National Monument in historic Belgravia suburb. Thirteen rooms, a pool and a tea room prove a bit of a squeeze. Serves an expensive dinner. ⑥.

Estate Private Hotel, 7 Lodge Rd (☎053/832 2668). The National Monument home of the Oppenheimer family before they moved to Johannesburg in 1915. The historical theme predominates, but the guesthouse has all mod cons, including a pool. ③.

Kimberley Club, 70–72 Du Toitspan Rd (☎053/832 4224). Run along the lines of a London club, though the rooms fail to match the grandeur of the rest of the building (see p.248). Filled with history and portraits of Cecil John Rhodes. ④.

Milner House, 31 Milner St (☎053/831 6405, *fires@kimnet.co.za*). High quality, well-run guesthouse in attractive surroundings in Belgravia area. ④.

ACCOMMODATION PRICE CODES

All the accommodation listed in the Guide has been categorized into one of nine price bands, as set out below. The rates quoted represent what you can expect to pay for much of the summer **per person**, and unless otherwise stated, are based on two sharing. Rooms are generally en suite. Expect prices in some areas to be significantly higher in peak season (Dec–Jan & Easter), and look out for discounts during the winter. For further details, see p.33.

① up to R50	⑥ R250–300
② R50–100	⑦ R300–400
③ R100–150	⑧ R400–500
④ R150–200	⑨ over R500
⑤ R200–250	

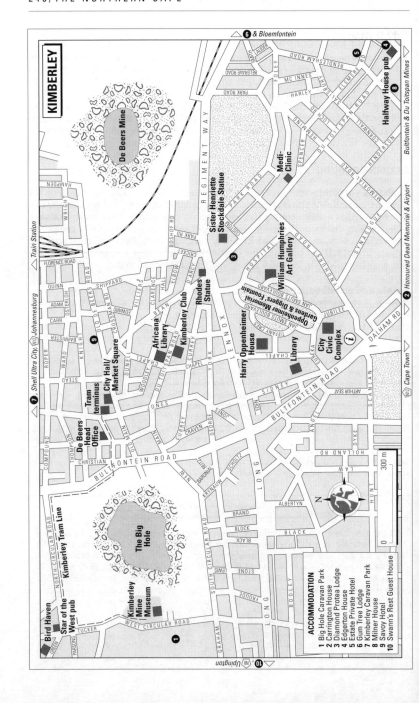

KIMBERLEY

De Beers Mine

△ **6** & Bloemfontein

Train Station

Halfway House pub

▷ Bultfontein & Du Toitspan Mines

◁ Shell Ultra City, ↖ Johannesburg

△ **7** Shell Ultra City

▷ Honoured Dead Memorial & Airport

◁ Cape Town

▷ **2** Honoured Dead Memorial & Airport

Medi-Clinic

Sister Henriette Stockdale Statue

William Humphries Art Gallery

Rhodes Statue

Africana Library

Kimberley Club

City Hall/Market Square

Tram terminus

De Beers Head Office

Harry Oppenheimer House

Oppenheimer Memorial, Diggers' Fountain & Gardens

Library

City Civic Complex

Bird Haven

Star of the West pub

Kimberley Mine Museum

The Big Hole

Kimberley Tram Line

△ Upington

▷ Upington

ACCOMMODATION
1 Big Hole Caravan Park
2 Carrington House
3 Diamond Protea Lodge
4 Edgerton House
5 Estate Private Hotel
6 Gum Tree Lodge
7 Kimberley Caravan Park
8 Milner House
9 Savoy Hotel
10 Swann's Rest Guest House

N

0   300 m

Savoy Hotel, 19 De Beers Rd (☎053/832 6211, fax 832 7021). Not in the best part of town, and very plain from the outside, but inside the *Savoy* retains an old-fashioned charm. ④.

Swann's Rest Guest House, 41 Swann's Way (☎053/861 3406). Two good-value, simple doubles with a kitchenette at the back of a suburban house, 2km from the centre. To get there follow R64 west out of town, turn left at Pickering and left again into Swann's Way. ②.

Campsites and budget lodging

Big Hole Caravan Park, West Circular Rd (☎053/830 6322). Privately run campsite located among the old mine heaps just beside Big Hole. Lush, neat and relatively quiet, with a pool, although the shade from the young trees isn't generous. There are rumours that a casino complex is to be built on the site. The office is open 6am–8pm. ①.

Gum Tree Lodge, Bloemfontein Rd (☎053/832 8577). Kimberley's only backpackers' lodge is an inconvenient 5km out of town, but is pleasantly shady and has a swimming pool. Dorms and more comfortable self-catering units are available, and there's an inexpensive restaurant next door. Dorms ①, units ②.

Kimberley Caravan Park, Hull Rd, next to De Beers Stadium (☎053/833 2582). Unappealing municipal campsite in an insalubrious part of town, with igloo-style cabins for rent. Camping and cabins ①.

The City

Many of Kimberley's main sights lie on or near **Du Toitspan Road**, which slices diagonally across the city centre and becomes one of the main arteries out of town to the southeast. The **Big Hole** – a must-see – lies just west of the centre, while the more open central business district (CBD) lies to the south of Lennox Road.

The Big Hole: Kimberley Mine Museum

Although the **Big Hole**, just west of the city centre, is neither the only nor even the biggest hole in Kimberley, it remains the principal attraction of the city. The only official way to see it is from inside the **Kimberley Mine Museum** (daily 8am–6pm; medium entry fee) on the western side of the hole. To get there, drive to West Circular Road, or take a tram from the City Hall (hourly at quarter past the hour 9.15am–4.15pm; R3 one way). The museum is spread out along the edge of the Big Hole and there are two viewing platforms, from where you can peer down into nothingness and look for the poetry

---

KIMBERLEY'S BIG HOLE

Where there is now a gaping five-hundred-metre-wide cavity was once a small hill on a typically dry, Northern Cape farm, which belonged to the brothers Johannes Nicolaas and Diederick Arnoldus de Beer. In the early 1870s, with diamonds known to be in the area, there were various work parties scratching around hoping for a lucky find. One, known as the Red Cap Party, led by Fleetwood Rawstorne, was working at the base of Colesberg *koppie* in July 1871. The story goes that they sent one of their cooks to the top of the hill as a punishment for being drunk, telling him, with a laugh and a clip round the ear, not to return until he had found a diamond. The unnamed servant duly came back with a peace offering, and within two years there were over fifty thousand people in the area frantically turning Colesberg *koppie* inside out. By 1914, when De Beers closed the mine, some 22.6 million tonnes of earth had been removed, yielding over 14.5 million carats of diamonds. Incredibly, the hole was dug to a depth of 240m entirely by pick and shovel, and remains the largest man-made excavation in the world. In its heyday, when tens of thousands of miners swarmed over the mine to work their ten-square-metre claim, and a network of ropes and pipes crisscrossed the surface, each day saw lives lost and fortunes either discovered or squandered. Once the mining could go no further from the surface, a shaft was dug to allow further excavations beneath it to a depth of over 800m.

and poignancy, which undoubtedly still lingers where mountains were moved in a belief in the power of wealth. Balanced on the lip of the crater on the far side is the now diminutive outline of the city, almost swallowed up by the size and silence of the hollow below it.

The rest of the museum comprises a large collection of **historic buildings**, many of them original from the days of Rhodes and Barnato, which were moved here from the city centre when development and demolition threatened. With old shops, churches, bars, banks and sundry other period institutions, including Barney Barnato's Boxing Academy, there is enough property to create a fairly complete settlement, and most of the fixtures, fittings and artefacts are genuine. You can walk down these old Kimberley streets, peer into shop windows and wander through a couple of the buildings, but for a "living museum" the atmosphere is somewhat soporific. One of the more engaging parts is an area where you can buy a bucket of alluvial river diggings and sift through it on old sorting tables, in the hope of finding one of the mock diamonds planted among the gravel, which you can then exchange for some eminently undesirable prizes, such as faded postcards of the museum or fluffy keyrings. Your chances of striking lucky are about one in five – much better odds than the original miners faced.

Market Square and around

At the heart of the city centre is **Market Square**, dominated by the white, Corinthian-styled **City Hall**. As well as being the hub of buying and selling during the early diamond days, the square was the scene of two occasions significant in South Africa's history: the public crushing of gold-bearing rock from the Witwatersrand that persuaded Rhodes, Barnato and others to further their investments in gold-mining; and the departure in 1890 of the Pioneer Column, which effectively established "white" Rhodesia by pursuing Rhodes' expansionist claims to the territory north of the Limpopo. Around the square, the sense of movement and commerce is perpetuated by a large taxi rank and an assortment of scruffy but colourful stalls and traders.

One block west of Market Square along the tramline, at 36 Stockdale St, is the head office of **De Beers**, a dignified but unremarkable old building rather swallowed up by the city around it. You can read the brass plates by the door, but the building is not open to the public.

The Kimberley Club and around

Not far southwest of Market Square, on Du Toitspan Road, is the two-storey **Kimberley Club**, founded in 1881 by the movers and shakers of the new settlement. The club was modelled on gentlemen's clubs in London, but its colourful, enterprising bunch of members ensured the place was more dynamic than stuffy. It was claimed that there were more millionaires to the square foot here than any other place in the world, and acceptance within the club is said to have been a significant carrot in Rhodes' wooing of Barnato in 1888 (that, and a cheque for £5 million). Although the present building is the third on the site, it was completed in 1896 and would have been known by Rhodes, whose presence seems no less dominant today than it was at the turn of the century, with countless portraits, busts and other memorabilia of the man in all parts of the building. As well as leather armchairs in the smoking lounge and marble in the hallway, there are plenty of fine antiques and a few quirky pieces, such as a weighing chair presented to the club by Lord Randolph Churchill, Winston Churchill's father. It is possible to look around or go for a drink in the **bar**, though you'll get a much less chilly reception if you introduce yourself at reception and pay due respect to the club's rules, which include no jeans and T-shirts, and no women in the bar – though this might be waived if a senior member gives permission. It's also possible to spend a night at the club (see "Accommodation" on p.245).

Across the road is the small but engrossing **Africana Library** (Mon–Fri 8am–12.45pm & 1.30–4.30pm), which specializes in historical material relevant to

Kimberley and the Northern Cape. Opened in 1887, it retains many original features and is worth peeping into – one of the librarians will show you around if you ask nicely. The library is one of the venues visited on the excellent Kimberley Ghost Trail (see p.251), which gives you a chance to look around the building at night and learn of the restless spirit of its first librarian.

The CBD

At the junction of Du Toitspan and Lennox roads stands a statue of **Cecil Rhodes**. Unusually, here he is portrayed astride a horse, although the tributes around the plinth spare little of the swagger common to most Rhodes memorials. Across the road in the grounds of St Cyprian's Cathedral, and a little more humble in tone, stands what is reputed to be the only statue of a nun in the world, depicting **Sister Henriette Stockdale**, a pioneer of nursing in South Africa.

Moving south of Lennox into the CBD area, you'll come to the **Oppenheimer Memorial Gardens**, which contain a bust of mining magnate Sir Ernest Oppenheimer and the striking **Diggers Fountain**. The combination maintains a balance of respect which Kimberley, to its credit, perpetuates between those who got dirt beneath their fingernails and those who made the money. The fountain depicts five miners holding high a massive sieve, and looks particularly impressive when floodlit at or after dusk. The tall building lurking above the gardens is **Harry Oppenheimer House** (HOH), the offices of De Beers' Central Selling Organisation, on the upper floors of which all of the company's South African-mined diamonds are assessed for caratage, colour, clarity and shape. So that this can be done in the best natural light, the building faces south and has special windows to eliminate glare. Not surprisingly, it isn't open to the public.

On the opposite side of the gardens to HOH lies an unexpected gem: the **William Humphreys Art Gallery** (Mon–Sat 10am–1pm & 2–5pm, Sun 2–5pm; free entry Wed, small fee other times), one of the country's top art galleries. Although dominated by European Old Masters when it opened in 1952, the collection has been moving with the times long enough to have established an impressively well-balanced representation of South African art, and shows no reservations about including traditional and contemporary work. The gallery was one of first places in the world to display **San rock** paintings as works of art rather than museum pieces.

Just south of the CBD, in the middle of a roundabout where Dalham and Memorial roads meet, is the **Honoured Dead Memorial**, a striking monument to the victims of the Kimberley siege during the Anglo-Boer War. Beside the memorial is the British gun used in the siege known as **Long Cecil** – built in the De Beers' workshops to respond to the Boer's Long Tom cannon.

Belgravia

About 1km southeast of the CBD, along Du Toitspan Road, lies **Belgravia**, the residential suburb where most of Kimberley's wealthy families lived. A stroll around these streets is a good way to get a feel for the more refined side of the diamond age. The focus of the area is at the junction of Du Toitspan and Egerton roads, where you'll find the historic **Halfway House** pub. The pub takes its name from the fact that it is situated halfway between the De Beers and Bultfontein mines, and gained fame as a drive-in (or, in those days, ride-in) pub frequented by the celebrities of the pioneer days. Sure enough, the sign swinging outside shows a badly drawn Cecil Rhodes atop his horse, holding a glass of beer – though presumably not just "The Half" the inscription hints at (Cecil not being one to do things in part measures). Happily, the pub has not fallen victim to tourist kitsch and is still a popular local drinking hole.

Next door is **Edgerton House** (Mon–Sat 10am–4pm), a National Monument built in 1901 that has been converted into an upmarket guesthouse with a tea room in the internal courtyard (see p.245). Across the road is the famous **McGregor Museum**

KIMBERLEY TOURS

One of the most impressive aspects of Kimberley is the number of fascinating **organized tours** on offer, well worth booking if you want to experience the full flavour of the city's unique history.

DE BEERS' DIAMOND MINES

Join an **underground tour** of two of De Beers' working diamond mines – **Bultfontein** and **Dutoitspan**, both on the outskirts of the city – and instead of being whisked around a sanitized visitors' centre, you get right to the working heart of the mine, amid the noise of turbines and engines, the dust, the mud, the heat and the thick air. After an introductory video and safety talk, visitors are kitted out with overalls, hard hats, torches and emergency oxygen packs – the same gear as the miners wear – and then taken down (in groups of about twelve) to a depth of 825m by the shaft lift. Once down, you'll be shown around caves where kimberlite is loosened by explosions, dragged out into trolleys, crushed and then taken to the surface for cleaning and sifting. In the event you spot a diamond while underground, De Beers will give you 20 percent of its value, more (they claim) than it could fetch on the black market. Don't get too excited, though; mostly all you'll see is grey clay dirt.

Tours (Mon & Wed–Fri 8am, Tues 9.30am; ☎053/842 1321) last three and a half hours and cost around R60, and you have to book beforehand. They're not a good idea for the timid or claustrophobic, and De Beers won't allow anyone under the age of 16 to go underground, but **surface tours** of the same mines (Mon–Fri 9am & 11am) are also available, lasting one and a half hours.

THE FEATHER, HOLE AND MALT TOUR

Also in the mornings, **The Feather, Hole and Malt Tour** shows you Kimberley from the back of a traditional horse-drawn wagon. This takes you to the Big Hole and past a number of the historic sights in the city centre, including Market Square and the De Beers offices, and ends with lunch at the historic *Star of the West* pub, still a digger's

(Mon–Sat 9am–5pm, Sun 2–5pm; small entry fee), housed in a grand building and named after an early mayor of Kimberley. Inside you'll find natural and cultural history collections, as well as an informative display on the siege of Kimberley, and – unusual still in South Africa – a well-balanced exhibition on the various ancestral roots of today's inhabitants of the Northern Cape. The museum also has a pleasant tea room and an informative tree and shrub trail. You can visit a couple of restored houses nearby, both on Lodge Road: **The Bungalow**, the mansion of mining magnate H.P. Rudd; and **Dunluce**, an elegant Edwardian home. Arrangements must be made at the museum if you want to see inside either, though you can walk past both, along with over thirty other historic homes and points of interest, on a self-guided **walking tour** of Belgravia, details of which can be obtained from the tourist information office (see p.244).

Adjacent to the McGregor Museum on Egerton Road is the **Duggan-Cronin Gallery** (Mon–Sat 9am–5pm, Sun 2–5pm; small entry fee), which despite its stuffy-sounding name includes a large collection of endearingly unsophisticated photographs taken by Alfred Duggan-Cronin, a night watchman for De Beers, portraying different aspects of the lifestyles of the indigenous people of South Africa.

Eating, drinking and nightlife

Kimberley's limited selection of **restaurants** is dominated by the ubiquitous steak-houses, and beyond the handful of historic **pubs**, which can be entertaining for their atmosphere and clientele, there is little in the way of **nightlife**.

favourite 100 years on. The tour departs from the Bird Haven aviary near the Big Hole at 9.30am, and costs around R120 per adult, including lunch. For bookings call ☎083/454 7047, or contact the tourist information office.

GHOST TOURS

As the light fades in early evening and the city centre empties, so the many restless spirits produced by over a hundred years of surreptitious diamond wheeling and dealing begin to make their presence felt. If you're brave enough to hear the stories, or simply like the idea of poking around some of Kimberley's most interesting buildings after hours, join a **Ghost tour** in the company of the city's resident ghost expert, who will show you scenes of strange encounters in places such as the Africana Library, the Regimental headquarters and the spooky Bungalow in Belgravia. Tours begin just before sunset at the Honoured Dead Memorial and last three to four hours. For details contact the tourist information office.

TOWNSHIP TOURS

Kimberley was the first settlement in South Africa to establish "locations" on its fringes to house the African and coloured labourers who worked on the mines. The present township, Galeshewe, offers an insight into the lives of many of Kimberley's disadvantaged residents, and the **township tour** also takes in some alternative historic sights – including the house and grave of Sol Plaatje, one of the first black Africans to write in English and a founding member of the ANC, and the house where Robert Sobukwe, founder of the Pan-African Congress (PAC), died. The tour also visits the !Xu and Khwe San communities, who were relocated near Kimberley after being disbanded from the South African Defence Force in the Eighties, whom they'd served as trackers in Angola and Namibia. The communities produce a range of traditional San and Bushmen crafts and artwork, which can be seen on the tour. For details contact Dirk Potgieter of Diamond Tours Unlimited (☎053/843 0017, mobile ☎083/265 4795, *dtours@kimnet.co.za*).

Barnato's, 6 Dalham Rd (☎053/833 4110). Predictable historic theme but decent, mid-priced food, close to the information office.

Halfway House Pub, corner of Du Toitspan and Egerton roads. Cecil Rhodes' old refreshment stop, and still a popular, unpretentious local. Pub lunches available, although *Umberto's* restaurant next door is perhaps better for a slap-up meal.

Keg & Falcon, corner of Du Toitspan and Memorial roads. Traditional-English theme pub that promises more than it delivers, but is inexpensive and very popular with locals.

Mario's, 159 Du Toitspan Rd (☎053/831 1738). In a small house across the road and just along from *Holiday Inn*, this medium-priced restaurant offers the best atmosphere in town. You can eat outside – although it fronts a main road. Friendly staff, and a big menu. Mon–Fri 11.30am–2pm & 6–10.30pm, Sat 6–10.30pm.

Old Diggers Restaurant, Bloemfontein Rd, next to *Gum Tree Lodge*. Large dining hall, serving up cheap, wholesome meals, principally for residents of the backpackers' lodge, at all hours of the day. Takeaway is available, and there's a bar.

Safari Steakhouse, corner of Transvaal/Jones and Old Main roads, Market Square (☎053/832 4621). Classic, popular steakhouse with medium prices that has been pumping out the protein for thirty years. Big on game: to order, simply point to the set of horns mounted on the wall to indicate which species you want. Among the imaginative menu is an elephant-sized, 1.1kg steak.

Star of the West, corner of West and North Circular roads. Near the Big Hole, Kimberley's oldest pub still serves beer to diggers after the diamond markets on Saturdays. This is a good place to eat or drink after a hard day's holing – and the solid, cheap pub lunches are a better option than the Mine Museum's tea room.

Tiffany's, in the *Savoy Hotel*, 19 De Beers Rd (☎053/832 6211). A meal at Kimberley's most formal restaurant doesn't come cheap – and the atmosphere can be a bit intimidating – but the food is good.

Umberto's, corner of Du Toitspan and Egerton roads. Next door to the *Halfway House Pub*, this regular Italian restaurant, with red-checked tablecloths, serves up decent pizza and pasta. The rest of the menu is slightly pricier. Closed Sun.

Listings

Airlines South African Express Airways are situated at the airport (℡053/838 3337).

Bus information Greyhound (℡053/831 4548); Intercape (℡021/386 4400); Translux (℡012/315 2333).

Emergencies Ambulance ℡831 1954; Fire ℡832 4211; Police ℡10111.

Hospitals The best hospital for visitors is the 24hr Medi-Clinic, 177 Du Toitspan Rd (℡053/838 1111).

Internet cafés The Conxion, New Park Mall, 1 Long St (℡053/831 6597, *markw@kimnet.co.za*); Small World Net Café, 42 Sidney St (℡053/831 3484, *training@smallworld.co.za*).

Pharmacy Piet Muller Pharmacy, 52 Market Square (℡053/831 1787), is open daily until 9pm.

Swimming Karen Muir Pool in Queen's Park, off Regiment Way, is an open-air pool. Open Sept–April.

Train information ℡053/88 2631.

Around Kimberley

The handful of interesting places around Kimberley include **Barkly West**, the town where some of the first diamond camps sprung up in the 1860s, and the archeological site at **Wonderwerk Cave**. Both lie off the **R31**, which runs northwest out of Kimberley in the direction of Kuruman. This is one of the roads in the region where you will see signs warning you not to exceed 60kph because of the danger of kudu leaping out of the bushes by the side of the road. Few drivers heed the signs, but the threat is a real one, particularly at night, as these large antelope have little judgement of the speed of a vehicle and will try to jump over the beam of headlights, often with fatal results – not just for the kudu. The mostly unremarkable landscape lying to the south of Kimberley along the N12 was the setting for one of the most dramatic campaigns of the Anglo-Boer War, and if such history appeals to you the scenery around **Magersfontein** can suddenly transform into an intricate and moving storybook.

Barkly West

Originally a convenient crossing point of the Vaal River known as Klipdrif, the small town of **BARKLY WEST**, 35km northwest of Kimberley, was the first important focus of the diamond rush, out of which rose the short-lived **Klipdrif Republic**, proclaimed by militant miners as British, Boer and Griqua authorities squabbled about who was to control the area. Later, political representation came in the form of Cecil Rhodes, who was the MP for the town up to and including his time as prime minister of the Cape Colony. Visibly poor, Barkly West is in a fairly sorry state today, although the alluvial beds along the river on the fringes of town are still being worked, and on Saturday mornings diggers come to sell their week's findings to licensed buyers at the **Diamond Market**. Some of the older diggers still prospect by hand, finding perhaps just five good stones in a year and always hopeful of one "big one". If you do want to investigate further – and it can't be denied that a rough romance still surrounds the whole business – snooping around on your own is unadvisable. The best way to explore is to join one of the fascinating insider **tours** of the alluvial diggings with Dirk Potgieter of Diamond Tours Unlimited (see "Kimberley Tours" on previous page). He will take you on half-day (R200) and full-day tours (R400, inlcudes lunch) to meet both the old hand-prospectors and the more modern operators – something you aren't be able to do on your own.

DIAMONDS ARE FOREVER

Diamonds originate near the centre of the earth as particles of carbon in the earth's mantle which are subjected to such high pressure and temperature that they crystallize to form diamonds. Millions of years ago the molten rock, or magma, in the mantle burst through weak points in the earth's crust as volcanoes, and it is in the pipe of cooled magma – called **kimberlite**, after Kimberley – that diamonds are found. Finding kimberlite, however, isn't necessarily a licence to print money – in every one hundred tonnes there will be about twenty carats (4g) of diamonds. The word "carat" comes from the carob bean, which, when dried, was used as a measure of weight, now standardized as 0.2g. (Carat has a different meaning in the context of gold, where it is a measure of purity.) De Beers estimate that fifty million pieces of diamond jewellery are bought each year, which represents a lot of marriage proposals.

Along the Vaal River, close to the area where alluvial diamonds are being mined, is an area that until recently was Vaalbos National Park. Opened to the public in 1994, it was one of only thirteen national parks in the country and home to a variety of animals, including the highly endangered desert black rhino, as well as a unique confluence of vegetation types. However, it was deproclaimed in 1999 amid a local outcry that accused people in high places in local government of being more interested in the diamonds that may still lie in its alluvial plains than in the protection of its wildlife and natural environment.

Wonderwerk Cave

If you're driving further along the R31 towards Kuruman, you will pass the intriguing **Wonderwerk** (Miracle) **Cave**, a major archeological site which has revealed some of the earliest evidence of the production of fire in the world. There is a small visitors' centre on the site, run by the McGregor Museum in Kimberley, and a **campsite** and self-catering **chalet** run by the local farmer (☎053/384 0680; ①–②). If there are archeologists working in the cave and you're interested enough in what's going on to ask a few questions, you're likely to hear some fascinating things. If there's no one around, you'll have to ask at the farm for the gate to be unlocked. A small admission fee is charged.

Magersfontein

Just over 30km south of Kimberley along the N12, the Anglo-Boer War battlesite at **Magersfontein** provides a poignant reflection on the area's blood-spattered past. This is where Boer forces put trench warfare into effect against British troops, with devastating results (see box, overleaf). Signposts point the way to a recently spruced-up **Visitors' Centre** (daily 8am–5pm; small entry fee), with tea room, viewpoint and various monuments situated on the western end of the line of hills. Out on the battlefield itself, now open *veld* with springbok grazing and the occasional car throwing up a plume of dust along the dirt road, the lines of **trenches** can still be seen, along with other memorials, including a pair of granite crosses marking the graves of Scandinavian soldiers who fought on the Boer side.

One of the most enjoyable ways of finding out more about the history is to book a one-day **battlefield tour** with Steve Lunderstedt (☎053/831 4006 or mobile ☎083/732 3189), a highly entertaining and well-informed military historian. The tours provide a vivid picture of the campaign, with trips to battle sites, fortifications and gun positions, and walks on the battlefields to get a sense of the terrain and look for old shells and other evidence of fighting.

THE KIMBERLEY CAMPAIGN

At the outbreak of the **Anglo-Boer War** the Boer forces identified diamond-rich Kimberley as an important strategic base, and quickly besieged the city, trapping its residents, including Cecil Rhodes, inside. In response, the British deployed an army under **Lord Methuen** to relieve the city. The army was compelled, by its size and lack of knowledge of the terrain, to advance from the coast along the line of the railway so that a supply of troops, water, food and equipment could be ensured.

Methuen first encountered Boer forces at Belmont, just across the Orange River. This encounter was followed by further battles at Graspan and Modder River, from where the Boers made a tactical withdrawal to Magersfontein, a range of hills about 30km south of Kimberley. Here, rather than defending the top of the ridge of hills, as was their ususal tactic, the Boer generals, under the leadership of General Cronjé but the tactical direction of **Koos de la Rey**, decided to dig a line of **trenches** along the bottom of the *koppie*. In the early hours of December 11, 1899, the British, led by the Highland Regiment fresh from campaigns in North Africa and India, and considered to be the cream of the British army, advanced on Magersfontein, fully expecting the enemy to be lined along the ridge. Just before dawn, as they fanned out into attack formation, four thousand Boers in the trenches just a few hundred metres away opened fire. The use of trenches was, at that point, a forgotten tactic in modern warfare, and the element of surprise caused devastation in the ranks of Highlanders. Those not killed or wounded in the first volleys were then pinned down by snipers for the rest of the day, unable to move in the coverless *veld* and suffering appallingly under the hot sun. The next day the British withdrew back to Modder River, and the relief of Kimberley – inside which relations between Rhodes and the leader of the British garrison were becoming fraught – was delayed for two months. The defeat was one in a series of three the British suffered within what became known as "Black Week", news of which sent shock waves through the British public expecting their forces to overrun the "crude farmers" before Christmas.

If you want to **stay** in the area instead of heading back to Kimberley, a good option is *Langberg Guest Farm*, 21km south of Kimberley on the N12 (☎053/832 1001, *getaway@langberg.co.za*; ②), a very hospitable B&B set in several Cape Dutch horse stables on a historic farm at the western end of the Magersfontein battlefield. The food here is excellent and the rooms good value.

THE KALAHARI

The Northern Cape has no shortage of dry, endless expanses, but the most emotive by far is the **Kalahari**. The very name holds a resonance of sun-bleached, faraway spaces and the unknown vastness of the African interior, something at once harsh and magical. The name derives from the word *kgalagadi* (place without water), and is used in a general sense to describe the semi-desert which stretches north from the Orange River to the Okavango Delta in northern Botswana, west into Namibia and east until the bushveld begins to dominate in the catchment areas of the Vaal and Limpopo rivers.

The Kalahari here is characterized by surprisingly high, thinly vegetated red or orange sand dunes scored with dry river beds and large, shimmering saltpans. Like most deserts (although this is strictly semi-desert), daytime temperatures are searingly hot in summer and numbingly cold at night in winter. North from the Orange, South Africa's largest river which flows defiantly through the parched regions, the land is populated only by tough, hard-working farmers and communities largely (although not wholly) descended from the nomadic Khoi. For many land-users, there is an increasing realization that **ecotourism**, rather than a First World luxury, may be the only viable option on huge areas of land where both stock farming and hunting provide at best a marginal living.

Upington, the main town of the area, stands on the northern bank of the Orange, at the heart of an irrigated corridor of intensive wheat, cotton and, most prominently, grape farms. At the far end of the farming belt, about an hour east, the Orange picks up speed, and froths and tumbles into a huge granite gorge at **Augrabies Falls**, a powerful spectacle and the focus of a growing national park.

The undoubted highlight of this area is the **Kalahari-Gemsbok National Park**, which occupies a spear of South African territory thrusting up between Namibia and Botswana. Together with the **Gemsbok National Park**, the adjoining protected area on the Botswana side, it forms part of the new **Kgalagadi Transfrontier Park**, the first such venture formalized in Africa, a vast desert sanctuary rich in game, well worth the long trek you'll have to make to get there. The options if you're coming to it directly from Johannesburg along the N14 highway are either to turn off at **Kuruman**, site of a famous nineteenth-century **mission station** established by Robert and Mary Moffat, along the R31 (a long, bleak dirt road which should only be tackled in a sturdy vehicle); or to travel on to Upington, the established gateway for the park, from where the road is tarred for two-thirds of the way.

Upington

As an inevitable focus of trips heading to the Kalahari-Gemsbok and Augrabies national parks, as well those to and from Namaqualand, **UPINGTON** is a good place to stop to gather supplies, organize a park tour or onward accommodation, or simply draw breath. Situated on the banks of the Orange River, it can also be a mellow spot, although savage summer temperatures mean you probably won't want to linger for much longer than is necessary. The climate doesn't necessarily improve once you leave, but at least you're on your way to something interesting.

Arrival and information

Arriving by **car**, you'll quickly find yourself in or near the centre of town, where parking is easy, although it's always worth hunting for a bit of shade. Intercape (☎054/332 6091) **buses** will take you to the *Protea* hotels, right in the heart of town, while **minibus taxis** tend to arrive at the railway station, a ten-minute walk away. Upington's **airport** (☎054/337 7900) is 7km northeast of town, on Diedericks Road.

Central Upington is compact and easy to get around, with most of the activity on the three main streets running parallel to the river. You'll find the helpful **tourist information office** in the Kalahari Oranje Museum complex on Schroder Street (Mon–Fri 8am–5.30pm, Sat 9am–noon; ☎054/332 6064). If you want to **book a tour** from Upington to either of the national parks, see the box on p.257. You can rent **4WD vehicles** from Walker's Midas, 53 Market St (☎054/332 4441), who offer good deals with unlimited mileage (they also rent out standard cars at decent rates). Avis **car rental** (☎054/332 4746) is based at the airport, and there are other car rental agencies in town, including Budget (☎054/332 4441) and Tempest (☎054/331 2268).

Accommodation

There are enough **places to stay** in Upington for you to find something appropriate, although bear in mind that tourism here is still geared to South African holidaymakers, and the tastes of international travellers are not always catered for or even understood.

Die Eiland, on an island in the river immediately opposite the town centre (☎054/334 0286). Huge, popular, and well-run resort with pleasant campsite and self-catering chalets, the best of which are right by the river and sleep four. Camping ①, chalets ②.

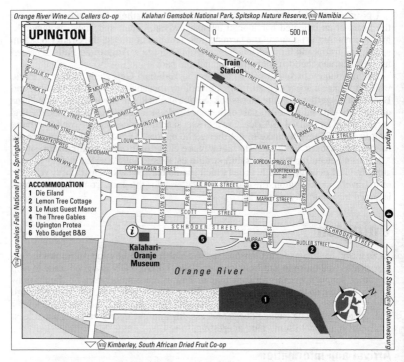

Orange River Wine △ Cellers Co-op   Kalahari Gemsbok National Park, Spitskop Nature Reserve,(N10) Namibia △

UPINGTON

ACCOMMODATION
1 Die Eiland
2 Lemon Tree Cottage
3 Le Must Guest Manor
4 The Three Gables
5 Upington Protea
6 Yebo Budget B&B

Kalahari-Oranje Museum

Orange River

▽(N10) Kimberley, South African Dried Fruit Co-op

Lemon Tree Cottage, 14 Budler St (☎054/332 1255). Comfortable self-catering apartment at the east end of the town centre (near the post office), in the grounds of an attractive house with a sultry tropical garden backing onto the river. ③.

Le Must Guest Manor, 12 Murray Ave (☎054/0332 3971, fax 332 5779, *lemusttravel@gem.co.za*). Tasteful, centrally located guesthouse in a two-storey Cape Dutch house on the riverbank. *Le Must Africa Lodge* has similarly elegant but less expensive rooms further from the centre at 26 Bult St. *Africa Lodge* ③, *Guest Manor* ④.

The Three Gables, 34 Bult St (☎054/331 1220). Decent B&B in a suburban area near the police station. One room in a mini-apartment in the large garden and one with a living room under the main house. ②.

Upington Protea, 24 Schröeder St (☎054/332 4414). More characterful of the town's two *Protea* hotels, with decent but unexceptional rooms, a few of which look out onto the river. A *Spur Steak Ranch* is downstairs. ③.

Yebo Budget B&B, 21 Morant St (☎054/331 2496). A pleasant house with spacious double rooms inside and a backpackers' dorm built on. Fairly quiet and relaxing, with a *braai* area and a pool. Dorm ①, doubles ②.

The Town and around

Upington's main disappointment is that you can see very little of the Orange River once you're in the town centre. The best place to glimpse it is from the grounds of the **Kalahari-Oranje Museum**, at the southern end of Schröder Street. The museum itself (Mon–Fri 9am–12.15pm & 2–5pm; small entry fee), based in the 1875 mission church which was the origin of the settlement here, tells a fairly predictable history. The grounds are pleasant enough, though – and you should look out for a quirky sculpture of a donkey. A couple of kilometres away at the other end of Schröder Street is an equally bizarre **statue of a camel**, which commemorates Upington's days as a frontier station, when the police – often mounted quite sensibly on camels – had to patrol large tracts of the wider Kalahari area, dealing variously with Griqua rebels, recalcitrant San bands and hostile German forces based in Namibian territory.

Thanks to irrigation schemes, Upington is surrounded by vineyards. Remarkably enough, ten percent of the country's grapes are grown in this stretch – mostly table grapes and dried fruit, but wine is also produced. **Factory tours** and tastings are available at both the Orange River Wine Cellars Co-op (Mon–Fri 8am–12.45pm & 2–5pm; free) in the industrial estate west of the town centre off Dakota Road, and the South African Dried Fruit Co-op (Mon–Fri 8am–12.45pm; free) on Louisvale Road, on the way out of town across the bridge.

Spitskop Nature Reserve

About 13km north of town along the R360, **Spitskop Nature Reserve** (dawn to dusk; ☎054/332 1336; small entry fee) offers an accessible taste of the semi-desert, although with its limited array of rather skittish antelope and other large game, the experience lacks the fullness you'll get when you venture further afield. The name Spitskop refers to a small rocky hill that offers some expansive and worthwhile views of the surrounding plains. At its base is a quiet **campsite** (①) and a simple **chalet** sleeping four (②), which are worth considering if you want the peace and quiet of being away from the town. There are hiking and mountain-bike trails throughout the reserve (staff will talk you through routes), and you can take game-viewing drives in your own car.

Eating and drinking

As the only large centre for hundreds of kilometres, Upington will seem like culinary heaven compared to the towns you'll pass through to get here. If ever conditions were right for you to appreciate a franchised **steakhouse**, this is it and, sure enough, they

---

KALAHARI TOURS FROM UPINGTON

Upington is a good place to arrange a **tour** of the North Cape's national parks. Most operators will be able to customize tours to suit your requirements. For details and prices, which vary depending on how many people are on the tour, phone the companies directly.

• **Adventure Runners** (☎011/839 4105). Canoeing and camel-back safaris on the Orange River below Augrabies Falls and into Northern Bushmanland.

• **Kalahari Adventure Centre** (☎ & fax 054/451 0177, *augrabies@cafedenet.co.za*). The outfit who offer the 8km Augrabies Rush above the falls also offer four-day canoe trails on the lower Orange and a livelier four-day whitewater rafting trip further along the Orange at Onseepkans Gorge, near Pella. They also have a four-day Kalahari Safari incorporating both national parks.

• **Kalahari Tours and Travel** (☎054/331 2252, mobile ☎082/493 5041, *kalaharitt @cafedenet.co.za*). Five-day budget tour of the Kalahari area; includes Augrabies Falls, canoeing on the Orange, with just over 24 hours in the Kalahari-Gemsbok park.

• **Molopo Safaris** (mobile ☎083/305 4227, *molopo@cafedenet.co.za*). A variety of tours offered by the acknowledged expert on 4WD in the area, including a three-day guided self-drive tour of the Kalahari-Gemsbok park and a longer safari with 4WD into Botswana. More upmarket, but well-run and authoritative.

• **Spitskop Tours and Safaris** (☎054/332 1336, *spitskop@cafedenet.co.za*). The next level up. Includes Augrabies Falls, rafting, and two days in the Kalahari-Gemsbok park. Led by a local farmer/hunter who is knowledgeable about the animals and North Cape area.

are lined up in anticipation in the town centre. Without doubt the best **restaurant** is *Le Must*, hidden behind some extravagant shrubbery at 11 Schröder St (☎054/332 3971), and serving up very imaginative South African and Provençal dishes.

For **coffee** or a snack, head for the *San Francisco* coffee shop, located in the mall bordered by Market and Hill streets, or, if your Afrikaans is feeling strong, *De Oude Kerkje Koffie Kôner* on the corner of River and Le Roux streets. Decent places to drown a **beer** include *Scotty's Bar* in the *Upington Protea*, 24 Schröeder St, and *O'Hagan's*, a few doors away.

On to the Augrabies Falls

From Upington, you're well-positioned to head to **Augrabies Falls National Park**, one of South Africa's most dramatic natural spectacles. The falls can easily be visited as a day-trip from Upington, although there are some decent accommodation both in the park itself and nearby. The route from Upington is west along the **N14**, following the Orange River and its rich fringe of vineyards, orchards and alfalfa fields. Along the road are two pleasant **campsites** situated on islands in the river: one at *Kanoneiland* (☎054/491 1147; ①) and the other at *Die Punt* (☎054/26472; ①), 20km further south.

Some 39km southwest of Upington, the road passes through **KEIMOES**, where, if you have time, it's worth driving to the top of **Tierberg Reserve**, a small *koppie* at the eastern end of town that commands impressive views over the riverine farming strip and the harsh semi-desert beyond.

The town of **KAKAMAS**, 32km from Augrabies Falls, offers a few options if you're looking for somewhere to **stay** near the park. Along Voortrekker, the shady main street, is the *Waterwiel Lodge* (☎054/431 0838; ②) and the friendly *Lapa-side* guesthouse (☎054/431 0150; ②). Alternatively, look out for the impressive *Vergelegen* guesthouse (☎054/431 0976, *vergelegen@electronet.co.za*; ③), by the roadside about 3km before you reach Kakamas, which has rooms around a courtyard and a restaurant and small shop attached. Slightly closer to the national park is *Ebenaeser Guesthouse* (☎054/431 1029; ②), set among the vineyards about halfway between Kakamas and the turning to Augrabies, while a fun place for those not demanding high levels of comfort is the *Kalahari Adventure Centre* (☎054/451 0177, *info@augrabies.co.za*), situated 12km from the park gates, where accommodation is available in tents, a tipee or unusual straw-bale rooms (all ①). To **camp** in Kakamas itself, follow the signpost to *Die Mas* (☎054/431 1150; ①), a secluded, privately owned camping and caravan site among the vineyards beside the river. The best **restaurant** in town is *Rodio*, in a modern mall behind the post office on Voortrekker.

Augrabies Falls National Park

Roaring out of the barren semi-desert just over 100km west of Upington, and sending great plumes of spray up above the brown horizon, is the most spectacular moment in the two-thousand-kilometre progress of the Orange River; the mighty waterfall still known by its Khoikhoi name, Aukoerebis, "the place of great noise".

At peak flow, the huge volume of water plunging through a narrow channel at the head of a deep granite gorge actually compares with the more docile periods at Victoria Falls and Niagara, although **Augrabies** lacks both the soul-wrenching grandeur of its larger rivals, and the prettiness of waterfalls that tumble from a greater height. However, it is free of rampant commercialization, and in its eerie desert setting, with the azure evening sky wide and smooth above, the falls provide a moving and absorbing experience.

The Falls

To **view** the falls, walk across the smooth granite domes beside the main rest camp to the fence along the edge of the gorge. The sides of the canyon are shaped like a smooth parabola and there are many tales of curious visitors going too far in their quest to peer at the falls and sliding helplessly into the seething maelstrom below. Although there is the odd miraculous survival – most famously a Scandanavian who was stripped of all his clothes by the force of the water before he was plucked out – over twenty have died since the national park was proclaimed in 1966. There is now a large fence, but ever since the suspension bridge across the gorge washed away there is no one spot where you can get a clear view of the main event, and the temptation to edge closer and closer to the edge of the gorge for a better look is strong. By being forced to try different viewpoints, however, including a dramatic spot very close to the frothing water just as it is about to launch itself over the falls, you end up with a better impression of the river and gorge as a whole.

The atmosphere, always noisy and awesome, is at its best near **sunset**, as the softer sun shines straight into the west-facing gorge and the echoing roar disappears off into a suddenly empty, ceilingless light-blue sky. To see more of the gorge, walk the short distance from the rest camp to **Arrow Point** or, if you're prepared to let the modern world intervene, drive on the link roads round to **Ararat** or **Echo Corner**.

The rest of the park

The rest of the park covers an extensive 184 square kilometres on both sides of the river. The land is dry and harsh, with plants typical of arid areas such as *kokerboom* (quiver tree), camelthorn and Namaqua fig providing sparse ground cover. The landscape is not without interest, however, and there are various striking rock formations in the park, notably some **potholes** scoured out by the river when it ran a different course to its present one, and **Moon Rock**, a huge dome of smooth, flaking granite rising out of the flat plains. If you drive on the (untarred) roads which go into the park you'll probably spot some of the resident fauna, notably **eland, klipspringer** and other small antelope. You are as likely to see the smaller animals, including dassie, mongoose and lizards, on foot as you wander around the falls and the camp.

Practicalities

The best time to visit Augrabies (daily: April–Sept 6.30am–10pm; Oct–March 6am–10pm; around R30) is from March to May, when the temperatures are slightly cooler and the river is at its maximum flow after summer rainfall up in the Lesotho catchment areas. Several **tours** run out of Upington (see box on p.257), but note that if you're coming independently, you'll have difficulty getting here without your own car as there's no public transport. It is possible to visit the park as a **day visitor**, a practical option if you're based in Upington or travelling on elsewhere, as in a couple of hours you can gather a good impression of the falls and gorge.

The **entrance gate** is 30km from the N14 along a good, tarred road; the park's **reception** (daily 7am–7pm; ☎054/451 0050) is a little way inside, and has some displays on the park. Facilities in the main camp include swimming pools, various levels of self-catering **chalets** and **cottages** (②–③), and a large **camping** and caravan area (①). Bookings are advised during school holidays (☎012/343 1991, *reservations @parks-sa.co.za*). Alongside the reception area is a shop, a self-service snack bar and a smart **restaurant** with views looking out over rocks towards the gorge.

Various **adventure activities** are promoted by the park, but none really match the adrenalin surge of the falls themselves. What can be fun is the "Augrabies Rush", a half-day trip on small rafts down 8km of increasingly swift river immediately above the falls, run by the *Kalahari Adventure Centre* (see above) for around R150.

On to Gemsbok

The journey to **Kalahari-Gemsbok National Park** is, whichever way you travel, a long, hot and weary one. You'll see plenty of the classic **red dunes** of the Kalahari, and every so often a huge, crazily paved grey saltpan, but the vegetation has been largely denuded and there is no shortage of desolate images, such as broken windmills and the rusting frames of motor cars, drowning in the desert sand.

From Upington, the R360 is tarred for 210km, after which it becomes dirt, while the longer approach via the R31 is tarred only between Kuruman and Hotazel. Drive carefully when you're on dirt roads, be extra alert at corners (where deep sand can build up), and beware of dust clouds when you pass another vehicle. It's also a good idea to reduce the pressure in your tyres by about half a bar before setting off. If you're just visiting the park, there's no need to go to the extra expense of renting a 4WD; a normal, reasonably strong car will do fine, but bear in mind that the higher the clearance the better – a car packed with four adults might struggle.

There are several **accommodation** options on the way, worth considering for a more homely experience before or after visiting the park. Remember, however, that the park's best **game viewing** is to be had first thing in the morning, so stopping en route isn't really an option if you're on a tight schedule. *Rooipan* (☎054902/91 2411; ③), is a farmhouse offering full board, as well as a strategically placed tea room, roughly halfway between Upington and the park, off the R360. At the turnoff, the *Yebo-Gogo* farmstall, a caravan brightly painted in the colours of the South African flag, is good for a drink or **snack**. Closer to the park, at **Andriesvale**, the *Molopo Lodge* (☎054/511 0008, *molopo@interkom.co.za*; ⑤) offers rondavels arranged around a very enticing pool, as well as camping sites (①). Andriesvale also has a **filling station** and a small shop. Some 7km east, along the R31 dirt road to Kuruman, is *Cromdale* (☎054902, extension 4; ②), which has a tea room and offers B&B in a small overnight cottage. Another 30km on is *Loch Broom* (☎054902, extension 91 6620; ③), a friendly guesthouse on a typical Kalahari farm.

Kalahari-Gemsbok National Park

The result of a formalization of a long-standing joint management arrangement between South Africa's **Kalahari-Gemsbok National Park** and Botswana's neighbouring **Gemsbok National Park** was the creation in 1999 of Africa's first official transfrontier park, named **Kgalagadi Transfrontier Park** after the ancient San description of the area. While the new park is a flagship for developing conservation policies in southern Africa and paves the way for other such parks, notably linking parts of Kruger National Park to protected areas in Mozambique and Zimbabwe, the recent changes are mostly symbolic, as almost all of the established tourist facilities are found in the South African section. The new park will be run as a single ecological unit and gate receipts shared, although the tourist facilities in the two separate areas will be run autonomously. It's inevitable, too, that the old names won't die away immediately, so expect to find the new park described by its former names for a few years yet.

The new park covers an area of over 38,000 square kilometres – nearly twice the size of Kruger National Park – and although the Kalahari-Gemsbok National Park is by far the smaller section, it still covers a vast 9500 square kilometres, bounded on its western side by the Namibian border, and to the south by the dry Auob River and a strip of land running parallel to this. In another recent development, this strip was returned to the local

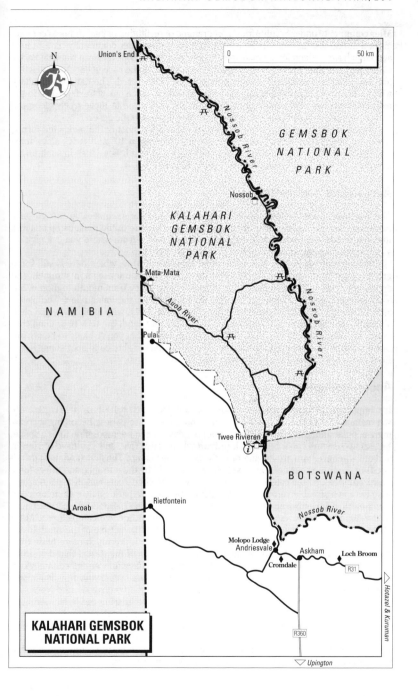

Mier community under South Africa's programme of restitution of land rights to communities that had lost land under the aparthied régime. The Mier community have in turn agreed to have the land jointly managed by themselves and South African National Parks, so the land remains part of the wildlife sanctuary, although the agreement also states that tourism opportunities for the local community will be explored. The national boundary with Botswana is along the dry Nossob River bed, along which one of the few roads in the park runs, but no fences exist along this line, allowing game to move freely along the ancient migration routes that are so necessary for survival in the desert.

The means of survival are very immediate criteria for most of the park's life forms, where any vegetation has to survive temperatures between 40° and 10°C, and a meagre rainfall of 200mm per annum. Life is not easy, and that it flourishes in such profusion and detail is the enduring wonder of the Kalahari.

Access and information

The two alternatives to making the long drive to Kalahari-Gemsbok are to go on a **package tour** (see p.257) or to **fly** by private charter plane to the main camp at Twee Rivieren (contact Walkers Fly-In Safaris; ☎082/820 5394), from where you can pick up a car by prior arrangement with Avis in Upington (see p.255).

The best time to visit the park is between **March** and **May**, when there is still some greenery left from the summer rain and the sun is not as intense as in summer. The only entrance is at **Twee Rivieren**, and opening hours vary from month to month, but if you arrive any time between 7am and 6pm, you'll find the gates open. The park's airstrip is here, as is the **Visitors' Centre** (☎054/561 0021), with exhibitions and slide shows worth checking out. All the roads in the park are sand, but they're in good condition, and a normal car will be perfectly adequate given that you're likely to be driving much slower than the 50kph speed limit to give yourself a chance to spot some game. **Fuel** is available at all three rest camps (see below).

Accommodation

It's important to **book your accommodation** (☎012/343 1991 or ☎021/22 2810, *reservations@parks-sa.co.za*) as far ahead as possible as the park is becoming increasingly popular and, especially during school holidays, it can be impossible to find space. For safety reasons you'll be given a **permit** when you arrive, and you have to sign in and out whenever you are leaving or arriving at a rest camp. The first (and most developed) of the three **rest camps,** Twee Rivieren is right by the entrance and offers functional but pleasant self-catering chalets (④), with thatched roofs and nice patio areas. Also here is a sizeable caravan and **camping** site (①), the park's only swimming pool, and a mediocre **restaurant** with inflexible opening hours (7.30–8.30am, noon–2pm & 6.30–8.30pm). A takeaway and a shop are nearby. The other two camps are at **Mata Mata**, 120km away at the end of the road which follows the course of the Auob River, and at **Nossob**, 160km along the Nossob River road. Both are much more basic than Twee Rivieren, but they hold so much of the raw flavour of the desert that it really is worth making the effort to get to one or the other. Both have fully equipped family cottages (③), simple three-person huts (②) and camping sites (①). If your time is limited, the shorter distance to Mata Mata makes more sense, but if you have longer Nossob is better both for atmosphere and game viewing: as well as hearing the lions roaring at night, you'll probably have your best chance of seeing them in this area. Not far from the Nossob camp is a water hole which has a hide overlooking it and is lit up at night. The only chance of **camping** outside the rest camps is on the Botswana side. You can get there via Twee Rivieren, but arrangements are through the Department of Wildlife and National Parks in Maun, Botswana (☎09267/66 0376).

The Park

Following the long slog to get to Twee Rivieren, be prepared to clock up even more mileage inside the park. The shortest circular game drive is over 100km long, not far short of the distance to Mata Mata rest camp. Although the network of roads through the park looks limited, it is in fact one of the most attractive things about Kalahari-Gemsbok. The main roads follow the **river beds**, and this is where the game – and their predators – are most likely to be. Water flows very rarely in the two rivers, but frequent **boreholes** have been drilled to provide water for the game. Larger **trees** such as camelthorn and *witgat* (shepherd's tree), offer a degree of shade and nutrition, and desert-adapted plants, including types of melon and cucumber, are a source of moisture for the animals. Both the outlying camps are located along the main roads which follow the river beds, so by making your way to them you're going through the best game-viewing areas.

Much of the park is dominated by **red sand dunes**, which, when seen from the air, lie strung out in long, wave-like bands across the ocean of desert. From your car, the perspective is a different one, as you are in the valley of the river bed. However, this doesn't prevent the path from offering one of the finest **game-viewing** experiences in South Africa – not only for the animals, but for the setting, with its broad landscapes, the crisp light of morning and the huge skies. **Photographers** especially prosper in the clear viewing and wonderful light, a fact you can confirm for yourself in the exhibition at the Visitors' Centre at Twee Rivieren camp or in any number of glossy coffee-table wildlife books.

The focus in Kalahari-Gemsbok is on game drives; there aren't many alternative activities on offer. During the main holiday season, short walks across the dunes are organized at Twee Rivieren as a way of seeing some of the smaller manifestations of life in the park, but you'll have to ask to find out whether these are available at other times.

Seeing the animals

The game-viewing highlights in Kalahari-Gemsbok are, inevitably, the predators, headed by the **Kalahari lion** and, enjoying rare status alongside the Big Five, **gemsbok**, the large, lolloping animal with classically straight, V-shaped horns. You won't find buffalo, elephant or rhino, but their presence is hardly missed. Of the remaining Big Five, the **leopard**, as elsewhere, is not uncommon, but manages to remain elusive. In the wide open spaces, with its light colours blending so well with the sandy environment, lion here have an image as noble and inspiring as anywhere in Africa. Although they are not considered a separate species, the Kalahari lions commonly have much darker manes than those found in the bushveld, and studies have shown their behavioural and eating patterns to be distinctively well-adapted to the semi-desert conditions here.

Beyond the Big Five, there is much to absorb you, both large and small, with various species of **antelope**, **hyena**, **jackal**, **bat-eared fox**, **cheetah**, and some extravagant **birdlife**, including raptors, bustards and ostrich.

The best time to take your game drives is as early as possible in the morning, when you're more likely to see game out in the open. The shortest drive you are likely to take will be four or five hours long, so an early start means less time outside as the desert sun approaches its zenith. The last couple of hours of light in the afternoon are also a good time for game (and for taking photographs), but it's a lot more relaxing to go out for a little foray from your base than to be en route for a new camp, destined to arrive just as it's getting dark. The middle section of the day, especially during summer, is a necessarily inactive time for both animals and humans, so don't plan too full a programme.

THE MOFFATS AND THEIR MISSION

Robert and Mary Moffat, newly married and envoys of the London Missionary Society, arrived in the Kuruman area in 1820, initially at a place rather charmingly mistranslated by early explorers as Lattakoo, about 14km from Kuruman. As a former market gardener, however, Moffat soon saw the advantages of irrigating the flow of The Eye of Kuruman, and began to build his mission on the closest land wide and flat enough to plough.

Moffat didn't clock up too many converts – by the time he had built his 800-seater church he had just nine – but the challenge of preaching and establishing a school inspired him not only to learn the local language, which he did by living for a period in a remote Tswana village, but also to attempt the daunting task of **translating the Bible** into Tswana, which he then published on an iron printing press, now on display in the old mission schoolroom.

The late nineteenth century was a time when the popular imagination of Victorian Britain about "Darkest Africa" was at its height and missionaries had the status of movie stars today. The Moffats may have lived for fifty years in a remote outpost of Africa, but they were treated as celebrities when they retired back to Britain in 1870, not least because of the continuing exploits of their son-in-law. The Mission at Kuruman, meanwhile, carried on until the passing of the Group Areas Act of 1950, which brought about the end of the school and the church as a functioning place of (multiracial) worship. The old Mission, neglected and forgotten, was revived in the Eighties as an interdenominational trust, and a retreat and conference centre has been built behind the old village, under the supervision of a permanent warden and volunteer staff.

Kuruman and around

Lying on the border between the Northern Cape and Northwest Province, the historic settlement of **KURUMAN** is an important stop on the way to the Kalahari-Gemsbok Park if you're travelling from Gauteng. The settlement grew up around **The Eye**, a natural spring which, since time immemorial and through drought and flood, has consistently delivered twenty million litres a day of crystal-clear water. The Eye was the focal point for a rather unsettled Tswana clan called the **Batlhaping**, whose chief, Mothibi, first invited missionaries to live among his people in the early nineteenth century, a decision that led to the building of the famous **Mission Station** by Robert Moffat, and the establishment of Kuruman as the "Gateway to the Interior" of darkest Africa.

Kuruman's town centre is pretty scruffy, dominated by cut-price chain stores, faceless bulk-buying supermarkets and litter-strewn minibus taxi ranks. The only sight of interest is The Eye, just along from the information office, and even here there's not much to look at: a moss-covered slab of rock dribbling water and a lily-covered pond surrounded by a high green fence, which you'll be charged a nominal sum to get past.

Moffat Mission Station

Of far greater interest than Kuruman itself, lying on the outskirts of town, just over 4km from the N14 along the R31 to Hotazel, is the **Moffat Mission Station** (Mon–Sat 8am–5pm, Sun 3–5pm; small entry fee). This collection of old stone-and-red-clay buildings was, for many years in the mid-nineteenth century, the focal point of that vague concept, the South African "Interior". It was here that a large, often gruff, energetic Scot, **Robert Moffat**, and his demure but equally determined wife, **Mary**, established a mission station (see box) where they lived for 50 years. During this time they produced the first Tswana Bible, a remarkable feat of publishing, and saw their eldest daughter, also called Mary, married to missionary/explorer, **David Livingstone**.

The Mission is a pleasant place in which spend a few hours wandering around. Charmingly overgrown and shaded by tall acacia and camelthorn trees, the old village includes the Moffat homestead, with furniture and exhibits inside, the schoolroom housing the Tswana printing press, and the large rough-stone church, with rows of pews standing on an uneven clay floor, huge rafters holding up a thatched roof and shafts of sunlight angling in through the small windows and split wooden door. In front of the homestead is the furrow that carried water from The Eye, and beyond that, in Mary Moffat's garden, is the stump of the almond tree (it was taken out by lightning) under which David Livingstone proposed to his future wife. It wasn't the last tree Livingstone (who had been recruited as a missionary by Robert Moffat during a lecture tour in Britain) was to make famous during his forays into darkest Africa. It was under a tree in Ujiji on the shores of Lake Tanganyika that he famously encountered H.M. Stanley, and when he died a few years later, in Ilala in present-day Zambia, his servants cut out his heart and buried it under a tree there. Appropriately, when the rest of his body returned to Britain for a state funeral at Westminster Abbey, one of the pallbearers was his father-in-law, Robert Moffat.

Practicalities

Ignore misleading street signs for the **tourist information office** (Mon–Fri 7.30am–1pm & 2–4.30pm; ☎053/712 1095); the building you want is on Main Road (the N14), between the main junction with Voortrekker (the R31) and The Eye. The office is located in the old *drostdy* (magistrate's house), which also has a pleasant **tea room** inside.

The cheapest **rooms** in town are at the Moffat Mission (☎053/712 1352; ①), in the conference centre just behind the old homestead. Bear in mind, however, that this a quiet retreat, not a lively hostel. For a bit more money, you might try *Janke Guest House*, 16 Chapman St (☎053/712 0949; ③), a large house obvious from the road as you head out towards the Mission, or *Nooitgedacht Guest House*, 5 Melville St (☎053/712 0904), which has a large garden with water from the Eye flowing past. You can **camp** at *Kuruman Caravan Park* (☎053/712 1479; ①), 500m from Main Road on the Kimberley road, although *Red Sands Country Lodge* (☎053/712 0033; ①), a **resort** set among some hills 15km along the N14 towards Upington, is a much more pleasant option if you avoid noisy weekends and school holidays. *Red Sands* also has chalets (③) and a restaurant.

The best of a very limited choice of **eating** places in Kuruman is *Over-de-Voor* restaurant, on Main Road, in a small white building with a green roof, across from The Eye.

On to Tswalu Private Desert Reserve

Some 60km north of Kuruman is a tiny settlement which vies with Pofadder as being the epitome of dead-end, deserted *dorps* in the Northern Cape: **Hotazel**. The town's name, coined by the first surveyors of the land, is its outstanding feature and, unless you're braving the long R31 to get to the Kalahari-Gemsbok park, you can get by with telling your friends: *"Sjoe, I was up in the Northern Cape, not far from that place called Hotazel. And boy, wasn't it just."*

The one other reason you might be out on this road is to get to the upmarket **Tswalu Private Desert Reserve** (☎053/781 9311, fax 781 9216, *tswalu@kimberley.co.za*), an impeccably stylish and expensive game lodge tucked under the Korannaberg Mountains, which rise to 1500m, not far from the tiny settlement of Sonstraal. The largest privately owned game reserve in South Africa, Tswalu was created by an English businessman, the late Steven Boler, who spent R50 million bringing nine thousand head of game to this desert setting, including **buffalo**, **lion** and, by special arrangement with the Namibian government, eight highly endangered **desert black rhino**. Part rich-man's dream, part dedicated wildlife protection project, and part glamorous safari experience, Tswalu is designed to compete with the finest of the private game lodges of the Kruger Park and Natal. A package stay here will put you in your own luxurious thatched stone house, complete with wooden deck giving splendid views of the Kalahari. Sumptuous meals, a swimming pool and game drives are included in the **price** – roughly US$400 per person per night, with a low-season rate of US$260 per night. Air transfers from Johannesburg are also available – contact the reserve for more details.

NAMAQUALAND

Namaqualand . . . tells the truth about the brevity of life, while offering flowers as symbols of hope and courage. We are able to believe that, like flowers buffeted, beaten and scarred by external forces, we can still attain moments of excellence and great beauty.

Freeman Patterson

Namaqualand is another of the regions in the Northern Cape with a name that conjures up a blend of desolation and magic. It is the land of the **Nama** people, Khoikhoi herders who were divided between the Little Nama, who lived south of the **Orange River**, and the Great Nama, who lived north of the river in what is now Namibia. Still sparsely populated, the region stretches south from the Orange to the empty **Knersvlakte** plains around Vanrhynsdorp, and from the **Atlantic coast** east to the edge of the winter rainfall area, somewhere beyond **Pofadder** in Bushmanland. Above all Namaqualand is synonymous with the incredible annual display of brightly coloured **wild flowers** which carpet the landscape in August and September, undoubtedly one of South Africa's most compelling spectacles. Outside the flower season – and it's worth noting that the "season" here is in August and September – swaths of orange, purple and white daisies are about the last thing you'd expect to emerge from the dry, empty landscape. Yet there is a tenacious beauty about the landscape, with mountain deserts, mineral-bearing granite hills, and drought-defiant succulents. An oft-quoted saying about the region, but one worth repeating, is that in Namaqualand you weep twice – once when you first arrive and once when you have to leave.

The area is reached by the **N7** highway which runs north from Cape Town. While flowers occur as far south as Darling (see p.228), the town of **Vanrhynsdorp** marks the start of the northern section of the flower area, with the region's capital, **Springbok**, well-placed right at its heart. From here roads lead north to the Orange River and Namibia, west to the coast at **Port Nolloth** and the remote but spectacular **Richtersveld National Park**, and east along the **N14** to Upington.

THE PRIVATE WORLD OF FLOWERS

The seeds of the multicoloured daisies, mesembryanthemums (*vygies*), aloes, gladioli and lilies, which make up the spectacular **flowers of Namaqualand**, lie dormant under the soil through the harshest droughts of summer, waiting for the rain that sometimes takes years to fall. Because different species – about four thousand are found in the area – react to different conditions, in any given place the flowers will come at different times each year, and any attempt to predict the venues of the best displays will always be fraught with uncertainty.

One of the keys is **winter rainfall**, unusual in semi-desert ecosystems, which is why the flowers appear only in August and September; and the other is **temperature**, which is why flowers rarely open before 10am and on cool or cloudy days the displays are muted. In simple terms, the flowers stay closed to protect their pollen from being blown away by the wind, which they assume is blowing if the temperature is below 16°C.

FLOWER TACTICS

A few days before you get to the flower areas, try and plan where the flowers are most likely to be. They follow the rainfall, so early in the season they will be out near the coast, moving steadily inland. Phone the tourist information offices in the area for guidance and for help organizing accommodation. Decide whether you'd rather stay on a farm or in one of the main centres, such as Calvinia or Springbok, from where you can follow a wider range of routes. You can also contact the central Flowerline in Cape Town (mid-July to early October; ☎021/418 3705) for help and information.

• Day by day, plan your route before you head out. Speak to your hosts, who often have inside information about the best spots on a particular day, or talk to the tourist information offices or Flowerline. Be warned, however, that their information is more public and you do sometimes get "gold rush" situations, with everyone flocking to certain places.

•Remember that the flowers open up around 10am and close between 3pm and 4pm, which gives you plenty of time for a good breakfast and to get yourself where you want to be. Because the flowers orientate themselves to face the sun, it's best to drive westwards in the morning, eastwards in afternoon, and generally from south to north.

•Get out of your car! All the most dedicated flower-watchers have muddy patches on their knees.

Although it goes without saying, don't pick the flowers. Take pictures or, if you're hopeless at that, buy a book such as the widely available *Garden of the Gods* by Freeman Patterson.

•Pack warm clothes, as it gets chilly at night.

•If it's rainy or dull, drive down to the coast, go for a walk in the mountains or improve your Voortrekker history in the museums in places such as Vanrhynsdorp, Calvinia or Springbok.

Northern Cape flower routes

Flower-viewing anywhere in Namaqualand demands that you spend a lot of time in your **car**, simply because the distances in this region are so great and because flowers can never be guaranteed and you may spend some time tracking them down. If you don't have a car your options are limited. Walking among the flowers is a highly recommended way of seeing them, but you have to get to them in the first place, and **bus tours** tend to be inflexible. **Cycling** is an option, although with accommodation at a premium in the flower season you'd need to organize your itinerary carefully, as it becomes a frustrating business when you're told that the best displays are 20km away.

The pre-eminence of the car means that the best way to approach the flower region is by thinking in terms of **routes**: either drives between two centres, or loops out from and returning to a specific town. Any route generally involves a combination of main roads to get to different areas and back roads to get into the countryside, where you can drive slowly or stop and get out to look at the flowers a bit more closely.

The flower areas of Namaqualand are most commonly approached from Cape Town and, while coming this far north involves a lot more time and effort than making one- or two-day trips out of Cape Town, the rewards are found in the variety of landscapes, and thus flowers, that you will encounter, the openness and breadth of the scenery and, perhaps above all, in realizing the vast geographical scope of this remarkable phenomenon.

Vanrhynsdorp to Springbok

Although not strictly part of Namaqualand and still within the Western Cape, the town of **Vanrhynsdorp** is really the gateway to the Northern Cape flower routes. It marks the crossroads between the N7 (the main road north) and the R27, which connects with

> Note that **phone numbers** for Vanrhynsdorp are due to change throughout 1999 and 2000. If you have any difficulties, call ☎1023.

Calvinia and ultimately Upington, on the northern fringe of the Great Karoo. The stretch of N7 between Vanrhynsdorp and **Springbok** eventually becomes attractive among the **Kamiesberg Mountains** between Garies and Springbok, although the 100km of **Knersvlakte** plains immediately north of Vanrhynsdorp can seem bleak and grey, particularly out of flower season.

Vanrhynsdorp and around

The main street in **VANRHYNSDORP** is Van Riebeeck, dominated by a tall church steeple at its far end. The town's **museum** is here (Mon–Fri 8am–1pm & 2–4.30pm), featuring a collection of old domestic and military pieces, neither compelling nor dreadfully dull and, as with many such places, there's always a bit of gentle fun to be had in looking out for poor English translations on the labels.

If you travel to the outskirts of town on Voortrekker Street, which runs parallel to and south of Van Riebeeck, you'll soon reach a succulent **nursery** (☎02727/91062) run by Buys Wiese, an expert in the succulents that grow in such profusion in the area. Around a third of the succulent species found in the world grow in this region, many of them endemic. You can buy plants at the nursery or, more practically for overseas visitors, obtain a permit for the three-kilometre-long **succulent trail**, situated 25km north of town off the N7 and a worthwhile diversion if you're travelling on that way. As well as displaying a fascinating range of succulents, the walk introduces you to the unusual **Knersvlakte**, the name given to the bleak plains covered in small white pebbles which lie to the north of Vanrhynsdorp. *Knersvlakte* means "plains of the gnashing teeth", and is taken to refer to the sound made by wagon wheels toiling across the fierce terrain, which you may notice bears a resemblance to the pebble-dash effect people pay large sums to have adorning their suburban driveway.

PRACTICALITIES

The first thing you come to after turning off the highway into town are two service stations, open twenty-four hours a day for fuel and food. The Shell garage is also the halt for **intercity buses** and **minibus taxis** departing for Cape Town, Springbok or Upington. There's a simple and friendly **tourist information office** (Mon–Fri 8am–1pm & 2–4.30pm; ☎ & fax 02727/91552) in the museum, on the right as you approach the church. Right beside this is the town's old gaol, now home to the *Jailhouse* (☎02727/91251), the best place to stop for a cup of tea or a hearty traditional **meal**.

If you're planning on **staying** more than one night, you're probably best off looking for somewhere on a farm or in the nearby mountains. The *Namaqualand Country Lodge*, Voortrekker St (☎02727/91633; ③), is the town's rather gloomy and plain **hotel**. Best of the **guesthouses** in town is *Van Rhyn's*, Van Riebeeck St (☎02727/91429; ②), which offers reasonable rooms in a converted stable. On the outskirts of town, the *Vanrhynsdorp Caravan Park*, Gifberg Rd (☎02727/91287), is reasonably quiet out of season and has a cheap **campsite** and self-catering **chalets** (all ①). Some 29km south of town, on the plateau of a nearby mountain, *Gifberg Farm* (☎ & fax 02727/91555; ①–②) has a large farmhouse and some old self-catering cottages to rent, as well as a network of paths and trails. A good base for finding flowers is the friendly *Aties Farm Guesthouse* (☎02727/91534; ③), signposted 7km south of town along the N7, and then signposted a further 7km along a dirt road.

Garies and Kamieskroon

North from Vanrhynsdorp the N7 carries on across the Knersvlakte, towards some distant hills, before passing **GARIES**, the first town inside the boundary of the Northern

Cape. A sleepy *dorp* for much of the year, Garies comes to life during the flower season, when the **Town Hall** is used as a flower information centre and casual market. There are a couple of **hotels**, of which the *Garies* (☎027/652 1042; ③) is reasonable. Further along Main Street, a left- rather than a right-hand turn if you're coming in from the N7 leads to a pleasant caravan park (☎027/652 1014) with a bit of grass for **camping** and some nice views up the Green Valley.

About 50km north of Garies, the village of **KAMIESKROON** is set among the Kamiesberg Mountains, beneath the rocky peak – or *kroon* – from which it takes its name. There isn't much to the village other than a pretty setting, the crisp air of the mountains and, in flower season, a sense of the privilege of being at the heart of the garden of the gods. As you come off the highway the village is to the right, while to the left is the *Kamieskroon* (☎027/672 1614, fax 672 1675, *kamieshotel@kingsley*.co.za; ④), seemingly an inauspicious wayside **hotel**, but in fact one of the few vibrant, creative nodes of Namaqualand. The hotel has become famous for running photographic workshops during the flower season (see box below), and is the centre for a growing number of activities in the surrounding Kamiesberg. The hotel also has a **camping** area (①), which is a much better option than the caravan park in the village.

Deeper into the mountains, at places east of Kamieskroon such as **Lelifontein** and **Nourivier**, the land is owned and farmed as a community project by the local Nama people, and in places you will see families living in traditional *matjieshuis* (reed huts). These settlements, many of which are still based around a mission, are connected by dirt roads, and so make good flower-viewing routes. A place worth going to in flower season, even if you're just passing through on the highway, is the **Skilpad Wildflower Reserve** (in flower season 8am–5pm; moderate entry fee), 7km to the west of Kamieskroon. The displays here tend to be more reliable than elsewhere, and this is one place where you will see great swaths of orange colour. There is a circular drive around the reserve, but only a few facilities, including toilets and a farmstall offering light meals. The reserve has recently been taken over by South African National Parks and may well undergo a name change, but while there are plans to increase its size, stock the area with animals, and open the reserve year round, there will be little change to what flower-seekers will find here in season.

Vanrhynsdorp to Calvinia

Heading **east from Vanrhynsdorp towards Calvinia** on the R27, you have a very clear impression of the sudden elevation of the land from the plains up to the Bokkeveld escarpment, which the road tackles by way of **Van Rhyn's Pass**, complete

---

KAMIESKROON PHOTOGRAPHIC WORKSHOPS

If you're in Namaqualand for the flowers, it's likely you'll take a few photos. Capturing the immensity and spectacle of the landscapes on film is no easy task though, and one way of improving your chances is to book a place on one of the popular **Photography Workshops** at the *Kamieskroon Hotel*. Here you'll learn about your camera, your eye, and the inspiring landscape and flora of Namaqualand, and hear the odd epiphany about the meaning of life. The residential courses last for a week, and involve lectures, tuition and field work under the instruction of the dynamic Colla Swart (whose family run the hotel) and the internationally renowned Canadian photographer **Freeman Patterson**, whose coffee-table book on the flowers of Namaqualand, *The Garden of the Gods*, is a classic portrait of the region. Although flowers are the principal focus, workshops are also held in the autumn (March & April), when field work takes place around the dunes on the Atlantic coast near Hondeklip Bay. The workshops are often booked out, so contact the hotel as far in advance as you can (☎027/672 1614, fax 672 1675, *kamieshotel@kingsley.co.za*; full board & tuition R3500).

GLENLYON

The old Bedford bus is called – naturally – Flora, and she is one of the great characters of Nieuwoudtville. Behind the wheel is another, **Neil MacGregor**, a man whose love and knowledge of the botany of the land he has farmed all his life has won him admiration not just in Namaqualand, but around the world. The visitors' book at **Glenlyon**, Neil and Neva MacGregor's farm just outside town, includes such names as David Attenborough, who came with the BBC Wildlife team to film *The Private World of Plants*, and Sir Ghilleam Prance, director of Kew Gardens in London. Each flower season, during the months of August and September, Neil and Flora take tours around the farm, a sixty-five-square-kilometre property where he breeds pure merino sheep and has been striving for three decades to prove that farming and the spectacular natural flora can flourish successfully alongside one another. The party piece at Glenlyon are orange bulbinellas, but Neil's enthusiasm and expertise soon have you down on your hands and knees examining all kinds of fascinating flowers. Tours lasts for two and a half hours and depart each day during the season at 2pm.; for details and prices, phone ☎02726/81200.

with a couple of neck-achingly tight hairpins near the top. There is an excellent viewpoint, signposted soon after you reach the plateau, which looks out over the plains. You'll notice (as the early settlers did, much to their relief, after hauling their ox wagons up the escarpment) that the vegetation on top of the plateau is suddenly more fertile.

Halfway between **Nieuwoudtville** and Calvinia, the R27 is joined by the **R364**, a dirt road which connects with **Clanwilliam** via the inspiring **Botterkloof** and **Pakhuis passes**. This is one of the more spectacular remote drives in the Western Cape area, particularly if there are flowers decorating the roadsides.

Nieuwoudtville

Ten kilometres on from the top of Van Rhyn's Pass, the R27 passes just to the north of attractive **NIEUWOUDTVILLE**, with its appealing collection of tin-roofed, honey-coloured sandstone buildings. On your left as you drive through on Voortrekker Road (the only tarred road), look out for a grand **church** set in a large plot of happily unkempt ground. An **information centre** (☎02726/81336) operates out of the house in the church grounds during flower season only and is a reliable source of local advice; year-round local **information** is best obtained at the *Smitswinkel* restaurant on Neethling Street. The flower season here is also notable for the highly recommended **tours** run by **Neil MacGregor**, one of the gurus of Namaqualand flowers, on his farm, Glenlyon (see box above).

Places to stay include the simple *Nieuwoudtville Hotel* (☎02726/81046; ②) and three pleasant guesthouses run by the *Smitswinkel* restaurant (☎02726/81535, fax 81426, *nieuvz@interkom.co.za*; ②). Just over 1km outside town is a pleasant **campsite**; book a spot here through the municipality office (☎02726/81316; ①). For somewhere to **eat**, head for the excellent *Smitswinkel* (open for lunch, afternoon tea and pre-booked dinners), or the *braai* house attached to the village store on the corner of Voortrekker and Nassau roads.

Around Nieuwoudtville

Some 2km east of Nieuwoudtville on the R27 is the town's **wild flower reserve**, an area which, because it is at the edge of the escarpment and receives unusually high rainfall, boasts over three hundred different species. Seven kilometres north from town, towards the settlement of Loeriesfontein, is **Bokkeveld Nature Reserve** and its ninety-metre waterfall which, when the Doring River is flowing between April and October, tumbles down into an impressive gorge where large raptors can sometimes be seen soaring around the tall cliffs.

Worthwhile for those who have a bit of time in the area, and also worth considering out of flower season, is a hike or visit to **Oorlogskloof Nature Reserve** (Mon–Fri 8am–4pm), perched on the edge of the escarpment south of Nieuwoudtville. The entrance to the reserve, which has various hiking and mountain-bike trails and natural swimming pools, is through **Arendskraal Farm**, to the east of Nieuwoudtville, but you must contact the conservator at the municipality office in town before visiting (☎02726/81159, after 4pm 81010), where you can also get maps.

Some of the farms around Nieuwoudtville offer **accommodation** in classic old thatched Karoo cottages, ranging from typically hearty farmhouse B&B to more basic self-catering rooms. *Kliprivier* (☎02726/81204; ①–②) and *Papkuilsfontein* (☎02726/81246; ①–②) are recommended.

Calvinia and around

Despite its stern name, bestowed by an early dominee, **CALVINIA** has quite an appealing prospect beneath the Hantam Mountains. The town acts as a service centre for a large area, but it isn't a place you'll want to spend a lot of time in, unless you are here for the flowers in the surrounding area. Outside flower season the **climate** can make the area fairly unwelcoming, with temperatures climbing towards 40°C during summer and dipping below freezing in winter, when snow is sometimes seen on the mountains.

The centre of Calvinia is dominated by the **Dutch Reformed church**, although it now has to vie for your attention with a cylindrical water storage tank dressed up as a huge red **postbox**, just along on Hope Street. The idea behind this was to create a tourist attraction, and however crass the concept it does turn heads. Letters and post-cards posted in the box will be stamped with a special postmark. Immediately opposite the postbox is a more serious attraction, **Hantam Huis** (daily 7.30am–5pm), the oldest building in Calvinia, which has won various awards for its restoration. Inside it's principally a tea room (see "Practicalities") and gift shop.

The large **Calvinia Museum** (Mon–Fri 8am–1pm & 2–5pm, Sat 8am–noon; small entry fee) is housed in a 1920 Art Deco synagogue on Church Street, a link to the sizeable Jewish community which once lived in town but has since melted away (one of its more famous sons is the Shakespearean actor Antony Sher, who was born in nearby Middlepost). Inside are some extensive displays of settler life, including old wooden flour mills, printing presses, huge forge bellows and no fewer than six pianos. There are also some bizarre exhibits, which include a black wedding dress and a display of *dagga* (marijuana) pipes. Predictably, a display cabinet displaying the memorabilia of the town's two rugby Springboks is as large as that showing San artefacts.

Practicalities

Despite its isolation, Calvinia is on a main cross-country route, and Intercape **buses** and **minibus taxis** travelling between Upington, Vanrhynsdorp and Cape Town stop at Trokkies Service Station at the western entrance to town. Tickets for the Intercape services are available in, of all places, the butcher's shop on Hope Street (☎0273/41 1073). You'll find the **tourist information office** (Mon–Fri 8am–1pm & 2–5pm, Sat 8am–noon; ☎0273/41 1712) in the museum, where staff give you details of the **flower routes** in the Hantam district.

The most characterful **accommodation** option is the collection of **old town houses** operated by Hantam Huis (☎ & fax 0273/41 1606; ③) – all wooden floors, lace curtains and quirky antique furnishings. The houses are self-catering, but you can make arrangements for meals; you rent by the room but you'll often end up with a house to yourself. Opposite Hantam Huis, another nineteenth-century building, 35 Water St, houses *Pionierslot Guesthouse* (☎0273/411263; ③) – the most pleasant **rooms** here are

---

| THE GREAT KAROO |

Strange though it may seem, the **Great Karoo**, the vast, dry, empty interior of South Africa was, some 250 million years ago, an equally vast inland lake. It was populated by tiny marine creatures and, around its fringes, dinosaur-like amphibians, some of which left footprints in the mud that have been preserved as fossils, making the area a fascinating one for paleontologists. The contrast now could hardly be greater, with slow creaking windmills struggling to bring water to the surface and the baked, brown-red earth roamed only by small herds of antelope or tough merino sheep.

Farmers here talk about the terrain in terms of hectares per sheep rather than sheep per hectare. The summer heat is fierce, the winter biting cold, the rain elusive, and the soil all but barren. Yet the Karoo has a special place for many South Africans, who take an almost perverse joy in the crisp air, the colours of the scattered *koppies* at sunset, the vastness of the pale sky, the depth of the darkness at night and the jostling galaxies of stars.

---

in the side annex. Elsewhere, the *Commercial*, Water St (☎0273/41 1020; ②) offers standard **hotel** rooms, and behind the bar is the engaging "tycoon of Calvinia", septuagenarian Cecil Traut, a man with a long grey beard, a soft voice and a collection of well over two thousand different ties, which decorate every wall, nook and cranny of the bar. The **camping and caravan park** (☎0273/41 1011; ①) is on the corner of Station and Hofmeyr streets, on the way through town towards the Upington road. *Hantam Huis* is the place to head for traditional **food**, while *Die Blou Nartjie* restaurant (closed Sat lunch & all day Sun; ☎0273/4114848) is a rather grander affair within *Pionierslot Guesthouse*. The *Paladium* café on Stigling Street sells tasty **ice cream**. Remember that the word for ice cream in Afrikaans is *roomys*, which, when writ large on a shop front, can cause some confusion if you're crawling around town looking for accommodation.

Into the Great Karoo

Just beyond Calvinia the road splits, with the R27 going north through **Brandvlei** and **Kenhardt** towards Upington, while the R63 goes west through **Williston** and **Carnarvon** to Victoria West and the main N12 route between Cape Town and Johannesburg via Kimberley. Other than their sheer isolation, these Karoo settlements throw up the odd interesting feature, such as ancient fossil remains and corbelled houses; whitewashed, beehive-like constructions built because of the lack of timber available for roofs.

South of Calvinia there is a remote area of land shaded on the maps as the **Tankwa-Karoo National Park**. It has been gazetted to protect a sector of succulent Karoo habitat, but is still in recovery phase after overgrazing by sheep and is not open to the public.

Springbok and around

SPRINGBOK is the main commercial and administrative centre of Namaqualand, and an important staging post on the N7. It lies around 550km from Cape Town, just over 100km south of the border with Namibia, and marks the junction with the **N14**, which runs right across the Northern Cape through Upington and ultimately on to Johannesburg. Springbok's great assets are its strategic position and reliable supply of good information, food and bed space.

Note that **phone numbers** for Springbok are due to change throughout 1999 and 2000. If you have any difficulties, call ☎1023.

The main action in town is centred on a mound of granite boulders called Klipkoppie (Rocky Hill), the site of a British fort blown up by General Jan Smuts' commando during the Anglo-Boer War. A short walk up Monument Street will bring you to the town's **museum** (Mon–Fri 8.30am–3.30pm; small entry fee) in an old synagogue, and a little way along from this at the back of town is the **Blue Mine**, the first commercial copper mine in South Africa, sunk in 1852, and reopened in 1998 to mine gemstones – previously ignored in the search for copper ore – for the Far East market.

Following the R355 past Springbok airport to the southwest of town for around 10km will take you to **Goegap Nature Reserve** (daily 8am–4pm; small entry fee), an important area described as "Namaqualand in miniature". The reserve incorporates the **Hester Malan Wild Flower Garden**, always a draw during the flower season. Two-day hiking trails, mountain bike trails and 4WD routes are on offer; the Visitors' Centre (8am–4pm; ☎0251/21880) can provide details. **Self-catering accommodation** is available in a couple of large chalets (②).

Practicalities

Flights from Cape Town arrive at Springbok's **airport** (☎0251/22380), 5km out of town along the R355 road to Goegap Nature Reserve. Intercape **buses** drop off in front of the *Springbok Lodge*, while the **minibus taxi** rank is on Landros Street, behind the First National Bank; VIP Taxis (☎027/851 8780) serve Port Nolloth, Upington and Kimberley. For **car rental** try Jowell's, Voortrekker Rd (☎0251/22061), or Richtersveld Challenge, Jurie Kotze Rd (☎0251/21905), for 4WD. Springbok's very useful **tourist information centre** (Mon–Fri 7.30am–4.15pm, daily during flower season; ☎0251/22011) is in the little Anglican church beside the post office on Namakwa Street. Another valuable source of local wisdom (and good **food**) is the *Springbok Lodge & Restaurant* on the corner or Voortrekker and Keerom roads. This local institution, whose owner, Jopie Kotze, sits rather like a godfather behind a counter at the back of the restaurant, is a hub for travellers, information-swapping and local chitchat. You could also try the *Melkboskuil Coffee Shop* (Mon–Fri 8am–5pm, Sat 8am–1pm) for tips on what to do locally, including advice on local hiking and mountain biking.

The cheapest and most original **accommodation** is at *Namastat* (☎0251/22435), a small cluster of *matjieshuis* (reed huts ①, wooden huts ②) 2km south of Springbok on the road in from the N7. There are shared washing facilities and a bar that serves traditional *potjiekos* meals in the evening. For **camping**, *Springbok Caravan Park* (☎0251/81584; ①) is 2km out of town along the R355 to Goegap, and has a swimming pool, but is near the noisy highway. Back in town, *Springbok Lodge & Restaurant* (☎0251/21321, fax 22718; ②) encompasses a variety of houses, mostly painted in white and yellow and including **dorms**, self-catering and large **doubles** with lounge, air conditioning and bath (all ②); go to Jopie's desk at the back of the restaurant to make arrangements. The smartest **hotel** is the Art Deco *Masonic Hotel*, Van Riebeeck St (☎0251/21505; ④), while *Naries Guest House* (☎0251/22462; ⑤), offers excellent dinner, bed and breakfast on a large farm 27km west of Springbok – perfect for flower season although you'll have to book well in advance to secure a room.

North to the Namibian border

Only 8km north of Springbok on the N7 is the slightly scruffy little town of **OKIEP**, which took over from Springbok as the copper-mining centre of Namaqualand in the 1880s. Miners and engineers from the tin mines in Cornwall arrived to help establish the mines, and you can still visit both the easily identified **smokestack** and **Cornish beam pump** beside it; visits are arranged through the *Okiep Country Hotel* (☎0251/41000), under the palm trees on the main street. The hotel itself is pleasant enough, with rooms in the main building (③) or in an annex (②).

Some 40km further north, **Stienkopf** marks the junction of the N7 with the **R382** to Port Nolloth and the **Richtersveld National Park**. Then, for the next 50km the N7 crosses some fairly bleak Namaqualand plains, before beginning to descend through a band of rocky hills, burnt black and ochre in the heat, and into a haunting pass with the Scrabble-winning name of **Vwfmylpoort**. The road then breaks through into the green flood plain of the **Orange River**, which marks South Africa's northern border with Namibia. The gathering of buildings on the South African side of the river is called **Vioolsdrif**, but there isn't much here apart from a filling station, a dusty store and a high-fenced government building.

A turning here along a dirt road traces the south bank of the Orange, 20km along which is a **campsite** right on the edge of the river, called *Peace of Paradise* (leave a message at ☎02521/8168; ①). It certainly lives up to its name, with some lush green grass to camp on, the meandering river to swim in and a bar serving ice-cold beer.

If you're going on into Namibia from Vioolsdrif you have to clear immigration and customs on both sides of the bridge; the border is open twenty-four hours a day. The town on the Namibian side, **Noordoewer**, has a collection of service stations and *Camel Lodge* (☎09264/63 297 171; ③), a hotel with a bar and restaurant that might be very welcome after the long, hot road.

Springbok to Upington

The **N14** from **Springbok to Upington** is long and, after leaving the mountains around Springbok, increasingly flat and empty. This is big telegraph-pole country: the more you can see stretching off to a shimmering horizon, the longer and straighter the road. The scarcity of trees means that a number of the poles have been adopted as hosts for huge brown **sociable weaver nests**, a distinctive feature of these arid northern regions.

Pella

Roughly 150km from Springbok is a turning to **PELLA**, an intriguing settlement established around a mission station. After the turning off the N14, take the right-hand fork after 3km and follow the dirt road for another 10km towards the range of mountains which are in fact following the course of the Orange River. Pella is a simple gathering of shacks, sandy roads and a few stone or brick buildings in the midst of which a striking yellow **cathedral** stands in an open, dusty white plot surrounded by stately date palm trees. The cathedral was built – remarkably – by a group of French missionaries in the 1880s who, lacking an experienced cathedral-builder in their group, used the *Encyclopédie des Arts et Métiers* for guidance. The surrounding attractive mission buildings are still home to a community of nuns, and the cathedral itself is in continual use. The two small **museums** among the mission buildings are of some interest; if they're not open, ask at the mission office.

On the corner where the road into Pella swings left to pass the mission you'll find the *Kultuur Koffie Kroeg*, a **coffee shop** run from a flimsy-looking reed house by a local woman and her daughters. With *kokkerboom* trunks for stools and coffee brewing on an open fire in the back yard, it's a triumph of local enterprise relished by the few visitors who make it this far. Very basic but authentic **accommodation** is available in *matjieshuis* (①) at the back of the *Koffie Kroeg*; the only real alternative is a **guesthouse**, 24km away at Klein Pella (☎054/971 0008; ②).

Pofadder

Back on the N14, and about 15km further on, the famously hot and remote town of **POFADDER** won't delay you for long, except perhaps to take a photo to prove you've been there. The name, much ridiculed by South Africans (it's Afrikaans for "puff adder", a particularly nasty snake found around the country), in fact refers to a nineteenth-century bandit called Klaas Pofadder, who spent most of his time on an island in the Orange River near Upington but had a hideout here. There is a **hotel** in town, the *Pofadder*, Voortrekker St (☎054/933 0061; ②), and a triangle of grass at the caravan park a couple of blocks away if you want to pitch a **tent** (☎054/933 0056; ①).

The West Coast

North from St Helena Bay, the hook of land 100km north of Cape Town, the long, lonely **west coast** of South Africa has two simple components: the cold, grey Atlantic Ocean, and the dominant sandveld vegetation, hardy but infertile. There isn't much more to the region: between the mouth of the Olifants River at Papendorp, parallel to Vanrhynsdorp, and the Orange River over 400km to the north, there is just one tarred road connecting the N7 highway to the coast, which leads to the only settlement of any significance, **Port Nolloth**.

Access to much of the coast is restricted due to **diamond-mining**, which has in many cases involved disturbance on a huge scale to the sandveld and coastal dunes. The first diamonds were discovered in Namaqualand in 1925, which confirmed that diamonds could be carried the length of the Orange, washed out into the ocean, and then dispersed by currents and the processes of longshore drift. Although inital prospecting was carried out along the course of the Orange and in the coastal dunes, it is the diamonds lying offshore on the sea bed that are now the more eagerly chased, mostly by boats operating with huge underwater "vacuum cleaners" and scuba divers working in often dangerous conditions underneath the boats.

During the flower season, the rains fall first on the coastal areas, and you can often see displays beginning about 20km inland, making the few roads down to the coast from the N7 worthwhile options for day routes. The dirt road through the **Spektakel pass** between Springbok and Kleinzee is one of the most spectacular drives in Namaqualand, and the **Anenous pass** on the R382 between Steinkopf on the N7 and Port Nolloth is also impressive. Along this road, too, you will see wandering herds of goats belonging to the pastoral **Nama** people who live in the area, as well as the intriguing peaks and intimidating valleys of the Richtersveld, the mountain desert which occupies the area immediately south of the Orange River.

Port Nolloth

PORT NOLLOTH is an odd but delightful place, where in the hazy, windblown sunshine the horizons are never quite in focus and the heavy fogs of the mornings shroud the town in a quiet eeriness. Populated by an eclectic mix of races and professions, including fishermen, diamond-boat-owners, fortune-seeking scuba divers, scuba-diver-seeking girls and a significant Portuguese community, Port Nolloth is a place with a whiff of mystery and excitement. Tales are thick about "IDB" (illegal diamond buying), and if you have an imaginative mind you'll find plenty to feed it on. Why, as locals will point out to wide-eyed visitors, are there four second-hand furniture shops and three second-hand car dealers in a town with only a few thousand people?

Attractions in town are limited, though a stroll to the **harbour** along the sand-strewn roads to the beach or the different parts of town always throws up a few memorable scenes. There is a small **museum** (Mon–Fri 8.30am–12.30pm) on the corner of the main road and Beach Road, with an adhoc collection of relatively interesting fishing castoffs.

A **minibus** to and from Springbok is run by VIP Taxis (☎027/851 8780). The best sources of local **information** are the museum and, immediately next door, *Bedrock*

CANOEING TRIPS ON THE ORANGE RIVER

One way to enjoy the majesty of mountain-desert landscape of the Richtersveld is to take a **canoe down the Orange River**. By the time it reaches northern Namaqualand the river is broad and easy-paced, so the few rapids you encounter tend to rouse you from slumber rather than quicken the pulse. Dramatic rock formations and varied birdlife are the highlights of the trip, but above all relaxation is the key. Trips from Noordoewer last four to six days, with camps set up by the riverbank en route, from around R250 a day. For more details, contact Felix Unite – pronounced "Unit" – (☎021/683 6433), or River Rafters (☎021/712 5094), both based in Cape Town.

Lodge (☎ & fax 027/851 8865; ①–②), which also makes a wonderful **place to stay**, in a stylish old beach house with wooden floors and laid-back staff. Alternatively, camping, backpacker rooms and a guesthouse are available at the *Richtersveld Experience Tours and Lodge* (☎027/851 8041; ①–③), on the left as you come into town from the east.

Despite the size of the town, the mix of people and professions keeps a generous range of **restaurants** in business. Best of the bunch is the cosy, relaxed *Pirate's Cove*, offering fish, meat and pasta dishes in a garage-type building opposite the *Scotia Inn*. There's also a good **espresso bar**, *Maresol*, on the main road.

North of Port Nolloth

Diamond activity is also much in evidence if you drive **north from Port Nolloth** towards the diamond town of **ALEXANDER BAY**, the most westerly point of South Africa, at the mouth of the Orange River. The town is run by the mining company Alexkor and was once closed to outsiders, but has recently opened to visitors, who are able to do such things as a diamond mine tour and follow walking trails around town and to the mouth of the river, noted for its birdlife. For details contact the **tourist information** centre (Mon–Fri 8.30am–4.30pm; ☎0256/831 1330).

The main reason for anyone to be coming along this road is en route to the Richtersveld National Park, and for those looking for a base either side of their visit to the park there is a very pleasant **place to stay** at *Brandkaros*, 27km from Alexander Bay (☎0256/831 1856; ①–②), a farm with chalets and a **campsite** 400m from the river.

Richtersveld National Park

The area of northwestern Namaqualand known as the **Richtersveld** covers an area roughly bounded by the Orange River to the north, the N7 to the east, the R382 to Port Nolloth to the south and the Atlantic Ocean on its western side. The **Richtersveld National Park**, created in 1991, covers 1600 square kilometres of the most dramatic parts of the region, tucked into an omega-shaped loop in the Orange, land impressive as much for its fierce hostility as its rugged scenery. Names such as Hellskloof, Skeleton Gorge, Devil's Tooth and Gorgon's Head are indicative of the austerity of the inhospitable brown mountainscape, tempered only by a surprisingly broad range of hardy succulents, mighty rock formations, the magnificence of the light cast at dawn and dusk, and the glittering canopy of stars at night. There is little fauna in the park other than lizards and klipspringers, although along the Orange there are is a surprisingly rich birdlife.

The rainfall in parts of the park is as low as 50mm per annum, making this the only true desert – and mountain desert at that – in South Africa. In summer the daytime heat can be unbearable, at night in winter the cold drops below freezing, and in spring a few flowers will sometimes make their miraculous appearance on the bare, burnt hillsides and sandy plains.

Practicalities

Facilities at Richtersveld are extremely limited – this is not the place for a casual visit. Normal (saloon) cars are not allowed inside the park; the only way to explore is in a **4WD** or a pick-up with a high enough clearance to handle the sandy river beds and rough mountain passes between the designated campsites. On arrival, visitors must report to the park headquarters, **Sendelingsdrift** (☎0256/831 1506; R30), 94km from Alexander Bay. No driving is allowed at night, and the only fuel available is at the park headquarters. It is recommended that you travel in groups of two vehicles.

Accommodation is in three **chalets** at Sendelingsdrift (②) or at the designated **campsites** (①) around the park, which have no shelter or facilities. Water is scarce, and only very limited stores are available at the park headquarters. It is possible to **hike** with a guide in the park between April and September along designated trails of one, two or three nights' duration.

The most popular time to visit is during the winter months, when the days are coolest. Avoid coming here in the summer, when temperatures have been recorded at over 50°C. For **bookings** contact the National Parks Board (Pretoria ☎012/343 1991, Cape Town ☎021/22 2810, *reservations@parks-sa.co.za*), and for more information contact the park itself.

Probably the most realistic way of seeing Richtersveld is as part of a guided **4WD tour**. The most experienced operation is Richtersveld Challenge (☎0251/21905, fax 81460), based in Springbok, while the Richtersveld Experience (☎ & fax 027/851 8041), based in Port Nolloth, is more dynamic, and organizes tours aimed at budget travellers. Both offer trips of varying lengths into the park and surrounding areas, and will be able to combine a trip with hiking or canoeing along a section of the Orange if requested. You can rent 4WD vehicles from either company, although prices don't drop much from the full guided tour, and you have to make sure you are fully equipped.

travel details

Trains

Kimberley to: Bloemfontein (daily except Sat; 2hr 50min) Cape Town (1 daily; 16hr 55min); Durban (Tues; 19hr 45min); Johannesburg (2 daily; 9hr 35min); Pretoria (2 daily; 10hr 35min)

Buses

Calvinia to: Cape Town (4 weekly; 5hr 45min); Upington (4 weekly; 4hr 45min).

Kimberley to: Cape Town (1 daily; 11hr 40min); Johannesburg (1 daily; 5hr 15min); Knysna (Thur and Sun; 11hr 5min); Pretoria (1 daily; 6hr 15min).

Kuruman to: Johannesburg (4 weekly; 6hr); Upington (4 weekly; 3hr).

Springbok to: Cape Town (4 weekly; 6hr 30min); Pretoria (4 weekly; 7hr)

Upington to: Calvinia (4 weekly; 4hr 45min); Cape Town (4 weekly; 10hr 30min); Johannesburg (4 weekly; 9hr); Pretoria (4 weekly; 10hr)

Flights

Kimberley to: Cape Town (1 daily; 2hr 10min); Johannesburg (4 daily; 1hr 15min).

Springbok to: Cape Town (1 daily Mon–Fri; 1hr 20min).

Upington to: Cape Town (4 daily Mon–Fri, 1 daily Sat & Sun; 1hr 50min); Johannesburg (6 weekly; 1hr 50min).

CHAPTER FOUR

THE EASTERN CAPE

Sandwiched between Western Cape and KwaZulu-Natal, South Africa's two most popular coastal provinces, the **Eastern Cape** has suffered a second-rate reputation as a place to visit – one that should be swiftly dismissed. With its one thousand kilometres of undeveloped **beaches** alone justifying a visit, sweeping back in immense undulations of vegetated dunefields, the province is actually one of the most rewarding regions in South Africa, combining geography, history, culture, wildlife and heritage in a way that is unique within the country.

Port Elizabeth is the province's commercial centre and transport hub, Principally used to start or end a trip along the Garden Route. **Jeffrey's Bay**, 75km to the west, has a fabled reputation among surfers for its perfect waves. East of the city, the **R72** coastal road, a great rolling journey, provides easy access to a series of unassuming resorts, all gloriously sited on euphorbia-clad hillsides at the mouths of lazy rivers. Alternatively, around an hour's drive inland, are two of the province's most significant game reserves, the only places in the southern half of the country that can provide serious game viewing: **Addo Elephant Park**, where sightings of elephants are virtually guaranteed; and the private **Shamwari**, the only game reserve in South Africa that's malaria-free throughout the year. The hinterland north of here takes in areas appropriated by English immigrants, shipped out in the 1820s as ballast for a new British colony: **Grahamstown**, a pretty university town, glories in its twin roles as the spiritual home of English-speaking South Africa and host to Africa's biggest arts festival. Close by, the giraffe, antelope and hippo country of the **Great Fish River Reserve Complex** is a marvellous tract of stony hills vegetated by monumental candelabra-like succulents and river courses lined with thorn trees.

The northwest is dominated by the spare beauty of the **Karoo**, the thorny, semi-desert heartland that drifts across much of central South Africa, a landscape that, for some, is the spiritual heart of South Africa. The rugged **Mountain Zebra National Park**, 200km north of Port Elizabeth, is a terrific place to watch herbivorous game in a stirring landscape of flat-topped mountains and arid plains stretching for hundreds of kilometres. **Graaff-Reinet**, a short step to the west, is the quintessential eighteenth-century Cape Dutch Karoo town, settled in the pleasing serenity of its whitewashed streetscape.

The eastern part of the province, largely the former Transkei, is by far the least developed, with rural Xhosa villages predominating. **East London**, the province's only other substantial city, sits on the cusp of the former "white" South Africa and the African "homelands", and also serves well as a springboard for heading north into the central region, where the principal interest derives from political and cultural connections. If you're interested in **Steve Biko**, the city holds several related sites, and you can easily take in his burial place in **King William's Town**. To the west is **Alice**, though it's less well known than its university, **Fort Hare**, which educated many of this century's African leaders, including Mandela. The only established resorts in this section are in the **Amatola mountains**, offering mossy coolness and indigenous forests that provide relief from the dry scrublands below. Tucked into the northeastern corner of the province, the **Drakensberg**, more commonly associated with KwaZulu-Natal, make a steep ascent out of the Karoo and offer trout-fishing, skiing in winter and ancient San rock-art. The focus of the area is the remote, lovely village of **Rhodes**, a long journey down a rough road, which rewards you with absolute tranquillity and big views from the roof of the province.

East of East London is the **Wild Coast Region**, the former Transkei, the poorest part of the poorest province, a fact that reflects its historic role as a dumping ground for black South Africans. The **Wild Coast Hotel Meander**, an organized walking trail, takes in a deserted stretch of cliffs and sands with convenient stops each night at small family resort hotels. In the rugged goat-chewed landscape further east, Xhosa-speakers live in mud and tin homesteads, scraping a living herding stock and growing crops. **Umtata**, the ugly former capital of the Transkei, is well worth passing through with speed, though if you're following in the footsteps of Mandela, **Qunu**, his birthplace west of the town, is an obvious port of call. However, most people venture into the region for the fabulously beautiful, hilly sub-tropical coast – the least developed in the country. From here, all the way to the KwaZulu-Natal border, dirt roads trundle down to the coast from the N2 to dozens of remote and indolent sub-tropical resorts, of which **Port St Johns** is the best known.

Some history

One reason the Eastern Cape has remained unvisited is its long **historical legacy** that carved up the region into black and white territories in a more consolidated way than anywhere else in the country. The stark contrasts between **wealth and poverty** that cut through the Eastern Cape were forged in the nineteenth century when the **British** drew the Cape colonial frontier along the Great Fish River, a thousand kilometres east of Cape Town, and fought over half a dozen campaigns (known as the Frontier Wars) to keep the **Xhosa** at bay on its east bank. In the 1820s the British shipped in thousands of settlers to bolster white numbers and reinforce the line. West of the Kei, you'll encounter fenced-off white farms, pretty historic towns and industrial development; while across the river, the scourges of imperialism and apartheid have left little but overgrazed communal lands dotted with traditional huts and skinny cattle.

Even for a country where everything is suffused with politics, the Eastern Cape's identity is excessively **political**. South Africa's black trade unions have deep roots in its soil, which also spawned many anti-apartheid African leaders, including former president **Nelson Mandela**, his apparent, **Thabo Mbeki**, and black consciousness leader **Steve Biko**, who died in 1977 at the hands of Port Elizabeth security police. The Transkei or **Wild Coast** region, wedged between the Kei and KwaZulu-Natal, was the testing ground for grand apartheid when it became the prototype in 1963 for the *bantustan* system of racial segregation. In 1976 the South African government gave it notional "independence", under the puppet leadership of the Matanzima brothers in the hope that several million Xhosa-speaking South Africans, who were surplus to industry's needs, could be dumped in the territory and thereby become foreigners in "white South Africa". When the Transkei was reincorporated into South Africa in 1994, it became part of the new Eastern Cape province, which is now struggling for economic survival under the weight of its apartheid-era legacy.

PORT ELIZABETH AND
THE WESTERN REGION

A city of flyovers and sprawling townships, **Port Elizabeth** is the industrial centre of the Eastern Cape, where African shanty dwellers scrape a living on the dust-and-plastic fringes of well-tended middle-class suburbs. In 1820, it was the arrival point for four thousand British settlers, whose immigration doubled the English-speaking population

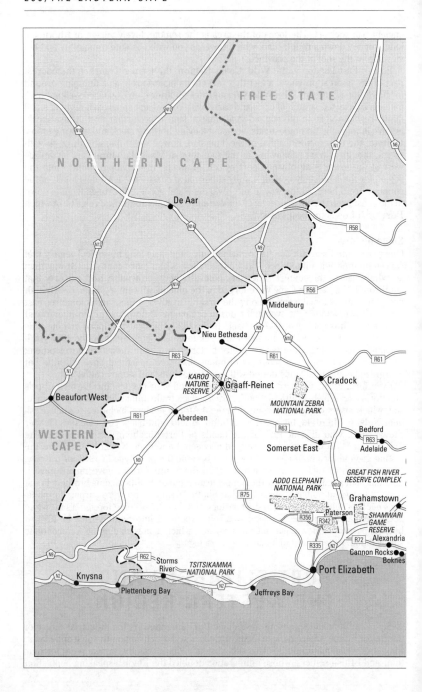

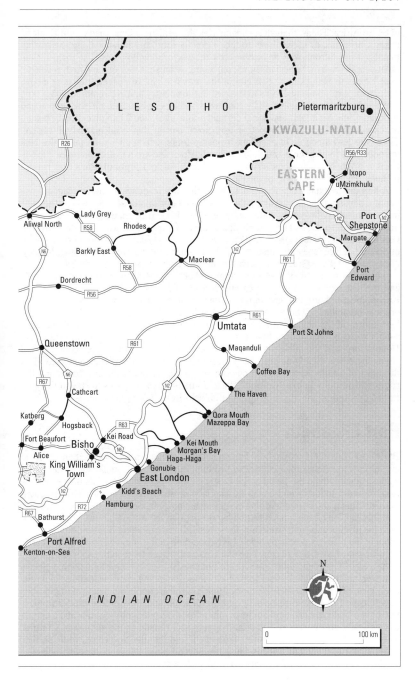

L E S O T H O

Pietermaritzburg

KWAZULU-NATAL

R26

R56/R33

EASTERN
CAPE

Ixopo
uMzimkhulu

Port
Shepstone

N2   N2

Lady Grey
Aliwal North   R58   Rhodes

Margate

Barkly East

N6

R58

Dordrecht

Maclear   N2

R61

Port
Edward

R56

Umtata   R61

Queenstown

R61

N6

Port St Johns

Maqanduli

R67

N6

Cathcart

N2

Coffee Bay

Katberg

The Haven

Fort Beaufort   Hogsback

R63

Kei Road

Qora Mouth
Mazeppa Bay

Bisho

N6

Alice   King William's
Town

Kei Mouth
Morgan's Bay
Haga-Haga

Gonubie

N2

East London

R67

Kidd's Beach

Bathurst

R72   Hamburg

Port Alfred
Kenton-on-Sea

N

INDIAN OCEAN

0   100 km

of South Africa. Today, their descendants risk the hellish national roads from Gauteng every Christmas, to speed down to the "Friendly City" and holiday along the institutionalized beachfront, with its burger bars and performing dolphins. The main reason most people wash up here is to launch out along, or finish, a tour of the **Garden Route**, Port Elizabeth being the largest city in the province and the prime transport nexus, with an airport, good road links to the rest of the country and car rental facilities. The port's industrial feel is mitigated by some outstanding city beaches, and should you end up killing time here (and you could certainly do worse), you'll find diversion in beautiful **coastal walks** a few kilometres from town and in the small **historical centre**. There are also a couple of excellent township tours, which give you one of the best introductions to apartheid and the new South Africa and are a welcome contrast to the Garden Route's beach focus. With time in hand, **Addo Elephant Park** is a recommended day's excursion out of the city.

A less urban experience than Port Elizabeth, for a few days at the seaside, are the handful of **resorts** to its east along the **R72 East London coast road**, where the roaring surf meets enormously wide sandy beaches, backed by mountainous dunes. The inland route to East London deviates away from the coast to pass through **Grahamstown**, a handsome university town, worth at least a night (more if you're interested in English settler history and the frontier conflicts with the Xhosa). Nearby, pretty settler villages trace the spread of the **1820 Settlers** into the interior.

A couple of hundred kilometres north from Port Elizabeth, an area of flat-topped hills and treeless plains opens out to extend across a third of South Africa. Its name, the **Karoo**, means "hard and dry" in the tongue of the Khoikhoi pastoralists, the region's original inhabitants, who were exterminated by Dutch frontiersmen. The oldest and best-known of the settlements here is the picture-postcard town of **Graaff-Reinet**, a solid fixture on bus tours. Just a few kilometres away is the awesome **Valley of Desolation**, and the village of **Nieu Bethesda**, best known for its eccentric Owl House museum. Nearly as pretty as Graaff-Reinet, though not as architecturally rich, the town of **Cradock**, to its east, has the added attractions of mineral baths and the rugged **Mountain Zebra National Park**. Some of the best places to stay in the *platteland*, or interior, are on sheep farms or in historically listed guesthouses.

Port Elizabeth

PORT ELIZABETH (commonly known as "PE") is not a place to visit if you're looking for cosmopolitan urban culture or beautiful buildings. The smokestacks along the N2 bear testimony to the fact that the Eastern Cape's largest centre has thrived on the back of heavy industry and cheap African labour, which accounts for it's deep-rooted trade unionism and strong tradition of African nationalism. So it may come as a surprise that this has long been a popular holiday destination for white Gauteng families – but then the town beachfront, stretching for several kilometres along Humewood Road, has some of the nicest, safest and cleanest **city beaches** in the country, thoroughly geared up with waterslides, and performing dolphins and snakes to keep the kids occupied.

As a city, PE is pretty functional. There's enough reason to linger for a couple of days however, and the city has some terrific accommodation and good restaurants in a relatively crime-free environment. Although much of the architectural beauty it might once have enjoyed has been ravaged by industrialization and thoughtless modernization, one or two buildings do stand out in an otherwise featureless **city centre**, and a couple of classically pretty rows of Victorian terraces still remain in the suburb of **Central**. There are also some creative **tours** around PE and into the townships, while further afield (but close enough for day-trips) are several good **game reserves**, including **Addo Elephant Park** and **Shamwari Game Reserve**.

For practical purposes, PE is one of the easist **entry points into South Africa**. Its small, newly established international **airport** lies just ten minutes from the compact and manageable city centre, which is itself the **transport hub** of the Eastern Cape, well served by flights, trains, buses and car rental companies. It's an admirable springboard, not just for exploring the Eastern Cape, but for launching out into the rest of South Africa.

Arrival and information

Port Elizabeth Airport (arrival and departure information ☎041/581 2984) is conveniently situated on the edge of Walmer suburb, 4km from the city centre. From here the reasonably priced Supercab Shuttle (☎041/457 5590) **minibus** will get you into town, stopping at all the main hotels, and making unscheduled stops on request. A metered **taxi** from the airport will cost you twice as much. **By train**, you'll arrive at the centrally located station (information ☎041/507 2222), from where you'll need to catch a bus or taxi to your accommodation. The Baz **backpacker bus** (☎021/439 2323, fax 439 2343, *info@bazbus.com*) will drop you off at any central location or accommodation. Arriving by **intercity bus** you can alight at Greenacres shopping mall in Newton Park suburb, 3km from the centre, or continue to the terminals of each of the lines (far more convenient if you're going to stay in the suburb of Central): Translux (☎041/507 1333) end at the train station; Greyhound (☎041/363 4555) finish nearby, in Fleming Street; and Intercape (☎041/586 0055) stop at 107 Govan Mbeki Ave. Of the **regional bus services**, the Leopard Express (☎041/484 1057) runs a weekend service (1 daily Fri–Sun) to and from Grahamstown, stopping at PE airport.

Information

The extremely helpful **Tourism Port Elizabeth** (Mon–Fri 8am–4.30pm, Sat & Sun 9.30am–4.30pm; ☎041/585 8884, fax 585 2564) has an office in the Donkin Lighthouse Building (itself a National Monument with a good, wide view from the top) on the Donkin Reserve in Central. It also has a satellite office, **Bay Tourism** (☎041/586 0773), on the corner of Brookes Hill Drive and Beach Road. Both offices offer a drop-in accommodation booking service for R40. A recorded touch-tone visitor **information service** (☎041/586 0773) provides up-to-date details of transport, tours, accommodation, what's on and eating out.

If you're spending any length of time in the city, **Braby's Map Book of Port Elizabeth** is invaluable. It's often out of stock at CNA newsagents, so you may need to go to the suburbs (see p.289) and try branches of Fogarty's Bookshop, at The Bridge shopping mall and Walmer Park Shopping Centre, or Exclusive Books, also at Walmer Park. The Automobile Association (☎041/363 1313) also has a good selection of maps at their shop in the Greenacres shopping mall.

City transport and tours

If you're staying in the the inner-city suburb of Central, exploring the city **on foot** is a realistic possibility. The self-guided **Heritage Walk** (map available at Tourism Port Elizabeth) takes you past interesting buildings, as well as nice cafés and pubs. However, for any serious exploration of PE, or for getting to and from the beachfront, **renting a car** is your best option, as the city's transit system leaves much to be desired (see "Listings", p.291). **Buses** operated by Algoa Bus Company, the municipal service, are inexpensive, but infrequent, running from the Market Square Bus Depot to the suburbs, the beaches and Greenacres shopping mall (timetable & route information ☎041/451 4241). The fifteen-seater Sunshine Passenger Service (☎042/293 1911, mobile ☎082/956 2687) offer a 24-hour door-to-door **shuttle bus**, though note that it

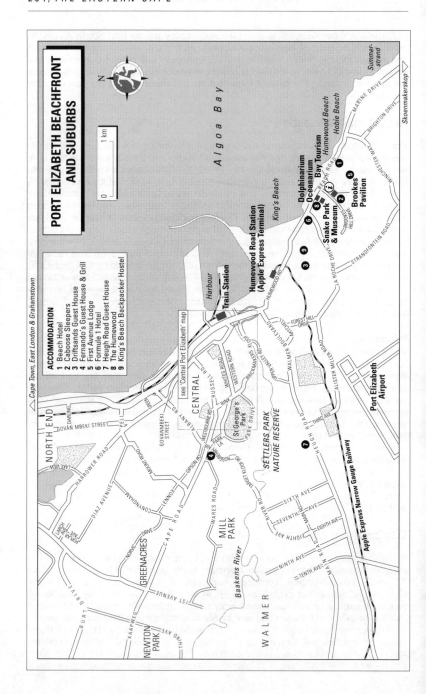

PORT ELIZABETH BEACHFRONT AND SUBURBS

N

0   1 km

Algoa Bay

ACCOMMODATION
1 Beach Hotel
2 Caboose Sleepers
3 Driftsands Guest House
4 Fernando's Guest House & Grill
5 First Avenue Lodge
6 Formule 1 Hotel
7 Heugh Road Guest House
8 The Humewood
9 King's Beach Backpacker Hostel

Cape Town, East London & Grahamstown

Summer-strand

Skoenmakerskop

MARINE DRIVE

BRIGHTON DRIVE

Hobie Beach

Humewood Beach

WINCHESTER WAY

Dolphinarium
Oceanarium

Bay Tourism

Snake Park
& Museum

Brookes Pavilion

BROOKES HILL DRIVE

BEACH ROAD

LA ROCHE DRIVE

STRANDFONTEIN ROAD

King's Beach

HUMEWOOD RD

Humewood Road Station
(Apple Express Terminal)

Harbour

Train Station

FOREST HILL DRIVE

MITCHELL

VALLEY ROAD

UPPER VALLEY RD

WALMER BOULEVARD

see 'Central Port Elizabeth' map

NORTH END

LAKE VIEW

GOVAN MBEKI STREET

HARROWER ROAD

DIAZ AVENUE

MOUNT ROAD

CONNYNGHAM

LENNOX

PELL

DARLING

STREET

GOVAN MBEKI STREET

CENTRAL

WHITES ROAD

WESTERN ROAD

ALBANY RD

RUSSELL RD

RINK

BRICKMAKERS KLOOF

St George's Park

PARK DRIVE

WESTBOURNE RD

PARK LA

LA

RICHMOND

ROSS

TARGET KLOOF

TARGET KLOOF RD

SETTLERS PARK
NATURE RESERVE

MILL PARK

WARES ROAD

CAPE ROAD

GREENACRES

NORWICH DRIVE

POPLAR AVE

LABORI AVE

HEUGH ROAD

ALISTER MILLER

THIRD AVE

MAIN ROAD

SIXTH AVE

SEVENTH AVE

EIGHTH AVE

RIVER ROAD

Baakens River

NINTH AVE

TENTH AVE

WALMER

Port Elizabeth Airport

Apple Express Narrow Gauge Railway

NEWTON PARK

KAAPWEG

BURT DRIVE

1ST AVENUE

THIRD AVE

charges for a minimum of two passengers. PE's **minibus taxis**, as elsewhere in the country, are racked by internal conflict and periodic internecine clashes around the main minibus taxi ranks. They do run from town to the beachfront on a regular basis, but are the least recommended way to travel. **Metered taxis** are reliable but more expensive (see "Listings", p.291). They don't have ranks so you'll need to phone for service, and if you're going to the bus or railway stations, or the airport, it's advisable to book ahead.

Tours

The best way to see Port Elizabeth is on one of the several excellent **bus tours** run by operators whose perspective on the culture and history of the city does not begin and end with the 1820 English Settlers. The following are highly recommended, offering a range of day- and night-trips around the city and the townships, longer jaunts to game parks, rock-painting excursions and eco-trails. For an insight into African Port Elizabeth, Gqebera Tours (☎041/581 2572, mobile ☎082/970 4037) goes to Walmer Township; Calabash Tours (☎041/585 6162, mobile ☎083/303 7553) outings include a well-researched, well-presented "Real City Tour"; Fundani Cultural Tours (☎041/463 1471, mobile ☎082/9646563) have an historic battlefields tour in their interesting itinerary; Tanaqua Indigenous Tours (mobile ☎083/270 9924) offer hiking and historical tours; and Pembury Tours (☎041/581 2581) run some wonderful big-game and explorer-type trips. All are knowledgeable and helpful, and the tours are a good way to meet locals.

Accommodation

The obvious, if most expensive, **place to stay** is at the **beachfront**, where hotels styled in a curious Thirties fusion of Art Deco and colonial architecture remain an intact and delightful local idiosyncrasy. Cheaper, but away from the sea, the well-preserved Victorian suburb of **Central** makes a pleasant alternative, with B&B accommodation and a few backpackers' lodges, and plenty of restaurants. There are a couple of excellent places in the less convenient (but greener) outlying suburbs of **Mill Park** and **Walmer**, plus a chance to stay with a family in an **African township** (see box overleaf).

During the December and January peak holiday period, the beachfront becomes the focus for most of the city's action, while February and March are much quieter yet still offer perfect beach weather. Note that PE is subject to **strong winds**; when these sweep across town the beachfront becomes a sandblaster, and you'd be better off booking into Central for the night – Algoa Leasing (☎ & fax 041/365 4086) is a central **booking agency** for the area.

ACCOMMODATION PRICE CODES

All the accommodation listed in the Guide has been categorized into one of nine price bands, as set out below. The rates quoted represent what you can expect to pay for much of the summer **per person**, and unless otherwise stated, are based on two sharing. Rooms are generally en suite. Expect prices in some areas to be significantly higher in peak season (Dec–Jan & Easter), and look out for discounts during the winter. For further details, see p.33.

① up to R50	⑥ R250–300
② R50–100	⑦ R300–400
③ R100–150	⑧ R400–500
④ R150–200	⑨ over R500
⑤ R200–250	

A SLICE OF TOWNSHIP LIFE

To experience life in one of the **African townships**, Fundani Lodge (☎041/463 1471, mobile ☎082/964 6563) offer a unique and very reasonably priced opportunity to enjoy football matches, traditional ceremonies and good African cooking, while staying with a family in the New Brighton, Zwide or Motherwell townships (R90).

Beachfront

Beach Hotel, Marine Drive, Humewood (☎ & fax 041/583 2161). Comfortable Thirties-style hotel, across the road from popular Hobie Beach. There's a great patio bar overlooking the sea, offering snacks, cocktails and cold beer. Ask about the weekend specials. ⑤.

Caboose Sleepers, Brookes Hill Drive, Humewood (☎041/586 0088, fax 586 0087). Tiny, wood-panelled rooms which sleep up to three people. The cramped sleepers are compensated for by a roomy, stylish lounge, sun deck and good self-catering facilities. ②.

Driftsands Guest House, 2 Marshall Rd, Humewood (☎041/586 0459, fax 585 6513). Recommended, cosy B&B run by friendly folk. ③.

First Avenue Lodge, 3 First Ave, Summerstrand (☎041/583 5173, fax 583 5176). Self-catering or B&B in this pleasant establishment with a pool. Airport transfers are available. ③.

Formule 1 Hotel, corner of Beach Rd and Laroche Drive (☎041/585 6380, fax 585 6383). Budget rooms with bath in this clean but rather impersonal hotel. ②.

The Humewood, 33 Beach Rd, Humewood (☎041/585 8961, fax 585 1740). Lovely rooms, a good bar, and a nice sun deck in a family hotel that has resisted modernization. ③.

King's Beach Backpacker Hostel, 41 Windermere Rd, Humewood (☎041/585 8113). In a former family home, and attracting a lively mix of young travellers. Camping facilities, 24hr check-ins, secure baggage- and mail-holding, self-catering kitchens and weekly rates. Dorms ①, doubles ②.

Central

Calabash Lodge, 8 Dollery St (☎041/585 6162). Cool simplicity, with cotton sheets and a touch of the ethnic in a stylish, well-located house, offering rooms with or without bath. This beats the rest of the town's budget accommodation hands down. ②.

Edward Hotel, Belmont Terrace (☎ & fax 041/586 2056). Edwardian landmark that has remained relatively intact, bang in the middle of historic Central. Great for a drink, tea, a ride in the vintage lift, and meeting people over breakfast, though the accommodation's not so hot. ④.

Global Backpackers, 75 Cape Road (☎041/374 3768, fax 374 8137). TV room, snooker table, fully equipped kitchen and *braai* area with airport transfers available. Dorms & doubles ①.

Jikeleza Lodge, 44 Cuyler St (☎041/586 3721, fax 585 6686, *winteam@hinet.co.za*). Port Elizabeth's best backpackers' lodge, with dorms and two doubles. Friendly, and a good source of local info. Dorms ①, doubles ②.

Millbrook House, 2 Havelock Square, Havelock St (☎041/585 3080, fax 582 3774). En-suite rooms at a charming B&B in Central's prettiest street. Situated in a Victorian house, there's a plunge pool, a *braai* area and airport transfers. ③.

Port Elizabeth Backpackers, 7 Prospect Hill (☎041/560 697, fax 585 2032, *pebakpak@global.co.za*). Basic accommodation (bring your sleeping bag) in a dorm sleeping eight, or doubles with bedding included. Continental breakfast and supper are extra. Dorms ①, doubles & family rooms ②.

Protea Lodge, 17 Prospect Hill (☎041/ & fax 585 1721). Nice old Victorian house in an interesting street in the middle of Central, with friendly staff. Twenty-four-hour check-ins, secure baggage- and mail-holding, and self-catering kitchens; weekly rates available. Shared toilet and washing facilities. Doubles ①.

The suburbs

Fernandos Guest House & Grill, 102 Cape Rd, Mill Park (☎041/373 2823, fax 374 5228). Popular string of Victorian houses offering reasonable rates, self-catering facilities and full board. ②.

Heugh Road Guest House, 55 Heugh Rd, Walmer (☎041/581 1007). Luxurious accommodation, close to the airport and at a reasonable price, in rooms built around a courtyard, each with its own private entrance and bath. Breakfast is extra. ③.

The City

Port Elizabeth's **city centre** is marred by the network of freeways perched on forests of concrete piles cutting a swath across the south of town and blocking off the city from the harbour. The city's white population retreated to the suburbs some time ago, taking the big department stores with them, and leaving the centre to African traders and township shoppers, who are slowly resuscitating the commercial spirit of former times.

City Hall and Central

The city's main street, which runs parallel to the freeway as it sweeps into town, has been renamed **Govan Mbeki Avenue** in honour of the veteran activist (father of South Africa's current president), who did time with Nelson Mandela. Fittingly, this is one of the few pockets of PE that retains its historic texture, with lovely old office buildings remaining intact save for their gaudy shop fronts. African traders dealing a pretty standard line in crochet tat and leather goods line up along the pavements giving the precinct a livelier feel than the deadly suburban malls.

Down Govan Mbeki, the symbolic heart of town is the **City Hall**, standing in **Market Square**, a large empty space surrounded by some striking mid-Victorian buildings, adjacent to the railway and bus stations on the edge of the harbour. But the dejection of the quarter, under the grimy shadow of a flyover, conspires against it ever pumping

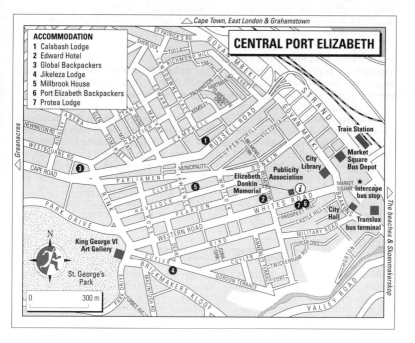

ACCOMMODATION
1 Calabash Lodge
2 Edward Hotel
3 Global Backpackers
4 Jikeleza Lodge
5 Millbrook House
6 Port Elizabeth Backpackers
7 Protea Lodge

CENTRAL PORT ELIZABETH

any real life into the district. Nevertheless, the **City Library**, on the corner of Whites Road and Govan Mbeki Avenue, is a real attraction, especially the second floor, with its beautiful stained-glass dome and windows and magical little balconies of bookshelves – a Victorian cathedral to the spirits of knowledge.

In stark contrast, the old Sanlam Building at 44 Strand St, was the notorious secret police centre where Steve Biko (see p.329) was tortured. In 1997 the building was renamed the **Steve Biko Building**, to mark the twentieth anniversary of his death. Now a boarding house mostly for students, the building has a small sixth-floor library with books, cuttings and photographs of Biko on view (sporadically open; small entry fee), in the same room where Biko was interrogated.

Heading west up hilly **Donkin Street**, past its exceptionally well-preserved Victorian street frontage, you'll come upon a curious stone pyramid which commemorates the city's namesake, **Elizabeth Donkin**. Elizabeth was the young wife of the Cape's acting governor in 1820, Sir Rufane Donkin; she died of fever in India in 1818.

Moving west from here through **Central**, up Havelock Street then south into Rink Street, you'll reach St George's Park and the **King George VI Art Gallery**, 1 Park Drive (Mon–Fri 8.30am–5pm, Sat 9am–4.30pm, Sun 2–4.30pm; free), which has an interesting collection of contemporary local work, visiting exhibitions and a small but good gallery shop selling postcards and local arts and crafts. **St George's Park** itself is a huge circular green, dominated by the St George's Cricket Ground, and includes a public swimming pool, a tiny but beautiful glasshouse and a couple of war memorials (one of them to horses that died under fire). North of Central's Russell Road boundary, you cross into **North End**, the city's industrial and administrative hub, where many fine old buildings were torn down to make way for the granite slabs of apartheid-era government offices. Worth a wander to get a feel of the city beyond the sanitized tourist haunts, North End is loud and lively, filled with African herbalists, Indian spice shops, gents' outfitters with impeccable window displays and snack bars selling mutton *rotis* and *bunny chow*.

The harbour, beachfront and around

The **harbour** area is an eyesore of oil-storage tankers immediately east of the train station, though this is due to change as it jumps on the bandwagon of waterfront developments – which started with Cape Town's V&A and works its way down the coast – and re-emerges as a tourist-friendly marina.

Just southeast of the harbour, on Humewood Road, **Humewood Road Station** is the starting point for the **Apple Express**, a beautifully restored steam train that usually runs on Sundays and occasional Saturdays during holidays (leaving at 9.30am) to Thornhill Village and other destinations, stopping on Van Staden's River Bridge, the highest narrow-gauge railway bridge in the world. After a leisurely lunch at Thornhill, the train trundles back to Humewood, arriving at 4pm. Tickets (R50) can be booked through Spoornet (☎041/507 2222) or Tourism Port Elizabeth (see p.283).

Even with the redevelopment, it's PE's wonderful **beaches** that offer its best hope of redemption, as the protection provided by Algoa Bay makes them safe for swimming

---

DIVING AROUND PE

Although the Indian Ocean around PE isn't tropically clear and warm, **diving** here is good, especially for soft corals. For dive courses, you won't do better anywhere along the South African coast than the five-star Pro Dive, at the Red Windmill, Beach Road, Summerstrand (☎041/583 5316, fax 583 5434, *prodive@intekom.co.za*), which is highly competitive at around R700 (excluding gear rental) for a three- to five-day course leading to an internationally recognized PADI certificate.

and clean enough to make **beachcombing** a pleasure. The beachfront strip, divided from the harbour by a large wall, starts about 2km south of the city centre at **King's Beach**, a built-up curve of strand with a children's paddling pool. The best place to swim and sunbathe, it only gets uncomfortably crowded at Christmas and on New Year's Day.

To its east is **Humewood Beach**, and across the road from that is a complex housing the **Port Elizabeth Museum** (daily 9am–5pm; small entry fee), which has a surprisingly good display on Xhosa people, and the **Oceanarium** (daily 9am–1pm & 2–5pm; dolphin shows 11am & 3pm; entrance fee), whose performing seals and dolphins attract hordes of excited children during the December holidays and also the displeasure of environmentalists. There's also a **Snake Park** (same hours & fee as Oceanarium), if you fancy gawping at imprisoned reptiles. Next door, **Brookes Pavilion** offers a variety of restaurants with great views. Beyond that, to the south, **Hobie Beach** and **Summerstrand** are great for walking and sunbathing.

Marine Drive continues down the coast as far as the suburb of **Schoenmakerskop**, along impressive coastline that alternates between rocky shores and sandy beaches. From Schoenmakerskop you can walk the eight-kilometre **Sacramento Trail**, a shoreline path that leads to the huge-duned **Sardinia Bay**, the wildest and most dramatic piece of coast in the area. To get there by road, turn right at the Schoenmakerskop intersection and follow the road until it signals left to Sardinia Bay.

The suburbs

PE's **suburbs** offer little to draw you away from the beachfront, unless you're a shopaholic, in which case you should make a beeline for **Newton Park**, 5km west of the centre and home to **Greenacres** and **The Bridge**, vast shopping malls to which all the city-centre department stores have relocated en masse. So strong is their status as the consumerist heart of Port Elizabeth that bus companies use Newton Park as an alternative terminus for travellers wishing to avoid the city centre.

Tranquil and leafy, 2km southwest of the centre, near the airport, **Walmer** suburb sits complacently between two irreconcilable landscapes. To its left, on the city side, is **Settlers' Park Nature Reserve**, with entrances on Park Drive and Third Avenue, which follows the Baakens River Valley from Valley Road, south of Main Street, to Newton Park, and has 54 square kilometres of indigenous growth and impressive cliffs. To its right lies **Walmer Township**, a dilapidated jumble of houses and shacks, divided from the mansions of Walmer's millionaires by a single strip of wasteland. Despite some small post-apartheid improvements, conditions here are generally appalling. The area is home to many of the domestic workers serving the suburban surrounds, and it's not unusual to find township cattle grazing on the wide grassy pavements which line Walmer's wealthy streets. A highly worthwhile **tour** can take you into the area (see "Tours", p.285).

Eating, drinking and nightlife

Port Elizabeth has no great culinary reputation, but there are some decent eateries, and at least you'll find places to suit most budgets, especially along the beachfront, and in Central, where there are more multiracial venues. Prices are much the same as the rest of the country, with fish an obvious choice. Apart from the hotel bars mentioned in the accommodation section, there are a few other passable joints for a **drink**, and a couple of nightclubs.

Restaurants

Aviemore, 12 Whitlock St (☎041/585 1125). Highly recommended (and expensive) restaurant in the centre, serving regional specialities, including springbok salad and seafood melange. Mon–Sat 6.30–10.30pm.

Coachman Steakhouse, 10 Lawrence St (☎041/582 2511). Off Russell Rd in Central, you'll find a good, mid-priced meat menu, and New Orleans whorehouse decor, which is curiously not at odds with the cosily middle-class clientele. Daily 7–11pm.

De Kelder, Marine Drive, Summerstrand (☎041/583 2750). Best food in town in a wine-cellar ambience, with a pricey menu. Specialities include seafood, steak, poultry and veal dishes, cooked in a European continental style. Daily 12.30–2pm & 6.30–10pm.

Don Carlos, 153 Russell Rd (☎041/585 2828). Delightful, unassuming little Spanish restaurant, run by an elderly couple from Barcelona. You can bring your own wine without an outrageous corkage added to the bill. Their paella specials are cheap and delicious. Ring for opening times.

Le Med, 70 Parliament St (☎041/585 8711). Medium to expensive eating in a lively atmosphere. Choose from fish dishes and unusual specialities, such as *tagine*, a Middle Eastern stew cooked in an earthenware pot. Booking is essential.

Lemon Tree, 58 Pearson St (☎041/586 4782). A pretty courtyard and verandah, together with some excellent light dishes makes this a good place for an inexpensive lunch. Daily 10am–4pm.

Nattis Thai Kitchen, 21 Clyde St (☎041/585 4301). Booking is essential at this scrumptious restaurant, and while it's expensive, Natti's magic cuisine is worth the price. Evenings only.

Rome, corner of Campbell and Russell roads (☎041/586 2731). Mouthwatering pizza made in a wood-burning oven and served in a laid-back atmosphere, at decent prices. Closed Sat & Sun lunch.

Tides, Summerstrand Village (☎041/583 4741). Good seafood and a great ambience make this one of the best of the seaside restaurants in town. Open daily for lunch and supper.

Zorba's, 68 Parliament St (☎041/585 2553). Varied, mid-priced menu includes tiger fish, stuffed squid and kebabs. There's a bar attached that stays open well after the restaurant has closed. Mon–Sat 6.30–10.30pm.

Bars and nightlife

Local live **music** is limited, most talented performers having taken off to the brighter lights of Cape Town. You'll find no shortage of Neil Diamond clones, though, crooning away at the steakhouses and tapas bars. Your best bet of catching something live is going to be one or two of the **bars** listed below, which occasionally have jam sessions; most bars stay open late if there's enough custom. The occasional **concerts** that come to PE's Opera House, and the odd **cabaret** at other venues, are listed in the daily *Eastern Province Herald*. The **cinema** situation is marginally better, with a good selection of current and art films showing at the Kine Park Cinema, 3 Rink St, Central (☎041/582 3311), and the usual Hollywood fare at the Nu Metro, Walmer Park Shopping Centre, Walmer (☎041/367 1102), and at the Ster Kinekor (☎041/363 0577), in The Bridge shopping complex – check the *Herald* for programme details.

The Boardwalk, The Boardwalk, Marine Drive, Summerstrand. A bar that's an incredibly popular summer spot and can get troublesome at night but boasts great sea views and a balcony.

Dockside Debbies, Bay Waterfront. The best bar in town occupies a quaint old dockside building with harbour views and is excellent for a sundowner or good pub grub. There are decks atop while life below stairs is a gloriously ramshackle affair of ancient, mouldering piers and garishly painted chairs rescued from an old lifeboat. There's a signposted entrance at the junction of Baakens and Valley roads.

Harry Casual Bar & Restaurant, 151 Heugh Rd, Walmer. Popular Walmer pub with pool tables. Indigo, Brookes Pavillion (☎041/586 1078). Dance club with visiting DJs. Popular – some say the only – place for PE youth culture.

Keg & Fox, 31 Clyde St, Central. Great selection of local and imported beers and lagers. Generous glasses of wine, tasty cocktail snacks, and a very pleasant atmosphere.

Razzmatazz, 4th Floor, Central House, Grace St, Central (☎041/585 1851). PE's greatest jazz venue hosts some of Cape Town's best musicians, as well as sessions with young locals in a suitably dark and smoky haze. Cheap, friendly non-racial vibe, with Wednesday the best night.

Tiko's, corner of Belont and Whites roads, Central. Laid-back joint with African decor, where you'll often catch great jam sessions of original live music as well as some covers. Sells cheap, late-night munchies.

Listings

Airlines SAA ☎041/507 1111.

Car rental Companies at the airport are: Aim (☎041/581 1798); Avis (☎041/581 1306, toll-free ☎0800/02 1111); Budget (☎041/581 4242); Hertz (☎041/581 6550, toll-free ☎0800/60 0136); Imperial (☎041/581 1268, toll-free ☎0800/13 1000); and Tempest (☎041/581 1256). Runabout Rentals, Kragga Kamma Rd (☎041/739 1009) rent out good second-hand cars and a 4WD – perfect for Addo Elephant Park.

Consulates British Consulate, First Bowring House, Ring Rd, Greenacres (Mon–Fri 9am–12.30pm; ☎041/363 8841, fax 363 8842).

Emergencies Ambulance ☎10177; Fire ☎55 1555; Police ☎10111.

Hospitals St George's (private), Park Drive, Settlers Park (☎041/392 6111); Provincial (state), Gibson Rd, Central (☎041/392 3911).

Laundries Automat, 6a Parliament St, Central; Rub & Tub, Rink House, 70d Clyde St, Central.

Pharmacy Mount Road Medicine Depot, 13 Lower Mount Rd (☎041/484 3838). Daily until 10.30pm.

Post office Brookes Pavilion, Humewood. Mon–Fri 9am–3.30pm, Sat 8.30–11am.

Taxis Good firms include Anchor (☎041/484 4798 extension 2); Hurters Taxis (☎041/585 5500); and Unicab (☎041/585 3030).

Travel agents Gentravel, 50a Pickering St, Newton Park (☎041/365 2344); and Pentravel, Walmer Park Shopping Centre (☎041/386 151, fax 386 162).

Around Port Elizabeth

In a region not generally noted for its wildlife, Port Elizabeth holds the ace as the nearest centre to **Addo Elephant Park**, one of South Africa's most rewarding game reserves and the only one of substance in the Eastern Cape. Also within easy striking distance is the private **Shamwari Game Reserve**, a luxury establishment boasting the "Big Five" (elephant, lion, leopard, buffalo and rhino) – though the lions are in pens. Southwest along the coast, **Jeffrey's Bay** attracts surfers the world over.

Addo Elephant Park

Addo Elephant Park (daily 7am–7pm; ☎042/233 0556; R12), 50km northeast of Port Elizabeth, should be your first choice for a day's trip out of the city, and also makes for a rewarding and peaceful overnight stop

The Addo bush is thick, dry and prickly, making it difficult sometimes to spot any of the 200–300 elephants; when you do, though, it's often thrillingly close up. The best strategy is to ask at the park's reception where the elephants have last been seen, and also to head for the elevated viewing platform to scan the bush for large grey backs quietly moving about. **Night drives** with a National Parks ranger, which cost R60, can be booked at reception if you're staying in the park (see below). Other animals to watch out for include **eland**, **kudu**, **buffalo** and **red hartebeest**.

A good break from waiting at waterholes or scouring the bush is to walk the six-kilometre circular **Spekboom Trail**, which takes you through the indigenous spekboom *veld* which predominates in the park. The walking is in an area fenced off from the elephants, and gives you a real feel of the landscape.

In the late Nineties, Addo began acquiring land with the aim of becoming the third-largest conservation area in South Africa, the Greater Addo National Park. It also will be the most diverse, with six of South Africa's seven biomes within its boundaries, the Alexandria coastal dunefield, two small islands, and a large tract of marine reserve. In addition to its famous elephants, the park will carry other mega-herbivores such as rhino and hippo, large predators including lions and cheetahs, the largest colony of African (jackass) penguins in the world, 400 species of birds, and an impressive array of indigenous plant species including cycads.

Practicalities

To **get to Addo Park** from Port Elizabeth, take the N2 in the direction of Grahamstown for about 50km, branching off onto the N10 for a further 20km and then turning left at the village of Paterson onto the R342. The National Park entrance is another 25km down this road. The network of roads within the park is untarred, but is in good condition. If you want to try a tour, most of PE's operators now include day and longer **organized trips** to Addo as part of their itineraries (see "Tours" on p.285).

Maps of the park are available at reception. **Accommodation** in the reserve is in fully equipped, self-catering forest huts (②); and two- or four-bedroom bungalows, including breakfast at the park restaurant (③), overlooking a small dam where animals come to drink and birds congregate. Camping is also available (①), and there's a swimming pool and tennis courts. **Bookings** are essential; contact South African National Parks (Pretoria: ☎012/343 1991, fax 343 0905; Cape Town: ☎021/22 2810, fax 24 6211, *reservations@parks-sa.co.za*). You'll find a decent **restaurant** (6am–8pm) next to reception, dominated by the head of an enormous stuffed elephant, and a small groceries shop next door for drinks, snacks and basic catering. The park map indicates the location of **picnic** and *braai* sites. If you're unable to secure accommodation inside the park you'll find reasonably priced **B&B** rooms at the *Sandflats Hotel* (☎042/235 1012, fax 235 1176), 500m west of Paterson on the R342, about twenty minutes by car from the National Park.

Shamwari Game Reserve

The private **Shamwari Game Reserve** (☎042/203 1111, fax 235 1224, *shamwaribooking@global.co.za*), 72km northeast of PE, is the only park in the Eastern Cape where you can currently see **lions** – even if they are kept in enclosures. The surroundings are marvellous, with dry hills and river-etched gorges stretching for miles. Safaris are aimed at the upmarket consumer, and if you're going to Natal or Mpumalanga you'd be better off spending your money in one of South Africa's great national game reserves. However, if you're only touring the southern provinces, or want to avoid the risk of **malaria** (there's none here at any time of year), Shamwari will provide a satisfactory safari experience.

Day packages include lunch and a three- to four-hour game drive, and start at R375 per person. If you're **overnighting**, the accommodation, in a choice of Victorian and Edwardian homesteads, gives Shamwari a vastly different flavour to the traditional tented safari camp – although you'll still get to go on game drives in open vehicles. The lodges have been restored to their original nineteenth-century splendour and prices start at R1500 per person, including accommodation, full board and game drives. Unlike the national parks, Shamwari is not a place you can just drop into, and **booking** is essential.

Jeffrey's Bay

The only place of any interest along the N2 as it stretches for 186km from Port Elizabeth to Storms River is **JEFFREY'S BAY** – at least if you happen to be a surfer. Some 75km west of Port Elizabeth, off the N2, J Bay, as it's known locally, is reputed to be one of the top three surfing spots in the world. Just thirty years ago, it consisted of nothing more than a few beachside shacks and a general store. Local residents, mostly conservative farmers, regarded the arriving surfers as lowlife, but were unable to ignore the commercial possibilities of their presence. Their contempt is visible in the town's design. Jeffreys is an irredeemably ugly dump, and the main street, **Da Gama**

Road, running the length of the town, consists mainly of cheap brick buildings devoid of any civic sensibility. The town's rising fame corresponded with the boom in coastal development in the Seventies, and its hills are littered with huge, tasteless, executive vacation homes and the retirement dwellings of wealthy folk who rent them out during holiday season at astronomical prices.

For **surfing aficionados**, however, these are trifling details, given the possibility of the perfect wave. If you've come to surf, head for the break at **Super Tubes**, east of the main bathing beach, which produces an impressive and consistent swirling tube of white water that attracts surfers from all over the world throughout the year. Riding inside the vortex of a wave is considered the ultimate experience by surf buffs, but should only be attempted if you're an expert. Other key spots are at Kitchen Windows, Magna Tubes, the Point and Albatross. Surfing gear, including wet-suits, can be rented from Billabong Country Feeling, Da Gama Rd (☎042/296 1797). In a league of their own, **dolphins** regularly surf the waves here, and **whales** can sometimes be seen between June and October. For the less agile, Main Beach (in town), and Kabeljous-on-Sea (a few kilometres north) are the main **bathing areas**, with some wonderful seashells to be found between Main and Surfer's Point. Rock **fishing** is very popular, as is **scuba diving**. Dives and equipment can be booked through ☎042/293 0218.

Practicalities

Getting to Jeffrey's Bay from PE without a car is straightforward. The Baz **backpacker bus** stops at J Bay on its daily trek in either direction between Cape Town and Port Elizabeth. Alternatively, the Sunshine Passenger Service will bring you here from PE (see p.283) for R40 (mninimum of two passengers).

The **tourist information office** (Mon–Fri 8am–5pm, Sat 9am–noon; ☎042/293 2588) on the corner of Da Gama and Dromedaris roads, publishes a wide-ranging list of **places to stay**. J Bay has two municipal **campsites**, both on the beach with access to surfing breaks. The *Kabbeljous Caravan Park*, on the corner of Da Gama Road and

---

SURFING ETIQUETTE

On the international surfer's map of the world, South Africa begins and ends at **Jeffrey's Bay**. Its legendary reputation was built on the Sixties cult movie *Endless Summer*, featuring surfer Bruce Brown trotting the globe in search of perpetual sunshine and the perfect wave (one of the breaks here is known as Bruce's Beauties). Although J Bay is by no means the best place to surf in South Africa – there are hundreds of good breaks up and down the coast between Cape Town and Durban – it is probably the place most single-mindedly devoted to the sport.

If you come here to surf, paddle-ski or boogie-board, you should take care to observe the fundamentals of **surfing etiquette**. On arriving at a new spot, always hang around the margins sussing out the scene, never intruding on someone else's patch and always remembering that you are a visitor. Surfers are highly territorial and there are clearly defined rules governing who takes precedence in the water. These often come down to proficiency. In the surfing pecking order, the rising stars are "grommets" or "surf rats", sixteen- or seventeen-year-olds who challenge the "old bullets" – twenty- or thirty-somethings whom they consider to be over the hill. Half-crazed rodeo riders of the swell, who take on large, seven-metre waves, are known as "hell men", while at the other end of the spectrum you'll find "doormats", "spongers" and "tea bags", who take to the sea on boogie- or knee-boards, and receive only marginally less contempt from surfers than paddle-skiers, who are termed "egg whippers" or "deckchairs". If you observe these conventions, the chances are you'll find South African surfers exceptionally friendly, ready to talk and happy to offer tips. And beginners will find it easy to locate someone willing to get them started for a small fee.

Kabbeljous Street (☎042/293 1111; ①), is close to the town centre, while the *Jeffrey's Bay Caravan Park*, on the corner of Da Gama Road and Friesland Street (☎042/293 1111; ①), is less central. **Budget** options are best booked in advance and include *Jeffrey's Bay Backpackers*, 12 Jeffreys St (☎042/293 1379; dorms ①), two blocks from Main Beach, with double-bed cabins, a bar, and bike and board hire. Other backpackers' lodges are *Island Vibe*, 10 Dageradd St (☎042/293 1625; ①), with camping in J Bay's best site, offering 180-degree views; the *Splash Inn*, 23 Diaz Rd (☎042/293 1375; ②), a small place with a sea view and self-catering accommodation; and *Rest Haven*, 20 De Reyger St (☎042/293 1248; ①), which rents out budget two-person flatlets.

You'll find more comfortable **cabins** at *Beach Cabanas*, 118 Da Gama Rd (☎042/293 2820; ②), but for a lot more luxury, head for *Diaz 15*, 15 Diaz Rd (☎042/293 1779; ④), with smarter two- and three-bedroom accommodation on Main Beach. Surfers who want to be near Super Tubes (the main surf beach), should try *Mount Joy Guest House*, 31 Mimosa St (☎042/296 1932; ③), three minutes from the beach and offering superb sea views.

For **eating**, J Bay has the usual collection of burger and steak bars, and lots of takeaway places. *Le Grotto*, in Da Gama Road, is famous for its cheap, 1kg steaks. The *Walskipper*, in Marina Martinique Harbour, offers luxurious and expensive seafood in an alfresco setting with lots of lovely homemade bread, pâtés and jams, while your main courses are cooked on an outside fire. *Breakers* is a popular eatery on Ferreira Street, which specializes in fish and game meats, and has a nice glassed-in patio. At the cheaper end, the *Sunflower*, 20 Da Gama Rd, offers breakfasts and some interesting pastas and salads, and also caters for vegetarians.

Port Elizabeth to Port Alfred

One of South Africa's most undeveloped stretches of **coast**, with wide beaches and exhilarating surf, stretches east from **Port Elizabeth** for a sandy 150km to **Port Alfred**. The sea temperature here is several degrees higher than around Cape Town (though not as warm as KwaZulu-Natal, and never tropically clear), and the beaches are a walker's paradise, with shells, birds and rock pools to detain you. The only problem is the **wind**, which often affects the whole Eastern Cape coast – particularly in the afternoon, so set out as early as you can. The weather is at its calmest from April to July, and while it's not hot enough to tan you'll certainly be comfortable picnicking or walking along the beaches. April to July is also the optimum season for scuba diving, with the water at its clearest.

The beaches can be deserted out of season, apart from the occasional growl of **4WD vehicles** embossing their heavy tread into the sands. The question of vehicles on beaches bitterly divides South Africans, with fishermen and the expensive-toy brigade defending their freedom to drive on the sands, and ecologists and strollers complaining of the disturbance they cause to coastal flora and fauna.

Thankfully, vehicles are banned on some parts of the coast, and you shouldn't encounter them on the **Alexandria Hiking Trail** – one of South Africa's best coastal walks over quite massive dunes. The twin resorts of **Bushman's River** and **Kenton-on-Sea**, each with a river dotted with boats, rocky coves and fabulous beaches for swimming and walking, are the most arresting spots along this coast. Most of the houses are holiday homes, unoccupied much of the year, belonging to white South Africans, but there is a fair bit of rentable **accommodation**, and the big plus of a regular bus service to Port Elizabeth or East London if you're without a car.

Alexandria State Forest and Diaz Cross

A fifty-kilometre tract of Eastern Cape beachfront is protected by the **ALEXANDRIA STATE FOREST** and can be walked on the circular two-day **Alexandria Trail**, one of

South Africa's finest **coastal hikes**, which winds through indigenous forest and across a deserty landscape of great hulking sand dunes, all the way to the ocean.

The thirty-five-kilometre trail starts at the Alexandria Forestry Station, 8km from the R72. The signposted turn-off is on the right, just before you reach Alexandria, 86km from Port Elizabeth. There's an **overnight hut** (①) at the station, for use at the beginning or end of the trail, and another at Woody Cape, both with mattresses and drinking water, but no cooking facilities. There is no public transport to the starting point, so you'll need to drive there. The hike is quite tough-going, especially along the windy dunes – the route markers in the sand can get blown over, obscuring the route – but in fine weather the isolated beaches are magnificent. You'll need to **book** one of the limited places on the trail through Alexandria Nature Reserve, PO Box 50, Alexandria 6185 (Mon–Fri 8am–4pm; ☎046/653 0601, fax 653 0302; R20) and, unless you get in well ahead, the trail tends to be full over weekends. The **forest** itself, with yellowwood trees trailing lichen, is accessible on a seven-kilometre day-walk from the forestry station, with a nice picnic and *braai* place.

ALEXANDRIA, a pineapple- and chicory-growing centre with a strip of shops and an imposing Dutch Reformed Church, is the closest town to the reserve. If you want a more comfortable night than the Alexandria hut can provide, *Heritage Lodge*, along the main street (☎046/653 0024, fax 653 0735; ③), is one of the few **places to stay**, and although its accommodation is nothing special the **restaurant** has a good reputation for lunches and dinners.

From Alexandria, a good dirt road takes you 18km through the State Forest and farmland to the coast at **Boknes**, a tiny resort that is the start of an hour-long beach walk eastwards to the monument of **Diaz Cross**, commemorating the Portuguese adventurer and explorer, Bartholomeu Dias, who rounded the South African coast in 1487 in search a profitable new sea route between Europe and the East. The first European to make recorded contact with the Khoikhoi, Dias was also the first to kill one of them. The cross, on a rocky promontory, marks the spot where he was forced by his crew to turn back to Cape Town, rather than face the journey eastwards. **Accommodation** along this stretch of coast is in short supply: the only place to stay is at **CANNON ROCKS**, 2km west of Boknes and 135km east of Port Elizabeth, where you'll find the thoroughly family-oriented *Cannon Rocks Holiday Resort* (☎046/654 0043, fax 654 0095) right on the beach. You can pitch a tent (①) or rent a luxury flat (⑤). Although there's a small shop, you're best off buying **supplies** from Alexandria, which is linked to Cannon Rocks by a tarred road.

Kenton-on-Sea and Bushman's River Mouth

Some 26km west of Alexandria, along two river valleys, are the resorts of **Kenton-on-Sea** and **Bushman's River Mouth**, perfect for a short beach holiday. A modest conglomeration of holiday houses served by a small collection of shops and places to eat, they're a good choice if you want to be somewhere undemanding and very beautiful – there's little to do here except enjoy the surf, the sandy beaches and dunes, wallow in big shallow tidal pools, and swim in the rivers. They don't see many foreign visitors and only locals pack in during the school holidays, so the rest of the year, especially during the week, you're assured of a quiet time. Note that while **swimming** in the rivers is great, you should avoid getting close to the entrance to the sea as strong riptides are frequent; swimming off the sea beaches is fine. If you want to spend time on Bushman's River, you can rent small **motor boats** from Kenton Marina (from R60 per hour; ☎ & fax 046/648 1223), well signposted off the R72, 300 yards up the R343 to Grahamstown. The Marina also rents out two-person beaver **canoes**, for paddling the 15km upriver from here that constitute the **Bushman's River Trail**. The trip, which passes through farm- and uncultivated land lined with cycads and euphorbias, and is filled with chattering birdlife, takes between two and five hours, depending on your fitness, the direction of the tide, and weather conditions. At the end of the trail there's a **hut** (book at the Marina; ②) that sleeps sixteen in bunks. Mattresses, cooking utensils, *braai* facilities and outdoor cold showers are provided, but you must bring your own sleeping bag and food as there are no shops or any other facilities here.

Kenton-on-Sea

Intercape **buses** pull into **KENTON-ON-SEA** at the shops next to Robby's Bottle Store on Kariega Road, the main route into Kenton off the R72. Facilities include a couple of restaurants, mini-supermarkets, a bank and cash machine, a post office and a filling station – all along Kenton Road, the main street.

Accommodation is in reasonably priced self-catering cottages, most of which provide breakfast as an extra. The cheapest beds in town are in **dorms** at the functional *Bushman's River Backpackers*, 49 Kenton Rd (☎046/648 2525; ①), the main drag, making it convenient for the village's sprinkling of shops and eateries, although it lacks a buzz. *The Bell*, 47 Northwood Rd (☎ & fax 046/648 1686) offers two immaculate units sleeping two to four (②), away from the beach and the river and close to the R72. In a fine location, five minutes' walk from the Kariega River, *Berribridge B&B*, 28 Oxford St (☎046/648 1048; ②) has three doubles sharing two bathrooms, set apart from the main house. *Burke's Nest*, 38 Van der Stel Rd (☎046/648 1894, mobile ☎082/577 2142; ②), has a cottage and a flatlet connected to a family home, a short amble from the Kariega River.

The best-located **eating and drinking** place in Kenton is *Homewoods*, 1 Eastbourne Rd, a restaurant and pub at the mouth of the Kariega River with two decks and grand views, where the run-of-the-mill fare includes steaks, fish and burgers. Downstairs, a joint with a younger feel, serves drinks and pizzas. Down Main Street there are a couple of other reasonable eateries, of which *Jody's Secret Garden* stays open during the day for good spinach and feta taremezinis and soups in a pleasant atmosphere that feels outdoors, even though it isn't; at night the *Pub & Grill* is a good bet for grills, hamburgers, chips and drinks.

Bushman's River Mouth

BUSHMAN'S RIVER MOUTH is a very similar resort, but it's a lot smaller. You can **camp** at the well-kept caravan park, 2 Loerie Rd (follow the signs from the turn-off to Bushman's from the R72), which is right in the centre (☎046/648 1227; ①) and a short walk to the river and sea. One of the few places to stay is the friendly *Bushman's River Mouth B&B*, 10 Hertzog St (☎046/648 2324; ②), which rents out two **rooms** with a shared bathroom in a family home. Renting a **cottage** is another option: enquire at the Kenton or Port Alfred agencies. In the tiny centre you'll find a large bottle store, a small supermarket and a decent **restaurant**, the *Bistro on the Square*, 1 Cycad St (☎046/648 1173; Mon & Wed–Sat 6.30pm–11pm), which specializes in kudu steaks and fresh fish, as well as prawns and mussels in season. Upstream along the Bushman's River and over the R67 is *The Sandbar Restaurant* (if you're coming along the R67 itself, take the Riversbend turn-off, west of Bushman's River Mouth), a modest pontoon that doubles up as a pub, and serves hamburgers, chips and excellent calamari. The views of the steep cliffs, thick with euphorbia, amply compensate for any lack of flair.

Port Alfred

Of all the settlements between Port Elizabeth and East London, only **PORT ALFRED**, midway between the two, can make any claims to a town life outside the holiday season, when for a few weeks its small centre is transformed into a hectic bustle of cars and people. For the rest of the year, its large retired white contingent and (even larger)

African population in the township are swelled every weekend by wetsuited surfers and partying university students from Grahamstown, less than an hour away.

Although it started life as a port for settler enterprises in the 1840s, Port Alfred was never quite suitable (the river kept silting up) and it quickly faded away into a resort. No large ships navigate the Kowie River, but plenty of **fishing boats** brave its turbulent mouth every day, watched by fascinated bystanders on the end of the pier. Nicknamed "Kowie" by locals, after the river, Port Alfred was named in honour of the second son of Queen Victoria, although he never actually made it here. The prince, who visited the Cape in 1870, cancelled a trip to Port Alfred at the last minute, because the prospect of an elephant hunt seemed more appealing.

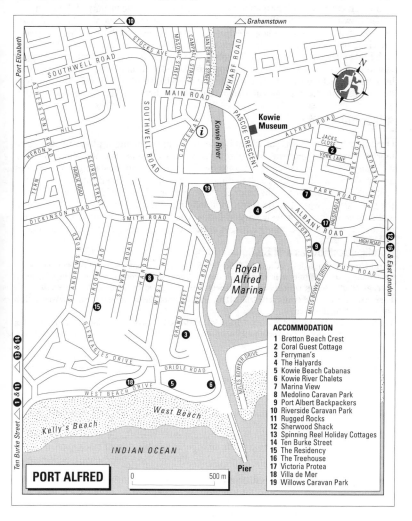

ACCOMMODATION

1 Bretton Beach Crest
2 Coral Guest Cottage
3 Ferryman's
4 The Halyards
5 Kowie Beach Cabanas
6 Kowie River Chalets
7 Marina View
8 Medolino Caravan Park
9 Port Albert Backpackers
10 Riverside Caravan Park
11 Rugged Rocks
12 Sherwood Shack
13 Spinning Reel Holiday Cottages
14 Ten Burke Street
15 The Residency
16 The Treehouse
17 Victoria Protea
18 Villa de Mer
19 Willows Caravan Park

PORT ALFRED

0   500 m

Arrival, information and orientation

Intercape **buses** travel in both directions between Port Elizabeth and East London (daily except Tues & Thurs), pulling into the *Halyards Hotel*, off the main coastal road on the east side of the Kowie River. From here, it's about ten minutes' walk to the helpful **tourist information** bureau (and tea shop), Causeway (Mon–Sat 10.30am–4.30pm; ☎046/624 1235), along the west bank of the Kowie River, and another minute or two to Main Street, the town centre, lined with banks and shops. While you can manage without a car, renting a **bike** is a good idea; you'll find a selection at Garro, 41 Van der Riet St (☎046/624 1882), directly accross Main Street from the tourist information bureau, where you can also get information about cycling **trails** in the vicinity of the town.

The **Kowie River** slices through Port Alfred, creating an **east** and **west bank**, with the town and most popular swimming **beaches** seated on the west, and the less-developed dunes stretching out along the east. The river is traversed by two bridges: a concrete bowstring-arch bridge that has become Port Alfred's symbol, and an older one, which leads straight into Main Street. Sadly, the natural lagoon was blasted away in the Eighties and replaced by a marina, floating with dozens of boats and artificial islands dotted with Toytown holiday homes. The *Halyards Hotel* and a pub constitute the town's ersatz, caged-in waterfront.

Accommodation

Outside school holidays, you should have no problem finding a **place to stay**. The tourist information bureau (see above) publishes a useful list of accommodation, including B&Bs and self-catering cottages. The priciest and most-sought-after places are on **West Beach**, while you'll find more affordable accommodation back from the seafront and particularly in the older and slightly more characterful areas on the hill on the east side of town. Most B&Bs are indicated from the main roads with official brown signs, making them relatively easy to find. If you're on a budget and value seclusion, one of the several self-catering cottages at **Salt Vlei** is an option worth considering.

Hotels, guesthouses and B&Bs

Coral Guest Cottage, Jack's Close (☎ & fax 046/624 2849). Reasonably priced B&B on one of the East Bank hills, a 20min walk from East Beach. Comfortable rooms with bath in a restored corrugated-iron settler cottage. You can expect to be pampered by the ebullient owner. ③.

Ferryman's, Beach Rd (☎ & fax 046/624 1122). Pleasingly old-fashioned hotel, close to West Beach and overlooking the river. ③.

The Halyards, Royal Alfred Marina, Albany Rd (☎046/624 2410, fax 624 2466). Smartest hotel in town, with smart decor, but you could be anywhere in the world. Sometimes offers massive discounts (over 50 percent) out of season. ⑤.

The Residency, 11 Vroom Rd (☎046/624 5382, *residency@imaginet.co.za*). Spacious, beautifully restored Victorian house on the West Bank with views across the dunes to the sea. Lemon-yellow wood-panelling, large comfortable beds, fine attention to detail, and breakfast served on the verandah make this one of the most stylish stays in town. ③.

Victoria Protea, corner of Albany Rd and Halstead Lane, just up the hill from the Marina (☎046/624 1133, fax 624 1134). Reliable and comfortable, mid-range hotel that won't deliver any surprises. Ask about discounts for two-night stays during quiet periods. ⑤.

Villa de Mer, 22 West Beach Drive (☎ & fax 046/624 2315). Ostentatious and rather kitsch guesthouse with a courtyard swimming pool, it's major recommendation being that it's one of the few places in town actually along the beachfront – visible through its enormous picture windows. ④.

Camping, budget and self-catering

Bretton Beach Crest, Freshwater Rd, Salt Vlei, 3km west of West Beach (☎046/624 1606). Well-kept if basic cottages that sleep three, set in dune bush, right on the seaside. A casual place that's ideal if you want to spend dawn to dusk in your swimming gear. ①.

Kowie Beach Cabanas, West Beach (book through Moore & Gardner, ☎046/624 2404). Luxury two-bedroom maisonettes that sleep four, in a prime spot and consequently in the thick of holiday activity. Bring your own linen or rent it through the agent. ②.

Kowie River Chalets, West Beach (☎046/624 4182). Port Alfred's most luxurious self-catering units sleeping two to six, in timeshare timber chalets on stilts with terrific views. Close to the river mouth and a stone's throw from the sea. ②.

Marina View, top of Park Rd, above the Marina (☎046/624 4180). Self-catering flats for two to six, nudging the lower end of their price range, with great views and a nice garden with a *braai* area, a 20min walk to the beach or town. ②.

Medolino Carvan Park, Prince's Ave, Kowie West (☎046/41651). Good camping facilities, self-catering chalets (bring your own towels) and a pool in a shady spot protected from the wind by its trees. Camping ①, chalets ②.

Port Alfred Backpackers, 29 Sports Rd (☎046/624 3020, *bapack@imaginet.co.za*). No great shakes as hostels go, but well located near East Beach and the Intercape bus stop. ①.

Riverside Caravan Park, Mentone Rd (☎046/624 2230). Small caravan park where you can rent small two-bedroomed chalets, but there's no camping. Peacefully set next to the river (but 3km from the town and beach) it faces onto a wetland. You can rent boats to explore the waterways. Bed linen can also be rented, but you bring your own towels. ②.

Rugged Rocks, Salt Vlei (☎046/624 3112, after 5pm ☎624 1276). Roughly 4km from the town centre, at a rocky beach, with large discounts out of season. Bring your own bedding, and choose from ropy old cottages sleeping six, or new four-bed wooden chalets sleeping four. All accommodation ②.

Sherwood Shack, Seafield road, signposted off the R72, 22km east of Port Alfred (☎046/675 1090, fax 624 2272, *src@imaginet.co.za*). Large dorms and two self-catering doubles on a farm, away from the coast. Emphasis is on getting to know the local area, with pineapple "safaris", trips to collect shellfish for feasts, and jaunts to Kleinemonde beach or the Fish River wetland. The owner is closely involved in an upliftment scheme teaching computer skills to people from the Port Alfred and Kenton African townships, and visitors are welcome to help – a terrific opportunity to meet members of disadvantaged communities outside a tourism framework. ①.

Spinning Reel Holiday Cottages, Freshwater Rd, Salt Vlei, 3km west of West Beach (☎046/624 4281). Next door to and identical to *Bretton Beach Crest*. ①.

Ten Burke Street, 10 Burke St, Salt Vlei (evenings only ☎046/622 5975, *witt@intekom.co.za*). Cheerful salmon pink cottage with a blue roof set in a large garden, just ten minutes' walk from a secluded, rocky section of beach. The unit sleeps four, comes fully equipped, including linen and a TV, and is rented out for a minimum of two people for two nights. ②.

The Treehouse, follow signs to Three Sisters Horse Trail farmhouse, 14 kilometres east of Port Alfred on the East London road (☎046/675 1269). A retreat for the adventurous, beside the Riet River in a cabin built into a fallen yellowwood tree and set on a hiking trail, with a beautiful *braai* area. It's a 1.5-hour hike from the main farmhouse, carrying all your supplies; the return route, along the Kleinemonde River, lasts 2.5 hours. There's no electricity, and lighting is by gas lamp; bring your own sleeping bags and food. The house sleeps up to eight, but is rented to one party (minumum of two). Not recommended in poor weather. ②.

Willows Caravan Park, Riverside, off the R72, by the bow-arch bridge (☎046/624 5201). Camping at the most central of the caravan parks, alongside Children's Beach and five minutes' walk from West Beach. ①.

The Town and its beaches

Port Alfred's attractions are firmly rooted in its **beaches** and the **Kowie River**. The town itself has little else to offer, apart from functional shopping in its one main street and a couple of open-air shopping malls. Of passing interest is the tiny **Kowie Museum**, in Pascoe Crescent (Mon–Sat 9.30am–12.30pm; free), on the east side of the old bridge, featuring sepia photographs of Port Alfred before the marina and its mansions gobbled up the magnificent lagoon.

Beach life is focused on popular **West Beach**, where the river is sucked out to sea and the breakers pound in. From the café and stone pier, you'll get blasts of sea air watching surfers riding the waves at the river mouth, and fishing boats making dramatic entries into the river from the open ocean. Fifteen minutes' walk west along the beach takes you to **Kelly's Beach**, where you can swim safely in a gentle bay. **East Beach**, reached from the signposted road next to *Halyards Hotel*, is the best walking beach, with a backdrop of hilly dunes stretching as far as you can see into the distance. For toddlers, the safest and most popular spot is **Children's Beach**, a stretch of sand close to the town centre along a shallow section of river, reached from Beach Road, a few hundred metres from the arched bridge.

Port Alfred is home to the reputable **Kowie Dive School** (☎046/624 2213), based at the *Halyards*. Boats go out to Fountain Rocks, and to a couple of nearby wrecks. Don't expect to see crystal waters and fluorescent fish (the Indian Ocean isn't tropical here), but you will come across colourful underwater denizens in the slightly murky water, as well as beautiful corals and sponges. For under R1500, you can qualify in a week for an internationally recognized **diving certificate** here.

Canoe trips, nature trails and riding

The two-day **Kowie Canoe Trail**, a 21-kilometre paddle up the Kowie River, is a much-sought-after trip and one of the only self-guided canoeing and hiking trails in South Africa (elsewhere you're accompanied by a nature conservation officer). Much of its charm is its colourful birdlife, and the landscape – hills of dense, dry bush that slope down to the river. You **stay overnight** in a hut in the **Horseshoe Bend Nature Reserve**, where the river loops around in a brown, curving horseshoe. From here you can explore the forest on foot, and climb up the steep escarpment to get an impressive view over the horseshoe. The biggest difficulty on this trip is the tide – make sure you check the tide table in the local *Kowie Announcer*, and paddle with the flow, going up the river when the tide is coming in, and back to Port Alfred when the river is flowing out. If it's windy, stay close to the shore and ensure your gear is in waterproof bags. **Booking** is essential (☎046/624 2230) and, while weekends are almost always full, weekdays out of school holidays are easy to get, and cost R50 per person, including accommodation.

If the trail is full, you can get a taste of the landscape **on foot** by driving to the reserve and taking the two-hour circular walk that traces its way through thick bush to the Kowie River and along its banks. Look out for primeval **cycads**, some as much as a thousand years old, in the riverine woodland. It's not unusual to see tortoises, monkeys, bushbuck and duikers. By *bakkie* or 4WD, you can reach the reserve, 5km out of Port Alfred along the Bathurst Road. Turn left at the "SANTA" sign and follow the rough road down to the picnic sites, after getting a permit from the rangers. The other access point is 3km before you reach Bathurst, on a dirt road signposted "Waters Meeting", which takes you to the top of the escarpment for a postcard view of the horseshoe. If you're feeling energetic, you can walk down through the forest to the river to get a real feel of the landscape.

Port Alfred has two **riding** establishments. Glenhope Riding, off the Bathurst Road (☎046/625 0866), is based on a pineapple farm and has first-rate horses and fabulous views to the sea; and The Three Sisters Horse Trail, signposted 14km east of Port Alfred off the R72 towards East London road (booking essential, ☎046/675 126; R75 per 90min), which has access to one of the loveliest stretches of the coast in the region. They also offer a couple of night hikes along the Riet and Kleinemond rivers; a one-night trail, staying in *The Treehouse* (see p.299); and a two-night one that continues from there onto *Kajak Camp*, from where you canoe up the Klienemond River.

An ambitious **long-distance hike** linking farms and beaches around Port Alfred is an option if you have more time. Hikers will start at *Bushman's River Backpackers* in Kenton (see p.296), walk along the beach to Port Alfred and continue to *The Treehouse*, just east of Port Alfred (see p.299), ending up at *Sherwood Shack* in Port Alfred (see p.299). The route passes along some of the most sensuous coastline in South Africa and, apart from the odd fisherman's 4WD vehicle, you should find the beaches deserted for a substantial part of the way. Contact Ed Cutten at *Sherwood Shack* for further details and booking (see p.299).

Eating

Port Alfred offers **fresh fish** galore, but the real surprise, and the biggest treat in town, is a private house serving authentic **Thai** food.

Butlers, 25 Van der Riet St (☎046/624 1398). Next to the river, this is the town's swankiest restaurant, and is good for fish.

Dulce's, Campbell St, town centre. The only place in town for halfway decent coffee and sandwiches.

Guidos on the Beach, Main Beach. Pizzas, pasta and booze at a young place with atmosphere on the beachfront, with an upstairs deck for watching the surf, but service isn't their strong point.

Papa Charlies, Arcade, 33 Van der Riet St (☎046/624 4653). The best-value takeaway in town is their freshly fried fish (while you wait) and chips which comes with a small helping of salad.

Ying Thai Restaurant, 6 York Rd (☎046/624 1647). On the east side of town, and serving the best food in Port Alfred; outstanding, authentic Thai cuisine served in a front room of a private home. Booking essential. Fri & Sat evening only.

Grahamstown

Just over 50km inland from Port Alfred, but worlds apart in terms of ambience, **GRA-HAMSTOWN** struggles to project an image of a cultured, historic town, quintessentially English, Protestant and refined. Dominated by its cathedral, university and public schools, this is a thoroughly pleasant place to wander through, with well-restored colonial **Georgian** and **Victorian buildings** lining the streets, and pretty suburban gardens. Every July the town hosts an **arts festival**, the largest of its kind in Africa and purportedly second largest in the world (after Edinburgh).

As elsewhere in South Africa though, there's an alternative reality of conquest and dispossession. Climb up Gunfire Hill, where the fortress-like 1820 **Settlers Monument** celebrates the achievement of South Africa's English-speaking immigrants, and you'll be able to see Makanaskop, the hill from which the **Xhosa** made their last stand against the British invaders. Strewn on its slopes and in its valleys are the desperately poor ghettos, where their descendants live in a town almost devoid of industry. Marking the gap are the Kowie Ditches (which you'll cross if you take the old East London Road out of town), a waterway that ran red with Xhosa blood in the 1819 battle of Grahamstown.

Despite all this, and the constant reminders of poverty, Grahamstown makes a good stopover, and the perfect base for excursions: a number of **historic villages** are within easy reach, some **game parks** are convenient for a day or weekend visit and, best of all, kilometres of **coast** are just 45 minutes' drive away. Cupped in a valley surrounded by hills, Grahamstown itself is compact; you'll only need a car to get out of town.

Some history

Grahamstown's sedate prettiness belies its beginnings as a **military outpost** in 1811. **Colonel Graham** made his name here (and gave it to the town), driving the Xhosa out of the Zuurveld, an area between the Bushman's and Fish rivers. The Fish River, 60km east of Grahamstown, marked the eastern boundary of the frontier, with Grahamstown as the capital. The ruthless expulsion of the Xhosa sparked off a series of nineteenth-century **Frontier Wars**.

A line of **forts** was built to defend the frontier, subsequently developing into the settlements, which now include Fort Beaufort, Fort Hare and Peddie, but these alone

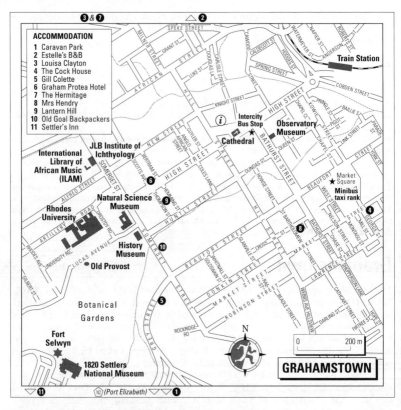

ACCOMMODATION
1 Caravan Park
2 Estelle's B&B
3 Louisa Clayton
4 The Cock House
5 Gill Colette
6 Graham Protea Hotel
7 The Hermitage
8 Mrs Hendry
9 Lantern Hill
10 Old Goal Backpackers
11 Settler's Inn

GRAHAMSTOWN

were not enough to hold the line, and the British decided to reinforce the frontier with a human barrier. With the promise of free land, they lured the dispossessed from a depressed Britain to occupy the lands west of the Fish River. In the migration mythology of English-speaking whites, these much-celebrated **1820 Settlers** came to take on a larger-than-life status as ancestors to whom many trace back their origins. However, far from the hoped-for paradise, the settlers, ill-equipped to deal with the rigours of their new life, found themselves in a nightmare; the plots given them were too small for cattle in the harsh Eastern Cape, and unsuitable for crops; drought, floods and disease were a constant problem, and the threat of Xhosa attack never far away.

Not surprisingly, many settlers abandoned their lands and headed to Grahamstown in the early 1820s. This brought prosperity and growth to the town, which enjoyed a boom in the 1840s, when it developed into the emporium of the frontier. Xhosa traders came to barter ivory and hides for beads, buttons and brass wire, while some colonists, who had persisted with farming in the surrounding district, traded **wool** from Spanish merino sheep which thrived in the Eastern Cape.

Arrival and information

Grahamstown is on the N2, 127km from Port Elizabeth and is roughly an equidistant twelve hours by bus from Cape Town, Johannesburg and Durban. Translux, Intercape and Greyhound **buses** stop outside the Conference Centre on the corner of Bathurst and High steets. The Leopard Express **minibus**, which irregularly connects Grahamstown with the airport at Port Elizabeth, terminates in Hill Street, diagonally opposite the Cathedral.

The **train station** is at the bottom of High Street, but sees only one train a day, a branch-line service connecting to the Johannesburg/Port Elizabeth line. Grahamstown is easily covered **on foot**, and the central accommodation and tourist information office are easily and safely reachable, but if you want a **taxi** use the reliable Beeline (mobile ☎082/652 0798), the only licensed company in town. The helpful **tourist information** bureau (Mon–Thurs 8.30am–5pm, Fri 8.30am–4pm, Sat 9–11am; ☎046/622 3241, fax 622 3266) High Street, next to the City Hall, has useful information on accommodation if our recommendations are full.

Accommodation

The only time you may have difficulty finding **a place to stay** is during the festival in July, when you'd be well-advised to book as early as March. Country Hospitality East Cape (☎046/622 8055) can arrange **bookings** for places in town as well as farms in the surrounding area. If you've just arrived from the Garden Route or one of the more popular tourist areas of South Africa, you'll find prices very reasonable. Grahamstown has the distinction of hosting the only backpackers' lodge in the country in an historic gaol, where you sleep in a cell. That apart, the most notable and choicest places to stay are in historic houses, and there's a good selection of hotels. You also have the opportunity to stay in an **African home** in the township (see box below) – something that remains all-too-rare in the "New South Africa".

The Town

Caravan Park, on the right of the N2 as you come into town from Port Elizabeth (☎046/622 9112). Nicely located next to wooded hills, and an easy walk to town. Besides camping, there are rondavels with bunks and self-catering chalets sleeping five (bring your own linen). ①–②.

Lantern Hill, 2 Thompson St (☎ & fax 046/622 8782). A couple of unpretentious, homely double rooms with access to a kitchen for self-catering in a family home just off High St. ③.

The Cock House, 10 Market St (☎046/6361295, fax 636 1287). Plush rooms in a beautiful Victorian country house, considered the town's top stay. Among its satisfied guests it counts Nelson Mandela, who has stayed here on two occasions. ④.

Gill Colette, 6 Grey St (☎046/622 2746, fax 636 1496). Two fully equipped self-catering apartments opposite the Botanical Gardens, an easy walk to the centre. ②.

Graham Protea Hotel, 123 High St (☎046/622 2324, fax 622 2424). Overpriced given its impersonal ambience, but the most central of Grahamstown's hotels, a stone's throw from the University. Ask about low-period discounts. ⑤.

GRAHAMSTOWN EAST HOMESTAYS

Under apartheid there were no B&Bs in the "African areas" of South Africa, and these days they are a rarity. There are signs, however, that the situation is slowly changing, and spending even a little time in one of the townships will give you a different perspective on the country and take you off the beaten tourism track that has always been the exclusive preserve of white operators. Grahamstown provides the ideal opportunity to do this conveniently without having to traipse too far (the townships are less than ten minutes' drive from the centre). Eastside Accommodation (contact Mfundo Draai, ☎046/637 1897, fax 622 5847) can place you with an hospitable Xhosa family in Grahamstown East, where you will be taken good care of. Expect to pay around R65 per person a night for B&B.

The Hermitage, 14 Henry St (☎046/636 1503). The best-value B&B in town, with bed and sitting room suites in a luxurious and stylish historic house. There are only two rooms, so book ahead. ③.

Mrs Hendry, 8 Bartholomew St & 1 Sheblon Lane, off Cross St (☎046/622 9720). Reasonably priced settler cottages (both National Monuments) in the old part of town, with yellowwood stripped floors. ③.

Old Gaol Backpackers, Somerset St (☎046/636 1001). Dorms and doubles in the dark cells of an old jail built in 1824. A truly atmospheric experience that may well prove too claustrophobic for some. ①.

Settlers' Inn Hotel, off the N2, next to 1820 Settlers Monument (☎046/622 7313). Just out of town, with a motel feel, peaceful surroundings, a nice garden and pool. ④.

The Town

Reminders of the **colonial past** are everywhere in central Grahamstown, not just in the architecture, but also the street names of Cape governors and soldiers: Cradock, Meyer, Somerset, Stockenstrom and Cuyler. The University itself, of course, is named after Cecil John Rhodes (see p.244).

High Street

Virtually all the shops and banks you'll need are down **High Street**, Grahamstown's major shopping axis. Running from the station at its seedier east end, it continues past the Cathedral at the junction of Hill Street, terminating at the 150-year-old Drostdy Arch, the whitewashed entrance gate to the former courthouse, now of Rhodes University. The terraces of the nineteenth-century buildings lend a graceful air to High Street. You'll also see hawkers on the pavements selling small bags of fruit and vegetables, and may see young Xhosa men in new caps and jackets, with red clay on their faces, signifying that their initiation period is over. At the centre of the street is the **Cathedral of St Michael and St George**, opened in 1830 and, like many churches in the area, a refuge for women and children during the Frontier Wars. Inside, on the right as you come in, is a quietly ironic memorial tablet to Colonel John Graham, who commanded the frontier.

Rhodes University and the museums

Strung along Somerset Street, which runs at right angles to the top (west end) of High Street, is **Rhodes University** and a succession of modest museums – all are covered by a convenient multi-entry ticket, and can pleasantly take up a morning.

If you've time for only one, head for the **Natural Science Museum** (Mon–Fri 9.30am–1pm & 2–5pm, Sat & Sun 2–5pm), just south of the University entrance on the same side of the street. The display of Eastern Cape fauna and flora from 250 million years ago is excellent, with intriguing plant fossils and bones of dinosaurs, which once roamed these parts. Also worth a look is the **gallery** of the curator who worked for 48 years at the museum, which houses his personal collection of objects in beautiful old teak display cases.

Next door, the **History Museum**, which once housed a dusty collection of 1820 Settlers memorabilia, nineteenth-century paintings and antique firearms, has been sold off to Rhodes University, though it is mooted that its contents will be relocated to the Science Museum – enquire there for an update.

Beyond the Drostdy Arch, tucked behind some buildings at the corner of Somerset and Prince Alfred streets, is **ILAM**, the International Library of African Music (Mon–Fri 8am–5pm; free; ☎046/636 8557). An absolute treasure trove of recordings of traditional African music from southern Africa, as well as Zaire, Rwanda, Uganda and Tanzania, the library also sells cassettes on request, and there's a collection of over 200 traditional instruments on view and for sale. Phone beforehand to be shown around (from R80), and to get a demonstration and chance to play some instruments with astonishing African music expert Andrew Tracey. Reasonably priced instruments, handmade using high-quality timber, can be bought from their **workshop** in Froud Street.

On the same side of the road, the **JLB Smith Institute of Ichthyology** (Mon–Fri 8.30am–1pm & 2–5pm; free) is named after the Rhodes University scientist who shot to fame in 1939 after identifying the coelacanth, a "missing link" fish, caught off the East London coast, and thought to have been extinct for fifty million years. In the foyer are two huge stuffed specimens, with fins that look like budding arms and legs. Far from being extinct, plenty of coelacanths have now been spotted by deep-sea divers; their preferred dwelling is in the pressurized, pitch-dark depths of the Indian Ocean around the Comoros Islands. There are no known colonies of them off the South African coast, they can't survive in aquaria, and it's still not known exactly how they reproduce.

Heading back down High Street and right onto Bathurst Street will bring you to the **Observatory Museum** (Mon–Fri 9.30am–1pm & 2–5pm; small entry fee), a fun display in a restored building that was the part-home and part-shop of a notable watchmaker and jeweller during the mid-1850s. Also well worth a visit is the unusual rooftop Victorian **camera obscura**, which projects magnified images of the streets below, onto a wall. It's best seen on clear day, when the reflections are crisp and clear.

The Old Provost, Monument and Botanical Gardens

One of Grahamstown's rewarding short walks starts at the **Old Provost** in Lucas Avenue, on the edge of the Botanical Gardens and University, and heads up through the gardens to the 1820 Settlers Monument, on the hill above. Built as a prison last century, the whitewashed stone Provost is now a craft shop. Next to it you'll find some graves of British soldiers, killed by Xhosa warriors.

Looming on Gunfire Hill, the **1820 Settlers Monument**, built in 1974 to commemorate the British settlers, is an ugly fortress-like building, supposedly fashioned to look like a ship. The best reason to trudge up here is for the panoramic views, or to see something at the Monument Theatre (see p.306). Women should avoid wandering around the gardens alone, especially in the evenings, as there have been some muggings and rapes.

Xhosa Grahamstown

Xhosa Grahamstown starts buzzing around **Market Square**, off Beaufort Street, where you'll see hawkers by the dozen and a busy minibus-taxi rank. In the late 1820s, the square was the trading venue for ivory, hides, wool and farm produce. If you're in the area, it's worth walking west of Market Square to see the restored **1820 Settlers cottages** in Cross and Bartholomew streets, some flat-roofed and double-storeyed, others with pitched tin roofs.

Beaufort Street, the main road for traffic passing through, leads up the hill towards the townships on the eastern side of town. At the top, the road cuts through a hill of white clay, where Xhosa people scratch out pigment for face markings. From this cutting, looking into the valley, well away from the squatters' shacks, you'll see some roughly made traditional huts, used during the seclusion period, when young men, **amakweta**, are inititated. All over the Eastern Cape, it's not unusual to see *amakweta* on the roadside wearing very little and smeared in white clay, which signifies that they've just been circumcised and initiated into manhood (Nelson Mandela went through the same ordeal, as a Xhosa speaker).

Beyond the cutting lies the treeless **Kings Flats** township where the **Umthathi Self-help Project** teaches people how to grow vegetables and raise chickens. Umthathi's office in Grahamstown train station (☎046/622 4450) can arrange **township tours** that include a traditional Xhosa lunch with a local African family, in a clean, bright township house. The money goes to the family and it's a great way to experience black South Africa authentically and in safety.

Eating and drinking

Eating prospects in Grahamstown are far from exciting, but at least one good pub, a decent coffee shop, and a couple of restaurants with pleasant settings, all go some way towards making up for the workaday fare. If you're **self catering**, the Home Industries shop on Hill Street is great for homemade pies, seasonal fruit and vegetables, and venison and ostrich eggs for gigantic omelettes (all their produce comes from local farms).

Restaurants, tea shops and pubs

The Blue Room, 127a High St. You may find yourself accidentally sitting in on a tutorial at this thoroughly convivial upstairs venue frequented by university staff and students. Excellent for light meals, interesting sandwiches, bottomless cups of coffee and the birds-eye view down High Street.

The Cock House, corner of Market and George streets (☎046/636 1295). Grahamstown's smartest restaurant in the town's top guesthouse with Provençal cuisine on its medium-priced menu. Booking advised.

La Galleria, 13 New St (☎046/622 2345). Highly recommended, moderately priced Italian restaurant run by Italians. Closed Sun.

Peppers, 28 New St. Hardcore drinking spot with a pool table, where town and gown mingle.

Pop Art Cafe, New St, opposite *La Galleria*. Grahamstown's most self-consciously stylish pub, where art students posture and cocktails are *de rigueur*. A juke box with a decent selection of modern and retro sounds is an added attraction.

The Rat & Parrot, New St. Jekyll and Hyde of a venue that's a lively student bar and restaurant by day, but becomes unpleasantly rowdy by night. Come for the decent food, notably dishes cooked and served in individual pots, or *potjies* (the seafood *potjie* is outstanding).

Redwood Spur, High St, near the cathedral. Reliable American-style food, with big salads and late-night bottomless coffee, served with a smile by clean-cut young waiters.

Settlers Inn, just behind the Monument, off the PE road. Grahamstown's best outdoor venue, in large gardens around a pool and duck pond, affording views that skim across the roofs of the town. Passable steaks, fish and other standard cheap- to medium-priced fare, this is the best place for a bite if you've got kids. If you're on foot, you can get there by walking up through the Botanical Gardens.

Entertainment

As home to the country's premier arts festival, and dominated by Rhodes University, you might think Grahamstown is going to be a bustling centre of nightlife, culture and entertainment. But you'd be sadly wrong. Outside the hectic festival fortnight in July, the town relies on its two **cinemas** to deliver its only regular evening entertainment. Of these, The Galaxy, based at the 1820s Settlers Monument, is the more salubrious and attempts to screen imaginative fare in addition to the usual Hollywood offerings.

However, because of the university connection, the town *is* periodically treated to a more exciting range of events than you'd be likely to find in the average Karoo *dorp*. You may stumble into town when there's something exceptional going on, so keep your eyes peeled. The two main venues for **live performances** are the Monument Theatre, and the Rhodes University Theatre, where the Drama Department puts on productions from time to time. Well worth catching is anything staged by solo-artist **Andrew Buckland**, a local actor who has made an international reputation in the world of physical theatre.

The university's Music Department also puts on eclectic and fairly regular classical **music concerts**, while local rock and folk musicians sometimes perform at *The Blue Room*. Black musicians also sometimes hit town, performing at the town hall or venues

THE GRAHAMSTOWN FESTIVAL

Every July, Grahamstown bursts to overflowing, with visitors descending for the annual Standard Bank National Arts Festival – usually called the **Grahamstown Festival**, or more simply The Festival. The hub of the event is the 1820 Settlers Monument, which hosts not only big drama, dance and operatic productions in its theatres, but also art exhibitions and free early evening concerts. Grahamstown's festival proper began in 1974 when the Monument building was opened; today, it's the largest arts festival in Africa, and even has its own fringe festival. For eleven days, the town's population doubles to 100,000, with seemingly every home transformed into a B&B and the streets alive with colourful food stalls. Church halls, parks and sports fields become flea markets and several hundred shows are staged, spanning every conceivable type of performance.

The published festival programme is bulky, but absolutely essential, and it's worth planning your time carefully to avoid walking the potentially very cold July streets, snooping around the markets and seeing nothing of the festival proper. The programme includes jazz, classical music, drama, dance, cabaret, opera, visual arts, crafts, films and a book fair. While work by African performers and artists is well-represented, and is perhaps the more interesting aspect of the festival for tourists, festival-goers and performers are still predominantly white. If you don't feel like taking in a show, the free art exhibitions at the museums, Monument and other smaller venues are always worth a look.

For more **information and bookings**, contact the Grahamstown Foundation, PO Box 304, Grahamstown 6140 (☎046/622 7115, fax 622 4457).

in the African townships. To find out **what's on** when you're in town, check the fly-posters down High Street and also look in *Grocott's Mail*, the local rag, which comes out on Tuesday and Friday afternoons. Another source of information is *GOG – Good Old Grahamstown*, a monthly booklet available from the tourist information bureau.

Around Grahamstown

From Grahamstown, it's a short journey to the **coast**: Port Alfred and Kenton-on-Sea are both less than an hour by car (see p.296), and each has a historic settler village en route – **Bathurst** and **Salem** respectively. A bit further afield, you can meander down dirt roads, pausing at old settler churches and graves, and end up at the Great Fish River Wetland Reserve (see p.322), which has a magnificent beach and river frontage.

Grahamstown is also close to a couple of fine **wildlife reserves**, especially good for getting a look at the striking, dry bush particular to this area, and at some of the wildlife which, little over a century ago, roamed the land freely. *Old Gaol Backpackers* (see p.304) can help arrange excursions to its sister hostel in **Mpofu Game Reserve**, and if you have your own transport, the highlight is the **Great Fish River Reserve Complex**, a rambling wilderness slaked by the Great Fish and its tributary, the Kap. Its appeal lies in its neglected feel – the roads can be rough at times – when held up against either Addo Elephant Park or the upmarket Shamwari Game Reserve, its cross-section of game, and the beauty of its landscape.

Bathurst and around

Historically a significant centre, **BATHURST**, 45km south of Grahamstown, is today little more than a picturesque straggle of houses, gardens and curiosity shops. Nevertheless, for anyone with the remotest interest in the settler trail it's an intriguing place, the highlight being the **Toposcope**, a monument that indicates the locations of the original settlers' farms, and St John's. The *Pig and Whistle Hotel*, on the corner of the Grahamstown road as you drive into Bathurst, started life as a smithy in 1821, with an inn attached a few years later; they can provide maps and directions to historical sites. The water-powered **Bradshaw's Wool Mill** is a pleasant two-kilometre walk from the *Pig and Whistle,* and marks the spot where South Africa's wool industry started.

If you've got children with you, the setup at **Summerhill Farm** (see below) will appeal to them, with an outsized yellow and green plastic pineapple museum plonked in the middle of a field full of the genuine items, as well as a pool and a playground. The area is a major farming district for the fruit and if you've ever wondered how they're grown, this is the place to find out.

Practicalities

You'll find **self-catering accommodation** at *Hayhurst,* midway through Bathurst on the Port Alfred Road (☎046/625 0856, *hayhurst@intekom.co.za;* ①), in two converted railway buses, with kitchens and bath, in a garden with a pool. For **B&B**, the two cottages at *Cosy Corner,* Hill St (☎ & fax 046/625 0955; ②), are good value, with a pool and *braai* facilities; they're also available as fully equipped self-catering units. If you're looking to stay at the *Pig and Whistle* (☎046/625 0673; ③), ask for one of the old **rooms** upstairs, furnished with period pieces. The town's most luxurious accommodation is offered by the very child-friendly *Summerhill Farm* (☎046/625 0833, fax 625 0621, *pineapple@imaginet.co.za;* ③), landmarked by its enormous plastic pineapple, along the main Port Alfred road (the R67). Best here are the B&B en-suite units in the original farmstead, with double beds, sitting areas and bunks for kids. There's a pool and you're free to explore the farm. Out of town is the upmarket *Findon Guest Farm* (☎046/624 2368; B&B ③): head south for 8km toward Port Alfred, then take the signposted turn-off. The proprietors are master chefs, so you can enjoy three really great meals a day, plus there's a bar – though, paradoxically, it's also a health farm offering acupressure, cleansing diets and medicinal herbs grown on the property. You can use their mountain bikes on the farm's cycling trails.

When it comes to **eating and drinking,** the atmospheric *Pig and Whistle* is a favourite weekend spot for locals to down a beer or five. Across the road, the *Bathurst Arms* serves pub lunches, and has a few tables in the garden. *Summerhill Farm* has a bar and a mid-priced restaurant for lunches and dinners, including English-style fish, chicken and meat, plus veggie meals. On Sundays they do a self-service carvery that needs to be booked (see above).

Salem and around

Grahamstown's closest nature reserve, **Thomas Baines** (daily dawn–dusk; free), is a hilly area 15km south of town on the road to Kenton-on-Sea. The main attraction here is **Settler's Dam**, good for picnics, *braais* and wandering around the vicinity of the dam. Walking elsewhere isn't permitted, as rhino and buffalo hang out in the thick, prickly bush. During late afternoons, you're very likely to see antelope grazing on open spaces.

SALEM, 20km southwest of Grahamstown along the same road, is a scrawny collection of settler homesteads dating back to 1822, surrounded by khaki scrub and arranged around a village green, dotted some Sundays with the bleached whites of local cricket teams. Salem's centrepiece is a little whitewashed **church**, which is now a National Monument and worth a brief visit, though there's nowhere to get anything to eat or drink. Inside, a plaque commemorates Quaker **Richard Gush**, whose descendants still live in the hamlet. During the Sixth Frontier War, local settlers took refuge in a stone church, where they were confronted by Xhosa raiders. Fed up with the ceaseless conflict, Gush stepped out unarmed to confront the Xhosa about their grievances. On being told they were driven by hunger, he went inside and, to the irritation of his fellows, returned with armloads of food. The town was subsequently left in peace.

Moving on from Salem, halfway to Kenton-on-Sea is Belton Hiking Trails (☎ & fax 046/622 8395; ①), who offer cheap dormitory **accommodation**, and self-catering facilities in a converted farmhouse. If the place is not booked out, you could get a room to yourself, though you'll need sleeping bags. The main point of coming here is for the several **hiking trails** on the farm, the longest taking you along cliffs and down to the Bushman's River. A further 6km on is the far more upmarket *Kariega Park* (☎046/636 1049, fax 636 2288, *kariega@yebo.co.za*), a privately run and delightful game reserve, with balconied lodges set in the bush. Lodges have three or four bedrooms and are rented out on a fully inclusive basis that includes all meals and game drives (⑦), or as B&B (⑤) or self-catering (④) units. The main activity is walking through the reserve looking for its varied range of herbivores that include giraffes, going on game drives or evening river booze cruises. You can also go swimming in the river or swimming pool.

The Great Fish River Reserve Complex

Thirty-four kilometres north of Grahamstown on the Fort Beaufort Road (the R67), lies the huge **Great Fish River Reserve Complex**, an amalgamation of three separate reserves covering 430 square kilometres . Provided you're ready to rough it, Great Fish is the Eastern Cape's most rewarding wildlife destination after Addo (see p.291), despite the notable absence of lions. A far cry from the well-tended game parks of Mpumalanga or KwaZulu-Natal, it has no shops or restaurants and the roads are often poor, but it's wild and very beautiful. Along the banks of the Fish and Kat rivers stands of thorn trees afford welcome shade during the summer heat, while in the parched areas away from the rivers, the striking landscape of cliffs and dense valleys is overgrown with scrubby bush, thick with succulents, euphorbias and aloes. The varied terrain supports an abundant range of **game** (although not in large numbers) including small predators such as black-backed jackals and larger ones like hyenas and rarely seen leopards. Among the trees and bushes you'll see several species of browsers and grazers, from blesbok to nyala, including numerous white rhinos, a handful of elephants, and warthogs by the dozen. A few snorting hippos while away their days in the rivers, and along the banks you may see waterbuck; look out for vervets in the trees.

Access

Self-driving is the only way to visit the Complex, most easily reached from the tarred R67, which connects Grahamstown to Fort Beaufort and provides **access** to the two entrances on the western flank: **Kamadolo Gate** in the south and **Sam Knott Gate** in the north. The R345 runs through the eastern section of the reserve, connecting the N2, at a point around 70km east of Grahamstown (just beyond the town of Peddie) with Alice (see p.332); this reasonable dirt road takes you to **Charles Tinley Gate**, the park headquarters (office daily 8am–5pm, gate open 24hr; ☎040/653 8010). The Great Fish River and its tributary, the Kat, flow in a series of sinuous oxbows to segment the reserve into three, so you can't always count on getting from one section to another in an ordinary vehicle, particularly when the river levels rise to flood the fords. If you do intend driving through the reserve, either enquire at headquarters about conditions before leaving or take a direct route to your destination. **Roads in the reserve** are dirt tracks and are frequently poor, so you'll have to drive carefully and slowly.

Accommodation

There's a limited selection of lodges and cabins in each of the reserve's three sections. Staff are on hand at the lodges to cook for guests, inlcuded in the price, and you pay a

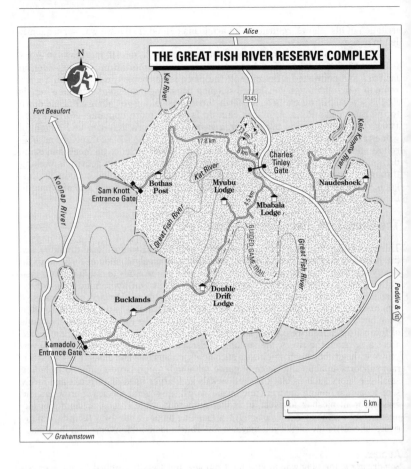

THE GREAT FISH RIVER RESERVE COMPLEX

N

Fort Beaufort

Kat River

R345

Keiskamma River

17.8 km

Kat River

Charles Tinley Gate

Naudeshoek

Bothas Post

Sam Knott Entrance Gate

Myubu Lodge

Mbabala Lodge

Koonap River

Great Fish River

4.5 km

GUIDED GAME TRAIL

Great Fish River

△ *Peddie & N*

Bucklands

Double Drift Lodge

Kamadolo Entrance Gate

0   6 km

▽ *Grahamstown*

minimum charge based on a group of four, with the exception of Botha's Post, where it's two. All bookings (except Bucklands) are through Eastern Cape Tourism Board in Bisho (☎040/635/2115, fax 636 4019).

In the **eastern section** (east of the Fish River), *Mbabala Lodge* (③) lies 2km south of Charles Tinley Gate, offers five doubles and is charged out to a single party at a time. Thirteen kilometres southeast of the gate, on the banks of the Keiskamma river, Naudeshoek has a single log cabin that sleeps six (②). At Mvubu, 9km southwest of the gate, there are four twin-bedded chalets (②) sharing a communal kitchen, dining area and plunge pool. There are also six rustic maisonette-style family chalets (③) right on the Great Fish, each sleeping two adults and two children.

In the **southwestern section** (the closest one to Grahamstown), *Double Drift Lodge* (①), 16km northeast of Kamadolo Gate, is a basic place with five doubles, perched on the north bank of the Great Fish. Also accessible through Kamadolo Gate is the privately owned *Bucklands Farm* (☎ & fax 046/622 8055, *buck@imaginet.co.za*), in a small salient with 17km of its own river frontage, technically outside the reserve. There's a large modern prefab house (②) in the farmyard for rent with single beds and bunks, which is equipped for self catering.

Finally, in the **northwestern section**, 3km inside the reserve from Sam Knott Gate, at Botha's Post, you'll find four self-catering cabins (②) that sleep four, each with en-suite shower, toilet and kitchenette.

Game viewing and activities

Most people coming to the reserve want to see **hippos** – a relatively rare sight in the Eastern Cape. To do so, report to Charles Tinley Gate and ask for an armed ranger to take you on the **guided game trail**, which runs along the northern bank of the Great Fish from *Double Drift Lodge*. Despite their cumbersome appearance, hippos can be extremely dangerous and are responsible for more deaths in Africa than any other animal. If you're staying at *Bucklands Farm*, you can arrange a similar outing through the owner, Lynne Philips. *Bucklands* also lay on excellent guided day- and night-time **game drives**.

If you're **self-driving**, your best bet is to make for the **Nyathi** loop, in the north-eastern section of the reserve, where game tends to concentrate. The best time to see the animals is early morning and late afternoon; at midday the animals duck into the deep shade of trees and bushes, where you won't see them. This is your cue to head for the terrific picnic spot near Double Drift, on the south bank of the Great Fish, under the shade of huge acacia trees.

If this all sounds too sedentary, there's always the option of **whitewater rafting** down the Great Fish. River Rafters, 45 Kendal Rd, Diep River, Cape Town (☎021/712 5094, fax 712 5241, *rafters@mweb.co.za*), organize weekend trips from September to May, including shooting the rapids, abseiling and game drives, for a minimum of nine people. You have a choice of staying at *Double Drift Lodge* (R350) or the Mvubu chalets (R415); prices are all inclusive.

Inland to the Karoo fringes

Travelling between Grahamstown and the towns of Cradock and Graaff-Reinet (the Eastern Cape's two most-visited Karoo towns), you'll be heading into **sheep farming country**, with the occasional *dorp* rising against the horizon, offering the chance to soak up the feel of an archetypal Eastern Cape one-horse outpost. The roads are quiet, and lined with rhythmically spaced telephone poles. Along the shimmering roadsides, people trudge long distances in the heat to unimaginable destinations in the middle of this vast emptiness. Dun-coloured sheep, angora goats and the odd springbok graze on brown stubble, and you'll often see groups of charcoal and grey ostriches in the *veld*, once farmed to satisfy an Edwardian feather fetish, and now reared to cater for a fashion for lean and healthy meat.

Adelaide, Bedford and Somerset East

The R63 west from Fort Beaufort (see p.334) brings you to **ADELAIDE**, a tiny Victorian market centre named after one of Queen Victoria's daughters. Arranged around a square, the tiny hamlet is dominated by the *Adelaide Century Lodge* (☎046/684 1058; ②), which is no bad reason to **stay overnight**. Life centres around its bar, outside which you'll see local farmers' *bakkies*, loaded with patient sheep waiting for their owners to quench their thirst after a tough morning at the stock sales. Many of the hotel's original Victorian trimmings are still in place, including a dining room, which serves solid steak and fried **lunches**.

Twenty-two kilometres west of Adelaide, in the foothills of the Kaga Mountains, is **BEDFORD**. Once the realm of Xhosa Chief Phato, it became one of the little "English" towns Cape governor Sir Harry Smith had promised to create. Now a drive-through place as you come off the road from Grahamstown, it nevertheless has some attractive settler buildings. In the mountainous backdrop you'll find some **farmstays**, most notably *Cavers*, 16km north of Bedford (✆ & fax 046/685 0619; ⑤), a working settler dairy farm tucked away in a pretty valley in the mountains. It has a thatched two-bedroomed cottage with its own garden, and the use of a swimming pool and tennis courts; walks on the property give you the chance to see antelope and myriad birds. You need to book in advance, when the owners will give you directions.

Just under 60km west of Bedford lies **SOMERSET EAST**, a town that gets chewing during its *biltong* festival in June, and where Afrikaans matrons with tight perms, cardigans and plump brown arms stroll the main street. The historical part of the town merits a visit. Down Beaufort Street, on an axis with the white-spired Dutch Reformed Church is the **Somerset East Museum** (Mon–Fri 8am–1pm & 2–5pm), whose most interesting feature is the building itself, once the home of a Victorian pastor, and today with rose-petal jam for sale, attesting to a once isolated "civilized" life in this strange, dry land. Somerset's second attraction is the **Walter Battiss Art Gallery** (Mon–Fri 10am–1pm & 2–5pm), in a handsome two-storeyed house on the corner of Beaufort and Poulet streets. Inside you'll find a very uneven collection of drawings and paintings by one of South Africa's best-known modern artists. It's worth a visit though; Batiss is noted for his sense of humour, which shines out even in this collection.

Cradock and around

CRADOCK, 240km north of Port Elizabeth, lies in the Karoo proper, the semi-desert heartland of South Africa, with knee-high bush, clear dry air and an enormous sense of space, reaching over horizons of slaty mountains. It makes a great stopover on the Port Elizabeth to Johannesburg run, not least because of the excellence of its accommodation in historical houses, and also for the **Mountain Zebra National Park**, which despite having no big cats is one of the country's top game parks.

On the surrounding sheep farms, you'll see the silvery **windmills** which have become an unofficial symbol of Cradock. Xhosa hawkers (often kids) stand along the main road around the city limits, selling intricately crafted wire model windmills, whose blades really do spin in the breeze. You're unlikely to see these anywhere else in South Africa apart from in Johannesburg galleries and on TV, where they first hit national stardom in a mobile phone advert.

Poverty, the motivation for this home industry, has overshadowed Cradock since the Frontier Wars of the last century and the subjugation of the Xhosa people that continued right up to the Nineties. Against this history of conquest, the town has provided fertile grounds for **resistance**: some members of the ANC were based in and around the town, and almost single-handedly kept the organization alive during the Thirties. In 1985, Cradock hit the headlines when anti-apartheid activist **Matthew Goniwe** (see box on p.314) and three of his colleagues were murdered.

Political controversy is also the theme at Cradock's biggest attraction, **Schreiner House**, 9 Cross St (Mon–Fri 8.45am–12.45pm & 2–4.30pm; small entrance fee). The house is dedicated to the life of the remarkable writer Olive Schreiner, best known for her novel *The Story of an African Farm* (1883), the first work of imaginative power in South African literature. It was remarkable enough for a woman from the conservative backwoods of nineteenth-century Eastern Cape to write a novel (it was published under the pseudonym Ralph Iron), but even more amazing that she espoused ideas considered dangerously radical even a century later. While in London looking for a publisher, Schreiner mixed with the likes of Havelock Ellis and Eleanor Marx, returning to South Africa at the turn of the century to campaign for universal franchise for men and women

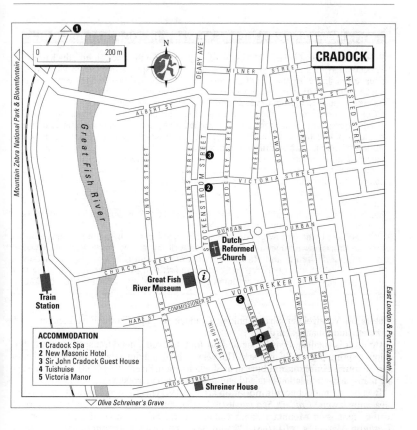

irrespective of race. After a life of campaigning, Schreiner died in Cape Town in 1921 and is buried near Cradock on the Buffelskop peak, overlooking the Great Fish River Valley. Her **burial site** has become something of a place of pilgrimage and details of how to get there are available from the tourist information bureau (see overleaf), along with a photocopied Ordnance Survey map. You'll need a car to get to the starting point, and you should allow a good half-day for the trip, which involves a very stiff climb.

Cradock's other highlights include the **Dutch Reformed Church** at the upper end of Church Street, based on London's St Martin's in the Field and completed in 1868, and a hot sulphur spring-fed **swimming pool**, Marlow Road (4.5km from town), which has indoor and open-air pools, and is a great place to relax after a long journey. The **Great Fish River Museum** behind the Town Hall (Tues–Fri 8am–1pm, Sat 8am–noon) is housed in an 1849 Dutch Reformed Church parsonage and depicts the early history of Eastern Cape pioneers.

Practicalities

Daily **trains** (information ☎048/801 8202) from Port Elizabeth to Johannesburg arrive at Cradock Station at the south end of Church Street at 7pm in the evening, and far less conveniently at 4.30am going the other way. Translux **buses** pull in daily at Struwig

MATTHEW GONIWE AND THE SLAYING OF THE CRADOCK FOUR

Even by apartheid standards, 1985 was a dark year for South Africa. In July, the hawkish President P.W. Botha declared a state of emergency in response to a nationwide wave of popular resistance. By the end of the year, over five hundred people had been killed in police action. In this maelstrom of repression, **Matthew Goniwe** and three other Eastern Cape leaders from Cradock died in "mysterious" circumstances.

Goniwe, a prominent member and rural organizer for the United Democratic Front (UDF; a proxy organization for the then-banned ANC), left Vergenoeg township on the outskirts of Cradock early on June 27, 1985. Accompanied by **Fort Calata**, **Sparrow Mkhonto** and **Sicelo Mhlauli**, he was heading for a UDF meeting in Port Elizabeth. The four were never to return. On their way home, they were ambushed, murdered and their bodies burnt and spread several kilometres apart. The nature of the murder indicated considerable planning and resources. A highly publicized inquest in 1989 could not find the necessary evidence to incriminate apartheid government forces. In May 1992 a chilling document leaked to the anti-apartheid *New Nation* newspaper revealed that a signal had been sent by Commandant du Plessis to General van Rensberg calling for Matthew Goniwe to be "permanently removed from society".

On the basis of the *New Nation* document, the inquest was reopened in 1993, and found that the assassins were members of the South African Defence Force. Dramatically, in 1997, during the **Truth and Reconciliation Commission** hearings, five members of the Port Elizabeth security police applied for amnesty to the Commission, confessing to the killings and explaining how they intercepted the car and murdered the Cradock Four.

Motors on Voortrekker Street, linking Cradock to Cape Town, East London, Port Elizabeth and Johannesburg.

Cradock is small and easily handled **on foot**, but you'll need transport to get to the sulphur spring pool or Zebra Park. The very helpful and desperately overworked one-person **tourist information** bureau in Stockenstroom Street (☎048/881 2383) can supply maps, accommodation lists and and information on farmstays.

Best bet for budget **accommodation** are the B&B chalets sleeping two to four at the pleasantly lawned *Cradock Spa* (☎048/881 2709; ②), 4.5km north of town on the road to the signposted Mountain Zebra National Park. For more comfort, head for the *Tuishuise*, Market St (☎048/881 1322, fax 881 5388, *tuishuise@global.co.za*; ④), a street of one- to four-bedroomed Victorian houses furnished with period decor. Other good options include the *Sir John Cradock Guest House*, Stockenstroom St (☎048/881 1443; ②), which has nicely furnished rooms with bath and a small garden. Of the two hotels, the old and characterful *Victoria Manor*, Market St (☎048/881 1322, fax 881 5388, *tuishuise@global.co.za*; ③), under the same ownership as the *Tuishuise*, is the nicer, while the *New Masonic Hotel*, Stockenstroom St (☎048/881 3115; ②), offers standard bed and breakfast but no funny handshakes. Out of town, the most accessible farmstay, with the least expensive B&B rooms outside Cradock, is *Bergendal* (☎048/881 4416 or 881 2239; ②), 12km south of town off the main Port Elizabeth road, on an angora goat and ostrich ranch.

The town's most notable **restaurant** is the *1814* (☎048/881 5390), with a distinctive sloping red roof standing out on Main Road. Here you'll find tasty breakfasts, lunches and teas with an Afrikaans bias. For more predictable fast food, cross the road for the *Steer*, part of the ubiquitous burger and chips chain. Along similar lines and a good bet for a pit stop if you're passing through is *Fraser's Grill* (☎048/881 1497), a favourite with local families in the Total filling station complex on Voortrekker Street. For something more exciting, make for *Lemoenhoek* (☎048/881 2514), 5km south of town on the R337 (the Mortimer road), where you can sit down to a high-quality four-course *boerekos* menu elevated with a soupçon of French sophistication.

Mountain Zebra National Park

When the **Mountain Zebra National Park** (daily: May–Sept 7am–6pm; Oct–April 7am–7pm; ☎048/881 2427) was created in 1937, there were only five Cape **mountain zebras** left on its 65 square kilometres. If that wasn't bad enough, four of them were males. At the time, environmental issues were far from being vote-winners; indeed, one cabinet minister dismissed the threatened animals as "a lot of donkeys in football jerseys". Miraculously, conservationists managed to cobble together a breeding herd from the few survivors on surrounding farms, and the park now supports several hundred of them, while also translocating healthy numbers to different corners of South Africa, thus securing their future.

For **game viewing**, the park has a couple of good part-tar, part-gravel loop roads forming a rough figure of eight. Most rewarding is the northernmost route, 14.5km long, which circuits the Rooiplaat section where the plains game tend to congregate. As well as zebra, keep an eye out for **springbok, blesbok** and **black wildebeest**. The introduction of **buffalo** in May 1998 and plans to bring in **cheetahs** and **rhinos**, adds to the wildlife interest, but has ended hiking in the park, one of its previous highlights. Unlike docile Asian water buffalo, their African cousins have a reputation for extreme aggression and rancour, which instils justified fear in even hardened hunters. Note that despite this, official literature still refers to three-day hikes and waymarked trails, information you should discount as, besides two short waymarked walks near the camp, you're no longer allowed to wander around freely on your own.

Practicalities

Mountain Zebra National Park is 26km west of Cradock. To get there by **car**, head north out of Cradock on the N10, turning west after about 6km onto the Graaff-Reinet Road. After a further 5km, turn left at the National Park sign onto a good gravel road, which reaches the park gate after a further 16km.

The park has **accommodation** in twenty comfortable two-bedroomed cottages (③), all of which have outstanding mountain views and their own kitchens and bathrooms. The price includes breakfast in the camp restaurant. There's also a good **campsite** (①), but the unrivalled highlight of the park's lodgings is the self-catering **Doornhoek Guest House** (③, based on a minimum of four), a beautifully restored Victorian homestead set in splendid isolation with great Karoo views across a small lake to the chain of scrubby hills that sweep around it. Extremely comfortable, it sleeps six people in three en-suite bedrooms furnished with antique beds. For **bookings** contact South African National Parks (Pretoria ☎012/343 1991, fax 343 0905; Cape Town ☎021/22 2810, fax 24 6211; *reservations@parks-sa.co.za*). A twenty percent discount on accommodation and camping is available from June to September, excluding school holidays (when the park is always booked out).

A small **shop** at reception sells basics, souvenirs, alcohol and soft drinks, but if you're staying for a few days you should stock up in Cradock. There's a reasonable licensed **restaurant**, a post office, a filling station and a lovely swimming pool set among huge rocks, all near reception.

Graaff-Reinet

It's little wonder that the tour buses pull in to **GRAAFF-REINET** in their numbers; this is a beautiful town, and one of the few places in the Eastern Cape where you'd want to wander freely day and night, taking in historical buildings and the odd museum, have a meal or a drink and stroll back to your accommodation. You don't even need a car to get to the town's sights.

Established in 1786, Graaff-Reinet is one of the oldest towns in South Africa, and much of its historical centre is intact. Exploring its charms takes at least a day and many people stop over en route from Johannesburg to the Garden Route. December is the busiest month, and you should definitely book well ahead if you want to stay over. Graaff-Reinet has a large population of Afrikaans-speaking coloured people, mostly living on the south side of town, some of slave origin, others the descendants of indigenous Khoi and San who were forced to work on frontier farms. The dry mountains surrounding the town are part of the **Karoo Nature Reserve**, whose main attraction is the **Valley of Desolation**, a B-movie name that disguises an impressive reality. The rocky canyon, echoing bird call and expansive skies of the valley, shouldn't be missed.

Some history
By the late eighteenth century Dutch burghers had extended the Cape frontier northwards into the Sneeuwberg Mountains, traditionally the stomping ground of Khoi pastoralists and San hunter-gathers. Little more than brigands, the settlers had become accustomed to raiding Khoi cattle and attacking groups of San, killing the men and abducting women and children to use as farm and domestic labourers. Friction escalated when the Khoi and San retaliated and, in 1786, the Cape authorities sent out a *landdrost* (magistrate) to establish **Graaff-Reinet**, from where he would administer the surrounding area and pacify the frontier.

Nine years later, *landdrost* Honoratus Maynier, following orders to stop vigilante rule by the white settlers and to curb the maltreatment of Khoi and San servants, was forced out of town at gunpoint by a group of burghers, bandying catch phrases from the recent French revolution. Declaring South Africa's **first Boer republic**, they complained that Maynier was "protecting the Hottentots and Kafirs against the Boers".

In 1800 Maynier was again put in charge of Graaff-Reinet and colonial control over the district was slowly consolidated, with vast tracts turned over to grazing sheep. The 1850s' **wool boom** brought prosperity to the town and established a pattern of farming and land ownership which continues today.

Arrival and information

Translux **buses** between Johannesburg and Port Elizabeth, and Intercape buses connecting Jo'burg with the Garden Route towns, pull in daily at Kudu Motors, 84 Church

---

ROBERT SOBUKWE AND THE AFRICANISTS

One of Graaff-Reinet's most brilliant and frequently forgotten sons is **Robert Managaliso Sobukwe**, founder of the Pan Africanist Congress (PAC). Born in 1923, Sobukwe won a scholarship to Healdtown, a boarding school near Fort Beaufort, going on to Fort Hare University (see p.331), where he joined the African National Congress Youth League. After graduating in 1947, he became a schoolteacher and then a lecturer at University of the Witwatersrand. A charismatic member of the Africanist wing of the ANC, who even the ultra-apartheid prime minister B.J. Vorster acknowledged as "a man of magnetic personality", Sobukwe questioned the organization's strategy of co-operating with whites, and formed the breakaway PAC in 1959. The following year he launched the nationwide **anti-pass protests**, which ended in the Sharpeville massacre and his imprisonment on Robben Island for nine years. In 1969 he was released under a banning to Kimberley, where he died in 1978. Five thousand people attended his funeral in Graaff-Reinet. Unlike some of his current followers in the PAC, who have not always held back from anti-white rhetoric, Sobukwe was not a racist, maintaining rather that whites were capable, in time, of becoming genuine Africans.

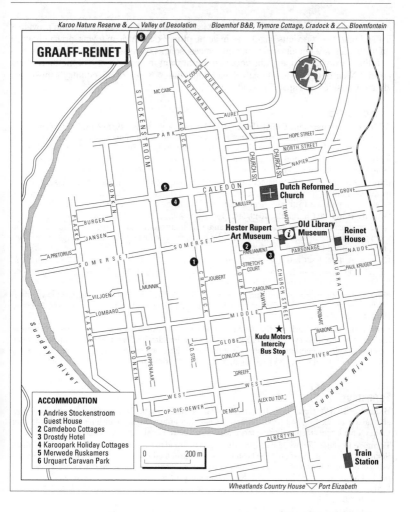

St, a stone's throw south from the historical centre. However, for tickets and timetables you'll need to go to the **tourist information** bureau (Mon–Fri 8am–1pm & 2–5pm, Sat 9am–noon, Sun 10am–noon; ☎049/892 4248), in the Old Library Museum on Church Street. This is also the place for **maps** and details on accommodation, including a list of more than a dozen people running B&Bs from their homes.

Accommodation

Graaff-Reinet has plenty of decent **places to stay** in the centre, the nicest being in listed historic buildings. There's a well-maintained **campsite** on the edge of town, with good-value chalets, and a cheap rooming house closer to the centre. Staying in a private house can work out less expensive than a guesthouse, and many houses have pools, *braai* facilities and welcome kids, though you'll have less privacy. The tourist bureau can provide a list and map (see previous page) – as in some other South African towns, private houses offering B&B are not allowed to put up notices, so it's pointless looking without these.

If the Karoo landscape grabs you, you might want to head for one of the **farmstays** around Nieu Bethesda and Graaff-Reinet, and witness some of the country's most dazzling night skies and spacious landscape.

In the centre

Andries Stockenstroom Guest House, 100 Cradock St (☎ & fax 049/892 4575). Handsome listed house with air-conditioned rooms that has twice won the Automobile Association award for the best guesthouse in South Africa, a couple of streets back from the *Drostdy Hotel*. Worth staying just for the evening meals – outstanding French-Karoo cuisine with imaginative game and mutton dishes and scrumptious desserts. You're unlikely to eat better anywhere in the Karoo. ④.

Camdeboo Cottages, 16 Parliament St (☎049/892 3180, fax 891 0919). Bang in the historical centre, these fully equipped nineteenth-century self-catering cottages built around a courtyard are smallish but pleasant (with hot-water bottles in winter), and couldn't be better located. ②.

Drostdy Hotel, 30 Church St (☎049/892 2161, fax 892 4582, *drostdy@intekom.co.za*). Elegant Cape Dutch landmark in a prime location, with a candle-lit dining room, shady gardens and fountains. The rooms, in terraced artisan cottages behind the hotel, are comfortable but small. Larger rooms are pricier and breakfast is extra. ③ & ⑤.

Karoopark Holiday Cottages, 81 Caledon St (☎049/892 2557, fax 892 5730). Modern complex of self-catering cottages set in a garden with a pool, plus dinky budget units that are perfectly adequate for an overnight stay. Cottages ③, budget units ②.

Merwede Ruskamers, 100 Caledon St (☎049/892 3749). The least expensive rooms in town, offering doubles and mini-dorms. Perfectly clean but a trifle dingy, and there are no cooking facilities. Dorms & doubles ②.

Urquhart Caravan Park, on the outskirts of town, at the extension of Stockenstroom St, next to the Karoo Nature Reserve (☎049/892 2136). Large, well-maintained park with campsites and good-value rondavels, chalets and bungalows, next to the Sundays River. The bungalows are more roomy than the stuffy rondavels, and have linen, but you must bring your own towels. Camping ①, other accommodation ②.

Farmstays

Bloemhof Bed & Breakfast, 27km north of Graaff-Reinet on the N9, and 5km down a good gravel road (☎ & fax 049/840 0203). Grand, turn-of-the-century homestead built on ostrich-feather money, on a large sheep and game farm. Mid-priced Karoo lamb dinners available. ②.

Trymore Cottage, Wellwood Farm, off the N9, on the road to Nieu Bethesda, 31km north of Graaff-Reinet (☎ & fax 049/840 0302). Self-catering four-bedroomed cottage on a farm famous for its private collection of Karoo reptiles, merino sheep stud and orange grove. *Braai* packs are available on request as are evening dinners, with Karoo lamb or venison on the menu. The stunning fossil collection is not open to the public, but you can write for permission to see it (PO Box 204, Graaff-Reinet 6280). ③.

Wheatlands Country House, 50km south of town, and 8km off the R75 to Jansenville and Port Elizabeth (☎ & fax 049/891 0422). Five bedrooms in a 1912 manor house and working sheep farm, with large gardens. B&B ③, half board ④.

The Town

Graaff-Reinet's layout centres around the imposing 1886 **Dutch Reformed Church**, with its pointy steeple and cake-icing decoration. The town's main thoroughfare, **Church Street**, splits at either side of the church, heading northwest to the Valley of Desolation and northeast to Nieu Bethesda, Middelburg and eventually Johannesburg. On either side of Church Street, little roads fan out, lined with whitewashed Cape Dutch, Georgian and Victorian buildings – it's in these parts that you'll find the town's museums, restaurants and most attractive buildings.

Church Street itself bustles with antique shops and businesses with Karoo-inspired names, such as Merino Pharmacy and Kudu Motors. One block south of the church is the **Old Library Museum** (Mon–Fri 8am–1 & 2–5pm, Sat 9am–noon, Sun 10am–noon), which doubles up as the tourist information bureau. The only attraction here is the collection of **fossil skulls** and skeletons of reptiles that populated the marshes, lakes and pools of prehistoric Karoo, some 230 million years ago. These Karoo dinosaurs were entombed in mud, and their bones became embedded in the present-day Karoo shale. The fossils were collected from the hills and sides of river channels in the surrounding area. There's an even better collection on Wellwood Farm (see *Trymore Cottage* under "Accommodation" opposite), but you'll need to write for permission to see it.

Next door, in a restored 1821 mission church with Dutch gables, is the **Hester Rupert Art Museum** (Mon–Fri 10am–noon & 3–5pm, Sat & Sun 10am–noon), which features a representative selection of work by South African artists (primarily white) active in the mid-Sixties. Much of it is dreary and derivative of European art, but a few pieces stand out. Look out in particular for Cecil Skotnes's woodcuts, the strong expressionistic work of Johannes Meintjies, and Irma Stern's very appealing paintings.

Opposite the Art Museum stands the graceful, whitewashed **Drostdy Hotel**, a historical building in its own right, as the former residence of the *landdrost*. Most of the hotel guests are housed behind the main building, in Stretch's Court, a cobbled lane of nineteenth-century cottages with brightly coloured shutters. It hasn't always been so twee: Drostdy's slaves used to dwell here and, after slavery ended in 1838, their descendants stayed on until they were kicked out under the 1950 Group Areas Act (when the area was zoned for whites only).

From the front steps of the Drostdy, you can look down Pastorie Street, lined with Cape Dutch buildings, to **Reinet House** (Mon–Fri 8am–12.30pm & 2–5pm, Sat 9am–noon, Sun 9am–noon), Graaff-Reinet's finest museum. Formerly a parsonage, it was built in 1812 in the traditional Cape Dutch H-plan, with six gables and a spiral stairway leading to the garden. Essentially a period house museum with wooden floors and airy rooms, it's filled with covetable furniture and intriguing household objects. Strangely enough, the museum is the only place allowed to distil an illicit home-brewed spirit called "Withond" (white dog), which has an exceptionally sharp bite. Little bottles of the clear liquor, labelled with a picture of a bull terrier, are sold at the front desk.

Eating and drinking

You'll find a fair number of centrally located **restaurants** and **tea shops** catering for Graaff-Reinet's many visitors. The culinary highlight is unquestionably the *Andries Stockenstroom Guest House* (see "Accommodation" opposite), but you need to be staying there to enjoy its cooking, which attracts gourmands from across the country.

Ambrosia Steakhouse, 30a Parsonage St. Steaks and hamburgers with a take-away section and an outdoor beer and coffee terrace. Daily 9am–10pm.

Desert Springs Spur, 22b Church St. Safe, standard steaks and burgers from one of the country's biggest fast-food franchises.

Drostdy Hotel, 30 Church St. Unrivalled garden setting for drinks or tea. Rather formal dinners in the grand dining room, offering a pricey English-style set menu, with the odd Afrikaans speciality thrown in. Their buffet lunches and breakfasts are better value.

Iets Anders, 3 Parsonage St. Daytime café/bar serving reasonably priced Afrikaans specialities, such as *bobotie* and rice, tomato *bredie* done in a *potjie* (a three-legged pot), hearty breakfasts, sandwiches, hamburgers, homemade ginger beer and cakes including syrupy *koeksisters* and *melktert*.

Kliphuis, 46 Bourke St. Open during the day only, this is a good place for tea and sandwiches or a light lunch, with the advantage of pavement tables. Closed Sun.

Karoo Nature Reserve and the Valley of Desolation

The low-lying **Karoo Nature Reserve** (daily dawn–dusk; free; ☎049/892 3476) totally surrounds the town, with its entrance lying 5km north of Graaff-Reinet's centre, off the Murraysburg Road. Its indisputable highlight is the strikingly deep **Valley of Desolation**. By car, follow the narrow tarred road that starts at the reserve's entrance and ascends up the bush-flecked mountainside, passing a series of viewpoints, up to the cliffs overlooking the Valley. Late afternoon is the best time to enjoy the scenery, when the tinted sun saturates the ochres and reds of the rock towers that soar from the valley floor. The views from the lip of the canyon, beyond the rocks and into the plains of Camdeboo, are truly thrilling, and even better when you tune into the echoing bird calls, especially when you see black eagles circling the dolomite towers, scanning the crevices for prey. There's a forty-five-minute looped **walk** along the canyon lip, well marked with a lizard emblem. For longer trails, and **staying overnight** in a hiker's hut (with a *braai* area), you'll need to book at the Department of Nature Conservation, Bourke St (☎049/892 3453), where you can also pick up detailed **maps**.

Nieu Bethesda

There's a mystique about the Karoo being at the unfathomable heart of South Africa, and if you want to get a sense of that dry, timeless centre **NIEU BETHESDA** is the place to do it. Winding into the mountains 50km north of Graaff-Reinet, much of the Karoo's attraction lies in its spareness, set against expansive skies. Nieu Bethesda is drier and dustier than you may find palatable, however, especially in midsummer when it boils with harsh, bright light. There are no streetlamps, and on winter nights temperatures plummet to zero and the sky fills with icy stars.

Most people come to Nieu Bethesda to marvel – or shudder – at the **Owl House**, River Street (daily 9am–5pm; R7; ☎049/841 1603), once the home of Helen Martins, a reclusive artist who expressed her disturbing and fascinating inner world through her surroundings. Every corner of the house and garden has been transformed to meet her vision, and the walls inside the house glitter and prickle with crushed glass. At the back of the house, trapped by a stone wall and high chicken wire, are hundreds of glass and cement sculptures – camels, lambs, sphinxes and human figures. Owls with large eyes gaze from her tin-roofed verandah. Martins never exhibited or courted publicity, though since her death in 1976 many have visited the museum and pondered on her life in this Karoo backwater. South African playwright Athol Fugard, who loves the Karoo and has a house in Nieu Bethesda, used her life and creative toil to talk about himself in his celebrated play, *The Road to Mecca*.

Owl House aside, the whitewashed village has plenty of charm. It's a tranquil place, accessible on a good gravel road, with the sound of spring water flowing down furrows into the little windmilled allotments. An archetypal Karoo *dorp*, its minuscule white population of around two dozen has been split since the Seventies between hippie outsiders, attracted by the region's isolation, and conservative locals. Nearby, a few hundred coloureds somehow manage to eke out a living in this ungiving environment. Making the most of the creative forces and lack of distractions, the **Ibis Gallery** on the main road (☎049/841 1623; free) hosts first-rate exhibitions of contemporary South African art, some of it generated locally, and runs workshops in creative writing, printmaking, painting and drawing.

The **Compassberg Mountain**, one of the highest peaks in the Eastern Cape and part of the Sneeuberg range, dominates the Nieu Bethesda skyline, and can be climbed. Contact Idil Sheard for details of **trails** (☎04984/22418), all operated from private farms.

Practicalities

Nieu Bethesda is 23km off the N9 between Graaff-Reinet and Middelburg. There's a **village shop** and butcher on the main road, but if you're self-catering you should stock up elsewhere, especially for fresh fruit and vegetables, which are scarce in the Karoo.

There's a good selection of **places to stay**. The Ibis Gallery (see opposite) offers self-catering accommodation at *Arthur's Cottage* (①), a compact garden flat next door. Best of the guesthouses is *Huis Nommer Een*, Murray St (book through the *Village Inn*, New St, ☎049/841 1635; ②), with three spacious rooms furnished in South African country style, a farm-style kitchen, and a handsome verandah. Another option is *Stokkiesdraai Guest House*, Murray St (☎049/841 1658; ②), with a two-bedroomed self-catering Karoo cottage. If you want to stay on a farmhouse, head for *Weltevreden Farm* (☎049/841 1400; ②), 13km north of the village, in the Sneeuberg Mountains, which has two self-catering cottages, hiking and riding. Alternatively, try the friendly *Doornberg Farm* (☎ & fax 049/841 1401; ②), which has a pub and serves evening meals, or you can self-cater; there's also a trampoline, pool, riding and hiking.

Given how tiny Nieu Bethesda is, it's surprising to find any **restaurants** at all, but you actually have a choice. The cosy *Stokkiesdraai Country Kitchen*, Martin Street (☎049/841 1658), serves plain, home-cooked evening meals and Sunday roasts, but needs to be booked in advance. You can pop into *The Waenhuis*, in the main road, for dinner and drinks without a reservation, though their most popular dish is the satellite aerial, which caters to the village's sport junkies. During the day you can eat at the *Village Inn* (☎049/841 1635), along from the Owl House, in New Street. A good place for continental or English breakfasts, light lunches and teas, it also sells local crafts and books about the Karoo. The owner, Egbert, is a fund of **information** about the area, and also takes bookings for some guesthouses. In a similar vein, the *Bethesda Craft & Coffee Shop*, opposite the Village Inn, does excellent sandwiches on homemade bread and supports local crafts, which you'll find on sale, including patchwork bedcovers, sarongs, wire windmills and rusty metal constructions by a local sculptor who uses found objects.

EAST LONDON AND THE CENTRAL REGION

Some of the Eastern Cape's least-developed **coastline** lies between Port Alfred and East London, saved from the hands of developers because it fell into the neglected Xhosa *bantustan* of the Ciskei. **East London**, formerly a part of white South Africa, wedged uncomfortably between two ex-*bantustans*, is the largest city in the central region of the province, with excellent city beaches for surfing and swimming and good transport links to Johannesburg and along the coast. Heading inland from here, **Fort Hare University** near Alice has educated political leaders across the subcontinent, including Nelson Mandela, and has the country's finest collection of contemporary black South African art. Sweeping up from Fort Hare's valley, the gentle, wooded **Amatola Mountains** yield up to the dramatic landscapes of the **Eastern Cape Drakensberg**, which offer hiking, horse-riding and even skiing opportunities. Before white settlers (or even the Xhosa), arrived, these towering formations were dominated by **San hunter-gatherers**, who decorated the rock faces with thousands of ritual **paintings**, many of which remain surprisingly vivid, depicting a cosmology in which the spiritual world melds into everyday reality.

The Coast: Fish River Mouth to East London

Heading 38km east of Port Alfred, along the R72, you'll come to the **Great Fish River**, the boundary across which Britain drove the Xhosa in the Fourth Frontier War of 1811–12. It's a major landmark, cutting through a steep-sided valley shrouded in prickly, thick bush. During the apartheid years, the river became the frontier of the notionally independent Ciskei *bantustan*, whose multi-million-rand border post on the east bank of the river stood unused until the Nineties, when it became a rather pleasant roadside tea room.

The **Great Fish River Wetland Reserve** is a preserved wetland area between the R72 and the river mouth, beautiful for the mauves, yellows and browns of the plants and the prolific birdlife. There's nowhere to stay, apart from **camping** rough, for which the best spots are in the coastal bush near the beach, where it's sheltered from the wind; but there are no facilities, bar crummy toilets and cold running water, and often no one supervising or collecting fees. **Without a car**, this is the only place you'll get to in the vicinity of the Fish – walk down the hill from the *Fish River Sun*, where the Port Elizabeth to East London bus makes a stop (daily except Tues & Thurs).

Just across the Great Fish, conforming to the bizarre logic of apartheid, the luxurious *Fish River Sun Hotel* (☎040/676 1102, or central reservations ☎011/780 7800; ⑥) is where Eastern Cape whites could nip over the border to the South African-owned **hotel** to enjoy a spot of gambling, which was banned in "White South Africa". The *Sun* has arguably the best **golf** course in the country (open to non-residents) with stunning views of the river and beach. A few kilometres further east, the *Mpekweni Marine Resort* (☎040/676 1026, or central reservations ☎011/780 7800; ⑤) is very comfortable, but not as glitzy. Its position couldn't be better, though, with rooms close to the beautiful lagoon and beach, which the hotel has managed to procure for its own private use.

Hamburg

One of the few resorts along the Pineapple Coast that feels like real Africa is **HAMBURG**, a low-key village on a good dirt road, 14km off the R72. The route passes through **Xhosa settlements** and shanties, where you'll see traditionally decorated thatch and mud huts. Look out for animals wandering perilously into your way and strolling around Hamburg itself, lending the town a truly rural feel. With plots currently being snapped up, this run-down backwater looks set for a slick rash of development. Hamburg is renowned for **fishing** and the muddy-bottomed Keiskamma River is excellent for catching prawns. The sea offers a good beach break for **surfers**.

Public **transport** is limited to the Baz Bus (☎021/439 2323), which travels along the coast and makes a detour into Hamburg off the main coastal road whenever someone requests a pick-up or drop-off. There are only three **places to stay**, all with views over the wide, brown Keiskamma River and high olive hills, but also a three-kilometre walk to the beach. There's nothing at the beach except for a car park, broken-down toilets and miles of sand and sea. The *Hamburg Oyster Lodge*, Main St (☎ & fax 040/678 1020; ①), has closely packed bunks and double rooms, and allows **camping**. You can get **meals** here, including fresh oysters. *Clive's Place* (☎ & fax 040/678 1014), signposted from the main road, is a self-catering house that sleeps eight in dorms and doubles (both ①). For more comfort, the nearby *Hamburg Hotel* (☎040/678 1061, fax 678 1055; ③, includes dinner) has doubles with bath and views onto gardens, an outside bar deck and a pool. **Fuel** is available at the hotel. The *Oyster Lodge* runs river **booze cruises** 14km up the Keiskamma for up to eighteen passengers.

> ### THE SHIPWRECK TRAIL
>
> One of the most rewarding ways to explore this area of the coast is on foot. The **Shipwreck Hiking Trail** is an informal beach hike traversing the 64km between Great Fish River and Chalumna, along deserted beaches where you'll spot the odd shipwreck. The main walk takes three days and two nights (you can also do a shortened version). En route, the best **places to stay** are at **Kiwane**, which has basic chalets (①), **Hamburg**, with hotel and backpacker accommodation (see opposite), and **Birha** and **Mpekweni**, which have camping only (①). There's no one supervising the trail and no need to book, as numbers are not restricted. The wildest section is the beach between Hamburg and Kiwane, though there'll undoubtedly be some fishermen and 4WDs churning up the sand. Kiwane has an especially lovely lagoon. Although primarily a beach walk, light running or walking shoes are recommended, as you may have to walk upriver to cross the Great Fish at Hamburg if there are no boats around, and clamber on rocks if you're collecting oysters and mussels to eat. Take the usual precautions against the sun and, if possible, walk at low tide when the sand is firm and easy to stride along. Alternatively, base yourself at Hamburg, right at the centre of the trail, and embark on day walks from here.

East London and around

EAST LONDON, the second-largest city in the Eastern Cape, is the obvious jumping-off point for exploring the Transkei or the coast west to Port Elizabeth. It has good **connections** to the rest of the country by air, rail and coach, and you can enjoy some beach life here without a car. But without fine, warm weather, the city can be dreary. What does happen takes place along the beachfront, where there's a plethora of places to stay, eat and drink. **Nahoon Beach** is a great **surfing spot**, and the town has a dedicated and lively surfing scene. It's also gradually becoming a place for black holidaymakers – a post-apartheid phenomenon.

Away from the holiday strip, East London is dominated by an industrial centre served by **Mdantsane**, a huge African township, 20km from the city towards King William's Town. Apart from the active river port, there are several large factories, including Mercedes Benz, whose workers presented Nelson Mandela with a bright-red, top-of-the-range Mercedes as a coming-out-of-prison present.

Some history

East London began life as a permanent British settlement during the nineteenth-century **Frontier Wars**, when it was used as a beachhead to land military supplies needed to push back the Xhosa. British governor Sir Harry Smith, taken by its strategic possibilities as a port, optimistically called it **London** in 1848, after the capital of the Empire. Later it was changed to the Port of East London, not after London's East End, but because the port was on the east side of the Buffalo River. British connections are still obvious, though: East London's main thoroughfare is called Oxford Street and there's a Fleet Street and even a Belgravia suburb.

Before the British, and even the Xhosa, this was home to the **Khoikhoi** people, who called it Place of the Buffalos. In the past the Buffalo River teemed with game, but the animals were gradually killed off with the arrival of British hunters.

Arrival, information and orientation

East London's small **airport** (☎706 0211), a few kilometres west of the centre on the R72, connects the city to all major centres. The **airport shuttle** (mobile ☎082/569

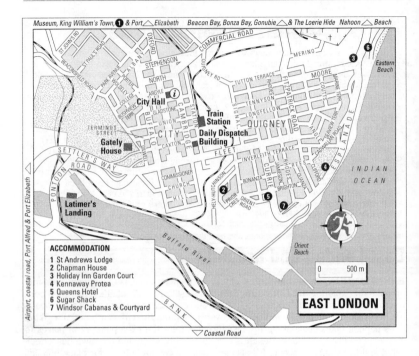

Museum, King William's Town, ❶ & Port △ Elizabeth   Beacon Bay, Bonza Bay, Gonubie △ & The Loerie Hide   Nahoon △ Beach

ACCOMMODATION
1 St Andrews Lodge
2 Chapman House
3 Holiday Inn Garden Court
4 Kennaway Protea
5 Queens Hotel
6 Sugar Shack
7 Windsor Cabanas & Courtyard

EAST LONDON

3599) meets all flights and drops off at the *Holiday Inn* near the beachfront. Coming in **by train** from Johannesburg, you'll arrive at the station on the eastern edge of East London's small business and shopping district. All three of the **intercity buses**, Translux from Durban, Intercape from Port Elizabeth, and Greyhound from Johannesburg, take you to the beachfront, dropping off at the coach terminal at Windmill Park on Moore Street. From the train station, it's a thirty-minute walk to the backpackers' hostel at Eastern Beach, and a slightly shorter stroll to Orient Beach. Buses are scarce, but there are metered **taxis** (see p.328) outside the station.

Like many South African cities, East London is gridded, sprawling and, with uncongested roads and easy parking, far more orientated to **driving** than walking. **Public transport** connects the African townships to the centre, via speeding minibus taxis, and buses link the city's two hubs, the **city centre** and **beachfront**, primarily at the beginning and end of the working day.

Maps and a comprehensive list of B&Bs are available from the helpful **tourist information bureau**, 35 Argyle St (Mon–Fri 8.30am–4.30pm, Sat 8.30–11am; ☎043/722 6015), behind the City Hall.

Accommodation

To get the best out of East London, **stay** either at the beachfront, or up the hilly and wooded east coast, towards Gonubie. If you're on your way to Port Elizabeth, there are a couple of convenient places just beyond the airport. East London fills up over the Christmas period, when prices rise sharply. For **backpackers** the only good lodge is *Sugar Shack*, at Eastern Beach, spectacularly situated in a former lifeguard's lookout. For **longer-term accommodation**, Eastern Cape Holidaymakers (☎043/726 0478, fax

726 0329), run an accommodation agency and also offer caravans, cottages and arrange hiking trails.

Beachfront

East London's **beachfront** sports graceless blocks of holiday apartments and functional hotels, redeemed only by their fabulous views of the Indian Ocean. The really cheap hotels are mostly filled with long-term residents, and are often rough drinking hangouts – best avoided.

Chapman House, 12 Ganteaume Crescent, Quigney (☎043/743 4134 or 743 4135, fax 726 9666). One B&B unit and a self-catering flatlet very close to Orient Beach. B&B ③, flat ②.

Holiday Inn Garden Court, Beachfront (☎043/722 7260, fax 743 7360). Close to Eastern Beach, and no surprises here in terms of price or decor. ⑤.

Kennaway Protea Hotel, Beachfront (☎ & fax 043/722 5531). Comfortable rooms in a reliable hotel with exceptional views. ③.

The Loerie Hide, 2B Sheerness Rd, off Beach Rd (☎ & fax 043/735 3206). Two cottages in the vicinity of Nahoon Beach, decorated in ethnic African and English country-cottage style, at the bottom of a garden that gives way to indigenous bushland.

Queens Hotel, 6 Currie St (☎043/722 3631, fax 722 3633). The only low-cost beachfront hotel worth considering, with ordinary rooms, and near the beach. ②.

St Andrews Lodge, 14 St Andrews Rd (☎043/743 5131, fax 743 9009, mobile ☎082/414 3360, *sandrews@iafrica.com*). Four comfortable en-suite units inside a suburban house and a garden cottage. There's a swimming pool and all units have separate entrances, plus TV and cooking facilities. B&B or self-catering ③.

Sugar Shack, Eastern Beach (☎ & fax 043/722 8240). Brilliantly located, right on the beach, and with terrific views. Bright dorms and outdoor relaxation area. Expect a lively surfing and partying crowd. Free pick-up is available from town or the station. ①.

Windsor Cabanas & Windsor Courtyard, George Walker Parade, Quigney (☎043/743 3220, fax 743 2225). Luxury Spanish-style, B&B pads near Orient Beach, with great views, where you can also self-cater (both ④). Also small claustrophobic budget rooms (②) with twin beds and no views, suitable only for an overnight stay.

Eastern suburbs and resorts

If the urbanity of the main beachfront doesn't appeal, your best bet is to head for the mostly white suburbs of **Beacon Bay**, **Bonza Bay** or **Gonubie**, close to the river and sea. Besides a couple of old-fashioned hotels, these areas have a good selection of smart **B&Bs** in private houses. You'll need your own transport to get there, unless you arrange to be picked up beforehand or take a taxi (from R60). East London's **campsites** are out this way too, near the water.

Blue Lagoon Hotel, Blue Bend Place, Beacon Bay (☎043/748 4821, fax 748 2037). Very pleasant accommodation set about by palm trees and close to the beach. Rooms are quiet and spacious with balconies looking onto the river, which you can reach via a short path that also leads to the beach. ③.

Dolphin Hotel, 85 Harewood Drive, Nahoon (☎043/735 1435, fax 735 4639). Plain, Fifities suburban hotel: the prim style gives no hint of the lush vegetation and wonderful beach just a 15min walk away. ③.

Gonubie Hotel, 141 Main Rd (☎043/740 4010, fax 740 2071). Attractive hotel on the point at Gonubie, a short boardwalk from the beach. ③.

Gonubie Resort & Caravan Park, 19km east of town off the N2 (☎043/740 2021). Sheltered camping spots, near the beach. ①.

Nahoon Caravan Park, Beach Road, Nahoon (☎043/705 2129, fax 743 4120). At the Nahoon estuary, the secure camping area nestles among riverine trees with plenty of grassy sites. A short walk to the river and a bit further to the open beach. There's a small shop, mostly open for ice creams and selling basics. You'll need your own transport or to take a taxi from the centre. ①.

Quintetta Guest Farm, Bonza Bay Rd, Beacon Bay (☎043/748 4729, fax 748 6727, *quinteta@iafrica.com*). Rural setting on a farm at the edge of the city limits, next to a golf course and pub, with horses and a pool, but 5km from the beach. Shared bath ②, en suite ③.

West of the city

If you're flying into the airport and don't fancy sampling East London itself, there are a couple of pleasant overnight stops which are on this side of town.

Kidd's Beach Hotel, Kidd's Beach (☎043/781 1715, fax 781 1852). Some 35km west of East London, this exceedingly old-fashioned place has cheap doubles and is a 10min walk to the beach. The resort itself has a Fifties ambience, great surfing and a crescent-shaped beach with a tea room. ②.

Lagoon Valley Holiday Resort & Caravan Park, Marine Drive (☎043/736 9753, fax 736 9796). Good, wholesome family-oriented establishment off the R72, on the banks of the Zaminyama River, with two-bedroom self-catering rondavels and no discos. From here you can walk for 1hr west along the beach to Cove Rock, best visited for all the sea birds that nest and gather on it, and the stupendous views you get by climbing onto it. ②.

The City

East London's drab city centre is dominated by **Oxford Street**, the main shopping and banking precinct, parallel to Station Street and the train station. Although a major traffic thoroughfare, it is largely deserted at night, when you shouldn't wander around alone. White East Londoners have abandoned the centre altogether, preferring to shop in the sanitized suburban malls.

Apart from a couple of handsome buildings, East London's Victorian heart has progressively been demolished. From the station, built on Station Street in 1877, you can walk a few blocks north up Cambridge Street to the city centre's principal landmark, the splendid terracotta and lace-white **City Hall**, opened in 1899. Its tall, colourful clock tower in an otherwise dreary lot of modernish buildings is a useful orientation point. Over the road is a rather wooden statue of martyred black consciousness leader **Steve Biko** (see p.329), a minor point of pilgrimage for visitors, unveiled by Mandela in 1997. Staying with the Biko theme, the **Daily Dispatch Building**, dressed in a surrounding colonial-style verandah, is also worth taking in, at the corner of Caxton Street and Cambridge Road. The newspaper, founded in 1879, made national headlines in the Seventies, when its then-editor, Donald Woods, earned the wrath of the apartheid government for being involved with Biko, who contributed to the newspaper under a pseudonym. Woods fled the country rather dramatically, after endless police harassment – a story told in the 1987 movie *Cry Freedom*.

One street north of here, Terminus Street leads to **Gately House** (Tues–Thurs 10am–1pm & 2–5pm, Sat & Sun 3–5pm; small entry fee), the Victorian home of the city's first mayor, John Gately. East of Terminus, across the railway line, is **Quigney**, an area of small colonial-style Victorian houses, some nicely restored with verandahs and corrugated-iron roofs, others run-down and cockroach-infested. Quigney slopes downhill to the **Esplanade** and **Orient Beach**, the safest place to swim and most easily reached along Currie Street, off Fleet Street. The city's best craft shop, stocking handmade African goods, is **Umzi Wethu Curio Shop**, 110 Moore St, uphill from the *Holiday Inn*.

The working dockland waterfront on the Buffalo River, characterful **Latimer's Landing** is 2km uphill from the centre. It's feeling the effects of a lack of business but still has a decent pub and restaurant, good for fresh fish. To get there, head west along Fleet Street towards the airport, and just before crossing the Buffalo Bridge head steeply down Pontoon Road. **Boat trips** from here head through the Buffalo harbour out to sea and along the beachfront shore. Yacht Miscky (☎043/735 2232) offers trips by arrangement.

A few kilometres north of the city centre, the **East London Museum**, Upper Oxford Street (Mon–Fri 9.30am–5pm, Sat 9.30am–noon, Sun 11am–4pm; entry fee) has a stunning collection of South Nguni beadwork, and contemporary wire sculpture, including an inventive wire car made by Mdantsane resident Phillip Ntliziywana. The museum's pride and joy, however, is its stuffed coelacanth, caught off the coast in the Fifties.

The beaches

East London's **Esplanade** loops from Orient Pier in a wide and beautiful sweep of rocks, beach and sand dunes to Eastern Beach, marred only by the motley assortment of holiday apartments, hotels and restaurants lining the beachfront. About thirty minutes' walk from the city centre, buses here are sporadic; there's no public transport along it, but it's easy enough to stroll from one end to the other

Tucked in next to Orient Pier, with dockland cranes poking their necks above the water, **Orient Beach** is a wonderful place to swim, though it looks a bit grim and industrial. The waves are gentle and the water and sandy beach are clean. Red-hatted lifeguards lend a sense of security, and there are changing rooms, and a couple of little pools for kids. You pay a small fee to enter the beach area during the day, but it's free after 5pm.

From Orient Beach, the sea-walled Esplanade continues northeast, along sand and black rocks, to **Eastern Beach**, with its high, bush-capped sand dunes. Although far more attractive, Eastern Beach is not really safe for swimming, and muggings have been reported here recently. Don't leave your stuff unattended, and give the beach a wide berth at night. Heading northeast beyond Bats Cave – a distinctive chunk of rock jutting out to sea – is popular **Nahoon Beach**, a long wash of sand, backed by dunes. This wonderful natural setting is superb for swimming and surfing, with some of the best waves in the world. However, Nahoon's image may be changing with the arrival of squatters who have established an area of makeshift homes with mountains of plastic bags in the tangled forest behind the dunes, edging onto the golf course and prestigious suburbs. Public transport is scant, but there are three **buses** a day from the Esplanade, or you can walk the 5km from the centre if you're feeling energetic. East of the Nahoon River, the coast curves into **Bonza Bay**, with kilometres of beach walks and a lazy lagoon at the mouth of the Quinera River. East London's best campsite, the *Nahoon*, is here (see p.325), nestling in the riverine trees.

Eating, drinking and nightlife

Although it's hardly a culinary capital, East London does have a couple of very decent places serving **fresh fish** in an outdoor setting: Latimer's Landing is the most congenial place to do this. **Drinking** spots abound, from beachfront sleaze at lowlife hotels to lively surfers' hangouts or swanky tipples overlooking the ocean. Some of the pubs double up as **live music** venues, as well as offering a bite to eat.

Beachfront

Buccaneer's Pub, Eastern Beach, next to *Sugar Shack*. Lively bar that buzzes till the early hours, with occasional live music on Wed, Fri and Sat. During the day there are fantastic views for watching the rodeo riders of the surf. Good pub fare includes their fish and chips and, best of all, the chicken schnitzel.

The Hideaway, Lock St Gaol, Fleet St, a couple of blocks up from Orient Beach. The only sit-down curry house in East London serves cheap but mouthwatering *rotis*. Lunchtimes only.

Mignon's, Esplanade on the Orient Beach side of the Aquarium. Best Italian-style ice cream in town, with tea, coffee, cakes and savouries also on offer. Don't leave without trying the chocolate fudge cake, topped with chocolate *gelato*. Daytime only.

Monte Rio Spur, Esplanade, just above the Orient Beach car park. Good-value, predicatble American-style burgers, steaks and salads.

Movenpick, upstairs at the paying entrance to Orient Beach. The best restaurant in East London with an outstanding Swiss chef who cooks up a seafood storm. Smart, but reasonably priced.

Numbers, King's Entertainment Centre, Esplanade. The only dance venue on the beachfront has an excellent lighting rig and occasionally holds thirty-something nights.

O'Hagan's, Esplanade, midway along, next to the Aquarium. Spectacular setting on a terrace which juts out over the waves. Even when the weather is bad you can watch the surfers through the huge picture windows, but the food is unexciting and overpriced, while the service is indifferent.

Quarterdeck, Orient Beach, overlooking the paddling pool. Acually the informal part of the *Movenpick*, served by the same kitchen and consequently one of the best beachside places for a quiet drink, with "catch of the day" fish served daily at reasonable prices.

Central and Quigney

Casbah Restaurant, *King David Hotel*, Inverleith Terrace. Moderately priced, delicious food with a Middle Eastern touch, in a lacklustre hotel.

Country Rose Coffee Shop, Caxton House, Caxton St. The centre's nicest coffee shop, a stone's throw from the *Daily Dispatch* newspaper. Open sandwiches, gooey cakes, quiches, coffee and *rooibos* tea. Daytime only.

Dave's Kitchen, Pearce St. Centrally located, casual and friendly – good for pizzas and the like.

Jade Garden, Pearce St, next to *Dave's*. The city's only Chinese restaurant, with moderate prices and wonderful beef in black-bean sauce and great fried *won ton*.

Latimer's Landing and Nahoon

Churchill's Pub, Beach Rd, Nahoon. Relaxed, English-style pub, where reasonably priced bangers and mash and cottage pie are on the menu.

Tug & Ferry, Latimer's Landing. Great for its location next to a functioning river port, an English-themed pub with a deck for watching the low-key bustle. Pub grub includes a good beer and steak pie as well as really fresh line fish. There's a large selection of draught beers on tap and fires indoors for chilly winter days. Lunch and eves.

Listings

Car rental Avis (☎043/736 2250), Imperial (☎043/736 2230).

Emergencies Ambulance ☎10177; Fire ☎722 1212; Police (Flying Squad) ☎10111.

Garages Stirling Motors, 8 Old Transkei Rd, does repairs and is open 24hr.

Hospitals Frere Hospital (state), Amalinda Drive (☎043/709 1111); St Dominics (private), 45 St Mark's Rd (☎043/743 4303).

Laundries Washing Well, Currie St, or Laundromat (coin-operated washing machines and ironing) at the Edcott Centre, Oxford St.

Pharmacies John Forbes, 205a Oxford St (☎043/722 2062; till 10pm); Hylton Boyd, 211a Oxford St (☎043/722 4368; till 11pm).

Taxis Springbok ☎043/722 4400.

Train information ☎043/704 2742.

Travel agents Rennies Travel, Caxton House, Terminus St (☎043/726 0698).

The Amatola Mountains

Most visitors drive quickly through the scrubby, dry impoverished area between East London and the **Amatola Mountains** proper, to reach the cool forests and holiday lands at the Hogsback. It's really worth deviating en route, though, to see the marvellous collection of African art at Fort Hare University, visit apartheid martyr Steve Biko's grave in King William's Town, and to take in bits of East Cape history, if you have the inclination.

King William's Town

More commonly and simply known as King, **KING WILLIAM'S TOWN**, 56km north-east of East London, started life as a military frontier and missionary outpost, and today has a large population drawn from the former Ciskei. If you're passing through, there's enough of historical interest here to satisfy at least half a day. To get a feel for **Xhosa history**, head for the **Kaffrarian Museum** (Mon–Fri 9am–12.45pm & 2–5pm; small entry fee) in Alexandra Road; the Xhosa Gallery has unusually good displays, including full accounts of the British tactics and campaigns which crushed the Xhosa. Traditional culture is well represented, with contemporary exhibitions on current building styles. Don't miss Phillip Ntliziywana's imaginative bus and car sculptures made from wire and discarded bits and pieces.

Two blocks north of the museum, off Albert Road, is the nineteenth-century **Edward Street Cemetery**, notable for the story it tells of the conflicts in the area. Besides a memorial to those killed in the innumerable Frontier Wars against the Xhosa, there is an open piece of ground on the far side of the cemetery which marks a mass grave. This is where hundreds of Xhosa were buried, their bodies emaciated as a result of the 1857 **Cattle Killing**, when many Xhosa people destroyed their cattle at the behest of the prophetess Nongqawuse – she promised that this would finally drive out the British (see p.348).

STEVE BIKO AND BLACK CONSCIOUSNESS

Steven Bantu Biko's brutal interrogation and death while in police custody triggered international outrage and turned opinion further against the apartheid regime. His death was followed by the banning of the Black Consciousness organizations, and helped lead to the imposition of a mandatory arms embargo against South Africa by the United Nations Security Council.

Born in 1946 in **King William's Town**, Biko's political ascent was a swift one, due in no small part to his eloquence, charisma and focused vision. While still a medical student at Natal University during the late Sixties, he was elected president of the exclusively black South African Students' Organisation (SASO) and started publishing articles in their journal, fiercely attacking white liberalism. In an atmosphere of repression – both ANC and PAC leaders were serving hefty sentences at the time – Biko's brand of **Black Consciousness** immediately caught on. He called for blacks to take destiny into their own hands, to unify and rid themselves of the "shackles that bind them to perpetual servitude". He became honorary president of the Black Peoples' Convention, an umbrella organization which attracted mainly young intellectuals and professionals. From 1973 onwards, Biko suffered banning, detention and other harassment at the hands of the state. In 1974, he defended himself in court, presenting his case so brilliantly that his profile in the international press soared.

Barred from straying out of King William's Town, Biko continued working and writing, frequently escaping out of his confinement. In 1976, black outrage burst into the open with the Soweto riots, when school pupils took to the streets to protest against the imposition of Afrikaans as the language of instruction in their schools. The police boot went in hard: hundreds were killed and imprisoned, and the search for "agitators" led to Biko's hundred-and-one day detention. In August the following year, he was stopped at a roadblock near Grahamstown (outside his restricted area), taken to Port Elizabeth, intensively interrogated and tortured. On September 12, 1977, he died from a brain haemorrhage, sustained at the hands of security police. No one was held accountable. Diplomats from thirteen Western countries joined the thousands of mourners at his funeral in King William's Town.

> **Phone numbers** in King William's Town are due to change throughout 1999 and 2000. If you encounter any difficulties phone the directory enquiry service on ☎1023.

About fifteen minutes' walk north of the Kaffrarian, the **Missionary Museum** in Berkeley Street (Mon–Fri 9am–1pm & 2–5pm; small entry fee) is mainly of interest for the glimpse it gives into early educational institutions in the Eastern Cape, where South Africa's first black professionals were schooled and, indeed, many of the new nation's current heavyweights, including Nelson Mandela himself.

King's only other attraction of note is **Steve Biko's grave**, a couple of kilometres out of town, tucked away at the end of a dirt track that branches off the end of Cathcart Street. It's a moving place, and the grave is much humbler than you'd expect for such an important figure in black politics. The polished, charcoal-coloured tombstone sits quietly among the large patch of paupers' graves that make up Ginsburg Cemetery. To get there, take Cathcart Street south out of town (towards Grahamstown), turning left onto a road signposted to the cemetery, after the bridge (just before the turn-off to your right to Alice). Biko is buried roughly in the middle of the graveyard, but there are no markers, so you have to walk through till you find it.

King is also the place to set out on all or part of **the Amatola Hiking Trail**, which starts from Maiden Dam, just outside town, and continues as a five-night/six-day hike into the mountains (see p.333).

Practicalities

Alexandra Road is the town's main drag, where you'll find a twenty-four-hour filling station and signs for King's **tourist information** bureau (Mon–Fri 8.30am–5.30pm, Sat 8.30am–1pm; ☎043/642 3391), which is in the public library opposite the Kaffrarian Museum, and can provide an accommodation list. The **minibus taxis** rank in Cathcart Street, with connections to East London and the rest of the Eastern Cape.

The cheapest **accommodation** in King is in two doubles and a **dormitory** (both ①) in some converted outhouses at the *Keiskamma Ecotourism Network*, 9 Chamberlain St (☎043/642 2571, fax 642 2571). These are available to hikers embarking on the Amatola Trail (see p.333) or backpackers just overnighting in town. Two pleasant **B&Bs**, both in Victorian houses are the centrally located *Bramble Hill*, 3 Upper Mount St (☎ & fax 043/642 3369; ③), and *Dreamers Guest House*, 29 Gordon St (☎ & fax 043/6423 012; ②), just off Alexandra Road, which has a pool, and real log fires in winter. Of the town's **hotels**, the *Grosvenor Lodge*, Taylor St (☎043/642 1440, fax 24772; ④), near the Kaffrarian Museum, is the most salubrious; next best is the *Crown*, Wodehouse St (☎043/642 3025; ③). At the edge of town is King's little-used caravan park and **camp-site** (①); ask at the information bureau whether it is currently safe to camp there.

For **eating and drinking**, *Archie's Pub & Pizzeria* in Taylor Street is popular, while *St Louis Spur*, in a prime spot at the corner of Alexandra Road and Cathcart Street, serves up the usual steaks and hamburgers. *Nando's* is a handy fast-food joint on Alexandra Road.

Bisho

Of little aesthetic interest in itself, **BISHO** is nevertheless worth the six-kilometre detour from King, if only for its curiosity value and ostentatious architecture. Now the provincial capital of the Eastern Cape, the town is beset by dreary Eighties monumental town planning. The brainchild of Lennox Sebe, the apartheid *bantustan*'s first "president", the architecture achieves the improbable feat of blending banality with grandiosity. Sebe is said to have been inspired by ancient buildings in Israel – quite possible given his strong links with the country, which provided arms and military training for his fiefdom.

As you approach Bisho, the **stadium** on the left is a grim reminder of apartheid atrocities. During the constitutional negotiations in 1991, Ciskei troops opened fire on a group of ANC supporters who were attempting to hold a rally at the sports ground. The protest centred around the continuing repression in the Ciskei, where the ANC was still outlawed. Twenty-eight were killed and two hundred injured. The outrage provoked by the massacre effectively spelt the end of the apartheid-backed Ciskei and was a milestone marking the demise of the old order.

The new order, embodied in the **Provincial Legislature** buildings, is a short hop from the town centre, but is grim and not worth the detour, despite its importance to the province. For a bit of light relief, you could nip over to the casino at the plush *Amatola Sun* (☎040/639 1111; ⑥), the only **place to stay** in Bisho, and a few hundred metres from the Legislature. **Minibus taxis** ply the route between King William's Town and Bisho.

Fort Hare

Despite decades of deliberate neglect and relegation after 1959 to a "tribal" **university** under apartheid, **FORT HARE**, 64km west of King William's Town, is assured a place in South African history. Established in 1916 as a multiracial college by missionaries, it became the first institution in South Africa to deliver tertiary education to blacks. Many prominent African leaders, including Zimbabwe's president Robert Mugabe and Tanzania's Julius Nyerere came here for their tertiary education. But most famous, of course, is **Nelson Mandela** (see p.356), making this an essential port of call if you're following Mandela's footprints. Sadly, though, the Wesley Residence from whose window the young Madiba reputedly used to climb to go ballroom dancing, has been pulled down. The spot it occupied is now the lawn just to your right as you enter through the main gate. **Freedom Square**, at the centre of the campus, is worth a visit to recall the many scenes of protest at the University – this is the spot where several members of the present government cut their teeth politically.

It's possible to visit **Beda Residence** where Robert Mugabe studied, though the dormitory where he stayed has been converted into single rooms. This is one of the pleasanter old residences; some of the others are pretty dilapidated owing to underfunding during the apartheid years. Virtually all students live on campus as Alice, the adjacent town, is too undeveloped to offer much in the way of digs.

If you have even the slightest interest in African art, take advantage of Fort Hare's **De Beers Art Gallery** (Mon–Fri 8am–5pm, Sat 8am–1pm; free). From the outside, the cylindrical gallery resembles a high-security bank vault, which is perhaps appropriate. Once inside, you're faced with a veritable treasure trove of contemporary black southern **African art** – one of the most significant and least publicized collections anywhere. Pioneers of black painting, including Gerard Sekoto and Pemba, are represented, and you should look out for the lively oils of Dan Rakgoate. There are some stunning sculptures: Uneas Sithole's elongated *Is my friend the chameleon hiding?*; Percy Konqobe's *Ntsikana and his cow*; and Sydney Kumalo's *Robot man*. Also unmissable is the sequence of fifteen woodcuts by Lucky Sibiya called *Umabatha*, the Zulu adaptation of *Macbeth*. You'll have to make an appointment to see Fort Hare's **ethnographic collection** – a major museum of traditional crafts and artefacts, with all sorts of rare and valuable pieces, but neither well-displayed in a permanent place nor publicized.

Practicalities

Ideally you'll have your own **transport** to reach Fort Hare, a couple of kilometres east of Alice on the R63, although from King William's Town there are **minibus taxis** to

Alice (see below) that conveniently drop off passengers at the University gates. A visit is best done as a day-trip from Grahamstown or East London, or as part of an excursion to the Hogsback. With the virtual lack of **accommodation** in Alice, you're better off staying either in Fort Beaufort or Hogsback – the choice of many of the University's lecturers.

Tours of the University and art gallery should be arranged beforehand through the University's public relations department (Mon–Fri 9am–5pm; ☎040/602 2239; free). Getting into the University past the security personnel at the main gates can be tricky, especially outside term time. Be polite and persistent: the art gallery, at least, is meant to be open for visits every day. If you haven't arranged a visit in advance, or you find the gallery closed, head for the public relations office at the entrance of the main administration buildings and ask someone to open up.

Alice

A handful of photogenically decaying colonial houses with peeling corrugated-iron roofs, and balconies smothered in creepers, constitute the main interest in **ALICE**. It's the closest town to the university, but can in no way be called a university town. The lengthy decay of the village reflects the second-class status accorded the university under Afrikaner Nationalist rule. There's one hopelessly tiny bookshop, a depressing reflection of local poverty and the high cost of books in South Africa, which puts them beyond the reach of the majority of the population – even the fifty percent who are literate. Alice's two **hotels** are little more than run-down carousing joints. Of the two, the *Amatola* is favoured for drinking by university staff and students.

Just 1km east of the town centre is **Lovedale College**, older than Fort Hare, and no less significant in educating Africans. Built in 1842 as a Presbyterian mission station, it was soon educating the country's first black professionals, and became an important publishing centre. The Xhosa language was first translated into written form here, and one of Lovedale's students, J. Tengo Jabavu, was the founder of South Africa's first weekly African-language paper, *Zabantsundu*. With the passing of the Bantu Education Act under the apartheid government, Lovedale was closed . Now that the college is in use again, as a high school, you can drive in and look at the Victorian buildings, but the actual site doesn't have any displays or information – for that, visit the Missionary Museum in King William's Town (see p.330).

Hogsback

Made sweeter by the contrast with the hot valleys below, **HOGSBACK**, 32km north of Alice (and 145km from East London), offers cool relief after hauling through prickly, overgrazed country. For whites hankering after a British past, this village in the Amatola Mountains represents a corner of England, a fantasy fed by mists, pine plantations and exotic trees such as oak, walnut and azaleas, and guaranteed snowfalls each winter. In fact, the real attraction of the place is the **Afro-montane cloud forest**, singing with bird calls and gauzy waterfalls, and populated by the odd troop of **samango monkeys**, which survive on the steep slopes above the pine plantations. Winding your way up the mountains on the road from Alice, you'll have a good view of the forest, dense with yellowwood, stinkwood and Cape chestnut.

Hogsback is a great place to spend an unchallenging couple of days, with plenty of walks, good air and many places to stay. The name of Hogsback, which applies to the area as much as to the village, comes from the high rocky ridge (actually three peaks) resembling a bushpig's spine, which runs above the settlement. Hogsback can be wet and cold, even in summer, so bring a warm pullover, sturdy shoes and rain gear all year round.

THE AMATOLA TRAIL AND ZINGCUKA LOOP

Ranked among South Africa's best forested mountain walks, the **Amatola Trail** is a tough but fabulously beautiful five-night trail. Starting at Maiden Dam in the Pirie Forest, some 21km north of King William's Town, it stretches for 105km to end up at Hogsback. There are huts with mattresses and *braai* facilities at each designated nightstop along the way – some have showers.

The main attraction of this walk is the dense, high forest, and the numerous waterfalls, rivers and bathing pools. There are also a number of shortened versions of the trail, but these can only be done outside of school holidays, or at short notice if the huts are not filled. Best of the shortened trails is the 36km **Zingcuka Loop** from Hogsback, which scales the Hogsback itself, and has you walking along streams much of the way, past idyllic waterfalls and pools. Right in the forest at the base of a cliff, the overnight hut has the luxury of a primitive shower, and firewood.

To go on one of these trails, you'll need well-broken-in boots, plus waterproofs, and warm clothes – you could get rained on between October and March. **Book** through the Keiskamma Ecotourism Network, 9 Chamberlain St, King William's Town 5600 (☎ & fax 043/642 2571). The complete trail costs around R150.

The hamlet itself is strung out along 3km of gravel road, with lanes branching out on either side to hotels and cottages. The closest thing to a **centre** is the small conglomeration of a general store, post office, filling station and some nearby craft shops. Hogsback has its own **indigenous craft** you'll find nowhere else in the country: prepare to be pestered by Xhosa kids selling the characteristic unfired clay horses and hogs with white markings. Storm Haven Crafts, in the main road, has some nice stuff, and doubles up as Hogsback's tourist information bureau (see "Practicalities").

Hogsback is prime **rambling** country with relatively easy, short trails, with way-marked routes indicated by hogs painted onto trees. For a rewarding taste of indigenous forest, the Contour Path above the campsite makes an easy, one-hour walk. From this path, there is a route going steeply up **Tor Doone**, which overlooks the settlement, and is the easiest summit to climb. One of the most rewarding waterfall trails is the one-hour steep downhill walk (two hours there and back) to the spendid **Madonna and Child waterfall**. A number of short and long routes, including the Amatola Trail and Zingcuka Loop (see box above), are detailed in inexpensive **guidebooks** available at the village shops.

Practicalities

It's worth spending a night or two in Hogsback, but you'll need a **car**, as no public transport serves the village, though it's worth noting that a cheap shuttle connects *Sugar Shack* in East London (see p.325) with the *Away With The Fairies* hostel (see below); phone either establishment to make arrangements (you needn't be staying). On the main road, Storm Haven Crafts is also the town's **tourist information** bureau (☎ & fax 045/962 1050), and can supply accommodation details.

Places to stay are plentiful, but the village tends to fill up during holidays and weekends, when you'll need to book ahead. At the budget end *The Amatola* (☎ & fax 045/962 1059), on the main road, has a hikers and backpackers' **dorm** (①) and individual rondavels (②). More unequivocally geared to the backpacker scene is *Away With The Fairies* **hostel**, Hydrangea Lane (☎045/962 1031), first turning on your right and signposted as you drive into Hogsback, a large converted house on a sizeable property with fabulous views of the Tyumi Valley. Small dorms sleep three to eight guests and there's a double in the house and one in a garden cottage (both ①). Bikes are available to rent, horse-riding can be arranged and there's jamming every evening.

Best value of the **self-catering** bunch are *Petersfield* (☎ & fax 045/962 1159; ②), a four-bedroom rondavel in a lovely garden with streams and an orchard, and the cottages at *The Edge* (☎ & fax 045/962 1159; ②). Both places are a couple of kilometres off the main road, and need to be booked in advance. For more luxury, head for *Hyde Park Chalets*, Dinwiddie Lane (☎045/962 1069; ③). Of the **hotels**, *King's Lodge*, along the main road (☎045/962 1024, fax 962 1058; half board ⑤), is a bright, wood-panelled establishment that has the best food and bar, as well as two self-catering units (③).

Hogsback has a general **shop** selling basic supplies. For **meals**, *Woodlands*, on the main road, is excellent, but is closed Tuesday and only does evening meals on Friday and Saturday. Otherwise, it's down to *King's Lodge*.

Fort Beaufort

A farming town at the heart of a citrus and wool district, **FORT BEAUFORT**, 80km northwest of King William's Town, is nothing to get excited about. Your most likely reason for a close encounter is because you're passing through on your way from Grahamstown or East London to Katberg or Mpofu Game Reserve. Having said that, Fort Beaufort does have a reputation throughout the Eastern Cape for its lusciously sweet oranges; should you find yourself here in winter, look out for African traders selling them by the sackful for a song, at the main crossroads out of town.

Founded as a link in the chain of forts built along the eastern frontier that formed a buffer against the Xhosa, Fort Beaufort's moment in history came in 1845, when a Xhosa man called Tsili stole an axe from a shop here, precipitating the bloody **War of the Axe** – the Seventh Frontier War. The theft provided a pretext for the British to act on a growing and expedient belief among whites that Xhosa land would be put to better use in their own hands. In 1847, after literally bringing the Xhosa chiefs to their knees (forcing them at bayonet point to kiss his boots), Governor Harry Smith told the vanquished that their land would be divided into counties, towns and villages bearing English names. "You may no longer be naked and wicked barbarians," he informed them, "which you will ever be unless you labour and become industrious."

The axe shop is still here, as is the 1830 officer's mess, now the highly eccentric **Fort Beaufort Museum**, which doubles up as a tourist office and resembles a bric-a-brac shop. Interesting items include a painting by the Victorian documentary oil colourist, Thomas Baines, and a proclamation by Sir Harry Smith inviting anyone with a gun to take pot shots at the Xhosa, with the incentive that they could keep any cattle they rustled. The other notable historical building is a **Martello Tower**, still intact and exactly the same as those built two hundred years ago along the British coastline to keep out the French. The underworked tourist office will direct you there and fill you in on local history.

Practicalities

The **tourist office** (☎046/645 1555), in Fort Beaufort Museum, can provide lists of places to stay. For **accommodation** in town, head for Durban Street, where you'll find the unexceptional *Savoy* (☎046/645 1146; ③), not far west of the museum on the other side of the road, with a couple of reasonable **B&Bs** nearby. A number of working merino and citrus estates in the district offer **farmstays**, amongst the nicest being the self-catering units at *Millbank*, an old settler homestead 24km out on the Queenstown Road (☎046/645 2912; ②), where you can stroll through orange groves on the farm.

The best **eating** place in town is *Helena's*, opposite the *Savoy* in Campbell Street, a daytime venue that serves light meals and sandwiches. If you're just stopping at Fort Beaufort to fill up, the *Pondorosa Café*, next to the Total garage on the Queenstown road, is a friendly and serviceable place for takeaways, as is *Champs*, Campbell St, which does reasonable burgers. Better than the lot is the *Country Club*, outside town on the R67 north to Queenstown, a farmers' hangout that does good steaks and pizzas and has a bar. Outdoor seating overlooks a golf course and has views of the surrounding hills.

Mpofu Game Reserve, Fort Fordyce and Katberg

If you want somewhere like the Hogsback, but without the hype, you'll find it in the undeveloped mountainscapes of **Mpofu** and **Fort Fordyce reserves**. Both are within spitting distance of Fort Beaufort, yet less than an hour's drive transports you dramatically from parched scrubby lowlands into high country, broken with cliffs and draped with indigenous forests. Facilities are fairly basic, but the plus is that the area draws far fewer visitors than the Hogsback and feels far more pristine.

Mpofu Game Reserve
More developed than Fort Fordyce, **Mpofu Game Reserve**, 21km northwest of Fort Beaufort, is a 75-square-kilometre tract of land with spectacular views over the Katberg Mountains. The steep terrain and changing rainfall generates a varied habitat that supports a respectable cross-section of herbivores including white rhino, giraffe, waterbuck, warthog, and a wealth of antelope including springbok, kudu, eland, reedbuck and lechwe. Baboons, vervet monkeys, black-backed jackals, caracals and ostriches are also here. A number of **trails** from ninety minutes to a full day provide the means to experience the countryside on foot. To **get there**, take the Lower Blinkwater/Post Retief turn-off to the left, 13km from Fort Beaufort, and continue for a further 8km to the entrance gate.

When it comes to **accommodation**, the reserve has the rare distinction of a backpackers' **hostel** on site – *Mpofu Backpackers*, with a dorm (①) that sleeps ten in bunks. It's pretty rustic, with no electricity: lighting is by paraffin, toilets are long drops and there are bush showers (hoisted buckets). You can also **camp** for next to nothing (①) and use their facilities. Booking through *Old Gaol Backpackers* (see p.304) in Grahamstown, who can also advise on how to get there. More salubrious are the fully equipped self-catering *Mpofu* and *Ntloni* **lodges** (minimum charge for four people; ②–③) in the northern section of the reserve, with beds for ten and eight people. These should be booked through the Eastern Cape Tourism Board in Bisho (☎040/635 2115, fax 636 4019).

Alternatively, and especially useful if you're without transport, there's **Waylands Farm**, a large, working stock-farm on a north-facing slope of the Katberg, 40km north of Fort Beaufort. *Katberg Backpackers*, on the farm (☎046/684 0151, fax 684 0881, *waylands@eastcape.net*), have doubles and four-bed **dorms** (①) in the original 1850s homestead; in the nearby art noveau farmhouse there are more upmarket **B&B** rooms (④) with four-poster beds, yellowwood floors and panelled walls, though with shared bathrooms. The farm arranges **hikes** and **game drives** in Mpofu, guided horse trails and mountain biking on its grounds, occasional art and music workshops, and has a resident practising herbalist and reflexologist. To get there, call *Katberg* to arrange a pick-up from Fort Beaufort, available for a small charge; the Magic Mountain Bus shuttle bus, which runs between East London and Katberg, is also based here (for information call *Katberg*, or mobile ☎082/972 3681). If you're driving, continue for 30km through the Mpofu Game Reserve from the entrance; at the T-junction, turn right towards Post Retief and drive for about 10km to Post Retief Country Club. From here take the right fork and continue for another 10km and you'll see Waylands signposted to your left.

Fort Fordyce
The change in scene as you leave the flat Karoo scrub of Fort Beaufort and climb the Amatola Escarpment to the reserve of **Fort Fordyce** (headquarters ☎046/684 0792) is dramatic. The distance is surprisingly short (a mere 24km northwest of Fort Beaufort),

but the drive takes a tortuous 45 minutes on a good day. If you're looking for simplicity and solitude it's certainly worth the effort, and during the week you're quite likely to find yourself alone.

Once there, steep cliffs and *kloofs* fall away to valleys vegetated by grassveld and indigenous forest that includes milkwood, yellowwoood and knobthorn trees – pine plantations are being harvested to allow the native species to regenerate. There are small numbers of **game**, including bushpigs, zebras, baboons and black wildebeest. The main activity here is hiking along four circular **trails** of between five and ten kilometres, including one going through a thick forest, along a stream and over grassland. **Horse-riding** is available (notify the reserve headquarters in advance) at R12 an hour or R50 for the whole day.

To get there from Fort Beaufort, take the R67 towards Queenstown. After 12km, the reserve is signposted to your left, after which it's another 12km along a dirt track to the headquarters. The last 8km of this are steep and the road is poor; allow 30 to 45 minutes for this section. There's absurdly cheap **accommodation** – some of it quite basic – at three separate sites in the reserve. All have cooking and ablution facilities, as well as linen, cooking utensils, crockery and cutlery; just bring your own food and towels. You pay for a minimum of four people, but it's still cheaper than a single dorm bed in most backpackers' lodges. *Louries Rest*, next to the park headquarters, is a huge comfortable cottage intended for large groups. It's the only one with electricity, plus it's got a large garden and outdoor seating with intoxicating views across the valleys. A few kilometres away, on the edge of the escarpment, *Phakamisa House*, the most rudimentary of the three, has basic solar electricity, which runs out a couple of hours into the evening, though there's a gas lamp. A similar distance away, there are slightly less basic facilities at *Harris Hut*, a timber chalet in a clearing right on the forest fringe, from which you can walk straight onto one of the trails. All **bookings** should be made through the park's headquarters.

Katberg

KATBERG, an area of mountains and indigenous forest west of Hogsback, is a sort of poor relation of that same village, since it fell into the former Ciskei and never developed into a residential area. To get there, take the R67 from Fort Beaufort towards Queenstown; after 40km, take the dirt road signposted to the *Katberg Protea* for 13km. It's essentially a weekending spot, with only one **place to stay** – the *Katberg Protea* itself (☎040/864 1010, fax 864 1014; full board ⑤), a mountain resort offering horse-riding, tennis and pleasant, shady gardens. The hotel is also visitable for **tea** or a **meal** if you just want to pop in after exploring the rich indigenous forest, on a variety of one-to four-hour walking **trails** or **horse-rides**. Maps and information are available from the hotel.

East London to Aliwal North

Besides the mountainous scenery of the Amatolas, there's little to encourage a stop along the N6 highway from East London en route to Johannesburg until you reach the inviting **hot springs** of **Aliwal North**. The road traverses a region which was once home to **German settlers**. Between 1857 and 1859, over four thousand Germans arrived in the Eastern Cape, initially drawn from a German regiment fighting for the British in the Crimea, and brought in by the Cape Governor to act as a buffer against the Xhosa. The once-cohesive German-speaking community has long been diluted, and the last settler farms were abandoned in the Eighties when the area came under the auspices of the Ciskei government.

Queenstown and around

There's no reason at all to pause in **QUEENSTOWN**, a sizeable workaday shopping and administrative centre, 190km north of East London, serving a large and poor black rural community and white stock-farmers. However, if you're here for the night on a cross-country journey, the **Lawrence de Lange** and **Longhill nature reserves** (both free), just out of town in the mountains, are worth a visit. Entrance is free and there are rhino, zebra, wildebeest and a wide variety of antelope in the park, as well as picnic sites in the Longhill section of the reserve. From Cathcart Road, the main street, head out of town on Kingsway and Hangklip roads, and look out for signs to the reserve.

The **tourist information centre**, 8 Owen St (Mon–Fri 8.30am–4pm; ☎045/893 2265), behind the town hall represents the surrounding Stormberg region, and can help with finding a place to stay and posts up an emergency B&B list after hours. The best **place to stay** is in the middle-class suburbs above the railway line, where you'll find some excellent B&Bs. *Carthews Corner*, 1 Park Ave, Blue Rise (☎ & fax 045/838 1885; mobile: 082 492 1547; ③) has garden cottages, a pool and *braai* facilities, and secure off-street parking – they can recommend other places if they're full. It's not advisable to **camp** in the run-down caravan park next to the busy East London road. Reliable **eating** comes down to steaks at the *Spur*, Cathcart Rd, and *O Hagan's*, 14 Robinson Rd; or the *Chinese Continental Restaurant* in Pick and Pay Mall, Cathcart Rd.

Dramatic scenery surrounds Queenstown in the shape of tawny grass-covered mountains and rocky outcrops. Carnarvon Estates (☎ & fax 045/856 0011; half board ④), 50km north of Queenstown on the N6, is the most established of several **game farms** in the area; here you can go on botanical walks and see seventeen species of antelope and 250 bird varieties, with accommodation in a luxury farmhouse lodge with seven en-suite bedrooms, or a garden cottage suitable for a couple.

Aliwal North

ALIWAL NORTH, 158km north of Queenstown, on the Orange River, borders Free State province and has a distinctly Afrikaner flavour. The town's name celebrates the smashing of the Sikhs at Aliwal in India in 1846 by the governor of the Cape Colony, Sir Harry Smith. (Aliwal South was the former name of Mossel Bay in the Western Cape.) More relevant to its Afrikaans character is the town's part in the **Second Anglo-Boer War**, when the Boers under General Olivier occupied the town and declared the Republic of Oliviersfontein in 1900. What remains of the short-lived republic is a sobering memorial to the Boers who died in concentration camps set up by the British. Historic interest aside, the main reason to come to Aliwal North is for its **curative mineral waters**, 3km from the centre, which merit a restorative stopoff.

The town is effectively divided into two: the central area dominated by the N6 traffic, and the area built up around the spa, which, although ugly, has the best places to stay, shop and eat. The **Spa** (7am–10pm; entry fee), signposted off the N6 and R58, centres around an Olympic-sized outdoor pool with palm trees and green lawns – perfect for swimming and relaxation. The indoor pools are much warmer, but not quite hot enough in winter. Admission also gives you access to the modest gym and tennis courts, but you'll need your own racquet and balls.

At the southern edge of town, signposted off the N6, is a heavy-handedly symbolic **Boer War Concentration Camp Memorial**. On the site of two camp cemeteries, the memorial looks like a prison or crematorium from the outside. Inside, the walls are plastered with handmade grave stones of the 716 people who died (many of them Afrikaner children), from the terrible conditions in the tented camps set up by the British.

Note that **phone numbers** in Aliwal North are due to change throughout 1999 and 2000. If you encounter any difficulties, call ☎1023.

Arrival, information and accommodation

Translux and Greyhound **buses** between Port Elizabeth/East London and Johannesburg pull in daily at *Nobby's Restaurant* in Somerset Street; **tickets** can be bought at Dampier Motors in the same street. The **tourist information office**, 97 Somerset St (☎0551/3567), can supply **maps** and lists of places to stay in the North Eastern Cape and over the river in the Eastern Free State mountains.

Most of the town's **accommodation** is clustered around the spa. There is a reasonable hotel in the centre, but this is only worth considering if you're not taking the waters.

Aliwal Spa, De Wet Drive (☎0551/2951, fax 3008). Municipally run outfit with a huge caravan park, camping and run-down bungalows. Also municipally run, but spanking new, are nice timber self-catering cottages set on a lake 8km beyond the campsite, known as *Islands*. When booking, ask specifically for these cottages – the best place to stay in Aliwal North. ②.

Balmoral Hotel, Somerset St (☎ & fax 0551/2453). The only central hotel, on the main road through town, with spacious en-suite rooms and a serviceable restaurant. Not the place to stay if the sound of big trucks bothers you. ③.

Buffelsbron Chalets, 35 Dan Pienaar Ave (☎0551/3129). Fully equipped and spotlessly clean self-catering brick chalets sleeping four to six people. ②.

Thatchers Spa Hotel, 14 Dan Pienaar Ave (☎0551/2772, fax 42008). Over the road from the spa, offering the best-value hotel rooms in town with a fair bit of comfort, including electric blankets in winter and tea-making facilities in the en-suite rooms. ③.

Umtali Motel, Dan Pienaar Ave (☎ & fax 0551/2400). At the end of the avenue, this is the smartest hotel, but it's a bit characterless and you'll need transport to get to the spa from here. ④.

Eating

If you're staying at the spa, you won't have to stray very far for something to **eat**; *Green Trees* is conveniently located right next to the pool, and serves up decent sandwiches, pancakes, burgers, omelettes and Cokes, from 8am to 8pm. Opposite the spa entrance, in Dan Pienaar Avenue, the smart *Pink Lady Steakhouse* offers reasonably priced fish and steak main courses. Back in the centre, the nicest place is *Kunsgallerie*, opposite the *Balmoral* in Somerset Street, which serves up good teas and light lunches, in a craft shop.

The Eastern Cape Drakensberg

The **Eastern Cape Drakensberg** are the highest and most extensive mountain chain in the country, stretching east across Lesotho and up the west flank of KwaZulu-Natal into Mpumalanga. Although known misleadingly as South Africa's "little Switzerland" in tourist brochures, they are wonderful African mountains, horse-brown in winter and full of **San rock paintings**, sandstone **caves** and craggy sheep **farms**. One of the country's best-preserved and prettiest Victorian villages, **Rhodes** is the obvious goal in the region, and makes a good base for riding, walking, skiing and trout fishing. While it's very cold, dry and sunny in the winter, summer is idyllically green, with river pools to swim in. There are some appealing cottages for rent on farms, and a number of **hiking trails**, many of which offer the opportunity to see rock paintings and sleep in enormous caves. Since there is no national park in the Cape Drakensberg, activities are all done through private farms. For **bird-watchers**, the region is especially good for raptors (notably the rare lammergeier and Cape vulture), as well as orange-breasted rock jumpers and ground woodpeckers.

From Aliwal North to Rhodes Village

LADY GREY, 50km east of Aliwal North and 5km off the R58, is the only place worth a stop en route to Rhodes, with one **hotel**, the *Mountain View Country Inn*, signposted from Botha Street (☎051/603 0421, fax 603 0114; ③), which has nice old-fashioned rooms with great views. The staff keep a list of **walks** to help you explore the surrounding peaks, and the owners can organize **fly-fishing**. Besides walking, the town's attractions amount to a visit to the tiny **museum** at the Dutch Reformed church, dominated by a Victorian horse-drawn hearse and more like a curiosity shop under dust covers than anything else. It is open by arrangement only, through the hotel. The first minister of the Dutch Reformed church was a Scot, **David Ross**, who used to preach both in Afrikaans and English. His anti-imperialist views got him imprisoned by the British during the Anglo-Boer War, after which he apparently never spoke his native tongue again.

Some 79km southeast of Lady Grey, **BARKLY EAST** serves a large surrounding farming community, and is the last place to get money and fill up your car if your destination is Rhodes. Don't expect much help from the **tourist information bureau**, which doubles up as the manual telephone exchange in the municipal offices. There is nothing at all to do in the town, so unless night is falling push on for another ninety minutes to Rhodes. The sixty-kilometre dirt road to Rhodes is tortuous and rough with sheer, unfenced drops – definitely not recommended in the dark or mist. The very comfortable *Elanli Guest House*, 33 Cole St (☎045/971 0185; ③), in a Victorian house on the signposted road to Elliot, provides the best **accommodation** in Barkly. There's also a little-used **campsite** (①), 100m off to the right as you hit town from Lady Grey.

Rhodes and around

Some 60km northeast of Barkly East, **RHODES** is almost too good to be true – a remote and beautiful village girdled by the Eastern Cape Drakensberg. Few people actually live here: like other villages in this region, Rhodes was progressively deserted as residents gravitated to the cities to make a living, leaving its Victorian tin-roofed architecture of gracious houses stuck in a very pleasing time warp. Today its *raison d'être* is as a low-key holiday place for people who appreciate its isolation, wood stoves and restored cottages. Although electricity reached the village a few years ago, very few establishments have it, and paraffin lamps and candles are the norm.

Given that Rhodes is not on the way to anywhere (on some maps it doesn't even appear), it is a place to go to for a few days, rather than an overnight stop. While nights are cool even in summer, in winter they are freezing, and there's no central heating, so pack warm clothes. The *Rhodes Hotel*, a general shop and a garage are at the heart of the village, which is not much more than a few crisscrossing gravel roads lined with pine trees. The trees were donated in the 1890s, so the story goes, after a group of scheming townsfolk hoped to extract a slush fund from **Cecil Rhodes**, by changing the village's name in his honour. All they got from the astute entrepreneur was a sackful of seeds. While there is a post office and payphone, there are no banking facilities and no public transport in or out of the village.

Rhodes is busiest in the winter when **skiers** use it as a base for the Tiffendell slopes (see box overleaf), an hour's 4WD drive into the highest peaks of the Cape Drakensberg. December to May are the best months for swimming, trout fishing and hiking, all of which are easy to do using the village as a base. The rivers jump with rainbow and brown trout, stocked in the Twenties. This is one of the best places in the country to **fly-fish**, with all the solitude and glorious landscape you could hope for. Advice about where to fish can be given by the *Rhodes Hotel*; better still you can go out for a day or longer with Dave Walker of *Walkabout* (see p.341), who can organize permits which give you access to 150km of river, but you'll need all your own gear.

TIFFENDELL SKI RESORT

Tiffendell, South Africa's only **ski resort**, promotes itself as a little Switzerland, with Alpine ski lodges and European instructors on the slopes. However, it's essentially a venue for for fun-loving South Africans, most of whom are conspicuous consumers after a nonstop party (packages tend to include free booze from lunch to midnight). The resort is enormously successful, and for foreign visitors it provides, if nothing else, a quirky experience of Africa.

Skiing at Tiffendell is on **artificial snow** (despite regular winter falls, the real snow melts too quickly to provide a reliable piste). You can rent everything you need at the resort at about R220 per day. If you've never skied, this is a good place to take **lessons**, and at around R300 per day all-inclusive it's very reasonable. Three-day, fully inclusive packages, including on-site accommodation, work out at around R1200 per person. Day visitors need to book, as there is a maximum of 180 people on the slopes per day. The season runs from May 30 to August 31. **Book** through *Tiffendell*, 14 Fairway Ave, Linksfield North 2191 (☎011/640 5160, fax 485 2915, *tiffendell@global.co.za*).

The only on-site **accommodation** is at the lodge, which is usually full. Rooms are small and functional, with shared washing facilities. Many people stay at Rhodes village, one hour's 4WD across mountain passes, or on guest farms in the area. Of these, one of the nicest is *Burnbrae Mountain Hideaway*, PO Box 123, Barkly East 9786 (☎04542, ask for 7403; mobile: 083/308 5172; ④), 15km from Tiffendell, which also offers self-catering (②). On the farm there are rock paintings and caves you can hike to and, in the summer, trout fishing and riding. *Fetcani Glen*, PO Box 88, Barkly East (☎04542, ask for 7412) offers similar attractions with a rambling five-bedroomed farmhouse for rent and a beautiful river cutting through a sandstone gorge on the property.

The shortest route for **getting to Tiffendell** is via Rhodes, but the road is steep and needs 4WD at all times. The alternative starts 23km north of Barkly East, and if the road is wet or snowy needs a 4WD vehicle for the last 19km. If you don't have the right transport, both the *Rhodes Hotel* and Henri Reeders (☎04542, ask for 9120) do daily transfers to the resort from Rhodes.

Rock-art sites

Rhodes is a good base for exploring millennia-old **San rock paintings**, the majority of which are on surrounding private farms which can be visited with the farmers' permission (some farms also take guests). The National Monuments Council (☎021/462 4502, fax 462 4509) in Cape Town has a comprehensive list, and Rhodes locals can point you to local farms, such as Buttermead and Hillbury, which have their own paintings.

There are two sites accessible from Rhodes, which you can drop in on without prior arrangement. **Martin's Hoek** farm, 16km from the village, is worth a visit, not just for the well-preserved, photogenic paintings, but for the lovely, lonely valley you have to drive though to get there. The signposted turn-off to Martin's Hoek is 8km from Rhodes on the road to Barkly East. From the turn-off it's another 8km to the site, with parking and a couple of picnic tables. The paintings, which are fenced off, are on the cliff face opposite the parking area. It's a ten-minute uphill scramble, much easier than it first appears, with views out onto the rough and streaky sandstone peaks. Local farmer Vasie Murray (☎04542, ask for 7012) does **tours** of the Martin's Hoek site. A second site, at **Denorben Farm**, 32km from Barkly East, offers the longest series of San paintings in the country. It's only 1km to the farm from the main road, and the long, painted panel is behind the house, at the bottom of the garden. A nominal entry fee is charged and there's a helpful information sheet on the images, many of which are confusing. Don't miss the impressive (unpainted) cave in the farm yard – it's common practice for farmers in the area to use overhangs as cosy sheep pens and sheds.

Rock-art had an essentially religious purpose, usually recording experiences of trance states. Shamans' visions often included powerful animals like the eland, which you can see depicted at both Denorben and Martin's Hoek, and whose power shamans were able to access for healing. A dying eland is a metaphor for the shaman who enters a **trance** and takes on aspects of an animal. At Denorben there's a half-animal, half-human figure, an image of transformation during the trance state. Also at Denorben are painted figures dancing, clapping and singing, in the process of inducing trance. For more details on rock-art, see p.413.

Accommodation

Gateshead Lodges, PO Box 267, Barkly East 5580 (☎045/971 0233). Several farmhouses and cottages on huge properties in marvellously remote and rugged territory, all within a large radius of Rhodes. Some cater specifically for fly-fishing, hiking, riding or bird-watching, while a few have caves and rock paintings on the property. All are clearly detailed in a pamphlet available from the above address. ②.

Ramseys, PO Box 1, Rhodes (☎04542, ask for 9240). *Ramseys* rent out a couple of cottages in the village, and a draughty former parsonage with single beds and bunks in large rooms. ②.

Rhodes Hotel, Main Rd (☎04542, ask for Rhodes 21). Decorative exterior and charming Victorian furnishings. Quiet horses are available for renting, there are tennis courts and the owner is a trout-fishing guide. Full board ④.

Rubicon Flats, PO Box 5, Rhodes (☎04542, ask for 9002). The best-value, and the warmest, place in town, this handsome old schoolhouse has been converted into self-catering rooms, each with an anthracite burner, and simple dorms. The owner also rents out self-catering cottages in the village. All accommodation ②.

Walkabout, signposted off the main road (☎04542, ask for 9203). Relaxed house with a few guest rooms. Friendly owner, Dave Walker, knows a good deal about the area and can organize almost any activity, including fly-fishing and horse-riding. Half board ③.

Eating and drinking

For **eating**, your best choice is the *Walkabout*, which does home-cooked meals, and, if booked in advance, vegetarian food. Cheapest of all are the ready-cooked meals, such as curry and rice, from local farmer's wife Marian Henning (☎04542, ask for 9013), who'll deliver to your door. **Drinking** comes down to the *Rhodes* bar, one of the most atmospheric bars in the country. It's decorated with the horns of Wydeman, the leader ox of the supply wagon from Barkly East, who dropped dead outside the hotel in 1896, and smoky relics of the days when this was a frontier town of gamblers, cattle rustlers and bar-room shoot-outs, line the walls.

Naude's Nek and the route south

The most exhilarating drive out of Rhodes is along **Naude's Nek**, the highest mountain-pass road in the country, connecting Rhodes with **Maclear** to the south, in a series of snaking hairpin bends and huge views. If you're chiefly looking for scenery, it's not essential to do the whole route to Maclear. Many people go from Rhodes to the top of the pass and back as a half-day trip, the highlight of which is to make a call from the highest phone (with a crank handle) in the country, in a corrugated-iron booth in the middle of a sheep pen at the top of the pass.

While it's only 30km from Rhodes, the journey can take a couple of hours to the Nek because so many changing vistas en route demand stops. You don't need a 4WD, but if you feel precious about your car don't attempt this route, as the road is harsh. The surface deteriorates from the top of the pass to Maclear, with sharp stones and a hump down the centre of the road, which may scrape the bottom of your vehicle, and is definitely impassable after snow. If you're wanting to use this route into the Transkei and KwaZulu-Natal, check with the *Rhodes Hotel* as to the current state of the road (see above).

If you're not aiming for the Transkei, you can loop west from Maclear, at the bottom of the escarpment, and take the tarred R56 towards **Dordrecht** and the N6. The string

NORTH EASTERN CAPE TRAILS AND HIKES

The **North Eastern Cape** is prime **walking** country, with expansive skies and long views across the mountains. There is no national park, so all walks have to be done (and booked) on private property, but are very reasonably priced for that. Three of the best trails are listed below.

•**Ben Macdhui Hiking Trail**. A three-day circular trail along a 51-kilometre route involving about eight hours' walking each day. Begins and ends at Rhodes village with highlights that include magnificent mountain scenery, wild flowers, waterfalls, the chance to see rare mountain birds (such as the bearded vulture) and climb Ben Macdhui, the highest mountain (3000m) in the Eastern Cape. Accommodation is in an old farmhouse and a mountain hut, both equipped with beds, mattresses, drinking water, long-drop toilets, a gas stove, kettle, pans, basin and a coal stove for heating. Rhodes village makes a convenient place to stay at the start and finish of this hike. Book through Gideon van Zyl, PO Box 299, 5580 Barkly East (☎04542/7021 or 9212).

•**Woodcliffe Farm**. A variety of one- to four-day trails on a farm, 22km north of Maclear, on the Naude's Nek Road. Highlights include stunning Drakensberg scenery, rock-art, dinosaur footprints on the Pot River and 185 bird species. Accommodation, in a self-catering cottage, can be used as a base for day-walks or at the start of a longer hike, while cave overhangs can be used on longer hikes. Maps are provided and planning advice is available for a route matching your fitness and time available. Book through Phyll Sephton, PO Box 65, Maclear 5480 (☎ & fax 045/932 1550).

•**Kranskop Hiking Trail**. One- to two-day hike on a farm, 33km north of Dordrecht, on the Barkly East Road. Highlights include some beautiful *kloofs*, sleeping overnight in a sandstone cave, and seeing some San rock-art. Accommodation at the start or finish of the trail is in a comfortable rustic farm cottage sleeping twelve. Beds, mattresses, pillows, hot water, stove, fridge, lamps, candles and a coal stove are provided. Farm milk and meat are available. Book through Frans Slabbert, PO Box 85, Dordrecht 5435 (☎045/944 1014).

of small towns along the the R56 from Maclear to Dordrecht are unmemorable trading centres, with nowhere to stay. All along the route though, the high Drakensberg march along, providing a dramatic backdrop to the journey. **Sheep farming** is the mainstay of white farmers in the region, though rampant stock theft is putting many out of business. One farmer has employed armed San ex-trackers from a defunct unit of the South African army to patrol his farm.

The R56 gives access to a couple of **hiking trails** with farm cottages for rent in the southern part of the Cape Drakensberg, notably **Woodcliffe** near Maclear, and **Kranskop** near Dordrecht, both of which have caves and rock paintings (see box above). If you're simply overnighting, or visiting rock-painting sites, *Peddlars*, PO Box 607, Elliot 5460 (☎045/931 2315; half board ④), at the bottom of Barkly Pass, is a good **place to stay**, with motel-style rooms on a farm.

THE WILD COAST REGION

The **Wild Coast region** is aptly named: this is one of South Africa's least tame areas – a vast stretch of undulating hills, lush forest and spectacular beaches skirting a section of the Indian Ocean notorious for its harrowing shipwrecks. The sense of wildness goes beyond the landscape, for this is the former **Transkei homeland**, a desperately poor region that during apartheid was disenfranchised and turned into a dumping ground for Africans who were either too old or too young for South African industry to make use of. Few whites live in the Wild Coast region; nearly everyone is **Xhosa**, and those in rural areas live mostly in traditional rondavels that dot the landscape for as far as the eye can see.

Despite the obvious hardship, it's refreshing – at least for visitors – to find that rural areas are still communally owned rather than parcelled up into private farms. Instead of the fenced-off spaces edged by squatter camps that you find in most of rural South Africa, here the land is unfenced and fully inhabited.

The **N2** highway runs through the middle of the region, passing through the old Transkei capital of **Umtata** and a host of unremarkable smaller towns along the way. Northwest of the N2, towards the Lesotho border and the Drakensberg mountains, you'll find beautiful hilly country and endless little villages, but the lack of accommodation and poor roads make travelling here difficult.

Far more accessible is the **coastal region**, which runs from just north of East London to the mouth of the **Mtamvuna River**. With its succession of great beaches, hidden reefs, patches of subtropical forest, rural Xhosa settlements and the attractive little towns of **Coffee Bay** and **Port St Johns**, which are both popular with backpackers, this region is one of the finest areas to visit in the Eastern Cape. In addition, there are some beautiful, state-run **nature reserves** along the coast; if you only have time to visit one or two, head for **Cwebe**, with its pretty waterfalls, lagoon, abundant birdlife and comfortable bungalow accommodation, or **Hluleka**, with its outstanding beaches and shoreline.

Wild Coast practicalities

Most roads in the Wild Coast region are **untarred** and, while generally passable in an ordinary car, they invariably take their mechanical toll. Always carry a tool kit, a spare tyre (preferably two), and take the roads slowly. Watch out for livestock on all Wild Coast roads, including the N2, and avoid driving in rainy weather and at night. **Public transport** throughout the region is poorly maintained and, except for the routes between Port St Johns and Coffee Bay, can be very time-consuming and occasionally dangerous. You're best off in your own vehicle, or relying on the Baz Bus, which covers a fair amount of territory in this region.

It's wise to book **accommodation** in advance: the Umtata-based Wild Coast Reservations (see p.354) is useful if you are planning to stay in several places on your journey. Even better is the superbly well-informed and efficient **Wild Coast Holiday Reservations** (☎043/743 6181, fax 743 6188, *meross@iafrica.com*), based in East London, which, apart from being able to arrange places to stay, is unsurpassed when it comes to organizing **activities** in the region, including hiking. There a number of good backpackers' lodges throughout the coast, and plenty of campsites. Although security is no longer the worry it once was, **camping in rural areas** is not advisable – if you want to stay among the rural Xhosa, the safest way to do so is with a guide.

To visit the region's **nature reserves** you'll usually need to book in advance. However a word of caution: the post-apartheid reorganization in the Wild Coast, combined with a bankrupt provincial administration and a disintegrating civil service, can make it exceedingly difficult to make arrangements. Provided you are resourceful, you should overcome these bureaucratic obstacles – an effort worth making as the region's wildernesses are exceedingly beautiful. We have provided the most up-to-date booking information available at the time of writing for each reserve.

One highlight of many people's visits to the Wild Coast region, especially the Port St Johns area, is the ready availability of high-quality **cannabis** (*insango* in Xhosa). Be warned, though, that cannabis is as illegal here as anywhere else in South Africa and that the former Transkei police are trying to prove their worth to the national force with regular busts. Avoid the temptation to buy in large quantities, as it often turns out that the few tourists who have run into trouble in the region were trying to do just that.

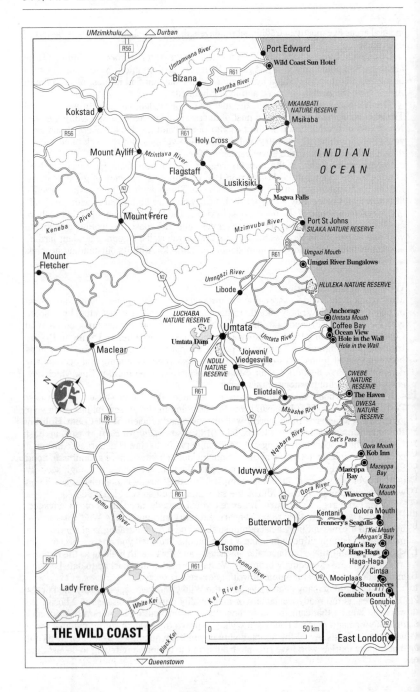

UMzimkhulu△ △Durban

R56

Port Edward
● Wild Coast Sun Hotel

Umtamvana River

R61

Bizana

Mzamba River

Kokstad

MKAMBATI
NATURE RESERVE
Msikaba

R56

R61

Holy Cross

INDIAN
OCEAN

Mount Ayliff Mzintlava River

N2

Flagstaff

Lusikisiki

Magwa Falls

Mount Frere

Keneba   River

Mzimvubu River

Port St Johns
SILAKA NATURE RESERVE

Mount
Fletcher

R61

Umgazi Mouth
● Umgazi River Bungalows

Umngazi River

N2

Libode

HLULEKA NATURE RESERVE

LUCHABA
NATURE
RESERVE

Anchorage
● Umtata Mouth
Coffee Bay
Ocean View
Hole in the Wall
Hole in the Wall

Maclear

Umtata Dam

Umtata

Umtata River

Jojweni/
Viedgesville

NDULI
NATURE
RESERVE

CWEBE
NATURE
RESERVE
● The Haven
DWESA
NATURE
RESERVE

R61

Qunu

Elliotdale

Mbashe River

N

N2

Nqabara River

Cat's Pass

Qora Mouth
● Kob Inn

Idutywa

Mazeppa
Bay

Mazeppa
Bay

R61

Qora River

Nxaxo
Mouth
Wavecrest

Kentani

Qolora Mouth

Tsomo River

Butterworth

Trennery's Seagulls

Kei Mouth
Morgan's Bay

Tsomo

Morgan's Bay
Haga-Haga
Haga-Haga

R61

Tsomo River

Cintsa

R61

N2

Mooiplaas

Buccaneers

Lady Frere

White Kei

Gonubie Mouth

Gonubie

Kei River

N2

THE WILD COAST

0   50 km

East London

Black Kei

▽Queenstown

A WALK ON THE WILD COAST

If you've got the time, an excellent way to take in the splendours of this coast is to hike it. The fourteen-day **Wild Coast Hiking Trail**, which runs from the Mtamvuna River to the Kei River, covers some of the most superb coastal scenery in the country. However the trail is poorly marked and years of neglect have left facilities along the way in a state of dereliction. A more realistic option is to do short day walks from resorts or towns along the coast where you can benefit from local knowledge of conditions. If you still want to undertake longer sections of the route, it's essential you plan well. A good starting point for information about the many pecularities of this wonderful trail is the authoritative and widely available *Complete Guide to Walks and Trails in Southern Africa* by Jaynee Levy.

A better-organized and more accessible alternative is the recommended **Wild Coast Hotel Meander**, which covers a 55-kilometre section of the coast from Qora Mouth to Morgan's Bay over an easygoing five days (six nights). Despite being packaged, this is still an adventurous excursion with some moderate challenges such as river crossings and hiking over headlands, though it poses no great difficulties to anyone of average fitness. Accommodation is at hotels along the route (*Kob Inn, Mazeppa Bay, Wavecrest, Trennery's* or *Seagulls* and *Morgan's Bay*), where you eat breakfast and dinner. They will also provide a picnic lunch for each day's walk and together with your personal effects, this is all you have to carry. You can go it alone, but the organizers recommend using trained local guides, who are members of the local community and are familiar with each stretch of the trail. **Bookings** should be made through Wild Coast Holiday Reservations (see p.343). The whole deal, including transfers between East London airport and the Wild Coast, five nights accommodation, all meals and the services of guides, costs around R1800 per person for a minimum of four, but reduces if there are more participants.

The southern coast: East London to the Mbashe River

Once you get beyond the holiday resorts between East London and the Kei River, all within an hour's drive of East London, and cross what was once the border of Transkei, you'll find that the atmosphere changes completely. The rest of the southern Wild Coast is densely populated, with barely a hillside not liberally coated with brightly coloured rondavels facing east to the rising sun. Most of the region's resorts lie between East London and the Mbashe River, almost always at the end of difficult dirt roads that are mercifully not too far from the N2 highway. **Qolora Mouth**, where you can take fascinating trails that explore the tempestuous history of the region, is definitely worth a visit, while the **Cwebe Nature Reserve** stands out for its easy accessibility and the bonus of a comfortable hotel.

Cintsa, Haga-Haga and Morgan's Bay

By far the best of the smattering of resorts between East London and the Kei River are to be found at Cintsa and Morgan's Bay. To find **CINTSA**, take the Brakfontein exit (no. 26) off the N2, travel down the highway back towards East London, take the next exit on your left, marked "East Coast Resorts" and follow the road for 16km until you see a sign pointing to Cintsa West and Cintsa Bay. Alternatively, you can take the **Baz Bus** (☎021/439 2323) to *Buccaneer's Backpackers* (☎ & fax 043/734 3012, *bucb-p@iafrica.com*) **hostel**, primarily aimed at backpackers, with good dorms (①) and excellent self-contained doubles (②); there is also a family cottage for four (②). Set next to the beach amidst the dune forest (and with a swimming pool), they offer a variety of sports and activities including surfing, a climbing wall, forest hiking and river cruises. It's self-catering, but inexpensive breakfasts and dinners are available in its pub and café. It also lays on *shebeen* outings, trips to a local black school, beach horse-rides, game viewing in the Double Drift reserve and tours in the Transkei. For something to eat, *Fred's Bar* (closed Tues), a ten-minute walk away in Cintsa East, serves up steaks and burgers, while the convivial *Steve's Bar* (closed Sun evening & Mon) in Cintsa West, adds fish and chips to this repertoire.

The next resort north of Cintsa is **HAGA-HAGA**, 72km from East London, excellent for beach walking, though not as pretty as Cintsa. It's dominated by the box-like but beautifully located *Haga-Haga Resort* (π & fax 043/841 1670, *hagahaga@hinet.co.za*; ③). Enquire about weekend deals out of season.

At beautiful **MORGAN'S BAY**, 90km from East London, two rivers converge in an estuary that carves out a passage through forested dunes. Here you'll find the *Morgan's Bay* (π & fax 043/841 1062, *mb.hotel@mweb.co.za*; full board ④), a friendly, family-oriented **hotel** with good food and a gorgeous beach right next to the hotel; there are cheaper rooms that share washing facilities, as well as camping (①). A hike from the hotel leads over some grassy knolls to the fifty-metre-high Morbay Cliffs, an excellent vantage point for spotting dolphins and, in season, whales. The bay is pounded by massive breakers, but the estuary provides a safe and tranquil place for toddlers to paddle.

There's no coastal road between Citsna and Haga-Haga or Morgan's Bay, but the route can be walked as part of the **Strandloper Trail**, that takes in 56km of beach as it wends its way from Kei Mouth to Gonubie. It lasts five days, with four nights in communal huts; bookings (R140) should be made through Wild Coast Holiday Reservations (see p.343).

Kei Mouth

The Kei River marks the beginning of the Wild Coast proper, and **Kei Mouth** provides the tranquil setting for the first three of a succession of old-fashioned family hotels that span the coast's length. Only one hour's drive from East London and its weekend holidaymakers, this area has become amongst the most manicured of the coast, and if you have the time you'll find it more rewarding to continue further north instead. To get to the Kei Mouth, turn off from the N2 at Mooiplaas, about 42km from East London. Ignore the turn-off to Haga-Haga and continue through pleasant grasslands for roughly 33km, until you reach the coast.

Accommodation includes the *Kei Mouth Beach* (π & fax 043/841 1017, *kmbeach@iafrica.com*; ③), a comfortable hotel close to the beach, offering rooms looking onto the sea, as well as deep-sea fishing and river cruises; the *Kei Sands* (π043/841 1011, fax 841 1248; ②), freshly refurbished self-catering beachfront apartments with a nice sun-deck and swimming pool and a restaurant on the premises; and the *Suncoast Cabanas* (π & fax 043/841 1102; ②) in the main road, where you'll find nine thatched, self-catering cabanas arranged around a pleasant pool, 300m from the river and 500m from the beach.

Butterworth

BUTTERWORTH, the oldest town in the Transkei, is located near the site of the Gcaleka chief Hintsa's Great Place, and was founded by Methodist missionaries in 1827. The town, known to Xhosa as Gcuwa (after the river running through it), derives its English name from the then-treasurer of the Wesleyan Mission Society, Reverend Butterworth, and was selected as the focal point of Transkeian industrial development in the Seventies, with its new industries drawing thousands of workers from the surrounding countryside. Most of the industries have now closed, but the people are still living in sprawling townships and squatter camps around the town, where unemployment is worryingly high.

Whilst Butterworth itself is unattractive and a bit chaotic, with tatty department stores and supermarkets filled with shoppers, the nearby **Bawa Falls** on the Qolora River, which have a sheer drop of nearly 100m, are spectacular and well worth a visit. The poorly maintained dirt track which leads to them is just west of town past the Shell filling station, but numerous twists and turns make the falls quite hard to find, so you will probably need to ask directions.

Practicalities

Butterworth is on the N2, just over 100km from East London, and if you are coming from there it is worth stopping off at the helpful **tourist information** bureau in the old border post on the Kei River, about halfway between the two towns, which has a good range of leaflets as well as reasonably priced Xhosa jewellery and fabrics.

The well-signposted road to Kentani and the Wild Coast is at the eastern end of Butterworth, past the Gcuwa bridge, and winds through the sprawling Zitulele Industrial Township, where the tar stops and gives way to a potholed dirt road, which is being tarred, that continues all the way to the coast. Butterworth's **bus** station is at the western end of town, next to the Shell garage, from where numerous buses and increasing numbers of **minibus taxis** run to East London, Umtata and Kentani. Daily Greyhound and Translux **buses** both stop just off main road on Merriman Street, which is just before the Gcuwa bridge.

The N2 highway runs through Butterworth and is lined with **takeaways**, beer halls and filling stations. The only decent **accommodation** in town is the *Wayside Protea* (☎047/491 4615), reached by turning right down King Street off the main road, and taking the first right into Sauer Street, where you will see the hotel on your left. The rooms are comfortable and are a fair bit cheaper over weekends (②) than during the week (④). The hotel has safe underground parking, and a good **restaurant** serving lunchtime buffets and à la carte evening meals. The one drawback is that the hotel is right next to a busy taxi rank that swarms with people until late into the evening. The *German Restaurant* (☎047/491 3852), just off the Kentani road at the eastern end of town, serves good-value steaks and German dishes.

Qolora Mouth

Heading east from Butterworth, and far more secluded than Kei Mouth, beautiful **Qolora Mouth** (roughly pronounced "kalocha" – the 'r' in Xhosa is like the 'ch' in loch), is best explored on one of the excellent **guided trails** run by two local residents: Trevor Wigley and Allan Burmeister. The trails include a popular three-hour walking and boating trip to the "gates" – the short, towering corridor of rock face that the Qolora passes through on its way to the sea. There's also a trail that explores the enormously varied shell life of the seashore and some of the coastline's many **shipwrecks** – including the *Jacaranda*, a liner that went down in 1971 and whose rusting hull can still be clearly seen. If contacted in advance, Trevor can arrange a visit to a local *igqirha*, or traditional spiritual doctor, who enacts a typical consultation.

The spot on the Gxara River (which runs between the Qolora and the Kei), where the prophetess Nongqawuse had disastrous visions that induced the Xhosa to kill their cattle (see box overleaf), is not far away, and Allan, who also works at the East London Museum, offers a ten-kilometre hike to the spot, providing lively historical commentary along the way. For the historically minded, there's a trail tracing the major **battle grounds** of the Final Frontier War between the Xhosa and the British in 1878. The Xhosa have not earned the same military reputation as the Zulu in European folklore,

THE GREAT CATTLE KILLING

The 1850s were a low point for the Xhosa nation: most of their land had been seized by the British, drought was withering their crops, and cattle-sickness was decimating their precious herds. In 1856, a young woman called **Nongqawuse**, whose uncle Mhlakaza was a prophet, claimed to have seen and heard ancestral spirits in a pool on the Gxara River who told her that the Xhosa must **kill all their remaining cattle** and destroy their remaining crops. If they did this, claimed the spirits, new cattle and crops would arise, along with new people who would drive the whites into the sea.

As news of her prophecy spread, opinion was sharply divided amongst the Xhosa, with those whose herds had been badly affected by cattle-sickness most inclined to believe the young prophetess. A turning point came when the Gcaleka paramount chief Sarili visited Nongqawuse, became convinced she was telling the truth and ordered his subjects to start the killing. Thousands of cattle were killed but when the "new people" failed to materialize on the expected day, the unbelievers who had not killed their herds were blamed. By February 1857, the next date for the appearance of the new people, over 200,000 cattle had been slaughtered and their corpses were festering everywhere. When the new people failed once more to materialize, it was too late for many Xhosa. By July there was widespread starvation, with 30,000 of an estimated population of 90,000 dying of hunger.

The British administration saw the famine as a perfect way to force the destitute Xhosa into working on white settlers' farms, and the Cape governor Sir George Grey closed down feeding stations established by missionaries to speed up the process. At the same time, he laid the blame for the disaster on Xhosa chiefs, and imprisoned many of them on Robben Island.

Not surprisingly, the 1856 cattle killing is often used by whites as evidence of the folly of black superstition. The Xhosa, however, have a different interpretation: "*Intombi kaMhlakaza yathetha ubuxoke*" goes the song – meaning "Mhlakaza's girl told lies".

yet during this campaign they fought and held their own for a time against soldiers hardened in warfare in the African bush. This trail involves travelling in a 4WD vehicle and is thus more expensive than the others. All the trails can be **booked** through *Seagull's* or *Trennery's* (see below), or the East London Museum (☎043/743 0686).

Practicalities

The easiest way to **get to Qolora Mouth** is to cross over the Kei Mouth on a small boat (which you can take your car on) that operates from 6am to 6pm in summer and from 7am to 5.30pm in winter. After disembarking, continue for another 10km on the dirt road to Gxara, where you should turn right and drive for a further 7km to the sea.

Qolora Mouth has two decent full-board **resorts**: *Seagull's* (☎047/498 0044; ④), near the rocky shoreline, and the more luxurious *Trennery's* (☎047/498 0004; ④), tucked away behind a fringe of sub-tropical forest, with a great swimming pool. Both are popular with South African families. The only budget option is *Allan's* (☎043/743 0686, evenings 748 1299; ③), a ramshackle self-catering seaside cottage owned by tour guide Allan Burmeister.

Nxaxo Mouth

Nxaxo Mouth, just north of Qolora, is a tranquil location with fascinating **mangrove swamps** that teem with wildlife. It's an ideal place for hiking, shoreline fishing and general relaxation, as well as the more strenuous activities of canoeing, waterskiing and deep-sea fishing. All of this can be arranged through the only **accommodation** available, the *Wavecrest* (☎047/498 0022; ④), a cluster of pleasant bungalows and family rooms that have recently been renovated, and a restaurant with a menu that's more imaginative than that of most along the Wild Coast.

To get there, return to Kentani and take the dirt road signposted to Nxaxo. This road is in poor condition, so take it slowly – and don't take it at all if it is raining hard and you do not have a 4WD vehicle.

Mazeppa Bay and Qora Mouth

Two of the best places for **fishing** and general relaxation on the Wild Coast lie further northeast from Nxaxo. To get to **MAZEPPA BAY**, take the signposted road from Kentani, and shortly after going through a spectacular narrow ridge – **Cat's Pass** – with great views of the surrounding countryside, take a signposted turn-off to the right and continue along a rough road to the coast. The *Mazeppa Bay* (☎047/498 0033; ④) offers full-board **accommodation** in comfortable cabanas or family rooms in the hotel, and has the added attraction of its own island, which is connected to the mainland by a suspension bridge. Surfing is good near the bay, but Mazeppa is frequented by hammerhead sharks, so take care.

Northeast of Mazeppa, **QORA MOUTH** has a good beach and a lagoon where you can swim, and is accessed by continuing past the Mazeppa Bay turn-off for around 30km along a potholed dirt road to the coast, passing through hilly lowland dotted with rondavels, river gorges and patches of subtropical forest. **Accommodation** is at the *Kob Inn* (☎ & fax 047/499 0011, *kobinn@iafrica.com*; ④), which features cosy, thatched bungalows, a well-stocked bar with stunning views of the sea, and a breathtaking swimming pool built into the tidal rocks. Staff can arrange a boat and fishing tackle, and can also equip you for canoeing, waterskiing and boardsailing. There is a small ferry across the mouth that can transport you to some good hiking trails along the coast, grassland and nearby forest patches.

Idutywa and around

The small town of **IDUTYWA**, 35km north of Butterworth on the N2, is only a place to head for if you are short of fuel, or very hungry and tired. On the main road going through town you'll find passable *Max Frango's* and *Kentucky Fried Chicken* **takeaways** and the *Idutywa* (☎047/427 1040; ③), a quiet **hotel** that is the only good place to stay on the main road between Butterworth and Umtata. Though the mattresses in the rooms are poor, the hotel is clean and its Fifties furniture lends the place a modest charm. The hotel's **restaurant**, the only one in town, serves a typical South African selection of steaks and grills.

A few kilometres east of town, a right-hand turn leads to **Colleywobbles**, the name given by British soldiers to a particularly tortuous and fascinating stretch of the Mbashe River about 10km down the dirt track. The river reaches the sea 50km further east, disgorging between the **Cwebe** and **Dwesa** nature reserves, but the best way for you to reach these two beautiful places is by continuing for another 60km or so along the N2 until **Jojweni** (sometimes still called by its former name of Viedgesville), and turning right down the Coffee Bay road.

Dwesa Nature Reserve

North of Qora Mouth, the **Dwesa Nature Reserve** (daily 6am–6pm; ☎ 047/499 0020) is in the throes of a protracted dispute over land ownership, which has rendered its

SOME XHOSA TRADITIONS

The Wild Coast region is largely populated with **rural Xhosa**, who still practise traditions and customs that have faded in more urban areas. Many people, for example, still believe that the sea is inhabited by strange people who do not always welcome visitors, which explains the relative scarcity of the activities you would normally find thriving among seashore-dwelling people, such as fishing and diving.

Initiation for teenage boys and young men is still common. Young men usually leave their homes to stay in "circumcision lodges", dress in distinctive white paint and costumes and learn the customs of their clan. At the circumcision ceremony the young men are expected to make no sound while their foreskin is cut off (with no anaesthetic) with a single slice of a knife. After the ceremony, they wash off the paint and wrap themselves in new blankets, and all their possessions are thrown into a hut and set alight – they must turn away from this and not look back. There follows a feast to celebrate the beginning of manhood and the start of a year-long intermediary period during which they wear ochre-coloured clay on their faces. After this, they are counted as men. Boys who have gone through the experience of initiation together are supposed to remain bonded at a deep level for the rest of their lives.

Like other African peoples, although they believe in one God, uThixo, or uNhkulukhulu (the great one), many Xhosa also believe that their **ancestors** play an active role in their lives. However, the ancestors' messages are often too obscure to be understood without the aid of specialists, or *amagqira*.

The Xhosa are patriarchal by tradition, with women's subordinate status symbolized by *lobola*, the dowry payment in cattle and cash that a prospective husband must make to her parents before he can marry her. If the woman is not a virgin, the man pays less. Married Xhosa women have the same right as men to smoke tobacco in **pipes**, and can often be seen doing so, with the pipes' long stems designed to prevent ash falling on babies suckling at their breasts. Pipes are shared between people, but each person must have their own stem, not just for matters of hygiene but also to prevent witchcraft: bits of the body make the most effective poisonous medicines against people, and that includes hair, skin and spittle.

The Xhosa did not wear cloth until it was introduced by Europeans, when it was quickly adopted. Today, what is now seen as traditional Xhosa cloth is almost always worn by women, mostly in the form of long skirts, beautifully embroidered with horizontal black stripes placed at varying intervals, which display themselves to subtle effect when the person wearing them is walking. Bags in matching colours with long shoulder straps are popular accessories, especially at weddings, when people put cash gifts inside them. The breasts of unmarried women were traditionally uncovered, while those of married women were usually covered with beads or matching cloth. These days, most women wear T-shirts. Almost all women, however, still cover their heads with scarves which are intricately tied to form two peaks above the forehead. The **traditional colours** of the Thembu and Bomvana clans are red or orange, while the colour of the Pondo and the Mpondomise clans is light blue. In practice, these traditions are not always observed, and married women from a number of clans often wear white instead.

future uncertain. The reserve is still very much visitable and safe, but its facilities and trails have fallen into disrepair. This is a shame, because Dwesa *should* be one of the best places to stay on the coast, with rare animals like tree dassies and samango monkeys, pristine forest, grassland and coastline, and well-sited – though run-down – fully equipped self-catering wooden chalets (①). There's also a campsite. To **stay** at Dwesa you should ideally book ahead, but the system is rather haphazard and not entirely reliable. You could try just turning up, but either way make sure you have some fall-back plan for the night. To get to the reserve, turn south off the N2 at Idutywa towards the coast. The road forks right to *Kob Inn* and left to Dwesa.

Cwebe Nature Reserve

North of the Mbashe River from Dwesa, the **Cwebe Nature Reserve** (daily 6am–6pm) makes up for its lack of big game with its dense subtropical forest, brimming with flora and fauna. Stinkwood and samango monkeys, both of which have all but disappeared from most of southern Africa's east coast, are to be found here via a poorly maintained network of trails. Thankfully, the trail to the beautiful **Mbanyana Waterfall** is in good shape, and you should find it easily walkable from the *Haven* (see below) if the ground is dry. The remaining section of the reserve comprises rolling grassland and a long stretch of wonderful dune-filled shoreline lying in the shadow of the Mbashe lighthouse.

The privately owned *Haven* has **bungalows** dotted fairly close together on the fringes of a small golf course that is regularly grazed by **wildebeest**, and are a short walk through milkwoods to the sea. Book through the *Ocean View* (see overleaf). The well-signposted **road to Cwebe**, though untarred, is in good shape and you should be able to drive it at regular speed. Take the Coffee Bay turn off the N2 at Jojweni and continue for another 20km to a tarred turn to the right with a small sign pointing to the *Haven*. You'll know you've gone too far if you go past a sign on the Coffee Bay road saying "Coffee Bay 54km". The road continues to small **Elliotdale**, the main administrative centre in the communal lands of the Bomvana people. Once through the town, turn off at a sign claiming the *Haven* to be 69km away onto a dirt road. In fact, it's much less than that and you should reach the reserve in less than an hour.

Hole in the Wall

The village of **HOLE IN THE WALL** has grown up on the shoreline near the large cliff that juts out of the sea a short distance from the Mpako River mouth, from which it gets its name. The cliff has a tunnel at its base through which huge waves pound during heavy seas, making a great crashing sound that has led the Xhosa to call it esiKhaleni (the place of sound). As well as good fishing and safe swimming, there are spectacular **hikes** all around, including a coastal walk to Coffee Bay.

A hotel, with limited sites for four tents, is the sum of the village's **accommodation** options. The *Hole in the Wall* (☎ & fax 043/575 2001) is a collection of simple but comfortable full-board (④) or self-catering (③) cottages. The self-catering units are fully equipped and you can also eat in the hotel's restaurant. To get to Hole in the Wall by **minibus taxi** from Umtata you'll need to take a taxi to Mqanduli, on the Coffee Bay road, and then one to Hole in the Wall. By **car**, take the Coffee Bay road and turn right at the Hole in the Wall turn-off, from where it is another 15km along a potholed dirt road to the village.

Coffee Bay and around

The densely populated, gentle hills of **COFFEE BAY**, known to the Xhosa as Tshontini after a dense wood that grows there, mark the traditional boundary between the Bomvana and Pondo clans of the Xhosa nation. Despite the absence of nature reserves, the combination of easy access from an excellent tarred road all the way from the N2, nearby attractions like the famous Hole in the Wall (see above) and a laid-back, relaxed atmosphere, mean that Coffee Bay attracts more and more visitors every year. New backpackers' lodges have sprung up to accommodate the influx, but the village retains its feeling of idyllic obscurity. Neither the swimming nor fishing are particularly good, and though the surfing is supposed to be the best on the Wild Coast the main attractions here are the **coastal hikes**, part of the Wild Coast Hiking Trail (see p.345), which take you through Xhosa villages through beautiful hilly countryside; ask your accommodation for directions, as the trails aren't well marked or maintained. The walk to Hole in the Wall is particularly outstanding: head south along the track from Coffee Bay, and turn left at a small sign just past the Telkom tower, from where it's another 5km along the coast. You can watch **traditional dancing** on request at Nomande Madlalisa's *Bayview Restaurant* (☎047/575 2004) on the way out of Coffee Bay, and dine on inexpensive, sumptuous traditional Xhosa meals, based mostly around meat stews.

Practicalities

There are plenty of **minibus taxis** running from Umtata to Coffee Bay. The **Baz Bus** will deposit you in Qunu, from where you can arrange for staff from *Coffee Bay Backpackers* to pick you up. The drive by **car** is a fast and easy one along a good tarred road from the Jojweni junction with the N2, but the river leading to the village itself is frequently impassable, so you will probably have to park your car on the other side (where it should be quite safe), and wade across with your luggage.

Accommodation is at a traditional full-board hotel, the *Ocean View* (☎047/575 2005; ④), a short distance from the rest of the village and a stone's throw from the sea, with the only **restaurant** for kilometres around. None of the backpackers' lodges (all ①) has its own phone, but you can leave messages at the hotel. The scruffy but cheerful *Coffee Bay Backpackers* offers dorms, doubles, camping and a lively bar, but can only just cope with the number of visitors it attracts. Nearby, *Woodhouse Backpackers* is an attractive wooden complex with a good kitchen and a cosy bar, basic dorms and small doubles with mattresses but no beds. *White Clay Backpackers* is a short walk from the village, in an isolated spot overlooking the sea, and offers comfortable dorms and one double. The municipal **campsite** (with cold water only; ①) is superbly located in a patch of semi-forest by the sea, and has campsites and huts intended for those walking the Wild Coast Hiking Trail (see p.345).

Umtata River Mouth

The **Umtata River** disgorges a short distance from Coffee Bay into another soothing lagoon that is the site of a **hotel**, the *Anchorage* (☎0475/44 2012; head office ☎ & fax 047/534 0061), where you can either stay in old-fashioned but reasonably comfortable bungalow accommodation with half board (④), self-catering (②), or camping (①). A good way to see the surrounding area's gentle hills, coastal forest and shoreline is on **horseback**, which the hotel can arrange for you.

Getting to the river mouth **from Coffee Bay** involves negotiating the short but difficult coastal road and following signs to Umtata Mouth. First head back on the Umtata road from Coffee Bay for a short distance, and then take the Mdumbi turn on the right, just past the police station. **From Umtata**, you should follow the road to Port St Johns, turning right towards Ngqeleni, and right again at the turn-off to Umtata Mouth.

Hluleka Nature Reserve

One of the loveliest of the Wild Coast nature reserves, **Hluleka Nature Reserve** (daily 6am–6pm; small entry fee) consists of coastal forest whose coral trees flower scarlet in July and August, a strip of grassland and outstanding sandy beaches interspersed with rocky outcrops tattooed with extraordinary wind-shaped rock formations. Although Hluleka's trails are poorly maintained and frequently end up as dead ends, the reserve is sufficiently small that you can usually afford to get a little lost for a while. In the grassland strip you're likely to encounter wildebeest and maybe some of the zebra and blesbok that also roam the area.

Accommodation is in two sets of chalets (①), one on stilts overlooking the sea and the other further up the hill, in the forest. Both are spacious but poorly equipped and subject to electricity curfews, so bring candles. You'll also need all your own food, though you may be able to buy fish from local fishermen if you tell the reserve's staff, who will tip them off. **Fishing permits** should be arranged via the Nature Conservation Office in Umtata (see below)

You can reach Hluleka along the difficult coastal road from Coffee Bay. After heading back on the Umtata road from Coffee Bay for a short distance, take the Mdumbi turn on the right, and continue for some 30km, when signs to Hluleka appear. Alternatively – and more easily – you can take the Hluleka turn on your right off the road from Umtata to Port St Johns (there is one before and one after Libode), and continue for another 70km to the coast.

Umtata and around

Straddling the Umtata River and the N2 highway, the fractious, shambolic town of **UMTATA** is the former capital of the Transkei and is the Wild Coast region's largest town. Unfortunately it's a pretty ugly place, its litter-strewn streets lined with nondescript Seventies office buildings and throbbing with pedestrians. However, the town is useful for stocking up and drawing breath for the next stage of your journey. If you're travelling by car and heading on to the Wild Coast, Umtata is also your last chance to ensure that your vehicle is in good enough shape to cope with the generally poor state of Transkei's roads.

Some history

The Umtata River was traditionally the boundary between the Thembu and Pondo clans of the Xhosa nation, with the Thembu to the south and the Pondo to the north. Whites farmed by the river from the 1860s, and after Britain acquired Thembuland in 1875. Umtata was established as the site of one of its four magistracies. From 1976 until 1994, Umtata was the capital of the Transkei homeland and still has a parliament building – now defunct – a smattering of showcase big buildings and a reputation for some of the most corrupt officialdom in South Africa.

Arrival and information

The small **Umtata Airport** (☎047/536 0023) lies 10km west of town on the Queenstown Road. There is no public transport from the airport, but you can rent a car from here (see p.316). Greyhound and Translux **buses** pull in at Shell UltraCity, from where you'll need to get a minibus taxi to the town centre. Coming from the direction of Durban, the Baz Bus stops at *Steers* restaurant at the Circus Triangle Mall for backpackers going to lodges in Port St Johns, at Shell UltraCity for those going to Hole in the Wall, and further southwest at Qunu for those going to Coffee Bay (coming from Port Elizabeth the order is reversed). Transtate buses and most **minibus taxis** stop near the train station, to the south of the city centre, at a rank straddling Edward and Alexandra streets.

You'll find Umtata's **tourist information** bureau (Mon–Fri 8am–4.30pm; ☎047/531 2885) on the corner of York Road and Victoria Street, with useful **maps** and staff who know the area well. Downstairs, the **Nature Conservation Office** (Mon–Fri 8am–4.30pm; ☎047/531 2711), is the place to book for accommodation in Silaka and Hluleka nature reserves, both reached by heading south out of town on the R61. Here you can pick up **maps** of the areas you want to visit and buy a helpful booklet about the

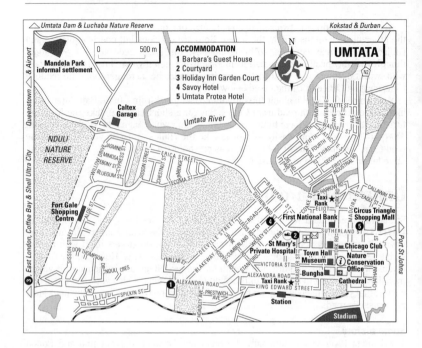

whole coastal strip. **Wild Coast Reservations**, 3 Beaufort St (daily 8am–6pm; ☎047/532 5344, fax 532 3766), can arrange accommodation at resorts and hotels throughout the region.

Accommodation

Most of Umtata's **accommodation** is pretty dismal, and budget options are few and far between. **Camping** at Umtata Dam (see opposite), just northwest of town, is not advised after reports of theft. However, there is a handful of reasonable hotels in the centre of town.

Barbara's Guest House, 55 Alexandra Rd (☎047/531 1751, fax 531 1754). Decent establishment with 30 rooms with or without bath, used mainly by business travellers, with a swimming pool, TV lounge and a bar with pool table, where you can have good pub lunches. ④–⑤.

Courtyard, corner of Sutherland St and Savoy Terrace (☎ & fax 047/531 0791). A part of the *Savoy*, with brand new rooms, and one of the few options in Umtata that is both cheap and recommended. ③.

Holiday Inn Garden Court, N2 (☎047/537 0181). Large modern building on the way out of Umtata, with a stylish pool, slot machines, a chic cocktail bar and a respectable restaurant. The rooms are unremarkable, though, and all the singles face the car park. ④.

Savoy Hotel, corner of Sutherland St and Savoy Terrace (☎047/531 0791). Elegantly decaying hotel with good rooms and a restaurant with a steak-dominated set menu. There are three bars: a smart private one, a public bar with pool tables, and a Xhosa bar at the back. ③.

Umtata Protea Hotel, corner of 71 Sutherland St and Madeira Street (☎047/532 5654, fax 531 0083). Unimaginative hotel offering decent rooms, excellent service, good views of Umtata if your room is high enough up, reliable food and safe parking. ⑤.

The Town and around

Central Umtata comprises a small grid of busy streets bursting with pedestrians and lined with dull office buildings interspersed with the odd older architectural gem. One of these is the elegant **town hall** on Leeds Street, with a fine clock stuck at nearly 6pm, which looks down onto a war memorial and pleasant gardens. One block south, oppo-site the tourist office, stands the town's small and neglected **museum** (Mon–Fri 8am–4.30pm; free), which has fairly informative displays of traditional Xhosa costume, local geology and an exhibit on the ANC that stops before the 1994 elections.

Continue further south to the corner of Owen and Alexandra streets for a peek at the distinctive, mustard-coloured old **parliament**, or *bungha*, built in 1927. The debating chambers are now closed, but the rest of the building is still being used as municipal offices and you can wander inside. One block east, on the corner of Alexandra and York streets, is an elegant sandstone Anglican **cathedral**, sadly permanently closed. A major taxi rank straggles along the opposite side of Alexandra Street, and behind it is the small **stadium** used by the Umtata Bucks soccer team. If you are in town for a few days and the weather is good, head for the pleasant open-air **swimming pool** (daily 9am–12.30pm & 2–4.45pm; small entry fee) at the western end of Sutherland Street, near the junction with Stanford Terrace.

Qunu

A little over 20km west of Umtata are the scattered dwellings of **Qunu**, which consti-tute the humble birthplace of **Nelson Mandela** (see box overleaf). Since Mandela was born here, the big changes in Qunu have been the N2 highway which now thunders through it, and a large and rather plain **presidential palace**, which you may photo-graph but not enter.

Nearby nature reserves

Though they can't compete with the wonderful subtropical forest reserves of the Wild Coast, the three small reserves close to Umtata are worth investigating if you're in town for a few days. **Umtata Dam** (daily 6am–7pm; small entry fee), a few kilometres north-west of town, is a tranquil spot, popular with anglers. To get there, take the Queenstown road and turn right after the Caltex garage past the Dela school. After this, turn left onto a dirt road at a sign pointing to the "Eastern Cape Appropriate Technology Unit", drive past the growing shanty town on your left, and take the first right turn after the bridge.

To get to the **Luchaba Nature Reserve** (daily 6am–7pm; small entry fee), turn left at the dam gates at a sign marked "boating and yachting" and continue for another 2km. This somewhat drab grassland reserve flanks the dam and has blesbok, wildebeest and diverse birdlife, but no accommodation.

Roughly 3km south of Umtata, the **Nduli Nature Reserve** (daily 8am–6pm; small entry fee) is a pleasant patch of bushveld which is home to a variety of antelope, includ-ing blesbok and impala, as well as wildebeest, but has no accommodation. To get there, take the first turn right off the N2 out of Umtata after Sissons Street, onto an unmarked road; from here, it's a short distance to the gate.

Eating and nightlife

As well as the hotel restaurants, of which those at the *Protea* and *Holiday Inn* are the best (see opposite), there are a limited number of good **places to eat** in Umtata. *La Piazza* (☎047/531 0795), in Fort Gale shopping complex, does varied and tasty Italian-based food, with a good range of salads, in a friendly, family-oriented setting. Of the fast-food

NELSON MANDELA AND THE QUNU CONNECTION

Nelson Rolihlahla Mandela was born near tiny **Qunu** in the even tinier village of Mvezo on July 18, 1918. His father was a member of the Xhosa royal house and a custodian of Xhosa history – he was also chief of Mvezo, until he crossed swords with the local white magistrate over a minor dispute concerning an ox. After his sacking, the family moved to a small *kraal* in Qunu, which Mandela remembers as consisting of several hundred poor households.

Mandela is often called **Madiba** – the name of his family's subclan of the Thembu clan. The name Nelson was given to him by a schoolteacher, and Rolihlahla means "pulling the branch of a tree" or, more colloquially, "troublemaker". Mandela has said that at home he was never allowed to ask any questions, but was expected to learn by observation. Later in life, he was shocked to visit the homes of whites and hear children firing questions at their parents and expecting replies.

Shortly after his father died, Mandela was summoned from Qunu to the royal palace at Mqhakeweni, where he sat in on disputes in court and learnt more about Xhosa culture. At 16 he was initiated – and burnt with shame for a long time afterwards at the cry he had let slip out when circumcised. He enrolled in Clarkebury, a college for the Thembu elite, then the Wesleyan college of Healdtown at Fort Beaufort, and finally the celebrated Fort Hare in Alice (see p.331), which has educated generations of African leaders. He was expelled from Fort Hare after clashing with the authorities and returned to Mqhakeweni. In 1941, faced with the prospect of an arranged marriage, he ran away to Johannesburg and there immersed himself in politics.

It was only in 1990 (at the age of 72) when, released from prison, Mandela was able to return to Qunu, visiting first the grave of his mother, who had died in his absence. He noted that the place seemed poorer than he remembered it, and that the children were now singing songs about AK47s and the armed struggle. However, he was relieved to find that none of the old spirit and warmth had left the community, and he arranged for a palace (or "country house" as he called it) to be built there. This palace has become the venue for Mandela's holidays and family reunions and has a floor plan identical to that of the house in Victor Verster prison where Mandela spent the last few years of his captivity. In his autobiography he writes: "The Victor Verster house was the first spacious and comfortable home I ever stayed in, and I liked it very much. I was familiar with its dimensions, so at Qunu I would not have to wander at night looking for the kitchen."

chains, *Nando's*, 85 York Rd, opposite the town hall, is the best, serving up the usual tasty grilled chicken meals. If you're just passing through and want a bite before pressing on, the *Whistle Stop*, at the Shell Ultra City filling station complex, is an excellent option for a snack and to freshen up. In addition, you'll find **street vendors** on the corner of Sutherland and Sprigg streets near the *Protea*, selling tasty dishes like *boerewors* and *pap*. Umtata has a thriving **nightlife**, but exploring it without a local escort isn't recommended. The notable exception is *Chicago*, on the corner of York Road and Leeds Street, opposite the Old Mutual building, which is open every night and plays a wide variety of sounds to a relatively mellow crowd.

Listings

Banks First National Bank, corner of Sutherland Street and York Road; Standard Bank, corner of York Road and Leeds Street. Expect large queues. Where you find banks, you'll also find ATMs.

Car rental Avis (☎047/536 0066), at Umtata Airport.

Emergencies Ambulance ☎22222; Police ☎10177 or ☎31 1333 (Flying Squad).

Garages Fort Gale Motors (☎047/532 3882), on the Queenstown road.

Hospitals St Mary's Private Hospital, 30 Durham St (☎047/531 2911).

Nature Conservation Office, corner of York Road and Victoria Street (☎047/531 2711).
Travel agents East West Travel, 1 Toyi Properties, Victoria St (☎047/532 2928), can arrange flight bookings, intercity bus travel and hotel accommodation in the region.

Port St Johns

The sixty-kilometre drive to **PORT ST JOHNS** from Umtata is one of the best journeys in the Wild Coast. After passing tiny **Libode**, with its small hotel and restaurant, you start the dramatic descent to the coast, passing by craggy ravines and epic vistas of forest and rondavel-spotted grassland. The road runs alongside the Mzimvubu River for the last few kilometres, giving you a perfect view of the Gates of St John, before reaching the town's square and taxi rank.

Port St Johns is a favoured destination for young backpackers, who are drawn by its stunning location at the mouth of the Mzimvubu River, dominated by Mount Thesiger on the west bank and Mount Sullivan on the east, and the copious quantities of strong cannabis that are grown around here. Even if the latter isn't your cup of tea, the town's famously laid-back atmosphere may tempt you to stay for longer than you intended. Port St Johns also has good fishing and swimming beaches, a wider choice of accommodation than anywhere else on the Wild Coast, and an excellent tarred road all the way into town.

Some history

The origins of Port St Johns' name is something of a mystery but may derive from the sixteenth-century Portuguese ship, *São João*, which was wrecked nearby, leaving around four hundred survivors to complete a seven-hundred-kilometre walk to Mozambique. Only eight survived and one of those was shipwrecked again near the Umtata river mouth two years later. He reportedly died of despair, unable to face the trek to Mozambique once more.

In 1878, in an effort to reduce gunrunning from the harbour, a representative of the Cape governor bought a fifteen-kilometre stretch of the river from the shore inland, and the land on the western side from the Pondo for R2000. While he was waiting for the money, an armed force arrived from Natal and annexed the eastern side of the river. A compromise was found by making Port St Johns a crown colony in its own right, though this was rescinded when the whole of Pondoland was annexed by Britain in 1895.

The area was then known for its **tobacco**, which was exported from Durban and East London. During the negotiations for the Act of Union (see p.690), the Transvaal demanded the cessation of the trade to allow its white tobacco growers to expand their business without competition. The Cape Colony obliged and in 1906 stopped exporting tobacco. Local farmers responded by switching to **cannabis** (*insango*), supplying the growing numbers of men from the area going to work on the Witwatersrand mines. Today, the cultivation and trade are as strong as ever, which may explain the presence of so many white South African hippies in the town.

Arrival and information

The Baz Bus drops off at Shell Ultra Cityin Umtata, from where you are met by the daily **Backpacker Shuttle**. The shuttle arrives at around 12.30pm and returns at 3pm; in Port St Johns it pulls into three of the backpacker hostels (*Port St Johns, Second Beach,* and *Amapondo Beach*) and costs R30. For a small additional fare it will drop you off at any of the other accommodation in town. Port St Johns is also easily reached by **minibus taxi** from Umtata: plenty run from the *Steer's* restaurant at the Circus Triangle Mall.

If you're travelling **from KwaZulu-Natal** to Port St Johns by public transport, an alternative route is to go via the *Wild Coast Sun* (see p.361), Bizana and Lusikisiki. This journey is most easily done by catching the Grimboys bus from Durban, which runs daily directly to Port St Johns. **Driving from Durban**, you should follow the same route, continuing along the coast after Port Shepstone to Port Edward, rather than striking inland on the N2. Sticking to the R61 is by far the most direct route and is tarred all the way, bar the final 18km stretch from Lusikisiki.

There's a **tourist information bureau**, with a coffee shop selling crafts, at *Outspan Inn*, and a number of lodges keep copies of a helpful hand-drawn **map** of the town by a local resident. Some lodges have also compiled their own information, the most comprehensive being provided to guests at *Port St Johns Backpackers*.

Accommodation

Port St Johns has the best selection of **accommodation** on the Wild Coast, with a healthy number of backpackers' lodges, old-fashioned hotels and nearby farm accommodation. For a memorable **township** experience, you can stay with the gregarious Ms Constance Duna in the Port St Johns township (or "location", as they call it here) perched up on the hill between Port St Johns and Second Beach: you'll need to book with *Port St Johns Backpackers* and pay in advance.

Amapondo Beach Backpackers, Second Beach (☎047/564 1582, mobile 082/459 6500). Lively hostel with a popular bar on the main swimming beach, some 5km from town. A free shuttle heads into the centre each morning. Six-bed dorms ①, doubles ②.

Franco's (no phone). Rustic farm with huts for visitors northeast of town amidst lovely countryside, overlooking the Umtafufu estuary, with many Xhosa living nearby whom the owner knows well. A pleasant 4hr walk from Port St Johns and a very restful place to stay. Bring your own bedding and food, and a guide to show you the way – *Port St Johns Backpackers* can arrange this. ①.

The Jetty (☎047/564 1072). Tranquil self-catering lodge (though meals are available) on the Umzimvubu's eastern bank catering mainly to anglers and travelling reps. A short distance from the Pondoland bridge and Lusikisiki road, it offers five en-suite rooms, an ample bar and choice fishing spots. You can rent boats for fishing trips or river cruises. ②.

The Kraal, near Mpandi (bookings ☎043/683 2384, fax 683 2098, *alliedin@iafrica.com*). Four traditional huts, each sleeping four people, on community land well off the beaten track, leased to a backpacker hostel. Efficiently run and wonderfully set right on the beach, there's no electricity or flushing toilets (enviroloos are in use), and showers and washing facilities are in reed huts. Meals are available and you can often get crayfish, oysters and mussels. There are beach hikes, snorkelling, surfing, dolphins and whale-watching in season. A hostel bus usually picks up passengers from the Baz Bus at Shell Ultra City in Umtata; phone in advance to check.

Lily Lodge, signposted off Second Beach Rd (☎ & fax 047/564 1229). Best known for its great seafood restaurant, this lodge has well-equipped and comfortable brick cottages set in a luxuriant subtropical garden, very close to Second Beach. ③.

The Lodge, Second Beach Rd (☎047/564 1171). Charming and secluded hotel at the end of Second Beach Rd, with three tasteful rooms and the best wine and cooking in Port St Johns. Booking essential. B&B ③.

Outspan Inn, behind the Outspan store, past the town hall on the road to First Beach (☎ & fax 047/564 1057). B&B with wonderfully decorated en-suite rooms, some with high beds that give a sea view. The restaurant is one of the better places to eat in town. ④.

Port St Johns Backpackers, Berea Rd, first right off the main road after the post office (☎047/564 1517). Comfortable facilities at a mellow hostel, staffed by friendly folk who really believe in what they're doing. Evening meals often feature fish *braais*, crayfish and mussels. They can also arrange guided two-to-three night trips into the villages and overnight visits to a traditional healer, and will drive you to Silaka Nature Reserve (see opposite). Camping, dorms & doubles ①.

Second Beach Backpackers, Second Beach (booking through *Port St Johns Backpackers*). Small and friendly backpacker hostel right on the beach, where the focus is more on learning about local culture. Two small dorms sleep no more than nine people, there's an honesty bar and meals are available. ①.

Second Beach Cottage, last driveway on right along the Second Beach road (☎ & fax 047/564 1266, *2ndbeach@wildcoast.co.za*). A secluded house with two doubles sharing bath and another en suite, plus two self-contained and well-equipped garden flats. The beach, conveniently at the bottom of the sub-tropical garden, is reached by means of a jungly walkway. ①–②.

Umngazi Bungalows, Umngazi River mouth, just west of Port St Johns (☎ & fax 047/564 1115). This smart resort is arguably the best-designed and best-equipped along the Wild Coast, though the rooms are small; those with river and sea views are more expensive. The beach and pool are inviting and the buffet spread is particularly good. It's signposted off the R61, about 10km out of Port St Johns towards Umtata; from the sign it's another 11km along a pot-holed dirt track. Full board ④–⑤.

The Town and around

Although there is nothing much to see in town, Port St Johns is still a nice place to take a leisurely stroll, particularly during the early evening, when many residents are doing the same. The town's main attractions are its two beaches; **First Beach** is along the main road from the post office and offers good fishing, while **Second Beach**, 5km along a road off a right turn past the post office, is a fabulous swimming beach. Most people rarely go anywhere else, though the rocky coastline into the **Silaka Nature Reserve** (see below) and as far as the **Umngazi River Mouth** provides wonderful walks, as do the endless stretches of pristine beach east of the Mzimvubu River. The Mzimvubu is muddy in summer, disgorging topsoil washed down the Drakensberg from Lesotho, but cleans up dramatically in winter, when it is clear and good for fishing.

Both the mountains of the **Gates of St John** merit a clamber to the top, from where you get a superb view of the lush surrounding landscape. The paths can be hard to find, though, and you'll be best off with a guide or at least a decent map. For trips into the Pondo heartland of **Mtambalala**, contact David and Steve (call the backpackers' lodges, or mobile ☎083/305 2213), two local residents who'll take you to stay with locals and hike to the stunning **Magwa Falls** and beyond. They can also arrange visits to a nearby traditional healer.

For **crafts**, check out Pondo People on the east side of the Mzimvubu River across the Pondoland bridge; the speciality here is immaculate bead jewellery and clothing. Jakotz, next to The Lodge on Second Beach, sells African printed clothes, while Bayou, 5km up the Umtata road has a colourful selection of batik clothes, handmade furniture and herbal products.

Silaka Nature Reserve

Just south of town, the **Silaka Nature Reserve** (daily 6am–6pm; small entry fee) is a small reserve with a dramatic coastline, and comprises the idyllic **Third Beach**, dense tropical-forest areas – through which there are good trails – and a handful of animals, including zebra and wildebeest. **Accommodation** is in spacious self-catering chalets (①) surrounded by grassland; book through the reserve. The reserve's hiking huts, intended for those walking the Wild Coast Hiking Trail (see p.345), are attractively located near Third Beach. To **get to the reserve**, travel down the Second Beach road from Port St Johns and then up the treacherously steep dirt road to the reserve's office. If you are staying at *Port St Johns Backpackers*, the owner will drive you to the office, from where you'll have a very pleasant walk back along the coastline.

Eating and drinking

You'll have to search a bit for decent places to **eat and drink** in Port St Johns. If you're self-catering the picture is a lot brighter, with plenty of tempting local produce, including tropical fruits and fresh fish (sold on the beach), guaranteeing you won't go hungry.

Lily's Restaurant, Lily Lodge, signposted left off Second Beach Rd as you head out of town (☎047/564 1229). On the way to Second Beach, this is the best restaurant in the area, serving up a set menu that often includes delicious and reasonably priced seafood. Enjoy the perfect view from the sun deck while you're eating. Closed Mon.

Outspan Inn, behind the Outspan store, past the town hall on the road to First Beach. Near the town hall, this spacious restaurant has an interesting and inexpensive menu, but not much custom. Good place for blowout breakfasts. Closed Sun evening.

Hippo's, on the main road, very near the Second Beach turn-off. Popular with locals, and serves inexpensive traditional dishes such as *samp* and bean stews.

The Lodge, Second Beach Rd (☎047/564 1171). Tiny hotel restaurant at Second Beach serving good seafood and European meals, with fine wines to wash it all down. Booking essential.

The northern Wild Coast and the KwaZulu-Natal enclave

For many visitors to the northern part of the Wild Coast, the main draw is the *Wild Coast Sun*, a hotel and casino on the border of KwaZulu-Natal. However, the stretch of coast from Port St Johns to the Mzamba River by the *Sun* is outstandingly beautiful, with three of only five waterfalls in the world that fall over 100m directly into the sea, as well as countless deserted beaches and cosy bays. The best way to see it is to walk though you can drive, with some difficulty, to the **Mkambati Nature Reserve**, which contains a good portion of this coast.

The **Lusikisiki** road from Port St Johns to the *Wild Coast Sun* via Bizana makes an interesting alternative to the N2 for getting from the Eastern Cape to KwaZulu-Natal. Inland, the road through the Eastern Cape enclave in KwaZulu-Natal takes you into the rolling hills of **Ixopo**, made famous by Alan Paton's novel, *Cry the Beloved Country*.

Mkambati Nature Reserve

The largest of the Wild Coast reserves, **Mkambati** (daily 6am–6pm; small entry fee; ☎0475/64 1115;), covering eighty square kilometres, consists almost entirely of grassland, though it is flanked by the forested ravines of the Msikaba and Mtentu rivers, and a ravishing coastline of rocky promontories and deserted beaches. The park has plenty of **game**; you are likely to see eland, hartebeest, wildebeest and blesbok, as well as Cape vultures. The highlight, though, is the Mkambati River itself, which flows through the middle down a series of striking waterfalls, of which the **Horseshoe Falls** near the sea are the most spectacular.

Accommodation is either in the main lodge – available for a minimum of five people – which has double rooms with bath (②) or in self-catering cottages and rondavels (①). There's an unimpressive **restaurant** in the main lodge. Bookings must be made through the Nature Conservation Office in Kokstad (☎037/727 3844).

To get to **Mkambati** from the N2, take the Flagstaff turn-off between Mount Ayliff and Kokstad, and just before Flagstaff, look out for signs to the Holy Cross Hospital and Mkambati. From there, a poor-quality dirt road, impassable in a standard car during rainy weather, takes you past the hospital to the reserve.

North to the Wild Coast Sun

The road from Port St Johns to the small, unremarkable town of **LUSIKISIKI** is untarred and hard to negotiate in wet weather for the first 16km, but tarred for the rest of the way to the *Wild Coast Sun*. Beyond Lusikisiki, the hills of Pondoland seem to stretch for miles, punctuated 50km later by the small village of **Flagstaff**. Roughly

30km further on, a junction leads back to the N2, and 20km beyond that through heavily populated hillsides is the busy town of **BIZANA**, 60km from the coast in an area where both **Oliver Tambo** and **Winnie Madikizela-Mandela** were born. The *Bizana Hotel* on the left side of the main road has a quiet **restaurant** serving good-value steaks and curries, but is not recommended as a place to stay.

Some 60km further along is the opulent *Wild Coast Sun* (☎039/305 9111, fax 305 1012), in a well-chosen location by the Mzamba River mouth. Despite its tacky Pacific island-themed decor, some of the hotel complex is quite pleasant. Most people are here to gamble, but an impressive games arcade, ten-pin bowling, pony rides and minigolf are also on offer. **Accommodation** is in small, well-equipped rooms, with some suites looking onto the sea (⑨). You can **eat** tasty (if overpriced) fish steaks at the *Driftwood Terrace*, which has a fantastic sea view.

Opposite the complex is the **Mzamba Crafts Market**, arranged in a circle to resemble a traditional *kraal*. The central shop sells authentic crafts from all over southern Africa for reasonable prices, with local ones the cheapest, particularly the grasswork. Reject goods are on sale in the outlying huts for even better prices. **Taxis** and **buses** stop outside the market on their way to Bizana and **Port Edward** in KwaZulu-Natal.

Mount Ayliff and Mount Frere

The quickest and busiest way from the Eastern Cape to KwaZulu-Natal is on the N2, passing by the scraggy towns of Mount Frere and Mount Ayliff, before reaching **Kokstad** and the provincial boundary. From the road you'll see hillsides dotted with densely packed dwellings. Closer inspection reveals that the hillsides are not coping well with the strain, as there are massive dongas creating scar-like craters in many places where huge volumes of topsoil have simply been washed away. **Mount Frere** is about 100km from Umtata, and is called *kwaBhaca* in Xhosa, meaning "the place of the Bhaca", for it was here that many of those who ran south from the Zulu king Shaka ended up, earning the name *amaBhaca*, "the people who hide". Today, Mount Frere is a fairly rough town and you'd be wise to pass swiftly through. The small trading-station town of **MOUNT AYLIFF**, 44km further on, though not ideal either, nonetheless offers the decayed, colonial *Mount Ayliff* (☎039/254 0050; ①), with basic **hotel** rooms that look out onto a large, rambling garden, and an inexpensive **restaurant**.

The Eastern Cape enclave in KwaZulu-Natal

The **Eastern Cape enclave in KwaZulu-Natal** for many years sat uncomfortably with the crass ethnic categorizations of past regimes, and the legacy of this lives on today. The people living in the enclave, whose main town is uMzimkhulu, are a mixture of Zulu, Pondo, Bhaca and Griqua, economically tied in the main to Pietermaritzburg and Durban. The apartheid regime yoked them with the Transkei, ostensibly on the grounds that most were Pondo, and thus part of the Xhosa nation, but in fact to tap them as a cheap labour reserve. Controversially, the area was included in the Eastern Cape when the boundaries were redrawn after the 1994 elections, in part because many in the area support the ANC and did not want to be part of a province ruled by the Zulu nationalist Inkhata Freedom Party.

The enclave is reached by turning off the N2 onto the R56 at the Stafford's Post junction towards **Ixopo**. It's scenic and pleasant enough to drive through, though not a good place to travel around in, and desperately poor, despite its extensive cornfields. **uMzimkhulu** is a busy transport centre, with a large taxi rank by its Shell garage and plenty of fast-food outlets to feed hungry passengers, most of whom are going to and from **Pietermaritzburg** and **Durban**. After passing the remnants of a small border post just east of the town, you will find yourself back in KwaZulu-Natal, a short distance from Ixopo.

travel details

All major transport in the Eastern Cape runs between Port Elizabeth and East London – the two hubs of the province. In addition to train, intercity bus and air services, there are backpacker buses and scheduled minibuses making additional connections to one or two smaller centres. Failing these, the option remains of cheap and frequent (though unscheduled and less comfortable or safe) minibus taxis.

Trains

Two mainline trains, the *Amatola* from East London, and the *Algoa* from Port Elizabeth, connect the Eastern Cape with Johannesburg and Pretoria, both stopping along the way.

East London to: Bloemfontein (daily; 13hr); Johannesburg (daily; 20hr); Pretoria (daily; 21hr 30min); Queenstown (daily; 4hr 30min).

Port Elizabeth to: Bloemfontein (daily; 11hr 30min); Cape Town (Sun only; 24hr); Cradock (daily; 4hr 30min); Johannesburg (daily; 18hr); Pretoria (daily; 19hr 30min).

Intercity buses

The main bus routes run from Port Elizabeth (up the N10) and East London (up the N6) to join the N1 via Bloemfontein to Johannesburg and Pretoria; and along the coast to Cape Town in the west and Durban in the east. An alternative route goes inland through the Little Karoo to Cape Town.

East London to: Alexandria (5 weekly; 3hr 15min); Aliwal North (daily; 5hr); Bloemfontein (daily; 7hr 30min); Cape Town (1–2 daily; 14hr); Durban (2 daily; 9hr); Grahamstown (2 daily; 2hr); Johannesburg (daily; 13hr); Kenton-on-Sea (5 weekly; 3hr); King William's Town (2–3 daily; 45min); Knysna (1–2 daily; 7hr 30min); Mossel Bay (1–2 daily; 9hr); Paarl (5 weekly; 14hr 30min); Plettenberg Bay (1–2 daily; 7hr); Port Alfred (3 daily; 2hr 30min); Port Elizabeth (3 daily; 4hr); Port Shepstone (2 daily; 8hr); Pretoria (daily; 14hr); Sedgefield (1–2 daily; 8hr); Storms River (1–2 daily; 6hr); Swellendam (1–2 daily; 11hr) Umtata (2 daily; 3hr 30min); Wilderness (1–2 daily; 8hr 30min).

Port Elizabeth to: Alexandria (5 weekly; 1hr); Bloemfontein (1–2 daily; 10hr); Cape Town (6–7 daily; 11hr); Durban (2 daily; 13hr 30min); East London (3 daily; 4hr); George (6–7 daily; 4hr 30min); Graaff-Reinet (5 weekly; 3hr 30min); Grahamstown (2 daily; 1hr 30min); Jeffrey's Bay (2 daily; 45min); Johannesburg (3–4 daily; 16hr); Kenton-on-Sea (5 weekly; 1hr 30min); Knysna (6–7 daily; 3hr 30min); Mossel Bay (6–7 daily; 4hr 30min); Paarl (4 weekly; 10hr); Plettenberg Bay (6–7 daily; 3hr); Port Alfred (5 weekly; 1hr 45min); Port Shepstone (2 daily; 12hr); Pretoria (1–2 daily; 17hr); Sedgefield (6–7 daily; 3hr 30min); Stellenbosch (6 weekly; 10hr); Storms River (6–7 daily; 2hr); Umtata (2 daily; 7hr 30min); Wilderness (4 daily; 3hr 30min).

Umtata to: Cape Town (1–3 daily; 17hr 30min); Durban (3 daily; 5hr 50min); East London (1–2 daily; 3hr); Johannesburg (2 daily; 12hr 45min); Port Elizabeth (daily; 5hr 40min); Pretoria (daily; 13hr 45min).

Backpacker bus

The Baz backpacker bus plies the coastal route daily between Port Elizabeth and Cape Town. It also goes all the way through to Durban four times a week.

Port Elizabeth to: Durban (5 weekly; 15hr 30min); East London (1–2 daily; 2hr 30min); George (daily; 7hr 45min); Jeffrey's Bay (daily; 1hr 45min); Knysna (daily; 6hr 30min); Mossel Bay (daily; 10hr 15min); Nature's Valley (daily; 4hr 30min); Oudtshoorn (daily; 9hr); Plettenberg Bay (daily; 5hr 30min); Port Alfred (4 weekly; 2hr 15min); Port Shepstone (4 weekly; 14hr); Umtata (4 weekly; 8hr 30min); Wilderness (daily; 7hr 15min).

Flights

East London to: Cape Town (1–4 daily; 2hr); Durban (2–3 daily; 1hr); Johannesburg (5–6 daily; 1hr 20min); Port Elizabeth (1–4 daily; 45min).

Port Elizabeth to: Bloemfontein (2 daily Mon–Fri; 1hr 20min); Cape Town (3–5 daily; 1hr 15min); Durban (4–5 daily; 1hr 10min); East London (2–3 daily; 45min); George (3 weekly; 1hr); Johannesburg (7–10 daily; 1hr 30min).

Umtata to Johannesburg (12 weekly; 1hr 30min).

CHAPTER FIVE

KWAZULU-NATAL

KwaZulu-Natal, South Africa's most African province, has everything the continent is known for – beaches, wildlife, mountains and accessible ethnic culture – a combination no other province can match. It's also the country's most turbulent region, wracked by political violence that has riven its Zulu majority in a low-key but deadly war of attrition and vendetta – one you're unlikely to encounter as it takes place in remote rural villages.

Among white South Africans, KwaZulu-Natal is well known for its subtropical **coastline**, which offers a temperate climate even in the winter, when the Cape can be showered by an icy downpour. This is where you'll find Africa's most developed beaches, in a 250-kilometre ribbon of holiday homes that stretches along the shore from the Eastern Cape border in the south to the Tugela River in the north.

At the ribbon's centre lies **Durban**, the industrial hub of the province and the country's principal harbour. Apart from Cape Town, Durban is the only major city in South Africa that warrants a visit in its own right. British in origin, it carries a heady mixture of cultural flavours derived from its Zulu, Indian and white communities. You'll find palm trees fanning Victorian buildings, African squatters living precariously on truncated flyovers, high-rise offices towering over temples and curry houses, overdeveloped beachfronts, and everywhere an irrepressible fecundity.

Paradoxically, while the coasts on either side of Durban – known as the **North and South coasts** – are South Africa's busiest and least enticing, north of the Tugela River are some of the most remote and pristine shores in the country. Here, **Maputaland**, a patchwork of wetlands, freshwater lakes, wilderness and Zulu villages, meets the sea at a virtually seamless stretch of sand that begins at the St Lucia Estuary and slips across the Mozambique border at **Kosi Bay**. Apart from southern **Lake St Lucia**, which is fairly developed in a low-key fashion, Maputaland is one of the most isolated regions in the country, traversed only by dirt roads. The reward at the end of one such track is **Rocktail Bay**, a dreamscape of tropical vegetation, tepid water and soft sands stretching as far as you can see in either direction. South Africa's best snorkelling and scuba diving lies just south of here, along the coral reefs off **Sodwana Bay**.

KwaZulu-Natal's marine life is matched on land by its **game reserves**, some of which are beaten only the Kruger National Park, and easily surpass it as the best place in the continent to see both black and white rhinos (though Kruger is better if you're bent on seeing lions and elephants). Concentrated in the north, just west of Maputaland, the reserves tend to be compact and beautiful places with some of the most stylish game-lodge accommodation in the country. Most famous and largest of the reserves is the **Hluhluwe-Umfolozi Park**, trampled by a respectable cross-section of wildlife that includes all of the Big Five. The low-key **Mkuzi** and **Ndumo** game reserves are two of South Africa's best destinations for bird-watching, while near the northern provincial border, most surprising of them all is the little-known **Itala Game Reserve**, a mountainous delight that year after year wins awards for its top-class accommodation.

The interior, north of the Tugela River, marks the **KwaZulu-Natal Battlefields**. This heartland of the nineteenth-century Zulu kingdom saw gruesome battles between Boers and Zulus, British and Zulus and finally Boers and British. Today the area can be

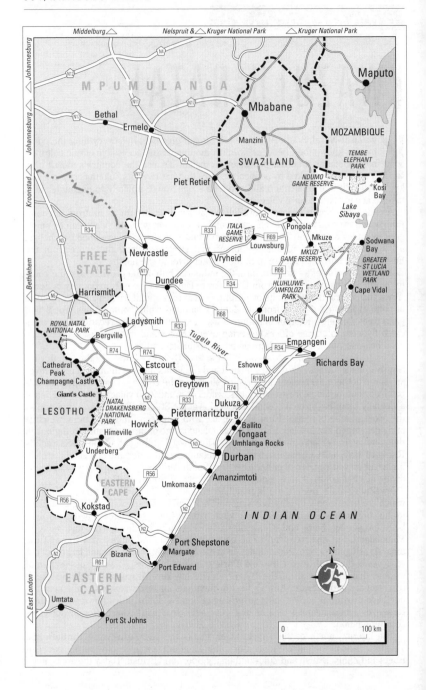

KWAZULU-NATAL CONSERVATION SERVICES

KwaZulu-Natal, particularly Maputaland, incorporates some of South Africa's regions most densely packed with game parks, designated wetlands and wilderness areas. All the public resorts described in this chapter fall under the **KwaZulu-Natal Conservation Services** and, unless otherwise stated, **hutted accommodation** at these should be booked in advance through KwaZulu-Natal Conservation Services Reservations, PO Box 13069, Cascades, Pietermaritzburg 3202 (☎033/845 1000, fax 846 1001), or in person at Tourist Junction, Old Station Building, 160 Pine St, Durban (☎031/304 4934). **Camping** reservations and **late bookings** for hutted accommodation must be made through the relevant camp.

explored through battlefield tours – a memorable way of taking in some of South Africa's most turbulent history.

Since the nineteenth century, when KwaZulu-Natal was one of the most missionary-trammelled regions in the world, the **Zulus** have captured the popular imagination of the West and remain one of the province's major pulls for tourists, despite the fact that you're as likely to encounter a Zulu dressed in jeans in Jo'burg as someone in traditional garb in KwaZulu-Natal. You'll find constant reminders of the old Zulu kingdom and its founder Shaka, including an excellent reconstruction of the beehive-hutted capital at **Ondini** and the more touristy **Shakaland**, near Eshowe.

The area south of the Tugela, designated in the mid-nineteenth century as "white man's country" and consolidated a century later under apartheid, represents the most English area of South Africa and is the least compelling section of the province, though it is known for some fabulous stays in country houses. The **Midlands'** rolling green sugar estates, polo clubs and rather contrived arts and crafts routes pale by comparison with the drama of the rest of the province, but it is extremely pretty.

From the Midlands, South Africa's highest peaks sweep west into the soaring **Drakensberg** range, known to the Zulus as the "Barrier of Spears". Protected by a chain of KwaZulu-Natal Conservation Services reserves, you'll find rest camps from where you can launch out on walks into the mountains or head out for ambitious hikes in the High Berg. With relatively little effort you can reap the huge reward of crystal rivers tumbling into marbled rock pools, peaks and rock faces enriched by ancient San paintings. The most elemental area of all KwaZulu-Natal, the Berg sees dramatic thunderstorms in summer, with lightning flashing across huge charcoal skies.

KwaZulu-Natal experiences considerable variations in **climate**, from the occasional heavy winter snowstorms of the Drakensberg to the mellow, sunny days, pleasant sea temperatures and good surfing a couple of hundred kilometres away along the coast. This makes the region a popular winter getaway, but in midsummer (Jan, Feb & Dec) the low-lying areas, including Durban, the coastal belt and the game reserves, can experience an uncomfortably high humidity.

DURBAN

Up to the Seventies, **DURBAN** was white South Africa's quintessential seaside playground – a status fostered by its tropical colours, oversized vegetation and an itinerant population of surfers, hedonists and holidaying Jo'burg families. Then, in the Eighties, the collapse of apartheid population-influx controls saw a growing stream of Africans flood in from rural KwaZulu-Natal – and even from as far afield as Zaire – to stake their claims in the city centre with shantytowns and cardboard hovels that reveal the reality of one of the most unmistakably African conurbations in the country.

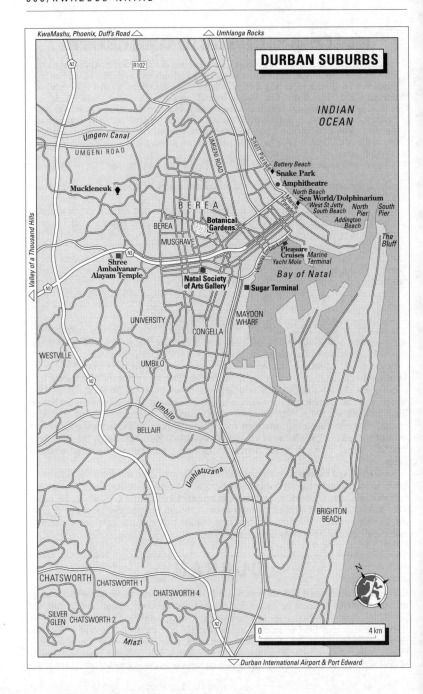

DURBAN SUBURBS

N2

R102

INDIAN OCEAN

Umgeni Canal

UMGENI ROAD

UMGENI ROAD

Snell Parade

Battery Beach

♦ Snake Park

● Amphitheatre

North Beach

Sea World/Dolphinarium

West St Jetty

South Beach

North Pier

South Pier

Addington Beach

The Bluff

Muckleneuk ♦

B E R E A

BEREA

Botanical Gardens

MUSGRAVE

N3

Pleasure Cruises

Yacht Mole

Marine Terminal

Victoria Embankment

Shree Ambalvanar Alayam Temple

N3

Bay of Natal

Natal Society of Arts Gallery

■ Sugar Terminal

UNIVERSITY

MAYDON WHARF

CONGELLA

WESTVILLE

UMBILO

N2

Umbilo

BELLAIR

Umhlatuzana

BRIGHTON BEACH

N

CHATSWORTH

CHATSWORTH 1

CHATSWORTH 4

SILVER GLEN

CHATSWORTH 2

N2

Mlazi

0 ——— 4 km

South Africa's third-largest city is a thriving industrial centre and the largest port in Africa, kept afloat by its **harbour**, which creates a photogenic place for meandering or eating and drinking at the dockside. Durban's second-largest population group, **Indians**, arrived here in the nineteenth century to work on the province's sugar plantations, and their mosques, bazaars and temples, festooned with wildly coloured deities, stand juxtaposed to the Victorian buildings that mark out the colonial centre.

The city's main interest lies not in its seaside, but its gritty urbanity, a seemingly endless struggle to reconcile competing **Indian**, **African** and **English cultures** and to keep the rampant vegetation at bay. There's enough here to keep you busy for a few days, looking at mosques, exploring the Indian area around Grey Street, or passing by the Dalton Road Zulu Market. However, most people come to Durban because it provides a logical springboard for the KwaZulu-Natal game parks, the Drakensberg and the Battlefields. Durban is well connected to the rest of South Africa by air and through intercity buses and trains, and some international flights touch down here.

Some history

Less than two hundred years ago, Durban was known to Europeans as **Port Natal**, a lagoon thick with mangroves, eyed by white adventurers who saw business opportunities in its ivory and hides. In 1824, a British party led by **Francis Farewell** persuaded the Zulu king, **Shaka**, to give them some land, which they planted with the Union Jack. Not long after, the British went on to rename the settlement **Durban** after Sir Benjamin D'Urban, governor of the Cape Colony, whose support, they believed, might not come amiss later.

Britain's tenuous colonial toehold looked threatened in 1839, when **Boers** trundled over the Drakensberg in their ox waggons and declared their Republic of Natalia nearby. The threat was compounded the following year, when a large force of now-hostile Zulus descended on the settlement and razed it, forcing the British residents to take refuge at sea in the *Comet*. Taking advantage of British absence, a group of Boers annexed Durban, later laying siege to a British detachment. This provided the cue for a much-celebrated piece of Victorian melodrama – familiar to every English-speaking school child in South Africa – when teenager **Dick King** heroically rode the 1000km from Durban to Grahamstown in ten days to alert the garrison there, which promptly dispatched a rescue detachment to relieve Durban.

While two-hundred-year-old Cape Town was on its way to becoming a cosmopolitan centre in the 1840s, Durban had a population of barely over one thousand who lived a basic existence in a near wilderness roamed by lions, leopards and hyenas. Things changed after Britain formally annexed the **Colony of Natal** in 1843; within ten years large-scale immigration of settlers from the mother country had begun. Over the next couple of decades all the niceties of English life – horse-racing, postal deliveries, two-storey houses and newspapers – started to make their appearance.

The promise of the industrial age, heralded in 1852 with the arrival of the first steamship, the *Sir Robert Peel* in Durban, actually pointed to the settlement's Achilles heel: the sand bar across the harbour mouth which prevented large vessels from entering. Work to clear it went on throughout the 1850s and beyond, while in 1860 the first railway tracks in town were laid and over three hundred indentured **Indian labourers** arrived to work in the KwaZulu-Natal cane fields, planting the seeds for South Africa's lucrative **sugar industry** and the city's now substantial Indian community.

The British **conquest of the Zulus** in 1879, and the imposition of taxes on them, paved the way for their enforced entry into South Africa's growing cash economy and saw many heading north in the 1890s to work on the Gauteng goldfields, while others were drawn south to enter Durban's expanding economy. In 1895, the completion of the railway connecting Johannesburg and Durban accelerated the process of migrant labour, which still carries hundreds of thousands of Zulu workers to Johannesburg every year. This link to South Africa's industrial heartland, and the opening of Durban's harbour mouth to large ships in 1904, ensured the city's eventual pre-eminence as South Africa's principal harbour.

In 1922, in the face of growing Indian and African populations, Durban's strongly English city council introduced **legislation** to restrict the sale of land in the city to whites, predating Afrikaner-led apartheid by 26 years. During the boom years of World War II, Africans flooded into the city in yet greater numbers, leading to calls, which were ignored, for their recognition as permanent residents.

As **apartheid** began being strictly enforced in the Fifties, Durban saw a decade of ANC-led **protests**, starting with the country-wide Defiance Campaign in 1952 (see Contexts, p.693) and reaching a peak in 1959 when *shebeen* queens (African women operating speakeasies) took to the streets and attacked municipal beer halls in protest at police harassment. The ANC was quick to seize this localized momentum and dovetailed it into nationwide marches and protests that led to nearly three years of turmoil, culminating in the government clampdown of 1961, when the authorities swamped the streets with troops, declared a state of emergency, and banned the ANC. Left with no peaceful option, the ANC formed its armed wing, Umkhonto we Sizwe, with plans for a nationwide **bombing campaign** that, by accident, was initiated one day earlier than planned with an explosion in Durban on December 15, 1961. In the comprehensive swoop that followed, the government put most of the ANC's activists behind bars, effectively paving the way for a decade of unopposed apartheid.

Durban scored another first in 1973, when workers in the city initiated a wildcat strike, despite a total ban on black industrial action, heralding the rebirth of South Africa's **trade unions**, reawakening anti-apartheid activity and sparking the final phase of the country's road to democracy.

By the Eighties, Durban had become the busiest port in Africa. By the close of the twentieth century, it was said to be the fastest-expanding city in the southern hemisphere, with thousands of people throwing up rude shacks in any open space or living rough in unimaginable numbers in the city centre.

Arrival

As a major industrial city and gateway to the country's densest ribbon of holiday beaches, along the North and South coasts, Durban is served by international and domestic flights, intercity buses, backpacker buses, trains, and the ubiquitous informal minibus taxis.

The airport

Durban International Airport (arrivals & departures ☎031/408 1066), 14km south of the centre on the Southern Freeway, receives flights from Europe, neighbouring countries and all the main centres inside South Africa; the domestic and international terminals are in the same building. **Bus services** leave every hour (5.50am–7pm; ☎031/201 1133) from outside the domestic terminal and go to the SAA building on Aliwal St, corner of Smith St, in the city centre (a 20min journey). For a small extra charge the bus will take you on request to any of the central or beachfront hotels. More expensive is the Super Shuttle (☎031/267 1548), which must be booked 24 hours ahead and will pick up from either terminal and take you to anywhere in Durban. The shuttle is a better option than the rather unsalubrious **taxis** that rank outside the terminal exits. A **bank** at the international terminal keeps normal banking hours, and also opens whenever there are international arrivals.

Durban station

The Trans-Natal service from Johannesburg (a 24hr jouney), and the interminable Trans-Oranje (over 36hr), both roll into the grim **New Durban Station** (☎031/361

USEFUL BUS ROUTES FROM THE CITY CENTRE

•**To North/South Beach** (daily: every 10min 6.20am–5.35pm, every 15min 5.35pm–6.25pm, every 30min 6.25pm–10.55pm). Mynah buses leave from St Andrews Street, on the north side of Albert Park, which stretches down to the Victoria Embankment at the western edge of the city centre (an inner-city strip of high-rise apartments best avoided at night, especially if you're carrying tourist trappings such as cameras). From here they turn north into Russell Street, before running all the way east along West Street to Marine Parade, where they either strike north as far as Battery Beach, or south as far as Addington Beach. Boards on the front of the bus indicate whether they are bound for North or South Beach. On their return trip, buses head through the centre along Smith instead of West Street.

•**To the Berea – "Musgrave–Mitchell Park Circle"** (Mon–Fri every 10min, Sat slightly less frequent, Sun hourly; 6.30am–7pm). Mynah buses leave from the Pine Street bus depot and head west down Smith Street to the Berea, taking in Florida Road (restaurant strip) and Musgrave Road (Musgrave Centre), before returning to the city centre via Berea Road.

•**To Natal Society of Arts Gallery**. Aqualine buses (route 86/87) leave from the Pine Street bus depot and go to Glenmore, via Bulwer Road, for the NSA Gallery (Mon–Fri every 15min 6.50–8.35am, every 30min 8.35am–5pm; Sat less frequent; Sun 3 daily 7am–5.30pm).

7609), off NMR Avenue, just north of the main commercial centre. From here you can catch one of the Mynah **buses** (see "City transport" overleaf), which leave every fifteen minutes from outside the station, for the ten-minute ride into the city centre, pulling in at the Pine Street bus depot, just east of Tourist Junction (see "Information" overleaf) in the same street. A more expensive and convenient option is to take one of the metered **taxis** that rank inside the station complex.

Intercity buses

Two of the main country-wide **bus operators**, Greyhound (☎031/309 7830) and Translux (☎031/361 8333) end their runs at the **Motorcoach Terminal** attached to the New Durban Station complex. The Margate Mini Coach (☎039/312 1406), from the South Coast, pulls in both here and outside domestic departures at Durban airport.

Two **minibus shuttles**, Rollercoaster Taxi (☎031/233 3706) and Rasool's (☎031/208 0919), each run a door-to-door service twice a day (pickup 5–6.30am & 5–6.30pm; a 6–7hr journey) in each direction between Johannesburg and Durban and will drop you anywhere in Durban. A number of other small companies operating limited routes within the province use other arrival points: the Cheetah Coach (☎033/342 0266), from Pietermaritzburg, lets passengers off at the airport and outside the Local History Museum on Aliwal Street; the Umhlanga Express (☎031/561 2860), from Umhlanga Rocks, drops off at a number of points in Durban, the most central of which is opposite Tourist Junction (see "Information" overleaf); Sunbird Tours (☎031/409 5489), from Richards Bay and the North Coast, winds up at the Pine Street bus depot; and the Baz Bus (☎021/439 2323, fax 439 2343, *info@bazbus.com*), from Port Elizabeth, and from Johannesburg via either Swaziland and Zululand, or the Northern Drakensberg, stops at all the Durban backpackers' lodges.

Long-distance minibus taxis

Long-distance **minibus taxis** from Gauteng arrive opposite the Umgeni Road entrance to the train station, while those from the South Coast and Transkei terminate at Berea Road in the Warwick Triangle area at the west of the city centre – both are very busy points, so take care of your baggage. From both places, city-centre and beachfront accommodation is a fairly brisk walk away. If you're planning on staying in the Berea, catch a Mynah bus to Smith Street and the main bus depot, from where you'll be able to get another Mynah bus connection.

Information and city transport

The obvious first port of call for information is the central **Tourist Junction**, Old Station Building, 160 Pine St (Mon–Fri 8am–5pm, Sat 9am–2pm; central switchboard ☎031/304 4934, fax 304 3868, *funinsun@iafrica.com*), which houses Durban Unlimited (the city's tourist bureau), the KwaZulu-Natal Conservation Services (see p.365) and the National Parks booking offices, accommodation agents, and a couple of travel agents who can book intercity coaches and **tours**.

Durban Unlimited can provide brochures and free maps of the city centre, but if you're planning on staying a while it's worth investing in one of the several street **map books** covering the city and suburbs in detail. MapStudio produce a range of maps, from mid-priced fold-out plans of the city to pricier charts that include the surrounding area. The best selection is at Adams Bookshop, 341 West St (☎031/304 8571), in the centre, or at Exclusive Books, Lower Level, Pavilion Shopping Centre, (☎031/265 0454), in the suburb of Westville. You can also pick up maps at any branch of the CNA chain.

While **buses** cover the centre, beachfront and the Berea, you'll find it more difficult to get **public transport** to the suburbs. If you're **driving**, you'll find Durban fairly easy to negotiate, though traffic on the freeways can be fast and aggressive.

Buses

Durban's most useful urban transport is the cheap and regular **bus** system operated by Mynah (☎031/309 4126) and Aqualine (☎031/309 4142), who cover the central districts, including the city centre, the beachfront and the Berea. If you want to get out to the more far-flung suburbs, Durban Transport Municipal Buses (☎031/309 4126), are quite functional though less salubrious and not as frequent. For quick and easy reference to **times and routes**, pop into the Pine Street bus depot, which is adjacent to The Workshop mall and is the starting point for local bus services.

Tuk tuks and mozziecabs

Cheaper than taxis, though more expensive (and convenient) than buses, **tuk tuks** are Asian-style three-wheel motorized rickshaws, while **mozziecabs** are Suzuki jeeps fashioned to resemble the original tuk tuks. Both will take you anywhere in central Durban. The vehicles can take up to six people and work out cheaper the more of you there are in a group. Tuk tuks rank 24 hours a day at the *Beach Hotel*, opposite the Aquarium on Marine Parade, while Mozziecabs (☎031/303 6137) must be contacted in advance for a pick-up.

DURBAN FERRIES

Scheduled **ferries** don't constitute a comprehensive form of transport in Durban. However, the *Ferry Fun Rides* hopper ferry, operated by Bay Services (daily every 30min 10.30am–6.30pm; ☎031/301 1953) offers rides along the northern harbour, serving the restaurants and pubs, starting from in front of *Café Fish* ferry jetty on the Esplanade. The *Sarie Marais* (☎031/305 4022) runs reasonably priced cruises around the harbour (daily at 11am) and deep-sea outings at 11.30am and 2.30pm from the Gardiner Street jetty. The *Sarie Marais* runs additional services during peak season.

DURBAN TOURS

One of the safest and easiest ways to get under the skin of ethnic Durban is on a **guided tour**, which can get you into African and Indian areas or out-of-the-way places.

•**Hamba Kahle Tours**, Tourist Junction, 160 Pine St (☎031/305 5586). Options include a three-hour tour of Durban's townships, including Phoenix, where Gandhi lived, and a longer tour that takes in township *shebeens* and includes some partying.

•**Strelitzia Tours**, 23 Serpentine Drive, Westville (☎031/266 1904, fax 266 9404). Daily minibus trips around the major sights, the centre and the Berea, as well as trips further afield to the game parks and the Battlefields.

•**Tekweni Eco Tours**, 169 Ninth Ave, PO Box 47773, Greyville (☎031/303 1199, fax 303 4369, *tekweni@global.co.za*). Drive and walk into the heart of the city and through informal settlements before joining locals for a Zulu meal and beer at the *shebeen*, or into local nature reserves and the Valley of a Thousand Hills. They also run camping safaris into the Drakensberg.

•**Tourist Junction** (see opposite). Staff here can arrange a number of excellent outings, including walking tours of the Grey Street area, city centre and historical tours.

Minibus taxis

Minibus taxis, which have a high accident rate, can be hailed down along any busy road – although they bear no obvious identification, you can usually recognize them by the frighteningly loud music blaring from their sound systems. To get to town or the beachfront from any of the suburbs, stand along the sidewalk and signal assertively with an index finger. Minibuses follow set paths, (you can get off at any point by asking the driver); once in the city centre, they follow West Street to the beachfront, but turn south into Marine Parade as far as Addington Beach.

Car and bike rental

The easiest way to explore Durban is by **car**. The city's freeways are well signposted, and careful map reading makes getting around pretty straightforward. You need to plan ahead, though, as Durban drivers are fast and there's no time to dither at lane changes and junctions. **Cycling** is fine along the beachfront, but hazardous on any major road. There are several car and bicycle **rental companies** in Durban; to find out who's currently operating and where to get the best deal, either pick up one of the brochures at Tourist Junction or look in the *Yellow Pages*. We've recommended some larger operators in "Listings" (p.390).

Accommodation

Durban's **accommodation** is concentrated along the **beachfront**, where sleek towers of chain hotels with sea views and swimming pools offer comfortable but pricey places to stay. Far more affordable are the scores of self-catering **apartments** (some with sea views, others a block or two back), which can be exceptional value for several people sharing. Staying at the beachfront ensures you're close to the action and only a few minutes from the central business district, and the area is well served with buses and taxis. Accommodation tends to be scarce during school holidays, and much more expensive in the peak holiday month of December.

The **city centre** is an obviously convenient location to stay, but it's not great at night, when the streets are deserted and potentially menacing. Taking private taxis or tuk tuks to your doorstep is recommended if you're returning to your hotel after dark. An alternative to the city centre and beachfront is the cool and leafy **Berea** residential area,

ACCOMMODATION PRICE CODES

All the accommodation listed in the Guide has been categorized into one of nine price bands, as set out below. The rates quoted represent what you can expect to pay for much of the summer **per person**, and unless otherwise stated, are based on two sharing. Rooms are generally en suite. Expect prices in some areas to be significantly higher in peak season (Dec–Jan & Easter), and look out for discounts during the winter. For further details, see p.33.

① up to R50
② R50–100
③ R100–150
④ R150–200
⑤ R200–250
⑥ R250–300
⑦ R300–400
⑧ R400–500
⑨ over R500

ten minutes west of the centre and with excellent restaurants and cafés. You'll find the best backpackers' lodge here, as well as a couple of other budget guesthouses, and B&Bs where you can smell the frangipani and tropical scents on balmy nights.

Beachfront

The Balmoral, 125 Marine Parade (☎031/368 5940, fax 368 5955). Dark timbers and historical photographs of Durban when the wetlands were king create a serious, colonial atmosphere. The verandah is magnificent for sipping drinks on balmy summer nights while watching the buzz along the Marine Parade and the ocean beyond. ⑥.

The Beach Hotel, 107 Marine Parade (☎031/337 5511, fax 337 4222). Bland but spacious rooms with great views. The major drawcard is the lively walk-side verandah that buzzes with punters from the hotel's pubs and restaurants. ④.

The Blue Waters Hotel, 175 Snell Parade (☎031/332 4272, fax 337 5817). Delightful Fifties Durban extravaganza opposite Battery Beach, with mangroves on the pavement and plush furnishing inside. The leisure lounge has great views onto the oceanfront. ⑤.

Durban Beach Youth Hostel, 19 Smith St (☎031/332 4945, fax 368 1720, *durban.beach.hostel-dk@pixie. co.za*). One minute's walk from the sea, with a travel centre on the premises, as well as internet and access. Dorms ①, doubles ②.

The Edward, Marine Parade (☎031/337 3681, fax 332 1692). Crystal chandeliers, dense colonial-style ambience and sea-view balconies make this Art Deco mansion the *grande dame* of the beachfront. The ladies' bar downstairs leads out onto a cool verandah. ⑧.

Golden Sands Holiday Apartments, 95 Snell Parade (☎031/368 2995, fax 337 1825). Functional self-catering apartments saved entirely by the (more expensive) rooms with magnificent sea views. Conveniently opposite North Beach and the Amphitheatre, the rooms are good value if there are three of you, and downright cheap for four or five sharing. ②.

Holiday Inn Garden Court – Marine Parade, 167 Marine Parade (☎031/337 2231, fax 337 4640). Crisp mirage with a cool through-breeze and tropical vegetation offering respite against the summer heat. While all the rooms face the sea, those on the top floors are best, and the vista from the thirtieth-floor swimming pool is fabulous. A back entrance across from Victoria Park provides handy access to the city centre. ⑤.

Impala Holiday Flats, 40 Gillespie St (☎031/332 3232). Large family apartments and bachelor units sleeping two to six people, one block back from South Beach, close to the Wheel Shopping Centre. ②.

Palace Protea Hotel, 211 Marine Parade (☎031/332 8351, fax 332 8307). Modern Art Deco landmark on Durban's Golden Mile, offering self-catering apartments opposite the Durban Fun Fair, and good access into the city centre along East St. ②.

Seaboard Protea Hotel & Holiday Flats, corner of West and Point roads (☎031/337 3601, fax 337 2600). Three-star hotel rooms and self-catering holiday apartments sleeping up to four, equidistant between the beach and town, in a tall block offering east-facing sea views. ③–④.

Silversands, 16 Erskine Terrace, South Beach (☎031/332 7391, fax 332 7814). Along the far end of Addington Beach, near the Addington Hospital, these spacious apartments sleeping two to six people (and cheaper for more sharing) are clean and comfortable. ②.

City centre

Albany Hotel, 225 Smith St (☎031/304 4381, fax 307 1411). Centrally situated budget hotel accommodation right next to the Playhouse Theatre Complex, and a stone's throw from harbour. Also across the road from the Natural Science Museum and Durban Art Gallery. ②.

Banana Backpackers, 61 Pine St, 1st Floor, Ambassador House (☎031/368 4062). Stuffy dorms and doubles in an old Durban building with a congenial courtyard. In the heart of the city, very close to Tourist Junction and the bus terminal. ①.

Durban International Backpackers and Youth Hostel, 31 Aliwal St (☎031/305 9939, *dbackpackers@eastcoast.co.za*). Some 110 beds, with fairly squashed doubles, triples and a dorm within walking distance of the Dick King statue, Tourist Junction and the beaches. Security, self-catering, fax and email facilities. All accommodation ①.

Hotel Formule 1, corner of NMR Ave and Jeff Taylor St (☎031/301 1551). No frills at this clean, budget hotel right next to the train station, with a flat room-rate making it only slightly pricier than a backpackers' hostel if there are two or three of you. ②.

The Royal Hotel, 267 Smith St (☎031/304 0331, fax 307 6884). Durban's finest hotel, and a local institution in the city centre. It's used mainly by business visitors, but is worth considering if you can afford five-star splendour and fancy the liveried service. The legendary *Ulundi* Indian restaurant is also here. Enquire about special discounts that are often available. ⑨.

The Berea and Morningside

Big J's Backpackers, 47 Essenwood Rd, Berea (☎031/202 3023). Funky spot in a prime area, with a swimming pool, bar, sundeck, herb garden, skateboards and bodyboards for use by guests. Fourth night free to Baz bus passengers. They pride themselves on being the only accommodation to stock Rizlas. Camping and dorms ①, doubles ②.

The Elephant House, 745 Ridge Rd, Berea (☎031/208 9580). B&B in Durban's oldest house, built in 1850 as a hunting lodge, in the tranquil part of the Ridge where the vegetation has won the day. The owners have a good collection of African literature. ④.

Florida Lodge, 258 Florida Rd, Morningside (☎031/312 9436). Well-situated and extremely cheap guesthouse along lively Florida Rd, with direct bus routes into town. Parking space and TV lounge. Room-only rate. ②.

Hotel California, 170 Florida Rd, Morningside (☎ & fax 031/303 1146). Genteel architecture and multiple eateries in an establishment above *Lams Restaurant* and *Bonkers* club, in the heart of the Florida Road nightlife strip. Avoid staying Wednesday nights if loud music is not your scene, as this is the night *Bonkers* sizzles. Breakfast extra. ③.

Meg's B&B, 12 Nutall Gardens, Morningside (☎031/312 9045). Dignified opulence at a B&B in a quiet part of Durban, with rich colours, generous bedding and original South African artwork. ④.

Napier House, 31 Napier Rd (☎031/207 6779). Clean, crisp rooms with the ambience of a country estate and an expansive view over the city. ④.

Nomad's Backpackers, 70 Essenwood Road, Berea (☎031/202 9709, mobile 082/920 5882, *nomads@zing.co.za*). One of Durban's best hostels, this is a short walk from the most upmarket shopping centre in town, on a main bus route (a 10min ride from the beach and Golden Mile). A black-bottomed swimming pool, a pool table, the *Bambooza Pub*, and friendly hosts who cook up a mean Durban curry, all add to the attractions of this highly recommended establishment. Dorms ①, doubles ②.

Tekweni Backpackers, 9th Ave, Morningside (☎031/303 1433, fax 303 4369). Favourite Durban backpacker spot in a converted old house, well situated just off Florida Road. The atmosphere is chilled-out, and the bar serves drinks on a shady, cool verandah. Guests have the use of the kitchen, pool room, swimming pool and leisure lounge. Dorms ①, doubles ②.

The City

Durban's **city centre**, confined by the Bay of Natal to its south and the beaches of the Indian Ocean to its east, grew around the arrival point of the first white settlers. The remains of the historical heart, some monumental Victorian and Edwardian buildings, including the City Hall, are concentrated around **Francis Farewell Square**,

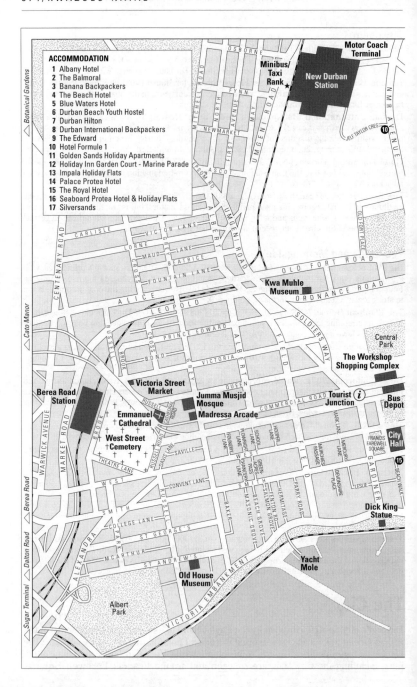

ACCOMMODATION
1 Albany Hotel
2 The Balmoral
3 Banana Backpackers
4 The Beach Hotel
5 Blue Waters Hotel
6 Durban Beach Youth Hostel
7 Durban Hilton
8 Durban International Backpackers
9 The Edward
10 Hotel Formule 1
11 Golden Sands Holiday Apartments
12 Holiday Inn Garden Court - Marine Parade
13 Impala Holiday Flats
14 Palace Protea Hotel
15 The Royal Hotel
16 Seaboard Protea Hotel & Holiday Flats
17 Silversands

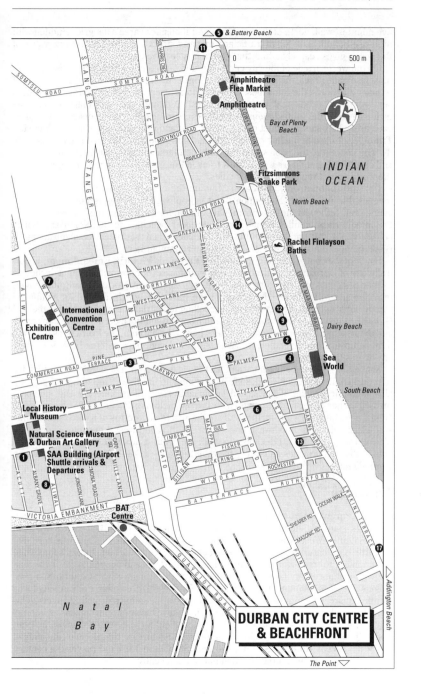

△ **⑤** *& Battery Beach*

⑪

0   500 m

SOMISEU ROAD

SOMISEU ROAD

STANGER

STANGER

SIR HARRY CRES

BRICKHILL ROAD

MOLYNEUX ROAD

SNELL PARADE

UPPER MARINE PARADE

PAVILION TERR.

● **Amphitheatre
Flea Market**

● **Amphitheatre**

*Bay of Plenty
Beach*

N

**INDIAN
OCEAN**

OLD FORT ROAD

BRICKHILL ROAD

BAUMANN ROAD

BOSCOMBE PLACE

MARINE PARADE

UPPER MARINE PARADE

GRESHAM PLACE

■ **Fitzsimmons
Snake Park**

⑭

North Beach

🏊 **Rachel Finlayson
Baths**

⑦

ALIWAL

WALNUT ROAD

STANGER

PRINCE ALFRED

JOHN MILNE ROAD

NORTH LANE

MORRISON
LANE

WEST LANE

HUNTER LANE

EAST LANE

MILNE LANE

SOUTH LANE

■ **International
Convention
Centre**

■ **Exhibition
Centre**

③

PINE
TERRACE

PINE

FAREWELL

WEST

PALMER

PINE

⑯

PALMER

SEA VIEW

⑫

⑨

②

④

Dairy Beach

● **Sea
World**

COMMERCIAL ROAD

PINE

PALMER

WEST

SMITH

FRED

PECK RD

WEST

TYZACK

LESLIE

MARINE PARADE

South Beach

■ **Local History
Museum**

■ **Natural Science Museum
& Durban Art Gallery**

■ **SAA Building (Airport
Shuttle arrivals &
Departures**

①

⑧

ALBANY GROVE

ALIWAL

MONA ROAD

JONSSON LANE

CATO MILLS LANE

CATO

SQ.

TIMBER

ROY RD

MAZEPPA

GULL

CREEK

SILIGAN

FISHER

PICKERING

WINDER

ROCHESTER

RUTHERFORD

POINT ROAD

⑥

⑬

BAY TERRACE

SHEARER RD.

MASONIC RD.

VICTORIA EMBANKMENT

■ **BAT
Centre**

●

QUAYSIDE ROAD

OCEAN WALK

ERSKINE TERRACE

PRINCE

POINT ROAD

⑰

△ *Addington Beach*

*N a t a l
B a y*

**DURBAN CITY CENTRE
& BEACHFRONT**

▽ *The Point*

five minutes' walk north of the bay. The central business area's flat grid, studded with high-rise buildings, is full of traffic and one-way street systems, and with no views of the ocean gives scarcely a hint that you're in a seaside city.

On the western side of the city centre, around Grey and Victoria streets, is Durban's most fascinating area, the **Indian district**. This is where you'll find a pulsing warren of bazaars, alleyways, the Juma mosque and Victoria Street market, as well as Zulu traders selling *umuthi* (traditional herbal medicines). Although the laws that enforced the divide between the white-dominated business centre and the Indian district have gone, each area still bears a distinct feel. Further west and deeper downtown, the **Warwick Triangle**, situated in the hub of taxi ranks and bus depots, seethes with ceaseless activity. The poorest of the poor spend the nights on their market stalls here under plastic and cardboard, and *shebeens* do a brisk trade in this great African interchange of one of the world's most rapidly urbanizing cities.

Durban's **beachfront**, or Golden Mile, on the eastern edge of the centre, is the magnet that pulls thousands upon thousands of white Jo'burgers down to "Durbs" every year. Although the beachfront's reputation for growing crime has sent many of the middle-class families scurrying out to safer beaches up the North and South coasts, you'll still find one of the city's greatest, and best-used, concentrations of restaurants and a surfeit of tacky family entertainment here.

South of the centre, skirting the north of the bay, is **Victoria Embankment**, historically one of Durban's most desirable residential areas but now witnessing a decline as former residents attempt to escape its city-rim apartment blocks. The Embankment provides access to the northern side of the **harbour**, which, despite its handful of trendy pubs and restaurants, offers a compelling industrial marinescape that is the real economic hub of the city. Protruding south from the southern corner of the city centre and the beachfront to enclose the northern half of the harbour, the **Point** is a seedy red-light peninsula that nevertheless has a couple of decent pubs and the best view of the city across the water.

Rising above the flat city centre and harbour is the **Berea**, a desirable residential district on a cooler ridge, which, despite its proximity to the centre, has luxuriant gardens alive with the sounds of birds, and fashionable restaurants, cinemas and shopping malls. Further afield lie the **western suburbs**, including Pinetown, Westville, Kloof, Gillitts and Hillcrest, while further still are the apartheid **ghettos** of KwaMashu, Inanda and Clermont to the northwest, and Umlazi to the southwest – dormitory towns for blacks who commute vast distances to work every day. **Cato Manor**, the closest township to the city, provides an easily accessible vignette of South Africa's growing urban contradictions.

The centre

Francis Farewell Square, a sultry palm-fringed garden overlooked by some fine old buildings, stands at the heart of colonial Durban. Hemmed in by the centre's two main thoroughfares, West Street to its north and Smith Street to its south, it was here that the British adventurists, Francis Farewell and Henry Fynn, set up Durban's first white encampment to trade ivory with the Zulus. Today, down-and-outs enjoy its lawns, dotted with statues of city fathers, while the yellows and blues of the **Cenotaph**, a marvellous Art Deco monument to the fallen of World War I, creates an eye-catching focus for the square. The granite obelisk is decorated with ceramics depicting angels delivering the soul of a dead soldier. Regarded initially by Durban's prim citizens as improperly vibrant, it clearly also offended an anti-apartheid activist, who bombed it in 1984. Today the monument is intact. North of Farewell Square are the pathetic remnants of the **Natal Great Railway Station**, 160 Pine St, built in 1894 and recycled a century later as shops and the Tourist Junction information centre.

City Hall and around

East of the cenotaph, the imposing neo-Baroque **City Hall**, erected in 1910, is the monumental centrepiece of the city-centre area and now houses the **Natural Science Museum** (Mon–Sat 8.30am–4pm, Sun 11am–4pm; free) on its ground floor. Along with an array of stuffed animals (useful if you want to bone up on your mammals before heading north to the game reserves), is the "KwaNunu" section, featuring oversized insects such as cockroaches – all a little too close to home for anyone living in Durban, where such creatures, known as "Durban prawns", are an ongoing menace and a constant topic for urban legends.

A far better reason to cross the City Hall's threshold is to visit the **Durban Art Gallery** (Mon–Sat 8.30am–4pm, Sun 11am–4pm; free) upstairs, which has a fine collection that includes Art Nouveau glassware by Lalique, bronzes by Rodin and Victorian paintings, but is most notable for its pioneering vision in the Seventies in becoming the first gallery in the country to collect **black South African art**. This approach has since been expanded into the recognition of indigenous craft as an art form of equal status with painting or sculpture, which is why the gallery has an outstanding collection of *hlabisa* baskets, a refined form indigenous to KwaZulu-Natal. In no way to be confused with cheap souvenirs bought at roadside stalls, *hlabisa* represents a traditional craft, revived in the province around two decades ago, and now highly sought after by galleries and collectors worldwide. Although this is traditionally a woman's activity, one of the most highly regarded proponents of *hlabisa* is a man, **Reuben Ndwandwe**.

Northwest of the City Hall, the **African Art Centre**, on the first floor of Tourist Junction, Old Station Building, 160 Pine St (Mon–Fri 8.30am–5pm, Sat 9am–1pm, Sun 8am–12.30pm; ☎031/304 7915; free), is the heart of Durban's artistic life, where many rural artists sell their work. Primarily a gallery and shop, the centre is also involved in work to move rural craftsmen away from the production of curios and towards artistic expression. Tito Zungu, who draws pen-and-ink aeroplanes and boats; Bheki Myeni, who sculpts wooden insects; and Mzwakhe Mbatha, originally an airline cook, who now carves wooden aircraft, are a few artists who have gained recognition through this centre.

East of the City Hall, on the corner of Smith Street, the **Local History Museum** (Mon–Sat 8.30am–4pm, Sun 11am–5pm; free), with its entrance in Aliwal Street, occupies the Old Courthouse. Durban's first two-storey building, it was erected in 1866 in the Natal Verandah style, characterized by wide eaves to throw off heavy subtropical downpours. The atmosphere is somewhat austere, but, if you want to see a reconstruction of Henry Francis Fynn's wattle-and-daub hut, Durban's first European structure, then this is the place to come.

North of the Local History Museum, along Aliwal Street, is **The Workshop Mall**, which sounds more interesting than it proves to be, although it does provide parking and every type of shop you're likely to need, conveniently close to Tourist Junction. On its north side, **Central Park**, with a lovely mosaic water fountain as its focus, offers a large green space. The **Exhibition Centre** in nearby Walnut Road, to the east, is the venue for a busy Sunday flea market, where you can pick up trinkets, authentic didgeridoos and (a hot tip if you need footwear) handmade leather shoes and hiking boots from the Ground Cover workshop in the KwaZulu-Natal Midlands. The market's popularity is paradoxically its drawback, and you'll need to shop quickly to avoid getting smeared by *boerewors* rolls or getting crushed.

Kwa Muhle Museum

North of the Exhibition Centre, at 130 Ordnance Rd, is Durban's newest and most fascinating museum, the **Kwa Muhle** (daily 8am–4pm). This is the country's only museum devoted to it's twentieth-century urban social history, and should not be missed if you have the slightest interest in understanding modern South Africa. Permanent exhibitions include one on the Durban System, which enabled the city council to finance the administration of African affairs without ever spending a penny of white ratepayers' money. It achieved this by granting itself a monopoly on the brewing of sorghum (a type of grain) beer, which it sold through vast, African-only municipal beer halls. The resulting revenue was used to ensure that blacks lived in an "orderly" way. The exhibit also illustrates the Pass System, one of the most hated aspects of apartheid, through which constant tabs could be kept on Africans and their influx into the urban areas. Look out, too, for photographs of life in the single-sex, artificially tribalized worker hostels, which deliberately sowed divisions among blacks and played its part in much of the current violence in South Africa.

Grey Street and around

Moving west to where **Grey Street** draws a north–south line across the city, the pace accelerates perceptibly, and you leave behind the formal city centre for the densely packed warren of shops and living quarters of Durban's central **Indian district**, the best place in town to sample local spicy food (see "Eating and drinking", p.384). Post-1910 Union style architecture is well-preserved here and, along with minarets and steeples, it punctuates the skyline with an eclectic roofscape. Down at street level, the cultural blend is rich, with African sidewalk vendors selling herbs, fruit and trinkets outside the Indian general dealers and spice merchants.

On the corner of Grey and Queen streets is the **Juma Musjid Mosque** and its gilt-domed minarets, completed in 1927 and the largest mosque in the southern hemisphere. It's the area's focal point, although Muslims are a minority among Durban's predominantly Hindu Indian population. You're welcome to enter the mosque, but make sure you leave your shoes at the door. The colonnaded verandahs give way to the alley of the bazaar-like **Madressa Arcade** next door, which provides tantalizing glimpses through mountains of coloured plastic bowls and draped bolts of cloth into general dealers cluttered with aluminium pots and kettles, and Indian traders peddling kerosene lamps, tailor-made outfits and beads. The arcade emerges with a start into Cathedral Street, dominated by the **Emmanuel Cathedral**, built in 1902 in the Gothic revival style.

North across Queen Street, the **Victoria Street Market** is a bright building with purple minarets, where traders sell curios and spices with labels that include "mother-in-law exterminator". The fish market downstairs can provide some hectic drama, particularly on Saturdays when the stall holders compete to shed their stocks before the Sunday close-down.

Moving west, towards the fag-end of town (where it hits the railway tracks), African hawkers unable to afford official stalls gather on **Russell Street**, where they scrape an existence trading *umuthi*, used goods or anything that will raise a few bucks. Extreme poverty dictates that they spend nights on their market pitches in plastic and cardboard hovels, because the minibus taxi fare to any of the township areas would cost an entire day's takings. West of Russell Street and jammed between the railway tracks and the N3 freeway into town, **West Street Cemetery** is zoned according to religion, with many of the city's colonial big names buried here, such as Durban's first mayor, George Cato, and the Victorian documentary painter, Thomas Baines. In the Muslim section some tombstones are inscribed "*hagee*" or "*hafez*", the former indicating someone who has been to Mecca and the latter an individual who managed to memorize the entire Koran.

If the crowds feel too intimidating – and there is always the risk of mugging – you can explore this area on one of the reasonably priced daily **walking tours** from Tourist Junction (see box, p.371).

Warwick Triangle

In an Africanized *Bladerunner* setting west of Grey Street, concrete freeways run overhead chaotic roadways and minibus taxi ranks; here you'll find Durban's real urban heart of hawkers, shacks and *shebeens*. You'll need to be bold to explore the **Warwick Triangle**, which lies between Berea Road, Brooke Street and Cannongate – police advise tourists to always go in a group, to leave cameras behind and to wear nothing snatchable.

The gateway to the triangle is across Brooke Street – known until 1988 as Slaughterhouse Road, because butchers slaughtered livestock here – and then through the Berea station concourse and across the Market Road footbridge to the market area between Market Road and Warwick Avenue. The station concourse, which services African townships, pumps with reggae and the music of popular South African musicians such as Dube, while hawkers sell baseball caps, patent leather shoes and tortoise shells. As you move across the footbridge, take a look at the truncated flyover alongside the station, going nowhere, but now the site for shacks. On a buttress at the end of the flyover, an eight-metre mural of the African goddess Nomkhubulwana stretches out her arms in a gesture of greeting and protection.

Durban's major fruit, vegetable and flower **market** is between Warwick Avenue and Market Road, operating in the early morning only, with selling extending well beyond its walls in a dense mass of vendors. Shopping is frenetic; take your own basket and load up with the cheapest produce in town, from aubergines and jackfruit to beetelnut leaf for red-stained lips and a two-minute rush.

Victoria Embankment and the harbour vicinity

The **Victoria Embankment**, or the Esplanade, running along the harbour edge south of the city, is Durban's palm-lined city avenue, connecting Point Road in the east to Maydon Wharf Road (which leads to the container terminal piers and the dry dock off Bay Road) in the west. During the city's early development in the nineteenth century, the Embankment was the prime residential area and it's here, one block north at the east end of the road, that the **Old House Museum**, 31 St Andrews St (Mon–Sat 8.30am–4pm, Sun 11–4pm; donation), is sited. Once the home of Sir John Robinson, who became Natal's first prime minister in 1893, the renovated settler house serves as a reminder of Durban's colonial heritage.

About 500m east along the Embankment you'll hit the entrance to the **Yacht Mole**, a slender breakwater jutting into the bay and home to the Point and Royal Natal Yacht clubs and the upmarket *Café Fish* bar and restaurant, which specializes in great seafood (see p.385). A walk along here to look at the amazing variety of craft provides a photogenic view of Durban from across the water and a breather from the city traffic. A little further east along the dockside, a statue of **Dick King** re-enacts his heroic ride to save Durban (see p.367), and if you keep going in the same direction along the Embankment you'll reach the **BAT (Bartle Arts Trust) Centre**, a focal point for arts in the city. This industrial-chic arts development and community venue right on the dockside offers a concert hall, practical visual art workshops, classes and exhibition galleries while the *Zansi Bar and Restaurant,* and the *Intensive Care Coffee Shop* provide a magnificent lookout for watching the passing harbour scene.

Back on the Esplanade, heading east towards the Stanger Street intersection, enter the Harbour at Port Entrance no. 3 and follow the signs to the **Ocean Terminal Building**, which harks back to the romantic days of sea travel and is one of Durban's architectural masterpieces. Formerly the harbour reception building, this is now the headquarters for Portnet, the public utility that maintains South Africa's harbours. Although you can't enter the building, the view from outside it at night, looking back onto the city, is spectacular.

Striking south from from the city centre and Winder Street, the eastern extension of Victoria Embankment, **Point Road**, known in its heyday in the early 1900s as Africa's most exciting thoroughfare and Durban's hottest red-light district, cuts down the **Point**, the northernmost of the two arms that enclose the Bay of Natal to contain

Durban's harbour. At the city end of the road are cheap and tawdry hotels that rent out rooms by the hour, late-night takeaways, loud drunks and scantily clad women lingering by the roadside.

Maydon Wharf wraps around the harbour's western edge in a photogenic complex of functional industrial architecture, most notable of which are the three dramatic sugar silos at the **Sugar Terminal**, 57 Maydon Wharf Rd, which are dedicated to storing Durban's white gold (one of the city's biggest revenue-earners) and whose design has been patented and used internationally.

Inland from the Sugar Terminal, across the Southern Freeway, the Dalton Road area clings closer to the city centre than any other African residential area. Craftsmen toil in the dingy hive of activity that constitutes **Dalton Road Market**, turning out traditional Zulu costume and regalia including *amabheshu* (leather aprons), shields, *izimboko* (staffs), dancing sticks and beadwork. Every Saturday night, the *Dalton Road Men's Hostel* comes alive with *isicatamiya* concerts (see p.386), which start around midnight and continue into the small hours. The concerts are competitions in which groups sing in unaccompanied harmony. This genuine Durban experience, not aimed at tourists, would be worth catching, but it's not advisable to come to this ropy part of town at night (doors open around 11.30pm) unless you know someone involved.

The beachfront

Durban's **beachfront**, a high-energy holiday strip just east of the city centre, is South Africa's most developed seaside, and one to avoid unless you enjoy unabashed kitsch and garish amusement parks. This six-kilometre stretch from the Umgeni River in the north to the Point in the south was traditionally called the **Golden Mile**, but is fast becoming known as Mugger's Mile, which is why so many middle-class Gauteng families are breaking the habit of generations and deserting the beachfront for the safer (white, middle-class) sands north and south of Durban.

Addington Beach, the southernmost swimming strand and a favourite spot for apprentice sufers, with a smaller swell, draws Durban families to its wide expanse of sand and lawns for sunbathing. Just north lies **South Beach**, the busiest beach in South Africa, which packs tight at peak times, and nets visitors with the start of the beachfront tourist tack: a refreshment and shopping complex and the dubious attraction of Sea World Durban (daily 9am–9pm; dolphin shows 10am, 11.30am, 2.30pm; shark feeding Tues, Thurs & Sun 12.30pm; R27), with its tropical aquaria, tanks of sharks, and performing dolphins, seals and penguins.

Further along Marine Parade, you'll find paddling pools, fountains, stepping stones, bridges, an aerial cableway and amusement rides. The only redeeming feature along here is the saltwater **Rachel Finlayson Baths** (☎031/337 2721), which offer sheltered swimming and sunbathing. Next is **Dairy Beach**, so called because of the milking factory that once stood here; now known as one of the country's best surfing beaches, it's also home to the Oceans Entertainment Centre, whose bars and restaurants are popular with the surfer-groupie crowd.

Dairy Beach adjoins **North Beach** and the adjacent **Bay of Plenty**, both of which make up the venue for the international Gunston 500 surfing contest held every July. North Beach is Durban's prime angling, bathing and surfing beach, made even more popular by the presence of hip bars and restaurants. Between Snell Parade and the pedestrian walkway at the Bay of Plenty is the **Amphitheatre**, the venue for Sunday flea markets, where local hawkers are joined by travelling merchants from Zimbabwe, Malawi and as far afield as Kenya, who trundle down the continent to sell their wares, trading for two weeks, before returning to restock. Any surplus goods are sold at cost to the Zulu traders who line the whole Marine Parade. The rickshaws also gather here, with their ornate carriages and elaborately decorated Zulu pullers decked out in beads

---

BEACHFRONT SAFETY

Durban's **beaches** are notorious hunting grounds for sharks – though not of the piscean variety. **Muggings** are common, though frequently avoidable if you take precautions. Despite repeated warnings, tourists continue to venture onto beaches wearing expensive watches and jewellery and carrying large wads of cash – highly attractive bait. On the beachfront you should stay in a group, and at night never go out alone, no matter how enticing the seafront seems on a balmy evening. Street children are an occupational hazard in most South African cities and they positively thrive on the rich pickings of Durban's beachfront. No matter how small they look, make no mistake – many are skilful pickpockets and accomplished bag-snatchers.

---

and streamers. Just north of the Bay of Plenty, on the corner of Snell Parade and Old Fort Road, is the **Fitzsimmons Snake Park** (daily 9am–5pm; R10), which offers the chance to gawp at reptiles in cramped glass boxes. Continuing north, the beachfront hype steadily diminishes with the less frenetic **Battery Beach**, with its good swimming and fewer crowds.

The Berea

West of the city centre, high on a ridge that cuts north–south, the **Berea** is Durban's oldest and most desirable residential district, where mansions and apartment blocks enjoy airy views to the harbour and the sea. Its palmy avenues provide an alternative focus for accommodation, eating and entertainment, away from the torrid atmosphere of the city centre and beachfront.

Undulating **Ridge Road** cuts a six-kilometre axis through the Berea from the Umgeni River in the north to the University of Natal. South of the N3, which passes through the Berea to the city, and east of Ridge Road, the **Natal Society of Arts Gallery** (Tues–Fri 10am–6pm, Sat & Sun 10am–4pm; free), or NSA, adjacent to Bulwer Park, provides a breezy venue for taking in fortnightly exhibitions of work by local artists and for relaxing in a great coffee shop. Designed for the local climate, the Nineties building is a spacious mass of interlinked volumes, divided by a timber screen that forms a verandah. The gallery shop has a good collection of original art pieces and cheaper, jazzy creations.

In **Upper Berea**, north of Berea Road, the **Botanical Gardens**, on the corner of Edith Benson and St Thomas roads, offer a pleasantly shady break from the surrounding urban torpor, with cool paths, excellent picnic spots, a lovely tea house and a magnificent orchid collection. Established in 1849, the gardens are famous for their cycad collection, which includes *Encephalartos woodii*, one of the rarest specimens in the world. A notice board outside the entrance advertises forthcoming functions, including Natal Philharmonic Orchestra **concerts**, which are regularly held here.

Heading north for several blocks up Musgrave Road and west into Marriott Road, on the corner of Essenwood Road you'll find another magnificent garden at **Muckleneuk** (by appointment only, ☎031/207 3432, *harkness@kcc.und.co.za*; tours R15), the turn-of-the-century Cape Dutch-revival former homestead of sugar baron Sir Marshal Campbell and home to the outstanding Campbell collections. This is Durban's premier museum, and holds one of the finest private collections of Africana in the country, including material relating to KwaZulu-Natal's ethnic heritage. The **Killie Campbell Africana Library** is well known for its comprehensive collection of books, manuscripts and photographs, while the **William Campbell collections** comprise artworks and excellent examples of Cape-Dutch furniture. The **Mashu Museum of Ethnology**, also on site, consists of a superb collection of Zulu crafts, that includes tools, weapons, beadwork and pottery.

OFF THE BEATEN TRACK: A DIY DURBAN TOUR

Some quintessential Durban experiences rarely make it into the pages of tourist brochures, but with a little effort and some courage you can get a glimpse of KwaMashu township, visit the place where Gandhi dreamed up passive resistance, witness the epic religious ceremonies of the Zulu-Christian Shembe sect and walk among the serene buildings of Inanda – a nineteenth-century seminary for Zulu girls.

A word of **warning** before you leave: self-driving through some of the areas covered here carries a certain risk and you'd be advised to go with someone familiar with the road and local customs – and be particularly aware here of the national penchant for car-jacking. Check with Tourist Junction (see p.370) for the best **maps** to use.

Heading out of town towards the North Coast, take the M19 along Umgeni Road past the Durban City Dump. Once along the M19 West, take the North Coast R102 turn-off leading to KwaMashu/Phoenix/Duff's Road. As the Duff's Road turn-off approaches, look up to the prominent hillside for Dookie Ramdaari's **Aeroplane House**. An affluent Indian bus builder with a taste for the unconventional, Ramdaari was a voracious traveller with a passion reflected in his first home built in the form of a ship – sailing east out of Duff's Road Indian township. Poised for take off, his current abode, the Aeroplane House, has wings, an undercarriage, a television room with row seats in the tail and a superb lounge in the cockpit.

Further on to Inanda you'll pass the black township of **KwaMashu** on your left, separated by the Phoenix Industrial park buffer strip from Phoenix itself, established in the late Fifties to house the forced-removal residents of Cato Manor. It displays all the unimaginative planning typical of such low-cost housing schemes, as does Umlazi, its counterpart to the south of Durban. The area is a sea of hills, vegetation and colour, which makes it tempting to romanticise the tropical poverty of the locality.

A turn-off to the right indicates "Bhambayi", (the Zulu approximation of Bombay), denoting Gandhi's **Phoenix Settlement** on the eastern edge of the vast Inanda squatter camp. Phoenix is the site of a self-help scheme established by Mohandas Gandhi soon after his arrival in Durban in 1903. It was from here that he began to forge his philosophy of passive resistance and it's a sad irony that violence brought it to ruin in 1985 when squatters from the adjacent camp spilled over and looted and razed the settlement. Of Gandhi's house, **Sarvodaya** ("a place for the upliftment for all"), only the foundations remain, although the printing press still stands, albeit in ruins, a melancholic reminder of the spirit and community of the area. The area now hums with traders along the roadside selling anything from water to hair makeovers or "Durban poison" – a highly sought-after type of *dagga* (marijuana).

Cato Manor

A short drive west of the city centre takes you through **Cato Manor**, a graphic slice through Durban's twentieth-century history, where you can see the juxtaposition of African squatter camps, Hindu temples and entropic vegetation mingling in the heart of the city's middle-class suburbs. A large area in a valley below the Berea, Cato Manor was named after Durban's first mayor, **George Cato**, who arrived here in 1839. During the first half of this century, the district was home to much of Durban's Indian community, who built temples on its hills. They were later joined by Africans, who were forced into crowded slums because of the shortage of housing. In 1949, a petty incident flared up into Durban's worst **riot**, when thousands of Africans attacked Indian stores and houses, leaving 142 people dead.

Because Cato Manor was bang in the middle of white suburbs, the apartheid government began enforcing the Group Areas Act in the Sixties, and moved Africans north to KwaMashu and Indians south to Chatsworth, leaving a derelict wasteland guarded only by the handful of Hindu temples left standing. The vacuum was filled again in the

The M25 continues to **Ekupakumeni** ("the elated place"), where two "stars" are laid in stone in the hilly landscape marking the spots where meteorites from the 1906 Halley's Comet struck the earth. This is also the site of the **Shembe settlement**, established by the Holy Church of Nazareth as a refuge for Africans dispossessed as a result of the Land Act of 1913. According to the founding history of the church, its prophet, Isaya Shembe was "called" in 1910 to the summit of a mountain outside Durban where he vowed before God to bring the Gospel to the Zulus. The church drew membership from rural people whose lives had been blown apart by colonization and who were eager to embrace Christianity but were unwilling to give up traditional customs. Shembe brought about a rich religious synthesis that rejected drinking, smoking and cults while encouraging a work ethic that centred around crafts, leading to a sect that now has tens of thousands of adherents. Continuing to the Inanda police station at the top of the hill, turn left to descend into the valley and cross the Umhlanga River bridge. At the next intersection take the dirt road to the left, past the sports field, and turn left to view **Ebuhleni**, where every July, devotees of the Holy Church of Nazareth gather for a month of worship. Ignoring the dirt road turn-off, head straight on to reach the Inanda Dam. The deep gorge to your left is the **Inanda Falls**, where the Shembe have baptismal ceremonies, which visitors are welcome to attend.

At the entrance gates to the settlement, rows of tables display what appear to be religious knack-knacks for sale to tourists, but to the converted of Shembe are actually revered religious artifacts. These include holographic images of Isaya Shembe, and key rings with religious icons embedded in perspex. A range of traditional outfits are sold in the village – from men's ceremonial skirts to the magnificent headdresses of the women. The settlement resembles an emerging medieval city, replete with winding pathways negotiating the narrow spaces between buildings. Many homes are owned by believers who come to Ebuhleni only at festival times – timeshare Zulu-style. On these occasions, the men and women live on different sides of the village, and the unmarried maidens live in a separate enclosure.

Sticking with the topic of unmarried maidens, make your way back to the M25, and continue to the **Inanda Seminary** along a well-indicated route. An institution for girls, the seminary was established in 1869 by Daniel Lindley, an American missionary and pastor of the Voortrekkers, and played a pioneering role in the liberation of Zulu women. Dignified old buildings give the place a permeating serenity. Staff members have always been drawn from all race groups and it is speculated that this is why the school received no funding from the apartheid educational authorities after 1957. The story of Inanda between 1869 and 1969 is recounted in a book by Agnes Wood, *Shine Where You Are*. To return to Durban, simply turn tail and head east along the M25.

late Eighties, when Africans pouring into Durban set up the closely packed tin shacks that line Bellair Road, which winds its way through Cato Manor's valley.

Along this interesting and safe drive it's well worth stopping to visit the **Shree Ambalvanar Alayam Second River Hindu Temple**, a National Monument in Bellair Road, which has no number but is on your right (just before the Edwin Swales freeway), if you're coming from town. The building is a 1947 reconstruction of the first Hindu temple in Africa, built in 1875 on the banks of the Umbilo River and subsequently destroyed by floods. The facade is adorned with a pantheon of wonderfully garish Hindu deities and the beautifully carved entrance doors are the originals salvaged from the flood. Around Easter every year the temple hosts a **firewalking festival** in which unshod devotees walk across red-hot coals to emerge unscathed. Visitors are welcome to join the melee of thousands of worshippers who come to honour the goddess Draudpadi. To get to Bellair Road, leave the city centre on the M13, take the Brickfield Road exit and then turn left into the M10; this becomes Bellair Road.

Eating and drinking

Eating out is a favourite pastime in Durban, whether you're a suburbanite relishing the seafood of a swanky restaurant, or an African worker shelling out a few rand for a filling Indian take away. Although you'll find all types of cooking here, **Indian** food is what Durban excels at – hardly surprising for a city with one of the largest Indian populations outside Asia. Perhaps less obviously, Durban also has some fine **Portuguese** restaurants, serving cuisine often imported from Mozambique, with highly spiced *peri-peri* dishes, of which chicken is the most common variety and prawns the tastiest. And of course, in this port city, **seafood** is excellent.

For a city that prides itself on its dedication to hedonism, Durban turns in disappointingly early, **closing time** for most restaurants being around 10.30pm. A notable exception is *Legends* in the Musgrave Shopping Centre, which is open past midnight. The best areas for restaurants are the city centre, along the beachfront and the Berea district. Prices are generally very reasonable, though you'll pay more for seafood. For Indian food, the best selection is in the Grey Street area; for fish, there's no better venue than the industrial marine landscape of the harbour. It's a good idea to **phone** before you set out, as opening hours tend to change frequently.

Durban's big contribution to the national fast-food scene is *bunny chow*, a cheap and filling scooped-out half-loaf of bread traditionally stuffed with curried beans, but now available with an array of mutton, vegetable, beef or even tinned fish curries. In a similar vein are curries wrapped in *roti* (a traditional Indian pancake). Down at the African markets and around the taxi ranks, you'll find *shisanyama* outlets, where you can buy a hunk of meat cooked on an open fire.

If you're **self-catering**, you can buy groceries at any of the supermarket chains which you'll find in shopping malls. **Tropical fruit** such as mangoes, papayas, bananas, lychees, pineapples, guavas and granadillas are available in season from supermarkets and street traders and at the Indian market off Warwick Avenue. In summer, try masala pineapple – cubes of the skewered fruit sprinkled with red-hot spices.

Beachfront

The Chartroom Smorgasbord, *The Edward*, 149 Marine Parade (☎031/337 3681). Delicious breakfasts on the terrace and very good smorgasbord lunches at one of the beachfront's hotels, where you'll find a magnificent and reasonably priced spread of seafoods, including crayfish oysters and kalamari. Open daily.

Joe Kool's Bar & Grill, 137 Lower Marine Parade (☎031/332 9697). Trendy, ultra-clean eatery and pub right on the beach, with pool tables and first-class live music.

City centre

Aangans, 86 Queen St (☎031/307 1366). Wildly exotic but totally authentic and phenomenally cheap Indian cuisine, which you're encouraged to eat with your hands. Specials include the marvellous *malai kofta* (cottage cheese and potato dumplings filled with mixed fruit and cream in a cashew nut gravy), and their outstanding Butter Chicken. Also famous for their Tandoori chicken, *tikka* and *parata*. Closes 8.30pm.

Manjras, 56 Cathedral Rd (☎031/306 0860). Highly affordable Indian cooking from the self-proclaimed "biryani kings", in a great location adjacent to the Juma Mosque near Grey Street, one of the most exciting parts of the city. Closed 2–3pm Sat.

O Pescador, 52 Albany Grove (☎031/304 4138). As the name suggests, seafood is the speciality at this moderately priced Portuguese restaurant, serving outstanding crab, complete with nutcracker and bib. Their starters are recommended, as are their mussels in onion and tomato sauce. Closed Sun.

Patel's Vegetarian House, (☎031/306 1774) Rama House, Grey St. One of the few places where Indians go to buy sweetmeats, and among the original homes of *bunny chow*.

Villa D'Este, corner of Davenport and Bulwer roads. (☎031/202 7920). One of the oldest and best places in town for seafood, with dollops of Italian charm and an expensive menu. Closed Mon.

Victoria Embankment and the harbour

Café Fish, Yacht Mole, Victoria Embankment (☎031/305 5062). Beautiful and moderately priced restaurant looking out onto harbour, which specializes in great seafood – eating the catch of the day is *de rigueur*.

Charlie Crofts Wharfside Diner, 18 Boatsman Rd, Maydon Wharf (☎031/307 2935). Right by a slipway in the industrial section of the harbour, their spicy kalamari grill is first-class.

The Famous Fish Co, North Pier, end of Point Rd (☎031/368 1060). Perfectly positioned at the port entrance, this seafood restaurant is recommended for the wonderful views of ships navigating the harbour mouth. Try their oysters with lemon tequila.

The Berea and Morningside

Baan Thai, 138 Florida Rd, Morningside (☎031/303 4270). Unfailingly excellent Thai food including *Ton Yum* soup and steamed mussels, outshone only by their honeyed duck, at surprisingly moderate prices.

Blue Zoo Café, 6 Nimmo Rd, Berea (☎031/303 3568). Varied and unusual menu featuring delicious Cajun chicken, steaks, fish and salads with mango and chilli dressings. Beautifully located in Mitchell Park Gardens, with moderate prices. Closed Mon & Sun.

EatCetera, 45 Windermere Rd, Morningside (☎031/303 3078). Stylish decor and extreme, far-out menu with sizzlers and nouvelle cuisine. Closed Sun.

El Turko, 413 Windemere Rd, Morningside (☎031/312 7893). Cosy restaurant with pavement seating and a recommended *meze* platter with fiery olives and moderate prices. "Turkish Tigers" (vodka, condensed milk, cream and cinnamon) are worth trying to fire you up. Closed Sat lunch & all day Sun.

Gulzar, 69 Stamford Hill Rd, Morningside (☎031/309 6379). Durban's classiest Indian restaurant dishes up magnificent curries and tandooris amid Moorish decor and tasteful Oriental carpets.

Indian Delights, 374 Brickfield Rd, Overport (☎031/293 038). Strictly vegetarian menu offering *puri-patha*, made of leaves, spread with a batter and spice, cut and fried and served with *roti*. Choose a sweetmeat to sample from the carnival of colours.

Roxy, Marriott Road (☎031/309 1837). Late night coffee shop/pub, with an excellent range of coffees, plus flavoured macadamia nuts and delicious cappuccino truffles. Live music and backgammon boards.

Two Moon Junction, 45 Windermere Rd, Morningside (☎031/303 3078). Reasonably priced Mediterranean cuisine, including *vermicelli*, salmon, brilliant strawberry and gooseberry salads and *millefleur* filo pastry dessert served in a techno-industrial aesthetic of steel bar-tops covered in fake Friesland cowhide set against a Corinthian column. Closed Sun.

Upstairs, 2a Avondale Centre, Morningside (☎031/312 9134). *Dim sum* starter with mouthwatering arrangement of sweet and hot sauces, spring rolls and assorted appetizers make this moderately priced Chinese cuisine worth travelling for. Order 24 hours ahead for their exotic Peking duck dish, consisting of smoked duck and skin served separately as a starter and reappearing as part of the stir-fry main meal. Closed Mon.

Coffee and snack shops

Café Geneve, 1st Floor, 384 Smith St (☎031/301 3102). Specialist coffee shop with excellent brews, and meals including burgers, prawns, steaks and fish curries. A cool refuge from Durban's humidity. 7am–late.

Clancey's on the Berea, Price Waterhouse, Silverton Rd (☎031/202 8270). Durban's top deli serves up a generous café au lait that requires both hands. A fine after-movie venue and popular with the city's jewel-bedecked nouveau riche for Saturday breakfasts of croissants and jams. 7am–late. Closed Sun.

Java Java Cyber Café, 13 Marriott Rd, Berea (☎031/309 1575, *javajava@sprintlink.co.za*). Durban's relaxed vegetarian cybercafé in a converted old-style house is an alcohol-free zone, where the only mind-altering substances are their shelves of Marxist books and net-surfing. Mon–Sat 9am–midnight, Sun 10am–midnight.

Loafers Bakery & Coffee Shop, 514 Windermere Rd (☎031/232 100). Light and airy venue, popular with Durbanites for Sunday morning breakfast. Budget but first-class full English breakfast. Daily 7am–4pm, Sat closes 3pm.

Takeaways

Charlie Croft's Wharfside Diner, 18 Boatsman Rd, Maydon Wharf (☎031/307 2935). Noted for its dockside setting and deli, where you can pick and mix your own starter and pay by the weight.

Sunrise Chip N' Ranch, 89 Sparks Rd, Overport. Fastest and tastiest *bunny chows* in town, 24 hours a day to take away, at rock-bottom prices.

Victory Lounge, corner of Grey and Victoria streets. Hot and spicy *bunny chow* to take away in the Indian quarter of the city centre.

Nightlife and entertainment

Durban is the grunge capital of South Africa and you'll find plenty of live **indie music** on offer, much of it derivative of European or North American trends. More interesting, but less accessible, are some of the **Zulu forms** such as *isicathamiya* and *maskanda*. On the **jazz** scene, the city's most indigenous offering is a spicy combination of American mixed with township jazz, Zulu forms and classical Indian music. Look out for performances by Gathering Forces II, featuring Darius Brubeck (son of Dave) and the classically trained Indian musician Deepak Ram.

The best place to hear **classical concerts** by the Natal Philharmonic Orchestra – more for the tropical ambience than the quality of performance – is at a sundowner concert held in the Botanical Gardens or the Kingsmead Cricket Grounds. Check for listings and adverts in the press or on the notice board in the Gardens.

Durban has a fairly well-established and lively **gay scene**, with a handful of excellent nightclubs where heteros are also welcome.

For details of **what's on**, the *Mercury* is the better of Durban's two English-language dailies, the *Daily News* has a comprehensive section on forthcoming events. *Natal on Saturday* gives an update on the latest drinking spots as well as where to go and what to do, while the Johannesburg-based weekly *Mail & Guardian* covers Durban nightlife in its What's On section towards the back of the paper.

Bars

Africa Tavern, 9 Ridge Road, Durban North. Ethnic hangout with serious local flavour, buffalo heads on walls, and food like South African *potjiekos*, crocodile, shark fillets, langoustines and ostrich. Mixed live music.

Gerry's Irish Tavern, 793 Jan Smuts Highway, Sherwood. Fun spot favoured by expats, with congenial host who occasionally bursts into song. Live music and outside deck for summer days and evenings.

Horse With No Name, Greyville Race Course, Mitchell Crescent, Greyville. Pub/restaurant that's a well-known hangout for divorcees, where, during night racing, you can place your bets with barmen as the horses thunder past. Great fun, and live music most nights.

Scallywags, Shop 2, Boscombe Terrace, off Brickhill Road. Festive pub with lots of expats, where you can watch British soccer and enjoy good bar meals. Live music three or four nights a week.

Thirsty's, King's Battery Development. Worth it for the harbour view alone, or go for the beer garden with a variety of imported beers and scampi baskets to whet the appetite. Weather permitting, seafood, fresh from the fishing boats moored alongside, grilled on deck.

Victoria Bar, Point Road. Seedy but highly popular Portuguese venue good for boozing and watching sport on TV. *Catembe* (cola and wine) is a house speciality, as is the excellent prawn curry and *peri-peri* chicken.

Clubs

Angelos, West Street Mall near beachfront, live music from all over South Africa. Only club in town open Wednesday night.

Bourbon Street, 123 Argyle Road, Greyville. Popular under-30s hangout with normal and shooter bars, and specials like Pigs' Nite (Tues) where your cover charge allows you to drink all you like before midnight. Also fun "foam parties" on Saturday nights.

Club 330, Point Road. Durban's definitive techno-rave club. Dress code is high fashion, accessories are body piercing, spring water and tiger balm ointment. Sat only, from 11pm.

Club Zoom, Dick King Street. In the city centre, with its mirror halls, this culturally mixed nightclub has a magnificent bar.

Crash!, main concourse of Durban Station. Brimming with young babes and the funkiest DJs in town.

Jamie's, 39 Pine Street. One of the few alternative venues in Durban, with retro, grunge and New Romantic sounds.

Stringfellas, corner of Point Rd and West St. In the city centre, this Indian club has two discos, two bars and a comfy seating area. Every second Sunday features *bhangra*, the Indian rave culture that continues to take Durban by storm.

Gay spots

Axis, Gillespie Street, beachfront. Durban's premier gay nightclub grooves to the sounds of disco classics.

Garth's, Avonmore Centre, Berea. One of Durban's late-night spots is a cosy place for cakes, coffee or drinks, and, proprietor willing, piano recitals. With eccentric crockery, embellished wall hangings and comfy chairs, this place feels a bit like home.

4-Play, Beachview Mall. Trashy hangout with live jazz on Wednesday nights, drag shows on Fridays and karaoke on Sunday nights.

Jazz

BAT (Bartle Arts Trust) Centre, Small Craft Harbour, entrance opposite Hermitage Lane, off Victoria Embankment. Probably the best jazz venue in Durban, with a free sundowner jazz concert on the deck every Friday, 5–6pm. On Friday and Saturday nights, top local and international jazz musicians play in Bat Hall. In the *Zansi Bar* restaurant there's live music on Fridays 7–10pm, and on Sundays 4–9pm. R20 cover charge, includes a light meal.

The Rainbow, 23 Stanfield Lane, Pinetown (☎031/729 161). From Afro-fusion to jazz, on occasional Sunday lunchtimes. Check press for programme details.

Theatre and cinema

There are two major **theatres** in town: the Playhouse Drama Theatre, 231 Smith St (☎031/260 2296) a mock-Tudor building that tends to host middle-of-the-road productions, but also sees performances by the resident progressive Playhouse Dance Company; and the Elizabeth Sneddon Theatre, University of Natal, on South Ridge Road (☎031/260 2296), a modern venue for university and visiting productions, which also hosts Monday lunchtime concerts, including Zulu traditional *maskanda* and piano recitals.

As far as movies go, the best and most convenient **cinemas** are the multiscreen complexes at the Musgrave Centre on Musgrave Road and the The Workshop Mall in the city centre. There are no art-house cinemas in Durban, but the Musgrave occasionally screens film-festival releases.

Outdoor activities

Durban's generous climate and beachside location foster a wide variety of **outdoor activities**. Not surprisingly for a city with such a British heritage, **cricket** and **horse-racing** are high on the agenda of spectator sports; the Kingsmead Cricket Ground, 2 Kingsmead Close (☎031/337 9703), is the principal cricket venue for local and international matches and is home to the **KwaZulu-Natal** provincial cricket team. You'll also have plenty of opportunity to watch **rugby** in season at King's Park Stadium, Walter Gilbert Rd, Stamford Hill (☎031/312 6368), which is the home to the local Sharks. **Horse-racing** is popular: the main season runs from May to August. and centres around the course at Greyville, Avondale Rd (☎031/309 4545). The Rothmans "July at Greyville" is South Africa's premier horse-racing event, drawing bets from across the length and breadth of the country and wildly exhibitionist fashions in the spectator boxes.

Surfing

Far more than a pastime, **surfing** in Durban amounts to an entire way of life. Night surfing competitions draw enormous crowds, as does the annual **Gunston 500**, the world's longest-running professional surfing competition, held here every July. During this month, the city goes surf mad, with a large expo displaying the latest in equipment and accessories.

The current favourite spot for surfers is **North Beach**, while a good place to pick up surfing gear is the Safari Surf Shop, 28 Somtseu Rd (☎031/337 2176), where Spider Murphy, South Africa's top board-shaper, will custom-make your board. This is a good opportunity to buy a world-class board far more cheaply than anything you'll find in Europe or North America. Island Style Surf Shop, 121 Old Fort Road, Marine Parade (☎031/305 4505), is a good bet for accessories. To **rent** boards, contact Surf Zone at the Ocean Action Centre (☎031/368 5818).

Diving and swimming

Diving is an obvious and pleasurable activity in KwaZulu-Natal's subtropical waters, but is somewhat limited immediately around Durban. The best diving sites around town are Vetches Pier, at the southern tip of Durban's beachfront, and Blood Reef at the tip of the Bluff. Further along the coast, Aliwal Shoal along the South Coast (see p.394), and Sodwana up the North Coast (p.436), are superb. **Scuba trips** can be arranged through Underwater World, 251 Point Rd (☎031/332 5820) or 3 Elements Xtreme Sports (see opposite).

If you fancy doing some laps, Durban's largest **swimming pool** is the heated King's Park Olympic Swimming Pool (☎031/312 0404) on NMR Avenue, between Argyle and Battery Beach roads in Stamford Hill. Convenient for the Berea are Sutton Park Baths, Stamford Hill Rd (☎031/303 1823), while the seawater Rachel Finlayson Baths, Lower Marine Parade (☎031/337 2721), are handy if you're staying near the beachfront.

Bird-watching and hiking

Bird-watching, a major activity in the green fringes of the city, is being encouraged by the Durban Metropolitan Open Space System (DMOSS), a project linking all the city parks via narrow green corridors. Promising spots include the Manor Gardens area; the Botanic Gardens, Botanic Gardens Rd; the Berea; Burman Bush, to the north of the city; Pigeon Valley, below the University of Natal; the Umgeni River Mouth; Virginia Bush, on the road to Umhlanga Rocks; and the Havana Forest in Umhlanga, where the spotted thrush and green coucal have been seen. Also worth a visit is the **Umgeni River Bird Park**, 490 Riverside Road, Durban North (daily 9am–5pm; ☎031/571 4600), which has a fantastic free-flight bird show twice-daily, with spectacular specimens as well as a vast collection of indigenous and exotic birds, including flamingoes, finches, magpies and macaws. There's a tranquil tea garden as well. For organized bird-watching outings and courses, contact the **Wildlife Society of South Africa**, 100 Brand Rd, Glenwood (☎031/201 3126).

You can arrange **hiking** in the relatively close **Drakensberg** through one of the several hiking clubs that organize expeditions to Injasuti, Cathedral Peak and the Southern Berg. These can be contacted through the Wildlife Society of South Africa (see above), which organizes a variety of bush outings; non-members are welcomed. For kitting up, head for the Quarter Master Store, The Workshop Mall, 99 Aliwal St (☎031/305 3087), and Bushwackers, 110 Pavilion Shopping Centre, Spine Rd, Westville (☎031/265 0102).

Extreme sports

3 Elements Xtreme Sports, 41 Glendowan Rd and 142 Percy Osborn Rd, Morningside (☎031/303 6359), run one- and two-day trips, including rock climbing for beginners and advanced practitioners; rapp jumping (extreme abseiling); sky diving; boulder clambering; hunting; and splat ball.

ZULU CRAFTS AND CURIOS

Durban's huge range of galleries, craft shops and markets make it one of the best centres in the country to pick up **Zulu crafts**. Traditional works include a range of functional items, such as woven beer strainers, grass brooms and basketry that can be extremely beautiful when well-crafted. Other traditional items are beadwork, pottery and Zulu regalia, of which *assegais* (spears), shields, leather kilts and drums are a few examples. However, drastic social changes in South Africa over the last century have affected the Zulus along with every other South African – black and white. The availability of cheap plastic crockery and enamelware has significantly eroded the time-consuming production of traditional ceramics and woven containers for domestic use. Instead, these personal household items are now frequently churned out en masse for sale to curio hunters who are indifferent to the authenticity or quality of what they are buying.

Fortunately the news isn't all bad and, although urbanization has stifled the production of much traditional craft, it has thrown up creative adaptations making use of new materials, or old materials used in new ways. Among these are beautifully decorated black and white **sandals** made from recycled rubber tyres, wildly colourful **baskets** woven from telephone wire and *sjamboks* (whips) decorated with bright insulation tape. On the more frivolous side are a whole genre of affordable curios that break away from the stereotypes of tribal woodcarvings and masks, and marry industrial materials with rural life or rural materials with industrial life. Attractive tin boxes made from flattened oil cans, chickens constructed from sheet plastic, and aircraft and little 4WD vehicles carved from wood are some of the results.

If you're serious about buying something really good, there is an entire movement of **master craftspeople** drawing on traditional forms to produce objects of the highest quality, many of which are sought after by art collectors. Among these many excellent craftworkers are woodcarver Vuminkosi Zulu; scrap-metal car sculptor Nkosinathi Gumede and potter Nesta Nala – track them down through the Natal Society of Arts shop in the Berea (see p.381).

Shopping

As one of South Africa's major cities, Durban is a good centre to pick up general supplies and local books and records. But it's for **crafts and curios** that it scores particularly highly, being the largest city in KwaZulu-Natal, home turf to the Zulus, who produce a dazzling range of handmade goods (see box above). The best places to browse for crafts are in the downtown markets, the weekend flea markets and the specialist shops around the city.

Books and music

Adams & Co, 341 West St (☎031/304 8571). In the city centre, this is Durban's oldest book store, and has an excellent selection of books on the history of Durban and KwaZulu-Natal.

Exclusive Books, Lower Level, Pavilion Shopping Centre (☎031/265 0454). Durban's flashiest general book store, where browsers are welcome to pore over titillating coffee-table books. Closes 11pm Sat.

Ike's Bookshop, Boulevard Level, Overport City, corner of Sydenham and Ridge roads (☎031/208 2565). Tiny second-hand bookshop, with an interesting range of items covering KwaZulu-Natal's history and the fauna and flora of the area.

Look and Listen, Lower Level, Pavilion Shopping Centre (☎031/265 0826). Durban's best-stocked music shop, with a comprehensive range of indigenous music from the whole continent, including local favourites such as Ladysmith Black Mambazo and Hugh Masekela.

Crafts and curios

African Art Centre, 160 Pine St, Old Durban Station, 1st floor (☎031/304 7915). A gallery and shop well worth visiting for its traditional and modern Zulu and Xhosa beadwork, beaded dolls, wire sculptures, woodcuts and tapestries.

The Bat Shop, The BAT Centre, Harbourside, off Victoria Embankment (☎031/332 9951). Contemporary works with an excellent collection by African artists, in a bright and colourful venue with masterful wireworks and robust ceramics. Closes 4pm Sat.

Deco Jazz, 515 Currie Rd, Berea (☎031/203 3968). Eco-friendly, animal-skin-inspired prints on rich cotton fabrics, and a range of functional accessories direct from the studio. Leopard, zebra and giraffe motifs add up to a cacophony of colours, stripes, dots and spots.

NSA Gallery Shop, NSA Gallery, Bulwer Rd, Berea. In a gallery building, this menagerie of hand-crafted goods includes a wonderful selection of functional art, including pewter cutlery, etchings and paintings.

Tourist Junction Shop, 160 Pine St (☎031/304 7915). Quality African artefacts, from Zulu basketwork to tribal masks and weaving.

The Workshop Mall, corner of Commercial and Aliwal streets. In part of the old station building, this is the city centre's largest shopping mall, and is a handy place to shop for gifts, souvenirs and curios.

Fleamarkets

South Plaza Market, Durban Exhibition Centre, Walnut Rd, City (☎031/301 9900). Over 500 indoor and outdoor stalls. Sun.

Farepark Market, corner West and Farewell streets (☎031/368 2190). Permanent stalls in rustic cabins. Daily.

Essenwood Fleamarket, Berea Park, Essenwood Rd. Upmarket stalls, in beautiful park setting, on the Berea. Sat.

Listings

Airlines British Airways/Comair (☎031/303 5885); South African Airways (☎031/250 1111); SA Airlink (☎031/450 3388).

Banks First National Bank, 32 West St, Marine Parade (☎031/337 9464), has extended hours for changing foreign currency. Mon–Fri 9am–7pm, Sat 8.30am–6pm, Sun 10am–3pm.

American Express 350 Smith Street (☎031/301 5551). Mon–Fri 8.30am–4.30pm, Sat 8.30am–noon.

Bicycle rental Cycle-Logic, 34 Cato St (☎031/332 2955).

Camera repairs Camera Clinic, Shop 4, Standard Bank Centre, 135 Musgrave Road (☎031/202 5396). Repairs and services of all photographic and video equipment.

Car parks The most convenient central ones are at Pine Arcade, at the west end of Pine St, and in The Workshop Mall, on the corner of Commercial Rd and Aliwal St.

Car rental Avis (toll-free ☎0800/02 11 11); Berea (☎toll-free 0800/33 38 11); Budget (toll-free ☎0800/01 66 22); Europcar (toll-free ☎0800/01 13 44); Imperial (toll-free ☎0800/13 10 00); Rent & Drive (☎031/332 2803); Tempest (toll-free 0800/03 16 66); and Windermere (☎031/312 0339). Berea also rent minibuses, and camper-vans are available from Britz Africa (☎031/72 9326) or the considerably cheaper Bobo Campers (☎031/464 8633).

Consulates UK, 19th Floor, Marine Building, 22 Gardiner St (☎031/305 2929); USA, Durban Bay House, 333 Smith St (☎031/304 4737).

Emergencies Ambulance ☎10177; Fire ☎031/361 0000; Police (Flying Squad) ☎10111; Rape Crisis ☎031/312 2323.

Hospitals The main state hospital is the central Addington, Erskine Terrace, South Beach (☎031/332 2111), which offers a cheap 24hr emergency ward, but the level of care cannot be guaranteed. A preferable alternative is Entabeni Private Hospital, 148 South Ridge Rd, Berea (☎031/204 1300), which has a casualty unit and can also treat minor conditions, but where you will have to pay a deposit on admission and settle up before leaving town. A convenient option is South Beach Medical Centre, Rutherford St (☎031/332 3101, 24hr), which has a pharmacy, doctors, an optician, a dentist, a physiotherapist, as well as aromatherapy, reflexology and homeopathy.

Laundries Musgrave Laundromat, 2nd Level, Musgrave Centre (☎031/201 1936), and Econ-O-Wash, Ground Floor, Berea Centre, Berea Rd (☎031/201 0834) are both convenient for the Berea. Mont Blanc Laundromat, 54 Gillespie St, is within walking distance of the beach.

Left luggage Durban Station has inexpensive left-luggage facilities on the first floor (daily 6am–6pm).

Pharmacies Medicine Chest, 155 Berea Rd, Berea (daily 8am–midnight; ☎031/305 6151); Daynite Pharmacy, corner of West St and Point Rd (daily 7.30am–11pm; ☎031/368 3666), which does free deliveries; and Mediquick Pharmacy, 98 Overport Drive, outside Overport City Shopping Centre, Berea (8am–10pm; ☎031/209 3456), which delivers anywhere in town for a nominal charge.

Post office Main branch, corner of Gardiner and West streets, has a poste restante and enquiry desk. Mon–Fri 8.30am–4.30pm, Sat 8.30–11.30am.

Taxis Aussies (☎031/337 4232); Eagle (☎031/368 1706); Swift (☎031/332 5569); Zippy (☎031/202 7067).

AROUND DURBAN

The **North** or **South coasts** around Durban make an obvious and easy day/weekend trip out of the city if you want quieter beaches. The coast around Durban, with its easy access to Johannesburg, warmest waters in the country and decidedly tropical feel, has primarily been developed for white South African families on holiday. It's not at all unpleasant, or even remotely congested like, say, the Mediterranean – there are kilometres of sandy beaches backed by wild banana trees, and the chance to spot dolphins, especially along the North Coast – but in a country with so many spectacular landscapes and wild places to visit, its blandness pales by comparison.

The South Coast draws diving enthusiasts to **Aliwal Shoal**, one of the country's top dive spots near Umkomaas, and is also notable for two nature reserves in the south: Oribi Gorge, inland from Port Shepstone, where you can overnight or visit by steam train; and Umtamvuna, inland from Port Edward, best visited to do day-walks along the Umtamvuna River.

Unless you're travelling to or from the Eastern Cape, the North Coast is preferable to the South Coast – it's a lot less built-up and tacky. **Umhlanga Rocks**, an upmarket resort less than half an hour's drive from Durban on the N2, offers beach walks, as well as great places to have a drink or meal, and gaze at the sea, and indeed is an alternative to staying in Durban itself. Further up the coast are a string of resorts which get more low-key the further north you go, all with sandy beaches and large tidal rock pools to swim in. Inland is sugar cane country, with a couple of upmarket guesthouses living up to the colonial-style grandeur of the early sugar barons. The old road north, the **R102**, which takes an inland route, is far more interesting than the coastal road, giving access to visiting Indian temples at **Tongaat**, the grave of one of the ANC's best-loved leaders, Albert Luthuli, at **Groutville**, and the Shaka memorial and museum, as well as the bustling Indian and African markets, at **Dukuza**.

Heading 80km northwest from Durban is **Pietermaritzburg**, the provincial capital, with an excellent art gallery and some interesting red-brick Victorian architecture combining with a vibrant mix of Zulu and Indian culture. Sampling Pietermaritzburg can be combined with the all-time favourite day-trip out of Durban – the **Valley of a Thousand Hills** – visitable by driving along the Old Main Road (R103) towards Pietermaritzburg. The outing to heady viewpoints of the folded hills amounts to taking in some great scenery and stopping for snacks or pub lunches along the way, or doing a bit of Zulu craft shopping.

Beyond Pietermaritzburg, and definitely more of a weekend stay than a day-trip, are the Natal **Midlands**, with appealing Drakensberg foothill scenery, trout fishing, numerous craft shops, and a number of hotels, guesthouses and cottages catering especially for the weekend trade. Although it's very pretty, the area is probably best experienced through the windows of your vehicle, as you head towards the real reward of the region, the stunningly beautiful Drakensberg Mountains.

Valley of a Thousand Hills

The evocatively named **Valley of a Thousand Hills**, 45km from Durban, makes for a picturesque drive along the edge of densely folded hills where Zulu people still live in traditional homesteads, and which visitors rarely venture into. The spectacular land-

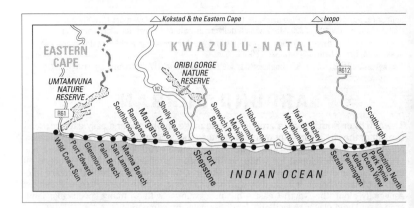

scape goes some way to soothing any misgivings you might have about ethnographic "game viewing", but it's only worth a special effort if you're not exploring the KwaZulu-Natal interior, where scenes like this occur in abundance. The trip to the valley and back can be easily done in half a day, and there are sufficient attractions laid on along the route to extend it to a full day's outing.

To reach the valley **by car**, head inland from Durban along the N3, following the Pinetown signs. At the Hillcrest/Old Main Road turn-off, turn right over the freeway onto the Old Main Road (R103) and continue along here to follow the scenic valley route. Pass the Fainting Goat Centre, and you'll soon reach **Phezulu Safari Park**, an African curio shop and a focal point of the drive. Here you'll find a reconstruction of a pre-colonial Zulu village, where you can watch touristy, but nonetheless spirited displays of **Zulu dancing** (daily 10am, 11.30am, 1.30pm & 3.30pm), set against the dramatic horizon of the valley. Part of Phezulu's untamed Africa setup is the Safari Park (daily 9am–4.30pm), which brings you close to deadly serpents – though they're tucked away in cramped little glass boxes – and other penned animals. Give it a miss if you're heading onto the real game reserves, just a few hours away.

Follow the road for another 5km to the small settlement of **DRUMMOND** and the old-fashioned tin-roofed *Drummond Arms Restaurant & Pub*, (☎ & fax 0325/34201), good for tea and scones, pub **lunches**, as well as its Sunday carvery, all accompanied by breathtaking views. The building is distinguishable by its bright green roof.

If you don't have your own transport, you can join one of the daily **tours** of the Valley offered by Tekweni Eco Tours in Durban (see p.371). Alternatively, take a vintage **train trip** with Umgeni Steam Railways (☎031/702 6734), which boasts one of the largest collections of historic locomotives and coaches in the southern hemisphere. From Durban, regular runs go to the Valley of a Thousand Hills; if you're a steam-head, it's also worth finding out about their get-togethers for train buffs.

The South Coast

The **South Coast**, the 160-kilometre seaboard from Durban to Port Edward on the Eastern Cape border, feels like a ribbon of seaside suburbs; thousands of families from the interior have jostled to build holiday homes along what is the closest stretch of sand to Johannesburg. But with truly exceptional beaches in northern Zululand and not far away in the Eastern Cape, it's difficult to justify coming to the South Coast unless you're travelling through KwaZulu-Natal and want to stay at the beach outside Durban. This

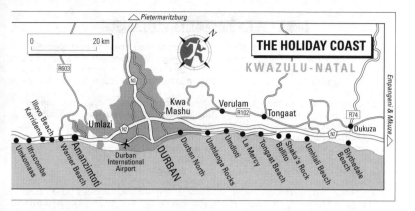

may be especially tempting in the winter months when it's much warmer and sunnier along this stretch than anywhere else in the country.

South Coast beaches are sandy and backed by luxuriant wild banana trees wedged between the holiday developments. Many shelve steeply into the powerful surf – so you need to restrict swimming to where it's indicated as safe. Away from the sea, the land is very hilly and green, dotted with sugar cane fields, banana plantations and palm and pecan nut trees. Gardens are bright with exuberant flowering trees and shrubs, and in some places alive with monkeys.

Transport from Durban and Johannesburg to the South Coast is good (see overleaf) and there are plenty of caravan parks next to the beaches, a couple of backpackers' lodges and a good number of mid-priced places to stay. **Margate**, 133km from Durban, is the transport and holiday hub of the area, with plenty of resorts lying to the east and west of it. **Port Shepstone**, 117km south of Durban, is the grim industrial and administrative centre along the coast, while **Oribi Gorge Nature Reserve**, just 21km inland from Port Shepstone, has lovely forest hikes and good-value accommodation.

Amanzimtoti, Warner Beach and Umkomaas

Some 27km south of Durban and just minutes from Durban Airport, **AMANZIM-TOTI** (Zulu for "sweet waters") earned its name, according to tradition, because it was here that King Shaka slaked his thirst, in the river that took the same name. Toti, as the resort is known to locals, is the largest town along the upper South Coast, yet feels more like a beachside suburb than a place in its own right. Outside weekends and school holidays – when its high-rise holiday developments are full to bursting point – it's worth coming here for a day's swimming and lounging on Nyoni Rocks beach.

If you're looking for somewhere to **stay**, however, **WARNER BEACH**, 3km further south, is the place to head for. Far less developed than Amanzimtoti, Warner Beach offers some excellent surfing spots, as well as good swimming and a large tidal pool that's safe for children. Overlooking the beach, *Angle Rock Backpackers*, 5 Ellcock Rd (☎031/916 7007, fax 916 7006, *anglerock@iafrica.com*), is a cut above the average **hostel**, with a swimming pool, four dorms (①) and three doubles (②) – all en suite with marble bathtubs. The atmosphere is supremely relaxed, and you may end up staying longer than you planned. The lodge offers free use of surfboards and canoes. Warner Beach has a handful of decent pubs and **restaurants**: *The Reef*, Kingsway, is good, and offers discounts to *Angle Rock* guests.

Roughly 16km further down the coast, **UMKOMAAS**, a faded town of buildings with corrugated-iron roofs, exudes an atmosphere that is more laid back still. Perched on a headland with outstanding views across the sea, this is essentially a retirement village with beaches that are periodically discoloured by effluent washing down the Mkomazi River from the Saiccor cellulose mill, just upriver. For **diving** enthusiasts, Umkomaas is the perfect point to set out for **Aliwal Shoal**, a scattered reef quite close to the shore and one of southern Africa's top dive sites. On the beachfront, the Whaler Dive Centre, Roland Norris Drive (☎039/973 1562, fax 973 1564; ③), offers a wide range of diving activities with self-catering **accommodation**. If you prefer other people to do the cooking, notify them beforehand and they can arrange breakfasts at the restaurant next door. Their Open Water diving course leads to an internationally recognized certificate and costs around R1000 (excluding accommodation). The best time to dive is between May and September, when visibility is at its best. Rewards for experienced divers include sightings of whale sharks, ragged-tooth sharks, potato bass, manta rays and eels, as well as shoals of tropical fish, corals and anemones.

Scottburgh to Port Shepstone

A further 9km south brings you to **SCOTTBURGH**, the oldest town along the South Coast and one of the most appealing because of its sheltered and lawn-covered beach fringes. The *Cutty Sark*, on the beachfront (☎039/976 1230; ③), offers reasonable hotel **accommodation**, while camping and self-catering are available at the nearby *Scottburgh Caravan Park* (☎039/976 0291, fax 976 2148; ①–②), on the seafront and a short walk from the shops. The park is huge, and during school breaks you're likely to be swamped by family holiday makers, but outside these periods it's less hectic.

One of the few **backpackers' lodges** on the South Coast is *Club Tropicana Youth Sanctuary,* PO Box 359, Annerley 4230 (☎039/681 3547, fax 682 6022, *roy1@iafrica.com*; ①), some 51km south of Scottburgh. Signposted off the N2, it's 12km beyond **Hibberdene** on a farm that's a couple of kilometres inland from attractive **Banana Beach**. Unlike the Durban backpackers' lodges, there's no party scene here, but the lodge does offer access to rural Zulu areas where you can meet people on more equal terms, rather than in the artificial environment of a theme-park Zulu village set up for tourists. The owners have good contacts with local chiefs, diviners and people practising traditional medicine, and are also involved in small-scale farming projects in areas dev-astated by apartheid and, more recently, the fighting between Inkatha and the ANC. Accommodation at the base camp at the main farm is in basic dorms and doubles (both ①), cheap evening meals are available and there are facilities for self-catering. But the real action takes place at **satellite camps** in a number of surrounding villages, where trained Zulu guides take guests through their paces, milking cows, herding cattle, shooting with slings, or carrying pails of water with the women. At night you'll be enter-tained by tales around the camp fire. It's an engaging way to learn about rural KwaZulu-Natal life, although there's no pressure to take part in any of the more socially minded activities; if you wish you can simply hang out and spend your days on Banana Beach. The Baz **bus** delivers you right to the doorstep of *Club Tropicana*, while the Margate Mini Coach takes passengers from Durban and drops them off a short walk away.

At the first set of traffic lights after Hibberdene you'll be in **Umtentweni**, where there's another backpacking set-up, *The Spot*, Ambleside Rd (☎039/695 1318) From here you just cross the lawn and you're right on the beach. The lodge has a dorm sleep-ing fifteen (①), plus doubles (②), or you can camp. Amenities include a bar and they rent out surfboards and fishing rods. Nearby you can charter boats to take you dolphin-and (in season) whale-watching, and can arrange abseiling at Oribi Gorge.

One unremarkable resort after another follows the shoreline from Hibberdene to grit-ty, sprawling **PORT SHEPSTONE**, a dismal place where you won't want to linger for long, although there are a couple of reasonable **beaches** just south of the town centre, and it's the gateway to the nearby Oribi Gorge Nature Reserve (see below). The town is also the place to hop on one of the *Banana Express* steam train journeys (see box below).

Oribi Gorge Nature Reserve

Twenty-one kilometres inland from Port Shepstone is **Oribi Gorge Nature Reserve** (8am–4.30pm; R8), the South Coast's most compelling attraction: a compact and high-ly scenic area of cliffs rising from vast chasms and jungly forest traversed by the fast-flowing Umzimkulu and Umzimkulwana rivers.

A circular scenic drive descends from the rest camp into the Umzimkulu Valley, where a picnic site sits on the riverbank. Here the road winds upward again through thick forest before leaving the park and skirting north past the *Oribi Gorge Hotel* turn-off and then back to the reserve. There are numerous other idyllic picnic spots on the riverbanks (don't swim here as bilharzia parasites are present in the water) and way-marked **hikes** ranging from thirty-minute to day-long excursions leading to dizzying look-out points or through the forest (the reserve office can provide hiking maps). A fine one-hour **walk** starts from the Umzimkulu car park and picnic site, crosses the river and heads immediately up some steps into the forest. You can hear the river through the dense vegetation, but you'll only see it when it opens out quite dramatical-ly to reveal **Samango Falls** and a perfect little rock-bounded sandy beach.

THE BANANA EXPRESS

A steam **train**, the *Banana Express*, Princess Elizabeth Drive, Port Shepstone (☎039/682 4821), chugs from Port Shepstone to the hamlet of Paddock along a scenic narrow-gauge railway three times a week. On the outward stretch it's a ninety-minute journey along the coastline and inland through banana groves and sugar-cane plantations, and costs R24 in tourist class and R36 in first (recommended). The whole journey, which includes a 550-metre climb through green hills dotted with traditional Zulu villages, costs R80, and lasts six hours (departs Wed & Fri at 10am). A shorter trip to the village of Iztosha, lasts nine-ty minutes altogether (departs Thurs 11am).

Wildlife in the reserve includes bushbuck, common reedbuck, blue and grey duiker, but not oribi, which have left for the succulent shoots of the surrounding sugar cane plantations. You're more likely to hear than to see the shy samango monkeys, hiding in the high canopy of the forest, and although leopards are present it's probable that they'll see you before you catch sight of them.

Practicalities

Travelling **by car** to Durban from the Eastern Cape along the N2, you'll find the reserve just a few hundred metres off the main road. You can also get here by **steam train** from Port Shepstone on the *Banana Express* (see box on previous page), though this is more of an excursion than a convenient means of transport.

The nicest **accommodation** is in the KwaZulu-Natal Conservation Services huts (②) in the rest camp at the head of the Umzimkulwana Gorge, peering into the chasm of Oribi Gorge itself. There's a swimming pool here, and all crockery, cutlery and bedding is provided. A camp chef is available to cook meals if you bring your own ingredients. For **booking** ahead, and this is recommended, contact the Conservation Services (see p.365). Alternatively, you can stay in the old-fashioned, colonial-style *Oribi Gorge* (☎039/687 0253, *jeffery@iafrica*; ③), a **hotel** some 16km from the rest camp, off the Oribi Flats road, which offers good-value rooms, meals to suit most budgets and a pleasant outdoor tea area. From here you can arrange to tackle the world's highest commercial abseiling (110m), whitewater rafting, scuba diving, deep-sea fishing, plane flips through the gorge, hiking trails, and bird-watching.

The Hibiscus Coast

The 44km of coast from Port Shepstone to Port Edward has been dubbed the **Hibiscus Coast** because of its luscious, bright gardens, luxury suburbs, beachside developments and attractive caravan parks. Although the whole area, the centre of which is at Margate, is built-up, the Hibiscus Coast gets nicer the further south you go, escaping the development.

Uvongo

Some 12km south of Port Shepstone, **UVONGO** is where the Vungu River narrows into a gorge and crashes down a **waterfall** before opening out onto a broad sandy beach. The waterfall is definitely the town's biggest attraction; elsewhere, tatty cliff-top developments have destroyed much of the natural vegetation. To see the falls, take the path from the bottom of the cliffs to the rear of the beach and follow the steps in the corner away from the river, following it through some undergrowth until you reach the viewpoint on a ledge. Uvongo's pleasant beach is the site of a daily market where Zulu women sell fruit, crafts and good-quality basketwork.

One of the most comfortable **places to stay** is *Glyndale Guest Lodge*, just east of the beach (☎039/315 0918; ③), with a good full-board rate outside school holidays and nice gardens, a swimming pool and an excellent sea view. Nearby, the *Uvongo Beach Lodge*, Pioneer Rd (☎039/315 0013, fax 315 1748; half board; ④), is a bit old-fashioned and gloomy, but it's very cheap and is only a ten-minute stroll from the beach. If you're after a cottage for a weekend or short break, contact the Holiday Cottage Accommodation Bureau, PO Box 151, Uvongo 4270 (☎039/315 0423).

The best **place to eat** is the *Pavilion*, a restaurant right on the beach with a curving glazed frontage looking out to sea.

Margate

The brash, built-up holiday town of **MARGATE**, 12km south of Uvongo, is the South Coast's undisputed tourism hub. Connected by daily direct SAA **flights** with

Johannesburg and by **buses** with Gauteng and Durban (see p.394), Margate is as far as you'll get down the South Coast using public transport and has become a last bastion for white holiday-makers retreating from the beaches closer to Durban. A cacophony of high-rise apartments, fast-food outlets, and ice-cream parlours, it doesn't offer much in the way of undiscovered coves or hidden beaches, but its big plus point is that out of peak season you'll find a wide choice of good-value places to stay.

It's worth making use of Margate's **tourist information bureau** on the beachfront (Mon–Fri 8.30am–4pm, Sat 9–11am; ☎039/312 2322), which can provide details of accommodation and general information about the whole South Coast area. Without a car, you'll find getting around the town easy enough using **tuk tuks**, which must be booked in advance (☎083/272 9593).

Accommodation includes *Margate Backpackers*, 14 Collis St, Manaba Beach (☎039/312 2176, fax 312 2048), which is almost on the beach and only 200m from a great tidal pool. There are dorms (①), doubles (②) and camping (①), and the hostel has a big self-catering kitchen, a pool table and pinball machines. A budget alternative is the *De Wet Caravan Park*, St Andrews Ave, along the beachfront (☎039/312 1022; ②), where you'll find fully equipped two-berth caravans and grassy campsites. A little more expensive, but closer to the centre, is *Skipper's*, Lagoon Rd (☎039/315 1223, fax 315 1231; ③), an old-fashioned, but clean and well-maintained boarding house popular with backpackers and South African families, overlooking the beach amusement park. Also excellent value is the more comfortable *Suntide*, Duke Rd (☎039/317 4010; ②–③), a hotel with modern self-catering apartments in a quiet stretch right on the beach. The only drawback is that most doubles face onto the car park; you're best off paying a little extra and, even if there's only two of you, taking a larger, sea-facing four-bedder. The very comfortable *Margate*, Marine Drive (☎039/312 1410, fax 317 3318; ④), is near the centre of town, right on the beach and often offers discounts.

Southbroom, Palm Beach and Port Edward

Some 11km beyond Margate, **SOUTHBROOM** is known disparagingly as "Houghton-by-Sea" after Johannesburg's wealthiest suburb, which allegedly relocates here en masse in December. The town is predominantly a sumptuous development of large holiday houses set in expansive gardens that, out of season, can feel quite deserted. Huge dunes covered by lush vegetation sweep down to the sea and there are good long walks along the shore although heading out alone isn't advisable along this coastline for safety reasons. The best place for swimming is **Marina Beach**, 3km south of Southbroom Beach. Southbroom is home to the area's most upmarket **hotel**, the tranquil *Country Lodge*, signposted off the R61 to Port Edward (☎039/316 8380, fax 316 8557; ⑤), a romantically secluded place surrounded by forest, away from the beachfront buzz.

Heading closer to Port Edward, which marks the border with the Eastern Cape, you'll soon get to one of the quietest spots along the South Coast: **PALM BEACH**, a rocky beach bordered with banana palms with a tidal pool for swimming.

The main attraction of **PORT EDWARD**, 9km further on, is its proximity to the Umtamvuna Nature Reserve (see overleaf). Nevertheless, it's a fairly relaxed and pleasant resort, with some nice sandy beaches. There are some some good **places to stay** near the beach. *Windwood Lodge*, Owen Ellis Drive (☎039/313 2169, *woodldg@iafrica.com*; ③), is a smart, family-oriented guesthouse some 500m from the seafront. If you can handle the institutionalized flavour, the *Port Edward Holiday Resort*, Owen Ellis Drive (☎039/313 2333, fax 313 2296; ②), which is mainly used by the South African Police Service for rest and recreation for their staff, has a perfect setting along the seafront and is close to the swimming beach, with cheap caravans, camping, rondavels and chalets ideal for families. Facilities are available for handicapped visitors.

Moving west from Port Edward, the only **public transport** is the minibus taxis that form a lively rank on the R61 just outside town, collecting passengers for the Eastern

Cape, many heading across the old Transkei border to gamble at the *Wild Coast Sun* casino (see p.361).

Umtamvuna Nature Reserve

Some of the best nature walks in the whole of KwaZulu-Natal are to be found at the **Umtamvuna Nature Reserve** (daily: April–Aug 7am–5pm; Sept–March 6am–6pm; small entry fee), about 8km north of Port Edward. Extending 19km upriver along the tropical Umtamvuna River and the forested cliffs rising above it, the reserve is well known for its spring flowers, and the sunbirds and sugar birds feeding on the nectar. Also here is a famous colony of rare Cape **vultures**, though to see where they nest you'll have to be prepared for a whole day's walk. Waymarked paths are dotted throughout the reserve.

Umtamvuna is off the R61 to Izingolweni, signposted near Port Edward. If you want to **stay** overnight, head for one of the pleasant options nearby. *Umtamvuna River Lodge*, Old Pont Rd (☎039/313 2313, *riverlodge@iafrica.com*; ③), has ten good B&B rooms set amidst tranquil forested surroundings on the banks of the river, inside the reserve, which is home to three hundred species of birds; water-skiing is available, and there are nature trails. *Old Pont Holiday Resort*, Old Pont Rd, Banners Rest (☎039/313 2211, fax 313 2033; ②), is also on the banks of the river, has a swimming pool and is a good spot for fishing, with canoes for rent if you want a paddle. Six- and four-berth caravans and camping are available, as well as six-person rondavels, and there's a café and a useful shop selling basics.

On the same street, and halfway between these two places, is the excellent *Old Ferry* **restaurant** (☎039/313 2410), which serves fine breakfasts, lunches, dinners and teas. You can sit upstairs on a thatched, open-air deck with fantastic views of the Umtamvuna River and enjoy tasty salads and reasonably priced main courses, including oxtail stew and vegetarian dishes.

North of Durban: the Dolphin Coast

The **Dolphin Coast** is the appealing name given to the eighty-kilometre stretch along the coast north of Durban, from Umhlanga Rocks to the mouth of the Tugela River. This narrow continental shelf combines with warm, shallow waters to create ideal conditions for attracting bottle-nosed dolphins all year round to feed. Though the chances of sighting a cetacean are fairly high, you'd be unwise to base a visit solely around the possibility.

Less tacky and developed than the South Coast, the North Coast attracts an upmarket breed of holidaymaker, especially to the main resorts of **Ballito** and **Salt Rock**. If an easy beachside holiday close to Durban is what you're after, **Umhlanga Rocks**, less than half an hour's drive from the centre of the city, and served by public transport, is the best choice. The beaches here are long, steep and sandy, backed by banana palms, with warm strong surf, and shark nets to protect swimmers.

Rolling in from the coast are hills of **sugar cane** plantations, the main industry of the area (it was barons who established the first holiday retreats along the coastline). Driving along the roads here you'll be competing with long transport trucks, which litter the tarmac with dry stalks and strands of cane.

The Dolphin Coast is still pretty well dominated by whites; the inland towns of **Verulam**, **Tongaat** and **Dukuza** have substantial Zulu and Indian populations, but their lack of facilities for travellers makes it hard to spend much time in them.

Umhlanga Rocks

UMHLANGA ROCKS, 20km from the centre of Durban, is a substantial settlement with a permanent population of around 50,000, which merges with the suburb of

Durban North, and makes a good day out from the city if you're after a beach walk, swim and a meal, or even an alternative place to stay. The town's main attraction is as a swish resort offering hotel-based holidays in its seven large (and numerous smaller) establishments. Apart from the pleasant, sandy **beach** dominated by a red-and-white lighthouse, the town's main focus is the shopping area along Chartwell Drive, where you'll find a collection of smart, well-stocked malls.

A couple of kilometres north of Umhlanga's centre, signposted off the N2, the **Natal Sharks Board**, Umhlanga Rocks Drive (☎031/566 1001; small entry fee), shows an intriguing, if slightly mawkish, multiscreen audiovisual (Mon noon, 1pm, 2pm & 3pm, Tues–Thurs 9am, noon, 1pm, 2pm & 3pm; Sun 2pm), which disabuses any notions of sharks as the hooligans of the oceans and plugs the work of the Board in maintaining Natal's shark nets. You can also see a dissection of one of the sharks that has recently fallen foul of the nets (Tues–Thurs 9am & 2pm; entry fee). Although these nets protect swimmers all along the coast, they are controversial: endangered turtles and dolphins also die in them, and by killing sharks the natural balance of the inshore ecosystem is affected. The Sharks Board is now investigating an electronic shark barrier that might improve the situation, while still ensuring safe swimming. Without your own transport, the best way to get to the Sharks Board is by one of the tuk tuks that rank outside the Umhlanga Publicity Association (see below).

Practicalities

The Sugar Coast Tourism Association, Chartwell Drive (Mon–Fri 8.30am–4.30pm; ☎031/561 4257), is a useful source for **maps and information** about attractions up the coast. Outside, you'll find the **tuk tuk** rank and the ticket kiosk and **bus** stop for the Umhlanga Express (☎031/561 2860), which runs five times every weekday to the Tourist Junction in central Durban.

The *Beverly Hills Sun*, Lighthouse Rd (☎031/561 2211, fax 561 3711; ⑨), is without doubt the flashiest **place to stay** but should be bypassed in favour of the *Oyster Box* (☎031/561 2233, fax 561 4072), on the opposite side of the road. The oldest hotel on the Dolphin Coast, it oozes a more established elegance for less than half the price, with a choice of rooms facing the sea (⑦) or less expensive ones that don't (⑤). The *Box* is also a great place for **tea or drinks**; you can sit on the outside terrace and gaze at the ocean. There are a few good-value, recommended **B&Bs** including *Sylvan Grove*, 49 Sylvan Grove (☎031/561 5137, fax 561 6698, *sylvangrove@mweb.co.za*; ③), which offers convenient transfers from Durban airport, and sleeps eight in en-suite rooms, with great breakfasts; and *Jessica's B&B*, 35 Portland Drive (☎ & fax 031/561 3369; ③), which can accommodate eight in two self-contained flats. *Honey Pot Cottage*, 11 Hilken Drive (☎031/561 3795, fax 561 2088, *sugarfld@iafrica.com*; ③), north of the M4, has B&B en-suite units for two, set in gardens with a swimming pool.

Among the surfeit of cheap fast-food outlets you'll find a handful of good **restaurants**, including *Cottonfields*, 2 Lagoon Drive, a popular local bistro and bar whose menu features *potjiekos* served in a small three-legged cast-iron pots. For recommended Greek food and exceptionally friendly staff, try *Ambrosia*, Chartwell Drive. If you can afford to splash out, look no further than *Razzmatazz*, at the *Umhlanga Sands Hotel*, Lagoon Drive. The restaurant has a great outdoor deck, and a prodigious reputation for its eclectic cuisine, which ranges from springbok fillets to Indonesian-style langoustines.

Umdloti, La Mercy and Tongaat

North of Umhlanga, the blur of development unexpectedly opens out into sugar cane hills and subtropical coastal vegetation. Plans for a big new international airport at La Mercy will certainly change this rural ambience, so get here while you can. **UMDLOTI**, just 6km north of Umhlanga, has a safe swimming beach, as well as a fabulous natural rock pool, great for swimming or snorkelling on the calm inside of the shallow reef. A couple of kilometres further along at **LA MERCY** is a recommended **restaurant** – the long-established *Sea Bell*, a slightly tatty curry house under a dingy hotel, which is noted for its piquant prawns (there's also a vegetarian alternative) and marvellous sea views, from where you can occasionally sight dolphins.

Tongaat Beach, 12km further up the coast, is monopolized by the slighly old-fashioned *Westbrook Beach* (π & fax 032/943 2021; ④), a **hotel** worth visiting for its **restaurant** with outdoor seating, casual atmosphere and superb wild oysters. The hotel also has its own wide beach and a swimming pool. A popular spot with **surfers** is the break at Westbrook Beach, just south of the parking area.

TONGAAT itself is a couple of kilometres inland from here across the N2 highway, a barrier between the coastal resorts and the gritty workings of Natal's sugar industry. Arriving in town you'll be confronted by a massive **sugar mill** pumping pungent white smoke from its towering chimneys, and people walking down the road chewing stalks of sugar cane. The town, fronted by neglected imitation Cape Dutch cottages, has long associations with South Africa's Indian community and boasts a handful of garish temples. The most distinguished of these is the small but awesome **Shri Jugganath Puri Temple**, off the main road, on the corner of Catherine and Plane streets. A whitewashed, phallic building tipped by deities on each corner, and surrounded by mango trees, the temple is dedicated to Vishnu and is a National Monument, built at the turn of the century by the Sanskrit scholar Pandit Shrikishan Maharaj who came to Natal in 1895. To get to the temple, take the R102 towards Durban, turn right into Ganie Street at the first traffic lights after the police station, then left into Plane Street and left again into Catherine Street.

Ballito and Shaka's Rock

There's nothing very African about **BALLITO**, a Mediterranean-style resort 43km up the coast from Durban, with a splurge of time-shares, high-rise holiday apartments and shopping malls by the sea. Nevertheless, it's a pleasant enough place, with a beach offering safe swimming and full-time lifeguards, and a couple of natural rock pools for bathing – one at Ballito itself, and the other at the far northern end of Ballito beach, near the Santorini development. The area is also well known for its luxury guest houses on wealthy sugar estates, set back from the coast and all signposted from the N1.

The excellent Dolphin Coast Publicity Association (π & fax 032/946 1997), just behind the BP service station as you enter town, has an up-to-date list of B&Bs and can supply **information** about the surrounding area. The cheapest **place to stay** is the central *Dolphin Coast Backpackers*, 10 Edward Place (π032/946 1644), in a massive house that accommodates twenty people in **dorms** (①) and an en-suite double (②), with space for many more camping in the garden (①). Situated on a good surfing and swimming beach, the hostel can help arrange boat charters for swimming with dolphins. *Dolphin Holiday Resort*, a well-shaded **campsite** (①) and collection of self-catering cottages (②) on the corner of Compensation Beach Road and Hillary Drive (π032/946 2187, fax 946 3490), has no sea view but is a five-minute walk from the beach. *Shorten's Country House*, Compensation Beach Rd (π032/946 1140, fax 946 1144, *sch@icon.co.za*; ⑦), a historic colonial homestead with fourteen luxury rooms surrounded by wonderful gardens, makes an elegant stay, while the swishest establishment in the vicinity is *Zimbali Lodge* (π032/538 1007, fax 538 1019, *info@sunint.co.za*; ⑨), 1km south of Ballito, set in lush subtropical coastal forest in the heart of a network of wetlands. Antelope are frequently seen, the butterflies, such as the citrus swallowtail, are larger than life, and the birdlife is prolific – you might even see the rare spotted narina trogon. Accommodation is in luxury suites attended by private butlers, and you can avail yourself of clay pigeon shooting,

THE WILDLIFE
OF EAST AND
SOUTHERN AFRICA

A ROUGH GUIDE

This field guide provides a quick reference to help you identify the larger mammals likely to be encountered in East and Southern Africa. It includes most species that are found throughout these regions, as well as a limited number whose range is more restricted. Straightforward photos show easily identified markings and features. The notes give you clear pointers about the kinds of **habitat** in which you are most likely to see each mammal; its daily rhythm (usually either **nocturnal or diurnal**); the kind of **social groups** it usually forms; and general **tips about sighting** it on safari, its rarity and its relations with humans.

⬕ HABITAT ◪ DIURNAL/NOCTURNAL ⬕ SOCIAL LIFE ☑ SIGHTING TIPS

Photographs © Bruce Coleman Picture Library. Text © Rough Guides, 1996.

Baboon *Papio cynocephalus*

◪ open country with trees and cliffs; adaptable, but always near water

◪ diurnal

◪ troops led by a dominant male

☑ common; several subspecies, including Yellow and Olive in East Africa and Chacma in Southern Africa; easily becomes used to humans, frequently a nuisance and occasionally dangerous

Eastern Black and White Colobus
Colobus guereza

◪ rainforest and well-watered savannah; almost entirely arboreal

◪ diurnal

◪ small troops

☑ troops maintain a limited home territory, so easily located, but can be hard to see at a great height; not found in Southern Africa

Patas Monkey *Erythrocebus patas*

◪ savannah and forest margins; tolerates some aridity; terrestrial except for sleeping and lookouts

◪ diurnal

◪ small troops

☑ widespread but infrequently seen; can run at high speed and stand on hind feet supported by tail; not found in Southern Africa

Vervet Monkey *Cercopithecus aethiops*

◪ most habitats except rainforest and arid lands; arboreal and terrestrial

◪ diurnal

◪ troops

☑ widespread and common; occasionally a nuisance where used to humans

P R I M A T E S

**White-throated or Sykes'
Monkey/Samango**
Cercopithecus mitis/albogularis
◼ forests; arboreal and occasionally
terrestrial
◼ diurnal
◼ families or small troops
☑ widespread; shyer and less easily
habituated to humans than the Vervet

Aardvark *Orycteropus afer*
◼ open or wooded termite country; softer
soil preferred
◼ nocturnal
◼ solitary
☑ rarely seen animal, the size of a small pig;
old burrows are common and often used
by warthogs

Spring Hare *Pedetes capensis*
◼ savannah; softer soil areas preferred
◼ nocturnal
◼ burrows, usually with a pair and their
young; often linked into a network,
almost like a colony
☑ fairly widespread rabbit-sized rodent;
impressive and unmistakable kangaroo-
like leaper

Crested Porcupine
Hystrix africae-australis
◼ adaptable to a wide range of habitats
◼ nocturnal and sometimes active at dusk
◼ family groups
☑ large rodent (up to 90cm in length),
rarely seen, but common away from
croplands, where it's hunted as a pest

PRIMATES – AARDVARK – RODENTS

Bat-eared Fox *Otocyon megalotis*
■ open country
■ mainly nocturnal; diurnal activity increases in cooler months
■ monogamous pairs
✔ distribution coincides with termites, their favoured diet; they spend many hours foraging using sensitive hearing to pinpoint their underground prey

Black-backed Jackal *Canis mesomelas*
■ broad range from moist mountain regions to desert, but drier areas preferred
■ normally nocturnal, but diurnal in the safety of game reserves
■ mostly monogamous pairs; sometimes family groups
✔ common; a bold scavenger, the size of a small dog, that steals even from lions; black saddle distinguishes it from the shyer Side-striped Jackal

Hunting Dog or Wild Dog
Lycaon pictus
■ open savannah in the vicinity of grazing herds
■ diurnal
■ nomadic packs
✔ extremely rare and rarely seen, but widely noted when in the area; the size of a large dog, with distinctively rounded ears

Honey Badger or Ratel
Mellivora capensis
■ very broad range of habitats
■ mainly nocturnal
■ usually solitary, but also found in pairs
✔ widespread, omnivorous, badger-sized animal; nowhere common; extremely aggressive

African Civet *Civettictis civetta*
◪ prefers woodland and dense vegetation
◪ mainly nocturnal
◪ solitary
☑ omnivorous, medium-dog-sized, short-legged prowler; not to be confused with the smaller genet

Common Genet *Genetta genetta*
◪ light bush country, even arid areas; partly arboreal
◪ nocturnal, but becomes active at dusk
◪ solitary
☑ quite common, slender, cat-sized omnivore, often seen at game lodges, where it easily becomes habituated to humans

Banded Mongoose *Mungos mungo*
◪ thick bush and dry forest
◪ diurnal
◪ lives in burrow colonies of up to thirty animals
☑ widespread and quite common, the size of a small cat; often seen in a group, hurriedly foraging through the undergrowth

Spotted Hyena *Crocuta crocuta*
◪ tolerates a wide variety of habitat, with the exception of dense forest
◪ nocturnal but also active at dusk; also diurnal in many parks
◪ highly social, usually living in extended family groups
☑ the size of a large dog with a distinctive loping gait, quite common in parks; carnivorous scavenger and cooperative hunter; dangerous

WEASEL RELATIVES - SPOTTED HYENA

Caracal *Caracal caracal*

◨ open bush and plains; occasionally arboreal

◨ mostly nocturnal

◨ solitary

☑ lynx-like wild cat; rather uncommon and rarely seen

Cheetah *Acionyx jubatus*

◨ savannah, in the vicinity of plains grazers

◨ diurnal

◨ solitary or temporary nuclear family groups

☑ widespread but low population; much slighter build than the leopard, and distinguished from it by a small head, square snout and dark "tear mark" running from eye to jowl

Leopard *Panthera pardus*

◨ highly adaptable; frequently arboreal

◨ nocturnal; also cooler daylight hours

◨ solitary

☑ the size of a very large dog; not uncommon, but shy and infrequently seen; rests in thick undergrowth or up trees; very dangerous

Lion *Panthera leo*

◨ all habitats except desert and thick forest

◨ nocturnal and diurnal

◨ prides of three to forty; more usually six to twelve

☑ commonly seen resting in shade; dangerous

CATS

Serval *Felis serval*

⊠ reed beds or tall grassland near water

⊠ normally nocturnal but more diurnal than most cats

⊠ usually solitary

☑ some resemblance to, but far smaller than, the cheetah; most likely to be seen on roadsides or water margins at dawn or dusk

Rock Hyrax or Dassie *Procavia capensis*

⊠ rocky areas, from mountains to isolated outcrops

⊠ diurnal

⊠ colonies consisting of a territorial male with as many as thirty related females

☑ rabbit-sized; very common; often seen sunning themselves in the early morning on rocks

African Elephant *Loxodonta africana*

⊠ wide range of habitats, wherever there are trees and water

⊠ nocturnal and diurnal; sleeps as little as four hours a day

⊠ almost human in its complexity; cows and offspring in herds headed by a matriarch; bulls solitary or in bachelor herds

☑ look out for fresh dung (football-sized) and recently damaged trees; frequently seen at waterholes from late afternoon

CATS - HYRAX - ELEPHANT

Black Rhinoceros *Diceros bicornis*
- ■ usually thick bush, altitudes up to 3500m
- ■ active day and night, resting between periods of activity
- ■ solitary
- ✔ extremely rare and in critical danger of extinction; largely confined to parks where most individuals are known to rangers; distinctive hooked lip for browsing; small head usually held high; bad eyesight; very dangerous

White Rhinoceros *Ceratotherium simum*
- ■ savannah
- ■ active day and night, resting between periods of activity
- ■ mother/s and calves, or small, same-sex herds of immature animals; old males solitary
- ✔ rare, restricted to parks; distinctive wide mouth (hence "white" from Afrikaans *wijd*) for grazing; large head usually lowered; docile

Burchell's Zebra *Equus burchelli*
- ■ savannah, with or without trees, up to 4500m
- ■ active day and night, resting intermittently
- ■ harems of several mares and foals led by a dominant stallion are usually grouped together, in herds of up to several thousand
- ✔ widespread and common inside and outside the parks; regional subspecies include *granti* (Grant's, East Africa) and *chapmani* (Chapman's, Southern Africa, right)

Grevy's Zebra *Equus grevyi*
- ■ arid regions
- ■ largely diurnal
- ■ mares with foals and stallions generally keep to separate troops; stallions sometimes solitary and territorial
- ✔ easily distinguished from smaller Burchell's Zebra by narrow stripes and very large ears; rare and localized but easily seen; not found in Southern Africa

Warthog *Phacochoerus aethiopicus*

⬛ savannah, up to an altitude of over 2000m

⬛ diurnal

⬛ family groups, usually of a female and her litter

☑ common; boars are distinguishable from sows by their prominent face "warts"

Hippopotamus *Hippopotamus amphibius*

⬛ slow-flowing rivers, dams and lakes

⬛ principally nocturnal, leaving the water to graze

⬛ bulls are solitary, but other animals live in family groups headed by a matriarch

☑ usually seen by day in water, with top of head and ears breaking the surface; frequently aggressive and very dangerous when threatened or when retreat to water is blocked

Giraffe *Giraffa camelopardalis*

⬛ wooded savannah and thorn country

⬛ diurnal

⬛ loose, non-territorial, leaderless herds

☑ common; many subspecies, of which Maasai (*G. c. tippelskirchi*, right), Reticulated (*G. c. reticulata*, bottom l.) and Rothschild's (*G. c. rothschildi*, bottom r.) are East African; markings of Southern African subspecies are intermediate between *tippelskirchi* and *rothschildi*

African or Cape Buffalo *Syncerus caffer*

■ wide range of habitats, always near water, up to altitudes of 4000m

■ nocturnal and diurnal, but inactive during the heat of the day

■ gregarious, with cows and calves in huge herds; young bulls often form small bachelor herds; old bulls are usually solitary

✔ very common; scent much more acute than other senses; very dangerous, old bulls especially so

Hartebeest *Alcelaphus buselaphus*

■ wide range of grassy habitats

■ diurnal

■ females and calves in small, wandering herds; territorial males solitary

✔ hard to confuse with any other antelope except the topi/tsessebe; many varieties, distinguishable by horn shape, including Coke's, Lichtenstein's, Jackson's (right), and Red or Cape; common, but much displaced by cattle grazing

Blue or White-bearded Wildebeest
Connochaetes taurinus

■ grasslands

■ diurnal, occasionally also nocturnal

■ intensely gregarious; wide variety of associations within mega-herds which may number over 100,000 animals

✔ unmistakable, nomadic grazer; long tail, mane and beard

Topi or Tsessebe *Damaliscus lunatus*

■ grasslands, showing a marked preference for moist savannah, near water

■ diurnal

■ females and young form herds with an old male

✔ widespread, very fast runners; male often stands sentry on an abandoned termite hill, actually marking the territory against rivals, rather than defending against predators

Gerenuk *Litocranius walleri*
◨ arid thorn country and semi-desert
◪ diurnal
◨ solitary or in small, territorial harems
☑ not uncommon; unmistakable giraffe-like neck; often browses standing upright on hind legs; the female is hornless; not found in Southern Africa

Grant's Gazelle *Gazella granti*
◨ wide grassy plains with good visibility, sometimes far from water
◪ diurnal
◨ small, territorial harems
☑ larger than the similar Thomson's Gazelle, distinguished from it by the white rump patch which extends onto the back; the female has smaller horns than the male; not found in Southern Africa

Springbok *Antidorcas marsupalis*
◨ arid plains
◪ seasonally variable, but usually cooler times of day
◨ highly gregarious, sometimes in thousands; various herding combinations of males, females and young
☑ medium-sized, delicately built gazelle; dark line through eye to mouth and lyre-shaped horns in both sexes; found only in Botswana, Namibia and South Africa

Thomson's Gazelle *Gazella thomsoni*
◨ flat, short-grass savannah, near water
◪ diurnal
◨ gregarious, in a wide variety of social structures, often massing in the hundreds with other grazing species
☑ smaller than the similar Grant's Gazelle, distinguished from it by the black band on flank; the female has tiny horns; not found in Southern Africa

Impala *Aepyceros melampus*

◩ open savannah near light woodland cover

◪ diurnal

◩ large herds of females overlap with several male territories; males highly territorial during the rut when they separate out breeding harems of up to twenty females

☑ common, medium-sized, no close relatives; distinctive high leaps when fleeing; the only antelope with a black tuft above the hooves; males have long, lyre-shaped horns

Red Lechwe *Kobus leche*

◪ floodplains and areas close to swampland

◪ nocturnal and diurnal

◩ herds of up to thirty females move through temporary ram territories; occasionally thousand-strong gatherings

☑ semi-aquatic antelope with distinctive angular rump; rams have large forward-pointing horns; not found in East Africa

Common Reedbuck *Redunca arundinum*

◩ reedbeds and tall grass near water

◪ nocturnal and diurnal

◩ monogamous pairs or family groups in territory defended by the male

☑ medium-sized antelope, with a plant diet unpalatable to other herbivores; only males have horns

Common or Defassa Waterbuck
Kobus ellipsiprymnus

◩ open woodland and savannah, near water

◪ nocturnal and diurnal

◩ territorial herds of females and young, led by dominant male, or territorial males visited by wandering female herds

☑ common, rather tame, large antelope; plant diet unpalatable to other herbivores; shaggy coat; only males have horns

IMPALA – REEDBUCKS – WATERBUCKS

Kirk's Dikdik *Rhincotragus kirki*

- scrub and thornbush, often far from water
- nocturnal and diurnal, with several sleeping periods
- pairs for life, often accompanied by current and previous young
- ✔ tiny, hare-sized antelope, named after its alarm cry; only males have horns; not found in Southern Africa except Namibia

Common Duiker *Sylvicapra grimmia*

- adaptable; prefers scrub and bush
- nocturnal and diurnal
- most commonly solitary; sometimes in pairs; occasionally monogamous
- ✔ widespread and common small antelope with a rounded back; seen close to cover; rams have short straight horns

Sitatunga *Tragelaphus spekei*

- swamps
- nocturnal and sometimes diurnal
- territorial and mostly solitary or in pairs
- ✔ very localized and not likely to be mistaken for anything else; usually seen half submerged; females have no horns

Nyala *Tragelaphus angasi*

- dense woodland near water
- primarily nocturnal with some diurnal activity
- flexible and non-territorial; the basic unit is a female and two offspring
- ✔ in size midway between the Kudu and Bushbuck, and easily mistaken for the latter; orange legs distinguish it; only males have horns; not found in East Africa

DWARF ANTELOPES – BUSHBUCK ANTELOPES

BUSHBUCK ANTELOPES

Bushbuck *Tragelaphus scriptus*

■ thick bush and woodland close to water

■ principally nocturnal, but also active during the day when cool

■ solitary, but casually sociable; sometimes grazes in small groups

✓ medium-sized antelope with white stripes and spots; often seen in thickets, or heard crashing through them; not to be confused with the far larger Nyala; the male has shortish straight horns

Eland *Taurotragus oryx*

■ highly adaptable; semi-desert to mountains, but prefers scrubby plains

■ nocturnal and diurnal

■ non-territorial herds of up to sixty with temporary gatherings of as many as a thousand

✓ common but shy; the largest and most powerful African antelope; both sexes have straight horns with a slight spiral

Greater Kudu *Tragelaphus strepsiceros*

■ semi-arid, hilly or undulating bush country; tolerant of drought

■ diurnal when secure; otherwise nocturnal

■ territorial; males usually solitary; females in small troops with young

✓ impressively big antelope (up to 1.5m at shoulder) with very long, spiral horns in the male; very localized; shy of humans and not often seen

Lesser Kudu *Tragelaphus imberbis*

■ semi-arid, hilly or undulating bush country; tolerant of drought

■ diurnal when secure; otherwise nocturnal

■ territorial; males usually solitary; females in small troops with young

✓ smaller than the Greater Kudu; only the male has horns; extremely shy and usually seen only as it disappears; not found in Southern Africa

Gemsbok *Oryx gazella gazella*

▣ open grasslands; also waterless wastelands; tolerant of prolonged drought

▣ nocturnal and diurnal

▣ highly hierarchical mixed herds of up to fifteen, led by a dominant bull

✔ large antelope with unmistakable horns in both sexes; subspecies *gazella* is one of several similar forms, sometimes considered separate species; not found in East Africa

Fringe-eared Oryx *Oryx gazella callotis*

▣ open grasslands; also waterless wastelands; tolerant of prolonged drought

▣ nocturnal and diurnal

▣ highly hierarchical mixed herds of up to fifteen, led by a dominant bull

✔ the *callotis* subspecies is one of two found in Kenya, the other, found in the northeast, being *Oryx g. beisa* (the Beisa Oryx); not found in Southern Africa

Roan Antelope *Hippotragus equinus*

▣ tall grassland near water

▣ nocturnal and diurnal; peak afternoon feeding

▣ small herds led by a dominant bull; herds of immature males; sometimes pairs in season

✔ large antelope, distinguished from the Sable by lighter, greyish colour, shorter horns (both sexes) and narrow, tufted ears

Sable Antelope *Hippotragus niger*

▣ open woodland with medium to tall grassland near water

▣ nocturnal and diurnal

▣ territorial; bulls divide into sub-territories, through which cows and young roam; herds of immature males; sometimes pairs in season

✔ large antelope; upper body dark brown to black; mask-like markings on the face; both sexes have huge curved horns

ORYXES – ROAN ANTELOPE – SABLE ANTELOPE

Grysbok *Raphicerus melanotis*

- ■ thicket adjacent to open grassland
- ■ nocturnal
- ■ rams territorial; loose pairings
- ☑ small, rarely seen antelope; two
  subspecies, Cape (*R. m. melanotis*, South
  Africa, right) and Sharpe's (*R. m. sharpei*,
  East Africa); distinguished from more
  slender Steenbok by light underparts;
  rams have short horns

Oribi *Ourebia ourebi*

- ■ open grassland
- ■ diurnal
- ■ territorial harems consisting of male and
  one to four females
- ☑ localized small antelope, but not hard to
  see where common; only males have
  horns; the Oribi is distinguished from the
  smaller Grysbok and Steenbok by a black
  tail and dark skin patch below the eye

Steenbok *Raphicerus campestris*

- ■ dry savannah
- ■ nocturnal and diurnal
- ■ solitary or (less often) in pairs
- ☑ widespread small antelope, particularly in
  Southern Africa, but shy; only males have
  horns

Klipspringer *Oreotragus oreotragus*

- ■ rocky country; cliffs and kopjes
- ■ diurnal
- ■ territorial ram with mate or small family
  group; often restricted to small long-term
  territories
- ☑ small antelope; horns normally only on
  male; extremely agile on rocky terrain;
  unusually high hooves, giving the
  impression of walking on tiptoe

beach or forest walks, steamrooms, massages, and pedicures. Even if the accommodation is beyond your budget, it's worth stopping off here for a meal in the **restaurant**, a cup of tea or, best of all, a sundowner in the bar, which is raised on stilts overlooking the fourteenth fairway of the golf course, and rewards you with soaring views across the Indian Ocean. In Ballito itself, the best place to eat is *Mariner's*, Ballito Shopping Centre, Compensation Beach Rd, which serves pricey but outstanding seafood.

Some 49km north of Durban, the rather tame coastal resort of **SHAKA'S ROCK** feels at odds with the name of Shaka, whose warrior reputation reverberated across southern Africa in the nineteenth century. More or less a continuation of Ballito, Shaka's Rock is dominated by the *Salt Rock*, Basil Hulett Drive (☎032/525 5025, fax 525 5071; ⑤), a **hotel** built and still run by the Huletts, one of the region's biggest sugar dynasties. The beach here is good for swimming, and guests can go on daily excursions diving with the dolphins. Adjoining the hotel is its **caravan park** (②), situated on grassy terraces. Two tidal pools, great for swimming, are built into the rocks below the hotel; this is where Zulu women are reputed to have collected salt in King Shaka's day. An even better tidal rock pool is at Thompson's Bay, built on an elevated rocky platform with changing rooms and big enough for anyone wanting to swim serious lengths. To get to Thompson's Bay, simply walk back along the beach, towards Ballito.

Dukuza and Groutville

You'll get far more of a sense of Shaka's legendary status as founder of the Zulu state by heading inland along the R102 to **DUKUZA** (still widely known by it's pre-1994 election name, Stanger), which has a special place in the cosmology of Zulu nationalists. Roughly 70km north of Durban, Dukuza is the site of the Zulu king's last *kraal* and the place where he was treacherously stabbed to death in 1828 by his half-brother Dingane, who succeeded him. Shaka used his exceptional military talents to build up the Zulu state into the greatest power in southeast Africa by the mid-1820s – creating disquiet even among the British with their mighty army. The warrior-king is said to have been buried upright in a grain pit, and is commemorated by a small park and **memorial** in Couper Street, bang in the centre of town. Near the memorial is a rock with a groove worn into it – supposedly where Shaka sharpened his spears. These days, the park is the venue for a semi-religious pilgrimage by modern-day **Zulu warriors** from all over the country – members of the fiercely Zulu nationalist Inkatha Freedom Party (IFP), which controls the province. Every year, on September 24, they gather here to be addressed by their leader, **Chief Mangosuthu Buthelezi**, a mercurial figure who started his political life as an ANC member, but later fell out with the organization and is now playing the Zulu nationalist card in his bid for provincial autonomy.

At the rear of the memorial park, the **Dukuza Interpretative Centre** (Mon–Fri 8am–4pm, Sat & Sun 9am–4pm; free) has a small display on Shaka and a very good fifteen-minute audiovisual display, as well as craftspeople at work and traditional meals. Nearby, the lively **Dukuza Market** in Market Road, off King George Road, is where Zulu and Indian traders sell fresh spices, herbs, fruit and vegetables, not for the benefit of tourists (you're unlikely to meet any here) but simply for local consumption.

Some 8km south of Dukuza on the R102, just across a rusty bridge over the Mvoti River, tiny **GROUTVILLE** is remarkable mainly for the grave of **Albert Luthuli**, one of South Africa's greatest political leaders. A teacher and chief of the Zulus in Groutville, Luthuli became President General of the ANC in 1952. He espoused a non-violent struggle against apartheid and was awarded the Nobel Peace prize in 1960, which at home earned him a succession of banning orders restricting him to the Dukuza area. In 1967 he died in mysterious circumstances in Dukuza, apparently knocked down by a train. The chief is buried next to a whitewashed, nineteenth-century corrugated-iron mission church. Luthuli's life is recounted in his moving autobiography, *Let My People Go*.

Blythedale and Zinkwazi

The closest stretch of sand to Dukuza is at **BLYTHEDALE**, some 8km away, where a ban on high-rise construction has preserved the deserted appearance of its endless **beach** and kept buildings screened behind the curtain of thick coastal vegetation. Swimming here is possible; shark nets are up between December and April and lifeguards on duty in season. As with many spots along the KwaZulu-Natal coast, you're likely to see local fishermen trying their luck for shad, garrick, kingfish and barracuda. There's **camping** and a small self-catering log cabin at *La Mouette Caravan Park*, 1 Umvoti Drive (☎032/551 2547; ①), just back from the beach, and **cottages** to rent at *Mini Villas* across the road (☎032/551 1277, fax 551 1628; ②). Slightly smarter cottages in a nicer setting are rented out by Mr Pelser at *Bush and Beach*, 71 Umvoti Drive (☎032/551 1496, fax 551 1546; ③–④). You'll also find reasonably priced **rooms** with en-suite showers at *Baroque B&B*, 14 Dolphin Crescent (☎032/551 5272; ③), 150m from the beach.

The northernmost and least-developed beach resort along the Dolphin Coast is **ZINKWAZI**, 13km beyond Blythedale, with mobile-home **chalets** (③) and **campsites** (①) set in lovely riverine gardens on the Zinkwazi River Estuary (☎032/485 3340, fax 485 3340). Boat trips along the river are recommended for bird-watching enthusiasts.

Harold Johnson Nature Reserve

Abutting the Tugela River is the **Harold Johnson Nature Reserve** (daily dawn–dusk; entry fee), signposted 24km north of Dukuza off the N2. With its well-preserved coastal bush, steep cliffs and gullies, this is a fine place to come for a day's visit or an overnight **camp** (☎032/486 1574; ①); it's possible to simply turn up, but there are no shops or facilities, so be sure to stock up in Dukuza beforehand. At the main picnic site and parking area, you'll find a cultural **museum** housed in huts and featuring good displays of Zulu beadwork and aspects of Zulu society. You can follow the two-kilometre "Remedies and Rituals" **trail**, which starts from the picnic site and takes you through plants whose medicinal uses you can read about. Alternatively, pick up the *Thukela Trail* booklet and follow a walk which highlights various historical sites in the reserve, most of them connected to the Anglo-Zulu War of 1879 and Ultimatum Tree. This wild fig tree, all but demolished in a cyclone in 1987, was where the British issued their ultimatum to King Cetshwayo in 1878, part of which required the Zulus to demobilize their standing army. The British used his non-compliance as an excuse to attack the Zulus and crush their independence. The remains of Fort Pearson, from which the British launched out to invade Zululand, are also on the trail.

Pietermaritzburg

Although **PIETERMARITZBURG** (often called Maritzburg) sells itself as the best-preserved Victorian city in South Africa, with strong British connections, not that much of its colonial heritage remains, and it's actually a very South African city. **Zulus** make up the largest community, with people of **Indian** descent coming second, and those of **British** extraction a minority – albeit a high-profile one. This multiculturalism, together with a substantial student population, add up to a fairly lively city that's also relatively safe and small enough to explore on foot.

Only 80km inland from Durban along the fast N3 freeway, Pietermaritzburg is an easy day's outing from the coastal city, and one you can do taking in the Valley of a Thousand Hills (see p.392) along the way. Maritzburg is also well positioned for an overnight stop on your way to the Drakensberg (see p.410) or the Battlefields in the Ladysmith (see p.453) vicinity.

Some history

Pietermaritzburg's **Afrikaner** origins are reflected in its name; after slaughtering three thousand Zulus at the Battle of Blood River, the Voortrekkers established the fledgling **Republic of Natalia** in 1839, naming their capital in honour of the Boer leaders Piet Retief and Gerrit Maritz. The republic's independence was short-lived, and four years later **Britain** annexed it and spent the rest of the century transforming Pietermaritzburg into an English town stamped with all the grandeur and pomposity of empire. Even as the Afrikaners trekked north to escape the irksome British, English settlers were arriving from the south to swell the city's population, and during the closing decade of the nineteenth century Maritzburg was the most important centre in the colony of Natal with a population of nearly 10,000 (more than Durban at that time).

Indians arrived at the turn of the twentieth century, mostly as indentured labourers but also as traders. Among their number was a young, little-known lawyer called **Mohandas Gandhi**, who was to become a thorn in the side of the British in India. He later traced the embryo of his devastatingly successful tactic of passive resistance to an incident in 1893, when he was booted out of a first-class train compartment at Pietermaritzburg Station because he wasn't white.

Pietermaritzburg is the provincial capital of KwaZulu-Natal, but its exact status is ambiguous, as Ulundi, in the former KwaZulu *bantustan*, is currently tussling to be recognized as the political centre of the province.

Arrival and information

Daily flights from Johannesburg, used mainly by business travellers, arrive at the city's **Oribi airport** (☎033/61542), south of the town centre. The only means of getting from here to town is by taxi. It's far easier to fly into **Durban airport** (see p.368), which is connected twice daily to Pietermaritzburg by the Cheetah **shuttle bus** (☎033/342 0266). The journey takes about 75 minutes and the bus drops off outside the *Imperial Hotel*, 224 Loop St. The Cheetah also picks up passengers in the centre of Durban, outside the local history museum in Aliwal Street. Greyhound, Intercape and Translux **intercity buses** pull in at the bus terminal on the north side of the information bureau, on the corner of Longmarket Street and Commercial Road. From here you can walk to the most central of the city hotels or take a taxi, which is also your best option to get to the suburban B&Bs. If you're staying at either of the two backpackers' lodges, you can arrange for staff to pick you up. The Baz **backpacker bus** drops off at any of the central places to stay.

Arriving **by train**, you'll find yourself at the station (☎033/958 2350) at the unsavoury southwest end of Longmarket Street, one of the main city thoroughfares. The station's down-at-heel environs make it advisable to arrange beforehand to be collected, particularly at night.

The **tourist information bureau**, Publicity House, on the corner of Longmarket Street and Commercial Road (Mon–Fri 8.30am–4.30pm, Sat 8.30am–12.30pm; ☎033/345 1348), has a good selection of books and accommodation leaflets and you can buy tickets for Translux and Greyhound buses in the same building. If you're planning on staying any length of time and will be travelling into the suburbs, a fold-out **map** of the whole city will come in handy. The best place to find these is at Shuter & Shooter, 230 Church St, which also stocks travel guides, natural history field guides and books covering Natal history.

The hectic minibus **taxi rank** is outside the tourist information bureau, and stretches from the bus terminus right down the block (destinations are posted outside the taxis). **Metered taxis** should be booked in advance (see "Listings", p.408), and in this compact city are unlikely to break the bank.

Accommodation

Pietermaritzburg has the whole gamut of **accommodation**, ranging from a good backpackers' lodge – conveniently located for the station and the central nightspots – to self-catering places and cheap B&Bs around the university on the south side of town, and more comfortable B&Bs in the lush northern suburbs – ideal if you're in a car. You'll also find a handful of good-value hotels in the city centre.

African Dreamz, 30 Taunton Rd, Wembley (☎033/394 5141, fax 345 5937). One mini-suite in a family home on a large property 2km from the centre, where you can self-cater or get breakfast. Guests have use of the garden on a stream as well as the tennis court and swimming pool. ②.

Ascot Inn, 210 Woodhouse Rd, Scottsville (☎ & fax 033/67958). Complex of comfortable mock-colonial cottages set on large lawned property, next to Scottsville race course and the N3. Swimming pool. ②.

Brevisbrook, 28 Waverleydale Rd, Boughton (☎033/344 1402, fax 345 3293). Three en-suite rooms with private entrances and use of a swimming pool and *braai* area in a large garden. Breakfast can be served on the patio. ③.

City Royal Hotel, 301 Burger St, City centre (☎033/394 7072, fax 394 7080). Pietermaritzburg's only four-star hotel is in a Thirties building that has been fully modernized and caters mainly to business travellers. Ask about their substantial discounts, offered over weekends and during school holidays. ④.

Crossways Country Inn, Old Howick Rd, Hilton (☎033/343 3267, fax 343 3273, *crossways@futurenet.co.za*). Roughly 9km north of Pietermaritzburg, and a fine choice if you want to be out of town. Modelled on an English country pub, with nice old furniture, this is also a good place to stop off for teas and lunches. ③.

Duvet and Crumpets, 1 Freelands Place, Wembley (☎ & fax 033/394 4133). Self-catering or B&B in a simple but pleasantly furnished mini-apartment in a Thirties family home. ②.

Imperial Hotel, 224 Loop St, City centre (☎033/342 6551, fax 342 9796). Popular with business travellers, this grand red-brick hotel is looking a bit past its prime with a huge entrance foyer, large rooms and heavy staircases. ⑤.

M'sunduzi Lodge, 82 Henderson Rd, Athlone (☎ & fax 033/394 4388). A cut above the other B&Bs, this offers very comfortable, well-furnished mini-apartments with views across the city, attached to a sociable private house. Guests have use of a bar, Jacuzzi and swimming pool – next to which huge breakfasts are served. ④.

Rehoboth Cottages, 276 Murray Rd, Hayfields (☎033/396 2312, fax 396 4008). Bright and cheerful mock-Victorian self-catering cottages set in large gardens 6km south of the centre. A full English breakfast can be served, as an extra. ②.

Sunduzi Backpacker Lodge, 140 Berg St (☎033/394 0072, *sunduzi@hotmail.com*). Party atmosphere at this centrally located lodge close to all the town nightspots. Choose from the family house, where bedrooms have been turned into dorms, or camping in the garden. Cheap meals (vegetarians catered for) are available, as are free pick-ups from the train or bus station. Friendly staff can help you arrange trips around the country. ①.

Tudor Inn, 18 Theatre Lane (☎033/342 1778, fax 345 1030). Immaculate and comfortable rooms at this little inn right in the characterful central Lanes area, run by a Portuguese proprietor who has created a European ambience. Each room has a small lounge area, phone and TV. ③.

The City

Most places of interest in Pietermaritzburg are within easy walking distance of the centre's heart, which is crossed by the junction of **Commercial Road** and **Longmarket Street**, slicing across it from the train station in the southwest. The inevitable old

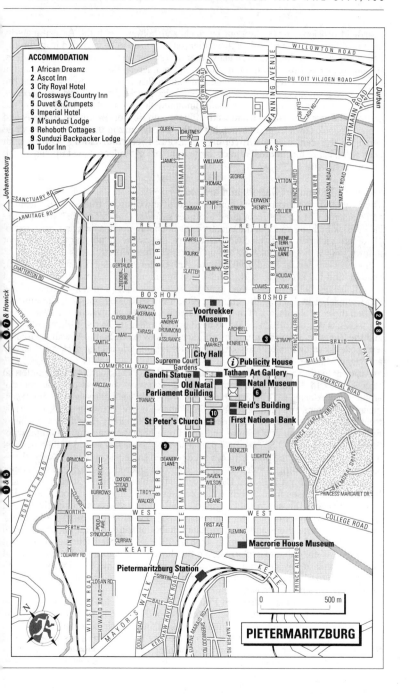

ACCOMMODATION

1 African Dreamz
2 Ascot Inn
3 City Royal Hotel
4 Crossways Country Inn
5 Duvet & Crumpets
6 Imperial Hotel
7 M'sunduzi Lodge
8 Rehoboth Cottages
9 Sunduzi Backpacker Lodge
10 Tudor Inn

PIETERMARITZBURG

apartheid divisions are marked out by roads and railways, with the African majority crammed into townships south of the station, as they used to be excluded from the city centre. By contrast, Indians were allowed to bring their business into the city fringes, but only as far as Boshoff Street, northeast of Commercial Road. Around here, and in the nearby Asian suburbs of Woodlands, Mountain Rise and Willowton, you'll find the greatest concentration of shops selling cheap spicy snacks like *rotis* and *bunny chows*, as well as the city centre's mosques and Hindu temples. On the hills, northwest of the centre, the predominantly white and affluent suburbs of Wembley, Athlone and Montrose look down from their heights at the sweaty buzz in the valley below, while south of the centre, the **University of Natal-Pietermaritzburg campus**, in Scottsville, is the magnet that attracts large numbers of students to set up digs in the suburban houses.

City Hall, Tatham Art Gallery and around

The **City Hall**, on the corner of Commercial Road and Church Street, once made international fame when it was recognized by Ripley's *Believe it or Not* as the "largest work-laden brick building south of the equator". It's definitely worth a look as a great example of late Victorian red-brick civic architecture, self-assuredly holding the prime spot in town, with wonderful detailing and an impressive fifteen-metre clock tower.

Across Commercial Road, the **Tatham Art Gallery** (Tues–Fri 10am–5pm; free), another fine brick edifice, is the undoubted highlight of Pietermaritzburg's formal attractions and houses one of the country's best collections of international and local art. Completed in 1871 as the Supreme Court of the Colony of Natal, the building formed the central complex of the capital's defences when an invasion was feared during the Zulu War of 1879. In 1990, the building became home to the Tatham collection and the Zulus finally made it inside, with artworks by black South Africans exhibited alongside those by Pablo Picasso, Graham Sutherland, Edgar Degas, David Hockney and Henri Matisse.

Adjacent to the Tatham, firmly rooted on the corner of Longmarket and Commercial streets, the **Old Natal Parliament Building** represents a typical piece of imperial architecture. Started in 1889 for Queen Victoria's Jubilee, it borrows the grand language of columns and pediments from the Roman Empire. Standing amid the formal front gardens is a statue of the unamused "Queen Empress" wielding a distinctly Freudian combination of a sceptre and orb. From here, heading down **Longmarket Street** as far as Chapel Street, you'll pass a series of attractive period buildings, most notable of which are: the **post office**, a solid dressed stone pile built in 1903; the three-storey **Reid's Building**, a little further along and considered a daringly tall skyscraper in its day; and the **First National Bank**, even further along, which dates from 1903 and had its facade chosen from an Edwardian catalogue and shipped out from the mother country. Between this section of Longmarket and Church streets is the tightly gridded warren of alleyways known as the **Lanes**, a mostly pedestrianized quarter of lawyers' offices, takeaways, shops and an inordinate number of hairdressers. The area, which was the financial hub of Natal from 1888 to 1931 and housed four separate stock exchanges, is enjoyable to explore during the day but is a notorious stamping ground of pickpockets, so stay alert and don't come here after dark. Any of the Lanes will bring you through to Church Street, which is worth wandering along back up to Commercial Road to take in some more period buildings.

On the corner of Chapel Street, **St Peter's Church**, completed in 1857, was the base for Bishop John Colenso after he was kicked out of the Church of England for his liberal theological ideas and his role in championing the Zulu cause against the British. As you head up Church Street, back toward the City Hall, you can't miss the **Gandhi Statue**, unveiled on June 6, 1993, on the centenary of his being thrown out of a first-class train carriage at Pietermaritzburg station because he wasn't white. Adjacent to

Gandhi, the **Supreme Court Gardens** on the corner of Commercial Road and Church Street, are filled with monuments to pugnacious Britons who died fighting against the Zulus, the Boers and other European powers in two world wars.

The museums

On the corner of Longmarket and Boshoff streets, the **Voortrekker Museum** (Mon–Fri 9am–4pm, Sat 8am–noon; free), centres on the original Church of the Vow, built in 1838 by Boers in honour of their victory over the Zulus three years earlier at the Battle of Blood River. The church was their part of a bargain allegedly struck with God (see p.452). The museum connects with the Voortrekker roots of Pietermaritzburg and is worth a fleeting visit to gain a little insight into life on trek. The most interesting items are the home-made children's toys and beautifully embroidered *kappies* (hats) which the women used to shield themselves from the sun. Across the lovely courtyard garden is the reconstructed house of **Andries Pretorius**, leader of the Voortrekkers at Blood River and the force behind the establishment of the Boer Republic of Natalia. The thatched house, originally built in 1846, is appealing for its sheer simplicity, which stands in contrast to fussy Victorian fashion.

Less inspiring is the **Natal Museum**, 237 Loop St (Mon–Sat 9am–4.30pm, Sun 2–5pm; small entry fee), one block east of the Old Natal Parliament, with an uncompelling collection of stuffed animals, dioramas, a small dinosaur display and a reconstruction of a late Victorian Maritzburg street. The best reason to visit is for the display of African sculpture, crafts and masks from across the continent, the highlight of which is a golden stool taken by British invaders as booty from the Asante people of Ghana.

Continuing down Loop Street for about 1km, you'll reach Pine Street, on the corner of which is the **Macrorie House Museum** (Mon 11am–4pm, Tues–Thurs 9am–1pm; small entry fee), a beautiful two-storey Victorian house with intricate wrought-iron detailing. The house, which contains furniture and relics of early British settlers, was built in 1862 and became the home of Bishop Macrorie from 1869 to 1891, after he arrived to take over from Bishop Colenso. Striking northwest up Pine Street brings you to the classically Victorian **Railway Station** at the end of Church Street. Although a little neglected in this now seedy part of town, the station remains notable for its alternating courses of red-brick and stone facings and for its fine wrought-iron lacework dripping from the forecourt eaves. As you enter the concourse, a small plaque on your left, just before the platform, records (yet again) that this was where Gandhi was thrown off a train for trying to occupy a first-class compartment reserved for whites.

ALAN PATON

Writer, teacher and politician **Alan Paton**, best known for his first novel *Cry, the Beloved Country*, was born in Pietermaritzburg in 1903. His visionary book, which focused international attention on the plight of black South Africans, was published in 1948 – the same year the National Party assumed power and began to put apartheid in place. Despite selling millions of copies worldwide, Paton's book coincided with a rising tide of repression inside the country and he entered politics to become a founder-member of the non-racial and fiercely anti-apartheid Liberal Party. He was president of the party from 1960 until 1968, when it was forced to disband by repressive legislation forbidding multiracial political organizations. Paton died in Durban in 1988, having published a number of works, including two biographies and his own autobiography. The following year the **Alan Paton Centre** (visits by appointment, ☎033/260 5926) was established at the University of Natal's archives building at 165 King Edward Ave. The Centre includes Paton's re-created study, personal memorabilia and documents.

Eating, drinking and nightlife

Pietermaritzburg has a fairly good choice of **restaurants**, as well as a handful of decent **nightclubs** and **pubs**, particularly along Commercial Road. Nightlife in the town centre is mostly white-dominated.

The two **cinema** complexes – the Nu Metro, in the Cascades Centre, McCarthy Drive, in the northern suburbs, and Ster-Kinekor, 50 Durban Rd, in Scottsville – show mainstream releases. The university's Hexagon and Churchill **theatres** host occasional productions – check the *Natal Witness* newspaper for details.

Restaurants and cafés

Café du Midi, 262 Boom St (☎033/394 5444). In an old house with an outdoor garden serving moderately priced Mediterranean-style food. Good for outdoor coffee during the day.

Els Amics, 380 Longmarket St (☎033/345 6524). Maritzburg's oldest restaurant in a colonial house is a popular place with a pleasant atmosphere, good prices and a varied menu. Closed Mon & Sun.

Kara Nichha's, 470 Church St (☎033/342 8015). Excellent, very cheap Indian takeaways, including filled *rotis* and Indian sweets.

Restaurant da Vinci, 117 Commercial Rd (☎033/345 6632). Rowdy American-Italian place with cheap pasta dishes and live music on Sunday evenings.

Tatham Art Gallery Coffee Shop, Commercial Rd. Best place in town for coffee and light lunches in the old Supreme Court, right in the centre, opposite the tourist information bureau. Closed Mon.

Tropicana, 418 Longmarket St (☎033/345 0051). Popular with Indian families, and serving up cheap curries and an extensive menu of burger and steak grills with chips.

Turtle Bay, 7 Wembley Terrace, Wembley, just off the N3 circle (☎033/394 5390). Excellent but pricey seafood restaurant in the northern suburbs.

Upper Crust, Longmarket St, opposite the taxi rank (☎033/342 7625). Good for a range of bread and imported foods, such as olive oil and Swiss chocolate, with home-baked pastries and pies. Open until 9pm daily.

Bars and nightclubs

Buzz Bar, 204 Longmarket St. Lively nightspot with an emphasis on white South African music.

Cafe 21, 50 Durban Rd, Scottsville. Bands occasionally play at this day and evening café near the university, worth checking out if you're staying in the area.

Crowded House, 124 Balhambra Way, and Commercial Rd. Pleasant indoor and outdoor bars which attract a late-twenties crowd.

Keg and Elephant, 80 Commercial Rd. Cheap pub meals popular with a racially mixed crowd of students and townsfolk.

McGinty's Irish Pub, 50 Durban Rd, Scottsville. Fairly smart pub with occasional live Irish music.

Listings

Emergencies Ambulance ☎11 0177; Police (Flying Squad) ☎10111; Rape Crisis ☎033/342 5276.

Hospital For medical emergencies, contact Mediclinic, Payn St (☎033/342 7023 or 342 7024).

Laundry The Wash Tub, Shop 2, Park Lane Centre, Commercial Rd (☎033/345 74580; daily 7.30am–6.30pm).

Pharmacy PMB Medicine Depot, 33 Commercial Rd (☎033/342 4581; Mon–Fri 9am–8pm, Sat 9am–5pm, Sun 10am–1pm & 3–9.30pm).

Taxis Junior Taxi Service, 391 Berg St (☎033/394 5454); Unique Taxis, 524 Khans Rd (☎033/391 1238).

The Midlands

For most travellers, the verdant farmland that makes up the **Midlands** is picture-postcard terrain, whizzed through on the two-hour journey from Durban or Pietermaritzburg to the Drakensberg Mountains. There's really not much reason to dally here, unless you've time to kill, money to spend and fancy taking in the region's quaint, English-style country inns, tea shops and craft shops. From 1842 to 1897, battalion after battalion of British troops marched through the Midlands during a succession of wars to pacify first the Zulus and later the Boers. The region plays up its **British** connections, with trout fishing clubs, polo clubs (over eighty percent of the country's clubs are based here), posh boarding schools and old-fashioned country hotels. The cosy image is deceptive: security fences erected around most farms indicate deep levels of black resentment, with theft common and murder of white landowners not unusual.

Public relations consultants in the Midlands have been working overtime and have dreamt up the **Midlands Meander**, a route that takes in a number of dispersed craftspeople, hotels and other minor attractions along a series of very attractive back routes. The scenery and little stopoffs are more appealing than any of the Midlands towns, which you can comfortably bypass in the certainty that you're not missing much. A number of upmarket country hotels offer plush accommodation, and there are B&Bs and self-catering cottages for cheaper stays. A free **map** outlining the attractions on this trip is available from most information bureaus throughout the vicinity.

The Midlands has an interesting historical footnote. Heading north out of Pietermaritzburg on the N3 through the Midlands, you're roughly tracing **Nelson Mandela's last journey** as a free man before being arrested in 1962 and imprisoned for 27 years. **Howick**, 18km northwest of Pietermaritzburg, is recorded as the place where his historic detention began. The actual spot is on the R103, 2km north of a sideroad heading to the Tweedie junction. On the run from the police, Mandela had been continuing his political activities, often travelling in disguise – a practice that earned him the nickname of the "Black Pimpernel". On this occasion he was masquerading as the chauffeur of a white friend, when their car was stopped on the old Howick road, apparently because of a tip-off. A memorial unveiled by Mandela himself in 1996 marks the unassuming spot, along farmland between a railway line and the road.

Midlands practicalities

For self-catering **accommodation** in the Midlands, try KwaZulu-Natal Conservation Services (see p.365), or contact Underberg Hideaways, 27 Ashby Rd, Pietermaritzburg 3201 (☎033/344 3505, fax 344 2133), an agency renting out cottages (mostly costing less than R150 per person) on farms throughout the region.

Nottingham Road, 25km north of Howick along the R103, makes a good orientation point for the Midlands, and has a couple of excellent country hotels. In the town centre, the *Nottingham Road*, 26 Nottingham Rd (☎033/263 6151, fax 263 6167; ③), reputedly has the oldest pub in the province, dating back to 1854. The hotel has retained the character of a coaching inn and features hand-coloured portraits of British officers from the Zulu Wars. Just south of town, *Rawdon's*, Old Main Rd (☎ & fax 033/263 6044, *rawdons@futurerest. co.za*; ⑥), is a gracious, thatched, English-style country estate looking onto its own trout lake with welcoming log fires for cool misty days and airy verandahs for the hot summer. Although this is a pricey place to stay, it's also highly tranquil, and has an atmospheric pub with an on-site brewery and a pleasant tea room – both of which are open to passers-by. For something more remote, head 22km west of Nottingham Road on the signposted Loteni road, and turn off after 17km onto the D544. This will take you to rustic *Bramleigh Manor* (☎033/263 6903), a large, thatched B&B guesthouse(④) facing onto its own yellowwood and blackwood forests with trout fishing, bird-watching, horse-riding, boating and sail-boarding, and two splendidly isolated self-catering cottages (③).

For **eating and drinking**, *Rawdon's* (see previous page) is excellent, as is the *Rose & Pig* (☎033/263 7369), a pleasant pub with indoor and outdoor seating in the tiny hamlet of **Rosetta**, 6km north of Nottingham Road on the R103.

THE DRAKENSBERG

The **Drakensberg**, South Africa's premier mountain wilderness, hugs the border with Lesotho for some 240km north to south, and is mostly a vast national park. The highest range in southern Africa, the "Dragon mountains" (or, in Zulu, the "barrier of spears") reach their highest peaks along the border with Lesotho. The mountain range is actually an escarpment separating a high interior plateau from the coastal lowlands of Natal, and is the source of many streams and rivers which flow out to the sea. Although this is a continuation of the same escarpment that divides the Mpumalanga highveld from the game rich lowveld of Kruger, and continues into the northeastern Cape, when people talk of the Berg, they invariably mean the range in KwaZulu-Natal.

For elating scenery – massive spires, rock buttresses, wide grasslands, glorious waterfalls, rivers, pools and fern-carpeted forests – the Drakensberg is unrivalled. This is a **hikers'** paradise, all the better for being wild, unpopulated and imbued with an intensity which is effortlessly spiritual. It's also a fly-fishing fantasy; **angling** at Loteni, Kamberg, Cobham or Giant's Castle costs R25 per day, by permit only from the Conservation Services (see p.365), and the bag limit is ten trout per day. You'll need to bring all your own gear.

The Drakensberg is one of the richest **San rock-art** repositories in the world. Over six hundred sites have been recorded, featuring more than 22,000 individual paintings by the original inhabitants of these mountains. You won't see anything like this number, as they are hidden all over the mountains, but there are three easily accessible caves at **Giant's Castle**, **Injusuti** and **Kamberg**. One of the best and most up-to-date introductions to rock-art is the slim booklet by David Lewis-Williams, *Rock Paintings of the Natal Drakensberg*, published by the University of Natal Press, available from most decent bookshops.

There are no towns close to the mountains; instead the park is hemmed in by rural African areas – former "homeland" territory, unsignposted and unnamed on many maps, but interesting places to drive through and take in a slice of traditional **Zulu life**, complete with beehive-shaped huts.

In terms of **weather**, summers are warm but wet, with some cracking thunderstorms and misty days that block out the views. Winters tend to be dry, sunny and chilly, and you can expect freezing nights and, on the high peaks, occasional snow. The best times for hiking are probably the transitional periods – spring or autumn.

Getting to the Drakensberg

There is no connecting road system through the Drakensberg, so it's not possible to drive from one end to the other. Besides **Sani Pass** in the south, which takes you into Lesotho on a hairpin dirt road requiring a 4WD vehicle, roads to the mountains branch off westwards from the N3, between Pietermaritzburg and **Ladysmith**, and come to a halt at various KwaZulu-Natal Conservation Services camps. There is no public transport to any of these.

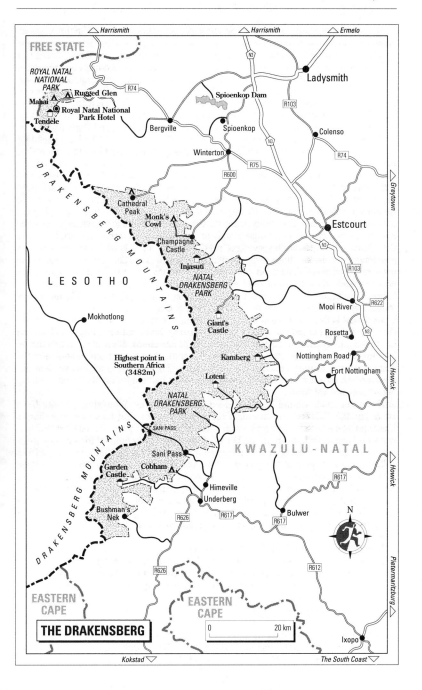

THE DRAKENSBERG

The most practical way of **visiting the Drakensberg** is to base yourself in the northern, central or southern section of the mountains, staying either in the self-catering and camping options provided by KwaZulu-Natal Conservation Service, or in one of several hotels that offer full-board rates. Without your own car, you'll have to go for the hotel or backpacker lodge option. Nearly all hotels in this area offer transfers from the Greyhound or Translux **bus** terminals in Estcourt or Ladysmith. The Baz Bus drops off at *Berg Backpackers* (see below); their Durban–Jo'burg route goes via Winterton for the Northern Drakensberg; or Mooi River and Estcourt for the Central Berg. The highest concentration of hotels and resorts is in the **Central Berg** area, midway between Johannesburg and Durban.

The nearest commercial centres lie on or just off the arterial N3, and are useful for stocking up on supplies, filling up your car or arranging transport into the mountains. Largest and least appealing of these is **ESTCOURT**, 88km north of Pietermaritzburg, home to a cold-meat factory that processes bacon, which, when the wind blows, perfumes the town with the whiff of an all-day fry up. Some 23km south of town, signposted off the R103, near Mooi River, is *Berg Backpackers* (☎033/263 2214; ①), a choice **hostel** with 24-hour check-in, offering dorms, doubles with fireplaces and camping (all ①), plus cheap meals. The Baz bus stops at the *Wimpy* in Mooi River, where you can be met by the hostel. The farmhouse stands on 200 hectares of forest and farmland near the Giant's Castle Game Reserve (see p.417) and the focus is on hiking, plus there's abseiling, trout fishing, horse-riding, sailing, and walks to see San rock paintings on the property. A crane rehabilitation centre on the farm gives you the chance to see blue, crowned and wattled cranes – all endangered – while eland, reebok, leopards and baboons roam the hills and stalk the rocks. If you want to get into the big mountains though, you still have to enter the national park at Giant's Castle.

WINTERTON, 43km north of Estcourt, along the R74 as it deviates westwards off the N3, is a tiny hamlet with a useful **tourist information bureau** (Mon–Fri 8.30am–5pm, Sat 8.30am–1pm; ☎036/488 1180), some shops, filling stations and banks. The **museum** (Mon–Fri 9am–3pm, Sat 9am–noon), signposted from Colenso Rd, the main drag next to the municipal offices, definitely justifies a stop for its excellent displays on San rock-art and coverage of the Boer War Battlefields in this vicinity, notably Spioenkop and Vaalkrans.

If you get stuck around here and need a **place to stay**, Winterton's *Bridge Hotel* (☎ & fax 488 1554; ③), on the main road, is one option, but far more appealing is *Ukuthula Bush Camp*, Skietdrift Farm (mobile ☎082/773 9914, fax 031/2093679), a working farm outside town on the banks of the Tugela. Accommodation consists of a huge, single self-catering cabin sleeping fourteen and divided into cubicles (①); a self-catering cottage that sleeps eight (②); and B&B rooms in the farmhouse itself (③). The camp organizes walks up the river and into the mountains, plus, as they're on the Battlefields route, they also trail to Spioenkop and Buller's Cross monuments. Other activities include riding, white-water canoeing, tubing, and fishing. Collection for backpackers can be arranged from Winterton. To get there, take the R23 to Ladysmith, then turn right at the signposted Skietdrift road; the camp is around 20km down this route.

Bergville, 23km north of Winterton, is another tiny village, notable primarily for being the last place to stock up before heading on to the Royal Natal National Park. Apart from the helpful **Drakensberg Tourism Association** (Mon–Fri 9am–4pm, Sat 9am–noon; ☎ & fax 036/448 1557) in Tatham Road, there's not much to keep you here.

Hiking in the Drakensberg

Whether you choose to take your time on easy walks or embark on a challenging three- or four-day trip into the mountains, **hiking** in the Natal Drakensberg is one of South Africa's top wilderness experiences. The marvel of setting out on foot in these mountains

THE SAN AND THEIR ROCK PAINTINGS

Southern Africa's earliest inhabitants and the most direct descendants of the late Stone Age, the **San**, or Bushmen, lived in the caves and shelters of the Drakensberg for thousands of years before the arrival first of the Nguni people and then white farmers. There is still some disagreement over what to call these early hunter-gatherers. Many liberal writers use the word "Bushmen" in a strictly non-pejorative sense – though the word was originally deeply insulting. Several historians and anthropologists have plumped for "San", but, as the term refers to a language group and not a culture, this isn't strictly accurate either. Since there is no agreed term, you'll find both words used in this book.

The San hunted and gathered on the subcontinent for a considerable period – paintings in Namibia date back 25,000 years. In the last two thousand years, the southward migration of Bantu-speaking farmers forced change on the San, but there is evidence that the two groups were able to live side by side. It was when white settlers began to annex lands for hunting and farming that tension built up. As the San started to take cattle from farmers, whites began to regard these people as vermin, and felt free to hunt them in genocidal campaigns in the Cape, and later in other areas, including the Drakensberg, until the San were literally wiped off the South African map.

San **artists** were also **shamans**, and painted trance-induced images, mostly depicting their **spiritual beliefs**. Interpreting their paintings of hunting, dancing and animals as realistic narratives of everyday life in the Drakensberg is thus quite pointless: to get the most out of the works, you'll have to dig a little deeper. J. Lewis-Williams (see "Books", p.737) makes the point that when we see a lamb in a stained-glass window in an old church we don't think of it as depicting a food source in past centuries, but know that it symbolizes Christ as the lamb of God; in a similar way, San art is metaphorical.

It's easy and rewarding to pick out some of the most significant elements in San paintings. The **medicine** or **trance dance** – journeying into the spiritual world in order to harness healing power – was the Bushmen's most important religious ritual and is depicted in much of their art. Look out for the postures which the shamans adopted during the dance, including arms outstretched behind them, bending forward, kneeling, or pointing fingers. Dots along the spine often relate to the sensation of energy boiling upwards, while lines on faces or coming out of the nose usually depict nosebleeds – a common side effect of the trance state. Other feelings experienced in trance, such as elongation, attenuation or the sensation of flight, are expressed by feathers or streamers.

To enter the spirit world, shamans often tapped into the power of certain **animals**. You'll see the spiral-horned **eland** depicted in every cave – not because these antelope were prolific in the Berg, but because they were considered to have more power than any other animal. Sometimes the elands are painted in layers to increase the store of potency. In any of the caves open to the public, you'll see fascinating figures in the process of transforming into their power animal. Besides antelope, other animals associated with trance are honeybees, felines, snakes and sometimes elephants and rhinos.

It's difficult to **date** the paintings in the Drakensberg with accuracy, but the oldest are likely to be at least eight hundred years old (although Bushmen lived in the area for thousands of years before that) and the most recent are believed to have been painted after the arrival of white people towards the end of the nineteenth century. The depictions of horses, cattle and white settlers, particularly in the Southern Berg, mark the end of the traditional way of life for the Drakensberg Bushmen, and it is possible that the settlers were painted by shamans as a supernatural technique to try to ward off people who destroyed them with all-too-real bullets.

Paintings weather and fade, many have been vandalized, and well-meaning people dabbing water on them to make them clearer, or touching them, has also caused them to disappear – so never be tempted.

is that you're unlikely to encounter vehicles, settlements, or even other people, and the scenery is nothing short of sublime.

The Drakensberg is divided into the High Berg and Little Berg, according to altitude. In the **High Berg**, you're in the land of spires and great rock buttresses, where the only places to sleep are in caves or, in some areas, huts. You'll need to be totally self-sufficient and obey wildnerness rules, taking a trowel and loo paper with you and not fouling natural water with anything – which means carrying water away from the streams to wash in. Both mountaineers' huts and caves must be booked with whichever KwaZulu-Natal Conservation Services office you launch out from, and you'll also need to write down your route details in the mountain register. Slogging up the passes to the top of the mountains requires a high degree of fitness, some hiking experience and a companion or guide who knows the terrain.

If you're not bothered about reaching high peaks, the **Little Berg**, lower down, with its gentler summits, rivers, rock paintings, valleys and forests, is no less remote or beautiful. The Little Berg is also safer, and easy enough to explore if you're averagely fit. If you don't want to carry a backpack and sleep in caves or huts, it's quite feasible to base yourself at one of the Conservation Services camps and set out on day-hikes, of which there are endless choices. It's also possible to do a two-day walk from one of the camps, spending one night in a cave; two highly recommended bases for walking are **Injasuti** in the Giant's Castle Game Reserve (see p.417), or **Tendele** in the Royal Natal National Park (see p.420). If you want the added luxury of spending your nights in a hotel, you could do no better than basing yourself in the **Cathedral Peak** area at the *Cathedral Peak Hotel* (see p.420).

Each of the Conservation Services offices sells **books** on Drakensberg walks, as well as *Slingsby* **maps** (1:150,000), though some of the paths indicated have now disappeared. One of the best guides is David Bristow's *Drakensberg Walks*, published by Struik and available from the Conservation Services shops and many book stores. The book outlines 120 walks (with maps), which vary in length from an hour to several days, and it's small enough to carry around with you.

If you want to hike up to the **High Berg**, and don't feel confident to tackle the terrain, or are alone, Stef Steyn (☎033/330 4293, *info@kzntours.co.za*) specializes in **guided hiking tours**; if he's not available, try Andrew Anderson, at Zulu Parks and Wildlife Safaris (☎033/343 4127, *zulusaf@iafrica.com*).

At any time of year the **weather** can change rapidly, so always take sufficient clothing and food – including a hat; the sun is fierce and bright, even in winter. And it goes without saying that you should use tried and tested, well-worn hiking boots.

The Southern Berg

Although for the most part the **Southern Berg**, the closest mountains to Durban and Pietermaritzburg, lacks the drama and varied landscape found further north, its outstanding highlight is the hair-raising **Sani Pass**, a precipitous series of hairpins that twist to the top of the escarpment up to the highest point in southern Africa reachable on wheels. The Southern Berg, with its extensive grasslands, is also the terrain of the highly recommended **Giant's Cup Hiking Trail** (see opposite), the only organized trail in the Drakensberg and an exhilarating introduction to the mountains.

Although Sani Pass is the Southern Berg's most popular destination, further north the KwaZulu-Natal Conservation Services offer campsites and cottages at **Cobham**, **Loteni** and **Kamberg**, and plenty of opportunity for trout fishing. Despite its isolation, even without transport the Pass is accessible via transport links and with a couple of hostels.

Underberg and Himeville

The main access into this part of the Drakensberg is along the **R617**, which strikes out west off the N3 north of Pietermaritzburg (take the Bulwer/Merrivale exit).

GIANT'S CUP HIKING TRAIL

The sixty-kilometre, five-day **Giant's Cup Hiking Trail** is the only laid-out trail in the Drakensberg and makes an excellent introduction to the mountains. The trail starts at the Sani Pass road, leading through the foothills of the Southern Drakensberg and winding past eroded sandstone formations, overhangs with San paintings, grassy plains, and beautiful valleys with river pools to swim in. No single day's hike is longer than 14km and, although there are some steep sections, this is not a difficult trail – you need to be fit to enjoy it, but not an athlete. The trail is restricted to thirty people per day and tends to get booked out during holiday periods; **booking** should be made through the KwaZulu-Natal Conservation Services (see p.365), who provide a map and a trail booklet. The trail costs R40 per person per night.

The **mountain huts** at the four overnight stops have running water, toilets, tables and benches, and bunks with mattresses. It's essential to bring a camping stove, food and a sleeping bag. The trail can be shortened by missing the first day and starting out at Pholea Hut, an old farmhouse where you spend the night, then terminating one day earlier at Swiman Hut, close to the Conservation Services office at Garden Castle. You can also lengthen the trail by spending an extra night at Bushmen's Nek Hut, in an area with numerous caves and rock-art sites.

Giant's Cup Trail is linear, so you'll need to arrange **transport** at the end of the hike to get back to where you parked. This should be arranged through the Underburg **tourist information**, who can pick you up at Himeville or Underberg, or move and store your car if you're driving.

UNDERBERG on the R617, is the main gateway, with a good **supermarket** for stocking up and some emergency services should you run into difficulties in the mountains. You can't miss the **tourist information office** (☎033/701 1419, fax 701 1471, *ecosse@yebo.co.za*) in Underberg, as the village is tiny. There's also a **pharmacy**, the Sani (☎033/701 1034; after hours 701 1955) and a private **hospital**, the Riverview (☎033/701 1516) for 24-hour emergencies. The Automobile Association offers a 24-hour breakdown service (☎033/702 1305).

HIMEVILLE, 4km north of Underberg, and the last village you'll find before heading up Sani Pass, also has a **supermarket** as well as the decent *Himeville Arms* (☎033/702 1305; ④), a country **inn** at the centre of the village, which makes a good stopover before the final haul to the mountains. They also offer 4WD trips, horse-riding, tennis and golf.

Sani Pass

SANI PASS, the only road from KwaZulu-Natal into neighbouring Lesotho, connects South Africa to the tiny highland outpost of **Mokhotlong** in Lesotho (see p.645), once known as the "loneliest settlement in Africa" and still no great metropolis. But it's the pass itself, which zigzags into the clouds, that draws increasing numbers into the High Berg. Sani Pass is the only place in the KwaZulu-Natal Drakensberg range where you actually can drive up the mountains – though you'll need a 4WD vehicle to negotiate the road and a passport to cross the **Lesotho border** (8am–4pm). If you don't have your own transport, consider booking a tour with one of the handful of operators (see overleaf) running journeys to the "roof of Africa".

Access and information

For all its isolation, Sani Pass is fairly straightforward to get to. Transport is available on Sani Pass Carriers **buses** (☎ & fax 033/701 1017, after hours ☎701 1030, *sanipasscarriers@wandata.com*), based in Underberg, who offer reduced rates for hostel, hotel and B&B guests. They ply the route from Pietermaritzburg (R95) or central Durban (R100) to Underberg or Himeville, where you can be met by your hotel or hostel; they also run between Underberg and Kokstad for a similar rate, if you're heading onward to the Eastern Cape. Their schedules, drop-off points and routes are a bit fluid, so it's best to ring beforehand to get the latest **timetables**.

Thaba Tours (☎033/701 1419), based in Underberg, offer several **tours**, including a daily jaunt into Lesotho, where they take you by 4WD to the highest point on the Sani/Mokhotlong Road to visit shepherds and learn about their lifestyle; they also organize horse-riding trails and walking trips to see rock-art. It's also possible to do Sani Pass as a worthwhile day-trip from Durban, with Strelitzia Tours (☎031/861 9040), which includes a visit to a Lesotho village, where you get to taste homemade sorghum beer and lunch at the *Sani Top Chalet*.

Accommodation

You'll find most **accommodation** at the foot of the mountains, just before the pass hair-pins its way up to the top. Closest to the start of the pass is *Mkomazana Youth Hostel*, Sani Pass Rd (☎033/702 0340, *theholm@iafrica.com*; all accommodation ①), offering self-catering in four- and six-bed dorms, a huge 30-bed dorm, doubles with shared toi-lets and washing facilities, plus two fully equipped houses sleeping eight; meals can also be arranged. The hostel is also near the start of Giant's Cup Hiking Trail (see box on previous page), and you can safely leave your car here before setting out on the trek. Less ambitious walks into the mountains begin on the property, which has its own river and waterfall. A little further down the road, dorms and doubles are on offer at *Sani Lodge Backpackers Hostel* (☎033/702 0330; ①), which has pleasant verandahs and lawns where meals are served all day, and a mean reputation for cakes. It's good for walking to waterfalls and rock paintings – they can supply packed lunches – plus there's horse-riding and mountain biking. Tours into Lesotho are also on offer, and you can stay in a nearby homestead to experience ordinary Zulu life. Nearby, and far more comfortable, the *Sani Pass Hotel* (☎033/702 1320, fax 702 0220, *sanipasscon@futurenet.co.za*; ⑥) offers full-board and plenty of extras – including sauna rooms and horse-riding and ten-nis facilities. If you're after a serious hiking vibe, but with a relaxed atmosphere, head for *Sani Top Chalets* (see p.646), at the top of Sani Pass, just inside Lesotho. For week-end breaks or longer, contact Underberg Hideaways (☎033/344 3505, fax 344 2133), who co-ordinate privately rented **cottages** and **farmstays** in this area.

North of Sani Pass: Loteni and Kamberg

Well off the beaten track, along dirt roads and seldom explored by foreign visitors, the two KwaZulu-Natal Conservation Services camps at **Loteni** and **Kamberg** (both daily: April–Sept 6am–6pm; Oct–March 5am–7pm; small entry fee) are worth ventur-ing into for their isolated wilderness, good trout-fishing and, at Kamberg, some exquisite San rock paintings. **Booking** is through Conservation Services central bookings (see p.365).

In a valley in the foothills of the Berg, **LOTENI** is tranquil and beautiful, with water-falls, grasslands and the lure of fishing in the Loteni River, which flows through the reserve and is stocked with brown trout. The **Settler Museum** is worth a quick once-over; it's housed in the original stone buildings belonging to the Root family who left Britain in the nineteenth century and farmed here for two generations before the area was proclaimed a reserve, and Arnold Root became the first warden. Displays include waggons, farm tools and period furniture, re-creating early settler life.

It's possible to **get there** by car via either Nottingham Road, 76km to its northeast, or from Himeville 74km to the southeast. You'll need to bring all your own **supplies**, or visit the trading store, 10km before you reach the **camp** (☎033/702 0540), for basics. There are twelve cheap but comfortable self-catering chalets (②), each sleeping up to six and with its own well-equipped kitchen and bathroom, and a small campsite (①). Best of all here is *Symes's Cottage*, a stone farmhouse, with a majestic outlook, its own trout lake and grounds traversed by bushbuck and eland. The cottage sleeps ten, and there's a minimum charge of R360.

The best reason to visit **KAMBERG**, 42km west of Rosetta, is for the rock-art at one of the three caves in the Drakensberg open to the public. At **Shelter Cave** (also known as Game Pass Cave), images of stylized figures in trance states and large, polychrome eland dance across the wall. The paintings can only be visited with a guard. You can arrange this beforehand, or join one of the guided tours which depart from the rest camp on Sundays at 9am (R25) – the walk there and back takes around three hours following a contour path through grasslands. There are other less distinct paintings, which you can visit at will for free, near the waterfall.

Kamberg's **rest camp** (☎033/263 7251; ②–③) consists of chalets, huts, and a rustic cottage that includes the services of a cook. There's no camping, but you can book to stay in one of the caves. As the nearest supplies are at Rosetta, you'll need to bring all your own food and drink. Walks from here are undemanding and very scenic, and there's a four-kilometre **trail** with handrails for **wheelchair-users** and the **visually impaired**.

The Central Drakensberg

The **Central Drakensberg** incorporates four distinct areas, all clearly signposted from the N3 and the R615. **Giant's Castle**, the site of a beautiful game reserve, is where you'll find the popular Lammergeyer bird hide and access to important San rock paintings. More San art is at **Injasuti** to the north, principally a hiking destination and definitely the place to head for if you're after utter wilderness. Far more accessible and tourist-trammelled is **Champagne Valley**, with a healthy number of full-board hotels with ample sporting facilities, while to the north, and out on a limb, the hotel at **Cathedral Peak** is the best place to base yourself for some serious walking.

Giant's Castle Game Reserve

GIANT'S CASTLE GAME RESERVE (daily: April–Sept 6am–6pm; Oct–March 5am–7pm; small entry fee) was created to protect the dwindling numbers of **eland**, which occurred in great numbers in the Drakensberg before the arrival of colonialists. The reserve is also home to antelope of the montane zone: oribi, grey rhebok, mountain reedbuck and bushbuck. Despite its four dozen mammal species and around 160 bird species, this is not a traditional game park – the way to see the wildlife here is by walking or hiking through the terrain, not by driving around in a car. There are no roads inside the reserve apart from access routes, which terminate at the two main Conservation Services camps – **Giant's Castle** and **Injasuti**. The reserve is bordered to the west by three of the four highest peaks in South Africa: Mafadi (the highest at 3410m); Popple Peak (3325m) and the bulky ramparts of Giant's Castle itself (3314 m).

One of the big attractions at Giant's Head is the thrilling **Lammergeyer Hide** (May–Sept Sat & Sun only), where you can see the rare lammergeyer, Cape vulture, black eagle, jackal buzzard and lanner falcon, attracted by the carcasses of animals put out by rangers during the winter. The lammergeyer, a giant, black and golden bird with massive wings and a diamond-shaped tail, was thought to be extinct in southern Africa until only two decades ago. Today the bird is found only in mountainous areas such as the Himalayan foothills, and in South Africa only in the Drakensberg and Maluti mountains. The lammergeyer, a scavenger, is an evolutionary link between eagles and vultures. In order to visit the hide (from R30 per person), you'll have to **book** as much as a year in advance through Giant's Castle Game Reserve, PO Box X7055, Estcourt 3310 (☎036/352 4617).

Giant's Castle has one of the three major **rock-art sites** open to the public in the Drakensberg, with over five hundred paintings at **Main Caves**, about a half-hour's easy walk up the Bushman's River Valley. There's a small entry fee to the fenced in caves, and self-guided tours with some interpretative materials on site.

If the Conservation Services accommodation is full, you'll have to head for the one **hotel** that gives access to the reserve: *White Mountain Lodge*, Giant's Castle Hutted Camp Rd (☎036/353 8644, fax 353 8437; ②–③), 34km on tar from Estcourt. The hotel offers full-board accommodation and self-catering cottages, and is in the foothills and close to Zulu villages and farmlands, so while the area is pretty, it is neither grand nor remote.

Giant's Castle

The most comfortable of the reserve's **rest camps**, *Giant's Castle Hutted Camp* (bookings through KwaZulu-Natal Conservation Services; see box on p.365) has self-contained and recently revamped **bungalows** (③) with wonderful picture windows looking out to the peaks and cosy open fireplaces. They vary in size, sleeping from two to eight people and are self-catering, though you can eat at the buffet-style **restaurant** if you don't want to cook. A **coffee shop** serves snacks, lunches and evening meals (but no breakfasts). The **camp store** sells frozen meat for *braais* and some tinned food and beers, but it's preferable to stock up before getting here. The reserve's only **filling station** is here, at the main entrance.

There are fabulous **hiking trails** from the camp, with some of the best-located and -equipped hiking **huts** (①) in the Berg at *Meander Hut*, *Giant's Hut* and *Bannerman's Hut*. The only drawback is that there is no campsite at *Giant's Castle Hutted Camp*, so if you plan to do an overnight hike in the mountains you'll need to book into one of the their bungalows for the first or last night of your trail.

Injasuti

Some 50km from both Winterton and Estcourt, **INJASUTI** is a hikers' dream. You can walk straight out into the mountains (there are ten different day-hikes, lasting from one to seven hours), swim in the rivers or look at rock-art. One of the best day walks is up Van Heyningen's Pass to the **View Point** – the friendly folk at reception will direct you. It's also supremely relaxing and beautiful. To **get there**, take the indicated turning off the R615, which takes you along 30km of dirt road, passing through **Zulu villages** with traditional beehive huts along roads that are frequently blocked by groups of Nguni cattle.

If you have even a passing interest in **rock-art**, don't miss the paintings at **Battle Cave**, so named because of a series of paintings that apparently depict an armed conflict between two groups of Bushmen. There are estimated to be over 750 beautifully painted figures of people and animals in this extensive cave, though many are faded. They're also fenced off, and can be visited only in the company of a Conservation Services guide, who sets out most days at 8.30am on the three- to four-hour walk. Once at the cave, the guard will play a recorded commentary that explains the paintings. Lewis-Williams has argued that, contrary to popular belief, the battle scene is unlikely to depict a territorial conflict, because there is no evidence that such conflicts ever took place in a society that was very loosely organized and unterritorial. Instead, he claims, the paintings are about the San spiritual experience and shamanic trance, the battles taking place in the spiritual realm where marauding evil shamans shoot arrows of "sickness", while good shamans attempt to fight them off.

The only **accommodation** in this section of the mountains is in a KwaZulu-Natal Conservation Services camp, which has no-frills cottages (②) and a campsite (①). There's no restaurant and only a very basic little **shop**, so you'll need to bring all your own supplies (though it does sell beer). Most people come here with the express purpose of taking to the hills and camping in one of the designated **caves**, which must be booked at reception and have absolutely no facilities. **Bookings** should be made through the Conservation Services (see p.365).

Champagne Castle and Champagne Valley

CHAMPAGNE CASTLE, the second-highest peak in South Africa, provides the most popular view in the Drakensberg, with scores of resorts in the valley cashing in on the soaring backdrop. The name, so the story goes, derives from an incident in 1861, when a Major Grantham made the first recorded ascent of the peak, towing his batman, who inadvertently dropped the bottle of bubbly and christened the mountainside.

These days, champagne tends to be enjoyed within the confines of the hotels down in the **Champagne Valley** by cityslickers who refuse to follow in the major's footsteps, preferring to enjoy their tipple in comfortable surroundings. This overcivilized area, which lies outside the KwaZulu-Natal Conservation Services reserve, is best avoided if you want to hike from your doorstep – you'll have to drive along the R600 through the valley to Monk's Cowl, from where plenty of hikes set off into the mountains. It's an easy 32km all the way from Winterton, and has facilities absent in other parts of the Drakensberg, such as a supermarket, liquor store, greengrocer, laundry and a couple of restaurants, all indicated along route.

The **Ardmore Ceramic Art Studio** (daily 9am–4.30pm; ☎036/468 1314), 5km down off the R600, indicated between the *Nest Hotel* and the *Drakensberg Sun*, is one of the highlights of the valley. The studio was started in the Eighties by fine-arts graduate Fée Halsted-Berning with trainee Bonnie Ntshalintshali, a young Zulu girl suffering from polio. By 1990 they had collected a clutch of awards for their distinctive ceramic works, and the studio now has around forty people creating beautiful sculpture and crockery with wildly colourful and often impossibly irrational motifs that have included rhinos dressed as preachers, administering the sacrament to a congregation of wild animals.

Accommodation

You shouldn't have any problem finding a **place to stay** in Champagne Valley: numerous hotels, family resorts and B&Bs are signposted off the R600. Perhaps the nicest **hotel** – though not the smartest – is the steadfastly old-fashioned *Champagne Castle* (☎036/468 1063, fax 468 1306; ⑤–⑥), closest of the hotels along the R600 to the hiking trails beginning at Monk's Cowl. The hotel, which still insists on collar and tie for dinner, has comfortable en-suite chalets set in lovely gardens with a swimming pool, and a rate that includes three English-style (rather stodgy) meals a day. The more expensive rooms have better views.

For backpackers' and B&B **accommodation**, *Inkosana Lodge* (☎ & fax 036/468 1202; ②–③), halfway along the R600 from Winterton to Monk's Cowl, offers unpretentious, ethnic-style rooms, with beautiful indigenous gardens and a bit of a retreat-centre feel. Self-catering is available, and the lodge can provide free transfers from Winterton and up to the Berg trailheads. *Inkosana* also has a studio and shop with a great selection of handpainted duvet covers, tablecloths and throws, which they're happy to post on to you. More expensive, *Ardmore Guest Farm* (☎036/468 1314, fax 468 1242; ③–④), also signposted off the R600 midway from Winterton to Monk's Cowl, is a thoroughly hospitable B&B on a farm, with accommodation in rondavels or inside the main house, attached to the Ardmore Ceramic Studio (see above) and offering en-suite rondavels. Guests eat together from marvellous hand-crafted crockery made on the farm. *Ardmore* also operates **horse trails** in the Drakensberg foothills for experienced and novice riders, lasting from two hours to three days.

There are no Conservation Services chalets, only a **campsite** (☎0364/68 1103; ①) at Monk's Cowl, at the end of the road through the valley, which serves as the trailhead for numerous hikes.

Cathedral Peak

North of Monk's Cowl and the Champagne Valley resorts is the Mlambonja River Valley and *Cathedral Peak Hotel* (☎ & fax 036/488 1888, *cth@ls.lia.net*; ⑤–⑥), the closest **hotel** in the Drakensberg to the mountains, and within the KwaZulu-Natal Conservation Services protected area. Rates are for half board. There are no other hotels in the vicinity, so the views are perfect. The *Cathedral Peak* is well signposted, 44km from either Winterton or Bergville, mostly on a dirt roads through Zulu villages, with the last 15km of road tarred.

Hiking trails start right from the hotel, which provides maps and books. One of the most popular day-walks is to the beautiful **Rainbow Gorge**. This eleven-kilometre round trip takes four to five hours, and follows the Ndumeni River with pools, rapids, falls, lichens, mosses and ferns to detain you. The hike can be wet, so wear proper walking boots. The hotel also operates guided trips up **CATHEDRAL PEAK** itself, a free-standing pinnacle sticking out of the five-kilometre-long basalt Cathedral Ridge. You should expect the ten-kilometre round trip to take nine hours, which includes plenty of time at the top to revel in the views. It's a very steep climb, and the final section beyond Orange Peel Gap should only be tackled by experienced climbers – you'll probably be quite satisfied to stop at this point. The peak looks nothing like a cathedral (its Zulu name, Mponjwane, means "the horn on a heifer's head").

The only other place to stay is the small Conservation Services **campsite** (☎0364/88 1880; ①), opposite the Mike's Pass guardhouse, about 4km before the hotel, although a major new camp, *Didima*, began construction in 1999. For the latest information and reservations, contact the Conservation Services (see p.365). The theme of the camp will be the San people and their rock-art, and will incorporate a sound-and-light interpretation centre as well as a restaurant. The guardhouse is the place to buy a permit to drive up **Mike's Pass**, a ten-kilometre twisting forestry road which takes you to a car park from where, on a clear day, you'll get outstanding views of the entire region. There's a scale model on top to help identify the peaks. An ordinary car will make the journey when the weather is dry and the road is hard, but you'll need a 4WD when it's wet.

The Northern Drakensberg

The dramatically beautiful **Northern Drakesnberg** consists mainly of the **Royal Natal National Park**, with a few resorts scattered around the fringes and Zulu villages pressing around the borders. The Tugela River and its bouldered gorge offer some of the most awe-inspiring scenery in the area, while the Amphitheatre, the main geographical feature, is a striking, five-kilometre rock wall over which the Tugela plunges. With a complete cross-section of accommodation, the Northern Berg is a very desirable area to visit. The best place to get a real feeling of these pristine mountains and valleys is at **Tendele**, the main KwaZulu-Natal Conservation Services camp, with chalets but oddly enough no camping.

Royal Natal National Park

The **ROYAL NATAL NATIONAL PARK** (daily 24hr; small entry fee), 46km west of Bergville, is famed for its views of the **Amphitheatre**, a crescent-shaped rock edge of the escarpment that virtually encloses the park, and probably appears on more posters and postcards and in more books than any other single feature of the Drakensberg. Almost everyone does the **Tugela Gorge walk**, a fabulous six-hour round trip from Tendele, which gives close-up views of the **Amphitheatre** and the **Tugela Falls** plummeting over the 500-metre rock wall.

The park itself is at the northern end of the High Drakensberg, tucked in between Lesotho to the west and Free State province to the north, and is the closest section of the Berg to Johannesburg. The three defining peaks are the Sentinel (3165m), the Eastern Buttress (3048m) and the Mont Aux Sources (3282m), which is also where five rivers rise – hence its name, given by French missionaries in 1878. The park was established in 1916 but only earned its royal sobriquet in 1947, when the British family paid a visit.

Access and information

The best way to get into the Royal Natal is with your own transport; the route comprises tarred roads all the way. Coming from Durban along the N3, take the Winterton/Berg resorts turn-off and follow the clear signposts through the village of **Bergville** to the park entrance, some 46km away. Several of the resorts offer transfers from Bergville or the N3 if you book ahead and notify them, but they tend to be expensive.

Although there are plenty of **Zulu** settlements en route, Bergville is the nearest place to stock up on supplies; there's a basic **provisions store** at the *Royal Natal National Park Hotel*, where you can buy bread, milk, meat, sugar and tinned food. The **visitors' centre** adjacent to the hotel sells books, maps, a good selection of hiking boots, and frozen and smoked trout.

Accommodation

KwaZulu-Natal Conservation Services **accommodation** consists of two campsites and the hutted camp. **Bookings** for chalets should be made through the Conservation Services (see p.365), while camping should be arranged locally. The only private hotel inside the park, and creating a centre of sorts, is the *Royal Natal National Park Hotel*. Outside the park, just before you reach the entry gate, from Bergville, a well-signposted dirt road heading north is the location for the handful of resort-style hotels in the area.

OUTSIDE THE PARK

The Cavern (☎036/438 6270, fax 438 6334). Off the R74 on the way to the resort. The most tucked-away of the hotels, the *Cavern* is family run, has an old-fashioned feel with adequate rooms, and is very much a South African weekend getaway with a swimming pool, horse-riding, Saturday night dances, a TV room; it's a full-board rate, and is cheaper during the week. Transfers from the Durban/Johannesburg buses at the N3 cost R220 per return trip and must be booked beforehand. ⑨, cheaper during the week.

Hlalanathi Berg Resort (☎036/438 6308, fax 438 6852). Some 10km from the *Royal Natal*, this is a family resort offering camping, self-catering thatched chalets, which sleep from two to six people, and offer trampolines, swimming pool, TV room as well as a sit-down and take-away restaurant serving cheap burgers, sandwiches and more substantial meals. During school holidays they insist on a five-night minimum stay. Camping ①, chalets ②.

Mont-Aux-Sources Hotel (☎ & fax 036/438 6230). Roughly 4km from the park, this smart but impersonal hotel has views of the Amphitheatre behind scrawny villages and cattle-chewed hillsides. ⑦.

INSIDE THE PARK

Mahai Campsite (☎036/438 6303, fax 438 6231). Adjacent to the the Royal Natal, this huge campsite set along the river caters for up to four hundred campers and attracts hordes of South Africans with their tents and caravans over school holidays and weekends. From here you can strike straight into the mountains for some of the best walks in the Berg. ①.

Royal Natal National Park Hotel (☎036/438 6200, fax 438 6101). Old-fashioned place with decent rooms and pleasant gardens, though its dinner, bed and breakfast rate is not cheap. It's well situated for hiking, though the views from the hotel itself are disappointing – you'd hardly realize you're so close to the famous vistas. The hotel has a smart-casual dress rule (no jeans, T shirts or open shoes) after 6pm. Its lease expires in 2000, when it will be closed and a new Conservation Service development put up. ⑥.

Rugged Glen Campsite, signposted 4km from *Mahai* (☎036/438 6303, fax 438 6231). A smaller and quieter campsite than *Mahai*, but the views and walks aren't as good. The *Mont-Aux-Sources Hotel* is an easy walk away – handy if you want a substantial meal. ①.

Tendele Hutted Camp (☎033/347 1981, fax 347 1980). At the end of the road, right in the mountains, this is one of the most-sought-after places to stay in South Africa, with splendid views of the Amphitheatre and excellent walks right from your front door. Accommodation is in comfortable en-suite units, the cheapest of which have hotplates, fridges, kettles, toasters and eating utensils. If you opt for the more luxurious cottages or lodge, chefs are on hand to cook for you, though you need to bring the food. There's a small shop for supplies, but it's best to stock up beforehand. You can walk or drive the couple of kilometres to the the hotel for a meal, but you'll need to be smartly dressed. ④–⑤.

THE ZULULAND COAST
AND GAME RESERVES

In startling contrast to the intensely developed 250-kilometre ribbon of the Holiday Coast, which runs north and south of Durban, the seaboard to the north of the Dolphin Coast drifts off into some of the wildest and most breathtaking sea frontage in South Africa – an imprecisely defined area known as **Maputaland**. Roughly speaking, Maputaland is the funnel-shaped slab wedged into the corner formed by Swaziland and Mozambique in the north, and confined to its east and west between the N2 and the coast.

If you've travelled along the Garden Route and wondered where stereotypical Africa was, the answer is right here in this tight patchwork of wilderness and **ancestral African lands**. The figures speak for themselves: Maputaland has more *nyangas* and *sangomas* (traditional healers and spirit mediums) per head than anywhere else in the country. With one healer for every 550 people – compared with one Western-style doctor to 18,000 people – **traditional life** is hanging on in this forgotten corner of sub-Saharan Africa's most industrialized country.

It's only since the Sixties that **navigable tracks** have twisted their way through Maputaland's grasslands and tangled forests, and even today there's no tarred road leading all the way from the N2 to its 200km of virtually uninterrupted beachfront, most of which is still only accessible with a 4WD vehicle.

Driving for less than three hours on the N2 north from Durban gets you into the **big game country** of Hluhluwe-Umfolozi, which rivals even the Kruger National Park in beauty and a sense of the wild. Drive the same distance, but turn right instead of left at the Mtubatuba junction, and you'll hit the southernmost extent of South Africa's most satisfyingly "tropical" **coast**, protected all the way up to Mozambique by wetland reserve and marine sanctuaries. The coast gets remoter and more exhilarating the further north you head, with South Africa's best upmarket beachside stay at **Rocktail Bay**, near Mozambique, where fewer than two dozen fortunate castaway guests have kilometres of rolling dunes and coastal forest to themselves.

So far the only major development blighting the area is the large modern industrial port of **Richards Bay**, 185km north of Durban, nudging the southern edge of Maputaland. But with the possibility of a continuous strip of resorts all the way from Durban to the Mozambique border, there are real fears for the whole of this fragile ecosystem. Large mining interests have their eye on tearing at the titanium-rich dunes of the St Lucia Wetland, and there's talk of constructing a massive harbour at the remote mouth of the Kosi River in the far north.

Conservationists are hoping that the nomination of the area as South Africa's first **World Heritage Site** will stave off environmentally destructive developments, but

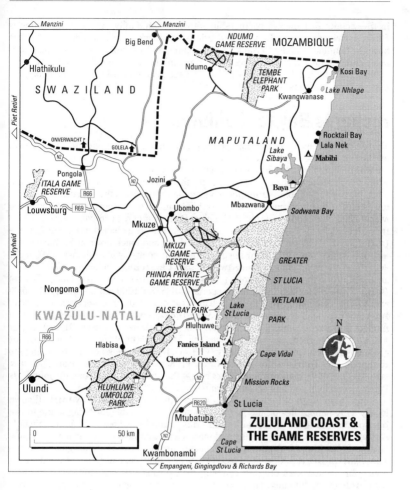

Empangeni, Gingindlovu & Richards Bay

conservation and poverty sit uncomfortably here; for **indigenous people** struggling to sustain a livelihood, the sight of visitors in their air-conditioned vehicles raising dust in their backyard leaves a bitter taste. In the past, African farmers were banned from planting crops in the wetlands, traditional fishermen were arrested for casting their nets on waters they believed to be theirs, and cattle herders had their livestock confiscated if they wandered into certain areas. It's not surprising that for some local people eco-tourism equals dispossession. This tension is one reason why **theft** is very high in the area. No matter how deserted a place looks, don't be lulled into leaving cameras or other valuables where they can be easily snatched.

Some locals, however, have responded more positively to the influx of visitors and Zululand is one of the best areas to buy **crafts**. Even on remote roads, you'll come across stalls with beautiful carvings, often suspended like windchimes from their roofs or from trees. Objects include platters, sticks or, in a more contemporary vein, models of little 4WD vehicles. More positive still is the growth of eco-tourism projects in the vicinity that involve partnership with the community. An example of this is **Phinda Private Game Reserve**, a seriously upmarket park near Mkuzi that has brought tangible benefits to the local community and suggests a way in which business, communities and the environment can gain mutual benefit from tourism.

Note that the northern KwaZulu-Natal coastal region is **malarial**. For details on necessary precautions, see "Health" on p.17.

Richards Bay to Hluhluwe

There's no conceivable reason for spending time in either **Empangeni**, 173km north of Durban, or **RICHARDS BAY**, 12km east, on the coast. Two modern industrial sprawls that are the only centres of any size in the vicinity, they are completely at odds with the remote and pristine coast to the north and should be given short shrift, even if you happen to be making **transport** connections here. Given that you can avoid these towns on the Baz **backpacker bus**, which links up with transport to points along the Maputaland coast and to Hluhluwe-Umfolozi Park, you only need come here if you're **flying** into Richards Bay and plan on renting a car to make a quick getaway. SA Express (☎035/786 0301) fly twice daily from Johannesburg and touch down at **Richards Bay airport** (☎035/786 0301), 6km north of the town centre, while Metavia (☎035/552 9624) also fly from Johannesburg twice a day. **Car rental**, including 4WD, can be arranged from the airport through Avis (☎035/552 6555, fax 786 0053), Budget (☎035/786 0986, fax 786 0985) and Imperial (☎035/786 0309, fax 7860462). The only way to get to Richards Bay from Durban is on one of the bus services, or by car. **Intercity buses** all arrive at the *Steers Steak House*, next to the Total filling station in Anglers Rod Street: Sunbird Tours (☎031/945 489) and Greyhound (☎031/309 7830 or ☎035/722 6474) each run from Durban, and Translux (☎011/774 3333 or ☎031/361 8333) go to Durban from Johannesburg/Pretoria. If you're stuck here for the night, the **Richards Bay Tourist Information** (Mon–Fri 8am–4pm, Sat & Sun 10am–2pm; ☎ & fax 0351/788 0040, *rbtour@uthungulu.co.za*), at the Small Craft Harbour, off John Ross Parkway, can help you find accommodation.

Some 26km north of Richards Bay, the tiny village of **KWAMBONAMBI** (known locally as Kwambo) lies on the Baz **bus** route, and is notable for being home to two **backpacker lodges**, which both offer trips around the area. The predominantly African hamlet is safe and friendly and makes a preferable base to the less appealing village of Hluhluwe for exploring St Lucia and the Hluhluwe-Umfolozi game reserve. The *Amazulu Lodge*, 5 Killarney Place (☎035/580 1009, fax 580 4707), is an upmarket house for backpackers offering camping (①), dorms (①) and double rooms (②), some with air conditioning. The hostel also has a swimming pool, sauna and a Jacuzzi, with golf next door, but the biggest pull of the place is the fact that the staff offer day safaris to the Hluhluwe-Umfolozi Game Reserve and boat safaris on the St Lucia Estuary, as well as diving trips to Sodwana Bay. *Cuckoo's Nest*, 28 Albizia St (☎035/580 1001, fax 580 1002) congenially hosted by expats, has A-frame doubles (②), camping (①), plus some dorms (①), plus a great tree-house double (②). The *Cuckoo's Nest* offers day or overnight trips to Hluhluwe-Umfolozi Game Reserve, snorkelling at Cape Vidal or the eastern shores of St Lucia, boat tours on the St Lucia Estuary, and diving at Sodwana. They also do visits to a Zulu gospel church with a full choir on Sundays.

Another 25km further north, **MTUBATUBA** (often shortened to Mtuba), is a centre for the local sugar cane industry. An interesting place, with lots of herbalists, traditional healers and a Zulu market, it's situated at the crossroads of the R618 with the N2, and offers the enticing choice of heading west for Hluhluwe-Umfolozi Game Reserve or east to the St Lucia Estuary – both an easy twenty minutes away. It has a couple of good

places to stay: *Wendy Country House*, 3 Riverview Drive (☎035/5501 1527, *wendybnb@iafrica.com*; ③), is set in an acre of lush gardens with a swimming pool. They offer tours of the area, including cruises on the St Lucia Estuary, boat trips to Charter's Creek and, in season, trips to watch turtle-egg laying. *The Circle*, Lot 92, Umkuhla Crescent (☎035/5500 660, fax 5501 209; ③) is a tranquil place, with forest walks and an array of wildlife activities organized by the host, who's fluent in Zulu and knows the area like the back of his hand.

Nearly 60km north of Mtuba, just off the N2 is the straggling village of **HLUH-LUWE**, a much less attractive place than either Kwambo or Mtuba. A few shops service the surrounding game farms and there's a **tourist information office** at 15 Main St (☎035/562 0352). Definitely worth checking out here is Ilala Weavers, five minutes' drive from Hluhluwe, a hub of community projects that sells well-priced traditional **crafts** in a cheerful atmosphere. If you want to visit a Zulu theme park, **Dumazulu Traditional Village** has displays of energetic Zulu dancing, beer brewing, spear and basket making. Nearby, on the Bushlands Road, you can **stay** at *Isinkwe Lodge* (☎ & fax 035/562 2258), 14km south of Hluhluwe and on the Baz bus route. It's a definite rival to the lodges in Kwanbonambi, but with more of a rustic feel, with birds and monkeys larking about on its 22 hectares of indigenous bush. There are dorms, wooden cabins and camping (all ①), as well as more comfortable doubles (②) in the lodge. Very reasonably priced meals are on offer, or you can self-cater and eat in the massive *boma*. The lodge does tours in open-topped 4WD vehicles to Hluhluwe-Umfolozi and Mkuzi, as well as to Cape Vidal and Lake Sibaya, plus fairly priced transfers on Sundays and Thursdays from Sodwana Bay or the Engen Garage in Hluluwe.

Hluhluwe-Umfolozi Park

Hluhluwe-Umfolozi (daily: April–Sept 6am–6pm; Oct–March 5am–7pm; R30 per vehicle, R7 per person) is KwaZulu-Natal's most outstanding game reserve, and rated by some above even the Kruger. While it certainly can't match Kruger's sheer scale (Hluhluwe is a twentieth of the size) or its teeming game populations, its relatively compact 960 square kilometres have a wilder ambience. This has something to do with the fact that, besides **Hilltop** – an elegant hotel-style rest camp in the northern half of the park – none of the other rest camps are fenced off, and wild animals are free to wander through. The vegetation, with subtropical jungly forest in places and Tarzanish monkey ropes dripping over the rivers, adds to the sense of adventure.

Until recently the park was two distinct entities – hence its tongue-twisting double-barrelled name – and the two sections retain their separate characters, reinforced by a public road slicing between them. The southern or **Umfolozi section** takes its name from a corruption of *mfulawozi*, a Zulu word that refers to the fibrous bushes that grow along its rivers. The topography here is characterized by wide, deep valleys incised by the Black and White Mfolozi rivers, with altitudes varying between 60 and 650 metres. Luxuriant riverine vegetation gives way in drier areas to a variety of woodland, savannah, thickets and grassy plains.

The notable feature of the northern **Hluhluwe section** is its river of the same name, so called because of the dangling monkey ropes that hang from the canopy of the riparian forest. A slender, slithering waterway, punctuated by elongated pools, the Hluhluwe rises in the mountains north of the park and passes along sandbanks, rock beds and steep cliffs in the game reserve before seeping away into the St Lucia wetlands to the east. The higher ground is covered by *veld* and dense thicket, while the well-watered ridges support the softer cover of ferns, lichens, mosses and orchid.

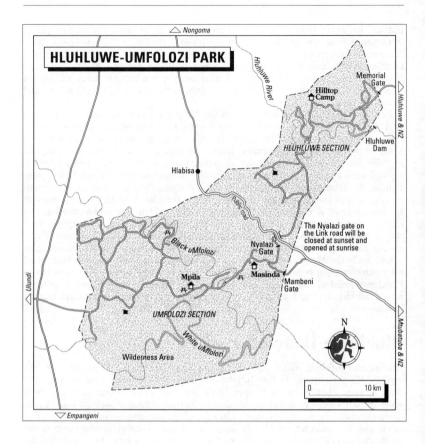

HLUHLUWE-UMFOLOZI PARK

Nongoma

Hluhluwe River

Memorial Gate

Hilltop Camp

Hluhluwe & N2

HLUHLUWE SECTION

Hluhluwe Dam

Hlabisa

Public road

Black uMfolozi

The Nyalazi gate on the Link road will be closed at sunset and opened at sunrise

Nyalazi Gate

Masinda

Mpila

Mambeni Gate

Ulundi

UMFOLOZI SECTION

White uMfolozi

Wilderness Area

N

Mtubatuba & N2

0   10 km

Empangeni

Some history

The sense of pristine wilderness you get at Hluhluwe-Umfolozi is entirely illusory – the result of careful **management** since the Fifties. Despite being the oldest proclaimed national park in Africa (it was created in 1895), Hluhluwe-Umfolozi's future as a game refuge has hung by a thread on several occasions in the last two hundred years. In the nineteenth century the park lay at the very centre of the **Zulu kingdom** and Umfolozi was the private hunting preserve of the Zulu king, Shaka. During Shaka's reign between 1818 and 1828 the area saw the most sustained campaign of hunting in Zulu history, but this was nothing compared to the destruction caused by white men in the twentieth century, when the park was twice de-proclaimed under pressure from neighbouring farmers whose cattle were being infected by **nagana**, a disease transmitted by tsetse flies from wild to domestic stock. Between 1929 and 1950 a crusade of game **extermination** was launched to wipe out the disease and saw 100,000 head of game from 16 species fall to the gun. Rhinos alone were spared.

It was only in 1952, when the park was handed over to the newly formed **KwaZulu-Natal Conservation Services**, that the slow process of resuscitation to the threadbare game reserve began. This was done with considerable flair and has been topped by the brilliant success of re-establishing its white rhino population from twenty animals at the turn of the century to nearly two thousand today. In 1994 the **white rhino** became the first species to be removed from the World Conservation Union's endangered list. Their survival is down mostly to efforts by conservationists in the Hluhluwe-Umfolozi Park, which has become the world's breeding bank for these animals.

Access and information

There is no public **transport** into Hluhluwe-Umfolozi. The only way of getting here without your own car is on one of the **tours**, such as those operated by the backpacker lodges in Kwambonambi, Mtubatuba or Hluhluwe (see pp.424–5). Access to the park is via one of three **gates**, two from the east along one of the two tarred roads that lead straight off the N2 into the park, and the other from Ulundi in the west. The R618, which begins 23km north of Kwambonambi, reaches **Mambeni Gate** after 27km, providing access to the southern section of the park. Some 46km beyond the R618, an unclassified but signposted and tarred road takes you via **Memorial Gate** into the northernmost section of the park. A third gate, **Cengeni**, is accessible along a thirty-kilometre dirt road from Ulundi to the west. You cannot enter the park from the public road connecting Hlabisa and Mtubatuba, which slices through its centre. Maps and information, including details of guided walks, are available at the receptions of *Hilltop* and *Mpila* camps.

Accommodation and eating

Accommodation is available at three public rest camps. **Bookings** for accommodation should be made through KwaZulu-Natal Conservation Services (see p.365). Camping should be arranged locally.

Rest camps in the (southern) **Umfolozi section** are at **Masinda**, near the Mambeni Gate, which has just six four-bedded units, communal ablution facilities and a kitchen where camp chefs cook food from ingredients that you provide, and at **Mpila**, in the centre of the section. Mpila commands excellent views of the surrounding wilderness and has twelve one-roomed huts with four beds each (②), communal ablutions and, like Masinda, cooks on hand to prepare your food. Mpila also has two self-contained three-bedroom cottages for seven people (④). Six self-catering chalets accommodate five people each (③). **Meal preparation times** from the central kitchen at both existing camps are daily 6.30–9am, noon–1.30pm and 4–7.30pm. There are no fences around the Umfolozi camps, so take care when walking around, particularly at night. A tented camp accommodating 22 people is in the pipeline.

The northern **Hluhluwe section** has just one camp, **Hilltop**, one of the best you'll find at any game reserve in the country. Set high on the edge of a slope, with sweeping views across the park's hills and valleys, it has modern, comfortable and varied accommodation, with twenty budget **rondavels** (③) that share communal ablutions and kitchen facilities; 27 en-suite **two-bed chalets** (⑤) with bar fridges, tea- and coffee-making facilities, and some with kitchenettes; and twenty **four-bed chalets** (⑤), with the same facilities. There's also a pleasant **restaurant**, the *Mpunyane*, plus the *Uzavolo Bar Lounge*, both attached to the central block. Hilltop is surrounded by an electric fence, which keeps out most animals. You may, however, come across nyala, zebra and other herbivores grazing around the chalets – all wild animals are potentially dangerous and should be treated with respect.

Game viewing and activities

Despite its compact size, Hluhluwe-Umfolozi is home to 84 mammal species and close on 350 varieties of bird. The Big Five are all here and it's no exaggeration to say that this is the best place in the world to see **rhinos** both black and white. **Lions** had become extinct in Umfolozi until 1958, when a black-maned male made an appearance, apparently having traversed the 400km from Mozambique. Females were later introduced and today there are around seventy of the big cats in the reserve, although they're not easy to see and their future hangs in the balance.

Other **predators** present are cheetah, leopard, spotted hyena and wild dog. **Herbivores** include blue wildebeest, buffalo, giraffe, hippo, impala, kudu, nyala and zebra. When it comes to **birds**, there are over a dozen species of **eagle**, as well as other **raptors** including hawks, goshawks and honey buzzards. Other larger birds include ground hornbills, vultures, owls and herons, and there are hundreds of other beautiful species to look out for. **Reptiles** number in the sixties, including crocodiles and several types of venomous snake, none of which you're likely to see. Along the Hluhluwe River, keep an eye open for the harmless monitor lizards, which resemble miniature dragons.

Where Hluhluwe-Umfolozi really scores over the Kruger is in the variety of activities on offer. Apart from **self-driving** around the park, there are also **self-guided walks** near several of the rest camps, **guided trails** in the company of an armed field ranger, and guided **night drives**. South Africa's first wilderness trail started in Umfolozi, and the reserve has remained one of the best places in South Africa for taking a walk on the wild side. Four-night **wilderness trails**, on which gear is carried by pack donkeys, leave from the base camp – you sleep under canvas for the next two nights, returning on the fourth to base. These all-inclusive trails, which must be booked through the KwaZulu-Natal Conservation Services (see p.365) run from March to November and cost around R1000 per person. Shorter weekend trails are a bit cheaper, at around R620 per person for two nights in the bush.

The Greater St Lucia Wetland Park

Five distinct ecosystems make up the **Greater St Lucia Wetland Park**, a 2750-square-kilometre patchwork of separate pieces locking together the St Lucia Reserve, St Lucia Park, False Bay Park, St Lucia Marine Reserve, Sodwana Bay National Park, Cape Vidal State Forest, Mkuzi Game Reserve, and other interlinking areas. Planned developments will make this the third-largest protected area in the country – it's already one of the most fascinating. The Wetland Park's origins as several separate reserves is readily apparent in the fact that few internal roads link one area to another, and each section is reached by a separate road that spurs off the N2.

The most striking feature is the 360-square-kilometre **Lake St Lucia**, South Africa's largest inland body of water, formed 25,000 years ago when the oceans receded. The lake is flanked by mountainous **dunes** covered by forest and grassland, whose peaks soar to an astonishing 200m above the beach to form a slender rampart against the Indian Ocean. Aside from the lake and dune ecosystems, the reserve protects a **marine zone** of warm tropical seas, coral reefs and endless sandy beaches; the **papyrus and reed wetland** of the Mkuze Swamps, on the north of the lake; and on the western shore dry **savannah** and **thornveld**. Any one of these would justify conservation but their confluence around the lake makes this a world-class wilderness.

St Lucia

It's a little strange to find a town inside a wilderness reserve, and there's nothing contemplative about **ST LUCIA**, which lies at the mouth of the **St Lucia Estuary** in the extreme south of the park. Reached after 32km at the end of the R620 east of Mtubatuba, the town becomes so hectic in midsummer that it could put you off northern KwaZulu-Natal altogether. Fortunately it's singularly atypical of the area. Everything in St Lucia centres around **angling**: you can't miss the plethora of tackle and bait shops, seafood restaurants and vehicles buzzing up and down the main street bristling with fishing rods, beers and men. Speedboats and jet skis surge through the water and 4WDs tour the beaches, an unpleasant white South African habit which you see wherever beaches are big and wild. A spin-off is that out of season, when the hordes of anglers have left, there's plenty of accommodation across a broad range of budgets.

The town takes its name from the estuary, whose mouth was reached by Portuguese explorers in 1576, and which they named Santa Lucia. During the second half of the eighteenth century, landlocked Boers made attempts to claim the mouth as a port but were pipped at the post by the British, who sent the HMS *Goshawk* in 1884 to annex the whole area, which then developed as a fishing resort. In the Twenties the town got its first hotel and in the Fifties it was connected to the mainland by a bridge.

St Lucia's best feature is the **estuary**, hidden behind the buildings along the main drag, and easy to miss if you drive quickly through. The main reason to fetch up here, however, is to get to **Cape Vidal** (see overleaf), the real prize of the area, inside the **St Lucia Wetlands National Park**, where strictly limited accommodation may necessitate basing yourself in St Lucia town.

The Town

If you end up spending any time in St Lucia, one of the best things you can do is go on a one-and-a-half-hour **guided lake cruise** on the KwaZulu-Natal Conservation Services's *Santa Lucia* (R46 adults, R27 children). From the deck you stand a good chance of seeing crocodiles and one of the eight hundred hippos that spend their days wallowing and snorting in Lake St Lucia, as well as pelicans, fish eagles, kingfishers and storks. Cruises leave daily at 8.30am, 10.30am and 2.30pm from the launch site next to the bridge on the west side of the estuary, and on Saturdays at 4pm there's a **sunset cruise**. **Bookings** are essential in peak season and can be made though the Conservation Services Office (see below).

Fishing and cruising aside, the **St Lucia Crocodile Centre** (daily 8am–4.30pm, crocodile feeding Sat 3pm; small entry fee), at the park gate at the north of town on the road to Cape Vidal, is worth an hour of your time if you have any interest in natural history. Rest assured that this isn't another of those exploitative wildlife freak-shows found throughout South Africa, but a serious educative spin-off of the Conservation Services's crocodile conservation campaign. Up until the end of the Sixties, crocodiles were regarded as pests, and this led to a hunting free-for-all that saw them facing extinction in the area. Just in time, it was realized that the reptiles have an important role in the ecological cycle, and the Conservation Services began a successful **breeding programme**, returning the crocs to the wild to bolster numbers. The Crocodile Centre aims to rehabilitate the reputation of these maligned creatures, with informative displays and an astonishing cross-section of species (although only the Nile crocodile occurs in the wild in South Africa) lounging around enclosed pools. There's also a very good **bookshop** at the Centre, with items on natural history and cheap but informative booklets about the local coastal and wetland ecology.

Practicalities

The St Lucia Publicity Association, on the corner of Mackenzie Street and Katonkel Road (Mon–Fri 8am–5pm, Sat 8am–noon; ☎035/590 1075) isn't that hot on **information** about the town, but operates a very useful accommodation-finding service. For information about the Wetlands National Park your best bet is the Conservation Services office (daily 8am–4.30pm; ☎035/590 1340, fax 590 1343), at the south end of Pelican Road.

Out of season, cheap **accommodation** isn't hard to find. *Pumula Lodge*, 25 Pelican St (☎ & fax 035/590 1328, mobile ☎082/321 4424), has clean basic self-catering en-suite doubles (①) at backpacker prices in a family house, with breakfast a bit extra; they also have a self-catering lakeside chalet (②). *Jo a Lize*, Mackenzie St (☎035/590 1085, fax 590 1224), has self-contained, self-catering flats (②) and tiny but clean en-suite B&B units (③); in the same street, the *Boma Hotel* (☎ & fax 031/562 9505; ③), has spacious, luxury self-catering cabanas, some of which have balconies with wonderful views of the estuary, plus there's a pool, wooden sundecks and *braai* stands. The most comfortable B&B in town is *Kingfisher Lodge*, Mackenzie St (☎035/590 1015; ④), the only lodge overlooking the estuary, with African-themed chalets, which may mean a stuffed buffalo head glaring down at you from the walls. They don't cater for backpackers and there's no self-catering – guests eat at the restaurant next door. Firmly on the Baz bus backpacker route is the good *Bib's International Backpackers*, Mackenzie St (☎ & fax ☎035/590 1360, *webmaster@backpackafrica.com*), a thatched lodge with camping (①), basic doubles (②) and slightly more expensive self-catering private rooms (③), and facilities such as microwaves, laundry and pool tables. On offer are daily trips to the game reserves, snorkelling at St Lucia, Wetlands trips, crocodile and hippo launch-trips, hiking trails, and bird-watching to tick off some of the 430 species in the area. At the same address, *Grunter's* is ideal for families, with cheap four, six and ten-bed chalets (①), all self-catering with TVs and *braai* stands, and set under big, old shady trees.

For **eating**, the best place is the *North Coast Restaurant,* Mackenzie Street, which serves good, reasonably priced seafood. If you want to enter the spirit of the place and catch your own fish, head for the Bait and Tackle Shop, also in Mackenzie Street, which sells rods, tackle and (should you fail to hook anything) fresh fish, as well as all the spices and condiments you'll need for a fish *braai*.

Cape Vidal

Another popular fishing spot, **CAPE VIDAL** (daily: April–Sept 6am–6pm; Oct–March 5am–7pm; R30 per vehicle, R7 per person) has the edge over St Lucia in that it's more difficult to reach and numbers are limited to just one hundred day-visitors' vehicles, while accommodation for overnight stays is limited to KwaZulu-Natal Conservation Services facilities. The only way of getting there is via St Lucia, from where you take a rough dirt road north for 32km, navigating along a narrow bridge of land between the lake on the west and the Indian Ocean on the east. This one- to two-hour journey passes through pine plantations, open grassland and wetland areas.

Even if you aren't a keen angler, there's enough stunning wilderness at Cape Vidal to get lost in or to keep you chilling out for several days. The sea is over the dunes, minutes from the Conservation Services accommodation. An offshore reef shelters the coast from the high seas, making it safe for **swimming**, and if you're keen on **snorkelling** an underwater extravaganza of hard and soft corals and colourful fish awaits. Burly anglers who use the rocks for casting their lines into the wide ocean may look at you in disbelief if you go looking into the tiny water worlds of the **rock pools**, but you'll be rewarded with sightings of seaweeds, snails, crabs, sea cucumbers, anemones, urchins and small fish.

Large mammals and fish move just offshore in open seas beyond the reef. Cape Vidal is an excellent place for shore sightings of **humpback whales**, which breed off Mozambique, not far to the north in winter. In October they move south, drifting on the warm Agulhas current with their calves. If you're lucky you may see these and other whales from the vantage of the dunes, but without binoculars they'll just look like specks on the horizon. A **whale-watching tower**, reached through the dune forest south of the rest camp, provides an even higher viewpoint. Eighteen-metre plankton-feeding whale sharks, the largest and gentlest of the sharks, have been sighted off this coast in schools of up to seventy at a time, and manta rays and dolphins are also common in these waters.

Practicalities

If you're planning to stay overnight, and this is highly recommended, prebook your **accommodation** before trawling out. There are only eighteen six-bed chalets (③) and twelve eight-bed Swiss-style log cabins (②), all of which are en suite and fully equipped at the service camp – all you need to bring is your own food and drink. Cabins are serviced and cleaned every morning by camp staff. There's also a campsite with space for fifty tents, in the dune forest near the beach (①), where facilites extend to ablutions. Construction of a new safari camp has begun and the campsite is being upgraded. On **arrival** at Cape Vidal, report to the Conservation Services Office (daily 8am–12.30pm & 2–4.30pm).

Reservations for cabins and chalets should be made through the Conservation Services (see box p.365). **Bookings for campsites** is vital during school holidays and over long weekends and can be made in writing up to one year in advance through the Officer-in-Charge, Cape Vidal, Private Bag X01, St Lucia Estuary 3936 (☎035/590 1404, fax 590 1300). Although **petrol** and firewood can be bought at Cape Vidal, for all other **supplies** the nearest place to stock up is St Lucia.

The Western Shore

The **Western Shore** of Lake St Lucia marks the old seashore, harking back for aeons to a time when the ocean level was 2m higher than it is today. Decayed matter from marine animals has created a rich soil that once supported an extensive array of animal life, and although the Big Five were shot out ages ago there are still **birds** and over a hundred species of **butterfly** flitting about. Among the **herbivores** are suni, Africa's smallest antelope, as well as nyala and red duiker. With no dangerous predators apart from **crocodiles** (take care along the shore), the inland bushveld and woodlands are safe for walking without a guide.

The main activities along the Western Shore, which is accessible only in your own vehicle, are **fishing** and **bird-watching**. Most camps also have **waymarked trails** that make a thoroughly enjoyable way, if you're moderately energetic, to explore the lakeside vegetation and birds. You should also keep an eye open for game, especially the water-loving reedbuck that take refuge in the swamps.

Charter's Creek

Primarily an anglers' retreat, **CHARTER'S CREEK** (April–Sept 6am–8pm; Oct–March 5am–8pm; small entry fee), which lies at the southern end of the lake, is also excellent for **bird-watching** and has two half-day **trails**. The major attraction here is the camp, situated on a cliff edge with views across the lake. From here you can spot waterfowl and flamingos – even pelicans make an appearance – while permanent residents include hippos and crocodiles. The seven-kilometre **Isikhova Trail** and the five-kilometre **Umkhumbe Trail** both leave from the camp and shouldn't take more than two to three hours to complete. The trails take in typical Western Shore coastal forest and provide the opportunity to spot small **game**, including the tiny red duiker, with its short, backward-pointing horns. Other species occasionally encountered include mongooses, bushbuck, jackals, bushbabies and, commonest of all, vervet monkeys.

To **get there**, turn off the N2, some 20km north of Mtubatuba and follow the signs all the way to Charter's Creek, via the Nyalazi river halt. **Accommodation** is in a choice of a seven-bedded cottage (③), and huts (②) – ten four-bedded, fourteen three-bedded and one two-bedded – all of which are fully equipped. Servicing and cooking is done by camp staff, though this is being phased out to make it self catering, and you must provide your own food. Although you can't swim in the lake, there's a pool at the camp for cooling off in. **Bookings** should be made through the KwaZulu-Natal Conservation Services (see box on p.365).

Fanies Island

Not an island at all but part of the Western Shore, approximately 20km north of Charter's Creek as the crow flies, **FANIES ISLAND** (April–Sept 6am–8pm; Oct–March 5am–8pm; small entry fee) looks out onto reeded islands between networks of waterlogged paths worn away by hippos. The views are magnificent across the reed beds to the grasslands, forests and misty hill-like dunes of Cape Vidal on the coast. The large croc population here makes bathing or paddling out of the question. Like all the Western Shore camps, Fanies Island is much favoured by anglers, but this is one of the most secluded, and attractively positioned.

Even if you're not fishing, it's a tranquil enough place to spend time, with a couple of walking trails to help you explore. The five-kilometre **Umkhiwane Trail** can be completed in two hours and goes through forest, open grassveld and swamp forest, and is highly recommended for bird-watching. Hippos, vervet monkeys, bushbuck, warthog, reed buck and waterbuck are among the common mammals you stand a good chance of seeing. The **Umboma Trail** is shorter, wending its way through forest and back to camp along the lake shore.

To **get there** follow the instructions for Charter's Creek, but 20km north of Mtubatuba, take the undesignated tarred road that sours east from the N2. Eleven kilometres from the N2, the route splits into two dirt roads; take the northernmost one for 14km to reach Fanies Island. The route is well signposted. **Accommodation** is in a seven-bedded cottage (③); and twelve fully-equipped two-bedded rondavels (②) with their own fridges, but sharing an ablution block and a kitchen, where your food is prepared by camp chefs (though this is being phased out). There are twenty shady **campsites** (①) for which **reservations** should be made through the Camp Manager, Fanies Island, PO Box 1259, Mtubabtuba 3935 (☎035/550 1631). All other accommodation should be booked through the KwaZulu-Natal Conservation Services (see p.365). **Fuel** is available at the camp, as is a limited range of basic foods, but you'll be far better off stocking up in Hluhluwe or Mtubatuba before you come.

False Bay Park

Situated about 20km north of Fanies Island, **FALSE BAY PARK** (April–Sept 6am–8pm, Oct–March 5am–8pm; small entry fee) perches on the west shore of a small, lozenge-shaped waterway connected to Lake St Lucia by a narrow steep-sided channel known colourfully as "Hell's Gates". Excellent for bird-watching, it's a quiet place, which doesn't see many tourists or even anglers despite offering opportunities to fish for both freshwater and marine species, as well as Cape salmon. The park gives an excellent, low-key experience of the lake, which you can get onto with **launch tours**. If you want to get out into the bush, the eight-kilometre **Dugandlovu Trail** and the ten-kilometre circular **Mpophomeni Trail**, will easily keep you busy for a couple of days. Both are clearly waymarked, pass through a variety of terrain and offer the opportunity of seeing birds and a decent variety of antelope and other small mammals such as jackals, mongooses, servals, genets, warthogs and vervet monkeys. If you're not so energetic, there's the shorter six-kilometre **Ingwe Trail**, which runs alongside the lake.

To **get there**, turn off the N2 towards Hluhluwe 49km north of the Mtubatuba turn-off, and continue east for 4km until you reach Hluhluwe. Continue through the village to a T-junction at the end of the road and follow the signposts for 15km to the False Bay gate. There's a **campsite** (①) at Lister's Point about midway down the west shore of False Bay, which has communal ablutions, but you must supply everything else. About

8km to the south, *Dugandlovu Rustic Camp* has four basic, four-bedded-huts (②) with cold showers, toilets, gas cookers and paraffin lamps. If you want hot water, the camp has big, fat, three-legged pots which you can put on the fire to heat water, then lug into the shower. You must bring all your own gear, including linen and sleeping bags. **Bookings** for both camps must be made through the Officer-in-Charge, False Bay Park, PO Box 222, Hluhluwe 3960 (☎035/562 0425).

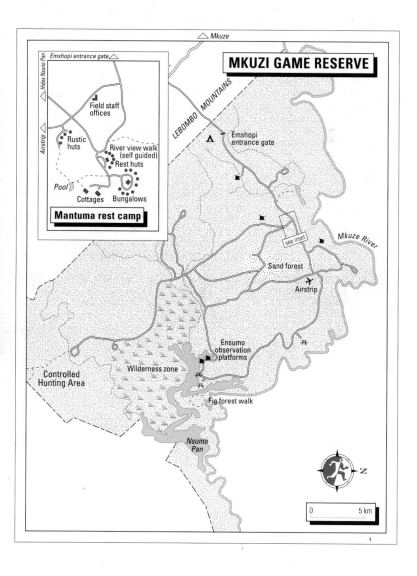

Mkuzi Game Reserve

Mkuzi Game Reserve (April–Sept 6am–6pm, Oct–March 5am–7pm; R30 per vehicle, R7 per person) is a major component of the Greater St Lucia Wetland Reserve, connected to the coastal plain by a slender corridor through which the Mkuze River flows before emptying itself in Lake St Lucia. Reached across the Lebombo mountains, 28km from Mkuze village on the N2, the reserve has no lions, but a rich cross-section of mammals covering 78 species inhabits its confines. It's for its varied and highly beautiful countryside and the avifauna that the reserve really rates – this is among the top spots for bird-watching in the country, with an impressive 430 species on record. Some of the prizes include Pels fishing owl and Rudd's apalis, a small insect-eating bird with a very restricted distribution. Even if you know nothing about birds, you're likely to appreciate one of Africa's most colourful here - the lilac breasted roller.

Defined to the west by the Lebombo mountains, Mkuzi marks the final haul of the coastal plain that stretches down the east of the continent from Kenya. The landscape varies from wetlands consisting of seasonal flood plains floating with waterlilies, reed beds and swamps, to savanna covered with grass. Elsewhere you'll come across stands of acacias (thorn trees) and in the south across the Mkuzi River you can wander through the cathedral-like fig forest that echoes to the shriek of trumpeter hornbills.

Access and information

There's no public **transport** into Mkuzi, and if you don't have your own vehicle you'll need to latch onto one of the **tours** that start in **Mkuze**. The village has a few shops for supplies, a garage for petrol or repairs and the very pleasant *Ghost Mountain Inn* (☎ & fax 035/573 1025; ⑤) signposted off the N2, which is great for a drink or meal and a dunk in their pool, even if you aren't staying. The hotel has information about tours, including straightforward half- or full-day **game drives** with Maputaland Tours, who are based here (☎ & fax 035/573 1025), for which you should expect to pay R80–175 depending on numbers.

If you're **self-driving**, the easiest way to get to the reserve is to leave the N2 at Mkuzi and follow the signs along a good dirt road for 28km to **Emshopi Gate**. An alternative route, which leaves the N2 further south, 35km north of Hluhluwe village, involves a lot more driving on dirt and doesn't knock off that much distance. For navigating your way around the park, the **reception office** (☎035/573 0003) provides a clear map that shows all routes and distances and gives general information about the park.

Accommodation

A **campsite** (①) is situated right at Emshopi Gate, while **Mantuma**, the main public rest camp, 9km into the park in the northern section, has a range of **accommodation**. Cheapest are the three-bedded rest huts (②) with shared ablution facilities and a kitchen, where a cook prepares your food for you. The most enticing units are the large traditional walk-in en-suite safari tents (②), each with its own roofed, but open-sided kitchen across the way. Nearby are three- and five-bedded en-suite bungalows (③–④) and a couple of seven-bedded cottages (④). All units are fully equipped and you need only bring food and drink. **Reservations** for camping should be made through the Camp Superintendent, Mkuzi Game Reserve, PO Box X550, Mkuze 3965 (☎035/573 004); all other accommodation must be booked through the KwaZulu-Natal Conservation Services (see p.365).

There's a **fuel pump** at the entrance gate where you can fill up your car, and a **shop** that sells basic supplies and books at the camp reception, but you should really stock up in Mkuze village before heading out here.

Game viewing and activities

Of the predators, **cheetah** and **leopard** are present but rarely glimpsed; you stand a better chance of seeing fox-like black-backed **jackals**. The obvious draw-card of Mkuzi, however, are its black and white **rhinos**. The **impala** antelope will also be hard to miss, and you should catch sight of the large, spiral-horned **eland** and **kudu**. **Baboons** and **vervet monkeys** are generally found rustling around in the trees and making a nuisance of themselves on the ground, while at night you could be treated to the eerie call of the thick-tailed **bushbaby** from the canopy.

Some 84km of road traverse Mkuzi, but one of the best ways to see game is to stay put and wait for the animals to come to you. With exactly this in mind, several **hides**, marked on the map given out at reception, have been erected at artificial waterholes and on the edge of pans. All animals have to drink at some time, particularly in the drier months when naturally occurring water is scarcer, so you're bound to have a relaxed and interesting time at a hide if you chill out with a pair of binoculars and a good field guide.

The two hides at **Nsumo Pan**, in the southern section of the park, apart from overlooking a very beautiful natural waterway, are superbly placed for observing waterfowl. The picnic site at Nsumo is one of the few places in the game reserve where you may leave your car and it makes a great place to stop and eat. Between July and September, if conditions are right, you can catch up to five hundred **birds** on the water at one time. Flocks of pelicans and flamingos make their appearance, as do kingfishers, fish eagles, waders, ducks, geese and countless other species.

From Nsumo you can embark on the three-kilometre self-guided **Mkuzi Fig Forest Trail** – another highlight of the reserve. Follow the signs from the car park to the Mkuze River, which can be crossed using a suspension bridge if the flow is too fast to allow rock-hopping. **Sycamore fig forest** is one of the rarest types of woodland in South Africa, and the stands of massive trees give the forest a gentle green glow. Look out for the flashing red flight feathers of fruit-eating **birds** like the purple-crested lourie or green pigeons and listen for the tap-tap of golden-tailed woodpeckers on the trees. **Monkeys** and **baboons**, which pass through from time to time pose no threat, except to steal your food, but you should keep alert to the possibility of encountering **black rhinos** or **hippos**, both of which are potentially dangerous and should be given a wide berth.

If you wish to explore other parts of Mkuzi on foot, you can go out on two-hour **conducted walks** with a field ranger. Many of the older rangers speak very little English and their main function is to protect you. Current Conservation Services policy, however, is to employ younger guides who speak English well and have a knowledge of the environment, so check out the situation when you book your walk at the rest-camp reception. More ambitious **three-day bushveld trails** are also available from March to November. On these, you'll be based at the trails camp in a remote part of the park, from which daily walks are accompanied by a well-informed field ranger and a game guard. The trails cost around R900 per person, which includes all meals and accommodation, but you must bring your own snacks and drinks. For booking and further information, contact the Conservation Services (see box, p.365).

Also not to be missed, and indicated on the map you'll get at the entrance gate, is a small **Crafts Centre**, where you can buy some great, inexpensive Zulu crafts made by people in the area.

Phinda Private Game Reserve

Although it's not one of the great South African game-viewing destinations, **Phinda Private Game Reserve**, on a 15,000 hectare ranch at the southern end of Mkuzi Reserve, is certainly a contender for the most stylish. The reserve offers a good chance of seeing **lion, cheetah** and both varieties of **rhino** on your game drives, but you can't help feeling it's all a bit too well-managed. At the moment the property is too small to sustain a self-regulating wildlife ecology, but if, as is hoped, it becomes integrated with surrounding parks (as has happened around the Kruger National Park) this could change dramatically.

Phinda is interesting, however, as an **eco-tourism** experiment based on the philosophy that to conserve wildlife in Africa it is necessary to bring tangible benefits to local communities. Not only has degraded farmland been returned to wilderness (*phinda* means "return" in Zulu), but more people now work providing services to tourists than were employed when it was ranchland.

Whatever Phinda may lack as a wildlife destination is made up for abundantly by the sheer panache with which it provides fine-tuned luxury and hospitality to its upmarket clientele. **Accommodation** is at four lodges, with *Mountain Lodge* providing vistas of the Lebombo range and the nearby St Lucia coastal plain; *Rock Lodge* embracing a more intimate experience, with just six stone and glass chalets suspended off a cliff face; *Forest Lodge* offering stunning Afro-Japanese-style stilted timber houses, each tucked away discreetly among bush and trees; *Phinda Vlei Lodge*, in a sand forest on the edge of a pan system, with highly polished timber and glass chalets. The **food**, described as "eclectic pan-African", is excellent. All game drives or walks are accompanied by well-informed expert guides, who are as good as any you'll find in South Africa.

Prices start at US$430 per person inclusive of all meals and game activities. **Bookings** should be made through Conservation Corporation Africa, Private Bag X27, Benmore 2010 (☎011/784 7077, fax 784 7667, *reservations@conscorp.co.za*), or through one of the specialist travel agents listed in "Basics". Unlike public parks, Phinda's wilderness is only open to its resident guests and you'll be given detailed instructions on **how to get there** when you make your booking.

Northern Maputaland

Northern Maputaland, roughly the region north of Mkuzi Game Reserve, is the remotest region of South Africa, mostly accessible only along dirt roads that work their tortuous way to the coast. For much of this area, a 4WD vehicle is essential and it's best to travel in two vehicles as there's nowhere to get repairs done and facilities are poor.

Some 11km north of **Mkuze** village, the longest tarred road in Maputaland snakes north and then east for 133km, before stopping abruptly at the busy, run-down settlement of **Kwangwanase** (Manguzi on some maps), 24km short of the coast. As it turns toward the sea, the road brushes past a short track that leads up to **Ndumo Game Reserve** and 8km later the entrance gate to Tembe Elephant Park, both hanging down from the Mozambique border. The latter is a very underdeveloped conservation area, to which only the dedicated go, as only five, private 4WD vehicles are admitted per day. It's far easier to see elephants elsewhere, such as the Kruger Park (see p.573). From Kwangwanase, 26km beyond Tembe, a road heads for Kosi Bay and the Mozambique border.

To the south of Tembe, roads branch off this tarred spine, leading to **Mbazwana**, a tiny settlement that gains some status from being poised between **Sodwana Bay** to the south and **Lake Sibaya** to the north. Mbazwana can be reached by striking south off the tar at **Jozini**, a small, dog-eared town that will seem like a thriving metropolis next to anything you're going to encounter beyond.

Sodwana Bay

A tiny scoop in the Zululand Coast, **SODWANA BAY** (daily 24hr; small entry fee) 19km south of Mbazwana along an unexpected interlude of tar, is the only breach in an almost flawless length of strand that extends from St Lucia for 170km to Kosi Bay. It's the fortuitous convergence of the bay, which makes it easy to launch boats, with the world's southernmost coral reefs that makes Sodwana the most popular base in the country for **scuba diving** and the most popular KwaZulu-Natal Conservation Services resort. Because the continental shelf comes extremely close to shore with near-vertical drops less than 1km away, it offers very deep waters, much loved by anglers, who gather here to launch out for some of South Africa's best **game fishing**.

When there's no one around, Sodwana Bay is paradise: a truly magnificent place with tepid waters, terrific sandy beaches, forest hikes, relaxed diving or snorkelling and plenty of cheap and basic accommodation. Over weekends and during school holidays, however, the picture changes, with fashion-conscious Jo'burgers tearing down to show off their designer wetsuits, while thick-set anglers from Gauteng, Free State and Mpumalanga kick up some sand with their heavy tread, drink themselves into a stupor and turn the beach into a massive 4WD car park. A gentler presence from mid-November to February are the leatherback **turtles**, which make their way onto Sodwana's beaches to reproduce, as they've been doing for the last 60,000 years (see p.441).

Access and accommodation

There is no public **transport** to Sodwana, although Coral Divers (see "Diving" below) meets the Baz **bus**, when it pulls into the village of Hluhluwe on its four-times-a-week run from Durban. Alternatively you can make arrangements through Kwambonambi-based *Amazulu Lodge* (see p.424), which organizes diving trips. **Hitching** is possible, but even if you do succeed in thumbing a lift there the place is so spread out that getting around on foot is a major hassle. The park takes in the bay itself, while the desultory collection of shops and an upmarket lodge that pass for the **town** are 8km to the west, back along the Mbazwana Road. One shop though, opposite the Conservation Services Office and park entry, sells **food** and other camping basics. It closes at around 4.30pm, so don't leave your purchases until you return from the beach. **Petrol** is also available.

Most **accommodation** is inside the park and tends to be pretty basic, apart from ten five-bedded (③) and ten eight-bedded (③) fully equipped **log cabins** provided by Conservation Services. Although the cabins are pricey for just two people because there's a minimum charge, they work out quite reasonably if there are three or more of you. There are also a staggering 446 **campsites** (①), which are levied at a minimum fee of R100 per site during public and school holidays as well as Friday and Saturday nights; the seasonal population explosion allegedly gives Sodwana the largest campsite in the southern hemisphere. **Bookings** for chalets should be made through the Conservation Services (see p.365); for campsites contact The Officer-in-Charge, Sodwana Bay National Park, Private Bag 310, Mbazwana 3974 (☎035/571 0051, fax 571 0115).

Apart from these, you can rent very basic **timber huts** (①) or bell tents on timber decks from the dive operators, when they aren't taken by scuba clients, with large communal kitchens and *braai* areas, and cohorts of monkeys and birds in the trees shading the camps. These are offered by Coral Divers and Sodwana Dive Retreats (see "Diving" below for details). The only **hotel** accommodation is at the expensive *Sodwana Bay Lodge & Hotel Resort* (☎031/304 5977, fax 306 4847; ⑦), 8km from the bay, with a dinner, bed and breakfast rate for rooms, and less if you're in one of the six or eight bed comfortable en-suite reed chalets with thatched roofs and decks. The hotel also rents out a private, self-catering house, sleeping four (③).

Diving

Unless you're a keen angler, the principal reason to come to Sodwana is for the **diving** off its coral reefs. More commonly found further north, coral reefs and bright tropical fish thrive here in the warm waters carried down the coast by the Agulhas Current.

Both soft and hard **corals** robe the rocks with their convolutions and delicate formations and their range of textures, shades and colours. The waters are clear, silt-free and perfect for spotting some of the 1200 varieties of **fish** that inhabit the waters off northern KwaZulu-Natal, making it second only to the Great Barrier Reef in its richness.

The reefs are reached on dive boats, which smash a path through the surf. Closest to the bay, most commonly visited and consequently most stressed, is **Two Mile Reef**, which is 2km long, 900m wide, plumbs depths of between 9m and 34m and still offers eminently satisfying dives. Among the others is **Five Mile Reef**, which is further north and is known for its miniature staghorn corals, while beyond that **Seven Mile Reef** is inhabited by large anemone communities and offers protection to turtles and rays, which may be found resting here.

Of the **dive operators** at Sodwana, only Sodwana Dive Retreats (☎031/307 4902 or 307 4903, fax 571 0042), based at *Sodwana Bay Lodge & Hotel Resort*, offer tuition leading to an internationally recognized **certificate**. If you want to learn to scuba dive in South Africa, this is unquestionably the best place to do it. They also do **dive packages** for people with open-water certificates, starting at R950 per person for three dives and two nights, hotel-style accommodation over a weekend on a half-board basis. A self-catering budget version, staying in tents or very basic timber cabins (bring your own towels and sleeping bag), is also available. A slightly nicer alternative, in more salubrious huts, again self-catering, is offered by Coral Divers, P/Bag 310, Mbazwane 3974 (☎082/556 2474, fax 035/571 0042), which has two-bedded huts (Mon–Wed ②; Thurs–Sun ③) and tents (Mon–Wed ①; Thurs–Sun ②) and packages for qualified divers, starting at R450 for three nights and five dives over a weekend. Both companies offer discounted rates during the week and rent out full diving kit.

Snorkelling, turtle tours and the Mngobolezeni Trail

If you don't want to go the whole hog with diving, you can still enjoy excellent **snorkelling** at Jesser Point, a tiny promontory at the southern end of the bay. Just off here is **Quarter Mile Reef**, which attracts a wide variety of fish, including moray eels and rays. Low tide is the best time to venture out – a sign on the beach indicates daily tide times. You can buy competitively priced snorkels and masks from the **dive shop** at *Sodwana Bay Lodge & Hotel Resort* (see "Access and accommodation" on previous page) and they may be prepared to rent these as well as wet suits during off-peak periods.

During December and January, when loggerhead and leatherback turtles (see p.441) come to nest and lay their eggs on the beach, KwaZulu-Natal Conservation Services operate well-informed guided **turtle tours**. Bookings for these must be made at the park reception, near the entrance gate and cost R70 per adult and R35 for children; it's half-price if you take your own 4WD vehicle.

The starting point for the five-kilometre circular **Mngobolezeni Trail** is just across from the park reception and winds its way through a variety of habitats, including woodland, to the coastal lake that gives the hike its name. Arrows and signs indicate the way – but take care not to get sidelined down one of the many game tracks that crisscross it. The walk takes around three hours and there's no drinkable water along the way, so you should take refreshment. **Crocodiles** live in the lake, as do hippos, who leave the water to feed, usually at dusk. If you encounter a hippo on land, treat it with the utmost respect: hippos are responsible for more human deaths than any other African mammal. Avoid getting between a hippo and its line of retreat, which will generally be the most direct route to the safety of the water. If you do disturb one, find a tree to hide behind or, even better, to climb!

Apart from hippos, you may be lucky enough to see some of the other animals that inhabit the dune forest and its surrounds, among them bushbuck, duiker (red and common), reedbuck and Tonga squirrels. An informative booklet, *Mngobolezeni Trail*, interprets points of interest along the way, and is available from the park reception.

Lake Sibaya and Baya Camp

On a windless day, **LAKE SIBAYA**, 10km due north of Sodwana, appears glassy, azure and flat. The waters are so transparent that when the Conservation Services do a hippo census they just fly over and count the dark blobs that are clearly visible from the air. South Africa's largest natural freshwater lake, it covers 77 square kilometres and is fringed by white sandy beaches that disappear into densely entwined forest. From the margins, timid crocodiles cut the lake surface, exchanging the warmth of the sun for the safety of the water. This is not an unpopulated wilderness: the lake fringes are dotted with traditional African lands and villages.

The only **accommodation** on the lake is at *Baya Camp*, on its western shore, 16km north of Mbazwana along a dirt track that traverses thick sand in places; although you won't need a 4WD vehicle to get here, because of the thick sand elsewehere you'll need one to explore the forest areas around the lake. Three four-bedded and four two-bedded huts (②), connected by boardwalks, are each equipped with a handbasin with cold running water. The lounge, dining, kitchen and ablution facilities (with hot water if there's been enough sun to power the solar panels) are all shared. **Meals**, using your own food, are prepared by camp staff. **Reservations** can be made up to six months in advance through the KwaZulu-Natal Conservation Services central office (see p.365). Don't just turn up expecting to find a vacant chalet, because if they're full you'll end up driving to the nearest hotel in Mkuze, some 111km away. There are no **facilities** apart from those already mentioned: the nearest shops and fuel are in Mbazwana, but you'd be better off stocking up at a larger centre, such as Mkuze or Jozini.

Boredom is a potential hazard in staying at Lake Sibaya, so consider coming here only if you're in a contemplative frame of mind as there's little to do apart from watch the hippos and crocs on the lake, survey the birdlife or embark on an exceptionally easy-going three-kilometre **circular walk** that starts from the viewing platform behind the camp. Nearby are two hides, and **bird-watching** can be rewarding with close on three hundred species present. Needless to say, with crocs and hippos lolling about, swimming in the lake would not be wise.

Mabibi

On the west side of Sibaya, **MABIBI** is probably the most remote and idyllic campsite in South Africa, made all the more appealing by the difficulty of getting there. Situated in luxuriant subtropical forest, about 20km from Sodwana up the coast towards Mozambique, the ten **campsites** (①) perch on a plateau at the top of monumental dunes that slide sharply down to the sea. The camp is protected from the winds by the dune forest and a boardwalk leads down the duneside to the **sea** – a walk that takes about ten minutes. This is one of the most undisturbed sections of coast in KwaZulu-Natal, and outside school holidays you stand a fair chance of having a perfect tropical beach all to yourself. You won't get the frenetic activity of outboard motors and 4WD vehicles found at Sodwana and other spots to the south, because they're banned within the Maputaland Coastal Forest Reserve, which Mabibi falls under.

The sea here is excellent for **surf angling** and the **snorkelling** matches that at Sodwana, with a rich tropical marine life thriving on the coral reefs offshore. A number of mammals live in the forest, but most of them – bushbabies, large-spotted genets and porcupines – only come out after dark, while others like suni and samango monkeys tend to be shy. Vervet monkeys, on the other hand, are fairly bold and you're bound to encounter a troop breezing through if you stay for more than a day.

The best **access** to the camp is along the tarred Kwangwanase (also called Manguzi) road from the N2, some 11km north of Mkuze. At the Manzengwenya intersection, turn right and follow the Mabibi signboards. Because this final 45km from the junction is along gravel and thick sand tracks, a 4WD vehicle, or at least one with high clearance such as a *bakkie* (pick-up truck), is essential. The closest **shops and fuel** are at Mbazwana, 60km to the south. The campsites can be **booked** up to six months in advance through the KwaZulu-Natal Conservation Services central office (see box on p.365).

Rocktail Bay

South Africa's most sublime beachstay lies about 40km north of Mabibi along the coast at **ROCKTAIL BAY**, an even less accessible stretch of sand and sea that is restricted to guests who are prepared to shell out for the undeniable privilege of staying at the upmarket *Rocktail Bay Lodge*. Few parts of the South African coastline are as unspoilt as the beaches around here, and although there's no big game to pull in the punters, the bird-watching is excellent and you could see a number of rare and sought-after species, among them the green twinspot, green coucal, grey waxbill, purple-crested and Livingstone's louries as well as the Natal robin and emerald cuckoo. A rare and prized bird to spot is the palmnut vulture.

Supreme idleness is one of the big attractions of the place, but if you're feeling perky you can go **snorkelling** in the bay at low tide (fins and snorkels are available to guests), walk in the coastal forest, join an excursion to Black Rock or Lake Sibaya and go onto the beach to watch turtles during the summer egg-laying season. **Surf fishing** for shad, springer, kingfish, bonefish, stumpnose, barracuda and blacktail is another possibility.

Accommodation is in ten reed and thatched chalets with private toilets and showers raised on stilts into the forest canopy, each with its own wooden deck. This is the ideal place to get away: there's no phone, limited solar electricity (about 3hr per day), and the last few kilometres are so heavy going that you leave your vehicle at the Coastal Forest Reserve office and have to be ferried in by 4WD. **Prices** inclusive of all meals and activities come to R875 per person and can be booked through Wilderness Safaris, PO Box 78573, Sandton, 2146 (☎011/883 0747, fax 883 0911, *info@sdn.wilderness.co.za*).

Ndumo Game Reserve

One of the most beautiful of the KwaZulu-Natal reserves, **NDUMO** (daily dawn–dusk; R30 per vehicle, R7 per person) peers across the flood plain into Mozambique to the north and up to the Lebombo Mountains in the south. Its northern extent hugs up to the **Usutu River**, which rises in Swaziland and defines South Africa's border with Mozambique. The turn-off to the reserve is 56km along the tar north of Jozini, with the final 15km along a rough gravel track.

No great volume of animals trammel the reserve, but the beauty, solitude and prolific birdlife here make this a good place to head for if you're not simply into the game of ticking off your list of **mammals** to see. That's not to underplay the 62 mammal species (including buffalo, jackal, wildebeest, giraffe, hippo, hyena, zebra and both species of rhino) here, but they may be more difficult to see than elsewhere. For bird-watchers, though, Ndumo is in the premier league, ranking among the country's bird-watching top spots. Of the staggering 420 different varieties that have been recorded here, among the "target" **bird species** for enthusiasts are the African broadbill, pink-throated twinspot, Pels fishing owl, gorgeous bushshrike, cuckoo hawk, southern banded snake eagle and the palmnut vulture.

As in other public game reserves, you can **self-drive** around some areas, one of the highlights being the trip to **Redcliffs**, where there's a picnic site with a towering vantage point that offers soaring views across the Usutu River into both Swaziland and Mozambique. KwaZulu-Natal Conservation Services do open-topped 4WD outings in

---

MAPUTALAND'S TURTLES

The whole of the Maputaland coast is excellent for spotting **loggerhead** and **leatherback turtles** when they come ashore every year between October and February to breed, but Rocktail Bay is probably the best spot of all. Turtles from as far afield as Malindi in Kenya (3500km to the north) and Cape Agulhas (2000km west along the South African coastline) converge on the beaches of Maputaland to lay their eggs. Sea turtles have survived virtually unchanged for almost a hundred million years and it's reckoned that loggerheads have been using Maputaland's beaches to lay their eggs for 60,000 years.

When the female turtle's eggs are ripe she heads for the beach to lay her eggs. It is believed that the turtles are lured onto the beach by a hormone that oozes from the beach, a scent that they follow. The scent is believed to have been programmed into their subconscious while they were in their eggs. The myopic turtle, whose eyes are adapted to underwater vision, pulls herself along the beach in the dark until she encounters an obstruction such as a bank or a log, where she begins digging a pit using her front flippers until she has scooped out a nest big enough to hold her own volume. She then digs a flask-shaped hole about 50cm deep and lays her eggs into this, a process which takes about ten minutes.

The female turtle fills the hole and covers it with sand using her front flippers, disguising the place where the eggs are stored, and returns to the sea. After about two months the eggs hatch, and when the temperature drops below 28°C the entire clutch of hatched turtles will simultaneously race down the beach to the ocean. Only one in five hundred will survive to return. Once in the ocean, the hatchlings swim out to sea where they are either carried away by the Agulhas current into the Atlantic or along the Indian Ocean coast.

As the turtles are easily disturbed, only park officials are allowed on the beaches at night, escorting groups of visitors to watch the turtles.

---

the mornings and evenings to the lovely **Inyamiti pan**, which are inhabited by hippos and crocodiles and receive visits from an array of waterfowl. Guided **walking trails** are also available.

The small **public rest camp** is sited on a hill and has several old, but well-maintained two-bedded **huts** (③), each with a fridge and handbasin with cold water. Ablutions are shared and camp chefs prepare your food for you; meals are taken communally in the dining room. A shop near the entrance gate sells basic **supplies**, but you'd be better off stocking up en route in Mkuze village. **Bookings** should be made through Conservation Services central office (see p.365).

The private **Ndumo Wilderness Lodge** consists of a series of luxury en-suite safari tents on decks overlooking a beautiful pan in an area of the reserve closed to the general public. The units are connected by boardwalks on stilts above the flood level of the pan. The lounge area is an open-sided deck that jetties out towards the water and offers fabulous views of its crocodile-infested waters and the perfect vantage from which to watch water birds with a pair of binoculars. The lodge also lays on **game drives** and informative **guided walks**, including to Inyamiti pan, that help to give a more rewarding experience of the wild. Prices inclusive of all meals and game activities come to R875 per person per day. Bookings can be made through Wilderness Safaris, PO Box 78573, Sandton 2146 (☎011/883 0747, fax 883 0911, *info@sdn.wilderness.co.za*).

Kosi Bay

The northernmost place along the KwaZulu-Natal coast, **KOSI BAY** is at the centre of an enthralling area of waterways fringed by forest. Despite the name, this is not a bay at all, but a system of four lakes connected by narrow reed channels which eventually empty into the sea at Kosi Mouth. You will only be able to get to the mouth itself if you have a 4WD and are extremely intrepid.

One of the most striking images of Kosi Bay is of mazes of reed fences in the estuary and other parts of the lake system. These are **fish kraals** or traps built by local Tonga people, a practice that has been going on for hundreds of years. Custom has made the method of harvesting sustainable, because trap numbers are strictly controlled; they are passed down from father to son and designed to only capture four percent of the fish that pass through.

Staying at Kosi Bay, you're likely to feel yourself frustratingly aground and won't so much as glimpse the coast unless you sign up for the four-day **Amanzimnyama Trail**, which is one of the few ways for the general public to see South Africa's northernmost section of the Indian Ocean. The circular hike begins at the base camp on the west shore of Nhlange and passes through beautiful coastal forest, along the beach, through cycad and giant raffia palm groves. In summer there's the chance of seeing turtles on the beach. Beds, pots, cookers, ablution facilities and limited water are available at night stops along the route, but there's no electricity or refrigeration and you must bring your own eating utensils, food, bedding, torches and snorkelling gear. Mosquito repellent is recommended and this is one of the few parts of the country where it's advisable to use water purification tablets. **Bookings** for the trail, which costs R250 per person, should be made through KwaZulu-Natal Conservation Services central office (see p.365).

A highly recommended alternative way to explore the area is on a **tour** guided by members of the local community, who can show you the lakes and the fish traps. Trips start just outside the rest camp from the reserve **office** (☎035/592 0236), where you can gather more **information**, or contact the Group for Environmental Monitoring Issues, who will be abreast of any community projects (☎011/403 7666, fax 403 7563, *gem@wn.apc.org*), at Kosi Bay.

Kwazulu Natal Conservation Services rent out **accommodation** at their rest camp on the west shore of Nhlage, the largest of the lakes, in a two-bedded (②), five-bedded (②) and a six-bedded lodge (③). There's a small campsite (①) nearby and a private lodge is in the pipeline. A little back from the "bay" itself, further private accommodation is available at *Kosi Bay Lodge* (enquiries: ☎ & fax 035/592 0037; bookings: 031/266 4172, fax 031/266 9118; ②–③), 500m from the lake, in basic four- or six-bedded reed chalets. There's a bar with a viewing deck and a restaurant serving run-of-the-mill fare. *Phambuka* (☎ & fax 035/591 0052) is closer to the ocean itself, near the sublime Kosi Mouth, which is accessible by 4WD only; the camp is tented and limited to 24 people, either self catering (④) or fully catered (⑥). There's great snorkelling and swimming in the estuary, and long walks on deserted beaches.

Itala Game Reserve

West of Maputaland and close to the Swaziland border, the small **Itala Game Reserve** (daily: April–Sept 6am–6pm; Oct–March 5am–7pm; R30 per vehicle, R7 per person) is little known, despite being one of the country's most spectacularly scenic places to watch wildlife. The reserve's relative youth (it was only proclaimed in 1972) may be why it is frequently bypassed by visitors, who rush for the big names such as Kruger and Hluhluwe-Umfolozi. This could soon change, especially as Itala's main camp, **Ntshondwe**, wins awards year after year as the best game-reserve rest camp in South Africa. Itala is notably mountainous and the terrain extremely varied; contained within a protective basin are numerous cliffs and rock faces.

If you're obsessed with seeing the Big Five, Itala is not the place to visit as the king of the beasts is notably absent here, even though the other four make periodic appearances. Come instead for the most relaxed, uncrowded and beautifully set game viewing you'll get in southern Africa. Like the rest of the KwaZulu-Natal game reserves, Itala is excellent for white **rhinos** and there is ample sufficiency of **plains game**, including zebras and giraffes. Of the **predators**, you could, if you're very lucky, bump into brown hyenas, cheetahs and leopards. But the best idea is to throw away your mammal check list and take a slow drive around the mountains into the valleys and along the watercourses. Because there are no lions, the game is relaxed, and on a quiet weekday watching **animal behaviour** can be pretty fascinating. Slow down, keep your eyes open, and you may recognize a rhino male defending his territory, or two young giraffes testing their strength with neck wrestling. One of the most rewarding **drives** is along Ngubhu Loop, with a detour to Ngubhu picnic site. You can get information and maps from the reception at *Ntshondwe* chalets.

There are some **self-guided trails** into the wooded mountainside above *Ntshondwe*, which give the chance to stretch your legs if you've spent a morning driving around. **Day and night drives** in open vehicles can be booked through *Ntshondwe* reception at a cost of R60 per person.

Practicalities

There's no public **transport** into the park, or even near to it, so self-driving is your only option. The main rest camp, **Ntshondwe**, 7km beyond the entrance gate, is ingeniously camouflaged against a high plateau with views at the foot of huge cliffs. There are no lawns or gardens; each chalet is surrounded by indigenous bush through which paved walkways weave their way around granite rocks and trees to the main reception area, which has a small shop, a restaurant, and bar with a deck overlooking a waterhole.

Accommodation at *Ntshondwe* is in one-bedroom chalets, either catered for (④), in which case you eat in the restaurant, or self-catering units (③), with two bedrooms, a fully equipped kitchen, lounge areas and verandahs. If you want an extremely pared-down bush experience, you won't beat the marvellous *Doornkraal* **campsite** (①), shaded by thorn trees and ilala palms, on the banks of the Mbizo River. Expect no frills here – it's cold showers in reed enclosures and cooking over wood fires, the only concession to civilization being a flushing toilet. There are also three, secluded self-catering **bush camps**, which only one party at a time uses, sleeping four to ten, each with the services of a private game ranger for walks. They're suitable if you're in a group, as there is a minimum charge, working out at around R170 per person if you meet the required number of people. Each one is pretty fabulously set and is a great bush experience since you're aware of no one apart from your party. **Bookings** for chalets and camps should be made through the Conservation Services (see p.365); for camping, contact the Officer-in-Charge, PO Box 42, Louwsburg 3150 (☎034/907 5239, fax 907 5303).

If you're happy to shell out, eat in *Ntshondwe*'s à la carte **restaurant**, which serves a surprisingly varied range of foods from *escargots* (not giant land snails fortunately) to steaks. Don't bother with self-catering unless you're a vegetarian (meat-free meals aren't always on the menu), as you'll need to get **supplies** before you come – the camp shop is poorly stocked with fresh foods and specializes in frozen meats and beers, which is great only if you plan to live on *braais* alone. **Louwsburg** has a very small general dealer that's a little better, but you'd be wise to pick up supplies at Vryheid, Pongola, Mkuze or one of the larger villages en route. A cosy **bar** serves drinks, appreciated all the more outside on the deck, overlooking the waterhole and across the valleys.

CENTRAL ZULULAND AND THE BATTLEFIELDS

Central Zululand – the Zulu heartland – radiates out from the unlovely modern town of **Ulundi**, some 30km west of the Hluhluwe-Umfolozi Park. At the height of its influence in the 1820s and 1830s, under King Shaka, the core of the Zulu state lay between the **Black Mfolozi River** in the north and in the south the **Tugela**, which discharges into the Indian Ocean, roughly 100km north of Durban.

Despite being a beautiful area of dry thornveld, large hills and big views, Central Zululand tends to be visited as a series of routes taking in museums and Battlefield sites. The Zulu heartland, where you'll find **museums** relating to local history and culture, is concentrated just to the west of the Hluhluwe-Umfolozi Park, King Shaka's personal hunting preserve. The heartland can be taken as a side-trip from a visit to Hluhluwe-Umfolozi or Itala Game Reserve, which lies about 150km north of Ulundi.

Contained in a relatively small area to the west of the heartland are series of **battle sites** from wars fought in the nineteenth century, first between Zulus and Boers, then Zulus and the British and finally between the Boers and Brits. If it sounds boring, it needn't be, particularly if you're interested in history and in modern South African politics. But you'll be wasting your time if you attempt this area on you own: all you'll see is empty *veld* with a few memorials. Far better is to join a tour with one of the several excellent **guides** who make it their business to bring it all alive (see p.450).

The Zulu Heartland

Don't expect to see "tribal" people who conform to the Zulu myth outside **theme parks** such as Shakaland. Traditional dress and the **traditional lifestyle** are largely a nineteenth-century phenomenon, deliberately smashed by the British at the turn of the century, when they imposed a poll tax that had to be paid in cash – thus ending Zulu self-sufficiency, generating urbanization and forcing the Africans into the modern industrial economy, where they were needed as workers.

You will find beautiful crafts, at which Zulu society excels, the best examples being in museums such as the little-known but outstanding **Vukani Collection** in Eshowe. Also worth checking out is the reconstructed royal enclosure of Cetshwayo, the last king of the independent Zulu, at **Ondini**, near Ulundi.

Some history

The truth behind the Zulus is difficult to isolate from the mythology, which was fed by both the Zulus themselves as well as white settlers. Accounts of the Zulu kingdom in the 1820s rely heavily on the diaries of the two adventurers **Henry Fynn** and **Nathaniel Isaacs**, who portrayed King Shaka as a mercurial and bloodthirsty tyrant who killed his subjects willy-nilly for a bit of fun. Despite their attempts to cover up their profligate disregard for the truth, a letter from Isaacs to Fynn was uncovered in the Forties. In it he encourages his friend, who was en route to London to publish his memoirs, to depict the Zulu kings as "bloodthirsty as you can, and describe frivolous crimes people lose their lives for. It all tends to swell up the work and make it interesting."

A current debate splits historians down the middle about the real extent of the **Zulu empire** during the nineteenth century. Some now question the conventional wisdom that Shaka was the "African Napoleon", a military genius who transformed the politics of nineteenth-century South Africa. What we do know is that in the 1820s Shaka consolidated a state that was one of the most powerful political forces in the subcontinent, and that internal dissent to his rule culminated in his assassination by his half-brother **Dingane** in 1828.

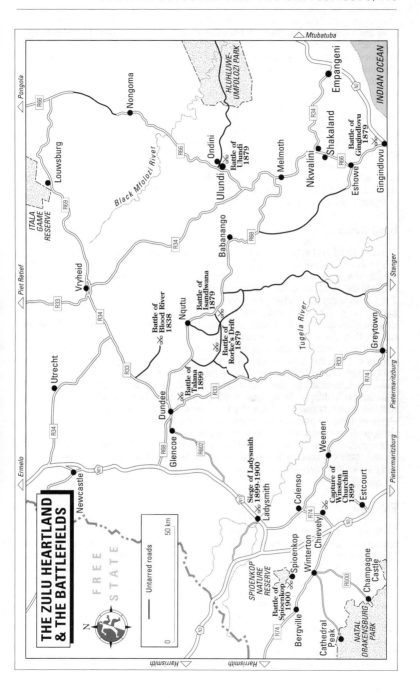

THE ZULU HEARTLAND & THE BATTLEFIELDS

△ *Mtubatuba*

HLUHLUWE UMFOLOZI PARK

INDIAN OCEAN

Nongoma

Empangeni

R66

R69

Louwsburg

R66

Ondini

Battle of Ulundi 1879

Shakaland

Battle of Gingindlovu 1879

ITALA GAME RESERVE

Ulundi

Melmoth

Nkwalini

Eshowe

Gingindlovu

R34

Black Mfolozi River

R66

Empangeni

△ *Pongola*

△ *Piet Retief*

Vryheid

R34

Babanango

R68

Battle of Isandlwana 1879

△ *Stanger*

R33

Battle of Blood River 1838

Nqutu

Battle of Rorke's Drift 1879

Tugela River

Greytown

Utrecht

R33

R34

Battle of Talana 1899

R33

R33

R74

△ *Pietermaritzburg*

R34

Dundee

△ *Ermelo*

R68

Glencoe

R602

Newcastle

N11

Siege of Ladysmith 1899-1900

Ladysmith

Weenen

△ *Pietermaritzburg*

FREE STATE

Colenso

Capture of Winston Churchill 1899

Estcourt

Spioenkop

Winterton

Chievely

N3

Battle of Spioenkop 1900

SPIOENKOP NATURE RESERVE

R600

Champagne Castle

Bergville

R74

Cathedral Peak

NATAL DRAKENSBERG PARK

N

50 km

Untarred roads

0

▽ *Harrismith*

▽ *Harrismith*

In the 1830s, pressure from whites exacerbated internal tensions in the Zulu state and reached a climax when a relatively small party of Boers obliterated Dingane's army at **Blood River**, leading to a split in the Zulu state, with one half following **King Mpande**. Collapse threatened when Mpande's sons Mbuyazi and Cetshwayo led opposing forces in a pitched battle for the succession. **Cetshwayo** emerged victorious and successfully set about rebuilding the state, but too late. Britain had already determined that its own interest would best be served by a confederated South Africa under its own control and a powerful Zulu state wasn't going to be allowed to stand in the way. On the banks of the Tugela River, the high commissioner, Sir Bartle Frere, delivered a Hobson's choice of an **ultimatum** that Cetshwayo should dismantle his polity or face invasion.

In January 1879, the British army crossed the Tugela, and after a humiliating defeat of a massive British veteran force at Isandlwana the tide turned against the Zulus. By the end of July, Zulu independence had been snuffed and Cetshwayo was being held prisoner in the Castle in Cape Town.

Gingindlovu

At **GINGINDLOVU** (shortened to Ging by local whites) the Zulus attacked a British relief column on April 2, 1879, as it was marching on Eshowe to relieve a siege. In one of the decisive battles of the Anglo-Zulu War, the colonial invaders delivered a crushing defeat to the Zulus that destroyed their morale, with the loss of only thirteen British lives. The following day the advancing British column continued on and successfully raised the Eshowe siege. There's nothing much to see in Gingindlovu, which is 50km north of Dukuza along the R102, but it makes as good a base as any to explore the Zulu heartland and the Battlefields, and has the advantage of being a mere 15km from the coast.

The Baz backpacker **bus** pulls in and can drop you off at either of the two excellent **places to stay**, the cheaper being the eccentric and thoroughly entertaining *Inyezane Backpackers* (☎083/255 7345) on a sugar farm just outside town; phone ahead for directions. Accommodation consists of a series of eclectically decorated rondavels, where you can stay in dorms (①) or doubles (②); camping (①) is also available. The hostel is well known for its **mud baths**, and you can also learn to make your own curios out of elephant dung, or play traditional musical instruments. Also on a sugar estate, but at the opposite extreme with its old-fashioned elegance, in a grand homestead that resembles something out of *Gone with the Wind*, is *Mine Own Country House* (☎035/337 1262, fax 337 1025; ⑥), 4km north of Gingindlovu on the R102. It's 15 minutes from the beach and offers a golf course, en-suite rooms, well-tended gardens, a swimming pool and tennis courts.

Eshowe

Visitors generally give **ESHOWE** a miss on their way to the more obvious drama of the old Zulu capital at Ondini and the Battlefields, but the place deserves more than a passing glance as it offers a gentle introduction to the **Zulu heartland**. Apart from its attractively organic setting, interlacing with the Dhlinza Forest, this town, 22km inland from Gingindlovu, houses one of the finest historical and contemporary collections of Zulu crafts, has a half-decent museum and offers exceptional tours that take you under the skin of a modern KwaZulu-Natal country town. As befits a forested town in the heart of Zululand, its name has an onomatopoeic Zulu derivation evoked by the sound of the wind blowing through the trees.

Graham Chennels, former mayor and current proprietor of the *George Hotel* in Main Street (see opposite), leads enthusiastic **tours** of Eshowe, taking in the white, coloured and African areas as well as the rural surrounds. This is one of the best and easiest ways of understanding exactly how segregation worked under apartheid, and one of the most optimistic views of South Africa's future you're likely to find.

The Vukani Collection and Zululand Historical museums

One very good reason for coming to Eshowe is for the little-advertised **Vukani Collection Museum**, Osborn St (☎0354/75274, curator 74902; Tues & Thurs 9am–1pm, other times by request), which happens to be the largest and among the best collections of traditional **Zulu arts and crafts** in the world, containing over 3000 pieces. Ask around for directions. If you have any interest in local material culture this is an essential port of call. Better still, arrange a guided **tour** (free) by the highly knowledgeable curator, who can put the items into a cultural and social context. On view you'll see a huge range of **baskets**, something Zulu culture excels at (and examples of which are held in many major international art collections), each made for a specific purpose. There are also carvings, clothing, beadwork, tapestries and some outstanding ceramics, including works by **Nesta Nala**, one of the leading contemporary proponents of the form. After seeing the bench-mark examples here, you'll have a good idea about the quality of basketry and crafts you'll see for sale as you work your way around Zululand.

Also worth a visit is the **Zululand Historical Museum** (daily 9am–4pm; entry by donation), housed within the limewashed crenellations of **Fort Nongqayi**. The collection is eccentric and informative by turns, but never dull. Among the displays is furniture belonging to **John Dunn**, the only white man to become a Zulu chief and, incidentally, also to take 49 wives, so becoming the progenitor of Eshowe's coloured community, many of whom still carry his last name. You can also see Zulu household artefacts, the replica of a silver beer mug given by Queen Victoria in London to Cetshwayo, the last king of the free Zulus in 1882, and displays on Zulu history. One of these covers the Bambatha Rebellion, in which Fort Nongqayi saw action, putting down the last armed resistance by Africans till the formation of the ANC's armed wing in the Sixties.

The large grounds around the museum are a great place to have a picnic. A twenty-minute trail leads to the **Mpushini Falls** and there's a one-hour self-guided walk through the majestic **Dhlinza Forest**, which has some hides where you can look out for forest birds.

Practicalities

The Translux **intercity bus** stops in front of the City Hall on its three-times-a-week haul between Pretoria/Johannesburg and Richards Bay, and the Baz **backpacker bus** also passes through town on its Durban–Johannesburg route.

The cheapest **accommodation** in town is at *Zululand Backpackers* (part of the *George Hotel*), 38 Main St (☎035/474 4919 or 42894, fax 474 1434), which has camping (①), small dorms (①) and doubles (②) in a beautifully cared for hostel. Outside, there's a big fig tree under which you can have meals and chill out. The hostel offers cultural encounters where you can meet rural Zulus at traditional wedding ceremonies and *sangoma* (diviner) rituals. There's also rapp jumping, abseiling (extreme abseiling), mountain biking, canoeing, hiking, waterfalling and rock sliding, plus there's a large swimming pool. The *George Hotel* itself (☎035/474 4919; ③) is good value, with comfortable en-suite rooms with TVs. *Forest Ledge*, 128 Main St (☎035/474 4079, fax 474 1908; ②), has fully equipped, self-catering units close to the forest and the falls, while *Amble Inn*, 116 Main St (☎035/474 1300; ③), has eleven rooms and its own **restaurant**, which serves English-style meals.

Shakaland and Simunye

North of Eshowe, the winding R66 leaves behind the softer vistas of the Dhlinza Forest, the citrus groves and green seas of cane plantations and looks across huge views of the valleys that figure in the creation mythology of the Zulu nation. In no time you're into thornveld (acacias, rocky kopjes and aloes) and **theme park** country. Most accessible of these "Zulu-village hotels" is **SHAKALAND**, Norman Hurst Farm, Nkwalini (☎035/460 0912, fax 460 0842, *shakares@iafrica.com*), 14km north of Eshowe off the R68, which just about manages to remain on the acceptable side of exploiting ethnic culture, but isn't quite as "authentic" as its publicity materials claim.

Built in 1984 as the set for the wildly romanticized TV series *Shaka Zulu*, Shakaland's management was taken over in 1988 by the Protea hotel chain. What the brochures don't tell you is that the village is a reconstruction of a nineteenth-century Zulu *kraal* (homestead) and is quite unrepresentative of how people live today. However, Shakaland does offer the chance to sample Zulu food in a spectacular dining area. **Tours** for day visitors (daily 11am & 12.30pm; R115) begin with an audiovisual about the origin of the Zulus, followed by a guided walk around the huts, an explanation of traditional social organization, taking in a beer-drinking ceremony, buffet lunch with traditional food, including a good choice for vegetarians among the spread, and concluding with some energetic dancing. **Accommodation** is available in comfortable traditional beehive huts (⑤) with untraditional luxuries such as electricity and en-suite bathrooms. All activities are included in the price and you get to see a Zulu courting ritual, stick fighting and spear throwing.

In a different league, **SIMUNYE** (☎035/450 3111, fax 450 2534; ⑤), along the D256, off the R34, and 6km from Melmoth, offers a far more authentic experience of Zulu culture, introducing guests to contemporary ways of life as well as traditional customs. Visitors are conveyed to the camp by horse or on an ox-waggon and while there you'll get to see dancing, visit a working *kraal* and meet local people. **Accommodation**, which is full board, is either in stone and thatched huts at the main camp, which overlooks the Mfule River, or at a *kraal* in a beehive hut or rondavels – either way there's no electricity.

Ulundi and Ondini

Some 83km north of Eshowe on the R66, **ULUNDI** is the former capital of the KwaZulu *bantustan* and lies at the centre of the **Makhosini Valley** (Valley of the Kings), which holds a semi-religious status among Zulu nationalists as the birthplace of the Zulu state and the area where several of its founding fathers lived and are now buried. Now that KwaZulu has been reintegrated with Natal, this rather unattractive modern town is tussling with Pietermaritzburg for pre-eminence in the province, but for the moment the two are joint capitals – a fact that brings joy to no one except the airlines that have to ferry provincial legislators from one centre to the other. There's nothing in Ulundi itself that is worth stopping for, apart from its historical connections.

The **Battle of Ulundi Memorial**, just outside town on the untarred road to the Cengeni Gate of the Hluhluwe-Umfolozi Park, is the poignant spot that marks the final defeat of the Zulus. An understated small stone structure with a silver dome houses a series of plaques listing all the regiments on both sides involved in the last stand of the Zulus on July 4, 1879. The rectangular park around the memorial marks the site of the hollow infantry square adopted by the British and supported to devastating effect by seven- and nine-pounder guns.

By far the most interesting sight around here is the **Ondini Historical Reserve** (Mon–Fri 8am–4pm, Sat & Sun 9am–4pm; small entry fee), a few kilometres further along the road, which houses the reconstruction of the royal residence of **King Cetshwayo**, a site museum and a cultural museum. In 1872 Cetshwayo succeeded to the Zulu throne and set about rebuilding the Zulu state, which had been fracturing since the 1850s. His success at achieving this proved to be his undoing, because the British didn't want a strong united Zulu kingdom standing between them and their aim of a confederated South Africa under the Union Jack. After the decisive Battle of Ulundi, the royal residence at Ondini was razed to the ground and Cetshwayo was captured. Still puzzled by Britain's actions, Cetshwayo wrote to the British governor in 1881 from his exile at the Castle in Cape Town: "I have done you no wrong, therefore you must have some other object in view in invading my land." The *isigodlo*, or **royal enclosure**, has been partially reconstructed with traditional Zulu beehive huts, which you can wander round, while the site museum has a model showing the full original arrangement. Among the items in the **Cultural Museum** is a major bead collection, which is pretty interesting if you're into ethnic arts and crafts.

A **picnic site** has been provided in the extensive grounds of the reserve and there's **camping** (①) and accommodation in the traditional *umuzi* (homestead) in a group of beehive **huts** (①–②) inside a stockade with beds and communal kitchens, with ablution facilities outside. **Bookings** for these should be made through the Clerk of the KwaZulu Monuments Council, PO Box 523, Ulundi 3838 (☎035/879 1223 or 879 1854).

The Battlefields

Most of the major KwaZulu-Natal Battlefields lie in the northwestern corner of the province, where first the Boers came out of the mountains from the northeast into Zulu territory and inflicted a severe defeat on the Zulus at **Blood River** in 1838, 13km southeast of the tiny town of Utrecht. Some four decades later the British spoiled for war and marched north to fight a series of battles against the Zulus, the most notable being at **Isandlwana** and **Rorke's Drift**, southeast of Dundee.

Twenty years on Britain again provoked war, this time against the **Boers** of the South African Republic and the Orange Free State to the north and west. The Second Anglo-Boer War (also known as the South African War) was fought over control of the Gauteng goldfields. British troops were landed at Durban, in the British colony of Natal, and boldly marched north. Britain, accustomed to fighting enemies without firearms, believed the campaign would be quick, cheap and over by Christmas. But in the early stages of the war the huge but lumbering British machine proved no match for the mobile Boers who fought a guerrilla campaign that checked the advance of the redcoats in northern KwaZulu-Natal.

At **Ladysmith** the British endured months of an embarrassing siege, while nearby at **Spioenkop** bungling British leadership snatched defeat from the jaws of victory. Although the Empire successfully struck back, it took three years for it to subdue the South African Republic and the Orange Free State, two of the smallest states in the world, after committing half a million troops to the field in an operation that was the costliest campaign since the Napoleonic Wars nearly a century earlier.

Isandlwana and Rorke's Drift

On January 22, 1879 the British suffered one of the most humiliating defeats in their colonial history when virtually their entire force of 1200 men at **Isandlwana** was obliterated by a "bunch of savages armed just with sticks". That same evening, honour was restored when a motley group of British veterans and sick successfully defended the field hospital at **Rorke's Drift**, just across the Buffalo River from the site of the earlier disaster, against the same advancing Zulu force, a sequence of events heavily romanticized in the Sixties film *Zulu*, which made the reputation of an ever-grateful **Michael Caine** and led him to "thank God for the Zulus."

If you're only planning to take in one Battlefield site, then Isandlwana should be that one, and once you're making the effort you really should take in Rorke's Drift as well to complete the day. Isandlwana is just over 130km northwest of **Eshowe**, but the clos-

GOING INTO BATTLE

There's little point in wandering around the Battlefields without a guide; all you'll see are stretches of *veld* and the odd memorial. Going along with a qualified **guide** will infinitely enhance your experience. Our recommended guides specialize in different battle sites, usually those closest to their base. You should expect to pay in the region of R250 and over for a day-trip.

Battlefield and Zulu Heartland Guides

Fred Duke (☎034/980 7835). Specializes in the Zulu Battlefields in the Vryheid area, namely the sites at Hlobane, Kambula, Ulundi and Blood River as well as the Route Prince Imperial and the Anglo-Boer War. Tours cost R250 per person.

Evan Jones, PMB Heritage Tours, PO Box 1380, Cascades 3203 (☎ & fax 033/344 3260, *heritage.battlefield@futurenet.co.za*). Extensive tours of the Battlefields conducted by a guide with a vast repository of knowledge, who breathes life into the battles and their theatre of activity. A two-day trip for four costs R1320 each and includes accommodation at the fabulous *Lennox Guest Cottage* (see p.452), meals, transport, entrance fees and transfers to and from Pietermaritzburg.

David Rattray, PO Box 3016 Rorke's Drift (☎ & fax 034/642 1843). Consummate story-teller, who infuses his accounts of Rorke's Drift and Isandlwana with emotion more than anyone else. In 1997, Britain's Prince Charles was fortunate enough to be taken around by Rattray, who grew up around Isandlwana and has a prodigious knowledge of the area. This could easily be the best live performance you attend in South Africa. The Isandlwana and Rorke's Drift combined tour costs R250 per person. Rattray has problems with his voice, which means you may get another guide, but it's worth making an effort to ensure that he's leading the tour on the day you go.

Maureen Richards (☎033/342 8253). Former curator of the Ladysmith Siege Museum and expert on the Anglo-Boer Battlefields, Spioenkop and Colenso, offering entertaining and highly informative tours. Tours are R500 per group.

John Turner, PO Box 10, Babanango (☎035/835 0062, fax 835 0160). Highly qualified as a natural scientist, with a degree in animal behaviour, Dr Turner is able to combine tours of Hluhluwe-Umfolozi game reserve and ecological topics including birding and basic tree identification, with Zulu historical sites and the Anglo-Zulu Battlefield. Tours cost around R190 per person (plus R540 fuel costs per group) and include lunch and all entrance fees.

Foy Vermaak, PO Box 1358, Dundee 3000 (☎ & fax 034/212 1925). Based close to Isandlwana and Rorke's Drift sites, in which he specializes. The rate is R300 per party, irrespective of size; you pay for the entrance fees, your own packed lunch, which he can provide, and he travels in your car.

Do-it-Yourself

If you can't afford a guide, the next best thing is to buy an **audiotape** to listen to in your car. These are available from reception at the Talana Museum (see p.452). David Rattray's excellent set of tapes *The Day of the Dead Moon*, covering Rorke's Drift and Isandlwana, is available from CNA newsagents or directly from Rattray (see above). The most authorititive book about the Anglo-Boer War is the highly entertaining *Boer War* by Thomas Pakenham (see p.733).

est town of any size is **Dundee** about 70km to its west. Both Isandlwana and Rorke's Drift are eerily beautiful places, which you can visit and walk around on your own, but far more rewarding is to join a **tour** with one of the excellent Battlefield guides, who can really paint a word picture of the battle against the mute landscape (see box above).

For somewhere to stay in the vicinity, you could do worse than the blink-and-you've-missed-it village of **BABANANGO**, 92km northwest of Eshowe, which consists of a shop or two and the *Babanango Hotel*, 16 Justice St (☎035/835 0029; ④), a small atmospheric country **hotel** whose rate includes dinner, bed and breakfast. Backpackers are also accommodated at a bargain rate (②) that includes breakfast, though it remains a mystery as to how its renowned, but tiny, *Stan's Pub*, manages to cram in its **drinking** clientele. The hotel has a 4WD vehicle to take guests to the Battlefields, game reserves or to a bush camp where you can go on trails and rough it among the thorn trees. A quieter option is *Babanango Valley Lodge* (☎035/835 0062, fax 835 0160; half board ⑧), situated on a Natural Heritage Site and signposted 4km west of Babanango on the R68, deep in one of the most beautiful valleys anywhere, where you can be taken on walks to expore the *veld*, rocks and river. Accommodation is in pleasant en-suite rooms set in the garden, and there's a swimming pool. The owner, Dr John Turner, is a registered guide (see opposite).

A couple of other good alternatives in beautiful countryside exist. Near the minuscule settlement of **HELPMEKAAR**, along the R33 south of the Rorke's Drift battlefield and 30km south of Dundee, *Penny Farthing* (☎ & fax 034/212 1925; ③), is a historic pioneer farm still furnished with a lot of original objects and generations of hunting trophies, set in an area of big open grasslands, hills with walks and hiking trails on the farm. Host Foy Vermaak is a Battlefields guide (see opposite) who enjoys fireside chats on the subject and has a personal collection of memorabilia.

The ultimate Battlefields stay is at *Fugitives' Drift Lodge* (☎ & fax 034/642 1843; full-board ⑨), 9km north of Rorke's Drift, where you're hosted by David Rattray (see box, opposite). Located on a huge game farm, the lodge overlooks the drift where British survivors of Isandlwana fled across the Buffalo River. Rooms are in individual cottages that open onto lawns and gardens, and guests eat together in a central dining room.

Isandlwana

Dominated by an eerie hill, the **ISANDLWANA** Battlefield, off the R68 between Nqutu and Babanango (daily 8am–5pm; small entry fee), remains unspoilt and unchanged apart from some small homesteads and the graves of those who fell. A small **interpretation centre** houses artefacts and mementos.

The monumental bungling and the scale of the Zulu victory over the British sent shock waves back to London. Following the British ultimatum to the Zulus, three colonial columns were sent to invade Zululand. King Cetshwayo responded by sending a force against each of these. On January 21, 1879, Zulu troops encamped 6km from Isandlwana Hill, where one of the British columns had set up camp. Unaware of the Zulus over the brow, the British commander took a large detachment to support another British force, leaving the men at Isandlwana undefended and unfortified.

Meanwhile, a British scouting party rode to the brow of a hill and were stunned to find the valley filled with 20,000 Zulu soldiers sitting in utter silence. Because of a superstition surrounding the phase of the moon, the Zulus were waiting for a more propitious moment to attack. On being discovered, they rose up and converged on the British encampment using the classic Zulu "horns of the bull" formation to outflank the unprotected British who they completely overran. Few of the 1200 British forces survived.

The British press at the time demonized the Zulus for disembowelling the dead, which must have made a pretty ghastly sight in the aftermath of the battle. In fact the practice had a religious significance for the Zulus, who believed that it released the spirit of the dead.

Rorke's Drift

RORKE'S DRIFT is the most rewarding Battlefield to visit on your own on account of its excellent **field museum** and interpretation centre (daily 8am–5pm; free). An atmospheric new road connects it with Isandlwana, 15km to the east.

Despite Cetshwayo's express orders to his men not to attack Rorke's Drift, a number of hot-headed young men were so fired up by their victory at Isandlwana and eager to "wash their spears" that they pushed on and attacked the hospital. For twelve hours spanning January 22 and 23, 1879, just over a hundred British soldiers (many of whom were ill) repulsed repeated attacks by four thousand Zulus, thus saving tattered British honour and earning eleven Victoria Crosses – the largest number ever awarded in one battle.

While you're here, it's also worth taking in the **Rorke's Drift ELC Craft Centre** (Mon–Fri 8am–4.30pm, Sat 10am–3pm), which is known for its hand-printed fabrics and tapestries depicting rural scenes.

Dundee and the Talana Museum

Some 32km west of the Rorke's Drift turn-off, along the R68, **DUNDEE** is a one-trick coal-mining town you can safely miss because its single draw-card, the **Talana Museum** (Mon–Fri 8am–4pm, Sat 10am–4pm, Sun noon–4pm; small entry fee), is 2km outside town on the R33 to Vryheid. The museum itself is excellent, consisting of nine historic buildings still standing from the time of the Battle of Talana Hill – the first engagement of the Anglo-Boer War, in 1899, and a landmark for the British army, which wore khaki for the first time.

The museum is scattered around the grounds in a series of whitewashed buildings under shady blue gums, the most interesting being **Talana House**, which gives information about northern KwaZulu-Natal conflicts, including Anglo-Zulu, Zulu-Boer and Anglo-Boer wars. Displays included weapons and uniforms, but most evocative are the photographs, which really personalize the wars. Even if you're not deeply interested in military history, you're bound to find some fascinating detail, such as the POW camps Boers were exiled to in far-flung parts of the Empire, including St Helena and the Far East. Often-neglected aspects of the Anglo-Boer War, including the roles of Africans and Indians, also get some coverage. In a photograph of Indian stretcher-bearers, you may be able to spot the youthful Mohandas Gandhi, who carried wounded British soldiers off the Spioenkop and Colenso Battlefields. The museum also has the lovely *Miners Rest Tea Shop*, which makes a far preferable stop for a **drink** and a **snack** than anywhere in town.

If you're looking for **accommodation** in the vicinity, try the excellent *Lennox Guest Cottage* (☎ & fax 034/218 2201, mobile 082/574 3032; half board ⑤), by the museum and at the foot of Talana Hill. Run by former rugby Springbok Dirk Froneman and his wife, Salome, the B&B is unpretentious and comfortable, with excellent cooking.

Blood River and Vryheid

You can't fail to be amazed by the monument at the **Blood River Battlefield** (daily 8am–5pm; small entry fee), 48km from Dundee on the way to Vryheid off the R33, which of all the Afrikaner quasi-religious shrines across the country definitely takes the biscuit. A replica *laager* of 64 life-size bronze waggons stands on the site where on December 16, 1838 the Boers defeated a Zulu army. During the apartheid years, this date was celebrated by Afrikaners as the **Day of the Vow**, a public holiday honouring a supposed covenant made by the Boers with God himself that if he granted them victory, they would hold the day sacred. Afrikaners still visit the monument on this day, but under the new government the public holiday has been recycled as the **Day of Reconciliation**.

Back on the R33, it's 56km east to **VRYHEID** (Freedom), one-time capital of the Nieuwe Republiek (New Republic), which for many whites, who refuse to fly the new South African flag, still represents some kind of Boer stronghold. Unless you're **stopping for the night** at the highly recommended *Villa Prince Imperial*, 201 Deputation St (☎034/983 2610; ④), clearly signposted from the main street, there's little reason to dally. The villa is a breath of French air in the heart of redneck country, offering twelve en-suite rooms with baths or (less expensively) showers, a swimming pool, billiard room and bar. The owner, Alain Delvilani, is a knowledgeable (and Satour-registered) Battlefield guide. There is also a **Zulu art gallery** on the premises, with the only display in northern KwaZulu-Natal of authentic and very beautiful antique Zulu beadwork, as well as works by young Zulu artists.

Ladysmith and around

LADYSMITH, 61km south of Dundee on the N11, owes what modest fame it has to one of the worst sieges in British military history nearly a century ago, and more recently to **Ladysmith Black Mambazo**, the local vocal group that helped Paul Simon revive a flagging career in the mid-Eighties. Now one of South Africa's best-known black groups, Mambazo are rarely at home, but the new **Cultural Centre and Museum** honours their status as local heroes. The longer-established reason to hang out here is to explore the Anglo-Boer War in the **Ladysmith Siege Museum**, monuments and the surrounding Battlefields.

Some 40km south of Ladysmith, near **Chievely**, is the spot where an armoured train carrying **Winston Churchill** was blown up by Boers, leading him to develop a fair respect for them, and when he returned to England he reported to his incredulous colleagues that they were a more formidable opponent than they (or he) had ever imagined.

Some history

"[Ladysmith] is famous to the uttermost ends of the earth: centre of the world's attention, the scene of famous deeds", wrote Winston Churchill, in his earlier incarnation as a young, gung-ho journalist covering the Anglo-Boer War for the *London Morning Post*. The **siege** began on November 2, 1899 and lasted 118 stinking days of filthy drinking water, as 12,000 British troops suffered the powerlessness and indignity of being pinned down by undisciplined farmers, who took regular pot shots at the town. It was one of three sieges (the others being at Kimberley and Mafikeng) that kicked off the early stages of the war and shocked a British establishment that had fully expected to give the Boers a jolly good hiding and have the troops home by Christmas.

Arrival and information

Of the **intercity buses** Greyhound (☎036/637 4181) pulls into Ted's Service Station on its Johannesburg–Durban route and Translux (☎036/637 1111) breaks its Bloemfontein–Durban run at the **train station** (☎036/637 7273), 500m east of the town hall. Daily trains arrive from Johannesburg and Durban, but arrival and departure times make taking the train an unrealistic option unless you're pressed. It's pretty easy to walk around Ladysmith's small centre, which is fortunate as there's no **public transport**.

THE UNKNOWN SOLDIERS

Africans are rarely mentioned in the context of the Anglo-Boer war, a confrontation fought in a theatre where eighty percent of the population was black. Although both sides denied that Africans served on their side, the **British** employed around 100,000 both as labourers and under arms, while the **Boers** had at least 10,000 blacks on their side – often press-ganged into service. After the war, the British denied recognition to Africans who had seen service with them, to the extent that Sir George Leuchars, Natal Minister for Native Affairs, blocked them from receiving their campaign medals on the grounds that it would "irritate" the Boers – to whom the British were now nuzzling up.

The **tourist information bureau**, Town Hall, Murchison St (Mon–Fri 9am–4pm, Sat 8am–1pm; ☎036/637 2992), has a good selection of literature on the Battlefields.

The Ladysmith Community Tourism Organization (☎036/637 2231 or 637 4922) offer **guided tours** that include a visit to Umbulwane (Small) Mountain, which was used by the Boers to shell the town but also has deeper connections with the San. The outing continues with a visit to the African township, including the place where local boy and world boxing champ, Sugarboy Malinga first trained, and ends at a tavern where you can quaff beer, chat and listen to local music.

Accommodation

There are plenty of **places to stay** in Ladysmith, some of them plugging right into the Battlefields scene, with proprietors offering themselves as "Battlefields hosts" who you can come back to in the evening and discuss the day's experiences.

The Aloes Game Farm and B&B, 33km from Ladysmith, signposted a further 6km south of Colenso on the R103 (☎036/422 2834, fax 422 2592). Farmstay in a thatched cottage, sleeping five, with fishing, and mountain biking, close to Weenen Game Reserve and the Drakensberg. Breakfast costs extra. ②.

Battlefields B&B, 25 Cove Crescent (☎ & fax 036/631 2585). Gracious home in quiet peaceful neighbourhood. ②.

Bullers Rest Lodge, 61 Cove Crescent (☎036/637 6154, fax 637 3549). Smart thatched establishment on a ridge overlooking town. ④.

Hunters' Lodge, 6 Hunter St (☎036/637 2359, mobile ☎083/627 8480). Lovely old home in a peaceful neighbourhood with three single and three double rooms, all en suite. ③.

Lera's Place, 16 White Rd (☎036/631 2893). Fully equipped, self-catering unit in a lovely garden with safe parking. Also has *braai* facilities. ②.

Mac's Nest, Heronmere Farm, 5km from town on Windsor Dam Rd, off the R103 to Harrismith (☎036/635 4093, mobile ☎082/802 1645). Homely B&B on a smallholding with scenic sunsets, first-rate cooking and a small brass foundry. Prolific birdlife, small antelope and pleasant meanders. ③.

Mambasa Hutted Camp, adjoining Spioenkop Nature Reserve, off the R600 between Ladysmith and Winterton (☎036/488 1003, fax 488 1116). The least expensive accommodation in the Ladysmith Battlefields area, in traditional Zulu beehive huts on the banks of the Tugela River. Furnished only with beds and mattresses, there are paraffin lamps, open fires for cooking meals, a deep freeze, hot and cold running water and flush toilets in a communal ablution block. Canoes and rubber tubes are available for use on the river. ①.

Royal Hotel, 140 Murchison St (☎ & fax 036/637 2176 or 637 2177 or 637 2178). In the heart of town, the original historic hotel that harboured the town's most privileged during the siege and was regularly shelled by the Boers is now a three-star establishment catering mainly to travelling reps. It's full during the week, which makes booking essential at any time of year. ④.

Spioenkop Game & Safari Lodge, adjacent to the Spioenkop Nature Reserve, (☎036/488 1404). Choice of self-catering or B&B rooms in two cottages. Guided tours of Spioenkop Battlefield, sunset cruises, fishing, canoeing, birding and game viewing on offer. ③.

Tugela Game Ranch Bush Camp, 33km south of Ladysmith (☎036/422 2592, fax 422 2532). Fully equipped rondavels overlooking a bass dam with game drives, game viewing, nature walks, fishing and bird-watching. ②.

The Town

Along **Murchison Street**, the main artery running through Ladysmith, you'll find banks, the post office and shops as well as the the main tourist attractions. Of these the **Ladysmith Siege Museum** (Mon–Fri 8am–4pm, Sat 9am–1pm; small entry fee), next to the Town Hall, on the corner of Queen and Murchison streets, stands out as an essential starting point for any tour of the Anglo-Boer Battlefields. This compelling little museum tells the story of the war through text and photographs, conveying the appalling conditions during the siege as well as key points in a war that helped shape twentieth-century South Africa, paving the way for its unification. The museum is also a good source of books about the war, written from both the British and Boer points of view. The neighbouring **Town Hall**, where the British were to "thank God we kept the flag flying" after the seige, is also worth a peek for its collection of photographs depicting the town's history up to the present.

Right behind the Town Hall and Siege Museum stands the **Cultural Centre and Museum**, 25 Keate St (Mon–Fri 9am–4pm, Sat 9am–1pm), housed in a lovely classic Victorian colonial house. Opened in 1997, when Ladysmith Black Mambazo were granted the freedom of the town, life-size cut-outs of the group dominate a mock stage in the Ladysmith Black Mambazo Hall – the first room to the left of the foyer, which is filled with the strains of their stirring choral music. Other rooms display artefacts from the town's various cultures, tributes to local high fliers – such as world boxing champion Sugarboy Malinga – and work by local artists. For kids, the Jungle/Discovery room offers an adventure into a tropical world with bugs and all, where they are encouraged to touch the exhibits.

Back on Murchison Street, 600m southwest of the Town Hall, is **All Saints** Anglican church, a Victorian Gothic edifice, built from chiselled shale in 1882 after the contemporary English style, with extensions carried out in 1902 as a memorial to those who died during the siege. Take a step inside to see a plethora of military memorials and some nice stained-glass windows.

Retrace your steps to the Town Hall, and diagonally opposite stands the **Royal Hotel**, where the more privileged of the besieged passed their time, including Leander Starr Jameson and Frank Rhodes (brother of the more famous Cecil), who routinely lunched there. Both had been involved, in 1895, in an attempt to overthrow the Boer government, which was why some believed that the Boers regularly shelled the hotel around lunchtime.

Head down Queen Street away from the *Royal Hotel* to Forbes Street, where a **statue of Gandhi** stands in front of the unprepossessing Vishnu Temple. Although the monument depicts Gandhi in his persona as the saintly Mahatma, his associations with Ladysmith go back before he had earned that title, to the Boer War, when he enrolled in the British army as a stretcher-bearer and trained members of Ladysmith's Indian community to do likewise. Gandhi, still at an early stage of his political learning curve, believed that by showing the British that Indians were loyal subjects they would grant independence to India.

Around the **Forbes and Lyell streets** areas, near the temple, Ladysmith presents an altogether more African face, thronging with people around the taxi ranks and informal market stalls set up on empty plots dotted between run-down Indian shopping malls, where people jive to the rhythm of backstreet music bars and mothers shop with babies strapped to their backs.

The Muslim side of Ladysmith is represented by the **Soofie Mosque**, across the Klip River in Mosque Road, in the Indian suburb of Rose Park, said (most notably by the Publicity Association) to be the most beautiful mosque in the southern hemisphere.

Eating and drinking

The siege is over and horse is off the menu, but the *Royal Hotel*, with its three **restaurants**, is still the best place to eat in town. Less formal is the *Guinea Fowl Steakhouse*, Alfred St, noted for its spare ribs, while *Savanna's Fast Foods*, Oval Shopping Centre, Murchison St, does the best Indian takeaways in town, serving cheap filled *rotis* and *biryanis* until 7pm. *Wimpy*, 7 Murchison St, is the only place to eat in a hurry and it stays open until 8pm.

Spioenkop

Spioenkop Battlefield lies 35km west of Ladysmith and is set in the Spioenkop Nature Reserve (daily: April–Sept 6am–6pm, Oct–March 6am–7pm). Bloodiest of all the Boer

War battles, Spioenkop took more British lives than any other and taught the British command that wars fought by means of set-piece battles were no longer viable. After this, the guerrilla-style tactics of modern warfare were increasingly adopted.

Some 1700 British troops took the hill under cover of a mist without firing a shot, but were able to dig only shallow trenches because the surface was so hard. When the mist lifted they discovered that they had misjudged the crest of the hill, but their real failure was one of flawed command and desperately poor intelligence. Had the British reconnoitred properly they might have discovered that they were facing a motley collection of fewer than 500 Boers with only seven pieces of artillery, and they could have called in their 1600 reserves to relieve them. Despite holding lower ground, the Boers were able to keep the British, crammed eight men per metre into their trenches, pinned down for an entire sweltering midsummer day, while the Boers pounded them and shot at any helmet that peered over the trenches. Around six hundred British troops perished and were buried where they fell on the so-called "acre of massacre".

Meanwhile the Boers, who were aware of the 1600 British reinforcements at the base of the hill, had gradually been drifting off, and by the end of the day, unbeknownst to the British, there were only 350 Boers left. In the evening the British withdrew, leaving the hill to the enemy.

travel details

As the economic centre of KwaZulu–Natal, Durban is also its transport hub, with the majority of links into the province beginning or ending here. For travellers, the most useful mode of transport could be the **backpacker buses**, which provide access to interesting destinations not on other regular routes.

Trains

Durban to: Johannesburg (1 daily; 15hr); Pietermaritzburg (1 daily; 2hr 10min).

Buses

The main **bus lines** serving the principal routes from Durban to Johannesburg or Cape Town are Translux (☎031/361 8333) and Greyhound (☎031/309 7830). Supplementary services are offered twice daily by Sunbird Tours (☎031/409 5489), up the north coast to Richards Bay; and one to two times daily down the South Coast as far as Margate, by Margate Mini Coach (☎039/312 1406).

Durban to: Ballito (6 weekly; 35min); Bloemfontein (2–3 daily; 10–12hr); Cape Town (3 daily; 20hr); East London (2 daily; 9hr); Dukuza (6 weekly; 1hr); Empangeni (2–3 daily; 2–3hr); Gingindlovu (2 daily; 1hr 30min); Grahamstown (2 daily; 12hr); Harrismith (7 daily; 4hr 30min); Johannesburg (8 daily; 11hr 30min); Kimberley (2 weekly; 11hr·30min); Knysna (2 daily; 15hr);

Ladysmith (4 daily; 3hr 30min); Margate (1–2 daily; 2hr); Melmoth (6 weekly; 4hr); Pietermaritzburg (9 daily; 2hr 15min); Plettenberg Bay (1 daily; 14hr 30min); Port Elizabeth (2 daily; 13hr 30min); Port Shepstone (3–4 daily; 1hr 30min); Pretoria (8 daily; 9hr); Richards Bay (2–3 daily; 2hr 30min); Sedgefield (2 daily; 15hr); Umhlanga Rocks (6 weekly; 15min); Umtata (2 daily; 6hr); Vryheid (1 daily; 6hr).

Margate to: Durban (1–2 daily; 2hr); Johannesburg (4 weekly; 8hr 30min); Pretoria (4 weekly; 10hr).

Pietermaritzburg to: Bloemfontein (2–3 daily; 8hr 30min); Cape Town (4 daily; 19hr); Durban (9 daily; 2hr 15min); Johannesburg (6–7 daily; 7hr); Kimberley (3 weekly; 10hr); Ladysmith (2 daily; 2hr); Pretoria (6–7 daily; 8hr).

Richards Bay to: Durban (2–3 daily; 2hr 30min); Johannesburg (6 weekly; 9hr 30min); Pretoria (6 weekly; 10hr).

Backpacker buses

The **Baz Bus** (☎021/439 2323, fax 439 2343, *info@bazbus.com*) follows routes specifically designed to take in places of interest that link with hostels rather than covering commuter routes. From Durban the Baz follows three routes. Its route **to Port Elizabeth** goes along the KwaZulu-Natal south coast, through the Transkei (giving access to the Wild Coast) and on to East London and finally Port Elizabeth passing en route through Warner Beach, Port Shepstone, Kokstad, Umtata, Cintsa, East London, Hamburg and Kenton-on Sea. In Port Elizabeth you can connect with another Baz the following day to continue on to Cape Town via the Garden Route. The bus **to Swaziland** travels principally along the N2 up the KwaZulu-Natal north coast, passing through Ballito, Gingindlovu, Eshowe, Richards Bay, Kwambonambi, St Lucia, Hluhluwe (which gives access to Sodwana Bay), Mkuzi and in Swaziland, Manzini and Mlilwane. The following day the same bus continues on **to Johannesburg/Pretoria** via Nelspruit (which provides access to the Kruger National Park); from there it completes the leg in a single day and passes along the west side of the province, giving access to the Drakensberg and passing through Pietermaritzburg, Howick, Mooi River and Harrismith.

Durban to: Ballito (4 weekly; 45 min); Cintsa (5 weekly; 6hr 30 min); East London (5 weekly; 9hr 45min); Eshowe (4 weekly; 2hr); Gingindlovu (4 weekly; 1hr 30min); Hamburg (5 weekly; 10hr 45min); Harrismith (4 weekly; 7hr); Hluhluwe (4 weekly; 7hr 15min); Howick (4 weekly; 2hr 30min); Johannesburg (4 weekly; 9hr); Kenton-on-Sea (5 weekly; 11hr 30min); Kokstad (5 weekly; 3hr 40min); Kwambonambi (4 weekly; 4hr); Manzini (4 weekly; 10hr 30min) Mkuzi (4 weekly; 8hr); Mliliwane (4 weekly; 10hr 30min); Mooi River (4 weekly; 3hr); Pietermaritzburg (4 weekly; 2hr); Port Alfred (5 weekly; 11hr 45 min); Port Elizabeth (5 weekly; 13hr 30min); Port Shepstone (5 weekly; 1hr 30min); Pretoria (4 weekly; 10hr); Richards Bay (4 weekly; 3hr); St Lucia (4 weekly; 5hr); Umtata (5 weekly; 5hr 45 min); Warner Beach (5 weekly; 30min).

Minibus shuttles

Two **minibus shuttles, Rollercoaster Taxi** (☎031/233 3706), and **Rasool's** (☎031/208 0919), run a door-to-door service twice a day (pickup 5–6.30am & 5–6.30pm; 6–7hr) in each direction between Jo'burg and Durban and pick up anywhere in Durban and drop off anywhere within central Jo'burg and the surrounding suburbs. Apart from a halfway break in Harrismith to stretch your legs, there are no intermediate stops.

Flights

Durban to: Bloemfontein (8 weekly; 1hr 20min); Cape Town (11–14 daily; 2hr 15min); George (3 weekly; 3hr); Johannesburg (21 daily; 1hr 10min); Pietermaritzburg (5 weekly; 25min); Plettenberg Bay (3 weekly; 2hr 50min); Port Elizabeth (7 daily; 1hr 20min); Ulundi (16 weekly; 40min).

Margate to: Johannesburg (1 daily; 1hr 30min).

Pietermaritzburg to: Durban (2 daily; 25min); Johannesburg (6 daily; 2hr 15min); Ulundi (2 daily; 1hr 30min).

Richards Bay to: Johannesburg (2–4 daily; 1hr 20min).

CHAPTER SIX

FREE STATE

One of South Africa's most scenic drives, the Highlands route, skirts the mountainous eastern flank of the **Free State,** the traditional heartland of conservative **Afrikanerdom**, which lies landlocked at the centre of the country. The **Eastern Highlands**, which sweep up to the subcontinent's highest peaks in the Lesotho Drakensberg, are worth the detour off the more humdrum N6 if you're driving from Johannesburg to Port Elizabeth (or possibly even Cape Town). And many travellers prefer it as a more circuitous, but unquestionably quieter and more enjoyable, route between KwaZulu-Natal and the Garden Route, with the bonus that you avoid the potholes and errant cattle of the N2 through the Transkei. The eastern Free State is also the **gateway to Lesotho**, with border posts close to each of the small towns on the South African side. You may well end up spending a night in one of them – no hard task since they're very pretty, surrounded by mountains and cherry farms, and offer decent B&Bs.

The highlight of the Eastern Highlands is the **Golden Gate National Park**, designated a national park not for its wildlife, but because of the beauty of the Maluti

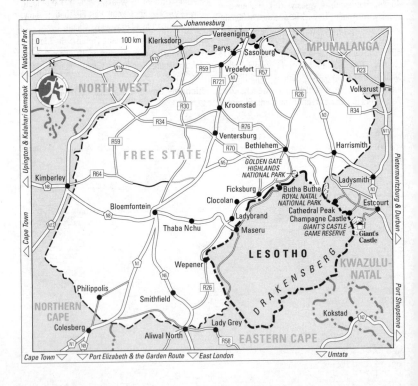

Mountains with their stripy red sandstone outcrops. It's an easy three- to four-hour drive from Johannesburg, and from here you could do a round trip of the Highlands, taking in Lesotho as well. A fully tarred road runs inside Lesotho's border, mirroring the Highlands route, though quite different in the slices of rural Lesotho life you'll see.

Southeast of Golden Gate you can drive to the **Sentinel car park** via the worth-while **Basotho Cultural Village** and **Phuthadijhaba**, and hike up to the highest plateaus of the **Drakensberg**, an easier way than starting from a much lower altitude in the Royal Natal National Park. West of the park is **Clarens**, by far the nicest of the string of towns that runs along the Lesotho border, with a distinctly arty feel, and some of the country's best riding at Bokpoort Farm. For young travellers, party-goers and ageing hippies the real focus of the region is **Rustler's Valley**, west of Clarens, where you can ride, hike in the hills or simply hang out on a truly magnificent farm.

In the rest of the province, there's some relief to be had, in the flat farmlands rolling away into miles of bright-yellow sunflowers, mauve and pink-petalled cosmos, maize and wheat fields glowing under immense blue skies. It's this area which the ever-gracious Nelson Mandela described as gladdening his heart "no matter what my mood. When I am here I feel that nothing can shut me in, that my thoughts can roam as far as the horizons."

Some history

Intriguing though it sounds, the name "Free State" is little more than a reminder that you're in redneck country. For nearly 150 years, the only people who were free in the Free State were its **white settlers**, who in 1854 were granted independence from Britain in a territory between the Orange and Vaal rivers, where they created a Boer Republic called the **Orange Free State**. The "Orange" part of the name came from the Orange River, which in its turn was named in 1777 by Colonel Robert Gordon, commander of the British garrison at the Cape, after the royal Dutch House of Orange.

The system of government in the republic, inspired by the US Constitution, was highly democratic – if you were a white male. Women couldn't vote and Africans had no rights at all, and were even forbidden from owning land. Two expansionist military campaigns were launched in 1858 and 1865 to drive out independent **Basotho** people from fertile lands along the Caledon River, which had been their home since the sixteenth century. Many Basotho under paramount chief **Moshoeshoe** retreated to strongholds in the Drakensberg (see p.620). The thousands who remained were reduced to squatters, sharecroppers and labourers who faced poor wages on the 15,000 thinly distributed white farms.

Even by apartheid standards, the Orange Free State was bad news, being the only province to ban anyone of Asian descent from remaining within its borders for longer than 24 hours. Africans fared little better and in 1970, under the grand apartheid scheme, a tiny barren enclave wedged between Lesotho, KwaZulu-Natal and the Free State became **QwaQwa**, a "homeland" for Southern Sotho people. As a result of forced clearances from white-designated areas, its population swelled from 24,000 to nearly half a million in the two decades after 1970, creating one of the worst rural slums in the country. Many men were forced to seek work as migrant labourers in the Gauteng gold mines. Another tiny area around Thaba Nchu, 63km east of Bloemfontein, was part of Bophutatswana, the Tswana *bantustan*, which became nominally independent from South Africa in 1977, but was never more than a series of disconnected fragments scattered all over the country, the capital at Mmabatho, in another shard of land in Northwest Province.

The *bantustans* have since been reincorporated into South Africa, and after an ANC landslide in Free State province in the 1994 elections, the "Orange" part of the name, with its Dutch Calvinist associations, was dropped.

BLOEMFONTEIN

BLOEMFONTEIN isn't a place anyone actually visits, but because it lies at the crossroads of South Africa many travellers end up here to break a journey across the country. You're unlikely to be wracked by regret if you give the city a miss, but once here you'll find enough diversion for an afternoon – maybe even a day – in its surprisingly fine **Oliewenhuis Art Gallery**, set in beautiful gardens, and in the unmistakably provincial **President Brand Street**, lined with its mixed bag of handsome, sandstone public buildings.

As an overnight stop, the city fulfils its functional role admirably, providing an apparently disproportionate quantity of accommodation at reasonable prices – a result of its importance as the only centre of any size in a thinly spread province. People home in from all over the Free State for hospital treatment, for the university (highly regarded for its medical school) and its several boarding schools. It's also the seat of the provincial parliament and the judicial capital of the country – a sop tossed out to draw it into the Union when South Africa federated in 1910.

Bloemfontein's urban origins go back to 1846 when **Major Henry Warden** was dispatched to establish a fort and residency here to enforce British control over the unruly Boers, Griquas and Basotho, who were in a constant state of conflict. Knocking their heads together proved fruitless and he was withdrawn in frustration eight years later and the territory left to the Boers, who set up the capital of their republic here, using a schoolhouse built by Warden in 1849 as the **First Raadsaal** (parliament).

Arrival and information

Translux (☎051/408 3242), Intercape (☎051/447 1435) and Greyhound (☎051/447 1558) **buses** pull in at the central bus terminal in the new tourist complex at the east end of Park Avenue, opposite the swimming pool. This is also the place to find the **tourist information bureau** (Mon–Fri 8am–4.15pm, Sat 8am–noon; ☎051/405 8490, fax 47 3859, *bloem@internext.co.za*) where you'll get **maps** of the city.

Few travellers fly into **Bloemfontein Airport** (☎051/433 2901), 10km east of town on the N8, although there are scheduled flights between here and the major cities. There are no shuttle buses from the airport into town, so your only choice is to phone for a fairly expensive **taxi**, or **rent a car** here (see "Listings" on p.467 for details of both). By **train**,

---

GAUTENG TO BLOEMFONTEIN: SOME ROUTE TIPS

The great plus of taking the **N1** from Johannesburg to Bloemfontein is that it's the fastest way of covering the distance – and there's a lot to be said for getting the journey over with as quickly as possible. This is no scenic route, however, especially the Gauteng section and the northern Free State area, which is full of ugly industrial towns. Toll booths are strategically positioned at intervals along the N1, but the charge hardly makes it worth taking free detours. **Kroonstad**, 207km south of Johannesburg, is the biggest town along the N1 before you get to Bloemfontein. The Kroon Park, a large, popular resort beside a river, with a swimming pool, offers a pit stop if you want to cool off or get something to eat.

The alternative route from just south of the provincial border to Kroonstad goes via **Parys**, first along the R59 and turning onto the R721 at Vredefort, 13km south of Parys. But while Parys is quite green and pleasant, you're very likely to get stuck behind slow traffic, whereas the N1 at this point is still straight, smooth and wide.

The further south you go, the flatter the Free State becomes, and there's an exceptionally long, dull stretch between **Ventersburg** and Bloemfontein – with no services, a one-lane road and not a lot going for it.

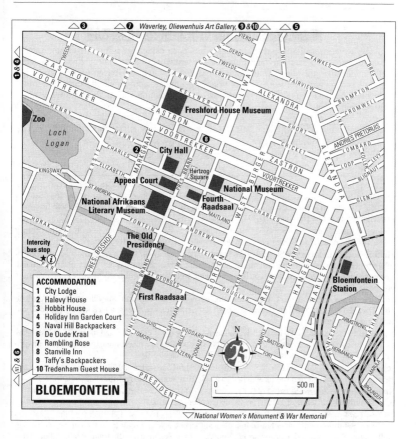

ACCOMMODATION
1 City Lodge
2 Halevy House
3 Hobbit House
4 Holiday Inn Garden Court
5 Naval Hill Backpackers
6 De Oude Kraal
7 Rambling Rose
8 Stanville Inn
9 Taffy's Backpackers
10 Tredenham Guest House

BLOEMFONTEIN

▽*National Women's Monument & War Memorial*

you'll arrive at Bloemfontein Station (☎051/408 2946) in Harvey Road at the east end of Maitland Street and by minibus taxi, you'll be dropped off at the rank in Hanger Street, one block west of the station. The area around the station and the minibus taxi rank is regarded by some residents as the dodgiest in the city centre, but there have been few actual incidents. Stay alert, and avoid the area at night if you can. Fortunately, metered taxis usually rank outside the train and at the bus station; alternatively, you can phone for one.

Accommodation

Bloemfontein bears the distinction of having *Hobbit House*, which has been voted South Africa's best guesthouse. Also here is some of the cheapest overnight **accommodation** in South Africa, mainly concentrated around the hospitals, in Universitas suburb to the west of the city centre, and around Oranjesig to its south. However, you're best off heading for the nicer and more central suburbs of **Westdene** and **Waverley**, both north of the centre and easily reached on foot.

City Lodge, corner of Zastron St and Parfitt Ave, Westdene (☎051/447 9888, fax 447 5669, *cl/bloem@citylodge.co.za*). Unremarkable but good value, with cheaper rates at weekends, just outside the centre. Serves excellent breakfasts, and is handy for shops, restaurants and cinemas. ③.

De Oude Kraal, 35km south of Bloemfontein on the N1 off the Riversford exit (☎051/564 0636, fax 564 0635). Restored original farmhouse famous for the Afrikaner opulence of its meals, with fireplaces in each en-suite room. Half board ⑤–⑥.

Halevy House, Markgraaff St (☎051/448 0271, fax 430 8749). City institution in a turn-of-the-century hotel. The beautiful facade hides a down-at-heel reality that's passable, given the price. ②.

Hobbit House, 19 President Steyn Ave, Westdene (☎ & fax 051/447 0663). A luxurious establishment full of beautiful and comfortable antique furniture, with teddy bears tucked into every bed under hand-made quilts. With only five rooms, you'll need to book well in advance. Excellent three-course dinners are available. ⑤.

Holiday Inn Garden Court Bloemfontein, corner of Zastron and Melville streets, Westdene (☎051/447 0310, fax 430 5678). Best of the posh hotels, with large rooms, a nice swimming pool, and weekend discounts. ④.

Naval Hill Backpackers, Delville Rd, as you turn into the old waterpump station (☎051/447 4413, fax 430 7962, *discover@iafrica.com*). Clean dorms (but no doubles) in a nicely done up late nineteenth-century pumping station with washed orange walls. Linen available. ①.

Rambling Rose, 77 President Reitz St, Westdene (☎051/447 1634, fax 430 5713, *rosie@internext.co.za*). Bright, comfortable garden rooms attached to a suburban house with a swimming pool. ③.

Stanville Inn, 85 Zastron St (☎051/447 7471, fax 447 7514). Tiny, well-maintained rooms in a five-storey apartment block, on a busy road but providing excellent value. ②.

Taffy's Backpackers, 18 Louis Botha St, Waverley (☎ & fax 051/436 4533, ask for Vilna; *web@lantic.co.za*). Salubrious suburban house in a pleasant street, a 15min walk from the centre, with a big, well-equipped kitchen and a large garden. Ring for a free pick-up from the train or bus station. They also arrange transport into Lesotho. Small dorms (①), doubles (②) and camping (①) in the garden.

Tredenham Guest House, off Eeufees Rd, just north of town (☎ & fax 051/433 1285). Colonial English farmhouse built in 1925, now Afrikaner-owned and furnished in period style. Good meals and relaxing atmosphere in a rural area, despite its proximity to the town centre. The more expensive inside rooms are by far the best. ③–④.

The City

For a city with a countrywide reputation as the bumpkin capital of South Africa, Bloemfontein turns out to be quite agreeable, with a slightly unreal character due to the way so many of its late nineteenth- and early twentieth-century **public buildings** pay a pick'n'mix homage to Mediterranean, British, Renaissance and classical influences. An almost nonexistent public transport system poses few obstacles to getting around; the central area can easily be crossed on foot in ten minutes.

City Hall and around

For the most rewarding stroll in the centre, head down **President Brand Street**, starting at the north end on the corner of Charles Street, where you'll see the **City Hall**, a monumental structure designed in the "new tradition style" by Gordon Leith, a former employee of Sir Herbert Baker, and built in 1934. On the opposite side of President Brand Street, **Hertzog Square** honours the dubious achievements of Boer general, high court judge and Afrikaner nationalist **J.B.M. Hertzog**, who founded the National Party in 1914, went on to become prime minister of the Union of South Africa in 1924 and was responsible for harsh segregationist legislation, including the stripping of voting rights from Africans in the Cape in 1936. Across the square at 36 Aliwal St, the **National Museum** (Mon–Sat 8am–5pm, Sun 1–6pm; small entry fee) is worth sticking your nose into for the rather good dinosaur fossil collection, the living beehive and an outstanding reconstruction of a turn-of-the-century Bloemfontein street. There's a general dealer, pharmacy, doctor's consulting rooms and a family scene that captures in frozen diorama a father telling off his son under a stern portrait of President Steyn, who looks on approvingly. The museum's tea room is a good place to take a break.

Returning to President Brand Street, south of the City Hall you'll come to the highest court in the country, the Roman-style **Appeal Court of South Africa**, built in 1929. Staring at it from across the road is the **Fourth Raadsaal**, regarded as the "architectural jewel" of the province. An imposing sandstone and red-brick building, typical of Free State construction of the period, the Raadsaal was the last parliament building of the independent Orange Free State republic (it's now the provincial legislature), and was built in 1890 in a style that manages to get away brilliantly with merging Greek, Roman and Renaissance elements.

National Afrikaans Literary Museum

One block south of the Appeal Court is the **National Afrikaans Literary Museum** (Mon–Fri 8am–noon & 1–3.45pm, Sat 9am–noon; free), in the Old Government Building, on the corner of President Brand and Maitland streets. Inside, an endless stream of offices have been reconstructed as the studies of the luminaries of Afrikaans writing, with name plates on the doors which make you feel rude for not knocking before going in. Look out for the display on **Eugene Marais**, the remarkable polymath who was active around the turn of the century and wrote a couple of trail-blazing natural histories on termites and baboons. Lawyer, poet of stature and journalist, he contributed articles to the *Observer* and *The Times* in London and to the Reuter news agency. Also represented are the "Sestigers" (generation of the Sixties), including novelist **Andre Brink**, who was loudly critical of apartheid, especially after the Seventies, and poet **Breyten Breytenbach**, who went into exile in Paris in 1961. Breytenbach returned to South Africa under cover in 1975 to gain support for Okhela, a largely white section of the ANC, and was captured by the South African authorities and imprisoned for seven years, leading to the publication after his release of *The True Confessions of an Albino Terrorist*. Towards the end of the museum, a couple of rooms are devoted to displays of Afrikaans as a language of oppression, where coloured South Africans make their eleventh-hour appearance. One of the leading lights of coloured Afrikaans (which has its own distinct character) is the poet **Adam Small**, who in one display describes the predicament of being a member of an oppressed community, while at the same time being a speaker of Afrikaans, the language regarded during the uprisings of the Seventies as the language of white persecutors. "I grew up with Afrikaans. Afrikaans is part of my culture," he is quoted as saying, "and when people said to you that Afrikaans was the language of the oppressor it was very painful, because it was also the language you got from your parents, it was your mother tongue and it was beautiful and full of humanity."

The Waterfront and Zoo

Having witnessed the huge success of the Victoria and Alfred Waterfront in Cape Town, every city in the country seems eager to bound onto the bandwagon, and Bloemfontein is no exception. Nevertheless, the Bloemfontein **Waterfront**, opened in 1998 on Loch Logan in King's Park, a couple of blocks west of the National Afrikaans Literary Museum, is a refreshing addition to the city, bringing with it new movie houses, pubs and restaurants in a pleasantly sited outdoor environment. It has also become flavour of the moment for nightlife. Adjacent, also in King's Park, the **Bloemfontein Zoo** (daily: summer 8am–6pm; winter 8am–5pm; entrance fee) is not bad as far as zoos go and is a reasonable place to catch African wildlife, but obviously offers no contest when compared to seeing animals under the more stimulating conditions of a game reserve.

The Supreme Court, Old Presidency and First Raadsaal

Carrying on south down President Brand Street to the corner of Selborne Street, opposite the Fire Station, the **Supreme Court**, completed in 1906, stands on the site of the home of the Fischers, a prominent Orange Free State Afrikaner family, whose heir, lawyer Bram Fischer, betrayed his Afrikaner tribal roots and defended Nelson Mandela during the 1963 Rivonia Trial (see p.694). After Mandela was found guilty and handed a life sentence, it was discovered that all the time Fischer had secretly been the leader of the proscribed Communist Party, and he too was jailed for life, later being released to die at home of cancer.

The **Old Presidency** (Tues–Fri 10am–noon & 1–4pm, Sat & Sun 2–5pm; free), on the opposite corner, was built on the site of the home of Major Henry Warden, the founder of Bloemfontein. Built in 1861 in "Scottish baronial style" as the official seat of the head of the republic, the Presidency is surprisingly plain, due as much to the impecunious condition of the state coffers as to the severe Calvinism that characterized the Boer republics. While you can go inside, you aren't going to get much of an idea of how the president lived because virtually none of the original furnishings remain. Turning east after the Old Presidency into St George's Street, you'll come to the **First Raadsaal** (Mon–Fri 10.15am–3pm, Sat & Sun 2–5pm), the oldest-surviving building in Bloemfontein. Built in 1849 by Major Warden as a school, the building was later used as a Dutch Reformed Church and venue for public meetings. At independence in 1854 it became first a meeting chamber for Free State Volksraad ("people's assembly") and subsequently reverted to a schoolhouse and church.

National Women's Monument and War Museum

Just over 2km south of the centre, along Monument Street, across the train tracks in an ugly industrial part of town, the solemn sandstone needle pointing skywards marks the **National Women's Monument and War Museum** (Mon–Fri 9am–4.30pm, Sat 9am–5pm, Sun 2–5pm; small entry fee), a memorial to the 26,370 Afrikaner women and children who died in British concentration camps during the second Anglo-Boer War. It's impossible to overestimate the depth of the scar left on the Afrikaner psyche by the concentration camps – probably the single most divisive issue between English and Afrikaans-speaking white South Africans, with reverberations even today. At the foot of the monument lies buried **Emily Hobhouse**, a British woman who energetically campaigned on behalf of the Boer internees. The interest of the adjacent museum lies principally in its status as a record of apartheid propaganda. The suffering it depicts isn't exactly untrue, just a little heavy handed in its unrelenting dioramas of dignified Boers suffering at the hands of faceless British bastards. Two cursory panels on concentration camps for Africans (never widely publicized in South Africa in the old days), tacked on at the end, are a post-apartheid afterthought that at least provides a partial record of the more than 14,000 black South Africans who died incarcerated. Some visual relief to death and suffering is offered by a room near the entrance of the museum, lined with brilliant ceramic-tile tableaux, depicting scenes from the Anglo-Boer War. The tiles were discovered and brought here in 1969 after being uncovered when wallpaper was stripped off the walls of the Transvalia Theatre in Rotterdam, the Netherlands – an indi-

J.R.R. TOLKIEN

Bloemfontein's biggest surprise is that it's the birthplace of **John Ronald Reuel Tolkien**, author of *Lord of the Rings* and *The Hobbit*, a fact which the city seems curiously reluctant to publicize. Elsewhere, you're bound to come across wild claims that Tolkien's experience of the South African landscape inspired him to create the world of Bilbo Baggins. In fact, nothing could be further from the fantastical realm of mountains, forests and supernatural beings of *The Hobbit* than the flatness of the Free State and the down-to-earth Calvinism of its farming community. Some accounts claim that he was inspired by the Natal Drakensberg, while others say it was the Amatola Mountains around Hogsback. Both areas do have an otherworldly magic – the only problem is that Tolkien departed South Africa for good when he was 3 years old, never having set foot outside Bloemfontein.

Tolkien's father, Arthur, left his native Birmingham, where he worked for Lloyds Bank, for the better prospects of the colonies. He eventually rose to manager of the Bank of Africa in Bloemfontein, where J.R.R. was born in 1892, in a house that stood on the corner of West Burger and Maitland streets, a couple of blocks east of President Brand Street. When Arthur Tolkien died in 1895, his wife returned to England with her two infant sons, and their house was later torn down to make way for a Bradlow's showroom, part of a cheap, nationwide furniture chain.

cation of how the war rallied the popular imagination in Europe on the side of the Boers.

Oliewenhuis Art Gallery and Freshford House Museum

The real highlight of Bloemfontein's museums is undoubtedly the **Oliewenhuis Art Gallery** on Harry Smith Street (Mon–Fri 8am–5pm, Sat 10am–5pm, Sun 1–5pm; free), the former residency of South African presidents when they rolled into town, about five minutes north of the centre by car. The collection is housed in a beautifully light neo-Cape Dutch manor set in large, attractive gardens that dissolve into wild bush traversed by short walking trails. The lightness of it all seeps into the gallery interior and creates an airy ambience for browsing through a surprisingly good range of **South African sculpture** and **painting**. Particularly satisfying is the landscape collection, which includes the strong, flashing strokes of a Van Gogh-esque interpretation of one of the city churches by **Bertha Everard**, and a **Thomas Baines** documentary painting of Bloemfontein as a tiny settlement in 1850. If you don't want to take in the culture, you can always have tea at the café under the trees on the lawn by a fountain – the most harmonious location in town.

Also to the north of the city centre, but not quite as far, **Freshford House Museum**, 31 Kellner St (Mon–Fri 10am–1pm, Sat & Sun 2–5pm; small entrance fee), makes a lightweight but enjoyable visit, especially if you're interested in **interiors**, as it has been refurbished impeccably in Victorian and Edwardian style. One highlight is a room authentically – and daringly – decorated in lime green, with three distinct William Morris wallpapers: one pattern up to the dado rail; another from there to the picture rail; and the third above that.

Eating and drinking

While Bloemfontein is no culinary capital and there are no regional specialities to sample, you can certainly have a good and inexpensive **meal** out, mostly in the city centre or the nearby suburbs of Westdene and Waverley, which are close to most of the accommodation. You'll also find the usual steakhouse chains scattered around the centre and in the shopping malls. For gluttonous **breakfasts**, the *City Lodge* and *Holiday Inn Garden Court* hotels (see "Accommodation", p.462) are always good bets.

Restaurants and cafés

Acropolis, CR Swart Building, Elizabeth St (☎051/447 0464) Revolving restaurant that's Bloemfontein's most stylish eatery, with decor based on London's *River Cafe*. Soaring city views and wholesome Greek-style food are both good reasons to come here.

Barba's Café, Mimosa Mall, Kellner St (☎051/448 4406). Good Greek food, a diverse cocktail menu and the best coffee in town at this venue near the university, which draws the young and trendy to linger amid the starkly fashionable decor.

Bon Appetit, 110 Voortrekker St. Adjoining an art gallery, this is the best place in the centre for daytime coffee and meals. The food is Mediterranean alfresco style and their dish of the day is reliably good.

Beef Baron, 22 Second Ave (☎051/447 4290). True to its name, this is the place to come for beef, where your mug-shot could join those of other carnivores who downed 1.5kg steaks and survived. The wine cellar is excellent.

Café Oliewenhuis, Harry Smith St, signposted off the R700. Tables in the formal gardens at the back of the gallery, leading onto a nature reserve, make this Bloemfontein's nicest place for a relaxing outdoor tea or lunch. Though the food itself is nothing to write home about on the whole, this is definitely *the* place for Sunday afternoon tea and cake.

District Six, 24 West Burger St (☎051/430 4440). Very affordable and freshly prepared Cape Cuisine matching anything you'll find in Cape Town, including curries and *masala snoek*. Ring ahead to check their hours.

Harbour Fish Market, 19a Second Avenue (☎051/448 4084). Surprisingly, for the most landlocked city in the country, this Greek seafood restaurant has an unusually wide variety of well-prepared fish served in a warm atmosphere.

Mystic Boer, 84 Kellner St. Knowingly kitsch, this one-off alternative and trendy Afrikaner venue is somewhere you can catch live performances, enjoy a drink and eat pizzas and vegetarian meals from their reasonable pub menu.

Oude Kraal, 35km south of town on the N1 (☎051/564 0636). Sunday lunch buffet blowout of rich, fattening Afrikaner-style food in lovely surroundings. Booking as far ahead as possible is mandatory to join the feast.

Roma Coffee Bar, 24 West Burger St (under *District Six* restaurant). Daytime only venue for good filter coffee and their legendary two-tone chocolate cake baked by a schoolgirl who won't divulge the recipe.

Sondeblom, 49 Second Ave. Eclectic coffee shop open evenings serving coffees with liqueur and basic meals.

Nightlife and entertainment

Finding out what's going on in Bloemfontein can be a problem for visitors, as there's no English-language newspaper. *Taffy's Backpackers* (see "Accommodation", p.462) is always a good source of information on up-to-the-minute drinking spots, but generally speaking **nightlife** is a pretty tame affair. For something quite different that you won't catch anywhere else in the country, the *Mystic Boer* has to be the place to head if you have only one night in town; while among the handful of bars in the centre worth checking out, *Barba's Café* (see "Restaurants and cafés" above) is a lively place for a drink, while *Déjà Vu*, at 158 Voortrekker St, is a bar/nightclub favoured by bikers and punky types and is good for dancing.

The most interesting of Bloemfontein's handful of **theatres** is the Observatory, on the crest of Naval Hill, just north of the centre, because it's situated inside a real observatory in the city's nature reserve, which supports a few giraffe and some antelope. The most presitigious theatre is the Sand du Plessis, on the corner of Markgraaff and St Andrew streets. The recent removal of a prominent statue of H.F. Verwoerd, the arch-theorist and practitioner of apartheid, from in front of the theatre, ruffled local right-wing feathers. Bloemfontein has several **cinemas**, mostly in suburban shopping malls; the Mimosa Mall in Westdene has seven cinemas, and Noordstad in Eeufees Road (R700) has four, all showing standard, mainstream movies.

Listings

Airlines South African Airways, St Andrew's St (☎051/447 3811).

Car rental Avis (☎051/433 2331); Budget (☎051/433 1178); Hertz (☎051/433 4018); and Imperial (☎051/433 3511). All are represented at the airport.

Emergencies Ambulance ☎10177; Fire ☎10178; Police (Flying Squad) ☎10111; Rape Crisis ☎447 6678.

Hospitals The main state hospital is *Universitas*, which offers a free 24hr emergency ward, but you may wait hours and the level of care is variable. Far better, if you can afford it or have travel insurance, is one of the private hospitals. These are *Hydromed*, Kellner St (☎051/404 6666), and *Rosepark*, Fichmed Centre, Gustav Crescent (☎051/422 6761).

Pharmacies Medirex Pharmacy, Southern Life Building, Maitland St (Mon–Sat 8am–10.30pm, Sun 9am–10.30pm; ☎051/447 5822).

Post office Main branch, corner of East Burger and Maitland streets (Mon, Tues, Thurs & Fri 8am–4.30pm, Wed 8.30am–4.30pm, Sat 8am–noon).

Taxis Rosestad (☎051/436 5901) and Silverleaf (☎051/430 2005). Majakathata (☎051/447 0877) minibus taxis are good for long-distance travel.

Train information Spoornet ☎051/408 2941.

South from Bloemfontein

Two major routes splay out and head south from Bloemfontein, the **N6** to the Eastern Cape via Aliwal North (see p.337) and the **N1** to the Western Cape via Colesberg (see p.175). Nothing much happens along either route apart from a couple of quirky small towns. Along the N6, **SMITHFIELD**, a tiny *dorp* 145km from Bloemfontein, makes a good place to break a journey along the N6 if only to stay at the pleasant *Artists' Colony Guest House* (☎ & fax 051/683 1138, *colony@global.co.za*, ③), with rooms in two en-suite cottages, one of which is a listed building. You can either have a continental breakfast in your room or repair to the nearby *Colony Room* (☎051/683 0021, *colony@global.co.za*), a restaurant along the N6, off Juana Square, for something with more substance. Noted for its Smithfield Omelette, distinguished by its grilled topping, this is also a fully licensed establishment that serves pub lunches and dinners.

PHILIPPOLIS, 168km south of Bloemfontein along a slight detour off the N1 between Trompsberg and Colesberg, is the place where **Sir Laurens van der Post** (see box above) grew up. The road is quiet and typical of the upper Karoo, with a bit of distant

---

THE GRIQUAS

In the early nineteenth century, roving bands of cattle-herders and raiders with a reputation for horsemanship and fierce independence appeared on the eastern edge of the Cape Colony around the Orange River. They called themselves, with some pride, "Bastaards", being mixed descendants of European, Khoikhoi, Asian and African people. The missionaries who persuaded them to establish settlements at places such as Griquatown, Campbell and Philippolis also took exception to their name, which was changed to **Griqua**. Though Griqualand West was still theoretically independent, clashes with the Boers and squabbles over land ownership when diamonds were found in their territory saw them turning to the British for protection, faith which was all too hastily swallowed up by the gorging Cape Colony.

In 1861 three thousand Griquas from Philippolis under their leader Adam Kok III trekked across the Drakensberg to southern Natal to found **Griqualand East**, a pocket of land on the far side of the Drakensberg, south of Natal. That settlement failed, and slowly the Griquas dispersed and became subsumed into the wider coloured community, although there are still odd pockets of their descendants living in various places around the Northern, Western and Eastern Cape provinces.

LAURENS VAN DER POST

Growing up in Philippolis, **Laurens van der Post**, the famous explorer, writer, soldier and philosopher, learnt of the stories and legends of the "Bushman", or San people who had once lived in the area but had been forced by the advance of African and European settlers into the northern deserts. "What drew me so strongly to the Bushman was that he appeared to belong to my native land as no other human being has ever belonged," he says, as he became entranced by the self-sufficient yet intensely spiritual and aesthetic way they lived. It prompted him to take a famous journey in search of the last remnants of the San, one he recorded in a book and film called *The Lost World of the Kalahari*. This narrative, along with a sequel called *The Heart of the Hunter*, was one of the first to prick the Western conscience with the idea that such a primitive "tribe" had anything to teach it. Van der Post was a Japanese prisoner of war during World War II – the book he wrote about his experiences, *The Seed and the Sower*, was made into the film *Merry Christmas, Mr Lawrence*. He lived in both London and South Africa, and died in 1996, aged 90.

scenery and the scattered signs of a scattered population. There isn't much to the town, although it was one of the first settlements north of the Orange River, established in the 1830s and named in honour of **Dr John Philip**, the British cleric who set up a mission station here. Way ahead of his time, Philip actively campaigned for the full integration of former slaves, Africans and coloured people into the white economic and social system, which he believed was the only way of ensuring peace, justice and stability.

Among the attractive old buildings that line the few streets is a small, white, flat-roofed house just before the post office on Voortrekker Street, the main thoroughfare running through the village, which has a plaque indicating that it was (according to tradition) the house of **Adam Kok III**, leader of the Griqua (see previous page).

There is an **information desk** and **accommodation** at *Die Basotho* guesthouse and tea room on Kok Street, which runs parallel to Voortrekker (☎051/773 0157, ③). The other guesthouse in town, the *Van der Post Guest House* (☎051/773 0324, ④) on Colin Fraser Street, is the old **van der Post family home**. A self-catering residence, (though breakfast is included), it only accepts one party at a time, which allows for some privacy, and there is a small archive about the writer and his family inside, although you can only have access to the house if you are a guest. Laurens, the thirteenth of fifteen children, was born on a farm outside town in 1906 and moved here when he was still very young. In *The Lost World of the Kalahari* he writes: "I was born near the Great River, in the heart of what for thousands of years had been great Bushman [San] country." Great River was a direct translation of "Gariep", the name the Khoi had used before the arrival of white settlers.

At the end of Voortrekker Street is the large **Dutch Reformed Church**, built on the site of the original Griqua mission station. Another good reason to take the Philippolis diversion is the chance to take a good look at the mighty **Orange River** – it's easier to stop and contemplate the river on a quiet country road than flashing over it at 120km per hour as you do on the highway.

THE HIGHLANDS ROUTE

Hugging the Lesotho border for 280 tarred kilometres from **Phuthadijhaba** (Witsieshoek) in the north to Wepener, beyond Ladybrand in the south, the **Highlands Route** offers one of South Africa's most scenic drives, taking you through massive rock formations streaked with ochre and red, cherry orchards and sandstone farming towns. Wedged into a corner between Lesotho and northern KwaZulu-Natal, Phuthadijhaba is the gateway to the Sentinel, the easiest route onto the **Drakensberg Escarpment**, the roof of southern Africa. Not far to the west is the highlight of the region, **Golden Gate**

Highlands National Park, encompassing wide open mountain country. The park is an easy three- to four-hour drive from Johannesburg, which means you could use it as a first- or last-night stop if you're arriving or leaving from Johannesburg and don't want to spend the night in the city. Nearby, the **Basotho Cultural Village** is worth visiting to gain insight into Basotho traditions. The closest town to the Golden Gate is **Clarens**, a centre for arts and crafts and the most attractive of all the villages along the route.

Basotho Cultural Village

The **Basotho Cultural Village** (Mon–Fri 9am–4.30pm, Sat & Sun 9am–5pm; entry fee; ☎ & fax 058/721 0300, *basotho@dorea.co.za*), 20km east of Golden Gate National Park and signposted from the main road, is in the QwaQwa National Park, which abuts Golden Gate and caters to sanitized curiosity about traditional people's lives – in this case the **Basotho** people, who have lived in the vicinity for centuries and have a close affinity to people living just across the border in Lesotho. The main display at the village is a **courtyard of Basotho huts** from the sixteenth century to the present day, with people outside in traditional dress, playing different roles. Visitors get to meet the chief, hear musicians play, see a traditional healer throwing the bones and get the chance to sample traditional beer. Although the whole setup is contrived, the half-hour tour can be good fun. The beautiful vernacular architecture of the huts, from organic, circular, six-teenth-century constructions to square ones with tin roofs and bright interior decor influenced by Boer scissorwork, is well worth seeing. Also interesting is the *litema*, or external decoration on houses, put on by women and still visible in rural Lesotho and Free State. The decoration varies from repeat patterns scratched into the mud-coloured plasterwork to vivid, modern motifs. While you're here, you can book to go on the intriguing two-hour **Matlakeng Herbal Trail**, guided by a traditional healer who gives an informed introduction to *veld* herbs. The tour also takes in a well-preserved **rock painting**. **Riding** on Basotho ponies is possible, but must also be booked beforehand.

There's a limited amount of very reasonably priced **accommodation** available in a couple of thatched, stone huts (②) with external toilets and washing facilities. A two-plate electric cooker and kettle are provided, along with basic utensils, and linen, blankets and towels. Views from the shuttered windows across the QwaQwa National Park are awesome, and this is a great place to stay, with an endless choice of casual walks. Don't expect to be looked after though, and be warned that the village is largely deserted at night, when the workers head back to contemporary urban Sotho life in Phuthadijhaba. A **curio shop** sells some quality local crafts (look out for raffia mats and baskets and the conical straw hats unique to this area and Lesotho), and the open-air **restaurant** serves teas and traditional food.

Phuthadijhaba and around

The only reason you're likely to drive through **PHUTHADIJHABA** (still sometimes called Witsieshoek), roughly 2km off the R712 and east of Golden Gate, is to reach the Witsieshoek Mountain Resort and the Sentinel car park, the easiest hiking access onto the High Drakensberg escarpment. Phuthadijhaba itself is rather bleak and functional, home to light industry and brick matchbox houses. In contrast to the emptiness of the landscape around Golden Gate, in Phuthadijhaba you'll see minibus taxis zipping around, and people and animals walking on the roadsides past shacks, their tin roofs weighted down against the wind with stones. Phuthadijhaba was the artificially created capital of the former **QwaQwa** *bantustan*, and references to that miserable episode are still to be found in road signs and around town.

Signposted from here, the road to Witsieshoek culminates, about 15km from the town, in a fork, one branch of which ends at **Witsieshoek Mountain Inn** and the other at the **Sentinel car park**. The road is tarred until the final few kilometres. On maps it

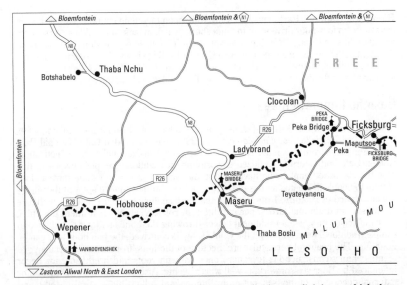

looks as if the Royal Natal National Park and Witsieshoek are adjoining – which they are, via footpaths up and down mountains – by road the journey is about 100km, into KwaZulu-Natal and around the high peaks.

HIKING UP THE DRAKENSBERG ESCARPMENT

South Africa's most spectacular mountain views are from the **Drakensberg Escarpment** and the top of the **Amphitheatre**. Both of these require a high level of fitness if approached from KwaZulu-Natal (see p.412), but can be achieved relatively easily via the Free State from the Sentinel car park to a chain ladder, which gets you to the bottom of the final short onslaught on **Mont aux Sources**, the highest peak on the Escarpment (3278m). The ladder is reached after a tough ten-hour climb from the *Mahai* campsite in the Royal Natal National Park, or a 2.5-hour walk from the Sentinel car park (8km from Witsieshoek Mountain Resort) in the Free State. Set out early so you have the whole day for the excursion onto the Escarpment. A three-kilometre walk from the car park brings you to the foot of the thirty-metre high chain ladder, from whose top you can climb to the summit of Mont aux Sources. The downside of this short cut is that you'll find litter and other environmental degradation around the ladder, although no more than one hundred people are allowed up per day. Don't be lulled by your apparently easy conquest: it's always the Berg's prerogative to have the last word. Always tackle the magic ladder with enough food, water, clothes and a tent in which to sit out violent storms.

If the mountain bug has bitten, you can engage on some serious **hikes**, including a two-week trek along the Escarpment plateau to Sani Pass in the southern Drakensberg, or a five-day, 62-kilometre Escarpment traverse, sleeping in caves, from the Sentinel car park to Cathedral Peak in the Natal Drakensberg Park, roughly 40km southwest, taking in the most dramatic parts of the Berg. For any of these hikes, you'll need a map and the excellent *Drakensberg Walks* by David Bristow (see "Books", p.737), available in most bookshops. If you're starting a big hike at the Sentinel car park, you'll find accommodation in a mountain hut there, where 24-hour security protects vehicles. The hut has no hot water or electricity, so you may be better off at the more comfortable *Witsieshoek Mountain Inn* (see opposite). To book for the car park hut and one of the hundred places a day allocated to climb the chain ladder, contact the Basotho Cultural Village (see previous page).

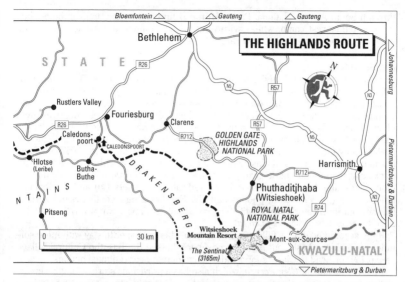

Witsieshoek Mountain Inn (☎058/713 6361 or 713 6362, fax 713 5274) represents one of the great lost opportunities of South African architecture, with the most spectacular setting of any mountain resort in the country but possibly the worst planning. **Accommodation** has been placed just below the brow of a plateau, thus denying guests one of the best views in the entire Drakensberg. Still, you can always walk out into the mountains to take in the views, and the functionality of the rooms is made up for by friendly service. The best rooms are the more expensive ones with views onto the Sentinel (half board ④). There is an overnight hikers' hostel (①), which sleeps twelve and has electricity and hot water – but you need your own sleeping bag.

Golden Gate Highlands National Park

Roughly 300km northeast of Bloemfontein on the R712, **Golden Gate Highlands National Park** (open daily; no entry fee) is Free State's only national park and was proclaimed for its outstanding beauty, rather than its wildlife. Although **eland**, **zebra**, **mountain reedbuck** and **black wildebeest** roam the hillsides, the real attraction here is the unfettered space, eroded sandstone bastions and seamless blue skies. These rocks, grassy plateaus and incised valleys belong to the Drakensberg range, characterized here by spectacular yellow and red cliffs and overhangs. Sandwiches of purples, reds and ochres stripe the massive rocks, where you'll usually find butter-coloured segments at the top, because the softer, terracotta sandstone tends to erode more quickly.

A number of roughly hour-long **rambles** into the sandstone ravines start from a direction board near the footbridge at the *Glen Reenen* campsite. There aren't many medium-length hikes in the park, the only exception being a half-day walk up **Wodehouse Kop**, which offers great views and is more physically challenging than any of the short rambles. The most strenuous hike is the two-day circular Rhebok Trail, which tackles the highest and lowest points of the park. Because the trail is so demanding you'll need to stay the previous night at *Glen Reenen*, where the trail begins, to make an early start (see "Practicalities" below). The Rhebok mountain hut on the trail provides basic accommodation for hikers. Bookings for the trail and hut must be made through South African National Parks. **Horse-riding** is on offer, and can be booked through either rest camp, while **swimming** in the summer is possible in a natural waterfall pool close to *Glen Reenen* campsite.

Practicalities

Golden Gate is almost equidistant and easily reached from either Bloemfontein or Johannesburg, which is 320km to its north on good, tarred roads. There are no entry gates to the park. **Accommodation** is at two rest camps, close to one another and both right on the R712, a fact which, combined with the ease of access, deprives them of any sense of being wilderness retreats, though both have lush settings amidst the sandstone bastions. Cheaper of the two is *Glen Reenen*, with a **campsite** (①), which at peak holiday times becomes little more than a car park jammed with Afrikaner families and their caravans, and closely packed en-suite rondavels with kitchenettes (②). *Brandwag*, the more upmarket camp about a kilometre to the west, is a blot on the fabulous landscape, but offers well-equipped self-catering chalets (③) and comfortable hotel rooms (④) with bath, phones and TV. For **bookings** contact South African National Parks (Pretoria ☎012/343 1991, fax 343 0905; Cape Town ☎021/22 2810, fax 24 6211; *reservations@parks-sa.co.za*).

If the accommodation is full or you want somewhere cheaper to stay with more solitude, consider the basic, but highly atmospheric huts at the Basotho Cultural Village (see p.469) or head to Clarens for a wider range of more conventional options.

Fuel is available at *Glen Reenen*, which also has a provisions store selling basics, as well as frozen *braai* packs, firewood and alcohol. Your only choice for eating out here is at the unexceptional restaurant at *Brandwag*. Alternatively, you could drive into nearby Clarens.

Clarens

Some 20km west of Golden Gate Highlands National Park lies the tree-fringed village of **CLARENS**, the most appealing of the settlements along the Highlands Route. Founded in 1912, Clarens is especially remarkable for its dressed stone architecture, which glows under the sandstone massif of the **Rooiberge** (Red Mountains) and the **Malutis** to the southeast. The best time to see the village is in spring, amid the blossoming fruit trees, or in autumn, when the poplar leaves turn golden russet. Throughout the year though, Clarens's relaxed air makes it a rare phenomenon in the Free State – a *dorp* you'd actually want to explore, or sip a sidewalk lager and simply hang out in.

By a slightly tortuous set of associations, Clarens was named after the Swiss town where **Paul Kruger**, president of the South African Republic, ended his days. Kruger led a campaign in the Free State in 1865 against the Basotho under paramount chief Moshoeshoe and defeated them. Fate was fickle, and at the turn of the century, when Kruger found himself on the losing side against the British in the second Anglo-Boer War, he fled to Switzerland to live out his days in Clarens, where he died in 1904. Despite the Boer connection, Clarens has shed its redneck ties to become an **arts and crafts centre**, with a number of studios and shops peppering the streets. If you arrive around lunchtime on a weekend there's a chance you'll catch some local live music at one of the streetside cafés on **President Square**, the effective town centre in the middle of Main Street.

Any among the several **galleries** along Main Street and around President Square is worth a visit if you're after gifts or souvenirs; look out for the local Basotho tapestries, baskets and traditional hats. A real treat is the Di Mezza & De Jager Trading Store, which you can reach from the main road northwest to Bethlehem, taking the Maluti Lodge turn-off. This is one of the few places in South Africa outside a museum where

FARMSTAYS AND HORSE-RIDING AROUND CLARENS

Horse-riding is big along the Eastern Highlands and a couple of **farms** near Clarens, both excellent family destinations, provide outstanding riding onto the Drakensberg Escarpment, from where you can gaze across into Lesotho and at southern Africa's highest peaks.

One of the most interesting farms is friendly **Bokpoort** (☎ & fax 058/256 1181, mobile ☎083/628 5055, *bokpoort@iafrica.com*), set in brilliant hiking country but more notable for its riding. The B&B accommodation (③) in farmhouse outbuildings is pretty basic, with brunch served in a converted shearing shed. There are also a couple of self-contained, self-catering, en-suite "mountain" huts (②) with basic cooking facilities, as well as backpacker/hikers' dorms (①) in an old sandstone barn and space for camping (①), with a pleasant communal cooking and eating place. Reasonably priced meals can be ordered from the farmhouse kitchen, while a small shop sells basics.

Bokpoort's big draw is the truly memorable **Western-style riding** in deep, comfortable cowboy saddles on sure-footed horses. Short rides from the farmhouse take in San rock paintings, swimmable river-pools, and the chance of seeing eland, zebra and springbok on the adjoining game farm. Better still, owners Christo and Sunette lead two- or three-day riding trails into the mountains adjoining Lesotho. You carry your own bedroll and waterbottle on your horse and sleep on your saddle blanket in a remote mountain hut. A packhorse brings the food, and you ride about six hours a day. Book well in advance for the longer trails; fully-catered weekend trails start at just under R600, or there's a budget version for almost half the price, where you sleep in their backpacker dorms and bring your own food. More affordable still are their combined riding/hiking weekends, which work out at around R165 per person; you bring your own food, and accommodation is in dorms. Trout fishing, mountain biking and game drives are also available, and if you fancy doing the whole survivalist thing they also offer archery lessons and target practice with a .22 rifle.

Riding is also available at **Schaaplaats Cottage & Ashgar Connemara Stud** (☎058/256 1176, fax 256 1258; ①–②), right in the mountains, 6km south of Clarens off the R711 to Fouriesburg. An establishment with a more English flavour, this turn-of-the-century farm has a sandstone thatched cottage that sleeps five and an extremely cheap but basic shepherd's hut above the homestead. From here you can go on terrific mountain hikes, visit Boer War graves, San rock paintings and go horse-riding. There's also a chance to brush up your equestrian skills, as the owner is a qualified riding teacher.

you're likely to catch an old-time general dealer that has barely changed in half a century. The shop is stocked to the brim with shelves of provisions, lamps, bicycle parts, sweets and colourful blankets, which are traditionally worn like cloaks by Basotho people in the district. The **blankets** make outstanding souvenirs if you're after something authentic.

Practicalities

When people in Clarens refer to "town", they mean Bethlehem, the largest centre of any size in the vicinity, some 30km to the north. Clarens itself has few facilities, no bank or large supermarket, but there's plenty of **accommodation**, both in the village (all signposted off Main Street and all easily walkable) and on surrounding farms. The cheapest place to stay is the *Clarens Inn*, Van Reenen St (☎058/256 1119), run by a musician and artist, with the choice between a functional dorm with a communal kitchen (①), or a self-catering unit sleeping six in two bedrooms (②). *Cottage Pie*, 89 Malherbe St (☎058/256 1214, ②), a B&B with self-catering garden chalets, is the town's premier guesthouse, offering breakfast on the patio and views onto a stream and the dramatic cliffs that surround the village. *Christine's*, Villiers St (☎058/256 1077, ②), is a friendly place with two B&B rooms with access to a shady garden. More conventional motel-style accommodation, with phones and TVs in each room, is available at the *Country Lodge* (☎ & fax 058/256 1354, ③), a resort on the edge of town, signposted just off the R712 to Bethlehem. In a similar vein, but smarter and more modern, the *Maluti Mountain Lodge* next door (☎058/256 1422, ④) is the most expensive place to stay in town, and offers pleasant rondavels in the garden.

Of the half-dozen or so **eating and drinking** places in Clarens, the *Street Café Restaurant* on Main Street is the busiest, owing to its reasonably priced pizzas, snacks, steaks and salads, and the 107 (at last count) varieties of local and imported beers on offer. For a full-blown meal, head next door to the *Guinea-Feather*, Clarens's top restaurant, where you can sit outdoors and enjoy a mid-priced menu that includes oxtail in red wine sauce, trout, curries, pizzas and game. Breakfasts and teas are also available here from 8am onwards. For venison and decent pub lunches, the *Maluti Mountain Lodge* is another good bet.

Fouriesburg and around

The funny little town of **FOURIESBURG**, 36km from Clarens on the R711, was given its name because of the high density of people named Fourie who were farming in the district. The hamlet hit the big time briefly in 1900, when it was proclaimed capital of the Orange Free State after Bloemfontein fell to the British in the Anglo-Boer War. Nothing much seems to have happened since, and one hundred years later they still haven't got round to rescinding the proclamation – so technically it's still the provincial capital. Overshadowed by the **Maluti Mountains** and the **Witteberge** (White Mountains), Fouriesburg serves as a decent overnight stop, with some good accommodation.

The nicest **place to stay** is the *Fouriesburg*, 17 Reitz St (☎058/223 0207, fax 223 0257; ③), a small, wonderfully antiquated hotel with a green, low-slung corrugated iron roof and comfortable rooms leading off the street-facing verandah. The owners let you rummage through the wine cellar to pick a bottle for dinner. Just under 2km out of town and signposted from the centre, the **Meiringskloof Nature Reserve** (☎ & fax 058/223 0067) offers one of the few places worth **camping** (①) along the Highlands Route, and also a few stone self-catering chalets (②). Set in a sandstone *kloof* with plenty of trees, a swimming pool and a small grocery shop, the reserve (best avoided during holidays, when it gets packed) is the starting point for a number of short **hikes**, and the five-day **Brandwater trail** (phone for details). More upmarket is *Wyndford Holiday Farm* (☎058/223 0274, fax 223 0664; ④–⑤), just before the Caledonspoort border post, 9km from Fouriesburg. Popular with South African families, this is a fairly staid place proclaiming "old-fashioned Christian values", and offers thatched rondavels (with bath) in pleasant gardens at a rate that includes all meals and teas.

Rustler's Valley

In contrast to the conservatism of Fouriesburg, **Rustler's Valley** (☎ & fax 051/933 3939, *wemad@rustlers.co.za*), 27km to its south and well signposted off the R26, has set itself up as the New Age epicentre of South Africa. Located in a beautiful valley in the foothills of the Maluti Mountains, it brings together a mixture of rave culture, Gaia philosophy, and plain old-fashioned hippiedom. In this alternative getaway you need to be ready to submit to the wound-down atmosphere, in which everything is slow and haphazard, including the service. This, and the poor road, make it an unsatisfactory overnight stop, but if you can stay for a few days you're likely to have a highly sociable time. Scheduled events take place about once a month (calendar available via email), and there's horse-riding, hikes, swimming in the dam, and bass and trout fishing. The biggest crowd-puller is the **Easter Festival**, which draws in hordes of young South

Africans to listen to music, get down and chill out. By European or North American standards, the festivals are nothing special, but the setting certainly is, and for South Africans it's one of the country's major *jorls* (parties). **Accommodation** ranges from camping (①), backpacker dorms (①), teepees (②) and en-suite doubles (②), to thatched rondavels with bath (③) set among peach trees and decorated with goblins and fairies. A kitchen is available for backpackers only; everyone else must rely on the bar and **restaurant**, which serves good vegetarian food but isn't cheap. **Getting there** without your own transport entails finding your way to Ficksburg (see opposite), from where staff at Rustler's can pick you up. When you phone to book your accommodation, ask for the best way to get to Ficksburg from where you are. If you're driving, take care over the last section of dirt road, which in parts is pretty appalling.

Next door to Rustler's, in the same beautiful valley, and well signposted, is *Franshoek Polo Lodge* (☎ & fax 051/933 3938, mobile ☎082/659 1966, ⑤). It's a more staid, but quite relaxed guest farm, ideal for horse-riding (you can even have polo lessons on the polo field). **Accommodation** is in pleasantly furnished rooms in a country-cottage style, without the frilly bits. Rates include a communal three-course farm dinner around a single table. While you're here, you might want to explore the eight- or fourteen-kilometre **hiking trails** on the farm, which take in a couple of spectacular sandstone overhangs that were used by San hunter-gatherers and later by Boer families hiding out during the Anglo-Boer War.

Ficksburg

FICKSBURG, 48km south of Fouriesburg, is the closest town to Rustler's Valley and the centre of South Africa's cherry and asparagus farming. The town's sandstone architecture gives it a pleasant ambience and this is a good place to make a stop halfway down the Highlands Route. An annual **Cherry Festival** in the third week of November is the highlight of Fickburg's calendar and features a marathon, floats, stalls, a "cherry queen" competition and a popular beer festival.

The cheapest way to stay here is by **camping** at *Thom Park* (☎051/933 2122, ①), a caravan park bang in the centre of town, on the corner of Bloem and McCabe streets. Nearby, *Bella Rosa*, 21 Bloem St (☎ & fax 051/933 2623, ③), is a hugely popular and exceptionally well-priced pair of Victorian sandstone houses with ten nicely furnished **rooms**, all with baths, telephones and TVs. Dinner is available but must be booked, and tea is served on the very pleasant verandah. An alternative is *Green Acorn*, 7 Fontein St (☎051/933 2746, ③), which has decent rooms with baths. As a last resort, you'll find rooms at the *Hoogland*, Market Square (☎05192/2214, ③), which also has a glassed-in coffee terrace upstairs and an unexceptional pizzeria around the corner. Preferable options for **eating** are the *Bella Rosa* (Mon–Fri till 10pm), which is licensed and serves above average English-style food; and the family-oriented *Bottling Co*, corner of Piet Retief and Erwee streets (☎051/933 2404, closed Sun evening & Mon), which also serves booze and does steaks, pastas, chicken and fish.

Clocolan and around

A tiny farming town dominated by its enormous grain silos, **CLOCOLAN**, 33km south of Ficksburg, has little to offer travellers aside from a visit to the **Lethoteng Weavers**, in a house on the main road. The weavers are Southern Sotho women who use angora rabbit and wool to produce lively tapestries based on traditional geometric motifs and imaginative illustrations of everyday life. To get to the main point of interest around here, you need to head some 9km out of town to **Tripolatania Farm**

Note that **phone numbers** for Clocolan and Ladybrand are due to change throughout 1999 and 2000. If you have any difficulties, call ☎1023.

(☎05191/2475), the site of the **Tandjiesberg rock paintings**, some of the best examples of San art in the Free State. Panel after panel of rock paintings are overpainted with animal, human and supernatural motifs, which are interpreted in an excellent monograph available from the Bloemfontein Museum (see p.463) and sometimes from the farmer, from whom you have to collect keys and pay a small fee to get to the paintings.

If you're simply passing through, Clocolan's best overnight **accommodation** is at *Makoadi B&B* (☎051/943 0273, ②) on Makoadi Farm, clearly signposted 1km southwest of town along the R26, where three spacious rooms (with bath) off a verandah are furnished with antique farm items, ball and claw baths, and have original mud and dung floors. For longer stays, two outstanding farm cottages are to be found some way out of town. The first, *Evening Star Cottage* (☎051/932 3212, ③), 13km from Clocolan west on the R703, is a romantically secluded self-catering thatched cottage tucked into a rocky outcrop, with French doors opening onto a balcony with views of farmlands and mountains. Lamps, candles and a mosquito net set the tone, and cooking is done on a fire outside in a beautiful rocky sitting area. The only drawback is that the toilet and bathroom are down the outside stairs, rather than en suite. The farm has a good **hiking trail** and serves tea in a converted monastery with an overgrown garden, where the owner sells her pottery. Another recommended getaway is the rustic *De Hoek* (bookings through *Jacana Country Retreats*, ☎012/346 3550 or 346 3551; ②–③), a four-bedroom house on a sandstone ridge with brass beds (bring your own bedding), dung floors, rough white walls, paraffin lamps (no electricity) and cooking on a coal stove. Two circular one-day **hiking trails** are available exclusively for *De Hoek* guests.

Ladybrand

LADYBRAND, just over 40km south of Clocolan, and on the main route into Lesotho, is one of the only towns in the Free State which is expanding, with a huge turnover of foreign currency in the local bank. This is due not to tourism, but to the Highlands Water Scheme across the nearby border in Lesotho (see p.619). The town gets its name from the mother of Johannes Brand, who was elected President of the Orange Free State four times after 1864. If you've got time to kill, it's worth popping to the **Catherina Brand Museum** in Church Street (Mon–Fri 10am–noon & 2–4pm; free) to see the small archeological exhibition, which displays fossils and stone tools found in the area, as well as reproductions of some of the rock paintings on Tripolitania Farm (see previous page). Other exhibits include a record of the Free State's oldest operating newspapers, and some historical background on Ladybrand.

Many of the foreign engineers and technicians working on the Highlands Water project in Lesotho choose to stay in Ladybrand rather than Maseru, so **accommodation** is in high demand, and doesn't come cheap. The only budget option is *Leliehoek Resort* (☎05191/40654), 2km south of the town hall, a rather run-down park with camping (①) and self-catering chalets (②). As to B&Bs, nothing along the Highlands Route can touch *Cranberry Cottage*, 37 Beeton St (☎05191/2290, fax 41168, *crancott@lesoff.co.za*, ④), which offers comfortable country-style rooms and excellent dinners, with vegetarians well catered for. Under the same ownership, and a touch less expensive, are the equally imaginative self-catering units at the *Railway Station* (③), quirkily located in the refurbished ticket office, stationmaster's office and waiting rooms on the Ladybrand

Station platform, which no longer serves passengers but occasionally sees goods trains trundle by. The owners act as an unofficial tourist information centre and are able to give guests **information** on pony trekking and rock-art sites.

When it comes to **eating**, Ladybrand shapes up well for a *dorp*, offering pasta, pizza and good Irish coffee from an Italian chef at *Imperio Romano*, in Church Street. Good home cooking can be found at *Die Dorphuis*, 13 Joubert St, a restaurant in an old converted house, where the Greek salad and steak are particularly recommended. For light meals, teas and coffees, *Zabi's Coffee Shop*, also on Church Street, is a good daytime venue for milkshakes, toasted sandwiches and coffee, while *Cranberry Cottage*, 37 Beeton St, does excellent breakfasts and four-course dinners.

travel details

Trains

Bloemfontein to: Cape Town (Fri; 20hr 45min); Durban (Tues; 16hr); East London (daily; 14hr 15min); Johannesburg (daily except Sat; 13hr); Port Elizabeth (daily; 12hr 15min); Pretoria (daily except Sat; 15hr 45min).

Buses

Bloemfontein to: Cape Town (4 daily; 11hr); Durban (2–3 daily; 9hr); East London (daily; 7hr 10min); Graaff-Reinet (5 weekly; 7hr); Grahamstown (daily; 7hr 30min); Johannesburg (4–5 daily; 6hr); Knysna (5 weekly; 11hr); Mossel Bay (5 weekly; 9hr 30min); Oudtshoorn (5 weekly; 8hr); Pietermaritzburg (2–3 daily; 8hr); Port Elizabeth (1–2 daily; 9hr); Pretoria (4–5 daily; 7hr).

Flights

Bloemfontein to: Cape Town (3 daily; 2hr 20min); Durban (2–3 daily; 1hr 15min); Johannesburg (9 daily Mon–Fri, 3 daily Sat & Sun; 1hr 10min); Port Elizabeth (1–2 daily; 2hr 20min).

CHAPTER SEVEN

GAUTENG

Gauteng means "Place of Gold" in Sotho, and no wonder: South Africa's smallest region comprises only 1.5 percent of its landmass, yet contributes over 40 percent of the GDP. Founded in 1994, this relatively new province is home to eight million people, and encompasses a section of the Magaliesberg mountains to the east, the gold-rich Witwatersrand to the south and west, on which are situated Johannesburg and Pretoria, and a host of grim satellite industrial towns.

Although lacking the spectacular attractions of the Cape Province or Mpumalanga, Gauteng has a subtle character all of its own. Startling outcrops of rock known as *koppies*, with intriguing and often lucrative geology, are set in open grassy plains of deep-red earth, and the usually mild climate is broken occasionally by spectacular summer lightning storms, which can unleash torrents of water over the Transvaal plains within seconds. The area is also prone to drought, and the water supply is a constant and worsening problem. Yet the light, particularly at dawn and dusk, is a photographer's dream, rendering serene and compelling even the starkest of industrial landscapes.

The beating heart of Gauteng is **Johannesburg**, whose origins lie in the exploitation of **gold**. In keeping with its tough mining origins, this is a hectic, sometimes dangerous city, home to extreme contrasts of wealth and poverty. Most visitors leave as quickly as they can, but if you do stick around, you'll soon start to absorb its distinctive pleasures; this highly cosmopolitan city is home to some of the liveliest townships, and most vibrant cultural life in South Africa. Some 50km north lies dignified **Pretoria**, the country's administrative capital and historically an Afrikaner stronghold, but today increasingly international. Pretoria is near enough to the airport to offer an alternative to Johannesburg, if you're looking for somewhere more peaceful to stay.

The section of the **Magaliesberg Mountains** which creeps into Gauteng is a magnet for Johannesburgers desperate to escape the city's pollution and stress. Although the hills can be crowded, there's ample opportunity for nature trailing and hiking. Southeast of Johannesburg lies the little-known **Suikerbosrand Nature Reserve**, a pleasant surprise for those in search of game viewing, with zebra, cheetah and red hartebeest among its varied inhabitants. Gauteng also has some of the most ancient archeological sites in the world, and trips to the **Melville Koppies**, with traces of Iron Age communties, and the astonishing **Sterkfontein Caves**, where the remains of pre-human primates have been found, are easily made from Johannesburg.

The wealth of the region may lie in gold, but since 1945 the **manufacturing industry** has far surpassed the profits of mines. This was a natural consequence of mining, as both the mines and their workers and families needed a wide range of goods. Mining profits enabled the necessary investment, and today there is more manufacturing in Gauteng than anywhere else in Africa. The mining industry is meanwhile in trouble: rising fixed costs and the fall in the value of gold mean that more and more mines are sliding into unprofitability. This has led to redundancies – the industry's workforce has shrunk from 700,000 to 330,000 in fifteen years, exacerbating Gauteng's unemployment problems.

Until 1994, much of the province, especially Pretoria, was renowned for white support for the restoration of apartheid, as proposed by the Conservative Party. But the elections of that year saw the **ANC** win control of the province convincingly, and just as

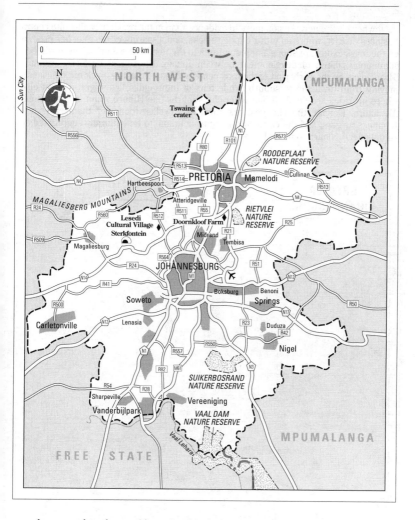

new faces populate the corridors of political power, so blacks are also making steady inroads into positions of influence in business, finance and industry, where the true power of the province lies.

JOHANNESBURG

Fast-paced, frenetic **JOHANNESBURG** has had a reputation for immorality, greed and violence ever since its first plot auction in December 1886. Today, with a new political division ensuring that formerly white areas are administratively yoked with the black townships, the city is also struggling to cope with a dramatic change in racial composition.

Nowhere is the new tension more in evidence than in the previously all-white central business district, where an influx of poor blacks, and a soaring crime rate, has prompted the mass exodus of shops and restaurants to the northern suburbs. There will be a continuous ribbon of development between Johannesburg and Pretoria, originally 54km apart, by the early part of the next century. Meanwhile, the black middle class is moving from township to suburb, while tens of thousands of immigrants from elsewhere in Africa are flooding into inner-city suburbs like Hillbrow and townships like Alexandra. Despite the changes, few township dwellers consider themselves true Johannesburgers, and the city's communities continue to be culturally segregated; as an outsider, it's hard to make inroads.

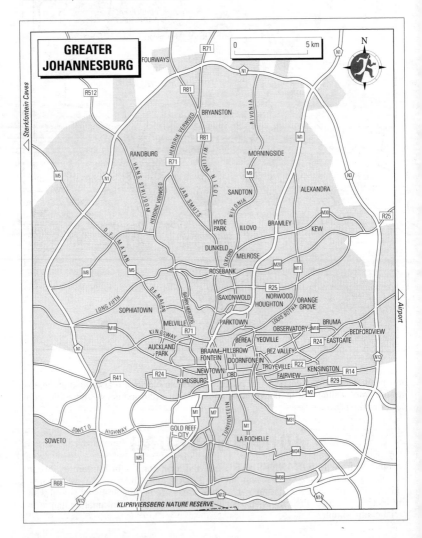

Johannesburg's contrasts are some of the most extreme in the world; poverty-stricken and overcrowded Alexandra is surrounded by some of the richest suburbs in South Africa, and downtown hundreds of homeless struggle to survive in the shadow of the continent's richest Stock Exchange. The contrast between suburb and township is mirrored nationwide, but is more extreme here because of the intense wealth of many of the suburbs, and the sheer size of the townships and their satellite squatter camps. Yet the city as a whole continues to suck in people and skills from all over the country, making it the financial, commercial and cultural powerhouse of South Africa.

A unifying strand through many lives, rich and poor, is the urgent desire to get ahead. Johannesburg is a profoundly entrepreneurial place, from its street hawkers to its boardroom executives. But it's not all about making money. In the evening, the city's renowned nightlife swings into action: Johannesburgers tend to party as hard as they work. The signals for the future are mixed, with everyday events confirming both bright optimism and deep cynicism. But it is this tension that gives the city its edge, making it amongst the most stimulating and provocative places in Africa.

Some history

Johannesburg dates back to 1886, when Australian prospector **George Harrison** found the main Witwatersrand gold-bearing reef. Almost immediately this quiet area of the Transvaal was swamped with diggers from near and far, and a tented city sprang up around the site. The Pretoria authorities were forced to proclaim a township nearby: they chose a useless triangle of land called the Randjeslaagte, which had been left unclaimed by local farmers. **Johan Rissik**, the surveyor, called it Johannesburg, either after himself, the chief of mining, Christiaan Johannes Joubert, or ZAR president Paul Johannes Kruger.

Mining magnates such as Cecil Rhodes and Barney Barnato possessed the capital necessary to exploit what was the world's richest gold reef, and their **Chamber of Mines**, founded in 1889, attempted to bring some order to the digging frenzy, with common policies on recruitment, wages and working conditions. In 1893, due partly to pressure from white workers, and with the approval of the ZAR government, the chamber introduced the **colour bar**, which excluded black workers from all but manual labour.

By 1895, Johannesburg's population had soared to over 100,000, many of whom were not remotely Boer and had no interest in the ZAR's independence. Kruger and the burghers saw in these *uitlanders* (foreigners) a possible danger to their political supremacy, and denied them the vote, despite the income they generated for the state's coffers. Legislation was also passed to control the influx of blacks to Johannesburg, and Indians were forcibly moved out of the city into a western location. Before long, large shanty-towns filled with blacks and Indians were springing up on the outskirts of Johannesburg.

In 1900, during the Anglo-Boer War, Johannesburg fell to the British, who had been attempting to annex the gold-rich area for some time. High Commissioner Sir Alfred Milner imported whiz kids from Oxford and Cambridge as his "kindergarten" to modernize the city. They lived in Parktown, and commissioned their houses from the celebrated English architect, **Sir Herbert Baker** (see p.498). At the same time, more black townships were established: **Sophiatown** was set up in 1903 in an area previously used for dumping sewage, and **Alexandra** was established two years later. Bubonic plague erupted on the northern fringes of the city in 1904, providing justification for the authorities to burn several Indian and African locations, including **Newtown**, just west of the centre.

Meanwhile, white mine workers were becoming unionized, and outbreaks of fighting over pay and working hours were a frequent occurrence. Their poorly paid black counterparts were also mobilizing; their main grievance was the ruling that skilled jobs were the preserve of white workers. Resentments came to a head in the **Rand Revolt** of 1922, after the Chamber of Mines, anxious to cut costs, decided to allow blacks into the skilled jobs previously held only by whites. White workers were furious: street battles broke out and lasted for four days. Government troops were called in to restore order and over 200 men were killed. Alarmed at the scale of white discontent, Prime Minister Jan Smuts ruled that the colour bar be maintained. Throughout the Twenties, the government passed laws restricting the movement of blacks.

During the Thirties, the township of **Orlando** became established southwest of the city, with accommodation for 80,000 blacks; this was the nucleus around which **Soweto** evolved. By 1945, 400,000 blacks were living in and around Johannesburg – an increase of 100 percent in a decade. In August 1946, 70,000 African Mineworkers Union members went on strike over working conditions. The government sent police in, and twelve miners were killed and over 1000 injured. Informal settlers on municipal land attempted a rent boycott that year, proclaiming "Asinamali!" ("We have no money!"). They were ignored, and non-rent payers were evicted. During the Fifties, *kwela*, a black urban culture unique to Johannesburg, began to emerge in the townships, and the new marabi jazz was played in illegal drinking houses called *shebeens*.

Forced removals, particularly from Sophiatown, began in 1955. Thousands were dumped far from the city centre, in the new township of Meadowlands, next to Orlando. Sophiatown was crassly renamed Triomf (triumph). The **ANC** found its mass base during this period, proclaiming the **Freedom Charter** in Kliptown, Soweto, that year. The Fifties was also the era of *Drum Magazine*, which revealed a sophisticated black Johannesburg culture, and introduced a host of talented journalists, like Can Temba and Casey "Kid" Motsisi, to the city and the world. *Mbaqanga* music emerged, with its heavy basslines and sensuous melodies capturing the bittersweet essence of life in the old townships.

The formation in 1972 of the **Black Consciousness Movement** (BCM) rekindled political activism, particularly among students in Soweto. On June 16, 1976, student riots erupted in the township, and the unrest spread nationwide (see p.695). The youth's war against the State escalated in the Eighties, resulting in regular **"states of emergency"**, during which the armed forces had permission to do anything they liked to contain revolt. Towards the end of the decade, the government relaxed "petty" apartheid, turning a blind eye to the growth of "grey" areas like Hillbrow – white suburbs where blacks were moving in.

The three years after **Nelson Mandela**'s release in 1990 saw widespread political violence on the Rand right up until the day before elections. However, as elsewhere in South Africa, the election on April 27, 1994 went off peacefully. The ANC won comfortably in Johannesburg, and, as expected, consolidated their hold on power in 1999, albeit to the sound of grumbling from some elements of their constituency about corruption, unemployment and crime.

Despite that, the late Nineties have seen the city move into a new era. The pace of life shows no signs of relenting, and a broadening international outlook means that the city is now a recognized stopover in the world tours of top music and cultural acts. **Sport** too ranks highly: Ellis Park was the scene of South Africa's emotional victory in the 1995 Rugby World Cup, the IAAF World Cup was held at the neighbouring athletics stadium in 1998, and the massive FNB soccer stadium, which fills to capacity for local derbies or international fixtures, is the focus of South Africa's bid to host the 2006 soccer World Cup. Indeed, Johannesburg dominates the country's soccer scene, with the nation's two biggest teams, the Kaiser Chiefs and Orlando Pirates, based in Soweto.

Arrival and information

Johannesburg's large **International Airport** (flight information ☎011/975 9963), once known as Jan Smuts, lies 20km east of the city. There's a range of options for getting from the airport into the city or suburbs. Of the scheduled **bus services**, Impala (every 45min 6.15am–10pm; a 30min journey) will take you to Park Station in the city for around R40. If your destination is the northern suburbs, you'll find it easier to take the Magic Bus (every 30min 5.30am–9.30pm, a 30min journey), which costs about R65. Get tickets for both serivces at the companies' desks in the domestic arrivals foyer.

The more expensive hotels often offer **courtesy buses**, while most backpackers' hostels and some smaller guesthouses or B&Bs arrange **pick-ups**. Depending on your length of stay these may be free; otherwise they tend to cost no more than the scheduled bus service. Touting at the airport by backpackers' hostels has been aggressive at times recently – sidestep the mayhem by pre-booking.

Taking a **taxi** from the airport is convenient and safe, but be sure to take a metered Johannesburg airport taxi or a reputable tour/transfer operator and make sure the

---

SAFTEY AND CRIME IN JOHANNESBURG

With its extremes of poverty and wealth and its brash, get-ahead culture, it's perhaps hardly surprising that Johannesburg can be a dangerous place. As in all major cities, taking sensible precautions is likely to see you through safely, although the presence of illegal firearms makes taking extra care especially important.

If you're wandering around on foot, the crime you are most at risk from is **mugging** (sometimes, but not always, violent), and some areas carry a much higher risk than others. Be particularly alert when exploring the central business district (CBD), Braamfontein and Newtown, although the introduction of tourist police in these areas has made things a bit safer. Joubert Park, Hillbrow and Berea are regarded at present as no-go zones, and although Yeoville and Observatory are safer, you still need to be wary. You are very unlikely to be mugged in Melville, Parktown or Rosebank. In high-risk areas, do your best not to look like a tourist. Study maps beforehand (not on street corners), try not to ask for directions from passers-by and don't walk around with luggage. Try to look into the crowds coming your way, to see if there are any groups of young men (the main offenders) moving as a block. If you're carrying valuables, leave a portion of them easily available, so that any mugger is likely to be quickly satisfied and not investigate you further. Never resist muggers; running like hell can work, but some have guns, which you won't know about until too late.

You are unlikely to be mugged on **public transport**, but, as always, it's wise to stay alert, especially around busy spots such as Park Station and bus stations or taxi ranks. Waiting for buses in the northern suburbs is generally safe.

Don't expect too much from the **police**. Police on the street are rare, and normally have other distractions than keeping an eye out for tourists. In the city centre you can make use of City Ambassadors, identified by their yellow caps and bibs. These are people hired by a partnership between local government and local shops and businesses to provide an anti-crime presence on the street. Some are better trained than others to help tourists, but you can always approach them if you want to know where somewhere is, or if you think you're being followed. You can ask them for an escort, although as they're assigned to different segments of the city you may find yourself being passed from one to another, and of course having an escort does mark you out as a nervous tourist.

If you're driving around, you're at risk of **car-jacking**, although staying in a hotel minimizes this risk (car-jackers tend to trail victims on their way home). Always keep all car doors locked and windows up – never wait in an unlocked car while a friend goes into a shop. Leaving or returning to your car are the most dangerous times, so keep a good lookout, seek out secure and preferably guarded parking, and don't dawdle. Stopping at traffic lights, particularly at night, can also make you vulnerable – though driving through them is riskier because of cars coming the other way. At traffic lights, keep a good distance between you and the car in front, check your mirrors often, and keep your foot hovering over the accelerator. Repeat to yourself the mantra "Most people are never car-jacked."

Finally, don't let paranoia ruin your stay in the city. Remember that most Jo'burgers have no intention of doing you any harm at all. The best thing is to do as they do: juggle your fear and your bravado, without letting one swamp the other.

driver knows where you're going before you set off. There are normally plenty of taxi touts hanging around the airport – you can normally discuss a price quite civilly with them, but if you feel hassled, say that you're not interested. Be prepared to pay at least R80 per person for most destinations. If you want to prearrange a taxi, Airport Link (☎011/792 2017) charge R130 for the first person and R35 for each additional passenger.

Greyhound (☎011/830 1301), Intercape (☎012/654 4114) and Translux (☎011/774 3333) **buses** and **intercity trains** (☎011/773 2944) arrive at Park Station in the centre of town. From here, you're best off – and safest – taking a taxi to your final destination or arranging a pick-up with your accommodation. Buses and minibuses run from the station to virtually everywhere, but finding out about them can be confusing and waiting around, especially surrounded by luggage, can be risky.

Information

Tourism Johannesburg's main office is in the Village Walk Mall in Sandton (Mon–Fri 8am–4.30pm; ☎011/784 1352), which is fine if you're staying in the Northern suburbs and feel drawn to shopping malls during the day, but not all that handy if you're not. They also have offices with a more limited array of leaflets and information at Park Station (Mon–Fri 8am–4.30pm; ☎011/773 3994) and on the ground floor of the Calton Centre (Mon–Fri 8am–4.30pm; ☎011/331 2041) in the heart of the CBD. Another mall-bound option if you want to browse brochures not just on Johannesburg but the rest of the province (including Pretoria) is to visit the smart new offices of **Gauteng Tourism** (daily 8.30am–5pm; ☎011/327 2000), situated above *Jaspers* restaurant in the Rosebank Mall in Rosebank. In the international arrivals hall of the airport there are two information offices: Info Africa (daily 5am–9pm; ☎011/390 9000) is large but tired; better is **Satour** (daily 7am–9pm; ☎011/970 1669), with brochures on Johannesburg and other parts of South Africa.

Free **maps** are available in various forms from the information offices, but they normally only cover the CBD and parts of the northern suburbs. To get around other parts you'll need a detailed street guide; the hefty *Witwatersrand Street Guide* is best, available from CNA newsagents.

City transport

Johannesburg's **public transport system** leaves much to be desired: it's slow, unreliable, and after commuting hours practically nonexistent. **Cars** are the order of the day, especially for those living in the suburbs. If you're not driving, though, don't despair: with patience and a bit of stamina, it is possible to negotiate your way around the city using the buses, and some areas are easily explored **on foot**. You're highly unlikely to want to use the city's **train** system, which has a poor reputation and very limited services.

Cars and private taxis

By far the best way to explore Johannesburg is in your own **car**. Although road signs can be poor, and local drivers pushy, the grid system at least removes some of the eccentricities that plague other big-city road networks. Familiarity with a few key roads and careful map reading before you set out makes getting around relatively straightforward. The **M1** connects the centre to the northern suburbs, flying over Newtown, through Braamfontein and Parktown, and heading into Houghton and Sandton, eventually turning into the N1 for Pretoria. Heading south, the M1 is one of the best routes to Soweto. The next artery west of the M1, also useful for heading north, is **Oxford Road**, which starts off in Parktown, and becomes Rivonia Road once it enters Sandton. West again is **Jan Smuts Avenue**, which passes through Rosebank and Dunkeld, before hitting Sandton.

The city is relatively well served for **car rental** (see "Listings", p.512). Local companies are the best bet: most offer good prices and old cars, which are less likely to be stolen. For longer stays, **buying a car** is a practical option; the weekly *Junk Mail* has a large selection of private sales – expect to pay upwards of R20,000 for a decent vehicle. You can resell through *Junk Mail*, too, if you have a contact telephone number.

For short journeys around the city, use **private taxis**, which must always be telephoned in advance (see "Listings" p.512.). A journey to the CBD from the northern suburbs will cost at least R100.

Buses

Johannesburg's **buses** (many of which are double-deckers), offer the safest and cheapest public transport during weekdays. Most bus routes start and end at the main terminus (☎011/838 2125) in Vanderbijl Square, off Eloff Street, in the city centre; this is also where you can pick up timetables and route maps.

Buses only run between the suburbs and the centre, so are useless for getting from one suburb to another, unless they both lie on the same route to town. In a close reflection of their commuter role, most buses stop by 6.30pm, though a small number keep going until 9.30pm. Weekend services are poor, with very few routes in action and waits of at least one hour between buses.

Minibus taxis

Even cheaper than buses, **minibus taxis** cover a far wider area, and can be picked up at ranks, or hailed mid-route by either raising your forefinger (if you're heading into town), pointing downwards (if you want to go uptown) or pointing towards yourself (if you want Park Station). The drawbacks, however, are worth bearing in mind; cramped cars, hair-raising driving, frequent accidents and petty criminals working the major taxi ranks have combined to deter most white Jo'burgers from using this mode of transport. If you do want to try one out, you'd be wise to wait at a smaller taxi rank, or wave one down en route – but never with bulky baggage. Most backpacker lodges know nearby useful routes and pick-up points and can give you a few tips.

Accommodation

Johannesburg has **accommodation** to suit every budget, and finding a room is usually not a problem. Where you decide to stay will depend less on availability than on the length of your visit and how concerned you are about safety. As a basic rule of thumb, the further from the city centre you are, the safer but more soulless the suburb. Remember also that the more upmarket it is, the harder it is to be without a car.

ACCOMMODATION PRICE CODES

All the accommodation listed in the Guide has been categorized into one of nine price bands, as set out below. The rates quoted represent what you can expect to pay for much of the summer **per person**, and unless otherwise stated, are based on two sharing. Rooms are generally en suite. Expect prices in some areas to be significantly higher in peak season (Dec–Jan & Easter), and look out for discounts during the winter. For further details, see p.33.

① up to R50	⑥ R250–300
② R50–100	⑦ R300–400
③ R100–150	⑧ R400–500
④ R150–200	⑨ over R500
⑤ R200–250	

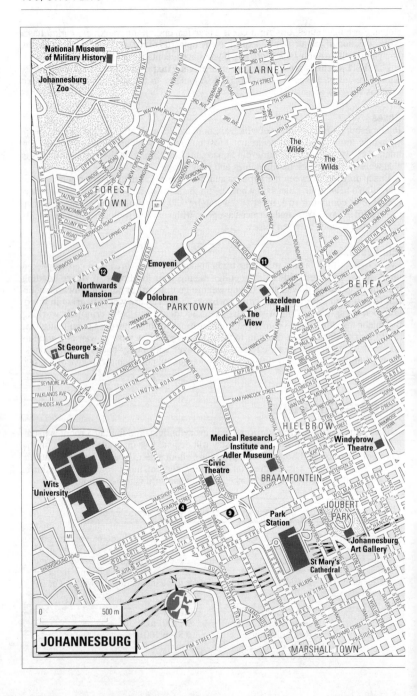

JOHANNESBURG

National Museum of Military History

Johannesburg Zoo

KILLARNEY

The Wilds

The Wilds

FOREST TOWN

BEREA

12 Northwards Mansion

Emoyeni

11

Dolobran

PARKTOWN

Hazeldene Hall

The View

St George's Church

HIELBROW

Medical Research Institute and Adler Museum

Windybrow Theatre

Civic Theatre

BRAAMFONTEIN

Wits University

4

9

JOUBERT PARK

Park Station

Johannesburg Art Gallery

St Mary's Cathedral

MARSHALL TOWN

0   500 m

N

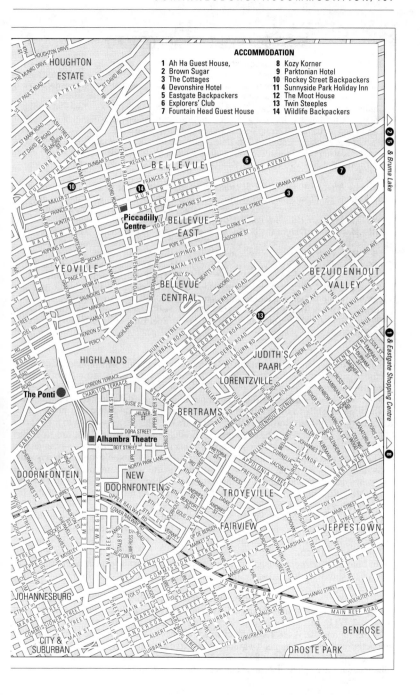

ACCOMMODATION

1 Ah Ha Guest House,
2 Brown Sugar
3 The Cottages
4 Devonshire Hotel
5 Eastgate Backpackers
6 Explorers' Club
7 Fountain Head Guest House
8 Kozy Korner
9 Parktonian Hotel
10 Rockey Street Backpackers
11 Sunnyside Park Holiday Inn
12 The Moot House
13 Twin Steeples
14 Wildlife Backpackers

JOHANNESBURG TOURS

One good way of taking in Johannesburg's main attractions, especially if you're here on a short stay, is to take one of the many **tours of the city** on offer. In addition to those listed below, most of the operators of tours of Soweto (see p.503) also offer various forms of city tours, and will pick you up from prearranged spots.

Chamber of Mines, 5 Hollard St, Marshall Town (☎011/498 7100). Tours of all the major mining houses, including Anglo-American and Anglo-Vaal. The day starts at 7.30am and is mainly taken up with a descent into the mine itself, where you'll witness blasting and hacking first-hand. You'll hear fulsome technical explanations, and will go on a quick whip round the mine compounds, which are still largely ethnically segregated. The day finishes with a large meal in the mine clubhouse – worlds apart from the miners' canteen. R150.

Dumela Africa (☎083/659 9928, *dumela@netactive.co.za*). Highly recommended city tours taking in the contrasting suburbs, including Sophiatown and the CBD, downtown walking tours and longer trips to the struggle sights around Jo'burg, Soweto and Pretoria. Half-day excursions cost R150–200, full days around R300.

Bill Harrop's Original Balloon Safaris (☎011/705 3201, fax 705 3203, *travelsa@iafrica.com*). Expensive but wonderful waft over the Magaliesberg Mountains in a balloon early in the morning. You can't rely on the wind, of course, so you may end up not going on the day you've booked. From R1015, includes champagne breakfast.

Parktown Tours, Parktown & Westcliff Heritage Trust, Northwards, Rockridge Rd, Parktown (☎011/482 3349). Informative tour of the Parktown mansions, with guides decked out in head-turning nineteenth-century regalia. R50.

Springbok Atlas Tours (☎011/396 1053). One of South Africa's major tour operators, offering bus tours of Johannesburg, Soweto, Gold Reef City and nearby parks. From R200 for a day tour.

There are few places to stay in the **CBD**, most hotels having joined the exodus to the northern suburbs. North-east of the CBD, **Yeoville** has the best range of **budget accommodation**, and attracts lively crowds of backpackers. Nearby **Observatory** is quieter, with larger houses, and is a good place to be based if you like action, but not all the time. Slightly to the south of these suburbs, and immediately east of the CBD, **Kensington** and **Bezuidenhout (Bez) Valley** are established areas close to the centre, but with less local action. The area around **Eastgate** and **Bruma Lake** are safer but more self-contained around their vast eponymous shopping centres.

The safest areas to stay– but also the blandest – are undoubtedly the **northern suburbs**, also handy for public transport. **Rosebank** is the most convenient for access to downtown, and is a good place to eat out or shop. Further to the west, off Barry Hertzog Drive, **Melville**, with its friendly cafés, is the most characterful and hip of these suburbs, while **Parktown** is worth considering for its great location on a ridge overlooking the city and its fine colonial mansions. Further north, **Sandton** has a wealth of pricey chain hotels aimed at business executives, and as a result prices here are higher than elsewhere. West of Sandton, **Randburg** is less expensive but a bit isolated from the best parts of the city.

Tourist infrastructure in the **townships** is minimal. In Soweto there are now a couple of hotels and a guesthouse, but the most rewarding way of experiencing the township is to stay with locals, something best arranged through an experienced tour operator (see p.503).

As an important destination for business travellers, Johannesburg is peppered with hotels run by large multinational chains such as *Holiday Inn* (central reservations ☎0800/11 7711), *Protea Hotels* (central reservations ☎0800/11 9000 and *Formule 1* (central reservations ☎011/440 1001), all of which offer predictable and adequate, if entirely characterless rooms if you need a quick fix. If you're looking for a wider choice, the B&B Association (☎011/482 2206 or 803 7170), handles bookings for around sixty B&Bs in the Johannesburg area on its lists and rooms can be booked through its central phone line.

CBD, Braamfontein and Berea

Devonshire Hotel, corner of Melle and Jorissen streets (☎011/339 5611, fax 403 2495). The best views in Braamfontein from rooms at this smart executives' hotel, equipped with several bars and restaurants. ④.

Parktonian Hotel, 120 De Korte St, Braamfontein (☎011/403 5740, fax 403 2401, *park@ilink.nis.za*). A member of the Protea hotel group, rather characterless but well-equipped suites aimed mainly at business travellers. ⑥.

Yeoville and Observatory

Brown Sugar, 75 Observatory Ave, Observatory (☎ & fax ☎011/648 7397). Infamous backpackers' hostel located in bizarre ex-drug baron's mansion on Observatory Ridge. Management promise to embroil you in Jo'burg's lively nightlife as quickly as possible. Not for the faint of heart – head here for action rather than comfort. ③.

The Cottages, 30 Gill St, Observatory (☎011/487 2829, fax 487 2404). Thirteen superb cottages perched on the Observatory ridge, with a countrified atmosphere and organized hikes from the lush two-acre plot to the top of the *koppie*. Self-catering or B&B, with evening meals available on request. ④–⑤.

Explorers' Club, 9 Innes St, Observatory (☎011/648 7138, fax 648 4673, *info@explor.co.za*). Dorms and doubles in what is probably the best hostel in the area, with a fine verandah, pool, garden and a useful travel centre, all a 15min walk from Rockey St's bars and clubs. Ask about their essential Jo'burg night tour. ①–②.

Fountain Head Guest House, 52 Urania St, Observatory (☎011/487 3564, fax 648 8009). Comfortable rooms in a stunning, Italian-style villa on Observatory ridge, with immaculate gardens and fountains, and great views. ④.

Rockey Street Backpackers, 34 Regent St, Yeoville (☎011/648 8786, fax 648 8423, *bacpacrs@icon.co.za*). Friendly, neat and well-run hostel five minutes from Rockey St, with dorms and doubles, a well-informed travel centre, a bar and a tiny swimming pool. French and German spoken. ①–②.

Wildlife Backpackers, 105 Hunter St, Bellevue (☎011/648 1072, fax 648 5636, *wildlife-backpackers@milkyway.co.za*). Slightly frenetic hostel with a tiny kitchen and no pool, but decent bar and *braai* area and located only one block from Rockey St. ①–②.

Eastern suburbs

Ah Ha Guest House, 17a Talisman Ave, Bedford View (☎011/616 3702, fax 615 3012, *ahhalux@global.co.za*). Silly name, but comfortable double rooms and self-catering suites, as well as a decent swimming pool, at this pleasant guesthouse. ④.

Airport Backpackers, 3 Mohawk St, Rhodesfield, Kempton Park (☎011/394 0485). Handily placed for the airport, with free pick up and drop off. Respectable backpackers' hostel with useful travel information. ①.

Eastgate Backpackers, 41 Hans Pirow St, Bruma (☎011/615 1092, fax 615 6229). Located on suburban street near Eastgate and Bruma shopping complexes. Often busy and lively, with dorms and doubles, a swimming pool and a small bar. ①–②.

Emerald Guest House, 5 Blouborsie St, Van Riebeeck Park, Kempton Park (☎ & fax ☎011/393 1390, *emerald.g.h@intekom.co.za*). Unstartling but helpful suburban B&B with pool and secure parking, located close to airport. ④.

Kozy Korner, 10 Milner Crescent, Kensington (☎011/615 5159, fax 453 9923). B&B with cosy beds in five plain rooms. Perfect for bus trips to the Eastgate shopping centre, or into town. ④.

Twin Steeples, 100 Ascot Rd, Judith's Paarl (☎011/614 8978, fax 614 7529). Wonderful old listed building, now converted into a B&B, and the most stylish accommodation in the area. ③.

Northern suburbs

Backpackers' Ritz, 1A North Rd (off Jan Smuts Ave), Dunkeld West (☎011/327 0229, fax 327 0233, *ritz@iafrica.com*). Busy northern-suburbs mansion with pool, gardens and a good bar, popular with overlanders. Camping is allowed on the grounds. ①–②.

Coopers' Croft, 26 Cross St, Randburg (☎011/787 2679, fax 886 7611, *cprscrft@global.co.za*). Friendly B&B with pool and tennis courts located near to Randburg's Waterfront restaurants and bars. ③.

Don Apartments (☎011/442 7495, fax 442 8040). Custom-built blocks of self-catering apartments located in Rosebank and Sandton; all are secure, tastefully furnished and well equipped. ⑤.

Happy Valley Backpackers Lodge, 86 Nanyuki Rd, Sunninghill Park (☎011/807 0972, *happyval@global.co.za*). Situated a long way north of the city, just beyond the motorway ring near Midrand. Large thatched house with dorms and doubles and space in extensive gardens for camping. ①.

The Grace in Rosebank, 54 Bath Avenue, Rosebank (☎011/280 7200, fax 280 7474, *gracesres@grace.co.za*). One of the most luxurious yet individual hotels in town, used mainly by upmarket business travellers. ⑨.

Kew Youth Hostel, 5 Johannesburg Rd, Kew (☎ & fax ☎011/887 9072). The city's only black-owned hostel offers mostly dorms, plus a few doubles, and has few facilities apart from a swimming pool. Visitors are not allowed after 10pm. ①–②.

The Melville House, 59 6th Ave, Melville (☎011/726 3503, fax 726 5990, *happy@iafrica.com*). Smartly run and well-priced guesthouse with a great little garden and tastefully decorated rooms. Well located with easy access to Melville's cafés and restaurants. ③.

Melville Turret Guesthouse, 118 Second Ave, Melville (☎011/482 7197, fax 482 5725, *turret@totem.co.za*). Classy and stylish accommodation entirely in keeping with its location in trendy Melville. Free transfer from airport for stays of two nights or more. ④.

The Moot House, 47, The Valley Rd, Parktown (☎011/646 9843). B&B in a flat attached to a 1906 Herbert Baker house, said to be where the Articles of Union were drawn up, set in a large garden with pool. ③.

Sunnyside Park Holiday Inn, 2 York Rd, Parktown (☎011/643 7226, fax 642 0019). Elegant, if somewhat anonymous hotel in one of Parktown's finest buildings, formerly a governor's residence. ⑦.

Sans Souci Hotel, 10 Guild Rd, Parktown West (☎011/726 6393, fax 480 5983). Wonderful old building on the Parktown ridge, with well-stocked bars, a swimming pool and a soothing garden. The rooms are in a Sixties extension, but are pleasant enough. Good-value buffet and restaurant lunches. ③.

Ten Bompas, 10 Bompas Road, Dunkeld West (☎011/327 0650, fax 447 4326, *tenbomp@global.co.za*). Quiet, intimate and stylish upmarket hotel, with each of its ten rooms done by a different interior designer. ⑨.

Zoo Lodge, 233A Jan Smuts Ave, Parktown North (☎011/788 5182, fax 788 3292, *zoolodge@iafrica.com*). Large, relaxed hostel with some oversized dorms but other better dorms and doubles, along with two pools and a large garden with camping space. Good transport links and Rosebank's shops and nightlife are nearby. ①–②.

Soweto

Nge Khethu Guest House, 1132 Diepkloof Extension, Phase III, Soweto (☎011/985 9403). Soweto's first guesthouse, located in a well-sized house in one of the township's safer and leafier suburbs. Rooms are adequate without being luxurious, but the hospitality is warm and genuine – the linked garage bar always livens up when word gets round that there are visitors staying. ③.

Maweni, 1309 Red Pear St, Protea Glen, Soweto (☎011/986 1142, fax 986 2119). A comparatively huge, white, modern mansion with pool, sauna and open balconies, owned by the late Godfrey Maloi, the "godfather of Soweto". Half board ⑦.

The City

Johannesburg is large, sprawling and poorly planned, with few conventional sights and a bewildering number of districts. The **central business district (CBD)** is where you'll find the city's most ostentatious buildings, serving mining, finance or the State, and a burgeoning multiracial street life, with office workers rubbing shoulders with hawkers, shoppers and gangsters. Across the train lines to the north lies **Braamfontein**, home to the highly rated University of Witwatersrand and, further north still, opulent **Parktown**, the original home of Johannesburg's richest residents.

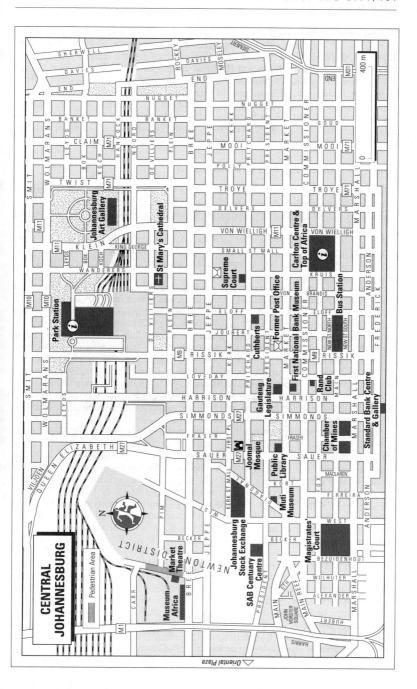

The seemingly endless **northern suburbs** that stretch from here to Pretoria throw up a few pleasant surprises, notably leafy **Melville**, with its lively parks and cafés, and Rosebank, the city's nicest place to shop. East of the centre, the buzzing inner-city districts of **Joubert Park**, **Berea** and **Hillbrow** are packed with migrants from all over the continent, while nearby **Yeoville** and **Observatory** exude a trendy ambience, with their lively ethnic mix and abundance of elegantly decaying houses. Further east still, the suburbs such as **Bezuidenhout (Bez) Valley** were, during apartheid, predominantly Portuguese, and today offer some great restaurants and bars. Southwest of the city centre lies another world: the vast **townships** of Soweto, Thokoza and Khatlehong, previously no-go zones for travellers, but today safe to explore with a reliable guide.

The CBD, Newtown and Braamfontein

With its towering office blocks and frenetic street life, it's easy to see why downtown Johannesburg has been dubbed "Africa's Manhattan". Unlike Manhattan, however, the **central business district** offers little beyond impressive office buildings to detain you, and the fact that it's one of Johannesburg's most crime-ridden areas means you can't afford to blank out as you stare up at the soaring skyscrapers. That said, the CBD is refreshingly multiracial; the sustained capital flight over the past few years has seen upmarket restaurants and shops replaced by a plethora of street traders, lending the area a bustling and genuinely African feel.

The **Carlton Centre**, which stands roughly halfway down Commissioner Street, is a good place to start explorations. The main attraction of this fifty-storey building is its top-floor **Top of Africa** lookout point (daily 9am–7pm; moderate entry fee), which offers the most breathtaking views of Johannesburg you'll get. Six blocks west of here, on the corner of Loveday Street, the grandiose **Rand Club** (visits by prior arrangement, ☎011/834 8311 to make arrangements) is where mining magnates have been coming to dine and unwind for nearly a century. Completed in 1904, the building is actually the fourth one to occupy the site, as each successive club was replaced to reflect the owners' growing wealth. Four blocks south, going down Simmonds Street, on the corner of Frederick Street, lies the **Standard Bank Centre**, which houses one of the best contemporary art galleries in South Africa, with changing exhibitions (Mon–Fri 8am–4.30pm, Sat 9am–1pm; free).

Moving west from Simmonds and Main streets leads to the forbidding **Magistrates Court** on West Street. The court holds bitter memories for many because of its role during apartheid, and is struggling to restore credibility. **Diagonal Street**, is one of the most fascinating areas in the CBD, is two blocks north. A jumble of street traders and shops, some of which date back to the 1890s, sell traditional medicines (*umuthi*), Sotho blankets and inexpensive household items, giving the street a very African buzz. Worth looking out for is the **KwaZulu Muti Museum of Man and Science** at no. 14, where all kinds of traditional medicines can be bought, often manufactured from the dried animal skins that hang from the ceiling. One block north is the incongruous sight of the **Johannesburg Stock Exchange**, towering above the noise and bustle. With world markets now hooked up to massive computer systems, there's little to see inside, and in fact this most telling of Johannesburg's contrasts will soon be lost when the Stock Exchange relocates to opulent Sandton (planned for 2000), confirming that suburb's designation as the new financial centre of South Africa.

Heading back east along Market Street, you soon reach the solemn **Public Library**, on the corner of Sauer Street (Mon–Sat 9am–5pm; free), and the recently revamped **Gauteng Legislature**, formerly the City Hall, on the corner of Harrison Street. The museum itself is dull, but the exterior facade, built in 1902, is worth a pause. The former **Post Office** is one block east on the corner of Rissik Street. When this was completed in 1897, it was the tallest building in the city, and is still impressive, despite being dwarfed by later additions to the skyline. Whilst basically neo-Baroque in style, it has quirky Dutch touches, primarily in its gabling. The fourth floor and clock tower are later additions, timed to coincide with the accession of British king, Edward VII, in 1902.

Two of the last survivors of the CBD's department stores are reached by continuing east until you hit the busy bus ranks of Eloff Street, and then heading north for two blocks until Pritchard Street. Here you will find Cuthberts, which opened as a shoe shop in 1904, and Markham's, built in 1886. Completing the tour, the **Rand Supreme Court**, two blocks further east on Pritchard Street, was once another hated symbol of oppression, but has been making a new and better name for itself since 1994, with landmark rulings on the new constitution.

Newtown

Just west of the city centre, **Newtown** is an area of redevelopment where some of Johannesburg's most vibrant cultural hot-spots are found alongside derelict factories and areas of wasteland. The main draw is its **Cultural Precinct**, a cluster of buildings lying under the M1 highway, designed to inject some life into the area, and to some extent succeeding. At its heart is the large and excellent **Museum Africa**, 121 Bree St (Tues–Sun 9am–5pm; R2), housed in the city's former fruit and vegetable market. The museum has three permanent exhibitions and numerous temporary displays. Most successful is "Johannesburg Transformations", a major exhibit with recreations of shacks and tenements (weird to find them in a musuem if you have just come from one), along with well-selected soundtracks from musical giants of the past, like *kwela* maestro Spokes Mashiane, and a plausible text. The overall effect is impressive and this is probably the best opportunity you'll have to get a sense of the city's history, up to and including the developments of the last decade. Less successful is the **Bensusan Museum of Photography**, which grandly aspires to be a "newseum of the present and future" but adds up to little more than a selection of cameras, holograms and CD ROMs – though camera buffs may find it rewarding. The **Museum of South African Rock Art** has few original paintings, as most of them are still on rocks scattered around South Africa, but there are some convincing replicas – which are as close as you'll get to the real thing without a hike up country. A useful text gives background on the artists and their work.

Next door, in the Market Theatre building (see p.510), is the **Rembrandt van Rijn Gallery** (Tues–Sat 10am–10.30pm; free), Johannesburg's foremost non-commercial art gallery, with adventurous displays of fresh artistic talent. Outside there's a worthwhile collection of shops, places to eat and drink, and *Kippies*, South Africa's most famous jazz venue (see p.507). The cultural centre continues south of Jeppe Street, with a live music venue (*Megamusic*), a dance rehearsal and performing space called the **Dance Factory**, and the **Electric Workshop**, which is used for the annual Arts Alive Festival (see box on, p.509). One of the city's better **flea markets** takes place every Saturday outside the theatre (see "Shopping").

On the corner of President and Bezuidenhout streets is the **South African Breweries (SAB) Centenary Centre** (Tues–Sat 10am–5pm; R10). A lengthy ninety-minute tour takes you through 6000 years of brewing history, which begs the question why SAB's ubiquitous end product, the anaemic, fizzy Castle lager, is so disappointing. Still, the reconstructed gold-rush pubs and Sixties *shebeen*, along with the greenhouse where sample crops of barley and hops grow, are fun, and from the balcony of the *Tap Room* bar you can watch the city rush by. Moving southwest, over President and Main streets, you'll come to the infamous **John Vorster Square**, site of the Johannesburg police headquarters, where anti-apartheid activists were detained and tortured, and some fell to their deaths having "jumped" from the tenth floor. After this, it's a pleasant relief to find the remains of the old Indian neighbourhood just further west, where

Jeppe Street turns into Minnaar Street. A busy commercial street ends up at the **Oriental Plaza**, an Indian-owned shopping complex, selling everything from suitcases and bric-a-brac to fabrics and spices. This is just about all that remains of Newtown's once-thriving Indian community, most of whom were forcibly removed in 1904 to make way for whites.

Braamfontein
The only time you're likely to visit **Braamfontein**, which starts at the main train station, and extends north as far as Empire Road, is for its transport facilities at Park Station. The only other attractions marginally worth a visit are the **Civic Theatre** in Rissik Street, which hosts some of Johannesburg's best theatrical, musical and dance productions (see p.510), and the **University of the Witwatersrand**, otherwise known as "Wits", which lies in Braamfontein's northwest corner, on the corner of Jorissen Street and Jan Smuts Avenue. The university has played an important role in the country's history, educating many future leaders, and acting as a site of major intellectual and political struggles. Contained within its grounds, in Senate House, is the **Gertrude Posel Gallery** (Mon–Fri 10am–4pm; free), which has an extensive and interesting collection of traditional African art.

The inner-city suburbs: Joubert Park, Hillbrow and Berea

Johannesburg's **inner-city suburbs** are multicultural, and crime-ridden. These were the "grey areas" of Johannesburg, where apartheid first started to break down in the Eighties. The police turned a blind eye as large numbers of blacks started moving into these previously all-white areas from the townships. Today, most whites have left, and migrants from all over the continent, but especially Nigeria and the Congo Republic, have flooded in. The noise and street life can be intimidating at first, but these districts offer a fantastic insight into Johannesburg's changing racial composition. All three suburbs have their moments of architectural excellence, though their hectic street life may leave you disinclined to savour them at leisure.

Joubert Park
Joubert Park meets the CBD at Bree Street and extends as far as Smit Street, with the only inner-city green space, the park itself, its natural centre. Named after General Piet Joubert (who lost the South African Republic general election to Paul Kruger in 1893), the park, with pleasant fountains and a conservatory, is always filled with people, but most white South Africans avoid it for fear of mugging.

In the south of the park stands the **Johannesburg Art Gallery** (daily except Mon 10am–5pm; free), an elegant, predominantly nineteenth-century building that is among the most progressive galleries in the country. If you're planning to walk there, it's probably best to find a City Ambassador willing to escort you; otherwise get a taxi to drop you off at the main entrance on Klein Street or make use of the gallery's secure parking. The regular exhibits inside include vast wooden sculptures by the visionary Venda artist Jackson Hlungwani that tower up to the gallery's ceilings. Elsewhere, the gallery shows a very South African mixture of African artworks and artefacts from the ceremonial to the purely decorative, and a range of European paintings, including some minor Dutch Masters. The special exhibitions are usually good, too; consult the *Mail & Guardian* newspaper for details.

At the park's southwest corner, on the corner of De Villiers and Wanderers streets stands the grand **St Mary's Cathedral**, built in 1926 and designed by Sir Herbert Baker (see p.498), but now largely deserted by its white patrons. Another Baker work stands northwest of Joubert Park, up Hospital Hill; the gracious **Medical Research Institute** was the architect's parting gesture before leaving for England. Look out for the bronze sculpture on the dome of the tower – a globe supported by three serpents. In the Institute's grounds, the **Adler Museum of the History of Medicine** (Mon–Fri 9am–4pm; free), includes recreations of an *umuthi* shop and an early twentieth-century pharmacy, along with a somewhat disturbing recreation of an early dentist's surgery. The main part of the museum has a bizarre selection of medical gadgets, including the world's first iron lung. There are plans to relocate the museum to Wits University Medical School in Parktown – phone ☎011/489 9482 for the latest.

Hillbrow and Berea

Smit Street, which runs north of Joubert Park, marks the boundary with infamous and densely populated **Hillbrow**, dominated by multistorey apartment buildings, all crammed with people. Traditionally, Hillbrow attracts the city's new immigrants. Immediately after the World War II, the typical immigrant was English, Italian or East European. These days, Africans from all over the continent are arriving in their numbers, lending the area a uniquely pan-African atmosphere, with music from Lagos to Kinshasa pumping from the bars and clubs. Along the many side streets, the scene is distinctly seedy, with drug pushers hanging outside gaudy strip joints. The main thoroughfares, with their markets, clubs and bars, teem with activity, but the suburb is widely recognized as a **no-go area** for tourists, and your best chance to experience it is to visit one of the better-known nightclubs or bars in a group and accompanied by a knowledgable local.

If you're in the area, keep an eye out for Hillbrow's most famous apartment building, the **Ponti** or "le petit Kinshasa", the round tower visible from miles around that is home to many of the suburb's Congolese immigrants. Also worth a look is the lovely mock-Tudor **Windybrow Theatre**, tucked away on the corner of Nugget and Pietersen streets. The theatre was built in the Twenties, and performances are still held there regularly (see p.510); there's no problem attending shows here if you can get dropped off at the front door.

Berea is mostly residential, dominated by tower blocks crammed with people. Its streets are increasingly monopolized by dealers and prostitutes, and most people who can afford to move away are doing so.

The eastern suburbs

Amongst the oldest of the city's suburbs, and home for years to Johannesburg's Jewish and Portuguese communities, as well as its bohemian whites, the eastern suburbs of **Yeoville** and **Observatory** have changed dramatically in recent years. Thousands of blacks, rich enough to avoid Hillbrow but too poor for the northern suburbs have arrived here from the townships, and lend the area a vibrant, frenetic street life. Should the fast pace start to grate, you can always head for the pleasant open space at **Bezuidenhout Park**.

Yeoville and Observatory

Lying east across the Harrow Road from Berea, and due north of Troyeville, **Yeoville** is Johannesburg's most vibrant and multiracial area. Despite the dire predictions of the whites who feel muscled out of the area, it's also still a relaxed and reasonably safe place to explore; the many restaurants and bars that line popular **Rockey Street** are filled with hip twenty-somethings of all races, and the street life, though bustling and occasionally seedy, is not aggressive.

Yeoville used to be predominantly Jewish, but now its spacious houses and Fifties apartment blocks are filled with a wider mix of people, ranging from young artists to yuppies – more black now than white – who like the area's bohemian ambience. A visit here will definitely take you along the stretch of road which starts out from Berea as

Raleigh Street and becomes **Rockey Street**, where you might want to stop in one of the many bars or cafés. The street markets, hawkers and interesting shops along here offer ample opportunity for browsing and bargain-hunting. Rockey Street itself is fine to walk at night, though women should avoid doing so on their own. At weekends the street is the closest Johannesburg gets to a carnival atmosphere. Trouble, when it surfaces, is usually connected to the drug dealers who frequent the parallel streets. Don't try to purchase anything from them and they should leave you alone.

Just before Rockey Street becomes Raleigh Street, you'll find a decent **park** at Yeoville Square, with a pleasant – and safe – public swimming pool next to the police station. At the bottom end of Yeoville on Harley Street stands an onion-shaped water tower, known simply as the **Yeoville Tower**. Built by Germans in 1914, it has miraculously escaped demolition during the city's many architectural purges, and remains one of the most bizarre and photogenic monuments you'll come across in Johannesburg.

At the other end of Rockey Street lies **Observatory**, whose leafy, residential streets are still dominated by affluent whites. There's not a lot to see here, but a pleasant walk can be had if you start at the end of Rockey Street, where Observatory Avenue starts, and wander east to Bezuidenhout Park.

Bezuidenhout Park and Bruma Lake

Further east again from Observatory are two of Johannesburg's best open spaces. **Bezuidenhout Park**, along Observatory Street, is popular with locals, especially at weekends, when large numbers park cars inside, turn up their hi-fis and drink the day away. The original homestead of the Bezuidenhouts, who owned the farm, is in the park, but is not open to the public.

Just east, across Queen Street, lies **Bruma Lake**, a shopping development around an artificial lake which, although relatively new, already appears decayed. The main attraction here is the vast, bustling **flea market** on Ernest Oppenheimer Drive (Tues–Fri 9.30am–6pm, Sat 8.30am–6pm, Sun 9am–6pm), one of the best places in Johannesburg to find curios, as long as you don't mind the pseudo-traditional dance troupes entertaining you as you browse. Just east again, off the R24, towards the airport, the ugly **Eastgate Shopping Centre** is reputedly the largest mall in Africa, and is much favoured by visitors from all over southern Africa.

The northern suburbs

Safe, prosperous and packed with shops and restaurants, the **northern suburbs** seem a world apart from the CBD and its surrounds. The name is actually a catch-all term for the seemingly endless urban sprawl that runs over 30km from Parktown almost as far as Pretoria. With the notable exception of Alexandra, this is a moneyed area, where plush shopping malls and well-tended parks are often the only communal meeting points, and most streets have a fortress-like appearance with high walls, iron gates and barbed wire used by the majority of home-owners to advertise how security-conscious a life they lead. Despite the often numbing sheen of affluence, however, interesting pockets do exist and, as most of the suburbs are close to major arterial roads, they are easily explored by car.

Parktown

Parktown, the first elite residential area in Johannesburg, lies northwest of Hillbrow, over Empire Road. The first people to settle here were Sir Lionel Philips, president of the Chamber of Mines, and his wife Lady Florence. In 1892, seeking a residence that looked onto the Magaliesberg rather than the mine dumps, they had a house built on what was then the Braamfontein farm. The rest of the farm was planted with eucalyptus trees and became known as the Sachsenwald Forest, some of which was given over

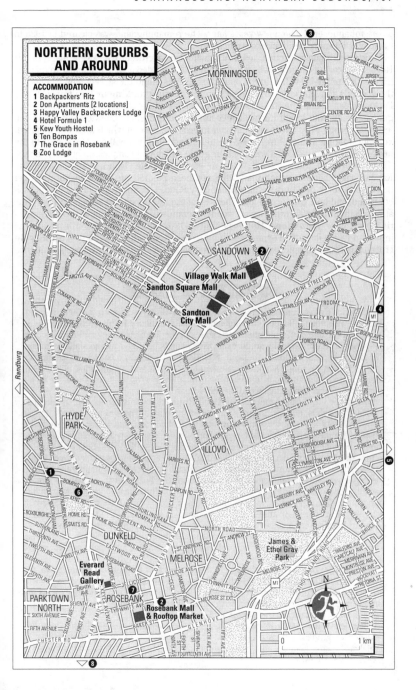

NORTHERN SUBURBS AND AROUND

ACCOMMODATION
1 Backpackers' Ritz
2 Don Apartments [2 locations]
3 Happy Valley Backpackers Lodge
4 Hotel Formule 1
5 Kew Youth Hostel
6 Ten Bompas
7 The Grace in Rosebank
8 Zoo Lodge

to the Johannesburg Zoo a few years later. The remaining land was cleared in 1925 to make way for more residential developments.

Parktown's main attraction lies in its distinctive **architecture**, given shape by Sir Herbert Baker (see below), whose arrival in 1902 heralded a style particular to this district, which today is evident in the opulent mansions lining the streets. You can take in the grounds and interiors of Parktown's highlights via a **walking or bus tour** with the Parktown & Westcliff Heritage Trust (Mon–Fri 9am–1pm; R50; ☎011/482 3349). Their guides, decked out in full Edwardian costume, are extremely knowledgeable and will lead you through the lavish grounds and mansions, some of which are quite inspired. You can walk the routes covered by the tours unguided, but without any access to the houses (the Trust publish a walking tour guide which you can pick up quite cheaply).

For your own tour, a good place to start is **Ridge Road**, just north of the Randjeslaagte beacon, which marks the northern point of old Johannesburg. To get there, turn north off Louis Botha at Boundary Road, which is a small road that is easily missed, and take the second left. The best of the houses on this street are **The View** at no. 18, built in 1897, with carved wooden verandahs and an elegant, red-brick exterior. Next door, **Hazeldene Hall** was built in 1902 and features cast-iron verandahs imported from Glasgow. Turning north into **York Road** will take you past **Sunnyside Hotel**, a massive complex which Lord Alfred Milner used as his governor's residence

SIR HERBERT BAKER

South Africa's most famous architect, **Sir Herbert Baker**, was born in Kent, England, in 1862. The young Baker's training included apprenticing to his architect uncle in London at the age of 17, and attending classes at the Royal Academy and Architectural Association, where he took care to make the contacts he would use so skilfully in later life. By the time he left for the Cape in 1892, Baker was already a convert to the new so-called **Free Style**, which advocated an often bizarre, but roughly historical eclecticism. The young architect's favourite influences, which would crop up again and again in his work, were Renaissance Italian and medieval Kentish.

Once in the Cape, Baker met up with **Cecil Rhodes**, and this connection, assiduously cultivated, established him as a major architectural player. The second Anglo-Boer War began in 1899 and Rhodes, assuming eventual British victory, sent Baker off to study the classical architecture of Italy and Greece, hoping that he would return able to undertake the mission of creating a British imperial architecture in South Africa. Baker returned to South Africa deeply influenced by what he had seen. He was summoned by **Lord Alfred Milner**, the administrator of the defeated Transvaal, to fulfil Rhodes' hopes, and took up the challenge with enthusiasm. Baker began with the homes of the so-called "kindergarten": the young men, mostly Oxford- and Cambridge-educated, whom Milner had imported to bring British-style "good governance" to the defeated territory. The result was the **Parktown mansions**, the opulent houses which line the roads of Johannesburg's wealthiest suburb. In adherence to the architectural creeds he had learnt in England, Baker trained local craftsmen and used local materials for these mansions. He also pioneered the use of local *koppie* stone, lending a dramatic aspect even to unadventurous designs.

Baker's major public commissions were the **St George's Cathedral** in Cape Town, the **South African Institute for Medical Research** in Johannesburg, and the sober, assertive **Union Buildings** in Pretoria, which more than any other building express the British imperial dream – obsessed with classical precedent, and in a location chosen because of its similarity to the site of the Acropolis in Athens.

Baker left South Africa in 1913 to design the Secretariat in New Delhi, India. He returned to England on its completion, where he worked on South Africa House in Trafalgar Square, London, and was knighted in 1923. He died in 1946, and is buried in Westminster Abbey.

from 1900. The road curves to the left into Jubilee Road, with several palaces on its northern side; the neo-Queen-Anne-style **Emoyeni**, at no.15, built in 1905, is especially striking. At the corner of Jubilee Road and Victoria Avenue stands **Dolobran**, a weird and impressive house, also built in 1905, and with a perfect verandah, wonderful red-brick chimneys, red Marseilles roof tiles, and hallucinatory stained glass.

Crossing over the busy N1 onto **Rock Ridge Road**, you'll reach the **Northwards Mansion**, home of the Parktown Trust, and built by Sir Herbert Baker in 1904. Baker's own residence is further along the road at no. 5, with a weighty wooden door at its entrance and a Roman-style atrium on the second floor. Rock Ridge leads to Eton Road and more Baker works: the attractive **St George's Church** and its rectory, which mix Kentish and Italian features and were built in local rock.

Zoo Lake and Houghton

Roughly 2km north of Parktown, off Jan Smuts Avenue, **Johannesburg Zoo** (daily 8.30am–5.30pm; admission fee), is home to over three thousand species, including polar bears. Despite recent attempts at revitalization, a sad air pervades, making this a good place for a melancholic wander, but not much else. Next door, and of greater interest, is the **National Museum of Military History** (daily 9am–4.30pm; small entry fee), where amongst the tanks, guns and uniforms you'll find a display on **Umkhonto we Sizwe (MK)**, the armed wing of the ANC, although the other liberation armies are conspicuous by their absence. The display focuses on the wing's commander, Joe Modise, now Minister of Defence. Opposite the zoo, on the west side of Jan Smuts Avenue, is the artificial but pleasant **Zoo Lake**. The park here is a popular walking spot and occasionally hosts outdoor performances, including an all-day music event every September during the Arts Alive festival (see p.509).

Moving east towards the lower end of **Houghton**, there's another green oasis in the **Houghton Wilds**. Far from wild, this is in fact a landscaped park covering rugged *koppie* outcrops either side of Houghton Drive (also known as the M31), just south of the junction with the M1. The park is excellent for strolling (but definitely not for women alone). You can follow a good trail northwards from the Wilds that runs along the Sandspruit stream to the **James and Ethel Gray Park**. Named after a city councillor and his historian wife, this contains the **Polish Memorial**, which is dedicated to the victims of Stalin's Katyn massacre of 1940 in Poland. There is a restful bird sanctuary, too, though it is not immune to the traffic roar. You can continue the trail from here into Sandton and beyond. Houghton is one of Johannesburg's wealthiest and greenest suburbs, where Nelson Mandela lives in a large white mansion dubbed Casa Graça after his third wife, Graça Machel. Interestingly, it was the country's only constituency to return an anti-apartheid MP, Helen Suzman, between 1961 and 1974.

Melville

By far the most appealing of the northern suburbs, **Melville** lies west of Parktown and is best reached by car from the Kingsway Road (the western extension of Empire Road). The suburb's villagey atmosphere has proved highly attractive to the stressed ranks of Johannesburg's upwardly mobile, who are steadily buying up the property here. The main streets, especially 7th Street, are worth lingering in for their inviting coffee shops, restaurants, second-hand bookshops and quirky antique dealers.

The **Melville Koppies Nature Reserve**, just north of the suburb, contain archeological remains of both stone and Iron Age settlements, including smelters, which can be viewed on the third Sunday of every month, between September and May (☎011/888 4831; free). Plans are afoot to develop this valuable site and increase access. The reserve is part of the large Jan van Riebeeck Park, that runs north and west for several kilometres, and also contains the **Johannesburg Botanic Gardens** in its northeast corner. Bonsai and herbal gardens, and a 24-acre rose garden (allegedly the largest in the world), plus plenty of open space, makes this a good place for walks and picnics.

Sophiatown

East of Melville is the suburb of **Sophiatown**, architecturally unremarkable but redolent of the destructiveness of apartheid. It was here that **Archbishop Trevor Huddleston**, the English cleric who established the Anti-Apartheid Movement, worked in the Fifties. For many years, Sophiatown was one of the few places within the city where blacks owned property, and as a result it became a melting pot of music, dance, culture and liberal thinking on issues of politics and race. In the Sixties the suburb was designated a white area by the government, who sent in the bulldozers, scattering the inhabitants to Soweto regardless of their claim to the land, and, with a degree of irony, if not fatalism, renamed the suburb Triomf, a name that remains on many maps and signboards. Although the name Sophiatown has now been reinstated, nothing of the original suburb remains apart from one house and **Christ the King** Anglican church, from where Trevor Huddleston conducted his ministry. When he died in 1998, his ashes were brought from London to be scattered in Sophiatown.

Sandton and Randburg

Some 20km north of the CBD, **Sandton** is the archetypal northern suburb. It is outrageously rich, with plush shopping centres and endless rows of lavish houses protected by sophisticated security systems. In recent years it has become the retreat of choice for banks and large corporations fleeing the CBD, and however overpowering the office blocks seem now, there is little doubt that they will be humbled by those which will rise from the various building sites at work now. A stroll through the linked **Sandton City** and **Sandton Square** shopping centres, complete with a pseudo-Italian piazza and attendant restaurants and cafés, is perhaps the best way to appreciate the wealth of this suburb, and the type of people who inhabit it.

Further west, fast-developing **Randburg** is known primarly for its **Waterfront** on Republic Road. Themed restaurants, bars, amusement arcades and shops, along with cinemas and a flea market, have been built around an artificial lake in a crude attempt to cash in on the success of the Cape Town Waterfront. The most recent attempt to brighten things up is a spectacle called **Liquid Fireworks** (nightly 7.30 & 8.30pm), which involves a series of fountains illuminated by multicoloured lights.

Alexandra

The contrast between **Alexandra** (just east of the M1) and the suburbs that surround it could hardly be greater. This intensely crowded, desperately poor black township somehow avoided the forced removals of former governments. Despite the simple grid design its map suggests, the township is actually a bewildering maze of smashed-up streets, filled to bursting point with people.

Alexandra's overcrowding has worsened since the mass influx of Mozambican informal dwellers (squatters) in the late Eighties. The squatters' shacks, known to Alexandrans as *Maputo*, are perched precariously on the banks of the Jukskei River, which runs through the township, and get swept away in heavy rains. Politically militant since the **bus boycotts** of the Forties, when mass action here prevented bus companies from raising their fares, Alexandra has long been an ANC stronghold, and paid dearly for it until the collapse of apartheid. Political violence is now a thing of the past, but the deprivation and crime remain; this is not a place to visit without a local guide. The inaccessibility is frustrating, as Alexandra has the best nightlife in the northern suburbs and good street markets. If you can't visit in person, tuning into its entertaining community radio station will at least give you a feel of this lively, though poverty-stricken suburb (see p.508). An indication of the will of the authorities for Alexandra to develop is that it was chosen as the site of the athletes' village for the 1999 All African Games.

South of the CBD

The suburbs immediately **south of the city centre** were traditionally the preserve of the white working class, but since the repeal of the Group Areas Act in 1990 blacks have started moving in and, unusually in contemporary South Africa, many are wealthier than the original residents. Aside from **Gold Reef City**, the only attraction of this area is the sizeable **Klipriviersberg** nature reserve, just south of the N12, in Winchester Hills. Few Jo'burgers know about this undeveloped, unspoilt parkland, which provides wonderful views of the city to the north. To get there, take the N1 heading south, turn left into Columbine Avenue (M68), and then right a kilometre or two further, at Ormonde Street.

Gold Reef City

Gold Reef City (daily except Mon 9am–5pm; R40), 15km south of the city centre, is where old Johannesburg meets Disneyland; a large, gaudy entertainment complex built around the old no. 14 shaft of the Crown Mines. If you can take the tackiness and piped ragtime music, there are some points of interest at what is essentially a theme park, notably the **old gold mine** itself, which you can descend 200m into and get at least an inkling of how it is to work underground. Keep an eye out, too, for the tribal dancing that happens five times a day, as the dancers are excellent, even if their routines are a travesty of the real thing.

The museums dotted around the complex are generally disappointing, with the possible exceptions of those dedicated to early Johannesburg, such as Olthaver and Nourse House. Otherwise, the most enjoyable thing to do in Gold Reef City is check out the **rides** (all included in the entrance ticket): easily the best are The Golden Loop and Thunder Mountain. In the unlikely event that you want to stay the night, the *Gold Reef City Hotel* (☎011/496 1626; ⑦) offers Victorian-themed decor, complete with a saloon, mock-oil lamps, and four-poster beds in the bedrooms. The restaurant serves a decent though pricey buffet.

To get to Gold Reef City, take the M1 heading south, and turn off at the Xavier Street exit. Otherwise, join one of the many tours that go there, who advertise in nearly every hotel lobby.

Soweto

South Africa's most famous township, **SOWETO** (short for South West Townships) is home to its most extreme contrasts. The area has the only street in the world where two Nobel Peace Prize winners once lived, yet suffers one of the highest rates of murder and rape in the world; it is the richest township in South Africa, but has some of the most desperate poverty; it is the most political township, yet has the most nihilistic youth.

Soweto is huge, stretching as far as the eye can see, with estimates of its population ranging between three and four million. Like any city of that size, it is divided into a number of different **suburbs**, with palpably middle- and upper-class neighbourhoods among them. On first sight it appears as an endless jumble of houses and shacks, overshadowed by palls of smoke. Once inside, parts of it have a villagey feel, especially if you are exploring on foot; and unlike anywhere else in Jo'burg, Sowetans will often stop to greet you or to chat, regardless of your colour.

Most of Soweto's **tourist highlights** are famous for historical reasons and are physically unimpressive. That history, however, is enthralling, not least because here it is told with a perspective and context rarely found in the rest of South Africa. For visitors it means an insight not just into a place famous from Eighties news bulletins for funerals and fighting, but into a way of life most Westerners have rarely, if ever, encountered.

A visit to Soweto with one of the many **tours** (see box opposite) is the single most popular attraction in Johannesburg. Where once these had a whiff of daring and originality, a well-trodden tourist trail has developed, and unless you're content to follow the herds of minibuses and coaches around the conventional sights, it's well worth using an operator who will mix the highlights with lesser known sights. And where once taking yourself to Soweto would have meant a display of bravado bordering on the foolhardy, it's now possible to **drive** there, though you'll need good navigational skills (the lack of obvious landmarks amidst the mile upon mile of bungalows can be highly confusing; Umtata Kraal, or Tourism Johannesburg office, can recommend maps) and to stick to the main sights – exploring less-visited areas by yourself, or going after dark, isn't recommended for safety reasons. However, your time will be your own, and you'll be able to check out the growing number of bars and eating places catering to tourists. Taking a **minibus taxi** to Soweto is more confusing than dangerous, as it isn't always easy to ascertain which part of the township it's heading for, for which reason it's not recommended. The best place to pick up **information** about visiting on your own is from Tourism Johannesburg at Ubuntu Kraal, on Senokonyeana Street in Orlando West (Mon–Fri 8.30am–4.30pm; ☎011/982 1050).

Orlando West and Dube

Set in the northern part of Soweto, **Orlando West** and **Dube** qualify as two of its more affluent suburbs, with a number of sights and the greatest concentration of places to eat and drink. Orlando East, across Klipspruit Valley from Orlando West, was the first part of Soweto to be established in 1932, and the area is fairly easily accessible off the Soweto Highway (M70). Here, **Hector Petersen Square** (daily 9am–5pm; small entrance fee), named after the first student to be killed in the 1976 uprising (see box on p.504.), has a memorial to Petersen and the other students who died. Around this, in steel containers, are photographs of the riots, taken by famous black photographers, including Peter Magubane and Sam Nzima.

Nearby is **Vilakazi Street**, a few hundred yards to the southwest, once home to Nelson Mandela and Desmond Tutu. Mandela's bungalow is where he lived with Winnie in the late Fifties and early Sixties, before his imprisonment on Robben Island, and where Winnie lived until exiled to the Free State (from which she returned to an imposing brick house with high walls and security cameras, just down the road). On his release, Nelson insisted on returning to his old home, but its smallness and lack of security proved too much of a strain, and he moved out of Soweto. Opened up by Winnie, tours of the old bungalow, **Mandela house** (daily 10am–4.30pm, admission fee), mix fascinatingly mundane memorabilia and large amounts of pro-Winnie propaganda.

About 1.5km away, near the junction of Klipsruit Valley (the M10) and Potchefstroom (the M68) roads, is **Regina Mundi Church**, Soweto's largest Catholic church and the focus of numerous gatherings in the struggle years. Again, its impact owes more to historical aura than anything particularly notable about its features, though with so few large buildings in the township it achieves a certain presence. Inside, look out for the **art gallery** displaying and selling the work of various Sowetan artists. Regina Mundi and the thousands of churches around the township play a vital role in understanding Soweto. Church services here, as in all townships, are friendly affairs, with liberal doses of fantastic music and, depending on the denomination, religious ecstasy too. Be prepared to give at least a small testimony (a

---

SOWETO TOURS

The most common – and safest – way to **visit Soweto** is with a tour operator. By far the oldest, biggest and slickest operation is Jimmy's Face to Face Tours, Budget House, 130 Main St, Johannesburg (☎011/331 6109, fax 331 5388). Jimmy pioneered tours into the township, and his operation has grown steadily over the years. Imbizo Tours (☎ & fax ☎011/838 2667, mobile ☎083/700 9098) run by the irrepressible Mandy Mankazana, provide stiff competition. Mandy is a mine of information and contacts, and her three-hour day tours and four-hour night tours of Soweto are excellent. Tours can be customized, and Imbizo also organize evening *shebeen*-crawls lasting up to five hours, depending on your stamina. Indicate what kind of company you would like to keep, from politicians to sports fanatics, and Mandy will select an appropriate venue.

As well as the well-established operators there are smaller, more flexible outfits offering imaginative **alternative tours**. Abantu Tours (☎011/648 7066 or mobile ☎082/459 3335) offer jazz outings, walking around Orlando West and Diepkloof, visits to Sowetan artists and stays with locals. African Travelogue Tours (☎011/794 4888 or mobile ☎082/675 4416) do a nightclub tour, plus an all-day tour incorporating a church service in the morning and jazz in the afternoon; they can also arrange for you to join some Sowetan musicians for a jamming session.

Before you go to Soweto on any kind of tour, it's worth preparing yourself for the fact that as a tourist you will always stand out, and that there's a good chance you'll be in the company of at least one other group of tourists. Most outfits are keen for you to "meet the people", though they all tend to visit the same shanty towns and *shebeens*, and you'll find that resulting conversations sometimes turn to you leaving a donation, tipping casual guides or buying local craftwork. While this gets a few tourist dollars directly into the townships, it often leaves visitors feeling pressurized and vulnerable. Ask your guide about the best way to deal with this in different situations.

---

brief rundown of your spiritual life to date). Services last several hours, but no one will think it a crime if you leave before the end.

Other tourist attractions will undoubtedly develop, such as **Freedom Square** – currently a combination of wasteland and taxi rank – in **Dube**, where the ANC's Freedom Charter was proclaimed to thousands in 1955. In the meantime many visitors enjoy paying a visit to the various **shebeens**, restaurants and even coffee shops that are making a big effort to attract outsiders as well as locals. We've listed the best in "Eating and drinking", p.506.

Eating and drinking

Despite the multiracial nature of Johannesburg, cultural interaction was obstructed for so long that a cuisine unique to the city has never emerged. However, you will have no problem finding almost every other variety of food – and French, Italian and Portuguese **restaurants** are particularly popular. Service almost everywhere is famously poor, but complaining can help. For eating on the run, keep an eye out for *African Hut*, a take-away chain with exotic African delicacies such as tripe and ox hoof, and *Nando's*, the Portuguese takeaway.

Not surprisingly for a city with such tough mining origins, **drinking** has always played a major part in Johannesburg's social life, often to the exclusion of all else. In most cases, bars are still male-dominated and for regulars only, but things are changing, especially in mixed areas like Yeoville. In the older suburbs the bars still front onto the street, while in the northern suburbs you'll need to look for them in shopping centres, where the modern trend for combination café/bar/restaurants, open most hours, is now encountered widely.

THE SOWETO UPRISING OF 1976

The **student uprising** that began in Soweto in June 1976 was a defining moment in South African history. The revolt was sparked off by a government ruling that **Afrikaans** should be used on an equal basis with English in black secondary schools. Whilst this was feasible in some rural areas, it was quite impossible in the townships, where neither pupils nor teachers knew the language.

On June 16, student delegates from every Soweto school launched their long-planned mass protest march through the township and a rally at the Orlando football stadium. Incredibly, details of the plan were kept secret from the omnipresent *impimpis* (informers). Soon after the march started, however, the police attacked, throwing tear gas and then firing. The crowd panicked, and demonstrators started throwing stones at the police. The police fired again. Out of this bedlam came the famous photograph of Hector Petersen, bleeding at the mouth, being carried by a friend, while a young girl looks on in anguished horror.

The police retreated to Orlando East, and students rushed to collect the injured and dead, erect barricades, and destroy everything they could belonging to the municipal authority, including beer halls. The attacks heightened the antagonism between the youth and many older people who thought that class boycotts were irresponsible given the students' already dismal employment prospects. Students responded angrily, accusing their elders of inactivity in the face of oppression, which they attributed in part to drunkenness. In a society that has traditionally regarded respect of the old by the young as sacrosanct, this was an historic departure and its effects still reverberate throughout South Africa's townships.

In the days following June 16, all Soweto schools were closed indefinitely, thousands of police were stationed throughout the township, and police brutality continued unabated. In the face of worldwide condemnation, the government insisted that there was no real problem, ascribing the violence to Communist agitation. As evidence, it cited the clenched-fist salutes of the students, though this was really an indication of their support for the Black Consciousness Movement, founded by Steve Biko (see p.329). Meanwhile, rebellion spread to other townships, particularly in Cape Town. In Soweto, schools did not reopen until 1978, by which time many students had abandoned any hope of formal education. Some had left the country to join the military wings of the ANC and PAC. Others stayed at home, forming "street committees" to politicize and police the communities. Others drifted into unemployment.

Now the armed struggle is over, the problems that face the students of 1976 are manifold. As their parents warned, their lack of qualifications count against them in the job market, even if June 16 is now a national holiday, during which they are praised for their role in the struggle. The street committees have dissolved, but the guns remain. This generation needs better prospects if these weapons are ever to be silenced.

CBD and Braamfontein

Countless takeaways and fast-food outlets serve the thousands of office workers and shoppers in the **CBD** and **Braamfontein**, but there are also a few restaurants and bars which have survived the changing times and are worth searching out. **Chinatown** in the CBD is a reliable stand-by if you get stuck, and the **Newtown Cultural Precinct** is a good place to find a range of food and a lively atmosphere at most times of the day and night.

Delhi Palace, 41 Central Rd, Fordsburg (☎011/838 6740). Near the Oriental Plaza and Newtown, this is one of the few good Indian restaurants in town, serving excellent tandooris and northern Indian dishes. No alcohol. Closed Mon.

Gramadoelas at the Market Theatre, Wolhuter St, Newtown (☎011/838 6960). Pleasant and popular spot specializing in Cape and African dishes, but not cheap. Closed Sun & Mon lunch.

Horror Café, 15 Becker St, Newtown (☎011/838 6735). Unusual two-storey venue beside the SAB centre, with regular live music, a good bar and decent food.

Kapitan's, 11a Kort St, CBD (☎011/834 8048). Located upstairs in a decrepit-looking building near Diagonal St, and gloomy and kitschy inside, but a Jo'burg classic serving delicious South African curries. Mandela's favourite when he worked as a lawyer nearby in the Fifties – his letter from prison holds pride of place. Lunchtime only Mon–Sat.

Kofifi, Newtown Cultural Precinct, Newtown. Lively bar and restaurant directly opposite the Market Theatre, serving inexpensive burgers and simple African dishes. Occasional live music.

Tong Lok, 7 Commissioner St, CBD. One of the best restaurants in Chinatown, and inexpensive too. Try *custard kok*, *beef congee* and other specialities. Closed Sun.

Northern suburbs

The **northern suburbs** have Johannesburg's highest density of pleasant cafés and top-class restaurants, though many of them are tucked away in shopping malls where franchised chains tend to breed alarmingly. The best selection of original eateries here are in **Rosebank** and **Melville**, which also have the best nightlife.

Bodega, Standard Bank Building, corner of Tyrwhitt and Cradock avenues, Rosebank (☎011/447 3210). Reasonable, fairly priced and often original Mediterranean food at this swish restaurant where diners come to see and be seen. Closed Sun.

Buzz 9, corner of 7th St & 3rd Ave, Melville. Seriously stylish bar, though everyone seems to relax after one or two of the speciality cocktails. Vibe carries on late into the night.

The Carnivore, Muldersdrift Estate (☎011/957 2099). On the D.F. Malan extension, past Randburg and Honeydew. Join white South Africans as they guzzle crocodile, giraffe, ostrich and buffalo, along with more humdrum fleshy fare. As much as you can eat for a reasonable set price of around R80.

Catz Pyjamas, 12 Main Rd, Melville. Nothing impressive about the food or prices, but it's open 24hr a day, and at its most interesting when the clubs spill out in the wee small hours.

The Codfather, 1 First Ave, corner of Rivonia Rd, Morningside (☎011/803 2077). Just north of Sandton, you select your fresh fish, then watch it scaled, filleted and cooked, with delicious results. Daily noon–10pm.

Cranks, The Mall, Cradock Ave, Rosebank (☎011/880 3442). The restaurant that made Thai food funky, now cooking up a storm with its Bangkok go-go bar theme. Menu extends to Vietnamese and Indonesian dishes, and there's live music Friday and Saturday nights. No reservations.

Global Wraps, 7th St. Take-away tortillas with tasty fillings – imaginative and great value at under R15.

Hard Times Café?, 63a 4th St, Melville. Quiet café, with a pinball machine and hearty, inexpensive meals. Daily 10am–2am.

Horatio's Fish Restaurant, corner of 7th St & 3rd Ave, Melville (☎011/726 2247). Seafood restaurant more at home on a rickety, barnacle-crusted pier. Expensive but original and a long-standing favourite. Closed Sat lunchtime & Sun.

Ile de France, Cramerview Centre, 277 Main Rd, Bryanston (☎011/706 2837). In the far northern suburbs, just south of the N1 ring road. Expect expensive, excellent French provincial cooking in pleasant, spacious surroundings. Closed Sat lunchtime & Sun.

Iyavaya, 14/15 Mutual Sq, 169 Oxford Rd, Rosebank (☎011/327 1312). Johannesburg's best-known African restaurant, with tasty, well-priced pan-African cuisine, with dishes including *mopani* worms, *mohodu* (black tripe) and Rooibos Tea Jelly.

Jimmy's Killer Prawns, Piazza Centre, corner of Jan Smuts Ave & Republic Rd, Randburg (☎011/886 8844). Good seafood and wines, while the views of the city lights are much preferable to the glitz of the nearby Waterfront. Closed Sat lunchtime & Sun evening.

Koala Blu, 9 7th St, Melville (☎011/482 2477). Fashionable restaurant serving fine Thai food in a relaxed setting. The chicken with cashew nuts is outstanding. Closed Mon & Sat lunchtimes & Sun.

Linger Longer, 58 Wierda Rd West, Wierda Valley West, Sandton (☎011/884 0465). Very classy French/Oriental cuisine from an award-winning chef. Closed Sat lunchtime & Sun.

Ohsho, Upper Level, Rosebank Mall, Rosebank (☎011/442 9109). Exquisitely prepared (and expensive) Japanese food in stylish and comfortable surroundings.

Osteria Tre Nanni, 9 Grafton Ave, Parktown North (☎011/327 0095). Near Zoo Lake, this is one of Jo'burg's best Italian restaurants, with a range of food from northern Italy, and a comfortable ambience. Great home-made *grappa* liqueurs round off the evening. Book ahead.

Pomegranate, 79 3rd Ave, Melville (☎011/482 2366). High quality, innovative international menu with Thai overtones, set in a typically charming Melville house. Closed Sat lunchtime & Sun.

Radium Beer Hall, 282 Louis Botha Ave, Orange Grove (☎011/728 3866). More famous as a pub and club playing a mostly reliable selection of grooves, from rock to soul, and into *mbaqanga* and *kwaito*, but the varied menu offers a steady stream of inexpensive specials, and is particularly good for fish. Closed Sun.

Sam's Café, 11 7th St, Melville (☎011/726 8142). Mostly Mediterranean dishes, reliably tasty and good value (particularly the specials). Closed Sat lunchtime & Sun.

Willoughby & Co, Hyde Park Corner, Hyde Park (☎011/447 5187). A wide selection of fresh fish cooked with considerable panache, for moderate prices. Closed Mon evening.

Eastern suburbs

The **eastern suburbs** are a lot less showy than those in the north, and here you'll find Johannesburg's best-value restaurants and most of its hippest bars. **Yeoville** and **Troyeville** are the areas to head for; Yeoville for its wide range of international cuisine and lively bars, and Troyeville for its very decent Portuguese restaurants, and somewhat more staid bars.

Bob's Bar, 76 Op de Bergen St, Troyeville. Late-night, well-decorated haunt of Troyeville's white alternative set. Screens B-movies at weekends. Closed Tues.

Gerhard's Bar, 128 Sivewright Ave, New Doornfontein. The walls of this old bar are covered in wonderful original photographs of Johannesburg, perfectly complementing its white, older clientele.

Gillooly's, Gillooly's Farm, Boeing Rd, Bedfordview (☎011/453 80252). The moderately priced food is nothing special, but the setting is – a Cape Dutch-style farmhouse in a pleasant open space.

Milky Way Internet Café, 206 Times Square Building, on the corner of Raleigh and Fortesque streets, Yeoville (☎011/487 3608, *info@milkeyway.co.za*).

Rooftop Bar, 26 Rockey St, Yeoville. Above *Tandoor*, 26 Rockey St, Yeoville. Reliably grooved music including reggae, a pool table, pinball and mixed clientele.

Slowcoach, 65 Raleigh St, Yeoville. Calm Forties station carriage, a good antidote to the street. Open til midnight. Closed Mon.

Time Square Café, Time Square, Raleigh St, Yeoville. Tolerable Yugoslav and Israeli cuisine. Open til 3am.

Tre Gatti, 28a Bezuidenhout St, Troyeville (☎011/614 8537). Portuguese-owned, but also serving inexpensive, good-quality Italian food, to eat in or take away. Closed Mon.

Southern and western suburbs

Decent restaurants are thin on the ground in the **southern suburbs**. What you will find, especially in **Soweto**, are some great **bars**, ranging from the most basic to the fantastically opulent. The **western suburbs**, meanwhile, are home to a handful of classic Portuguese and Indian restaurants.

Blue Fountain, Mapetla, Soweto. Run by the notorious Godfrey Moloi, with a fountain in the middle, mirrors, rows of spirits, ice-cold beers, and a young, chic crowd.

Edwaleni, 2358 Koma Rd, Rockville, Soweto (☎011/984 7371). Along with *Wandie's*, probably the most respectable restaurant in the township, though a lot less touristy.

Palazzo Di Stella, Mncube Dr, Dube. "Stella's Palace", and the lady herself presides over a great venue for pizzas, lively drinking and Sunday afternoon jazz sessions.

Pappies Tavern, Dlamini II, Soweto. Excellent *shebeen*, with a relaxed, soul-oriented music policy, and a good-humoured crowd.

Shakara, Jabulani Shopping Centre, Jabulani Ext. 1, Soweto. Large, safe bar on the Shebeen Route with a good local feel and meals available.

Soweto Cappuccino, 11787 Mtipa St, Orlando West Ext. Attracted lots of publicity as Soweto's first Italian-style coffee bar, but it's hard to fault for good coffee, light meals and yuppie quotient.

Wandie's, 618 Dube, Soweto. Classic *shebeen*, deservedly visited by every tour operator. Still used by locals, though now predominantly a food place rather than a drinking venue.

Entertainment, nightlife and culture

Johannesburg has always had the best **entertainment** and **nightlife** in South Africa: the city draws top performers from all over the world, and its audiences are the most sophisticated around. The best way to find out **what's on** is to keep your ears open listening to the local radio stations (see overleaf) and your eyes open for roadside posters and leaflets. *SA Citylife* magazine has a good blend of features and listings, but only comes out monthly; the *Mail & Guardian* newspaper publishes decent weekly listings and articles on the main events. The daily *Star* newspaper tracks mainstream cinema and theatre. Tickets for most events can be booked from Computicket (☎011/445 8000).

Live music: jazz, blues and rock

Although Johannesburg dominates the South African **music scene**, the city's lack of venues means that good music is often hard to track down, even at weekends. Large concerts tend to happen at the Standard Bank Arena in Ellis Park or the FNB Stadium on the way to Soweto. Medium-sized acts generally play in the Newtown Cultural Precinct, especially at the *Megamusic Warehouse*. Newtown and the northern suburbs are where you'll find live **jazz**, while **kwaito** bands pull enthusiastic crowds in Hillbrow and Yeoville. Music from the rest of Africa is filtering through slowly, with **Congolese bands** gigging regularly. In Soweto, live music is infrequent due to a venue shortage, but there are hundreds of excellent clubs and all-night street parties. A number of bars and clubs have occasional live acts and are a good source of more mainstream sounds – see "Eating and Drinking" p.503. and "Clubs" overleaf.

CBD, Newtown and Braamfontein

Kippies, Market Theatre/Newtown Cultural Precinct, corner of Bree and Wolhuter streets (☎011/834 4714). *Kippies* has played host to South Africa's finest jazz acts for years, and continues to do so – not bad for a former municipal toilet. It's tiny, so bands are best seen during the week, though the weekend vibe is one of the city's great cultural experiences.
Megamusic Warehouse, Market Theatre/Newtown Cultural Precinct, corner of Bree and Wolhuter streets (☎011/834 2761). With good acoustics, but lousy ventilation, this venue attracts some excellent and varied acts, such as Mahlathini and Busi Mhlongo.

Yeoville and Hillbrow

Jahnito's Live House, 43 Rockey St, Yeoville (☎011/648 9288). At the east end of Rockey St, just before the road turns residential. Small, but squeezes in two stages, one with live Central African sounds, the other playing R&B and reggae. A good early evening place.
Tandoor, 26 Rockey St, Yeoville (☎011/487 1569). Yeoville's main live-music venue is pretty good, if a bit seamy. The eclectic music selection veers towards the townships and the Congo.

Northern suburbs

Bassline, 7 7th St, Melville (☎011/482 6915). Small, wine-bar-style venue that has the most innovative selection of jazz and African bands in the city, and is reasonably priced.
The Blues Room, Village Walk Mall, Sandton (☎011/784 5527). A reliable venue for some of the best blues to be found in town. Quite smart (as you'd expect for Sandton), but also refreshingly mixed and lively.
Morgan's Cat, Randburg Waterfront, Randburg (☎011/886 4408). Rock and pop bands play for free to suburban teenagers in a rather synthetic environment.
Roxy's Rhythm Bar, *Melville Hotel*, 20 Main Rd, Melville (☎011/726 6019). Veteran establishment hosting local indie bands; the rooftop bar is great for hot summer nights.
206, 206 Louis Botha Ave, Orange Grove (☎011/728 5333). Friendly and reliably happening space featuring local and international blues and jazz bands.

Clubs

Johannesburg is the country's most desegregated city, which has improved nightlife greatly. Add to that the stylish fashion sense of many Johannesburg *jollers* (good-timers), and their celebrated love of a party, and you have the main ingredients for a memorable night out. **Hillbrow** and **Yeoville** are the heart of serious clubland, where you'll find an eclectic mix of disco, soul, hip-hop, *mbaqanga*, *kwaito* and Zairean *souk-ous*. These sounds are now filtering through to the predominantly white **northern suburbs,** where rock and indie sounds once dominated, with Rosebank generally the location of the livliest night-time action.

Raves take place every weekend in ever more unusual venues. Entrance is expensive, but the sessions go on all night. They are almost exclusively white. Tickets and information are available from Bizarre Generation, corner of Rockey and Raymond streets, Yeoville (☎011/648 7808).

CBD, Braamfontein, and Newtown

Carfax, 39 Pim St, Newtown (☎011/834 9187). Seriously hip venue offering performance art, jazz bands and highly rated resident DJs.

Da Flava, 22 Claim St, CBD. Popular venue playing fresh hip-hop, bubblegum and *kwaito* to a well-dressed party crowd.

ESP, 96 End St, Doornfontein. Full-on rave scene at this popular club on the edge of the city centre.

Therapy, 39A Juta St, Braamfontein. Gay nightclub big on rave, house and techno. Sat night only.

LOCAL RADIO

In recent years the **airwaves of Johannesburg** and the nation have been transformed by the granting of over eighty new licences countrywide. In Gauteng most stations are on FM, and while reception is often poor and presentation amateur, the best stations have an energy and vitality lacking in their more established competitors. They all have community obligations, which are discharged more dutifully by some than by others, but most rely on DJs to attract their audience. Listening to the radio is one of the essential ways to pick up Jo'burg's vibe: the following is a selection of the current favourites.

ALX FM, 89.1FM. Broadcasts out of the Alexandra township and can be picked up in most northern suburbs and some eastern ones. It focuses on township issues, but avoids excessive worthiness, and plays a fine selection of soul, R&B, reggae, *kwaito* and gospel, making it one of the most musically reliable stations around.

Khaya 96.9FM. Where you go when you're too old and boring for YFM. A mellower mix of mainstream *mbaqanga* and jazz, with good information on what's playing live around the city. Can be picked up city-wide.

New Panhellenic Voice, 823MW. Broadcasts in vernacular only to Johannesburg's sizable Greek population. Wonderful Greek music is the compensation for those who don't speak the language.

Radio 702, 702MW. Well-established local talk-radio station famed for its lively discussion programmes and excellent presenters. Also good for local news.

Soweto Community Radio, 105.8FM. Lots of community information and discussion, mostly in African languages and Sowetan slang. There's plenty of excellent South African gospel on Sundays; otherwise, the staples are American soul, *kwaito* and *mbaqanga*. Can only be picked up in Soweto and adjoining suburbs.

Voice of Soweto, 87.6FM. Soweto's finest DJs spin some great sounds. As they say in Jamaica, "a dem have the tunes, sah!", and so they do. Can only be picked up in Soweto and adjoining suburbs.

YFM, 99.2FM. The only place to have your dial if you're under 21. A blistering introduction to the upwardly mobile young black culture of Johannesburg, with wall-to-wall *kwaito*, slick news bulletins and risqué phone-ins.

Yeoville and Hillbrow

Base, corner of Twist and Kotze streets, Hillbrow. A heavy sound system and an excellent chill-out balcony overlooking the busy street. At weekends, this club pulls a well-dressed, cosmopolitan crowd, and plays soul and *kwaito*, occasionally live. Single women can get pestered, but generally it is safe.

Chez Ntemba, corner of Claim and Kotze streets, Hillbrow. The rooftop beer garden adds an unusual twist to this lively nite spot playing *kwaito*, *kwasa kwasa* and US imported sounds.

Polli Polli, Hunter St, Yeoville. Large, mainstream nightclub near Rockey St, with mixed crowds at the weekend and a lively vibe.

Northern suburbs

Calabash, Benmore Gardens, Benmore Rd, Sandton. Hard-core venue for serious R&B and funk, popular at weekends with a smart, young black set. The mid-weekWest African theme nights are worth checking out.

The Foundation, Shop 5, Cargo Corner, Keyes Ave, Rosebank. House, garage and funk at this trendy venue with a slightly older crowd than other clubs in the area.

Hoods, 1 Hood Ave, Rosebank. Unremarkable venue but popular with students, featuring resident DJs and regular live music.

Hysterix, Randburg Waterfront, Randburg (☎011/787 0754). Jo'burg's only dedicated stand-up comedy club, though it sometimes struggles to live up to its name.

Krypton, Constantia Centre, Tyrwhitt Ave, Rosebank. Fashionable gay and bi club, but open to all, playing imported house from garage to trance. Wed–Sat.

The Palladium, New Constantia Centre, corner of Tyrwhitt and Jan Smuts avenues. Large venue at the heart of Rosebank's night scene. Mainstream R&B, soul and *kwaito*.

Classical music, theatre and dance and film

The Civic Theatre in Braamfontein and the Market Theatre in Newtown are Johannesburg's premier venues for **theatre** and **opera** productions, but there are several other good venues, and the city is blessed with some innovative companies, including the Johannesburg Youth Theatre. South Africa's **National Symphony Orchestra** (☎011/714 4501) plays regularly at Linder Auditorium in Parktown. Johannesburg **dance** is going through a revival: key players are the Moving into Dance Academy, which is rearing new generations of South African choreographers, and the Dance Factory in the Newtown Cultural Precinct, with several dance companies revolving around it.

Alhambra, 109 Sivewright Ave, Ellis Park Precinct (☎011/402 6174). Three theatres in this attractive complex hosting large musicals and shows, from stand-up comedy to drama.

The Dance Factory, Newtown Cultural Precinct, Newtown (☎011/716 3891). Giving dance some oxygen in downtown Jo'burg. Interesting but irregular programme – check local papers for details.

Johannesburg Civic Theatre, Loveday St, Braamfontein (☎011/403 3408). A good mix of mainstream shows and more adventurous productions at this impressive, four-stage venue.

Market Theatre, Newtown Cultural Precinct, Newtown (☎011/832 1641). Venue for some of Johannesburg's finest stage productions and top-grade visiting music acts; celebrated for its innovative community theatre, and the odd costly epic.

Tates Theatre Café, Randburg Waterfront (☎011/789 4949). Cabaret venue with an entertaining line up of regular performers and touring acts.

Theatre on the Square, Sandton Square, Sandton (☎011/883 8606). One of the few theatres in the northern suburbs, though only open sporadically.

Windybrow Theatre, corner of Nugget and Pietersen streets, Hillbrow (☎011/720 7009). Staging mainly community theatre, throughout the year. The theatre's finest moment is its arts festival every March.

Film

The multi-screen Nu-Metro and Ster-Kinekor **cinemas** control the movie market and can be found all over the city, especially in shopping malls. Good listings can be found in the *Mail & Guardian* newspaper, published on Fridays. Independent and foreign films can be found at the following:

Rosebank Cinema Nouveau, Mall of Rosebank, Rosebank (☎011/880 2866). Presents itself as the *grande dame* of the avant-garde, and screens a hip selection to a discerning audience.

Northcliff, corner of Weltevreden and Arbor streets, Blackheath (☎011/782 6816). Off DF Malan, just before the N1 highway, showing a good selection of art-house movies.

Sandton Select, Sandton City, corner of Rivonia and Sandton streets, Sandton (☎011/784 3113). Pleasant cinema with a good programme, surrounded by over twenty other screens showing mainstream movies.

Village Walk Nu-Metro, Village Walk Mall, Rivonia Rd, Sandton (☎011/883 9558). One arts screen squeezed between the action movies, in a rather nondescript uptown mall.

Shopping

With its vast availability of goods, Johannesburg is a magnet for consumers from all over the subcontinent, who zoom down the highways to stock up before heading back the same day. For visitors, the city is the best place in South Africa to find **arts and crafts**, with excellent flea markets and galleries offering a plethora of goods, some of a very high quality. As the queen of **mall culture**, Johannesburg is also home to over twenty major malls (daily 8am–6pm), most of which are depressingly anonymous. A handful, however, (listed below), are so plush and enormous that they merit a visit in their own right.

Malls

Hyde Park Mall, Jan Smuts Ave, Hyde Park. Trendy and upmarket, awash with swanky cafés and *haute couture* outlets. The excellent Exclusive Books chain have a branch here.

Randburg Waterfront, on Republic Rd, Randburg. Built around an artificial lake, with restaurants, a flea market and a cinema alongside the clothes shops and chain stores.

Mall of Rosebank, corner of Baker and Cradock streets, Rosebank. One of the city's nicest malls, with exclusive boutiques, craft shops and – unusually – outdoor cafés, restaurants and walkways.

Sandton City Shopping Centre, corner of Sandton Drive and Rivonia Rd, Sandton. This enormous mall is worth a visit for its sheer size and mind-boggling abundance of shops, cinemas and attractions, including some good bookshops and African art galleries Linked to the seriously opulent Sandton Square mall.

Craft shops and markets

Art Africa, 62 Tyrone Ave, Parkview (☎011/486 2052). Good selection of innovative and more familiar items, many ingeniously created out of recycled material.

Diagonal Street, CBD. The best place in South Africa to buy Sotho blankets, also good for *umuthi* medicine and herbal cures particular to this part of the world.

Everard Read Gallery, 6 Jellicoe Ave. Beautiful arts and crafts, but expensive.

M2 Highway, CBD. Informal market stretching for large tracts underneath this major artery, a few blocks south of Anderson St. Most stalls specialize in *umuthi*, but there are plenty of local crafts as well.

Mai Mai Bazaar, Albert St, underneath the M1, CBD. Once a migrants' hostel, now a great daily market selling Zulu crafts, medicines, food and clothes mainly to the local Zulu community.

Market Africa, Newtown. The city's liveliest flea market, next to the Market Theatre. Rifle through colourful blankets from Mali, Congolese masks and statues, and more. Sat 9am–4pm.

Rosebank Rooftop Market, Mall of Rosebank, 50 Bath Ave, Rosebank. Entertaining place where you can browse through an impressive array of cottage-industry crafts and clothes. Sun 9am–5pm.

Rural Craft, Shop 42E, Mutual Gardens, Rosebank (☎011/788 5821). Non-profit-making city outlet for various craft co-operatives around South Africa – a refreshing alternative to hard-sell pavement hawkers. Mon–Fri 8.30am–5pm, Sat 8.30am–2.30pm.

Music shops

Johannesburg is a good place to pick up a wide range of **African music**; the CBD (especially) has dozens of small shops selling cassettes of South African and American sounds. The Musica chain of shops are the most prevalent, and concentrate on soul and rock import CDs, with small selections of local music.

Bizarre Generation, corner of Rockey and Raymond streets, Yeoville. Best rave shop in Johannesburg.

Cadence Tropical, Time Square, Yeoville (☎011/648 7957). South Africa's finest stockist of Central and West African music, and *the* place to find out about clubs currently playing these sounds. Closes at 10pm.

Kohinoor, 54 Market St, CBD. Excellent vinyl selection, as well as a range of tapes and CDs. The focus is on jazz, but you'll find all manner of South African styles here, ranging from gospel to *maskanda* and *mbaqanga*.

CD Wharehouse, Mutual Square, Rosebank. Best selection of CDs in Johannesburg, with all the latest local sounds and helpful staff.

Listings

Airlines Air Afrique, Sanlam Arena, 10 Cradock Ave, Rosebank (☎011/880 8537); Air Botswana, FedLife Building, 257 Oxford Rd, Illovo (☎011/447 6078); Air France, Oxford Manor, Oxford Rd, Illovo (☎011/880 8040); Air Malawi, Vasco da Gama House, Ernest Oppenheimer Dr, Bruma (☎011/662 0466); Air Namibia, Dunkeld Place, 12 North Rd, Dunkeld West (☎011/442 4461); Air Zimbabwe, Finance House, Ernest Oppenheimer Dr, Bruma (☎011/615 7017); Alitalia, Oxford Manor, Oxford Rd, Illovo (☎011/880 9254); American Airlines, Dunkeld Crescent (West), Albury Rd, Hyde Park (☎011/880 6370); Balkan Airways, Norwich Life Towers, 13 Fredman Drive, Sandton (☎011/883 0957); British Airways/Comair, 158 Jan Smuts Ave, Rosebank (☎011/441 8600); Canadian Airlines, Everite House, De Korte St, Braamfontein (☎011/339 4865); Lufthansa, 22 Girton Rd, Parktown (☎011/484 4722); Olympic Airways, JHI House, Cradock Ave, Rosebank (☎011/880 1614); Qantas, c/o British Airways (☎011/441 8600); Royal Swazi Air, Finance House, Ernest Oppenheimer Dr, Bruma (☎011/616 7323); SA Airlink, South African Airways & SA Express Airways Park, Jones Road, Johannesburg International Airport (☎011/978 1111); Sun Air, Jet Park, Johannesburg International Airport (☎011/923 6300); Virgin Atlantic, Hyde Park Shopping Centre, Jan Smuts Ave (☎011/340 3400).

American Express Nedbank Gardens, 33 Bath Ave, Rosebank (Mon–Fri 8.30am–4pm, Sat 9am–noon; ☎011/880 8382); and Sandton City Shopping Centre, Sandton Dr (☎011/883 1316).

Bureau de change. Foreign exchange is available 24hr at Johannesburg International Airport.

Bookshops Exclusive have branches at Hyde Park Corner, Jan Smuts Ave (☎011/325 4298), Sandton City (☎011/883 1010), and Killarney Mall, Houghton (☎011/686 0931); and Facts & Fiction are at Rosebank Mall (☎011/447 3028), The Firs Mall, Rosebank (☎011/880 7833), and Sandton Square (☎011/784 5418). For a good second-hand selection try Yeoville Books, 27a Rockey St, Yeoville (☎011/648 2002), or Huxley's, 31 Tyrwhitt Ave, Rosebank (☎011/447 4292). The Bookdealers mini-chain specializes in second-hand books and remainders, and is staffed by enthusiasts; find them at 12 7th St, Melville (☎011/726 4054), and 29 Mutual Square, Rosebank (☎011/442 4089).

Car rental Protea (☎011/402 6328); Tempest (☎011/402 7100, toll-free 0800/031 666); Dolphin (☎011/394 6605, toll-free 0800/01 1344); Imperial (☎011/337 2300, toll-free 0800/13 1000); and Budget (☎011/392 3929, toll-free 0800/016 662). For cheaper, local deals try Apex (☎011/402 5150), Eco Rent A Car (☎011/965 1029), Afro Auto Rent (☎011/792 8240) or Dorset (☎011/614 1177).

Cricket Wanderers Stadium, off Corlett Drive, Illovo (☎011/788 1008). Site of international test matches and good for idling away an afternoon during the season. Corlett Drive is reached either from the M1 or Oxford Road.

Emergencies Ambulance ☎999; Fire ☎011/624 2800; Police ☎10111; Rape Crisis ☎0800/012 322.

Hospitals State-run hospitals with 24hr casualty departments include Johannesburg Hospital, Parktown (☎011/488 4911); JG Strijdom, Auckland Park (☎011/489 1011); Hillbrow, Hospital Rd, Hillbrow (☎011/720 1121); and Baragwanath, Zone 6, Diepkloof, Soweto (☎011/933 1100). Private hospitals include Millpark Hospital, Guild St, Parktown (☎011/480 5600); and Morningside Clinic, off Rivonia Rd (☎011/282 5000), in Morningside, near Sandton.

Internet cafés *Milky Way Internet Café*, 206 Times Square Building, corner of Raleigh and Fortesque streets, Yeoville (Mon–Thurs 8.30am–10pm, Fri 8.30am–midnight, Sat 9am–7pm; ☎011/487 3608, *info@milkeyway.co.za*); and *Internet Virtual Café*, Bruma Board Walk Shopping Centre, Bruma Lake (Mon–Thurs 9.30am–10pm, Fri & Sat 9.30am–midnight, Sun 10am–8pm; *cafe@virtualcafe.co.za*).

Poste restante Avoid the main poste restante post office on Jeppe St, as it's in an unsafe part of town. Make arrangements instead with your accommodation, or use Amex.

Rugby Ellis Park, just off Bertrams Road in Ellis Park (☎011/402 8644), is a South African rugby shrine, particularly since the triumph of the national team in the 1995 World Cup. It's also home ground to the provincial Gauteng Lions team. Ellis Park comes into its own during major fixtures, where the atmosphere is electric. A number of buses run there.

Soccer The FNB Stadium, off the Soweto Highway, on the NASREC road, is the premier venue; tickets are cheap, and there is safe parking. Orlando Stadium, in Orlando, Soweto, also hosts major games, though it's more run-down and less safe than the FNB. Ellis Park is also occasionally used for big games.

Swimming Pools include the superb, outdoor, Olympic-sized Ellis Park pool (Sept–March Mon–Fri 6.30am–9pm, Sat & Sun 6.30am–6pm), and decent pools in Bezuidenhout Park (Sept–March Mon–Fri 9am–5.50pm, Sat & Sun 9am–6pm), on Rockey St in Yeoville (Sept–March Mon–Sat 7.30am–6pm, Sun 8.30am–6pm), and in most middle-class suburbs.

Taxis Maxi Taxis, Yeoville (☎011/648 1212), rank in Cavendish St, and are the most reliable for almost all parts of town. Otherwise Rose Radio (☎011/725 1111 or 725 3333), Good Hope (☎011/725 6431) and Metro (☎011/484 7975) cover most of the city. Taxis often also wait outside the large hotels.

Train information For the half-hourly service to Pretoria, phone ☎011/773 2944.

Around Johannesburg

Johannesburgers wanting to get away from it all tend to head for the **Magaliesberg Mountain** range, which stretches from Pretoria in the east to Rustenberg in the west. Don't expect to see a horizon of impressive peaks: much of the area is private farmland running across rolling countryside, although there are some impressive *kloofs*, as well as numerous resorts and hotels to cater for the weekend crowds.

The **Suikerbosrand Nature Reserve**, 40km south of Johannesburg, is the biggest and best nature reserve in Gauteng, offering interesting archeology and good hikes.

Even more impressive, archeologically, are the world-renowned **Sterkfontein Caves**, where 3,000,000-year-old hominid bones were found recently, and the overcommercialized **Kromdraai Caves**, both of which are near the West Rand town of Krugersdorp, near Johannesburg.

Immediately east and west of the city, grim industrial towns such as Boksburg and Springs offer little to entice. The one exception is **Benoni**, in the east, where an excellent mining museum, the **Benoni Museum**, on the corner of Elston Avenue and Rothsay Street (Mon–Fri 9am–4.30pm; free), features intriguing exhibits on mining strikes in the late nineteenth and early twentieth century.

Suikerbosrand Nature Reserve

Though hardly in the same league as the epic parks of Kruger and the like, the **Suikerbosrand Nature Reserve** (Mon–Fri 7.15am–4pm, Sat & Sun 7am–5pm; ☎011/904 3930; small entry fee), south of Johannesburg, is attractive nonetheless, and easy to get to from the city. The beautiful Suikerbosrand mountain range dominates the reserve, but you'll find gentle grassland plains too, with antelope, zebra and wildebeest, and even the odd cheetah and leopard.

The **visitors' centre**, at the entrance to the reserve, can supply maps and guidebooks. Next door, the **Diepkloof Farm Museum** is worth a visit, as careful renovation has ensured that the farm buildings look pretty much as they did when they were first built in 1850. The farm was worked by one Gabriel Marais, who participated in the Great Trek, but it was burnt by British soldiers in the Anglo-Boer War, and remained neglected until the Seventies, when it was renovated. Most of the exhibits are aimed at Afrikaner children, and try to enthuse them about their fast-disappearing rural culture. However, other brief displays dwell on the sixteenth- to nineteenth-century settlements of Sotho and Tswana people, which were extensive, and have been excavated nearby.

You can **explore the reserve** on foot or by car, following a network of trails. Several hiking trails include overnight accommodation in camps (book at the visitors' centre). Alternatively, you can book out the very basic meditation hut, 18km from the visitors' centre. There's no electricity, but it's definitely quiet and undisturbed.

To get to the reserve and farm, take the N3 south of Johannesburg, and turn right onto the R550. The turn to the reserve is a few kilometres along the road, on your left.

Sterkfontein, Kromdraai and the Rhino and Lion Nature Reserve

Just over 40km west of Johannesburg lie the **Sterkfontein Caves** (daily except Mon 9am–4pm; ☎011/956 6342; small entry fee), Gauteng's oldest archeological site. Millions of years old, the caves are believed to have been inhabited by pre-human primates who lived here up to 3.5 million years ago. They first came to European attention in 1896, when an Italian lime prospector, Martinaglia, stumbled upon them. Martinaglia was only interested in the bat droppings, and promptly stripped them out, thus destroying the caves' dolomite formation. Between 1936 and 1951, archeologist Dr Robert Broom excavated the caves and in 1947 found the skull of a female hominid that was over two million years old. Archeologists have nicknamed it "Mrs Ples". In 1995, another archeologist, Ronald Clarke, found "Little Foot", the bones of a 3,000,000 year-old walking hominid, with big toes that functioned like our thumbs do today. The latest discovery, in 1998, was of the oldest complete skeleton yet found in the world.

Fossilized wood samples and animal remains suggest that the area was once a tropical forest inhabited by lots of "Little Feet", as well as giant monkeys, long-legged hunting hyenas and sabre-toothed cats. One million years later, in a much drier climate, toolmaking hominids had arrived on the scene, along with ostriches, horses and pigs. It seems likely that the caves were still being lived in when Mr Martinaglia came upon them.

Informed **guided tours** every half-hour take you around the main features. **To get to the caves**, travel west out of Johannesburg on the R47, until the R563 junction – about 40km. Turn right, and just over 2km further along is a sign on the right to the caves.

Equally old, but more commercially developed, the **Kromdraai Caves** (daily 9am–4pm; ☎011/957 0106; moderate entrance fee), a few kilometres away, are billed as "wonder" caves. Expect carefully placed lighting inside, which often appeals to children, but far less substantial tours. These caves were mined for lime in the 1890s, which killed their dolomite production too. To get there, take the DF Malan Drive out of Johannesburg, and turn left at the Kromdraai junction, some 2km after crossing the R28.

You can also visit the Kromdraai Caves via the **Rhino and Lion Nature Reserve** (daily 8am–5pm; ☎011/957 0109; moderate entrance fee), which is a very short drive away. The reserve has ten white rhino, and plenty of wildebeest, hartebeest and giraffe, as well as antelope, lions, cheetahs and wild dogs in large enclosures. It's pleasant, but not likely to hold you for more than an hour or two, though you can stay in a self-catering chalet sleeping four if you pre-book (②). The reserve's restaurant serves hearty (if unimaginative) meat dishes.

All three attractions now fall within an area called the **Kromdraai Conservancy**, which centres on a pleasantly rural **information office** and craft shop (daily 8am–7pm; ☎011/957 0034) located 3km from the Sterkfontein Caves. Here you can organize tours, hikes, horse-riding, trout fishing and a visit to the Old Kromdraai Gold Mine, the first mine on the Witwatersrand.

Magaliesburg Village and around

Named after Mohali Mohale, a chief of the Po clan of the Ndebele people, **Magaliesburg Village** is a functional, though not wildly attractive village, serving its purpose well – that is, providing stressed city-dwellers with accommodation and facilities amid the fresh mountain air. If you plan on a jaunt up here, be sure to book **accommodation** ahead, especially at weekends. The nicest (and priciest) place to stay by far is *Mount Grace*, Rustenburg Rd (☎014/577 1350, fax 011/880 3282; ⑦–⑧), magnificently located on a hilltop, and offering immaculate and stylish rooms. The restaurants here are superb, and classical concerts are held outside during the summer. If that's full, you could try the *Magaliesburg Country Hotel*, Rustenburg Rd (☎ & fax 014/577 1109; ⑥), in the heart of the village, which is comfortable and has a good restaurant. For B&B, *Out of Africa* (☎ & fax 014/577 1126; ⑤–⑦) offers luxury cottages by the river, tastefully decked out with antique furniture and original art. For a better feel of the rolling, open landscapes of the countryside, *Wind in the Willows* (☎014/557 3401, fax 557 3404; ④) is a well-run guesthouse set on a horse stud 15km west of the village along the R509, from which it's signposted, with good trails nearby for horse-riding or hiking.

The village lies on the R24, west of Krugersdorp. For a day-trip from Johannesburg, you can travel here by **steam train**: the Magalies Express (☎011/888 1155) runs most weekends, and the fares for the three-hour return journey are quite reasonable at around R100, with lunch at the *Magaliesburg Country Hotel* included in the price.

PRETORIA

Gauteng's two major cities are just 50km apart, but could hardly be more different. **PRETORIA**, or ePitoli as it is known in the townships, has throughout much of its history been the epitome of staid traditionalism, with its graceful government buildings, wide avenues of purple flowering jacarandas, and staunchly Boer farming origins. Yet, although South Africa's administrative capital is seen by many South Africans as a bastion of **Afrikanerdom**, with its notorious supreme court and massive prison, things are changing. Ever since the nation's re-acceptance into the international arena, Pretoria has become increasingly cosmopolitan, with a substantial diplomatic community living in Hatfield, east of the city centre. Furthermore, most Pretorians are not Afrikaner, but Sotho and Ndebele, and the change of government has brought many more well-educated and well-paid blacks into the ranks of civil servants living in the capital. The city's Afrikaner community is hardly monolithic, either: as well as the stereotypical khaki-shorted rednecks, there are thousands of students, an active art scene and a thriving Afrikaans gay and lesbian community.

Pretoria is near enough to Johannesburg's airport to provide a practical alternative base for exploring Gauteng. The main attractions are that it's safer and less spread out than Johannesburg, there is at least a sprinkling of things worth seeing, and the nightlife of Sunnyside and Hatfield is energetic and fun. As well as the **Union Buildings** and **Church Square**, **Melrose House** is interesting and the **Police and Correctional Services museums** are compellingly bizarre. The city is unquestionably more boring than Johannesburg, but due to the risks associated with Johannesburg's excitements this is a price you might be willing to pay.

Some history

Unlike Johannesburg, Pretoria developed at a leisurely pace from its humble origins as a **Boer farming community** on the fertile land around the Apies River. When the city was founded in 1855 by **Marthinus Wessel Pretorius**, who named it after his father, Andries Pretorius, it was intended to be a unifying hub around which the new South African Republic (ZAR) would prosper. Embodying the Afrikaner conviction that the land they took was God-given, Pretoria's first building was a church. The town was then laid out in a grid of streets wide enough for teams of oxen brought in by farmers to turn corners.

In 1860 the city was proclaimed the capital of the new ZAR, the result of tireless efforts by Stephanus Schoeman to unite the squabbling statelets of the Transvaal. From this base, the settlers continued their campaigns against local African peoples, bringing thousands into service, particularly on farms. Infighting also continued amongst the settlers, and violent skirmishes between faction leaders were common. These leaders bought most of the best land, resulting in the dispossession and embitterment of many white trekkers, and the large-scale massacre of the wild animals of the region, particularly its elephants.

The British annexed Pretoria in 1877, and investment followed in their wake. Although it prospered and grew, farmer **Paul Kruger**, who was determined not to be subjugated by the British again, mobilized *commandos* of Afrikaner farmers to remove them. This resulted in the first Anglo-Boer War (1877–81). After defeat at Majuba on the Natal border, the colonial government abandoned the war and ceded **independence** in 1884.

Paul Kruger became ZAR president, and ruled until 1903. However, his mission to keep the ZAR Boer was confounded by geology. The discovery of **gold** in the Witwatersrand precipitated an unstoppable flood of foreigners. Kruger's policy of taxing the newcomers, while retaining the Boer monopoly on political power, worked for a while. Most of the elegant buildings of Church Square were built with mining revenues, while the Raadsaal (parliament) remained firmly in Boer hands. At the same time, the ZAR's military arsenal grew, largely thanks to imported German weapons.

ZAR independence ended with the second Anglo-Boer War (1899–02), but despite the brutality of the conflict Pretoria remained unscathed. With the creation of the **Union of South Africa** in 1910, the city became the administrative capital of the entire country. In 1913 Sir Herbert Baker built the epic Union Buildings to house the civil service, and some ministries, including the office of the president, are still there today.

In 1928, the government laid the foundations of Pretoria's industry by establishing the **Iron and Steel Industrial Corporation** (Iscor), which rapidly generated a whole series of related and service industries. These, together with the civil service, ensured white Pretoria's quiet, insular prosperity. Meanwhile, increasing landlessness amongst blacks drove many of them into the city's burgeoning **townships**. Marabastad and Atteridgeville are the oldest, and Mamelodi is the biggest and poorest.

After the introduction of apartheid by the National Party in 1948 (see p.692), Pretoria acquired a hated reputation amongst the country's black population. Its **supreme court** and **central prison** were notorious: the source of the laws and regulations that made their lives a nightmare. As the poet **Mzwahke Mbuli** expressed it, in exasperation:

Central Prison – in Pretoria
Pass laws – in Pretoria
Pretoria – why you?

Mandela's inauguration at the Union Buildings in 1994 was the symbolic new beginning for Pretoria's political redemption. The change won't happen overnight, but there are signs that things are moving in the right direction, not least in the lively cultural and social scene which is fast becoming one of the city's defining characteristics.

Arrival, information and city transport

The nearest airport to Pretoria is **Johannesburg International Airport** (see p.482) some 50km away. From here, the only way to reach Pretoria is via one of the hourly **Pretoria-Airport Shuttle** buses, which arrive downtown at Sammy Marks Square via Church Square. The journey takes about an hour and costs around R50 one way. If you're arriving by **train** you'll alight at Pretoria Station (☎012/334 8470), designed by Sir Herbert Baker, to the south of the city centre; **intercity buses** stop beside the station building.

Pretoria's main point of **information** is the helpful Tourist Information Centre on Church Square (daily 8am–5pm; ☎012/337 4337), where you can pick up *Time Out*, a free monthly publication handy for restaurant listings. **Satour** also has its offices in the centre, and provides information and booking facilities by phone for the whole country (☎012/347 0600).

Pretoria's city centre is easily explored on foot, but public transport is useful if you are heading slightly further afield. For journeys to the suburbs, you'll need the municipal **bus** services, which start in **Church Square** (where there's a bus information office, ☎012/308 0839), and spread outwards. You buy the tickets – which are never more than a few rand – when you get on. Timetables are available from Church Square, the buses themselves and from pharmacies.

The best place to catch **minibus taxis** is from the corner of Jacob Maré and Bosman streets, just north of the railway station, though you can hail them from anywhere. As in Johannesburg, you can't hail metered **taxis**, but you'll usually find one on or near Church Square. Alternatively, cabs can be booked ahead by phone (see "Listings", p.527).

Accommodation

Pretoria has plenty of soulless modern hotel complexes that range from the moderately to the expensively priced; the Tourist Information Centre can provide you with detailed and updated lists. Nicer by far is to stay at one of the few **hotels** and **guesthouses** with genuine character, some of which are listed opposite. For backpackers, the quality of the **hostels** in Pretoria is high. Bear in mind that apart from **Sunnyside**, **Arcadia** and **Hatfield**, everywhere outside the townships dies at night.

Arcadia Hotel, 515 Proes St (☎012/326 9311, fax 326 1067). Centrally located but a little over-priced, especially as there's no pool. Rooms are comfortable and the restaurant reliable. ④.

Batiss Guesthouse, 3 Fook Island, 92 20th St, Menlo Park (☎ & fax ☎012/46 7318). Very comfortable B&B accommodation in the original home of eccentric artist Walter Batiss. Expect brightly painted floors, unusual decorations and a distinctly Greek feel. ④.

Hotel 224, corner of Leyds and Schoeman streets (☎012/44 5281, fax 44 3063). Single and double rooms in this fairly characterful mid-range hotel near the Union Buildings, with a restaurant and bar attached, and safe parking. ②.

Kia Ora Backpackers, 257 Jacob Maré St (☎012/322 4803, fax 322 4816, *kia-ora@global.co.za*). A neat, comfortable hostel with excellent doubles and average dorms in a well-positioned spot next door to Melrose House, with a bar featuring live music. ①–②.

La Maison, 235 Hilda St, Hatfield (☎012/43 4341, fax 342 1531). Very pleasant guesthouse with six immaculately tasteful rooms, lovely gardens and an outstanding restaurant. ⑥.

Malvern Guesthouse, 575 Schoeman St (☎ & fax ☎012/341 7212). Small B&B handy for Arcadia's restaurants, and popular with students. Rooms are clean, with shared bath, but no TV. ③.

Mazuri Backpackers, 503 Reitz St, Sunnyside (☎ & fax ☎012/343 7782, *bogbrush@pixie.co.za*). The most easy-going hostel in town, with dorms and doubles across two houses, a plunge pool and a friendly owner. ①.

Mutsago Guesthouse, 327 Festival St, Hatfield (☎012/43 7193, fax 43 7635). Good B&B with pretty rooms and a nice swimming pool, near the university and a large shopping centre. ④.

North South Backpackers, 355 Glyn St, Hatfield (☎012/362 0989, fax 362 0960, *northsouth@smartnet.co.za*). The best-positioned hostel for the lively Hatfield nightlife, with dorms and doubles, located in a large, quiet suburban house with a great garden and pool. ①–②.

Orange Court Lodge, corner of Vermeulen and Hamilton streets, Arcadia (☎012/326 6346, fax 326 2492). Self-catering suites in one of the oldest buildings in Pretoria. It's pleasant and secluded, despite being off a main road. Breakfast is available, and there's safe parking. ④.

Pretoria Backpackers, 34 Bourke St, Sunnyside (☎012/343 9754, fax 343 2524, *ptaback @hotmail.com*). Well-located for nightlife, and the knowledgeable owner runs the best tours of the city and surrounding attractions. The property, offering dorms and doubles, is a little cramped, and with so many backpackers about a pool would improve things. Offers a daily shuttle to Johannesburg International Airport (R50). ①–②.

Ronde Geluk, 570 Pretorius St, Arcadia (☎ & fax 012/341 9221). Wonderful thatched cottages sleeping two to four, hidden away in central Pretoria, each self-contained and beautifully decorated. Breakfast is included in the price. ③.

Victoria Hotel, corner of Scheiding and Paul Kruger streets (☎012/323 6052, fax 323 0843). Historic building opposite the railway station, once the railway workers' bar, now offering plush accommodation and often filled with upmarket travellers taking luxury trains to Cape Town. ⑦.

Word of Mouth, 430 Reitz St (☎012/343 7499, fax 343 9351, *wom@mweb.co.za*). Friendly but slightly down-market hostel with some wooden Wendy Houses in the garden masquerading as doubles. Best thing is *Drum and Art Lounge* drum workshop next door. ①–②.

The City

Pretoria's city centre is compact grid of wide, busy streets, and is easily explored on foot. Its central hub is **Church Square**, with other historic buildings and museums close by. To the north lie the vast Zoological Gardens, well worth a visit, while over in the east the Arcadia district is the site of the city's famous **Union Buildings**. Head south on any of the diagonal streets to explore **Sunnyside**, home to the city's friendliest street culture. Further east, **Hatfield**, close to Pretoria University, is where students and yuppies throng the latest bars and restaurants, as well as being the home of Pretoria's diplomats, who live in the swankiest houses in town. You need to travel 15km east out of town to find the sprawling township of **Mamelodi**; Pretoria's other major township, **Atteridgeville**, is equally far out of town to the west, off the N4, or R104, on the way to the Hartbeesport Dam and Sun City.

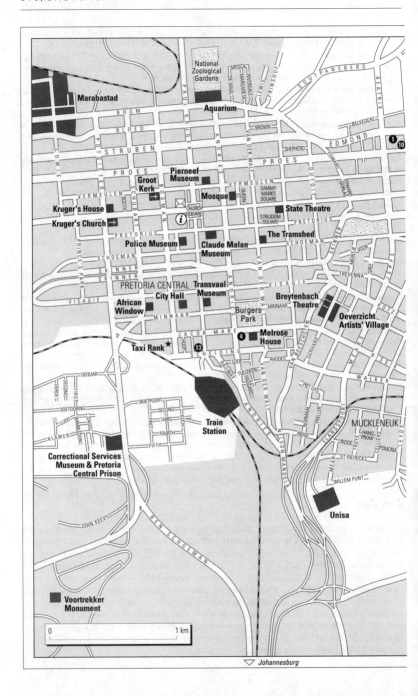

Marabastad

National Zoological Gardens

Aquarium

Groot Kerk

Pierneef Museum

Mosque

Kruger's House

Kruger's Church

State Theatre

The Tramshed

Police Museum

Claude Malan Museum

PRETORIA CENTRAL

African Window

City Hall

Transvaal Museum

Breytenbach Theatre

Burgers Park

Oeverzicht Artists' Village

Melrose House

Taxi Rank ★

Train Station

Correctional Services Museum & Pretoria Central Prison

MUCKLENEUK

Unisa

Voortrekker Monument

0   1 km

▽ *Johannesburg*

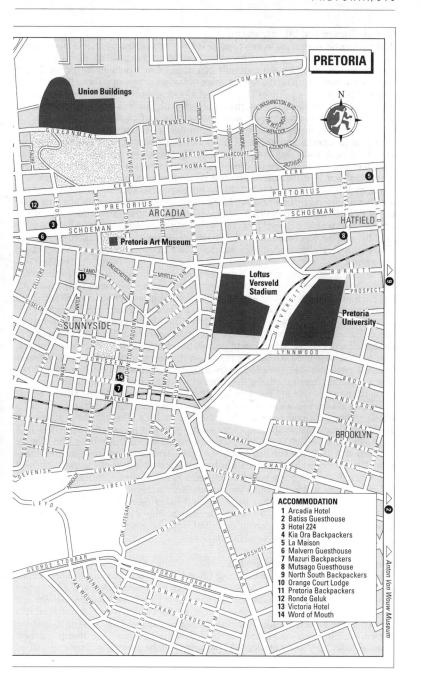

PRETORIA

N

Union Buildings

TOM JENKINS

S WASHINGTON BLVD

THE ROTUNDA

WENLOCK

PERIGO

EASTWOOD

CUSTODIAN

BALMORAL

DUMBARTON

COLROYN

ROTHSAY

GOVERNMENT

GEORGE

MERTON

THOMAS

PINE

EAST CLYFFE

BLACKWOOD

AUBRE

KERK

KERK

FESTIVAL

HILDA

PRETORIUS

PRETORIUS

LEYDS

WESSELS

ARCADIA

ORIENT

SCHOEMAN

HATFIELD

SCHOEMAN

BECKETT

TARENTAAL

ARCADIA

Pretoria Art Museum

PARK

PARK

BURNETT

TROYE

CELLIERS

LAND

LINDSCHOTEN

VALLEY

MYRTLE

ANTON

MAPLE

BRECHER

VILLA

KIRKNESS

UNIVERSITY

PROSPECT

Loftus
Versveld
Stadium

Pretoria
University

ESSELEN

BOURKE

WATER

SPUY

VERDOORN

BOND

SUNNYSIDE

LEYDS

DWARS

RELLY

JORISSEN

JOHNSTON

MELVILLE

RIVIER

COMPANY

HUGH

LYNNWOOD

BROOKS

REITZ

WALKER

JOHN

ORMOND

PHILLIP

ANDERSON

MURRAY

BEREA

MIDDELBERG

LOVEDAY

DOUGAL

SMITH

COLLEGE

MACKENZIE

BROOKLYN

RIDGE

KRUIN

MARAIS

CAMERON

MARAIS

WILLIAM

DEVENISH

LUKAS

ARNOLD

SIBELIUS

NICOLSON

CHARLES

LEYDS

DR LATEGAN

MACKIE

KOM NGN WILHELMINA

BOSHOFF

TOTIUS

GEORGE STORRAR

GEORGE STORRAR

VAN WOUW

WENNING

LANE

BRONKHORST

FRANS OERDER

EIPDOL

ESSEMA

ACCOMMODATION
1 Arcadia Hotel
2 Batiss Guesthouse
3 Hotel 224
4 Kia Ora Backpackers
5 La Maison
6 Malvern Guesthouse
7 Mazuri Backpackers
8 Mutsago Guesthouse
9 North South Backpackers
10 Orange Court Lodge
11 Pretoria Backpackers
12 Ronde Geluk
13 Victoria Hotel
14 Word of Mouth

Anton Van Wouw Museum

Church Square and the city centre

Attractive, pedestrianized **Church Square** is Pretoria's central point, and a good place to start exploring the city. It was here that Boer farmers *outspanned* their oxen when they came into town for the quarterly Nagmaal (Holy Communion) of the Dutch Reformed Church, turning the square temporarily into a campsite. Today this spot continues to be a meeting point for Pretorians of all races, many of whom you'll see lounging on the grass in the sun, gathering to protest with placards and singing, or simply watching it all go on while sipping coffee at the cultured *Café Riche*.

Nearly every important white meeting, protest or takeover the city has known happened in Church Square; the ZAR Vierkleur ("four colours") flag was lowered here in 1877 to make way for the Union Jack, only to rise again in 1881, after the British eviction from the republic; the British flag flew again in 1900 but was lowered for the last time in 1910; Paul Kruger was proclaimed head of state in the square four times, and 30,000 crammed it in 1904 for his memorial. Such historical resonances are viewed differently by Pretoria's black community, and the square's central **statue of Paul Kruger** – the work of Afrikaner sculptor Anton Van Wouw – is for many an unwanted relic of a dismal past. Van Wouw had to work fast: Kruger hated posing and the sculptor had little time with him. Nevertheless he still managed to produce this frighteningly miserable representation, set above four rugged Voortrekker archetypes.

The continental-style square is surrounded on all sides by some of the most impressive buildings in South Africa. Look out first for the old **Raadsaal** (parliament) on the southwest corner of the square, built in neo-Renaissance style in 1891, and still exuding the bourgeois respectability yearned for by the parliamentarians of the ZAR. Next door is the **Netherlands Bank Building**, now home of the tourist information office. Unbelievably, it took a gathering of 10,000 people in 1975 and five years of deliberation to reverse a decision to demolish this building and its two neighbours. The Art Nouveau **Café Riche** (see p.525), on the corner of Church Street, operates as an informal tourist information centre for the square, and you can buy a booklet or hire a cassette player explaining the history and architecture of the square.

On the opposite side of Church Street is the imposing **General Post Office**, beside which is a **Stamp Museum** (Mon–Fri 7.30am–4pm; free), which displays over half a million stamps, including a rare Cape Triangle of 1853. The grandiose **Palace of Justice**, on the northwest side of the square, was started in 1897, and used, half-completed, as a hospital for British troops during the second Anglo-Boer War. After its completion in 1902, the building was home to the Transvaal Supreme Court for many years. The new court is an ugly box which you will find sitting squatly in a street behind the Palace. It's worth going round to the back, as recent demolition has revealed the Palace's original rear facade and a fine balcony. Next to this is the **Reserve Bank** building, designed in distinctive style by Sir Herbert Baker (see p.498). Other buildings of note around the eastern and northern side of the square include the **Tudor Chambers**, built in neo-Tudor style in 1904, and the neoclassical **Standard Bank** building, built on the site of the old Grand Hotel.

Sammy Marks Square and around

Moving east from Church Square, along Church Street, will take you towards Sammy Marks Square. Just before you get there, a left turn into Queen Street and a further left turn along a passage-way halfway down the block reveals the unexpected site of a bright white **mosque** sitting askew of its surroundings so as to face Mecca. Pretoria's Muslims, who reportedly got on well with Kruger, acquired the site in 1896, and the current building was constructed in 1927 by Cape artisans. The mosque is now hemmed in by ugly tower blocks, but is somehow all the more indomitable for that.

Garish **Sammy Marks Square** itself is named after the founder of South African Breweries (SAB), who was a patron of the city. Apart from the chain stores, the only thing worth checking out here is the excellent **library** (Mon–Fri 8am–5.50pm, Sat 8am–12.50pm; ☎012/313 8956) geared to adult education, with every available space decked out in Pretoria's trademark purple.

Cross Church Street for a brief taste of ghastly **Strijdom Square**, dominated by a vast and horrific bust of the man himself, encased in a modernistic arch. Prime minister from 1954 to 1958, Strijdom strongly supported apartheid and was a firm believer in "white supremacy". Some say it's high time the statue was replaced by a memorial to the victims of the random shooting at minibus taxis here by a right-wing delinquent namesake, Barend Strijdom, in 1993.

Paul Kruger's House and around

To find **Paul Kruger's House** (Mon–Sat 8.30am–4pm, Sun & public holidays 11am–4pm; R5), head west along Church Street from Church Square, crossing Bosman and Schubart streets. Kruger's House was built in 1884 by the English-speaking Charles Clark, described by Kruger as one of his "tame Englishmen", who mixed his cement with milk instead of water. Inside, the museum is rather dull, though you may find some of Kruger's effects interesting, like his large collection of spittoons. The *stoep* (verandah) is the most famous feature of the house, for here the old president would sit and chat to any white who chose to join him. Out at the back is Kruger's private railway coach, built in 1898, which he used during the second Anglo-Boer War.

Opposite is a characteristically grim Reformed church known as **Kruger's Church**. You'll find the **Groot Kerk (Great Church)**, on the corner of Vermeulen and Bosman streets, more impressive. There's no need to go inside, but have a look at its strikingly ornate tower, one of the finest in the country.

A little further away, south along Bosman Street, then left into Pretorius Street and right into Volkstem Street, you will find the unmissably kitsch **Police Museum** (Mon–Fri 8am–3.30pm, Sat 8.30am–12.30pm, Sun 1.30–4.30pm; free). Amid the tacky re-creations of South African murders that made tabloid headlines, and scores of weapons old and new, are the latest exhibits, added since 1994, and by far the most interesting. You'll find re-creations of the 1961 Sharpeville shootings, the murder of Black Consciousness leader Steve Biko in 1977, the 1992 Bisho massacre, and the assassination of the ANC military leader Chris Hani in 1993. Each of these except the last were perpetrated or orchestrated by the police, and the exhibits are there to signal self-reflection and commitment to change.

Burgers Park and the Museum Mall

South from Church Square lies a precinct of museums and open spaces that has drawn complimentary comparisons with Washington DC's Smithsonian Institute. On Jacob Maré Street between Andries and Van der Walt streets is the restful **Burgers Park** (daily 8am–6pm; free), named after ineffective ZAR president Thomas Burgers, who ruled between 1873 and 1877. The park has a good botanic garden, a quirkily designed curator's house and a pavilion at its centre, once the preserve of brass bands and all-white tea parties, but now multiracial and a good place to relax. A tea room in the centre of the park, *Café Wien*, serves up undistinguished light meals and refreshments made up for by the pleasant surroundings.

Opposite the park's southern border, **Melrose House**, 275 Jacob Maré St (Tues–Sun 10am–5pm; moderate entry fee), is an overdecorated Victorian house with a wonderful conservatory, interesting exhibitions, and a great African arts and crafts shop. The house was built in 1884 for local businessman George Heys, who made his money running mailcoach services. Lord Kitchener used the house during the second

Anglo-Boer War, and the treaty of Vereeninging that ended hostilities was signed inside. Outside, a sumptuous tea garden serves up cakes and scones.

Head west of Burger Park along Minnaar Street, and then turn right into Paul Kruger Street and under a huge whale skeleton for the grand **Transvaal Museum** (Mon–Sat 9am–5pm, Sun 11am–5pm; moderate entry fee), Pretoria's oldest museum, dedicated to natural history. Among the huge number of stuffed animals, models of dinosaurs and displays aimed with kids in mind are wonderful fossil remains, some over one million years old. In the Austin Roberts Bird Hall, you'll find an informative exhibit on South Africa's many species of birds. For the dedicated, a permanent geological exhibition has as many rock samples as you could possibly wish for.

Opposite the museum at the far end of a series of fountains and well-tended flower beds is the **City Hall**, with its eclectic mix of Greek and Roman architectural styles, and two rather good statues of Andries and Marthinus Pretorius immediately outside. The next large block to the west is taken up by the latest addition to the Museum Mall, **African Window** (daily 9am–4pm; moderate entry fee), accessed from Visagie Street. This large, airy exhibition space has adopted a very modern attitude to the museum culture, with generous room given to temporary museums and interactive exhibits appealing to all ages. Permanent exhibitions include "Access to Power", which displays and explains San rock-art, and the engaging "People's Choice", where groups of local people, including township women's groups and schoolchildren, have been invited to select objects from the museum's vast collection of some 3 million pieces. There's also a coffee shop and an attractive craft shop.

North of Church Square

North of Church Square, busy Proes and Struben streets are filled with cut-price stores, black shoppers and minibus taxis heading for the townships. Watch out for the gangs who work these streets, as a number of tourists have been mugged here.

Head across Bloed and Boom streets for the **National Zoological Gardens** (daily 8am–5.30pm; moderate entry fee), which is spacious and surprisingly good, housing rare species of antelope, a white rhinoceros, and a wide selection of South American as well as African animals. It's well worth trying to book on one of the **night tours** (R30; ☎012/328 3265), starting at 6pm on Wednesdays, Fridays and Saturdays, when you'll see some of the zoo's freakiest creatures at their most active. Next door, the **Pretoria Aquarium** (daily 8am–5pm; moderate entry fee) is less impressive, but nonetheless has plenty of beasts, some very weird and highly poisonous. Hawkers sell curios outside, but you're better off heading a few blocks west for the bustling market at **Marabastad**, the city's first "non-white" area. While you're here, don't miss the intricately decorated Hindu **Mariammen Temple**, right next to the market.

Arcadia and the Union Buildings

Head east along Vermeulen or Church streets, and you'll soon reach the **Arcadia** district, where Pretoria's **Union Buildings**, the headquarters of the South African government, perch majestically on the main hill. Designed by Herbert Baker in 1910, allegedly to symbolize the union of Briton and Boer, the lashings of colonnades and lavish amphitheatre seem instead to glorify British imperial self-confidence. Nelson Mandela had an office inside, and the Buildings were famously the site of his inauguration in 1994. This was perhaps the first time their imperialist symbols were transformed, not least by the African praise-singers who delivered their odes from the amphitheatre, proclaiming Mandela as the latest in a long line of African heroes from Shaka to Hintsa, and beyond. You can walk around the buildings and their gardens, and if you're a particular enthusiast of Baker's work and the Union Buildings in particular, tours called The Baker's Dozen are run by the talkative Leone Jackson (around R50; ☎012/344 3197).

South of the Union Buildings, the **Pretoria Art Museum**, corner of Schoeman and Wessels streets (Tues & Thurs–Sat 10am–5pm, Wed 10am–8pm; small entry fee), houses an excellent selection of South African art and Dutch Masters, as well as some black artists, including Ephraim Ngatane. There is a small gallery (same hours; free) just beyond the main entrance which is worth popping into for its contemporary exhibitions and small café.

Sunnyside and Hatfield

Southeast of the centre, desegregated **Sunnyside** is one of the few areas of Pretoria that feels vaguely African, with lively street life, distinctive old houses and a multitude of cafés. Don't miss **Oeverzicht Artists' Village**, on the corner of Kotze and Gerard Moerdyk streets, a collection of attractive old cottages with interesting craft shops and restaurants. Nearby, **Breytenbach Theatre,** 137 Gerard Moerdyk St, said to be haunted by the ghosts of those who died there when it was a hospital for Germans, hosts mainly student productions. The tiny **Die Teaterhuise** is around the back of the street. **Esselen Street** is Sunnyside's busiest thoroughfare, brimming with restaurants, bars and street hawkers. Nearby, the **Loftus Versveld Stadium** hosts major rugby games.

Continuing east to **Hatfield**, **Pretoria University** houses a fantastic art collection, viewable by appointment only (☎012/420 3100). The collection includes seventeenth- and eighteenth-century furniture, Dutch Masters and beautiful ceramics from Europe and China. Some of the Chinese ceramics date back to the Han dynasty (206BC–221AD). The only art you can see without an appointment are the minimalist and metallic sculptures of Eduardo Villa in the Old University Library, which aren't really worth the effort. Otherwise, stroll to Park, Burnett and Hilda streets to reach a plethora of studenty cafés, bars and restaurants, which have developed in the last few years into Pretoria's livliest area, with the trendiest hangouts and nightlife.

To visit the elegant house and museum of acclaimed Afrikaner sculptor **Anton van Wouw**, 299 Clark St (Tues–Fri 10am–4pm, Sat 10am–noon; free), you'll need to head southeast of the university to the wealthy suburb of **Brooklyn**. Van Wouw was responsible for most of the brooding effigies of Afrikaner public figures from the 1890s to the Thirties that are scattered around the country, including the Kruger statue in Pretoria's Church Square (see p.520). His most famous work is the Voortrekker Monument, further south of the city (see below). The museum, designed by the celebrated architect Norman Eaton in 1938, houses a collection of his smaller pieces. Van Wouw's figures tend to be placed in rural settings, but here you'll find two striking, non-rural pieces, one of a mine worker and another showing an accused man, standing in the dock. Keep an eye out too for *The Guitar Player*, a feisty-looking woman strumming away with a trace of a smile on her face.

South to the Voortrekker Monument

Travelling south towards Johannesburg on Preller Road, you can't miss the enormous and head-shakingly ugly **UNISA**, South Africa's largest university. Over 300,000 students are enrolled here – though most of them are on correspondence courses. Inside, on the fifth floor, there's a very good **art gallery** (daily 10am–4pm; ☎012/429 3111; free), which hosts some of Pretoria's most innovative exhibitions, as well as a permanent collection exhibiting young South African talent of all races. Telephone in advance to make sure the curator is here.

On the outskirts of Pretoria, west of UNISA, the chilling **Correctional Services Museum** (Tues–Fri 9am–3pm, Sun 10am–3pm; free), at Pretoria Central Prison, is well worth a visit. Make for Potgieter Street, which runs vertically three blocks west of Church Square, and stay on it while it becomes the R101 to Johannesburg. You'll see the notorious prison, where many famous political prisoners were held (and many executed), on your right. Be prepared to walk past depressed-looking visiting relatives on your way in. Inside the museum you can see artworks made by prisoners, including a life-size statue of a destitute man crawling towards an expressionless prison warder, who has his arms outstretched, ready to correct him. There are also exhibits of knives concealed in Bibles and shoes, files in cakes and so forth. Most alarming by far are the group photos of various forbidding-looking prison warders through the ages, which seem a strange sort of propaganda for the prison service.

Continue out on the R101 and follow the signs to view the famous **Voortrekker Monument and Museum** (daily 9am–4.30pm; moderate entry fee). This striking, austere block of granite was built in 1940 to commemorate Boer victory over the Zulu nation at Blood River on December 16, 1838, and its symbolism is crushingly heavy-handed. The monument is enclosed by reliefs of ox wagons, with a large statue of a woman standing outside, shaking her fist at imaginary oppressors. Inside, a series of moving reliefs depict scenes from the Great Trek. Outside, hidden by some trees, are two pint-size replicas of the huts of Zulu kings Dingane and Cetswayo. Incidentally, the first ever Afrikaans pornographic magazine, *Loslyf*, created a sensation in 1995 when it used the monument as the backdrop to a centrefold spread, causing outrage among those Afrikaners who still make a pilgrimage here every December 16.

Eating and drinking

Pretoria has plenty of good **restaurants**, but prices, especially in the centre, tend to be high. If you're on a budget, head for the suburbs of Sunnyside and Hatfield, where the choice is wider. The city's top restaurants are mostly in Arcadia and the outer suburbs. **Cafés** are numerous and varied; you'll find particularly attractive ones in Hatfield. Pretoria is a drinking town and has a host of **bars** to meet demand. Forget the bland ones that fill the city centre, and head for those in Sunnyside or Hatfield. Segregation has started to break down, but most bars are predominantly white. The bulk of the black community's drinking is still done in the townships, where *shebeens* abound.

Restaurants

Bacini's, 216 Esselen St, Sunnyside (☎012/341 0689). Popular, inexpensive Italian restaurant, with reasonably tasty dishes.

Brasserie de Paris, 525 Duncan St, Hatfield (☎012/362 2247). Faithful reproduction of the classic Parisian café, with a pleasant terrace, spacious interior, moderate prices and a great menu. Closed Sat lunchtime & Sun.

Chagall's, 924 Park St, Hatfield (☎012/341 7511). Chic, expensive restaurant, with excellent food, wines to match, and a lovely setting a few kilometres out of town. Closed Sat lunchtime & Sun.

Die Werf, Plot 66, Olympus Rd, Pretoria East. A hearty selection of South African dishes at this popular, good-value restaurant.

Gerard Moerdyk, 752 Park St, Arcadia (☎012/344 4856). Beautifully prepared South African cuisine served at a price amidst lavish surroundings. Choose from ostrich, springbok pie and other intriguing dishes. Closed Sat lunchtime & Sun.

Hillside Tavern, Rynial Building, 320 The Hillside, Lynnwood (☎012/47 5119). Moderately priced restaurant, celebrated locally for its steaks.

Hong Kong, Shop 23, Brooklyn Mall, New Muckleneuk (☎012/46 9221). Reliable, mid-priced Chinese food in inauspicious surroundings.

La Madeleine, 258 Esselen St, Sunnyside (☎012/44 6076). Expensive, truly delicious dishes ranging from Provençale to quasi-Japanese. Booking essential. Closed Sat lunchtime & Sun

La Perla, 211 Skinner St (☎012/322 2759). In the city centre, serving classic, moderate-to-expensive European fish dishes like *bouillabaisse*, and line fish *grenobloise*. Closed Sat lunchtime & Sun.

Mostapha's, 478 Duncan St, Hatfield (☎012/342 3855). The fame of Mostapha, once chef to Moroccan royalty, spreads far across Gauteng. Tasty and moderately priced.

Safrika, Maroelana Shopping Centre, Maroelana St, Hazelwood (☎012/46 9269). Best African restaurant in Pretoria, though a little way from the centre, with plain decor but a wonderfully tasty and authentic buffet in the evening. Closed Mon & Sun.

Santorini, Brooklyn Plaza, 521 Fehrson St, Brooklyn (☎012/346 3672). Very decent, inexpensive Greek restaurant recently moved from busy Sunnyside to more refined Brooklyn.

Sirocco, 109 Gerard Moerdyk St, Sunnyside (☎012/341 3785). Restored Sunnyside house, providing an excellent setting for consistently good, moderately priced Mediterranean cuisine.

Bars and cafés

Café Riche, 2 Church Square West, city centre (☎012/328 3173). One of the finest cafés in the country, with a Continental atmosphere and a quirky events programme, including late-night philosophical discussions and Sunday brunch on Church Square. Daily 6am–midnight.

Ed's Diner, Hatfield Galleries, Burnett St, Hatfield. Fifties nostalgia identical to other *Ed's Diners* around the world, heaving with students in the evening when the in-house disco cranks up.

The Grapevine, 204 Sunnyside Galleries, Esselen St, Sunnyside. About the best bar on the street, with generally mellow and cheerful regulars.

Keg and Hound, 107 Arcadia St, Hatfield. Bearable themed British pub. Good selection of beers.

News Café, Hatfield Square, Burnett St, Hatfield. Popular bar and café in the heart of Hatfield, serving breakfasts and brunches from 9.30am at weekends, and decent food well into the night all week.

Star City Disco, corner of Bosman and Jacob Maré streets, near the bus station. Major black hangout, especially at weekends, when good music and beer flow freely. Take a cab there and back.

Tings and Times, Hatfield Galleries, Burnett St, Hatfield. One of Pretoria's happening bars, popular with students, but also a wider clientele who come for the easy-going style, the vibe, and great reggae.

Nightlife and entertainment

Pretoria lacks the rich **arts and music** scene of Johannesburg, and on weekends that's where locals tend to head. However, if you're here on a brief visit, you should find enough to satisfy, especially in **Sunnyside**, where Esselen Street and the surrounding area have the city's highest concentration of **nightclubs** and **music venues**. This is also where you'll find a thriving number of gay clubs, which work hard to keep Pretoria's gay community in the city over the weekend. Things are very different in Mamelodi and Atteridgeville, where plenty of small clubs play South African and soul sounds.

Theatre and cinema

Pretoria's main venue for **theatre**, **opera** and **classical concerts** is the State Theatre, Church St (☎012/322 1665), which also has a good workshop. Nearby in Church Square, the Basement Theatre below *Café Riche* (☎012/328 3173) is an elegant, compact venue with a good record of adventurous productions. For lively student productions, head for the Breytenbach, Gerard Moerdyk St, Sunnyside (☎012/44 4834), beside the Oeverzicht Artists' Village. Die Teaterhuise, off Gerard Moerdyk St, Sunnyside (☎012/322 1665), is a tiny venue still establishing itself but promising great things.

Pretoria's **cinemas** carry the typical selection of Hollywood fare, and the city is amongst the first to receive new releases. For big releases, the Nu-Metro in Sammy Marks Square (☎012/326 6614) is reliable, and you'll find branches of Ster-Kinekor at Beatrix Street in Arcadia (☎012/341 7568), and Jeppe Street in Sunnyside (☎012/44 4069). Back in the centre, on the corner of Schoeman and Van der Walt streets, the cinema in The Tramshed (☎012/320 4300) screens decent non-mainstream films. *The Pretoria News* is good for theatre and cinema **listings**, while the national *Mail & Guardian* is covers the visual arts, theatre and major musical events.

Live music and clubs

Bootleggers, Glenwood Centre, Glenwood Rd, Lynnwood Glen (☎012/47 2025). Live music by frequently dodgy acts, so phone first.

Crossroads Blues Bar, The Tramshed (upper level), corner of Schoeman and Van der Walt streets (☎012/322 3263). Hip, downtown venue, in the same complex as the cinema, hosting rock and blues bands.

DNA, 600 Van der Walt St. Popular Friday night club playing funk and progressive house. On Saturday night, Orange plays garage and hard house.

House of Blues, corner of Gerhard Moerdyck and Kotze streets, Sunnyside (☎012/322 5400). Relaxed, arty bar and venue for live jazz, folk and world music on Wed & Sat night.

Tequila Sunrise Café, Village Centre, Esselen St, Sunnyside. Nice little venue featuring young bands. Musical proficiency isn't a high point here, but there's usually a good vibe.

Upstairs at Morgan's, Burnett St, Hatfield (☎012/362 6610). Live music Mon–Sat, from some of South Africa's hottest bands to run-of-the-mill fare. Frequent party nights, promotions, and popular with students.

The Yearling, corner of Rissik and Mears streets, Sunnyside. Latest contender for the title of flashest and busiest gay club in town, with guest DJs starring at weekends.

The Viper Room, 57 Esselen St, Sunnyside. Occasional venue for live music, but better known as an alternative club.

Listings

American Express 4 Brooklyn Mall, 338 Bronkhorst St, New Muckleneuk (travel section: Mon–Fri 8.30am–5pm; foreign exchange: Mon–Fri 9am–4.30pm; ☎012/346 3580, after hours 082/901 5910).

Banks Most banks are around Church Square and along Church St.

Buses North Link Transport (☎012/315 2333 or 315 3481).

Bookshops Exclusive Books, Sunnypark Centre, Esselen St, Sunnyside (☎012/44 1118) is the best.

Camping/hiking Trappers Trading, 79 Sanlam Centre, 252 Andries St (☎012/320 0247), is the best place in town to buy outdoor and camping gear.

Car rental Avis, 70 Schoeman St (☎012/325 1490); Budget, 456 Church St East, Arcadia (☎012/323 3658); Dolphin, Orange Court Lodge, Vermeulen St (☎012/326 3715); Imperial, corner of Pretorius and Potgieter streets (☎012/323 3259); and Tempest, 186 Struben St (☎012/324 5007).

Embassies and consulates Australia, 292 Orient St, Arcadia (☎012/342 3740); Canada, 1103 Arcadia St, Hatfield (☎012/422 3000); Ireland, Tulbagh Park, 1234 Church St, Colbyn (☎012/342 5062); Lesotho, 343 Pretorius St, Momentum Centre, 6th floor, West Tower (☎012/322 6090); Malawi, 770 Government Ave, Arcadia (☎012/342 0146); Mozambique, 199 Beckett St, Arcadia (☎012/343 7840); Namibia, 702 Church St, Arcadia (☎012/344 5992); Swaziland, Infotech Building, 1090 Arcadia St, Arcadia (☎012/324 5782); UK, 255 Hill St, Arcadia (☎012/43 3121); USA, 877 Pretorius St, Arcadia (☎012/342 1048); Zambia, 353 Sanlam Building, Festival St, Hatfield (☎012/342 1541); Zimbabwe, 798 Merton St, Arcadia (☎012/342 5125).

Emergencies Ambulance ☎012/644 4515; Fire ☎012/323 2781; Police ☎10111 or 326 2222; Rape Crisis ☎0800/012 322.

Flea markets Hatfield Flea Market, Hatfield Plaza, every Sun, is Pretoria's best flea market, with crafts, bric-a-brac and lively banter.

Hospitals Hospitals with 24hr casualty services include Pretoria Academical Hospital, Doctor Savage Rd (☎012/329 1111); Pretoria West, Trans Oranje Rd (☎012/386 5111); and the private Starcare Muelmed, 577 Pretorius St, Arcadia (☎012/44 2362).

Intercity buses Intercape (☎012/654 4114), Greyhound (☎012/323 1154) and Translux (☎012/315 2333) have their terminal and office beside the train station. North Link Transport (☎012/323 0379), run buses to Pietersburg and the north from Bosman St, between Church and Pretorius streets.

Internet cafés *Net Café*, Hatfield Square, Prospect St, Hatfield (Mon–Sat 10am–3am; Sun 10am–2am; *www.netcafe.co.za*); *Odyssey*, corner of Burnett and Festival streets, Hatfield; *Tramshed Internet Café*, Tramshed Shopping Centre, Schoeman St (daily 9am–11pm).

Laundries De Luxe Drycleaners, 479 Pretorius St, city centre (☎012/44 2251).

Pharmacies Berea, 8 Rissik St, Sunnyside (☎012/44 7109); Station, 509 Paul Kruger St (☎012/323 1238); and in every shopping mall.

Police The central police station is on the corner of Pretorius and Bosman streets (☎012/326 2222).

Taxis The best local firm is Rixi Mini Cabs (☎012/325 8072); others include City Taxis (☎012/321 5742); and Five Star (☎012/320 7513).

Tours Packers Safaris (☎012/343 9754), based at *Pretoria Backpackers*, run the best budget tours of the city, as well as trips to Sun City and an Ndebele Village. Walking Treks & Tours (☎012/542 2641) offer walks around Church Square and the city centre. Yakhe Tours & Safari (☎012/800 4198 or 083/727 9899), run by Pretoria's first registered black guide, do day and night trips to Mamelodi township, plus general and jazz tours.

Train information For the half-hourly service to Johannesburg, phone ☎012/315 2268. The luxurious Blue Train runs to Cape Town on Tues, Thurs & Sat, via Jo'burg (☎012/315 2436), while the even more sumptuous Rovos Rail Trains (☎012/323 6052) travel to Cape Town, via Jo'burg, and Victoria Falls.

Around Pretoria

The most absorbing sight around Pretoria is **Doornkloof Farm**, former home of Prime Minister Jan Smuts. East of Pretoria, the mining town of **Cullinan** harks back to the pioneering days of diamond prospecting a century ago, while the **Tswaing meteorite crater** and nearby **Mapoch Ndebele Village** are efforts by disadvantaged communities to create a worthwhile tourist attraction in their area; to the west. however, the **Hartbeesport Dam** and nearby **Lesedi Cultural Village** have become rather unfortunate victims of their own popularity.

Doornkloof Farm and Rietvlei Nature Reserve

Doornkloof Farm in Irene, just south of Pretoria, was once the home of **Jan Smuts**. The museum here (Mon–Fri 9.30am–4.30pm, Sat & Sun 9.30am–5pm; moderate entry fee), tends toward hagiography but does shed some light on one of South Africa's most enigmatic politicians (see box, p.229). The massive library heralds his intellectual range and numerous mementos confirm his internationalism. Other displays focus on him as one of the most successful commanders of Afrikaner forces during the Anglo-Boer Wars. Also worthwhile is the 2.5km Oubas Trail from the house to the top of a nearby *koppie*, a walk the nature-loving Smuts took every day. To get to the museum, travel south from Pretoria on the M18 or R21 for about 20km, and take the turn-off to Irene.

The **Rietvlei Nature Reserve** (Mon–Fri 8am–6pm, Sun 6am–6pm; R10), on the other side of the R21, is unspectacular but does at least offer Burchell's zebra, rhino and antelope, and plenty of birdlife.

Cullinan

Popular with tourist coaches, but worth considering if you're not visiting Kimberley, **CULLINAN** lies 50km east of Pretoria. It was in the town's Premier Mine, still working today, that the world's largest diamond, the 3106-carat Star of Africa, was discovered in 1905. The De Beers mine dominates the small town, but the oldest buildings, many from the turn of the century, are being used to cater to the swarming tourists, preserving a leafy, cultured atmosphere. Unless you take a **surface tour** of the mine (Mon–Fri 10.30am & 2pm, Sat 10.30am; R30) there isn't much to do other than wander around, though a couple of pleasant places to **eat** include the *Station Steakhouse* in the old railway station. You can **stay** at *The Oak House* (☎01213/40083; ④), Cullinan's second-oldest building, attractively set on Oak Avenue, leading up to the mine.

Tswaing Crater and Mapoch Ndebele Village

Some 40km north of Pretoria, located off the M35, **Tswaing Crater** (daily 7.30am–3pm; moderate entry fee) is one of the youngest and best-preserved meteorite craters in the world, a five-hundred-metre-wide depression created around 220,000 years ago. Tswaing means "place of salt" in Tswana, and the rich deposits of salt and soda around the edge of the shallow crater lake have attracted people from earliest times; artefacts up to 150,000 years old have been discovered here. A simple visitors' centre marks the start of a seven-kilometre trail to the crater and back, while a shorter walk goes to a viewpoint on the crater rim.

Ten kilometres west of Tswaing is **Mapoch Ndebele Village** (daily 10am–4pm; moderate entry fee), where the houses and enclosures are painted with the colourful geometric patterns for which the Ndebele are famous, often incorporating modern aspects such as telephones and the South African flag. These, and the equally colourful beadwork, both among South Africa's most distinctive art forms, are always done by women. Unlike other Ndebele villages, Mapoch is relatively uncommercialized, and little attempt is made to cover up the less traditional parts of the village. You are expected to pay for a guide (around R10–20) in addition to the admission charge.

Hartbeespoort Dam and Lesedi Cultural Village

In the Magaliesberg mountains west of Pretoria, the man-made **Hartbeespoort Dam** has the potential to be a pleasant escape from the urban sprawl of Gauteng. Unfortunately, large numbers of Gauteng's inhabitants have already had the idea, and the dam and its surrounds have been thoroughly mauled by camping and picnic sites, animal parks, cableways, mini-resorts and endless ranks of arts and craft emporiums. At weekends, the mid-week jams of Sandton and Randburg are simply transferred to the countryside, and petrol-heads scream up and down the dam on jet skis in much the same way as they do the the M1 in urban 4WDs.

Slightly more interesting, though hardly more inspiring, **Lesedi Cultural Village**, off the R512 south of Hartbeespoort, crams four cultural villages into one bewildering experience, with the Zulu, Pedi, Xhosa and Basotho all represented. The steady flow of tourists and their money ensures that the huts, corals, costumes and displays are lively and colourful. You can join a **traditional African feast** (lunch or dinner), with post-prandial singing and dancing, and **stay a night** with a Lesedi family (☎01205/51394; ④).

travel details

Trains

Johannesburg to: Bloemfontein (1 daily; 13hr 20min); Cape Town (1 daily; 29hr 30min); Durban (1 daily; 13hr 30min); East London (1 daily; 19hr 45min); Kimberley (1 daily; 8hr 15min); Messina (1 daily; 15 hr); Nelspruit (1 daily; 9hr 45min); Port Elizabeth (1 daily; 20 hr); Pretoria (32 daily; 1hr 30min).

Pretoria to: Bloemfontein (1 daily; 14hr 50min); Cape Town (1 daily; 28hr); Johannesburg (32 daily; 1hr 30min); Kimberley (1 daily; 10hr 35min); Messina (1 daily; 14 hr); Nelspruit (1 daily; 8hr 20min).

Buses

Johannesburg to: Bloemfontein (3–4 daily; 5–6hr); Cape Town (3–5 daily; 16–18hr); Durban (6 daily; 8–11hr); East London (1 daily; 11hr 30min); Kimberley (3–4 daily; 6–8hr); King William's Town (2 daily; 12hr 15min); Klerksdorp (3–5 daily; 2–4hr); Knysna (2–3 daily; 14–16hr); Kuruman (1 Tues, Thurs, Fri & Sun; 8hr 15min); Ladysmith (1 daily; 6hr 30min); Louis Trichardt (1 Tues, Thurs, Fri & Sun; 4hr 15min); Mossel Bay (1–2 daily; 14hr 30min); Nelspruit (1 daily; 5hr); Newcastle (1 daily; 4hr 45min); Oudtshoorn (1–2 daily; 13hr); Pietermaritzburg (7 daily; 6–8hr); Pietersburg (1–2 daily except Sat; 3hr 45min); Plettenberg Bay (1 Tues & Fri; 15hr 30min); Port Elizabeth (2–4 daily; 13–15hr); Potchefstroom (1–3 daily; 1hr 30min); Pretoria (over 70 daily; 1hr); Queenstown (2 daily; 10hr); Rustenburg (1 daily; 2hr); Umtata (1 Mon, Wed, Fri & Sun; 12hr 45min).

Pretoria to: Aliwal North (2 daily; 9hr); Beaufort West (3–5 daily; 12–13hr); Bloemfontein (3–4 daily; 6–7hr); Cape Town (3–5 daily; 17hr); Durban (6 daily; 9hr); East London (1 daily; 12hr 30min); Ermelo (1 daily; 4hr 20min); George (1–2 daily; 16hr); Graaff-Reinet (2 daily Mon–Sat; 11hr 45min); Harrismith (1 daily; 4hr 45min); Johannesburg (over 70 daily; 1hr); Kimberley (3–4 daily; 7hr); King William's Town (2 daily; 13hr 25min); Klerksdorp (3–5 daily; 3hr–4hr 30min); Knysna (2–3 daily; 16hr); Kuruman (1 Tues, Thurs, Fri & Sun; 9hr 15min); Ladysmith (1 daily; 7hr 30min); Louis Trichardt (1 Tues, Thurs, Fri & Sun; 5hr 15min); Mossel Bay (1–2 daily; 15hr 35min); Nelspruit (1 daily; 4hr); Newcastle (1 daily; 4hr 45min); Oudtshoorn (1–2 daily; 14hr); Pietermaritzburg (7 daily; 7hr 15min); Pietersburg (1–2 daily except Sat; 3hr); Plettenberg Bay (1 Tues & Fri; 16hr 30min); Port Elizabeth (2–4 daily; 16hr); Potchefstroom (1–3 daily; 2hr 30min);

Queenstown (2 daily; 10–11hr); Umtata (1 Mon, Wed, Fri & Sun; 13hr 45min).

Flights

Johannesburg is a major international point of entry into South Africa, with flights from all around the world. The city is also an important centre of the domestic network, and you can fly to virtually anywhere in the country from here. Services include:

Johannesburg to: Bloemfontein (6 daily; 1hr 10min); Cape Town (20–26 daily; 2hr); Durban (17–22 daily; 1hr); East London (3 daily; 1hr 25min); Hoedspruit (1 daily; 1hr); Kimberley (4 daily; 1hr 15min); Manzini (1 daily except Thurs & Sun; 1hr); Mmabatho (1 Mon–Fri; 1hr); Nelspruit (3–6 daily; 1hr 50min); Pietersburg (3 daily Mon–Fri, 1 daily Sat & Sun; 50 mins) Port Elizabeth (6–9 daily; 1hr 40min); Upington (1 daily Mon–Sat; 1hr 50min).

CHAPTER EIGHT

NORTHWEST PROVINCE

S outh Africa's **Northwest Province** is one of the country's most-visited but least-understood regions – renowned, among tourists at least, for the famously vulgar **Sun City** resort and Big Five **Pilanesberg Game Reserve**, but not much else. Few people venture beyond these attractions to explore this area in greater depth; consequently, it can be curiously rewarding to do so. There's a myriad of little *dorps* scattered throughout the region where few whites are fluent in English, and most blacks speak only Tswana. Outside the main cities, the old-fashioned hospitality you'll encounter, along with the stillness and tranquillity in the endless stretches of grassland and fields of *mielies* (sweetcorn) are a refreshing change after hectic Johannesburg.

Northwest Province extends west from Gauteng to the Botswana border and the Kalahari desert. Along the province's eastern flank, essentially dividing Northwest from Gauteng, loom the **Magaliesberg Mountains**, one hundred times older than the Himalayas and these days dotted with holiday resorts for nature-starved Jo'burgers. If you're driving from Johannesburg to Cape Town and can afford a bit of meandering, try taking the **N12** through Northwest via Kimberley (in Northern Cape); the road follows the Vaal River for hundreds of miles, and once you're past uninspiring **Potchefstroom** and **Klerksdorp**, a detour to the riverbanks provides a lovely breather, particularly to **Bloemhof** for its quiet nature reserve which teems with birdlife. The province also has a healthy number of **game lodges**, where, depending on your budget, you can view game from a luxurious verandah, or camp in the bushveld under the stars.

The N4 from Pretoria will lead you to **Rustenburg** and its windswept **nature reserve**, where you can hike high enough to gaze down onto the shimmering plains beneath. **Groot Marico**, further west, is a friendly *dorp* with powerful home-brews and laid-back people to share them with. Nearby, the **Madikwe Game Reserve** is set to become one of South Africa's finest wildlife spots.

Relentless sun alleviated only by torrential rain makes summer in Northwest something of an endurance test: aim to come here in spring or autumn. Camping is especially rewarding in this part of South Africa; pitching a tent in the stillness of the *veld* allows you to savour the sense of timelessness before you head off once more.

Some history

San hunter-gatherers were Northwest's first inhabitants: they were displaced some one thousand years ago by Iron Age peoples from the north, who pitched their first settlements on low ground near watercourses. By the sixteenth century, these settlements had developed into stone-walled towns on hilltops; the largest, Karechuenya (near Madikwe), was estimated by a Scottish observer in 1820 to have at least 20,000 inhabitants – more than Cape Town had at that time. By the nineteenth century, the dominance of the Rolong, Taung, Tlhaping and Tlokwa clans was established. European observers classified them all as **Tswana**, but it's unclear whether these people regarded themselves as very different from people further east classified as "Sotho".

The outbreak of intense **inter-clan violence** in the early 1800s was due to displacements caused by white settler expansion, and the new availability of firearms. Victory went to those who made alliance with the new arrivals, whether **Griqua** from the Northern Cape, or **Afrikaners** from further south. The Tlhaping were soon driven out, eventually finding their way to Zambia. Mzilikazi's Ndebele ruled the region in the 1820s and 1830s, but they too were forced out, this time to modern Zimbabwe. The victories of the remaining clans were short-lived: their Griqua and Afrikaner allies soon evicted them from their land and forced them into service.

Potchefstroom and **Klerksdorp** were the first towns established here by the Afrikaners, and more followed, each forming the nucleus for a quarrelsome ministate. In 1860 these mini-states amalgamated to form the **South African Republic** (ZAR), with Pretoria as its capital. The first Anglo-Boer War raged from 1877 until British defeat in 1881, with most of the province unaffected. In 1885, the British successfully fought the Afrikaners of the Goshen republic near Mmabatho and established the protectorate of north and south Bechuanaland – the north later became Botswana, while the south was annexed to the Cape Colony by Cecil Rhodes in 1895. British intervention meant that some land remaining in Tswana hands stayed that way, but by then the clans had lost almost everything. When **gold** was discovered on the Witwaters and and around Klerksdorp, Tswana men left in droves to work in the mines.

Of far greater impact was the **second Anglo-Boer War** (1899–1902). As well as the celebrated **siege of Mafikeng**, where British and Tswana forces held out for 217 days against Afrikaner troops there were protracted and nasty skirmishes up and down the Vaal River. Both Afrikaner and Tswana had their lands torched, and many were thrown into concentration camps by the dreaded Lord Kitchener.

The Union Treaty of 1910 left the province as the western part of the Transvaal, firmly in Afrikaner hands. Its smaller *dorps* soon became bywords for rural racism, epitomized in the 1980s by the fascistic AWB led by **Eugene Terreblanche**, whose power base was here. The migration of so many Tswana men and the lack of industrial development impeded the growth of a black working class in the province, which is why Northwest played a relatively minor role in the national struggle against apartheid.

The **Bophuthatswana** *bantustan* – or "Bop" – was created in 1977 out of the old "native reserves", the poor-quality land into which Tswana had been forced. Far from being a long-awaited "homeland" for blacks, Bop proved to be a confusing amalgamation of enclaves, ruled by the corrupt **Lucas Mangope**, who grew rich on the revenues from **Sol Kerzner**'s casinos in Sun City and the discovery of platinum. Bophuthatswana's short life came to an end with the elections of 1994, but its legacy lives on in the form of its notoriously corrupt civil servants, many of whom have kept their jobs in the new regime. Since Bop's capital, **Mmabatho**, has been absorbed into Mafikeng, the capital of Northwest, these people have found the transition an easy one, and whilst there have not yet been scandals on a par with the Eastern Cape (which absorbed two *bantustans*), it is an ironic outcome, particularly for those who risked their lives fighting the Mangope regime.

The Magaliesberg

Given that large parts of the province are empty and flat, Northwest's most distinctive asset is the **Magaliesberg mountain range**, which gets its name from the Tswana chief **Mogale** of the Kwena clan. Kwena people lived here from the seventeenth century until 1825, when most of them were forced out by the Ndebele chief Mzilikazi.

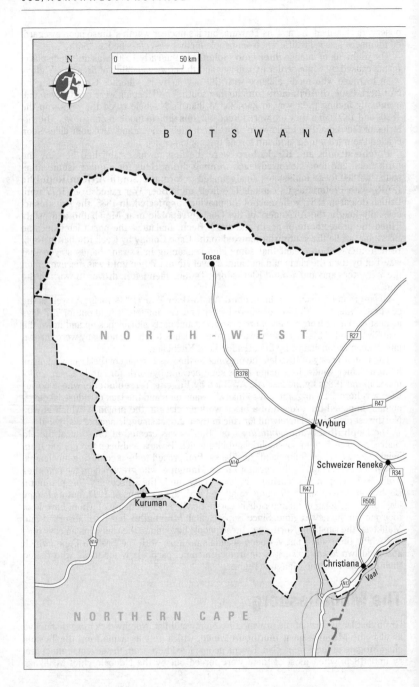

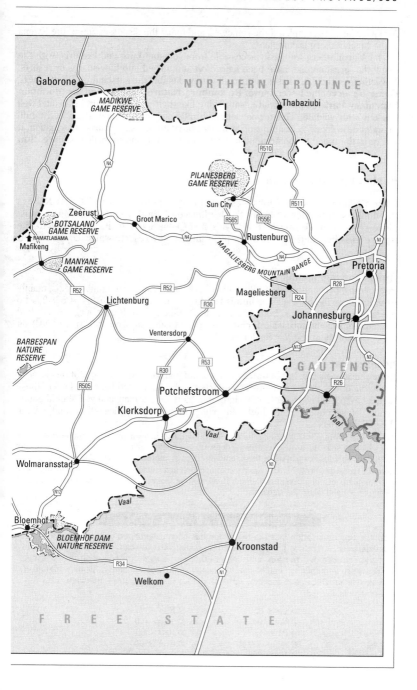

Afrikaner farmers completed the removals, and today the dispossession of the Kwena in the Magaliesberg is complete.

The Magaliesberg are easily accessible from Johannesburg and Pretoria, with the result that great chunks have been fenced off and turned into time-shares or resorts. Nevertheless, there are oases of unspoilt nature, notably the outstanding **Pilanesberg Game Reserve**, the lesser-known **Rustenburg Nature Reserve** and the **Mountain Sanctuary Park**, all preserved in something like their previous natural state and well stocked with wildlife. The towns dotted throughout the mountains are fairly dull, though you're likely to want to stop at **Rustenburg** for its useful tourist information. If you're in the mood for some mind-boggling architecture and touristic opulence, **Sun City** provides the perfect gateway to Pilanesberg.

Rustenburg and around

Some 120km northwest of Johannesburg, the mining town of **RUSTENBURG** has the dubious distinction of being the birthplace of **Paul Kruger**, the ZAR's most famous president. However, the town's main appeal lies in its proximity to the **nature reserve**, and for the many pleasant country resorts which lie in the surrounding hills.

Arrival and information
Public transport connections to Rustenburg are poor. Apart from minibus taxis, mainly from Pretoria, the only regular **bus** is run by Elwierda Tours (☎012/664 5880), who operate a daily service from Pretoria to Mafikeng via Rustenburg. You'll find Rustenburg's useful **tourist information office** (daily 8am–7pm; ☎014/597 0904) on the corner of Kloof and Van Staden streets.

Accommodation
Rustenburg has a handful of **hotels** in town, but you'll get the most out of this area by staying in one of the many **country resorts** nearby (and listed below). Many of these do not have street addresses; we've indicated them on our map, and you should phone before you set out. Avoid the B&Bs advertised in the tourist office – they tend to be in the dull suburbs.

Amble Inn (☎014/534 0608). Self-catering chalets southeast of town, in a pretty mountainside setting which, despite the owners' enormous dogs, is very restful. Follow the N4 to Pretoria, turning right at the sign for Rex and left at the Kromriver turn-off; continue for about 10km. ②.

Ananda Hotel (☎014/597 3875). Cosy accommodation in a fantastic spot, with a variety of sports, a swimming pool and a decent restaurant. Head west on Malan Road, and at the T-junction out of town turn left and follow the signs. ④.

ACCOMMODATION PRICE CODES

All the accommodation listed in the Guide has been categorized into one of nine price bands, as set out below. The rates quoted represent what you can expect to pay for much of the summer **per person**, and unless otherwise stated, are based on two sharing. Rooms are generally en suite. Expect prices in some areas to be significantly higher in peak season (Dec–Jan & Easter), and look out for discounts during the winter. For further details, see p.33.

① up to R50	⑥ R250–300
② R50–100	⑦ R300–400
③ R100–150	⑧ R400–500
④ R150–200	⑨ over R500
⑤ R200–250	

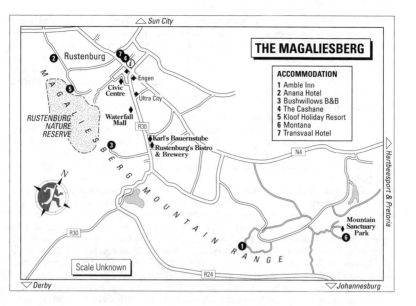

Bushwillows B&B Waterkloof Farm, south of town off the R24 (☎ & fax 014/537 2333). Attractive, well-run B&B, with a pool, on a farm beside the nature reserve 10km from Rustenburg town centre. ③.

The Cashane, corner of Steen and Van Staden streets (☎014/592 8541). One of the two hotels in the centre of town, and offering comfortable rooms with TV. There's a reasonable restaurant attached, but no pool. ③.

Kloof Holiday Resort (☎014/594 1037). Uninspiring housing estate layout, made up for by the magnificent hill towering above, which is within hiking distance. During school holidays the resort gets packed. The F chalets are the nicest and cheapest. Follow the directions for *Ananda* (opposite). ③.

Montana (☎014/534 0113). Eight self-contained cottages sleeping two to four on a long, thin, hikeable strip of the Magaliesberg. Cottages 6 and 7 have the best views. Follow the N4 to Pretoria, turning right at the sign for Rex and left at the Kromriver turn-off; continue for about 20km. ④.

Transvaal, 33 Prinsloo St (☎014/592 9351). Pleasant enough hotel in town, but with a loud disco downstairs that throbs with music all night on Fri and Sat. ②.

The Town and around

There's not much to see in Rustenburg itself, apart from a compelling **Dutch Reformed Church** on Burger Street, and a mediocre **museum** (Mon–Fri 8.30am–4.30pm, Sat 9am–1pm, Sun 3–5pm; free), which contains a battered old ZAR flag.

Some 4km southwest of town, **Rustenburg Nature Reserve** (Mon–Fri 7.30am–4pm, Sat & Sun 10am–1pm; small entry fee; ☎014/533 2050) spans a spectacular portion of the Magaliesberg, and offers sweeping views and great hikes over terrain spotted with rock formations created by millennia of erosion. You'll find dry *veld* too, and streams coursing through the valleys that have generated a lush botany all of their own. Scattered around the reserve are aloes indigenous to the Magaliesberg, and the discreet *frithiapulchra*, a succulent with only its leaf tips exposed, flowering between November and March. Rustenburg is home to a host of **antelopes** – klipspringer, mountain reedbuck, sable and impala – and also **zebras**, and the many hilly crags are perfect for predatory birds – keep a lookout for the rare **black eagle** and **Cape vulture**, as well as parrots and paradise flycatchers.

The reserve can be explored on a day- or overnight hike. For **day-hikes**, head south out of town on Wolmarans Street and, some way down, take the left turn into Boekenhout Street, which leads to the reserve gate. From here, the road winds dramatically up to the mountaintop, where you'll find the **visitors' centre**, with useful maps and information on hikes and trails, as well as **camping** (①) and *braai* facilities. The three-hour "Peglerae" interpretive trail takes in most of the reserve's best features, and the Parks Board puts out a good booklet to go with it.

To hike **overnight** at weekends you must book in advance, but during the week overnight huts are often available at short notice. Make for the **northern gate** by heading south out of Rustenburg on Smit Street, turning right some way down onto Wildevy Street, and then following the road to the gate. The huts have firewood and cooking utensils, but you bring the food. The hikes last two days and two nights, with a leisurely nine-kilometre walk on the first day and, slightly more strenuous, a twelve-kilometre one on the second.

Smaller than Rustenburg Nature Reserve, but a gem nonetheless, **Mountain Sanctuary Park** (March–Aug 8am–5.30pm; Sept–Feb 8am–6.30pm; entry fee; ☎014/534 0114), about 50km east of Rustenburg, has been allowed to return to a wilderness state, and is dotted with bilharzia-free streams safe for swimming in, and spectacular *kloofs* and gullies. You'll find klipspringer, rhebok and duiker wandering freely, and thousands of birds flying overhead. Chalets (②) and caravans (①) are available for **overnight stays**, but bring your own bedding. There's an extraordinary **swimming pool** by the caravans, which gives the impression that you're on the edge of a precipice as you look out into the valley below. The simplest way to **get to the park** is to take the N4 as far as the Marikana turn-off, and then turn right (instead of left to Marikana). Once on this road, take the second dirt-track turning on your left and continue for about 3km.

Boekenhoutfontein Farm (Mon–Sat 8am–1pm, 2–5pm, Sun 9am–1pm, 2–5pm; small entry fee), home of Paul Kruger, lies some way out of town, signposted 20km north of the town – a short way from the R565, on the way to Sun City. Built in 1875, this is a plain house with flamboyant Victorian wallpaper. The main exhibits are the Kruger family Bible and grim-faced portraits of his clan.

Eating and drinking

Eating in the centre of Rustenburg is limited to a snack or grill; for anything more substantial, the obvious place to head is the new Waterfall Mall, on the edge of town along the R30 (signposted as the Johannesburg road), where the predictable range of pizza/pasta restaurants and steakhouses captivates locals. A little further out on the same road, the more individual *Karl's Bauernstube* (closed Mon, Sat lunch & Sun evening) serves up delicious Austrian and German food and beers and is reasonably priced, while *Rustenburg's Bistro & Brewery* next door is essentially a drinking establishment, but offers reasonable meals.

Sun City

A surreal pocket of concrete and tinkling gaming machines in the endless bushveld of the northwest, **SUN CITY** consists of four hotel/resorts tightly packed together with golf courses, water parks and entertainment centres. Despite its enduring appeal to holidaying South African families and somewhat bemused foreign visitors, it has fallen on hard times now that **gambling** is legal in South Africa. When entrepreneur Sol Kerzner began building the vast complex some twenty years ago, however, when the area was part of the Bophuthatswana *bantustan*, it was one of the few places in the country to throw dice legally. Thousands visited from "across the border" to sample Kerzner's blend of gambling, topless shows and over-the-top hotels. During apartheid, the resort played host to a series of high-profile rock concerts, with artists such as Elton John taking the stage despite the cultural boycott in operation at the time. These days, although the crowds have diminished, Sun City's bizarre and unique attractions haven't faded, and if you're in the area it's well worth popping in for a gawp, especially if you're travelling to Pilanesberg Game Reserve.

Arrival and information

You can **fly** to Sun City's small airport (roughly 7km away), from Johannesburg on SA Airlink (☎011/978 1111). Daily Sun City **buses** drive from Johannesburg (book through Computicket, ☎011/445 8000) and Pretoria (book through Tourist Rendezvous, ☎012/313 7980). If you're **driving** from Johannesburg, it's easier to take the R24 towards Rustenburg until you meet the N4, and then take the next right turn, the R565, which goes through Boshoek to Sun City. From Pretoria, follow the N4 past the Brits turn-off, and turn right onto the R556; from here it's roughly 70km to the resort. A popular option, particularly if millionaire status is still a little out of reach and you just want to sample the phenomenon, is to join a **day tour** here from Pretoria or Johannesburg. A large number of operators based in these cities offer trips, with prices varying depending on the target market.

Entrance to Sun City costs R40, R30 of which you get back in Sunbucks, the Sun City currency, used to pay for most things inside, including restaurant meals. Arriving by car, drive right into the complex and head for the parking places nearest the Entertainment Centre. If you've arrived by plane or bus, use the free **monorail** that runs from the entrance to the **Welcome Centre** (☎014/557 1544). This is a good starting point for an exploration of Sun City (which, though it looks huge, is easily explored on foot), and can provide plenty of maps, leaflets and details of special offers. You can also book **game drives** into the Pilanesberg Game Reserve at the Safari Desk here (☎014/552 1561).

Accommodation

All accommodation can be booked at Sun International Central Reservations (☎011/780 7800).

The Cabanas (☎014/557 1000). Practical for families, this cluster of self-catering holiday chalets offers the most inexpensive accommodation in Sun City. Moderately priced restaurants, an adventure playground and good indoor pool complete the picture. ⑤.

Cascades Hotel (☎014/557 1000). After the *Palace*, this is the resort's most comfortable place to stay. Next door to the Entertainment Centre, it's a stylish high-rise, with "designer-tropical" decor, a mini rainforest and aviary, and outside lifts offering splendid views of Sun City and the surrounding hills. The inviting pool and bar are for residents only. ⑨.

Palace of the Lost City (☎014/557 3133). Fantastically opulent hotel based on the theme of an African palace, with stunning carvings and sculptures, jungle murals and ultra-plush rooms. A stay here is bank-breakingly expensive but pretty unforgettable, and there are two outstanding restaurants. Room prices range from $400 to $4000 a night, payable in foreign exchange only.

Sun City Hotel (☎014/557 1000). Near the resort entrance, and housing the main casino and nightclub. If you can handle the tackiness and sound of slot machines, this hotel is worth considering for the well-furnished rooms and three decent restaurants. ⑦.

The resort

The undoubted showpiece of the resort is the **Lost City**, separated from the rest of Sun City by an entrance fee (R40) and the vibrating Bridge of Time. On entering, you'll be met by **Valley of the Waves**, a gigantic pool area designed to look like a beach, complete with sand, palm trees and a wave machine which produces a two-metre-high break suitable for surfing. By far the best thing about Sun City, the Valley has two fabulous waterslides, Viper and Mamba, which send you spinning down a dark tunnel on an inflated tyre at a truly terrifying speed.

Looking onto the water is the staggering *Palace of the Lost City* (see previous page). Despite the laughable mythology about it being part of a lost civilisation, the *Palace* is breathtaking in concept and execution: a soaring, distinctively African edifice covered in elaborate woodcarvings and glowing mosaics, with beautiful, palatial interiors. You can pop in for a drink if you're not staying, or you join one of the daily **Sun City tours** (2pm from the Welcome Centre; small entry charge) for a more thorough snoop.

The **Entertainment Centre** is the focal point of the rest of Sun City. Here you'll find rows of bleeping slots faithfully fed tokens by their determined flock, and banks of arcade games. The centre's **cinema** has the best movie selection in Northwest, and the **concert hall** hosts regular beauty contests, music and sports events, which have improved since the lifting of the cultural and sports boycotts in the Nineties. If you're after something to **eat**, there is a wide choice of decent restaurants, snack bars and coffee shops dotted around the resort.

Watersports from windsailing to powerboating are offered at Waterworld, a large, artificial lake near the *Cabanas* hotel, and you'll also find tennis courts, a fitness centre and three golf courses, including the internationally renowned Gary Player Country Club.

Pilanesberg Game Reserve

Home to a huge variety of southern African animal life, the **Pilanesberg Game Reserve** (daily: April–Aug 6am–5.30pm; Sept–March 5.30am–7pm; R15 per person, R10 per car) is Northwest's biggest tourist draw. Don't let the crowds put you off though: this huge, well-managed park offers game-viewing thrills aplenty, with a good chance of seeing all of the **Big Five**, along with **hippo**, **giraffe** and **cheetah**, as well as a vast range of **birdlife**. If you've only limited time in South Africa, and are based in Johannesburg, this is definitely the place to come to see some game.

Pilanesberg is the site of an earthquake that erupted some 1300 million years ago in what is now Lake Mankwe. Before the eruption, the magma's pressure cracked the earth's surface into unusual concentric circles. After the eruption, the earth's crust collapsed into the resulting underground vacuum, which squeezed the remaining magma into the cracks. The magma solidified, and now constitutes the park's many beautiful hills, which are in some ways Pilanesberg's finest feature, though often ignored by visitors more interested in scouring their slopes for wildlife. These hills were home to **Tswana** people until the Seventies, when Operation Genesis saw huge numbers of animals shipped from all over the country to create an impressive wildlife reserve.

You'll need at least a day to do Pilanesberg justice. If you're driving, aim to travel at under 20km per hour and allow plenty of time if you want to catch sight of the animals. An excellent **map** and **guidebook** are available at the information centre at reception explaining the various habitats, enabling you to plan your journey around what you most want to see. Bear in mind that other drivers have this map too, and areas recommended for popular animals tend to become congested. The most sought-after big animals are lion, elephant, white and black rhino, hippo, giraffe, buffalo, cheetah, leopard and the most recent introduction, wild dog. The majority of antelope species are here too, along with hundreds of bird species and snakes. At night, some fantastic creatures emerge, including the civet, porcupine and caracal, though their dislike of the large vehicles with spotlights used for night rides mean you will be lucky to catch a glimpse of them.

Practicalities

The main entrance to Pilanesberg is the **Manyane Gate**, on the eastern edge of the reserve. Driving **from Rustenburg**, you'll need to follow the R510 to Thabazimbi, and take a left turn near Mogwase. **From Sun City**, which is nestled in the southern border of the reserve, the nearest entrance is the **Bakubung Gate** west of the resort on the R565. The park's **reception** at the Manyane Gate (daily 7am–6.30pm; ☎014/555 5351) provides useful maps and leaflets. In the centre of the park, the **Pilanesberg Centre** (same hours) features displays and maps, and there is a shop selling tea, coffee and snacks.

Pilanesberg is easily explored in your own car, especially with the official map. The various picnic spots and hides dotted around are ideal for breaking the drive. Alternatively, you can book **game drives** (2.5hr; from R80)with Gametrackers, who have a desks at Manyane (☎014/555 6136) and Sun City (see p.537), a good way to see the Big Five. They also operate **hiking trails** (from R100) in the reserve, which give you a genuine feel for the bush and the chance to stand close to large and potentially dangerous animals, fortunately in the company of an armed warden. Also available are **night drives** (from R80) and, for a hefty R1350 per person, you can waft above the park on a four-hour **balloon safari**, which includes food and drink.

ACCOMMODATION

Pilanesberg has large numbers of day visitors – many from Sun City – and like any other decent game reserve you'll get most from it if you're able to stay a little bit longer and put yourself in pole position for the best game-viewing time, at dawn, before the day visitors arrive. Pilansberg has a well-developed range of **accommodation** available, from the upmarket *Kwa Maritane* and *Tshukudu* lodges to traditional national park campsites, although the best-value options are the small camps in the heart of the park, with permanent tents. **Bookings** for everywhere except *Bakubung, Kwa Maritane* and *Tshukudu* must be made through Golden Leopard Resorts (enquiries ☎014/555 6135; bookings ☎011/406 3443, fax 406 3405, *jhb@marketel.co.za*).

Bakgatla Complex, near the Manyane Gate. Well-situated, self-catering chalets sleeping five and an area for caravans and camping, all set among weird-looking hillocks. Camping ①, chalets ④.

Bakubung Lodge (☎014/552 1861). On the southern edge of the park, just west of Sun City. The highlight at this large, modern lodge is the hippo pool, a stone's throw from the restaurant. Rooms are pleasant if bland, and guided walks and game drives are on offer. ⑨.

Bosele Group Centre. Inexpensive dorms with shared kitchen facilities and use of the pool, shop and restaurant at neighbouring *Manyane Resort*. ①.

Kololo Hilltop Camp. Nestled in the park's beautiful western hill ranges, this small camp has four two-person tents and rustic kitchen and refrigeration facilities. With its wonderful views and detached feel, this is probably the best-value accommodation in the park. ④.

Kwa Maritane Lodge (☎014/552 1820). In the southeast corner of the park, near Pilanesberg Airport, this upmarket resort feels somehow detached from its fabulous surroundings. Full-board, plenty of facilities, and game drives. ⑨.

Mankwe Camp, by Mankwe Lake, in the centre of the park. Another simple, pleasant camp with eight four-person safari tents in a lovely setting. No electricity and only *braai* sites for cooking. ④.

Manyane Resort, just by the Manyane Gate. The low cost and convenience compensate for the distinctly un-bushlike atmosphere of the park's main camp. There's a bar and restaurant, pool, gym and mini-golf. Thatched chalets with kitchen ④, camping stands ①.

Metswedi Wilderness Hide, in the northern hills of the park. Luxurious, fully catered safari camp with outstanding views. ⑦.

Tshukudu Lodge (☎014/552 1861). The most upmarket and expensive lodge in Pilansberg. Gaze out at big game from your verandah in an outstanding setting in the southwest of the park. Picturesque thatched huts offer luxury accommodation (sunken baths, roaring log fires), and the high price includes all meals and game drives. ⑨.

The Central Region

Thanks to its scrawny and desolate dryness, Northwest Province's **Central Region** feels especially remote. **Mmabatho**, once the capital of Bophuthatswana and now incorporated into neighbouring **Mafikeng**, capital of Northwest, forces reluctant bureaucratic pilgrimages on people from all over the province but the linked town remains profoundly uncosmopolitan. The city's monthly *What's On* magazine invariably reveals "not much", and the same is true, only more so, of **Zeerust**, **Groot Marico** and **Lichtenburg**. The region's appeal lies elsewhere, in the brooding plains and lush river valleys of Marico and the rarely visited game reserves, including **Botsalano** near the Botswana border. Then there are the remains of the rich but depressing history of the region, centring on the relentless dispossession of the Tswana, but also including the famed **siege of Mafikeng** during the second Anglo-Boer War, and the incredible **Lichtenburg diamond rush** of 1926. Finally, there are the people: local Tswana and Afrikaners are both short on English but long on hospitality, at least to visitors.

Groot Marico

GROOT MARICO, resting contentedly by the banks of the Marico River, just south of the N4 and 90km west of Rustenburg, gained fame through Herman Charles Bosman's short stories based on his time as a teacher here. The town's handful of attractions include the **Art Factory** (Mon–Sat 9am–5pm) on the main street, where you can pick up local Tswana cultural artefacts, along with any local news worth knowing about what's going on. Also worth a visit are the remains of **Tshwenyane** and **Karechuenya**, two Tswana towns built in the sixteenth and seventeenth centuries. They lie 36km northwest of town, on the Orion Farm (☎01428/23350), which is reached by taking the signposted turn-off from the Zeerust–Gaborone section of the N4, about 16km from Zeerust. If there are just one or two of you, enlist the help of Marico's information centre (see below) for transport. There's a display on these archeological findings at the Mafikeng Museum (see p.543).

Although prone to stultifying heat, particularly in summer, the hills of the Marico district are good for hiking, and when it all gets too much you can make for the river for cool relief. The water of the **Marico Oog**, a spring some 20km south of town, is particularly clear and refreshing: festooned with water lilies and surrounded by beautiful dolomitic rocks, it makes a tranquil place for a picnic.

Most **minibus taxis** travelling along the N4 from Pretoria to Gaberone or Pretoria will stop at the Groot Marico turn off (a 20min walk south of the village) on request, but you'll find it easiest to reach Groot Marico by **car**. The town's idiosyncratic but friendly and dedicated **information centre** (☎014/503 0010, mobile ☎083/272 2958), marked by a small signpost along the main street from the *Bosveld Hotel,* is open most hours of the day and night, but if it's closed call in at the *Art Factory.* The *Bosveld* has Groot Marico's only public bar, where white locals, inspired by beer, brandy and their own good humour, have been known to dance traditional Afrikaans two-steps; for **accommodation** go a few doors further along Paul Kruger Street to *Lavender Guest House* (☎082/822 8397; ②), which has four rooms and a typically warm, hospitable welcome. For the more adventurous, a **farmstay** can be booked through the information centre. The nicest **camping** spots around here are at *Salileni Farm*, 3km south of

Note that **phone numbers** for Groot Marico are due to change throughout 1999 and 2000. If you have any difficulties, call ☎1023.

town, by the river (☎014252, ask for 114), and near the **Marico Dam** (☎014252, ask for Gronum Loots, 1303), north of town, where hot water and electricity are available. At weekends the dam is a magnet for local *braais*, fishing, drinking and watersports.

Zeerust and around

The large and unprepossessing regional centre of **ZEERUST**, 40km west of Groot Marico on the N4, is essentially a supplies town, and only worth stopping at on the way to Gaborone or one of the surrounding game reserves. There's an annual **mampoer festival** (check with the Groot Marico tourist information office for dates); otherwise, shops aside, there's precious little to see. Just outside town, the **Abjasterkop** is a striking, pointed hill which

---

MAMPOER

Mampoer is the Afrikaans word for the fearsomely strong distilled alcohol so beloved by Marico locals for many years. Any fruit can be used to make *mampoer*, but peach is the most traditional: until 1878, much of Northwest's farmland grew peach trees solely devoted to this purpose. Things changed with the ZAR government's distilling tax, and new licensing system in 1894, and thousands of *mampoer* stills were destroyed. A few, however, escaped detection. One farmer, we are told, cleaned out his entire drainage system but made no attempt to conceal his fifteen barrels of *mampoer*. The inspectors found the barrels, split them open and poured the entire contents down the drain. Meanwhile, the canny farmer had his family stationed in the field where the pipe ended up with every container the household possessed, and managed to recover fourteen of the fifteen barrels.

To make *mampoer*, distillers put the fruit in a copper still and allow it to ferment until the juice is settled, at which point they light a fire under the still. A copper pipe leads from the top of the still to a drum filled with cold running water, which it coils inside. As the juice heats up, steam gathers at the top of the still and comes down the pipe, condensing when it reaches the coil in the drum. This liquid is distilled once more, this time over a low, slow fire. In the old days the alcohol content was measured by throwing a chunk of lard into a sample. If it floated halfway, the *mampoer* was perfect.

The drink is celebrated in Herman Charles Bosman's short story, **Willem Prinsloo's Peach Brandy**, set in the Twenties:

". . . we arrived at Willem Prinsloo's house. There were so many ox-waggons drawn up on the veld that the place looked like a laager [circle of wagons]. *Prinsloo met us at the door.*

'Go right through, kerels,' he said. 'The dancing is in the voorhuis [barn]. *The peach brandy is in the kitchen.'*

Although the voorhuis was big, it was so crowded as to make it almost impossible to dance. But it was not as crowded as the kitchen. Nor was the music in the voorhuis – which was provided by a number of men with guitars and concertinas – as loud as the music in the kitchen, where there was no band, but each man sang for himself.

We knew from these signs that the party was a success.

When I had been in the kitchen for about half an hour I decided to go into the voorhuis. It seemed a long way, now, from the kitchen to the voorhuis, and I had to lean against the wall several times to think. I passed a number of men who were also leaning against the wall like that, thinking. One man even found that he could think best by sitting on the floor with his head in his arms.

You could see that Willem Prinsloo made a pretty good peach brandy."

If you want to sample *mampoer*, either head for Pieter Roets's Vergenoeg Farm (open most days, closed evenings) a few kilometres south of Marico along the untarred main road, where you can cautiously pick up a bottle of barbed-wire entwined, eighty percent proof *Doringdrood*, or to Tienie Zwart's Driefontein Farm, 2.5km beyond the Groot Marico turn-off on the N4, where you can see the stuff being made.

rewards a quick scramble or a more serious hike. You can park at the *Abjasterkop Hotel* (☎018/642 2008; doubles ③, rondavel ②, camping ①), 2km east on the N4, and ask the manager for directions. The hotel itself is in a magnificent hilly setting, ideal for hiking, and is the best **place to eat** in the area, with a restaurant with an à la carte menu, and a good bar. Also near Zeerust is the **Klein Marico Resort** (☎018/646 0146; small entry fee; chalet ③, camping ①), which occupies a beautiful position high above the town. There are enough **antelope** to justify the entrance cost, and you'll find a restaurant serving moderately priced meat dishes. The ugly brick chalets mercifully do not intrude on Klein Marico's soothing midweek tranquillity. To get there, head back to Groot Marico on the N4, turn off at the Total Garage and continue for 4km.

Madikwe Game Reserve

The main attraction in this northeastern section of the province is north of Zeerust along the N4, which leads to Gaborone, the capital of Botswana. Here you'll find one of the least known of South Africa's large wildlife areas, **Madikwe Game Reserve**, established in 1991 and now run by Northwest Parks Board. At 600 square kilometres, Madikwe is larger even than her sister reserve in the province, Pilansberg, and in South Africa only Kruger and Kalahari-Gemsbok national parks cover a greater area. Thanks to Operation Phoenix, a massive programme of reintroduction, the largely low-lying plains of woodland and grassland of Madikwe are amply stocked with the Big Five and hundreds of other species, including spotted hyena, giraffe, cheetah and wild dog.

Plans for the reserve include initiatives to involve communities living in the vicinity, but for now the only practical means of visiting is to **stay overnight**. *Mosetlha Bush Camp* (☎011/802 6222, *bushwise@netactive.co.za*; ⑨), in the centre of the reserve, offers the most rustic accommodation, in simple raised log cabins, with an emphasis on game walks as much as drives. Alternatively, there are two upmarket lodges: *Tau Lodge* (☎018/365 9027; ⑨), on the northern edge of the reserve, boasts spectacular views over a large waterhole visited frequently by the animals, including lion, who have been known to make a kill while guests looked on from their grandstand vantage. *Madikwe River Lodge* (☎014/778 0891, fax 778 0893; ⑨) is smaller and enjoys a more intimate setting on the lush Marico River, offering luxury chalets with wooden decks reaching out over the water. Rates at all three include full board and game drives.

Mafikeng and Mmabatho

The twin towns of **MAFIKENG** and **MMABATHO** offer a unique portrait of both the vision of apartheid and the deep contradictions it rent in the geography and mindset of South Africa. On the one hand, it's most famous for Baden-Powell and the Boer **siege** of 1900 (see box opposite), and in many ways it's a typical colonial settlement, serving a wide area of farmland, possessing a smattering of graceful buildings, its entrenched whites living in dull suburbs, and a centre used increasingly as a shopping and transport hub by blacks from the surrounding area. Yet less than 5km away, but a world apart in appearance, values and atmosphere, is **Mmabatho**, designated capital of the former homeland of Bophuthatswana, and a showcase for the grandiose visions of Bop dictator **Lucas Mangope**. The troop of white elephants constructed by Mangope on the back of revenues generated from Sun City, from huge government offices to the towering sports stadium, along with the wide boulevards that connect them, are undoubtedly worth experiencing, even if the wiser course for finding somewhere to stay or eat and drink is to retreat to the Mafikeng side. Although the twin cities are the capital of Northwest Province, and despite the fact that Mmabatho's notoriety as the epitome of homeland-hypocrisy will linger, both are often simply called Mafikeng.

Mafikeng

Mafikeng's smattering of historic buildings make for a pleasant stroll. Starting from Victoria Street, four blocks north of Main Street, look out for the **Victoria Hospital**, which was pounded during the siege of 1900, and the elegant **St Joseph's Convent**. Three blocks south, on Martin Street, stands the splendid **St John's Anglican Church**, designed by Sir Herbert Baker and built in 1902. Nearby is the town's main attraction, the **Mafikeng Museum** (Mon–Fri 8am–4pm, Sat 10am–12.30pm; free), which has some intriguing exhibits on the San, with a range of the poisons and weapons that they hunt with, and photos of hand signals San make to each other when hunting in their customary silence. Tswana exhibits include a life-size recreation of a traditional hut, complete with stylish trademark enclosed porch, and samples of pottery and beadwork. An extensive display of herbs and medicines throws up some interesting specimens, including the sweet violet with five times the Vitamin C content of oranges, and a relative of the potato called the mandrake, with awesomely hallucinogenic powers. The **Mafikeng Siege** is given a room of its own, filled with classic British imperial memorabilia, including a tattered flag, ration book, diaries and a wonderful collection of photos. Extensive quotations from Peter Warwick's *Black People and the SA War 1899–1902* intersperse the exhibits, offering a subversive account of the events. The Tswana writer and activist Sol Plaatje lived in Mafikeng for many years, and wrote a diary of the siege (see box below), and he receives a full, informative display. Keep an eye out too for the fascinating exhibit on Mafikeng and the railways, which provides evidence of the connection between their spread from Cape Town and Rhodes' mission to colonize Africa.

The only other sight in Mafikeng worth a visit is the **Cemetery** on Carrington Street, in the town's northwestern corner, next to the sleepy railway sidings. Dusty and unkempt, it counts amongst its headstones white iron crosses marking the graves of British soldiers. Some were casualties from the siege, and others are from the many other battles waged by the British against the Afrikaners and Tswana. Until the 1980s this was a whites-only cemetery, and still commemorates only the Europeans who died during the siege.

THE SIEGE OF MAFIKENG

Mafikeng was **besieged** within three days of the start of the second Anglo-Boer War (1899–1902) by generals Snyman and Cronje. **Colonel Robert Baden-Powell** (founder of the Boy Scouts) had the task of defending the town. This he did for 217 days, from October 16, 1899 until May 17, 1900, when relief arrived from Rhodesia and from the south. In the process, Baden-Powell became a British household name and hero, exemplifying imperial ability and courage under fire.

Mafikeng was strategically irrelevant to the war, and Baden-Powell's real achievement was to distract the six thousand Afrikaners besieging the town from fighting elsewhere. He relied heavily on the Barolong people for defence, labour and reconnaissance, but failed to record this either in his dispatches to London or in his memoirs. The Barolong received far fewer rations than the British and over one thousand subsequently died of starvation, yet none received any of the £29,000 raised in Britain for the rehabilitation of Mafikeng. To add insult to injury, not one Barolong was decorated for bravery, in contrast to the plentiful medals dished out to the British regiments, and none of the promises Baden-Powell made about land grants to them were ever kept. An important legacy of the involvement of the black population was the diary of the siege kept by **Sol Plaatjie**, one of the first black writers to make an impact on English literature, who was later to become one of the founder memebers of the ANC.

Mmabatho

Mmabatho was created from nothing in 1977 as the capital of the new "independent homeland" of Bophuthatswana. The city prospered fast, both from the discovery of platinum and the revenue from Sol Kerzner's gambling resort. Under the direction of Bop president Lucas Mangope, the capital became an ostentatious attempt to show off what a prosperous independent African state could become, though in practice it demonstrated a bloated and surreal quasi-state, riddled with corruption and egocentricity. Huge buildings were constructed for the burgeoning civil service; brand new casinohotels catered to the new black elite, as well as South Africans chasing the illicit thrills denied them across the border; and money was poured into bizarre enterprises, including a sports stadium with 80,000 seats but scarcely any shade, and a state-of-the-art **Recording Studio**, which has been highly regarded but little used by the world's rock and pop stars. One of the more positive legacies of those days is the impressive **Mmabana Cultural Centre**, on the outskirts of Mmabatho, at the southern end of the Mangope Highway. The centre offers a wide range of social and educational services, mostly to Tswana children, and can be visited by prior arrangement (☎0140/24100).

Practicalities

SA Airlink (☎011/978 1111) operate two daily flights from Johannesburg to **Mmabatho International Airport**, roughly 17km from the town centre. From here, you'll have to rent a car to get downtown, as there's no public transport. Daily Elwierda **buses** (☎012/664 5880) from Pretoria stop in both Mafikeng, by the train station, and Mmabatho, and there are also services run by Mmabatho Bus Services (☎018/381 2680), from Megacity Shopping Mall. To get here **by car**, take the R27 from Zeerust and Vryburg, or the R52 from Lichtenburg. Mafikeng is only 25km from the Ramatlabama border post with Botswana. For getting around, **minibus taxis** making the short hop from Mmabatho's Megacity Shopping Mall stop in Mafikeng at the railway station, and at the corner of Warren and Shippard streets.

The **tourist information office** (Mon–Fri 8am–4.30pm; ☎018/381 3155) is in Mafikeng, in a new thatched complex beside the entrance to *Cook's Lake Campsite*, off Voortrekker St, on the far side of the railway track from the town centre.

In Mafikeng, the best budget **accommodation** option is at *The Surrey*, 32 Shippard St (☎018/381 0420; ②), which is central but rather run-down. Also central are *Royal Palm Guest House*, 79 Sheppard St (☎018/381 2218; ③), with good-value B&B, and the *Windsor Hotel Lodge*, 39 Tillard St (☎018/381 1150; ③), one of Mafikeng's best places to stay – though the rooms vary considerably, so ask to see yours before checking in. If you've got a car, it's worth staying a little way southeast of Mafikeng, in tiny **Rooigrond**. Here, the delightful *Hope Fountain Guest Farm* (☎018/645 0781; ②) offers cosy chalets in semi-rural surroundings, with breakfast included. To get there, turn off the R503 at the "*Sehuba Protea*" sign, from where it's indicated. The only **campsite** near town is *Cooke's Lake Camping Ground* (①), south of Mafikeng off the R503, with basic facilities but a noisy roadside location.

In Mmabatho, the *Molopo Sun*, University Rd (☎018/382 4184; ④), offers comfortable rooms and a restaurant and pool. The rooms of the grander *Mmabatho Sun* (☎018/389 1111; ⑦), on Voortrekker Road – which connects Mmabatho to Mafikeng – are surprisingly poky for a casino-dominated hotel, but its three restaurants, two bars, two swimming pools, sauna and spa are some compensation. Probably the most interesting option in Mafikeng are the attractive and comfortable thatched chalets beside the *Bop Recording Studios* (☎018/386 2609; ④), located off Voortrekker Rd just before the *Mmabatho Sun*, available to travellers as long as they haven't been booked up by travelling rock stars and their entourages (which isn't all that often).

If you're looking for something to **eat**, the most reliable options are the upmarket restaurant in the *Mmabatho Sun*, or the more casual *O'Hagan's Pub and Grill*, a kilometre

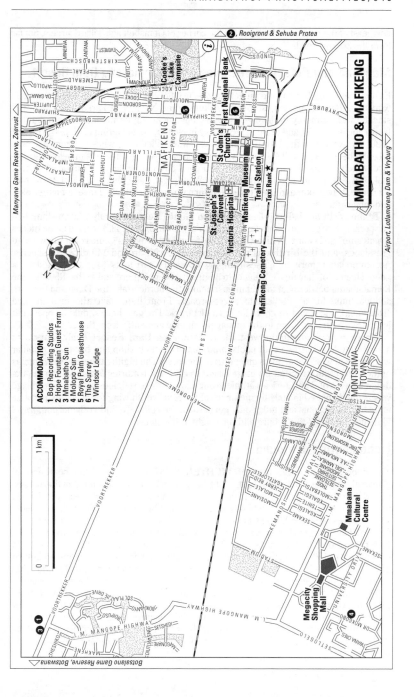

△ *Manyane Game Reserve, Zeerust*

2, *Rooigrond & Sehuba Protea*

Airport, Lotlamoreng Dam & Vryburg ▷

▽ *Botsalano Game Reserve, Botswana*

MMABATHO & MAFIKENG

ACCOMMODATION
1 Bop Recording Studios
2 Hope Fountain Guest Farm
3 Mmabatho Sun
4 Molopo Sun
5 Royal Palm Guesthouse
6 The Surrey
7 Windsor Lodge

First National Bank
St John's Church
Mafikeng Museum
Train Station
Taxi Rank
St Joseph's Convent
Victoria Hospital
Mafikeng Cemetery
Mmabana Cultural Centre
Megacity Shopping Mall

1 km
0

northeast of the centre of Mafikeng, on the corner of Gemsbok and Tillard streets, not far from the Zeerust road.

Manyane and Botsalano reserves and Lotlamoreng Dam Resort

East of Mafikeng, 10km along the R49 to Zeerust, lies **Manyane Game Reserve** (daily 6am–6pm; R10 per person, R5 per car). Run by the Northwest Parks Board, it's well stocked with primarily herbivorous plains game, including **rhino** and **buffalo**, but the landscape is a bit flat and drab. You can **stay** in pleasant self-catering chalets (☎018/381 6020; ②). Nearby is the **Wondergat**, a deep, water-filled cave whose bottom has only recently been reached. If you swim you might feel the warm stream 20m below the surface, which makes the water sparkle. On a good day, particularly in summer, this area makes a fine picnic spot. To reach the Wondergat, take the first right turn after Manyane, travel 4km and then take a left turn down a dirt track. Travel a further 8km and turn right.

To the north of Mafikeng lies **Botsalano Game Reserve** (daily 7.30am–4pm; R10 per person, R20 per car; camping ①, safari tent ③; ☎018/386 2433), whose name means "friendship" in Tswana. **White rhino**, **giraffe** and other plains game roam the wooded grasslands, and the **birdlife** is pretty impressive, with around 140 different species. Accommodation here comprises camping (①) and safari tents (③), and you stand a good chance of having Botsalano to yourself. To get there, take the R503 to the Ramatlabama border post for 20km; just before the border, take the Dinakana turn-off, and continue for about 7km to a crossroads. From here, take the turn marked "Dinakana", and travel another 7km up a dirt track. The gate here should be open. If it isn't, drive a further 12km to the management gate and enter from there.

Closer to town, and to the west, the **Lotlamoreng Dam Resort** (daily 7am–noon; small entry fee) has two cold pools, *braai* stands, a tuck shop and bar that's popular with locals at weekends, but is quiet during the week. The highlight here is the remains of the Credo Mutwa Cultural Village inside its grounds, featuring *kraals* built in the traditional styles of South Africa's ethnic groups, and bizarre religious statues. The village was badly damaged in 1994 by members of the ANC youth wing for allegedly perpetuating tribal divisions, and today only goats roam the ruins. To find Lotlamoreng, travel 5km along the R27 to Vryburg and turn right at the signs.

Lichtenburg and around

The deeply conservative *dorp* of **LICHTENBURG** lies some 65km southeast of Mmabatho on the R503, close to the N14 highway which connects the Northern Cape to Gauteng. Lichtenburg's name means "place of light"; when the town was proclaimed in 1873, it was hoped that the new settlement would bring some light to this forsaken spot. Progress was deadly slow until 1926, when a Tswana labourer on the Elandsputte farm of Jan Voorendyk discovered a **diamond**. News spread fast, and by 1927 the Lichtenburg diamond diggings were 36km long and around 1.5km wide. Incredibly, a shantytown of 150,000 people had sprung up by then, sporting over 200 diamond-buying offices. The quantity of diamonds discovered here threatened the diamond market, but De Beers bought nearly every one to maintain its monopoly and the diamonds' worth.

The shantytown was famed for its **dust**, which was alleged to waft from Lichtenburger mouths as they spoke. By 1935, the rush had petered out, but a few prospectors continued working the diggings right up until 1993. Today only one company still works the diggings; you can watch its men in action by following the R505 north of Lichtenburg towards Zeerust, and turning left just before the Bakerville turn-off.

DIGGING FOR DIAMONDS

"Once you have found your first diamond, you will never give up looking." *Digger proverb*
According to digger mythology, all that anyone needs to find diamonds are a claim, a pick, a shovel, a wheelbarrow, and the luck of the gods. In practice, however, extra equipment comes in pretty handy. First off, you'll need a *dummy*, which is a swinging sieve in a frame that gets rid of larger stones. After this, you'll need a *washing machine*, which mixes the gravel left by the dummy with muddy water, its rotating arms and teeth holding the mixture in suspension. The diamonds and heavier gravel sink to the bottom, and the lighter gravel, called *tailings*, floats to the top and is poured out. Another sieve separates the tailings from the water, which is reused. After the washing machine, the remaining gravel is poured into a *sluice* and then a *washing tub*, which removes the last of the water, and grades the gravel into three sizes. These are then pored over with a knife, in the hope that this time there will be a diamond. In 1926, at the time of the Lichtenburg diggings, all this equipment cost around £600, which effectively meant you needed a diamond to pay for it.

In De La Rey Square, the **Lichtenburg Museum** (Tues–Fri 10am–noon & 1–5pm, Sat 10am–1pm; free) is worth a visit for its display on **General Koos De La Rey**, who tried and failed to capture Lichtenburg from the British in 1900. De La Rey was one of the Boer "bitter enders", who only stopped fighting in 1902 with the greatest of reluctance, and is credited with the re-invention of trench warfare (see p.254).

Accommodation is limited, the only hotel being the rather grim *Elgro* (☎018/632 3051; ③), on Republiek St, though far more comfortable is the *Melville*, 20 Melville St (☎018/632 3514; ②), a B&B with a small art gallery attached. For **eating and drinking**, you could try the *Spur* steakhouse next door to the *Elgro*, or *O'Hagan's* pub on Melville Street. Marginally better than both is the *Taverne*, 145 Melville St, where you can tuck into a reasonably priced steak and dessert.

Nearby nature reserves

The **Lichtenburg Nature Reserve** (Mon–Fri 8am–4pm, Sat & Sun 8am–6pm; entry fee; ☎018/632 2818; rooms ②) operates as a game-breeding farm, and as a result has an unusual selection of wildlife, including an excellent vulture restaurant in its small forest. The vultures usually feed in the afternoon, but enquire at the gate for precise times if you enjoy the sight of birds devouring raw flesh. Less gory are the hundreds of birds you can watch from the hide by the lake. **To get to the reserve**, take the R505 north of the town to Ottoshoop and Zeerust, turning left 2km later at the easily missed signpost, and go under the railway bridge. The reserve is another 2km further on.

About 100km southwest of Lichtenburg on the N14 near Delareyville, you'll find the **Barberspan Nature Reserve** (☎053/948 1842; daily), a large, natural wetland that sits in striking contrast to the fields of *mielies*, and is home to tens of thousands of birds, including flamingos, herons, storks and ibis.

Along the Vaal River

The mighty **Vaal** (or Lekwa) was the historic boundary between the Orange Free State and the South African Republic (ZAR). Still the provincial boundary, separating Northwest from the Free State, today the Vaal runs alongside the N12 highway between Johannesburg and Kimberley. The landscape here is dominated by flat maize fields, but being close to the river is a bonus, providing you with opportunities for timely sorties from the beaten track.

Potchefstroom

One of the largest and oldest towns of Northwest, **POTCHEFSTROOM** is a classic Afrikaner settlement, with main streets wide enough to turn a wagon in, a large square and plenty of churches. Founded by Voortrekker leader **Andries Potgieter** on the banks of the Mooi River in 1837, Potchefstroom means "stream of chief Potgieter". Once the capital of the ZAR, today "Potch" is best known for its university, which has known some turbulence between black and Afrikaner students since blacks were admitted in the Nineties, but the presence of a large student population does means that parts of town enjoy a youthful and energetic vibe.

The main highway cuts through town, leaving the central area with little of the charm you'd expect of such an old settlement. Kerk Street, at right-angles to the highway, is now an inelegant shopping arcade, although parallel Greyling Street is the site of the old *landdrost* and post office; Potchefstroom played a major role in the ZAR's postal services, and black runners were employed here to deliver mail as far away as what is now Mpumalanga province, hundreds of kilometres distant. The **Potchefstroom Museum**, Gouws St (Mon–Fri 9am–5pm; free), houses one of the few remaining Voortrekker wagons used at the Battle of Blood River in 1838, when Voortrekkers defeated the Zulus.

Away from the centre and away from the main highway, Potch takes on a much more appealing demeanour, especially around the univeristy area. Tom Street boasts an impressive avenue of oak trees that leads all the way to the university precinct, known as the Bult, where you'll find attractive old buildings and functional new ones, along with the buzz of university life. It's a long walk from the centre – you'll need to drive or cycle here – and some nearby attractions include **Pretorius House** (Mon–Fri 10am–1pm & 2–4pm; small entry fee), Van der Hoff Rd (an extension of Kerk St), the former home of Marthinus Pretorius, the ZAR's first president. It's a beautiful old house with whitewashed walls, green doors and a thatched roof, and is typical of nineteenth-century Afrikaner dwellings. Inside, you'll find dour photos and ornate wallpaper, minimal furnishings and a family Bible. On the opposite side of the street stands the **Totius Museum** (Mon–Fri 10am–1pm & 2–4pm; free), recreated to be as it was when the poet lived here a century ago. Totius was a key figure in the Dutch Reformed Church and Afrikaans language movement: as well as establishing the church's theological college in Potchefstroom, he was one of the first poets to publish in Afrikaans, and translated the Bible into Afrikaans between 1923 and 1933. The most striking part of the museum is the poet's tome-filled study, but look out too for paintings by the celebrated and controversial Jacob Pierneef, which were especially dedicated to Totius.

Practicalities

Potchefstroom is well served by public transport. Daily Translux, Greyhound and Intercape **buses** stop on Potgieter Street, near the tourist information centre, on their route between Cape Town and Johannesburg via Kimberley. **Trains** from Cape Town and Johannesburg terminate at the train station west of the city centre (train information ☎018/299 3205). Like many university towns, the classic way of **getting around** in Potch is by bike – to rent them, head for Dingo Cycles in the Cachet Park Shopping Centre, Tom St (☎018/293 2456).

There's a helpful **tourist office** in a new building next to the Town Hall, corner of Kerk and Potgieter streets (Mon–Fri 7.45am–1pm & 1.45–4.30pm; ☎018/299 5130), which has maps and leaflets about the town. The only budget **place to stay** is *Lake Recreation Resort* (☎018/299 5474; ①), north of the town centre on Tom Street, where you can rent a self-catering bungalow or **camp** amid good facilities beside a lake. Otherwise there's the large, plain *Elgro Hotel*, 60 Wolmarans St (☎018/297 5411; ③), near the centre, though a better option would be one of the B&Bs scattered around town – *Ou Drift* (☎018/297 4939; ⑤), by the banks of the Mooi river, is comfortable and relaxing.

The best place for **eating and drinking** is the university area. Here, at the heart of Die Bult complex, Tom St, is the great *Akker Coffee House*, open for most of the day and night, and, more importantly, the best place to hang out. For livelier action the *Bourbon St Brewery*, also in Die Bult, has live music at weekends and serves pub grub, while for more conventional fare the familiar line up of pizza/pasta restaurants and steak houses are well represented at the Riverwalk Centre, Potch's main mall, off Potgeiter Street on the Johannesburg (east) side of the town centre.

Klerksdorp and around

Nondescript **KLERKSDORP**, 25km down the N12 from Potchefstroom, is a busy agricultural and mining centre near some of the world's largest gold mines. The only significant attraction here is the **Klerksdorp Museum** at the corner of Margaretha Prinsloo and Lombard streets (Mon–Fri 10am–1pm & 2–4.30pm, Sat 9.30am–noon, Sun 2–5pm; free). Hardly surprising for a former prison, this is a fairly creepy place, with displays of flogging equipment, solitary confinement and the like, very effective in evoking the once-grim conditions. The courtyard has been converted into a standard Afrikaner museum, complete with waggon and candle-making displays .

Some 11km northwest of Klerksdorp, the **Faan Meintjes Nature Reserve** (daily 10am–3pm; ☎018/462 7805; R12; caravan stands ①, chalets ②), has few carnivores of note, but plenty of **white rhino**, **giraffe** and **antelope** wandering its bushveld terrain. To reach the reserve, head north on Van Riebeeck (R30), which is also called Church Street, south of the N12, and turn right at the signpost a few kilometres later, along Brady Lane. There are **San rock paintings** nearby on the Bosworth farm, which you can visit by appointment through the owner of the *North Hills Country House* (see below).

Practicalities

Daily Translux, Greyhound and Intercape **buses** stop on Church Street on their way between Cape Town and Johannesburg via Kimberley. The **train station** is just off Margaretha Prinsloo Street, a few blocks east of the city centre, with daily arrivals from Cape Town and Johannesburg (train information ☎018/406 2022).

Klerksdorp's **best place to stay** is unquestionably the *Fountain Villa Guest Lodge*, 21 Hendrik Potgieter Rd (☎018/464 1394 or mobile ☎082/466 4001; ③), a superb house in the old town sporting elegant turrets and wooden lattice work, and featuring an outstanding **restaurant** in the converted stables, where there are also a couple more rooms. Further out, on the road to the Faan Meintjes reserve, the *North Hills Country*

AFRIKANER MUSEUMS

The former Transvaal and Orange Free State are filled with museums dedicated to the preservation and propagation of **Afrikaner mythology**. Typically, exhibits will include mementos from the Great Trek (waggons are particularly prized); displays of farm-life domesticity such as butter-churning and candle-making; children's toys (generally toy waggons made from bones); photos of Afrikaner generals from the Anglo-Boer Wars, with accompanying text about the "War of Liberation"; tattered Afrikaner flags, rifles and bullet belts; details of Afrikaner casualties of concentration camps and, finally, a plaque to tell you where the town's 1938 Voortrekker centenary monument is.

Many museums have recently had their grants cut, and widening the focus to include African culture is their only chance of renewing their financial lifeline.

House (☎018/468 6416; ④) provides comfortable rooms, excellent German cooking (with good dishes for vegetarians), and doubles up as an Arabian stud farm.

The road to Kimberley

Once past Klerksdorp, the N12 passes through vast stretches of maize-growing country. There are no big towns until **Kimberley** in the Northern Cape, and you'll find yourself passing through a succession of sleepy *dorps*. A string of small nature reserves on the banks of the Vaal and the excellent *Lindbergh Safari Lodge* provide good opportunities to break up your journey.

Wolmaransstad and around

WOLMARANSSTAD, 90km southwest of Klerksdorp on the N12, consists of little more than two or three streets with a handful of shops. There's a scraggy **campsite** off the R504 on the way to Leeudoringstad, but the nicest attraction in these parts is the *Lindbergh Safari Lodge* (bookings ☎011/884 8923, *lindbergh@iafrica.com*; ⑦-⑧), where you can get a tantalizing glimpse of how the Northwest *veld* looked before maize took over, when it was thronging with birds and wildlife. Set in a small nature reserve, the beautiful thatched lodge looks out onto a watering hole popular with wildlife, enabling indolent game viewing from an armchair. The rooms are luxurious, and there's a simple bush camp if you'd rather self-cater. The main attraction of the lodge is that the absence of predators makes it safe to wander on foot, and get close up to the giraffe, antelope and other plains game. To reach *Lindbergh*, turn right onto a dirt road, off the N12 some 20km south of Wolmaransstad, and follow the signs to Rietpan, and then to Leeufontain. The lodge is about 15km from the main road in all, but the roads are bad and signposting poor, so aim to travel during the day.

Further down the road, the *Buisfontein Safari Lodge* (☎018/598 6704; ③) is a collection of thatched chalets with a good restaurant attached. For a taste of the Vaal River, continue past Leeudoringstad and head east a few kilometres, avoiding the R504, to Bothaville for the *Wolwespruit Nature Reserve* (☎053/433 1706; ①), which has a good **campsite** and some **stone cottages**.

Bloemhof and Christiana

Heading further down the N12, tiny **BLOEMHOF** is an agricultural town that also serves as a stopover for buses on the long haul between Johannesburg and Cape Town. Laid out by one James Barkly on his farm in 1866, the town was named after a garden of flowers cultivated by his daughter. Greyhound **buses** arrive and leave from the Trek Garage on Prince Street; Intercape from outside the Volkskas Bank on the main street; and Translux buses from outside the post office. The only decent **place to stay** is the *Bloemhof* (☎053/433 1211; ②), on the main street, offering rooms with TV and bath, and an adjoining windowless restaurant serving standard meaty fare. Ignore signs to a B&B on a side street, as it's situated right next to a particularly smelly factory.

Even smaller than Bloemhof, **CHRISTIANA** is just over 50km further south, its few shops straggled out along the main road. **Accommodation** is limited to the tolerable *Christiana* (☎053/441 2326; ②), on the main street, which has a **restaurant** serving grills, and two bars: one decorated for whites; the other windowless, shed-like, and for blacks. There's a decent **campsite** on the banks of the Vaal, with showers, *braai* facilities, and incredibly noisy birds. Across the river in the Free State, on the road to Hertzogville, are stunning **San rock carvings** said to be over 7000 years old. Sadly interspersed with pathetic graffiti, some carvings depict wildlife, whilst others are abstracts. You can find the carvings on the *Stowlands-on-Vaal Farm* (☎053/441 3054), where the owner is planning to erect rondavels.

t r a v e l   d e t a i l s

Trains

Bloemhof to: Cape Town (1 daily; 19hr); Johannesburg (1 daily: 5hr); Klerksdorp (1 daily; 2hr); Potchefstroom (1 daily; 3hr).

Klerksdorp to: Cape Town (1 daily; 23hr); Johannesburg (1 daily; 3hr 30min); Potchefstroom (1 daily; 50min).

Potchefstroom to: Cape Town (1 daily; 24hr); Johannesburg (1 daily; 2hr 20min); Klerksdorp (1 daily; 50min).

Buses

Bloemhof to: Cape Town (1 Mon, Wed & Fri–Sun; 13hr 45min); Johannesburg (2–3 daily; 3–4hr); Kimberley (2–3 daily; 2hr); Klerksdorp (2–3 daily; 2hr); Potchefstroom (2–3 daily; 2hr).

Christiana to: Cape Town (1 Tues & Sun; 12hr 15min); Kimberley (1–2 daily; 1hr 30min); Klerksdorp (1–2 daily; 2hr); Johannesburg (1–2 daily; 5hr); Potchefstroom (1–2 daily; 3hr).

Klerksdorp to: Cape Town (1–2 daily; 15hr); Johannesburg (3–4 daily; 2hr); Kimberley (2–3 daily; 4hr); Potchefstroom (3–4 daily; 45min).

Mafikeng to: Johannesburg (1 daily; 3hr); Rustenburg (1 daily; 1hr).

Potchefstroom to: Cape Town (1–3 daily except Tues; 16hr); Johannesburg (3–4 daily; 2hr); Kimberley (2–3 daily; 4hr 15min); Klerksdorp (3–4 daily; 45min) .

Rustenburg to: Pretoria (1 daily; 2hr); Mafikeng (1 daily; 1hr).

Sun City to: Johannesburg (2–3 daily; 2hr); Pretoria (1 daily; 2hr).

Zeerust to: Pretoria (1 daily; 3hr 15min).

Flights

Mafikeng to: Johannesburg (1–2 daily; 1hr).

Sun City to: Johannesburg (1–3 daily; 35min).

CHAPTER NINE

MPUMALANGA AND THE KRUGER NATIONAL PARK

Mpumalanga, "the land of the rising sun" to its Siswati- and Zulu-speaking residents, extends east from Gauteng to Mozambique and Swaziland. To many visitors the province is synonymous with the **Kruger National Park**, the real draw of South Africa's east flank, and one of Africa's best game parks. Kruger occupies most of Mpumalanga's and Northern Province's borders with Mozambique, and covers over 20,000 square kilometres – an area the size of Wales or Massachusetts. Unashamedly populist, Kruger is the easiest African game park to drive around in on your own, staying at one of its many well-run rest camps. Joined to its west, a number of **private reserves** offer the chance to escape the Kruger crush – at a price – with well-informed rangers conducting safaris in open vehicles.

Apart from the irresistible magnet of big-game country, Mpumalanga also has some spectacular scenery in the mountainous area known as the **Escarpment**, a couple of hours' drive west of Kruger and easily tacked onto a visit to the park. With the exception of **Pilgrim's Rest**, none of the Escarpment towns merits exploration, but they make good night stops to and from Kruger, and there are some famously stunning views as you drive around, where the bottom drops out of the mountains and hits the Lowveld. The most famous viewpoints – **God's Window, Bourke's Luck Potholes** and **Three Rondavels** – are along the lip of the Escarpment, which can be driven as a 156-kilometre looped day-trip from Sabie. The views of **Blyde River Canyon** are most famous of all and, while you can't drive into the canyon, there are some fabulous hiking opportunities in this area.

Jammed between the mountains and Kruger are the former African **bantustans**, created under apartheid: Lebowa for Sotho speakers and Gazankulu for Shangaan- and Tsonga-speaking people. The poverty of these artificial statelets was exacerbated in the Eighties, when hundreds of thousands of Mozambicans fled into Gazankulu to escape the civil war in Mozambique. Even today, Mozambicans attempt to cross illegally into South Africa, braving lions, National Parks officials and anti-poaching units in Kruger in a quest to reach the "golden city" of Johannesburg.

For overseas visitors, the **route** is usually the other way round, starting from Johannesburg and heading through the unappetizing industrial corridor traversed by the N4 as it races to **Nelspruit**, the modern capital of Mpumalanga, which is served by buses to Johannesburg, an airport and car rental facilities. From here the N4 continues

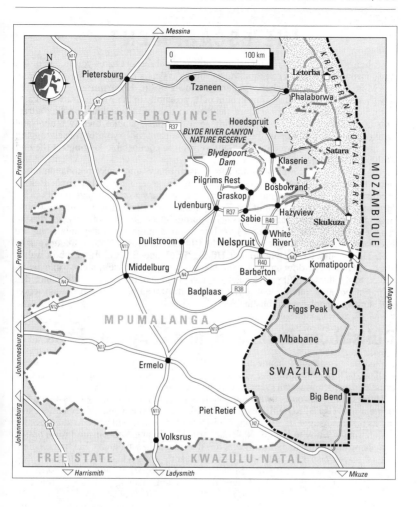

to the **Mozambique** border. This route gives you access to the southernmost part of Kruger; from Nelspruit it's 62km to Malelane Gate and 51km to Numbi Gate. Nelspruit also connects with the road south through **Barberton** to Swaziland.

Descending the Escarpment on one of four mountain passes takes you into the tropical-fruit-growing and bushveld country of the Lowveld, with impressive views back towards the towering massif of the Escarpment. A number of places close to the **Blydepoort Dam** at the foot of the Blyde River Canyon can be taken in as bushveld breaks on the way to or from Kruger. In the same vicinity, around the tiny centre of **Hoedspruit**, roughly 90km via an eastwardly arching route from the Escarpment, a number of small **game farms** offer cut-price game experiences that are good for an overnight stop but shouldn't be confused with the real thing. This you'll find nearby at the far pricier game lodges in the Manyeleti and Timbabavati private game reserves as well in Kruger itself.

THE ESCARPMENT

Four hours' drive east of Johannesburg International Airport takes you to one of the city's favoured mountain retreats: the waving grasslands and luxury guesthouses of the Mpumalanga Drakensberg, generally known as the **Escarpment**. This region mostly sees travellers purely on account of its proximity to the Kruger National Park, but it holds some of the most dramatic views in the country and its unfailing attraction is that they can be enjoyed with so little effort. Unlike the KwaZulu-Natal Drakensberg, this section of the range is one you can tour in your own car, stopping at one of the tourist towns for lunch and retiring to comfortable lodgings at the end of the day.

The little forestry towns of **Sabie** and **Graskop** have ample accommodation for all budgets and are convenient bases for exploring the area, but only **Pilgrim's Rest**, a reconstructed mining settlement from turn-of-the-century gold-rush days, merits a visit for itself. The overriding pull of the Escarpment is the **Blyde River Canyon**, whose dizzying views into one of the world's great gorges appear in every other South African tourist brochure. Most commonly gazed into from a number of viewpoints along the Escarpment lip, it can also be seen from the **Blyderivierspoort Nature Reserve** at its foot. The five-day **Blyderivierspoort Hiking Trail**, one of South Africa's best walks, starts at **God's Window** on the lip and takes in all the major viewpoints, while giving access to the flora and (if you're quiet and lucky) fauna of the reserve, which includes zebra, hippo, kudu and the entire range of South African primates – baboons, vervet and samango monkeys and bushbabies.

Dullstroom, Lydenburg and Long Tom Pass

Some 209km east of Johannesburg the R540 branches off the N4 at nondescript **Belfast**, to head into the hills, where the typical highveld countryside is covered by grasslands which wave tall green in summer, turning russet in winter.

Unless your passion is fly-fishing, chances are you'll find the tiny crossroads settlement of **DULLSTROOM**, 35km north of Belfast on the R540, just about as exciting as its name suggests. However, Dullstroom can be a useful place to stop over for a night on your way to Kruger National Park. The cheapest **accommodation** option is to camp at the village dam (①), which is decent and has ablutions, but there a number of places also rent out rooms; the pleasantly cool, Victorian *Dullstroom Inn*, Teding van Berkhout St (☎013/254 0071, fax 254 0278; ④) is one of the least expensive. Of the upmarket country lodges that cater to fly-fishing enthusiasts, the most luxurious is *Walkerson's Country Manor* (☎013/254 0246, fax 254 0260; half board ⑨), 20km north of Dullstroom on the R540. This is a small, sixteen-room hotel on a nature reserve, which provides exclusive fishing for its guests in its ten dams and 2km of river frontage. One notch down, the *Critchley Hackle Lodge*, Teding van Berkhout St (☎013/254 0145, fax 254 0262; half board ⑧), is a country-style hotel with stone and brick cottages, each with a fireplace. Less pricey still, *The Poacher*, 66 Hugenoten St (☎013/254 0108, fax 254 0068; ④), is a small, friendly lodge with four rooms, plus dam and river frontage and a tackle shop. Dullstroom's best-known **restaurant**, *Tonteldoos*, in the main street, draws out gourmands from Jo'burg just for lunch but appears to be losing its former touch. The deli at the front of the restaurant stocks smoked trout and other delicacies. Less formal, and good for refreshments and weekend evening meals, is *Rose Cottage* on Critchley Common, the crossroads that constitutes the effective village centre.

Some 58km north of Dullstroom, functional **LYDENBURG** is the site of one of South Africa's major archeological finds, replicas of which are on display at the

Lydenburg Museum (Mon–Fri 9am–noon & 2–4.15pm, Sat & Sun 10am–4pm; small entry fee) in the Gustav Klingbiel Nature Reserve, 3km out of town along the R37 to Sabie. The **Lydenburg Heads**, seven ceramic masks that date back to the fifth century, are some of the first figurative sculptures in southern Africa, and they are rather beautiful, probably ceremonial and definitely unique. As well as replicas of these heads (the originals are in the South African Museum in Cape Town), there are excellent displays of human activity in the vicinity over the past million years or so.

Striking east from Lydenburg, the R37 twists its way up **Long Tom Pass**, which takes its name from the Scheider siege guns used here by the Boers during the 1899–1902 Second Anglo-Boer War against the British. Known as Long Toms because of their elongated necks, the artillery pieces were able to throw a 43kg shell a distance of 10km. You can still see the holes blasted by retreating Boers into the series of switchbacks cutting up the pass, known as the Staircase.

Sabie, Pilgrim's Rest and Graskop

Only three towns occupy the heights of the Escarpment and of these **Sabie** is the largest, its personality split between serving the surrounding agroforestry industry, while trying to please the tourists that make it their base. Of the other two, **Pilgrim's Rest** unashamedly plays to the tour buses, pushing hard with its restored gold-rush buildings and themed museums, while the relatively uninteresting timber centre of **Graskop** is desperately working at its potential in an attempt to lay its hands on those elusive tourist bucks.

Sabie and around

SABIE is the centre of Mpumalanga's agroforestry industry, and with 450 square kilometres under active cultivation is dubiously proud of lying at the heart of South Africa's largest artificial forests. The extensive pine plantations look painfully monotonous next to the rich, jungly variety of the remaining pockets of indigenous woodland. Before the foresters arrived, Sabie made its name as a gold centre, with a lucky strike in 1895 at the Klein Sabie Falls. Mining stopped halfway through the twentieth century, and today the gold prospectors have been replaced by escapees from hectic Johannesburg, who make a living here running restaurants, B&Bs or craft shops. Sabie's compact size, slow pace, mildly arty ambience and gentle climate make it a congenial base – as long as you have your own transport – for exploring the Escarpment.

ACCOMMODATION PRICE CODES

All the accommodation listed in the Guide has been categorized into one of nine price bands, as set out below. The rates quoted represent what you can expect to pay for much of the summer **per person**, and unless otherwise stated, are based on two sharing. Rooms are generally en suite. Expect prices in some areas to be significantly higher in peak season (Dec–Jan & Easter), and look out for discounts during the winter. For further details, see p.33.

① up to R50	⑥ R250–300
② R50–100	⑦ R300–400
③ R100–150	⑧ R400–500
④ R150–200	⑨ over R500
⑤ R200–250	

Arrival and information

Public **transport** to Sabie is limited to the thrice weekly door-to-door service operated by Arrow Trekkers (☎011/425 2385, fax 425 1096, mobile ☎083/442 2477) from Pretoria/Jo'burg (they'll pick up non-backpackers for a fee); otherwise, the only way to get here is in your own car. The town lies on the R37, beyond Long Tom Pass. You'll find at least three privately run tourist information bureaus in Main Road, all touting information on accommodation and activities. The official **information office** is the Sabie Publicity and Marketing Association (☎013/764 2090, fax 764 2533, *spma@global.co.za*), in the centre of the village, next to the town hall and library. Sondelai Travel & Information (☎013/764 3492), at the Forestry Museum, Tenth Ave, just off Main Street, corner of Ford St and Tenth Ave, is useful if you're keen on **fly-fishing**, as they can issue permits, arrange rod and tackle rental and offer tips on the best places to fish.

Accommodation

You'll find a good supply of reasonably priced **accommodation** in Sabie, though prices can rise dramatically during South African school holidays. Avoid the rock-bottom B&Bs listed at all the information bureaus if you can: most of them offer no privacy.

Artist's Cafe, Hendriksdal, 15km south of Sabie along the R37 (☎013/764 2309). Colonial Africa in the beautifully converted station buildings of Hendriksdal siding, which still has goods trains trundling along its tracks. The stationmaster's house has been converted into a first-class restaurant. ④.

Castle Rock, 2km west of the centre on the Old Lydenburg Rd (☎013/764 1242). Ageing municipal caravan park with the cheapest campsites in town, pleasantly sited along a river, but beginning to suffer from neglect. ①.

Hillwatering Country House, Marula St, off Main St (☎013/764 1421, fax 764 1550). English country decor, antiques and a fabulous breakfast make this Sabie's ultimate overnight experience. The owner is a chef of note, so it's worth ordering dinner here to top it all off. ④.

Jock of the Bushveld, off Main Rd (☎013/764 2178, fax 764 3215). Well-maintained but unexceptional caravan park in the centre with backpackers' dorms and basic self-catering, en-suite chalet rooms. ①–②.

The Kranz, third turning left off the R537 at the airport sign (☎013/764 1330, fax 764 3135). Good-value accommodation in a comfortable house with shared bathroom (②); or the choice of en-suite rooms, rooms in a cottage, or a deluxe suite with a view over a cliff (③).

Merry Pebbles Holiday Resort, 2km west from the centre on the Old Lydenburg Rd (☎013/764 2266, fax 764 1629). Rated the third-best caravan park in the country and the pick of the Sabie self-catering establishments, with camping and self-catering, en-suite chalets. ①–②.

Misty Mountain Lodge, 24km southwest of Sabie on Long Tom Pass (☎013/764 3377, fax 764 1482, *mystymtn@iafrica.com*). Pleasant, newly refurbished B&B units (with self-catering available), some with splendid views across pine plantations into the valleys. Trout fishing on the property with rods and flies for rent at a nominal rate, and well-placed for walks into indigenous forest. ④.

Sabie Rest Camp, Sixth St, opposite the Toyota filling station (☎013/764 2182). Basic dorms with bunks at a central place that has a swimming pool, bar and TV room. ①.

Villa Ticino, corner of Louis Trichardt and Second streets (☎013/764 2598). Extremely hospitable Swiss-owned B&B with a terrace looking onto the hills, and a guest lounge with a pool table. Winter discounts. ③.

The Town and around

Sabie is segmented by **Main Street** (the continuation of the Long Tom Pass from Lydenburg), which meanders into the town centre where it hits **Main Road** at right angles. At the junction of the two, the compact **St Peter's**, an English-style country church designed in 1912 by Sir Herbert Baker, hides in a dense, verdant garden dominated by a gigantic jacaranda tree, which confetties the lawn with mauve petals in early summer.

A large number of **waterfalls** drop down the slopes just outside Sabie. Just 7km from town, down the Old Lydenburg Road (which culminates in a dead end), you can take in three of the most impressive: **Bridal Veil**, **Horseshoe** and, appropriately at the end of the road, **Lone Creek Falls**. Loveliest and easiest to reach of the three, Lone Creek is conveniently accessed down a paved, circular path that crosses a river and works its way back to the car park. More thrilling still are the 70-metre-high **Mac Mac Falls**, which are about 13km north of Sabie along the Graskop road. Shimmering with dewy rainbows, the falls tumble into an inviting pool which is unfortunately fenced off. They were named after the many people of Scottish descent who died looking for gold in the area and whose names appear on dozens of tombstones in the vicinity.

On the way to Lone Creek, *Sabie Horse Trails* (☎013/764 1011 ext 205, after hours ☎764 3324) offers **horse-riding** outings from one hour to two days, depending on your level of experience. Along the same stretch of road you can stop off for a day's **trout fishing** along the Sabie River (see "Arrival and information" opposite for details of permits).

Eating and drinking

Sabie has a couple of very memorable **restaurants**, some relaxed places for light meals or drinks and one or two places you'd probably rather forget.

Artists' Café, Hendriksdal, 15km south of Sabie along the R37 (☎013/764 2309). The owners of this restaurant in converted station buildings cook up a real storm. Their Italian-style dishes are especially recommended. Prices are high, but the art-gallery setting and great atmosphere guarantee a memorable lunch or dinner. Booking essential.

Café Mocha, Main St. Daytime venue dishing up traditional South African food like *bobotie*, Cape curries, malva pudding and an extraordinary wine list featuring choices from the smaller Cape estates.

Loggerhead Restaurant, corner of Main and Old Lydenburg roads. Pick of the bunch and reasonably priced, the *Loggerhead* is known for its trout dishes and imaginative menu, which includes items such as pork fillets stuffed with spinach and cheese, biltong salad, deep-fried ice cream cooked in filo pastry, and a good Cape wine list.

Petena Pancakes, Main St. Cheap but unremarkable creperie with outdoor seating, serving pancakes with savoury mince or fish as well as sweet fillings.

Woodsman Restaurant, corner of Main and Mac Mac roads (☎013/764 2204). Greek food, including vegetarian *meze*, plus local specialities such as ostrich and trout, at a licensed restaurant with a beer garden and a good Cape wine list.

Zeederburg Coach House, Ford St. Restaurant and coffee house-cum-pub in an old colonial house with a verandah which attracts a laid-back crowd.

Pilgrim's Rest

Hiding in a valley 35km north of Sabie, **PILGRIM'S REST**, an almost too-perfectly restored gold-mining town, is an irresistible port of call for the scores of tour buses that meander through the Escarpment's passes every day. A collection of red-roofed corrugated-iron buildings, including a period bank, a filling station with pre-1920 fuel pumps and the wonderful Royal Hotel brimming with Victoriana, the place is undeniably photogenic, but you can't help feeling there's not much substance behind the romanticized gold-rush image, a suspicion that is confirmed when the village nods off after 5pm once the day-trippers have been spirited away.

Some history

Pilgrim's Rest owes its origins to South Africa's first **gold rush**, which predates the uncovering of the great Gauteng seams. In 1873 Alex "Wheelbarrow" Patterson discovered gold in the creek and tried but failed to keep his discovery secret. By the end of the year, Patterson had been joined by 1500 diggers hectically working 4000 claims. Far from the pristine little village of today, the **Pilgrim's Rest diggings** were the site of gruelling labour and unhygienic conditions. Many diggers arrived malnourished, suffering from dysentery and malaria after punishing treks through the

Lowveld. Those who survived could expect drab lives in tents or, if they struck lucky, more permanent daub and wattle huts. The diggings were bought up by the Transvaal Gold Mining Estates (TGME) in 1896. In 1972 the TGME closed down its Beta Mine and Pilgrim's Rest was handed over to the provincial administration. In the Eighties the whole settlement was declared an historic monument. Hidden behind the hill to the southwest of town, away from tourist eyes, mining continues, with functional buildings, cyanide-filled slimes dams and great red scars hacked into the hillside in pursuit of the precious metal, indigenous forest that got in the way having been bulldozed out of existence.

Orientation, information and accommodation

Pilgrim's Rest stretches along its one main road and is divided into Uptown and Downtown. **Uptown**, to the east, centres around the *Royal Hotel* and the **tourist information centre** (daily 9am–12.45pm & 1.15–4.30pm; ☎013/768 1211), which can provide details on accommodation and the surrounding area. Uptown has the greatest concentration of shops and restaurants and consequently draws the bulk of tourists. **Downtown**, or Lower Town, just 1km to the west, has a more down-to-earth atmosphere – though many visitors slip in and out of Pilgrim's without realizing that this area even exists.

Although Pilgrim's Rest is by far the prettiest of the Escarpment towns, it has very little **accommodation**. In Lower Town, the self-catering *District Six Miners' Cottages* (☎013/768 1211; ②) offer authentic two-bedroomed Twenties workers' houses with verandahs overlooking the town and mountains; these are among the best places to stay on the Escarpment, and are extremely well priced. Book ahead, as there's no on-site office. The *Pilgrim's Rest Caravan Park* (☎013/768 1367), also in Lower Town, has a grassy campsite (②) with a river running through it, as well as fully equipped tents (②). The *Royal*, Main St, Uptown (☎013/768 1100; ⑦), is an atmospheric hotel that dates back to the gold-rush days and brims with luxurious Victoriana.

The Town

Apart from souvenir hunting and lingering in the cafés and tea shops, the main activity in Pilgrim's is visiting its handful of **museums**. **Tickets** for all these must be bought at the tourist information office before heading out (see above). You can whip through the three modest town "museums" in a matter of minutes, as they amount to little more than rooms reconstructed as they were in the gold-rush days. More interesting are those out of the centre. To get a really authentic impression of the gold-mining days, head for the open-air **Diggings Site Museum** on the eastern edge of town on the Graskop Road (tours only, daily at 10am, 11am, noon, 2pm & 3pm), where you can see demonstrations of alluvial gold-panning and get a bit of a garbled guided tour around the bleak diggers' huts, remnants of workings and machinery from the early mining days. By contrast, if you want to see how those at the top lived, visit **Alanglade**, just west of the Downtown area (guided tours only, Mon–Sat 2pm), the reconstructed home of the former general manager of the mine. The house has a wonderful collection of early twentieth-century British fashion and decorative arts and shows a sheltered way of life far removed from either Africa or mining.

Eating and drinking

Pilgrim's Rest has plenty of restaurants and tea shops to provide for the daily influx of visitors using Graskop or Sabie as their base. Of the **places to eat** in Uptown, only the *Digger's Den*, a lively, canteen-style place attached to the *Royal* (see above), is open all day and every evening. For lunches the choice is wider: *Chaitow's*, a small café opposite the hotel, serves pricey but tasty pastas and pizzas, as well as smoked trout fillets and pâté. For something more exciting, head for *Edwin Wood's Wine Cellar*, below their wine shop on Main Street, which serves the best Cape wines with cheese platters and, their speciality, smoked wildebeest. There are a few more daytime places along the Downtown section of the main drag: *Scott's Café* serves light meals and has a pleasant bar; *Pilgrim's Pantry*, known for its home-baked pies; *Jubilee Potters & Coffee Shop* does chicken and burgers; and the *Vine* has national specialities such as *bobotie* or oxtail and *samp* on the menu and stays open till 7pm.

Graskop

Some 15km southeast of Pilgrim's Rest, **GRASKOP** owes its place on the tourist map to *Harrie's Pancake Shop*, which serves much-imitated but rarely rivalled crepes, and attracts all the tour buses doing the Escarpment viewpoints. The town itself is exceedingly ordinary, with timber trucks rumbling heavily through, and nothing at all to see in the centre. Its location, however, as the closest town to the Blyde River Canyon, which lies to the north, goes some way towards compensating, and the growing number of artists, together with a small gay community, are helping to shift Graskop's lumberjack image.

Practicalities

Graskop Information Centre, in the Spar Centre (Mon–Fri 8.30am–5pm, Sun 9am–5pm; ☎013/767 1833) is useful, principally for helping with **accommodation**. At the budget end is the *Graskop Backpackers*, corner of Eeufees and Blood River streets (☎013/767 1761, *graskop@global.co.za*; ②), occupying a two-storey house converted into dorms, as well as the property next door, where there are doubles, some en suite. Camping (①) is allowed on the large shady lawn and bedding can be rented at a small charge. Given its size, Graskop has a surprisingly large crop of self-catering places, starting with the budget *Municipal Tourist Park*, on the corner of Louis Trichardt Ave and Hugenote St (☎013/767 1126; ②), which has slightly dour chalets and rondavels. In a similar vein, the *Graskop Log Cabin Village*, Oorwinning St (☎013/767 1974, fax 767 1975; ②–③), is right in the centre of town and has a swimming pool but no views, unlike the *Panorama Rest Camp* (☎ & fax 013/767 1091; ②), just outside town on the road to Hazyview, which has campsites and a variety of units sleeping two to eight people and gardens looking out over the Escarpment. Across the road, *Kloofsig Chalets* (☎013/767 1489, fax 767 1322; ④) make up for their slightly less spectacular siting with more modern and luxurious units and offer discounts when they're not too busy. The only conventional **hotel** in town is the delightful *Graskop*, on the corner of High St and Louis Trichardt Ave (☎ & fax 013/767 1244; ④), which from the outside looks like a bog-standard travelling-salesmen's joint, but hides an attractive interior of African baskets, fabrics and sculptures and airy rooms decorated with considerable flair.

For **eating**, you won't get better than the legendary *Harrie's*, Louis Trichardt St, which has a nice outdoor terrace, serves sweet or savoury pancakes, and has an inside dining room with a roaring log fire in winter. *The Lonely Tree*, on the corner of Louis Trichardt and Kerk streets, works hard to compete, with pancakes, chocolate cake, filter coffee and good service, while *Eastern Delights*, a small groceries shop next to the Total garage in Main Street, does cheap Indian takeaways, including vegetarian options.

For more substantial meals, *Leonardo's*, Louis Trichardt St (☎013/767 1076), is one of the few places open in the evening and serves up average pizzas and pasta; while the *Garret*, Oorwinning St (☎013/767 1573), inside an old train behind the Spar superette, has an extensive menu from *boerekos* to prawns.

Blyde River Canyon and Blydepoort Dam

There are few places in South Africa where you enjoy more dramatic scenery and hardly leave your car than the **Blyde River Canyon**, which drops sharply away from the Escarpment into the Lowveld, and is weathered out of strata of red rock and colossal formations. Protecting it, the **Blyde River Canyon Nature Reserve** (also known as Blyderivierspoort Nature Reserve) stretches from a narrow tail that tickles Graskop in the south and broadens itself into a great amphitheatre partially flooded by the **Blydepoort Dam** about 60km to the north. The views of the canyon are wonderful from both above and below, but the nicest way to take in the vistas is on an easy half-day's drive along the canyon lip.

Canyon viewpoints

Some 3km north of Graskop, the road branches and the easterly R534 takes a fifteen-kilometre loop past a series of intoxicating viewpoints with surprisingly banal names. The road winds through pine plantations until it comes to the turn-off to the **Pinnacle**, a gigantic quartzite column topped with trees, that thrusts out of a ferny gorge. After another 4km the road reaches **God's Window**, one of the most famous and consequently most developed of the viewpoints, with toilets and specially constructed stalls for curio sellers. The sheer drop, with views onto the Lowveld, makes God's Window well worth the effort to get to. The looping road returns to rejoin the R532, which from here heads north for 28km beyond the turn-off to reach **Bourke's Luck Potholes** – strange, smoothly scooped formations carved into the rocks at the confluence of the Treur and Blyde rivers by water-driven pebbles. The best view of all lies 14km beyond, at the **Three Rondavels**. The name describes only one small feature of this cinemascope vista: three cylinders in the shape of ships with the meandering Blyde River twisting its way hundreds of metres below. No photograph does justice to the sheer enormity of the view, punctuated by one series of cliffs after another buttressing into the valley.

The only place in the nature reserve where you can **stay** is *Aventura Blydepoort* (☎013/769 8005, fax 769 8059, *aventura@iafrica.com*; Fri & Sat ③, Sun–Thurs ②), 5km north of the turn-off to the Three Rondavels lookout. The resort has comfortable, self-contained and fully equipped cottages, a swimming pool, supermarket, bottle store and filling station, but a bit of an institutionalized atmosphere, which is nevertheless ideal for children.

Three Rondavels to Blydepoort Dam

The ninety-kilometre drive from the Three Rondavels viewpoint to the base of the canyon affords spectacular views of the Escarpment cliffs rising out of the Lowveld and is easily incorporated into your itinerary if you're heading for Kruger. The drive winds west to join with the R36 and heads north to begin its descent through the Abel Erasmus Pass and then the J.G. Strijdom Tunnel, which plunges through the mountain, with the wide Lowveld plains opening out on the other side. The road takes a wide arching trajectory to circumnavigate the canyon.

Along the R527, near its junction with the R36, the **Monsoon Gallery**, 29km west of Hoedspruit, makes a good place to pause on your journey. This great African arts and crafts shop has an absorbing selection of authentic material, including ironwork and woodcarving from Zimbabwe, superb tapestries from the Karosswerkers factory near Tzaneen, Venda pots and jewellery. Linked to the gallery is an outstanding **place to eat** – *Mad Dogz Café* (☎015/795 5425), where breakfasts, lunches and teas are available

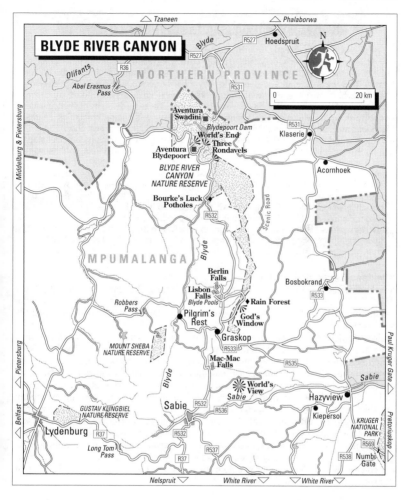

every day. Part of the same outfit, you'll also find a farm stall, an **information bureau** and very comfortable (and stylish) **B&B** accommodation at the *Blue Cottages* (☎015/795 5114; ③). You can have a medium-priced dinner from *Mad Dogz*, served in your garden under candle-light.

Roughly 15km further east, the untarred Driehoek road hives off to the south past the *Aventura Swadini* resort and on to the Blydepoort Dam. Alternatively you can continue on the R531 for a further 12km and take the tarred turn-off to the southwest, which leads straight down to the dam. At a dead end along this road, the **Blyde River Canyon Visitors' Centre** (daily 7am–5pm) has interesting displays on local ecology and a useful model of the canyon that helps you get orientated. The best reason to come here though is for the vistas across the flooded valley below and for the excellent prospects for spending the night close to indigenous bushveld at the foot of the mountains.

BLYDERIVIERSPOORT HIKING TRAIL

The only way to get directly into the canyon from the Escarpment is by walking there, and the five-day **Blyderivierspoort Hiking Trail** is a great way of doing this. Although the 65-kilometre route requires a fair degree of fitness, the gradients aren't generally too taxing and the walk could be undertaken by a hardy novice. The hike starts at God's Window, 5km north of Graskop, and works its way north, finally ending up at the Blydepoort Dam in the valley, 38km from Hoedspruit. There's a diversity of plant and animal life along the way and, even though the nature reserve's hippos, crocodiles, zebras, baboons and monkeys aren't that easy to spot, this is certainly your best shot.

Accommodation is provided along the way in four fully equipped huts that can sleep up to thirty people (the maximum allowed on the trail), with flush toilets, cold showers and firewood. You must carry all your own food. For somewhere to stay near the start or end of the trail, see the Graskop and Blyde River Canyon accounts. As the start and finish of the trail are 150km apart by road, you'll need to have access to two vehicles or make arrangements to get back to your starting point. Take note, too, that although the trail starts in malaria-free terrain, you will be ending up in the Lowveld, where this mosquito-transmitted **disease** is a potential hazard, especially in summer.

Reservations can be made up to six months in advance through the Officer-in-Charge, Blyderivierspoort Nature Reserve, Private Bag X431, Graskop 1270 (☎013/769 6031).

Blydepoort accommodation

Reached along the same road as the visitors' centre, *Aventura Swadini* (☎ & fax 015/795 5141), has 78 **chalets** (Sun–Thurs ③; Fri & Sat ④) that sleep up to six and a **campsite** (①) with stunning scenic surrounds, but a similar institutional feel to its sister resort on the mountain. A number of short trails start from here and you can take cruises on the Blydepoort Dam. Far more intimate, and highly recommended for a quiet and spectacular retreat, is the nearby *Trackers* (☎015/795 5033, fax 793 1689), which has an assortment of accommodation on a marvellous farm full of indigenous bushveld vegetation (as well as zebra and antelope) abutting the canyon's cliffs: camping (①), a backpacker house with a dorm and six doubles (①), self-catering chalets (②) and half-board (④). A trained botanist, who lives on the farm, runs highly recommended, informative and inexpensive **guided walks** through the indigenous vegetation. To get to *Trackers*, turn south into Driehoek road (as for the *Aventura* resort) and continue for a little over 6km, then follow the "D Rushworth" sign on your right to get to the homestead. *Trackers* can also direct you to *Candle Cottage* (②), a **forestry bungalow** on the edge of the canyon with views across to the Kruger National Park. From the cottage, which sleeps eight people in three rooms and comes fully equipped, you can set off on trails through rainforest.

THE LOWVELD

The **Lowveld**, wedged between the Mpumalanga section of the Drakensberg and the Mozambique coastal plain, is a sub-tropical region of savannah that stretches north as a narrow strip, then opens out into Northern and Northwest provinces and engulfs most of Zimbabawe, Zambia and Central Africa. Closely associated at the turn of the century with fortune-seekers, hunters, gold-diggers and adventurers, these days the Lowveld's claim to fame is its proximity to the Kruger National Park and the adjacent private game reserves. Although several of the towns wrapping around the game park fringes are pleasant enough, most people are here to get into big game country.

Largest of the Lowveld towns (and the capital of Mpumalanga), **Nelspruit** lies on the N4, five hours' drive from Johannesburg and accessible by air and bus (with buses to

Maputo as well), making it the transport hub of the region. From Nelspruit, you can head south for 32km to **Barberton**, an attractive settlement in the hills with strong mining connections, or continue for another 41km to **Swaziland**. East from Nelspruit the N2 strokes the southern border of the Kruger, providing easy access to its Malelane and Crocodile Bridge gates, the latter of which is just 12km north of **Komatipoort**, a humid frontier town that guards the border with **Mozambique**.

Heading north from the provincial capital, the R40 passes through **White River**, **Hazyview**, **Klaserie**, **Hoedspruit** and **Phalaborwa**, a series of small towns, all of which are springboards into the Kruger (each in close proximity to its own Kruger entrance gate); are well supplied with accommodation; and with tours available from some, can make good bases for sorties into the game reserve (see p.573). Hoedspruit and Phalaborwa actually fall within Northern Province, but for the sake of continuity have been included in this chapter.

Note that the Lowveld area is **malarial**. For details on necessary precautions, see p.17.

Nelspruit

Mpumalanga's provincial capital, **NELSPRUIT**, 358km east of Johannesburg on the N4, is a traditionally conservative Afrikaner town fast transforming itself into one of South Africa's most relaxed and racially integrated cities. The town's importance lies in its status as the business capital of the province, but it is also a gateway into the southern part of Kruger Park, and has the province's best **transport connections**.

Arrival and information
Daily flights from Durban, Johannesburg and Maputo on Metavia Airlines (π013/741 3142) and SA Airlink (π013/741 3557) arrive at **Nelspruit International Airport**

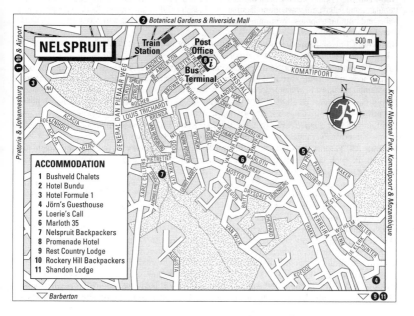

(☎013/741 3557), 12km southwest of town. This grandly named landing strip is served by the **car rental** offices of Avis (☎013/741 1087) and Budget (☎013/741 3871) – pretty handy as there's no transport into town. Camper van and 4WD vehicles are available from Mashona (☎013/741 4447), also at the airport. Greyhound (☎013/753 2100), which has its office in the Promenade Centre, as well as Intercape and Translux **intercity buses** from Johannesburg stop outside the *Promenade Hotel* in Louis Trichardt Street. The Baz **backpacker bus** drops off at the town lodges on its four-times-weekly trip (both directions) from Mbabane (Swaziland) and Jo'burg. Arrangements can be made with hostels in Hazyview (see p.569) to pick you up from Nelspruit. **Minibus taxis** generally rank on the corner of Andrew and Voortrekker streets, a block south of the Nelspruit Station.

Daily Spoornet **trains** between Johannesburg and Komatipoort (continuing on to Maputo three times a week) stop at **Nelspruit Station**, off Andrew Street at the north end of the town centre. Coming from Jo'burg the train arrives at 3.20am; it's more practical to travel in a westerly direction, and services leave Maputo at 8.30am (Mon, Wed & Fri), arriving in Nelspruit at 8.30pm.

There's an excellent **tourist information bureau**, shop 5, Promenade Centre (Mon–Fri 8am–5pm, Sat & Sun 9am–4pm; ☎013/755 1988 or 755 1989, fax 755 1350), next to the *Promenade Hotel* in Louis Trichardt Street, which can provide **maps** and information about the town. Staff can also arrange bookings for Kruger rest camps. Around Louis Trichardt, the main street, you'll find everything you need, from travel agents for arranging tours, to massive supermarkets for stocking up for a trip into Kruger.

Accommodation

Nelspruit's **accommodation** tends to be geared to business travellers and rooms are on the pricey side. If you're on a tight budget, head for the better-value options away from the centre or to the *Hotel Formule 1*, which offers the cheapest beds in town.

Hotel Bundu, 11km from Nelspruit off the R40 to White River (☎ & fax 013/758 1221 or 758 1222). Popular, good-value family accommodation in an old-fashioned country hotel, decorated with animal hides and hunting trophies. Swimming pool, horse-riding and hiking trails to caves with rock paintings. Camping ①, huts ③.

Bushveld Chalets, Kaapschehoop Rd, 6km from Nelspruit (☎013/741 5058, fax 741 3219). Small, self-catering en-suite chalets near the airport. ②.

Hotel Formule 1, corner of N4 and Kaapschehoop Rd (☎013/741 4490, fax 741 4491). The only budget beds in the centre are in no-frills, en-suite boxes, which make for a functional night stop. Continental breakfast is available for small extra charge. ②.

Jörn's Guest House, 62 Hunter St (☎ & fax 013/752 3855). Good B&B run by a former hotelier in a private house, with a nice garden offering Lowveld views and a swimming pool. ④.

The Loerie's Call, 2 Du Preez St (☎ & fax 013/752 4844). Modern house with pool offering en-suite rooms with private verandahs looking onto the Crocodile River Valley. ④.

Marloth 35, 35 Marloth St (☎013/752 4529). Cheapest of Nelspruit's B&Bs, featuring simple furnishings in cool, ceramic-tiled rooms, with breakfast served outdoors under sun umbrellas. Swimming pool and *braai* facilities. ②.

Nelspruit Backpackers, 9 Andries Pretorius St (☎013/755 4429). Former guest house, next to a nature reserve, now converted into a hostel with one large and several small dorms (①) and doubles (②). Also offer budget trips to Kruger and the Blyde River Canyon.

Promenade Hotel, Louis Trichardt St (☎013/753 3000, fax 752 5533). Nelspruit's smartest hotel is aimed primarily at business people but has the advantage of being bang in the centre of town. ④.

The Rest Country Lodge, Uitkyk Rd, 10km from Nelspruit (☎ & fax 013/744 9991 or 744 9992). Each luxury suite in this modern, purpose-built lodge has its own balcony with beautiful views over the Lowveld. Swimming pool, sun deck and verandah. ⑥.

Rockery Hill Backpackers, Mataffin Rd, about 12.5km southwest of town along the Kaapschehoop road, just beyond the airport (☎ & fax 013/741 5011, *1483140@beltel.co.za*). Choose from camping, dorms, double cabins or an en-suite cottage on a farm with a communal kitchen and campfire cooking but no electricity. The owners can usually arrange transfers and do budget Kruger tours. All accommodation ①.

Shandon Lodge, 1 Saturn St (☎ & fax 013/744 9934). Rooms with private entrances arranged around a swimming pool in well-established and large suburban home run by friendly hosts who provide good food. ④.

The Town and around

Nelspruit grew in the 1890s as a base for transport riders, farmers and prospectors, but there is little evidence of these historic origins. Most of the old buildings have been ripped out and replaced by shopping malls and freeways, and the town has a bustling and mildly prosperous feel, mostly due to the fact that it is a major commercial centre, not only for the Lowveld, but also for shoppers from Swaziland and Mozambique.

The town centre, roughly six streets crisscrossed by another half dozen, could hardly be easier to get around. The N4 from Johannesburg to Komatipoort sweeps through town, briefly pausing to become **Louis Trichardt**, Nelspruit's main street, before reassuming its identity as the national highway.

Apart from the shops and supermarkets, Nelspruit's major attraction lies just outside of town: the **Lowveld National Botanical Garden** (daily: May–Sept 8am–5.15pm; Oct–April 8am–6pm; small entry fee). Some 5km north of Nelspruit off the R40 and set on the banks of the Crocodile River, the garden comes a close second to Cape Town's Kirstenbosch Gardens. Natural waterfalls and walks through humid rainforest make a very pleasant break from the boiling midday heat. If you've been to Kruger, you'll have a chance to look at some of the same **trees** here, helpfully identified with labels. The plants are grouped according to habitat, and the garden specializes in **cycads** from around the world. There is also a grove of baobabs from South Africa and other African countries. A useful brochure sold at the entrance gate has a map showing the highlights of the garden and the paths through it.

The **Riverside Mall** complex on the other side of the river from the Botanical Gardens comprises a casino, a large shopping centre and a hotel. Over the road is the **Crocodile River Snake and Reptile Park** which is worth a visit if you don't mind seeing reptiles in cages.

Eating and drinking

Most of Nelspruit's **restaurants** are buried in shopping malls, where you'll find all the usual steakhouses and fast-food chains. *Spur*, in the Sanlam Centre on Louis Trichardt, is good for salad selections and burgers, and you'll find spicy Portuguese-style chicken takeaways at *Nando's* in Brown Street off Louis Trichardt. *Café Mozart*, Promenade Centre, Louis Trichardt Street, does quiches, coffee and tea, and there's the *Steer* steakhouse in the same mall. For a more expensive and imaginative meal, head for *Costa Do Sol*, in Nel City, on the corner of Kruger and Louis Trichardt streets, which serves good Portuguese and Italian dishes. **Drinking** is done mostly at the restaurants or at the *Hotel Promenade* in the centre.

Listings

Emergencies Ambulance ☎013/10177; Fire ☎013/753 3331; Police ☎10111.

Hospitals Nelmed Clinic (☎013/755 2672) is open 24 hours a day and is suitable for non-emergency treatments. For urgent consultations contact Nelspruit Private Hospital (☎013/744 7150).

Laundry The Laundrette (open daily), is at the Youth Centre along the N4, next to Joshua Doore on the corner of Paul Kruger and Louis Trichardt streets.

Mozambique Embassy, Brown St (013/752 7396), for visa applications.

Post office The main post office, in Voortrekker St, is open 8.30am–4pm.

Taxis City Bug (☎013/744 0128) runs tuk-tuk shuttle services around the centre and to the suburbs.

South from Nelspruit: Swaziland via Barberton

Provided you have your own transport, **Barberton** makes a more relaxed staging post than Nelspruit for journeys between the south of the Kruger National Park and Swaziland. The closest and most beautiful route into **Swaziland** from Barberton is through the border crossing at Bulembu (8am–4pm), but the road is poor and should be avoided unless you're in a 4WD vehicle, or a fairly tough car in the dry season. A more practical option is to enter Swaziland via the Ngwenya/Oshoek (7am–10pm) or Jeppe's Reef/Matsamo (8am–4pm) border posts. There is no organized transport to Swaziland from Barberton.

Barberton

BARBERTON lies 36km south of Nelspruit and has a colonial backwater charm, a handful of historical sights, tropical vegetation and an attractive setting in a basin surrounded by mountains. The town began its urban existence after Auguste Robert ("French Bob") discovered **gold** in 1883 on a nearby farm. Despite his attempts to keep the news to himself, other diggers realized something was up when French Bob began building a canal to his claims. The following year, **Graham Barber** discovered another incredibly rich gold reef and got his name hitched to the town at a riotous christening using a bottle of gin. An influx of shopkeepers, hoteliers, barmen and prostitutes, followed by ministers of religion whiffing the ripe scent of sin, soon joined the diggers in the rude tent, tin, thatch and mud frontier town, with nearly every second building functioning as a boozing joint. During the fabulous **boom** of the 1880s the mines slipped out of the grasp of the small-time prospectors and came under the control of the large corporates that still own them today.

Arrival and information

No scheduled public **transport** comes into Barberton: the closest transport hub is Nelspruit, from where you'll need to find a minibus taxi for Barberton. The excellent **tourist information bureau**, Crown St (Mon–Fri 8am–1pm & 2–4.30pm, Sat 8.30am–noon; ☎013/712 2121), can find you accommodation in the area, or point you to local walks, as well as supply you with reams of brochures and maps covering the whole province.

Accommodation

Because it's a bit off the main trail, Barberton is short on **places to stay**, but the prospects get better as you head a little out of town.

Fountain Baths Guest House, 48 Pilgrim St (☎013/712 2707). Pleasant rooms and self-catering mini-apartments for two, with a garden edging onto the hills and a swimming pool. ②.

Jock of the Bushveld Huts, Nelspruit Rd, 4km from town (☎013/712 4002, fax 712 5915). Reasonably priced thatched self-catering chalets, huts and a guesthouse, sleeping two to six, on a lychee and mango farm, with horse-riding, swimming and microlight flights on offer. ②.

Kiaat Cottage, 6km from Barberton on the Agnes Mine road (☎013/712 4067). Self-catering cottage tastefully furnished and with magnificent views of the De Kaap Valley. ②.

Old Coach Guest House and Restaurant, 13km north of Barberton on the R38 to Kaapmuiden (☎013/719 9755, fax 719 9637). Comfortable twin and double en-suite rooms at an establishment set in its own grounds with a pool. The licensed restaurant has a terrace looking onto spactacular mountains. A convenient stop en route to the southern Kruger rest camps or Swaziland.③.

The Phoenix, 20 Pilgrim St (☎013/712 4211, fax 712 5741). Barberton's only hotel has a long corridor of standard en-suite rooms, where the noise of television seeps through doors. ③.

Weston Cottage, 17km west of Barberton on the R38 to Badplaas (☎013/712 3920). Cottage that sleeps four on a big cattle farm, done out in frilly florals and with self-catering and B&B rates. ②–③.

The Town

There are seven working **mines** around Barberton, and each has its own club and entertainment scene, which means you won't find miners packing out public bars as in the wild days of old. Neither do the mines run tours; since they are all fully operational, there's no time to humour a few visitors. However, there is one small-time prospector and hotelier outside Barberton (see box, below) who will give you a go at gold-panning, swilling water and sand in a big dish to watch for the telltale thread of gold appearing in the dark sand.

You can explore the mining history of the town at the **Barberton Museum**, 36 Pilgrim St (Mon–Fri 9am–4pm, Sat & Sun 9am–1pm & 2–4pm; small entry fee), three blocks east of the tourist information bureau. In a well-designed, modern building, the museum has good displays on the gold-rush era and, if phoned in advance, staff can do a gold-panning display for groups.

While you're here, pick up the map showing the location of the **Victorian houses** that fall under the museum's supervision and make a good excuse to wander some of the streets and enjoy the flamboyant gardens. Built for a wealthy middle-class family and restored to its 1904 grandeur, **Belhaven House**, 18 Lee Rd, is a five-minute walk north from the museum and has an intriguing frontage, but is not always open. Further up Lee Road, **Fernlea House** (Mon–Fri 9am–12.30pm & 1.30–4pm; small entry fee) is a wood and iron structure, while **Stopforth House**, 18 Bowness St, to the east, is the most interesting of the three, and a guard can take you through the house at 10am, 11am, noon, 2pm and 3pm. The original wood and iron house and outbuildings were built by James Stopforth, a local baker and general dealer.

Eating and drinking

Barberton's best place to **eat** is the cheap and friendly *Co-Co Pan* in Crown Street, which dishes up straightforward hamburgers, steaks and omelettes. Your best shot at meeting locals is to head downstairs to the lively **pub** below the restaurant. Next to the tourist information bureau on Crown Street is the pleasant *Victorian Tea Garden*, with a white gazebo straight out of a London park, and good tea and light snacks served outdoors. The *Old Coach Guest House* (see opposite), 13km from town, is recommended for its good cooking and beautiful surrounds.

GOLD-PANNING AND HIKING AT BARBERTON

Unlike at Pilgrim's Rest, where you'll have to be content with merely watching how panning was done, at Barberton you can try it yourself on trips operated by Danny Brink (☎013/712 6289). He can extend the tour to **Eureka City**, an 1880s mining settlement that died forty years later. Eureka hasn't been reconstructed the way Pilgrim's Rest has and you'll only see walls and foundations, but you drive through a real mine to get there.

To get a sense of what the old mines were like, the two-kilometre circular **Fortuna Mine Hiking Trail**, just south of town, takes you through a disused tunnel built to transport gold-bearing ore to the Fortuna Mine. The actual tunnel is 600m long and you'll need to take a torch. The trail, which starts at the car park off Crown Street to the south of town, goes through an attractive area of identified indigenous trees before entering the tunnel, and once you're through you get good views of Barberton and the De Kaap Valley.

East from Nelspruit: Komatipoort and the Mozambique border

Heading east from Nelspruit, the N4 roughly shadows the progress of the **Crocodile River**, which traces the southern boundary of Kruger National Park on its journey to the Indian Ocean through Mozambique. For 58km to the tiny settlement of **Malelane**, the road travels within view of the Crocodile's riverine forest, passing by lush, sub-tropical farmlands and the grey Dali-esque formations of granite *koppies*. Some 4km further on, the road turns off to Kruger's **Malelane Gate**, which is the most convenient entry point for *Berg-en-Dal* rest camp (see p.580). A signpost 12km east of Malelane indicates *Buhala Country House* (☎013/790 4372, fax 790 4306, *buhala@lbm.co.za*; ⑦), a fabulous **guesthouse** on a mango, sugar cane and papaya farm, set high on the banks of the Crocodile, with views across the slow water into Kruger. Trips into Kruger can be arranged from here for around R350 per person.

Komatipoort

Of all the towns along the Kruger fringes, **KOMATIPOORT**, 87km east of Nelspruit, owes its frontier character least to tourism and far more to the fact that it stands at the cusp between one of Africa's richest countries and one of its poorest. The exotic flavour of this small, rambling town comes from its dusty streets dotted with small-time market traders selling tiny piles of tomatoes and onions, the vivid green of the surrounding cane plantations and the colourful wraps of Mozambican women. Despite a slightly seedy edge and the unshakable whiff of wheeling and dealing in sweaty hotel bars, it's a safe and friendly place, where you can enjoy a hint of what lies in Mozambique, just across the Crocodile River.

Komatipoort's **Ressano Garcia** border post is the bottleneck through which hundreds of dispossessed **Mozambicans** attempt to squeeze their way each day to get to the "gold-paved streets" of Johannesburg. Some who get turned back will chance their lives attempting to steal in elsewhere through the wilds of Kruger, while the luckier ones who already have jobs on the mines pass through, drinking their earnings on the thrice-weekly train that takes them home to Maputo and returns this way with a fresh cargo of labour. Unless you're flying, this is the only major South African gateway into Mozambique. A favoured holiday playground for white South Africans and Rhodesians up until the Seventies, when it gained majority rule, Mozambique was brought to its knees by a devastating, apartheid-sponsored war that brought tourism to an end for nearly two decades. Peace has thankfully returned and travellers are again beginning to explore and are returning with positive tales to tell.

Practicalities

Greyhound, Translux and Intercape **intercity buses** all pass through town on their way between Jo'burg and Maputo (via Nelspruit), stopping at the border post outside town. A daily train from Johannesburg arrives at **Komatipoort Station**, Nichol St, and there are the ubiquitous **minibus taxis** from Nelspruit. If you're planning on heading into Mozambique, contact Mozambique Tours (☎013/790 8000 or 790 8222; ask for Carl Parsons), which can advise on visas and travel.

Places to stay include *Komati Holiday Resort* (☎013/790 8040; ②), roughly 2km out of town, which has self-catering en-suite timber cabins (each with a double and two singles) set among indigenous thorn and fever trees and camping. To get there, take the N4 towards Nelspruit for about 200m out of town and turn right at the Shell garage, following the signs to the resort. The only upmarket place to stay is the motel-style *Border*

Country Inn (☎013/790 7328, fax 790 7100; ④), 3km out of town just before the border – a convenient stop if you want to make an early start into Mozambique in the morning.

Komatipoort's big surprise is its humdinger of a **restaurant**: the *Tambarina* (☎013/790 7057) in Rissik Street, a Mozambican-style cantina that captures the taste and feel of the former Portuguese colony, with vibrantly tropical decor and a courtyard shaded by mango trees.

North from Nelspruit: Kruger's western flank

The **R40** heads north from Nelspruit along the western border of the Kruger National Park, passing through prosperous tropical-fruit-growing farmlands and poverty-stricken former black "homeland" areas. Guesthouses, many of them fairly upmarket, pop up all along the way to Hazyview until you reach the densely populated former *bantustan* areas around **Bosbokrand** (also known by its English name, Bushbuck Ridge). Roadside lodgings reappear once you reach Klaserie, which lies on the border of Mpumalanga and Northern Province. Many of them are on game farms – poor cousins to the pricier lodges right inside the game reserves to the east.

North of the Mpumalanga border you'll pass by little towns en route to the central section of Kruger National Park and the Manyeleti and Timbabvati private game reserves. If you're coming down the Escarpment along the R36/R527 from the Blyde River viewpoints, after about 75km you'll encounter a fork in the road. The more northerly road leads to **Hoedspruit** and **Klaserie**, both of which lie in the heart of bushveld **game farm** country where budget game viewing is offered, though these are no substitute for the big game country of Kruger and its adjacent private reserves. Much further north and generally accessed from Pietersburg on the N1, **Phalaborwa** is unavoidable if you're heading into central Kruger through Phalaborwa Gate.

Hazyview

HAZYVIEW, 43km north of Nelspruit, is little more than a sprawl of shops buzzing with minibus taxis and small market stalls selling fruit and goods to the surrounding African community. The village's only interest lies in the fact that, just 19km from Numbi Gate, it's perfectly positioned for access to the game-rich southern section of Kruger National Park. This is one of the best bases for visitors who aren't spending the night in the park itself and would prefer to come home after a hard day's game viewing to hotel comforts. **Day-trips into Kruger** can be arranged through Welcome Tours & Safaris, on the road to Paul Kruger Gate – see p.578 for details.

Practicalities

No public **transport** comes into Hazyview, but if you're staying at one of the local backpackers' lodges you can arrange to be collected from Nelspruit.

The village has a wide range of **accommodation**. At the bottom end of the scale, the *Kruger Park Backpackers*, Main Rd (☎ & fax 013/737 7224, *krugback@mweb.co.za*), is pleasantly located under shady bushveld trees and offers campsites, dorms, rondavels and, nicest of all, Zulu beehive huts (all ①). There's a swimming pool and they run organized tours into Kruger from here, Jo'burg or Pretoria. In a similar vein, *Big Five Backpackers* (☎013/737 6098, fax 011/622 3668), 2km outside town on the White River road, has dorms (①) and doubles (②) in stone buildings with thatched roofs on a massive banana plantation with big views, as well as offering budget camping tours of Kruger, which is just 18km away. Staying at the old-fashioned but comfortable *Numbi*, Main Rd (☎013/737 7301, fax 737 7525), won't break the bank either if you camp (①) or stay in their bungalows (③) – the place also has conventional hotel rooms (④). *Tembi*, along the R40, just north of the Sabie River (☎013/737 7729, fax 737 7036; ③) has reasonably priced en-suite B&B rooms.

For somewhere out of the ordinary, make for *Thulamela*, 1km down White River Road, off the R40 (☎ & fax 013/737 7171, *info@thulamela.co.za*; ⑤), which is run by a dietician who serves healthy breakfasts and puts you up in en-suite timber cottages, each with its own deck, Jacuzzi and bushveld views. Ask about weekday discounts. Additional luxurious accommodation is offered at *Hippo Hollow Country Estate* (☎013/737 7752, fax 737 7673; ⑤), along the R40 to Paul Kruger Gate, just south of town, with thatched cottages on the banks of the Sabie River featuring a communal eating, reception and bar area. Trips into Kruger with Welcome Tours leave from here every morning. Hazyview's most upmarket country lodge is the *Rissington Inn*, just south of town (☎013/737 7700, fax 737 7112; ④–⑤), which has a handful of plush rooms set in the gardens of a large homestead with a swimming pool and excellent food. To get there from Hazyview, take the R40 south and turn right at Kiaat Park, after the Haze Nissan garage on the left-hand side of the road.

All the hotels have unexceptional, mid-priced **restaurants** open to the public.

On to Klaserie

The only reason you're likely to find yourself heading along the R40 from Hazyview is to gain access to the private game reserves – **Sabi Sand**, **Manyeleti** or **Timbavati** – that join up with the western flank of Kruger (covered on p.586). These reserves can also be reached via the more scenic routes along the Escarpment, but the Lowveld route isn't without its interest, if only as an antidote to the sanitized worlds of Kruger and the mountain resorts.

After Hazyview the R40 passes through irrigated farmlands and low hills dotted with bushveld trees. As you approach **Bosbokrand**, 28km to its north, the corridor between the Escarpment and big game country changes, with the sudden appearance of shantytowns, busy roads, overgrazed lands and dense settlements interspersed with the odd papaya and banana tree. Also known as Bushbuck Ridge (a direct translation from the Afrikaans), the town's name comes from the hilly finger that extends east from the Escarpment. Any bushbucks that might once have wandered here have long since been displaced by the cattle and goats that have chewed away the surrounding vegetation and now spill out into the roads.

Despite the fact that maps indicate little or no habitation, the busy and sometimes hazardous road passes through the former *bantustan* of **Lebowa**, where the people live crammed at a density six times greater than the provincial average. **Klaserie**, 42km north of Bosbokrand, lies in the middle of game farms and sits poised on the border between Mpumalanga and Northern Province. Head east from here for **Orpen Gate**, 45km away, which gives access to the rewarding central section of Kruger National Park.

Hoedspruit

Lurking in the undulating Lowveld, straight up the R40 from Klaserie, with the hazy blue mountains of the Escarpment visible on the distant horizon, is the small service centre of **HOEDSPRUIT**. The town lies at the heart of a concentration of **private game reserves** and lodges. There aren't any sights here; the only reason you'll be passing through is on your way to Kruger or to stay in one of the game lodges, which, invariably, you will have booked long before you reach the area.

Generally what's on offer around Hoedspruit is a more affordable taste of the bush. As the price drops, however, so do a few other things, most importantly the quality of the game you're likely to see. What you do still get is a degree of pampered living, privacy and the opportunity of guided game viewing, all of which can intensify your experience of the bush immeasurably when you get to Kruger.

Practicalities

Daily scheduled **flights** from Johannesburg on SA Express arrive at Eastgate Airport (☎015/793 3681), some 14km south of Hoedspruit. For **car rental**, Budget (☎015/793 3681) have an office at the airport. For transfers to game lodges from here, contact Eastgate Lodge Transfers (☎015/793 3678). Hoedspruit itself is little more than a collection of gun shops, liquor stores, service stations and the odd grocery shop. The **Central Lowveld Tourism Association** (☎015/793 2418), which has no official office, will be able to give you advice over the phone about the different game lodges.

Around Hoedspruit

As this is an area where animals are taken very seriously, it's not surprising to find the **Moholoholo Wildlife Rehabilitation Centre** (tours 9.30am & 3pm; moderate entry fee; booking essential, ☎ & fax 015/795 5236), on the R531 between the R40 and R527, about 3km from the tarred turn-off to the Blydepoort Dam. Ex-ranger Brian Jones has embarked on an individual crusade to rescue and rehabilitate injured and abandoned animals, notably raptors, but also lions, leopards and countless others. The centre is part of a wider reserve and both night drives and early morning walks are offered. You can also make an easy tour of the rehabilitation cages and pens. Game-lodge-style fully-catered **accommodation** (⑦), including three meals, a night drive and an early morning walk, is available.

Along similar lines, although larger in scale, is the **Hoedspruit Research and Breeding Centre for Endangered Species** (Mon–Sun 8.30am–4pm; ☎015/793 1633; entry fee), more commonly called the **Cheetah Project**, 20km south of Hoedspruit on the R40. Here a minibus will take you around a large number of pens and cages containing beautiful, silky-furred king cheetah, wild dog, blue crane and other endangered species bred for purposes of protection, restocking and research. While the centre gives you an opportunity to see some of these animals at close quarters, it does feel like a bit of a zoo and it can be tough work convincing yourself that it's all done in the name of science.

A worthwhile project is the **Nyani** Shangaan cultural village, (☎015/793 3816), 4km along the Guernsey Road which turns off the R40, 22km south of Hoedspruit. This is a genuine effort developed by Axon Khosa, a local Shangaan man, who asked his grandparents what the villages were like when they were children. He hosts visits along with his extended family of nine, taking visitors on a tour of the village and offering the option of a **meal**, which is usually a chicken dish with butternut, gem squash (a delicious local cricket-ball sized marrow), served with wild spinach and groundnuts mixed into *mielie pap* (maize meal). You can also **stay overnight** (②) in a hut with traditional dung floors and thatching (that looks untidy by comparison with the safari lodges but is authentically Shangaan). The walls are constructed with mud taken from termite mounds and are beautifully hand-decorated with white, orange and black motifs. You sleep on fold-up matresses and there are showers and toilets for the exclusive use of guests. If you want to spend time at Nyani, **booking** is essential as this isn't a casual drop-in place. The project is child-friendly and highly recommended if you're travelling with nippers. Nyani can also be taken in as part of a tour to the Kruger operated by Trans Frontiers Safaris (see Kruger "Tours and packages", p.578 for details).

Hoedspruit game farms

None of the following **game farms** have direct access to Big Five game viewing, but they're worth considering as relatively inexpensive and comfortable places to stay deep in the bush on your way to or from Kruger. A number of farms also offer specialist activities.

Eyrie Birding Lodge, 36km from Hoedspruit on the R531 (☎015/795 5775). Rather downhome accommodation in a fantastic, elevated position on the slopes of the Escarpment. Run by Dr Peter Milstein, one of South Africa's most knowledgeable experts on birds, and chosen by him as one of the finest bird-watching spots in the country. Full board ⑨.

Kwa-Mbili, Thornybush Game Reserve, 30km east of Hoedspruit (☎015/793 2773). Intimate, unpretentious lodge with vibrant African decor, bush cuisine and plenty of game in the vicinity. A maximum of ten guests are housed in chalets or luxury tents. Activities on offer include game viewing on foot and by mountain bike. Full board ⑨.

Marc's Camp, just over 6km along Guernsey Rd (☎015/283 2811). Fun and wacky place to stay, with accommodation up a stepladder in creaking tree houses above the Klaserie River. The rooms don't have electricity and bathrooms are shared. Game drives on a neighbouring estate are on offer. Full board ⑨.

Otter's Den, on R531 not far from junction with the R521 (☎ & fax 015/795 5250). Small and relaxing camp on a bush-covered island in the Blyde River recommended for fishing and bird-watching. There's also a river-fed rock swimming pool. Full board ⑦.

Tlhakan Chuni Camps & Trails, 10km north of Hoedspruit on the R40 (book through Central Lowveld Tourism Association, ☎015/793 2418, fax 793 1678). Basic but atmospheric reed-walled self-catering camp set on the riverbank by the confluence of the Blyde and Olifants rivers. The emphasis is on bird-watching and bushwalking. Minimum of four people ③.

Tshukudu, 4km north of Hoedspruit on the R40 (☎015/793 2476, fax 793 2078; *tshukudu@iafrica.com*). Family-run farm good for kids (baby sitters can be arranged), but not the place to come if you like your animals wild and hungry – here you might be accompanied on your early-morning game walk by cuddly, hand-reared lion cubs or a kindly elephant. The price includes two game drives. Full board ⑨.

Phalaborwa

The most northerly access to the central section of Kruger is at **PHALABORWA**, 74km north of Hoedspruit. The name means "better than the south", a cheeky sobriquet coined as the town developed on the back of its extensive mineral wealth. During the Sixties, the borders of the park near Phalaborwa suddenly developed a kink, and large copper deposits were found, miraculously, just outside the protected national park area.

The only reason you'll be in Phalaborwa is on your way in or out of Kruger, and there's little to divert you on your way through unless you need a bed for the night. However, keen golfers shouldn't miss the chance of a round in the company of big game at the signposted **Hans Merensky Country Club** (☎015/781 5931), where it's not unusual to see giraffes and elephants sauntering across the fairways. If you find yourself kicking your heels in the late afternoon you can whet your appetite before heading into the park with a short **microlight flight** over the park (contact ☎082 956 1502), or a sundowner **boat trip** with Jumbo River Safaris (☎015/781 6168, booking essential), which sets out at 3pm down the Olifants River and frequently encounters game, including elephants.

You may see dust-encrusted vehicles driving around town which have long aerials with small flags attached to the top of them – this is so that they don't get squished by the big trucks manoeuvring around the mines. Also unusual is the refugee camp on the outskirts of town, which has sprung up because illegal immigrants from Mozambique, only 60km away on the other side of Kruger National Park, use Phalaborwa as a navigation aid, guiding themselves by the smoke of the chimneys by day, and the lights by night.

Arrival and information

Regular SA Airlink (☎015/781 5823) flights arrive from Johannesburg at Phalaborwa **airport** (☎015/781 5823), very close to Kruger's Phalaborwa Gate, off President Steyn Street. The closest rest camps from here are Letaba, 50km into the park, and Shimuwini, 52km in. All Phalaborwa's **car rental** firms are represented at the airport:

Avis (☎015/781 5169), Budget (☎015/781 5404) and Imperial (☎015/781 2376). Phalaborwa Safaris (☎015/781 6247) offer transfers from the airport to game farms and lodges.

Phalaborwa has a good selection of **shops**, including the well-stocked Link pharmacy, open until 8pm, in the mall off Palm Street.

Accommodation

Phalaborwa has plenty of **places to stay**, but prices can be steep. *Elephant Walk*, 30 Anna Scheepers St (☎015/781 4758, fax 781 2758; ①), is a small and friendly backpackers' lodge with camping facilities and budget tours into Kruger on offer. They also have a fully-equipped self-contained flat (②) as well as two self-catering cottages (②) at Kruger's Phalaborwa Gate, which work out cheaper than staying in the park and are handy if all the accommodation on the other side is full. Equally relaxed, though a tad more upmarket, is *Sefapane Lodge*, Copper St (☎015/781 7041, fax 781 7042; ④), a collection of neat beehive huts which achieves the feeling of a comfortable rest camp, with a restaurant, a nice pool and a poolside bar. *Steyn's Cottage*, 67 Bosvlier St (☎015/781 2836; ③), is a fairly classy Victorian-style guesthouse, with a swimming pool, a tea garden and a restaurant, while the *Impala Protea Inn*, on the corner of Essenhout and Wildevy streets (☎015/781 5681; ④), is pretty characterful as *Proteas* go, and has a pool and a pleasant pub.

Eating and drinking

For a relatively small town, Phalaborwa has a good selection of **places to eat**. The restaurant at *Sefapane Lodge* is pretty decent, and its sunken **bar** beside the swimming pool is the most convivial in town. There are two independent restaurants on Rooibos Street: *Monroe's* serves inexpensive burgers, while the classier, though still moderately priced *Tiffany's* has a wide-ranging menu. You'll find the usual steaks on offer at the *Campico Spur*.

KRUGER NATIONAL PARK

Kruger National Park is arguably the emblem of South African tourism; the place that delivers what most visitors to Africa want to see – scores of elephants, lions and and a cast of thousands of other game roaming the savanna. A narrow strip of land hugging the Mozambique border, Kruger stretches across Northern Province and Mpumalanga, an astonishing 414-kilometre drive from Pafuri Gate in the north to Malelane Gate in the south, all of it along tar, with many well-kept gravel roads looping off to provide routes for game drives.

Kruger is designed for **self-driving** and **self-catering**, though the temptation is to drive too much and too fast, leading to fewer sightings, and rental cars tend to be low off the ground and aren't as good for game viewing as those used by lodges or tour operators. However, self-driving offers complete flexibility, and you can hop in a car knowing you'll find supplies once you arrive at most of the rest camps (though not much in the way of fruit or vegetables) – indeed it remains the only way of seeing Kruger's animals if you're travelling with children, as many lodges don't allow under-twelves. The park's popularity means that not only are you likely to share animal sightings with other motorists, but that **bookings** are at a premium, particularly during South African school holidays, and that at any time of year you may have to stay in whichever camp has accommodation, rather than in your first choice. Book as far in advance as possible.

More exclusively, Kruger comes pretty close to fulfilling *Out of Africa* fantasies in the **private game reserves** that rub up to its western flank – where you'll get luxury accommodation and food, but more importantly (especially if this is your first safari), qualified rangers to show you the game and the bush with only a tiny group of other guests.

The ideal is to do a bit of each, perhaps spending a couple of nights in a private lodge to "get your eye in" and a further two or so exploring the public section. But whatever you choose, be sure to relax and don't get too obssessed with seeing the Big Five. Remember that wildlife doesn't imitate TV documentaries and you're most unlikely to see lion-kills (you may not see a lion at all), or huge herds of wildebeest migrating across dusty savanna. There is always an element of luck involved in what you see, and this is exactly what makes game spotting so addictive. A few **game-spotting tips** are outlined on p.580, which can make a big difference to your trip.

Walking possibilities are limited, though many of the private reserves will offer escorted morning game walks. However, there are several three-night **wilderness trails** in different parts of the park, led by armed rangers – a fabulous way of getting in touch with the wilderness, but one you'll have to book for months in advance.

Note that Kruger National Park is **malarial**. For details on necessary precautions, see p.17.

Some history

It's highly questionable whether Kruger National Park can be considered "a pristine wilderness", as it's frequently called, given that people have been living in or around it for thousands of years. **San hunter-gatherers** have left their mark in the form of paintings and engravings at 150 sites that have so far been discovered and there's evidence of farming cultures at many places in the park. Around 1000 to 1300 AD centrally organized states were building stone palaces and engaging in **trade** that brought Chinese porcelain, jewellery and cloth into the area.

But it was the arrival of white **fortune seekers** in the second half of the nineteenth century that made the greatest impact on the region. The twentieth century has had an ambivalent attitude to the hunters, criminals and poachers (like the notorious ivory hunter Cecil Barnard), who made their livelihoods here, decimating game populations. Barnard's exploits are admiringly recounted in the *Ivory Trail* by T.V. Bulpin, while every other episode of the still-popular yarn, *Jock of the Bushveld*, set in the area, includes accounts of hunting. In the twentieth century African farmers were kicked off their traditional lands to create the park.

Paul Kruger, former president of the South African Republic is usually credited with having the foresight to set aside land for wildlife conservation. Kruger figures as a shrewd, larger-than-life figure in Afrikaner history and it was **James Stevenson-Hamilton**, the first warden of the national park, who cunningly put forward Kruger's name in order to soften up Afrikaner opposition to the creation of the park. In reality Stevenson-Hamilton knew that Kruger was no conservationist and was actually an inveterate hunter. Kruger "never in his life thought of animals except as biltong", Stevenson-Hamilton wrote wryly in a private letter.

Mammals, birds, reptiles and insects

Among the nearly 150 species of **mammals** which you may see in the park are cheetah, leopard, lion, spotted hyena, wild dog, black and white and rhino, blue wildebeest, buffalo, Burchell's zebra, bushbuck, eland, elephant, giraffe, hippo, impala, kudu, mountain reedbuck, nyala, oribi, reedbuck, roan antelope, sable antelope, tsessebe, warthog and waterbuck. The staggering 507 **bird species** include raptors, hefty-beaked hornbills, ostriches and countless colourful specimens.

Keep your eyes open and you'll also see a variety of **reptiles, amphibians** and **insects** – most rewardingly in the grounds of the rest camps themselves. Although the camps are fenced off from big game, there's always something to see up the trees, in the bushes or even inside your rondavel. If you spot a miniature ET-like reptile crawling upside down on the ceiling, don't be tempted to kill it; it's an insect-eating gecko and is doing you a good turn. If, however, you have a horror of insects or frogs, stay away from Kruger in the rainy season (Nov–March), when they're more in evidence.

When to visit

Kruger is rewarding at any time of the year, though each season has certain advantages and drawbacks. If you don't like the heat, avoid high **summer** (Dec–Feb), when on a bad day temperatures can nudge 45°C – though they're generally in the mid- to high thirties. Many of the camps have air-conditioning or fans and it's definitely worth considering renting an air-conditioned car. Throughout the summer (Nov–March) the heat can be tempered by short thunder showers. At this time of the year, everything becomes greener, softer and prettier, and from early November you're likely to spot cute young animals.

There's little rain from April to August, the cooler **winter** months, and the vegetation withers over this period, making it easier to spot game. Although daytime temperatures rise to the mid-twenties (days are invariably bright and sunny throughout winter), the nights and early mornings can be freezing, especially in June and July, when you'll definitely need warm clothes. Rondavels in the public rest camps are not heated. A definite plus of winter is the virtually total absence of mosquitoes and other insects.

Orientation

The public section of Kruger can be divided roughly into three sections, each with a distinct character and terrain. If you have limited time, it's best to choose just one or two areas to explore; but if you're staying for five days or more, consider driving its length slowly, savouring the changes in landscape along the way. The southern, central and northern sections are sometimes referred to as "the circus", "the zoo" and "the wilderness" – sobriquets that carry more than a germ of truth.

The **southern section** has the greatest concentration of game, attracts the highest number of visitors and is the most easily accessible part of the park if you're coming from Johannesburg, which is 478km away on the N4 national highway. The park headquarters (Skukuza) are here, with an airport, car rental facilities, a filling station, a car repair workshop, a car wash, bank, post office and doctor, as well as enough rondavels to accommodate one thousand people. The **central section** also offers good game viewing, as well as two of the most attractive camps in the park at **Olifants** and **Letaba**. The further north you go, the thinner both animal populations and visitors become, but it's the **northern section** that really conveys a sense of wilderness, reaching its zenith at the marvellously old-fashioned **Punda Maria** camp, which dates back to the Thirties.

Outside the public section, big-game country continues in several exclusive and expensive **private game reserves** clustering on huge tracts of amalgamated land to its west. The three major private reserves are **Sabi Sand** to the south and **Timbavati** and **Manyeleti**, adjoining the central section of the national park. Although they are privately owned, as far as animals are concerned the private and public areas are joined in an enormous, seamless whole. The only real difference is that private reserves are not places you drive yourself around in and they are for the exclusive use of private guests. If you do arrive here by car you'll leave it at the gate and not see it again until you leave.

Access

Without your own car, you've got three options for getting to Kruger: you can take one of the many **tours** on offer – some involving day-trips from points just outside the park, others involving camping inside the park; you can fly into the **airport** and rent a car; or you can stay in a private reserve and arrange to be transferred from one of the

Lowveld towns that is served by buses or planes (see p.589). However, flights to airports servicing Kruger, and car rental, are expensive, and there are no special deals.

By road

There are eight **entrance gates** along the western and southern borders of Kruger; where you enter will depend on where you're coming from and which camp you're heading to. **From Johannesburg**, the quickest way to get to Kruger is along the N4, which brushes along its southern boundary en route to Mozambique and quickly gets you close to the **southern gates** of Malelane, 411km away, and Crocodile Bridge, another 57km further on. These are also the closest if you're coming **from KwaZulu-Natal**, either via Barberton or Swaziland. If you've been exploring the **Blyde River Canyon** area, access is off the R538/R40 between White River and Klaserie to the **western gates** (Pretoriuskop, Paul Kruger, Orpen and Phalaborwa) leading into the southern and central sections of the park. The easiest way to get to the two **northern gates** on the west side is off the N1 from Johannesburg to Messina on South Africa's northern border, taking the R524 east at Louis Trichardt for Punda Maria Gate, or the R525, 58km further north, to Pafuri Gate (see p.584).

Remember if you're trying to get from one part of the park to another that although it's far more fun driving inside, the speed limit (50kph on tar, 40kph on dirt) makes it a slow journey – and you're bound to make loads of stops to watch animals.

By air

SAA (☎011/356 1111) **fly** out three times daily from **Johannesburg** to **Skukuza**, Kruger's headquarters. SA Airlink (toll-free ☎0800/11 4799) flies three times every weekday (and less frequently over weekends) from Johannesburg to **Phalaborwa** (see p.572), which lies just outside Phalaborwa Gate, and six times every weekday (less often over weekends) to **Nelspruit**, 45 minutes' drive from either Numbi or Malelane gates. SA Airlink also fly daily **from Durban** to Nelspruit. SA Express Airlines (☎011/978 6927, fax 978 5429) offer **fly-drive packages** (see below).

Car rental

For **car rental**, Johannesburg or Pretoria are obvious centres to make your arrangements, but closer to the Kruger you can sort out a vehicle at Nelspruit International Airport, 56km from Numbi Gate, through Avis (☎013/741 1087), Budget (☎013/741 3871) or Imperial (☎013/741 3120). Phalaborwa Airport also has branches of Avis (☎015/781 5169), Budget (☎015/781 5404) and Imperial (☎015/781 2376). At Skukuza Airport, inside Kruger, you'll find only Avis (☎013/735 5651).

Tours and packages

An increasing number of **tours** will get you into the Kruger – your best bet if you're not self-driving. As well as those listed below, it's also worth checking out the backpackers' lodges in the vicinity, most of which either operate budget safaris or have links to operators who do. In **Hazyview** contact *Big Five Backpackers* or *Kruger Park Backpackers* (see p.569); in **Nelspruit**, *Rockery Hill* and *Nelspruit* backpackers can both arrange tours (see p.564); and in **Phalaborwa** (see p.573), *Elephant Walk* does reasonably priced day-trips.

Bundu Bus Tours and Safaris (☎011/675 0767, fax 675 0769, mobile ☎082/567 7041, *sryan @bundusafaris.co.za*). Departuring from Jo'burg, a four-day, fully catered safari takes in the Escarpment, Timbavati game reserve, two nights in Kruger, a night drive and a walk with an armed ranger (R1050). They also do a six-day safari with two nights in Swaziland, visiting wetlands and game reserves in KwaZulu-Natal, and a Zulu cultural village (R1850).

Livingstone Trails (☎011/867 2586, fax 867 6774, *livtrail@global.co.za*). Four days, two spent inside the Kruger at campsites, plus a visit to a Ndebele cultural village and a jaunt around the Blyde River Canyon for around R850. Longer trips also available.

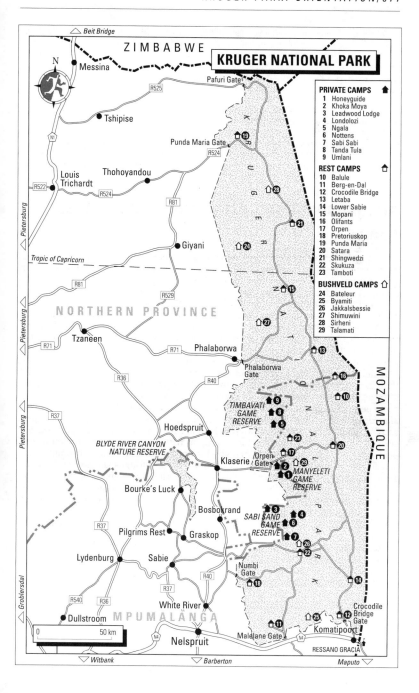

SA Express Airlines (☎011/978 6827, fax 978 5429). Fly-in safaris with a choice of accommodation. Their cheapest, from Jo'burg, includes two nights at *Skukuza* public camp, all meals and three game drives (R3486). Expect to spend around R1000 extra for one of the luxury private camps, or a cool R3500 or so more for the ultra-upmarket *Singita* camp.

Trans Frontiers Safaris (☎015/793 3816, mobile ☎083/700 7987). Good backpacker-friendly tours run by a couple with an outstanding track record. Four-night/five-day safaris from Jo'burg hostels, with some nights in huts at two camps on community land bordering the Kruger. Activities include walking in game country with an armed guide and drives into the Kruger. The last night is at the *Nyani* Shangaan village, with a traditional dinner and post-prandial singing and drumming. Good value at around R1800.

Welcome Tours, *Sanbonani Resort Hotel*, on the road between Hazyview and Paul Kruger Gate (☎013/737 7945, fax 737 6293, *fgrove@welcome.co.za*). Half-day (R350, excluding lunch – they pull into a rest camp, or bring your own) and full-day (R445, includes lunch) tours from Hazyview. Daily departures at 5–6am (depending on the time of year).

Accommodation: rest camps and bushveld camps

At most of Kruger's fourteen main **rest camps** the sounds of the African night tend to get drowned out by air conditioning and the merriment of *braais* and beer. It's not all bad news, though; at least you'll have all the facilities you could ever want on hand. Nearly all camps have electricity, public telephones, petrol stations, shops, restaurants, laundrettes and snack bars. Some also have pools and most offer night drives for viewing nocturnal animals on large trucks equipped with spotlights. Despite the suburban atmosphere, the rest camps can be very pleasant, with walks around the edges, labelled trees to help you identify what you see on drives, and plenty of birds and smaller creatures around the camps themselves. Several, including *Lower Sabie*, *Skukuza*, *Olifants* and *Letaba* have views onto rivers where, from a distance, you can see game coming to drink.

Kruger camps have a variety of accommodation. At most of them you'll find **thatched rondavels**, each with an outdoor eating area and facing communally towards each other rather than out towards the views. The best rondavels are on the camp perimeters or directly facing onto rivers. Nine of the rest camps have a **campsite** (with shared kitchen and washing facilities), which provide the park's cheapest accommodation (R40 to R75 for two people). Sites for **caravans** and **camper vans** are available wherever there's camping, cost up to R70 for two people and often have a power point. Some camps have **furnished safari tents** and **huts**, in configurations usually sleeping two to four people. Most of these have fridges and air conditioning, some come with basic crockery and cutlery, and all share communal kitchens and ablutions at prices ranging from R80 to R150 for two people. **En-suite chalets**, **rondavels** and **huts** come in several variations, ranging from those with just showers, toilets and fridges to ones fully equipped with kitchens. Prices range from R225 to R380 per couple, and often reflect how modern the camp is rather than the accommodation facilities.

For a more rustic (and pricier) experience, you'll need to head out to one of the handful of smaller **bushveld camps**, which dispense with all the niceties of shops and restaurants and get down to basics. These camps are more exclusive, being out of bounds to anyone not booked in to stay.

Southern Kruger rest camps

The so-called "circus" is the busiest section of the Kruger, with its hub at **Skukuza**, the biggest of all the Kruger camps and **Lower Sabie**, one of the most popular. Apart from containing some of the best places for seeing large quantities of game, southern Kruger is also easily accessed from Johannesburg along the N4. At peak times of year

KRUGER ESSENTIALS: THE PUBLIC SECTION

ACCOMMODATION BOOKINGS

Kruger's rest and bushveld camps are adminstered by South African National Parks. If you're planning on staying at the park over school holidays or weekends, book well ahead. Booking in writing opens thirteen months in advance; closer to the date, you'll usually find somewhere, especially at off-peak times, if you're not too particular about where you stay in the park. For **bookings** contact South African National Parks (Pretoria ☎012/343 1991, fax 343 0905; Cape Town ☎021/22 2810, fax 24 6211; *reservations @parks-sa.co.za*).

ENTRY GATE ADMISSION FEES

To enter Kruger, you pay a fee per person plus a charge for the vehicle.

Adult	R30
Child (2–15)	R15
Vehicle	R24
Minibus	R97

OPENING HOURS

Gates

Every rest camp is fenced off and has an entrance gate that's closed and opened at the times indicated below. You are required to return to your rest camp or leave the park prior to gate closing times. Except where specified, all times refer to both entrance and camp gates.

Jan	5am–6.30pm (camp); 5.30am–6.30pm (entry)
Feb	5.30am–6.30pm
March	5.30am–6pm
April	6am–5pm
May–Aug	6.30am–5.30pm
Sept	6am–6pm
Oct	5.30am–6pm
Nov & Dec	4.30am–6.30pm (camp); 5.30am–6.30pm (entry)

Reception at rest camps
8am–5.30pm

Shops
8am–half an hour after gate closing

Restaurants

Breakfast	7–9am
Lunch	noon–2pm
Supper	6–9pm

DRIVING

Speed limits are: 50kph on tar, 40kph on untarred roads and 10kph in rest camps. Speed traps operate in some parts of the park.
Approved roads only should be used. Don't drive on unmarked roads and never drive off-road.
Never leave your car (it's illegal and dangerous), except at designated sites.

this area can buzz with vehicles jostling to get up close to big cat sightings, which always appear to evoke poor human behaviour.

GAME-VIEWING TIPS

•**Binoculars are a must** for scanning the horizon when you're out viewing. Don't try consciously to spot animals – many are well disguised. Instead, watch for any movement or something that strikes you as a bit out of place.

•**Look out for other stopped cars**, which are often a good indicator of a game sighting.

•**Plan your game drive carefully** and invest in a detailed map of Kruger (available at virtually every rest camp). Use the map to choose a route which includes rivers or pans where you can stop and enjoy the scenery and birdlife while you wait for game to come down to drink, especially in the late afternoon.

•**Driving really slowly** pays off, particularly if you stop often. Switch off your engine when you stop, open your window and use your senses. Being in the bush isn't just about seeing animals: there are also the smells and sounds of the wilds, which complete the picture and provide useful clues. Twigs breaking or the alarm calls of animals can hint at something afoot.

•**Don't embark on overambitious drives** from your rest camp. You'll see as much game sitting quietly in your car as you would frantically driving around all day.

•**Take food and drink** with you. You don't want to have to break off that terrific lion-sighting because you're starving and can't miss lunch. Carry plenty of water to avoid dehydration or heatstroke. If you have your own teabags and milk you can make tea at the designated picnic sites, where there is always boiling water available, tables and chairs to enjoy your picnic in the wild, and *braai* places powered with gas.

•**Tuning into animal behaviour** can greatly enrich your experience and provides constant interest even on days when big cats stubbornly refuse to put in an appearance. Even commonplace species such as impala become fascinating when you understand what they're doing and why. Although the widely available *Safari Companion* by Richard Estes sounds like a manual on how to treat your porters, in fact it's an accessible and engrossing guide to the behaviour of African mammals (see "Books", p.737).

•**The best times of day** for game viewing are when it's cooler during the early morning and late afternoon. Set out as soon as the camp gates open in the morning and go out again as the temperature starts dropping in the afternoon. Take a siesta during the midday heat, just as the animals do, when they head for deep shade where you're less likely to see them.

•**Take an interest in geology, trees and birds** and you need never be bored because "there's nothing going on". The excellent *Make the Most of Kruger*, available at most rest camps, is well worth investing in for the basic interpretation it provides of the park ecology and for filling in those empty moments.

Berg-en-Dal

In the southwest corner of the park, **Berg-en-Dal** is one of the newest camps, built in the Eighties and with modern chalets that break with the Kruger tradition of thatched rondavels. Set attractively among *koppies* in a shallow grassy basin (its Afrikaans name means "hill and dale"), 12km northwest of **Malelane Gate**, the camp overlooks the Matjulu stream and dam, both of which can be reached by means of a walkway running along the perimeter fence. The modern, fully equipped chalets with terraces are widely spaced to provide privacy and are landscaped among indigenous bushveld vegetation. Facilities include a beautifully positioned swimming pool, a shop selling a good range of food, a licensed restaurant, a snack bar, a filling station and a laundry.

Crocodile Bridge

East of *Berg-en-Dal*, **Crocodile Bridge** is the least scintillating of Kruger's rest camps, and its position at the very southern edge of the park overlooking farmland does nothing to enhance your bush experience. Located at the **Crocodile Bridge Gate** on the north bank of the Crocodile River, the camp is reached via Komatipoort, 12km to its south on the Mozambique border. The main reason to spend the night here is if you're arriving late and don't have time to press on into the park. Facilities are limited to a laundry and filling station, and a shop selling the most basic of supplies. Accommodation is in en-suite huts that sleep two to three and have cooking facilities. If you're pushing north to *Lower Sabie*, it's worth taking the drive slowly, as this area, dotted with knobthorn and marula trees, is known for its herbivores, which include giraffe, kudu, steenbok, wildebeest, zebra, buffalo and waterbuck as well as ostrich, warthog and the magnificent black sable antelope. You should also keep your eyes peeled for predators such as lion, cheetah, hyena and jackal.

Lower Sabie

Some 35km north of *Crocodile Bridge*, **Lower Sabie** occupies game-rich country that places it among the top three rest camps in the Kruger for mammal-spotting. The surrounding open savanna and the camp's position on the banks of the Sabie River attract animals coming to drink and graze, and the terrain around here is rated among the most beautiful in the southern Kruger. Within kilometres of the entrance gate to the camp, a number of waterholes and dams populated with crocodiles and hippos make good spots to park and watch for game coming to quench their thirst. In the thorn thicket country hard by the west of the camp, you'll find promising terrain for catching sight of elephants moving between the trees as well as white rhino grazing on the sweet grasses, which also bring herds of buffalo and, in their wake, lions. Accommodation is in huts with shared ablutions as well as more expensive en-suite units with kitchens, some with river views. There's a restaurant, a cafeteria, a shop, a filling station and a laundry.

Pretoriuskop

Due west of *Lower Sabie*, but not directly connected to it, **Pretoriuskop** is reached via **Numbi Gate**, 9km to its west. Set in an area of sourveld, characterized by granite outcrops, tall grass and sickle bush favoured by mountain reedbuck, sable and white rhino, the camp is in an area stalked by lions, wild dogs and side-striped jackals. However, given the dense bush you'll be more likely to spot larger species such as kudus and giraffes poking their necks over the bushes. Accommodation consists of en-suite cottages and rondavels in addition to cheaper units with shared ablution and cooking facilities. The camp has a restaurant, a snack bar, a shop, a laundry, a swimming pool and a filling station. Night drives are on offer.

Skukuza

Kruger's largest rest camp, **Skukuza** lies at the centre of the best game-viewing area in the park. Its position can be a double-edged sword, because where you get large amounts of game, hordes of humans aren't far behind. *Skukuza* accommodates over one thousand people and resembles a small town. A sprawling collection of rondavels, it sits on the edge of the Sabie River, which is overlooked by a wide paved walkway furnished with park benches, from which you can watch crocodiles float by on the brown water looking like driftwood.

Skukuza is the hub of Kruger and has an airport you can fly into and a car rental agency. You can get repairs done here to your vehicle in the rest camp's garage and there's also a post office, a bank, a filling station, two restaurants, a cafeteria and a library at the central reception area. The closest entry point is through **Paul Kruger Gate**, 12km to the west, which in turn is 42km east of Hazyview. Accommodation is in a range of thatched, en-suite units, or more cheaply in some furnished East African-style tents in the caravan park, with shared ablutions and kitchens. Night drives and day drives in open vehicles can be arranged at the main complex, and cost around R60 and R100 per person respectively.

Central Kruger rest camps

Game viewing can be extremely good in the "zoo", with the area between *Skukuza* and *Satara* reckoned to be one of the global hot spots for lions. At **Olifants** you'll find the Kruger's most dramatically located camp, with fantastic views into a river gorge, while **Satara** is the second-largest and one of the most popular – its placement is ideal for making sorties into fertile wildlife country.

Orpen and Maroela

Like *Crocodile Bridge*, **Orpen** is located right by an entrance gate, 45km east of Klaserie, and is recommended mainly if you're arriving late and don't have time to make it further into the park before the camp gates close. *Orpen* is far preferable to its southern counterpart though, because although it's on the western periphery of Kruger, the substantial Timbavati Private Game Reserve lies to its west, so you're already well into the wilderness once you get here. Facilities are pretty basic, with a filling station and a reception that doubles up as a rudimentary shop. None of the accommodation is en suite and cooking is done in communal kitchens. The camp is small, peaceful and shaded by beautiful trees. If you want to camp you'll need to go to the small **Maroela** satellite camping area that overlooks the Timbavati River. It is situated approximately 4km from *Orpen* and has electricity. You must report to *Orpen* reception to check in before going to the campsite.

Tamboti

Not far from Orpen Gate into the park, **Tamboti** is reached by turning left 2km after *Orpen* and continuing for 1km. Kruger's only tented camp doesn't quite match up to its promise of a traditional East African safari. In it's favour though, its position on the banks of the frequently dry Timbavati River is superb, among apple leaf trees, sycamore figs and jackalberries. You'll often see elephants from your tent just beyond the electrified fence, digging in the river bed for moisture. This is why it's deservedly so popular – you'll have to book ahead to be sure of getting a place. Each walk-in tent has its own deck overlooking the river, but best of all are numbers 21 and 22, which enjoy the deep shade of large riverine trees, something you'll be grateful for in the mid-summer heat. All kitchen, washing and toilet facilities are in two shared central blocks and you bring all your own cooking and eating utensils. There are fridges and electric lights in the tents.

Satara

Due east of Orpen Gate, 46km straight along the tar, **Satara** ranks second only to *Skukuza* in size and the excellence of the game viewing in its surrounding grassy plains. Set in the middle of flat grasslands, the camp commands no great views, but is preferable to *Skukuza* because it avoids the feeling of suburban boxes on top of each other. Accommodation is in cottages which are arranged around lawned areas shaded by large trees, which provide some relief from the midday sun. Facilities include a restaurant, cafeteria, shop, filling station, laundry and vehicle repair workshop. About halfway along the tarred road between *Satara* and *Skukuza*, which is 92km to its south, the vicinity around Tshokwane picnic site reputedly has the highest concentration of lions in the world and is hence also a popular stamping ground for motorists. The area around *Satara* itself is usually rewarding for sighting grazers, such as buffalo, wildebeest, zebra, kudu, impala and elephant.

Balule

On the southern bank of the Olifants River, **Balule** is 41km north of *Satara* and 87km from Phalaborwa Gate. The only voltage you'll find at this very basic satellite to *Olifants*, 11km to the north, is in the electric fence that keeps out lions. The compact *Balule* has two sections, one consisting of six spartan rondavels and another of fifteen camping and caravan sites. Each section has its own communal ablution and cooking facilities. *Balule* takes its bushveld identity seriously and luxuries are kept to a minimum – as is the price: this is one of the few rest camps where, unless you're camping, two can stay for under R100. There are iron washstands with enamel bowls, no windows and you can forget about air conditioning. You'll have to bring your own crockery, cutlery and utensils. You need to report to *Olifants* at least half an hour before the gates close.

Olifants

Because of its terrific setting on cliffs overlooking the braided Olifants River, **Olifants**, is reckoned by many to be the best rest camp in Kruger. It's quite possible to spend hours sitting on the benches on the covered look-out terrace, gazing into the valley whose airspace is crisscrossed by Bateleur eagles and yellow billed kites cruising the thermals, while the rushing of the water below creates a hypnotic rhythm. The camp has a charmingly old-fashioned feel. Accommodation is in thatched, en-suite rondavels, with numbers 1 to 24 possessing superb views overlooking the valley; it's worth booking well in advance to get one of these. The river marks the division between rugged, rocky *veld* with ghostly fever trees growing along the riverbanks to the south and to the north mopane woodland which attracts the large antelope such as eland, roan, sable and tsessebe. Also around here is promising country for spotting elephant, giraffe, lion, hyena and cheetah, and you should look out for the tiny klipspringer, a pretty antelope that inhabits rocky terrain which it nimbly negotiates by boulder-hopping. A highlight of the area are some of the dirt roads which loop along the Olifants River. Facilities include a restaurant, a snack bar, a shop and a laundry.

Letaba

Set in mopane shrubland, **Letaba** is 34km north of *Olifants*, set beautifully on an oxbow curve along the Letaba River, a view which, sadly, very few of the rondavels enjoy. The restaurant does have great vistas of the floodplain, and you can spend a day just watching herds of buffalo mooching around, elephants drifting past and hosts of other plains game. The camp is old and quite large, a fact mitigated by large acacias and mopanes as well as ilala palms. *Letaba* is in the midst of good elephant country and has an interesting museum with exhibits on the life cycle of the large mammals as well as displays on the bull elephants with inordinately large tusks, who have trampled the area. Accommodation is in either en-suite rondavels or ones with shared ablution and cooking facilities as well as large furnished tents. All the usual restaurant, shopping and laundry facilities are here, as well as a vehicle repair workshop.

Northern Kruger rest camps

You won't find edge-to-edge game in the northern "wilderness", but crossing the Tropic of Capricorn after **Mopani** camp gives a symbolic boost to the idea that you're entering hot savanna country. The north is the least visited of Kruger's regions and creates the most convincing impression of African wilderness, especially once you hit **Punda Maria** camp, which feels like a real old-time outpost in the bush.

Mopani

Some 42km north of *Letaba*, **Mopani** is one of the newer camps in Kruger and overlooks the Pioneer Dam. A sprawling place in the middle of monotonous mopane scrub, its swimming pool provides cool relief after a long drive. Similarly, the dam, one of the few water sources in the vicinity, attracts animals to drink and provides an outstanding lookout for a variety of wildlife including elephant, buffalo and antelope. The modern en-suite accommodation, built of rough-hewn stone and thatch, is quite spread out and designed more for driving than walking. The restaurant is above the usual Kruger average and the bar has a good view across to the dam. Other facilities include a shop, a laundry and filling station, and you can go on organized night drives.

Shingwedzi

A fairly large camp featuring square, brick chalets and a few older, colonial-style white-wash and thatch bungalows, **Shingwedzi**, 63km north of *Mopani*, is sited in extensive grounds shaded by large mopane trees and palms. The dining room has a terrace, frequented by starlings and cheeky hornbills jostling to pounce on your food. From the terrace you get a long view down across the usually dry Shingwedzi River. Look out for the weavers' nests with their long, tube-like entrances hanging from the eaves outside reception and the cafeteria. Facilities include a restaurant, a cafeteria, a shop, a filling station and a swimming pool. Night drives are on offer.

Punda Maria and Pafuri

Kruger's northernmost camp, **Punda Maria**, 71km beyond *Shingwedzi*, is also the park's wildest and least visited. There's less concentration of game up here, but to aficionados, this is the real Kruger: a relaxed, tropical outpost near the Zimbabwe border, well away from the bustle of motorists. This isn't to say you won't see wildlife here (the Big Five all breeze through from time to time), it's simply that in its woodlands and dense mopane scrubland you have to work that much harder at game spotting. The real rewards of *Punda* are in its landscapes and stunningly varied vegetation types, with a remarkable nine biomes all converging here, which also makes it paradise for bird-watchers. Some of the accommodation is in the original Thirties huts that ought to be declared National Monuments but are in danger of being pulled down for modernization. All units are en suite and have fridges, while some have kitchens and the rest make use of communal cooking areas. The camp has a very simple restaurant, a small shop and a filling station. **Pafuri** picnic site, 46km north of Punda, should on no account be missed, as it's here that you'll experience the true richness of northern Kruger. The site is a large area under the shade of massive thorn trees, leadwoods and jackalberry trees on the banks of the Luvuvhu River and is the ultimate place for lunch. An interpretation board gives a fascinating account of human history in the area. There are *braai* facilities, a constantly boiling kettle to make your own tea and ice-cold canned drinks can be bought from the attendant.

Bushveld camps

Bushveld camps are far smaller, more remote and a whole lot more basic than the main rest camps. You won't find any shops or restaurants at these camps, but they are all within reasonable reach of larger rest camps – just in case you can't survive without a Coke. The appeal of the bushveld camps is that they get you away from day-to-day trivialities – and the tourist pack – and into the wilderness. The downside is that they all have **cottages** accommodating a minimum of four people, which means that you're going to pay at least R175 per person, and a lot more if there are only two of you and you're staying in one of the larger units that go for about R615–900 each. Because of their exclusivity, the camps get booked up quickly, so stake your claim as early as possible. Most offer game drives during the day and at night.

WILDERNESS TRAILS

Wilderness trails in Kruger won't bring you closer to game than driving would: the experience is really about getting closer to the vegetation and smaller creatures. Under the guidance of an experienced ranger, the two-day trails pass through areas of notable beauty that have a diverse plant and animal life. Groups (limited to eight people) spend three nights in four rustic, two-bed huts, served by reed-walled showers and flush toilets. Simple meals are provided. Trails cost in the region of R1100 per person fully inclusive.

The trails are closed over the Christmas school holidays and are heavily subscribed for the rest of the year. **Booking** in writing opens thirteen months in advance and is recommended if you have your heart set on a particular trail; contact South African National Parks (see p.579).

•**Bushman Trail** covers the southwestern section of the park, near *Berg-en-Dal* rest camp. The trail camp is in a secluded valley, characterized by granite hills. San paintings in many of the hill shelters are an added feature of the trail.

•**Metsimetsi Trail** operates midway between Skukuza and Satara, with the camp at the foot of a mountain and overlooking a small waterhole. Black rhino and large predators move through the undulating savanna and rocky gorges and ravines.

•**Napi Trail** sets out from a camp between *Skukuza* and *Pretoriuskop* into woodland bushveld. Undulating terrain and granite hills suit the area's resident population of white rhino, while black rhino, elephant, lion and buffalo are also often seen. Birdlife is prolific.

•**Nyalaland Trail** is based in the remote northern section of the park along the Madzaringwe Stream north of *Punda Maria*. The area is known for its fever-tree and baobab forests, prolific birdlife and spectacular views.

•**Olifants Trail** has its camp on the southern bank of the Olifants River, from which it offers a magnificent view of the river. Riverine bush and gorges characterize the terrain, and lion, buffalo and elephant are often seen.

•**Sweni Trail** camp overlooks the Sweni stream in the wilderness area near Nwanetsi and provides a view of marula and knobthorn savanna. A resident pride of lions pads about here and is frequently seen.

•**Wolhuter Trail** walks in the vicinity of *Berg-en-Dal* and *Pretoriuskop* camps in the southern section of the park, where rhinos are relatively common, as is a wide variety of other game.

Bateleur

About 40km southwest of *Shingwedzi* rest camp, **Bateleur** is well off the beaten track, in the remote northern section of the park on the banks of the frequently dry Mashokwe stream. The camp has a timber viewing-deck, excellently placed for vistas of game coming to drink at a seasonally full waterhole. The nearby Silver Fish and Rooibosrand dams also attract game as well as birdlife in prodigious quantities. Seven family cottages can accommodate up to 34 people. Each has its own kitchenette and fridge, with electricity provided by solar panels.

Byamiti

Byamiti is on the banks of the Mbyamiti River, about 41km northeast of the Malelane Gate and 26km west of Crocodile Bridge Gate. Its proximity to the latter is one of the main advantages of this very southerly camp. Another plus point is that the terrain attracts large numbers of game including lion, elephant and rhinos. Fifteen family cottages, all with fully equipped kitchens, can accommodate a maximum of seventy visitors.

Jakkalsbessie

On the bank of the Sabie River, some 7km north of *Skukuza* rest camp, near the airfield, **Jakkalsbessie** is one of the less remote bush camps and is periodically treated to the sound of aircraft taking off or landing at the *Skukuza* landing strip. Although it may be too close to the "city lights" of *Skukuza* for some, the camp is beautifully positioned and has easy access to some of the richest game country in Kruger. Eight thatched cottages with fully equipped kitchens can accommodate a maximum of 32 people.

Shimuwini

On the upper reaches of the Shimuwini Dam, which is filled by the Letaba River, **Shimuwini** lies about 50km from the Phalaborwa Gate on the Mooiplaas Road. In mopane and bushwillow country, with sycamore figs along the banks of the river, this camp is not known for its game but is a perennial favourite among bird-watchers. It's an excellent place for spotting riverine bird species, including fish eagles. Up to 71 people can be accommodated in the fifteen family cottages which come equipped with kitchens and with verandahs.

Sirheni

Sirheni is on the bank of Sirheni Dam, roughly 54km south of *Punda Maria*. It's a fine spot for bird-watching, with some game also passing through the area. The big pull, however, is its remote bushveld atmosphere in an area that sees few visitors. The fifteen one- or two-bedroom cottages, all equipped with kitchens, can accommodate eighty visitors.

Talamiti

Lying on the banks of the usually dry Nwaswitsontso stream, about 31km south of Orpen Gate, **Talamiti** is in the varied terrain of mixed bushwillow woodland that attracts giraffe, kudu, wildebeest, zebra and predators like lion, hyena and jackal, as well as rhino and sable. The camp has the capacity for eighty people in its ten six-bed and five four-bed cottages.

Private accommodation

Which **private camp** you choose depends largely on what type of safari you're after: a more rustic experience with no electricity and the sounds of lions roaring at night, or a highly luxurious hotel in the bush where food is as important as your bush experience. All the camps follow the same basic formula of full board, with dawn and late-afternoon game drives conducted by a ranger, assisted by a tracker, in open vehicles. Afternoon outings usually turn into night drives following sundowners in the bush, and you'll usually be able to fit in a walk as well.

Private camps aren't places you can casually pop into. You'll need to **book ahead** either directly through the contact addresses given here or through a specialist travel agent (such as those listed in Basics). There are scheduled **flights** from Johannesburg to Phalaborwa, Hoedspruit, Nelspruit and Skukuza, or from Durban to Nelspruit. Camps generally pick up guests from the airport. By car it will take five to six hours from Johannesburg; you'll be given detailed instructions on how to get to your camp when you book.

Prices quoted are **per person, per night**, sharing a double unit, including all meals (where relevant) and activities. At the rock bottom end (under R500) are extremely rustic places with the most basic of facilities, such as bucket showers. What they do give you is exclusive access to the best of South Africa's big game country. For the real safari experience, staying in more comfortable en-suite units where you're fed and pampered, expect to pay from just under R1000. It should be stressed, though, that such places are rare and need to be booked well ahead. The really snazzy places, which are by far the majority, weigh in from R1000 to anything upwards of R2500. On the whole, the huge price gulf between the bottom and top ends reflects the incidental extras, such as level of luxury and cuisine – and often simply reputation. All are en suite and have proper beds and a swimming pool unless specified.

Honeyguide

Manyeleti Game Reserve; PO Box 786064, Sandton 2146 (☎011/880 3912, fax 447 4326, *hguide@global.co.za*).
One of the best-value private reserves accommodates guests in large East African-style tents with beds. Each has a deck which overlooks a dry river bed fringed with riverine forest. Its two vehicles are in radio contact with each other and with neighbouring *Khoka Moya*, which multiplies your chances of a game-sighting. *Honeyguide* has access to 100 square kilometres of the Manyeleti, which it shares with *Khoka Moya*, and there are seldom more than three vehicles out at a time. Surprising touches for a budget camp include fine, custom-made linen, and tea brought to your tent in the morning. The food is good, the service excellent, the staff friendly, the game drives first class and the camp highly recommended at prices starting from R750. They also have the more basic *Outpost Camp*, which costs R400.

Khoka Moya

Manyeleti Game Reserve; PO Box 298, Hoedspruit 1380 (☎ & fax 015/793 1729, *khoka @country-escapes.co.za*).
An easy-going, tasteful game lodge taking sixteen guests and verging on the luxurious, but still affordable for its type. Accommodation is in comfortable huts connected by boardwalks set in semi-woodland savanna. Prices start from R720 for the original, unmodernized units, rising to R950 for the more luxurious newer ones.

They also run the *Trails Camp*, a very basic reed camp, elevated 2m in the air, deep in the bush beside a waterhole, with a bucket shower. The camp is rented out to a single group of four to eight people, with its own ranger, tracker and chef. An absolute steal at R300, including meals.

Leadwood Lodge

Sabi Sand Game Reserve; Exeter Game Lodges, PO Box 2060, Nelspruit 1200 (☎013/741 3180, fax 741 3183, *exeter@cis.co.za*).
Operated by Exeter Safaris, one of the few self-catering outfits is also one of the cheapest private camps. Accommodation is in five thatched, two-bed cottages dotted along the banks of the Sand River under jackalberry, leadwood and tamboti trees. The comfortably furnished air-conditioned units come with all cooking utensils; just bring your own food and drink. Full-time camp staff service the cottages and tend fires in the public area. Two daily game drives and a walk are included in the price, but you run the risk of these turning into a bit of a scrum as Leadwood shares traversing rights with Exeter's *Main Lodge* as well as two neighbouring outfits, all of which are liable to descend on the same game sighting. Costs start at R450, including game drives but no meals. For a minimum of eight and maximum of ten people they also have *Hunters' Lodge*, another self-catering outfit (R430). Book well ahead as their excellent value makes them highly popular.

Londolozi

Sabi Sand Game Reserve; Private Bag X27, Benmore 2010 (☎011/784 7077, fax 784 7667, *reservations@conscorp.co.za*).
Leopards are virtually synonymous with *Londolozi* and there are few places you'll stand a better chance of seeing these notoriously elusive stalkers in the wild. If you're

prepared to fork out large sums to see cats, there's no better place to do it than at one of *Londolozi*'s camps, each of which carries the imaginative stamp of Conservation Corporation Africa, whose hallmark is unapologetic indulgence with a green conscience. Biggest and least exceptional of the three is *Main Camp* (US$450), which accommodates twenty in comfortable chalets. The best thing about it is the wonderful outdoor dining room surrounded by woodland and jettying out over the Sand River basin. But once you're spending this kind of money you may as well go the extra hundred to stay in the more intimate surroundings of the smaller camps. *Bush Camp* accommodates sixteen people and has a beautiful swimming pool from whose deck you can lounge and look onto the river with rates starting from US$500, while most exclusive is *Tree Camp*, built into a riverbank amid indigenous woodland at US$550.

Ngala

Timbavati Game Reserve; Private Bag X27, Benmore 2010 (☎011/784 7077, fax 784 7667, *reservations@conscorp.co.za*).
Despite being a member of Small Luxury Hotels of the World, *Ngala* is actually rather large for a private game lodge, accommodating up to 42 people. Expect every indulgence you'd get at a top-quality hotel. Everything at *Ngala* conspires to feed "old Africa" fantasies, from thatched buildings crammed with stylish furniture and decorated with fine artefacts, right down to the silver and Villeroy and Boch crockery. Formal dinners (starched tablecloths and crystal wineglasses) by lamplight under the stars in the tree-canopied courtyard top off the day. Cottages US$400 and safari suite US$700.

Nottens Bush Camp

Sabi Sand Reserve; PO Box 622, Hazyview 1242 (☎013/735 5105, fax 735 5970).
Just over a decade old and still resisting the temptation to expand, this family-run outfit is one of the most popular small camps, but the fact that each evening is a hosted dinner party may not suit everyone. Accommodation for a maximum of ten is in double-bedded chalets lit by oil lamps, with tin roofs. The lack of electricity is an explicit part of the camp philosophy of bringing guests into contact with the bush and for the same reason game drives take place in one vehicle without the use of radio contact, which means that although the game here is excellent you stand a less than even chance of seeing the Big Five. To get closer to the wild, you can spend a night or two in their bush *boma* (open-topped enclosure). Evening meals are eaten around a large table, while breakfast and tea are served on a massive deck that acts as a viewing platform for the open plain that stretches out in front of the camp. From R1150.

Sabi Sabi

Sabi Sand Game Reserve; PO Box 52665, Saxonwold 2132 (☎011/483 3939, fax 483 3799, *sabisabi.com*).
Sabi Sabi is the largest outfit in the Sabi Sand Reserve and puts out more vehicles than any other, all in radio contact, so although your experience may be shared you stand an oustanding chance of seeing game, especially the Big Five. This isn't to say that it's simply about churning guests through; keen attention is paid to the particular interests of guests, whether birds, trees or the local ecology. *Sabi Sabi*'s trump card is that it has 10km of Sabie River frontage, which waters dense vegetation that in its turn attracts large numbers of animals and birds, including crocs, hippos and even leopards.

Selati Lodge (R2600) is the most exclusive, and the most exceptional, consisting of atmospheric stone cottages furnished with antiques that hark back to a fantasy "old Africa" of steam travel and pith helmets and great white hunters. The far larger *Bush* and *River* lodges (R2400) would suit visitors who feel comfortable being pampered in a hotel-style environment. *Bush Lodge* has 22 chalets and 5 luxury suites in bushveld overlooking a waterhole, and *River Lodge* has 21 chalets and 2 luxury suites on the banks of the

Sabi River. A cheaper and potentially more exciting option is the Ranger Training Experience (R1200), which caters to groups of four to seven participants, who spend a minimum of three nights in Nkombe tented camp deep in the bush. The food is good, the beds comfortable and bush showers and toilets are provided. The course includes instruction in flora and fauna, spoor identification and tracking skills, orienteering, bush survival techniques, ecology and habitat management, astronomy and 4WD handling.

Tanda Tula

Timbavati Game Reserve; PO Box 32, Constantia 7848 (☎021/794 6500, fax 794 7605, *res@ilink.co.za*).
One of the longest-established and friendliest Mpumalanga bush camps has accommodation in twelve en-suite, East African-style walk-in tents, each with its own private deck overlooking the riparian forest of the usally dry Nhlaralumi River. The thatched dining room and bar also overlook the dry river bed, to which the guests sometimes decamp for silver-service dining under the stars. A small waterhole and hide, on site, offer game-viewing opportunities without leaving the camp and there's a much-needed swimming pool for cooling off in the sweltering summer. R1560.

Umlani

Timbavati Game Reserve; PO Box 26350, Arcadia 0007 (☎012/329 3765, fax 329 6441, *umlani@cis.co.za*).
One of the least expensive bush camps gets down to basics with eight reed-walled huts overlooking the dry Nhlaralumi River. Each has an attached open-topped bush shower, heated by a wood boiler (there's no electricity) and the languid atmosphere is reinforced by hammocks hanging lazily from trees with a plunge pool to dunk in. Unusually for South Africa, the camp isn't fenced off, the emphasis being very much on a bush experience, with flimsy blinds over the windows. While it's not recommended if you freak out easily, there's barely another camp that will bring you closer to the feeling of being in the wild. There are guided morning walks to track game, and for an extra frisson you can spend the night alone, away from the camp in a stilted tree house overlooking a waterhole – highly recommended at full moon. An exceptional game experience, though the food isn't that great. R970.

travel details

Mpumalanga is primarily a self-drive province and, apart from flights serving *Skukuza* and small service towns close to the private reserves, scheduled transport amounts to a daily train service between Johannesburg and Nelspruit and, most practical of the lot, a daily Greyhound bus between the two cities. If you want to get to anywhere else in the province you'll need to use Nelspruit as a springboard and take minibus taxis.

Trains

Nelspruit to: Johannesburg (1 daily; 10hr); Maputo (3 weekly; 7hr); Pretoria (1 daily; 8hr).

Buses

Nelspruit to: Johannesburg (3 daily; 5hr); Maputo (2 daily; 4hr); Pretoria (3 daily; 4hr).

Backpacker bus

Nelspruit to: Johannesburg(4 weekly; 4 hr); Manzini (4 weekly; 2 hr 30min); Mbabane (4 weekly; 3hr 30min); Pretoria (4 weekly; 5 hr).

Flights

Nelspruit to: Durban (1 daily; 1hr 30min); Johannesburg (3–6 daily; 1hr 50min); Maputo (daily; 1hr 35min).

Hoedspruit to: Johannesburg (1 daily; 1hr).

Phalaborwa to: Johannesburg (1–3 daily; 1hr).

Skukuza to: Johannesburg (3 daily; 1hr 5min).

CHAPTER TEN

NORTHERN PROVINCE

T he **Northern Province** is South Africa's no-man's-land: a hot, thornbush-covered area caught between the dynamic heartland of Gauteng and, to the north, the Limpopo River, which acts as South Africa's border with Zimbabwe and, further west, Botswana. Towards the eastern side of the province is the game-rich lowveld, dominated by the seventy-kilometre-wide strip of Kruger National Park abutting the Mozambique border. This part of the Northern Province is covered in the previous chapter (see p.562).

Running through the centre of this no-man's-land is the **N1** highway, often called here the **Great North Road**. This is South Africa's umbilical cord to the rest of Africa, and the importance of the N1, and the weight of traffic which uses it, overshadow the rest of the province; indeed it's invariably the only part of the province most travellers see, with those travelling north eager to get to Zimbabwe, and those heading south impatient to reach Johannesburg.

The principal draws of the Northern Province lie in its three distinctive **mountain escarpments**, where the region's sense of wilderness is at its strongest. The most significant of these is the first rise of the **Drakensberg** escarpment, on its long and often spectacular sweep through South Africa. This north–south escarpment marks the descent from the highveld to the lowveld, but there is a lot to see in the mountains themselves, especially in the haunting, forested slopes of the **Letaba** area immediately to the east of **Pietersburg**, the provincial capital. This is a region of lakes, waterfalls, some excellent walking and comfortable country guesthouses.

On the otherwise unremarkable western side of the N1 lies the more sedate **Waterberg** massif, long a domain of cattle farming and hunting, which is fast becoming an important centre for conservation. In the north, lying parallel to the Limpopo and bisected by the N1, are the subtropical **Soutpansberg Mountains**, and the intriguing and still very independently minded **Venda** region, a former homeland, to the east. North of the Soutpansberg are wide plains dominated by surreal baobab trees, much in evidence along the N1 as it leads to the only (very busy) border post between South Africa and Zimbabwe, at Beitbridge.

Some history

It was across the Limpopo and into what is now the Northern Province that the first black Africans arrived in South Africa, sometime before 300AD. The various movements and migrations, and of course trading, ensured a fluidity in the people who established themselves here, and the historical and cultural ties to the north are, as you might expect, stronger in this region than in other parts of South Africa. Traditional arts and crafts such as **pottery** and **woodcarving** are still an important part of life; legendary figures such as the **Rain Queen** retain great potency, and even **witchcraft** is still encountered in many places.

The arrival of the **Voortrekker** ox-waggons in the early nineteenth century brought profound changes to the orientation of the region. Their route roughly followed what is now the N1, founding such towns as Warmbaths, Nylstroom and Pietersburg. Led by men such as Louis Trichardt, Hermanus and Piet Potgieter, Andries Pretorius and Paul Kruger, the Voortrekkers who ventured this far north were determined people, and

---

MALARIA IN THE NORTHERN PROVINCE

Parts of the Northern Province are malarial; you will need to take prophylactics, and exercise caution against mosquitoes if you are travelling in the lowveld, including Kruger National Park, or north of the Soutpansberg Mountains. The Waterberg and Letaba areas are not at present affected. However, the situation may change, and it's a good idea to double-check before you go. For reliable local advice contact the British Airways Travel Clinics in Cape Town (☎021/419 3172), Knysna (☎044/382 6366) or Johannesburg (☎011/807 3132).

---

their conflicts with the local peoples were notoriously bitter. At **Makapan's Cave** near Potgietersrus, thousands of Ndebele were starved to death by an avenging Boer commando, while further to the north Venda troops forced the Voortrekkers to abandon the settlement they had established at **Schoemansdal** in the Soutpansberg.

In the twentieth century, the **apartheid years** saw some large chunks of the province hived off as homeland areas, with Venda becoming nationally independent and Lebowa and Gazankulu self-governing. Now reformed as one, the contrasts between the old homelands and the white farming areas are manifest throughout the province. Indeed, in recent elections the Northern Province has returned the highest-percentage vote in the country for both the ANC and the right-wing Afrikaner Freedom Front.

THE CENTRAL REGION

The core of the Northern Province, at least in terms of density of settlement and land use, lies along the N1 **from Warmbaths to Pietersburg**. The dominance of farming here, however, means there is little by way of sights or diversions until you leave the highway and head for the mountains, either westward to the Waterberg (see p.604), or eastwards along the R71 from Pietersburg into the otherworldly **Letaba** area.

The Great North Road

In between Pretoria and Beitbridge, the N1 highway or **Great North Road** links a series of towns established by the Voortrekker settlers. Most of these are little more than service centres for the surrounding farmland, and as such few have any real attraction beyond what they offer on a practical level – somewhere to sleep, eat or pass through on the way to somewhere else. Although all have significant black populations, the prevailing flavour of the towns is strongly Afrikaner, with little in the landscape to lighten the sometimes uncomfortable tone this sets.

The southernmost of the towns, **Warmbaths** and **Nylstroom**, make a valiant attempt to rise above their mundane roots by catering for weekend and holiday tourists from Gauteng with a glut of unexciting family-oriented resorts; moving north, **Potgietersrus** is an infamous example of a town struggling to come to terms with the New South Africa, while the larger provincial capital, **Pietersburg**, offers a range of services but remains dominated by the highway. North of Pietersburg, there is a 100-kilometre stretch to Louis Trichardt and the Soutpansberg Mountains, an area covered separately (on p.609).

For all its grand title, the highway is rather a disappointment, although by South African standards it is fast and easy, if often busy. It's a **toll road** from just before Nylstroom to Pietersburg, and then again from Pietersburg to Louis Trichardt, and although it's possible to use alternative roads, the charges aren't crippling for a one-off journey, and don't merit skimping on.

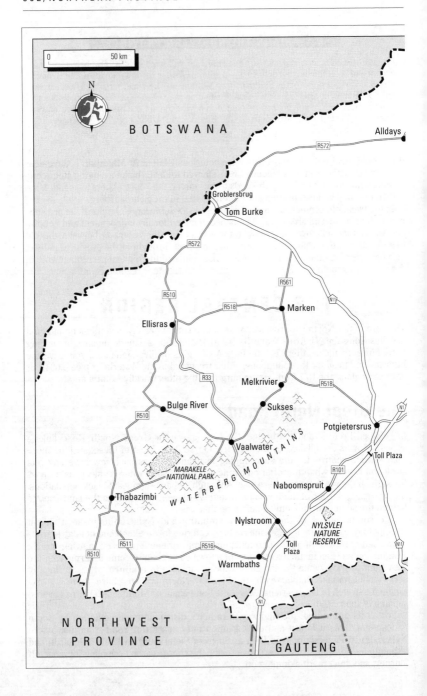

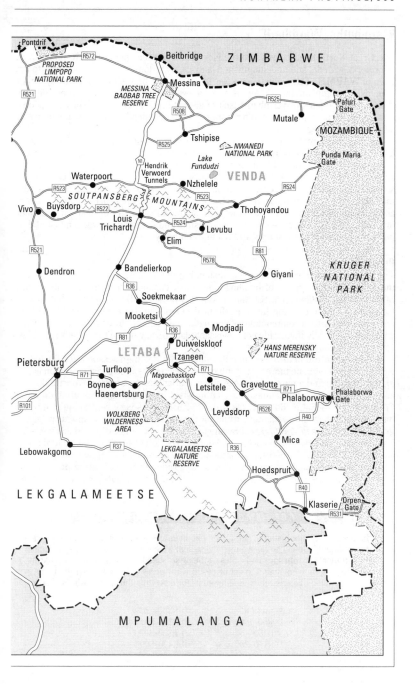

Warmbaths (Warmbad)

The Great North Road passes into the Northern Province approximately 40km north of Pretoria, with flat and undistinguished landscape predominating all the way up to the town of **WARMBATHS**, which lies a few kilometres to the west of the highway. Other than as a pitstop on the N1 or as the gateway to Thabazimbi and the southern Waterberg (see p.608), Warmbaths isn't of all that much interest, and for most people it is too close to Pretoria and too far from their ultimate destination to be much use as a base for exploring.

There is one point of interest in town: the **hot mineral spring**, from which the town takes its name, which has been engulfed by the sprawling Adventura Warmbaths watersports and leisure resort. This offers such things as waterslides and a water-skiing lake, and can attract up to 10,000 people a day during the holiday periods. You can see the source of the spring, which every hour pumps out 20,000 litres of water at 50°C, beside the entrance gate to the resort on Voortrekker Road. In the area surrounding the town, and in particular between it and Nylstroom, 30km to the north, there are any number of smaller holiday resorts – out of season dismal and deserted; at weekends and during school holidays, almost unbearably busy and noisy.

Practicalities

The **layout** of Warmbaths is quite confusing, but the town isn't large. Coming in from the south, the first group of buildings you meet contains the **tourist information office** (Mon–Fri 8am–5pm, Sat 9am–noon; ☎014/736 3694), one of the thatched A-frame buildings comprising the Waterfront development. Here you should be able to get some help with accommodation if you need it. Remember to be specific about what you want, especially if your idea of a pleasant place to stay doesn't involve waterslides, caravans and copious *braai* facilities.

Accommodation in town is generally quite pricey, and high-season rates (including weekends) will often be more than double low-season rates. The cheapest option is holiday flats: you'll find a number of these along Moffat Street, parallel to Voortrekker, or ask at the tourist information office. Otherwise, large, mustard-coloured *Elephant Springs Hotel*, 31 Sutter Rd (☎ & fax 014/736 2101; ④), is very central, quite hip and has a friendly bar and restaurant, while on the outskirts of town is an extravagantly grand B&B, *Chateau Annique*, off Swanepoel Street, (☎ & fax 014/736 2847; ④–⑤). The *Adventura Warmbaths* resort itself, Voortrekker Rd (☎014/736 2200, central reservations ☎012/346 2277; ③–④), has various chalets and hotel accommodation.

As a town by a main highway Warmbaths has a wide selection of **eating places**: your best bet is the *Lion and Elephant* pub in the *Elephant Springs Hotel*, where you can get

---

ACCOMMODATION PRICE CODES

All the accommodation listed in the Guide has been categorized into one of nine price bands, as set out below. The rates quoted represent what you can expect to pay for much of the summer **per person**, and unless otherwise stated, are based on two sharing. Rooms are generally en suite. Expect prices in some areas to be significantly higher in peak season (Dec–Jan & Easter), and look out for discounts during the winter. For further details, see p.33.

① up to R50	⑤ R200–250
② R50–100	⑥ R250–300
③ R100–150	⑦ R300–400
④ R150–200	⑧ R400–500
	⑨ over R500

good, cheap pub grub or a fuller restaurant meal. It has a deck if you want to have a drink outside, and the toilets have been creatively decorated with the pages of the Afrikaans farmers' weekly *Die Landbouweekblad*. At the *Waterfront* development there's an *O'Hagan's Irish Pub and Grill*; a couple of doors away is *Greenfields,* a restaurant that serves breakfast from 7am, and other meals through the day. There are various fast-food takeaways around the town centre.

Nylstroom

The most entertaining thing about **NYLSTROOM**, 27km north of Warmbaths on the R101, is the story behind its name. The legend goes that the first Voortrekkers discovered a reed-lined river, consulted their Bibles (the only reference books they carried) and decided that they had been travelling north for so long that they must surely be at the source of the Nile. The presence of a pyramid-shaped hill, Kranskop, the large mountain you can see clearly from the N1, only confirmed their theory.

The Little Nyl river (as it was dubbed) runs through the centre of the modern town, parallel to the wide main street, **Potgieter**. Along here, establishments like Ammo Africa and Trappers Trading Co, as well as an endless parade of orange dust-covered *bakkies*, proclaim the town's white farming roots. Interestingly, one of the more profitable local crops is table grapes, grown on large vineyards in the well-irrigated surrounding area.

Sights are few. In town there is a memorial **gateway** at the primary school (Laerskool) on Van Riebeeck Street that commemorates the women and children who died in a concentration camp sited there during the Anglo-Boer War. There's also, less predictably, a **mosque**, not far from the bridge over the river – testimony to the presence of an unexpectedly large Indian community.

Practicalities

In Nylstroom, the **accommodation** options are the *Eurosun* campsite (☎014/717 1328; ①), beside the stadium on the northern side of the river, or a rather sugary but civilized guesthouse, *Pink Gables*, 3 De Beer St, by the hospital on the Warmbaths road (☎014/717 5076; ③). There is a more upmarket country lodge, *Shangri-la* (☎014/717 5381, fax 717 3188; half board ⑧), at a turn-off 3km down the Eersbewoond road, a turning from the R33 between Nylstroom and the N1. It's pricey but comfortable; the surroundings are lush and it's filled with an eclectic mix of African memorabilia and interesting antique furniture.

There are **places to eat** in town along Potgieter and Voortrekker streets, most notably a plain restaurant, *Sparrow's,* 100 Potgieter St, and a slightly more lively place by the main crossroads on Potgieter which revels in the name *Mampoer Boer Pub and Grill*. There's a classier dining room at *Shangri-la Country Lodge*, though you must book ahead (☎014/717 5381).

Just outside Nylstroom, the *Thaba Kgatla* guest lodge (☎ & fax 014/717 3959; half board ⑦) is a "village" of Tswana huts built among the ruins of an 800-year-old Iron Age site. The attractive huts here have been designed to mix comfort with authenticity, but one unusual touch is that the owners of the lodge are making an attempt to breed the indigenous Western Sanga cattle and Pedi sheep, which the original inhabitants would have kept, not for meat but as a display of wealth.

Naboomspruit and Nylsvlei Nature Reserve

To the east of the N1, midway between Nylstroom and **NABOOMSPRUIT**, another resort-encircled highway town situated at the foot of the Swaershoek Mountains, is **Nylsvlei** – a 310-square kilometres nature reserve enclosing one of the most important

ARCHEOLOGICAL SITES IN THE NORTHERN PROVINCE

Across the Northern Province, excavations at a number of important **archeological sites** have helped piece together a picture of the different people who have inhabited the land for thousands of years. Some of the most interesting sites are at places where iron was smelted, as the development from what was essentially a Stone Age culture to an Iron Age culture, with its associated improvement in tools for cultivation and war, was a vital part of the migration of black tribes into South Africa around 1500 years ago. Although the iron itself seldom survives the processes of erosion, the presence of slag and other wastes normally provide the strongest clues. Some of the most revealing excavations have taken place at **Thulamela**, inside Kruger National Park not far from the Punda Maria gate, **Bakone Malapa** cultural village outside Pietersburg, **Makapan's Cave** near Potgietersrus, and **Masorini**, also in the Kruger park, not far from Phalaborwa.

The single most important site in the Northern Province is at **Mapungubwe** (Hill of the Jackals), situated by the confluence of the Limpopo and Shashi rivers where South Africa, Zimbabwe and Botswana meet. The site was only discovered in the Thirties, when a local farmer climbed the dome-shaped granite hill and found remains of stone walls, iron tools, graves, pottery and jewellery, including a tiny rhinoceros and a bowl, both made out of gold. It is now thought that the civilization which was centred at Mapungubwe later moved to the much more famous Great Zimbabwe. The area is now protected as part of the Limpopo National Park, although as yet there is no general access.

wetland areas in South Africa. When the Nyl River is in flood, the *vlei* can spread out to as much as 7km in width, attracting over 150 species of bird, including a number of the country's rarest indigenous water birds. As well as picnic sites and bird- and game-viewing routes there is also a simple camping site.

Potgietersrus

A further 50km north of Naboomspruit, also just off the N1, is **POTGIETERSRUS**, named after the Voortrekker hero Piet Potgieter, who died during a famous siege at Makapan's Cave in the hills that close in on the town to the north. The N1 formerly ran right through the centre of town, but the new highway smoothly by-passes it, an act you should have few qualms about following, unless you are bound for parts of the northern Waterberg or have a perverse attraction to check out one of the country's racist hot-spots.

In the mid-Nineties the town attracted worldwide publicity when white locals tried to prevent black children entering what had been all-white schools during the apartheid years. The dogged racism the issue highlighted caused uneasiness in South Africa, and earned the town the unenviable title of racist capital of South Africa. Certainly there's little doubt that the old thinking still dies hard in the town and its agricultural hinterland – something you'll still pick up from such things as "Club Members Only" signs over white-filled bars and intolerant squabbling over local services and amenities. On the other hand, blacks crowd the main streets with stalls and, despite the continual crawl of traffic, give the place a bustling, lively feel.

The one place worth stopping at is the **Arend Dieperink Museum** (Mon–Fri 8am–4.30pm; small entry fee), located in an old schoolhouse set back from Voortrekker Road (the main R101), behind the tourist information office. It has a substantial collection of ploughs, tractors, waggons and farm implements outside; inside is more interesting, with well-labelled displays on the significant archeological discoveries made at Makapan's cave, 19km north of Potgietersrus, including that of three-million-year-old fossils of *Australopithecus africanus,* a predecessor of *Homo sapiens.* For the moment, access to the cave itself is only by arrangement with the museum (☎0154/419 2244).

MAKAPAN'S CAVE (MAKAPANSGAT)

In 1854, bent on revenge after a party of Voortrekkers had been ambushed, a Boer commando cornered the clan of Ndebele chief Makapan in the hills to the north of Potgietersrus. Led by Piet Potgieter, the nephew of Voortrekker leader Hermanus Potgieter who had been skinned alive not long before by kinsmen of Makapan, the Boers besieged the chief and an estimated three thousand of his followers inside the network of caves which ran through the hills. With little food and almost no water, the imprisoned Ndebele became increasingly desperate, and eventually seven hundred besieged men rushed out towards a nearby stream, only to be mown down by the patient Boers. When the siege was finally broken after four weeks, hundreds of rotting bodies were found inside. The Boers lost only two men, one of them Potgieter, whose body was "heroically" retrieved by a young Paul Kruger. A rather one-sided account of the siege is available at the museum in Potgietersrus.

Practicalities

The local **tourist information office** (☎0154/419 2244) is on Voortrekker Road as you come into the main part of town from the south, between Kruger and Van Riebeeck streets. Most of the **accommodation** in Potgietersrus is in the form of travellers' overnight rooms, and as a result rates drop at weekends. There is an unappealing municipal caravan park (①) just off the N1 on the northern side of town, behind a parked steam locomotive. The cheapest place to stay is the block of apartment rooms at *Lonely Oak Lodge*, Van Riebeeck and Hodge streets (☎0154/491 4560; ②). On the northern edge of town, by the side of the main road, are a couple of travellers' hotels: *Oasis* (☎0154/491 4124; ③); and the ageing but respectable *Protea Park* (☎0154/491 3101, fax 491 6842; ④), which has a pool and a decent restaurant. North of town, signposted after 32km along the N1, is the *Ranch Hotel* (☎0152/290 5000, fax 290 5050, *reservations@theranch.co.za*; ⑤), a well-run, pleasant but pricey modern holiday hotel. On the southern side of the Nyl River, 10km south of Potgietersrus on the N1, is a homely B&B, *Jaagbaan* (☎0154/491 7833; ②).

Pietersburg

Lying almost dead central in the province of which it is the capital, **PIETERSBURG** is also the largest city on the Great North Road between Pretoria and the border. It's mostly an administrative and industrial centre, and much of its energy derives from the large volume of traffic moving through the city on the N1. But it does have a couple of quirky attractions, including an excellent museum, and if you're heading towards the Letaba area, the lowveld and central Kruger National Park, Pietersburg is also the point to connect with the R71 to Tzaneen and Phalaborwa.

Arrival and information

The city's former air-force base now operates as **Gateway airport**, located on the N1 5km north of the city. This is serviced by both domestic flights (SA Airlink ☎015/288 0166) and occasional international connections from neighbouring countries. All the city's **car rental firms** are located here: Avis (☎015/288 0171), Budget (☎015/288 0169) and Imperial (☎015/288 0097). **Taxis** are also available on ☎015/297 4493.

Daily **trains** to and from Messina stop at the train station on the northern edge of the city centre, just off the R521 (an extension of Market Street). All the intercity **buses** pass through the centre of town: Translux stop at the Big Bite on Grobler Street, Greyhound at the Shell Ultra City and the Zimmie Bus at the *Holiday Inn*.

Pietersburg may not be well-endowed with attractions, but it doesn't want for tourist information services. The best **tourist information office** is that run by the Pietersburg Marketing Company on the northern side of Civic Square (Mon–Fri 8.30am–4.00pm; ☎015/290 2010) – the best way to get to it is off Landros Mare Street. There are also more limited desks in the round building behind a statue of a donkey at the corner of Landros Mare and Vorster streets; at the nearby Irish House Museum on Market and Vorster; as well as a helpful budget travellers' tourist agent, SA Tours and Bookings, at 89a Schoeman St (☎015/297 0816, *satours@cis.co.za*).

Accommodation

The municipal camping and caravan park is situated beside Pietersburg Game Reserve on the edge of town; get to it by following Dorp Street south out of the city. While the proximity of the nature reserve doesn't really rub off, you can camp here and it has some inexpensive rondavels (①). Otherwise there are a range of options aimed at the passing business trade, including:

Arnotha's Lodge, 42 Hans van Rensburg St (☎015/291 3393). Cheap but not all that cheerful, offering a row of centrally located self-catering rooms open 24hr. ②.

Holiday Inn, corner of Vorster and Bok streets, (☎015/291 2030, fax 291 3150). A couple of blocks from Civic Square, with unremarkable but decent rooms and an outdoor pool. ④.

Kismet Guest House (☎015/293 8207). A row of plain but decent units situated directly off the N1 near the SAB plant north of town. ③.

Mrs B's Bed and Breakfast, 17 Welsford St, Bendor (☎015/296 1021). Unremarkable but inexpensive and hospitable suburban B&B with two twin bedrooms. ②.

Plumtree Lodge, 138 Marshall St (☎015/295 6153). Not far from the centre, probably the smartest and most comfortable lodge in town, with a pool, a big garden and cheaper rates over the weekend. ③–④.
Vivaldi Guest House, 2 Voortrekker St (☎015/297 0816). A friendly, well-kept guesthouse with six rooms in a pleasant part of town. Known for its hearty breakfasts and the parrots in the garden. ③.

The City and around

Pietersburg has a busy, compact CBD set out on a grid pattern, with layers of industry and suburbia tightly packed around it. It may not be the most inspiring spot, but much of the Northern Province's drive and enterprise emanates from its capital. At its heart, the **Civic Centre**, a park area bounded on two sides by Landros Mare and Vorster streets, has an incongruous but entertaining array of sculptures, statues and monuments, and a white church housing the small but absorbing **Hugh Exton Photographic Museum** (Mon–Fri 9am–4pm, Sun 3–5pm; free), which displays the early years of Pietersburg through the work of a local commercial photographer, who quite evidently had a knack for taking excellent portraits. Opposite the park, on the other side of Vorster, is the old shop frontage of the decent **Irish House Museum** (Mon–Fri 8am–4pm, Sat 9am–noon, Sun 3–5pm; free), the city's neat and thoughtfully laid-out history and natural history museum.

For those inspired by the sculptures of the Civic Centre there's a small **art museum** above the library on Schoeman and Jorissen streets, together with an annexe of outdoor, industrial-type modern sculptures in a park on the left as you leave town on the N1 heading north.

However, the one sight in Pietersburg really worth putting aside time to see is the **Bakone Malapa Museum** (daily except Mon afternoon 8.30am–12.30pm & 1.30–3.30pm; moderate entry fee), 9km southeast of town on the R37. This is an open-air museum displaying the traditional way of life of the local Bakone people, a grouping within the Northern Sotho. A village of huts has been built in the traditional style, and fourteen people live permanently on site, working on crafts such as pottery and leather-working through the day. One of them also acts as a guide, and will explain the different activities going on, as well as the architecture, history and legends of the site. It is a simple but genuine project, and one which succeeds in conveying some of the old way of life where many flashier examples have fallen short.

Eating and drinking

True to its functional role, Pietersburg has no shortage of standard chain **restaurants and takeaways**. The largest collection of these can be found at the Savannah mall, on the fringes of the city along the Tzaneen road – here your best bets are the *Villa Italia*, part of a small local chain of Italian restaurants, or *Mariner's*, offering well-packaged seafood fare, both found on the lower level. The one worthwhile place in town is *Tassels* (Tues–Sat 8am–10pm, Sun 8am–3pm; ☎015/291 1918), set in an older house on the corner of Voster and Dorp streets, where you can get good coffee and a range of attractive sandwiches and other snacks through the day, and full meals in the evening.

Letaba

The **Letaba** is a forested, lush, mountainous area east of Pietersburg which contrasts very sharply with the hot lowveld immediately east and the wide, flat bushveld to its west. It marks the first dramatic rise of the Drakensberg escarpment as it begins its sweep south through Mpumalanga, and in many ways is an attractive but less well-known alternative to the lush but crowded highlands of that province. The forestation begins around the mountain village of **Haenertsburg** and follows two very scenic parallel valleys to the largest centre in the area, **Tzaneen**. The colourful valleys are filled with still lakes surrounded by dark pine forests, sparkling rivers, misty peaks and,

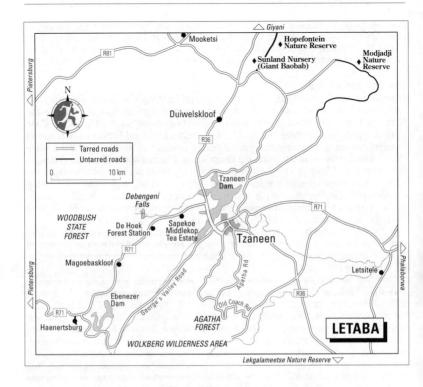

towards Tzaneen, intense subtropical crops such as tea, macadamia nuts and avocados. There are some very comfortable and beautifully located guesthouses, farmstalls and tea rooms, hiking trails and trout fishing, making the Letaba a highly soothing alternative to some of South Africa's more challenging environments.

Haenertsburg and around

The mellow village of **HAENERTSBURG** lies 60km from Pietersburg, high on a hillside looking down on the R71 as it winds down into the beginning of the thickly wooded Magoebaskloof valleys. Haenertsburg is an old gold-rush village, with wonderful views over the area they call the Land of the Silver Mist, and one **main street**, along which you'll find a small pub, a friendly tea room, *The Elms*, which also has a gift shop and is the place to buy trout and ask about trout fishing, and a useful **tourist information office**, Byadladi Tourist Association (Mon–Fri 8am–10pm; ☎015/276 4472, *bta@pixie.co.za*), where you can organize local accommodation or tours, or find out about good picnic spots and short walks in the area, including a tough one up to the **Iron Crown**, the peak above the village. Good **food** can be had during the day at *Picasso's Pancakes*, in a large wooden cabin beside the R71, and in the evenings at the *Atholl Arms* (☎015/276 4412), on the main street beside *The Elms*.

If you're planning to be in the area in May – a beautiful time with glorious autumnal colours in the valley – get details from Byadladi of the annual **music and cultural festival**, which sees national orchestras and choirs performing in unusual venues locally.

EASTER GATHERINGS

On the 60km between Pietersburg and Haenertsburg there are two huge, incongruous institutions, the **University of North** at **Turfloop**, and **Zion City Moria** at **Boyne**, identified by a huge Star of David on the hill above it. Each Easter, an incredible three million people gather here for the annual gathering of the Zion Christian Church, an independent, Africanized Christian Church. The symbols of followers of the church, a silver star or badge pinned onto the chest, and sometimes a grey peaked cap, are worn right across the northern areas of South Africa, and a certain amount of mystery and suspicion surrounds the movement. However, there isn't really anything to see other than during the Easter gathering, which is the one time you want to stay well clear, as three million people can cause some mighty traffic jams.

Georges Valley Road and the Magoebaskloof Valleys

Just east of Haenertsburg is a turning to the right off the main R71, which offers an alternative route to Tzaneen along the Georges Valley Road. There is, in fact, little to choose between the two options in terms of both distance and stunning scenery, and if you are spending any time in the area it's worth trying both.

The things to look out for along the Georges Valley Road are a **memorial to John Buchan**, the author who was captivated by the area when he came here not long after the Anglo-Boer War – "A place enchanted and consecrated," he described it – and the peaceful, almost Arthurian **Ebeneezer Dam**, a good spot for swimming and picnicking.

Staying on the R71 you come to the **Magoebaskloof Valleys**, named after the rogue chief Makgoba, who eventually had his head chopped off by an Impi serving under Abel Erasmus in 1895. About 4km beyond Haenertsburg is a turning to the **Cheerio Gardens**, where an annual Cherry Blossom Festival is held at the end of September. If you miss the festival it still isn't hard to imagine the lush subtropical landscape bursting into extravagant colour; the **Letaba Tourism Association** (☎015/307 4699, *bourdy@mweb.co.za*) can give you details of various private show gardens in the area. Along this same turning is another wonderful piece of backwoods life, at the tiny **Wegraakbos Dairy** (☎015/276 1811), where cheese is made in traditional style over an open fire in a huge copper cauldron. A visit is thoroughly recommended: tours, which cost a few rand, are at 9am, but you can visit the dairy throughout the day, and taste the cheese and walk around the farm and nearby woods.

As the R71 crosses over the Magoebaskloof pass it twists and turns impressively, with dark forests and long views alternating on either side. A sideroad leads into the **Woodbush State Forest**, where there is a network of roads (not all of them passable), various multi-day hiking trails and the famous **Debegeni Falls**, an attractive series of waterfalls, slithers and natural pools. There are some *braai* sites by the river (small admission fee), and you can swim in various places if you're careful, but the smooth, slippery rock is very dangerous and a sign indicates that a few folk who have tried the DIY waterslide haven't lived to recommend it.

Between the turn-off to Debengeni and Tzaneen the valley becomes broader, with huge stands of citrus, avocado and banana trees, as well as the rich green texture of tea bushes, covering the rolling hillsides. On the **Sapekoe Middlekop** tea estate not far from the junction of the R71 and R36, a winding road leads up to the **Pekoe View tea garden** (daily 10am–5pm) – the location of some of the best views in the whole valley. Tea and scones are always available, along with other snacks and drinks, packets of local tea and coffee can be bought in the shop, and there are also worthwhile factory tours (Tues–Sat 11am), on which you can see tea being picked, learn about different grades of tea, and take a look at the production process in the factory.

Accommodation

One of the main themes in the area around Haenertsburg and Magoebaskloof – and indeed around Tzaneen as well – is escape, and to that end there are a lot of attractive **places to stay**. Both the Byadladi Tourist Association in Haenertsburg, and the Letaba Tourism Association will be able to help you find somewhere suitable.

Simple self-catering lodges and guesthouses abound: 5km east of Haenertsburg at Den Eden farm off the R71, is a genuine *Log Cabin* (ask for Meinie de Villiers at ☎015/276 4242, mobile 083/269 3552; ②), set under some tall pine trees; off the same road, just before Haenertsburg, are *The Chalets* (☎015/276 4264; ③), various Swiss-style self-catering chalets in a scenic setting. *BaliWillWill Farm* (☎015/276 2212; ③), 1500m into the hills from Haenertsburg past the police station, offers B&B rooms in the farmhouse or in a simple self-catering flat. Moving up a notch, the *Magoebaskloof Hotel*, 10km east of town on the R71 (☎015/276 4276; ⑤), has probably the most spectacular view in the area from its front deck, but the rest, including a pub with an old red postbox outside, is fairly uninspired. Top of the range, and one of the finer country lodges in South Africa, is *Glenshiel*, 2km from Haenertsburg on the R71 (☎ & fax 015/276 4335, *glenshiel@global.co.za*; ⑧), full of roaring fires, deep sofas, antiques and fine food.

Along the George's Valley Road is an unusual and appealing backpackers' lodge, *Satvik* (☎015/307 3920, 082/853 6645, *satvik@pixie.co.za*; ①–②), 3km from Tzaneen in a group of old whitewashed farmworkers' cottages and set above a lake. The facilities, which include doubles and small dorms, are simple and rustic, but the paraffin lamps, outdoor showers and lakeside bar and cooking area make it is an atmospheric spot typical of Letaba, and one you could easily find yourself chilling out at for days on end.

Tzaneen and around

The dams and soaring gum forests surrounding **TZANEEN** are graceful and attractive. However, the town itself is fairly scruffy, well-endowed with shops and a useful transport hub, but worth avoiding as a place to stay. The one thing to see here is the **Tzaneen Museum** (Mon–Fri 9am–5pm, Sat 9am–1pm; small entry fee), situated in a tiny, four-roomed building in the grounds of the library at the top of Agatha Street. You'll need time: the dedicated curator and his assistants don't label any items, preferring to walk around with you and talk about the small but valuable collection, which includes sacred drums and other items associated with the Rain Queen. It's almost impossible to have a quick, casual visit, but it's essential to spare the time if you want to scratch a bit more deeply into the history and traditions of the region.

Practicalities

A daily **minibus**, operated by Northlink Tours (☎015/307 2950), links Tzaneen with Pietersburg and Johannesburg. The privately run **Tzaneen Tourism Information Centre** (Mon–Fri 8am–5pm, Sat 8am–11am; ☎015/307 1294), 23 Danie Joubert St, is a useful place to find out about local accommodation, as well as pick up advice on travelling to spots such as Modjadji, the Magoebaskloof Valleys and Kruger National Park. A couple of locals run **tours** to these: contact Letaba Active Tours (☎ & fax 015/307 1294), or Yvonne Clarke (☎015/307 2000). There are also a number of good local **mountain-bike routes** – ask at the information centre for more details.

Accommodation options in town aren't inspiring, especially in comparison to what is available in the surrounding countryside, and it's a better idea to head for the Magoebaskloof Valleys or take the road leading out of town into the Wolkberg Mountains to Agatha, which has some high-class country lodges and spectacular views out over the valleys and peaks of the escarpment (see opposite).

If you're not inclined to do this, or don't have the time (or money), there's a decent caravan park on Old Gravelotte Road, *Fairview* (☎015/307 2679; ①–②), which has inexpensive chalets; otherwise *Silver Palm Lodge* (☎015/307 3092, mobile ☎083/635 0556; ③) off Danie Joubert Street beside the Malaria Research Institute, has some decent modern units around a pool.

As for **food**, Tzaneen has a smattering of familiar takeaways and a few chain restaurants. The best in town is the *Villa Italia,* corner of Danie Joubert and Lannie streets, and there's a *Mariner's* seafood restaurant in the Oasis Mall. Near the museum there's a pleasant coffee shop, *Gazebo Gardens*, 30 Agatha St, set in an old Victorian garden.

Agatha

AGATHA, the wife of an early mining commissioner, gave her name to a high plateau overlooking Tzaneen, now covered in forest but a cool and attractive place, especially if you can rise to a night at one of the top-class guesthouses set along the edge of the ridge. The best value of these is *Kings Walden Estate*, 12km from Tzaneen up Agatha Road (☎015/307 3262; ④), a family-owned avocado farm with superbly lush gardens and four simple rooms. Turning left at the top of the hill, Old Coach Road leads to *The Coach House* (☎015/307 3641, fax 307 1466; ⑦–⑧), a classy, well-run establishment that's consistently quoted as one of the best small hotels in South Africa. The views from the breakfast balcony and pool area are breathtaking. In the opposite direction from the top of Agatha Road, *Sherwood's Country House* (☎015/307 5512, fax 307 4216, *sherc_h@mweb.co.za*; ④) is a more intimate but slightly less-well-bred rival. A less expensive, more down-to-earth alternative in the Agatha area is *Granny Dot's Country Spot* (☎015/307 5149, 083/702 3421; ③), a B&B close to the Rooikat Walking Trail (see box overleaf) with fine views and lush surroundings.

Modjadji Nature Reserve

The area around the rather downbeat village of **MODJADJI**, north of Tzaneen off the R36, is the home of the famous **Rain Queen**, the hereditary female monarch of a section of the Venda people whom legend maintains has the power to make rain, a useful talent in these often parched northern areas. Suitably, her home village is up in the mists on a mountain where a special form of ancient cycad, or tree fern, flourishes. The **Modjadji Nature Reserve** (daily 8.30am–4pm; small entry fee) protects these plants in an area set on the very top of the hill, and incorporates some fine views (often obscured by the wispy mist) and various short but pleasant, rather vaguely marked walking trails. There are a few facilities, such as a souvenir shop and information centre, which explains a bit more about the unique plants found here and, of course, the famous monarch, who in fact lives in a modern house in the village, set on the mountainside.

Around 20km away from the turning to Modjadji lies the **Sunland Nursery**, which has a massive baobab tree with a pub inside where the owner will serve you a draught beer and relate a few of the strange stories that attach to his odd location. He'll put his case for this being the largest baobab in the world, a claim also made for a few others around the Northern Province. Still, it's fun to visit, especially if you've got time for a few convivial drinks, though you have to pay to get in (R10). A few kilometres further down the same road is the five-hundred-hectare **Hopefontein Nature Reserve** (☎015/305 3607; ③), where you can stay in one of two tree houses or a rustic farmhouse. Phone beforehand if you want to stay.

Letsitele and around

LETSITELE is a small town 30km east of Tzaneen whose main function is as a waypoint to a few places of interest in the area of lowveld abutting the escarpment. To the south are the large nature and wilderness areas of **Lekgalameetse** and **Wolkberg**,

HIKING IN LETABA

One of the principal attractions of the Letaba area, especially given the spectacular scenery, deep forests and relatively cool air of the escarpment, is hiking. Of the **multi-day hikes**, the two most popular are the two-day Debegeni and three-day Dokolewa trails, which are well-marked and utilize well-kept forester's houses or log cabins (①–②) for the overnight stops – details from the state forestry organization, SAFCOL (☎013/764 1058). The two large protected areas in the southern parts of the Letaba also offer excellent walking: Wolkberg Wilderness Area (☎015/276 1303) has a campsite (①) at Serala Forest Station, which you get to from the Haenertsburg side, but few other facilities – it's meant to be wild and untamed; **Lekgalameetse Nature Reserve** (☎015/383 0015), reached from the R36 south of Tzaneen, encompasses the transition between lowveld and escarpment and has accommodation in simple log cabins (①).

If you're not on for such serious hiking, there are good **day-walks** in various parts of the Letaba: around Haenertsburg, through some of the last remaining indigenous forest, along the waymarked four-kilometre Lesodi Trail, beginning at Sandford Heights Nursery on the R71 past the Magoebaskloof Hotel; along the Rooikat Walking Trail, a circular forest trail on the Agatha ridge, also marked and begining near the *Coach House*; and at Modjadji Nature Reserve.

places to explore if you have a few days and a penchant for empty, green landscapes. Near Letsitele itself is one of the most interesting handicraft projects in the province, **Karosswerkers**, who produce intricate and striking embroidered ethnic place mats, cushion covers and wall hangings. You can arrange to see the workshops (call ☎015/345 1765), which employ over 150 locals, and you'll find their work on sale at the excellent Monsoon Gallery on the R527 west of Hoedspruit (see p.560). Another worthwhile project is Mahuka Crafts (☎015/303 0918), 17km from Tzaneen, where local Sotho and Shangaan women make felt and handpainted fabrics.

North from Letsitele a road leads to the **Hans Merensky Nature Reserve**, the location of an Aventura resort, *Die Eiland* (☎015/386 8759; ②–④), on the Letaba River, which has chalets offering various degrees of comfort. Also here is the **Tsonga Kraal Open-Air Museum**, one of the first working cultural villages of its kind but now overtaken by other similar projects in the province. Between the reserve and Letsitele there's a highly rated up-market game lodge, *Ndzalama* (☎015/307 3065, central reservations ☎011/883 9898, *ndzalama@zebra-rsa.co.za*), set on an 8000-hectare protected reserve, with rhino, elephant and various rare antelope. One outstanding feature of the reserve is the architecture of the lodge, bush camp and reconstructed Shangaan village, which have been beautifully designed to blend with the surrounding natural environment. Prices start at R450 for the bush camps rising to R1200 for the luxury Rock Lodge. Other game reserves in this area, including the Kruger National Park and its fringes, are described on p.571 onwards.

WATERBERG

And even now, . . . with the great gold-city belching its smoke almost within sight – even now, with invading civilization marching across the hills in seven-league boots, Waterberg still holds its charm.

Eugène Marais

Rising out of the plains to the west and north of the Great North Road, the **Waterberg** is one of the least-known and most intriguing of South Africa's significant mountain

A journalist who left South Africa to study law and medicine (simultaneously), in London during the 1890s, **Eugène Marais** was one of the most gifted yet troubled South Africans of his time. In the early 1900s he emerged as one of the first writers to make a literary mark in the "new" Afrikaans language, writing poetry and short stories. However, he also suffered from depression and ill health, and he retreated from his career as a lawyer to the remote Waterberg Mountains. His intense involvement with the natural world around him there led to the publication of two pioneering studies of animal behaviour: *The Soul of the Ape*, which was the result of some three-and-a-half years living in close proximity to a troop of baboons, and *The Soul of the White Ant*, a study of termites which argues that a termite nest is a single functioning composite similar to the human body. Still racked by ill health and increasingly addicted to morphine, he committed suicide in 1936.

massifs. Once a place of lakes and swamps – hence its name – the elevated plateau can often seem a place as dry and sparse of water as its surrounding northern bushveld; yet it harbours a diversity of vegetation and topography which supports cattle-ranching, little-trumpeted hunting concessions and, increasingly, some of the country's foremost conservation projects.

These have developed over recent years to the extent that some fifty percent of the Waterberg is now under formal conservation management. Indeed, the Waterberg is being mooted as an undiscovered alternative to the lowveld areas around Kruger National Park. However, while it has impressive credentials as a vast area of true wilderness, and is certainly less commercialized, the game is less rich than around Kruger. Rhino have been reintroduced, and elephant and lion are found in a couple of reserves, but otherwise the wildlife highlights are large antelope, giraffe, hippo and the presence of leopard, although it is worth pointing out that here you are much less likely to have to share your encounters with other people. It remains, also, an isolated region, detached from other main areas of interest and with scant transport links.

The largest single area is the new, but still mostly inaccessible, **Marakele National Park**, situated in the more mountainous southern section of the massif, but complemented by a patchwork of very dedicated private reserves around the central town of **Vaalwater**.

Northern Waterberg

The **northern section of the Waterberg**, centred on the small town of **Vaalwater**, is the beating heart of the region's conservation-centred approach to land use and tourism. The area can boast an embarrassing richness of reserves and game farms dedicated to the conservation ethic and offering absorbing bush experiences on most levels, from luxury lodges to inexpensive self-catering cottages and wilderness campsites.

The scenery in this part of the Waterberg is subtle rather than dramatic, but by staying here for a few days you can pick up the rich intensity of the bush and the thrill of being surrounded by it. The area also offers some exciting adventure activities, including bush hiking trails and some of the finest wilderness horse-riding in South Africa. For enthusiastic, organized and genuinely helpful local **information**, contact Clare Beith on ☎014/7552 ext 4021.

Vaalwater

The town of **VAALWATER** is a small farming centre, and for the visitor offers little more than an orientation point on the R33, which connects Nylstroom, just off the N1, with Ellisras, and marks the junction with the tarred road to Melkrivier and Marken – along which the main conservation areas of the northeastern Waterberg are located.

If you need **accommodation** in town, the best B&B here is at the *Zeederberg Cottages* (☎014/755 3862; ②), situated by a service station and an excellent craft shop on the northern side of town, at the junction where the R510 to Bulge River meets the R33 to Ellisras. Otherwise, there's *Bosveld Chalets and Caravan Park* (☎014/755 3696; ①–②), 165 Davidson Rd, a small campsite off a suburban side street with adequate if unexciting chalets. Rooms, a small restaurant and a lively locals' bar are at the *Vaalwater Hotel* (☎014/755 3686; ②), on the right-hand side as you come into town from Nylstroom. It subtitles itself the *International Hunter's Hotel*, which says quite a lot about what you can expect. If you are looking for **somewhere to eat**, there's a calmer atmosphere and reasonable range of meals at the *Waterhole Steakhouse* (☎014/755 3775), located in a the Village Square complex set amongst the gathering of shops by the Melkrivier turn-off.

If you're interested in finding out about **touring the Waterberg**, Brown's Safari Services (☎ & fax 011/957 2938, mobile ☎083/659 0039), can help with specialized or tailor-made tours, transfers, and other advice about the area.

Around Vaalwater: game reserves and farms

Most of the lodges in the Waterberg are relatively remote and quite small, so it's advisable to prebook somewhere to stay, at least for your first couple of nights, if you want to be sure of a room. Most lodges in private reserves usually include early morning and late-afternoon game drives or walks in their programmes, so it's worth arriving at a time when you can take full advantage of these. Game walks are an integral part of the Waterberg experience, and as such are definitely worth experiencing. All the luxury lodges will offer these in the company of a guide, while the less expensive accommodation can normally recommend good walking trails on their property or on private reserves nearby where access rights have been negotiated.

Generally you will find that "luxury" here is not as over-the-top as in more developed parts of the country, and that most of the lodges recommended have a down-to-earth charm and friendliness that more than make up for any lack of pampering.

Game lodges, reserves and self-catering

The Waterberg owes much of its credibility and profile to the conservation ideals of Lapalala Wilderness Area (☎011/453 7645, fax 453 7649), a 350-square-kilometre reserve masterminded by Clive Walker, a highly regarded South African conservationist and artist, which provides sanctuary for endangered and rare animals (see box, opposite). The up-market option here is to stay in the intimate and relaxed Rhino Camp (⑨), a tented **bush camp** right by the Lapalala River which includes full board and game drives in the rate. Much less expensive are a series of basic but remote self-catering bush camps (②) in different parts of the wilderness area, some of which have a wonderfully atmospheric setting that you can explore on foot by yourself. Lapalala is also the exclusive location of some top-notch horse safaris, run by Equus Horse Safaris (☎011/788 3923, *horsesaf@iafrica.com*), lasting between three and eight days

Apart from Lapalala, there's a wide range of attractive places to stay. At the top end of the scale it's worth bypassing the luxury lodges catering to larger numbers of visitors in favour of one of the more intimate, smaller **lodges** on strongly conservation-minded private reserves. A couple of these, both offering full board, are particularly good: *Mokolo River Nature Reserve* (☎0147552, extension Bulgerivier 1511, fax 082/899 1766; ⑦), above a gorge in the Mokolo River and run with a determined conviction about the primacy of animals and the bush, where you'll find both elephants and rhino, along with some very engaging, unpretentious hospitality; and the tranquil *Ant's Nest*

LAPALALA-PUTTING RHINOS FIRST

The **Lapalala Wilderness Area** was established in 1981 by Clive Walker and business-man Dale Parker, and has since grown sevenfold in size and developed into one of the foremost conservation projects in South Africa. It makes few bones about putting tourism well down its list of priorities: it was the first private game reserve in the country to obtain the highly endangered black rhino, when five were acquired from Natal Parks Board for R2.2 million. It also promotes education through the Lapalala Wilderness School, established in 1985 and each year introducing some 3000 children from all over Africa to the principles and practice of conservation during week-long courses in the heart of the wilderness area. Lapalala is also the mainstay of the growing Waterberg Conservancy, a close-knit association of conservation-centred landowners which now embraces some 1200 square kilometres of the northeastern Waterberg and hopes to be declared a UNESCO Biosphere. An excellent introduction to some of the achievements of Lapalala, and the personalities involved, is at the world's only dedicated **Rhino Museum** (Tues–Sun 9am–5pm), based in the old Melkrivier School, about 6km along the road to Lapalala off the Vaalwater to Marken tarred road.

(mobile ☎083/287 2885 or 456 1874, *horizon@waterberg*.net; ⑨), a converted farmhouse set deep in the bush with giraffe, gemsbok and blesbok, and drives, walks and horse-riding. The sense of sheer escapism here is clinched by the fact that the owners only ever host one couple or party at a time.

Much simpler and less expensive are various **self-catering chalets** and **cottages** which often make arrangements with larger farms or reserves nearby for game walks or drives. The best of these include *Cattlelands Cottage* (☎0147552, extension 4021; ④), a tasteful, comfortable cottage sleeping two with a plunge pool and a secluded bush setting; *Mount Leisure Bush Camp* (☎014721/927; ③), situated between Nylstroom and Vaalwater, whose chalets have an impressive mountainside location; *Le Thabo Pioneer Settlement* (☎0147522, extension 4013, or 012/55 5232, *Afrigraf@iafrica.com*), a collection of small log cabins on the banks of the Melk River near Lapalala; and *Kudu Canyon* (☎011/884 3662), with self-catering lodges (③), a private tented camp (④), lively game drives and boat trips on an adjoining dam.

If you want somewhere to **eat** try *Walker's Wayside* (☎0147552, extension 4041; closed Mon), a pub and restaurant popular with the locals, at the Rhino Museum near Lapalala. Here you'll find well-priced and tasty lunches and evening meals.

Activity-based game farms

While game viewing from a vehicle or on foot is a mainstay of most of the lodges and private reserves in the Waterberg, the area is also an excellent place to come if you're interested in doing something a little more energetic. The Waterberg is recognised as one of South Africa's finest locations for **horse-riding safaris**, a fact complemented by a couple of well-established and highly professional outfits. The more up-market of the two is Equus Horse Safaris, based in the Lapalala Wilderness Area (see opposite), who offer top-class riding out of an eight-bed luxury tented bush camp. Horizon Horse Trails (☎014755/3737, *tessa@smartnet.co.za*), based at *Triple B Ranch*, 25km from Vaalwater along the Melkrivier road, offer more down-to-earth, less luxurious safaris of one to three days, sleeping out in fly camps in the bush or in rooms in the farmhouse where the horses are stabled. This is a fun place for horse-lovers: other activities on offer include cattle-mustering, polocrosse and a cross-country course. For a touch more luxury, you can combine any of Horizon's activities with accommodation at *Ant's Nest* (see opposite). Other activities, including **mountain-bike trails** and "Hunt with a camera" **photographic safaris**, are available at *Waterberg Game Reserve* (☎083/630 3615; ③), which has self-catering cottages and a bush camp.

Incidentally, if you're visiting the *Triple B* ranch, take a look at the tiny stone **church** at Twenty-Four Rivers (on the edge of the ranch), designed by Sir Herbert Baker (see p.498). He was commissioned by two maiden aunts who expected that he would do it for free, since it was a place of worship. Their assumption was, unsurprisingly, not shared by Baker.

Southern Waterberg

The **southern parts of the Waterberg** boast more dramatic scenery than the land to the north, although they have fewer game lodges and are dominated by the burgeoning **Marakele National Park**, which, though one of the bright new stars among South African game reserves, is still raw and undeveloped for visitors.

The main road into the area from Vaalwater is the R510, although there is also good access from the east via Warmbaths and from the south along the R511 and R510, both of which connect with the N4 highway west of Pretoria.

Thabazimbi and around

The southern Waterberg centres around the town of **THABAZIMBI**, a place that lists mining and hunting as its core activities. Its name means "mountain of iron" and, while the town has a striking setting among some high peaks, it doesn't take too long to work out that large parts of the mountains have been dug up by the mines, well-sifted and then put back in place. Some locals have been heard to complain that they can feel the south wind blowing through town these days, something it never did before they rearranged the mountains.

There's not much point in hanging around, but if you need **accommodation** in town the *Hotel Kransberg* (☎014773/71586; ②), Deena St (off Eland Street), has rooms, while *Bonanza* (☎014773/71831; ①–②), signposted off the road towards Marakele National

---

HUNTING: A ROUGH GUIDE

To some it is barbaric blood lust, and to others it lies at the heart of conservation. The emotive issue of **hunting** is one you will encounter and hear vigorously debated in the Waterberg, as you will in many rural areas of South Africa where it is regarded as an essential part of life in the bush. It is also a multi-million-rand industry and, although you don't necessarily read about them in the guidebooks, there are many more hunting reserves in South Africa than there are eco-friendly game reserves.

In hunting reserves, the land is stocked with game specifically for the purpose of hunting, whereas in conservation-oriented game reserves the guiding principle is that tourists will pay simply to see the animals in their natural environment. However, wherever man has established artificial fences around a piece of land (which is just about everywhere), the idea of a completely natural environment is inevitably compromised, and intervention is necessary to maintain a realistic balance and diversity of nature within that area. Such intervention – "management" is a common euphemism – takes place even in the most conservation-oriented reserves. What is more at issue is the extent to which this process is commercialized. Some game reserves, knowing that they need to cull a certain number of animals, will allow paying clients to hunt for that quota, providing a valuable source of income for the reserve and its conservation ideals. However, inevitably this leads to grey areas. How many animals need to be culled, for instance, when there is money at stake? Whatever your beliefs, it is undoubtedly true that animals, many of them endangered species, are dying in large numbers in reserves all over South Africa, many of them needlessly, and many of them for profit.

Park on the edge of town, is an unsophisticated resort with campsites and chalets. **Places to eat** include the windowless *Rhino Restaurant* at the hotel, which offers meat galore, and the *Pizza Cabin* in the Carpe Diem Centre, off 13th (Dertiende) Street.

Around Thabazimbi

Just under 7km south of Thabazimbi is the **Ben Alberts Nature Reserve** (☎014773 71670; ①), which has a shady camping area, though the reserve isn't much to get excited about: as an adjunct to the mine, it is meant to act as a fig leaf to the towering man-made slag heap immediately behind. A further 15km south of town on the Rustenburg Road (R510) is the **Rhino Bushveld Eco-Park** (☎014773/71483, *viva.africa@pixie.co.za*; ③–⑥), a private reserve set in typical bushveld which is attempting to push eco-tourism hand in hand with "wildlife management" (ie hunting). The butchery by the entrance isn't a particularly encouraging sign; within the reserve, however, there are some reasonable bush camps (self-catering or full board) and bush hiking trails with simple mountain huts.

Marakele National Park

In the mountains to the northeast of Thabazimbi, **Marakele National Park** (daily: May–Aug 8am–5pm; Sept–April 8am–6pm) is one of South Africa's newest national parks, already an impressive 600 square kilometres, but still growing as more land around it is bought up. At its core are the Kransberg, a striking assortment of odd-shaped peaks, plateaus and cliffs. The diversity of land and altitude means that a variety of interesting plants, including ferns, orchids, and even some proteas and cycads, are found here, while the species of animals have already achieved an impressive breadth, with rhino, tsessebe, roan and sable antelope, red hartebeest and 800 breeding pairs of the endangered Cape vulture. Larger game such as elephant, rhino and lion have also been introduced, many of them from Kruger National Park.

The potential for the park is great, and it is destined to become a valuable and magnetic part of the efforts being made in conservation in the Waterberg as a whole. **Day visitors** are restricted to a small area of the park, although this does include Kransberg, where the outlook is inspiring. At present, however, the only place to **stay** is a tented camp situated on the banks of the Matlabas River, which you will need a 4WD vehicle to get to. Bookings for this can be made through the National Parks Board (☎012/343 1991 or 021/422 2810, *reservations@parks-sa.co.za*.).

THE FAR NORTH

The **northernmost part of the Northern Province** is a hot, green, undeveloped rural region with as much in common with Zimbabwe as with South Africa. The essential geographical features of the area are the **Limpopo River**, the border between South Africa and Zimbabwe (and, further west, Botswana), and the alluring **Soutpansberg Mountain range**, aligned east–west just to the north of the area's main town, **Louis Trichardt**. Both landmarks lie in the path of the N1 highway, still the main route through the area, which crosses into Zimbabwe at **Beitbridge**.

As a first impression of South Africa for visitors arriving from Zimbabwe, the far north cannot compete with the lure of attractions further south. Yet it is an area where the lack of sophistication and isolated history of the people and culture make absorbing contrasts to other parts of the country. Perhaps the most significant manifestation of the distinctness of the area is the **Venda** region, formerly an "independent" homeland under the apartheid regime. While economically impoverished, it (and its people) remains rich in tradition, art and legend. East of the Venda lands is the northern tip of

Kruger National Park, a less-visited but intriguing part of the park (covered on p.584); there are two entry gates to the park here, at **Punda Maria** and **Pafuri**.

The Soutpansberg area

The **Soutpansberg Mountains** have an unusual claim to distinction, named as they are after a set of saltpans – one of the flatter natural features known to man. The name came about after Voortrekker pioneers, under the leadership of Louis Trichardt, established their first settlement by the pans on the northern side of the mountain range. While the settlement soon relocated to Schoemansdal, on the southern side, the moniker stuck.

An impressive range of hills, particularly from the south, the Soutpansberg attract sufficient rainfall to create a subtropical climate, and lush farms along the southern slopes produce a range of exotic crops such as avocados, mangoes, bananas and macadamia nuts. In other parts the rocky *kloofs* and green hillsides offer some remote and unspoilt mountain retreats, shaded by up to 250 different species of tree, and the home of monkey, small antelope, foraging warthog and some noble raptors.

The N1 highway bisects the range, passing through the main town of the north, **Louis Trichardt**, situated in the southern shadow of the mountains, then climbing over a low pass and descending through a pair of tunnels on the northern side. Once over the escarpment the highway runs north across mostly empty baobab plains to **Messina** and the **Limpopo**.

Louis Trichardt

With the N1 sliding through town, it doesn't take much to miss **LOUIS TRICHARDT**, basically a practical place to stop at the junction of the road leading into Venda and to the Punda Maria gate of Kruger National Park. With little on offer further north at Messina, however, this is the last town with a reasonable selection of shops and services before you reach the border. A centre for the surrounding mountain and bushveld farms, it has hung onto its traditional role as a white bastion in the hostile north, and you'll find its white population overwhelmingly Afrikaans-speaking.

Practicalities

There is a well-organized and convenient **tourist information office** (Mon–Fri 8am–5pm, Sat 8am–1pm; ☎015/516 0040) beside Safari Motors, just off the highway at the most northerly of the three sets of traffic lights on the N1 as you come past town. The **train station** is at the southern end of Kruger Street. **Minibus taxis** for links into Venda and up to Beitbridge rank near the corner of Trichardt and Kruger streets. Greyhound and Translux **buses** stop at the information office and Northlink buses use the *Bergwater Hotel*.

The best **accommodation** in the area is out of town, mainly in the foothills of the Soutpansberg (see p.612), but there are a few inexpensive places you can stay here. The

---

ELEPHANT TALK: AFRICA'S SHITTIEST SOUVENIRS

One piece of modern Africana you shouldn't miss in Louis Trichardt is an unusual home industry – elephant-dung paper and products made by Lynne and Bruce Murray's **Elephant Talk**. They mix elephant-dung (personally gathered from the Tuli Block in Botswana) with recycled paper pulp to produce writing paper, cards and notelets. Made on their farm, Blair, in the Soutpansberg Mountains, you can see some of their range of guaranteed fragrance-free and biodegradable paper souvenirs in their shop, The Stamp Shop, 24 Rissik St, Louis Trichardt, or at the tourist information centre.

municipal caravan park is on Grobbelaar Street near the centre of town – it offers a bit of gloomy shade and grass for camping (①), but it's unattended and isn't really an attractive option. In town, the *Bergwater*, 5 Rissik St, (☎015/516 0262; ③), has some decent-sized and relatively modern rooms upstairs with views over a small lake. Off Rissik Street, the *Carousel Lodge*, Klein St (☎015/516 4482; ①–②), is an unglamorous alternative, but has adequate and inexpensive self-catering rooms and units, as well as a dorm. It can help organize tours and horseback and mountain-bike trails into the Soutpansberg.

Outside town, the small *Ben Lavin Nature Reserve*, signposted 8km south of town on the N1 (☎015/516 4534; ①–②), has a collection of larger antelope and giraffe, with a neat rest camp deep in the bush. It has walking and mountain-bike trails (bikes can be rented), self-catering cottages, luxury tents and space to pitch your own tent. The *Plaas Guesthouse*, 21km east of town along the R524 (☎015/516 4717; ③), is a very hospitable, friendly B&B on an avocado farm on the lush slopes of the Soutpansberg, with great breakfasts. There's also *Uitvlugt Cottage*, Roodewalpad St, 6km northeast of town (☎015/516 4468; ②), a simple and rather jumbled self-catering flatlet, but in a pleasant farmlands setting.

There are various familiar take-away **food** outlets around the grid-set town centre. For a sit-down meal, the *Shenandoah Spur* steakhouse is on Kroeg Street and Magistrate Avenue, while *Vino's*, a rather intimidating maroon-fronted bar and weekend nightclub on Trichardt Street, has an unexpectedly decent pub-type menu. There is also a pricier restaurant at the *Bergwater Hotel*.

Schoemansdal

Established by the first Voortrekkers to reach the Soutpansberg, **SCHOEMANSDAL**, off the R522 towards Vivo (Mon–Sat 9am–4pm; small entry fee), was abandoned around thirty years later, after it failed to stem attacks by Venda warriors. It was never again occupied. When control of the area was regained by the Zuid-Africaanische Republiek in 1898, a new settlement was established at Louis Trichardt, some 12km to the east, leaving Schoemansdal the only established Voortrekker settlement in the country not to become a modern town. Perhaps not surprisingly, the site of the historic village has been turned into an **outdoor museum of pioneering history**, with a number of old dwellings and buildings re-created and various aspects of settler life and domestic crafts on display. From the top of a wooden viewing platform you can make out the lines of grass where the streets of the settlement once were, as well as the archeological diggings which have been made on the site. It certainly paints a humble picture of pioneer Voortrekker life, and one that is not so readily evident in the collections of artefacts on display in dusty town houses. Having said that, the Schoemansdal museum is obviously dying a slow death of neglect, and has really become a place to absorb those interested in history rather than the wider audience it has the potential to attract.

Elim and around

Southeast of Louis Trichardt along the R578 lie some areas that used to form part of the self-governing homeland of Gazankulu (a Tsonga area), and they boast the leftover scruffiness and vibrant roadside action typical of such rural areas – most notably at **ELIM**, a cluster of stalls, minibuses and hoardings on the site of a long-established Swiss mission hospital. A short way from here, along the road to Levubu, is the modest but relaxing *Shiluvari Lakeside Lodge* (☎015/556 3406; ③), with lawns running down to the edge of Albasini Dam and views over the water to the Soutpansberg.

Continuing on the R578 from Elim crossroads, towards the town of Giyani, there are a series of rural arts and crafts workshops. This isn't strictly in Venda (see p.613), but the traditions and skills in arts and crafts are not dissimilar, and most of the workshops and small factories have simple, rural roots, making the trip to see them quite an adventure but definitely one well worth making. About 4km along this road, at the brow of a hill (directly opposite the road into Tsonga Textiles), the **Akanani development agency** is a small community centre with offices and workshops covering a range of practical subjects. This isn't a craft place, but they do have simple bunk rooms available (☎015/556 3133; ①) and will point you in the right direction for an interesting sunrise/sunset walk through the villages to nearby **Ribolla Hill**.

The Soutpansberg Mountains

Lush, rounded mountains rising to a height of over 1700m and cut by some dramatic outcrops of pinky-orange rock, the **Soutpansberg** seem to form a final barrier of colourful relief before the long hot plains either side of the Limpopo. Travelling north on the N1, you begin to climb immediately after leaving Louis Trichardt, up what becomes a narrow, winding road not easily negotiated by the heavy trucks which ply the Great North Road. Along this stretch you will pass a number of **hotels** that have used the lush surroundings to create a mountain-resort-type atmosphere. None are outstanding, and it is probably better to regard them as alternatives to a stopover in Louis Trichardt than attractions in their own right. The first two are on the southern side of the mountain range. The *Mountain View* (☎015/517 7031; ③), 9km north of town, is a little more pleasant, if slightly larger, than the *Clouds End* (☎015/517 7021; ③), 3km north of town. Also, just after the *Mountain View*, there is a turning (marked "Bluegumspoort") that provides a scenic drive along the face of the mountain range through stands of impressive eucalyptus. Once over the low pass, on the much less dramatic northern slopes, you'll find the well-run *Ingwe Ranch Motel* (☎015/517 7078; ③), which has a variety of rondavels and rooms, a coffee bar and one of the better restaurants in the area.

Mountain retreats

Beyond the well-worn route of the N1, you can get deeper into the more remote and wilder parts of the mountains if you have a couple of days to spare. Just south of Waterpoort, is the Sand River gorge, through which the rail line makes its pass through the mountains; here, approached from the southern side (29km west of Louis Trichardt on the R522) is the escapist *Medike Mountain Reserve* (☎015/516 0481; ②), with **accommodation** in thatched stone cottages and trails to see the rock-art, birdlife, wildlife and waterfalls in the surrounding area. Further west along the R522, along a turn-off 46km from Louis Trichardt, *Lajuma Mountain Retreat* (☎015/593 0352, mobile 082/200 3201; ②), situated by the top of Letjume, the highest point of the Soutpansberg, has two attractive thatched chalets perched on the mountainside, as well as simpler Victorian cottages tucked into the luxuriant tropical bush. Again, there are terrific opportunities to explore the slopes. On the north side of the mountains you can explore the salt pans that gave the range its name at *Bergpan Eco Resort* (☎015/593 0127) east of Waterpoort along the R523, where tours of the pans and a chance to experience salt-making are offered, along with hiking and a self-catering guesthouse (②). The tourist information office in Louis Trichardt holds details of other retreats.

North to the border

Once over the Soutpansberg, the N1 runs across some hot, mostly featureless plains of dense bush and baobab trees for some 60km before reaching the town of **Messina**, the last settlement before the Zimbabwe border at the Limpopo River. There isn't anything much else in the region, although the famous Iron Age site at Mapungubwe (Hill of the Jackals) is around 80km west of Messina, close to the confluence of the Shashe and

Limpopo rivers. This is set to become part of the ambitious Trans-Limpopo National Park, with links to nature reserves in Zimbabwe and Botswana, but as yet there's no public entry or facilities.

Messina

Floating rather oddly 18km south of the border, **MESSINA** is above all a mining town, although it does mop up a fair bit of the traffic passing through on the N1. The border at Beitbridge is not open 24 hours a day, so there's always call for accommodation and food, which Messina does offer, but without flourish.

The one thing of note around Messina is the **Baobab Tree Reserve** that encircles the town. Baobab trees, the legend says, God planted upside down, with their roots in the air. You don't find the trees in great stands but rather dotted around the bushveld, each one with a plate nailed onto it displaying its protected status. Many are over a thousand years old, and the largest have been hollowed out inside and used as houses, bars, shops and even toilets. There are quite a number of fine examples by the roadside on the N1, although many of these are covered in graffiti. The entrance to the reserve, which doesn't have any facilities, is a couple of kilometres south of town.

Practicalities

The town's caravan and camping park, which has some grass and shade and is reasonably well run, is on the left not long after you come into town from the south. Otherwise **accommodation** is a choice between *Günter's Country House* (☎01553/41019 or 40484; ③), 25 Irwin St (the R508 to Tshipise), a civilized, pleasant B&B with a pool; *Ilala Lodge* (☎015/534 3220; ③), situated in the baobab reserve 8km northwest of town, with secluded stone chalets with a pool; or, least expensive, the *Limpopo River Lodge*, on the N1 in the centre of town (☎015/534 0204; ②) – a plain travellers' hotel with a certain creaking character and a restaurant attached.

When it comes to **eating**, there are various takeaways, including a *Nando's*, at the elbow in the road close to the mine entrance. For sit-down meals, the *Buffalo Ridge Spur* franchise is by the N1 off Sam Street; there's also a steakhouse at *Mudzwiri Lodge*, by the mine on the northern side of town, plus a basic restaurant attached to the *Limpopo River Lodge*.

Beitbridge

On the South African side of the Limpopo there isn't much to **BEITBRIDGE** other than a tacky service station, a habitually long queue of trucks, some noisy minibus touts and the customs and immigration buildings (which include a duty-free shop). Two bridges cross the Limpopo (the river memorably described by Rudyard Kipling in *Just So Stories* as "great grey-green, greasy"), one for vehicles and one for pedestrians. The border is open 5.30am–10.30pm, but count yourself lucky if you get through without delay, hassle or hinderance. The only viable alternative if you want to get to Zimbabwe from South Africa is the Grobersbrug/Martin's Drift border (daily 8am–4pm), 150km northwest of Potgietersrus on the N11, although this means detouring through Botswana.

Venda

To the west and north of Louis Trichardt lies the intriguing land of the **VhaVenda** people, a culturally and linguistically distinct African grouping known for their mystical legends, political independence and their arts and crafts. Venda was demarcated as a homeland under the apartheid system in the Fifties, and became one of three nationally independent homelands in South Africa in the late Seventies. Of all the homelands, Venda was one of the least compromised, keeping both its geographic and cultural integrity, and largely being left to mind its own business during the dark years of apartheid. Its boundaries have regained their former fuzziness, within the Northern Province, but the region has retained its strong, independent identity.

Venda history and culture

The people who today call themselves **VhaVenda** are descended from a number of ancient groupings who migrated from the Great Lakes area in east-central Africa in the eleventh and twelfth centuries. Their identity gelled when a group under Chief Dimbanyika arrived at Dzata (which means "peace" in Venda) in the northern Soutpansberg, where a walled fort was later built. From here they consolidated their power in the region, fending off attack from a number of different African groupings (including the Voortrekkers, whom they harried from their settlement at Schoemansdal, just south of the Soutpansberg in 1867). Although the VhaVenda suffered a reverse at the hands of the Boers in 1898, the onset of the Anglo-Boer War prevented that victory being consolidated. The British had little interest in such a remote region, and were content to allow their administration to be run by the local chiefs, a system of self-government which, in one contrived form or another, lasted through the apartheid years until 1994.

The culture of the VhaVenda is a fascinating one, steeped in mysticism and vivid legend. One pervading theme is water – always an important concern in hot, seasonal climates, but in which Venda is unusually abundant. Lakes, rivers, waterfalls and lush forests all form sacred sites, while legends abound of *zwidutwane*, or water sprites, and snakes who live at the bottom of dark pools or lakes. You can still even find older people who hold a taboo against fish, partly because the animals live in water and partly because they believe that if you eat fish the crocodiles will go hungry and turn on other available food sources, such as humans.

Many VhaVenda ceremonies and rituals still hold great importance, with the most famous the python, or *domba*, dance performed by young female initiates. Naked but for jewellery and a small piece of cloth around their waist, the teenage girls form a long chain, swaying and shuffling as the snake winds around a fire to the sound of a beating drum – another sacred object in Venda – often for hours on end. Although it is well known, your chances of seeing it performed are limited – although dancing can always be arranged (at a price, and with notice). The genuine thing is most common during spring; Heritage Day around the end of August or the beginning of September is a good time for celebrations.

Thohoyandou

A fairly direct, if slightly chaotic, 70km west of Louis Trichardt following the southern edge of the Soutpansberg along the R524, the Venda capital of **THOHOYANDOU** is an ugly, dirty sprawl of broken concrete and undisciplined building glamorized by a money-spinning casino. Situated among the last of the foothills at the eastern end of the Soutpansberg, it's not a place you'll want to spend time in if you can help it; and if you're heading for Kruger, the R524 mercifully bypasses the town altogether.

The highlight of the capital, at least according to the tourist authorities, is the **Venda Sun hotel and casino** (☎0159/824600, central reservations ☎011/780 7800; ⑤), a clone of the gambling dens tacitly encouraged in the homelands by the apartheid government and lapped up by South Africans denied such illicit entertainment in their own country. It is set in the heart of the downtown area, surrounded immediately by trees, but not far beyond the road and tatty shopping mall. To get to it, turn left off the R534 coming from Louis Trichardt at the Delta/Toyota service station, and right at the third set of traffic lights. As a hotel, it has decent, if expensive, rooms and facilities include a pool.

The only reasonable alternative in town to the *Venda Sun* is *Bougainvillea Lodge* (☎0159/82 4064; ③), just up the hill from the *Venda Sun*, a simple motel-like travellers' stop. Some way out of town, though good for budget travellers keen to explore the region, is *Land of Legend Backpackers* (☎ 015/583 0033; ①–②), situated off the R524 about halfway between Louis Trichardt and Thohoyandou; free pick-ups from Louis Trichardt can be organized. Accommodation is in two dorms and a rondavel with a double. Facilties are for self catering, though meals can be arranged.

There isn't a wide choice of **places to eat** in Thohoyandou. In the shopping centre next to the *Venda Sun* there are a number of take-away food shops, including a *Nando's* and *KFC*. There is a pricier sit-down restaurant in the *Venda Sun* itself. **Minibuses** for Louis Trichardt leave from the large, chaotic taxi rank in front of the shopping centre.

Information – and seeing Venda

Like most of the other homelands of apartheid South Africa, Venda arrived in the new South Africa with a bloated and inefficient beaurocracy, and despite the restructuring of the provinces and tightening of budgets, many difficulties have lingered. Venda Tourism, ambitious even in its heyday, eventually crumbled in 1998, leaving vague promises of new provincial structures but very little of substantive help to the visitor to Venda. For now the best place to get **information** is from the tourist information office in Louis Trichardt (see p.610) or one of the established independent accommodation options, such as the *Venda Sun* or *Land of Legend Backpackers*. **Tours** of the area, including to Lake Fundudzi, are available from both establishments or the ebullient *Face Afrika Tours* (☎ & fax 015/516 2076, mobile ☎082/969 3270, *facaf@mweb.co.za*). Otherwise you'll find almost no tourist-oriented infrastructure whatsoever in Venda and a general lack of familiarity with visitors and what they might be looking for. However, it's a lot less dangerous to **travel independently** through Venda than many other places in South Africa, and the travelling can be wonderfully rough, raw and rewarding. But be prepared for the fact that you will be very much on your own.

Lake Fundudzi, the Sacred Forest and the Mabudashango Trail

Along the northern side of the Soutpansberg, through a valley traced by the R523 road from the N1 to Thohoyandou, is the most appealing core of VhaVenda history and

---

ANIMAL MAGIC

Along with their spiritual relationship with water-inhabiting creatures, the VhaVenda have an interesting affinity with a number of **animals** of the forests and mountains. The relationship is, in many ways, a lot less aggressive and more humanized than that found in other African peoples. With lions, the VhaVenda recall the story of their great leader Makado, who harried the Boer commandos from the north. He was captured and thrown into a lion pit in Pretoria, but, rather like Daniel in the Old Testament, the lions chose not to eat him. Around the hot spring at Mphephu the legend runs that a leopard controls the hillside, and that it's always wise practice to keep him informed about who's in the area. And towards the eastern end of the Soutpansberg range there is a Lion's Head-shaped hill (there are nice views of it across Vondo Dam, on the Thate Vondo pass road) called Lwamondo. It is inhabited by baboons, who are protected because they once warned the VhaVenda of an imminent attack from their enemies.

ARTS AND CRAFT IN VENDA AND GAZANKULU

The Venda and Gazankulu regions have established a strong reputation in **arts and crafts**. The best known of these are clay pots distinctively marked with angular designs in graphite silver and ochre. Also growing in status are woodcarvings, ranging from abstract to practical; though, while the best of these can be imaginative and bold, you will see a lot which are unfinished and overpriced. You'll also come across tapestries, fabrics, basketwork and painting.

One thing which adds to the attraction of the art and crafts of these rural regions is that you can still find it being made in the villages, using traditional techniques and skills. Finding your way to these villages, however, can be quite an adventure, as they are widely scattered, the roads are poor, and directions can often be vague and confusing.

In the fromer homeland of **Gazankulu**, the main route is along the R578 between Elim and Giyani. Travelling southeast from Elim crossroads, look out for a track leading up to the **Rivoni** workshop (opposite the turn to Waterval), where blind and other handicapped people make sisal mats, furniture, candles and coffins – a line that evidently does a roaring trade. There isn't a great deal to see, but the place is industrious and there is a small shop. Back on the R578, turn left at the brow of the next hill, then up a right-hand fork, to reach **Tsonga Textiles**, where screen-printed fabrics are produced and turned into such things as tablecloths, bedspreads and clothes.

The R578 then goes down a hill, at the bottom of which is a turning to Mbhokota village. Going along this, turning left at the T-junction and left again along a narrow track just past a small homestead with a busy garden, you'll find a run-down looking collection of buildings where **Twananani** textiles are made – attractive, funky hand-painted and batik garments with traditional African designs, made by around twenty people.

At the next junction off the R578 to Riverplaats, then along a right-hand fork, is the house and small workshop of Shangaan woodcarver **Jackson Thugwane**. He's an almost mystical figure, with pieces exhibited in major galleries around the country and in Europe; if he isn't there you won't find much to see; if he is, be prepared for a few absorbing hours of philosophy, theology, art and the state of the modern world. If you take the left-hand fork after the Riverplaats sign, you will eventually come to a village called **Mashamba** where villagers make clay pots in the traditional way. This is, however, a trek deep into the rural areas of Gazankulu and road conditions are fairly unreliable, so ask around for the latest.

In **Venda**, the villages are even more scattered and hard to find. There are a number of sites situated to the south of Thohoyandou, including the workshop of **Noria Mabasa**, whose clay and wood sculptures have become widely recognized around South Africa. Another place to look out for is **Mutale**, to the north of Thohoyandou, where traditional decorative drums are made. You can pick up a hand-drawn **arts and crafts map** of Venda at the tourist information office at Louis Trichardt; another option is to contact **Annette and Martin Kennealy** (☎0159/32096, mobile ☎083/326 2922), artists who are very knowledgeable about art (rather than crafts) in the area and can advise on what to look out for and where to find it.

legend. This is where you'll find the lush forests, waterfalls and mountains which give Venda its mystical atmosphere.

From Thohoyando, climb out of town to the north and then west, eventually shucking off the suburbs to get amongst the elevated green scenery which lies ahead so enticingly. You'll pass the **Vondo Dam**, created in the early Nineties and surrounded by pine forests, then climb over the **Thate Vondo Pass**, over the summit of which a small shack marks the entrance to a network of forest roads that take you into the area containing the most important lake in Venda, **Lake Fundudzi**, and the **Sacred Forest**, an area of dense indigenous forest which contains the burial ground of Venda chiefs. You can look at both from afar, but to get any closer is a matter of deep cultural sensitivity: you have to gain permission, which, without local leads to the right people, is not easy to do. Another thing that contributes to the mystery of the place is that there isn't a readily available map showing you the network of roads around the forest, and some of the roads require 4WD. If you want to see the area it's best to join a tour (see p.615) or make sure you've gathered information and advice beforehand.

One option well worth considering is the **Mabudashango Hiking Trail**, a four-day, fifty-five-kilometre walk that takes you as close as any road to the main highlights of the area, including Lake Fundudzi and the Sacred Forest. The trail is big on views – undoubtedly a spectacular aspect of the area, as well as lush vegetation and a real sense of the water-fed wonder of the sacred land. At each of the camps there is a shelter with water and toilet facilities; for details, contact the tourist information office in Louis Trichardt (see p.610).

Mphephu and Dzata

Heading west, the R523 crosses over the crest of the Thate Vondo pass and then follows the **Nzhelele River** down a valley of scattered but mostly unbroken settlement. About halfway along is a poorly signposted turning to **Mphephu Resort** (☎0159/730 321; ②), on the flanks of the Soutpansberg by a hot spring, and one of the few former Venda Tourism resorts that has so far remained open through the cutbacks. There are chalets here, as well as a rather unglamorous complex with a takeaway and a shop, but the pools fed by the hot spring can be pleasant if there aren't too many people around, and the setting is relaxed and away from the unpleasantness of Thohoyandou. There are in fact two springs – one within the resort and the other behind a reed screen just outside, which is used by locals – with a strict division of hours for men and women.

Not far west of Mphephu, on the northern side of the road, are the **Dzata ruins**, the remains of the royal kraal of the kings of VhaVenda, which date from 1400. They're very interesting historically, but, as with the rest of the tourism infrastructure, not very visitor-friendly. If you find the gate locked, you may need to toot your horn to rouse your gateman.

Further afield

The R525 runs across the Messina plains towards **Pafuri Gate**, the most northerly of the Kruger entrances, past which is a border post to Mozambique, although there is little beyond unless you're well equipped for adventure. If you need a **stay** over on your way to Kruger, there's an Aventura holiday resort at Tshipise (☎015/539 0624, central reservations 012/346 2277; ②–③). More worthwhile, *Waller's Camp* (☎0159/83802 or 083/255 8463, *wcamp@mweb.co.za*; self catering ④), at Mavhulani, just before you reach the Pafuri Gate. This is an attractive, open bush camp constructed from natural materials, from where you can set off in pursuit of the profuse local plants and wildlife, or relax by the river or pool. Full board arrangements can also be made.

travel details

Trains

One daily train travels in each direction between Johannesburg and Messina (a 17hr journey), calling at Pretoria, Warmbaths and Potgietersrus. Also from Jo'burg, one train a week stops at Louis Trichardt (9hr), Messina (12hr), and Pietersburg (6hr).

Buses

Greyhound, Intercape and Translux buses ply the N1 between Johannesburg and Beit Bridge, stopping at Warmkatus, Pietersburg, Louis Trichardt and Messina; most services carry on to either Bulawayo and Victoria Falls or Harare in

Zimbabwe. Northlink Tours connect Tzaneen and Johannesburg via Pietersburg. These and other routes are also covered by minibus taxis from any moderately sized town; the best way to find out where they're going and when they depart is to enquire at the taxi rank.

Beit Bridge to: Johannesburg (daily; 8–10hr).

Pietersburg to: Johannesburg (daily; 4hr); Tzaneen (daily; 1hr 45min).

Tzaneen to: Johannesburg (6 weekly; 6hr 15min); Pietersburg (daily; 1hr 45min).

Flights

Pietersburg to: Johannesburg (3 daily Mon–Fri, 1 daily Sat & Sun; 50min).

CHAPTER ELEVEN

LESOTHO

The most liberating aspect of the aptly named "mountain kingdom" of **Lesotho**, particularly if you have come from barbed-wire-mad South Africa, is its almost total absence of fences. This means you can wander at will, meeting as you do a people who are also some of the most hospitable of the region. The other thing you'll notice pretty quickly is that Lesotho is virtually treeless, with the exception of the invasive and water-hungry eucalyptus and the peach trees introduced by French missionaries a century ago. Indeed the country, once the grain basket of the region, is in deep ecological trouble, and acres of irreplaceable topsoil, loosened by decades of over-farming, are washed away down its rivers each year.

The **Lesotho Lowlands** form an east-facing crescent around the country, and are where you'll find all the nation's major towns, including the busily practical capital of **Maseru**, still recovering from widespread looting and burning in demonstrations in 1998, and a host of smaller settlements that began life as tax collection centres for the British administration. The Lowlands have other delights – the weaving crafts of **Teya-Teyaneng**, the extraordinary caves at **Mateka**, and **Thaba Bosiu**, the mountain fortress of Lesotho's founder, king Moshoeshoe I. But the true splendours of the country lie in its ruggedly beautiful **Highlands**, which are dotted with excellent and inexpensive accommodation. There you can visit the engineering masterpiece of the **Katse dam**, ski at **Oxbow**, fish from rivers everywhere, and above all wander the countryside, dividing your time between immaculately crafted dry-stone-walled villages and their relaxed inhabitants, and the peaceful solitude of the mountains.

Although the tarred **road network** is good and getting better, many Sotho still travel by **pony**. You can do the same, from pony-trekking lodges all over the country; along with hiking it's unquestionably the best way to see Lesotho. Most of Lesotho's over four hundred **San rock-art sites** and the many more **dinosaur footprints** can only be visited this way – although there are still plenty close by the roads which you can reach with ease if travelling by car.

Some history

Lesotho exists because of the determined efforts of one man, **Moshoeshoe I** (1786-1870), to secure land in the face of intense social upheaval and the insatiable land-hunger of others. Before the arrival of Moshoeshoe's ancestors around 900 AD, the San inhabited Lesotho's hills and mountains unchallenged. Today the San are gone, exterminated by the British led by one Colonel Bowker, who led the last of many missions against them in the highland region of Sehonkong in 1873. However, they have left their mark through rock paintings, glimpses of their tongue in the Sotho language, and traces of their features in some Sotho people.

The Sotho first settled the fertile plains that today form the Lesotho lowlands and the Free State, before going on to colonize the mountains. They farmed these plains relatively peacefully for centuries, but by Moshoeshoe's time, bandit clans from elsewhere had already forced thousands of Sotho off their land. Moshoeshoe proved his own marauding skills in 1809, when he rustled so many cattle from another chief that he was judged to have "shaved his beard"; Moshoeshoe is the "praise name" he earned for that feat – pronounced "Moshwehshweh", the name is supposed to represent the sound of

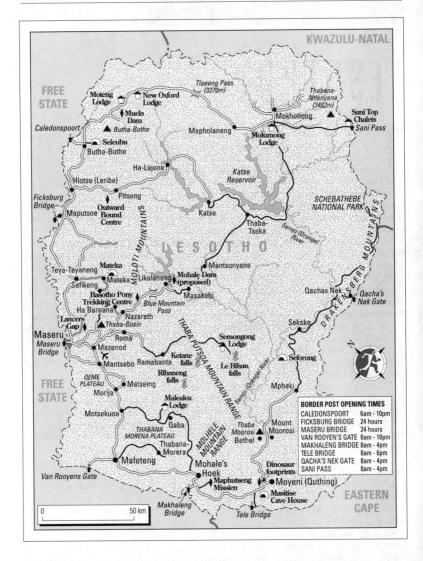

shaving. Moshoeshoe became a chief in 1820, based on top of a mountain near Butha-Buthe, where he became patron to many refugees in search of safety. However, after a particularly vicious attack on Butha-Buthe in 1824, Moshoeshoe decided it was no longer safe and trekked south with his followers in search of a better mountain. Moshoeshoe found one at Thaba Bosiu, which was subsequently attacked repeatedly but never taken. Moshoeshoe meanwhile expanded his kingdom by securing other clan chiefs as clients, at the same time earning a reputation for wisdom and generosity amongst ordinary Sotho that is almost mythical today.

Moshoeshoe had heard from travellers that **missionaries** brought peace, and so welcomed the arrival in 1833 of three from the Paris Evangelical Missionary Society (PEMS). Moshoeshoe established them in Morija, and took an active interest in their work, but never officially converted, despite their efforts. The missionaries established what is now the Lesotho Evangelical Church, second in size only to the Catholics in Lesotho, whose missionaries founded Roma in the 1860s (see p.635).

The kingdom was encroached by land-hungry whites from the 1840s, and the Orange Free State (OFS) government invaded in 1858, their soldiers destroying Morija and then launching a failed attack on Thaba Bosiu. They nonetheless captured plenty of farm land whose acquisition was sanctioned by a British treaty in 1860. In 1865, the OFS government cited Sotho cattle theft as the pretext for a new war, though few could deny Moshoeshoe's bitter assertion that "my great sin is that I possess a good and fertile country". The ensuing Seqiti War mainly involved the destruction of Sotho crops by Free State troops, an event which forced Moshoeshoe into a humiliating treaty in 1866 which signed over most of his remaining good land. Even this was not enough, and war resumed in 1867, halted only by the British taking over what was left of the kingdom as the protectorate of Basotholand in 1868. The Treaty of Aliwal North in 1869 restored Moshoeshoe's land east of the Caledon but left the rest with the Free State, where it has remained to this day.

Moshoeshoe died in 1870 and the British handed Basotholand to the Cape administration a year later, which began taxing its new subjects, establishing a series of hut tax collection points which have since grown into Lesotho's modest collection of small towns. In 1879, in a bid to tempt the OFS and Transvaal into federation, the Cape government decided to confiscate all Sotho firearms. The result was two years of raids and futile skirmishes, known as the **Gun War**, an expensive failure that brought down the Cape government and so outraged London that Britain resumed direct rule in 1884.

Along with Bechuanaland and Swaziland, Basotholand rejected incorporation into the union of South Africa in 1910, with **King Letsie II** instead helping found the South African Native National Congress (later the ANC) in 1912. During the following years, the monarchy and chiefs' position declined, partly because British reforms forced their uneasy conversion into a junior arm of the colonial civil service, but also because social changes at work in the region, like migration, urbanization and rising education levels, proved too much for chiefs and successive kings to adapt to. In 1960, when **Moshoeshoe II** was crowned king, independence politics were in full swing, spearheaded by Pan-Africanist Ntsu Mokhele's Basotho Congress Party (BCP), and rivalled by the more conservative Basotho National Party (BNP). The BCP easily won the 1960 elections, but the 1965 ones were narrowly won by the BNP, who duly led newly named Lesotho into independence on October 4, 1966. However, after losing in 1970, prime minister **Leabua Jonathan** annulled the result, declared a state of emergency, and carried on ruling until he was toppled in 1986 by **Major General Metsing Lekhanya**. Lekhanya ordered the expulsion of the ANC from Lesotho and signed an agreement that year with South Africa for the Lesotho Highlands Water Project (see p.647).

In 1990, Lekhanya sent Moshoeshoe into exile and installed his son **Letsie III** as king, but a year later Lekhanya was himself ousted by **Major General Phisona**, who then gave way to a democratically elected government led by Mokhele's BCP in 1993. There was no end to the turmoil, however, with Letsie dissolving the BCP government in August 1994 for alleged incompetence, although regional pressure soon forced the restoration of the government and constitution. Letsie stood down in favour of his father in 1995, but Moshoeshoe II died in a car crash the next year, and Letsie regained the throne rather sooner than he really desired.

The **elections** of 1998 were won in a landslide by Mokhele, this time at the head of the breakaway Lesotho Congress for Democracy (LCD), but opposition parties cried foul amid widespread allegations of vote-rigging. That July and August, large crowds gathered outside the Royal Palace in Maseru demanding the results be overturned; these protests

• **Accommodation** This is reasonably priced in Lesotho; you can get a double room for about M90 a person in most parts of the country, and for M140 a person in one of the middle-range hotels in Maseru. Be aware that most outside Maseru take cash only. The most common form of accommodation around the country is lodges, which vary in quality but tend to be rather bland, conventional hotels that get most of their business from conferences. Only a few lodges target travellers, but these – such as *Malealea Lodge*, *Fraser's Semonkong Lodge*, *Molumong Lodge* near Mohkotlong and *New Oxbow Lodge* – are relaxed, easy-going places that capture the feel of Lesotho very well.

• **Banks and exchange** These are found in all Lesotho's towns, but Maseru is the only place where it's easy to change money at them. Hours are Mon–Fri 8.30am–3.30pm, closing 1pm on Wed, Sat 8.30am–11am. Saturday is not a good day to do any banking, as the banks are invariably heaving with customers. Banks do not as a rule have ATMs, and any you do find are unlikely to accept foreign cashcards. The larger hotels in Maseru and the Lowland towns change money, but for ludicrously bad rates, making them very much a last resort.

• **Books** The glossy official tourist literature has useful phone numbers but is otherwise thin on facts, in which case you should turn to Marco Turco's *Visitor's Guide to Lesotho* (Southern, 1994), or the small *Backpackers' Guide to Lesotho*, self-published by Russell Suchet, who runs the *Sani Lodge*. Some South African backpackers' lodges have copies; otherwise contact him direct (see p.416). Some of the lodges stock a very good 1:250,000 topographical map of Lesotho, which you can also get at the Department of Land, Surveys & Physical Planning (see opposite), the only place where you can get the sort of detailed maps you need for serious hiking.

• **Camping** Freelance camping is possible all over rural Lesotho, provided you check with the local chief first; the virtual absence of fences in the country means you can roam, and pitch your tent almost anywhere. Some lodges allow camping in their grounds.

• **Costs** These are lower than South Africa's. Buying food and eating out are slightly less expensive, and so is public transport. Pony trekking costs about M100 a day at most of the lodges (see p.626). Imported items like film are more expensive in Lesotho than South Africa, and only reliably available in Maseru. A ten percent sales tax is applicable, and often not added to marked prices on menus or in supermarkets and shops.

• **Credit cards** Most major cards, such as Visa, Mastercard and American Express, are of limited use. Hotels and lodges geared to foreign visitors accept them, as do a few Maseru restaurants and the craft shops of Teya-Teyaneng. Otherwise you need cash for everything.

• **Currency** Lesotho's currency is the Maloti (M), divided into 100 lisenti, which is tied to the South African rand (R1 = M1). You can use rands in Lesotho, so you don't need to convert them beforehand, but you cannot use or exchange maloti anywhere outside Lesotho, so make sure you use them up or exchange them before leaving.

• **Embassies** South Africa, 391 Anderson St, Menlo Park, Pretoria (☎012/46 7648); UK, 7 Chesham Place, Belgravia, London SW1 (☎0171/235 5686); USA, 2511 Massachusetts Ave NW, Washington DC (☎202/797 5533).

• **Gay and lesbian** Same-sex relationships are not explicitly illegal in Lesotho, but they are not approved of either, so it is safer to avoid public displays of affection. There is a gay scene, but it is underground, so make use of South African gay contacts to find it.

• **Passports and visas** Visa requirements for the kingdom of Lesotho were in the habit of changing fairly often, but currently seem a little more settled. All

developed into a **mutiny** by Lesotho Defence Force soldiers, and in September, under the flag of a Southern African Development Community (SADC) **peacekeeping force**, South African troops crossed the border. Fierce fighting took place around military bases and

Commonwealth citizens, except those from India, Pakistan, Nigeria and Ghana, do not need visas, and nor do citizens of France, Germany, Ireland, Israel, Italy, Japan, the Netherlands, Spain, Switzerland and the USA. You may find that border officials, particularly at smaller entry points, do not know the new rules, and will demand a visa from you even if you do not need one. There is not much you can do about this, but since visas are available on the spot, and are relatively inexpensive (M20/R20 single-entry, M40 multiple entry), you may as well pay up. If you have travelled through a yellow-fever zone, you will need an International Certificate of Vaccination against yellow fever. The standard entry permit is for 14 days, but, should you need an extension, contact the Department of Immigration and Passport Services, Kingsway, Maseru (☎31 7339).

• **Phone numbers** To phone Lesotho from anywhere but South Africa, the country code is ☎266, followed by the number (note that there are no area codes); from South Africa, dial ☎09266. To phone abroad from Lesotho, dial ☎00, followed by the country and area codes and then the actual telephone number. To phone South Africa, first dial ☎0027, then the area code and phone number. To call collect, first call the operator, ☎100. Where area codes are indicated in the text, the number in question is a South African number, and you will need to prefix it with ☎0027 if calling from Lesotho.

• **Tour operators** The Lesotho Tourist Board (☎31 2896, fax 32 3638) can arrange tailor-made tours of the country. Lesotho Tours (☎ & fax 32 2782, mobile 85 7805) is run by a German living in Maseru. Alternatively, the *Malealea Lodge* (☎ & fax 051/447 3200) offers some innovative options, often involving pony trekking or 4WDs, while *Hotel Maluti Lodge* (☎78 5224, fax 78 5341) also offers specialized 4WD trips.

• **Water** Safe to drink out of the tap. Whilst Lesotho's rivers and streams are bilharzia-free, drinking from them is inadvisable without purifying the water first if you are in any doubt about what might lie upstream (eg people washing clothes, dead livestock).

HIKING IN LESOTHO

As an almost entirely fenceless country, and hospitable to boot, Lesotho is a **hiker's paradise**. It really is possible to set off into the hills and hike for as long as you like, with no prospect of an angry farmer yelling at you to get off his land – quite a change from South Africa. If you're camping, it's important to ask permission, preferably from the chief, although it's normally fine just to pitch your tent if there's no one around. A cosier alternative, where its available, is to stay in a rondavel, for which which you will definitely need to ask permission, and to pay a small offering – M10–20.

Always prepare adequately before setting out, and bring supplies for at least a day more than you think the hike will take. Lesotho's weather is notoriously fickle, and you should bring a sunhat and sunblock, as well as warm clothing and waterproofs, whatever the season. Other basics include a torch, plenty of food (there aren't many stores in very rural areas, and those there are don't often have much stock), a water container, water purifying tablets, an all-weather cooker with fuel (don't count on finding firewood), a genuinely waterproof tent, a sleeping mat and a warm sleeping bag. Also invaluable is a decent map and a compass. The 1:250,000 map available from the Basotho Hat Building in Maseru marks most trails and topography, although the really detailed 1:50,000 maps of specific regions of Lesotho, available from the **Department of Lands, Surveys and Physical Planning** (☎32 2376), on Lerotholi Road, near the corner of Constitution Road in Maseru, are far better. Be warned that in the highest reaches of the Drakensberg there are very few villages, and you can walk for days without seeing anyone. Lovely as this is, it is also risky, so make sure someone knows where you have gone, and don't hike there on your own.

at the strategically vital Katse Dam, but the delayed arrival of further peacekeeping troops from Botswana meant that Maseru was left unsecured, and demonstrators from the Royal Palace were joined by thousands of others from surrounding districts angry at

---

A SOTHO PROVERB

Lesotho's myriad of villages look peaceful enough, but as an outsider you never know the full story, as a proverb well-known in Lesotho (but surely universally true) points out: *Motse o motle kantle feela* ("A village is only beautiful on the outside").

---

what they regarded as South Africa's heavy-handed intervention. A large number of shops and offices in Maseru, as well as towns such as Mafeteng, were looted and burned. Elections are planned for early 2000, but there is every evidence that the political squabbling will continue until then, if not long afterwards. It would take exceptional circumstances, however, and some severe misjudgements from the peacekeeping troops of the SADC, for such serious violence to be seen again.

When to go

The Lesotho **winter** runs from May to July, when it often snows in the Highlands and sometimes in the Lowlands too, which is great for skiing and very picturesque. Although the days are usually crisp and warm, it does get extremely cold at night and ice can make driving hazardous in Highlands areas. **Spring**, between August and October, is a beautiful time, when the snow melts, new plants sprout up everywhere, and the fields are tilled again. November to January is **summer**, when Lesotho gets most of its rain, which is often torrential, turning dirt roads into mudslides. Still, when it isn't raining the weather is usually lovely and sunny and the landscape vivid shades of green. **Autumn** runs from February to April, and is one of the best times to visit the country, as it doesn't usually rain too much and it hasn't started to get really cold. Whatever the time of year, Lesotho can be very cold at night, particularly in the Highlands, and prone to rapid weather changes, for which it is always wise to be prepared.

Getting there

There are twelve **border posts** from South Africa into Lesotho – from the Free State, KwaZulu-Natal and the Eastern Cape. All the **Free State** border crossings, and **Tele Bridge** (daily 8am–6pm) in the Eastern Cape, cross over into the Lesotho Lowlands and are much more accessible than the others, which enter via the Drakensberg. The latter include the famous **Sani Pass** (daily 8am–4pm), which you need a 4WD to ascend, although alternative transport is provided by local backpackers' lodges (see p.415). The **Ficksburg Bridge** and **Maseru Bridge** crossings (both 24hr), are the busiest in the country.

The **drive** from Bloemfontein to Maseru is an easy 200km east along the N8. From Durban, turn off towards Ficksburg at Bethlehem, and then either cross the border at Maputsoe and drive down through Lesotho, or continue on to Ladybrand and cross the border at Maseru. Driving from the Eastern Cape to Maseru is more fiddly, and if you

---

LESOTHO PUBLIC HOLIDAYS

January 1 – New Year's Day
March 11 – Moshoeshoe Day
April 4 – Heroes Day
Good Friday
Easter Monday
Ascension Day (Thursday)

May 1 – Workers' Day
July 17 – King's Birthday
October 4 – Independence Day
December 25 – Christmas Day
December 26 – Boxing Day

want to stay on tarred roads for as long as possible, remain in South Africa at least until Wepener, from where you can cross into Mafeteng through the Van Rooyen's Gate **border post** (daily 6am–10pm), or continue through Hobhouse on the Ladybrand road, taking the right-hand fork to Maseru.

Lesotho's only international **airport**, Moshoeshoe I, is 18km south of Maseru, but scheduled flights are limited those run bySA Airlink (☎011/978 1111).

Getting around

Lesotho has a good tarred **road network**, though you can't avoid dirt roads when heading to more out-of-the-way places of interest. Wherever you travel, however, and especially when you make for the Highlands, twisting roads, fast minibus taxis and frequent encounters with road-side pedestrians and livestock make driving here tiring work. Of the main roads, the **northern route** is a continuous tarred road leading north from Maseru to Mokhotlong; the road to Sani from Mokhotlong is untarred but can be negotiated in a saloon car, but the fearsome Sani Pass itself can only be tackled with a 4WD. Striking off the northern route, the Hlotse to **Katse dam road** is tarred and of very high quality, though it goes over some punishing gradients. On the **central route**, the tar extends as far as the site of the new Mohale Dam around Likalaneng, and then reverts to dirt and gravel of sometimes poor quality as far as Thaba Tseka. The high-altitude route from here to Katse is also only for 4WD vehicles, although minibus taxis will tackle it. The southern route from Maseru is tarred as far as Mphaki, but is passable in an ordinary saloon car up to Qacha's Nek. The road to Sehlabathebe National Park is impassable without a 4WD, though again minibus taxis and buses somehow manage it.

If you've rented a car in South Africa, make sure the **insurance** covers you for travel in Lesotho. Some companies are reluctant to do this, because of the condition of many of the roads. **Fuel** costs roughly the same in Lesotho as it does in South Africa. The **speed limit** is 120kmh out of town, and 50kmh in urban areas.

Public transport covers Lesotho well. **Buses** are slower but safer than **minibus taxis**, but they are both very inexpensive. **Timetables** do not exist as such; the rule of thumb is to check the day before, and get to the bus station early if you have a long distance to travel, as long-distance transport usually leaves around 6am. If you're travelling short distances on the main tar and dirt roads, you shouldn't have to wait too long for a minibus taxi going your way.

Hitching is much safer in Lesotho than in South Africa and is a good way to get around. Some drivers expect payment, so you should negotiate this before you've travelled too far.

For **internal flights** you can charter planes out of Moshoeshoe I through Mission Aviation Fellowship based in Maseru (☎31 3640) who charge around M900 per hour for planes that can carry four to five people.

MASERU AND THE CENTRAL DISTRICTS

The most convenient entry point from South Africa, and the country's most sophisticated urban centre by far, **Maseru** is a good place to start exploring Lesotho. Apart from a few elegant colonial sandstone buildings, there is not a great deal to see here. A few burned-out shells of buildings, victims of the 1998 riots, make for rather eerie monuments to the political troubles of the small kingdom, but the pervading atmosphere is not hostile and travellers will probably feel more comfortable here than in most South African cities. There are plenty of bracing excursions into the hills and plateaus that

PONY TREKKING

Ponies were introduced to Lesotho in the nineteenth century, with one of the first given as a present to king Moshoeshoe I by chief Moorosi in 1829. Moshoeshoe learnt to ride that year, and rapidly acquired further steeds, which he distributed to his family and followers. By the time of Moshoeshoe's death in 1870, ponies were widespread throughout the kingdom and the Sotho had become expert riders.

Lesotho's ponies are famously hardy, capable of slogging away for hours and negotiating slippery rock passes. The Sotho rarely groom their ponies much, so they usually look pretty dishevelled, but that doesn't affect their performance in the hills, where for many locals they are the only form of long-distance transport.

A number of lodges offer pony trekking, for which no previous experience at all is needed. However, only a few are well-organized, with guides, routes and places to stay worked out in advance. Among the best places are the Basotho Pony Trekking Centre (☎31 72845), the *Malealea Lodge* (☎051/447 3200), and the *Semonkong Lodge* (☎051/933 3106). You might also consider trying the *Trading Post Guest House* (☎34 0202) in Roma, the *Molumong Lodge* (☎033/702 1050) near Mokhotlong, and the *Mount Maluti Hotel* (☎78 5224) in Mohale's Hoek.

Of the three most professional outfits, the Basotho Pony Trekking Centre is cheapest, at around M80 a day, although there are reports of declining standards. At *Malealea* and *Semonkong*, a beady eye is kept on the standard of both ponies and guides, which cost around M100 a day. One way to decide which place to go for is to first choose what kind of countryside you want to trek in. Semonkong, Mokhotlong and the area around the Basotho Pony Trekking Centre are all high up, above the sandstone and into the basalt (see box, p.639); most of the others are lower down, where conditions are usually less harsh for you, though harder on the ponies.

Wherever you go, make sure you bring a wide-brimmed sunhat, sun protection cream and waterproof gear, and, if you are staying somewhere overnight, a sleeping bag and mat, food, and something to cook it on. A luxury, but one you'll definitely appreciate, is some kind of balm to ease your aching limbs and buttocks, which will certainly be sore after a day's trekking, even if you are used to riding.

surround the city, including the one to Lesotho's most famous mountain Thaba Bosiu, the so-called Mountain of the Night where the founder of the nation, Moshoeshoe I, ruled for almost fifty years.

Roma, less than 40km from the capital along good roads, is the educational centre of the country, surrounded by beautiful sandstone hills and with an historic Catholic mission – the ascent from Roma deep into the Highlands to Semonkong, through several mountain passes, is one of the most striking in the country. **Semonkong** is famous for its mighty waterfalls, and you can visit another set, the **Ketane Falls**, by trekking westwards by pony from the delightful *Semonkong Lodge*.

Any car can manage the drive from Maseru along Lesotho's **central route** to the Basotho Pony Trekking Centre and the Mohale Dam construction site some way beyond. However, continuing further on over the epic **Central Mountain Range** requires a rugged vehicle that can handle the poor and rocky roads. Though the final destination of **Thaba Tseka** is unspectacular, the journey more than compensates, and from Thaba Tseka it is possible to continue along a difficult dirt road to Katse and its massive new dam (see p.647).

Maseru

Sprawling **MASERU** spills east from the Caledon River, which marks the border with South Africa, and is the nation's capital and only big town. Maseru's older buildings, as

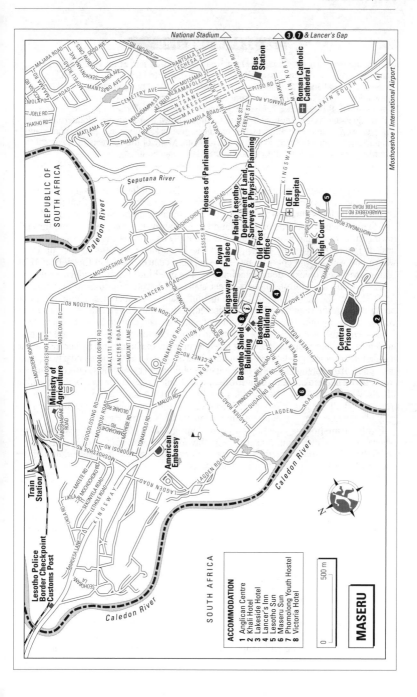

National Stadium △

△ ❸ ❼ & Lancer's Gap

Moshoeshoe I International Airport ▷

Bus Station

Roman Catholic Cathedral

REPUBLIC OF SOUTH AFRICA

Seputana River

Caledon River

Houses of Parliament

Radio Lesotho

Department of Land, Surveys & Physical Planning

Old Post Office

QE II Hospital ❺

❶ Royal Palace

High Court

Kingsway Cinema

❹

Basotho Shield Building ❽

Basotho Hat Building

Central Prison ❷

❻

Ministry of Agriculture

American Embassy

SOUTH AFRICA

Train Station

Lesotho Police Border Checkpoint Customs Post

Caledon River

Caledon River

N

ACCOMMODATION

1 Anglican Centre
2 Khali Hotel
3 Lakeside Hotel
4 Lancer's Inn
5 Lesotho Sun
6 Maseru Sun
7 Phomolong Youth Hostel
8 Victoria Hotel

MASERU

0   500 m

LEAVING MASERU

Orientation is fairly easy, as both **Main Road North** (A1) and **Main Road South** (A2), the two major roads out of town, begin life at the cathedral traffic circle, which is at the eastern end of Kingsway. There are a few fuel stations scattered along both for their first few kilometres. Public transport from Maseru to the rest of the country runs from the bus station off the Main Road North; just after the cathedral traffic circle, turn left into Pitso Road and you cannot fail to miss the huge sprawl in front of you. Rather than trying to work out the method in the madness, just ask around for where buses and minibuses to your destination currently run from. Many of the services to towns south of Maseru congregate a little way along the Main Road South.

well as some stylish new ones, are built from well-crafted local sandstone, now recognized as the town's vernacular building material, though a number of ill-thought-out concrete box buildings diminish the effect, and unfortunately dominate the skyline. Most of the daytime action happens on or around the Kingsway, the road which runs through town getting more and more downmarket and lively as it heads east towards the cathedral. It is along Kingsway, particularly in the less-affluent sections further up town, where you will see the charred shells of shopping centres looted in the riots of 1998. Some have been quickly demolished and redeveloped into bright, modern malls, but others provide a backdrop to lively street stalls and hawkers, who have undoubtedly profited from the demise of their more institutionalized competitors. The tension that brought about the riots has quickly dissipated, and as long as you take the precautions you would in any other city on the continent, you can walk around here comfortably.

Maseru is the best place in the country to do any **banking**, as the banks are the only ones in the country adept at handling foreign currency exchange, partly because of the number of aid workers who have been based here since the Seventies. The city's brand-new **post office** stands proudly on Kingsway amid a flurry of ambitious construction work. If you need to stock up on **supplies**, you should do so in Maseru before heading off elsewhere, although Maseru does not have the craft selection of Teya-Teyaneng. You can get all the **maps** you should need of Lesotho from Maseru, which is also the only place where you can book for the Sehlabathebe National Park.

Public transport is chaotic and crazily unregulated, but does at least go everywhere in the country from Maseru, invariably for low sums of money. You are only a short drive from some beautiful walking country, although the true splendours of the country lie further east and into the Highlands.

Some history
Maseru, which gets its name from the local sandstone from which it was first built, was established by the British as their administrative centre in 1869. Britain had annexed Basotholand, as it was then known, a year earlier (see p.621) and needed somewhere close to the Sotho royal stronghold of Thaba Bosiu that was relatively accessible from the Cape Colony.

Britain put as little effort into developing Maseru as it did the rest of the country, no doubt expecting it to become just a minor South African town when Basotholand was incorporated into South Africa – which is what the British intended. It's grown swiftly over recent years, not so much because it is booming economically but because the poverty in Lesotho's rural areas has driven people to the city in search of a better life. Few have found it yet, and the city has a high unemployment rate.

Maseru has been the location for most of the turbulence of post-independence politics, including two successful coups and several more unsuccessful ones – and, most recently, the serious disturbances that followed the disputed elections in 1998. However, the ensuing destruction is fast being cleared up and Maseru has all the marks of an upwardly mobile African city, with slick fashions and mobile phones much in evidence – even if they are sometimes spotted alongside blanket-wearing villagers and the occasional horse-drawn cart.

Arrival, information and getting around

Moshoeshoe I international **airport** is 18km southeast of Maseru off the Main Road South (A2); there are frequent, inexpensive minibus taxis and buses into town during the day and early evening (arrivals & departures, ☎35 0777). Private taxis are available but cost considerably more (around M40).

There are no **train** connections to Maseru; the nearest station is in Bloemfontein in the Free State. None of the big South African bus companies go to Maseru, but there are always the daily **minibus taxis**, which travel from Johannesburg, Bloemfontein and Durban, as well as a host of smaller places nearer Maseru. All of them stop at the border, which you must cross on your own. From there, you can easily find public transport into the centre of town.

You'll find the **Lesotho tourist information office** (Mon–Fri 8am–5pm, Sat 8am–1pm; ☎31 2896, fax 32 3638), at the western end of the town centre, on the main Kingsway road near the *Victoria Hotel*. Although underresourced, the staff are helpful and can give you a town map, flyers from the few resorts that consistently supply them, reasonably up-to-date information on hotel costs, and the odd glossy brochure. If you're planning on a visit to the Sehlabathebe National Park, you'll need to arrange bookings in Maseru; contact Sehlabathebe Reservations at the Ministry of Agriculture, on Raboshabane, off Moshoeshoe Road, PO Box 92, Maseru 100 (☎32 3600 or 32 2876).

To find out about most of the limited public entertainment Maseru has to offer, and for information about services aimed at visitors, pick up a copy of the monthly *What's On in Maseru*, from either the tourist office or the Copy Shop, corner of Kingsway and Old School Rd, which produces it.

Maseru is small enough for **walking around** to be no bother, though some accommodation is too far to reach easily on foot. Walking around after dark is risky. Plenty of **minibus taxis** go up and down the Kingsway and off into semi-urban areas, with each journey costing under M2. Otherwise, there are a few **taxi** companies you can try (see "Listings", p.632). **Driving** is straightforward in town, though often slow. Bear in mind that the Kingsway becomes a one-way street in the direction of the border from 7–9am each week-day morning. For **car rental**, see "Listings".

ACCOMMODATION PRICE CODES

All the accommodation listed in this chapter has been categorized into one of nine price bands, as set out below. The rates quoted represent what you can expect to pay for much of the summer **per person**, and unless otherwise stated, are based on two sharing. In Lesotho, rooms are generally not en suite. Expect prices in some areas to be significantly higher in peak season (Dec–Jan & Easter), and look out for discounts during the winter. For currency and further accommodation details, see p.622.

① up to M50		⑥ M250–300
② M50–100		⑦ M300–400
③ M100–150		⑧ M400–500
④ M150–200		⑨ over M500
⑤ M200–250		

Accommodation

Maseru is the only place in the country where there's much choice of **accommodation**, offering everything from camping and grim dorms to luxury suites in plush hotels. The most central options, on or near the Kingsway, are also the most practical if you don't have your own transport.

Anglican Centre, corner of Assisi and Lancer's roads (☎32 2046). Large and austere travellers' centre reasonably close to the Kingsway, though tricky to find, with spartan doubles equipped with elderly mattresses. Male and female guests are supposed to be housed in separate rooms, and there is a 7pm curfew, although a night watchman will normally let you in later. Ask for Mrs Mokoena if you want to stay. ①.

Khali Hotel, off Pioneer Rd (☎32 5800). Slightly dingy, but rooms are spacious, with TVs that broadcast the South African movie channel M-Net. You can camp here too, and there are condoms on sale at reception, which come in handy for some of the permanent guests. There are private and public bars. The hotel is 1500m south of the Kingsway; turn left off Pioneer Rd after the bridge. The bus/minibus taxi towards the *New Europa* takes you pretty close. Camping ①, rooms ②.

Lakeside Hotel, off Main Rd North (☎31 3646). Big, ugly, brick building on the edge of an industrial estate, though the rooms are OK, with en-suite bath, soft mattresses and TVs with M-Net. The restaurant does solid and inexpensive meals, but the hotel's main attraction is its occasional choral music shows and competitions. Turn right off Main Rd North at the junction marked for Mafeteng, and the hotel is 100m further on the left. ②.

Lancers Inn, Kingsway (☎31 2114, fax 31 0223). Very central, pleasant, sandstone building that escaped burning in the 1998 riots but was looted bare. The renovations are impressive and tasteful, and with comfortable rondavels and chalets with en-suite bath, grassy areas and a pool, this is one of Maseru's most characterful and pleasant places to stay. Has a good beer garden and restaurant. ④.

Lesotho Sun, off Nightingale Rd (☎31 3111, fax 31 0104). Behind the QEII hospital, this is the smartest hotel in town, accommodating visiting dignitaries and wealthy businessmen. It has comfortable if smallish rooms with TVs and all sorts of sports facilities, a pool, casino, cinema, and one of the best restaurants in town. ⑥.

Maseru Sun, Orpen Rd (☎31 2434, fax 31 0158). Decent, though box-like, rooms, in soothing well-tended garden surroundings that are popular with locals in the evening. A decent restaurant, and the slot machines are a big draw too. ⑤–⑥.

Phomolong Youth Hostel, Lancers Gap Rd (☎33 2900). Some way out of town, offering battered dorms with ancient mattresses. You can use the spartan kitchen, but meals are only provided for groups. Doors close at 10pm. Take the Lancers Gap turn off Main Rd North and carry on for 2.5km, where it's on the right in a low building surrounded by a fence. Not recommended unless you run out of alternatives. ①.

Victoria Hotel, Kingsway (☎32 2002 or 31 2922, fax 31 0318). Prominent city landmark with reasonable rooms, a popular dining room and bar with a terrace attached, from which you can watch Maseru go by beneath you. ④.

The City

Maseru's most famous landmark used to be the **Basotho Hat Building**, appropriately Basotho-hat-shaped, which stood on the corner of Kingsway and Orpen Road, opposite the *Victoria Hotel*. However, during the 1998 riots its thatched roof made for a spectacular bonfire, destroying the building. Undaunted, its resident craft shop relocated to the Basotho Shield building on the opposite side of the road, though plans to rebuild the Basotho Hat have been announced. A little way east along the Kingsway you'll find more crafts, mostly woven grass Sotho hats, sold on the pavements outside the tourist office, though further down Orpen Road there's a more upmarket selection at Mohair Cottage, a foyer boutique in the *Maseru Sun*. See p.641 for more on Lesotho's craft industry.

Walking from the Basotho Hat Building up the Kingsway, into the main part of town, look out for the Alliance Française in the interesting old sandstone library, corner of Pioneer and Kingsway, and the former Anglican church in a scruffy park area in front of *Lancers Inn* on your right, and then, to the left, the striking new **Post Office**, ready evidence of Maseru's intention to create an image of being a thoroughly modern African capital. Nearby are a number of single-storey sandstone buildings, many dating from the end of the last century, including the old Post Office building, gutted in the riots but suggested as a location for the tourist information centre. A little further up on the left, it's worth pausing to look at the old **Resident Commissioner's House**, now a government department, built in sandstone in 1891 and now restored, making it one of Maseru's finest buildings once again. The large Queen Elizabeth II Hospital is a short distance further up on the right. From here on the Kingsway is busier, its low-priced shops thronged by shoppers, and informal traders touting everything from Sotho fast food to cutlery made of galvanized iron. In a new mall on the left-hand side, just past the Sales House store, the Lesotho Blanket Company sells the best-priced Sotho blankets (see p.641) in Lesotho, while J's Music Bar, next door, has the widest selection of Sotho and South African music cassettes in town.

The Kingsway comes to an end at the traffic circle by the impressively large, though architecturally unremarkable, **Roman Catholic Cathedral**, and splits into Main Road North and Main Road South. Continue along Main Road North, turning right a few kilometres further on to reach Lancers Gap (see p.633), where the particularly striking mountain pass has good views over the town.

Eating, drinking and nightlife

Maseru has a better selection of **restaurants** than anywhere else in Lesotho, though a number of popular spots closed down following the riots. There's a range of familiar chain takeaways, including *KFC* and *Something Fishy*, along Kingsway, as well as plenty of inexpensive informal daytime takeaways and **snacks** to be had there and around the bus station. One place not to miss is the bakery beside *Lancers Inn*, where you can get delicious freshly baked loaves, muffins and other treats. **Nightlife** is considerably more limited, as there's only one nightclub and two cinemas. However, the club's a good one, and there are plenty of hotel bars if you're just after a drink or two.

Restaurants

China Garden, Orpen Rd (☎31 3915). Interesting, reasonably priced Chinese menu in a setting of faded opulence, but the food can take ages to appear on the table. Closed Sun.

Early Bird, off Kingsway, opposite the OK supermarket. Inexpensive fry-ups, chicken and pies to eat in or take away.

Lehaha Grill, *Lesotho Sun*, off Nightingale Rd (☎31 3111). An often busy restaurant serving a tasty but somewhat pricey range of continental dishes.

Maseru Sun, Orpen Rd. Choice of buffet or à la carte, with the buffet probably the better and certainly the healthier bet.

Penthouse, *Victoria Hotel*, Kingsway. Right at the top of the hotel, with a bird's-eye view of the town, this serves respectable Italian dishes, grills and seafood amidst great splurges of faded velvet decor. Closed Sat lunchtime & Sun.

Rendezvous, *Lancers Inn*, Kingsway (☎31 2114). Impressively renovated after the riots, with an African-themed, moderately priced menu.

Victoria, *Victoria Hotel*, Kingsway (☎31 2992). Standard and unexciting meaty fare or pizzas, but a spacious restaurant, and usually busy in the evening. Best visited when they serve curries (Mon) and traditional Sotho dishes (Wed afternoon).

Bars and nightlife

Maseru's **bars** are almost all attached to hotels or restaurants, with those at the *Victoria* and *Lancers* being among the most cheerful, though *Taverne d'Auberge*, a beer shack constructed from empty beer cans, is a funky recent addition outside the

Basotho Shield building, on the corner of Kingsway and Orpen streets. They also serve hamburgers and sandwiches. If you want to drink in more typically Sotho surroundings, you need to head out of the town centre a bit and make for any of the numerous informal bars scattered about the outskirts of town,

Maseru's **nightclub** options are limited to just the *Cross-roads Nite-club* (Thurs–Sun 9pm–late) under the *Victoria Hotel*. Fortunately, it's well worth checking out, both for the music and to see Maseru's youth strutting their stuff until the wee hours of the morning.

Otherwise, you have a choice of two **cinemas**, with the one at the *Lesotho Sun* screening mostly action movies (☎31 3111), and the Kingsway Cinema (☎32 5424) next to the *Victoria Hotel* offering a reasonable range of Hollywood releases, usually a few weeks after they've hit South Africa.

Listings

Adventure activities Lesotho isn't ideal for canoeing, as the rivers are only deep enough during the summer and there aren't many stretches of white water. But on the Phutiatsana River the water flow is good so you don't have to do much paddling. The Lesotho–Durham Anglican Link (☎ & fax 31 2614) run trips, and a few unhurried hours will end you up near Mazenod, from where they'll take you back to Maseru. Trips cost around M100 for a day. They can also organize rock-climbing.

Airlines Mission Aviation Fellowship (☎31 3640); SA Airlink, in Jo'burg (☎011/978 1111).

Airport Moshoeshoe I International Airport (☎35 0777).

American Express, beside Maseru Book Centre, Kingsway (☎31 2554, after hours ☎32 4760).

Banks Main branches of Lesotho Bank, Nedbank and Standard Bank are on Kingsway.

Books The best of Maseru's small range of bookshops, called simply The Book Centre, is on Kingsway, just past the Lesotho Bank.

Car Rental Avis, at the airport(☎31 4325/35 0328); Budget (☎31 6344).

Emergencies Ambulance ☎121; Fire ☎122; Police ☎123.

Hospitals Queen Elizabeth II Hospital, Kingsway (☎31 2501); Maseru Private Hospital, Thetsane Rd (☎31 3260).

Internet facilities Lesotho Office Equipment, Orpen Rd (Mon–Fri 8am–5pm; ☎31 6437)

Libraries American Cultural Centre, Options Building, Pioneer Rd; British Council, corner of Kingsway and Lerotholi Rd (☎31 2609); National Library, Kingsway.

Post office and stamps The grand new post office is prominent on Kingsway, and is open Mon–Fri 8am–4.30pm, Sat 8am–noon. Lesotho stamps are famous and highly prized; if you're a keen collector, contact the philatelic bureau on the first floor here.

Radio You can get better BBC World Service (90.2FM) radio reception here than anywhere else in Africa.

Swimming pool The pool at the *Maseru Sun* is normally open to non-residents. Check with reception and expect to pay around M10.

Taxis Hoohlo Bereng (☎32 4035); Max Taxis (☎32 5935); Moonlight Taxis (☎31 2695); Silver Star (☎31 1603).

Travel Agents Afric-Go-Tours (☎32 5367); American Express (☎31 2554); Execu Travel (☎32 5113).

Around Maseru

Although it doesn't make sense to spend much of your time in Lesotho in Maseru, if you can help it, you'll find a number of rewarding places to visit within only a short distance of the capital.

The Word, the Flesh and the Devil excursions

Just behind the *Lesotho Sun* hotel, there's an easily accessible climb to three peaks known locally as **the Word, the Flesh and the Devil**, a favoured hangout for snipers during the Gun War (see p.621). Walk between the fences separating the hotel and Friebel Houses, and straight up the hill past a succession of large boulders. After less than twenty minutes you'll reach the northernmost peak, the Word, where you'll find a survey beacon and excellent views of Maseru and the distant mountains. From there you can walk along the ridge to the other two peaks, the Flesh and then the Devil, though neither provide such good views.

Lancers Gap

Lancers Gap is an extraordinary ridge a short distance east from town, with a great gap in the middle through which the road passes, so named because a Lancers regiment was allegedly ambushed and defeated there during the Gun War. In fact, the regiment was ambushed somewhere else, but it doesn't really matter, as this is still a great place to scramble around and look out both on Maseru and the mountains in the east. To get there, take the Main Road North from Maseru, and turn right at the Lancers Gap turn. The ridge is a few kilometres further along, up a very steep incline which you ascend along a good-quality hairpin bend road.

TAKING THABA BOSIU (BY STRATEGY)

Fresh from conquering much of the flat land east of the Caledon in 1828, the Ngwane were the first to attack **Thaba Bosiu**, but were badly beaten, after which they never troubled **Moshoeshoe** again. The mixed-race Kora people also harried Thaba Bosiu in 1831, often making away with and enslaving the villagers living beneath it, but always driven off the mountain proper by Moshoeshoe's fighters. The warrior, **Mzilikhazi**, of the Ndebele, who later conquered much of modern-day Zimbabwe, tried to take the mountain the same year, but his men were defeated by the mass of great boulders flung down from the top by the Sotho; Moshoeshoe is reputed to have sent the Ndebele a large number of fat oxen after their defeat, an unprecedented move for a victorious chief – as if to say that he understood that their attack had been inspired by hunger and that he wanted to help them out. At any rate, Mzilikhazi never came back that way.

There followed a twenty-year period of relative calm, during which time, when Moshoeshoe was on the mountain, he would receive visitors in a beautifully tailored dark-blue military uniform, complete with cloak, and offer them tea from a prized china tea service. He allowed the French missionary, Eugene Casalis, to establish a mission at the bottom of the mountain in 1837, and employed him as his secretary and interpreter. In 1852, a British punitive force led by the Cape governor, Sir George Cathcart, didn't even make it as far as the mountain, instead being attacked a short distance away by a well-armed mass of Moshoeshoe's troops, who forced their hasty withdrawal. Afrikaner forces fighting for the Orange Free State (OFS) made a brief attempt on Thaba Bosiu in 1858, but came back in a more determined manner, armed with heavy artillery, in 1865, and began steadily shelling the mountain, launching two simultaneous assaults a few days later. Eight men made it to the top, but were seriously wounded as soon as they did so, and speedily retreated back down. A week later, more Afrikaner troops and the OFS president turned up, and another assault was launched. General Wepener led his men right to the top of the Khubelu Pass, but he was shot at the top and mortally wounded. The Sotho then pressed a counter-attack, and the Afrikaner forces withdrew. They continued the siege for a month, though, during which time most of the livestock on Thaba Bosiu died of hunger and the Sotho became so short of bullets that they melted down the shells being fired at them to make homemade ones.

Although they won this battle, the Sotho lost the war, and Moshoeshoe signed a humiliating treaty in 1866 which surrendered most of Lesotho's farmland to the OFS. Four years later, the old king died and was buried on the top of Thaba Bosiu. Since then, every Sotho king has been buried there, including the latest to die, Moshoeshoe II, in 1996.

Qeme Plateau

The large T-shaped **Qeme Plateau**, which measures over 25 square kilometres, is only a few kilometres south of Maseru, near the South African border. It provides superb vistas into the Free State and east into Lesotho and is a good place for a day-trip from the capital. The usual way to get there is by going along the Main Road South as far as Mantsebo, turning right at the crossroads, then turning left after a Frasers Store. Leave your transport there, look out for a diagonal line climbing the plateau from left to right and make for this. You soon hit a footpath which takes you to the top. To climb to the top and back takes three or four hours.

Alternatively, take United Nations Road (the new ringroad, accessible from Kingsway along Pioneer Road) out of Maseru, and follow it down until you meet the rise of Qeme. Here, a right turn along a dirt road heading towards Mokhalinyane takes you through beautiful countryside along the western part of the plateau. Look out for a cleft in the plateau's ridge, and park at its foot at the village of Ha Mapholo. Leaving your car here is quite safe. Walk through the village and make for the cleft; you'll find that the first part of the climb is pretty obvious, but two-thirds of the way up you'll need either inspired guesswork or the help of one of the many herd boys who are usually clambering around here with their cows and goats. The climb takes about two hours there and back.

Once at the top, the boulders and grasslands make for an excellent stroll and picnic spot, albeit not much else. Make sure you've left yourself enough time to get back down before dark. From Ha Mapholo, you can either return the way you came or carry on a few kilometres, at which point the road improves, finally taking you to Main Road South just north of Morija.

Thaba Bosiu

THABA BOSIU is Lesotho's most important historical sight, a steep mountain with a large flat top about 20km east of Maseru that was the capital of the kingdom in the days of Moshoeshoe I. Although it has been declared a world heritage site by UNESCO, nothing has yet been done to develop it, and there's not that much to see once you reach the top. However, it is a place of great significance to the people of Lesotho, and the burial ground of the country's kings, and as such is well worth a visit.

Moshoeshoe I trekked with his followers to Thaba Bosiu in 1824, in a bid to settle somewhere far from the warrior clans then terrorizing the flat plains to the north and west, and somewhere that would be extremely hard for anyone to capture. Thaba Bosiu, with its good grazing and seven or eight freshwater springs on top, fitted the bill, although it wasn't long before warrior clans, including Afrikaner ones, found their way here – although none were able to take the mountain, which has earned it, and Moshoeshoe, a good deal of mystique.

The name means "Mountain of the Night", perhaps because, as the legend has it, Moshoeshoe first arrived there at night. A more compelling reason, and the one most Sotho prefer, is that the mountain, which does not look particularly high or impressive by day, grows inexorably as night falls, becoming huge and unconquerable, before slipping back to more hill-like normality during the daytime.

There is a **tourist information** building (daily 8.30am–4pm), where you arrive, which will charge a small fee for information leaflets and an official guide who will show you around. He takes you up the **Khubelu Pass** where the Afrikaner General Louw Wepener was killed trying to storm the mountain in 1865 (see previous page), past the rock where Sotho warriors used to watch out for approaching enemy forces and to the remains of Moshoeshoe's European house, built for him by army deserters living on the mountain top. From there, it is a short walk to the slight remains of

Moshoeshoe's royal court and then to the royal graveyard. The tombs of Moshoeshoe I and most of the monarchs are marked with simple stone cairns, except the latest, of Moshoeshoe II, who was killed in a car crash in 1996, which is a more elaborate affair, adorned with plastic flowers. If you look to the east of the mountain, you get a great view of Qiloane, a strange cone-shaped mountain with a large nodule on the top, which apparently was the inspiration for the distinctive Basotho Hat – the national headware.

Around the other side of the mountain is a kind of cave village where the royal household used to hide during attacks, but which were lived in and decorated with rock paintings by the San who lived there before them. A guide who usually hangs around the Khubelu Pass can take you to them, and include a visit to the traditional healer (*sangoma*) who lives in one of the caves. The caves are about a four-kilometre drive from the Khubelu Pass, followed by a short walk.

Practicalities

To **get to Thaba Bosiu by car**, take the Main Road South, turning right where Thaba Bosiu is signposted. Follow this road through a dip down into a riverbed where the road is temporarily untarred, and all the way to a T-junction. Turn left at the junction and Thaba Bosiu is about 3km further along on the right. During the day a number of **minibus taxis** run between here and the main bus station in Maseru.

There is good **accommodation** next to the mountain at the *Mmelesi Lodge* (☎35 7215 or 35 7216, fax 31 2369; ②), probably the best-run Basotho-owned lodge in the country, which has a plush bar and pleasant restaurant serving moderately priced meat and fish dishes, and comfortable rondavels out the back with en-suite bathrooms.

Roma and Semonkong

Southeast of Maseru, the historic Catholic mission and university town of **Roma** is worth a stop, and the road from here to the town of **Semonkong** is an epic drive through the sandstone and stunning basalt peaks of the Thaba Pusoa range of the Lesotho Highlands, past a succession of remote and relaxed-looking villages filled with Lesotho's characteristic dry-stone-walled rondavels. The road ends at Semonkong, but one reward is the *Semonkong Lodge* – one of the best places to stay in the country, and only a short distance away is the spectacular Semonkong (LeBihan) Falls, which crash down from nearly 200m to the Maletsunyane River below.

Roma

About 30km from Maseru along a good road, the mission town of **ROMA** has a beautiful location in strangely sculpted sandstone foothills and is home to the unlovely campus of the **University of Lesotho**, which began life as Pius XII College, run by the Roman Catholic Church and, between 1964 and 1971, was the university of all three of the former British southern African protectorates, now Lesotho, Botswana and Swaziland. You can buy phonecards and make use of their public phone boxes, which are rare in Lesotho, but there's not much to see on campus, except of course the cream of Lesotho's young elite in action. A kilometre or so further up the road from the university, lined with a succession of schools and colleges, is **Roma Mission**, most of which was built in 1862. Though grander, and intentionally so, than its evangelical counterpart in Morija (see p.649), the mission is still a little run-down these days, and there's not much reason to linger – although its extension to accommodate the grave of one

DONGAS AND SOIL EROSION IN LESOTHO

Travelling around in Lesotho's scarred and treeless landscape, it's hard to believe that the country was once the grain basket of the region. Yet, during the nineteenth century, the kingdom exported food to the neighbouring Orange Free State (OFS) and to Kimberley and the Rand to feed the thousands of diamond- and gold-mine workers. The problems began with the expropriation of the best land by the OFS in the 1860s, which forced the Sotho to start farming hilly areas that had previously only been used for winter grazing. This process continues to this day, and you will even see crops being grown at over 2000m in districts like Semonkong and Mokhotlong. Mountains are no substitute for fertile plains, however, and Lesotho has been a net importer of food since the Twenties.

The ecological effect of the sustained and unrelenting cultivation of the Lesotho mountains has been devastating. Already poor soil fertility has plummeted and, more seriously, huge quantities of topsoil are simply washed away with each summer rains, often ending up as silt in the rivers of the Eastern Cape. In many places, so much topsoil has gone that great ravines called **dongas** have opened up. These, though they often look green enough, in fact tend to be so close to the surface rock that they are useless for serious cultivation.

Efforts have been underway to slow this process for some time, most noticeably through the neat terracing of fields set on hillsides, with layers of grass interspersed with the crops. For one of the best examples of how simply *dongas* can be reclaimed, ask to be shown the way to the Musi family *donga* in the village beside *Malealea Lodge* (see p.650). It's not difficult to spot – on a hillside of degraded cropland and bare earth, it is an oasis of fertility, lush greenness and birdlife.

Father Gerard is a classic of Catholic kitsch. Father Gerard was a founder member of the Mission and celebrated for restoring a young girl's sight through prayer, for which he has recently and posthumously been beatified (he died in 1940).

Practicalities

Several **buses** and many more **minibus taxis** travel daily between Maseru and Roma, which is one of the busiest public transport routes in the country. The journey costs around M5 whichever means you use. Once you're here, the Mission will reluctantly put you up if you beg them, but the best **accommodation** is undoubtedly at the *Trading Post Guest House* (☎34 0202; ①) at the western end of Roma. Built in 1903 as a trading store by the Thorn family, this self-catering guesthouse has been lived in by them ever since. You can camp, stay in rondavels, or in the house itself. They've added a swimming pool and can arrange pony trekking (M15 an hour) in the surrounding sandstone hills. To get there, look out for a sign on the right of the main road as you enter Roma from the Maseru side, marked *"Manonyane High School"* and the *"Trading Post,"* and travel 100m up the dirt road. Introduce yourself at the house or the trading store next door. The accurately named *Speak Easy Liquor Restaurant*, mainly used by students and opposite the university, is the only place to **eat** in Roma. It dishes up inexpensive, good-value food that you can wash down with a spectacular selection of alcoholic beverages that far surpasses anywhere in Maseru for choice. Right next door is the last place you can buy **fuel** before Semonkong.

Semonkong and around

The road from Roma to Semonkong is one of the most spectacular in Lesotho, with views galore as you climb higher and higher into the Highlands. Where the tarred road turns to gravel at Moitsupeli, look ahead towards the twin summits of the appropriately named **Thabana liMele** (Breast Mountains). The northern summit is climbable without special gear if you can find the cleft on its northern side. Just park at the next village of **Ha Dinzulu**, let people know where you are going, cross the Makhalaneng River and make your way up as far as you can. If you make it to the top, it's about seven hours there and back.

The road from Ha Dinzulu continues to climb until peaking at 2000m on Nkesi's Pass and then dropping down to the village of Ramabanta, where you cross the Makhalaneng River and then drive up to 3000m by Thaba Putsoa itself, before descending gently to the curiously straggled town of **SEMONKONG**. Inhabited only by the San until the 1880s, Semonkong began life after the Gun War as a refuge for displaced Sotho from the Lowlands. In town, you'll find a few basic stores, plenty of bars stocking a remarkable selection of beers and ciders, and even a post office and bank, though you can't rely on either for vital business. The roads in town are bad but not impassable, and it's worth going to the ubiquitous Frasers Store just to check out the Wild West style clientele, dressed mostly in blankets and gumboots, with their ponies hitched to a post at the entrance. If you're here in winter, try to catch the local horse races on the last weekend of every month.

Practicalities

Semonkong is about a six-hour **drive** from Maseru if you don't stop long in Roma. There are a couple of **buses** daily, which take considerably longer. If you miss the bus, you can always take public transport to Roma and then a minibus taxi from there, though these stop running by mid-afternoon. Alternatively, you can charter a **flight** to the airstrip in town from the Mission Aviation Fellowship from Maseru for around M600 (☎31 3640).

There's **accommodation** right next to the airstrip at the *Mountain Delight Lodge* (②), which offers pleasant rondavels and a bar. Far more soothing though, in a valley by the river on the outskirts of town, is the excellent *Frasers Semonkong Lodge* (☎ & fax 051/933 3106, *verney@lesoff.co.za*; ①–②), where you can light a *braai*, make use of the well-equipped kitchen, or just tuck into the lodge's excellent cooking. There's a great bar area with a pool table and a good selection of music (when the CD player is working) and friendly, laid-back management. You can camp, or stay in cosy dorms or doubles. Unusually for accommodation outside Maseru, the lodge takes Visa. The lodge will also arrange **pony trekking** for about M110 per day, with an extra M15 for each night you stay out in a village en route, and M30 per day for the guide.

Around Semonkong: Ketane and Semonkong falls

From Semonkong, it will take you a day's walk or pony trek west (see "Practicalities" above) over some pretty high mountains to the pristine 120-metre **Ketane Falls**. The Falls are inaccessible by any other means of transport, and the pony trek is reckoned to be one of the best in the country. They can also be reached in a popular four-day pony trek from *Malealea Lodge* (see p.650).

Rather easier to reach are the **Semonkong Falls**, a pretty five-kilometre walk from town through the maize fields and grazings that adorn the banks of the Maletsunyane River, though the path is slippery in parts. (It's possible to drive but you risk getting your car broken into if you go down to the bottom.) Also known as the LeBihan Falls, after the French missionary who was the first European to see them, the dramatic Semonkong (Smoking Water) Falls drop nearly 200m down a sheer and scary cliff surrounded on all sides by natural vantage points, and into an exotic and swimmable pool. There's a path down to the bottom which takes three or four hours there and back, though it's well worth the journey, particularly if you fancy the swim, or if you want to camp. The water at the foot of the Falls usually freezes by June, but the waterfall keeps going all winter, spraying the surrounding rocks with ice and forming an impressive ice cage over the pool.

The road to Thaba Tseka

Beyond the turn to Roma, the central A3 road runs over Lesotho's Central Mountain Range to the small district capital of Thaba Tseka, 175km from Maseru, and the countryside changes from cultivated Lowlands to more sparsely populated mountains.

The small village of **NAZARETH** is the first settlement you come to along this route. Here you'll find the *Tollgate Caravan and Camping Park* (☎37 0206; ①), the only official campsite in the country, but there's little happening here and the surrounding scenery is easily surpassed by what comes later. A few kilometres north of Nazareth are what were once some of the finest rock paintings in the country at **Ha Baroana**. The paintings are still impressive, with clearly discernible figures of animals, dancers and hunters, but they have been vandalized and washed away by child guides who throw water at them to make them clearer for tourists. To get to the paintings, either walk or drive north along a difficult dirt road to Ha Matela and walk the last 4km from there, or drive up the next turn to the left, also along a bad road, which takes you straight to the site.

After Nazareth, the main road then ascends steeply into the mountains through the 2268-metre-high **Bushman's Pass**. Along the way you may see young boys trying to sell lumps of quartzite and, much more worryingly, Lesotho's national flower, the protected and rare spiral aloe. Don't be enticed to purchase one, as it will only sustain the market in these unique plants – if you are interested in seeing one, you'd be much better off hiking into the mountains and finding one in the wild. A short while after the pass you find the ageing *Molimo Nthuse Lodge* (☎37 0211, fax 31 0318; ②), attractively perched by a stream in a tight fold in the surrounding hills. It's a good, comfortable place to stay, particularly if you are interested in trout fishing or hikes in the surrounding hills, though the moderately priced meals are rather mediocre.

The lodge is also the perfect stopping off point if you are on your way to the **Basotho Pony Trekking Centre** (☎31 7284), a short distance further up the road (2hr by bus from Maseru, less by car). This is about the least expensive place to pony trek in Lesotho, with a two-day/one-night trek for example costing only M125 per person, plus M10 for overnight accommodation. As usual, you need to bring all your supplies with you. A shorter trek, and also suitable for hiking (2hr each way), is to the impressive Qiloane Falls on the Makhaleng River, due north of the *Lodge* and Trekking Centre; the latter can provide information on directions.

The road carries on from here over the epic **Blue Mountain Pass**, more than 2600m high, from where you will find commanding views of the surrounding mountains, though the views are even better if you climb the hills on either side of the pass. From there, the road descends into the village of **Likalaneng**, where there has been a great deal of construction associated with the **Mohale Dam**, the second phase of the Lesotho Highlands Water Project (see p.648) that began with the Katse Dam. When this project is completed in 2004, water will flow by gravity from the dam down a forty-kilometre delivery tunnel to the Katse Dam. For now, however, you'll mostly see heavy lorries and rows and rows of new housing. For a good view of the progress of construction on the dam wall, take a left turn not long after the village out towards the control building, set prominently on a long spur of hillside.

Now a dirt road, the route rises once more to the village of **Marakabei** on the banks of the Senqunyane River, where you can buy fuel. The lodge marked on the roadside approaches to the village is closed. You can also buy fuel at **Mantsonyane**, about 20km

> ### SANDSTONE AND BASALT
>
> Lesotho is the only country in the world that lies entirely above an altitude of 1000m, and as such thoroughly deserves the name "the mountain kingdom". The Lesotho Lowlands would be Highlands anywhere else, and are made of **sandstone**. Right across the country, at about 1400m, the sandstone gives way to a dark grey rock called **basalt**, which was thrown up by volcanic eruptions several million years ago. Roughly marking the beginning of the Lesotho Highlands, basalt is a hard rock and resists erosion, unlike the sandstone, which has been carved by the wind over the millennia into an infinite variety of shapes that have rendered the hills the natural sculptures of the kingdom.

further east, where there are also a few take-away restaurants serving Sotho dishes, and some sparsely filled trading stores. This is as far as you can safely go with a car that doesn't have high clearance; if you still want to press on, there are buses going on to Thaba Tseka.

Thaba Tseka

The road into **THABA TSEKA** is a dramatic one, peaking in the heart of the Central Mountain Range at the Mokhoabong Pass (2880m) before descending to the town, which is over 2200m above sea level. Once here, though, you may wonder why you made the effort, as there is very little in this Eighties purpose-built administrative centre except buses to take you somewhere else. The only place to stay at is the self-catering Agricultural Training Centre (☎90 0304; ①), a long prefabricated building that's often full during the week. There are no restaurants in town, though there are one or two stores serving Sotho food to take away. There's no road south to Semonkong and the Sehlabathebe National Park, though there are hikeable trails if you have the time (for maps, see "Tips on Travel in Lesotho", pp.622-623). There is a road to Sani Pass from Thaba Tseka, but it is so bad that you should ask how it is beforehand and only attempt it in a high-quality 4WD vehicle, in which case it should be a spectacular ride.

The road to Katse is much better and, although you still shouldn't attempt it in an ordinary saloon car, there are a number of buses plying the route. From Katse there's a perfect tarred road to Hlotse in the north (see p.647). Otherwise, your only option is to go back the way you came, towards Maseru.

THE NORTHERN DISTRICTS

The route from Maseru to Sani Pass takes in the best of both Lesotho's Lowlands and Highlands, from the wind-carved sandstone hills on the way to **Teya-Teyaneng**, a hill town famed for its woven crafts, to the epic mountain passes of the "roof of Africa route" that runs from **Butha-Buthe** to Sani, and the new road from **Hlotse** across the Central Mountain Range to the Katse reservoir. There are plenty of fascinating out-of-the-way treats along the way, like the remarkable **cave houses** at Mateka, or the **dinosaur footprints** near the Tsikoane Mission, a short distance from Hlotse. You'll find plenty of good places to stay (though some take a little finding), particularly in the Highlands where a succession of well-located lodges make the perfect bases from which to hike the surrounding mountain countryside. A new attraction is the **Katse reservoir**, completed in 1997, which collects water from Lesotho's south-flowing rivers, thanks to a 185-metre dam wall. The road from Butha-Buthe climbs into the Highlands, past

Oxbow, one of southern Africa's few skiing venues, and is tarred all the way to Mokhotlong, deep in the highest of Lesotho's (and southern Africa's) highest mountains. A dirt road leads to the infamous **Sani Pass**, which provides the most dramatic entrance there is into South Africa, down the western reaches of the mighty Drakensberg.

Maseru to Hlotse

Sped through by most travellers on their way to the more spectacular regions of the Highlands, you'll find the lowland stretch between Maseru to Hlotse nonetheless has a number of attractions to offer, if you look for them. The caves at **Mateka** are architecturally the most fascinating in Lesotho and well worth a special trip, and the woven crafts in **Teya-Teyaneng** are of superb quality and design. The busy town of **Hlotse** has less of interest, but nearby is one of the largest collections of **dinosaur footprints** in the country.

There are two good roads from Maseru to Teya-Teyaneng. The most commonly used is the **Main Road North**, which takes you efficiently through the scenic, sandstone mountain-studded Lowland journey. Only a few kilometres after leaving Maseru, you'll come to the hexagonal, red-roofed *Palace Hotel* (☎50 0700, fax 50 0010; ②), whose rooms have opulent beds and decent bathrooms, but balconies with no divisions between the rooms, which makes the rooms less secure than they should be. The hotel restaurant serves steaks, chops and fish for moderate prices. The *Galaxy Nightclub,* next door, opens on Fridays and Saturdays till late, and fills up when there's something special on. From the hotel, it's only an hour's drive to T.Y., though it takes a little longer by bus.

A good alternative to the Main Road North, which takes you near the most fascinating caves in Lesotho, is the **Sefikeng Road**. To take this, you follow the Main Road North out of Maseru, and turn right after a short distance at the sign to Lancers Gap and Sefikeng; you soon find yourself on the Berea plateau, from where you can look down on the Lowlands to your left. At Sefikeng, turn left at the Paradise General Dealer, along a short patch of dirt track, and then onto the tar road towards Mateka.

Mateka

Getting to **MATEKA** by public transport or hitching is possible, but is an exercise in considerable patience. If you're driving, leave your car at Mateka, and enlist one of the many children usually hanging around to take you on the half-hour walk down the hill to the cave houses. The seven **cave houses** here have been sculpted out of mud under a huge rock overhang, and look more like igloos or West African mud architecture than anything you usually find in southern Africa. They are still being lived in, but their laid-back inhabitants don't mind you taking photographs, or simply goggling at what are the best-kept architectural secrets in the country.

Due to the tragic death of the chief and chief's son who were running it, the *Teng Lodge*, signposted from Mateka, is not really open, but if you make the tricky eight-kilometre journey here, across a seemingly impassable river (wade in first to check the depth, and take it at speed) and some dodgy stretches of dirt road, the new chief (who is the old chief's wife) will let you stay there for a donation only, and send someone round to give you hot water in the morning. You'll stay in a lovely rondavel looking out onto the Berea Mountains, but you'll need candles, food and cooking gear as the lodge has none of these. The chief can also provide a guide to take you to some remarkable, unvandalized San rock paintings about one hour's walk away, through gentle hills, maize fields and charmingly secluded villages.

Once you are back in Mateka, it is only a half-hour drive to T.Y., and if you are travelling under your own steam, you'll find the occasional minibus taxi or private vehicle plying what is a good, tarred road, though you will probably have to wait a while.

Teya-Teyaneng and around

TEYA-TEYANENG, which means "place of shifting sands" after the sometimes treacherous sandy patches on the nearby river, straggles out over a hill; it has a compact centre but suburbs that meander several kilometres north and east. The town is widely refered to simply as T.Y. The main reason for coming here, apart from to pass through on your way to the northern Highlands, is that it is the **crafts capital** of Lesotho, specializing in all manner of weavings, from luxurious jerseys to elaborately designed wall-hangings.

There are three **weaving outlets** in town. Setsoto Weaving (daily 8am–5pm), opposite the *Blue Mountain Inn* off a signposted road west of the main road, has a good selection, as well as crafts from elsewhere in the region, like Shona soapstone carvings from Zimbabwe and candles from Swaziland. Just before you reach T.Y., on the left of the main road from Maseru, look out for signs to the small showroom of

---

CULTURE AS FASHION: THE BLANKET AND THE HAT

In a region of Africa where **traditional dress** has all but died out, Lesotho stands out as the exception. It's true that the **mokorotlo** (the Sotho traditional hat) is not widespread these days, but you still occasionally see its distinctive cone and bobble in Lesotho, and in South Africa it is widely worn by Sotho migrant workers in the South Africa, where it is a convenient badge of ethnic distinction. Ironically, miners' hard-hats are often sported in Lesotho as a fashion item, often by younger brothers of Basotho men working in the South African mines. Modelled on the shape of the Qiloane mountain near Thaba Bosiu, and made of woven straw, the *mokorotlo* has become the standard Sotho souvenir, sold in every craft shop, usually for M25 or less.

More prevalent than the *mokorotlo* is the Sotho **blanket**, still worn all over the country. At the time when king Moshoeshoe I was presented with a blanket by European traders in 1860, there were hardly any in his kingdom, with people wearing *karosses* made of animal hides instead. However, by 1872 traders were reporting insatiable demand for the blankets. Made from high-quality woven cloth, they were originally manufactured in Birmingham, England, and are today made in Port Elizabeth, South Africa. The ubiquitous Frasers Stores, which you find all over the country, first established themselves by selling blankets, and still stock them today, although the Lesotho Blanket Company in Maseru (see p.631) is the cheapest place to buy them. Good ones (made of pure wool) cost about M200, and if you do buy one don't forget to buy an outsized safety pin to tie the blanket with.

The blankets are essentially practical; they keep the body at an even temperature except when it's really hot outside (although the Sotho wear them whatever the weather); they don't absorb much water, and they do not easily catch fire, which is handy when you are dozing by an open fire. Blankets are also associated with fertility, which is why some carry the design of a maize cob, a Sotho symbol of fertility and prosperity. Young brides are supposed to wear a blanket around their hips until their first child is conceived, and boys wear different blankets before and after circumcision.

Most blankets have stripes on them that are supposed to lie horizontally when you wear the blanket. A curious feature of the design of some blankets is their retention of British imperial symbolism. One popular design features a large crown at its centre; another shows warplanes sporting British military markings. However, although they always were (and remain) foreign imports, and are the commodities on which many European trader fortunes have been built, the blankets remain quintessentially Sotho, and a source of national pride.

Hatooa Mose Moasali (daily 8am–5pm), which translates as "women must stand up and work hard". This women's collective sells particularly beautiful weaving, though they keep a fairly limited range in stock. Their catalogue displays some very special wall hangings, which you need to order as they take a week or two to make. A short distance further on, also signposted but this time to the right off the main road, the pleasant sandstone Anglican St Anges Mission is home to Helang Basali Handicrafts (daily 8am–5pm). The showroom has an excellent selection of woven crafts, again including some very elaborate items, and in the workshop next door you can watch the craftswomen working on the wall hangings from great looms that stretch nearly to the ceiling.

Practicalities

T.Y.'s **bus and taxi ranks**, as well as plenty of **fuel stations**, are all on the side of the main road, alongside a number of undistinguished fast-food and take-away stores. There is plenty of **public transport** from T.Y. to Maseru, and further north to Hlotse and Butha-Buthe, and you rarely have to wait long.

You'll find the **post office**, which is reasonably functional, off the main road to the left, on the road that leads to the *Blue Mountain Inn* (☎50 0362; ②), the only **accommodation** in town. A spacious hotel with old-fashioned but comfortable cottages at the side to stay in, the *Blue Mountain* also has T.Y.'s only proper **restaurant**, which serves tasty, inexpensive meals with quite a good wine selection to accompany them, and the town's only **nightclub**, which is busy and recommended on a Saturday night. Both the private and public bars are popular too, and the large surrounding garden is a fine place in which to drink and relax.

Maputsoe

A rough, manufacturing-based border town opposite the South African town of Ficksburg, **MAPUTSOE** is not a good place to stay long, if you can avoid it. Fortunately, the border is open 24 hours a day, and there is lots of public transport to Maseru and Hlotse and the north, so you shouldn't have to linger.

The town's main streets are filled with migrant workers commuting between Lesotho and South Africa, among whom are an uncomfortable number of hustlers who can spot strangers in town a mile off. Many seem to congregate at Maputsoe's only **accommodation**, the *Sekekete Hotel* (☎43 0621; ②), near the border, usually filled with heavy drinkers and gamblers stuffing money into the slot machines. The hotel's plain but functional rooms are around the back, a short distance from the general commotion. The main street also has plenty of takeaways, of which the *Captain Dorego's* is probably the best. There's a 50kmh speed limit leaving town and plenty of police about, so take care if you are driving.

Hlotse (Leribe)

A dilapidated but pleasant little Lowland town named after the local river, **HLOTSE** was founded in 1876 by the Anglican missionary, Reverend John Widdicombe, and suffered repeated siege during the 1880 Gun War. Since then it has kept a low profile and, apart from a few shops and department stores, the only thing to see in town are the battered remains of a small military tower built by the British and now practically falling down.

There are, however, one or two local attractions, including a set of **dinosaur footprints** a few kilometres south of the town, left off the Main Road to T.Y., at the turn-of-the-century **Tsikoane Mission**. You'll need to climb up the rock overhang above the church, preferably with the help of a guide (ask at the mission), where you'll find over forty pretty clear imprints. Rather more accessible is **Leribe Craft Centre** (daily

8am–5pm), on the right-hand side as you head north, where the exit road from Hlotse meets the main road. Here you can buy mohair scarves, blankets and table mats, along with a small selection of other crafts, made by a team of local women, about half of whom have disabilities.

On the road **north of Hlotse** towards Butha-Buthe, you will see on your right the **Leribe plateau**, which gives the town its other name, and the **Leribe Mission**, founded in 1859 by François Coillard, at its foot. French and Sotho missionaries headed from here to modern-day Zambia in the 1870s, founding the Barotseland Mission there. The mission is only a short walk off the main road, though frankly there's not much to see there these days.

Practicalities

There's plenty of **public transport** in and out of Hlotse, and it stops just near the post office. For **something to eat**, you'll find Sotho restaurants dotted all over the town, where you can buy inexpensive *pap* and stew or chicken. Otherwise, there's the *Pelican Bar and Steakhouse* just off the main road, which serves inexpensive and sizeable meat dishes, or the restaurant of the *Leribe Hotel* (☎40 0559; ②), which is the town's main **accommodation**. At the hotel, you have a choice of rondavels or terraced rooms overlooking a pleasant garden, which are all fine except those with numbers in the thirties (they're next to a large and noisy tank). The somewhat staid restaurant serves moderately priced meat and fish dishes and the occasional vegetarian pasta, and also, unusually for Lesotho, filter coffee. The only other place to stay at in town is the Agricultural College (①) on the old road from Hlotse to Butha-Buthe, just before it meets the new road. There are basic dorms here and, though the college isn't really geared to taking in outsiders, its staff will let you stay if you ask nicely.

Butha-Buthe to the Sani Pass

The road from **Butha-Buthe** is the most popular route into the Lesotho Highlands and travels through some of the highest and most dramatic mountain passes in the country. Though there's not much to do in Butha-Buthe except stock up for the continuing journey, while the Butha-Buthe mountain just beyond, where **Moshoeshoe I** first ruled as chief before moving south (see p.620), rewards the steep climb with some great views.

Butha-Buthe and around

Not far from the Caledonspoort **border post** (daily 6am–10pm), and the last major town before the Highlands, **BUTHA-BUTHE** has a frontier feel. The main road is clustered with take-away restaurants and stores, and the pavements are filled with Highlanders here for their monthly shopping trip. The town was founded in 1884 because the local chief refused to go to Hlotse to pay taxes, necessitating a new tax centre nearer his residence. Butha-Buthe attracted traders from the outset, and is one of the few towns in Lesotho with much of an Indian community.

The **Butha-Buthe** (Lie Down) mountain, just north of town, is where Moshoeshoe I had his first stronghold before retreating to Thaba Bosiu in 1824 (see p.633). Though a stiff climb to the top, it is not really too difficult to ascend, which was one of the reasons the king felt obliged to move. Once at the top, you get tremendous views of the surrounding area. Not too far from here, 7km north of town on the Main Road, the **Sekubu caves** are 9km down a signposted dirt track. They're worth a look if you have the time; guides will point out some pretty good rock paintings but rather faint **dinosaur footprints**.

Practicalities

There is absolutely no shortage of **public transport** in Butha-Buthe, all of which congregates at the market in the centre of town. As well as buses and minibus taxis going to Maseru, Katse and Mokhotlong, you can also find buses going to Bloemfontein and Johannesburg.

The only **accommodation** in town is at the run-down *Crocodile Inn* (☎46 0223; ②), signposted off the main road on the left as you come in from Hlotse from the south. The hotel, which offers large rooms with thin walls but tolerable beds, has seen better days and fills up at weekends with dedicated drinkers who pursue their art in its various bars until well into the next morning. Food at the restaurant is inexpensive, but unimpressive and pretty slow in coming.

More pleasant, but much trickier to get to, is the self-catering *Ramakantane's Youth Hostel* (①), affiliated to the HI, 3.5km from town in the village of Ha Sechele. The hostel is pretty basic, with no electricity but gas instead for lighting and cooking; but the management is friendly and it's a good place to meet Sotho villagers and hike into the hills nearby. You can't drive there without a high-clearance vehicle, so the best thing is to walk. Turn by the Guys n'Gals store on the main road and it's about an hour's walk uphill from there. A further choice is the *Cindi Lodge & Supermarket* (☎46 0616; ①), 10km north of town, just by the Main Road. Despite its rough appearance, rooms here are basic but perfectly adequate; there's a bar with a pool table and two restaurants, one serving Sotho food and the other, decorated exclusively with mirrors, serving steaks and chops. The lodge is the last place to get fuel before Oxbow.

The road to Mokhotlong: Muela, Oxbow and the Moteng Pass

Just over 20km further along the road from Butha-Buthe, just after the small settlement of **Khukhaune**, a good tar road to the left leads up to **MUELA**, an integral part of the Lesotho Highlands Water Project (see p.648). Here the water flowing down the delivery tunnel from the Katse Reservoir powers an underground power station, which now supplies all of Lesotho's electricity, as well as a small surplus sold to South Africa. Previously Lesotho had to buy its electricity from South Africa, so in addition to the royalties received for water, this part of the scheme benefits the mountain kingdom to the tune of something like thirty million rand a year. At the **Muela Dam**, water enters a second delivery tunnel, which empties into the Ash River, near Clarens, which in turn feeds the Vaal Dam, the main water supply for Gauteng. There isn't a great deal to see here – the power station is well hidden inside the mountain and the reservoir is small, but the view of the surrounding mountains is worth pausing to admire. You can stop for a drink or a **meal** at the attractive new *Muela Lodge*, a small, thatched building on the right at a sharp left-hand bend in the road as you go along the good tar road that leads to Muela; planned rondavels should offer a pleasant place to **stay**.

The road from here into the Highlands is one of the most dramatic in Lesotho, passing through some particularly striking sandstone cliffs before finally climbing into the basalt. Some 10km or so on from Muela, up an increasingly winding route, you come to the unpretentious and quiet *Moteng Lodge* (☎460714; ②), set into the mountain, with rooms that are plain and ugly from the outside but reasonably cosy inside. The restaurant, which is rarely busy, serves inexpensive Sotho food, while the private bar's eatery offers fry-ups and steaks.

A further 20km, over the **Moteng Pass** (2820m) and through stunning mountains and ravines, each of which would make for perfect hiking (though there are no formal routes at all), you come to the *New Oxbow Lodge* (☎ & fax 051/933 2247; camping ①, doubles ③), whose alpine-style buildings have comfortable, warm rooms.

There's also a well-stocked bar, and a restaurant serving reasonably priced meals. You'll find good trout fishing on the Malimbamatso River, which flows by the lodge, and wonderful hiking in any direction. If you're coming here in winter, it's worth checking with the *Lodge* about the state of the roads, as they tend to ice over from April onwards. In fact, temperatures up here sometimes drop to below -20°C, so come prepared. If you are driving on from the lodge, remember that this is the last place you can buy **fuel** before Mokhotlong. There's **skiing** a few kilometres further along the road, in a wide development below the the Mahlasela Pass (3220m). Extravagant plans for a large development with proper lifts and chalets are occasionally rumoured, but for now the runs are short and the tows primitive – most visitors who venture this far in winter are South Africans simply intrigued to see snow. *Oxbow Lodge* rent skis for around M100 a day.

The road on to Mokhotlong is often called "the roof of Africa route", and it's easy to see why as you travel over a succession of ever higher passes, peaking at the **Tlaeeng Pass** (3270m), and passing through bleak, sparsely populated but entrancing mountain countryside. The road was recently tarred from *Oxbow Lodge* to Mokhotlong, which makes the journey a lot more feasible, although with the extremes of temperature experienced here the road is already breaking up in places. If you are adequately equipped, this district is tremendous hiking country, and you'll find the hardy locals who eke out a living here amongst the most hospitable in the country. About 40km from the Tlaeeng Pass, the descent to Mokhotlong begins, and most transport stops first at the small village of **Mapholaneng**, where there are two well-stocked bars. From here it's only 30km to Mokhotlong as the crow flies, though twists and turns in the road make the actual distance around 50km.

Mokhotlong

Perched on the banks of the Mokhotlong River, **MOKHOTLONG**, whose name means "place of the bald ibis" (although they are rarely seen these days), began life as a police post in 1905. Slowly, the post evolved into a trading centre for the Highlanders of the region, but remained cut off from the rest of Lesotho for years, with radio contact only established with Maseru in 1947. An airstrip was constructed in 1948 and a rudimentary road link built in the Fifties, but Mokhotlong continued to get the bulk of its supplies by pony from Natal, via Sani, for a long time afterwards. Even today, it looks, feels, and *is* remote, with locals usually riding into town for a shop and a drink on ponies, resplendent in their blankets.

Not much happens in town, which is dominated by hurriedly built and decidedly plain breeze-block buildings that compare unfavourably with the immaculately constructed dry-stone-walled dwellings of the surrounding countryside. On Tuesdays things liven up a bit, when Mokhotlong has its livestock sales. Or you can pick up decent cassettes, or just listen to the music blasting out from the Mamolibeli Music Shop on the main road at the western edge of town near the *Senqu Hotel*. But otherwise you'll find little to buy except for fast food from a few stores near the bus stops in the centre of town.

There's no public transport to Sani from Mokhotlong, but there are two daily **buses** that stop at Butha-Buthe, one leaving at around 6.30am and the other at 8.30am. Plenty of buses and **minibus taxis** run short distances, including the 15km or so to the *Molumong Lodge* (see below), often marked in the direction of "Ha Janteau".

Accommodation

There is a surprising amount of choice of **accommodation** in Mokhotlong: the *Senqu* is the best option in town, the Farmers' Training Centre the least expensive, but the nicest place in the area, for its location, facilities and relaxed atmosphere, is the *Molumong Lodge*, 15km southwest of town on the dirt road to Thaba Tseka.

Farmers' Training Centre (☎92 0235). A friendly place, but with limited bedding, hot water only if they are running a course, and no kitchen. You can camp here. Situated at the far eastern end of town, past the hospital, with a bright-red roof. Quite a walk, but you can get minibus taxis. ①.

Mokhotlong Hotel (☎92 0212). Reasonable though rather bare rooms with functional en-suite bathrooms looking out onto the mountains, and a public bar popular for its TV but with hardly any chairs. The restaurant serves moderately priced, unadventurous, meat-dominated meals. The hotel is at the end of the tarred section of the main road, just beyond the hospital, and unfortunately right next to a blood-stained informal abattoir. ②.

Molumong Lodge (☎0331/431 425). Set in a wonderful mountain location in the village of Ha Rafolatsane, and clearly marked "Molumong" on its red roof. Self-catering, with very cosy doubles and a great lounge to relax in, the lodge offers inexpensive pony trekking, and is a good place from which to explore and hike. Either take a bus or minibus taxi from Mokhotlong or, if you're driving, take the junction just before Mokhotlong to Sani Pass and then the first right. ②.

Senqu Hotel (☎92 0330). The smartest hotel in town, and the first you come to from the Butha-Buthe road, with comfortable rooms, strangely poky corridors, a TV in the public lounge, and tolerable food in its high-ceilinged, echoing restaurant. ②.

Sani and around

Branching off from the Mokhotlong road, 5km before the town, the rough gravel and dirt road to **SANI** twists its way in spectacular fashion for nearly 60km along the Sehonkong River, peaking at the **Kotisephola Pass** (3240m) before dropping to 2895m at **Sani Top**. There are plenty of rewarding hikes from Sani Top, including the twelve-kilometre one to **Thabana Ntlenyana** (3482m), the highest peak in the region, which is walkable in a day if you start early enough, and the tough but stunningly beautiful forty-kilometre **Top-of-the-Berg** walk to the Sehlabathebe National Park, which takes about four days.

Although the descent from Sani, down the infamous, hairpin-bend-filled Sani Pass, is just about possible in an ordinary car, you'd be much better off with a 4WD, and there is no way you can ascend the pass from the South African side without one. During the winter, the pass is frequently blocked with snow, and rain often renders it very slippery during the summer, so ring the chalet or lodge (below) in advance to find out conditions.

The only **public transport** from Mokhotlong to Sani is the odd minibus taxi. Otherwise you'll need to hitch, in which case you should make your way to the junction off the Mokhotlong Road as early as possible, or better still, arrange a lift in Mokhotlong the day before. From the South African side, Sani Pass Carriers (☎033/701 1017, mobile 083/555 5059, *sanipasscarriers@wandata.com*) have scheduled links between *Sani Lodge* (see p.416) and Pietermaritzburg, Durban and Kokstad. At the latter it meets the Baz Bus (☎021/439 2323) travelling between Johannesburg, Durban and Cape Town.

The **border** is open daily (8am to 4pm), and there's **accommodation** on both sides. On the Lesotho side is the popular *Sani Top Chalets* (mobile ☎082/574 5476, or contact Himeville information office ☎033/702 1158, *drakensburg.info@futurenet.org.za*; camping & dorms ①, doubles ②), where you can either self-cater or let them do the work. Book in advance, as it's often full, though you can camp in the chalet's grounds. The setting is superb, with commanding views of the mountains, and it has the highest **pub** in Africa. It's good for lunch, while in the evenings you can drink in front of the fire and watch the sunset over the mountain tops. In winter, if there's enough snow, skis and boots are on hire, and at other times you can take an overnight pony trekking trail with a guide. The *Chalets* do a daily return run between Himeville and the lodge, which can be useful if you need

transport, although it's also possible to hitch a lift or hop on one of the 4WD taxis which ply the route. Some way down the pass on the KwaZulu-Natal side is the excellent *Sani Lodge* (see p.416)

Katse and the Lesotho Highlands Water Project

The **Lesotho Highlands Water Project** is southern Africa's most ambitious engineering feat for decades, and its centrepiece, the **Katse reservoir**, with its huge dam, stands in stark contrast to the rural simplicity that surrounds it. The road built for the dam from Hlotse to Katse is a remarkable journey that's almost worth doing for the drive alone, although once you reach it the incongrous sight of such a large expanse of water deep in the Highlands offers some absorbing and impressive scenery. Once at Katse itself, you should also take a tour around the dam, whose sheer size and bulk linger in the mind long after the construction's vital statistics and the project's careful propaganda have faded.

The road to Katse

Once amongst the most inaccessible parts of the country, Katse's future has been changed forever by the Lesotho Highlands Water Project, not least by the transformation of its **road**, which used to be a rough track, into one of the best tarred routes in the country. The road begins at Hlotse, from where it is a speedy, unexciting run through the Lowlands to dreary **PITSENG**. Just north of Pitseng is a turn on the right to the *Outward Bound Centre* (☎40 0543), which runs week-long adventure activities for groups, including climbing, abseiling, hiking and kayaking. If really pushed for accommodation, you can probably arrange to stay in one of their very spartan dormitories (full board ③). Pitseng is an important centre for public transport, and is the place to catch a **bus** or **minibus taxi** to Katse, and to buy **fuel**, but apart from that there's absolutely no reason to hang around.

After Pitseng, just before the road starts to ascend steeply, there's a police barrier. If you're in a private car, an official will ask you to stop and may, depending on their mood, pry further about where you're going and what you've got in your boot. From here the road climbs to over 3000m at the **Mafika-Lisiu Pass** in under 30km, making it a punishing journey for most cars, most of which are lucky to make it out of second gear. Thanks to some remarkable engineering, the road twists and turns around the mountains, sometimes cutting through them, sometimes jutting out instead, leaving you suspended on the edge, a terrifyingly long way from the ground. There are plenty of places to stop and take in the view, though there have been reports recently of theft (in some cases armed) of tourists who have done just that, so keep a good look out if you stop, and your vehicle in view at all times.

After the Mafika-Lisiu Pass, you start descending to the small village of **HA-LEJONE**, at the northern end of the massive Katse reservoir. Though signposted as if it offers accommodation, the *Marmeso Lodge* is in fact just a good bar with a pool table and customers likely to offer you illicit diamonds, which you would do well not to buy. From Ha-Lejone, the road follows the reservoir, and just after the unmissable **Intake Tower**, which marks the point where the long tunnel carrying water to Gauteng begins, it crosses the water on the impressive new **Malibamatso Bridge**. From here, it climbs once more, reaching 2600m at the **Laitsoka Pass**, descends to the small village of Seshote, climbs again inexorably to the **Nkaobee Pass** (2510m), before descending to pass below the dam wall and reaching the now burgeoning town of Katse.

THE LESOTHO HIGHLANDS WATER PROJECT: THE HISTORY SO FAR

Lesotho's abundance of water but its shortage of cash, and Gauteng's monetary wealth but water poverty, are the stark facts that have led to the stunningly ambitious **Lesotho Highlands Water Project**. The essence of the project is to dam Lesotho's major rivers, most of which flow into the Senqu River (which South Africans know as the Orange River); then divert the water through specially constructed tunnels, via a hydroelectric power station at Muela near Butha-Buthe, to South African rivers; which carry it to the Vaal Dam; which then supplies Gauteng. For this, South Africa presently pays Lesotho royalties of around R12 million a month.

The treaty that started the project was signed in 1986, when South Africa had a government fond of imposing draconian states of emergency on its people, and Lesotho had a military dictatorship; unsurprisingly, popular consultation never featured very strongly in the treaty. There wasn't much of an assessment of the environmental impact of the project either, which is worrying in view of recently reported "seismic activity" induced by the reservoir, though the engineers have been busy assuring everybody that things are OK. Various compensation arrangements have been put in place for villagers whose homes, fields or grazing areas have been flooded, or who can no longer get from one side of the Katse valley to the other, though not unexpectedly there are grumbles that these promises have not been met. Meanwhile, the project marches inexorably forward, and it was no surprise that when South African peace-keeping forces entered Lesotho in 1998, one of their main priorities was to secure the dam. The fighting here was heavy, and there were more casualties among the rebel Lesotho soldiers here than anywhere else.

The initial treaty only committed the two parties to complete the first of four proposed phases of the project, after which there would be fresh negotiations and agreements, and it seems likely that when these happen both countries will have much more accountable governments than were in place in 1986. Phase 1a, which is now pretty much completed, consisted of the construction of the Katse reservoir and dam wall, the tunnels to South African rivers, and all the road infrastructure. Phase 1b will see the building of the Mohale Dam on the Senqunyane River (see p.638), which is due to be completed by 2004. After that, the new negotiations begin, but if all goes according to the original plan, the Senqu will be dammed in three separate places, with the water repeatedly diverted into the Katse reservoir, and the whole thing will be finished some time in the 2020s. Right now, however, the most impressive engineering feat is the dam wall itself, curved inwards for extra strength to such a degree that when you look down from the top you cannot see the rest of the wall, and experience the uneasy illusion of being suspended in space.

Katse and the dam

The town of **KATSE** is drab and boring, with uniform box-like houses arranged in an uninspired suburban manner. But the massive dam really is impressive, even if you aren't usually interested in engineering. To find out more, make for the blue pre-fab **visitor's centre** (Mon–Fri 8am–noon, 1–4pm, Sat & Sun 8am–noon), just before the town and dam, where you can take in a video about the development of the dam, as well as a rather bewildering relief model with flashing lights showing how water will be moved around the Highlands when (or if) the whole scheme, with five separate dams, is completed well into the next few decades. The centre can also provide someone to take you around the dam wall, which is 185m high and up to 60m thick and, if you are lucky, into some of its amazing network of tunnels.

The only **place to stay** in Katse is the *Katse Lodge* (☎91 0202; ②), with functional if well-kept rooms offering fine views of the reservoir and its impressive birdlife, and a surprisingly good restaurant serving a decent selection of inexpensive meals. Unfortunately, the lodge is small and still primarily intended for LHDA workers, so the staff only confirm your reservation a maximum of 48 hours before your arrival, and there's always a good chance that the place will be completely full. If it is, your only other option is to stay at the Agricultural Training Centre (☎90 0304; ①), which is a long drive on a terrible road in Thaba Tseka (see p.639). At least there is a steady stream of private and public transport from Katse to Thaba Tseka, so you should be able to find something going there, though rarely after 2pm.

For **boat trips** on the dam, which can include a *braai*, picnic and drinks, contact Alec in Maseru (mobile ☎083/250 8167). These operate from Ha-Lejone, at the northern end of the dam, rather than Katse.

THE SOUTHERN DISTRICTS

The **Southern Districts** of Lesotho hold some of the country's most dramatic countryside, perfect for pony trekking, which you can do from a number of scenically sited lodges. There are a number of small towns, some based around missions founded by the British in the last century – **Malealea** is probably the most handsomely situated, **Morija** the most historic. Further south, you can see **dinosaur footprints** at **Mohale's Hoek** and, more accessibly, at **Moyeni**, before moving on east to **Qacha's Nek** and the isolated delights of the **Sehlabathebe National Park** beyond, Lesotho's only national park.

Morija to Malealea

The main road south from Maseru, past the airport and the Qeme Plateau (see p.634), soon takes you to historic **Morija**, with its small cluster of mid-nineteenth-century buildings and the only museum in the country. A further 45km away, along a dirt road that gets increasingly scenic as you near your destination, the easy-going and smoothly run lodge at **Malealea** is the most attractive of its type in Lesotho. Set amid wonderful countryside, it's a perfect spot for hiking and well-organized pony trekking in wind-carved sandstone hills.

Morija

Just 44km from Maseru, **MORIJA**, the first mission to be established in Lesotho, in 1833, is a pleasant little town at the foot of the Makhoarane Plateau, housing the country's only museum and Lesotho's oldest building, church and printing press. Granted to three missionaries of the Paris Evangelical Missionary Society (PEMS), Eugene Casalis, Thomas Arbousset and Constant Gossellin, by King Moshoeshoe I, they gave the place the name that Abraham bestowed on the mountain where he was reprieved from killing his son by God (it means "God will provide"). Both easy to get to from Maseru with your own and public transport, with buses and minibus taxis running throughout the day in both directions, Morija is also a good spot to pick up transport going further south to Mafeteng and Mohale's Hoek.

The large, red-brick **mission church**, with its impressive teak-beamed roof, is almost always open. Begun in 1847, this is the third church built on this site, using the labour of Pedi economic migrants on their way to the Cape Colony, though its tall steeple was only built in 1905. You cannot, unfortunately, get in to see the historic **printing works** nearby, which have produced Sotho literature since the 1860s and the country's oldest newspaper, *Leselinyana la Lesotho* (Little Light of Lesotho), which has been in almost continual publication since 1863.

Most of Morija was razed to the ground by Afrikaner troops in 1858, and almost the only building left standing was the **Maeder House**, built in 1843 and now Lesotho's oldest building. Today, this simple stone house contains a small craft shop, selling inexpensive Sotho hats, dolls, carvings, tapestries and batiks. Close by, the **Morija Museum & Archives** (Mon–Sat 8am–5pm, Sun 2–5pm; M5) is a stimulating combination of a geological and fossil exhibition, ethnographic material and historic items of Moshoeshoe and his contemporaries, and a useful commentary on Lesotho's history and modern-day political issues. The geological and fossil displays are presented somewhat drily, although the dinosaur exhibits are striking, but you should find something of interest amongst the ethnographic and historical items, including a succession of treaties broken by the British, Moshoeshoe's china tea set, and a *khau*, the beautiful V-shaped neck ornament awarded to brave Sotho soldiers. The archives have yet to be fully organized and catalogued, but you are allowed to dip into them under supervision and see what you can unearth among the jumble of nineteenth-century missionary tracts and records and some valuable Africana. The museum also produces a **booklet**, *A Guide to Morija*, which tells you everything and more that you could possibly want to know about the town, including some pointers to nearby sites of interest. Browse through it in the museum's **tea shop** (Mon–Sat 9am–4.30pm, Sun 2–4.30pm), sitting either in the cool little rondavel or on the attractive lawns outside.

The best of the **walking trails** marked out from Morija takes about an hour there and back, and leads to a dinosaur footprint on one side of a large rock, halfway up the **Makhoarane Plateau**. To get there, make first for the *Ha Matela Lodge*, up the hill behind the museum, and from there head for the plateau, across a donga, following a succession of red arrows. Though a stiff climb to the rock, much of the path is sheltered by trees and the footprint itself is impressive, though rather faint.

The only **place to stay** in Morija is the self-catering *Ha Matela Lodge* (☎36 0306; ②), set in a pleasant and secluded spot at the top of the town on the way to the Makhoarane Plateau, and offering a small number of comfortable doubles in three houses, including one with a lovely verandah festooned with grapes in the summer. If you organize it beforehand, catering can be arranged with the tea room at the museum (③). The lodge can also arrange pony trekking for competitive rates.

Malealea

Further on, 85km from Maseru, there isn't much to **MALEALEA**, apart from the popular *Malealea Lodge* (☎ & fax 051/447 3200, *malealea@mweb.co.za*; dorms and camping ①, doubles ②, rondavels ③), which has a superb setting in the approaches to the Thaba Putsoa mountain range, and skilled, professional management, making it one of the finest places to stay in Lesotho. The lodge was originally a trading store, established by the British adventurer Mervyn Bosworth-Smith in 1905, and it was he who wrote the inscription "Wayfarer, pause and look upon a gateway of Paradise" at the mountain pass that takes you into the final stretch of the journey to the lodge. There is indeed a magnificent view from there, and if you have your own transport you would do well to heed his advice and pause a moment to take it all in. The current owners have extended the trading store and turned its back into backpackers' dorms and a dining room (you can also self-cater), and have built a series of sturdy, comfortable rondavels and doubles. Central to the complex is a great little bar with an open fire outside, around which local school children gather on some evenings to perform songs and dances for the guests.

Many visitors come to Malealea to hike, and the lodge has mapped out a series of trails, but the main activity is **pony trekking**. The lodge doesn't own the ponies, but acts as an agent for local horsemen who get the bulk of the money. It costs about M100 for a day trek, with the cost rising to M135 a day plus a small additional cost for staying in a village for overnight treks. Together with the horsemen, the lodge has worked out a series of guided trips, from short one-hour tours and half-days to as many days as your bottom and your wallet can stand. An excellent two-day adventure is the journey to the **Ribaneng Falls**, which takes you down and over steep sandstone valleys and hills. Although you need to take cooking and sleeping gear with you, the lodge ensures that there is an empty, well-kept rondavel with a gas cylinder in every village you stay in. If you have the time for a four-day journey, your guide will take you all the way east to the impressive Ketane Falls (see p.637) and back, while six days is sufficient for the return trip to Semonkong, both over some particularly beautiful mountains, and through quiet, friendly villages. A good, less pricey alternative to the pony trekking, which is quite hard on the body if you are not used to it, is simply walking and using a pony as a pack animal. The pony can carry four people's packs, provided they are not excessively heavy.

To get to Malealea by **public transport** from Maseru, take a bus or minibus taxi to Motsekuoa if you can find one, or Morija if you cannot, from where you can easily get one to Motsekuoa. During the day, there's quite a bit of transport from there heading towards Matelilie and the only possible slow bit is after you are dropped off at the junction to Malealea, which is about 8km away. However, almost all the vehicles going that way are likely to give you a lift to the lodge. There is frequently transport travelling between the lodge and Bloemfontein, via Wepener; ask about this when you make your booking.

Mafeteng, Mohale's Hoek and Moyeni

Though there is not much to detain you between **Mafeteng** and **Moyeni**, there are still some good walks in the sandstone hills that surround, including some that lead to interesting sets of **dinosaur footprints**. You'll also find the best meal for miles around at the *Hotel Mount Maluti*, where you can also hire ponies to explore the beautiful and little-visited Mokhele mountain range east of the town of **Mohale's Hoek**. Mafeteng, Mohale's Hoek and Moyeni are all close to the South African border, with Mafeteng the most practical one to use for border crossings, with the most public transport.

Mafeteng and around

The bustling town of **MAFETENG**, 20km from the Van Rooyenshek **border post** (daily 6am–10pm), is the first you come to in Lesotho if crossing from Wepener in the Orange Free State. It means "the place of Lefeta's people", after the son of a French missionary Emile Rolland, who was the district's first magistrate and was nicknamed Lefeta, or "he who passes", by locals, who regarded him as virtually Sotho except for the fact that he "passed by" initiation school.

Unfortunately a good deal of the town suffered in the 1998 riots, leaving the centre in quite a mess, but in any case the only building of interest in Mafeteng is the **council office** on the main street. It's worth a quick look for the carved animal heads studding its front wall, and a nice statue of a handlebar-moustached Cape Mounted Rifles soldier in the front garden. There are two good nearby excursions, though you'll need your own transport to get to them. The **Luma Pan**, 3km from town, attracts a good selection of birdlife; head for Wepener, and turn right down the first substantial dirt road you come to. About 20km east of Mafeteng, along a road that deteriorates past the village of Likhoele to the point that you're taking a risk in an ordinary saloon car, is the impressive **Thabana Morena Plateau**. Rising above a village of the same name, it rewards the steep climb with good views of the Free State plains to the west and the Thaba Putsoa mountains to the east.

Practicalities

As befits a border town, Mafeteng has a very busy **bus station** from where you can easily find transport north to Morija, Maseru and Malealea, and south to Mohale's

---

BOG STANDARD: THE NEW PIT LATRINE

A new feature of the Lesotho landscape are great numbers of improved **pit latrines** with white chimneys, which are easy to build and hygienic, but hardly to be found in neighbouring South Africa. Their main improvement on the old pit latrines, still in use in the Republic, is that they keep flies that have come into contact with human feces away from humans and their food. Flies are the big problem with pit latrines, as they invariably head for the latrine pit; but with this design once they are in the pit they never get out again.

Typically, flies enter the latrine when someone opens the door, and then fly down through the latrine seat and hole and then into the pit itself. With the old design, they would then fly out the way they came in, but with this one they are attracted by the light at the top of the chimney. However, they cannot escape from it, because of the chimney gauze. As long as people remember to close the lavatory seat and keep the latrine door shut, thus keeping light out of the latrine, this is pretty foolproof, keeping the flies buzzing harmlessly in the pit and chimney rather than on people's food or babies' mouths, and so preventing a great deal of unnecessary dysentery.

Hoek, Moyeni and beyond. There are various small **places to eat** by the bus station and on the main street, but otherwise the best choice is one of the hotels. For **accommodation**, there is the *Golden Hotel* (☎700566; ②), an anonymous-looking building offering adequate rooms and a small dining room serving meat dishes, to the right of the Main Road South from Maseru, just before you enter Mafeteng proper. Your other, rather better choice, is the *Hotel Mafeteng* (☎70 0236; ②), which looks like a Sixties airport control tower, and has pleasant rooms and cottages in a secluded garden with a good swimming pool. The restaurant serves a limited range of moderately priced meat dishes. You'll find the hotel signposted off the Main Road South to Mohale's Hoek.

Mafeteng's **nightlife** centres around the rather seedy, mirrored *Las Vegas* disco in the grounds of the *Hotel Mafeteng*, which blasts out soul and South African *kwaito* sounds until 4am on Friday and Saturday nights. Alternatively, the *Golden Hotel* sometimes has *famo* music – a folksy style with accordians and singing – on Saturday nights.

Mohale's Hoek

MOHALE'S HOEK, a short distance from the little-used Makhaleng Bridge **border post** (daily 8am–6pm), is a rather bedraggled little town, but with one of the best hotels in the area and some interesting sites in the attractive surrounding hills, including some well-preserved **dinosaur footprints**. Mohale was Moshoeshoe's younger brother, who was appointed by the king as part of his bid to wrest control of the district from chief Moorosi. There are still quite a few of Moorosi's Baphuthi clan here though, whose language is in some ways closer to Xhosa than Sotho.

If you desperately need to do some banking, you'll find the Standard and Nedbank **banks** more efficient than most banks outside Maseru, although changing money and travellers' cheques can still take some time. These are located on the main street, perpendicular to the main road through town. Otherwise, there's nothing to see or do here, but you'll find an excellent drive/walk to the **Mokhele Mountain**, about 10km east of town. Travel a short distance south on the main road to the little village of Mesitsaneng, and then head 7km east along a rough dirt track to the **Maphutseng mission**. Just before this historic French mission, which once hid locals in its roof from attacking Boers, turn right down a smaller track, and you'll see a plateau to the right a short walk away, where you'll find some **dinosaur footprints** and an inscription marking their "discovery" in 1959.

Practicalities

You'll find it hard to work out the system at the busy **bus station** in the centre of Mohale's Hoek, so instead just ask where the bus for your destination is standing. **Minibus taxis** congregate on the main street, and between them and the buses you should be able to find transport heading either north or south throughout the day.

The first **accommodation** you come to if entering Mohale's Hoek from the north is *Monateng Lodge* (☎78 5337, fax 78 5341; ②), but its rooms aren't very good and the lodge has been poorly built – though the public bar is lively and friendly. Much better is the central *Mount Maluti Hotel* (☎78 5224, fax 78 5341; ③), owned by a white family who have lived in the area for years and can offer plenty of good advice about what to see and do there, as well as arranging inexpensive pony treks and guides. They've also plotted an adventurous 4WD route through the southern Highlands, though to hire a 4WD vehicle you'd have to speak to Avis in Maseru (see "Listings", p.632). The hotel rooms are comfortable, with TVs, and there's a tennis court, pool and small garden, and a small but pleasant **campsite** (ask at the hotel reception). The highlight is its restaurant, which offers decent cuisine, even for vegetarians, at reasonable prices. It's a good place to stop off for a meal, or a cup of coffee. As usual, there are also plenty of inexpensive **places to eat** on the main street.

Moyeni and around

MOYENI (Place of the Wind), also known as Quthing, is a curious split-level town established by the British after the Gun War in 1884. The town itself is messy, though it has an attractive setting beside a river gorge, with views of the surrounding hills improving as you climb to the upper part of town. This has the police station, the main hotel, a large hospital and one or two pretty useless banks, while the lower half has most of the shops, fuel stations and is where you catch public transport. During the day, there are always plenty of **buses** and **minibus taxis** running north towards Maseru, far fewer running east towards Qacha's Nek, and one or two heading for the nearby Tele Bridge **border post** (daily 8am–6pm), from where you can pick up transport to Sterkspruit in the Eastern Cape.

The most easily accessible **dinosaur footprints** in Lesotho are very near the Moyeni's lower half. Just continue a short distance up the Main Road from the Moyeni turn and look out for an obvious orange, thatched building right beside the road on the left. This **visitor's centre** (daily 8am–4pm), a rare privilege for a historic site in Lesotho, is simple, and the man who works there will motion you towards the variety of clearly discernible prints in the hope of a small tip.

Also worth a visit is the **Masitise Cave House**, a few kilometres west of Moyeni to the right of the main road. Follow signs to the Masitise Primary and High schools, and at the high school ask for someone to show you the house, built into the cave by the French Protestant missionary family who lived here in the 1870s.

A little further on are some much-vandalized and greatly faded **rock paintings**. If you have made it this far, have a brief look also at the pleasant mission **church**, which has a fine bell tower but no bell to go with it.

Accommodation

The Catholic mission at Villa Maria is the only budget **accommodation** option, and there are two hotels in town. Neither is of particularly high standard, though the *Mountainside* just about wins on points for its more intimate and friendly atmosphere.

Mountainside Hotel (☎75 0257). Halfway between upper and lower Moyeni, this is a small hotel with mostly adequate rooms (check the mattress before you accept a room), half of which look onto the street, while the others are more secluded and quieter. There's a pleasant and cosy private bar, a friendly public one and a good restaurant with a tasty fixed menu that normally has something for vegetarians. ②.

Orange River Hotel (☎75 0252). An ungainly building decorated in Seventies-style in hessian and pine, which has the air of having seen little attention, and fewer guests, since. Rooms are reasonable but very stuffy, and some of the ceilings are in serious trouble. The tolerable restaurant looks out over upper Moyeni and has a good view of the surrounding countryside. To get to it follow the main road through town, almost to the top of the hill. ②.

Villa Maria Roman Catholic Mission (☎75 0364). Set in the grounds of the very grand two-towered church, the mission offers clean, inexpensive rooms with communal bathrooms. The complex is just west of Moyeni, to the right of the main road. ①.

Mount Moorosi, Qacha's Nek and the Sehlabathebe National Park

A far less-used route into the Highlands than the northern road from Butha-Buthe to Mokhotlong, the mountain road from **Mount Moorosi to Sehlabathebe** is ruggedly beautiful, with the added bonus of the mighty Senqu (Orange) River winding majestically alongside much of it. If the Katse dam builders have their way, the Senqu will in a few years be much reduced, but for now the chocolate-brown river is normally in full flood. The highlights along the route include **Thaba Moorosi**, the mountain where the outlawed chief Moorosi made his last stand against the British in 1879, the San caves at **Seforong**, and the remote, inaccessible, pristine national park of **Sehlabathebe** itself, the only national park in the country – perfect for fishing, bird-watching and kilometre-upon-kilometre of isolated hiking.

Mount Moorosi and around

Just over 40km on from Moyeni, along a decent tar road with fine views of the mountains and glimpses of the mighty Senqu (Orange) River, the small town of **MOUNT MOOROSI** clings to the mountainside and provides inhabitants of various local villages with a minibus taxi stop and shopping. The largest institution is Mitchell's Trading Store, which serves as the town's main store, garage and fuel station. Ask here if you want to park your car in the compound (where it should be safe) before taking the ferry across the Senqu to Bethel (see below).

Mount Moorosi is named after chief Moorosi, who moved to the region in the 1850s, living in the cliffs around the town. He was an ally of the San and had several San wives, but made an enemy of the British in the 1870s when they captured his son and Moorosi promptly captured him back. British troops retaliated by attacking his stronghold in 1879, but he held out for eight months, until finally captured when the soldiers used scaling ladders on the steep cliffs, and then cut off and publicly displayed his severed head. **Thaba Moorosi**, where the main battle took place, is a kilometre or so further along the main road on the right, and you'll find if you climb it that some stone slabs still bear the inscriptions of the soldiers sent to get the chief. It is quite a tricky climb, though, so be sure to let someone in Mount Moorosi know where you are going.

Bethel

An inexpensive minibus taxi ride from Mount Moorosi will take you a few kilometres along the main road to the ferry point on the Senqu River, below the towering cliffs of Thaba Moorosi. There are hopes that a road crossing will be built, but while that decision awaits, the simplicity of the brief rowing-boat crossing of the strongly flowing river is worth experiencing. Once on the other side, it is a four-kilometre walk to the village of **Bethel**, where there is a rather neglected large mission church and the much more proactive **Bethel Business and Community Development Centre** (①). Despite its rather cumbersome name, this is an innovative training centre, which teaches locals practical skills in solar technology, permaculture and market gardening. The fascinating thing about being here is that the centre is a thriving advertisement for the principles it expounds, with healthy crop fields and vegetable patches, rows of trees, well-designed buildings and solar power used for everything from the hot water to a satellite phone link-up for email. Facilities include a self-catering guest flat (①) and dormitories, and meals are available if arranged beforehand. Short-term visitors are welcome, but if you would like to stay longer, write to the centre at PO Box 53, Mount Moorosi 750, or email them (*bbcdc@maf.org*), as far in advance as you can. If you have a 4WD vehicle, an alternative to crossing by ferry is a two-hour drive along a route that leaves the tarred road on the western side of the bridge over the Senqu, between Moyeni and Mohale's Hoek.

Mphaki and around

Shortly after rounding Thaba Moorosi, the main road leaves the Senqu River, and heads swiftly into the Highlands through the impressive **Quthing Gorge**, peaking after about ten kilometres at the **Lebelonyane Pass** (2456m). The views are superb, but don't enjoy them too much if you are driving as there are no barriers to stop you plunging onto the slopes beneath. The road carries on through a series of attractive high-altitude valleys, before reaching the small village of **MPHAKI**, which has excellent accommodation at the Farmers' Training Centre (②), whose self-catering rondavels are far better equipped than most, as well as a pleasant guesthouse. If you don't fancy self-catering, the *Motsekuoa Liquor Restaurant* opposite the Centre provides inexpensive and tasty Sotho **food** as well as a good bar.

The tarred road continues for another 10km out of Mphaki, where it reverts to decent gravel. You'll find some interesting **San caves** a short hike off the road a few kilometres further on at **Seforong**, just before **Sekake**, though they do not – unusually – have rock paintings. At Sekake you can **camp** or **stay** at the atmospheric Christian Council of Churches Mission, a kilometre or so along a rocky track that leaves the main road at the *Hotline Restaurant*.

Qacha's Nek

Past Sekake, the road rejoins the southern banks of the Senqu, but deteriorates significantly in quality, though you can still make it with care in an ordinary vehicle. You'll find it a beautiful, undulating drive, amongst the loveliest in Lesotho, though once you reach the approach to **QACHA'S NEK** you'll see depressingly familiar soil erosion and dongas.

Qacha's Nek, named after chief Moorosi's son Ncatya, was an area famed for its banditry when the British founded the town in 1888, in an attempt to forestall the kind of trouble they had experienced with chief Moorosi. Many of the "bandits" were in fact desperate San, hounded out of everywhere they used to live and now with nothing to survive on. This left the British unmoved, and they hunted them to extermination throughout the 1860s. Moorosi's Baphuthi people had started moving there in the 1850s, rapidly wiping out all the game, and turning the land over to grazing and cultivation instead. The area has unusually high rainfall, and the weather conditions favour conifers, including a few massive Canadian redwoods, giving Qacha's Nek an atmosphere completely different from most of virtually treeless Lesotho.

There's nothing much to see in town, except the elegant **St Joseph's Church** at its eastern end, but the entire surrounding mountainous countryside is great for **hiking**. Qacha's Nek is also an important **border town** (daily 8am–6pm) and there is usually plenty of public transport heading west towards Moyeni, which leaves from the Shell garage in the centre of town. You can hear the minibus taxis a mile off, because they have cowbells tied to their fronts. You'll also find transport just over the border heading for the Eastern Cape town of Matatiele, from where it is a simple matter to find buses and minibus taxis going on to Kokstad and beyond.

The best **accommodation** in town is the *Nthatuoa Hotel* (☎950260; ②–③), which is the first building you come to on the left as you enter Qacha's Nek. The hotel offers four types of room, each more luxurious than the last, starting with a decent though smallish double and ending with a large, fancy suite. All tariffs include a substantial breakfast from a restaurant that serves the finest **food** in town (unless you are vegetarian, in which case there's nothing for you). Just past the hotel, and opposite the Farmers' Training Centre, ask your way to the excellent *Narna's Guest House* (☎95 0374; ①), which is close by. Though the owners don't speak much English and water supply is often a problem (as it is elsewhere in town despite the high rainfall), this is a friendly place with a good kitchen where you can either do your own cooking or just provide the ingredients and let the owner cook them up, for a small extra charge. Turn left past the fuel station in town for the *Central Hotel* (☎95 0224; ②) which despite its name is over a kilometre further on, nestled away next to the PEP department store. A sandstone building and full of character, the hotel has only six rooms and is often full. Even if you are not staying, it's worth visiting it at weekends for live music. There are a small number of inexpensive **places to eat** in the centre of town, but for more substantial meals you should really make for one of the hotels.

Sehlabathebe National Park

The only national park in the country, **Sehlabathebe National Park** (free) is remote and inaccessible, but predictably peaceful and beautiful. Set on the border with South Africa, in the eastern reaches of the Drakensberg, the park has a few game animals, and is better known for its birdlife, excellent trout fishing, waterfalls, and seemingly endless open spaces that make for perfect hiking. Once here (just turn up, and they'll let you in), you probably won't want to leave in a hurry, so bear this in mind when you book. Having said that, the weather can be so foul as to make you want to move on straightaway, with mists and rain emerging out of nowhere even on the finest days.

Sehlabathebe is managed by the Ministry of Agriculture, and is the subject of ongoing land disputes that primarily concern grazing access. The current state of affairs is a rather messy compromise, and you are likely to see herd boys grazing livestock all over the park, much to the irritation of environmentalists.

Practicalities

To **get to the park** from the Lesotho side you definitely need a 4WD. Failing that, there is a daily bus from Qacha's Nek to the village outside the park, which takes four to five hours; or you can sometimes hitch a lift from the junction about 11km from Qacha's Nek, but you are then faced with the problem of walking up the very steep 17km from the park entrance to the park's office. The only other way into the park from the Lesotho side is to walk the forty-kilometre "Top of the Berg" hike from Sani Top (see p.646). From South Africa, the only way in is a day's walk along the dramatic path starting at Bushman's Nek, which is a few hours' drive from Underberg and Himeville in KwaZulu-Natal.

To be sure of **accommodation** in Sehlabathebe's well-equipped and inexpensive lodge (①), book in advance in Maseru through *Sehlabathebe Reservations*, Ministry of Agriculture, on Raboshabane Road, off Moshoeshoe Road, PO Box 92, Maseru 100 (☎32 3600 or 32 2876). The easiest way to do this is in person when you are in Maseru. During the week, however, the lodge is rarely full, and even if it is, you can always camp (①). Neither the Ministry of Agriculture, nor the tourist information office nor the park office itself have any maps of Sehlabathebe; if you want to do some serious hiking, go to the Department of Lands, Surveys and Physical Planning in Maseru (see p.623), where you should be able to pick up some good, detailed maps of the area.

travel details

Buses

There is no such thing as a bus timetable in Lesotho, and the following information is intended just to give a rough idea of frequencies and journey times. Minibus taxis supplement bus services everywhere and ensure that you can always find some form of public transport on major routes, though the story is very different on minor routes off the tarred roads, where you can expect long waits. Because public transport is so erratic, it's usually a better idea to just make for the next town on and find something from there rather than getting a ticket all the way to your destination (unless there's only one a day); your bus will stop at the next town anyway, and wait for more passengers, and you might be able to get a minibus taxi in the meantime.

Butha-Buthe to: Hlotse (4 daily; 30min); Maputsoe (4 daily; 45min); Mokhotlong (2 daily; 7hr).

Hlotse to: Butha-Buthe (4 daily; 30min); Maputsoe (5 daily; 30min); Maseru (8 daily; 2hr).

Mafeteng to: Maseru (5 daily; 1hr 30min); Mohale's Hoek (5 daily; 45min).

Maputsoe to: Butha-Buthe (4 daily; 45min); Hlotse (5 daily; 30min); Maseru (8 daily; 2hr).

Maseru to: Hlotse (8 daily; 2hr); Mafeteng (5 daily; 1hr 30min); Maputsoe (8 daily; 2hr); Qacha's Nek (1 daily; 10hr); Roma (4 daily; 1hr); Semonkong (4 daily; 5hr); Teya-Teyaneng (8 daily; 45min).

Mohale's Hoek to: Mafeteng (5 daily; 45min); Moyeni (5 daily; 45min).

Mokhotlong to: Butha-Buthe (2 daily; 7hr).

Moyeni to: Mohale's Hoek (5 daily; 45min); Qacha's Nek (1 daily; 7hr).

Qacha's Nek to: Maseru (1 daily; 10hr); Moyeni (1 daily; 7hr).

Roma to: Maseru (4 daily; 1hr); Semonkong (4 daily; 4hr).

Semonkong to: Maseru (4 daily; 5hr); Roma (4 daily; 4hr).

Teya-Teyaneng to: Maputsoe (8 daily; 45min); Maseru (8 daily; 45min).

Flights

Maseru to: Johannesburg (2 daily Mon–Fri, 1 daily Sat & Sun; 1hr 10min).

CHAPTER TWELVE

SWAZILAND

ooking at a political map of South Africa, you could be forgiven for assuming that **Swaziland** was another bizarre product of South Africa's apartheid engineering. This small, landlocked kingdom, with a population of less than one million, lies in the spanner-like grip of Mpumalanga which surrounds it on three sides. But in fact, although South Africa's influence predominates, Swaziland was a British protectorate from 1906 until its full independence in 1968.

During the long years of apartheid, white South Africans regarded Swaziland as a decadent playground, where sinful opportunities (gambling, interracial sex and porn movies), forbidden by their Calvinist rulers, were freely available. This image is fading fast, and though Swaziland still feels a lot more commercialized than, say, Lesotho, its outstanding **scenery** makes it well worth a visit. The country spans a choice portion of the southern African highveld's descent into the eastern lowveld and is blessed with easily accessible areas of great natural beauty, including **five national parks**, some featuring big game. With a car and a bit of time, you can explore some of the less trampled reserves, make overnight stops in unspoilt, out-of-the-way settlements and, if you time your visit well, take in something of Swaziland's well-preserved **cultural traditions**.

Despite encroaching political dissent, Swaziland remains one of the world's few absolute monarchies, and **King Mswati III**, educated at Britain's elite Sherbourne college, regularly appears in the country's sacred ceremonies, bedecked in the leopard skins of his office, participating in a ritual dance or assessing the year's crop of eligible maidens as they dance before him. He might even choose to add a few to his collection of wives, carefully drawn from a wide selection of clans in order to knit the nation more closely together. If you can, plan to come to Swaziland for **Ncwala** (around the end of Dec or start of Jan) or **Umhlanga** (Aug or Sept); both ceremonies are as important to the Swazis as New Year is to the Chinese.

Laid-back **Mbabane**, the country's tiny capital city, makes a useful base from which to explore the attractive central **eZulwini Valley**, home to the royal palace and the **Mlilwane Wildlife Sanctuary**. With your own transport, or a bit of determination and public transport, you can venture further afield, heading into the highveld of the northwest, and up to the fantastically beautiful **Malolotja Nature Reserve**, with its fabulous hiking country, soaring valleys and cliffs.

If you are trying to get between northern KwaZulu-Natal and the Kruger National Park in South Africa, Swaziland offers a good, fully tarred **through route** via the Matsamo Border in the north and the Lavumisa and Mahamba borders in the south, passing by the Mkhaya Game Reserve and Big Bend. Approaching Kruger this way is a far more attractive option than skirting through the eastern parts of Mpumalanga.

Note that Swaziland's eastern lowveld, including Hlane Royal National Park and Mkhaya Nature Reserve, is **malarial** during the summer months (November to May). For details on necessary precautions, see p.17.

Some history

The history of Swaziland dates back to the **Dlamini** clan and their king, **Ngwane**, who crossed the Lubombo mountains from present-day Mozambique in around 1750.

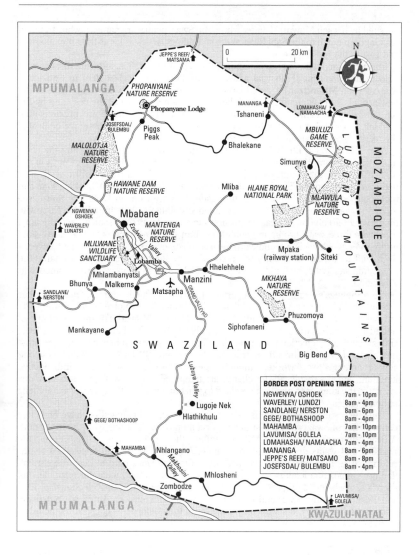

Pushed into southeast Swaziland by the Ndwandwe people of Zululand, the clan eventually settled at Mhlosheni and then Zombodze in the southwest, where Ngwane reigned precariously, under constant threat of Ndwandwe attack. His grandson, **Sobhuza I**, was forced to flee north from the Ndwandwe, but they in turn were defeated by the Zulu king Shaka in 1819. Sobhuza then established a new capital suitably far from Shaka in the eZulwini Valley, and made peace with the Ndwandwe by marrying the king's daughter.

Sobhuza's power grew as he brought more and more clans under his wing. His alliance with the newly arrived Afrikaners, forged out of mutual fear of the Zulu, was pursued by his son **Mswati II** (after whom the Swazi people are named), who stretched his kingdom north to the Sabi River and sent raiding parties as far as the Limpopo river and east to the Indian Ocean.

Europeans arrived in greater numbers throughout the 1880s, after the discovery of gold in neighbouring Transvaal and at Piggs Peak and Forbes Reef in Swaziland. Mswati's son **Mbandzeni** granted large chunks of his territory in concessions to the new arrivals, emboldening Britain to ignore his claims to most of the rest, and by the time Swaziland became a protectorate of South Africa in 1894 there was precious little land left. After their victory in the Second Anglo-Boer War, Britain assumed control of the territory and retained it until 1968.

After World War II the British invested in their protectorate, establishing the enormous **sugar plantations** on the northeast, and an **iron-ore mine** at Ngwenya in the highveld (today, the country's major export is sugar). Meanwhile, **Sobhuza II**, who had become king of the Swazis in 1921, concentrated on buying back his kingdom, and had acquired about half of it by the time independence came in 1968. The Swazi aristocracy managed the transition to independence skilfully, with its Imbokodvo party winning every parliamentary seat in the first elections. In 1973, a radical pan-Africanist party won three seats, prompting Sobhuza to **ban political parties** and declare a state of emergency which has technically been in place ever since. A parliament governs Swaziland today, but final authority rests with the king, who continues to name the prime minister (who, by tradition, is always a Dlamini) and approve or veto important legislation.

After Sobhuza's death in 1982, a period of intrigue ensued, with the Queen Mother Dzeliwe assuming the regency until deposed by Prince Bhekimpi, who ruled until 1985, purging all the opposition he could. The current king, **Mswati III**, the son of one of Sobhuza's 70 wives, was recalled from an English public school to become king in 1986, and parliamentary elections were held in 1987. New opposition began to emerge, most notably the **People's United Democratic Movement** (PUDEMO), which has strong support amongst Swazi workers, though in general Swazis are proud of their distinctive kingdom, and as a result calls for change are tempered by an unwillingness to show disloyalty to the king, or to expose Swaziland to what many see as the predatory ambitions of South Africa.

Thus the maintenance of tradition and appeals to broad nationalism have been key components of Swazi royalty's strategy to retain power. Relations with the new South African regime are uneasy: the ANC remembers the expulsion of its activists during the Eighties and wants speedy political change. Although Mswati III appears to favour reform, so far none has happened, and the authorities work hard to keep dissent bottled up – opposition leaders aren't able to speak freely in the media, for example, and there's sporadic police repression – and poor turnouts marked the "elections" of 1993 and 1998. Currently, Swaziland is the only country in southern Africa not practising multiparty democracy. It seems only a matter of time before it is coerced by the other regional powers into doing so.

When to go

Summers are hot, particularly in the eastern lowveld. **Winter** is usually sunny, but nights can be very chilly in the western highveld around the Malolotja Nature Reserve and Piggs Peak. In summer, rainfall is usually limited to short, drenching storms that play havoc with the smaller untarred roads.

Getting there

Of the eleven border posts serving traffic from South Africa, the main ones are **Ngwenya/Oshoek** (7am–10pm), which is closest to Johannesburg and is the easiest route to Mbabane; **Jeppe's Reef/Matsamo** (8am–8pm) in the northwest, which is handy if you're coming in from Kruger Park; **Mananga** (8am–6pm) in the northeast; **Lavumisa/Golela** (7am–10pm), in the southeast, close to the KwaZulu-Natal coast; and **Mahamba** (7am–10pm), in the southwest, off the N2 from Piet Retief in the KwaZulu-Natal interior. The northern crossing via **Bulembu** (8am–4pm) to Piggs Peak is perhaps the most spectacular in the country, but the bad road makes this journey hard going in an ordinary car. Crossing the border is usually very straightforward: you simply have to show your passport and pay the token E5 (R5) **road tax**.

Transtate **buses** from Johannesburg enter Swaziland through the Ngwenya/Oshoek border, stopping at Ermelo en route to Mbabane; and through Mahamba, stopping at Nhlangano and Hlathikulu. The Baz Bus runs eastbound from Jo'burg to Durban via Mbakane and then Manzini, where it arrives on Monday, Wednesday, Friday and Sunday; westbound, from Durban, it also stops overnight at *Swaziland Backpackers* in Manzini on Tuesday, Wednesday, Friday and Sunday, before carrying on to Mbabne and Jo'burg.

Swaziland has one **international airport**, Matsapha (often referred to as "Manzini"), between Mbabane and Manzini. Comair operate five **flights** a week from Johannesburg, while Royal Swazi Airways flies one to two times daily, to and from Johannesburg. Swazi Express Airways fly in from Durban on Mondays, Tuesdays, Thursdays and Fridays.

A new **train** service between Durban and Maputo travels through Swaziland, stopping at Mpaka, 35km east of Manzini. Departures from Durban are on Tuesdays and Fridays.

The national parks

Swaziland has six **national parks**, between them exemplifying the country's geographical diversity, and all offering good-value accommodation. The Swaziland National Trust Commission in Lobamba (see p.669) manages **Malolotja Nature Reserve** in the northwest highveld, **Mlawula Nature Reserve** in the eastern lowveld and the tiny **Mantenga Nature Reserve** in the eZulwini valley. Royal Swazi Big Game Parks (see p.664), in Mbabane's New Mall, run the **Hlane Royal National Park** in the lowveld, **Mlilwane Wildlife Sanctuary** near Mbabane, and the upmarket **Mkhaya Nature Reserve** between Manzini and Big Bend.

MBABANE AND AROUND

Tucked in the jumble of granite peaks and valleys that make up the Dlangeni hills, Swaziland's administrative capital, **MBABANE** (pronounced "M-buh-barn"), is small, relaxed and unpretentious, with a population of only 90,000. Just over 20km from Swaziland's western borders with South Africa, the city roughly marks the point where the mountainous southern African highveld descends briefly into middleveld, before bottoming out further east as dry lowveld. This is a good base from which to start exploring Swaziland, especially if you're without your own transport: the **Mlilwane**

TIPS ON TRAVEL IN SWAZILAND

• **Accommodation** at the mid- and upper range is generally better value than in South Africa. Backpacker and budget places are on a par with South Africa.

• **Banks** are easily found in the major centres. Opening hours are generally Monday to Friday, 8.30am to 2.30pm, with some branches open on Saturday from 8.30am to 11am. Most banks and hotels should be prepared to change travellers' cheques, but usually at poor rates of exchange. ATMs in Swaziland are usually only for Swazi bank account holders, but some are being upgraded and may accept international cards.

• **Camping** is possible near almost every tourist attraction and in all the national parks except for Mkhaya.

• **Currency** is the **lilangeni** – plural emalangeni (E) – which is tied to the South African rand (1 rand = 1 lilangeni). The rand is legal tender in Swaziland, so you won't have to change any money. Emalangeni are not convertible outside Swaziland. There is a shortage of change in Swaziland, so if you do exchange money ask for a good amount of low denomination notes.

• **Credit cards** such as Visa, Mastercard (Access) and American Express are widely accepted in hotels, restaurants and shops. The national parks are supposed to accept cards, but only Mkhaya can be relied upon to do so. If you're visiting any of the others, you'd be well-advised to carry cash.

• **Costs** are similar to those in South Africa, with food and fuel somewhat less expensive.

• **Phone numbers** The country code for Swaziland is ☎268, to be followed by the destination number (there are no **area codes**). The code for **phoning out from Swaziland** is ☎00, followed by the country and area codes and finally the destination number. To phone **South Africa**, dial ☎07. To arrange a **collect call**, dial ☎94. Country codes are the same as those dialled from South Africa (see p.45). All telephone numbers within Swaziland changed in early 1999 – we've given the new numbers, but if you experience difficulties phone **enquiries** on ☎919490.

• **Driving** is the best way to see Swaziland; distances are small, all the main tourist sites are near good, tarred roads, and the major gravel roads are in decent condition. Most dirt roads are passable with an ordinary vehicle in dry months. The authorities permit a **blood-alcohol level** in drivers which is double that permitted in South Africa, and enough to make you think twice about long drives at night. Also, the general **speed limit** of 80kph outside towns is universally ignored and very rarely enforced. Small **toll charges** are set to be introduced on the new highway between Mbabane and Manzini. For Swazi car rental, see "Listings" for Mbabane (p.667).

• **Passports and visas** – see p.13.

• **Tour operators** – see p.667.

Wildlife Sanctuary lies not far south, and the royal village of **Lobamba** makes an easy day's outing – vital if you're here when the Umhlanga or Ncwala ceremonies take place. There's not much to do in the city, but you should find it a more agreeable than hectic **Manzini**, especially if you need to change money, find a comfortable bed or plan your trip ahead.

AN ALTERNATIVE ROUTE TO MBABANE

While most visitors – and Transtate buses from South Africa – approach Mbabane from the Ngwenya/Oshoek border, a good **alternative route** is via the **Sandlane/Nerston** border post (8am–6pm), about 35km further south, and roughly 70km from the city. Although a longer journey, this road passes through some outstanding scenery and will take you past some excellent places to stay on the way.

Once past Nerston, where there are some interesting San paintings (ask at the church for someone to show you the way), the road plunges deep into the vast and beautiful **Usutu Forest**, which covers over ten percent of Swaziland. After some steep climbs, you'll start a

SWAZILAND ON THE INTERNET
http://www.swazi.com
Swaziland's official website is lively, colourful and packed with useful information, including hotel listings and alternative tours of Swaziland. You can also read the *Swazi Observer* newspaper online, or visit the "Artists on the Internet" page for a roundup of the country's arts scene.

http://www.biggame.co.sz
Practical information on Hlane, Mlilwane and Mkhaya parks, with links to the Swazi Trails site and details of tours.

http://www.swazitrails.co.sz
Details of a range of tours around Swaziland, including cultural, wildlife and adventure options.

LANGUAGE
Siswati greetings and responses

Hello (to one)	*Sawubona*
Hello (to many)	*Sanibona*
How are you?	*Kunjani?*
I'm fine	*Kulungile*
Goodbye (person leaving)	*Sala kahle*
Goodbye (person remaining)	*Hamba kahle*

Basics

Yes	*Yebo* (also a casual greeting)
No	*Ha*
Thank you	*Ngiyabonga*
Today	*Lamuhla*
Tomorrow	*Kusasa*
Yesterday	*Itolo*

Travel

Where is. . . ?	*Iphi I . . . ?*
Where can we stay?	*Singahlala hephi?*
Where are you going?	*U ya phi?*
How much?	*Malini?*

long descent to the factory town of **Bhunya**, whose hub is a belching pulp mill – reason enough not to linger. Press on for another 15km or so on the road to Mhlambanyatsi, taking care when crossing the single-lane bridge over the Lusutfu River. Just before Mhlambanyatsi is a fine **hotel**, *The Forester's Arms* (☎26084, fax 74051, *forestersarms@iafrica.com*; half board ⑤), set in a picturesque clearing in the surrounding woodland. Cosy rooms with wonderful mountain views and hearty **meals** make this a good place to stop over, and if you're here on a Sunday so much the better: this is when people from all over the country pour in to feast on the hotel's superb buffet and roast – you'll need to **book** ahead to be sure of a table.

Back on the road, **Mhlambanyatsi** itself has a small shopping centre and some filling stations, but little else. Keep going, as the road beyond it enters a beautiful, lush river valley, with traditional houses dotted all around; this is prime **hiking** territory, and a particularly spectacular umarked trail leads all the way to (but not into) the Mlilwane Wildlife Sanctuary (see p.670), although there are no facilities and you have to be pretty self-sufficient, asking at villages for somewhere to stay. Eventually the road breaks through the hills to the plateau on which Mbabane stands, where you can connect with the main routes to the centre of the country.

Arrival and information

Matsapha airport (☎518615), 35km southeast of Mbabane, just west of Manzini, is Swaziland's only international airport. There's no public transport from here into Mbabane, so if you haven't been able to arrange a pick-up with your hotel be prepared to take a **taxi** or **rent a car** (see p.667). You cannot change money at the airport, so have some rands or emalangeni handy.

Transtate (Jo'burg, ☎011/774 7768) **buses** from South Africa terminate some way out of town at the intersection of Usutu and Manzini roads, from where you should call a taxi, as the distance into town isn't walkable. The main bus station is off the Western Distributor Road, beside the Swazi Plaza mall, and from here you can take a bus to almost anywhere in Swaziland. **Minibus taxis** ply the Mbabane–Manzini route and rank on the west side of the bus station – this is also where you can rent a **private taxi** for local travel.

Mbabane's **tourist office**, Swazi Plaza (Mon–Fri 8am–5pm, Sat 8.30am–12.30pm; ☎4042531) has a good supply of **maps** and brochures and a free *What's On?* guide – very handy for information on forthcoming events. The **Royal Swazi Big Game Parks Office** (Mon–Fri 8am–4pm; ☎4044541, fax 4040957, after hours and weekends ☎61591, *reservations@biggame.co.sz*) in the New Mall has a similar selection of leaflets and very helpful staff, and handles booking for the national parks.

Central Mbabane empties out at night, and **muggings** are a risk for those wandering the streets alone. If you're going out after dark, arrange for a taxi to pick you up.

Accommodation

Mbabane's **accommodation** is somewhat limited, and some of the options in the lower price range are in a seedy part of town. However, there is a good backpackers' lodge near the centre and a handful of fairly decent **hotels** on and around Allister Miller Street. Most of the establishments in the eZulwini Valley (see p.667) are close enough to be considered as alternatives to those listed below. If you have trouble finding anywhere, staff at the tourist office should be able to help out.

Chillage Backpackers, 18 Mission St (☎4048342, *chillage@hotmail.com*). Friendly, if almost intimidatingly laid-back backpackers' lodge a ten-minute short walk north of the city centre, offering inexpensive dorms and doubles. Arranges alternative tours to a village and waterfall deep in the Swaziland wilderness, with accommodation in a remote farmhouse ("the Chillage in the Village") also available. Dorms ①, doubles ②.

City Inn, Allister Miller St (☎4042406, fax 4045393). City-centre hotel offering spacious, en-suite rooms, all with TV. Rooms near the bar can get noisy, so specify what you want. ③.

Hill St Lodge, Hill St (☎4046342). Basic rooms with shared bath in a quiet suburb west of Allister Miller St. ①.

ACCOMMODATION PRICE CODES

All the accommodation listed in the Guide has been categorized into one of nine price bands, as set out below. The rates quoted represent what you can expect to pay for much of the summer **per person**, and unless otherwise stated, are based on two sharing. Rooms are generally en suite. Expect prices in some areas to be significantly higher in peak season (Dec–Jan & Easter), and look out for discounts during the winter. For further details, see p.33 and 662.

① up to E50	⑥ E250–300
② E50–100	⑦ E300–400
③ E100–150	⑧ E400–500
④ E150–200	⑨ over E500
⑤ E200–250	

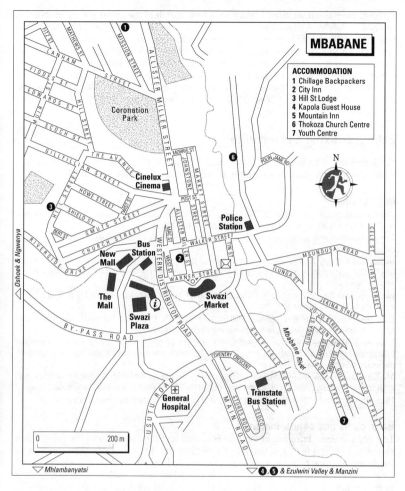

Thokoza Church Centre, Mhlanhla St (☎ & fax 4046681). Church mission, some way east of the city centre, offering drab but cheap two- or three-bed rooms. There is a 10pm curfew unless you make prior arrangements. The area can be rough at night. ①.

Youth Centre, Isomi St (☎4042176). Southeast of town in the Msundusa suburb, this evangelical centre offers cheap, basic rooms. Public transport to and fro is scarce, and it's quite a walk to the centre from here. ①.

The City

Mbabane's hilly **centre** is a pleasant jumble of office blocks, markets, plazas and shacks that you can very easily explore on foot – which is just as well, as driving here can be stressful without a sound grasp of the street layout. **Allister Miller Street** is the city's main thoroughfare, running south into the central business district (CBD), and lined in parts by colonial administrative buildings which are attractive to look at, but can only be entered on official business. The real hub of the city is **Swazi Market**, at the end of Allister Miller Street on the banks of the Mbabane River. Here you'll find neat rows of curio stalls with a colourful selection of handicrafts and, though prices aren't cheap, you can always haggle. Further into the market, fresh fruit and vegetable stalls make for a tempting browse (though prices here aren't negotiable).

Several blocks west of the market and the CBD, and southwest of the Western Distributor Road, are Mbabane's two major shopping malls, the **Swazi Plaza**, the more upmarket **Mall** and **New Mall** brimming with department stores, banks and restaurants.

Eating, drinking and nightlife

You'll find the ubiquitous *Spur*, *Steers*, and *KFC* in Mbabane, but the town also has a smattering of very good **restaurants**, as well as some lively **bars** and **clubs**.

Restaurants

Continental, Swazi Plaza (☎4043276). Cheap and cheerful pizzas and grills, with some outdoor seating. Closes 6.30pm Mon–Thurs & Sat, about 9.30pm Fri.

Copacabana, Alistair Miller St (☎4040692). Inexpensive Mozambique-influenced meals, with live music some nights.

Indingilizi Gallery & Restaurant, 112 Johnstone St (☎4046213). Very pleasant place to come for lunch. The restaurant is in the gallery's back garden, and serves light, wholesome dishes at reasonable prices.

Kowloon Fast Food, New Mall (☎4048637). Reliable Chinese takeaway, open till 8pm. There's also a branch on Allister Miller St.

La Casserole, Omni Centre, Allister Miller St (☎4046426). Upmarket but good-value restaurant specializing in German dishes, and offering vegetarian selections.

Lourenco Marques, Gilfillian St (☎4043097). Expect to pay upwards of E80 at this excellent Portuguese restaurant. Mouthwatering king-sized prawns are a speciality, and you can buy their explosive *peri-peri* sauce.

Mediterranean, Allister Miller St, just opposite the Cinelux cinema (☎4043212). Despite the name, this is an Indian restaurant serving up moderately priced wonderful dishes in a dark, cavernous setting.

Pizza Pasta, New Mall (☎4048628). Reliable, well-priced Italian fare and good coffee.

Bars, clubs and entertainment

The city's liveliest **bars** are in the *City Inn* hotel and the *Plaza Bar* in the Swazi Plaza complex. The best bet for action into the night is the *West End Girls* **nightclub**, above the *Yemfo* bar, reached down Western Distributor Road or West Street, where a good local band can normally be found at weekends. Most locals think nothing of travelling to happening spots along the eZulwini Valley or in Manzini, and for the best nightlife it's not a bad idea to follow them. Check the daily *Times of Swaziland* for details. **Women travellers** on their own are likely to encounter some harassment in bars and clubs, but the pestering probably won't be aggressive or persistent.

Mbabane has two **cinemas**, the Cinelux (☎4042818), a characterful time-warp near the junction of Gilfillian and Allister Miller streets, and Maxi Movies, in the Swazi Plaza. Their generally mainstream programmes are advertised in the daily papers and the *What's On?* guide.

Listings

Airlines Royal Swazi Airways, Swazi Plaza (☎4043486). Scan Air Charter (☎5184474) and Steffen Air Charter (☎3636531) are private airlines with light aircraft available for chartered flights and some scheduled services. There is no SAA representative in Swaziland.

Banks Most banks are lined along Allister Miller Street or in the Swazi Plaza. Branches include First National, Nedbank, and Standard. Hours are generally Mon–Fri 8.30am–2.30pm, Sat 8.30–11.00am.The best time to bank is a weekday morning.

Bookshops Websters, at 120 Johnstone St and in the New Mall, has the best general selection. There is also SNA newsagent (the Swazi equivalent of South Africa's CNA) in the Swazi Plaza.

Car rental Avis (☎5186226) and Imperial (☎5184393) are located at Matsapha Airport, and there is another Imperial agent at the Engen service station at the junction of the By-Pass Road and Main Road. Cheaper than either company is Affordable Car Hire (☎4049136) in the Swazi Plaza.

Embassies South Africa, New Mall (☎4044651); UK, Allister Miller St (☎4042581); USA, Warner St (☎4046441).

Emergencies Fire ☎4043333; Police ☎999 or ☎4042221.

Hospitals Mbabane Clinic Service (private), St Michael St (☎4042423); Government Hospital (public), Usutu Rd (☎4042111).

Internet facilities The *Internet Café* (*box31@icafe.co.sz*, or check out the Web site at *www.iafrica.sz.icafe*), at the Omni Centre, opposite the cinema on Allister Miller St. This isn't really a café – it's a room in a business centre – but it does offer access to the Internet, and is Swaziland's only public Internet facility.

Laundries Swaziland Steam Laundry & Dry, Allister Miller St, and in the Swazi Plaza.

Library Mbabane Library (☎4042633).

Pharmacy Mbabane Pharmacy, Allister Miller St; Philani Pharmacy, in the Swazi Plaza; and Green Cross, in The Mall.

Post office The main post office is on Warner St, and there's a smaller one in the Swazi Plaza. Mon–Fri 8am–4pm, Sat 8–11am.

Taxi Mbabane Taxis ☎4043084.

Tour operators Swazi Trails (☎ & fax 4162180, *tours@swazitrail.co.za*) run tours to the Lobamba royal village, game parks, nature reserves, craft centres, local villages and even a local *sangoma* (healer). They can also arrange horse-riding, hiking, mountain-biking and white-water rafting. Woza Nawe (☎4045218) is a smaller operation, offering more atmosphere-oriented trips to traditional homesteads and scenic spots.

The eZulwini Valley and Lobamba

Immediately southeast of Mbabane, the smooth, new, four-lane **MR3** winds downhill in a series of sweeping curves, made hazardous by crawling lorries and reckless minibus taxis, and then shoots off southeast towards Manzini. Unless you're bound directly for Manzini and beyond, however, the older and quieter **MR103** is the route to follow, linking most of the main sights of the scenic **eZulwini Valley** (Place of Heaven). Nestled within it are two of Swaziland's biggest tourist draws: the royal residences of **Lobamba** and **Ludzidzini**. Since the Sixties, a succession of casinos, strip joints, hotels and caravan parks have sprung up here, all catering for mainly South African tourists. Now that gambling is legal in South Africa, however, the number of pleasure-seekers has dropped and business is no longer booming. Behind the noise of the slot machines and karaoke, beautiful mountains soar and, stretching along the west side of the road, the lush **Mlilwane Wildlife Sanctuary** offers welcome respite, as well as a wide variety of wildlife.

Malagwane Hill and the eZulwini Valley Road

Soon after leaving Mbabane, the valley road begins its giddy descent down **Malagwane Hill**. At the top of the hill is a turn to the left for the elegant *Mountain Inn* (☎4042781; ⑨), wonderfully located and a great **place to stay**. The adjoining *Friar Tuck* **restaurant** is a bit dark, but serves up reliable buffet lunches and à la carte dinners. An alternative is *Kapola Guest House* (☎4043449; ④), located at the bottom of the hill, a large family home with four doubles and a pleasant breakfast balcony.

NCWALA AND UMHLANGA

The most sacred of Swaziland's ceremonies, with its timing determined by royal astrologers, **Ncwala** celebrates kingship, national unity and the first fruits of the new year. Around the time of the new moon in November, a group of selected men journey east to the ancestral home of the Ngwane on the shores of the Indian Ocean to collect foam from the waves. While they are there, the Ncwala ceremony begins, with songs and rituals performed until the afternoon of the December full moon, when the six days of the full Ncwala begin. Young Swazi men meet at **Lobamba** and are then sent away to gather branches of the *lusekwane* tree, from which they build a bower for the king. Warriors gather and sing songs that can only be sung at this time, while the king dances with them and eats the first fruits of the harvest. On the sixth day, objects representing the previous year are burnt on a massive bonfire, and prayers are offered to Swazi ancestors, asking them to put out the fire with rain. The ceremony ends amidst raucous singing, dancing and feasting. Visitors are allowed to attend most of Ncwala, but photography is prohibited during certain times (a free permit is also required; contact the Government Information Service, PO Box 338, Mbabane), so be sure to ask first to avoid having your camera smashed.

The **Umhlanga** is a **fertility dance** which gets its name from the large reeds gathered by young women and brought to the residence of the Queen Mother to repair her *kraal*, usually in late August or early September. The sixth and seventh days are the most spectacular: this is when you can watch the young women, dressed in elaborate and carefully coded costumes, sing and dance before the king and Queen Mother at Lobamba, giving the king an opportunity to pick **a new wife**. The former king, Sobhuza II, invariably plucked a new mate from the bevy of young beauties, but Mswati III has proved more restrained – no one has been chosen by him in the last few years.

As the highway begins to level out at the bottom of the valley, the first main exit leads to the old eZulwini Valley road, the **MR103**, which runs parallel to the mountains on the southern side of the valley. Shortly after joining this road is the *Mgenule* (☎4161041; ③), which has some rather run-down **self-catering** accommodation, offering rooms with kitchens but no cooking utensils. Next door, there's a pleasant and inexpensive tandoori **restaurant** with long, flexible opening hours that change pretty much according to demand.

Tea Road

Just over a kilometre beyond the *Mgenule* is a road to the left, signposted "Phangisa Gearbox & Brake Service". Following this will take you over the new highway and onto the **Tea Road** (so called because it's the route to the Tea estates), a truly spectacular thirty-minute drive into the mountains, ending up roughly 8km from Manzini, where it joins the MR3. Stay alert if you decide to get out of your car to take some photos, as there have been reports of gangs stealing from cars left unsecured on the roadside. Just as importantly, take care if the weather is wet, as the road can get slippery.

Opposite the turn-off to the Tea Road, safe, if unremarkable, **camping** and spartan rondavels are available at the *Timbali Caravan Park* (☎4161156; ①–②). Down the same turn-off as the *Timbali* you'll find one of Swaziland's swankiest **restaurants**, the *Calabash* (☎4161187), which serves an excellent range of fresh seafood and specializes in German, Swiss and Austrian dishes. Further up this road, *Martin's Bar & Disco* becomes pleasantly raucous and drunken at weekends, and if you're in the mood for partying will doubtless deliver a night to remember.

Continuing along the MR103 valley road, you'll soon come to **Cuddle Puddle** (daily 6am–6pm; E5), a beautifully warm pool of mineral waters surrounded by tropical vegetation and perfect for a dip on cool days – or even when it's raining. Immediately beyond this lie three *Sun* **hotels** offering their usual blend of comfort and anonymity.

The *Royal Swazi* (☎4161001; ⑨) is the smartest of the lot, with a fine swimming pool, a golf course, a good selection of restaurants and plenty of upmarket bars, as well as a swanky casino and a tatty adult cinema. Swazi Trails (see p.667) have an office in the hotel lobby. The other *Sun* options offer slightly better value: the *Lugogo* (☎4161550; ⑦) is blessed with a well-priced buffet that is particularly enticing at breakfast, and the *Ezulwini* (☎4161201; ⑦) has a beer garden open on Tuesday nights and serving the local Sibebe brew. In the same direction, just beyond the filling station and past the *Sun* hotels, the *1st Horse* **restaurant** (☎4161137) serves up very good Chinese meals and has a large bar. Opposite the filling station is an extended line of **craft stalls**, commonly signposted by one or two tour buses drawn up alongside. This is as good a place as any to find mainstream Swazi crafts such as wood and soapstone carvings, though you'll have to haggle to get the prices down to sensible levels.

The Mantenga road

More exclusive and individual crafts, such as fabrics, artworks and better carvings, can be found at nearby **Mantenga Crafts**, an attractive purpose-built village of craft shops signposted about a kilometre further along the road. After running past the unremarkable self-catering **chalets** (sleeping four to six) of *Smoky Mountain Village* (☎4161291; ③), the road leads through Mantenga Crafts to the beautifully located *Mantenga Lodge* (☎4161049, fax 4162516, *mantenga@iafrica.sz*; ④), with cosy chalets, for two to four people each, nestled on the hill rise and a good bar and **restaurant** with especially good views.

Keep going along this road for 1km, and you'll come to **Mantenga Nature Reserve** (daily 6am–6pm; small entry fee), which incorporates Swaziland's most authentic, and as yet unnamed **cultural village**. This open-air, living museum replicates a nineteenth-century Swazi homestead with sixteen beehive huts, all built in traditional style using wooden frames joined by leather strips, reed thatch, cow-dung and termite-hill earth. Cattle and goats wander about, and there are often demonstrations of traditional activities and crafts. The guides, who'll take you round on tours (free), are enthusiastic and informative, and you can even **stay** (☎4161013 or 4161151; ①) in one of three beehive huts if you're prepared to rough it, as there's no bedding, no electricity, and you cook on a campfire; the best place to get your supplies from is Mbabane. Although the cultural village is the main draw, the rest of the reserve shouldn't be ignored, as there are some pleasant **hikes** and a beautiful **picnic** and **swimming** spot with views of the ninety-five-metre **Mantenga Falls**, a fifteen-minute walk from the village along a jeep track.

The royal villages of Lobamba and Ludzidzini

Some 20km south of Mbabane, along the MR103, **LOBAMBA** was originally built in 1830 for King Sobhuza I, and was the royal *kraal* of Sobhuza II. The Houses of Parliament are situated here, and must be one of the few in the world to have cattle grazing undisturbed in surrounding fields. Next door, fascinating exhibitions of Swazi life can be found in the **National Museum** (Mon–Fri 8am–1pm & 2–3.45pm, Sat & Sun 10am–1pm & 2–3.45pm; small entry fee). They provide a helpful potted history of the country, with displays of cultural artefacts and wonderful old photographs of Swazi people and royalty, of Manzini and Mbabane when they were one-horse towns, of sweaty British administrators in full colonial regalia attending functions of the Swazi royal house, and much more. A natural history wing was also opened recently. The museum is the base of the **National Trust Commission**, PO Box 100, (Mon–Fri 8am–1pm & 2–3.45pm, Sat & Sun 10am–1pm & 2–3.45pm; ☎4161151, fax 4161875, *mantenga@sntc.org.sz*), which handles bookings for the Malolotja and Mlawula nature reserves (see p.675 and p.677).

CHOOSING THE KING

Swazi monarchs are always men of the **Dlamini** family, and over the course of their reign marry a number of women who are carefully selected from different clans in the name of national unity. In theory, the king marries women from increasingly important families as he goes along, which means that the son of the last wife is always a strong contender for the succession. In practice, however, other wives with older sons are also in with a chance, and this ensures turbulence and power-struggles every time the king dies. After his death, the royal council, or *liqoqo*, selects the new **Queen Mother**, who rules as regent until her son is old enough to take charge. She usually has to work hard to ensure her position against ambitious uncles. The main advantage of this awkward process is that by the time the new king is old enough to rule, he and his mother have generally garnered enough support for him to do so effectively.

Outside the museum stands a life-size re-creation of a traditional Swazi homestead. Remarkably, given their size, these huts are portable. Across the road is **King Sobhuza II Memorial Park**, a peaceful open space dedicated to the much-loved late king.

Lobamba's **Somhlolo stadium** is the country's venue for major events and football matches, which are usually highly entertaining. For a few emalangeni on a Sunday afternoon, you can treat yourself to violence-free games of occasional great skill, with a good-humoured and vocal crowd. Consult the local *Swazi Observer* and *Times of Swaziland* for details, or ask almost any male Swazi.

On the other side of the MR103 from Lobamba, the village of **LUDZIDZINI** is the royal *kraal* of the present king, Mswati III, and the Queen Mother. Unlike Lobamba, Ludzidzini cannot be visited or even photographed at all except during Ncwala (around New Year) and Umhlanga (end of Aug/early Sept) – at these times, you'd be mad to miss the place (see p.668).

Mlilwane Wildlife Sanctuary

A good alternative to staying in Mbabane or on the eZulwini strip is to head straight for the **Mlilwane Wildllife Sanctuary** (daily dawn–dusk; medium entry fee). The name Mlilwane refers to the "little fire" that appears on occasion when lightning strikes the granite mountains. With its relaxed, easy-going atmosphere and rich landscapes, this is one of Swaziland's most popular reserves, so it's a good idea to book ahead if you intend to stay overnight.

Mlilwane's **wildlife** is herbivorous in the main, including giraffe, zebra and bountiful numbers of antelope, but also the odd crocodile. Over 100km of road enable you to drive through the park to view game. Alternatively, guided walks and drives are available through the park office at the main rest camp; best of the self-guided **walking trails** is the Macobane Hill Trail, a gentle, three-hour hike through the mountains. The office can supply maps for all these. There are also **mountain-bike tours** (E45 per hour) and **horseback trails** (E200 per hour), both guided and both fairly relaxed ways of taking in the park's attractions. If you're feeling less energetic, you can pass the time watching **hippos** wallowing in the hippo pool, overlooked by the *Hippo Haunt* restaurant at the main rest camp. The hippos are fed every day at 3pm.

Practicalities

To get to **Mlilwane** take the turning from the eZulwini Valley road, signposted off the MR103 about a kilometre beyond the turn-off to Ludzidzini; from here it's 3.5km along a dirt road to the entrance gate. For **accommodation**, the park's main rest camp, about 1.5km from the gate, offers a variety of **self-catering** options, including a campsite, dorms (both ①), traditional beehive huts (②) and en-suite wooden huts (③), along with communal ablution facilities and a swimming pool. Situated in the nothern part of the sanctuary is *Sondzela* **backpackers' lodge** (④), a friendly place now firmly established on the backpacking circuit, while on a hilltop surrounded by woodland with fantastic views over valley and plains is *Reilly's Rock Hilltop Lodge* (⑤), offering **full board** for those seeking a more up-market experience. **Bookings** for all options should be made through Royal Swaziland Big Game Parks in Mbabane (see p.667). The only place to eat is at the inexpensive *Hippo Haunt* **restaurant**, at the main rest camp, where there's also a bar. For those who don't have their own **transport**, a shuttle bus (free) runs between *Sondzela*, the main rest camp and the entrance gate, and does a pick-up once a day from the Swazi Trails office at the *Royal Swazi Sun*.

Through the Malkerns Valley

Continuing on the road towards Manzini, a turn to the southwest roughly 5km beyond the road to Mlilwane (beside a row of shops and a petrol station) will take you to the scenic, pineapple-growing **Malkerns Valley**. There's a wonderful **restaurant** here, *Malandela's* (☎5283115; closed Mon), which serves hearty English cooking in a stylish setting with soothing views of the adjoining fields and the mountains in the distance. Next door, Tishweshwe Crafts has an enticing collection of **local handicrafts**, while the Gone Rural workshop makes and sells woven mats and baskets as part of a project developing traditional local handicrafts. A little further on, the village of **Malkerns** itself (which derives its name from a turn-of-the-century trader called Malcolm Kerns Stuart) holds few attractions, unless you have a particular interest in pineapple canning.

TED REILLY AND THE SWAZI NATURE CONSERVATION STORY

Swaziland owes the creation and survival of three of its major wildlife sanctuaries – Mlilwane, Mkhaya and Hlane – to **Ted Reilly**, who was born in Mlilwane in 1938, the son of a British Anglo-Boer War soldier who had stayed on. As Reilly was growing up, Swazi wildlife and its natural habitats were coming under serious threat from poachers and commercial farmers. In 1959, Reilly lobbied the colonial government to set aside land for parks but was defeated by farmers who wanted the land for commercial agriculture. Undeterred, he turned his Mlilwane estate into a park anyway, and set about cultivating a relationship with **King Sobhuza II**, who was having trouble himself with poachers at the royal estate in Hlane. After Swazi independence, Sobhuza became much more powerful, and Reilly's relationship with him lent weight to his nature conservation efforts.

Despite rickety finances, the **Mlilwane Wildlife Sanctuary** opened in 1963, and the re-stocking and reintroduction of species has continued ever since (today the reserve is ten times the size of the original sanctuary). Meanwhile, Sobhuza asked Reilly to help stamp out poaching at Hlane. Reilly's approach was to get tough, and the resulting shootouts earned him the praise of some, but the enmity of many. Matters came to a head in 1992, when, with the help of the South African Police Endangered Species Protection Unit, Reilly tracked down a poaching unit that had been operating in Mkhaya. In the ensuing gun-fight, one poacher was killed and another paralysed. Criticism of Reilly's tactics intensified.

Reilly's dependence on royal connections has also generated controversy: critics claim it has prevented the development of a single parks board and a participatory, grass-roots involvement in conservation that is the key to long-term success. Some also assert that Reilly subordinates wildlife management principles to the needs of the tourist industry. Reilly's answer to his critics is simply to point to the three game parks his company runs. It's a hard argument to defeat – without Reilly, the parks would not exist, and Swaziland and its visitors would be much the poorer for it.

Continuing on the road past Malkerns takes you to **Luyengo**, and then either to **Bhunya** or **Mankayane**, but a sharp left at the T-junction in Malkerns will bring you back onto the signposted Manzini road. Before you get to this junction however, there are several more **craft shops** lined along the road: Swazi Candles (daily 9am–1pm) sells a bewildering array of brightly patterned wax candles; Baobab Batik, 2km further along, sells all manner of colourful batiks. Beside this is *Nyanza Cottage* (☎5283090; ④), a B&B on a working farm linked to Nyanza Horse Trails, who offer cross-country and mountain rides lasting from half-an-hour to a whole day. If your appetite for crafts is still not satisfied, carry along to the Manzini road; 2km after the junction is the **Bethany Mission**, a collection of craft workshops selling fine woven cotton rugs.

Manzini

MANZINI is Swaziland's largest town and its commercial hub. Almost all the country's industrial and commercial sector is based in or around here, and the city is dominated by office blocks and malls that obscure the few attractive edifices. With a rising crime rate and an atmosphere far less relaxed than Mbabane, Manzini would be an eminently missable place were it not for its outstanding **market**, which operates every day except Sunday, on the corner of Mhlakuvane and Mancishane streets.

Much of Manzini's market is given over to the practicalities of life, such as fresh fruit, household goods and traditional medicines, but there's an upper section that spills onto the steps below and is devoted to crafts and fabrics. The **crafts** selection is bigger, more varied and much better value than any other market in Swaziland, while the **fabrics**, which are Zimbabwean, Zairean, and Mozambican, cannot be easily obtained anywhere else in the country.

Just north of the market, on Ngwane Street, stands **The Bhunu**, one of Manzini's new shopping malls, and handy for shops and restaurants. **The Hub**, south of the mar-

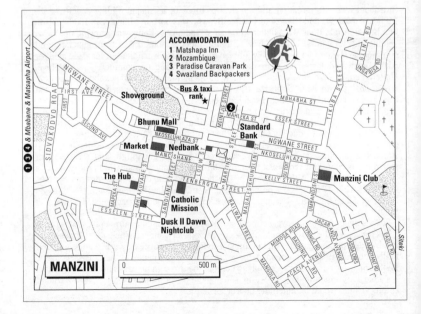

ket, on Mhlakuvane Street, is smarter and has a good supermarket and several restaurants and takeaways. Manzini's only other point of interest is its original **Catholic mission**, an elegant stone building (not open to casual visitors) opposite the new cathedral on Sandlane Street (parallel to Mhlakuvane Street).

Practicalities

Buses from all over the country and South Africa pull in at Manzini's busy main bus station at the end of Louw Street, just north of Ngwane Street. **Matsapha Airport** (☎5186155) lies 8km west of the city centre; if you're arriving here, you'll need to take a **taxi** into central Manzini. The centre itself is small enough to walk around.

Manzini has a limited selection of **places to stay**. Near the bus station, on the corner of Meintjies and Mahleka streets, the *Mozambique* (☎5052489, fax 5052586; ②) offers tiny rooms with paper-thin walls, but has a friendly bar and an excellent restaurant. Seven kilometres west of the city, on the road to Malkerns and eZulwini, is a recently upgraded backpackers' **hostel**, *Swaziland Backpackers* (☎5187255; ①), which operates as the overnight stop for the Baz Bus, and consequently attracts a fair amount of passing travellers stopping off to check out Swaziland for a couple of days. Nearby is the motel-like *Matshapa Inn* (☎5186888; ③), and a sparse **campsite**, *Paradise Caravan Park* (☎5184935; ①).

As well as the *Mozambique's* restaurant, other good **places to eat** in town include *Gil Vicente*, in the Ilanga Centre, Martin St (☎5053874; closed Mon), which serves up tasty Portuguese dishes; the *Mongolian*, Villiers St, where you'll find the best Chinese food in town; and the *Fontana de Trevi Pizzeria*, The Hub, Mhlakuvane St. The best **nightlife** is found at the *Dusk II Dawn* nightclub, Mhlakuvane St, which often attracts bands from South Africa at weekends and lives up to its name with some no-holds-barred Swazi partying.

PIGGS PEAK AND THE NORTHWEST

The highveld of **Piggs Peak** and the **northwest** is unquestionably the most beautiful region of Swaziland, with rolling hills perfect for hiking, countless sparkling streams, a sprinkling of waterfalls and, to round things off, some wonderful accommodation where you can relax after appreciating it all.

Approaches to Piggs Peak

Most visitors to the northwest enter Swaziland after going through the Kruger National Park (see p.573), but Piggs Peak is only 64km north of Mbabane and easily reached from there, too. The most spectacular – and rugged – entrance into the country is via the Bulembu road from Barberton in Mpumalanga (see p.566), which passes through Bulembu village on the way to Piggs Peak.

From Jeppe's Reef/Matsamo border

From the **Jeppe's Reef/Matsamo border** (8am–4pm), the road on the Swazi side is good all the way to Piggs Peak. Some 25km south of the border on this road is a good **place to stay**, the *Protea Piggs Peak Hotel & Casino* (☎4371104; ⑤), set in thousands of acres of mountainous pine forest. Despite the monolithic appearance of the hotel's exterior, the rooms have fabulous views, and there's an inviting swimming pool with a bar in the middle, plus a good buffet **restaurant**. You can buy hand-spun mohair products in the hotel lobby as well as from their source nearby.

Travel another 3km to reach a sign to the right pointing you to the private **Phophonyane Nature Reserve** (☎4371319), which is five slow kilometres away from the road. The reserve is small, but carefully laid-out **trails** ensure that there is plenty to see, including the Phopanyane waterfall on the reserve's eastern side. The vegetation is subtropical and attracts hundreds of colourful **bird species**. Animals include mongooses, bushbabies, otters and numerous snakes, but all are hard to spot. This is one of the most beautiful **places to stay** in Swaziland, offering cottages for four to six (⑤) with private kitchens and gardens, and safari tents sleeping two (④) next to the Phopanyane River, with a communal kitchen and washing facilities. If you can't afford to stay, it's still worth stopping here for a short hike in the reserve and a meal in its secluded, mid-priced **restaurant**. The pool, although chillingly cold, is cleverly blended into the rocks beside the tumbling river and has one of the world's great locations, looking out onto endless mountains and surrounded by luxuriant vegetation.

A few kilometres south of Phophonyane, 1km north of Piggs Peak, the turn-off to Kuthuleni is the start of a beautifully scenic fifty-kilometre drive along a good dirt road to **Bhalekane**. There isn't much in Bhalekane (except a prison), but you can proceed from here to Tshaneni and the **northeast** (see p.676), or head south through fairly remote territory to Mafutseni and then Manzini.

From Bulembu

The road from Barberton in Mpumalanga, to Piggs Peak via **Bulembu border post** (8am–4pm), is briefly tarred out of Barberton, but soon deteriorates as it passes through some of the most rugged country imaginable, with the road near the crossing in particularly poor shape. Looking up, you can see the Barberton–Havelock cableway, which carries asbestos from the nearby Havelock mine to South Africa. Once in Swaziland, the road soon passes through Bulembu, with Piggs Peak a further 20km away.

Piggs Peak

PIGGS PEAK, a small forestry town straggled along the main road, was named after a French prospector called William Pigg, who discovered gold nearby in 1884, where it was mined until the site was exhausted in 1954. Apart from the attractive surrounding countryside, there's nothing much to see here, but if you're heading to Mallotja Nature Reserve this is a good place to stock up on supplies.

The town's **bus station** and **market** are near the Total garage at the northern end of town, where there is also a small shopping centre with a **supermarket**. There are a couple of **banks** in the centre of town, but they are unused to foreign transactions, so either summon your patience or hold out until Mbabane. For an **overnight stay**, the *Highland Inn* (☎4371144; ③), in a pleasant colonial building on the southern edge of town, offers simple but comfortable rooms. Inside, the *Woodcutter's Den* **restaurant** serves up steaks and other fleshy fare at fairly reasonable prices. For a quick snack, *The Ranch*, in the town's shopping centre, dishes out fast food, while the *Pholani* **bar** nearby does plenty of trade, rocking until late on weekends.

On to Malolotja Nature Reserve

Driving south, you soon leave the pine plantations behind and pass into rolling highveld grassland, peppered with rural dwellings, with the stretch across the Nkomati River valley a particularly beautiful one. Alongside the road are curio stalls, often staffed by young children dressed in leaves to attract your attention. Also along this road is evidence of the construction work on the large **Maguga dam** project on the Komati River, which will radically alter the scenery of the river valley through flooding by the time it is completed early in the twenty-first century.

About 30km from Piggs Peak, just after Nkhaba, you'll reach the entrance to the Malolotja Nature Reserve. The main road continues south from here to join the Ngwenya–Mbabane road at Motshane (see p.676), 20km further on.

Malolotja Nature Reserve

Swaziland's least tourist-trampled park, the easy-going **Malolotja Nature Reserve** (daily: summer 6am–6.30pm; winter 6.30am–6pm; small entry fee; enquiries ☎4424241) offers awesome scenery and some of the finest hiking in southern Africa. This is a place to come for rugged, wild nature and a real sense of tranquillity, rather than for game spotting. The mountains here, among the oldest in the world (3.6 billion years old), are covered in grassland and graced by a myriad of streams and waterfalls, including the 95-metre-high **Malolotja Falls**.

Nearly three hundred species of **bird** are to be found in Malolotja, with an impressive colony of the rare bald ibis just by the waterfalls. You'll have to look harder for **game**, although wildebeest, blesbok and impala are often visible, and there are leopards and two very retiring elephants lurking somewhere in the gaping tracts of mountain and valley; in the friendly spirit of the reserve, a leaflet is handed out on arrival asking hikers to help the park's research by reporting any signs of the elephants, or of the rare eland introduced a few years ago. There is also the **Ngwenya Mine**, the world's most ancient at 43,000 years old, where workers once dug for specularite and haematite, which were then used as cosmetics and for religious rituals. To visit you must book a **guide** at least one night beforehand, although there's always a guide on duty at weekends, at an entry point at the south of the reserve near to Ngwenya Glass which is open between 8am and 4pm (see p.676). Note that this gate gives access to the mine only. Nearby, the **Forbes Reef Gold Mine** can be visited alone, but you'll have to take care on the slippery banks; you can find it using the map you get on arrival at the park entrance.

Malolotja's small network of roads pass some fine viewpoints and picnic sites, but to really savour this park's rugged wilderness – and see its waterfalls – you'll need to hike. A variety of **hiking trails** are laid out in the reserve, from easy half-day excursions to seven-day marathons, with accommodation available en route (see below).

Practicalities

Brochures and **maps** are available from the reserve's **office**, just inside the entrance gate. The office also issues permits for Hawane Dam Nature Reserve – useful if you're planning on heading there next. Hikers would do well to ask for the free *Hiking and Backpacking Guide*, which gives helpful information on hiking in the reserve.

Accommodation should be booked in advance through the National Trust Commission (see p.669). The main rest camp (①) has fifteen tent sites with *braai* areas but not much wind shelter, and hot water in a communal bath area. There is also an A-frame **chalet** (①), which sleeps up to six people, and five well-located log **cabins** (②), which can also house up to six people each. A small shop at the entrance sells basic **provisions**, but you would do better to stock up in Piggs Peak or Mbabane. Twenty **campsites**, with no facilities, are scattered around the reserve for those attempting longer hikes: you'll need to bring all your own equipment, including a cooker, as no fires are permitted.

If you're on a long hike during the summer, be prepared for blisteringly hot days. Temperatures drop dramatically in winter, when nights can be freezing.

Hawane Dam Nature Reserve

A few kilometres south of Malolotja, on the Mbabane road, lies the **Hawane Dam Nature Reserve** (☎4424241; Mon–Fri free, Sat & Sun E10), a small area around the northern end of the Hawane Dam protecting part of the Black Umbuluzi River wetlands. Hawane's main attraction is its wealth of **birdlife**, and there's a very helpful trail for bird-watching.

A little further on is **Hawane African Adventure Trails** (☎ & fax 4043375), sign-posted down a track, a good option if you fancy exploring the attractive surrounding countryside on horseback. They have a range of ponies and horses for trails lasting anything between a couple of hours and a week, as well as a base-camp with around half-a-dozen comfortable bee-hive **huts** for two (③), which are available even if you're not riding.

Back on the Mbabane road, *Hawane Park* (☎4044477; huts ①, chalets ②) is a simple and uninspiring resort looking back to Hawane Dam, though it does have a cosy bar and some soothing eastern views of spacious grassy plains dotted with gentle hills.

Ngwenya

The road from Piggs Peak meets the MR3 at the small settlement of **Motshane**, between the Ngwenya/Oshoek border post and Mbabane. A kilometre west of Motshane along this road is the Ngwenya Glass factory, where of one of Swaziland's best-known exports, **Ngwenya glass**, is made. Their products, which range from attractive wine glasses to endless trinkets in the shape of rotund animals, are made from recycled glass and are produced by highly skilled workers, and it's well worth stopping here just to see them blowing and crafting the glass from the viewing balcony above the roaring furnaces. The adjoining gift shop and **café** (Mon–Fri 7.30am–4pm, Sat & Sun 9am–4pm) are usually swamped by coach-loads of adoring tourists, who can further satisfy their craving for crafts a little further along from the factory at **Endlotane Studios** (Mon–Fri 8am–4.30pm, Sat–Sun 9am–5pm), where large and colourful tapestries are painstakingly woven from mohair wool spun on the premises. Nearby is an entrance to Malolotja Nature Reserve allowing access to **Ngwenya Mine** (see p.675).

THE NORTHEAST

Northeast Swaziland is dominated by sugar plantations that stretch far into the distance, shimmering from the constant water spray, wreaking havoc with the water table and leaving many locals without, but earning the country valuable foreign exchange. Three large tracts of bush – **Hlane**, **Mlawula** and **Mbuluzi** – have been preserved as wildlife and nature reserves, and these are the main attractions for visitors to this region. Mlawula takes in a small portion of the **Lubombo Mountains**, which run in a continuous line from north to south and form a natural boundary with Mozambique.

The most direct and obvious route to the reserves from Mbabane is to follow the signposted and tarred **Siteki road** for 100km. The **northern route** is a little over twice as long and is part gravel, but makes for a far more spectacular journey. Travel north to **Piggs Peak** from Mbabane, and turn right at the **Bhalekane** turn-off towards Bhalkane, roughly 1km later.

Tshaneni

The gravel road from Piggs Peak passes through some fabulous scenery before eventually winding up at the sugar town of **TSHANENI**. There's one **hotel** here, the *Impala Arms* (☎3131244; ②), where the rooms are plain but comfortable; the bar, which has a pool table, is filled with exuberant Swazi at weekends. If you need supplies, Tshaneni's Score **supermarket** will come in handy, and there is a Caltex **garage** nearby for fuel.

The **Mananga border post** (8am–6pm) is 5km north of here, from where the road leads to Komatipoort (see p.568). Heading south, however, the next town you'll meet is bougainvillea-festooned **Mhlume**, and 20km further on is a junction at Maphiveni, where a left turn to the north takes you to the **Lomahasha/Namaacha border post** with Mozambique (7am–4.45pm), another 20km away, while a right turn followed almost immediately by a signposted left takes you to Mbuluzi Game Reserve and Mlawula Nature Reserve.

Mbuluzi Game Reserve

Privately owned and little-known, **Mbuluzi** (daily 8am–5pm; E10 per person, E20 per vehicle; ☎3838861, *mbuluzi@iafrica.sz*) is about 1km off the Manzini–Lomahasha road, and straddles the road to Mlawula. It's set in classic lowveld bush, which means that it's hot in the summer, and filled with thorn trees. Currently the park is being restocked with game, including hippo and giraffe, which you can view in your own vehicle – as long as it's 4WD. From the park entrance you can rent vehicles for E150 per day, and hire guides for a negotiable amount. The absence of predators in Mbuluzi's southern portion means that you can walk along a network of **trails** in this section.

Mbuluzi's self-catering **accommodation** (⑤), for three- to eight people, is its finest feature: three large and comfortable lodges with verandahs overlook the Mlwawula stream, whose luxuriant vegetation attracts birds and animals which you can watch from the verandahs.

Mlawula Nature Reserve

The main attraction of the **Mlawula Nature Reserve** (daily dawn–dusk; E10 per person, E5 per vehicle) is the section of the **Lubombo Mountains** that runs along its eastern border and provides fantastic views of both Swaziland and the western fringes of Mozambique. Unique species of ironwood trees and cycads grow on the slopes, which can be easily hiked along a **trail** marked by a series of beacons, each of which can only be identified once you have reached the one before it (try not to find yourself searching for these at dusk). The trails wend their way around the river heading for caves, a waterfall and a rhino pool (although there are none left), and vary in length from two to eight hours.

The Mlawula stream and more substantial Mbuluzi River both flow through some spectacular valleys in this reserve, and early Stone Age tools over one million years old have been found along their beds. **Antelope**, **zebra** and **wildebeest** congregate near the water, but so do **crocodiles**, so resist the temptation to swim. Enquire at the gate for feeding times at the **vulture restaurant**, where you can watch the critters feeding on recently deceased carcasses.

Practicalities

Buses from Manzini travel to the Mlawula Nature Reserve once a day very early in the morning. To get here by **car**, continue past the Mbuluzi Reserve for a few kilometres until you see a sign pointing to the Mlawula Reserve on your right. You can pick up a daunting range of leaflets at the park gate, but no supplies, so stock up beforehand.

Accommodation should be booked through the National Trust Commission, in the National Museum at Lobamba (see p.669). Overnight **camping** on the trail has not been permitted since the camping hut was burnt down, apparently by Mozambican border-hoppers, but there is a shaded campsite (①) in the Siphiso River valley and a tented camp (①) where you can also use your own tent. The camp has one of the finest open-air bathrooms in southern Africa, consisting of a donkey-boiler, firewood, water and galvanized-iron washtubs, with a stunning view that looks west over the reserve and beyond, making it perfectly positioned for sunset. More comfortably (but less beautifully), you can stay in a **self-catering cottage** nearby (③).

Hlane Royal National Park

Some 67km northeast of Manzini is **Hlane Royal National Park** (daily dawn–dusk; small entry fee; ☎4044541), the largest of Swaziland's parks. Formerly a private royal hunting ground, the main attraction here is the presence of big game, including **elephant**, **rhino**, **lion**, **leopard** and **cheetah**. Hlane is also one of the best parks in southern Africa to view elephants and rhino **on foot** – an unforgettable experience – in the company of a guide (E15 per hour). These two species are in the northern area of the park, which you can also visit in your own vehicle, with or without a guide, and rhino-sighting is virtually guaranteed. Other animals in this section include giraffe, zebra and waterbuck.

Various **southern enclosures** contain the lion, cheetah and leopard, along with some more elephant and rhino; walking around here is out of the question, but you can go on a drive with a guide in your own car. There's also a **minibus** (E80) if you don't have your own transport. Although the enclosures guarantee lion sightings, the animals are well habituated to vehicles and look thoroughly bored by the whole experience – a pity, as the presence of lions in the country is meant to be the source of great pride to the Swazis, not least because they are the symbol of the king.

Practicalities
The **entrance** to Hlane is roughly 4km south of Simunye, off the Manzini–Lomahasha road. **Buses** between Manzini and Simunye stop at the park gate.

Hlane has two **accommodation** options, both of which must be **booked** through Royal Swazi Big Game Parks (see p.667) in Mbabane. The *Ndlovu* camp, near the gate and the various game enclosures, offers self-catering rondavels (①) and camping spots (①), but no electricity. Paraffin lamps are provided, and cooking is on an open fire. Near the campsite there is a large watering hole where you can sit and watch animals, including rhino, elephant and giraffe, coming to drink – it gets particularly busy at sunrise and sunset. The self-catering *Bhubesi* camp, with its three comfortable stone cottages (①) overlooking a dry river, is 18km from Ndlovu along a dirt track, and feels much more remote, though the cottages here have electricity.

Siteki
Perched spectacularly on a hillside and once the gateway to a busy border post with Mozambique, **SITEKI**, just over 30km south of Mlawula Nature Reserve, is a fairly lively regional centre. Although the border has now been closed for some years, Siteki remains busy, with a **bus station** that operates frequent services to Manzini, a colourful **market**, and a number of lively restaurants along the main street. Next door to the *Siteki* hotel, off the main road on the way out of town, is the headquarters of Litiko Letinyanga (☎3434512), a traditional healing organization, run by Dr Nhlavana Maseko, which seeks to improve the credibility of traditional healing with Western medical institutions. You may be able to arrange a session with a traditional healer, but you'll have to phone beforehand (ask for Betty).

There's only one **place to stay** – the *Siteki* (☎3434126; ③), which is nice enough, though the rooms feel a bit spartan. Downstairs, the hotel **restaurant** serves steaks and other meat dishes, and there's a great bar attached, which is popular with locals and gets very lively at weekends.

At the beginning of the road ascending to the town, you'll pass through a foot-and-mouth disease control **checkpoint**; the guards only check you on the way out, to confiscate any meat products that you might have tucked away.

THE SOUTH

Approaching Swaziland from one of its border crossings in the south is an excellent idea if you're heading on to Kruger National Park. The scenery, particularly along the drive from **Mahamba** to Manzini through the **Grand Valley**, is really superb, and the road passes near most of the historical sites of the Swazi royal house. The south is also home to the **Mkhaya Nature Reserve**, Swaziland's most upmarket reserve and a sanctuary for the rare black rhino.

From Mahamba to Manzini

The **Mahamba border crossing** (7am–10pm) is the nearest to Piet Retief in South Africa. Mahamba means "the runaways", which refers to nineteenth-century pretenders to the royal throne who ran here twice to escape retribution. The nearest major town is **NHLANGANO**, only 16km from the border. Nhlangano (the name means "meeting place", in honour of the meeting of British and Swazi monarchs George V and Sobhuza II in 1947) is a good place to change money and to catch **buses** to Mbabane and Manzini.

The town also has a couple of decent **places to stay**: the lively *Phoenix* (☎2078488; ②) on the main street offers en-suite rooms, while the upmarket *Nhlangano Sun* (☎2078211; ⑤), designed to resemble a ski resort, lies off a signposted turn-off just north of town and looks out onto the Makhosini Valley. Rooms are plush, and the hotel's reasonably priced **restaurant** is worth stopping in if you're just passing through. The hotel also has a casino.

The **Makhosini Valley**, 8km **east of Nhlangano** on the Mhlosheni road, is the site of the main **royal burial grounds**, which are guarded and tended by the Mduli clan, who prevent any disturbance to their eternal rest. This includes not cutting the grass, which means that the grounds now stand out as islands of forest in a sea of cultivated land. The Mduli people also grind the king's medicines and snuff, and have the interesting task of preventing any part of his body (including his faeces, semen, toe-clippings, etc) from being used for magical purposes.

A little further on is a turn on the south to **Zombodze**, King Ngwane I's first royal residence in modern-day Swaziland. It's badly signposted, so follow signs for the Ngwane High School, which is very close by.

Another 28km **north of Nhlangano**, along on a good road, is **HLATHIKHULU**, perched impressively high on a hill and providing cool relief after the murderous heat below. Ngwane's grandson **Sobhuza I** fled near here from the attacks of the mighty Ndwandwe king Zwide, to a place called kaPhungalegazi ("place of the smell of blood"), though nothing is now left of the *kraal* he erected here. Sadly for the town, the main road steams right by it, leaving it forlorn on a diversion to the right.

The Ngwane clan fought a murderous but inconclusive battle with the Zulu under King Dingane in the nearby **Lubuya Valley** in 1839. This quiet valley is barely populated and, though there's nothing to remind you of the battle that once raged here, it's a good place for a picnic and a stroll. To get to the valley from Hlathikhulu, take the first turning right after heading north towards Manzini, towards Lugoje Nek, and a left turn at the fork here brings you to the valley. The battle left Dingane's forces much reduced, making him an easy target for his brother Mpande the following year.

From Hlathikhulu, Manzini is 74km away, with the bulk of the drive passing along the **Grand Valley**, through which flows the sometimes mighty Mkhondvo River. The valley is hot, overgrazed and almost barren, but offers stunning hiking possibilities and stupendous views from a car.

From Lavumisa to Manzini

Travelling north from KwaZulu-Natal, you'll come to the **Lavumisa/Golela border post** (7am–10pm). The border is named after one of the wives of Sobhuza I, whose son Malambule tried to overthrow Sobhuza's successor, Mswati II. Golela, on the South African side, means "many animals", and indeed this area was once predominantly a hunting ground. Today, however, the animals have all but gone and there is little reason to linger, unless you are tempted by the prospect of a close encounter with one of the lions at **Nisela Safaris** (daily 8.30am–4.30pm; ☎3030247, fax 3030259). A small, new game reserve, it has thatched cabins (⑤), each sleeping four, a pool and a restaurant. Its animals, for understandable reasons of preservation, are kept apart from the lions, who prowl their own separate enclosure. Otherwise, press on towards Big Bend, crossing the Ingwavuma River just south of Nsoko, about 30km from the border, and follow the road parallel to the **Lubombo mountains**.

A few kilometres before Big Bend, you'll pass by **The Riverside**, a complex on the main road housing a functional **motel** (☎3636012; ②), a good Portuguese restaurant, a scruffy nightclub and, downstairs, Emoya Handicrafts, which has a small selection of good-value handicrafts. Next door is the Bushlands Butchery, where prices are so good that many South Africans drive here to stock up on meat. A kilometre further on is an outstanding **restaurant**, *Lubombo Lobster* (☎3636613), which serves a wonderful seafood curry.

BIG BEND itself, dominated by a huge sugar mill, is only worth visiting for its **hotel**, the *New Bend Inn* (☎3636337; ②), on a hill at the far end of town beyond the golf course. A slightly run-down colonial establishment with superb views of the valley and well-positioned bars, the hotel is a lively Swazi haunt on weekends, when major parties take place. The rooms are spartan but air-conditioned and perfectly comfortable, and the hotel **restaurant** serves tolerable curries and grills for around E25–40.

From the centre of Big Bend **buses** travel to Manzini and Mbabane, and north to Siteki (see p.678).

Mkhaya Nature Reserve

Roughly 30km north of Big Bend is **Mkhaya Nature Reserve**, situated along a turn-off from the brilliantly named village of **Phuzumoya** ("drink the wind") in classic lowveld scrubland, filled with acacia and thorn trees. A sanctuary for the rare **black rhino**, Mkhaya also accommodates **white rhino**, **elephant** and the near-extinct **roan antelope** and its other more numerous relatives, like nyala and eland. Rubbing shoulders with them are ample herds of **Nguni cattle** (see box below).

NGUNI CATTLE AND MKHAYA

The long-horned **Nguni cattle**, herded by the African clans when Europeans encountered them in the nineteenth century, were descendants of the early Iron Age herds. Although they are hardy, disease-resistant and well-adapted to their environment, white beef-farmers regarded them as too puny and unproductive for their industry, and replaced them with imported stock. By the Seventies, pure strains of long-horned cattle had virtually disappeared from Swaziland, and **Ted Reilly** initially purchased Mkhaya (see above) to save them. The sharp increase in the price of cattle feed in the late Seventies made the long-horns increasingly attractive commercially, enabling Reilly to sell them as pure bred breeding stock, using the money to fund the game acquisition programme at Mkhaya. Today, the cattle graze alongside zebra, wildebeest and antelope, just as they always used to.

WHITE-WATER RAFTING

One of the most exhilarating things you can do in southern Swaziland is to **white-water raft** on the beautiful Lusutfu River, near the Mkhaya Nature Reserve. The route runs for 15km in summer (a bit less in winter), and crosses over rapids classed in grades two to four. Anyone can tackle these rapids once they have had a safety briefing.

The scenery along the route is stunning, but hard to appreciate once you hit the rapids, which leave you paddling like crazy and doing your best not to fall in the water. Most people do capsize, but careful supervision ensures that everyone lives to tell the tale. Trips usually depart from the Mkhaya Game Reserve and cost around E100 a person, including a picnic lunch and evening sundowners. A package is available from the *Sondzela* lodge at Mlilwane (see p.671), which includes transport to and from the river, and two nights' accommodation at Mkhaya, for E300 – contact Royal Swazi Big Game Parks (see p.677) in Mbabane to make bookings.

Visits to Mkhaya must be booked in advance (see below), and you can't tour Mkhaya in your own vehicle, but must arrange to be met at the gate, from where there are two pick-ups daily (10am & 4pm; E185). The drive ensures that you see all the big game and a generous **lunch** is included in the price. For overnighters, morning and evening game drives are included in the accommodation price, as well as late-morning escorted walks that offer you the chance to get much closer to animals than you can in a vehicle.

Practicalities

You'll need to **book** your visit to Mkhaya through Royal Swazi Big Game Parks (see p.667) in Mbabane. Visitor facilities are definitely a cut above the norm, but you should be prepared to fork out for the luxuries. The reserve's main camp, *Stone Camp*, makes up for the lack of elevation in the reserve with an atmospheric bush setting beside the dry Ngwenyane river bed. There are two types of full-board **accommodation**: open-plan and open-sided thatched cottages; and luxury safari tents with en-suite toilets and showers. Cooking is done on a large campfire in the main part of the camp under the shade of a massive sausage tree (its seed pods look like sausages), and staff have been known to treat guests to an after-dinner concert.

travel details

Trains
Mpaka to: Durban (2 weekly; 16hr); Maputo (2 weekly; 6hr).

Buses
Big Bend to: Manzini (13 daily; 1hr 30min); Siteki (2 daily; 1hr 30min).

Manzini to: Big Bend (13 daily; 1hr 30min); Hlatsi (2 daily; 1hr 30min); Johannesburg (3 weekly; 8hr); Lavumisa (2 daily; 5hr); Mbabane (27 daily; 45min); Nhlangano (12 daily; 3hr 15min); Siteki (15 daily; 1hr 30min).

Mbabane to: Johannesburg (3 weekly; 7.5hr); Manzini (27 daily; 45min); Nhlangano (4 daily; 4hr); Piggs Peak (10 daily; 1hr).

Nhlangano to: Manzini (12 daily; 3hr 15min); Mbabane (4 daily; 4hr).

Piggs Peak to: Mbabane (10 daily; 1hr).

Siteki to: Big Bend (2 daily; 1hr 30min); Manzini (15 daily; 1hr 30min).

Baz Bus
Manzini to: Durban (4 weekly; 10hr); Johannesburg (4 weekly; 8hr).

Flights
Manzini to: Johannesburg (1–2 daily; 1hr).

PART THREE

THE
CONTEXTS

THE HISTORICAL FRAMEWORK

No account of South Africa seen from the tail end of the twentieth century can avoid talking about its most famous social invention, apartheid. While apartheid was never inevitable, its roots lie in its 350-year-old colonial history. The extreme legalized system of segregation and repression that was put in place in the second half of the twentieth century may not have been intended by the British authorities, but they nevertheless began the process in the nineteenth century with wars of conquest, laws to control the movement of labour and segregated reserves. South Africa's twentieth-century history has been about the rise to power of Afrikaner nationalism, its attempts to suppress African rights and the ultimate victory at the end of the century of multiracialism and democracy.

PREHISTORY

When our ancestors climbed down from the trees, it is quite likely they did it in South Africa – if a growing body of scientific evidence is to be believed. In 1924, the world's **oldest hominid remains** and the first-ever evidence of human-like creatures to be discovered in Africa were dug up in the Northern Cape and identified as a "fossilized monkey skull". After a stint as a humble paperweight, the fossil came

to the attention of Professor Raymond Dart at the University of the Witwatersrand, who identified the earthshaking find as an intermediate species between apes and humans, with a small brain but an upright posture. Still a little shaky on its feet, our ancestor trod the plains of eastern and southern Africa, perhaps three million years ago. Dart called it *Australopithecus africanus*: **Africa's southern ape**. After the emergence of *A. Africanus*, hominids spent the next couple of million years or so perfecting bipedal walking, tool-making, speech and got big-headed (a huge expansion in brain size took place) until they finally strode forth as *Homo sapiens*: the modern humans. Another first for South Africa was the unearthing of the oldest fossil evidence of *Homo sapiens* in a cave at the Klasies river mouth in the Eastern Cape, reckoned to be between 50,000 and 100,000 years old.

THE FIRST SOUTH AFRICANS

Rock-art provides evidence of human culture in the subcontinent dating back nearly 30,000 years and represents South Africa's oldest and most enduring artistic tradition. The artists were hunter-gathers, sometimes called bushmen but more commonly **San**, a relatively modern term from the Nama language with roots in the concept of "inhabiting or dwelling" to reflect the fact these were South Africa's aboriginals. The most direct descendants of the late Stone Age, San people have clung up to the present to a tenuous survival in tiny pockets, mostly in Namibia and Botswana, making theirs the longest-spanning culture in the subcontinent. At one time they probably spread throughout sub-Saharan Africa, having pretty well perfected their **nomadic lifestyle**, which involved an enviable twenty-hour week spent by the men hunting and the women gathering. This left considerable time for artistic and religious pursuits. People lived in small, loosely connected bands comprising family units and were free to leave and join up with other groups. In this egalitarian society, the concept of private property had scant meaning because everything required for survival could be obtained from the environment.

About two thousand years ago, this changed when some groups in northern Botswana laid their hands on fat-tailed **sheep and cattle** from northern Africa, thus transforming themselves into **herding communities**. The introduction of livestock had a revolutionary effect on social organization and introduced the idea of ownership and accumulation. Animals became a symbol of both wealth and social status and those who were better at acquiring and holding onto their animals gradually became wealthier. Social divisions developed, political units became larger and centred around a chief, who had important powers, such as the allocation of pasturage.

These were the first South Africans encountered by Portuguese mariners, who landed along the Cape coast in the fifteenth century. Known as **Khoikhoi** (meaning "men of men"), they were not ethnically distinct from the San, as many anthropologists once believed, but simply represented a distinct social organization. According to current thinking it was possible for Khoi who lost their livestock to revert to being San and for San to lay their hands on animals to become Khoi, giving rise to the collective term "Khoisan". This dynamic view of history is significant because it throws out the nineteenth-century idea that race was an absolute determinant of history and culture – a concept that found great popularity among apartheid apologists.

FARMS AND CRAFTS

Around two thousand years ago tall, dark-skinned people who practised mixed farming – raising both crops and livestock – crossed the Limpopo River into South Africa. San paintings from some time in the intervening period depict small ochre people and larger black ones in a variety of hostile and harmonious relationships, indicating contact between the two groups. These **Bantu-speaking** farmers were the ancestors of South Africa's majority African population, who gradually drifted south, to occupy the entire eastern half of the subcontinent as far as the Eastern Cape, where they were first encountered by Europeans in the sixteenth century.

Today there are four main **Bantu language groups** in South Africa; **Nguni** (comprising Zulu, Swazi and Xhosa) and **Sotho** (Sotho and Tswana) being by far the largest. The other two are **Venda** and **Tsonga**. Apart from highly developed farming know-how and a far more sedentary life than the Khoisan, the early Bantu speakers were skilled craftworkers and knew about mining and smelting metals, including gold, copper and iron, which became an impor-

tant factor in the extensive network of **trade** that developed.

The picture painted by the British of them as bloodthirsty Africans engaged in endemic internecine conflicts probably said more about the white colonizers than the Bantu speakers. The nineteenth-century traveller Ludwig Alberti underlined this fact when he observed that the Xhosa of the Eastern Cape "cannot be regarded as a warlike people; a predominant inclination to pursue a quiet cattle-raising life is much more in evidence amongst them".

THE CAPE GOES DUTCH

In the fifteenth century, Portuguese mariners under the command of **Bartholomeu Dias** became the first Europeans to set foot in South Africa. Marking their progress, they left an unpleasant set of calling cards all along the coast – African men and women they had captured in West Africa and had cast ashore to trumpet the power and glory of Portugal to the locals. Little wonder that their first encounter with the Khoi along the Garden Route coast was not a happy one. It began with a group of Khoi stoning the Portuguese for taking water from a spring without asking permission and ended with one Khoi main lying dead with a crossbow bolt through his chest – a rather disappointing start for friendly relations.

It was another 170 years before any European settlement was established in South Africa. In 1652 a group of white employees of the **Dutch East India Company**, which was engaged in trade between the Netherlands and the East Indies, pulled into Table Bay to set up a refreshment station to revictual Company ships trading between Europe and the East. There was no thought at the time of setting up a colony; on the contrary, the Cape was a rather bum posting, given to the station commander **Jan van Riebeeck** because he had been caught with his hand in the till by the company bosses. Van Riebeeck dreamed up a number of schemes to isolate the Cape Peninsula from the rest of Africa, including a plan to build a canal that would cut it adrift. In the end he had to satisfy himself with planting a **bitter almond hedge** (still growing in Cape Town's Kirstenbosch Gardens) to keep the natives at bay, symbolically representing an ambivalence about being European in Africa, which still haunts most white South Africans.

Despite van Riebeeck's view that the **Khoi**, who were already living at the Cape, were "a savage set, living without conscience", from the start the Dutch were dependent on them to provide livestock, which were traded for trinkets. As the settlement developed, van Riebeeck needed more **labour** to keep the show going, and bemoaned the fact that he was unsuccessful in persuading the Khoi to discard the freedom of their herding life for the toil of ploughing furrows for him. Much to his annoyance, the bosses back in Holland had forbidden van Riebeeck from enslaving the locals, and refused his request for slaves from elsewhere in the company's empire.

This led to the inexorable process of **colonization** of the lands around the fort, when a number of Dutch men were released in 1657 from their contracts to farm as **free burghers** on land granted by the company. The idea was that they would have to sell their produce to the company at a fixed price, thereby overcoming the labour shortage. The only snag with this was the land didn't belong to the company in the first place and the move sparked the first of a series of **Khoikhoi–Dutch wars**. Although the first campaign ended in stalemate, the Khoikhoi were ultimately no match for the Dutch, who had the tactical mobility of horses and the superior killing power of firearms. Campaigns continued through the 1660s and 1670s and proved rather profitable for Dutch raiders, who on one outing in 1674 rounded up eight hundred Khoi cattle and four thousand sheep.

Meanwhile, in 1658, van Riebeeck had managed to successfully purloin a shipload of **slaves** from West Africa, whetting an insatiable appetite for this form of labour. The Dutch East India Company itself became the biggest slave owner at the Cape and continued importing slaves, mostly from the East Indies, at such a pace that by 1711 there were more slaves than burghers in the colony. By the end of the eighteenth century there were almost 15,000 slaves and just under 14,000 burghers at the Cape. With the help of this ready workforce, the embryonic Cape colony expanded outwards and trampled the Peninsula Khoikhoi, who by 1713 had lost everything. Most of their livestock (nearly 50,000 animals) and most of their land west of the Hottentots Holland Mountains had been gobbled up by the Dutch East India

Company. Dispossession and diseases like smallpox, previously unknown in South Africa, decimated their numbers and shattered their social system. By the middle of the eighteenth century, those who remained had been reduced to a condition of miserable servitude to the colonists.

Impoverished whites living at the dog-end of colonial society also had few options, but these included the real possibility of dropping out of its grindingly class-conscious constraints. Many just packed up their waggons and rolled out into the interior, where they lived by the gun, either hunting game or taking cattle from the Khoi by force. Beyond the control of the Dutch East India Company, these nomadic **trekboers** began to assume a pastoral niche previously occupied by the Khoi. By the turn of the nineteenth century, trekboers had penetrated well into the Eastern Cape, pushing back the Khoi and San in the process. Not that the indigenous people gave up without a fight. As their lives became disrupted and living by traditional means became impossible, the Khoisan began to prey on the cattle and sheep of the trekboers. The trekboers responded ruthlessly by hunting down the San as vermin, killing the men and often taking women and children as slaves, bringing them to virtual extinction in South Africa.

After the **British occupation of the Cape** in 1795, the trekboer migration from the Cape accelerated. Britain was now undisputed as the world's dominant naval power. In the ferment that followed the French Revolution, it feared for the security of the Cape sea route to the East and therefore sent a few war sloops into Table Bay and informed the Dutch officials there that they were no longer in charge.

RISE OF THE ZULUS

While in the west white trekboers were migrating from the Cape colony, in the east equally significant movements were under way. Throughout the seventeenth and eighteenth centuries, descendants of the first **Bantu speakers** to penetrate into South Africa had been swelling their numbers and had expanded right across the eastern half of the country, where the rainfall was high enough for their mixed farming economy. By the turn of the nineteenth century the territory was brimming with people and cattle who were fast grazing it out, the limits of expansion having been reached. Exacerbating this was a sustained period of drought.

Nowhere was this more marked than in **KwaZulu-Natal**, where chiefdoms survived by subduing and absorbing their neighbours to gain control of pasturage, thus creating larger and more powerful groupings. By the early part of the nineteenth century two chiefdoms, the **Ndwandwe** and the **Mthethwa**, dominated the eastern section of South Africa around the Tugela River. During the late 1810s a major confrontation between them ended in the defeat of the Mthethwa.

Out of their ruins emerged the **Zulus**, who were to become one of the most powerful polities in southern Africa. Prior to the defeat of the Mthethwa, the Zulus had been a minor clan under their domination. Around 1816, **Shaka** assumed the chieftaincy of the Zulus, whose fighting tactics he quickly transformed, supplementing the Nguni's traditional long throwing spear with a short stabbing one suitable for close combat. The throwing spear rendered a warrior unarmed once he had thrown it and was relatively easily deflected by a cowhide shield, but with a **stabbing spear** he could keep on fighting indefinitely. Shaka also introduced the tactic known as the "horns of the bull" by which the enemy were outflanked by highly disciplined formations spreading out to engulf them by means of two wings. The manoeuvre was used to devastating effect against the British at the Battle of Isandlwana in 1879.

By 1820, the Zulus had incorporated the fragments of the Mthethwa and had defeated the Ndwandwe. By the middle of the decade they had formed a **centralized military state** with a 40,000-strong standing army. The nature of war in the east changed from the almost symbolic skirmishes that characterized Nguni raids up to the end of the eighteenth century to decisive battles in which massacres of women and children weren't unknown. Nevertheless, the real strength of the system lay in its ability to absorb the survivors, who became members of the expanding Zulu state. Throughout the 1820s Shaka sent out his armies to attack his neighbours and take their cattle. In 1828, in a palace coup, he was stabbed to death by a servant and his two half-brothers, one of whom, **Dingane**, succeeded him. Dingane continued with his brother's ruthless policies and tactics.

The rise of the Zulu state reverberated right across southern Africa and led to the creation of a series of **centralized Nguni states** as well as paving the way for Boer expansion into the interior. In a movement known as the **mfecane**, or forced migrations, huge areas of the country were laid waste and people across eastern South Africa were displaced, dispossessed and driven off their lands, either attempting to survive in small groups or banding together in larger political organizations to survive. To the north of the Zulu kingdom, another Nguni group with strong cultural and linguistic affinities with the Zulus came together under Sobhuza I and his son Mswati II, after whom their new state **Swaziland** took its name. A few hundred Zulus under the leadership of **Mzilikazi** had taken refuge in Northwest Province after rebelling against Shaka. By 1829 their numbers had swelled to around seventy thousand, but in 1838 they were routed by encroaching Voortrekkers, against whose firearms they proved no match. They relocated to southwestern Zimbabwe, where they re-established themselves as the **Matabele** kingdom. In the Drakensberg, on the west flank of KwaZulu-Natal, **Moshoeshoel**, another chief from humble origins, used diplomacy and cunning to build up his state from the ruins of the mfecane. By providing a haven to refugees, he was able to build up a substantial state from disparate Sotho groupings. Believing that "peace is like the rain which makes the grass grow", he kept no standing army, relying instead on opportunism and good-neighbourliness to survive.

THE GREAT TREK

Back in the Cape, many Afrikaners were becoming fed up with British rule. Their principal grievance was the way in which the colonial authorities were tampering with labour relations and destroying what they saw as a divine distinction between blacks and whites. In 1828 the **Cape Ordinance 50** gave Khoi residents and free blacks equality before the law, while the **abolition of slavery** in 1834 was the last straw. One Voortrekker wrote: "it's not so much their freedom that drove us to such lengths, as their being placed on an equal footing with Christians, contrary to the laws of God and the natural distinction of race".

In this spirit 15,000 Afrikaners (one out of every ten living in the colony) set out to leave the Cape and once and for all shake off the meddlesome British. When they arrrived in the eastern half of the country, they were delighted to find vast tracts of apparently unoccupied land. In fact, they were merely stumbling into the eye of the *mfecane* storm – areas that had been temporarily cleared either by war parties or by fearful people hiding out to escape detection. As they fanned out further they hit up against the Nguni states and a series of battles followed. By the middle of the nineteenth century, the Voortrekkers had consolidated control and established the two Boer states of the **South African Republic** (now Mpumalanga, Northwest and Northern provinces) and the **Orange Free State** (now Free State), both of whose independence was recognized by Britain in the 1850s.

Britain wasn't too concerned about the interior of South Africa. Apart from its strategic position, South Africa was a chaotic and undeveloped backwater at the butt-end of the Empire that was of scant interest back in London. At this time the United States, which was first settled by Britons a mere thirty years before the Dutch hit South Africa, had a population of over thirty million people of European extraction and 80,000km of railways compared with South Africa's 250,000 whites and 120km of railways. Things changed first in the 1860s, with the **discovery of diamonds** (the world's largest deposit) around modern-day Kimberley and even more significantly in the 1880s, with the **discovery of gold** at Witwatersrand (now Gauteng). Together these discoveries were the catalyst that transformed South Africa from an almost feudal farming society to an urbanized industrial one. In the process great wealth was made by capitalists like **Cecil John Rhodes**, traditional African society was crushed and the independence of the Boer republics ended.

Although the **Gauteng goldfields** were exceptionally well-endowed with ore, they were also particularly difficult to mine, requiring the sinking of deep shafts, which necessitated capitalist intervention. Exploiting the mines required costly equipment and cheap labour to operate it. Capital quickly flowed in from Western investors eager for big profits and even up until today the West has retained strong links with the South African mines. Gold transformed the South African Republic from a down-at-heel rural society into an industrial

nation that was the world's largest producer of gold.

Despite the benefits it brought, the discovery of gold was also one of the principal causes of the **Second Anglo-Boer War**. Gold-mining had shifted the economic centre of South Africa from the British-controlled Cape to a Boer republic, while at the same time Britain's European rival, Germany, was beginning to make political and economic inroads in the Boer republics. Britain feared losing its strategic Cape naval base, but perhaps even more important were questions of international finance and the substantial British investment in the mines. London was at the heart of world trade and was eager to see a flourishing gold-mining industry in South Africa, but the Boers seemed rather sluggish about modernizing their infrastructure to assist the exploitation of the mines.

In any case, a number of Britons had for some time seen the unification of South Africa as the key to securing **British interests** in the subcontinent. To this end, under a wafer-thin pretext, the Empire had declared war and subdued the last of the independent African kingdoms by means of the **Zulu War** of 1879. This had secured KwaZulu-Natal and meant that all the coastal territories of South Africa from Namibia round to Mozambique were under British control. All that remained was to bring the two Boer republics under the Union Jack.

THE ANGLO-BOER WAR

During the closing years of the nineteenth century Britain demanded that the South African Republic grant voting rights to British miners living in the country – a demand that, if met, would have meant the end of Boer political control over their own state. The Boers tuned down the request and war broke out in October 1899. The British command, which had been used to fighting colonial wars against enemies armed with spears, believed they were looking at a walkover; in the words of Lord Kitchener, "a teatime war" that would get the troops home in time to open their Christmas presents.

In fact the battle turned into the most expensive campaign since the Napoleonic Wars. During the **early phase** of the war the Boers took the imperial power by surprise and penetrated into British-controlled KwaZulu-Natal and the Northern Cape, inflicting a series of humiliating defeats. By June a reinforced British army was pushing the Boers back and once again the high command was talking about being home in time for their Christmas pudding. But the Boers fought on for another two years of protracted guerrilla war. **Lord Kitchener** responded ruthlessly with a scorched-earth policy that left the countryside a smouldering wasteland and thousands of women and children homeless. To house these thousands of dispossessed, the British invented the **concentration camp**, which took the lives of 26,370 Boer women and children. This episode wasn't quickly forgotten: for some Afrikaners it remains a major source of bitterness against the British today. Less widely publicized were the **African concentration camps** which took 14,000 lives. By 1902, the Boers were demoralized and split between those who couldn't face another winter of near starvation (the so-called "hands-uppers") and those who wanted to fight on ("the bitter-enders"). In May that year the Boer republics signed a treaty surrendering their independence in exchange for British promises of reconstruction. By the end of the so-called "teatime war", Britain had committed nearly half a million men to the field and lost 22,000 of them. Of the 88,000 Boers who fought, 7000 died in combat. With the two Boer republics and the two British colonies under imperial control, the way was clear for the federation of the **Union of South Africa** in 1910.

MIGRANT LABOUR AND THE BAMBATHA REBELLION

Between the conclusion of the Anglo-Boer War and the unification of South Africa, the mines suffered from a shortage of **unskilled labour**. Most Africans still lived by agriculture, either as tenant farmers on white farms or in reserves created by the colonial government. They had no need to desert their traditional farming way of life for a thankless existence in shantytowns far away from home. To counter this the government took measures to compel them to supply their labour. One method was the imposition of **taxes** that had to be paid in coin, thus forcing Africans from subsistence farming and into the cash economy, where they would have to earn a wage. Responding to one such tax, a group of Zulus protested in 1906 and refused to pay up. The authorities declared martial law and dealt mercilessly with the protestors, burning their huts and seizing all their possessions.

This provoked a full-blown rebellion led by Chief Bambatha, which was ruthlessly put down by the colonial authorities, with 4000 rebels dying in the process. This marked an end to armed resistance by Africans for over half a century. After the defeat of the **Bambatha Rebellion**, the numbers of African men from Zululand working in the Gauteng mines shot up by sixty percent. By 1909, eighty percent of adult males in the territory were absent from their homes and working as migrant labourers. **Migrant labour**, with its shattering effects on family life, became one of the foundations of South Africa's economic and social system, and was a basic cornerstone of apartheid.

KICK-STARTING AFRIKANERDOM

In a parallel development, large numbers of **Afrikaners** were forced to leave rural areas in the early part of the twentieth century. This was partly due to the aftermath of British scorched-earth tactics during the Anglo-Boer War, but also a result of overcrowding, drought and pestilence. Many Afrikaners joined the ranks of a swelling **poor white working class** that felt itself caught in a vice: victimized and despised on the one hand by the English-speaking capitalists who commanded the economy, and on the other under pressure from lower-paid Africans who were competing for their jobs.

In 1918 (the year Nelson Mandela was born) a group of Afrikaners formed the **Broederbond** ("the brotherhood"), a secret society to promote the interest of Afrikaners and to forge an Afrikaner republic in South Africa. It aimed to uplift impoverished members of the volk ("people") and to develop a sense of pride in their language, religion and culture. Ultimately the Broederbond was to dominate every aspect of the way the country was run for close on half a century.

During the Thirties, a number of young Afrikaner intellectuals travelled to Europe, where they were inspired by the jackbooted march of **fascism** in Portugal, Spain, Italy and Germany. This extreme manifestation of nationalism appeared to hold the key to realizing Afrikaner nationhood. It was around this time that Afrikaner intellectuals began using the term **apartheid** (pronounced "apart-hate", not "apart-hide").

Among the leading lights of apartheid who could be found kicking their heels in Germany in the 1930s were **Nico Diederichs**, who became Minister of Finance under the National Party government; **Hendrik Frensch Verwoerd**, apartheid's leading theorist and prime minister from 1958 to 1966; and **Piet Meyer**, controller of the state broadcasting service, who named his son Izan ("Nazi" spelled backwards – but he later claimed this was sheer coincidence). Meanwhile in 1939, the Broederbond kicked into action with a scheme that launched 10,000 Afrikaner businesses in the space of a decade. Some of these, such as Rembrandt Tobacco, Volkskas (the country's third largest bank), the Santam insurance company and Gencor (one of the five largest mining houses) are still among the leading players in South Africa's economy.

AFRICANS' CLAIMS

Despite having relied on African co-operation for their victory in the Anglo-Boer War and having hinted at enhanced rights for blacks after the war, the British excluded blacks from the cosy deal between Afrikaners and Britain that resulted in the unification of South Africa in 1910. It wasn't long in fact before the white Union government began eroding African rights. In response, a group of middle-class mission-educated Africans formed the **South African Native National Congress** (later to become the ANC) in 1912. The founders weren't interested in overthrowing the white government; they simply wanted recognition by white society. Middle-class blacks already enjoyed the vote in the Cape Province (now the Western, Northern and Eastern capes) on the basis of a **qualified franchise** according to education and property ownership, and the early African leaders wanted this to be extended to the rest of the country. Taking as their model the evolutionary growth of democracy in Britain, they hoped that this would eventually lead to universal suffrage.

In 1914, the leaders set off as a deputation for London, to protest against the **1913 Natives' Land Act**, which severely restricted property ownership by blacks. The trip was unsuccessful and the Land Act came into force and provided the legal foundation stone for the subsequent formalization of apartheid some 35 years later. The Act provided for the division of South Africa into distinct African and white areas, with blacks, despite constituting the overriding majority of the population, confined to less than ten percent of the land surface.

Through the early half of the twentieth century, the ANC remained a conservative organization unwilling to shift from a tactic of deputations to engage in active protest. This led to accusations that its leaders were "good boys tied to the apron strings of the white liberals". In response, a number of alternative mass organizations arose. Among the largest was the mighty **Industrial and Commercial Union**, an African trade union founded in 1919, which at its peak in 1928 had gathered an impressive 150,000 members. But in the 1930s it ran out of steam. The first political movement in the country not organized along ethnic lines was the **South African Communist Party**, which was founded in 1921 with a multiracial executive. While it never itself gained widespread membership, it became an important force inside the ANC.

Throughout the Thirties the ANC plodded on with speeches, petitions and pleas, which proved completely fruitless. They suffered a major setback in 1936 with the **termination of the African franchise** in the Cape Province. The ANC's response was to send a deputation to Prime Minister Hertzog to protest. Hertzog treated them abominably, not even offering them seats. "Well you've seen the newspapers," he told them dismissively. These events left the ANC crippled and hobbling impotently into the Forties.

World War II split Afrikanerdom. There were those like Prime Minister **Jan Smuts** who stood firmly in favour of joining the war alongside Britain. But for others, like **John Vorster**, Britain was the old enemy, so they supported Germany, some signing up with the **Ossewa Brandwag** (the "Ox-Wagon Torch Commando"), which carried out sabotage against the government. After the war there were hopes of reform from Prime Minister Smuts, who at the time was playing a leading role in the formation of the **United Nations**. Smuts even had a part in penning the Preamble to the Charter on Human Rights, but while his work for abstract "human rights" earned him a statue next to Winston Churchill outside Britain's parliament, he was in no hurry to grant such rights to the majority of South Africans. Even conservative African leaders were losing patience: one, Councillor Paul Mosaka, complaining that "we have been asked to co-operate with a toy telephone. We have been speaking into an appartus which cannot transmit sound."

YOUNG TURKS AND STRIKING

In 1944 a young hothead called **Nelson Mandela** got together with his friends **Oliver Tambo** and **Walter Sisulu** under the leadership of **Anton Lembede** to form the **ANC Youth League**. Strict Africanists, they refused to work with any other organizations – such as the Indian Congress. The League's founding manifesto criticized the ANC leadership as a group who regarded themselves as "gentlemen with clean hands". Lembede's radical brand of politics was based on his idea that "Africa is the black man's country". He continued: "We have inhabited Africa, our motherland, from time immemorial. Africa belongs to us."

The 1945 annual conference of the ANC adopted a document called "**Africans' Claims in South Africa**", which reflected an emerging politicization resulting from the experiences of the war and especially the defeat of fascism. The document demanded **universal franchise** and an end to the **colour bar**, which reserved most skilled jobs for whites. The Youth League was influenced by the industrial militancy it had witnessed during the war. Despite a ban on industrial action, between 1942 and 1944 there were sixty strikes. In 1946 the African Mineworkers' Union launched one of the biggest strikes in the country's history in protest against falling living standards. Virtually the entire Gauteng gold-mining region came to a standstill as 100,000 workers downed tools. Smuts sent in police who forced the workers back down the shafts at gunpoint.

In 1947, the ANC Youth League was thrown into confusion when Lembede died suddenly. He was succeeded by **A.P. Mda**, and **Nelson Mandela** took his first step into public life when he was elected general secretary of the organization. At the same time, the Smuts government was under pressure for change. Meanwhile, **European decolonization** was beginning in earnest, with Britain withdrawing from India in the same year. This seemed to have implications for political rights for black South Africans. But more important still was demography, with the relentless **influx of Africans** into the urban

areas breaking the traditional stereotype of them as rural tribespeople.

For years, the white government had been hinting at easing up on segregation, and even Smuts himself, who was no soft liberal, had reckoned that it was untenable and would have to end at some point. His deputy **J.H. Hofmeyr** had thrown caution to the winds and committed himself to scrapping job reservation, which excluded blacks from skilled jobs. "I take my stand on the ultimate removal of the colour bar", he went on record as saying. Playing for time, the government appointed the **Fagan Commission** to look into the question of the Pass Laws, which controlled the movement of Africans and sought to keep them out of the white cities unless they had a job. The laws led to millions of black South Africans being condemned to a ghetto existence in the rural areas, where there were no jobs, poverty reigned and infant mortality was high.

When the Fagan Commission reported its findings its 1948, it concluded that "the trend to urbanization is irreversible and the Pass Laws should be eased". While some blacks may have felt heartened by this hint of reform, this was the last thing many whites wanted to hear. For Afrikaners, the threat seemed particularly acute, and raised all sorts of fears about losing their identity and being swamped by blacks. For **white workers** the threat of losing their jobs to lower-paid African workers was a real one, while **Afrikaner farmers** were alarmed by the idea of a labour shortage due to Africans leaving the rural areas for better prospects in the cities.

Against this background of black aspiration and white fears, the Smuts government called a **general election**. The opposition **National Party** campaigned on a *swart gevaar* or "black peril" ticket which played on white insecurity and fear. The Afrikaner nationalists promised to satisfy a range of conflicting interests. With an eye on the vote of Afrikaner workers and farmers, they promised to reverse the tide of Africans coming into the cites and send them all back to the reserves. For white business they made the conflicting promise to bring black workers into the cities as a cheap and plentiful supply of labour.

On Friday May 28, 1948, South Africa awoke to the unthinkable reality of a **National Party victory** at the (whites-only) polls. Party leader

D.F. Malan was summoned to Pretoria by the governor-general to form a cabinet. On arriving by train at Pretoria station he told a group of ecstatic supporters: "For the first time, South Africa is our own. May God grant that it always remains our own. We Afrikaners are not a work of Man, but a creation of God. It is to us that millions of barbarous blacks look for guidance, justice and the Christian way of life."

Meanwhile, the ANC was riven by its own power struggle. Fed up with the ineffectiveness of the old guard, and faced with the rabid D.F. Malan, the Youth League staged a putsch, voted in their own leadership with Nelson Mandela on the executive and adopted the League's radical **Programme of Action**, with an arsenal of tactics that Mandela explained would include "the new weapons of boycott, strike, civil disobedience and non-cooperation".

THE FIFTIES: PEACEFUL PROTEST

During the Fifties, the National Party began putting in place a barrage of laws that would eventually constitute the structure of apartheid. Some early onslaughts on black civil rights included: the **Coloured Voters Act**, which stripped coloureds of the vote; the **Bantu Authorities Act**, which set up puppet authorities to govern Africans in the reserves; the **Population Registration Act**, which classified every South African at birth as "white, Native or coloured"; the **Group Areas Act**, which divided South Africa into ethnically distinct areas; and the **Suppression of Communism Act**, which made any anti-apartheid opposition (Communist or not) a criminal offence.

The ANC responded in 1952 with the **Defiance Campaign**, which kicked off with a letter to the government demanding the same civil rights for blacks that whites enjoyed. During the campaign, eight thousand volunteers deliberately broke the apartheid laws listed above and were jailed. The campaign rolled on through 1952 until the police provoked violence in October by firing on a prayer meeting in East London. A riot followed in which two white people were killed, thus appearing to discredit claims that the campaign was non-violent. The government used this as an excuse to swoop on the homes of the ANC leadership, resulting in the detention and then banning of over one hundred ANC organizers. **Bannings** were designed to restrict a person's movement and political activities. A banned person was prohibited from seeing more than one person at a time or talking to another banned person; prohibited from entering certain buildings; kept under surveillance; was required to report regularly to the police and could not be quoted or published.

The most far-reaching event of the decade was the **Congress of the People**, held near Johannesburg in 1955. At a mass meeting of nearly three thousand delegates, four organizations, representing Africans, coloureds, whites and Indians, formed a strategic partnership called the **Congress Alliance**. Explaining the historic significance of the meeting, ANC leader Chief **Albert Luthuli** commented that "for the first time in the history of our multiracial nation its people will meet as equals, irrespective of race, colour and creed to formulate a freedom charter for all the people of our country". The **Freedom Charter**, which was adopted at the Congress of the People, became the principal document defining ANC policy.

The government found the breadth of the movement and its principles of freedom and equality too much to stomach and they sent in the police to round up 156 opposition leaders who were charged with treason. Evidence at the **Treason Trial** was based on the Freedom Charter, which was described as a "blueprint for violent Communist revolution". Although all the defendants were acquitted, the four-year trial disrupted the ANC and splits began to emerge. From within the organization, a group of Africanists criticized the Freedom Charter because it promoted co-operation with white activists. At the 1958 ANC national conference they attempted to hijack the leadership, but when they failed they walked out and formed

THE FREEDOM CHARTER

- The people shall govern.
- All national groups shall have equal rights.
- The people shall share the nation's wealth.
- The land shall be shared by those who work it.
- All shall be equal before the law.
- All shall enjoy equal human rights.
- There shall be work and security for all.
- The doors of learning and culture shall be opened.
- There shall be houses, security and comfort.
- There shall be peace and friendship.

the **Pan Africanist Congress** under the leadership of the charismatic **Robert Mangaliso Sobukwe**. Upstaging the ANC, the PAC launched an anti-pass campaign ten days before a similar one planned by the ANC.

SHARPEVILLE

On March 21, 1960, Sobukwe and thousands of followers left home to present themselves without passes to police stations. Sobukwe gave strict instructions to keep the demonstrations peaceful and not to be provoked by anyone. Across Gauteng and the Western Cape there were demonstrations which in due course dispersed, but at **Sharpeville** police station, south of Johannesburg, the crowd refused to leave, despite being buzzed by low-flying Sabre jets. A scuffle broke out, the police panicked and opened fire, killing 69 and injuring nearly 200. Most were shot in the back.

In a rapid sequence of events, demonstrations swept the country on **March 27**, and ANC activist Oliver Tambo (later to become the ANC leader in exile until the release of Mandela) illegally left the country. The following day Africans staged a **total stay-away** from work and thousands followed Nelson Mandela and Albert Luthuli in a public pass-burning demonstration. The day after that the government declared a **state of emergency** and rounded up 22,000 people. One day later, the United Nations Security Council resolution called for the government to abandon apartheid, to which it reacted swiftly with bans on the ANC and PAC. It was now illegal to be a member of either organization. Among white South Africans there was near hysteria as the value of the rand slipped, shares slumped and some feared an imminent and bloody revolution.

Later that month, Prime Minister **Hendrik Verwoerd** was shot twice in the head by a half-crazed white farmer and many people hoped his death would provide a speedy retreat from apartheid. But Dr Verwoerd survived, with his prestige enhanced and his appetite for apartheid stronger than ever. More than anyone else Verwoerd made apartheid his own and formulated it into a coherent system based around the idea of **notionally independent bantustans**, in which Africans were to exercise their political rights away from the white areas. The underlying aim of the scheme was to divide Africans into distinct ethnic groups, thereby dis-

mantling the black majority into several separate "tribal" minorities, none of which on its own could outnumber whites.

After the banning of opposition in 1960, Dr Verwoerd pressed ahead with his cherished dream of an all-white **Afrikaner republic**, which he succeeded in achieving in March 1961 through a referendum. For his pains the Commonwealth Prime Ministers' Conference in London kicked the republic out of the British Commonwealth and Mandela called for a national convention "to determine a non-racial democratic constitution". Instead Verwoerd appointed one-time neo-nazi **John Vorster** to the post of Justice Minister. A trained lawyer, Vorster eagerly set about passing a succession of repressive laws that circumvented normal legal procedures and flouted all principles of natural justice.

Some in the ANC realized that the rules of the game had changed irrevocably. "The time comes in the life of any nation when there remain only two choices: submit or fight. That time has now come to South Africa. We shall not submit", Mandela told the world, before going underground as commander-in-chief of **UmkhontoWe Sizwe** (Spear of the Nation, aka MK), a newly formed armed wing involving ANC and Communist Party leaders. The organization was dedicated to economic and symbolic acts of sabotage and was under strict orders not to kill or injure people. Mandela operated clandestinely for a year, travelling in disguise, leaving the country illegally and popping up unexpectedly at meetings – all of which earned him the nickname, the "Black Pimpernel". In August 1962 he was finally arrested, tried and imprisoned. He was let out again briefly in 1963 to defend himself against charges of treason at the **Rivonia Trial**. Mandela and nine other ANC leaders were all found guilty and handed life sentences.

APARTHEID: THE DARK DAYS

With the leadership of the liberation movement behind bars, the Rivonia Trial marked the beginning of the decade in which everything seemed to be going the white government's way. Resistance was stifled, the state grew more powerful and for white South Africans, businessmen and foreign investors life seemed perfect. The panic caused by the Sharpeville massacre soon became a dim memory and confidence returned. For black South Africans poverty deepened – a state of affairs enforced by apartheid legislation.

There was a minor setback in 1966 when Dr Verwoerd was stabbed to death (and failed to return from the dead this time) in parliament by a messenger who went off the rails after a tapeworm had ordered him to do it, as he told doctors. The breach was filled by **Balthazar John Vorster**, whose approach was more pragmatic than that of Verwoerd. Not averse to travelling to Africa to shake hands with tame black leaders like Hastings Banda of Malawi in the interests of détente, his approach to black South Africans was rather less chummy. His premiership was characterized by an increased use of the **police** as an instrument of repression, while bannings, detentions without trial, house arrests and deaths of political prisoners in detention became commonplace.

The ANC was impotent, and resistance by its armed wing MK was virtually nonexistent. This was partly because up to the mid-Seventies South Africa was surrounded by sympathetic white regimes – in neighbouring Rhodesia and Mozambique – making it close to impossible to infiltrate combatants into the country. But as South Africa swung into the Seventies, the uneasy peace began to fray, prompted at first by **deteriorating black living standards**, which reawakened industrial action. **Trade unions** came to fill the vacuum left by the ANC and neither Vorster nor any of his National Party successors proved able to stem the escalation of strikes, despite all the repressive resources at their disposal.

However, it was the Soweto Revolt of June 16, 1976, that signalled the transfer of protest from the workplace to the townships, when black youths took to the streets in protest against the imposition of Afrikaans as a medium of instruction in their schools. The protest spread across the country after police opened fire and killed thirteen-year-old Hector Peterson during one march. By the following February, 575 people (nearly a quarter of them children) had been killed in the rolling series of revolts that followed.

Even in the face of naked violence, protest spread to all sections of the community. The government was forced to rely increasingly on armed police to impose order. Even this was unable to stop the mushrooming of new libera-

tion organizations, many of them part of the broadly based **Black Consciousness movement**. As the unrest rumbled on into 1977, the Vorster government responded by banning all the new black organizations and detaining their leadership. In September 1977, **Steve Biko** (one of the detained), became the 46th political prisoner to meet his end in jail at the hands of the security police. In place of the banned organizations, a fresh crop had sprung up by the end of the Seventies. The government never again successfully put the lid on opposition as it escalated through the Eighties. There were rent, bus and school **boycotts**, **strikes**, and **campaigns** against removals. By the end of the decade business was complaining that apartheid wasn't working any more, and even the government was starting to agree. The growth of the black population was outstripping that of whites; from a peak of 21 percent of the population in 1910, whites now made up only 16 percent. This proportion was set to fall to 10 percent by the end of the century. The sums just didn't add up.

TOTAL STRATEGY

It was becoming clear that Vorster's deployment of the police couldn't solve South Africa's problems, and in 1978 he was deposed by his defence minister **Pieter Willem Botha** in a palace coup. Under Vorster's premiership, Botha had turned the **South African Defence Force** into the most awesome military machine on the African continent and it became central to his strategy for maintaining white power. Botha realized that the days of old-style apartheid were over, and he adopted a two-handed strategy of reform accompanied by unprecedented repression. Believing there was a total onslaught on South Africa from both inside and outside the country, he devised his so-called **Total Strategy**.

In June 1980, MK, the ANC's armed wing, made an unscheduled reappearance when it successfully attacked the heavily guarded strategic oil refinery at **Sasolburg**, taking the government by surprise. The Eighties saw the growing use of sabotage against the apartheid state. During 1981 there were over ninety **MK armed actions** against police stations, railway lines, power plants, military bases and army recruiting offices. Attacks were often co-ordinated with protest campaigns: for example, buildings at the British Leyland plant were bombed when workers were on strike there. Botha began thinking about reforms and moved **Nelson Mandela** and other imprisoned ANC leaders from Robben Island to Pollsmoor Prison in mainland Cape Town.

At the same time, he poured ever-increasing numbers of troops into African townships to stop unrest, while using economic incentives to attempt to draw neighbouring countries into a "**constellation of Southern African states**" under South Africa's leadership. Between 1981 and 1983 the army was used to enforce compliance on every one of the country's neighbours. An undeclared war against **Angola** reduced a potentially oil-rich country to war-ravaged ruins, while a South African-sponsored conflict in **Mozambique** brought a poverty-stricken country to its knees. Nor was Botha averse to sending commando units across the borders into **Botswana**, **Zimbabwe**, **Swaziland** and **Lesotho** to attack and bomb South African refugees.

Botha hoped that by making a few reforms that tinkered with apartheid and by creating a black middle class as a buffer against the ANC, he could get the world off his back and stem internal unrest. In both he was wrong. Unrest continued unabated and he found himself having to rely increasingly on force. Detentions and executions of political activists increased (in contravention of the Geneva Convention) and heavy sentences were handed down in political trials. Used to maintaining control through the barrel of a gun, Botha was lost for any real political initiatives. Nevertheless, in 1983 he concocted what he believed was a master plan for a so-called **New Constitution** in which coloureds and Indians would be granted the vote. But before anyone got too excited he qualified this with the revelation that each group would be represented in separate chambers, which would have no executive power. Meanwhile, for Africans, apartheid would continue as usual.

Botha hoped for a tactical alliance between whites, coloureds and Indians in opposition to Africans. The scheme was a dismal failure that only served to alienate right-wingers, who saw it as selling out white privilege. As Botha was punting this ramshackle scheme, 15,000 anti-apartheid delegates met at Mitchell's Plain in Cape Town to form the **United Democratic Front** (UDF) at the biggest opposition gathering since the Congress of the People in 1955. Under a leadership that included ANC veterans, the UDF was a multiracial umbrella for 575 organizations. It endorsed the Freedom Charter and became a proxy for the ANC. Two years of strikes, protest and boycotts followed. But there were sinister stirrings when **Mangosuthu Buthelezi**, chief minister of the KwaZulu *bantustan* and leader of the Zulu nationalist **Inkatha** movement, told a rally of migrant workers in Soweto that "the UDF seems to be another force for disunity and cannot succeed without Inkatha. From now on Inkatha will adopt the attitude of an eye for an eye." Attacks by Inkatha members on UDF and ANC supporters became commonplace and have continued to the present. (Evidence in the Nineties pointed to support for Inkatha from elements in the apartheid security forces, including the supply of weapons.)

In the face of intensifying protest, the government looked for ways to respond, and between March and December it offered to **release Mandela** no fewer than five times, provided he agreed to banishment to the Transkei *bantustan*. Five times he refused and this cat-and-mouse game continued right through the Eighties as the pressure mounted and South Africa's townships became ungovernable. Towards the end of the decade the world watched as apartheid troops and police were shown regularly on TV beating up and shooting unarmed Africans. The **Commonwealth**, despite the concerted efforts of British Prime Minister Margaret Thatcher to stop them, condemned the apartheid government. The United States and Australia **severed air-links** and Congress defied President Reagan and passed the comprehensive Anti-Apartheid Act which promoted **disinvestment**. In 1985, the **Chase Manhattan Bank** announced that it would no longer be prepared to roll over its loan to South Africa. Over the next two years ninety US firms closed down their South African operations. An increasingly desperate Botha now modified his conditions for releasing Mandela, offering to "release Mandela if he renounces violence".

Mandela issued a moving reply, read by his daughter Zinzi to a crowd at Jabulani Stadium, in Soweto: "I am surprised by the conditions the government wants to impose on me. I am not a violent man. It was only when all other forms of resistance were no longer open to us that we turned to armed struggle. Let Botha show that he is different to Malan, Strijdom and Verwoerd. Let him renounce violence. I cherish my own freedom dearly but I care even more for yours."

As events unfolded, a subtle shift became increasingly apparent: Botha was the prisoner and he desperately needed Mandela to release him. On the one hand **black resistance** wasn't abating, while on the other Botha was facing a white **right-wing backlash**. At every by-election the ultra right-wing Conservative Party had been eroding government majorities. In the **1987 general election** the government polled just 52 percent while, so far to the right that it had slid off the political spectrum, the **Afrikaner Weerstand Beweging** (Afrikaner Resistance Movement, aka AWB) broke up National Party meetings and threatened civil war.

CRISIS

In 1986 Botha declared yet another **state of emergency** and unleashed a last-ditch storm of tyranny. There were **bannings** of people and meetings, and **shootings** by the police were carried out with impunity. There were **mass arrests**, **detentions**, **treason trials** and **torture**. Sinister hit squads were deployed to assassinate the UDF leadership. Alarmed by the spiral of violence that was engulfing the country, a group of South African businessmen, mostly Afrikaners, flew to Senegal in 1987 to meet an ANC delegation headed by **Thabo Mbeki**. A joint statement pressed for unequivocal support for a negotiated settlement.

Weeks after the world celebrated **Mandela's seventieth birthday** in July 1988 with a huge bash at London's Wembley Stadium, Mandela was rushed off to Tygerberg Hospital, suffering from tuberculosis. Although he was better by October the government announced that he wouldn't be returning to Pollsmoor Prison. Instead he was moved to a warder's cottage at Victor Verster Prison in Paarl. Outside the prison walls, Botha's policies had hit the buffers and even the army top brass were pushing for change. They told Botha that there could be no decisive military victory over the anti-apartheid opposition and the undeclared war in Angola was bleeding the treasury dry.

At the beginning of 1989, Mandela wrote to Botha from Victor Verster Prison calling for negotiations. "I am disturbed by the spectre of a South Africa split into two hostile camps – blacks on one side, whites on the other," he wrote. An intransigent character, Botha found himself with little room to manoeuvre. He had brought South Africa to a state of unprecedented crisis, yet he refused to change direction. When he was weakened by a stroke, his party colleagues moved swiftly to oust him and replaced him with **Frederik Willem De Klerk**.

Drawn from the conservative wing of the National Party, from the start De Klerk made it clear he was totally opposed to majority rule. But he inherited a massive pile of problems that could no longer be ignored: the economy was in trouble and the cost of maintaining apartheid prohibitive; the illegal influx of Africans from the country to the city had become an unstoppable flood; blacks hadn't been taken in by Botha's constitutional reforms; and even South Africa's friends were beginning to lose patience. In September 1989, US President **George Bush** let De Klerk know that if there wasn't progress on releasing Mandela within six months, he would extend US sanctions against South Africa.

De Klerk made a strategic calculation that the ANC was organizationally weak, having little internal base and having lost all its external support as a result of the enforced closure of its bases in Angola and Zambia, as well as having lost aid from eastern Europe with the collapse of the Iron Curtain regimes. He gambled on his own party's five-decade track record in gerrymandering and on his own ability to outmanoeuvre the ANC. In February 1990, De Klerk announced the **unbanning** of the ANC, the PAC, the Communist Party and 33 other organizations, as well as the **release of Mandela**. On Sunday February 11, at around 4pm, Mandela stepped out of Victor Verster Prison and was driven to City Hall in Cape Town, from where he spoke publicly for the first time in three decades. He told his supporters that the factors which necessitated armed struggle still existed, but that he believed that "a climate conducive to a negotiated settlement will exist soon".

That May, Mandela and De Klerk signed an **agreement** in which the government agreed to repeal repressive laws and release political prisoners, while Mandela persuaded the ANC to suspend the armed struggle. As events moved slowly towards full-blown negotiations it became clear that De Klerk still clung to race-based notions for a settlement. "Majority rule is not suitable for South Africa," he said, "because it will lead to the domination of minorities."

NEGOTIATIONS

The **negotiating** process which took place between 1990 and 1994 was fragile, and at many points a descent into chaos looked likely. Obstacles included ongoing violence linked to a sinister "**Third Force**" – elements in the apartheid security forces who were working behind the scenes to destabilize the ANC; **threats of civil war** from heavily armed right-wingers and a low-key war of attrition in KwaZulu-Natal between Zulu nationalists and ANC supporters had already claimed three thousand lives between 1987 and 1990.

In August 1990 this violence burst into the Johannesburg townships when gunmen opened fire on black commuters on a train. In June 1992, forty people were hacked to death in a midnight attack on a squatter camp near Johannesburg. Eyewitnesses reported seeing police trucks ferrying alleged Inkatha supporters to the area. When Mandela arrived at the scene a crowd of youths sang: "Mandela, you behave like a lamb while we are being slaughtered." This response was very much to the advantage of the National Party as it gave the impression of an impotent ANC unable to protect its supporters and with no power to stop the violence. Mandela responded by breaking off negotiations and launching a **campaign of mass action** to pressurize the government. On August 3 and 4, 1992, the ANC called the largest **strike** in South African history, when four million workers stayed away from work. Subsequently negotiations between the government and the ANC resumed and in October 1992, President De Klerk apologized (conditionally) for apartheid.

But in April 1993, it looked like the whole process was going to unravel with the **assassination of Chris Hani**, the most popular ANC leader after Mandela. Hani's slaying by a right-wing gunman touched deep fears among all South Africans. A descent into civil war loomed and for three consecutive nights the nation watched as Mandela appeared on prime-time television appealing for calm. This marked the

decisive turning point as it became apparent that the ANC president was able to hold the country together, while De Klerk kept his head down. Pushing his stategic advantage, Mandela swiftly called for the immediate setting of an **election date**. On June 3, 1993, the poll was proposed for April 27, 1994, and Mandela was able to tell his followers that "the countdown to democracy has begun".

By December 1993, South Africa had its first multiracial administration in 350 years, when the **Transitional Executive Authority** was installed. But this did nothing to stop the violence, which continued to endanger the transition, while Chief Buthelezi and the white right-wing continued to threaten civil war unless KwaZulu-Natal was given autonomy and the Afrikaners a *volkstaat* (homeland). Bloodshed and mayhem continued in KwaZulu-Natal and it looked like the election was going to be disrupted. In February 1994, the negotiating parties held fresh discussions to accommodate Chief Buthelezi and the right-wingers. But concessions accepting the principle of self-determination failed to draw either into the elections.

In March 1994, a popular uprising against the government of the **Bophuthatswana** *bantustan* resonated across South Africa. The territory's army and police mutinied and, in an attempt to shore up his regime, Chief Mangope asked the white right wing to help. Hundreds of armed AWB neo-nazis converged on the capital, Mmabatho, and South Africa watched as they were routed by the *bantustan* army. Televison images of armed white neo-fascists being ingloriously defeated by Africans put paid to any ideas about white invincibility and laid to rest the threat of a right-wing rebellion.

In response, the fractionally less right-wing **Afrikaner Volksfront** (Afrikaner Peoples' Front), an alliance of whites who wanted their own self-governimg homeland, announced that it would take part in the election, thus leaving Buthelezi isolated. Yet Buthelezi still insisted on boycotting the poll and threatened to lead a KwaZulu-Natal secession from South Africa. His supporters were whipped up into a frenzy of violence that swept across the province. The transitional government declared a **state of emergency** in KwaZulu-Natal and swamped the province with troops. One week before the election was due, the mercurial Inkatha leader agreed to take part.

THE 1994 ELECTION

Despite a last attempt by right-wingers to disrupt the election by bombing Johannesburg International Airport, the **election** of April 27, 1994, passed peacefully. At the age of 76, Mandela, along with millions of his fellow citizens, voted for the first time in his life in his country's elections. On May 2, De Klerk conceded defeat after an ANC landslide, in which they took 62.7 percent of the vote. Of the remaining parties, the National Party fared best with 20.4 percent, followed by Inkatha Freedom Party with 10.5 percent; trailing way behind were the Freedom Front with 2.2 percent, the Democratic Party with 1.7 percent, and the Pan Africanist Congress with 1.2 pecent. The ANC was dominant in all but two of the provinces, the National Party taking the **Western Cape** decisively and Buthelezi's Inkatha sweeping to a tight 50.3 percent majority in its **KwaZulu-Natal** heartland. However, one of the disappointments for the ANC was its inability to appeal broadly to non-African racial groups. Ironically, the National Party won an overwhelming proportion of this Indian, coloured and white support.

For the ANC, the real struggle was only beginning. It inherited a country of 38 million people. Of these it was estimated that six million were unemployed, nine million were destitute, ten million had no access to running water, and twenty million had no electricity. Among adult blacks, sixty percent were illiterate and fewer than fifty percent of black children under 14 went to school. The gap between black and white was still gaping. One indicator of this, infant mortality, ran at eighty deaths per thousand among Africans, compared with just seven among whites.

THE MANDELA YEARS: 1994–1999

Few people in recorded history have been the subject of such high expectations; still fewer have matched them; Mandela has exceeded them. We knew of his fortitude before he left jail; we have since experienced his extraordinary reserves of goodwill, his sense of fun and the depth of his maturity. As others' prisoner, he very nearly decided the date of his own release; as president, he has wisely chosen the moment of his going. Any other nation would consider itself privileged to have his equal as its leader. His last full year in power provides us with an occasion again to consider his achievement in bringing and holding our fractious land together.

Mail & Guardian, Dec 24, 1998

South Africa's first five years of democracy are inextricably linked to the towering figure of **Nelson Mandela**, who had the unenviable task of presiding over attempts to redress the atrocities and imbalances of racial oppression while simultaneously fostering reconciliation. On one hand he had to mollify the fears of many whites, who, having seen their political privileges stripped away, imagined an imminent collapse of lifestyle. And on the other, he had to temper the impatience of a black majority that, having finally achieved civil rights, found it hard to understand why economic advancement wasn't following quickly. The achievements of the government, however, were more uneven than those of its leader.

Soon after taking power, Mandela announced the **Reconstruction and Development Plan** (RDP), which set health, housing, education and economic growth as its priorities. This was to be realized in the electrifying of 350,000 homes in the ensuing year, the provision of decent education for all children, and in the building of 2.5 million houses by the end of the decade. But in August 1994, Mandela's keynote address, outlining the government's progress in its first hundred days of office, was greeted by industrial action protesting at the slow pace of change. By the end of 1997, only 350,000 houses had been built, though the introduction of clean, piped water, and electricity to over a million homes were significant successes.

Despite the victory of liberal democratic principles embodied in the 1994 election, South Africa still displayed a singular lack of the trappings associated with civil society. **Crime**, sensationalized daily in the media, continued to dog the country. In the closing stages of the ANC's first five years, the police were reporting an average of 52 murders a day, a rape every half hour (including a frightening rise in child rape), and one car theft every nine minutes. Simmering behind the scenes was a less obvious threat to the social fabric, a culture of **non-payment of municipal rates**. This had begun as a form of anti-apartheid political action during the Eighties, but by the post-apartheid era it had

THE TRUTH AND RECONCILIATION COMMISSION

As you type, you don't know you are crying until you feel and see the tears on your hands.

Chief typist of the transcripts of the TRC hearings, as told to Archbishop Tutu

By the time South Africa achieved democracy in 1994, it was internationally accepted that **apartheid** was, in the words of a UN resolution, "a crime against humanity," and that unspeakable atrocities had been committed in its name. But no one could have imagined how systematic, horrific and at the same time banal these atrocities had been.

This was only to emerge at the hearings of the **Truth and Reconciliation Commission** (TRC), set up to investigate gross abuses of human rights under apartheid. Under the chairmanship of Nobel Peace laureate, Archbishop **Desmond Tutu**, the commission was mandated to examine acts committed between March 1960, date of the Sharpeville massacre, and May 10, 1994, the day of Mandela's inauguration as president.

The objective of the TRC was to discover the **secret history of apartheid** (not to punish wrongdoers) and to gain "as complete a picture as possible of the nature, causes and extent of human rights violations". The main means of achieving this was through evidence given by victims and perpetrators. To facilitate this there was provision for **amnesty** to be granted in exchange for "full disclosure of all the relevant facts relating to acts associated with a political objective committed in the course of the conflicts of the past".

The commission began sitting in April 1996 under the glare of international TV cameras, and completed its hearings on July 31, 1998 (with ongoing investigations continuing until June 2000). Unique among the truth commissions of the late twentieth century, including those held in Latin America, the South African TRC operated **in public**, allowing all South Africans to share a knowledge of what had actually happened.

Among the deeply moving **testimonies** given by over 21,000 people were individual stories from parents, siblings and friends of those who had disappeared. Others gave gruesome accounts of torture, bombings and murders on an extensive scale. In his foreword to the TRC report, Tutu recalls "how at one of our hearings a mother cried out plaintively: 'Please cannot you bring back even just a bone of my child so that I can bury him'."

Leading members of the former government and the ANC appeared before the TRC, among them former president **F.W. De Klerk**. In May, 1996, he told the commission that he had not been aware of any atrocities committed under apartheid – a statement Archbishop Tutu said he found difficult to believe, especially given the avalanche of information available to De Klerk as president.

Further evidence of a systematic and brutal campaign of repression by the government came

---

become a way of life, with nearly eighty percent of township residents withholding payment.

In response, Mandela called for a **"new patriotism"** and attacked the "culture of rapacity" that appeared to underlie these problems. But a popular sense that whites weren't doing enough to redress the imbalances, and that many officials had forgotten about liberation and were simply riding the gravy train, did little to encourage a climate of probity. One well-publicized, but by no means isolated example of **corruption** involved the Reverend **Allan Boesak**. A founding member of the United Democratic Front and a stalwart of the liberation struggle, in 1999 he was found guilty of misappropriating over a million rands of Danish donor funding. That March, at a Human Rights Day rally, the then deputy president Thabo Mbeki acknowledged the extent of the problem and pledged to root out "those who have smuggled themselves into the ANC not to serve the people, but to pursue their own ends."

The overriding theme of the Mandela presidency was that of **reconciliation**. In 1995, he hosted a symbolic lunch for the wives of liberation leaders and ex-prime ministers and presidents, as well as taking tea with Betsie Verwoerd, widow of Hendrik Verwoerd. Perhaps the highlight of this policy was in May and June 1995, when the rugby union **World Cup** was staged in South Africa. The Springboks won – for many years an international pariah due to their whites-only membership – watched by Mandela, sporting Springbok colours. Rapprochement was also pursued with the **Inkatha Freedom Party (IFP)**, leading to a reduction in political violence in KwaZulu-Natal. The most significant side-show of the period was the **Truth and Reconciliation Commission**, which began sitting in 1996, set up to examine gross human rights abuses in South Africa between 1960 and 1993 (see box above).

On a more positive note, the **New Constitution**, approved in May 1996, ensured that South Africa would remain a parliamentary to light during a trial (incidental to the TRC) in September 1996 of former police colonel, **Eugene De Kock**, who was pleading in mitigation after being convicted on 89 charges of murder, gunrunning and fraud. He revealed that his activities were not the work of a rogue unit, but part of a well-coordinated campaign by the security forces, carried out with the full knowledge of the government, including presidents Botha and De Klerk.

After two-and-a-half years of hearings across the country, the TRC released its 3,500-page **report** on October 29, 1998. Unsurprisingly, the commission found that "the South African government was in the period 1960–94 the primary perpetrator of gross human rights abuses in South Africa, and from 1974, in Southern Africa". The TRC heard overwhelming evidence that from the Seventies to the Nineties the state had been involved in criminal activities including "extrajudicial killings of political opponents." Among the violations it listed were torture, abduction, sexual abuse, incursions across South Africa's borders to kill opponents in exile, and the deployment of hit squads. It also found that the ANC (and a number of other organizations, including the PAC and Inkatha) was guilty of human rights violations, though on nowhere near the scale of the government. The report acknowledged that the ANC had been waging a just war against apartheid but drew "a distinction between a 'just war' and 'just means'".

There was considerable **criticism of the TRC** from all quarters. Many people felt that justice would better have been served by a Nuremburg-style trial of those guilty of gross violations, but Tutu argued that this would have been impossible in South Africa, given that neither side had won a military victory. Defending the amnesty provisions, he pointed out that "members of the security establishment would have scuppered the negotiated settlement had they thought they were going to run a gauntlet of trials for their involvement in past violations."

The South African media has tended to give the impression that the Truth and Reconciliation Commission has led to a deterioration of race relations in South Africa (as if that were possible). However, a market research survey carried out for *Business Day* in August, 1998, found that attitudes to the TRC split along racial lines; eighty percent of black respondents believed that "the people in SA will now be able to live together more easily", while ninety percent of whites felt that the commission would not bring the races closer.

Responding to the lack of support for the TRC, and sometimes even active obstructivism from white leaders, Tutu remarked: "I have been saddened by a mean-spiritedness in some of the leadership of the white community. They should be saying: 'How fortunate we are that these people do not want to treat us how we treated them. How fortunate that things have remained much the same for us except for the loss of some political power.'"

democracy with an executive president. One of the most progressive constitutions in the world, it incorporated an extensive bill of rights. The main points were the outlawing of discrimination on the grounds of race, gender, pregnancy, ethnic or social origin, sexual orientation, disability, religion, belief, culture or language; protection of freedom of religion, belief, movement, association, expression and artistic creativity; prohibition of slavery, servitude, forced labour, torture, detention without trial, violence or cruel punishment; guarantee of the right to life, banning capital punishment but permitting abortion; and the appointment of a public protector to defend individuals against maladministration.

THE POST-MANDELA ERA

One of the president's most skilful achievements was to initiate the post-Mandela era while still in office, ensuring a seamless political transition for South Africa as it takes on the twenty-first century. By the middle of Mandela's

presidency, his deputy, **Thabo Mbeki**, had taken charge of the nuts-and-bolts running of the country, having already assumed the chairmanship of the ANC in 1993. At the 1997 ANC national congress he succeeded Mandela as the leader of the party, securing his position as the next president of South Africa.

If Mandela has associated himself with reconciliation, then Mbeki is the champion of **black empowerment** which he has wrapped in his notion of the "**African renaissance**". What exactly this entails is unclear, as Mbeki has so far failed to define its tenets. Some commentators suspect that leaving it vague is his intention – a means of being all things to all Africans. For some whites, this conjures up fears that reconciliation is over and that Mbeki will ruthlessly pursue a programme of **Africanization** that will see them marginalized and further stripped of privilege. Indeed, he has commented that "You can't say there must be reconciliation on the basis of the maintenance of the status quo."

Meanwhile, on the political left, socialists and trade unionists fear that the end of the ANC's whirlwind flirtation with redistribution has been replaced by a black empowerment agenda entailing the transfer of political and economic power from one bourgouisie (a white one) to another (a black one). In 1996 there was alarm from COSATU and the SACP – the ANC's alliance partners – when the party announced a strategy for job creation through growth, framed in neo-Thatcherite terminology of budget-deficit reduction and wage restraint. A month later, these fears were further fuelled by Mandela when he described **privatization** as "the fundamental policy of the ANC", sparking a one-day strike.

By 1999, however, Mandela's eye was firmly on his long-promised retirement to Qunu, the small village in the Eastern Cape where he had grown up, and he officially stepped down from the presidency to the inevitable panegyrics from around the world. The **general election** of June 1999 confirmed two of South African politics' most unwieldy aspects: the continued mass loyalty of the electorate to the ANC, and the lack of a potent opposition. Increasing their majority from the 1994 elections, Mbeki's ANC secured a fraction under two-thirds of the vote (266 seats), a mark that would have allowed them to tinker with the constitution. The real surprises came among the (admittedly far-distant) placings, with the **Democratic Party**, under the leadership of the feisty but eloquent and principled Tony Leon, becoming the official opposition with 38 seats – a huge rise of 31 seats on their disappointing 1994 performance. Leon's dynamic election campaign saw him emerge as the next best hope for large numbers of white South Africans, who deserted the National Party (restyled as the New National Party) in droves as their representation dropped from 82 to 28, four seats behind Mangosuthu Buthelezi's IFP.

With the most pressing focus of reconciliation in the country shifting from black-white tension to that between the ANC and IFP, **Buthelezi** was widely tipped to become Mbeki's deputy president. The Zulu leader, however, declined the significantly watered-down post, preferring not to trade-in IFP power in KwaZulu-Natal, still the most volatile and problematic of South Africa's provinces, and held onto his role as minister for home affairs. As a result Mbeki's **cabinet** was a distinctly loyalist one, from low-profile deputy president **Jacob Zuma** to retained finance minister **Trevor Manuel**. Much of the heat of the administration is likely to be generated by the more provocative postings of **Steve Tshwete**, sent in to deal with the recalcitrant reformers of the civil service in much the same way he had with white-dominated sports, and **Nkosazana Zuma**, the most powerful female politician in the country, whose appointment as minister for foreign affairs was described by Tony Leon as like "sending a bull into a china shop".

The process of transformation begun during Mbeki's deputyship looks set to continue during his presidency, changing the complexion of business, the civil service and politics to reflect gender and race distribution. One tool for achieving this is **affirmative action**, in which blacks and women are recruited in preference to white males (who have traditionally dominated politics and business). Mbeki has described this as not "a philosophy, not an end in itself, but an instrument to get a more equal society, broadly representative of South African demography". This has proved controversial, particularly among liberals, who criticize the policy for retrenching skilled whites and replacing them with untrained personnel, simply because they are black. They regard this as both patronizing and seriously damaging to the country's infrastructure, and argue that a longer-term strategy of skilling-up blacks, although slower, would lead to a sounder economy. Understandably, this is unappealing for most blacks, who would face the prospect of sacrificing their own advancement today in the interests of a better tomorrow for future generations.

South Africa's second five years of democracy will probably be even more crucial than the first five. With Mandela off the scene, the symbolic transfer of power that he embodied and his aura of near-saintliness can't be relied on to walk South Africa across any rough waters ahead. What will count is the ability of the government to steer South Africa through the vagaries of a globalizing economy while balancing the interests of entrenched white business with the aspirations of an ascendant black middle class. And, just as importantly, they must deliver something of substance to disadvantaged South Africans, who are becoming impatient to cash in their post-apartheid dividend.

WILDLIFE

There's nowhere better than South Africa to encounter African mammals. Kruger National Park, the biggest of several major reserves along the northern and eastern extremes of the country, is rated among the world's top wildlife reserves, both for its ease of access and its range of mammal species. Apart from offering thrilling experiences, the major South African reserves are islands of living archeology, hinting at the teeming life that moved across the subcontinent as far south as present-day Cape Town, before European settlers with firearms swept it to the margins of the country. Apart from Kruger, Kalahari-Gemsbok, Hluhluwe-Umfolozi and Pilanesberg parks, where you'll see the big five (lion, leopard, buffalo, elephant and rhino), over a hundred other reserves offer numerous smaller predators and dozens of herbivores, including endangered species, in invariably beautiful settings.

This account supplements the colour field-guide to "The Wildlife of East and Southern Africa" in the centre of the book (to which bracketed page numbers refer) and will help you get the most from watching both big game and smaller species. It aims to inspire you to go beyond checklists, to appreciate the interactions of the bush and help you get more out of your safari. Beyond the scope of this account are the hundreds of colourful **bird species** that are an inseparable part of the South African landscape and whose calls are a constant element of its soundtrack. An interest in these will add immeasurably to your experience. Some outstanding **field guides** are listed on p.737.

ECOLOGICAL ZONES

South Africa's ecological zones encompass a range of climate, topography and vegetation supporting a rich diversity of animal life. There are thornveld deserts, pockets of forest, tangles of subtropical vegetation, grassy savannas, mountainous peaks and several distinct coastal habitats. Geographically, South Africa is divided in two by successive mountain ranges that run in a huge arc from the Cape Peninsula to Mpumalanga, approximately parallel to the coast. This Great Escarpment divides the vast, drier interior plateau from the moister marginal zone that merges with the coastal belt. The plateau and coastal margin can each be divided up into a series of ecological zones, or biomes, which share a climate and similar vegetation.

THE LOWVELD

The **lowveld**, or bushveld, is immediately recognizable as the stereotypical African landscape of great plains, forming a backdrop for thousands of animals. It stretches down across a third of Africa, from Malawi into South Africa; here it forms a large, crescent-shaped swathe running parallel to the Limpopo River, and then sweeps down between the Drakensberg and the sub-tropical coastal strip that runs from the northern KwaZulu-Natal coast into the Eastern Cape as far as Port Elizabeth. Typical vegetation consists of mixed **savanna** and **dry woodlands** and includes deciduous broad-leafed trees such as **marulas**, whose fruit is highly sought-after by elephants.

The moister section of the lowveld, along the Mpumalanga and northern KwaZulu-Natal borders, is a subtropical region, with thorny **acacias**, stands of green-barked **fever trees** and the thick-set form of **baobabs**, with varieties of **palm** thriving in the river valleys.

In the drier transitional zones to the west, bordering the arid zone, succulent species such as **aloes** (with their red-hot poker flowers) and massive candelabra-tree **euphorbias** dominate a harsher landscape.

SUBTROPICAL LOWLAND

South of the Mozambique border, to the Great Fish River in the Eastern Cape, lies the narrow **coastal plain**, at an altitude of below 400m.

Once thickly forested, cane fields have replaced the indigenous woodlands, particularly in KwaZulu-Natal. However, one of the wildest environments in the country survives in Maputaland, where extensive **dunes** and **wetlands** constitute a transitional zone between the Mozambique tropics and subtropical KwaZulu-Natal. Some 21 ecosystems have been identified here.

With the notable exception of lions, you can expect to see a terrific array of wildlife, including aquatic and semi-aquatic species such as crocodile, hippo, terrapin, clawless otter, reedbuck and water monitor lizard. Giant forests on the protected west flank of its dunes provide refuge to red duiker, bushpig, and vervet and samango monkeys.

From southern KwaZulu-Natal into the Wild Coast of the Eastern Cape, dozens of major river courses have etched deep valleys that protect the remnants of dwindling forests. Nowhere is it more dramatic though, than at Oribi Gorge Nature Reserve, near Port Shepstone, where a 24km-long and five-kilometre-wide gorge is part of an environment that descends from **clifftop grasslands**, down **sandstone cliffs**, to dense **riverine forests**. Here you'll find bushbuck, cheeky vervets and shy samango monkeys, two species of the small duiker antelope, and with an eye to a meal, leopards.

THE FYNBOS REGION

Confined to a shallow southwestern corner of South Africa, the **fynbos region** extends in an inverse arc from the Olifants River in the north to Port Elizabeth in the east, and includes the Cape Peninsula. The region consists of the smallest and richest of the world's six floral kingdoms. A **heathland** system, it grows on the back of the Cape fold mountains that cut off the coastal belt from the semi-arid Karoo interior. Despite its diversity, fynbos is extremely nutrient poor and is unable to support a large biomass (it can't feed large organisms in great quantities). Although a reasonable cross-section of mammals, including lion and elephant, inhabited the zone when the first settlers arrived, they were relatively few in number and were soon wiped out in the localized area. One, the blue antelope, a large species related to the sable, was totally extinguished.

Most exciting of its mammals are the fairly numerous but infrequently seen Cape mountain leopards. The same species as those elsewhere in the country, they're smaller here – an adaptation to the scarcity of nutrients. Other predators include caracals, African wild cats, and jackals. The Cape of Good Hope Nature Reserve is one of the best places to get an idea of the fynbos ecological zone and is one of the areas where the endangered bontebok still survives, alongside baboons, porcupines and Cape mountain zebras. For more on fynbos see "Cape Town", p.117.

THE WESTERN ARID ZONE

The **western arid zone** creeps down from the north and includes the entire section of the Kalahari ecological zone that licks into the Northern Cape from Botswana, as well as the succulent Karoo zone along the west coast and the Nama Karoo zone in the extensive interior. Permanent surface water is almost totally absent throughout the zone – the Orange River is the only perennial watercourse in its entire vastness. The succulent Karoo coastal zone is a region of profuse succulents which explode into swathes of colourful flowers in August and September after the winter rains; the South African Kalahari is a lonely region of **red sandveld** punctuated with **camelthorn acacia** trees; and the Nama Karoo consists predominantly of wiry **dwarf shrubs** in flat country fringed with low **hills**.

Kalahari-Gemsbok National Park is the most notable game reserve in the western arid zone, rated by some as a rival to Kruger because of its wilder ambience and excellent wildlife. It's one of the few places in the country to see gemsbok, and you might also encounter lion, cheetah, jackal and bat-eared foxes among an impressive list of mammals. Only elephant and buffalo are notably absent.

The Karoo was once the theatre of swarming herds of migrating antelope including springbok and bontebok. Now they're only seen behind fences, where they are raised for their meat alongside millions of sheep. However, some species that once roamed the Karoo, including gemsbok, hartebeest and black wildebeest, have been reintroduced into the National Park, where they co-exist with survivors such as baboon, reedbuck, klipspringer and caracal.

THE HIGHVELD

The high-lying central plateau (generally 1200–1829m) of South Africa, known as the

highveld, takes in the territory south of Johannesburg, including the Free State east of Bloemfontein, and is defined in the south and east by the Great Escarpment. The ecological zone varies from flat grassy, treeless **plains** to the rugged **peaks** of the Drakensberg, where you'll find alpine-type vegetation above an altitude of 3000m. Most of the region is now covered by **semi-desert** scrub and **maize fields**, with indigenous vegetation surviving only around the peaks and in the rugged valleys. Of the mammals that once thrived here, only smaller species, such as caracal, mongoose and hare, have managed to cling on under the massive agricultural onslaught. However, at Suikerbosrand Nature Reserve, just south of Johannesburg, you can see once-endangered species such as blesbok, as well as cheetah, springbok, hartebeest, oribi, zebra, mountain reedbuck, rhebok, duiker, steenbok, kudu and brown hyena. One bird you could well see striding through cultivated fields is the blue crane, South Africa's national bird, which feeds on the seeds of standing crops. In the reserves of the Drakensberg, mountain-adapted antelope, such as klipspringer and mountain reedbuck, and baboon, porcupine and jackal all thrive.

AFRO-MONTANE FOREST

South Africa is one of the least forested countries in the world, a tiny fraction of one percent of its surface carrying indigenous woodland. **Afro-montane forest**, which requires high annual rainfall, exists only in isolated pockets, most famous of which is the Knysna Forest on the southern slopes of the Western Cape's Outeniqua Mountains. Best known for its **giant trees**, including yellowwood, stinkwood and ironwood, it also has leopard, bushpig, bushbuck, caracals and mongoose. Similar forest also survives in the Eastern Cape in the Katberg-Hogsback area and here baboon, vervet and samango monkeys, duiker, bushbuck and porcupine are common.

PRIMATES

Southern Africa has the lowest diversity of primates on the continent, a mere five species (compared with Kenya's twelve) excluding *Homo sapiens*. They include two varieties of bushbaby, two monkeys and one species of baboon – the largest and most formidable of the lot. Great apes such as gorillas and chim-

Page numbers below refer to the **colour guide** to "The Wildlife of East and Southern Africa" in the centre of this book.

panzees aren't found in the wild in southern Africa.

CHACMA BABOONS

Chacma baboons, *Papio ursinus* – cynocephalus – (p.2), the local subspecies of common savanna monkeys, are the primates most widely found in South Africa. Males can be somewhat intimidating in size and manner and are frequently bold enough to raid vehicles or accommodation in search of food, undeterred by the close presence of people. Baboons are highly gregarious and are invariably found in troops, which can number as few as fifteen to as many as a hundred, though around forty is common. Social relations are complex, revolving around jockeying to climb the social ladder and avoiding being toppled from its upper rungs. Rank, gender, precedence, physical strength and family ties determine an individual's position in this mini society, which is led by a dominant male. Males are unreconstructed chauvinists, and every adult male enjoys dominance over every female. Days are dominated by the need to forage and hunt for food; baboons are highly opportunistic omnivores who will as happily tuck into a scorpion or a newborn antelope in the bushveld as they will clean up the entire crop from an orange tree on a Garden Route citrus farm. Grooming is a fundamental part of the social glue during times of relaxation. When baboons and other monkeys perform this massage-like activity on each other, the specks which they pop into their mouths are sometimes parasites – notably ticks – and sometimes flecks of skin.

VERVET MONKEYS

Another widespread primate you're likely to see in the eastern half of the country, and along the coastal belt as far west as Mossel Bay, are **vervet monkeys**, *Cercopithecus aethiops* (p.2). Although happy foraging in grasslands, they rarely venture far from woodland, particularly along river courses. You can see them outside reserves, where they often live around farms and even come into suburban fringes, where opportunities for scavenging are promising. In the Eastern Cape, KwaZulu-Natal and along the

Garden Route you might see them hanging about along the verges of the coastal roads, risking their lives "playing chicken" with the traffic. Vervets are principally vegetarians but they are not averse to eating invertebrates, small lizards, nestlings and eggs, as well as processed foods like biscuits and sweets – when they can snatch them from visitors. Vervet society is made up of family groups of females and young defended by associate males and is highly caste-ridden. A mother's rank determines that of her daughter from infancy, and lower-ranking adult females being castigated if they fail to show due respect to these "upper crust" youngsters.

SAMANGO MONKEYS

In striking contrast with the cheekier, upfront disposition of vervets, the rarer **samango monkeys**, *Cercopithecus mitis* (p.3), are shy animals that may only give themselves away through their loud explosive call or the breaking of branches as they go about their business through the canopy. Although they bear a passing resemblance to vervets, samangos are larger and have long cheek hair that gives the passing appearance of Darth Vader. Found only in isolated pockets of KwaZulu-Natal, the Eastern Cape and Mpumalanga, they tend to hang out in the higher reaches of gallery forest, though on occasion they venture into the open to forage. Like vervets, they're highly social and live in troops of females under the proprietorship of a dominant male, but unlike their relatives they are more inclined to fan out when looking for food.

BUSHBABIES

With their large soft, fluffy pelts, huge, saucer-like eyes, large, rounded ears and superficially cat-like appearance, **bushbabies** are the ultimate in cute, cuddly-looking primates. Of the half-dozen or so species endemic to Africa, only the thick-tailed bushbaby, *Otolemur crassicaudatus*, and, about half the size, the lesser bushbaby, *Galago moholi*, are found south of the Limpopo. The former is restricted to the eastern fringes of the sub-continent, while the latter overlaps its range in the northeast and extends across the north of the country into Northwest Province.

If you're staying at any of the KwaZulu-Natal reserves, you stand a fair chance of seeing a bushbaby after dark as they emerge from the dense forest canopy, where they rest in small groups, for spells of lone foraging for tree gum and fruit. Even if you don't see one you're bound to hear their piercing scream cut through the sounds of the night. Unlike other bushbabies, including the lesser, which leap with ease and speed, *crassicaudatus* (thick tails) is a slow mover that hops or walks along branches, often with considerable stealth. Bushbabies habituate easily to humans and will sometimes come into lodge dining rooms, scavenging for tidbits; at *Rocktail Bay Lodge*, on the northern KwaZulu-Natal coast, Gremlin, a semi-tame bushbaby, periodically joins guests in their beds and has developed a penchant for sugar and booze.

CARNIVORES

Almost three dozen species of carnivore are found in South Africa, ranging from mongooses and weasels to hyenas, dog-relatives and seven species of cat.

DOG-RELATIVES

South Africa's five **dog-relatives**, *Canidae*, consist of two foxes, two jackals and the wild dog. The member of the *Canidae* you're most likely to see is the **black-backed jackal**, *Canis mesomelas* (p.4), found especially, though not exclusively, in the country's reserves. It bears a strong resemblance to a small, skinny German Shepherd, but with a more fox-like muzzle, and is distinguished from the grey **side-striped jackal**, *Canis adjustus*, by the white-flecked black saddle on its back, to which it owes its name. In South Africa, the side-striped is found only in and around Kruger and the extreme north of KwaZulu-Natal, and this is the only region where any confusion can arise. The fact that the black-backed seeks a drier habitat, in contrast to the side-striped's preference for well-watered woodland, is an additional identification pointer. Both are omnivorous, with diets that take in carrion, small animals, reptiles, birds and insects, as well as wild fruit and berries; and both are most commonly spotted alone or in pairs, though family groups are occasionally sighted.

The **bat-eared fox**, *Otocyon megalotis* (p.4), is found throughout the western half of the country and along the Limpopo strip and can be easily distinguished from the jackals by its outsized ears, its shorter, pointier muzzle and its considerably smaller size. The bat-eared's black Zorro mask helps distinguish it from the similar sized **Cape fox**, *Vulpes chama*, which inhabitats an overlapping range. Like other dogs, the bat-eared fox is an omnivore, but it favours termites and larvae, which is where its large radar-like ears come in handy. With these it can triangulate the precise position of dung beetle larvae up to 30cm underground and to dig them out. Bat-eareds tend to live in pairs or family groups, an arrangement that affords mutual protection.

Once widely distributed hunters of the African plains, **wild dogs**, *Lycaon pictus* (p.4), have been brought to the edge of extinction. For many years they were shot on sight, having gained an unjustified reputation as cruel and wanton killers of cattle and sheep. More recent scientific evidence reveals them to be economical and efficient hunters – and more successful at it than any other African species. They have only survived in the Kruger, and have been reintroduced into Hluhluwe-Umfolozi, though you'd be extremely lucky to see a pack trotting along for a hunt. Capable of sustaining high speeds (up to 50kph) over long distances, wild dogs lunge at their prey en masse, tearing it to pieces – a gruesome finish, but no more grisly than the suffocating muzzle-bite of a lion. The entire pack of ten to fifteen animals participates in looking after the pups, bringing back food and regurgitating it for them.

CATS

Apart from lions, which notably live in social groups, **cats** are solitary carnivores. With the exception of the cheetah which is anatomically distinct from the other cats, remaining members of the family are so similar that, as Richard Estes comments in *The Safari Companion*, big cats are just "jumbo versions" of the domestic cat, "distinguished mainly by a modification of the larynx that enables them to roar."

Perhaps it's just a question of size, but the most compelling of the *Felidae* for most people on safari are **lions**, *Panthera leo* (p.6) the largest cats, and indeed, the most massive predators in Africa. It's fortunate then that despite having the most limited distribution of any cat in South Africa, lions are the ones you're most likely to see. Of the public reserves, the Kruger and Kalahari-Gemsbok parks have healthy populations, and prides have been reintroduced into Hluhluwe-Umfolozi, where num-

bers are relatively limited. Lazy, gregarious and sizeable, lions rarely attempt to hide, making them relatively easy to find, especially if someone else has already spotted them – a gathering of stationary vehicles frequently signals lions. Seeing them hunt is another matter, and you're less likely to see David Attenborough-esque enactments of the chase. In fact their fabled reputation as cold, efficient hunters is ill-founded, as lions are only successful around thirty percent of the time, and only then if operating as a group. Males don't hunt at all if they can help it and will happily enjoy a free lunch by courtesy of the females of the pride.

The lion may be king, but most successful and arguably most beautiful of the large cats is the **leopard**, *Panthera pardus* (p.6), which survives from the southern coastal strip of Africa all the way to China. Highly adaptable, they can subsist in extremes of aridity or cold, as well as in proximity to human habitation, where they happily prey on domestic animals – which accounts for their absence in the sheep-farming regions of central South Africa, due to extermination by farmers. They're present in the rugged, mountainous southern areas of the Western Cape, but you are most unlikely to encounter these secretive, solitary animals here. Your best chance of a sighting is at the private lodges in Sabi Sands, abutting Kruger, both of which trade on their leopards being highly habituated to people. You'll need greater luck and sharper eyes to see them in the public reserves they inhabit, including the Kruger, Kalahari-Gemsbok, Hluhluwe-Umfolozi and Mkuzi. Powerfully built, they can bring down prey twice their mass and drag an impala their own weight up a tree. The chase is not part of the leopard's tactical repertoire; they hunt by stealth, getting to within two metres of their target before pouncing.

In the flesh, the **cheetah**, *Acionyx jubatus* (p.6), is so different from the leopard that it's hard to see how there could ever be any confusion. Cheetahs are the lightly built greyhounds of the big-cat world, with small heads, very long legs and an exterior decor of fine spots. Unlike leopards, cheetahs never climb trees, being designed rather for activity on the open plains. They live alone, or sometimes briefly form a pair during mating. Hunting is normally a solitary activity, down to eyesight and an incredible burst of speed that can take the animal up to

100kph for a few seconds. Because they're lighter than lions and less powerful than leopards, cheetahs can't rely on strength to bring down their prey, instead having to resort to tripping or knocking the victim off balance by striking its hindquarters and then pouncing. Once widespread across South Africa, now you'll only see them in a few reserves including Kruger, Kalahari-Gemsbok and Hluhluwe-Umfolozi.

The other *felidae* are usually classified as small cats, although the **caracal**, *Caracal caracal* (p.6), is a substantial animal. An unmistakeable and awesome hunter, with great climbing agility, it's able to take prey, such as adult impala and sheep, which far exceed its own mass of eight to eighteen kilogrammes. More commonly it will feed on birds, which it pounces on, sometimes while still in flight, as well as smaller mammals, including dassies. Found across most of South Africa, excluding KwaZulu-Natal, but not often seen, caracals live in the Mountain Zebra National Park (one of the best places to see them), Kruger, Giant's Castle, Cape of Good Hope, Karoo, and Kalahari-Gemsbok.

Long-legged and spotted, **servals**, *Felis serval* (p.7), are higher at the shoulder but lighter than caracals, and are equally rarely seen, although they are present in Mpumalanga and KwaZulu-Natal in the Kruger, Hluhluwe-Umfolozi and Giant's Castle. Efficient hunters, servals use their large rounded ears to pinpoint prey (usually small rodents, birds or reptiles), which they pounce on with both front paws after performing impressive athletic leaps.

Of the genuinely small cats, the **African wild cat**, *Felis lybica*, is distributed throughout South Africa and is easily mistaken for a domestic tabby, although its legs are longer and it has reddish ears. First domesticated six thousand years ago by the Egyptians, wild cats are so closely related to the domestic version that the two are able to interbreed freely. You're unlikely to encounter the compact small **spotted cat**, *Felis nigripes* (also known as the black footed cat), a beautifully spotted fluffy animal, which is so rarely seen that little is known about its behaviour in the wild.

HYENAS

The largest carnivores after lions are **hyenas**, and apart from the lion, the **spotted hyena**, *Crocuta crocuta* (p.5), is the meat-eater you will most often see. Although considered a scavenger *par excellence*, the spotted hyena is a formidable hunter, most often found where antelopes and zebras are present. Exceptionally efficient consumers, with immensely strong teeth and jaws, spotted hyenas eat virtually every part of their prey, including bones and hide and, where habituated to humans, often steal shoes, unwashed pans and refuse from tents. Although they can be seen by day, they are most active at night – when they issue their unnerving whooping cries. Clans of twenty or so animals are dominated by females, who are larger than the males and compete with each other for rank. Curiously, female hyenas' genitalia are hard to distinguish from males', leading to a popular misconception that they are hermaphroditic. They occur in Kruger, Hluhluwe-Umfolozi and Kalahari-Gemsbok parks, and north into East and West Africa.

The **brown hyena**, *Hyaena brunnea*, is restricted to parts of Namibia, Botswana, Zimbabwe and South Africa, where it's generally seen only in the northernmost regions. That it's usually seen singly also distinguishes this shaggier, slightly larger hyena from its spotted cousin.

The hyena-like **aardwolf**, *Proteles cristatus*, is smaller than the spotted hyena and far lighter (about two-thirds the height at the shoulder and roughly a tenth of its weight) as well as being less shaggy with vertical dark stripes along its tawny body. It is further distinguished from hyenas by its insectivorous diet and its particular preference for harvester termites, which it laps up en masse (up to 200,000 in one night) with its broad sticky tongue. Far more widely distributed in South Africa than the hyenas, this nocturnal animal is sometimes active in the cooler hours just before dusk or after dawn. Although they aren't often seen, keep an eye open at the Cape of Good Hope, Karoo, Mountain Zebra, Pilanesberg, Kruger, Hluhluwe-Umfolozi and Kalahari-Gemsbok reserves.

SMALLER CARNIVORES

Among the smaller predators is the unusual **honey badger**, *Mellivora capensis* (p.4), related to the European badger and with a reputation for defending itself extremely fiercely. Primarily an omnivorous forager, it will tear open bees' nests (to which it is led by a small bird, the honey guide), its thick, loose hide rendering it impervious to stings.

Small-spotted (or common) genets, *Genetta genetta* (p.5), are reminiscent of slender elongated cats, and were once domesticated around the Mediterranean (but cats turned out to be better mouse hunters). In fact they are viverrids, related to mongooses, and are frequently seen after dark around national park lodges, where they live a semi-domesticated existence. Found throughout the country, apart from KwaZulu-Natal, they're difficult to distinguish from the **large-spotted genet**, *Genetta tigrina*, which has bigger spots and a black (instead of white) tip to its tail. These are found in northeastern parts of the country, KwaZulu-Natal and along the coastal margin as far west as the Cape Peninsula.

Most species of **mongoose** (p.5), of which there are nearly a dozen in South Africa, are also tolerant of humans and, even when disturbed, can usually be observed for some time before disappearing. Their snake-fighting reputation is greatly overplayed: in practice they are mostly social foragers, fanning out through the bush like beaters on a shoot, rooting for anything edible – mostly inverterbrates, eggs, lizards and frogs.

One of the best places to see Cape **clawless otters**, *Aonyx capensis*, a large heavily built species, is in the Tsitsikamma National Park, where it feeds on crabs, fishes and octopuses and will commonly forage on cliff faces and in tidal pools. They are also common in the KwaZulu-Natal reserves and the Kruger.

The **civet** (or African civet), *civettictis civetta* (p.5), is a stocky animal resembling a large, terrestrial genet. It was formerly kept in captivity for its musk (once an ingredient in perfume), which is secreted from glands near the tail. Civets aren't often seen, but they're predictable creatures, wending their way along the same path at the same time, night after night.

ANTELOPE

Antelope are the most regularly seen family of animals in South Africa's game reserves, and you'll even spot some on farmland along the extensive open stretches that separate interior towns. South Africa has roughly a third of all antelope species in Africa. South African antelope can be sub-divided into a number of tribes, and like buffalo, giraffe and domestic cattle, they are ruminants.

BUSHBUCK TRIBE

Among the bushbuck tribe, it's generally only males that have horns, which are curved and spiralled. The exception is the eland, in which both sexes have straight horns (but still marked by distinctive spiralling). Bushbuck are the only non-territorial African antelope, and you'll see them in the shadows of thickets and bush cover, which they use for defence against predators.

Largest of the tribe, and indeed, the largest living antelope is the **eland**, *Taurotragus oryx* (p.14), which is built like an ox and moves with with the slow deliberation of one, though it's a great jumper. Once widely found, herds survive around the Kruger, Kalahari-Gemsbok and a tiny enclave in northern KwaZulu-Natal Drakensberg, plus they've been reintroduced to a number of other reserves throughout the country.

The magnificent **kudu** (known as the greater kudu in east Africa), *Tragelaphus strepsiceros* (p.14), is more elegantly built, and males are adorned with sensational spiralled horns that can easily reach 1.5m in length – it's these that you'll often see mounted in old-fashioned country hotels. Female groups usually include three or more members and will sometimes combine temporarily to form larger herds; males form similarly sized but more transient groupings, although it's not uncommon to encounter lone bulls.

Despite a distinct family resemblance you could never confuse a kudu with a **bushbuck**, *Tragelaphus scriptus* (p.14), which is considerably shorter and has a single twist to its horns, in contrast to the kudu's two or three turns. They also differ in being the only solitary members of the tribe, one reason why you're less likely to spot them. Apart from the major reserves, they're found in Addo Elephant and Greater St Lucia parks.

Nyalas, *Tragelaphus angasi* (p.13), are midway in size between the kudu and bushbuck, with which they could be confused at first glance. Telling pointers are their size, the sharp vertical white stripes on the side of the nyala (up to fourteen on the male, eighteen on the female) and in the males a short stiff mane from neck to shoulder. Females tend to group with their two last offspring and gather with other females in small herds of rarely more than ten. Males become more solitary the older they get. You'll tend to see males and females separately, as they only deliberately congregate for mating.

HORSE ANTELOPE

Restricted mainly to the Kruger, the **sable**, *Hippotragus niger* (p.15), is easily as magnificent as the kudu. A sleek, black upper body set in sharp counterpoint to its white underparts and facial markings, as well as its massive backwardly curving horns, make this the thoroughbred of the ruminants, particularly when galloping majestically across the savanna (though they prefer woodland). Highly hierarchical female herds number between one and three dozen, while territorial bulls frequently keep their distance, remaining under cover where you could easily miss them.

The **roan**, *Hippotragus equinus* (p.15), is very similar looking, but larger than a sable (it's Africa's second largest antelope), with less impressive horns and lighter colouring. You're more likely to see them in open savanna than sables.

Geographically more restricted, **gemsbok** (also known as the oryx), *Oryx gazella* (p.15), are only seen in South Africa in Kalahari-Gemsbok, the southernmost part of their range which stretches down from the deserts of Namibia and Botswana. If you encounter a herd of these highly gregarious grazers, you should be left in no doubt as to what they are. Like the roan and sable they have thick-set bodies and superficially similar facial markings, but their greyish fawn colouring, black and white underbody markings and long, slender, almost straight backward-pointing horns make them unmistakable. Gemsbok are highly adapted for survival in the arid country they inhabit, able to go for long periods without water, relying instead on melons and vegetation for moisture. They tolerate temperatures above 40°C by raising their normal body temperature of 35°C above that of the surrounding air, losing heat by conduction and radiation; at the same time they keep their brains cool by using cool blood from their noses as a coolant.

HARTEBEESTS

With their bracket-shaped, relatively short horns and ungainly appearance, **hartebeest** look vaguely like elongated cows – particularly their faces. All hartebeest are gregarious, but the exemplar of this is the **blue wildebeest**, *Connochaetes taurinus* (p.10), which, in East Africa, gather in hundreds of thousands for their annual migration. You won't see these numbers in South Africa, but you'll see smaller herds if

you go to any of the reserves in the northern half of the country or KwaZulu-Natal, as well as a number in the southern half, where they've been reintroduced. A particularly photogenic sight is wildebeest mingling with zebras, a habit said to be for mutual defence, though it may simply reflect the fact that they are both grazers and therefore hang around similar terrain. You're less likely to see **black wildebeest**, *Connochaetes gnou*, which were brought to the edge of extinction in the nineteenth century and now number around 3000 in South Africa, though you may find them in the Karoo and Mountain Zebra parks as well as Giant's Castle. You can tell them apart from their blue cousins by their darker colour (brown rather than the black suggested by their name) and long white tail.

Rather inelegant, like the wildebeests, the **red hartebeest**, *Alcelaphus buselaphus* (p.10), the extremely rare **Lichtenstein's hartebeest**, *Sigmocerus lichtensteinii*, and the **tsessebe**, *Damaliscus lunatus* (p.10), are all highly similar in appearance, but confusion is only likely to arise at the Kruger, the one place Lichtenstein's are found in the same range as tsessebes. The key distinction is in the horns, which in the hartebeest curve round to almost touch each other, while the tsessebe's are more splayed. Parks where you can see red hartebeests include Mountain Zebra, Karoo, Addo and Kalahari-Gemsbok.

The **blesbok**, *Damaliscus dorcas phillipsi*, and **bontebok**, *Damaliscus dorcas dorcas*, are near identical sub-species of the same animal and resemble darker, better-looking versions of the tsessebe. The largest bontebok population is at De Hoop Nature Reserve, with other members of the sub-species at the Cape of Good Hope Nature Reserve. Good places to see blesbok include Mountain Zebra National Park and Suikerbosrand Nature Reserve. After springboks, blesboks are the most important game-farm species in the country, and you may see them on Karoo farms.

DUIKER AND DWARF ANTELOPE

Duiker and the dwarf tribe are non-herding antelope that are either solitary or live in pairs. Despite their size, or perhaps because of it, males tend to be highly aggressive and are able to use their straight, stiletto-sharp horns to deadly effect.

The smallest South African antelope, the **blue duiker**, *Philantomba monticola*, weighs in at around 4kg, has an arched back and stands 35cm at the shoulder (roughly the height of a cat). Extremely shy, it is seldom seen in the southern and eastern coastal forests (as well as Ndumo Game Reserve) where it lives.

The slightly larger **red duiker**, *Cephalophus natalensis*, is three times heavier, and enjoys a similar environment to the blue, but only inhabits the woodlands and forest of KwaZulu-Natal.

The member of this tribe you're more likely to see, though, is the **common duiker** (sometimes called the grey duiker, reflecting its colouring), *Sylvicapra grimmia* (p.13), which occurs all over South Africa and is one of the antelope most tolerant of human habitation. When under threat it freezes in the undergrowth, but if chased will dart off in an erratic zigzagging run designed to throw pursuers off balance.

This type of fast darting movement is also characteristic of **dwarf antelope**, particularly the **Cape grysbok**, *Raphicerus melanotis* (p.16), and **Sharpe's grysbok**, *Raphicerus sharpii*, which bear a close resemblance to one another, but can't be confused because their ranges don't overlap. The Cape grysbok lives in the Western Cape fynbos belt (including Cape of Good Hope Nature Reserve and Addo), while Sharpe's occur in the northeastern corner of the country around the Kruger. Both are nocturnal and so are not often sighted.

A relative of the grysbok, the **steenbok**, *Raphicerus campestris* (p.16), is by far the most commonly sighted of all the dwarf antelope, and you can spot them by day or night all over the country (except parts of KwaZulu-Natal). Its large, dark eyes, massive ears and delicate frame give this elegant half-metre-high antelope an engaging Bambi-like appearance.

Another dwarf antelope you could well see is the **klipspringer**, *Oreotragus oreotragus* (p.16), whose Afrikaans name (meaning "rock jumper") reflects its goat-like adaptation to living on *kopjes* and cliffs – the only antelope to do so, making it unmistakeable. It's also the only one to walk on the tips of its hooves. Keep your eyes peeled at Kruger or Mountain Zebra parks (and other wilderness areas where there are rocky outcrops) for their large, bounding movements to scale steep inclines or their hopping from rock to rock.

The largest of the dwarves is the **oribi**, *Ourebia ourebi* (p.16), which could be taken for an outsized steenbok or a small gazelle, to which its faster smoother movements, when compared to other dwarves, are more akin. Only found in small pockets of KwaZulu-Natal, they live in small parties of a ram and several ewes. You may hear their their short sharp warning whistle as you approach, before you see them, although they will frequently stop after fleeing a little way to look back at you.

GAZELLE

Springbok, *Antidorcas marsupalis* (p.11), are said to have once migrated in their millions across the drylands of South Africa, but today their numbers are greatly reduced and the network of fences segmenting the country has ended such mass movements. South Africa's only gazelle, they are the most populous members of this tribe, whose several other species are found in East Africa. Their characteristic horns and dark horizontal patch on their sides, separating their reddish tawny upper body from their white underparts, are definitive identifiers. Tolerant of a wide range of open country from deserts to wetter savanna, you'll see these medium-sized antelope in reserves in the western arid zone of the country. The symbol of the national cricket and rugby teams, they're also raised on farms in this region for venison and hides. Springbok are recorded as having reached nearly 90kph and are noted for "pronking", a movement in which they arch their backs and straighten their legs as they leap into the air.

IMPALA

Larger and heavier than springbok, which they superficially resemble, **impala**, *Aepyceros melampus* (p.12) are a one-off antelope in a tribe of their own. Elegant and athletic, they are prodigious jumpers that have been recorded leaping distances of 11m and heights of 3m. Only the males carry the distinctive lyre-shaped horns. They are so common in the reserves of the northeast and of KwaZulu-Natal that some jaded rangers look on them as the goats of the savanna – a perception that carries more than a germ of truth as these flexible feeders are both browsers and grazers. Ewes and lambs form tight herds that can number over a hundred, moving about in a home range that may overlap the territory of several rams. During the rut, which takes place during the first five months of each year, these males will cut out harem herds of around twenty and expend considerable amounts of effort herding them and driving off any potential rivals.

NEAR-AQUATIC ANTELOPE

Of the near-aquatic Kob tribe, only the males have horns, but all species live close to water. Largest of the tribe, **waterbuck**, *Kobus ellipsiprymnus* (p.12), are sturdy antelope – 1.3m at the shoulder – with shaggy reddish-brown coats and a white horseshoe marking on their rumps. They're found sporadically in the northeastern reserves, always in proximity to permanent water close to woodland. Sociable animals, they usually gather in small herds of up to ten, and occasionally up to thirty.

Two closely related species, the **common reedbuck**, *Redunca arundinum* (p.12), and the slightly smaller **mountain reedbuck**, *Redunca fulvorufula*, both roughly two-thirds the height of waterbuck, are tan-coloured antelope. The common reedbuck favours a habitat of tall grass or reedbeds for refuge, while the mountain reedbuck inhabits hilly country with trees or grassy slopes.

All three species can be seen in suitable habitat in the Kruger, while the waterbuck and common reedbuck will also be sighted in the wetland reserves of KwaZulu-Natal, and the mountain reedbuck in the Mountain Zebra, Giant's Castle and Pilanesberg parks.

OTHER HOOFED RUMINANTS

Alongside cattle, sheep, goats and antelope, buffalo and giraffe are also hoofed ruminants – animals that have four stomachs and chew the cud. Bacteria in their digestive systems process plant matter into carbohydrates, while the dead bacteria are absorbed as protein – a highly efficient arrangement that makes them economical consumers, far more so than non-ruminants such as elephants, which pass vast quantities of what they eat as unutilized fibre. Species that concentrate on grasses are grazers; those eating leaves are browsers.

BUFFALO

You won't have to be in the Kruger or most of the other reserves in South Africa for long to see **buffalo**, *Syncerus caffer* (p.10), a common safari animal that, as one of the big five, appears on every hunter's shopping list. Don't let their resemblance to domestic cattle or water buffalo (to which they are not at all closely related) or apparent docility lull you into complacency; lone bulls, in particular, are noted and feared even by hardened hunters as dangerous and relentless killers. In other words, don't assume that because there are no carnivores about in some reserves that it's safe to go walking without a guide.

Buffalo are non-territorial and highly gregarious, gathering in hundreds or even sometimes thousands. Herds under one or more dominant bulls consist of clans of a dozen or so related females under a leading cow. You'll be able to spot such distinct units within the group: at rest clan members often cuddle up close to each other. There are separate pecking orders among females and males, the latter being forced to leave the herd during adolescence (at about three years) or once they're over the hill, to form bachelor herds, which you can recognize by their small numbers. Evicted old bulls (sometimes called "*daga* boys" on account of their penchant for mud baths), stripped of their social position and sex lives, understandably become resentful and embittered loners and are to be avoided at all costs. To distinguish males (as shown in the colour guide) from females, look for their heavier horns bisected by a distinct boss, or furrow.

GIRAFFE

Giraffe, *Giraffa camelopardalis* (p.9), are among the easiest animals to spot because their long necks make them visible above the low scrub. The tallest mammals on earth, giraffes spend their daylight hours browsing on the leaves of trees too high for other species; combretum and acacias are favourites. Their highly flexible lips and prehensile tongues give them almost hand-like agility and enable them to select the most nutritious leaves while avoiding deadly-sharp acacia thorns. At night they lie down and spend the evening ruminating. Non-territorial, they gather in loose, leaderless herds; if you encounter a bachelor herd look out for young males testing their strength with neck wrestling. When the female comes into oestrus, which can happen at any time of year, the dominant male will mate with her. She will give birth after a gestation period of approximately fourteen months. Over half of all young, however, fall prey to lions or hyenas in their early years. Kruger, Pilanesberg and KwaZulu-Natal parks are all good places to see them.

NON-RUMINANTS

Non-ruminating mammals have more primitive digestive systems than animals that chew the cud. Although both have bacteria in their gut that convert vegetable matter into carbohydrates, the less efficient system of the non-ruminants means they have to consume more raw material and to process it faster. The upside is they can handle food that's far more fibrous.

ELEPHANTS

Elephants, *Loxodonta africana* (p.7), were once found throughout South Africa. Now you'll only see them in a handful of reserves, notably the Kruger, Pilanesberg, Hluhluwe-Umfolozi, Tembe and Addo, the last of which protects the only population to survive naturally in the southern two-thirds of the country. Apart from this, one or two elephants may still survive in the Knysna forest, but their days are numbered and they are rarely, if ever, seen. Elephants are the most engaging of animals to watch, perhaps because their interactions, behaviour patterns and personality have so many human parallels. Like people they lead complex, interdependent social lives, growing from helpless infancy through self-conscious adolescence to adulthood. Babies are born with other cows in close attendance, after a 22-month gestation. Calves suckle for two to three years.

Basic family units are composed of a group of related females, tightly protecting their young and led by a venerable matriarch. It's the matriarch that's most likely to bluff a charge – though occasionally she may get carried away and tusk a vehicle or person. Bush mythology has it that elephants become embarrassed and ashamed after killing a human, covering the body with sticks and grass. They certainly pay much attention to the disposal of their own dead relatives, often dispersing the bones and spending time near the remains. Old animals die in their seventies or eighties, when their last set of teeth wears out and they can no longer feed.

Seen in the flesh, elephants seem even bigger than you would imagine. You'll need little persuasion from those flapping warning ears to back off if you're too close, but they are at the same time amazingly graceful. Silent on their padded, carefully placed feet, in a matter of moments a large herd can merge into the trees and disappear, their presence betrayed only by the noisy cracking of branches as they strip trees and uproot saplings.

DASSIES (HYRAXES)

Dassies look like they ought to be rodents, but amazingly, despite being fluffy and rabbit-sized, their closest relatives (some way back) are elephants rather than rats. Their name (pronounced like "dusty" without the "t") is the Afrikaans version of *dasje*, meaning "little badger", given to them by the first Dutch settlers. **Tree dassies**, *Dendrohyrax arboreus*, a rarely seen, solitary species, live along the Eastern Cape and southern KwaZulu-Natal coastal plains, where they take refuge in forest and thick bush.

In contrast, **rock dassies**, *Procavia capensis* (p.7), are widely distributed, having thrived with the elimination of predators. They hang out in suitably rocky habitat all over the country apart from north of the Orange River in the western half of the country and in the east along the northern KwaZulu-Natal coast. One of the most dramatic places you'll see them is sunning themselves along the rocky shore of the Tsitsikamma National Park, as breakers crash down ahead.

Like reptiles, hyraxes have poor body control systems and rely on shelter against both the cold and hot sunlight. They wake up sluggish and seek out rocks to catch the early morning sun – this is one of the best times to look out for them. One adult stands sentry against predators and issues a low-pitched warning cry in response to a threat. Dassies live in colonies of a dominant male and eight or more related females and their offspring.

RHINOS

Two species of rhinoceros are found in Africa: the hook-lipped or **black rhino**, *Diceros bicornis* (p.8), and the much heavier square-lipped or **white rhino**, *Ceratotherium simum* (p.8). Both have come close to extinction in the African wild and have all but disappeared. Happily, South Africa has bucked this continental trend and, due to timely conservation measures (especially in KwaZulu-Natal), it's the best place in the world to see both. Spend a day or two at

Itala, Hluhluwe-Umfolozi or Mkuzi reserves and you're bound to see one species or the other. Elsewhere, look for white rhinos at Addo and both varieties at Kruger and Pilanesberg.

"Hook-lipped" and "square-lipped" are technically more accurate terms for the two rhinos. "Black" and "white" are based on a linguistic misunderstanding – somewhere along the line, the German *weid,* which refers to the square-lipped's wide mouth, was misheard as "white". The term has stuck, despite both rhinos being a greyish muddy colour.

The shape of their lips is highly significant as it indicates their respective diets and consequently their favoured habitat. The cantankerous and smaller black rhino has the narrow prehensile lips of a browser, suited to picking leaves off trees and bushes, while the wide, flatter mouth of the twice-as-heavy white rhino, is more like a lawnmower and well-suited to chomping away at grasses. Diet and habitat also account for the greater sociability of the white rhino, which relies on safety in numbers under the exposure of open grassland; the solitary black rhino relies on the camouflage of dense thickets, which is why you'll find them so much more difficult to see.

Rhinos give birth to a single calf after a gestation period of fifteen to eighteen months, and the baby is not weaned until it is at a least a year old, sometimes two. Their population growth rate is slow compared with most animals, another factor contributing to their predicament.

HIPPOS

Hippopotamuses, *Hippopotamus amphibius* (p.9), are highly adaptable animals that once inhabited South African waterways from the Limpopo in the north to the marshes of the Cape Peninsula in the south. Today they're restricted to the northeastern corner of the country, with the most southerly indigenous population living in KwaZulu-Natal. You will find them elsewhere, in places where they've been reintroduced, such as the Double Drift Reserve in the Easten Cape. Hippos need freshwater deep enough to submerge themselves in, with a surrounding of suitable grazing grass. By day they need to spend most of their time in water to protect their thin, hairless skin. After dark, hippos leave the water to spend the whole night grazing, often walking up to 10km in one session.

Their grunting and jostling in the water may give the impression of loveable buffoons, but throughout Africa they are feared and rightly so, as they are reckoned to be responsible for more human deaths on the continent than any other animal. When disturbed, lone bulls, and cows with calves, can become extremely aggressive. Their fearsomely long incisors can slash through a canoe with ease, and on land they can charge at speeds up to 30kph and have a tight turning circle.

ZEBRAS

Zebras are closely related to horses and, together with wild asses, form the equid family. Of the three species of zebra, two live in South Africa.

The Burchell's or **plains zebra**, *Equus burchelli* (p.8), has small ears and thick, black stripes, with lighter "shadows" and survives in Mpumalanga, KwaZulu-Natal and along the Limpopo. Elsewhere it has been widely introduced and you'll see them in many reserves across the country.

The **Cape mountain zebra**, *Equus zebra zebra*, only narrowly escaped extinction, but now survives in healthy but limited numbers in the Mountain Zebra National Park in the Eastern Cape and other reserves in the southwest wherever there is suitably mountainous terrain. Distinguishing characteristics of the mountain zebra are the dewlap on its lower neck, the absence of shadow stripes, its larger ears, and stripes that go all the way down to its hooves – in contrast to the Burchell's whose stripes fade out as they progress down its legs.

Zebras congregate in family herds of a breeding stallion and two mares (or more) and their foals. Unattached males will often form bachelor herds. Among plains zebras, offspring leave the family group after between one and two years, while mountain zebras are far more tolerant in allowing adolescents to remain in the family.

PIGS

Two **wild pigs** are found in South Africa. If you're visiting the Kruger, Pilanesberg or the KwaZulu-Natal parks, families of **warthogs**, *Phacochoerus aethiopicus* (p.9), will become a familar sight, trotting across the savanna with their tails erect like communications antennae. Family groups usually consist of a mother and her litter of two to four piglets, or occasionally two or three females and their young. Boars join the group only to mate; they're distinguished from sows by their prominent face warts, which are thought to be defensive pads protecting their heads during often violent fights. Warthogs shelter in holes in the ground, usually porcupine or aardvark burrows, although they are quite capable of making their own – in fact, they are supreme diggers who routinely dig up nutritious bulbs.

Bushpigs, *Potamochoerus porcus*, are slightly more widely distributed than warthogs in South Africa, but because they're nocturnal forest dwellers, they aren't as often seen. Their northerly range overlaps with that of the hogs, but they also extend along the southern coastal woodlands of the Eastern Cape as far west as Mossel Bay. Much like hairier versions of domestic pigs, they live in harems called "sounders", consisting of a boar with several females and their piglets. Fathers drive out male offspring when they approach adolescence.

OTHER MAMMALS

Despite their common taste for ants and termites, their nocturnal foraging and their outlandish appearance, aardvarks and pangolins are quite unrelated. The **aardvark**, *Orycteropus afer* (p.3), is one of Africa's – indeed the world's – strangest animals, a solitary mammal weighing up to 70kg. Its name, Afrikaans for "earth pig", is an apt description, as it holes up during the day in large burrows that are excavated with remarkable speed and energy. It emerges at night to visit termite mounds within a radius of up to 5km, digging for its main diet. It's most likely to be common in bush country that's well scattered with termite mounds. Holes dug into the base of these are a tell-tale sign of the presence of aardvarks.

Pangolins, *Manis temminckii*, are equally unusual – scale-covered mammals, resembling armadillos and feeding on ants and termites. Under attack they roll themselves into a ball. Pangolins occur widely in South Africa, north of the Orange River.

A number of species of rabbits and hares bounce about the South African landscape, but the **scrub hare**, *Lepus saxatilis*, distinguished by its exceptionally long ears, is the commonest and one you'll undoubtedly see in scrubby, wooded country throughout the region. Wherever there's rocky terrain south of the Orange River and in KwaZulu-Natal, keep an eye open for **rock rabbits**, which look just like brown- and white-speckled domestic bunnies.

If you go on a night drive you'd be most unlucky not to see the glinting eyes of **springhares**, *Pedetes capensis* (p.3), which, despite their resemblance to rabbit-sized kangaroos, are in fact true rodents. In the western arid zone you'll spot **ground squirrels**, *Xerus inauris*, scurrying about during the day looking for roots, seeds and bulbs, while in the northeast, **tree squirels**, *Paraxerus cepapi*, enjoy a similar diet. The most singular and largest of the African rodents is the **porcupine**, *Hystrix africae-australis* (p.3), which is quite unmistakeable with its coat of many quills. Porcupines are widespread and present in most reserves, but because they're nocturnal, you may only see shed quills lying along the path or in front of their burrows.

Scores of different **bats**, either fruit or insect eaters, leave their roosts each night and take off into the South African night, but all you're likely to see of them is some erratic flying against a moonlit sky. The foxy-faced **Egyptian fruit bat,** *Rousettus aegyptiacus*, is virtually single-handedly responsible for pollinating baobab trees, thus keeping them from extinction. And while **rats and mice** are probably not what brought you on safari, it's worth noting that over forty different species are found in South Africa.

LITERATURE

Without apartheid, some critics have argued, there would not have been any South African literature. Apartheid has delivered ready-made plots and subject matter for gifted and mediocre artists alike. Stories of the white minority's psychological and political alienation versus the legitimate struggle of the oppressed majority, illegal and clandestine interracial relationships, and possibilities of reconciliation, revenge or revolution abound. With all these, apartheid and its colonial precursors have provided a truth stranger than many fictions. Produced by people with vastly different life experiences and subject to different political pressures over centuries, it is difficult to avoid distinctions between the literature of white and black South Africans.

During pre-colonial times there were a variety of oral literary forms, sometimes known as **orature**, in the southern African region. Orature was male-dominated, but women played a significant part in genres such as **praise poems**, equivalent to the heroic epic and folk tales. In contemporary South African orature there has been a further blurring of the boundaries of genre and gender. Women produce oral works at political gatherings, traditionally a male prerogative, while men and women participate in the **toyi-toyi**, a direct descendant of the war songs originally performed only by women to exhort men in battle, now most commonly associated with resistance and political rallies.

EARLY SETTLERS AND TRAVELLERS

From the sixteenth century onwards explorers such as Drake, Houtman and Hakluyt provided descriptions of the Cape, and in 1572, the Portuguese poet **Luis de Camoens** described his voyage (partly mythologized) in *The Lusiads*. **Jan van Riebeeck**, governor of the Dutch East India's station wrote a *Daghregister* (Journal), as did **Adam Tas**, one of the station's more rebellious subjects. As the territory passed between the various Dutch, French and British administrators, so arrived different residents and visitors. One such person was **Francois La Valliant**, an admirer of Rousseau, whose *Travels* is an example of how travellers of the past (and today) can live out their preconceptions for themselves and for their metropolitan audiences.

COLONIALISM AND TRANSITION

Published in 1883 under a male *nom de plume*, **Olive Schreiner**'s *The Story of an African Farm* is widely regarded as the first novel rooted in South Africa. It stands in marked contrast to the frontier tales of **Percy Fitzpatrick**'s *Jock of the Bushveld* (1907) and **Henry Rider Haggard**'s *Boy's Own*-style tales of colonial penetration and subjugation such as *King Solomon's Mines* (1885) or *She* (1887). Today these find direct and indirect descendants in Wilbur Smith, literary doyen of airport departure halls, and the late Sir Laurens van der Post, spiritual mentor to Prince Charles.

Christian mission education, the only early route to literacy for black South Africans, favoured men and prioritized the translation of biblical and religious texts, such as John Bunyan's *Pilgrim's Progress*, which appeared in Sesotho, Zulu and Xhosa. As a result, African women did not have the literary opportunities open to the playwright **H.I.E. Dhlomo**; the writer **Thomas Mofolo**, whose historical novel *Chaka* (1925) originally appeared in Sesotho and was translated into English, French, Italian, German, Yoruba and Afrikaans; or the journalist, translator and novelist **Sol Plaatje**. A founder member of the ANC, Plaatje's best-known works are *Mhudi* (1930) and *Native Life in South Africa* (1916). The former is the story of an African society in transition as it deals with the implications of the Afrikaner Great Trek and the social upheaval caused by the Zulu military state's raids and conquest. In *Native Life* Plaatje documented the disastrous effects on Africans of the 1913 Land Act. This law denied them access to the land of their birth after the Anglo-

Boer War, and the formation of the Union of South Africa had effectively resolved economic and political differences between the white settler interests and British imperial power.

JIM-COMES-TO-JO'BURG

The discovery of minerals and the growing urbanization and industrialization of South African society had a detrimental effect on African and Afrikaner rural society alike. From the white perspective, removal from the land threatened the "natural order" of race relations for landless Afrikaners and Africans arrived in the city as "equals". While the perceived threat to white civilization was greatly exaggerated, it had four significant consequences for white writers at the time: it shifted literary attention away from rural concerns towards urban-based issues, it provided the context for fears of miscegenation; it encouraged a re-examination of the image of Afrikaners; and it opened up new forms of narration.

Movement towards the city fostered what Nadine Gordimer later termed the **"Jim-comes-to-Jo'burg"** novel, in which a naive young African man moves from a protected and stable rural environment to city life and a variety of urban experiences and temptations. **Peter Abrahams'** contribution was *Mine Boy* (1946), often regarded as South Africa's first proletarian novel, while for **Alan Paton** the true nature of African culture was to be found in a rural setting and the *status quo ante*. Much later **Mtutuzeli Matshoba**'s short story "Three Days in the Land of a Dying Illusion", from his collection *Call Me not a Man* (1979), would invert and parody the genre.

MISCEGENATION AND ARCHETYPES

Roy Campbell (*Selected Poems*, 1981), subsequently associated with Iberian fascism, is the best-known poet of the interwar years. Like **Guy Butler** after him, he tended to equate Europe with history, development and rationalism, and Africa with unchanging archetypes. During this period **Sarah Gertrude Millin**'s fiction, particularly *God's Stepchildren* (1924), provided the starkest articulation of differences between Europe and Africa and white anxiety about the consequences of **miscegenation**. The basis for Millin's views lay in the notion of

"good" and "bad" blood, and in the fear that the (male) colonizer's possession and control of the colonial territories would simultaneously confirm his dominance and open him to control by the "heart of darkness". Millin of course did not even begin to contemplate "the horror" of miscegenation involving a black man and a white woman. **Ethelreda Lewis** offered a problematic variant on the theme of blood and civilization in *Wild Deer* (1933), the story of an African-American singer, modelled on Paul Robeson, who visits South Africa in search of spiritual renewal. He decides to uplift the "pure" and pre-urban African by impregnating "a carefully chosen virgin mate" and so pass on the benefits of his civilization while protecting the "kernel of primitive life".

With the repeal of the so-called Immorality Act in 1985, which forbade interracial sexual relations, miscegenation has lost its literary and political significance, though repackaged in the form of theories of hybridity and difference it is now making a fashionable return. **Stephen Gray**'s *Time of our Darkness* (1988) may well be the last serious work on the "immorality" subject tackled by **William Plomer** in *Turbott Wolfe* (1926), **Peter Abrahams** in *The Path to Thunder* (1948), **Alan Paton** in *Too Late the Phalarope* (1953), **Nadine Gordimer** in her short story "The Country Lovers" (1967), and **Athol Fugard**, one of South Africa's most famous playwrights, in *Statements After an Arrest Under the Immorality Act* (1974).

FROM DISPOSSESSION TO APARTHEID

The separation of **Afrikaners** from "their" land, and their participation in an industrializing economy largely controlled by English speakers, encouraged sentimental literary representations of Afrikaners. **Pauline Smith**'s work, such as *The Beadle* (1926) and her short story collection *The Little Karoo* (1925), inadvertently fostered the myth of the Boer as a landless, economically oppressed victim denied his language and culture. While **Herman Charles Bosman**'s short stories such as "Mafeking Road" (1947) and "A Cask of Jerepigo" (1964) also focus on rural Afrikaner life, they display far more irony. Narrated by one Oom Schalk Lourens, who in Mark Twain-like fashion is never fully aware of the implications of the stories that he tells, Bosman's humorous tales of backveld ambition, betrayal and desire presage the concerns and doubts about writing and the control of history, truth and identity that would increasingly characterize what the novelist **J.M. Coetzee** has called "white writing" – writing that articulates the "concerns of people no longer European, not yet African".

Alan Paton's Cry, the Beloved Country appeared in 1948, the year in which the Nationalist government came to power, and has been filmed twice. Despite its reputation as an anti-apartheid novel, Paton's representation of the Zulu language as the discourse of a past, heroic age, and the book's support for racial segregation, perpetuate nostalgic, pastoral myths of the "noble Zulu" found in the works of Wilbur Smith, Rider Haggard and that most Victorian of socialists, Friedrich Engels.

THE DRUM GENERATION

It is to the link between emergent, predominantly male **black writing and journalism**, centred on the Johannesburg-based **Drum magazine**, that the Fifties belong. The publication was one of the few outlets for black creative writers such as **Can Themba**, **Es'kia Mphahalele**, **Bloke Modisane** and **Todd Matshikiza**, many of whom chose to write short stories or autobiographical novels. Favoured because of its flexibility and compatibility with their fast-paced and fractured life styles under oppressive conditions, the short story has remained a popular medium for black and white South African fiction. The so-called **Drum generation** articulated black urban experience and aspirations, often in an Americanized B-movie style in journalism, fiction and drama such as King Kong, a musical based on the life of an actual boxer-gangster that helped to launch the singing careers of Thandi Klaasen, Dolly Rathebe and Miriam Makeba. **Z.B. Molefe**'s A Common Hunger to Sing (1997) gives them and successors such as Brenda Fassie, Sibongile Khumalo and Yvonne Chaka Chaka the recognition they deserve.

In general, there was little space for **women's journalism and fiction** at this time. Covering her pre-Botswana years in South Africa, **Bessie Head**'s posthumously published The Cardinals (1993) is a rare exploration of the problems faced by one of the few black women journalists during this period who made the transition to novel-writing.

While many of the Drum generation died relatively young and in exile, **Es'kia Mphahalele** has been a survivor. His Down Second Avenue (1959) is often viewed as the definitive text of an era characterized by black male autobiographies such as Tell Freedom (1954) by **Peter Abrahams**, **Bloke Modisane**'s Blame me on History (1963) and **Todd Matshikiza**'s Chocolates for my Wife (1961). Mphahalele's subsequent novels, The Wanderers (1971) and Afrika my Music (1984) recorded the fragmented experience of exile, that "soul-mutilating process" that has affected so many South Africans in the last sixty years.

Sophiatown, the last area in Johannesburg where Africans had freehold property rights, was the heartbeat of the Drum generation. **Jurgen Schadeburg**'s photographs, and a host of reminiscences of Drum and Sophiatown by figures ranging from **Anthony Sampson** in Drum: An African Adventure-and Afterwards to **Father Trevor Huddleston**'s Naught for your Comfort, are testimony to the fascination it held. Its nearest equivalent in Cape Town was District Six, a multiracial but predominantly coloured inner-city slum that provided the backdrop for the early work of three Cape Town writers **Richard Rive** (Buckingham Palace and District Six) in 1986, and **Alex La Guma** (A Walk in the Night) in 1962, and **Achmat Dangor**'s anthology Waiting for Leila (1981). Of more recent works, **Nomvuyo Ngcelwane**'s Sala Kahle, District Six (1998) recounts the life of its African residents, a community ignored or marginalized in most accounts, while **Linda Fortune**'s The House in Tyne Street (1996) is more idyllic. Set in the Sixties, but with little reference to the main political developments of the time, the autobiographical novel The Party is Over (1997) by veteran poet and novelist **James Matthews** recounts the frustrations of a black writer in a paternalistic, white-dominated world of arts and letters. Poetry of note in this period can be found in Sirens, Knuckles, Boots (1963), Letters to Martha (1968), by **Dennis Brutus**, who devoted considerable energy to ensuring South Africa's sporting isolation during the apartheid years, and **Arthur Nortje** in Dead Roots (1973). Like the short-story writer **Zoe Wicomb** in her collection of short stories, You Can't Get Lost in Cape Town (1987), Nortje was prepared to explore the more ordinary and less obviously political aspects of life in South Africa by focusing on inner worlds and on the issue of coloured identity as marginal to larger political and national questions, as **Mphahalele**, in *Man Must Live* (1947), and **Njabulo Ndebele**, in *Fools and Other Stories* (1983), had for African township life.

Rive wrote several Cape Town-based novels such as *Emergency* (1964), the latter about the events surrounding the declaration of a state of emergency in 1960. Several other novelists have set works in this and subsequent periods of repression: **Jonty Driver**'s *Elegy for a Revolutionary* (1969), **Lewis Nkosi**'s *The Rhythm of Violence* (1964) and **Alex La Guma**'s *In the Fog of the Seasons' End* (1972) for the Sixties; **Sipho Sepamla**'s *A Ride on the Whirlwind* (1981), **Mongane Serote**'s *To Every Birth Its Blood* (1981) and **Miriam Tlali**'s *Amandla* (1981) for the Soweto period; **Menan du Plessis**'s *A State of Fear* (1983), **Hein Grosskopf**'s *Artistic Graves* (1993), **Mandla Langa**'s *A Rainbow on the Paper Sky* (1989) and **Bridget Pitt**'s *Unbroken Wing* (1998) which continues the theme on a more personal note, for the late Eighties.

PRISON WRITINGS

Novels of resistance are inevitably accompanied by **prison writings**, and South Africa is not short of these. Among many books on the subject, **Albie Sachs**' *Jail Diary* (1966) and **Ruth First**'s *117 Days* (1982) record their detentions without trial in the early Sixties, while **Indres Naidoo**'s *Island in Chains* (1982) deals with his ten years on Robben Island after being arrested and charged with sabotage. Most prisoners served out their sentences, but Tim Jenkin, Alex Moumbaris and Stephen Lee managed to escape from Pretoria Central Prison where most white political prisoners were held. **Tim Jenkin**'s tale, *Escape from Pretoria* (1987) reads like a thriller, while in *The True Confessions of an Albino Terrorist* (1983) **Breyten Breytenbach** manages to combine political critique with grim humour. Not surprisingly, fictional accounts of prison such as **Alex La Guma**'s *The Stone Country* (1974) and **D.M. Zwelonke**'s *Robben Island* (1973) rely heavily on their authors' own experiences, but are complex narratives. In the realm of non-political prison writings, **Herman Charles Bosman**'s *Cold Stone Jug* (1971) provides an ironic and beautifully written foil to the seriousness of "correct" accounts.

South African writers are gripped by what Mphahalele has described as "the tyranny of place". All but one of **Alex La Guma**'s five novels are set in Cape Town, and they are linked by a steady evolution of political consciousness and organization. A journalist, writer and political activist from the Sixties until his death in Cuba in 1985, where he was the ANC's Chief Representative, his early works, *A Walk in the Night* (1962) and *And a Threefold Cord* (1964) explore individual acts of defiance against the state. His later novels, *In the Fog of the Seasons' End* (1972) and *Time of the Butcherbird* (1979), display more complex narrative structures and deal with collective resistance.

WHITE LIBERAL WRITING

If La Guma's concerns have been with the disenfranchised and the dispossessed, **Nadine Gordimer**'s novels and short stories stand as dispassionate and coldly sensual chronicles of the interior voice of white liberal and radical opposition to apartheid. They represent an alternative to Paton's stress on individual responsibility as the key to political change. Over the years Gordimer has moved from confessional, though not necessarily autobiographical, narratives such as *The Lying Days* (1953), to bolder and more complex explorations of time and psychological make-up, such as *July's People* (1991).

While the former explores the growing political awareness of her typical main character, a white middle-class woman resident in Johannesburg's prosperous suburbs, the latter is set in a post-revolutionary South Africa in which Maureen Smales, wife and mother to a white middle-class family, has become heavily dependent on July, their former "houseboy". The novel explores her search for political and personal liberation, part of which involves her efforts to confront and break with the emotionally fraught and contradictory personal and political dynamics so often associated with domestic service relationships in a colonial context. Her more recent *The House Gun* (1998) continues the exploration of white liberal consciousness and conscience in the post liberation period.

Gordimer is not the only white writer to explore the dilemmas of privilege and conscience. The **Sestigers** were an innovative group of Afrikaans writers prominent in the Sixties that included **Breyten Breytenbach** and **Andrè Brink**, who has acquired the reputation of being the foremost white literary opponent of apartheid. Brink's works explore notions of truth, history and freedom in the colonial setting through books such as *An Instant in the Wind* (1976), which rewrites the traditional frontier-explorer novel; *A Chain of Voices* (1982); *The Wall of the Plague* (1984); *An Act of Terror* (1991); and *Devil's Valley* (1998). In this he has much in common with Booker Prize winner and literary critic **J.M. Coetzee**'s first novel, *Dusklands* (1974). This book establishes psychological and behavioural parallels between America's presence in Vietnam and the behaviour of one Jacobus Coetzee during his South African frontier experience in 1760. Several of J.M. Coetzee's subsequent novels have used the perspective of a borderline psychotic narrator to explore the political and psychological damage caused by colonialism and apartheid. His *In the Heart of the Country* (1976) is narrated by an isolated spinster and plays ironically with the tradition of farm novels as represented by Olive Schreiner and others. *Waiting for the Barbarians* (1980), which takes its title from Cavafy's poem of the same name, occupies a more allegorical domain, with a narrator who is a bumbling magistrate wrestling with moral concerns in the outpost of an unnamed empire. *His Life and Times of Michael K* (1983) foregrounds the concern with allegory by making it a concern of one of the novel's characters.

An intellectually brilliant postmodern critic of apartheid, Coetzee has always distanced himself and his works from the demands of publishing in order to function as a "weapon of struggle". Though by describing himself in Dusklands, even parodically, as "one of the 10,000 Coetzees . . . that Jacobus Coetzee begat", he invites parallels with the self-hatred and self-obsession of Rian Malan's *My Traitor's Heart* (1990), which establishes its author in Calvinist style as the seventh-generation inheritor of the founding fathers' sins.

While white writing became increasingly introspective and its ventures into the interior shifted from geographical to psychological terrain, black writing faced an entirely different situation. Impeded by the exile of many artists, intimidated by trials and arrests, and censored by the state during a period of severe repression

in the early Sixties, it was largely dormant until the late Sixties and early Seventies. This period saw the growth of the Black Consciousness Movement and the increasingly effective organization of black workers, followed by the Soweto riots and the independence of Angola and Mozambique.

BEYOND SOCIAL REALISM

The dawn of the Seventies saw both white and black writing beginning to look beyond the conventions of social realism, but for very different reasons. In the case of white writing, **interiority** was a response to the dilemmas imposed by a conscience that could not be ignored and privileges that could not be sacrificed. For black writers, **poetry**, and free verse in particular, became popular because it facilitated indirect forms of political expression. Among the names associated with this phase **Oswald Mtshali**, *Drum* survivor **Casey Motsisi**, **Mafika Gwala**, **Don Mattera**, **Njabulo Ndebele**, **Mongane Serote**, **Mandla Langa**, **Gladys Thomas** and **James Matthews** from Cape Town are the most prominent. In subsequent decades, many of these also wrote short stories and novels.

Oswald Mtshali was working as a motorbike courier when his path-breaking *Sounds of a Cowhide Drum* appeared in 1971. For Mtshali and many of his contemporaries, a cultural nationalism that rejected "white" standards and asserted a specifically "black" aesthetic and identity was the route to political nationalism. They sharply criticized the self-destructive nature of township violence, and used the perspectives and experiences of children to point out the injustices and inequalities of apartheid. Like many of their predecessors Ndebele, Serote and Langa were forced to leave the country, but James Matthews stayed, and *Cry Rage* (1972), co-written with Gladys Thomas, still remains a powerful statement of black consciousness and protest poetry. Along with **Gcina Mhlope** and **Jennifer Davids**, Thomas was able to modify the traditional role of black women (at best) as significant but secondary figures in the national liberation struggle, typified by the idea of the powerful black woman as mother figure.

The early Seventies also saw a resurgence of **drama**. There were escapist and exploitative musicals such as *Ipi Tombi*, nostalgic and utopian works such as **Credo Mutwa**'s *uNosilimela* and **Gibson Kente**'s *Too Late* and *Survival*, both with strong political messages. For international audiences, however, **Athol Fugard** remains the most prominent South African playwright. Fugard would be the last to claim full responsibility for several of his works, which were produced under workshop conditions with actors such as John Kani and Winston Ntshona contributing their views and experiences to *Sizwe Bansi is Dead*, a play about strategies to avoid pass law controls, and *The Island*, based on Sophocles' *Antigone*. Continuing the tradition of collaborative production, *Ubu and the Truth Commission* (1998) combines the talents of writer Jane Taylor, artist William Kentridge and puppeteers Basil Jones and Adrian Kohler in a work that explores some of South Africa's less enviable qualities – evil, ultra-violence, cowardice and self-pity – in a work that reflects on a country dealing with the consequences of the Truth and Reconciliation Commission. This is also the subject of **Antjie Krog**'s *Country of My Skull* (1998), a multileveled and many layered account of more than two years' reporting on the Commission, from its legislative origins to testimonies of victims and perpertrators.

PEOPLE'S HISTORY

Launched in 1977, and capitalizing on the limited cultural and political space occasioned by the apartheid government's moves towards a policy of "repressive reform" in the post-Soweto period, **Staffrider magazine** was the most important literary development of the late Seventies. Taking its name and image from township slang for people (frequently black youth) who rode the overcrowded African sections of the racially segregated commuter trains by hanging onto the outside or sitting on the roofs, the magazine had two main objectives: to provide publishing opportunities for community-based organizations and young writers, graphic artists and photographers; and to oppose officially sanctioned state and establishment culture. Selections from the magazine between 1978 and 1988 appeared in *Ten Years of Staffrider* (1988). Initially based on a hands-off editorial policy, the magazine focused on "**people's history**", helping to retrieve hidden aspects of South Africa's past for a wider audience. The *Staffrider* tradition continues; Charles van Onselen's tome *The Seed is Mine* (1996), Isabel Hofmeyer's *We Spend Our Years as a*

Tale That is Told (1994) have been outstanding contributions to this genre.

The magazine also popularized a return to traditional conventions and forms of oratory such as **Nongenile Zenani** and **Harold Scheub**'s *The World and the Word* (1992) and **Sandile Dikeni**'s *Guava Juice* (1992). Much of the latter's poetry was delivered at opposition mass rallies and trade union launches. By contrast, **Mongane Serote**'s *Third World Express* (1992), his first published work since his return from exile, retains links with with an oral tradition but is more introspective than Dikeni's poetry. More recently, praise poets performed at the inauguration of President Mandela and the opening of the country's first democratically elected parliament.

From the Eighties onwards, debates around the political relevance of poetry became even more intense than those dealing with prose. Some of the more politically committed poets included **Kelwyn Sole** (*Blood of Our Silence*; 1988) and **Jeremy Cronin**, whose anthology *Inside* (1983) asks readers "To learn how to speak/With the voices of the land", return to introspective themes of language and the poet's sense of place. In *Even the Dead* (1997) Cronin searches for a moral community that incorporates the past and takes issue with the "smug rainbowism" of the new South Africa. Others, such as **Christopher van Wyk** with *It is Time to Go Home* (1979) and **Achmat Dangor** in *Bulldozer* (1983), retain a strident anger mixed with Cape Town's acerbic slang.

THE EIGHTIES AND NINETIES

By the mid-Eighties, international condemnation of apartheid and support for the liberation movement coincided with the growth of feminist theory and an expanding **feminist** publishing industry. These developments favoured the emergence of black South African women's autobiographies such as **Ellen Kuzwayo**'s *Call Me Woman* (1985) and **Emma Mashinini**'s *Strikes Have Followed me All my Life* (1989). This form has seen little development since the appearance of **Noni Jabavu**'s *Drawn in Colour* (1960) and *The Ochre People* (1963), in the early Sixties, and Sindiwe Magona's two autobiographical works *To My Children's Children* (1990) and *Forced to Grow* (1992) retain an American connection. In *Mother to Mother* (1998), she deals with the death of visiting

American scholar Amy Biehl, killed by black youths stirred up by "anti-white" slogans, through an address from one of the mothers of Biehl's killers to the mother of his victim.

The late Eighties was also a favourable period for the publication of black women's poetry in anthologies such as *Siren Songs* (1989) and *Breaking the Silence* (1990) or in individual collections such as Sobhna Poona's *In Search of Rainbows* (1990).

As the Nineties took hold, however, the politicized approach that saw publishers, writers and readers going for the "struggular" had to acknowledge the less dramatic and more byzantine process of negotiations towards a relatively peaceful transfer of power, and the emergence of splits and disagreements in the cultural sphere between the ANC and some of its internal supporters. In this context, **Phyllis Ntantala**'s *A Life's Mosaic* (1992) acknowledged personal concerns, **Mamphela Ramphele**'s *A Life* (1995) criticized ways in which the liberation struggle had been male-dominated, and **Barbara Schreiner**'s *A Snake with Ice Water* (1992), a collection of interviews, stories and poems by women about their prison experiences from the Sixties onwards, confronted the shame and sense of incapacity to which many women in the liberation struggle had been subjected.

Exile and **return** are themes with which several writers have dealt. **Breyten Breytenbach**'s *Dog Heart* (1998) recalls present and past Bonnievale, the village of his birth. In *The Naked Song and Other Stories* (1996) **Mandla Langa** explores the transition from exile to "home", while **Barry Feinberg**'s *Gardens of Struggle* (1992) covers 30 years of the poet's life, from exile in 1961 to return in 1991.

Good insights into the troubled psyche of the white South African male in a period of political transition include **Ivan Vladislavic**'s short-story collection *Missing Persons* (1989) and his novels *The Folly* (1993) and *Propaganda by Monuments and Other Stories* (1996), **Etienne van Heerden**'s *Mad Dog and Other Stories* (1992) and *Casspirs and Camparis* (1993) – casspirs are armoured personnel carriers used by the police and army – and **Mark Behr**'s *The Smell of Apples* (1995), which attached significance to the death of Hendrik Verwoerd, architect of apartheid, during their fictionalized child-

hoods. Behr's subsequent disclosure that he was a police informer during his days as an anti-apartheid student activist doubtless adds interest to this confessional narrative.

POLITICAL AUTOBIOGRAPHY AND BIOGRAPHY

The tradition of **political autobiography** is now well-established. *Let my People Go* (1962) by the late **Albert Luthuli**, former leader of the ANC, remains as compelling an explanation of the struggle for majority rule as Nelson Mandela's *Long Walk to Freedom* (1994). Dramatic political change and the acquisition of freedom has seen many politicians and public figures come and go. Inevitably this has encouraged several to write stories of the life they would like us to believe they led or, in the case of those involved in clandestine work such as **Ronnie Kasrils** (*"Armed and Dangerous"*: *My Undercover Struggle Against Apartheid*, 1993), **Joe Slovo** (*Unfinished Autobiography*, 1995) and **Natoo Babenia** (*Memoirs of a Saboteur: Reflections on my Political Activity in India and South Africa*, 1995), of the life they could not previously talk about in public. National secretary of the non-racial Federation of South African women in the Fifties, **Helen Joseph** was banned four times, jailed four times, on trial for four years and periodically unbanned. Her autobiography *Side by Side* appeared in 1986. Centrally involved in many of the inquests of the political detainees who died in South African jails, *No one to Blame?* (1998) by Advocate **George Bizos** provides a grim if illuminating complement to the life stories of those who survived torture and interrogation. **Bram Fischer**, member of an eminent Afrikaner family and a lawyer who defended Mandela and Sisulu in the Rivonia trial and member of the then banned SA Communist Party, was one of those who did not survive. Stephen Clingman tells his story *Bram Fischer: Afrikaner Revolutionary* (1998).

. . . AND BEYOND

South Africa's recently acquired political respectability has meant that writers of the formerly international polecat state can now, in Michael Ondaatje's phrase, become "international bastards" if they wish, as postmodernism and magical realism, sometimes in combination with autobiography, have become more popular and politically acceptable. **Ashraf Jamal** in *Love Themes for the Wilderness* (1996) has been quick to capitalize on the space available. Two novels by **Zakes Mda**, already recognized as a major playwright, *She Plays with the Darkness* (1995) and *Ways of Dying* (1995), can also be classified as **magical realism**. While the former may rely upon aspects of a traditional African culture with which many urbanized black South Africans have no contact, the latter explores some of the country's more bizarre forms of death from the perspective of a self-styled "professional mourner". With the differences between official and personal histories a subject of continuous negotiation, **Mike Nicol**'s *This Day and Age* (1992) makes a strong case for the integration of magical realism and **postmodern** techniques in pursuit of a new perspective on South African history. **Rayda**

Jacobs' novel *The Slave Book* (1998), set on the eve of slave emancipation, returns to earlier moments of political and personal freedom that invite comparison with the present. **Etienne van Heerden**'s *Kikuyu* (1999) is set on that sign of the times (but rarer in the Sixties) – a holiday farm in the Karoo. *On Soebatsfontein*, **Fabian Latsky**'s sheltered world of eccentric characters comes into contact with the rumblings of an increasingly unstable South Africa. **Tony Spencer-Smith**'s *The Stooping of Aquila* (1999) is an erotic thriller set in Cape Town, focusing on environmental issues, their growing prominence a sign of the region's tourist potential and of a shift in values away from overtly political concerns, in Hout Bay.

Meanwhile Wilbur Smith, and now his wife too, continue to churn them out . . .

Roger Field

SOUTH AFRICAN WRITERS

There's no better way to get under the skin of South Africa than through its writing. And, while no five extracts can ever hope to convey South African literature's richness and diversity, the ones we've selected can be useful as a taster of some of the country's unplumbed literary depths. What the writers below have in common is that, although they are well-known in South Africa, none is internationally a big-name author. For a more comprehensive survey of the literary landscape, see p.716.

STEVE BIKO

Charismatic Black Consciousness activist **STEVE BIKO** *(1946–77) died after police torture. These words, extracted from an interview some months before his death, give insight into Biko's extraordinary commitment to political change. The extract is taken from "I Write What I Like", a collection of non-fiction writing from 1969 to 1972. In 1973 Biko was banned and could no longer travel, speak in public or write for publication.*
Reprinted by permission of Bowerdean Publishers.

ON DEATH

You are either alive and proud or you are dead, and when you are dead, you can't care anyway. And your method of death can itself be a politicizing thing. So you die in the riots. For a hell of a lot of them, in fact, there's really nothing to lose – almost literally, given the kind of situations that they come from. So if you can overcome the personal fear for death, which is a highly irrational thing, you know, then you're on the way.

And in interrogation the same sort of thing applies. I was talking to this policeman, and I told him, "If you want us to make any progress, the best thing is for us to talk. Don't try any form of rough stuff, because it just won't work." And this is absolutely true also. For I just couldn't see what they could do to me which would make me all of a sudden soften to them. If they talk to me, well I'm bound to be affected by

them as human beings. But the moment they adopt rough stuff, they are imprinting in my mind that they are police. And I only understand one form of dealing with police, and that's to be as unhelpful as possible. So I button up. And I told them this: "It's up to you." We had a boxing match the first day I was arrested. Some guy tried to clout me with a club. I went into him like a bull. I think he was under instructions to take it so far and no further, and using open hands so that he doesn't leave any marks on the face. And of course he said exactly what you were saying just now: "I will kill you." He meant to intimidate. And my answer was: "How long is it going to take you?" Now of course they were observing my reaction. And they could see that I was completely unbothered. If they beat me up, it's to my advantage. I can use it. They just killed somebody in jail – a friend of mine – about ten days before I was arrested. Now it would have been bloody useful evidence for them to assault me. At least it would indicate what kind of possibilities were there, leading to this guy's death. So, I wanted them to go ahead and do what they could do, so that I could use it. I wasn't really afraid that their violence might lead me to make revelations I didn't want to make, because I had nothing to reveal on this particular issue. I was operating from a very good position, and they were in a very weak position. My attitude is, I'm not going to allow them to carry out their programme faithfully. If they want to beat me five times, they can only do so on condition that I allow them to beat me five times. If I react sharply, equally and oppositely, to the first clap, they are not going to be able to systematically count the next four claps, you see. It's a fight. So if they had meant to give me so much of a beating, and not more, my idea is to make them go beyond what they wanted to give me and to give back as much as I can give so that it becomes an uncontrollable thing. You see the one problem this guy had with me: he couldn't really fight with me because it meant he must hit back, like a man. But he was given instructions, you see, on how to hit, and now these instructions were no longer applying because it was a fight. So he had to withdraw and get more instructions. So I said to them, "Listen, if you guys want to do this your way, you have got to handcuff me and bind my feet together, so that I can't respond. If you allow me to respond, I'm certainly going to respond. And

I'm afraid you may have to kill me in the process even if it's not your intention".

HERMAN CHARLES BOSMAN

HERMAN CHARLES BOSMAN (1905–51), one of South Africa's most widely read writers, is best known for his wry and amusing short stories about Afrikaner life in the Groot Marico district of the then Western Transvaal, where he spent six months as a schoolteacher in 1925.

A BEKKERSDAL MARATHON

At Naudé, who had a wireless set, came into Jurie Steyn's voorkamer, where we were sitting waiting for the railway lorry from Bekkersdal, and gave us the latest news. He said that the newest thing in Europe was that young people there were going in for non-stop dancing. It was called marathon dancing, At Naudé told us, and those young people were trying to break the record for who could remain on their feet longest, dancing.

We listened for a while to what At Naudé had to say, and then we suddenly remembered a marathon event that had taken place in the little dorp of Bekkersdal – almost in our midst, you could say. What was more, there were quite a number of us sitting in Jurie Steyn's post office, who had actually taken part in that non-stop affair, and without knowing that we were breaking records, and without expecting any sort of a prize for it, either.

We discussed that affair at considerable length and from all angles, and we were still talking about it when the lorry came. And we agreed that it had been in several respects an unusual occurrence. We also agreed that it was questionable if we could have carried off things so successfully that day, if it had not been for Billy Robertse.

You see, our organist at Bekkersdal was Billy Robertse. He had once been a sailor and had come to the bushveld some years before, travelling on foot. His belongings, fastened in a red handkerchief, were slung over his shoulder on a stick. Billy Robertse was journeying in that fashion for the sake of his health. He suffered from an unfortunate complaint for which he had at regular intervals to drink something out of a black bottle that he always carried handy in his jacket pocket.

Billy Robertse would even keep that bottle beside him in the organist's gallery in case of a sudden attack. And if the hymn the predikant gave out had many verses, you could be sure that about halfway through Billy Robertse would bring the bottle up to his mouth, leaning sideways towards what was in it. And he would put several extra twirls into the second part of the hymn.

When he first applied for the position of organist in the Bekkersdal church, Billy Robertse told the meeting of deacons that he had learnt to play the organ in a cathedral in northern Europe. Several deacons felt, then, that they could not favour his application. They said that the cathedral sounded too Papist, the way Billy Robertse described it, with a dome three hundred feet high and with marble apostles. But it was lucky for Billy Robertse that he was able to mention, at the following combined meeting of elders and deacons, that he had also played the piano in a South American dance hall, of which the manager was a Presbyterian. He asked the meeting to overlook his unfortunate past, saying that he had had a hard life, and anybody could make mistakes. In any case, he had never cared much for the Romish atmosphere of the cathedral, he said, and had been happier in the dance hall.

In the end, Billy Robertse got the appointment. But in his sermons for several Sundays after that the predikant, Dominee Welthagen, spoke very strongly against the evils of dance halls. He described those places of awful sin in such burning words that at least one young man went to see Billy Robertse, privately, with a view to taking lessons in playing the piano.

But Billy Robertse was a good musician. And he took a deep interest in his work. And he said that when he sat down on the organist's stool behind the pulpit, and his fingers were flying over the keyboards, and he was pulling out the stops, and his feet were pressing down the notes that sent the deep bass tones through the pipes – then he felt that he could play all day, he said.

"I don't suppose he guessed that he would one day be put to the test, however."

It all happened through Dominee Welthagen one Sunday morning going into a trance in the pulpit. And we did not realise that he was in a trance. It was an illness that overtook him in a strange and sudden fashion.

At each service the predikant, after reading a passage from the Bible, would lean forward with his hand on the pulpit rail and give out the number of the hymn we had to sing. For years his manner of conducting the service had been exactly the same. He would say, for instance: "We will now sing Psalm 82, verses I to 4." Then he would allow his head to sink forward on to his chest and he would remain rigid, as though in prayer, until the last notes of the hymn died away in the church.

Now, on that particular morning, just after he had announced the number of the psalm, without mentioning what verses, Dominee Welthagen again took a firm grip on the pulpit rail and allowed his head to sink forward on to his breast. We did not realise that he had fallen into a trance of a peculiar character that kept his body standing upright while his mind was a blank. We learnt that only later.

In the meantime, while the organ was playing over the opening bars, we began to realise that Dominee Welthagen had not indicated how many verses we had to sing. But he would discover his mistake, we thought, after we had been singing for a few minutes.

All the same, one or two of the younger members of the congregation did titter, slightly, when they took up their hymn books. For Dominee Welthagen had given out Psalm 119. And everybody knows that Psalm 119 has 176 verses.

This was a church service that will never be forgotten in Bekkersdal. We sang the first verse and then the second and then the third. When we got to about the sixth verse and the minister still gave no sign that it would be the last, we assumed that he wished us to sing the first eight verses. For, if you open your hymn book, you'll see that Psalm 119 is divided into sets of eight verses, each ending with the word "Pouse".

We ended the last notes of verse eight with more than an ordinary number of turns and twirls, confident that at any moment Dominee Welthagen would raise his head and let us know that we could sing "Amen".

It was when the organ started up very slowly and solemnly with the music for verse nine that a real feeling of disquiet overcame the congregation. But, of course, we gave no sign of what went on in our minds. We held Dominee Welthagen in too much veneration.

Nevertheless, I would rather not say too much about our feelings, when verse followed verse and Pouse succeeded Pouse, and still Dominee Welthagen made no sign that we had sung long enough, or that there was anything unusual in what he was demanding of us.

After they had recovered from their first surprise, the members of the church council conducted themselves in a most exemplary manner. Elders and deacons tiptoed up and down the aisles, whispering words of reassurance to such members of the congregation, men as well as women, who gave signs of wanting to panic.

At one stage it looked as though we were going to have trouble from the organist. That was when Billy Robertse, at the end of the 34th verse, held up his black bottle and signalled quietly to the elders to indicate that his medicine was finished. At the end of the 35th verse he made signals of a less quiet character, and again at the end of the 36th verse. That was when Elder Landsman tiptoed out of the church and went round to the Konsistorie, where the Nagmaal wine was kept. When Elder Landsman came back into the church he had a long black bottle half-hidden under his manel. He took the bottle up to the organist's gallery, still walking on tiptoe.

At verse 61 there was almost a breakdown. That was when a message came from the back of the organ, where Koster Claassen and the assistant verger, whose task it was to turn the handle that kept the organ supplied with wind, were in a state near to exhaustion. So it was Deacon Cronje's turn to go tiptoeing out of the church. Deacon Cronje was head warder at the local gaol. When he came back it was with three burly Native convicts in striped jerseys, who also went through the church on tiptoe. They arrived just in time to take over the handle from Koster Claassen and the assistant verger.

At verse 98 the organist again started making signals about his medicine. Once more Elder Landsman went round to the Konsistorie. This time he was accompanied by another elder and a deacon, and they stayed away somewhat longer than the time when Elder Landsman had gone on his own. On their return the deacon bumped into a small hymn book table at the back of the church. Perhaps it was because the deacon was a fat, red-faced man, and not used to tiptoeing.

At verse 124 the organist signalled again, and the same three members of the church council filed out to the Konsistorie, the deacon walking in front this time.

It was about then that the pastor of the Full Gospel Apostolic Faith Church, about whom Dominee Welthagen had in the past used almost as strong language as about the Pope, came up to the front gate of the church to see what was afoot. He lived near our church and, having heard the same hymn tune being played over and over for about eight hours, he was a very amazed man. Then he saw the door of the Konsistorie open, and two elders and a deacon coming out, walking on tiptoe – they having apparently forgotten that they were not in church, then. When the pastor saw one of the elders hiding a black bottle under his manel, a look of understanding came over his features. The pastor walked off, shaking his head.

At verse 152 the organist signalled again. This time Elder Landsman and the other elder went out alone. The deacon stayed behind on the deacon's bench, apparently in deep thought. The organist signalled again, for the last time, at verse 169. So you can imagine how many visits the two elders made to the Konsistorie altogether.

The last verse came, and the last line of the last verse. This time it had to be "Amen". Nothing could stop it. I would rather not describe the state that the congregation was in. And by then the three Native convicts, red stripes and all, were, in the Bakhatla tongue, threatening mutiny. "Aa-m-e-e-n" came from what sounded like less than a score of voices, hoarse with singing.

The organ music ceased.

Maybe it was the sudden silence that at last brought Dominee Welthagen out of his long trance. He raised his head and looked slowly about him. His gaze travelled over his congregation and then looking at the windows, he saw that it was night. We understood right away what was going on in Dominee Welthagen's mind. He thought he had just come into the pulpit, and that this was the beginning of the evening service. We realised that, during all the time we had been singing, the predikant had been in a state of unconsciousness.

Once again Dominee Welthagen took a firm grip of the pulpit rail. His head again started drooping forward on to his breast. But before he went into a trance for the second time, he gave out the hymn for the evening service. "We will," Dominee Welthagen announced, "sing Psalm 119."

ALEX LA GUMA

ALEX LA GUMA *(1925–85) was the son of one of the leading figures in the black liberation movement. He was politically active against the apartheid government – among other things, helping with the Freedom Charter in 1956 – until he was put under house arrest in 1962. He and his wife fled the country in 1967 to the UK, then moved to Cuba where he was the ANC representative. His writing was banned by the white minority government.*

This extract is from La Guma's first work, a collection of short stories set in Cape Town's District Six, before the area was razed to the ground and declared an area for whites only.

A WALK IN THE NIGHT

Up ahead the music shops were still going full blast, the blare of records all mixed up so you could not tell one tune from another. Shopkeepers, Jewish, Indian, and Greek, stood in the doorways along the arcade of stores on each side of the street, waiting to welcome last-minute customers; and the vegetable and fruit barrows were still out too, the hawkers in white coats yelling their wares and flapping their brown paper packets, bringing prices down now that the day was ending. Around the bus-stop a crowd pushed and jostled to clamber onto the trackless trams, struggling against the passengers fighting to alight. Along the pavements little knots of youths lounged in twos and threes or more, watching the crowds streaming by, jeering, smoking, joking against the noise, under the balconies, in doorways, around the plate-glass windows. A half-mile of sound and movement and signs, signs, signs: Coca-Cola, Sale Now On, Jewellers, The Modern Outfitters, If You Don't Eat Here We'll Both Starve, Grand Picnic to Paradise Valley Luxury Buses, Teas, Coffee, Smoke, Have You Tried Our Milk Shakes, Billiard Club, The Rockingham Arms, Chine . . . nce In Korea, Your Recommendation Is Our Advert, Dress Salon.

Michael Adonis moved idly along the pavement through the stream of people unwinding like a spool up the street. A music shop was playing shrill and noisy, "Some of these days, you gonna miss me honey"; music from across the Atlantic, shipped in flat shellac discs to pound its jazz through the loudspeaker over the doorway.

He stopped outside the big plate window, looking in at the rows of guitars, banjoes, mandolins, the displayed gramophone parts, guitar picks, strings, electric irons, plugs, jews-harps, adaptors, celluloid dolls all the way from Japan, and the pictures of angels and Christ with a crown of thorns and drops of blood like lipstick marks on his pink forehead.

A fat man came out of the shop, his cheeks smooth and shiny with health, and said, "You like to buy something, sir?"

'"No man," Michael Adonis said and spun his cigarette-end into the street where a couple of snot-nosed boys in ragged shirts and homy feet scrambled for it, pushing each other as they struggled to claim a few puffs.

Somebody said, "Hoit, Mikey," and he turned and saw the wreck of a youth who had fallen in beside him.

"Hullo, Joe."

Joe was short and his face had an ageless quality about it under the grime, like something valuable forgotten in a junk shop. He had the soft brown eyes of a dog, and he smelled of a mixture of sweat, slept-in clothes and seaweed. His trousers had gone at the cuffs and knees, the rents held together with pins and pieces of string, and so stained and spotted that the original colour could not have been guessed at. Over the trousers he wore an ancient raincoat that reached almost to his ankles, the sleeves torn loose at the shoulders, the body hanging in ribbons, the front pinned together over his filthy vest. His shoes were worn beyond recognition.

Nobody knew where Joe came from, or anything about him. He just seemed to have happened, appearing in the District like a cockroach emerging through a floorboard. Most of the time he wandered around the harbour gathering fish discarded by fishermen and anglers, or along the beaches of the coast, picking limpets and mussels. He had a strange passion for things that came from the sea.

"How you, Joe?" Michael Adonis asked.

"Okay, Mikey."

"What you been doing today?"

"Just strolling around the docks. York Castle came in this afternoon."

"Ja?"

"You like mussels, Mikey? I'll bring you some."

"That's fine, Joe."

"I got a big starfish out on the beach yesterday. One big, big one. It was dead and stank."

"Well, it's a good job you didn't bring it into town. City Council would be on your neck."

"I hear they're going to make the beaches so only white people can go there," Joe said.

"Ja. Read it in the papers. Damn sonsabitches."

"It's going to get so's nobody can go nowhere."

"I reckon so," Michael Adonis said.

They were some way up the street now and outside the Queen Victoria. Michael Adonis said, "You like a drink, Joe?" although he knew that the boy did not drink.

"No thanks, Mikey."

"Well, so long."

"So long, man."

"You eat already?"

"Well . . . no . . . not yet," Joe said, smiling humbly and shyly, moving his broken shoes gently on the rough cracked paving.

"Okay, here's a bob. Get yourself something. Parcel of fish and some chips."

"Thanks, Mikey."

"Okay. So long, Joe."

"See you again."

"Don't forget the mussels," Michael Adonis said after him, knowing that Joe would forget anyway.

"I'll bring them," Joe said, smiling back and raising his hand in a salute. He seemed to sense the other young man's doubt of his memory, and added a little fiercely, "I won't forget. You'll see. I won't forget."

Then he went up the street, trailing his tattered raincoat behind him like a sword-slashed, bullet-ripped banner just rescued from a battle.

Michael Adonis turned towards the pub and saw the two policemen coming towards him. They came down the pavement in their flat caps, khaki shirts and pants, their gun harness shiny with polish, and the holstered pistols heavy at their waists. They had hard, frozen faces as if carved out of pink ice, and hard, dispassionate eyes, hard and bright as pieces of blue glass. They strolled slowly and determinedly side by side, without moving off their course, cutting a path through the stream on the pavement like destroyers at sea.

They came on and Michael Adonis turned aside to avoid them, but they had him penned in with a casual, easy, skillful flanking manoeuvre before he could escape.

"*Waar loop jy rond, jong?* Where are you walking around, man?" The voice was hard and flat as the snap of a steel spring, and the one who spoke had hard, thin, chapped lips and a faint blonde down above them. He had flat cheekbones, pink-white, and thick, red-gold eyebrows and pale lashes. His chin was long and cleft and there was a small pimple beginning to form on one side of it, making a reddish dot against the pale skin.

"Going home," Michael Adonis said, looking at the buckle of this policeman's belt. You learned from experience to gaze at some spot on their uniforms, the button of a pocket, or the bright smoothness of their Sam Browne belts, but never into their eyes, for that would be taken as an affront by them. It was only the very brave, or the very stupid, who dared look straight into the law's eyes, to challenge them or to question their authority.

The second policeman stuck his thumbs in his gun-belt and smiled distantly and faintly. It was more a slight movement of his lips, rather than a smile. The backs of his hands where they dropped over the leather of the belt were broad and white, and the outlines of the veins were pale blue under the skin, the skin covered with a field of tiny, slanting ginger-coloured hair. His fingers were thick and the knuckles big and creased and pink, the nails shiny and healthy and carefully kept.

This policeman asked in a heavy, brutal voice, "Where's your dagga?"

"I don't smoke it."

"*Jong*, turn out your pockets," the first one ordered. "Hurry up."

Michael Adonis began to empty his pockets slowly, without looking up at them and thinking, with each movement, You mucking boers, you mucking boers. Some people stopped and looked and hurried on as the policemen turned the cold blue light of their eyes upon them. Michael Adonis showed them his crumbled and partly used packet of cigarettes, the money he had left over from his pay, a soiled handkerchief and an old piece of chewing gum covered with the grey fuzz from his pocket.

"Where did you steal the money?" The question was without humour, deadly serious, the

voice topped with hardness like the surface of a file.

"Didn't steal it, baas (you *mucking boer*)".

"Well, muck off from the street. Don't let us find you standing around, you hear?"

"Yes (you *mucking boer*)."

"Yes, what? Who are you talking to, man?"

"Yes, baas (you *mucking bastard boer with your mucking gun and your mucking bloody red head*)."

They pushed past him, one of them brushing him aside with an elbow and strolled on. He put the stuff back into his pockets. And deep down inside him the feeling of rage, frustration and violence swelled like a boil, knotted with pain.

Reprinted by permission of Heinemann.

ANTJIE KROG

ANTJIE KROG *is an Afrikaans poet, novelist and journalist who reported on the Truth and Reconciliation Commission for the South African Broadcasting Corporation. She blends introspection and meditations on her Afrikaner origin, some of which she describes as "lies in this book about the truth", with reflections on the content and texture of experiences of a reporter on this harrowing 'beat'.*

COUNTRY OF MY SKULL

. . . And suddenly it is as if an undertow is taking me out . . . out . . . and out. And behind me sinks the country of my skull like a sheet in the dark – and I hear a thin song, hooves, hedges of venom, fever and destruction fermenting and hissing underwater. I shrink and prickle. Against. Against my blood and the heritage thereof. Will I forever be them – recognizing them as I do daily in my nostrils? Yes. And what we have done will never be undone. It doesn't matter what we do. What De Klerk does. Until the third and fourth generation.

Famished. Parched, one waits for Constand Viljoen's party [Freedom Front] to make its submission. They form a modest group.

Viljoen speaks as if he wants to capture something, bring something back, confirm some essence of Afrikanerhood that is wholesome. I want it too – but at the same time know it not to be. When Viljoen talks about how the British took away the land of the Boers, an English-speaking journalist mutters sarcastically, 'Ah shame!'

I cannot help it, I spit like a flame: 'Shut up, you! You didn't utter a word when De Klerk [leader of the National Party] spoke . . . Viljoen is at least trying.'

'You must be joking – this poor man is an anachronism.' My anger shrivels before his Accent. And his Truth.

Viljoen was the only political leader who requested that a special Reconciliation Commission be set up in future to deal with 'the hardening of attitudes I experience daily.'

After the first political submissions in August 1996 I interviewed Archbishop Tutu. 'Weren't you irritated that you had to listen to four versions of South Africa's past?'

He spreads his four skinny fingers under my nose. 'Four versions . . . four . . . exist of the life of Christ. Which one would you have liked to chuck out?'

I try another question. 'Why did the last part of the ANC's submission sound so paranoid? As if the whole world is in a conspiracy against Thabo Mbeki.'

Tutu tilts his head in surprise. 'You should be the last person to ask me this. You are sitting with me daily, listening to what happened in the past. Many people are the second and third generation of being persecuted. And if you don't know the past, you will never understand today's politics.'

A friend who has emigrated visits me in the office. She answers a call for me: 'It's your child. He says he's writing a song about Joe Mamasela and he needs a word to rhyme with "Vlakplaas".' She lowers the phone. 'Who is Joe Mamasela?'

A massive sigh breaks through my chest. For the first time in months – I breathe.

The absolution one has given up on, the hope for a catharsis, the ideal of reconciliation, the dream of a powerful reconciliation policy . . . Maybe this is all that is important – that I and my child know Vlakplaas and Mamasela. That we know what happened there.

When the Truth Commission started last year, I realized instinctively: if you cut yourself off from the process, you will wake up in a foreign country – a country that you don't know and that you will never understand."

Reprinted by permission of Random House SA.

MTUTUZELI MATSHOBA

MTUTUZELI MATSHOBA is a black writer who is well known in South Africa. The extract *below gives an idea of the conditions of life in the Transkei, the first artificially created homeland or bantustan, after it was notionally given "independence" in 1976. Kaiser Matanzima, the repressive first leader of the Transkei, imprisoned political opponents without trial and imposed emergency regulations which he renewed annually.*

THREE DAYS IN THE LAND OF A DYING ILLUSION

"Heh, heh," he had chuckled at my ignorance of the present world. "You don't know that Transkei is independent?"

"Independent from what, of what?"

"Of South Africa," and his eyes had completed the sentence with "bloody fool!"

"That's news to me," I said as sincerely as I could.

"You must have been in jail. Were you not in prison when Transkey got independence? Or maybe you were mad, at Sterkfontein."

"Maybe. If that's what you want – your fellow blacks to be in prison. What's the red tape?"

"Give me your pass."

Fortunately, for once I had it for identification purposes. What with everybody looking for "terrorists"under every stone. I gave it to him and he pages through it before throwing it back at me.

"You're Xhosa, neh?"

I nodded.

"Then go and apply for Transkei citizenship at Counter Six. Next!"

I could not suppress my indignation anymore. "When you look at me you imagine I could make an ideal Transkei citizen? When you arrive home this evening you tell your mother to apply for it so that she can go and learn witchcraft if she is not a professional already." I turned and stomped for the door without waiting for his reaction.

So there I was, rolling into Qamata with my third denomination comrades. The discussion petered out to a noticeable hush as everybody was diverted from the articulate lady by the crossing of an invisible Iron Curtain.

The soil was red, ironically reminding me of Avalon and Doornkop cemeteries back home, the land parched and scarred with erosion. In the first fields that we passed the maize had grown hardly a metre high. The weeds, blackjack outstanding, outgrew it. A woman in dusty traditional attire with a baby strapped to her back and two boys in inherited clothes following her, was searching for stems that might have been overlooked at harvest time.

We passed two cows shaving the roadside of sun-scorched grass.

"*Kakade*, what's the use of buying cattle that end up short of grass?" remarked one of my travelling companions.

"*Imfuyo* [stock] is no longer an investment these days," added another.

I had thought the animals looked acceptable. Perhaps that was due to my inability to judge good beef. However you looked at it, some of the animals that we saw were scrawny and others well-nourished. Probably the latter belonged to people who could afford to buy hay.

The mountains rose high, solid, silent and motionless until they melted into blue-grey and hazy horizons, the only sight that appealed magnificently to my eyes. Below them there were picturesque villages of perfectly circular, thatched rondavels whitewashed for about a foot just below the edges of the thatch and around the windows and doors. This architecture dotted the elevated parts of the landscape on both sides of the road for endless acres.

"*Awu*," someone ventured, "*esikaDaliwonga! Ilizwe lembalela* [a land of drought]. That is why he has left it to pick out the richest parts of the land for himself elsewhere; to bulldoze the people out of land that they inherited from their fathers."

"*Ewe. Natbi uyokusixina ngaphaya.*" [Yes. He also crowds us into the parts that remain ours.]

I was confounded by those words because they came from simple people. Things being taken for granted as they generally are, who could have expected them to nurture any misgivings concerning their share of that wilderness? I say wilderness because that was the most suitable description of what was unfolding before my eyes compared with the white-owned Free State country I had seen the previous day. Proof of its being wasteland lay in the

fact that they had surrendered to the inhuman migratory way of life rather than stay and try to eke out a living in their "homeland". It showed there was just no way to suck blood out of a stone. The illusion of freehold in a free land had long faded in the imagination of my cheated people. Independence, *uburu*, had come, avowedly to break the chains of blackness and drive away poverty. Instead it had brought an ominous fog of helplessness that hung over a land marred with eroded ravines which gave one a clear picture of what the earth might look like after an earthquake. From the silvery trickles that traced erratic courses on the sandy beds of some of the shallow dongas, I concluded that they had been rivulets many aeons ago.

The maize refused to grow higher than a foot without water and scientific agricultural methods. It would cost decades in time and billions of rands in the form of irrigation, fertilizer and technology before one would see any advance beyond cross-plantation on the slopes, which was the only scientific land treatment about which I could write home. Where would the billions come from? Obviously from "white South Africa" with her own sick economy.

If anybody out there had figured that he could temporarily depend on South Africa by sending people there as slaves, hoping that they would earn enough to be self-sufficient after some time, he had dreamt up a nightmare. Slaves don't earn anything; they live from hand to mouth. His country would forever remain both a labour reservoir and a vacuum to suck discarded human labour units out of the South African economy.

We passed a village with a dusty filling station or garage that might have been constructed from the home-made mudbricks of the rondavels. Even if I had a car and happened to have a breakdown near that place, I would never risk taking it there.

Reprinted by permission of Ravan Press in association with Rex Collings.

BOOKS

For a country with such a low proportion of its population reading regularly, South Africa generates a huge amount of literature, particularly about subjects the literate feel guilty about – namely, politics and history. Almost all the books listed below are in print, and those that are not, and which are published in either the UK or US, should be fairly easy to track down in second-hand bookshops. Those books only published in South Africa may prove hard to find outside South Africa itself. Where two publishers are given, the first is British, the second US.

HISTORY AND ANTHROPOLOGY

William Beinart, *20th Century South Africa* (OUP, UK). Useful and concise account of South African history this century, with an emphasis on economic history that manages to emphasize the essential without descending into tedium. His predictions for the future seem wobbly now, but there's nothing unusual about that.

Axel-Ivar Berglund, *Zulu Thought Patterns and Symbolism* (Hurst, UK). Sensitive and knowledgeable account of rural Zulu world views, related as they have been described to the author, with the minimum of interpretation from him tacked on. He does, however, set the scene well, and make thought-provoking connections between the various views expressed to him, whilst bending over backwards to avoid tedious judgementalism.

Philip Bonner, *Kings, Commoners and Concessionaries* (CUP, UK). The definitive history (so far) of nineteenth-century Swaziland, by a skilled historian with a gratifying grasp of the source material and mostly reliable judgement. Its one weakness is a lack of oral historical

research, though fortunately useful work has been done on this recently by the Swazi Oral History Project, based at the University there.

Emile Boonzaier, Candy Malherbe, Andy Smith and Penny Berens, *The Cape Herders, A History of the Khoikhoi of Southern Africa* (David Phillip, SA; Ohio University Press, US). Recently published and accessibly written account of the Khoikhoi people of southern Africa, successfully exploding the many prejudices and myths that surround them and exploring their way of life, their interaction with Europeans, and what remains of them today.

Jane Carruthers, *The Kruger National Park: A Social and Political History* (University of Natal, SA). Specialist history that deals with broad issues. By examining the scientific and ideological forces that gave rise to the Kruger National Park, this fascinating book asks important questions about our notions of nature and conservation.

Rodney Davenport *The Transfer of Power in South Africa* (Toronto University Press) Eminent liberal historian examines reconciliation in SA society since 1990 and explains how potential obstacles have been overcome.

Stephen Gill, *A Short History of Lesotho* (Morija, Lesotho). Thoughtful and well-informed account of Lesotho's history and the best single volume you'll find, written by the chief archivist at the Morija museum. Gill clearly loves Lesotho and has little sympathy for its many invaders but is a little over-generous in his account of Lesotho's missionaries.

Barbara Hutton, *Robben Island – Symbol of Resistance* (Sached Books UK; Mayibuye Books, SA) Fast, straightforward and illustrated account of Robben Island from prehistoric times to the present, with a good overview of prison conditions in the apartheid years.

Antjie Krog, *Country of My Skull* (Jonathan Cape, Times Books). A deeply personal rollercoaster and gripping account of the hearings of the Truth and Reconcilliation Commission by Afrikaner SABC radio journalist and poet. Krog reveals the complexity of horrors committed by apartheid, and also paints an admiring tribute to Commission head Desmond Tutu.

Hilda Kuper, *The Swazi, A South African Kingdom* (Saunders College Publishing, US). A combination of anthropology and history, written in the Sixties, whose theoretical perspectives seem pretty dated now, though Kuper's observations still sound sharp. Her political insight was often astute too, though she was too fond of the Dlamini royal house to provide much of a critical perspective on them.

Ben Maclennan, *A Proper Degree of Terror – John Graham and the Cape's Eastern Frontier* (Ravan, SA). Riveting account of the early nineteenth century in the Eastern Cape history, written with the cracking narrative pace of a novel.

Candy Malherbe, *Men of Men* (Shuter and Shooter, SA). Brief, simple and highly readable primer on the earliest inhabitants of the Cape, the Khoikhoi, who were systematically dispossessed, but have nevertheless left their mark on modern South Africa.

Hein Marais *South Africa, Limits to Change* (Zed Books) Readable assessment of why the privileged classes remain just that, and why the new government has followed relatively conservative economic policies.

Shula Marks and Stanley Trapido (eds) *The Politics of Race, Class and Nationalism in 20th century South Africa* (Longman, UK). Seminal collection of Marxist and left-leaning analyses of South African social and political trends this century, with an emphasis on the micro-study that stands in deliberate contrast to the sweeping liberal histories that have preceded it.

Noel Mostert, *Frontiers – The Epic of South Africa's Creation and the Tragedy of the Xhosa People* (Pimlico, UK). Academically solid and brilliantly written history of the Xhosa of the Eastern Cape and their tragic fate in the frontier wars fought against the British.

Credo Mutwa, *Indaba, My Children* (Payback Press, Grove Atlantic). Many of Africa's most enduring and entertaining legends, myths and stories vividly retold – and some would say reinvented – by enigmatic Zulu spiritualist Mutwa.

Dougie Oakes (ed), *Illustrated History of South Africa* (Reader's Digest, SA). Physically weighty, but written in a delightfully light style, this illustated history is an essential volume on the shelves of anyone seriously interested in the democratic history of South Africa.

Thomas Pakenham, *The Boer War* (Abacus, UK). Definitive liberal history of the Anglo-Boer War that reads grippingly like a novel, managing to maintain a panoramic sweep of events while homing in on the quirks and foibles of the individual player.

Jeff Peires, *The Dead Will Arise* (Ravan, SA) and *The House of Phalo* (Ravan, SA). The lead-

ing historian of the Xhosa people tells in beautifully readable prose the stories of the Eastern Cape before the arrival of whites as well as the impact of colonialism on their lives and society in these two books that rely on both written and oral sources.

Marjorie Shostak, *Nisa* (Earthscan, UK). A fascinating book – both bawdy and romantic – based on the life of a San woman in a hostile Kalahari environment.

Leonard Thompson, *A History of South Africa* (Yale UP, UK/US). Reliable and elegantly written, this is among the best introductions to its subject.

Laurens van der Post, *The Lost World of the Kalahari* (Penguin, UK). The author's almost spiritual quest to find, and film, San people still existing as pure hunter-gatherers. *The Heart of the Hunter* (Penguin, UK), is the sequel, although it can be read on its own, dwelling on the San he met and their mythology.

Nigel Worden, Elizabeth van Heyningen and Vivian Bickford-Smith, *Cape Town: The Making of a City* (David Philip, SA). Definitive and highly readable illustrated account of the social and political development of South Africa's first city from 1620 to 1899, written by three leading historians based at the University of Cape Town. A companion volume covers the twentieth century.

AUTOBIOGRAPHY AND BIOGRAPHY

Breyten Breytenbach, *True Confessions of an Albino Terrorist* (Faber & Faber, UK). In vividly poetic language, the exiled Afrikaner poet tells the entertaining story of his return to South Africa in 1975 - to be arrested and jailed for seven years.

Wilfred Cibane, *Man of Two Worlds* (Kwela Books, SA) Autobiography of Cibane's life from rural goatherd to cosmopolitan man of means and the cultural clashes that accompanied it.

Robin Denniston, *Trevor Huddleston, A Life* (Macmillan) Inspiring biography of the English churchman who worked among Johannesburg's urban blacks in the Fifties and later founded the Anti-Apartheid Movement.

Mark Gevisser, *Portraits of Power* (David Philip, SA). Forty profiles of South Africa's movers and shakers in the era of transition.

Sindiwe Magoma, *To my Children's Children* (David Phillip, SA). Fascinating autobiography –

initially started so that her family would never forget their roots – that traces Magoma's life from the rural Transkei to the hard townships of Cape Town, and from political innocence to wisdom born of bitter experience.

Nelson Mandela, *Long Walk to Freedom* (Abacus, UK). Superb best-selling autobiography of the South African president, which is wonderfully evocative of his early years and intensely moving about his long years in prison. However, when it comes to his love life, the byzantine intricacies of ANC politics during its long years as an illegal organization, and the story behind the negotiated settlement, Mandela is more diplomatic than candid. Mandela's generosity of spirit and tremendous understanding of the delicate balance between principle and tactics come out very strongly, and the book is without doubt essential reading for the new South Africa.

Emma Mashinini, *Strikes Have Followed me All my Life* (Women's Press, UK). Moving account of this diminuitive but unstoppable trade unionist, who defied both injustice in the labour market and the deep sexism of her colleagues during her tireless struggles from the Fifties to the Eighties.

William Plomer, *Cecil Rhodes* (David Phillip, SA). There are countless books on Rhodes, most of which feed the legend, although the distance of time has made some historians ready to regard him as a flawed colossus. This is a re-publication of one of the most critical accounts, written several decades ago, against the grain, by a South African poet-novelist, when colonialism was still regarded by many whites as a good thing. It pulls no punches in presenting Rhodes as an immature person driven by his weaknesses.

Richard Rosenthal, *Mission Improbable* (David Philip, SA). Fascinating account of and attempt to set up "talks about talks" between the ANC and P.W. Botha's government in Switzerland during December 1988, which were cut short by the latter's stroke.

Albie Sachs, *The Soft Vengeance of a Freedom Fighter* (David Phillip, SA). The ANC veteran relates the story of how, in exile in Mozambique, he was almost killed by a South African security police bomb. The book vividly traces his recovery and the mental difficulties he went through to emerge with a new vision of the struggle.

Anthony Sampson, *Mandela, The Authorised Biography* (Harper Collins, Knopf). Released to coincide with Mandela's retirement from presidency in 1999, Sampson's authoritative volume can compete with *A Long Walk to Freedom* in both interest and sheer poundage. Firmly grounded in the author's long association with his subject, as well as exhaustive research and interviews, it offers a broader perspective and sharper analysis than the autobiography.

TRAVEL AND GENERAL

Dan Jacobson, *The Electric Elephant* (Hamish Hamilton, UK). Jacobson, who left South Africa in the Fifties, returned in 1993 to travel from Kimberley in the Northern Cape to Victoria Falls, along the old "Great North Road", built by Rhodes and since trodden by generations of missionaries, colonists and freebooters.

Dervla Murphy, *South from the Limpopo: Travels through South Africa* (John Murray, UK). Fascinating bike journey through the new South Africa with a writer who isn't afraid to explore the complexities and paradoxes of this country.

Marco Turco, *Visitor's Guide to Lesotho* (Southern, SA). Exhaustive account of nearly every town and village on the main routes through Lesotho, accompanied by constant exhortations for readers to get out and meet the Sotho. Helpful in places, though rather indiscriminate.

Marco Turco, *Visitor's Guide to Swaziland* (Southern, SA). Turco travelled everywhere to write this book, including some really out-of-the-way places, though his account is marred by his tendency to recommend everything, no matter how dull it turns out to be when you get there.

FICTION

Tatamkhulu Afrika, *The Innocents* (Africasouth, SA) Set in the struggle years, this novel examines the moral and ethical issues of the time from a Muslim perspective.

Mark Behr, *The Smell of Apples* (Abacus, UK). Best-selling novel about a small white boy growing up in a military family under apartheid in the Seventies, and painfully resonant for many.

Herman Charles Bosman, *Unto Dust* (Human & Rousseau, SA). Superb collection of short stories from South Africa's master of the genre, all set in the tiny Afrikaner farming district of Groot Marico in the Thirties, with the narrator Oom Schalk Lourens revealing with deliciously wry irony the passions and foibles of his community.

André Brink, *A Chain of Voices* (Minerva, UK). Superbly evocative tale of Cape eighteenth-century life, exploring the impact of slavery on one farming family, right up to its dramatic and murderous end.

J.M. Coetzee, *Age of Iron* (Penguin, UK/US). Voted by writers in a *Mail & Guardian* poll to be the finest South African novel of the last ten years, this depicts a white female classics professor dying from cancer during the political craziness of the Eighties. She is joined by a tramp who sets up home in the garden, and thus evolves a curious and fascinating relationship that transforms her.

Achmat Dangor, *The Z Town Trilogy* (Ravan, SA). One of the best Cape Town writers, Dangor sets this trilogy in a town much like it, during one of apartheid South Africa's many states of emergency, which have started to burrow in intricate ways into the psyches of his characters.

Modikwe Dikobe, *Marabi Dance* (Heinemann, UK). Short novel celebrating the bittersweet nature of black Johannesburg life in the Thirties, where the daily humiliations of life are tempered by the prospect of wild *marabi* parties when the weekends come.

Nadine Gordimer, *July's People* (Penguin, UK/US). Liberal white family is rescued by its gardener July from revolution, and taken to his home village for safety, where Gordimer teases out the power dynamics of this fraught situation with customary insight and eloquence.

Alex La Guma, *A Walk in the Night* (Heinemann, UK). Evocative collection of short stories set in District Six, the ethnically mixed quarter of Cape Town that was razed by the apartheid government, by this talented political activist/author.

Dan Jacobson, *The Trap, and a Dance in the Sun* (David Phillip, SA). Two taut novellas in one volume, written in the Fifties, skilfully portraying the developing tensions and nuances of the white-versus-black lives of the era.

Anne Landsman, *The Devil's Chimney* (Granta, Penguin). A stylish and entertaining piece of magic realism about the Southern Cape town of Outshoorn in the days of the ostrich-feather boom.

Zakes Mda, *Ways of Dying* (OUP, UK). Winner of the 1997 M-Net Book Prize, this brilliant tale of a professional mourner is full of sly insights into the culture of black South Africa.

Thomas Mofolo, *Chaka* (Heinemann, UK). Thomas Mofolo was Lesotho's first great fiction writer, who wrote this epic tale in Sotho of the Zulu king Shaka in 1909, here portrayed as a man fatally controlled by his strong passions. The original English translation gave the text a misleadingly biblical slant, which has been corrected in this newer translation by Daniel Kunene.

Isaac Mogotsi, *Alexandra Tales* (Ravan, SA). Delightful tales of family life in the run-down, lively homes of Johannesburg's Alexandra township, all with a clever and provocative twist in the tail.

Es'kia Mpahalele, *Down Second Avenue* (Faber & Faber, UK). Classic autobiographical novel set in the Forties, where Mpahalele grew up in the impoverished township of Alexandra in a large extended family battling daily to survive the problems and injustices of the age.

Marlene van Niekerk, *Triomf* (Johnathan Ball, SA; Little, Brown & Co, UK). Award-winning Afrikaans novel translated into South African English as well as a less idiomatic form for the overseas market. Tells the colourful and tragic story of a family of poor whites living in the emblematic Johannesburg suburb of Triomf, built on the ruins of the black enclave of Sophiatown.

Alan Paton, *Cry, the Beloved Country* (Penguin, UK). Classic novel by one of South Africa's great liberals, describing with tremendous lyricism the journey of a black pastor from rural Natal to Johannesburg, depicted as a veritable Sodom and Gomorrah, to rescue his missing son from its clutches.

Kathy Perkins, *Black South African Women – An Anthology of Plays* (Routledge, UK) Groundbreaking collection of ten plays by a wide range of known and unknown playwrights such as Gcina Mhlope, Sindiwe Magona, Muthal Naidoo and Lueen Conning.

Sol Plaatje, *Mhudi* (Heinemann, UK). The first English novel by a South African writer, *Mhudi* is the epic story, set in the 1830s, of a young Barolong woman who saves her future husband from the raids of the Ndebele, at a time when the Afrikaner Great Trek had just begun. Plaatje was also a political activist and was one of the founder members of the ANC.

Linda Rode, *Crossing Over* (Kwela, SA) Collection of 26 stories by new and emerging SA writers on the experiences of adolescence and early adulthood in a period of political transition.

Olive Schreiner, *Story of an African Farm* (Penguin, UK/US). The first-ever South African novel, Schreiner wrote this in 1883 under a male pseudonym. Though subject to the ideologies of the era, the book nonetheless explores with genuinely open vision as it tells the tale of two female cousins living on a remote Karoo farm whose young lives are disrupted by an Irish traveller.

Sipho Sepamla, *A Ride on the Whirlwind* (Heinemann, UK). Set in the terrifying times of 1976 in riot-swept Soweto, Sepamla's novel explores the psychology of resistance and defiance amongst the angry township youth.

Mongane Wally Serote, *To Every Birth Its Blood* (Heinemann, UK). Serote's only novel is a powerfully turbulent affair that traces the evolution of a township man from someone interested only in jazz, drinking and sex, to political consciousness through the humiliations he is subjected to by the forces of authority.

Martin Trump and Jean Marquard (eds) *A Century of South African Short Stories* (Ad Donker, SA). Respectable selection of South Africa's finest short stories, including contributions from *Drum* writer Can Themba, Charles Bosman and Nadine Gordimer.

POETRY

Guy Butler (ed), *A Book of South African Verse* (Oxford, UK); **Jack Cope and Uys Krige** (eds), *The Penguin Book of South African Verse* (Penguin, UK). Early anthologies that, for better or for worse, "mapped" South African poetry. Butler's comment in his introduction – "Most of our poets have tried to belong to Africa and, finding her savage, shallow and uncooperative, have been forced to give their allegiance, not to any other country, but to certain basic conceptions" (read Europe) – remains controversial.

Tim Couzens and Essop Patel (eds), *Return of the Amasi Bird* (Ravan, SA). Comprehensive collection of black South African poetry, which stretches right back to the early colonial era and extends to the cries of liberation and beyond.

Leon de Kock and Ian Tromp (eds), *The Heart in Exile* (Penguin, UK/US/SA). Well-considered anthology of South African poems written

between the time of Nelson Mandela's release in 1990 and the democratic elections of 1994. An interesting balance of forward-looking and reflective work from some of the country's most accomplished poets.

Peter Horn, *The Rivers which Connect us to the Past* (Mayibuye, SA) Among SA's most prolific protest poets during the Seventies, with strong socialist convictions.

Lesego Rampolokeng, *Horns of Hondo* (Cosaw, SA). One of the most promising talents unleashed by the Congress of South African Writers (Cosaw). Rampolokeng speaks with a fiery township voice, his poetry flowing to dread rhythms of rap and dub.

Mongane Wally Serote, *Selected Poems* (Ad Donker, SA). The leading light amongst South Africa's many protest poets, with a work that ranges from early rage to incantations of freedom, leavened with humour and startling imagery.

Yvonne Vera, *Under the Tongue* (David Philip, SA) Long poem in novel form, concerned with the power of language to heal and facilitate self-transformation.

THE ARTS

Marion Arnold, *Women and Art in South Africa* (David Philip, SA). Pioneering work that reinterprets South African art history.

Basil Beakey, *Beyond the Blues: Township Jazz of the Sixties and Seventies* (David Philip, SA) Portraits of the country's jazz greats such as Kippie Moeketsi, Basil Coetzee, Abdullah Ibrahim (Dollar Brand).

Ian Berry, *Living Apart* (Phaidon, SA). Superbly evocative and moving photographs spanning from the Fifties to Nineties, which chart a compelling vision of the politics of the nation, but at a micro level, with a decidedly small "p".

Clive Chipkin, *Johannesburg Style* (David Philip, SA). Perhaps a contradiction in terms, but a fascinating study of architecture and society in the South African city.

J. Christopher, *The Atlas of Apartheid* (Routledge, UK). Detailed but accessible study of the policy and implementation of urban and regional planning that gave South African towns and cities their current form.

S. Francis and H. Dugmore, *Madam and Eve* (Penguin, SA). One of South Africa's leading cultural exports conveys the daily struggle between an African domestic worker and her white madam in the northern suburbs of Johannesburg in various volumes of telling and witty cartoon strips that say more about post-apartheid society than countless academic tomes.

J.D. Lewis-Williams, *Discovering Southern African Rock Art* (David Phillip, SA), and *Images of Power: Understanding Bushman Rock Art* (David Phillip, SA). Short, concise books written by an expert in the field, full of drawings and photos. It concludes that most of the paintings depict images seen while in a state of shamanic trance, and reflect a San world-view in which the spiritual and material were both a part of everyday life.

Z.B. Molefe, *A Common Hunger to Sing* (Kwela, SA). Large format, well-illustrated tribute to the achievements of the country's black women singers and the obstacles they have overcome.

Jurgen Schadeberg, *Sof'town: Images from the Black '50s* (Jurgen Schadeberg, UK). Classic black-and-white photographic studies of the *Drum* era of the swinging Johannesburg, where, if Schadeberg is to be believed, every black woman was a beauty and every black man a dude in a zoot suit.

Sue Williamson, *Resistance Art in South Africa* (David Phillip, SA), and *Art in South Africa: The Future Present* (David Phillip, SA). Taken together, these two volumes map the course of South African art from the early Eighties to the present day, with a thoughtful text that's minimal enough to let the artists' works speak for themselves.

Zapiro, *End of Part One* (David Philip, SA) Third collection of cartoons by the country's leading exponent, preceded by *The Hole Truth* and *The Madiba Years*.

SPECIALIST GUIDEBOOKS

GM Branch, *Two Oceans* (David Philip, SA) Don't be fooled by the coffee-table format; this is a comprehensive guide to Southern Africa's marine life.

David Bristow, *Best Hikes in Southern Africa* (Struik, SA). Well-written and reliable guide that does your homework for you, selecting the best trails from a confusingly extensive lot.

David Bristow, *Drakensberg Walks: 120 Graded Hikes and Trails in the 'Berg* (Struik, SA). An indispensable paperback for anyone exploring the Drakensberg, with detailed route instructions and informative background about the natural history of the massif.

Shirley Brossey, *A Walking Guide for Table Mountain* (self-published, SA). Useful and inexpensive guide to trails around the Table Mountain, with handy hand-drawn maps and a down-to-earth text.

Judith Hopley, *On Foot in the Garden Route* (self-published, SA). Excellent little guide that's perfect if you're planning on exploring the coasts and forest of the Garden Route on foot.

Jaynee Levy, *The Complete Guide to Walks & Trails in Southern Africa* (Struik, SA). Encyclopedic hiker's bible covering over 500 trails suitable for all abilities, with useful practical information about what to take and where to book. One to invest in if you're a keen trailist spending time in the country, but definitely not light reading to take for a walk.

Mike Lundy, *Best Walks in the Cape Peninsula* (Struik, SA). Handy, solidly researched guide to some of the Peninsula's many walks, and small enough to fit comfortably in a backpack while you are walking them.

Tony Pooley and Ian Player, *KwaZulu-Natal Wildlife Destinations* (Southern, SA). Comprehensive directory of every game and nature reserve in the province, with useful practical and background information.

Charles Stewart, *Rock and Surf Fishing* (Southern, SA). Uninspiringly written, but the author does appear to have tried his luck from nearly every available vantage point on the South African coast, and the book is a useful guide to what he has found out on the way.

Cornel Truter, *West Coast* (UCT, SA) The history, flora, industry, agriculture and tourism of this gaunt but beautiful stretch that is the opposite of the lush Garden Route.

BIRDS

Hugh Chittenden, *Top Birding Spots of Southern Africa* (Southern, SA). Essential companion guide for any keen bird-watcher, with information on spots, how to access them as well as a rundown on the common species and any specials to look out for.

Gordon Lindsay Maclean Roberts, *Birds of Southern Africa* (New Holland, UK). The definitive reference work on the subcontinent's entire avifauna population: if it's not in Roberts, it doesn't exist. Alas the weight of this tome makes it more of a book to consult in a library than to take on your trip.

Ian Sinclair, *Southern African Birds – A Photographic Guide* (Collins, UK; Struik, SA). Pocket-sized volume full of photos to help you bird-spot your way around the country, with pretty minimal textual accompaniment, rather short on interesting little facts about the birds in question.

MAMMALS

Richard D Estes *Safari Companion* (Russell Friedman Books, SA). A long-needed guide on how to understand African wildlife, with interesting and readable information on the behaviour and social structures of the major species.

Chris and Tilde Stuart *Field Guide to the Mammals of Southern Africa* (New Holland, UK). One of the best books on this subject providing excellent background and clear illustrations to help you recognize a species.

TREES AND PLANTS

L. McMahon and M. Fraser *A Fynbos Year* (David Phillip, SA). Exquisitely illustrated and well-written book about South Africa's unique floral kingdom.

Keith Coates Palgrave *Trees of Southern Africa* (Struik, SA). The authoritative book on the subject, but big and too heavy to carry around.

Eve Palmer *A Field Guide to the Trees of Southern Africa* (Collins, UK). Covers South Africa, Botswana and Namibia and is small and more practical to carry than Coates Palgrave.

WINE

David Biggs, *South African Plonk Buyer's Guide* (Ampersand, SA). Annually updated survey of the best of the cheap wines (under R20).

John Platter *South African Wine Guide*. Annually updated pocket guide to South Africa's current output, with reviews and rating by one of the country's top wine writers.

James Seely *The Wines of South Africa* (Faber & Faber, UK). Almost as definitive as it claims, this book tackles South African wine region by region, estate by estate, complete with tasting notes and recommendations. Written by an author who once imported wine to the UK for Harvey's, but now does so for himself, its a useful and inexpensive reference guide.

MUSIC

In a region dominated musically by Zaire's mighty rhumba sound, South Africa is the exception, not just for the remarkable profusion of local styles, but because of the power and influence of African-American music. Although Zairean musicians are now making inroads in Johannesburg, in most of South Africa it's American soul, r&b and hip-hop that appear to reign supreme, dominating both the airwaves and the music shops, and shaping black and coloured township cool. White people, as ever, have gone their own way, also looking outside the country for inspiration, but this time to the white British and American rock scene.

Nonetheless, despite countless predictions of its imminent demise, South African music lives on, reaching depths in the South African soul that imported music, no matter how cool, can never hope to touch. While Western fans could be forgiven for thinking that the **mbaqanga** or township jive, made famous by Paul Simon's Graceland album, and touring South African artists like the **Soul Brothers** and **Mahlathini** are at the music's cutting edge, in fact they are viewed in the country as distinctly old hat. Far and away the most popular music in the country is **gospel**. Also huge amongst township youth is **kwaito** or **d'gong**, a somewhat tinny South African variant of house that comes complete with its own dress codes and formation dancing styles. Meanwhile, thirtysomethings are more likely to top up their daily dose of American soul with **bubblegum**, the youth music of their day, essentially based on a mix of *mbaqanga* and disco, or the **reggae** of singers like Lucky Dube. In the rural areas and in the hostels, **neo-traditional music** holds sway, with songs accompanied by the accordion, guitar and a thumping bassline, constantly reworking themes of marriage, dowries, betrayal and village gossip. City sophisticates, particularly in Cape Town and Pretoria, tend to go for **jazz**, either of the old school, performed largely by those who went into exile in the Sixties and returned in the Nineties like **Hugh Masekela** and **Abdullah Ibrahim**, or of the new school, which draws heavily on American West Coast fusion sounds. Young whites have plenty of **alternative rock bands** to choose from, like **Urban Creep** and the immensely popular **Springbok Nude Girls**, and there's always at least one to see on the weekend in any of South Africa's major cities.

GOSPEL

Choral harmony and melody are perhaps black South Africa's greatest musical gifts to the world, and nowhere are they better manifested than in its **churches**. In the mainstream Catholic, Anglican and Methodist denominations a tradition of choral singing has evolved that has taken the style of European classical composers, such as Handel, but loosened it up, adding rhythm and some great dance routines. This type of choral singing is immensely popular, with regular competitions involving amazingly attired choirs – some of which are over one hundred strong. If you can't make it to a competition, you can watch the choirs every Sunday on television's SABC 1.

In the **Pentecostal** churches, the music is more American-influenced, with liberal spicings of "Hallelujahs" and "Praise the Lord"s. Even so, the harmonies and melodies remain uniquely South African and intensely moving. Pentecostal gospel music is the style you are most likely to find on cassettes, where you should look out for groups like **Pure Gold**, the **Holy Spirits** and the incomparable **Rebecca Malope** (see box, overleaf).

Also worth seeking out is **Zionist gospel**. The Zionist churches have more members than any other denomination in the country, who are required to donate ten percent of their income to the church, live an ultra-clean life and attend all the services and conventions, in distinctive long robes, often adorned with sashes. Their music is

REBECCA MALOPE

Diminutive **REBECCA MALOPE** is unquestionably South Africa's biggest music star. These days, she only plays in stadia, with nearly every concert a sellout. Every album she releases goes gold or platinum, popular magazines can't get enough of her photos, views and story, and everyone seems to know the lyrics to all her songs. Well, nearly everyone that is, for Rebecca Malope is virtually unknown outside the black community.

Rebecca's musical formula rarely varies. Her songs are anthems that manage to sound as though they have been around for ever, and to which you can sing along, wave your arms in unison, do nifty little dance shuffles, or simply weep tears of ecstatic joy – all of which you will see fans doing at her concerts.

Rebecca employs marvellous backing singers, the best of whom is **Vuyo**, a handsome, mischievous, pig-tailed and deep-voiced man who is now forging a successful solo career. Rebecca's competent, unobtrusive backing includes keyboardist **Zako**, who also produces her and writes most of her songs. Despite an obvious humility and a willingness to promote other talents, Rebecca remains the undisputed star, with a tremendous, soaring and sometimes husky voice, dramatic

gestures as she becomes possessed by the spiritual power her lyrics unleash, and a total commitment to her songs and the gospel message they convey.

The daughter of a Sotho father and Swazi mother, Rebecca was born in Nelspruit, Mpumalanga in 1969, and soon began singing in the local Assemblies of God church, where her grandfather was a pastor. Her initial recordings were mostly forgettable pop, but in Johannesburg she was spotted by Zako, and under his tutelage and because, she says, of letters from fans pleading that she sing God's songs, Rebecca returned to gospel in 1990, where she has since been amply rewarded. Denying that she is apolitical, Rebecca says she does sometimes sing at rallies, but will select songs that tell the politicians what she believes they need to hear.

Safely huge in South Africa, Rebecca is keen to make it internationally, but a European tour in 1997 made little impact, despite her producing some of her most intimate and powerful performances in years. She will no doubt try again, when audiences may be ready for the woman who in South Africa rests unchallenged as the reigning champion of the local music scene.

both inspirational and mournful, with a tonality all of its own, rendering it perfect for the moving night vigils that precede funerals, as well as for regular church services, held outside and often in parks, where you are welcome to watch as long as you do so respectfully. Zionist gospel cassettes are easily spotted, as their covers invariably feature the substantial performing choir in full robes, often with the preacher out in front in some suitably religious pose.

KWAITO

Kwaito, or **d'gong** as it is sometimes known, is South Africa's newest music and dance craze. International audiences more used to the good-time grooves and real instruments of Seventies *mbaqanga* and township jive seem to find little of merit in its sound, but devotees of house and drum'n'bass are more likely to lend it an appreciative ear. *Kwaito* is heavily influenced by both house and drum'n'bass, and its once rather thin production sound has become progressively heavier and more dubwise of late. In an accurate reflection of the current depressed and somewhat nihilistic mood of township youth

culture, *kwaito*'s vibe is usually downbeat and pretty mean, and the music carries a strong association with gangsterism and explicit sexuality. All this is more than enough to condemn it in the eyes of most older and God-fearing South Africans but matters nix ("nothing") to its young township fans, to whom *kwaito* embodies the style and groove of the new South Africa to such an extent that many are now almost entirely weaned off American soul music.

Kwaito, like all modern dance music, is pretty pointless without a party crowd to dance to it, and when you see the music in this context it starts to make sense. Black South Africans have a predilection for formation dancing, preferably with plenty of deft footwork and synchronized about-turns, and *kwaito* is perfect for this, with its *tsotsi-taal* (ghetto slang) lyrics contributing the necessary contemporary vibe, complemented in the dance by the distinctive *kwaito* fashion of the crowd – currently long trousers that are too short for the men and skimpy miniskirts for the women.

Kwaito music is like bubblegum (see opposite) in that no tune or performer lasts very long. There are some major stars to look out for though, including **Arthur**, who these days is as big a success as a producer as an artist; **TKZee**, who specialize in light, summery, R&B-influenced sounds; **Skeem**, who are among the more musical of the current *kwaito* crop and sing in a curious blend of coloured Afrikaans, English and *tsotsi-taal*; and the two big rival female outfits **Abashante** and **Boom Shaka**, who borrow liberally from current Jamaican ragga hits, adding sugary vocals and, on stage at least, large dollops of intense sexual athleticism.

BUBBLEGUM

Bubblegum is *kwaito*'s predecessor, and established the formula of ultra-contemporary throwaway music that loses its flavour after only a couple of plays, which is how it got its name. Essentially a mix of township jive and disco, bubblegum was the vehicle for success of a number of artists who now like to think of themselves as more serious performers, perhaps as an explanation for their rapidly declining popularity. Such artists include **Sipho "Hotstix" Mabuse**, who had a massive hit with the tune Jive Soweto in the Eighties but has now branched out into jazz and more pan-African sounds; **Sello "Chicco" Twala**, who today makes his bucks producing *kwaito* and **Yvonne Chaka Chaka**. Yvonne showed more foresight than most bubblegum artists in the late Eighties by assiduously cultivating a following in the rest of Africa, so that although she is barely rated in South Africa any more she can still draw a huge crowd in the rest of the continent. Her biggest hit, which still stands up to scrutiny, is *Umgqombothi*, which is all about the delights of traditional beer. Yvonne's big rival was always **Brenda Fassie**, a genuine pop star with a flair for both self-destruction and promotion, whose monster hits include *Too Late for Mama* and, to commemorate the release of Nelson Mandela, to whom she is related, *Black President*. Brenda has more recently been experimenting with Congolese **soukous** and duetted with Papa Wemba on her 1997 album *Now is the Time*. She has also dabbled in *kwaito* with varying degrees of success, but scored a phenomenal hit in 1998 with a classic bubblegum track called *Vuli Ndlela*, which is about the jealousies that get prompted by a township wedding.

RAP AND REGGAE

While **rap and reggae** are very popular in South Africa, particularly in the coloured community, credible local performers are a bit thin on the ground. By far the best South African rap group are the **Prophets of Da City**, who hail from the coloured townships of Cape Town, and have a distinctly political slant to their lyrics. The unquestioned king of the local reggae scene, though he has been pretty quiet recently, is **Lucky Dube**. Originally a township jive singer, his switch to Peter Tosh-style roots reggae in the early Nineties was an inspired one, and his album *Prisoner* became the biggest-selling South African album of all time. An energetic, disciplined and talented live performer, Lucky Dube can also come up with a falsetto like Smokey Robinson's, which adds a distinctly new twist to his otherwise familiar roots sounds.

NEO-TRADITIONAL MUSIC

The best way to see South African **neo-traditional music**, unless you're lucky enough to find yourself at an event where it's being performed live, is on SABC TV Channel 1's *Ezodumo* on Thursday nights, which is compulsory viewing in the few rural homesteads and hostels that have a television. The programme is a great showcase for the bands, all dressed in vaguely traditional attire, and usually consisting of a male lead vocalist, female backing singers and a small rhythm section, which often includes a concertina player. As with *kwaito*, the instrumentation is really just a backdrop to the lyrics – usually shouted at great speed – and the dance routines, which reveal grace of movement in even the largest of backing singers.

The king of neo-traditional music is undoubtedly **Thomas Chauke**, who is an *Ezodumo* regular, and probably the best seller in any of the neo-traditional genres, making heavy use of a drum machine, an electric keyboard and some often intricate lead-guitar work to complement his endless vocals.

Sotho neo-traditional styles have shown the least development over the years, largely because of a particularly conservative music policy on Radio Sotho during the apartheid era. Nevertheless, the basslines are good, and while you can take or leave the concertinas the

LADYSMITH BLACK MAMBAZO AND THE ISCATHAMIYA SOUND

The most famous of all South Africa's neo-traditional music is the great Zulu invention of **iscathamiya**, or *mbube*. Iscathamiya is an unaccompanied and distinctive choral singing style made famous in the West by **Ladysmith Black Mambazo**, most recently with the help of the baked beans manufacturer Heinz. The style began in the migrants' hostels after World War I, with the first hit going to Solomon Linda and the Original Evening Birds, whose song *Mbube* sold 100,000 copies, and has been used many times since, most recently in the Disney movie *The Lion King*, where it has been worked into the song *The Lion Sleeps Tonight*.

Although it enjoyed pan-ethnic popularity in the Forties and Fifties, in the Sixties *iscathamiya* reverted to its role as the defining sound of Zulu men's hostels. This was cleverly used by Radio Zulu to promote the apartheid concepts of rigid ethnic identity and ruralism, and the station encouraged and recorded songs that dwelt on

Zulu-ness, and the need to leave the cities and return to the rural areas. In 1973, Ladysmith Black Mambazo recorded their first album, *Amabutho*, which quickly sold 25,000 copies and have since recorded about forty others, all of which have gone gold. Following their collaboration with Paul Simon on *Graceland*, he produced their album *Shaka Zulu*, which sold 100,000 copies around the world, and took *iscathamiya* to the international stage.

Having flirted with the Inkhatha Freedom Party's Zulu nationalist politics in the late Eighties, today Ladysmith Black Mambazo prefer to dwell on religious matters, and keep their politics to calls for peace. Though non-Zulu speakers can appreciate the group's smooth dance steps, immaculate singing and vocal arrangements, the true glory of their music for the Zulu is the beauty of the lyrics, composed by Black Mambazo's gentle lead singer **Joe Shabalala**, who is surely one of South Africa's greatest living poets.

shouting is definitely first class. **Tau Oa Matshela** and **Tau Oa Linare** are groups to look out for.

You do not often hear Xhosa or Tswana neo-traditional sounds, but **Zulu music** is everywhere, both in its instrumental and a cappella form, known to the Zulu as *iscathamiya* (see box, above). A unique guitar-picking style (*ukupika*) is central to the instrumental sound, though it's often overshadowed these days by a hammily played electric keyboard. Each song starts with the *izihlabo* (an instrumental flourish), followed by the main melody, which is interrupted by the lead singer's *ukubonga*, a fast-spoken declamation, usually in deep rural Zulu, that always used to be some kind of praise poem, but could just as well in modern songs be a denunciation of a woman's cooking or the jealousy of a rival. For particularly fine examples of the art, look out for the singer **Phuz'khemisi**, whose cassettes are everywhere, particularly in KwaZulu-Natal.

JAZZ

Ever since its main exponents went into self-imposed exile in the Sixties, **South African jazz** has been the music most associated with the struggle against apartheid. Musically, though, the sound of the exiles represented a departure from the indigenous *marabi* jazz of

the Fifties (see below), and a move in the direction of the American avant-garde, as personified by Thelonious Monk, Sonny Rollins and John Coltrane. The two prime exponents of this new fusion were the **Jazz Epistles**, featuring Hugh Masekela, Jonas Gwangwa, Abdullah Ibrahim (then called Dollar Brand) and the great Kippie Moeketsi, and the **Blue Notes**, who included in their line-up Chris McGregor and Dudu Pukwana. Most of the Epistles left South Africa in 1960, and the Blue Notes left in 1964. During their exile, South African jazz musicians sought to reincorporate South African styles, and *mbaqanga* in particular, into their repertoire. Today, the exiled artists, including Miriam Makeba, are back home, at last receiving the recognition and respect they have long deserved. Some, like **Ibrahim** and **Winston "Mankunku" Ngozi**, continue to perform fairly regularly and you should catch them if you get the chance. Others have moved closer to politics, with Masekela working as a top-level cultural bureaucrat in Pretoria, and Makeba an ANC Member of Parliament in Cape Town, which leaves them too little time for practising or for original composition and innovation.

Ironically, you'll have more opportunity to hear **marabi jazz** than the old new-wave, thanks to the dedicated gigging of the elderly but tireless **African Jazz Pioneers** and **Elite**

Swingsters, often featuring Dorothy Rathebe on vocals. When it first emerged in the Twenties, *marabi* was the music of the black Johannesburg slums, played on pianos in *shebeens*. Always revolving around a simple three-chord structure, *marabi* developed in the 1930s, with guitars, banjos and concertinas added to the line-up. In the Forties, American swing jazz hit South Africa and it was the fusion of swing and *marabi* that led to *marabi* jazz.

A new generation of jazz musicians has emerged in South Africa, keen to move beyond nostalgia, *marabi* and Sixties-style avant-garde, often drawing instead for inspiration on American West Coast fusion, but their problem is that, so far, few South Africans have shown much interest in their efforts. Virtuoso pianist **Bheki Mseleku** has elected to stay in London, and the talented young bassist **Sipho Gumede**, despite the critical acclaim he has received, is struggling to find a decent audience at home. Pianist **Moses Taiwa Molelekwa** has taken an interesting route, fusing his jazz with jungle beats on the excellent 1998 album *Genes and Spirits*, that has certainly excited the critics if not huge numbers of the general public. You can almost always find modern South African jazz in either Johannesburg or Cape Town on virtually any weekend of the year, and sometimes mid-week too – you just need to check the press for details.

POLITICAL MUSIC

With the collapse of apartheid and the accession to power of the ANC, the heyday of South African **political song** has passed. With lyrics singing the praises of Umkhonto weSizwe (the armed wing of the ANC), or stating bluntly that "*uMama uyajabula uma ngibulala iBhunu*" ("My mother is happy when I kill a Boer"), the songs were performed during marches, demonstrations, rallies and most of all at the funerals of slain activists, usually accompanied by the *toyi-toyi*. This combination of a march and a dance is performed on the spot or on the move, with knees brought high, and is still widely used, but the old songs don't really fit any more, and you hear them less and less.

Mzwakhe Mbuli made his name in the Eighties as "the people's poet", performing his articulate and angry political poetry at countless rallies around the country. His house was firebombed by the authorities, and Mzwakhe himself was harassed and detained, but his poetry remained defiant, with titles like *Unbroken Spirit* and *Now is the Time*. In 1989, Mzwakhe correctly discerned the signs of the times, proclaiming in one poem that "the bull is dying at last, kicking at random", and in the following year, while celebrating Mandela's release, he urged prophetically: "When you vote and get elected, think of those who died."

After the 1994 elections, Mzwakhe was for a while a more contented man, asking his many disillusioned compatriots that "if this is not the time for happiness, when is?", but at the same time using his poetry to urge an end to social ills like criminality and drug addiction. However, for over a year now, Mzwakhe has been incarcerated in a maximum security prison in the company of apartheid mass murderers like Eugene de Kock, accused of armed robbery and repeatedly denied bail. Mzwakhe insists that he has been framed, and after long delay is now trying to prove it in court. Most of his former comrades in the ANC have notably refused to visit him in prison and he is reported to have prepared some incisive poetry for them if, and when, he is ever released.

BOEREMUSIEK

Boeremusiek is what is left of Afrikaans folk music, originating in Dutch and French folk music, but heavily influenced over the years by American country and hillbilly music, with the legendary **Jim Reeves** standing out as a major hero of the scene. These days, it's definitely easy listening, with the style's major current practitioner **Bles Bridges** known for throwing roses, Barry Manilow-style, to his adoring fans. However, the jazz-tinged concertina virtuosity of the veteran **Nico Carstens** can be interesting, particularly since his recent experimental fusions with *mbaqanga*, which he calls *Boereqanga*. **Koos Kombuis** champions a blend of rock and Afrikaans music, though the lyrics are the key thing here and just listening to the rather average instrumentation is not much compensation.

You can be sure of hearing traditional *Boeremusiek* at any Afrikaner day out in the *dorps*.

WHITE ROCK

It is the eternal lament of **white rock** musicians in South Africa that no one in Europe or

DISCOGRAPHY

BUBBLEGUM

Brenda Fassie, *Mama* (CCP, SA); Great late-Eighties tunes from South Africa's very own Madonna. *Now is the Time* (CCP, SA) serves up snatches of *kwaito* and soukous in the mix, while her latest, *Memeza* (CCP, SA) returns to more traditional bubblegum territory, and is her most successful album in years.

Sello "Chicco" Twala, *The Best Of. . .* (Teal, SA). A fair selection of Chicco's biggest bubblegum.

Yvonne Chaka Chaka, T*he Best Of. . .* (Teal, SA). Contains pretty much all the Yvonne you need to hear, packed with her Eighties hits.

GOSPEL

Choirs of South Africa, *Choirs of South Africa* (Roi Music, SA). Stirring gospel anthems delivered by mass choirs with exuberance and power. All that's missing is the visual spectacle of their members dressed in flowing garments and swaying to the mighty sounds.

IPCC, *Ummeli Wethu* (Gallo, SA). An excellent offering from one of South Africa's most popular gospel choirs, replete with charisma, powerful sounds and stunning melodies.

Lusanda Spiritual Group, *Ungababek'ityala* (Gallo, SA). Lusanda is a serious challenger for Rebecca Malope's position as South Africa's gospel queen, though her apparent mournfulness perhaps makes her a little less accessible to foreign ears.

Rebecca Malope, *Uzube'nami* (CCP, SA). Rebecca's main effort of 1996, and a stunning set of stirring anthems.

Rebecca Malope, *Shwele Baba* (CCP, SA). One of Rebecca's finest albums, with the title track a strong contender for her best-ever song and the rest of the cuts all pretty good too.

Pure Magic, *Ikhoni'mfuyo* (CCP, SA). Rebecca Malope's backing band, with lead vocals courtesy of her dashing sideman Vuyo Mokoena, and some powerful compositions. The band's most recent offering, *Likhon' Ithemba* (CCP, SA), follows the same route and has proved an equally impressive success in South Africa.

Amadodana Ase Wesile, *Morena U Ba Elele* (Gallo, SA). The latest offering of stirring anthems from this popular Methodist male choir, who wear blazers and red waistcoats, keep time by thumping a Bible, and can make huge congregations sway and sing as one.

Various Artists, *Gospel Spirit of Africa* (Gallo,SA). An excellent compilation of most of South Africa's top current gospel choirs, including Ladysmith Black Mambazo, the Holy Cross Choir, and the Holy Brothers.

JAZZ

Dollar Brand, *Voice of Africa, African Sun, Tetenya* and *Blues for a Hip King* (Kaz, UK). Virtually definitive four-album compilation of the best of Abdullah Ibrahim's (Dollar Brand) prodigious output, including the seminal *Mannenberg (Is Where It's Happening)*. *Township One More Time* (EMI, SA) is Ibrahim's latest offering, and as the title suggests, is a return to his older, more accessible ways. It includes a superb version of the anthem *Shosholoza*.

Errol Dyers, *Sonesta* (Nkomo, SA). Dyers is a smooth, fusion-oriented guitarist, whose work on this album tends to be too laid back for its own good, but comes to life for the superb Latin-influenced title track.

Sipho Gumede, *Down Freedom Avenue* (B&W, UK). Intriguing jazz-fusion from this accomplished bassist at the cutting edge of the new South African jazz sound.

Jazz Epistles, *Verse One* (Celluloid, France). Seminal recordings of this great South African jazz band, featuring Hugh Masekela, Kippie Moeketsi, Jonas Gwangwa and Dollar Brand.

Jazz Pioneers, *Sip 'n' Fly* (Flametree, UK). Well-paced old-style *marabi* jazz by the veterans of the art.

Sibongile Khumalo, *Ancient Evenings* (Sony, SA). Though a classically trained opera singer, Khumalo takes on both jazz and a variety of traditional melodies in this wonderful album that demonstrates clearly why she is currently one of South Africa's best-loved singers.

Winston Mankunku, *Yakal'Inkomo* (Polygram, SA). Coltrane's influence on this stalwart of the jazz scene is palpable, and successfully fused by Mankunku on this release with some classic township melodies.

Moses Taiwa Molelekwa, *Genes and Spirits* (Melt2000, UK). Fascinating jazz/drum'n'bass fusion by this talented young pianist who is already emerging as one of the finest jazz musicians of his generation.

Miriam Makeba and the Skylarks, *Miriam Makeba and the Skylarks* (Teal, SA). Two-CD set of 32 great recordings of South Africa's queen of song, from the Fifties.

Hugh Masekela, *The Collection* (Connoisseur, UK). Good budget-price compilation of Masekela's Sixties and Seventies hits. Masekela scored a deserved recent hit with *Black to the Future* (Sony, SA), which includes the excellent track *Chileshe* – an impassioned plea to his countrymen to discard their intense xenophobia towards African immigrants.

Philip Tabana and Malomobo, *Unh!* (Elektra Nonesuch), *Ke a Bereka* (Tusk, SA). The masterful guitarist with a sound and a style entirely his own does his individualistic take on Afro-jazz. The second release veers in a more traditional direction, but is still unmistakably Tabana.

KWAITO

Arthur, *Die Poppe Sal Dans* (CCP, SA). 1996 release of the man who came to fame with the controversial hit *Don't call me Kaffir*, this time stirring up a storm once more with *Voetsek* ("fuck off" in Afrikaans).

Boom Shaka, *Words of Wisdom* (Polygram, SA). Mostly fairly lightweight, but does include the group's notorious and funky rendition of the national anthem, which earned them the public condemnation of none other than Nelson Mandela.

Makhendlas, *Jammer* (CCP, SA). Features two massive hits, *Emenwe* and *Ayeye Aho*, from Arthur's brother, who tragically shot himself immediately after killing a troublesome fan after a gig in late 1998.

S'Bu, *Amalawyer* (Polygram, SA). Archetypal *kwaito* sounds from this popular artist, with a strong hook line and chorus, a catchy beat, and not much else. The title track draws its inspiration from black South Africa's new found interest in the law since the demise of apartheid.

TKZee, *Halloween* (BMG, SA). A solid offering from these popular *kwaito* artists, complete with their trademark catchy anthems and R&B-based sounds.

Various Artists, *Kwaito Hits* (EMI, SA). The first in what is likely to be a long line of compilations, and a very good one at that. Includes most of today's top *kwaito* artists, including Arthur, TKZee, Skeem and Abashante.

MBAQANGA

Mahlathini and the Mahotella Queens, *Thokolize* (Earthworks, UK). Perfect introduction to the Eighties sound of this most stomping of *mbaqanga* outfits.

Soul Brothers, *Jive Soweto* (Earthworks, UK). Good compilation of all the Soul Brothers tunes that matter, including their masterly title track that still goes down a storm in South Africa.

Various Artists, *Zulu Jive* (Earthworks, UK; Carthage, US). Good selection of early Eighties cuts, mostly from Zulul *mbaqanga* ace Joshua Sithole, as well as more traditional stompers from Aaron Mbambo and Shoba.

NEO-TRADITIONAL

Amampondo, *Drums for Tomorrow* (Melt2000, UK). South Africa's most famous marimba (xylophone) band deliver a fine and well-produced set here, full of their distinctive Xhosa melodies and powerful polyrhythms.

Bayete, *Umkhaya-Lo* (Polygram, SA). Not strictly neo-traditional this, but rather a seminal fusion of South African sounds with laid-back soul and funk, blended by lead singer Jabu Khanyile's unique mixing talent and spiced with his beautifully soothing vocals. Khanyile's latest offering, *Umathimula* (Polygram, SA), is less remarkable, but does include some fascinating *soukous* fusion.

Ladysmith Black Mambazo, *The Best of. . .* (Shanachie, US). Respectable introduction to a group who have never put a musical foot wrong, and whose back catalogue is gratifyingly mostly available.

Ringo, *Sondelani* (CCP, SA). A superb modern reworking of traditional Xhosa sounds by this bald Capetonian heart throb, including the hit track *Sondela*, undoubtedly South Africa's most popular love song.

Busi Mhlongo, *UrbanZulu* (Melt2000, UK). Classic Zulu *maskanda* from this powerful *sangoma* (traditional healer), immaculately produced by an innovative British label fast making a name for itself as one of the best sources of contemporary South African music around.

Various Artists, *The Heartbeat of Soweto* (Shanachie, US). Misleading title for this fine collection of Zulu, Shangaan and Tsonga traditional styles.

Various Artists, *Singing in an Open Space* (Rounder, US). Superb compilation of Zulu traditional styles by Gallo's guru Rob Allingham.

box continues overleaf. . .

POLITICAL MUSIC

Mzwakhe Mbuli, *Resistance is Defence* (Earthworks, UK). Great sample of the militant lyricism of the people's poet, including a moving ode to Mandela's release.

RAP AND REGGAE

Lucky Dube, *Prisoner* (Shanachie, US). South Africa's biggest-selling album ever, full of stirring Peter Tosh-style roots tunes.

Prophets of Da City, *Ghetto Code* (Polygram, SA). South Africa's rap supremos' most recent release, full of tough but articulate rhymes and some seriously funky backing tracks to wash them down with, all in true Cape Flats style.

WHITE ROCK

The Kerels, *Chrome Sweet Chrome* (Tic Tic Bang SA). A taste of grunge South African-style, with lyrics taking a wryly jaundiced view of the world, while the guitars thrash away in the background.

Tim Parr, *Still Standing* (Tic Tic Bang, SA). Celtic soul meets African rhythms on a celebratory, swinging album.

James Phillips, *Made in SA* (Shifty/Tic Tic Bang, SA). A collection of the best of this seminal singer, songwriter and bandleader, who died in 1995, going back to late-Seventies punk-style protest, to Eighties rock and Nineties R&B, tackling the complexities and nuances of South African society.

Pressure Cookies, *Swallow!* (Shifty/Tic Tic Bang, SA). All-grrrl group with sharply observed songs delivered in refreshingly bouncy manner.

Springbok Nude Girls, *Afterlife Satisfaction* (Sony, SA). One of South Africa's most popular white bands deliver an album mostly of derivative funk-rock, though some songs have bite.

COMPILATIONS

Various Artists, *From Marabi to Disco* (Gallo, SA). Quite simply the best South African music compilation around, with superb tracks and informative sleeve notes taking you from the Thirties to the Eighties.

Various Artists, *The Indestructible Beat of Soweto Volumes 1–4* (Earthworks, UK). Superb compilation, mainly featuring Eighties *mbaqanga*, along with a few more traditional samples. As the compiler Trevor Herman writes, "best heard loud and standing up".

America will take them seriously, and that 95 percent of South Africans will never be interested in what they are up to. Still, in the Eighties at least they had plenty to say, with **James Phillips** and his Afrikaans alter ego **Bernoldus Nieman** dishing up deranged tunes that laughed at and kicked against white orthodoxy, seeking refuge instead in the tried and tested formula of sex, drugs and rock 'n' roll. Today, apartheid is over and Phillips is dead, but the alternative white scene still looks healthy, despite the continued absence of decent sales. The **Springbok Nude Girls** are currently South Africa's most successful white rock band, and are building a following overseas among the increasing numbers of young whites who have recently emigrated, having already established a solid support base at home. The utterly derivative **Just Jinger** are also immensely popular, and the more interesting **Urban Creep** command a strong following. Worth checking if you get the chance are the Cape Town-based **Truly Fully Hey Shoo Wow Band**, whose great name accurately lists five of white Cape Town's favourite expressions, and whose exciting live act sometimes includes the near-legendary Duncan Dragon as a guest fire-eater. New bands spring up all the time in all the major cities, and even though most of their music is derivative and poorly executed, every so often you hit upon a gem that makes stomaching all the dross worthwhile.

LANGUAGE

South Africa has eleven official languages, all of which have equal status under the law. In practice, however, English is the lingua franca that dominates politics, commerce and the media. If you're staying in the main cities and national parks you'll rarely, if ever, need to use any other language. Afrikaans, although a language you'll rarely find any need to speak, nevertheless remains very much in evidence and you will certainly encounter it on official forms and countless signs particularly on the road; for this reason we give a comprehensive list of written Afrikaans terms you could come across.

With nine official indigenous African languages and several unofficial ones, unless you're planning on staying a very long time, there's little point trying to get to grips with the whole gamut, and even progressing beyond the absolute fundamentals of one of these languages is likely to be a challenge. Having said this, it's always useful to know a few phrases of the local indigenous language, especially **greetings** – a gesture that will always be appreciated even if you aren't able to carry your foray through to a proper conversation. For basic greetings in English and six other of the most commonly used languages, see the box overleaf.

The nine official **African languages** are split into four groups. **Nguni**, which consists of Zulu, Xhosa, siSwati and Ndebele; **Sotho**, which comprises Northern Sotho, Southern Sotho (or Sesotho) and Tswana; and **Venda** and **Tsonga**. Most people speak languages in the

first two groups. In common with all indigenous southern African languages, these operate under very different principles to European languages in that their sentences are dominated by the noun, with which the other words, such as verbs and adjectives, must agree in person, gender, number or case. Known as **concordal agreement**, this is achieved by supplementing word stems (the basic element of each word) with prefixes or suffixes to change meaning.

If you're in KwaZulu-Natal, it's worth investing in one of the Zulu **language cassettes** available in bookshops. These can easily help you to master the basic phrases we've listed. Tapes for other languages can be more difficult to come by, but it's always worth checking out bookshops.

ENGLISH

South African English is a mixed bag, one language with many variants. Forty percent of whites are mother-tongue English speakers, many of whom believe that they are (or at least should be) speaking standard British English. In fact, South African English has its own distinct character, and is as different from the Queen's English as is Australian. Its most notable characteristic is its huge and rich vocabulary, with unique words and usages, some drawn from Afrikaans and the indigenous African languages. The hefty *Oxford Dictionary of South African English* makes an interesting browse.

As a language used widely by non-native speakers, there is great **variation in pronunciation** and usage – largely a result of mother-tongue interference from other languages. Take for example the sentence "The bad bird sat on the bed", which speakers of some African languages (in which distinctions between English vowel sounds don't exist) might pronounce as "The bed bed set on the bed". While some English-speaking whites feel that their language is being mangled and misused, linguists argue that it is simply being transformed.

AFRIKAANS

Contrary to popular belief outside South Africa, the majority of **Afrikaans** speakers are not white but coloured, and the language, far from dying out, is in fact understood by more South Africans than any other language. It's the predominant

BASIC GREETINGS & FAREWELLS

ENGLISH	AFRIKAANS	NORTHERN SOTHO	SESOTHO	TSWANA	XHOSA	ZULU
Yes	Ja	Ee	E!	Ee	Ewe	Yebo
No	Nee	Aowa	Tjhe	Nnyaa	Hayi	Cha
Please	Asseblief	Hle. . /. . .hle	(Ka kgopo) hle	Tsweetswee	Nceda	Uxolo
Thank you	Dankie	Ke a leboga	Ke a leboha	Ke a leboga	Enkosi	Ngiyabonga
Excuse me	Verskoon my	Tshwarelo	Ntshwaerele	Intshwarele	Uxolo	Uxolo
Good morning	Goiemore	Thobela/dumela	Dumela (ng)	Dumela	Molo/bhota	Sawubona
Good afternoon	Goeiemiddag	Thobela/dumela	Dumela (ng)	Dumela	Molo/bhato	Sawubona
Good evening	Goeinaand	Thobela/dumela	Fonaneng	Dumela	Molo/bhota	Sawubona
Goodbye	Totsiens	Sala gabotse/ sepele gabotse	Sala(ng) hantle	Sala sentle	Nisale kakuhle	Sala kahle
See you later	Sien jou later	Re tla bonana	Re tla bonana	Ke tla go bona	Sobe sibonane	Sizobonana
Until we meet again	Totsiens	Go fihla re kopana gape	ho fihlela re bonana	Go fithlelela re bonana gape	De sibonane kwakhona	Size sibonane
How do you do	Aangename kennis	Ke leboga go le tseba	Ke thabela ho o tseba	O tsogile jang?	Kunjani	Ninjani?
How are you?	Hoe gaan dit?	Le kae?	O/le sa phela?	O tsogile jang?	Kunjani?	Ninjani?
I'm fine, thanks	Goed dankie	Re gona	Ke phela hantle	Ke tsogile sentle	Ndiphilile, enkosi	Ngisaphila

tongue in the Western and Northern Cape provinces, and in the Free State is the language of the media.

Broadly speaking, Afrikaans is a dialect of Dutch, which became modified on the Cape frontier through its encounter with French, German and English settlers, and is peppered with words and phrases from indigenous tongues as well as languages used by slaves. Some historians argue, very plausibly, that Afrikaans was first written in Arabic script in the early nineteenth century by Cape muslims.

Despite this heritage, the language was used by Afrikaners from the late nineteenth century onwards as a key element in the construction of their racially exclusive ethnic identity. The attempt by the apartheid government in 1976 to make Afrikaans the medium of instruction in black schools, which led to the Soweto uprising (see p.504), confirmed the hated status of the language for many urban Africans, which persists to this day.

THE NGUNI GROUP

In common with Southern Sotho, the **Nguni language group** contains a few clicks adopted

from San languages, which are difficult for speakers of European languages but can be mastered with practice.

Zulu (or isiZulu), the most widely spoken black African language in South Africa, is understood by around twelve million people. It's the mother tongue of residents of the southeastern parts of the country, including the whole of KwaZulu-Natal, the eastern Free State, southern Mpumalanga and Gauteng. Some linguists believe that Zulu's broad reach could make it an alternative to English as a South African *lingua franca*. Don't confuse Zulu with **Fanakalo**, which is a pidgin Zulu mixed with other languages. Still sometimes spoken on the mines, it is not popular with most Zulu speakers, though many white South Africans tend to believe it is.

For all practical purposes, **siSwati**, the language spoken in Swaziland, is almost identical to Zulu, but for historical reasons has developed its own identity.

The same applies to **Ndebele**, which shares around 95 percent in common with Zulu. It broke off from Zulu (around the same time as siSwati), when a group of Zulu-speakers fled north to escape the expansionism of Shaka. Ndebele is now spoken in pockets of Gauteng

AFRIKAANS SIGNS

Mans	Men	*Pad*	Road
Vrouens	Women	*Padwerke voor*	Road works ahead
Sentrum	Centre	*Pastorie*	Parsonage
Bed en Ontbyt	Bed and Breakfast	*Perron*	Platform (train station)
Derde	Third	*Plaas*	Farm
Dankie	Thank you	*Poskantoor*	Post Office
Doeane	Customs	*Regs*	Right
Drankwinkel	Liquor shop	*Ry*	Go
Droe vrugte	Dry fruit	*Singel*	Crescent
Eerste	First	*Slaghuis*	Butcher
Fruit	Vrugte	*Stadig*	Slow
Geen ingang	No entry	*Stad*	City
Gevaar	Danger	*Stad sentrum*	City/town sentrum
Grens	Border	*Stasie*	Station
Hoof	Main	*Straat*	Street
Hoog	High	*Strand*	Beach
Ingang	Entry	*Swembad*	Swimming Pool
Inligting	Information	*Toegang*	Admission
Kantoor	Office	*Tweede*	Second
Kerk	Church	*Verbode*	Prohibited
Kort	Short	*Verkeer*	Traffic
Links	Left	*Versigtig*	Carefully
Lughawe	Airport	*Vierde*	Fourth
Mark	Market	*Vyfde*	Fifth
Ompad	Detour		

GLOSSARY OF SOUTH AFRICAN TERMS

African	Indigenous South African, distinct from "black"
Apartheid	Term used from the Forties for the National Party's official policy of "racial separation"
Arvie	Afternoon
Assegai	Spears introduced by Shaka for the Zulu armies
Baai	Afrikaans suffix meaning "bay", used in place names eg Stilbaai
Bakkie	Light truck or van
Bantustan	Term used under apartheid for the territories such as Transkei reserved for members of the African linguistic groups
Bergie	A vagrant living on the slopes of Table Mountain in Cape Town
Biltong	Sun-dried salted strip of meat, chewed as a snack
Boerekos	Farm food, usually consisting of loads of meat and vegetables cooked using butter and sugar
Boerewors	Spicy lengths of sausage that are *de rigueur* at *braais*
Boland	Southern part of the Western Cape
Boy	Offensive term used to refer to an adult African man who is a servant
Braai	Barbecue
Bredie	Vegetable and meat stew
Bundu	Wilderness or back country
Bush	See *bundu*
Bushveld	Country composed largely of thorny bush
Cape Dutch	Nineteenth-century, whitewashed, gabled style of architecture
Ciskei	Eastern Cape region west of the Kei River declared a "self-governing territory" for Xhosa speakers in 1972 and now fully reincorporated into South Africa
Cocopan	Small tip truck on rails used to transport gold ore
Coloured	Mulattos or people of mixed race
Dagga	Marijuana
Dagha	Mud used in traditional indigenous construction
Dankie	Thank you (Afrikaans origin)
Dassie	Hyrax
Donga	Dry, eroded ditch
Dorp	Country town or village (Afrikaans origin)
Drift	Fording point in a river (Afrikaans origin)
Egoli	Zulu name for Johannesburg (lit: "city of gold")
Fanakalo	Unfashionable pidgin mixture of English, Zulu and Afrikaans taught to facilitate communication between white foremen and African workers on the mines or farms
Frikkadel	Fried onion and meat balls
Fundi	Expert
Fynbos	Term for vast range of fine leafed species that predominate in the southern part of the Western Cape (see p.117)
Gem squash	Orange shaped (and sized) marrow
Girl	Offensive term used to refer to an African woman who is a servant
Gogga	Creepy crawly or insect
Group Areas Act	Now defunct law passed in 1950 that provided for the establishment of separate areas for each "racial group"
Hanepoort	Delicious sweet dessert grape
Highveld	High-lying areas of Gauteng and Mpumalanga
Homeland	See *bantustan*
Hottentot	Now unfashionable term for indigenous Khoisan herders encountered by the first settlers at the Cape
Impi	Zulu regiment
Indaba	Zulu term meaning a group discussion and now used in SA English for any meeting or conference
Inkatha	Fiercely nationalist Zulu political party, formed in 1928 as a cultural organization
Is it?	Really?
Jislaaik	Exclamation equivalent to geez or crikey
Jol	Party
Just now	In a while

Kaffir	Highly objectionable term of abuse for Africans
Karoo	Arid plateau that occupies a large proportion of the South African interior
Khoi-Khoi	Self-styled name of South Africa's original herding inhabitants
Kloof	Ravine or gorge
Knobkerrie	Wooden club
Koeksister	Deep-fried plaited doughnut, dripping with syrup
Kopje	Dutch spelling of *koppie*
Koppie	Hillock
Kraal	Enclosure of huts for farm animals or collection of traditional huts occupied by an extended family
Kramat	Shrine of a Muslim holy man
Krans	Sheer cliff face
Lapa	Courtyard of group of Ndebele houses; also used to described an enclosed area where *braais* are held at safari camps
Lebowa	Now defunct homeland for North Sotho speakers
Lekker	Nice
Location	Old-fashioned term for segregated African area on the outskirts of a town or farm
Lowveld	Low-lying subtropical region of Mpumalanga and Northern Province
Malay	Misnomer for Cape Muslims of Asian descent
Mealie	See *mielie*
Melktert	Traditional Cape custard pie
Mielie	Maize
MK	Umkhonto we Sizwe (Spear of the Nation), the armed wing of the ANC now incorporated into the national army
Naartjie	Tangerine or mandarin
Nek	Saddle between two mountains
Nguni	Group of southeastern Bantu-speaking people comprising Zulu, Xhosa and Swazi
Nkosi Sikelel 'i Afrika	"God Bless Africa", anthem of the ANC and now of South Africa
Nyanga	Traditional healer
Pawpaw	Papaya
Pastorie	Parsonage (Afrikaans origin)
Platteland	Country districts (Afrikaans origin)
Poort	Narrow pass through mountains along river course
Pronk	Characteristic jump of sprinbok or impala antelope
Protea	National flower of South Africa
Qwaqwa	Now defunct homeland for South Sotho speakers
Raadsaal	Council or parliament building
Rest camp	Accommodation for visitors to national parks
Robot	Traffic light
Rondavel	Circular building based on traditional African huts
Rooibos tea	Indigenous herbal tea
SABC	South African Broadcasting Authority
Sjambok	Rawhide whip
Shebeen	Unlicensed tavern
Skelm	Villain
Snoek	Large fish that features in many traditional Cape recipes
Sosatie	Spicy skewered mince
Stoep	Verandah
Tackie	Sneakers or plimsolls
Township	Areas set aside under apartheid for Africans
Transkei	Now defunct homeland for Xhosa speakers
Tsostsie	Villain
Van der Hum	South African *naartjie*-flavoured liqueur
Velskoen	Rough suede shoes
Vetkoek	Deep-fried doughnut-like cake
Vlei	Swamp
VOC	Verenigde Oostindische Compagnie, the Dutch East India Company

and Northwest provinces as well as throughout southern Zimbabwe.

Xhosa is Nelson Mandela's mother tongue, which he shares with seven million other South Africans, predominantly in the Eastern Cape, but the language is also spoken by Africans in the Western Cape, most of whom are concentrated in Cape Town.

THE SOTHO GROUP

Northern Sotho, Southern Sotho (or Sesotho) and Tswana are members of the **Sotho language group**. As with the Nguni languages, the distinctions between these owe more to history, politics and geography than to pure linguistic factors; speakers of some Northern Sotho dialects can understand some dialects of Tswana more readily than they can other Northern Sotho dialects.

Northern Sotho dialects, which are numerous and diverse, are spoken by around 2.5 million people in a huge arc in the northwestern region of South Africa that takes in the country around the Kruger National Park, around to the Botswana border and south from there to Pretoria. **Southern Sotho**, one of the first African languages to be written, is spoken in the Free State, parts of Gauteng, as well as Lesotho and the areas of the Eastern Cape bordering it.

Tswana, also characterized by a great diversity of dialects, is geographically the most widespread language in southern Africa. The principle language of Botswana, in South Africa it's dialects are dispersed through the Northern Cape, the Free State and Northwest provinces.

INDEX

Stay in touch with us!

ROUGH*NEWS* is Rough Guides' free newsletter. In four issues a year we give you news, travel issues, music reviews, readers' letters and the latest dispatches from authors on the road.

I would like to receive ROUGH*NEWS*: please put me on your free mailing list.

NAME . . . .

ADDRESS . . . .

Please clip or photocopy and send to: Rough Guides, 62–70 Shorts Gardens, London WC2H 9AB, England or Rough Guides, 375 Hudson Street, New York, NY 10014, USA.

ROUGH GUIDES: Travel

Amsterdam
Andalucia
Australia

Austria
Bali & Lombok
Barcelona
Belgium &
  Luxembourg
Belize
Berlin
Brazil
Britain
Brittany &
  Normandy
Bulgaria
California
Canada
Central America
Chile
China
Corfu & the
  Ionian Islands
Corsica
Costa Rica
Crete
Cuba
Cyprus
Czech & Slovak
  Republics

Dodecanese
Dominican
  Republic
Egypt
England
Europe
Florida
France
French Hotels &
  Restaurants 1999
Germany
Goa
Greece
Greek Islands
Guatemala
Hawaii
Holland
Hong Kong
  & Macau
Hungary
India
Indonesia
Ireland
Israel & the
  Palestinian
  Territories
Italy
Jamaica
Japan
Jordan

Kenya
Laos
London
London
  Restaurants
Los Angeles
Malaysia,
  Singapore &
  Brunei
Mallorca &
  Menorca
Maya World
Mexico
Morocco
Moscow
Nepal
New England
New York
New Zealand
Norway
Pacific Northwest
Paris
Peru
Poland
Portugal
Prague
Provence & the
  Côte d'Azur
The Pyrenees
Romania

St Petersburg
San Francisco
Sardinia
Scandinavia
Scotland
Scottish Highlands
  & Islands
Sicily
Singapore

South Africa
Southern India
Southwest USA
Spain
Sweden
Syria
Thailand
Trinidad & Tobago
Tunisia
Turkey
Tuscany & Umbria
USA
Venice
Vienna
Vietnam
Wales
Washington DC
West Africa
Zimbabwe &
  Botswana

AVAILABLE AT ALL GOOD BOOKSHOPS

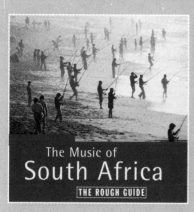

HOSTELLING
INTERNATIONAL

The last word in accommodation

Safe reliable accommodation
from $8 a night at over 4500 centres
in 60 countries worldwide

http://www.iyhf.org

the perfect getaway vehicle

low-price holiday car rental.

rent a car from holiday autos and you'll give yourself real freedom to explore your holiday destination. with great-value, fully-inclusive rates in over 4,000 locations worldwide, wherever you're escaping to, we're there to make sure you get excellent prices and superb service.

what's more, you can book now with complete confidence. our £5 undercut* ensures that you are guaranteed the best value for money in holiday destinations right around the globe.

drive away with a great deal, call holiday autos now on **0990 300 400** and quote ref RG.

holiday autos
miles ahead